T0180909

Communications
in Computer and Information Science   **828**

Commenced Publication in 2007
Founding and Former Series Editors:
Alfredo Cuzzocrea, Xiaoyong Du, Orhun Kara, Ting Liu, Dominik Ślęzak,
and Xiaokang Yang

More information about this series at http://www.springer.com/series/7899

Pushpak Bhattacharyya · Hanumat G. Sastry
Venkatadri Marriboyina · Rashmi Sharma (Eds.)

Smart and Innovative Trends in Next Generation Computing Technologies

Third International Conference, NGCT 2017
Dehradun, India, October 30–31, 2017
Revised Selected Papers, Part II

 Springer

Editors
Pushpak Bhattacharyya
Indian Institute of Technology Patna
Patna, Bihar
India

Venkatadri Marriboyina
University of Petroleum and Energy Studies
Dehradun
India

Hanumat G. Sastry
University of Petroleum and Energy Studies
Dehradun
India

Rashmi Sharma
University of Petroleum and Energy Studies
Dehradun
India

ISSN 1865-0929   ISSN 1865-0937 (electronic)
Communications in Computer and Information Science
ISBN 978-981-10-8659-5   ISBN 978-981-10-8660-1   (eBook)
https://doi.org/10.1007/978-981-10-8660-1

Library of Congress Control Number: 2018944386

This Springer imprint is published by the registered company Springer Nature Singapore Pte Ltd.
part of Springer Nature
The registered company address is: 152 Beach Road, #21-01/04 Gateway East, Singapore 189721, Singapore

Preface

These proceedings comprise the best research papers presented at the Third International Conference on Next-Generation Computing Technologies (NGCT 2017) organized by the School of Computer Science at the University of Petroleum and Energy Studies, Dehradun, India during October 30–31, 2017. The conference theme was "Smart and Innovative Trends for Next-Generation Computing" and all the tracks and sub-tracks focused on contemporary research in computing and information technology. NGCG 2017 offered a platform to researchers, experts, academics, and industry fellows to share and discuss their research findings with the aim of offering humans better daily living with the help of next-generation computing technologies. NGCT 2017 followed a strict peer-review process, with 135 top-quality papers being selected and presented out 948 submissions from various parts of the globe.

The present proceedings contain five parts, namely, "Smart and Innovative Trends in Computational Intelligence and Data Science," "Smart and Innovative Trends in Communication Protocols and Standards," "Smart and Innovative Trends in Image Processing and Machine Vision," "Smart and Innovative Trends in Security and Privacy," and "Smart and Innovative Trends in Natural Language Processing for Indian Languages."

We express our thanks to the university leaders, advisory and technical board members, keynote speakers, and Organizing Committee members. We extend our thanks to the conference sponsors IBM India, SERB-DST, DRDO, Springer, CSI, and IUPRAI.

April 2018

Pushpak Bhattacharyya
Hanumat G. Sastry
Venkatadri M.
Rashmi Sharma

Organization

Steering Committee

Chief Patron

S. J. Chopra   UPES, Dehradun, India

Patron(s)

Utpal Ghosh   UPES, Dehradun, India
Deependra Kumar Jha   UPES, Dehradun, India

Co-patron(s)

Kamal Bansal   UPES, Dehradun, India
Manish Prateek   UPES, Dehradun, India

General Chair

Pushpak Bhattacharyya   IIT, Patna, India

Honorary Chair(s)

Ajoy Kumar Ray   IIEST, Shibpur, India
Valentina E. Balas   Aurel Vlaicu University of Arad, Romania

Conference Chair

Hanumat G. Sastry   UPES, Dehradun, India

Conference Secretary

Venkatadri M.   UPES, Dehradun, India

Advisory Committee

William Stallings   Independent Consultant, USA
Sartaj Sahni   University of Florida, USA
Margaret Burnett   Oregon State University, USA
Luciana Salgado   Universidade Federal Fluminense, Brazil
Cristian Rodriguez Rivero   Universidad Nacional de Córdoba, Argentina
Ramachandran Venkatesan   Memorial University of Newfoundland, Canada
Vincenzo Piuri   The University of Milan, Italy
N. Subba Reddy   Gyeongsang National University, South Korea
Mohammed A. Aseeri   National Centre for Sensors and Defense Systems Technologies (NCSDST), Saudi Arabia

Pabitra Pal Choudhury	Indian Statistical Institute, Kolkata, India
Anirban Basu	CSI, India Council, Bangalore, India
Shekhar Sahasrabudh	ACM, India Council, Bangalore, India
Preeti Bajaj	IEEE, India Council, India
Akshaya Nayak	CSI, India Council, India
Sandhya Chintala	NASSCOM, Noida, India
Prosenjit Pal	Prophecy Sensorlytics, LLC, Bangalore, India
Hari Seetha	VIT University, Vellore, India
Jimson Mathew	IIT, Patna, India
R. Rajendra Prasath	Indian Institute of Information Technology, Chittoor, India
C. A. S. Murthy	C-DAC, Hyderabad, India
Kunwar Singh Vaisla	Uttarakhand Technical University, Dehradun, India
Vikram Bali	Panipat Institute of Engineering and Technology, Panipat, India
Jayraj Ugarkar	Infosys, Bangalore, India
Rajesh Khambayat	NITTR, Bhopal, India
Sanjay Sood	C-DAC, Mohali, India
Nikhil R. Pal	Indian Statistical Institute, Calcutta, India
Karunesh Arora	C-DAC, Noida, India
Sapna Poti	Kyungpook National University, NSDC, New Delhi, India
C. Rama Krishna	NITTTR, Chandigarh, India
Suman Bhattacharya	TCS, Bhubaneswar, India
V. S. K. Reddy	Malla Reddy College of Engineering and Technology, Medchal, India
Rathna G. N.	IISc, Bangalore, India
Rajesh Siddavatam	REVA University, Bangalore, India
Bhabatosh Chanda	Indian Statistical Institute, Kolkata, India
D. Vasumathi	Jawaharlal Nehru Technological University, Hyderabad, India
Vithal Madyalkar	IBM Innovation Center for Education, India
Ganesh Venkatesan	Elsevier, Chennai, India
Gopi Krishna Durbhaka	TCS Innovation and Transformation Group, Pune, India
Hema Gopal	TCS, India
E. Balagurusamy	EBG Foundation, Coimbatore, India
Yashavant P. Kanetkar	KICIT and KSIT, Nagpur, India
Ujjwal Maulik	Jadavpur University, India
Arindam Biswas	NSHM Knowledge Campus, Durgapur, India
Arindam Biswas	IIEST, Shibpur, India

Keynote Speakers

Pushpak Bhattacharyya   IIT Patna, India
Rajkumar Buyya   University of Melbourne, Australia
Valentina E. Balas   University 'AurelVlaicu', Arad, Romania
R. K. Shyamasundar   IIT Bombay, India

Technical Program Committee

Technical Program Chair(s)

Rashmi Sharma   UPES, Dehradun, India
Kamal Kumar   UPES, Dehradun, India
Sriparna Saha   IIT, Patna, India
Vinay Avasthi   UPES, Dehradun, India
Nitin   JIIIT, Noida, India

Editor(s)

Pushpak Bhattacharyya   IIT, Patna, India
Hanumat G. Sastry   UPES, Dehradun, India
Venkatadri M.   UPES, Dehradun, India
Rashmi Sharma   UPES, Dehradun, India

Members

William Stallings   Independent Consultant, USA
Sartaj Sahni   University of Florida, USA
Margaret Burnett   Oregon State University, USA
Luciana Salgado   Universidade Federal Fluminense, Brazil
Cristian Rodriguez Rivero   Universidad Nacional de Córdoba, Argentina
Ramachandran Venkatesan   Memorial University of Newfoundland, Canada
Vincenzo Piuri   The University of Milan, Italy
N. Subba Reddy   Gyeongsang National University, South Korea
Mohammed A. Aseeri   National Centre for Sensors and Defense Systems
                               Technologies (NCSDST), Saudi Arabia
Ankur Mani   University of Minnesota, USA
Ajith Abraham   Machine Intelligence Research Labs (MIR Labs),
                               Washington, USA
Ravi Muttineni   E2E INC, USA
Amit Cohen   Huawei Technologies, Israel
Kei Eguchi   Fukuoka Institute of Technology, Japan
Hussein A. Abbass   University of New South Wales, Australia
Vijay K. Vaishnavi   Georgia State University, USA
Arun K. Somani   Iowa State University, USA
Subramaniam Ganesan   Oakland University, USA
Jonathan Reichental   City of Palo Alto, USA
Kiran Thatikonda   Accenture, Houston, USA

Jerry Luftman   Global Institute for IT Management, USA
Dennis K. Peters   Memorial University, Canada
M. N. Hoda   BVICAM, New Delhi, India
C. V. D. Ramprasad   STPI, Hyderabad, India
C. S. R. Prabhu   NIC, Hyderabad, India
Prabir Kumar Das   STPI, Assam, India
Manisha Mohan   Tata Interactive, Mumbai, India
Sanjeev Asthana   I-Farm Venture Advisors Pvt. Ltd., Gurgaon, India
K. R. Murali Mohan   National Resources Data Management Systems,
                                   New Delhi, India
Pranay Chaudhuri   Heritage Institute of Technology, Kolkata, India
Niladri Chatterjee   IIT, New Delhi, India
Hemanatha Kumar   University of Mysore, India
Rajani Parthasarathy   Anna University, Chennai, India
Awadesh Kumar Singh   NIT, Kurukshetra, India
Himani Bansal   Jaypee Institute of Institute Technology, Noida, India
Suresh Gupta   Panipat Institute of Engineering and Technology,
                                   Panipat, India
Vijayakumari Gunta   Jawaharlal Nehru Technological University,
                                   Hyderabad, India
Sipra Das Bit   IIEST Shibpur, Howrah, India
Jaya Sil   IIEST Shibpur, Howrah, India
K. Chandrasekaran   NIT, Surathkal, India
S. Sampath   Madras University, Chennai, India
Lokanatha C. Reddy   Dravidian University, Kuppam, India
M. L. Saikumar   Institute of Public Enterprise, Medchal, India
K. K. Shukla   I.I.T., Varanasi, India
Umapada Pal   Indian Statistical Institute, Calcutta, India
S. Muthukumar   Indian Institute of Information Technology, Srirangam,
                                   India
Pabitra Pal Choudhury   Indian Statistical Institute, Kolkata, India
Anirban Basu   CSI, India Council, Bangalore, India
Shekhar Sahasrabudh   ACM, India Council, Bangalore, India
Preeti Bajaj   IEEE, India Council, India
Akshaya Nayak   CSI, India Council, India
Sandhya Chintala   NASSCOM, Noida, India
Prosenjit Pal   Prophecy Sensorlytics, LLC, Bangalore, India
Hari Seetha   VIT University, Vellore, India
Jimson Mathew   IIT, Patna, India
R. Rajendra Prasath   Indian Institute of Information Technology, Chittoor,
                                   India
C. A. S. Murthy   C-DAC, Hyderabad, India
Kunwar Singh Vaisla   Uttarakhand Technical University, Dehradun, India
Vikram Bali   Panipat Institute of Engineering and Technology, India
Jayraj Ugarkar   Infosys, Bangalore, India
Sanjay Sood   C-DAC, Mohali, India

Nikhil R. Pal	Indian Statistical Institute, Calcutta, India
Karunesh Arora	C-DAC, Noida, India
Sapna Poti	Kyungpook National University, NSDC, New Delhi, India
Suman Bhattacharya	TCS, Bhubaneswar, India
V. S. K. Reddy	Malla Reddy College of Engineering and Technology, Medchal, India
Rathna G. N.	IISc, Bangalore, India
Rajesh Siddavatam	REVA University, Bangalore, India
Bhabatosh Chanda	Indian Statistical Institute, Kolkata, India
D. Vasumathi	Jawaharlal Nehru Technological University, Hyderabad, India
Ganesh Venkatesan	Elsevier, Chennai, India
Gopi Krishna Durbhaka	TCS Innovation and Transformation Group, Pune, India
Hema Gopal	TCS, India
Brojo Kishore Mishra	C.V. Raman College of Engineering, Bhubaneswar, India
Souvik Pal	Elitte College of Engineering, Kolkata, India
Pooja Kamat	Symbiosis International University, Pune, India
Preeti Mulay	Symbiosis International University, Pune, India
Yogita Gigras	The Northcap University, Gurugram, India
Sudan Jha	Nepal Engineering College, Changunarayan, Nepal
Manjula Sanjay Koti	Dayananda Sagar Academy of Technology and Management Technical Campus, Bangalore, India
Bautu Elena	Ovidius University, Romania
K. Shashi Prabh	Shiv Nadar University, Dadri, India
Sunil Tekale	R&D Glenmark Generics Ltd., Mumbai, India
G. Sridevi	KL University, Guntur, India
Kiran Ravulakollu	Sharda University, Greater Noida, India
Zarinah Mohd Kasirun	University of Malaya, Malaysia
Akshaye Dhawan	Ursinus College, USA
M. S. Aswal	Gurukul Kangri University, Haridwar, India
Dilip Singh Sosodia	National Institute of Technology, Raipur, India
Atul Garg	Maharishi Markandeshwar University, Ambala, India
B. Surendiran	National Institute of Technology, Puducherry, India
Charu	Jaypee Institute of Information Technology, Noida, India
Vinay Nassa	South Point Technical Campus, Sonipat, India
Neeta Singh	Gautam Buddha University, Greater Noida, India
Sapna Gambhir	Maharishi Dayanand University, Rohtak, India
Deepti Mehrotra	Amity University, Noida, India
R. K. Yadav	JRE Group of Institution, Greater Noida, India

Gurpreet Singh	Giani Zail Singh Campus College of Engineering and Technology, Maharaja Ranjit Singh Punjab Technical University, Bathinda, India
Mangal Sain	Dongseo University, South Korea
Girish Kumar Sharma	Indraprastha University, New Delhi, India
Emmanuel Pilli	Malaviya National Institute of Technology, Jaipur, India
Himanshu Agarwal	Punjabi University, Patiala, India
Sarika Jain	Amity University, Noida, India
S. R. Balasundaram	National Institute of Technology, Trichy, India
Manu Sood	Himachal Pradesh University, Shimla, India
Sharad Saxena	Thapar University, Patiala, India
Anil Verma	Thapar University, Patiala, India
Asif Anwar Alig	Northern Border University, Arar, Saudi Arabia
Subodh Wairya	Uttar Pradesh Technical University, Lucknow, India
S. Mini	National Institute of Technology, Goa, India
Rabindra Jena	Institute of Management Technology, Nagpur, India
Ashutosh Gupta	MJP Rohilkhand University, Bareilly, India
Subodh Srivastava	Indian Institute of Technology, Varanasi, India
Shashidhar G. Koolagudi	National Institute of Technology, Surathkal, India
Shyamal Tanna	L. J. Institute of Engineering and Technology, Ahmedabad, India
Rambir Singh	Indraprastha Engineering College, Ghaziabad, India
Vinay Chavan	Seth Kesarimal Porwal College, Nagpur, India
Sujata Pandey	Amity University, Noida, India
Sridhar Vaithianathan	Institute of Management Technology, Hyderabad, India
Raman Chadha	Chandigarh Group of Colleges, Chandigarh, India
Rajeev Kumar	Jaypee University of Information Technology, Solan, India
Satish Chandra	Jaypee Institute of Information Technology, Noida, India
Zubair Ahmad Khattak	Iqra National University, Peshawar, Pakistan
Saru Dhir	Amity University, Noida, India
Kalpana Tiwari	Amity University, Noida, India
Paresh Virparia	S. P. University, Anand, India
Arputha Rathina	B. S. Abdur Rahman University, Vandalur, India
Promod Joshi	Amrapali Group of Institutes, Haldwani, India
Haribabu	BITS, Pilani, India
Rohit Khokher	Vidya College of Engineering, Meerut, India
Satish Chhokar	Rajkumar Garg Institute of Technology, Ghaziabad, India
Vinay Rishiwal	MJP Rohilkhand University, Bareilly, India
Inderjeet Kaur	Ajay Kumar Garg Engg College, Ghaziabad, India
Yashwant Singh	Jaypee University of Information Technology, Solan, India
M. Sandhya	B. S. Abdur Rahman University, Chennai, India

Tarun Gupta	Radha Govind Engineering College, Meerut, India
Satyanarayana Reddy	Cambridge Institute of Technology, Bangalore, India
Anil Kumar Dubey	Govt. Engineering College, Ajmer, India
Punyaban Patel	Mala Reddy Institute of Technology, Hyderabad, India
Hemant Sahu	Geetanjali Institute of Technical Studies, Udaipur, India
K. Ammulu	Dravidian University, Kuppam, India
Rajesh Mehta	Amity School of Engineering and Technology, New Delhi, India
B. V. Kiranmayee	VJIT, Nizampet, India
Manju Kaushik	JECRC University, Jaipur, India
Surendra Kumar Yadav	JECRC University, Jaipur, India
Naveen Hemrajani	JECRC University, Jaipur, India
Narendra Singh Yadav	JECRC University, Jaipur, India
S. Arvind	CMR Institute of Technology, Kundalahalli, India
T. Venu Gopal	JNTUH, Medak, India
D. Murali	MRCET, Hyderabad, India
Bhabatosh Chanda	ISI, Kolkata, India
Luciana Salgado	Universidade Federal Fluminense, Niterói, Brazil
Visvasuresh Victor Govindaswamy	Concordia University, Montréal, Canada
Phalguni Gupta	Indian Institute of Technology, Kanpur, India
Bimal Kumar Misra	BIT, Mesra, India
Hemraj Saini	Jaypee University of Information Technology, Waknaghat, India
Praveen Srivastava	Indian Institute of Management, Rohtak, India
Deepak Garg	Bennett University, Greater Noida, India
V. Singh Vr.	National Physical Laboratory, New Delhi, India
Mario Dantas	Universidade Federal De Santa Catarina, Trindade, Brazil
Maninder Singh	Thapar University, Patiala, India
Sunil Bhooshan	Jaypee University of Information Technology, Waknaghat, India
Prashant Deshmukh	Sipna College of Engineering and Technology, Amravati, India
Manoj Diwakar	Babasaheb Bhimrao Ambedkar University, Lucknow, India
Ashish Ghosh	ISI, Kolkata, India
Gagandeep Jagdev	Punjabi University, Damdama Sahib, India
Prasanta Jana	Indian Institute of Technology, Dhanbad, India
Brijendra Joshi	Military College of Telecommunication Engineering, Indore, India
Rajib Kar	National Institute of Technology, Durgapur, India
Rajeev Kumar	Teerthanker Mahaveer University, Moradabad, India
Durbadal Mandal	National Institute of Technology, Durgapur, India
Manas Patra	Berhampur University, Brahmapur, India

Jasbir Saini	DCR University of Science and Technology, Murthal, India
Abdus Samad	Aligarh Muslim University, Aligarh, India
Baldev Singh	VIT, Vellore, India
Harikesh Singh	Jaypee University of Engineering and Technology, Guna, India
Tarachand Amgoth	IDM, Dhanbad, India
Pallav Kumar Baruah	Sri Sathya Sai Institute of Higher Learning, Puttaparthi, India
Nagarajan Kathiresan	SIDRA Medical and Research Center, Qatar
Rajiv Pandey	Amity University, Lucknow, India
Fereshteh-Azadi Parand	Allameh Tabatabae'i University, Iran
Kanchana Rajaram	Anna University, Guindy, India
Diptendu Sinha Roy	National Institute Technology, Meghalaya, India
Shrikant Tiwari	Chhattisgarh Swami Vivekananda Technical University, Bhilai, India
Priyanka Tripathi	NITTTR, Bhopal, India
Ajay Pratap	Indian Institute of Technology, Patna, India
Xiao Zhang	Syracuse University, USA
Shashank Joshi	Bharti Vidyapeeth College of Engineering, Pune, India
Meenakshi Sood	Jaypee University of Information Technology, Solan, India
Rajeev Sharma	National Institute of Technology, Kurukshetra, India
Hiren Deva Sarma	Sikkim Manipal Institute of Technology, Rangpo, India
Satya Ghrera	Jaypee University of Information Technology, Solan, India
Arjun Singh	Manipal University, Jaipur, India
Sumit Srivastava	Manipal University, Jaipur, India
Manik Lal Das	DA-IICT, Gandhinagar, India
Sandeep Chaurasia	Manipal University, Jaipur, India
Vishnu Srivastava	CSIR CEERI, Chennai, India
Jyotirmoy Karjee	TCS Research and Innovation Lab, India
Arun Somani	Iowa State University, Iowa, USA
Chittaranjan Pradhan	Kiit University, Bhubaneswar, India
Bimal Roy	Indian Statistical Institute, Kolkata, India
Sangram Ray	National Institute of Technology, Sikkim, India
Vijay Bhasker Semwal	IIIT, Dharwad, India
Arun Mishra	Defence Institute of Advanced Technology, DRDO, Pune, India
Chhagan	University of Padova, Italy
Kharmega Sundararaj G.	PSN College of Engineering and Technology, Tirunelveli, India
Abhijit Das	CDAC, Silchar, India
Rajesh Bhat	IIIT Delhi, New Delhi, India
Preeti Gera	SGI, Gurgaon, India
Arvind Jain	RJIT, Tekanpur, India

Mantosh Biswas	National Institute of Technology, Kurukshetra, India
Srikanth	CDAC, Hyderabad, India
Shamanth Rai	Sahyadri College of Engineering and Management, Mangalore, India
Divya Rishi Sahu	SIRT, Bhopal, India
Raju Baraskar	RGPV, Bhopal, India
Rajeev Kumar Gupta	SISTec, Bhopal, India
Abhineet Anand	Galgotias University, Grater Noida, India
Indu Bhusan Lal	L. N. Mishra College of Business Management, Bihar, India
Manish Kumar	Vidya Vihar Institute of Technology, Bihar, India
Manish Saini	DCRUST, Haryana, India
Hitender Tyagi	Kurukshetra University, Kurukshetra, India
Seng Loke	Melbourne Burwood Campus, Deakin University, Burwood, Australia
Gang Li	Melbourne Burwood Campus, Deakin University, Australia
Ashok Kumar Saxena	Indian Institute of Technology, Roorkee, India
Rajdeep Chakraborty	Netaji Subhash Engineering College, Kolkata, India
Mahesh Kumar Porwal	Sree Chaitanya College of Engineering, Hyderabad, India
Gopalakrishnan T.	Bannari Amman Institute of Technology, Erode, India
J. Bhuvana	King Khalid University, Kingdom of Saudi Arabia
Shuchi Dave	Poornima College of Engineering, Jaipur, India
Harish Mittal	B.M. Institute of Engineering and Technology, Sonipat, India
Sonal Purohit	FMS-WISDOM Banasthali University, Banasthali, India
Nupur Srivastava	Poornima College of Engineering, Jaipur, India
Nidhi Mishra	Poornima College of Engineering, Jaipur, India
J. K. Deegwal	Government Engineering College, Ajmer, India
Ghanshyam Singh	Malaviya National Institute of Technology, Jaipur, India
Vipul H. Chudasama	Nirma University, Ahmedabad, India
Sathiyamoorthi	Sona College of Technology, Salem, India
Vrijendra Singh	Indian Institute of Information Technology, Allahabad, India
Rakesh Kumar Bansal	Maharaja Ranjit Singh Punjab Technical University, Bathinda, India
Savina Bansal	Maharaja Ranjit Singh Punjab Technical University, Bathinda, India
Saurabh Mukherjee	Banasthali Vidyapith, Jaipur, India
Arun Kumar Verma	MNIT, Jaipur, India
N. Narayanan Prasanth	National College of Engineering, Maruthakulam, India
Arvind Rehalia	Bharti Vidyapeeth, New Delhi, India

N. V. Ganapathi Raju	Gokaraju Rangaraju Institute of Engineering and Technology, Hyderabad, India
Anuradha Sharma	IIT, Delhi, India
J. A. Laxminarayana	Goa College of Engineering, India
Arun Kumar	Doon University, Dehradun, India
Arun Sharma	Indira Gandhi Delhi Technical University for Women, New Delhi, India
Chitra Ganesh Desai	Mit, Aurangabad, India
Sathyanarayana S. V.	JNN College of Engineering, Shimoga, India
H. N. Suresh	Bangalore Institute of Technology, India
Rinkle Rani	Thapar University, Patiala, India
Rashid Ali	Aligarh Muslim University, India
Angelina Geetha	B. S. Abdur Rahman University, Chennai, India
Natarajan Meghanathan	Jackson State University, USA
Sanjay Misra	Federal University of Technology, Nigeria
Majid Bakhtiari	University Technology Malaysia, Malaysia
Vigna Kumaran	Universiti Tenaga Nasional, Malaysia
K. Anitha Kumari	PSG College of Technology, Coimbatore, India
B. K. Sarkar	B.I.T., Mesra, India
T. Amudha	Bharathiar University, Coimbatore, India
Amandeep Singh Sappal	Punjabi University, Patiala, India
A. K. Mohapatra	Indira Gandhi Delhi Technical University for Women, New Delhi, India
Y. J. Nagendra Kumar	Gokaraju Rangaraju Institute of Engineering and Technology, Hyderabad, India
Om Prakash Sharma	Poornima College of Engineering, Jaipur, India
Rajesh Bodade	Military College of Telecommunication Engineering, Mhow, India
Lokesh Kumar Bansal	Skyline Institute of Engineering and Technology, Greater Noida, India
A. K. Verma	Thapar University, Patiala, India
Rahila Sheikh	Rajiv Gandhi College of Engineering Research and Technology, Chandrapur, India
Sarat Kr. Chettri	Assam Don Bosco University, Guwahati, India
Sagar Gulati	Technology Education and Research Integrated Institutions, Kurukshetra, India
Geeta Patil	Army Institute of Technology, Pune, India
P. M. Jat	DA-IICT, Gandhinagar, India
Anil Rajput	CSA Govt. PG Nodal College, Sehore, India
Gang Wang	Hefei University of Technology, China
Bharati Ainapure	MITCOE, Pune, India
Priyanka Sharma	Nirma University, Ahmedabad, India
Devendra Kumar Sharma	Meerut Institute of Engineering and Technology, Meerut, India
Geetali Banerji	Institute of Innovation in Technology and Management, New Delhi, India

Sanjeev Dewra	Shaheed Bhagat Singh State Technical Campus, Ferozepur, India
Hazman Yusoff	University Technology Mara Shah Alam, Selangor, Malaysia
Adel Alyan Fahmy	Nuclear Research Center, Atomic Energy Authority, Cairo, Egypt
Piyush Kumar Shukla	Rajiv Gandhi Technological University, Bhopal, India
Noor Elaiza Binti Abdul Khalid	University Technology Mara Shah Alam, Selangor, Malaysia
Rajni	Shaheed Bhagat Singh State Technical Campus, Ferozepur, India
Daya Gupta	Delhi Technological University, Delhi, India
Vandana Niranjan	IGDTUW, New Delhi, India
Jyotirmay Patel	MIET, Meerut, India
Soumen Bag	Indian Institute of Technology (Indian School of Mines), Dhanbad, India
Prabhat Verma	Harcourt Butler Technical University, Kanpur, India
Vitor Hugo Mendes Costa Carvalho	Polytechnic Institute of Cávado and Ave, Portugal
Pradeep Kumar	Maulana Azad National Urdu University, Gachibowli, India
Manoj Kumar Majumder	International Institute of Information Technology, Naya Raipur, India
Ram Shringar Rao	Indira Gandhi National Tribal University, Amarkantak, India
Surya Prakash	Indian Institute of Technology, Indore, India
Chandresh Kumar Chhatlani	Janardan Rai Nagar Rajasthan Vidyapeeth University, Udaipur, India
Satish Kumar Singh	Indian Institute of Information Technology, Allahabad, India
Ravi M Gulati	Veer Narmad South Gujarat University, Surat, India
Ajay Parikh	Gujarat Vidyapith, Ahmedabad, India
Vivek Jaglan	Amity University, Manesar, India
Jayant Umale	Pimpri Chinchwad College of Engineering, Pune, India
Shrivishal Tripathi	Indian Institute of Technology, Jodhpur, India
S. Ghosh	Galgotias University, Greater Noida, India
Manoj Kumar Gupta	KIET, Ghaziabad, India
Sajai Vir Singh	Jaypee Institute of Information Technology, Noida, India
Manoj Kumar Panda	G. B. Pant Engineering College, Garhwal, India
Dhaval R. Kathiriya	Anand Agricultural University, India
Nanhay Singh	Ambedkar Institute of Advanced Communication Technologies and Research, New Delhi, India
Pankaj Kumar	NIT, Rourkela, India
Vishal Nagar	Pranveer Singh Institute of Technology, Kanpur, India
Ashutosh Kumar Bhatt	Birla Institute of Applied Sciences, Nainital, India

Anand K. Tripathi	ITM Group of Institution Technical Campus, Gwalior, India
M. P. Singh	National Institute of Technology, Patna, India
Parminder Kaur	Guru Nanak Dev University, Amritsar, India
Rakesh Chandra Balabantaray	IIIT, Bhubaneswar, India
B. K. Singh	R. B. S. Engineering Technical Campus, Agra, India
R. K. Singla	Panjab University, Chandigarh, India
Devendra Tayal	Indira Gandhi Delhi Technical University for Women, New Delhi, India
Seema Verma	Banasthali Vidyapith, Rajasthan, India
Ashish Sureka	ABB (Research Lab), Bangalore, India
Brijesh Kr. Gupta	BRAANET Technologies Pvt. Ltd., Kanpur, India
T. Kalaiselvi	Gandhigram Rural Institute (Deemed University), Dindigul, India
Diwakar Bhardwaj	GLA University, Mathura, India
Jyoti Prakash Singh	National Institute of Technology, Patna, India
Ajay Verma	Dayalbagh Educational Institute (Deemed University), Agra, India
Tanvir Ahmad	Jamia Millia Islamia, New Delhi, India
Sandeep Paul	Dayalbagh Educational Institute (Deemed University), Agra, India
Ruchi Agarwal	Sharda University, Greater Noida, India
Sunil Sikka	Amity University, Gurgaon, India
Suraiya Jabin	Jamia Millia Islamia, New Delhi, India
Om Prakash Sangwan	Guru Jambheshwer University of Science and Technology, Hissar, India
Sanjeev Kumar	Dr. B. R. Ambedkar University, Agra, India
V. K. Jain	Mody University of Science and Technology, Lakshmangarh, India
Sounak Paul	Birla Institute of Technology International Centre, Oman
Ram K. Pathak	Dr. H S Gour University, Sagar, India
Koukopoulos Dimitrios	University of Patras, Greece
Sushil Kumar	Amity University, Greater Noida, India
Sudeep Tanwar	Nirma University, Ahmedabad, India
Sudipta Roy	Assam University, Silchar, India
Arup Kumar Pal	IIT (ISM), Dhanbad, India
Ashish Kumar	I.T.S. Engineering College, Greater Noida, India
Rudra Mohan Tripathy	Silicon Institute of Technology, Patia, India
R. K. Krishna	R. G. College of Engineering Research and Technology, Chandrapur, India
Amit Sharma	D. C. R. University of Science and Technology, Sonipat, India
Reena Pagare	MITCOE, Pune, India
Balachandra	MIT, Manipal, India

Dhirendra Mishra	Narsee Monjee Institute of Management Studies, Mumbai, India
Mayuri Mehta	SCET, Surat, India
Vimal Bibhu	Amity University, Greater Noida, India
Ningrinla Marchang	North Eastern Regional Institute of Science and Technology, Nirjuli, India
Nitin S. Choubey	MPSTME, Dhule, India
Mohand Lagha	University of Blida, Algeria
Prabhat Sharma	Visvesvaraya National Institute of Technology, Nagpur, India
S. G. Desai	SAL Institute of Technology and Engineering Research, Ahmedabad, India
S. K. Singh	Galgotia College of Engineering and Technology, Greater Noida, India
Brahmjit Singh	National Institute of Technology, Kurukshetra, India
P. Raghu Vamsi	Jaypee Institute of Information Technology, Noida, India
Neha Kishore	Chitkara University, Solan, India
Anil Kumar Yadav	UIET-CSJM University, Kanpur, India
K. Shahu Chatrapati	JNTU, Hyderabad, India
Nikhil Kumar Rajput	University of Delhi, New Delhi, India
Sanjeev Sofat	PEC University of Technology, Chandigarh, India
Dileep Kumar Yadav	Krishna Engineering College, Ghaziabad, India
Kuldeep Kumar	Birla Institute of Technology and Science, Pilani, India
Neetesh Kumar	ABV-Indian Institute of Information Technology and Management, Gwalior, India
Anil K. Ahlawat	KIET Group of Institutions, Ghaziabad, India
Dinesh Kumar Verma	JUET, Guna, India
Sunita Varma	S.G.S.I.T.S., Indore, India
Bipin K. Tripathi	H. B. Technical University, Kanpur, India
Ruqaiya Khanam	Galgotias University, Greater Noida, India
Zhi-Kai Huang	NIT, Nanchang, China
Niyati Baliyan	Thapar University, Patiala, India
Rakesh C. Gangwar	Beant College of Engineering and Technology, Gurdaspur, India
Lavika Goel	Birla Institute of Technology and Science, Pilani, India
R. Venkatesan	Sastra University, Thirumalaisamudram, India
Yogendera Kumar	Galgotias University, Greater Noida, India
K. Valli Madhavi	Chaitanya Engineering College, Visakhapatnam, India
Dilip Debnath	Galgotias University, Greater Noida, India
Ching-Hao Lai	Industrial Technology Research Institute, Taiwan, China
Hashmi S. Asrar	MGM's College of Engineering, Nanded, India
Abhishek Gupta	Poornima College of Engineering, Jaipur, India
Kamlesh Sharma	Lingaya's University, Faridabad, India
Vishal Bhatnagar	AIACT&R, New Delhi, India

Shelly Sachdeva	JIIT, Noida, India
Payal Pahwa	I.P. University, New Delhi, India
J. K. Rai	Amity University, Noida, India
Ajay Shiv Sharma	G.N.D.E.C., Ludhiana, India
Vishal Jain	Bharati Vidyapeeth's Institute of Computer Applications and Management, New Delhi, India
Ripu Ranjan Sinha	SS Jain PG College, Jaipur, India
K. Saravanan	Anna University, Tirunelveli, India
Prateek Jain	Lovely Professional University, Phagwara, India
O. P. Vyas	IIIT, Allahabad, India
Sanjay Kumar	G. B. Pant University of Agriculture and Technology, Pantnagar, India
Narendra Kohli	Harcourt Butler Technical University, Kanpur, India
Der-Chyuan Lou	Chang Gung University, Taiwan
Vishal Goyal	GLA University, Mathura, India
Rajesh Kumar Tripathi	GLA University, Mathura, India
Vikas Kumar	MIT, Moradabad, India
Shanmugam Raju	Amity University, Mumbai, India
Ranjeet Kumar	Indian Institute of Information Technology, Allahabad, India
Sanjeev Sharma	Rajiv Gandhi Technological University, Bhopal, India
Noor Zaman	King Faisal University, Kingdom of Saudi Arabia
Yu-Chen Hu	Providence University, Taichung, China
Misbhauddin Mohammed	King Faisal University, Saudi Arabia
Lenin Mookiah	Tennessee Technical University, USA
Sherin Zafar	Jamia Hamdard University, New Delhi, India
N. Sandhya	Vignana Jyothi Institute of Engineering and Technology, Nizampet, India
Harsh Achrekar	University of Massachusetts Lowell, Washington, USA
C. Kiran Mai	VNR VJIET, Hyderabad, India
M. S. V. Sivarama Bhadri Raju	SRKR Engineering College, Bhimavaram, India
Arvind Jayant	Sant Longowal Institute of Engineering and Technology, Sangrur, India
D. Manivannan	Sastra University, Thanjavur, India
B. Narendra Kumar Rao	Sree Vidyanikethan Engineering College, Tirupati, India
K. Saravanan	Anna University Regional Campus, Tirunelveli, India
U. Karthikeyan	Rajalakshmi Engineering College, Chennai, India
R. Balakrishna	Rajarajeswari College of Engineering, Bengaluru, India
V. Vidhya	Sri Venkateswara College of Engineering, Sriperumbudur, India
S. Vijayalakshmi	Galgotias University, Greater Noida, India
M. Sandhya	B. S. Abdur Rahman University, Chennai, India

K. V. S. N. Rama Rao	A.S.K. Battula Jawaharlal Nehru Institute of Advanced Studies, Hyderabad, India
Alexander Gelbukh	NLP Laboratory, Centro de Investigación en Computación (CIC) of the Instituto Politécnico Nacional (IPN), Mexico
P. Kumar	Rajalakshmi Engineering College, Chennai, India
Rishi Pal Singh	Guru Jambheshwar University of Science and Technology, Hissar, India
P. Alli	Velammal College of Engineering and Technology, Madurai, India
Santhi Thilagam	N.I.T.K, Surathkal, India
Kishore Kumar Senapati	Birla Institute of Technology, Mesra, India
Kiran Kumar Pattanaik	Indian Institute of Information Technology and Management, Gwalior, India
Jitender Rai	GGSIPU University, New Delhi, India
S. Geetha	VIT University, Chennai, India
Ranjit Rajak	Dr. Harisingh Gour University, Sagar, India
P. K. Jawahar	B. S. Abdur Rahman University, Chennai, India
Ramakanthkumar P.	R. V. College of Engineering, Bangalore, India
Hanumanthappa M.	Bangalore University, India
C. Tharini	B. S. Abdur Rahman University, Chennai, India
Ch. Bindu Madhuri	JNTU, Kakinada, India
A. Hemlata	Jabalpur Engineering College, Jabalpur, India
A. V. Krishna Prasad	M.V.S.R. Engineering College, Hyderabad, India
K. Sankar	Sri Venkateswara College of Engineering and Technology, Thiruvallur, India
Satyajee Srivastava	Galgotias University, Greater Noida, India
S. N. Panda	Chitkara University, Patiala, India
Sunanda Dixit	DSCE, Bangalore, India
K. Venkatachalam	VCET, Vasai, India
Alireza Haghpeima	Islamic Azad University of Mashhad, Iran
Chandra Kanta Samal	University of Delhi, New Delhi, India
G. Suseendarn	Vels University, Chennai, India
Manju Khari	Ambedkar Institute of Advance Communication Technologies and Research, Delhi, India
Aruna Devi	Surabhi Softwares, Mysore, India
Ashish Sharma	Jodhpur National University, India
R. V. Jaya Sree	Panimalar Institute of Technology, Chennai, India
Goutham Reddy Alavalapati	Kyungpook National University, South Korea
Prathamesh Karmakar	Veda Semantics, Bangalore, India
Kannan Sethuraman	Mavreic Systems Ltd., Chennai, India
Kamal Kant Sharma	Chandigarh University, India
Seema Maitrey	Krishna Institute of Engineering and Technology, Ghaziabad, India

Rajan Patel	Sankalchand Patel College of Engineering, Visnagar, India
Ankit Mundra	Manipal University, Jaipur, India
Raghvendra Kumar	LNCT Group of College, Jabalpur, India
Vithal Madyalkar	IBM Innovation Center for Education, India
Anita Sahoo	JSS Academy of Technical Education, Noida, India
Rama Challa	NITTTR, Chandigarh, India
Abishi Chowdhury	NITTTR, Bhopal, India
Shibendu Debbarma	Tripura University, Agartala, India
Suchi Johari	Jaypee University of Information Technology, Waknaghat, India
Sanjay Kumar	Pandit Ravishankar Shukla University, Raipur, India
Hari Mewara	Government Engineering College, Ajmer, India
Samaresh Mishra	KIIT University, Patia, India
Atul Sharma	Kurukshetra University, Kurukshetra, India
Vijander Singh	Amity University, Jaipur, India
Ankur Bist	KIET, Ghaziabad, India
Nguyen Cuong	Quang Nam University, Vietnam
Surinder Khurana	Central University of Punjab, Bathinda, India
Sanjaya Kumar Panda	Veer Surendra Sai University of Technology, Burla, India
Ashutosh Tripathi	Amity University, Jaipur, India
Mithun Mukherjee	Guangdong University of Petrochemical Technology, China
Vandita Singh	JEMTEC, G. Noida, India
Bhupendra Singh	CDAC, Noida, India
Pratiyush Guleria	NIELIT, DOEACC Society, India
Saiyedul Islam	BITS, Pilani, India
Rajat Saxena	Indian Institute of Technology, Indore, India
Debi Prasad Mishra	College of Engineering and Technology, Bhubaneswar, India
Suket Arora	Amritsar College of Engineering and Technology, Amritsar, India
Mohit Dua	National Institute of Technology, Kurukshetra, India
Ankit Jain	National Institute of Technology, Kurukshetra, India
Vijay Verma	National Institute of Technology, Kurukshetra, India
Sumit Yadav	Indira Gandhi Delhi Technical University for Women, New Delhi, India
Kaushlendra Pandey	Cental Institute of Technology, Kokrajhar, India
Bhawna Ahuja	Amity School of Engineering and Technology, New Delhi, India
Shaveta Tatwani	Amity School of Engineering and Technology, New Delhi, India
Gautam Kumar	Galgotias University, Grater Noida, India
Vishnu Pratap Patel	DRDO, Hyderabad, India
Priyank Jain	AVP, Barclays, Mumbai, India

Ashok Yadav	Amity School of Engineering and Technology, New Delhi, India
Mukul Kumar Yadav	DEITY, New Delhi, India
Neelam Choudhary	Suresh Gyan Vihar University, Jaipur, India
Deepak Agarwal	Poornima College of Engineering, Jaipur, India
Mayank Sharma	Poornima College of Engineering, Jaipur, India
Shakti Arora	Panipat Institute of Engineering and Technology, India
Rahul Hada	Criterion Networks, Bangalore, India
Neha Mathur	Poornima College of Engineering, Jaipur, India
Ashish Sharma	Maharaja Agrasen Institute of Technology, New Delhi, India
Anuj Aggarwal	KITM, Kurukshetra, India
Lalit B. Damahe	Yeshwantrao Chavan College of Engineering, Nagpur, India
Prashant Modi	U. V. Patel College of Engineering, Mehsana, India
Mukesh Kalla	SPSU, Udaipur, India
Debabrata Chowdhury	Kalyani Govt. Engineering College, Nadia, India
Nikita Chavan	G. H. Raisoni College of Engineering, Nagpur, India
Gurmeet Singh	KITM, Kurukshetra, India
Arun Malik	Lovely Professional University, Jalandhar, India
Kanwar Pal	G.L. Bajaj Institute of Technology and Management, Noida, India
Arvind Dhingra	Guru Nanak Dev Engineering College, Ludhiana, India
Arun Kumar M. V.	Bapuji Polytechnic, Davangere, India
Rajat Singh	Theem College of Engineering, Thane, India
Umesh L. Kulkarni	VIT Wadala, Vellore, India
Suhas Bhagate	D.K.T.E Society's Textile and Engineering Institute, Kolhapur, India
Aparajita Pandey	B.I.T., Mesra, India
Sanjeev Yadav	Govt. Women Engineering College, Ajmer, India
A. Sajeevram	VELS University, Chennai, India
Ashok Kumar	Govt. Women Engineering College, Ajmer, India
Supriya M.	Amrita School of Engineering, Bengaluru, India
G. Yogarajan	Mepco Schlenk Engineering College, Sivakasi, India
Swagata Paul	Techno India College of Technology, Kolkata, India
Rakesh Sharma	CRM Jat College, Hissar, India
Ashim Saha	National Institute of Technology, Agartala, India
Ashok Kumar	Ambala College of Engineering and Applied Research, Ambala, India
Arunvinodh C.	Al-Ameen Engineering College, Shoranur, India
Deepak Kumar	Panipat Institute of Engineering and Technology, India
Sandeep Singh Bindra	Panipat Institute of Engineering and Technology, India
Arun Rana	Panipat Institute of Engineering and Technology, India
Ashish Upadhyay	Alstom India, Bangalore, India
Ramkrishna Vadali	Pimpri Chinchwad College of Engineering, Pune, India
Ripon Patgiri	National Institute of Technology, Silchar, India

Neha Bajpai	CDAC, Noida, India
C. Radha Charan	JNT University, Hyderabad, India
Trupti Kodinariya	Government Engineering College, Rajkot, India
Deepa Abin	Pimpri Chinchwad College of Engineering, Pune, India
Dharmendra Gupta	Chameli Devi Group of Institution, Indore, India
Ashish Vashishth	KITM, Kurukshetra, India
Nihar Ranjan Roy	GD Goenka University, Gurgaon, India
Nandini Sharma	SRCEM, Palwal, India
Girish Paliwal	Amity University, Jaipur, India
Shrikant Ardhapurkar	Yeshwantrao Chavan College of Engineering, Nagpur, India
P. S. Bogawar	Priyadarshini College of Engineering, Nagpur, India
Nilesh Patel	JUET, Guna, India
Aditya Dev Mishra	Galgotias University, Greater Noida, India
Purnima Sharma	Mody University of Science and Technology, Lakshmangarh, India
Rohini G. Pise	Pimpri Chinchwad College of Engineering, Pune, India
Kalyani Pendke	Rajiv Gandhi College of Engineering, Nagpur, India
Chaitra D. Desai	REVA University, Bengaluru, India
Anita Thengade	MITCOE, Pune, India
Ahmed Mateen Buttar	University of Agriculture, Faisalabad, Pakistan
Archana Kadam	Pimpri Chinchwad College of Engineering, Pune, India
Rashmi Thakur	Thakur College of Engg and Technology, Mumbai, India
Vikram Singh	National Institute of Technology, Kurukshetra, India
Madhuri Sachin Wakode	Pune Institute of Computer Technology, Pune, India
Sumitra Purushottam Pundlik	MITCOE, Pune, India
Deepali Javale	MITCOE, Pune, India
H. R. Mhaske	Pimpri Chinchwad College of Engineering, Pune, India
Kranti Dive	MITCOE, Pune, India
Vimal Gupta	JSS Academy of Technical Education, Noida, India
S. Prakash	M.M.M. University of Technology, Gorakhpur, India
Manoj Kumar	Shri Mata Vaishno Devi University, Katra, India
Anagha Chaudhari	Pimpri Chinchwad College of Engineering, Pune, India
Sameer Saxena	Amity University, Jaipur, India
Xavier Arputha Rathina	B. S. Abdur Rahman University, Chennai, India
Ashok Kumar Sahoo	Sharda University, Greater Noida, India
Sangeetha B	PSG College of Technology, Coimbatore, India
Suman Saurabh	Sapient, New Delhi, India
I. Joe Louis Paul	SSN College of Engineering, Kalavakkam, India
Emmanuel Shubhakar Pilli	MNIT, Jaipur, India
Mahendra P. Dhore	Rashtrasant Tukadoji Maharaj Nagpur University Campus, India
R. V. Bidwe	PICT, Pune, India
Poulami Dutta	Techno India University, Kolkata, India

Joish George	KMEA Engg College, Aluva, India
C. M. Sharma	Bhagwan Parshuram Institute of Technology, New Delhi, India
Prasad Halgaonkar	MITCOE, Pune, India
Sumit Dhariwal	SGI, Bhopal, India
Abhishek Bajpai	SRM University, Lucknow, India
Manuj Aggarwal	ARSD College, New Delhi, India
Tarun Goyal	AIETM, Jaipur, India
Mohd Imran	Aligarh Muslim University, Aligarh, India
Rakesh Garg	Hindu College of Engineering, Murthal, India
Kailash Chander	Haryana Space Applications Centre (HARSAC)-DST-Govt. of Haryana, Hissar, India
Kapil Mehta	Gian Jyoti Group of Institutions, Shambu Kalan, India
Shivani	Dhi India Water and Environment Pvt. Ltd., India
Mradul Dhakar	Madhav Institute of Technology and Science, Gwalior, India
Rohit Beniwal	Delhi Technological University, New Delhi, India
Vedika Gupta	National Institute of Technology, Delhi, India
Amrit Pal Singh	Guru Govind Singh Indraprastha University, New Delhi, India
Surya Kant Singh	GLA University, Mathura, India
Syed Aamiruddin	Guru Govind Singh Indraprastha University, New Delhi, India
Swati Sharma	Delhi Technological University, New Delhi, India
Deepti Chopra	Indraprastha College for Women, New Delhi, India
Rohini Sharma Ohlan	Jawahar Lal Nehru University, New Delhi, India
Anuradha Singhal	University of Delhi, New Delhi, India
Swati Chauhan	K.I.E.T, Ghaziabad, India
Dinesh Kumar Yadav	University of Delhi, New Delhi, India
Vidhi Khanduja	NSIT, New Delhi, India
Sandhya Pundhir	Aligarh Muslim University, Aligarh, India
Jyoti Shokeen	MDU, Rohtak, India
Suvadip Batabyal	BITS PILANI, Hyderabad, India
J. K. Verma	Deen Dayal Upadhyaya College, New Delhi, India
Dheeraj Malhotra	Guru Govind Singh Indraprastha University, New Delhi, India
Sumit K Yadav	IGDTUW, New Delhi, India
Manish Kamboj	PEC University of Technology, Chandigarh, India
Prem Shankar	Delhi Technical University, New Delhi, India
Rashmi Sharma	KIET Group of Institutions, Ghaziabad, India
Satish Chhokar	RKGIT, Ghaziabad, India
Anju Saha	Guru Govind Singh Indraprastha University, New Delhi, India
Swati Chandurkar	Pimpri Chinchwad College of Engineering, Pune, India
Chandresh Kumar Maurya	IBM Research, Bangalore, India
Dhananjaya Singh	Delhi University, New Delhi, India

Jagdeep Kaur	The NorthCap University, Gurugram, India
Chandra Shekhar Yadav	SLIET, Longowal, India
Shailendra S. Aote	Rajiv Gandhi College of Engineering and Research, Wanadongri, India
Poonam Sharma	Sharda University, Greater Noida, India
Deepak Mehta	Lovely Professional University, Phagwara, India
Sarnam Singh	BHU, Varanasi, India
Shruti Jaiswal	Delhi Technological University, New Delhi, India
Amit Patel	RGUKT IIIT, Nuzvid, India
A. K. Maurya	Shri Ramswaroop Memorial University, Lucknow, India
M. V. Kamal	Malla Reddy College of Engineering & Technology, Hyderabad, India
Nicy Kaur Taneja	Media Lab Asia, New Delhi, India
Jyoti Sahni	The Northcap University, Gurugram, India
Priya Singh	Path Infotech, Noida, India
Gaurav Agrawal	Inderprastha Engineering College, Ghaziabad, India
Srishti Sharma	NSIT, New Delhi, India
Shivani Saluja	Gdgoenka University, Gurgaon, India
Vaibhav Muddebihalkar	Savitribai Phule University of Pune, Pune, India
Ramandeep Singh	Lewis University, Illinois, USA
Jobin George	GL Bajaj Institute of Engineering and Technology, Greater Noida, India
Narayan Chaturvedi	Graphics Era University, Dehradun, India
N. Suresh Kumar	Gitam University, Visakhapatnam, India
Rajesh Sharma	Dr. B.R. Ambedkar Govt. Polytechnic, Una, India
Rupesh Kumar Jindal	Sharda University, Greater Noida, India
Sunil Kumar Chawla	Chandigarh Group of Colleges - College of Engineering, Chandigarh, India
Tarun Kanti Bhattacharjee	C3I Healthcare Ltd, Hyderabad, India
Abhay Katiyar	Jabalpur Engg. College, Jabalpur, India
Anand Nayyar	KCL Institute of Management and Technology, Jalandhar, India
Sanjoy Debnath	PwC, Kolkata, India
Vivek Parashar	Amity University, Gwalior, India
V. Srihariraju	Parexel International, India
H. Marathe	Paladion Networks, India
Chintan M. Bhatt	Charotar University of Science and Technology, Changa, India
Srishti Sharma	The Northcap University, Gurgaon, India
Smith Gonsalves	National Cyber Defence & Research Centre, India
Arvind Kumar	Espire Infolabs Pvt. Ltd., Gurugram, India
Nitish Ojha	Chandigarh University, Chandigarh, India
Shaligram Prajapat	International Institute of Professional Studies Devi Ahilya University, Indore, India
Pooja Batra Nagpal	Amity University, Gurgaon, India

Anand Singh Gadwal	SIRT, Indore, India
Sirisha Velampalli	JNTU-K, Kakinada, India
Milan Goyal	Jaipur, India
Amit Andre	Vinsy, New Jersey, USA
Manisha Saini	G.D. Goenka University, Gurgaon, India
Manik Sharma	DAV University, Jalandhar, India
G. Suseendran	VELS University, Chennai, India
Tanupriya Choudhury	Amity University, Noida, India
Kamal Kumar Ranga	Delhi University, New Delhi, India
Aditya Patel	Relicmail Software Solution, Jabalpur, India
T. R. V. Anandharajan	Einstein College of Engineering, Tirunelveli, India
Navnish Goel	S. D. College of Engineering and Technology, Muzaffarnagar, India
Krishan Kant Singh Gautam	Shivaji College, Delhi, India
Sudhanshu Kumar Jha	National Institute of Technology Jamshedpur, Jamshedpur, India
Hariharan Ravi	St. Joseph's College of Commerce, Bangalore, India
Gopi Krishna Durbhaka	TCS, Pune, India
Kusum Yadav	University of Hail, Kingdom of Saudi Arabia
S. Balan	Government Arts College, Coimbatore, India
Jeevan Das Koli	Scientific Analysis Group, DRDO, New Delhi, India
Abdul Jabbar Shaikh Azad	Kasturi Shikshan Santha's Arts, Commerce and Science College, Pune, India
Rajarshi Bhatraju	IBM, Hyderabad, India
Hemant Gupta	Seven N India Pvt Ltd., Gurgaon, India
Rashmi Agrawal	Manav Rachna International University, Faridabad, India
Nisha Thakur	Armacell Pvt Ltd., Pune, India
Charu Sharma	IMS, Ghaziabad, India
Nilam Choudhary	VIT (East), Jaipur, India
Syed Abudhagir Umar	B. V. Raju Institute of Technology, Hyderabad, India
Shruti Mathur	JERC University, Jaipur, India
Shakti Ranjan	Emoksha, Chandigarh, India
Praveen Gupta	VIT East, Jaipur, India
K. M. Mehata	Hindustan University, Chennai, India
Chitra A. Dhawale	P. R. Pote College of Engineering and Management, Amravati, India
Anwesa Das	NFET, NSHM Knowledge Campus, Durgapur, India
Ajay Prasad	University of Petroleum and Energy Studies, Dehradun, India
Abhijit Kumar	University of Petroleum and Energy Studies, Dehradun, India
Inder Singh	University of Petroleum and Energy Studies, Dehradun, India
Kingshuk Srivastava	University of Petroleum and Energy Studies, Dehradun, India

Hitesh Kumar Sharma	University of Petroleum and Energy Studies, Dehradun, India
Madhushi Verma	University of Petroleum and Energy Studies, Dehradun, India
J. C. Patni	University of Petroleum and Energy Studies, Dehradun, India
Ankur Dumka	University of Petroleum and Energy Studies, Dehradun, India
Ved Prakash	University of Petroleum and Energy Studies, Dehradun, India
Monit Kapoor	University of Petroleum and Energy Studies, Dehradun, India
Rajeev Tiwari	University of Petroleum and Energy Studies, Dehradun, India
Neeraj Chugh	University of Petroleum and Energy Studies, Dehradun, India
Amitava Choudhury	University of Petroleum and Energy Studies, Dehradun, India
Susheela Dahiya	University of Petroleum and Energy Studies, Dehradun, India
B. Surekha	K.S. Institute of Technology, Bangalore, India
Neha Gulati	University Business School, Panjab University, Chandigarh, India
Pooja Jain	S.V.V.V. University, Indore, India
Bright Keswani	Suresh Gyan Vihar University, Jaipur, India
Sumitra Pundlik	M.I.T.COE, Pune, India
Amit Banerjee	Innovative Photonics Evolution Research Center, Shizuoka, Japan
S. Palaniyappan	TRP Engineering College, Tiruchirappalli, India
Neetu Mishra	IIIT, Allahabad, India
Akhilesh Kumar Sharma	Manipal University, Jaipur, India
Mohd Vasim Ahamad	University Women's Polytechnic, Aligarh, India
Atul M. Gonsai	Saurashtra University, Rajkot, India
Siddharth S. Rautaray	KIIT University, Bhubaneswar, India
Praveen Kumar	Amity School of Engineering and Technology, Noida, India
Manisha Rathee	NIT, New Delhi, India
Venkatesh Gauri Shankar	Manipal University, Jaipur, India
Ujjwal Maulik	Jadavpur University, India
Arvind Kumar	Government College, Solan, India
Swati Gupta	Panipat Institute of Engineering and Technology, Panipat, India
Narendra Kohli	Harcourt Butler Technical University, Kanpur, India
Ambika Annavarapu	Kakatiya Institute of Institute and Sciences, Warangal, India
Prachi Gupta	ICFAI University, Dehradun, India

Nitish Mittal	Noon.com, Dubai, UAE
Kannimuthu	Karpagam College of Engineering, Coimbatore, India
Pranjal Bogawar	R.T.M. Nagpur University, Nagpur, India
Wenjun Hu	Palo Alto Networks, Santa Clara, USA
Kalavathi P.	Gandhigram Rural Institute - Deemed University, Dindigul, India
Ashutosh Kumar Bhatt	Birla Institute of Applied Sciences, Bhimtal, India
Furkan Ahmad	AMU, Aligarh, India
Rajeev Gupta	Maharishi Markandeshwar University, Mullana (Ambala), India
Krishna Kumar Singh	RGUKT Nuzvid, India
E. Golden Julie	Anna University Tirunelveli, India
Chandra Kanta Samal	Delhi University, New Delhi, India
Neha Verma	VIPS, Affiliated to Guru Gobind Singh Indraprastha University, Delhi, India
Varsha Garg	Jaypee Institute of Information Technology, Noida, India
Mala Kalra	NITTTR, Chandigarh, India
Kumar Anurupam	Rgukt-Iiit, Nuzvid, India
Arputha Rathina	B. S. Abdur Rahman Crescent University, Chennai, India
R. China Appala Naidu	St. Martin's Engineering College, Hyderabad, India

Organizing Committee

Convener(s)

Hanumat G. Sastry	UPES, Dehradun, India
Venkatadri M.	UPES, Dehradun, India

Publication Chair(s)

Neelu Jyoti Ahuja	UPES, Dehradun, India
Raghvendra Kumar	LNCT Group, India
Hitesh Kumar Sharma	UPES, Dehradun, India

Web Master

Ravi Tomar	UPES, Dehradun, India

Joint Secretary(s)

Sunil Kumar	UPES, Dehradun, India
Ankit Khare	UPES, Dehradun, India

Technical Program Sub-Committee

Sumit Kumar	UPES, Dehradun, India
P. Srikanth	UPES, Dehradun, India
Aradhana Singh	UPES, Dehradun, India
Amitava Chowdary	UPES, Dehradun, India
Sunil Kumar	UPES, Dehradun, India
Ankit Khare	UPES, Dehradun, India

Members

Anurag Jain	UPES, Dehradun, India
J. C. Patni	UPES, Dehradun, India
Kingshuk Srivastava	UPES, Dehradun, India
Nilima Salankar Fulmare	UPES, Dehradun, India
Rajeev Tiwari	UPES, Dehradun, India
Shamik Tiwari	UPES, Dehradun, India
Susheela Dahiya	UPES, Dehradun, India
Tanmay Bhowmik	UPES, Dehradun, India
Abhijeet Kumar	UPES, Dehradun, India
Abhijit Kumar	UPES, Dehradun, India
Alok Jhaldiyal	UPES, Dehradun, India
Amitava Chaudhary	UPES, Dehradun, India
Ankit Vishanoi	UPES, Dehradun, India
Bhagwant Singh	UPES, Dehradun, India
Deepak Sharma	UPES, Dehradun, India
Gagan Deep Singh	UPES, Dehradun, India
Harvinder Singh	UPES, Dehradun, India
Neeraj Chugh	UPES, Dehradun, India
Nitin Arora	UPES, Dehradun, India
P. Srikant	UPES, Dehradun, India
Prashant Rawat	UPES, Dehradun, India
Sandeep Partap	UPES, Dehradun, India
Sandip Kumar Chaurasiya	UPES, Dehradun, India
Saurabh Jain	UPES, Dehradun, India
Saurabh Shanu	UPES, Dehradun, India
Vishwas Rathi	UPES, Dehradun, India
Varun Sapra	UPES, Dehradun, India
Ambika Agarwal	UPES, Dehradun, India
Anushree	UPES, Dehradun, India
Apurva Gupta	UPES, Dehradun, India
Aradhana Singh	UPES, Dehradun, India
Kalpana Rangra	UPES, Dehradun, India
Niharika Singh	UPES, Dehradun, India
Prerna Pandey	UPES, Dehradun, India
Richa Chaudhary	UPES, Dehradun, India

Roohi Sille	UPES, Dehradun, India
Ruchika Saini	UPES, Dehradun, India
Sachi Chaudhary	UPES, Dehradun, India
Shahina Anwarul	UPES, Dehradun, India
Sheetal Bisht	UPES, Dehradun, India
Shelly	UPES, Dehradun, India
Dhiviya Rose	UPES, Dehradun, India

Contents – Part II

Smart and Innovative Trends in Security and Privacy

Smart and Innovative Trends in Image Processing and Machine Vision

Contents – Part I

Smart and Innovative Trends in Natural Language Processing

Smart and Innovative Trends in Communication Protocols and Standards

IEEMARP: Improvised Energy Efficient Multipath Ant Colony Optimization (ACO) Routing Protocol for Wireless Sensor Networks

Anand Nayyar[1]($\boxtimes$) and Rajeshwar Singh[2]

[1] Desh Bhagat University, Mandi Gobindgarh, India
anand_nayyar@yahoo.co.in
[2] Doaba Group of Colleges, Nawanshahr, Punjab, India
rajeshwar.rajata@gmail.com

Abstract. Wireless Sensor Networks (WSNs) being special type of wireless communication networks, characterized via various specific features like Limited Memory, Energy, Less Processing power. In Wireless Sensor Networks, every sensor node actively participates in routing work by forwarding the packets from sender to receiver and the packet forwarding is entirely based on network topology. One of the most important issue surrounding WSNs is Energy Efficiency and Efficient Routing mechanism which should be dynamic and efficient enough to handle changing topologies. So, there is utmost need for optimization techniques which can lay the foundation of development of suitable routing protocol to attain energy efficiency and routing in sensor networks. Swarm Intelligence is one the most important technique which is highly considered for developing energy efficient routing protocols. Considering Swarm Intelligence, Ant Colony Optimization (ACO) technique is utilized to propose Energy Efficient protocol for WSN. In this paper, a Novel Energy Efficient Routing Protocol based on ACO for WSN is proposed i.e. IEEMARP (Improvised Energy Efficient Multipath Ant Based Routing Protocol). Hardcore testing of protocol proposed i.e. IEEMARP is done in different simulation scenarios using NS-2 simulator on varied parameters like Packet Delivery Ratio, Throughput, Routing Overhead, Energy Consumption and End-To-End Delay and performance is compared with other routing protocols like Basic ACO, DSDV, DSR, ACEAMR, Ant Chain, EMCBR and IACR. The results states that IEEMARP is almost 7 to 10 times better in different parameters. It has also been observed that IEEMARP routing protocol is also efficient in transmitting TCP packets.

Keywords: Sensor networks · Wireless Sensor Networks · ACO
Routing · Pheromone table · IEEMARP · Energy Efficiency · NS-2
ACEAMRA · IACR · EMCBR · Ant chain · DSDV · DSR · AODV
Routing protocol

© Springer Nature Singapore Pte Ltd. 2018
P. Bhattacharyya et al. (Eds.): NGCT 2017, CCIS 828, pp. 3–24, 2018.
https://doi.org/10.1007/978-981-10-8660-1_1

1 Introduction

Wireless Sensor Networks (WSN) [1–3] are sophisticated next generation sensor networks, integrating various technologies like Sensors, Wireless Communication Network, MEMS technology [4, 5]. WSNs encourage tons of novel and existing applications like Environmental Monitoring, Military, Health-care, industrial production, safe public transportation, smart homes and space technology [6]. Wireless Sensor Networks have enabled highly compact and self-autonomous sensor nodes, each node containing different sensors and have additional functionalities in terms of computation, communication and limited power supply [7]. Conserving energy and balancing power consumption among sensor nodes in entire network is the first and foremost goal to improve overall lifetime of sensor network.

Wireless Sensor Networks (WSNs) consists of few to tons of hundreds and thousands of sensors working cooperatively in particular geographic area to get live data from surroundings. Particularly, two types of sensor networks exist: Structured and Unstructured. In Unstructured WSN, nodes are installed in ad-hoc fashion and once deployed the network can perform monitoring and communication operations without any interference. This network face limitation in terms of failure detection as numbers of nodes is very large. In Structured WSN, few sensor nodes are installed after proper planning and the overall cost and maintenance of this type of network is usually very small.

WSN Technology offers unique advantages as compared to traditional networks in terms of less costs, scalability, efficiency, accuracy, robustness, flexibility and above all ease of deployment. WSN being promising technology to bring revolution in near future especially in terms of Medical technology, Smart Cities development in order to transform the world. Research in WSN aims to meet various limitations in terms of designing new concepts, improvising or developing new routing protocols, new applications development and innovating new algorithms.

WSN networks are highly mobile and dynamic, so finding the optimal path in terms of energy efficiency becomes highly complex. Every sensor node performs the task of routing the packets between source to destination node. As the network packets travel in network, various issues in terms of Packet Delay (Time taken by network packets to reach destination), Energy Efficiency (Battery consumed by sensor nodes to transport the packets), Packet Loss (Dropping of packets in transmission process), Latency and other issues occur which impacts the overall performance and reliability of network. So, sophisticated methodologies and measures are required to combat these issues to make WSN network overall dynamic, robust, energy efficient and highly scalable.

Routing is one of the central issues to be addressed and lots of researchers have proposed novel routing protocols. Data flow between sensor nodes is basically performed via conventional multipath routing protocols like AOMDV which uses same path for transmission in all scenarios. The shortcoming for using AOMDV routing protocol is excessive energy utilization, failure of nodes and partitioning of network which impacts the overall network. Todays, WSN network demand optimal paths changing as per transmission requirements, energy efficiency, less packet loss and proper load balancing. Swarm Intelligence oriented routing protocols [18, 19, 31, 32] -

Ant Colony Optimization, Bee Colony Optimization are best in terms of energy efficiency, packet transfer and load balancing. Ant Colony Optimization based techniques and methodologies [8] are used in several domains cum disciplines to find solutions to tough problems. ACO technique [10–12] basically revolves around studying the behavior and pattern of biological ants to search for food stuff roaming randomly in the environment and their collective behavior to transport the food from source to nest in optimal manner via Pheromone trail based technique.

Ant Colony Optimization (ACO) [9, 13, 14, 19, 29, 30, 39] is based on ants foraging behavior roaming arbitrarily in environment in search for food and upon discovering the food source, returning back to nest leaving behind a trail of chemical substance called "Pheromone" [15–17] for other ants to follow. As, other ants start moving, the routes longer from nest to source loose pheromone as pheromone evaporates guiding the ants to choose the best shortest path.

Stigmergy [20–22] is associated with two common words: "Stigma" and "Ergon" meaning "Stimulation by work". It is combination of Positive and Negative feedback, Multiple Interactions and Randomness.

Swarm Intelligence [19, 23–25] lays the strong foundation of algorithms for distributed optimization and control which ultimately leads to design and development of various routing algorithms/protocols for WSN.

Considering Swarm Intelligence based technique Ant Colony Optimization as prime source of motivation, we propose IEEMARP- ACO based routing protocol for sensor networks. The protocol is suitably evaluated in diverse scenarios using various simulation parameters. The results obtained via novel proposed protocol i.e. IEEMARP is compared with other existing novel routing protocols like Basic ACO, Ant Chain, EMCBR, ACEAMR, IACR protocol on various parameters. The results obtained show the proposed protocol i.e. IEEMARP is quite effective as compared to other protocols in selected schemes.

The Research paper is drafted in following sequence: Sect. 2 presents Literature Review. Section 3 underlines the Design Parameters, Algorithm & Overall scenario flow of IEEMARP Routing Protocol. Section 4 outlines Simulation based results and protocol performance analysis on diverse parameters. Section 5 is devoted to conclusion and future directions.

2 Literature Review

Ant Colony Optimization [14] is completely laid on Ant foraging. Ant Colony System [26–28] is strong example of distributed biological system by which ants via mutual cooperation complete complex tasks which a single individual is almost incompetent to complete. When ants move out from nest in real world environment, in search for food release chemical substance called "Pheromone" [33–35] which is highly volatile. The path is followed by large number of ants which raises the pheromone level and majority of ants follow the same path. Finally, ants will determine the optimal path via cooperation.

Gunes et al. [36] proposed Ant Colony Based Routing Algorithm (ARA). ARA, on-demand algorithm to Adhoc networks in which routing discovery totally relies on forward and backward ants. In Route discovery, ARA protocol broadcasts forward ants which carries a unique sequence number. If a node receives forward ant that it has never got, it creates a reverse path and rebroadcasts the ant to its neighbors. If the node has received duplicate ant, it will drop the ant. On reaching the destination, the forward ant transforms itself to backward ant and traverses the path to nest backwards. If the intermediate node receives the backward ant, it creates a path to destination node (including next hop, destination and pheromone) and continues the transmission along with reverse path. The intermediate nodes create the respective routing tables. The multipath to the destination node can be formed. Simulation results showed that ARA protocol is efficient as compared to DSR, AODV and DSDV routing protocol.

Shah and Rabaey [37] proposed Energy Aware Routing. The approach is highly useful for less energy and low bit rate networks. Simulation results presents EAR scheme produces an increase of overall 40% network lifetime increase as compared to DD routing scheme.

Hussein and Saadawi [38] proposed Ant Routing Algorithm for Mobile Adhoc Networks (ARAMA). When a node needs to establish a path to destination node, it transmits a forward ant to a neighbor node rather than flooding. Intermediate Node ID's are appended to forward ant along with other information like hops, energy left over, bandwidth, queue length. ARAMA is based on grade and the value is calculated by backward ant and saved in nodes. The formula of grade lies on link information such as energy. When backward ant reaches intermediate node, the pheromone values are updated. The backward ants are dropped on reaching the destination. The data gets transmitted in optimal path.

Camilo et al. [40] proposed Energy Efficient Ant Based routing (EEABR) protocol. Every sensor node in the network launches a forward ant at regular intervals to determine optimal route. Every ant carries the address of the last visited nodes. Every time, a node receives ant, it looks up the entry in routing table. If no loop exists, it adds the entry to the table the information of ant and timer restarts and forwards the ant to next hop. When the forward ant reaches the destination, it is converted to backward ant and lay the pheromone trail on every hop till reaches the nest. EEABR protocol is compared by author with BABR and IABR and results show EEABR is efficient in maintaining energy level of nodes in overall network.

Patel et al. [41] proposed EMCBR protocol. EMCBR is fast, scalable and avoids congestion, delay and improves overall QoS of routing in WSN.

Xia and Wu [42] proposed ACO-EAMRA. In this algorithm, the authors optimized state transition rule and global pheromone update rule. Two parameters q and qo were added in the algorithm to improvise the state transition rule and ants possibility to determine best route. The protocol modifies the pheromone of each edge. ACO-EAMRA Algorithm will repeat N number of times to get optimal global routing path.

Peng et at. [43] proposed IACR protocol. The protocol considers QoS along with balancing energy level of nodes. The protocol constitutes two parts: Route Discovery and Route Maintenance. The algorithm is preferred for performing real-time multimedia activities like Voice Streaming, Video Streaming.

3   IEEEMARP- Improved Energy Efficient Multipath Ant Colony Based Routing Protocol for Wireless Sensor Networks

In this section, IEEMARP- Energy Efficient Multipath Ant Colony Based Routing Protocol for Wireless Sensor Networks will be covered- Design Parameters, Algorithm, Protocol phases and Properties of protocol proposed.

3.1   Design Parameter

STEP 1:   Suppose S being the source node want to transmit some data D being destination node with considering all QoS parameters like Energy Efficiency, faster transmission rate, avoidance of delay and quality bandwidth. The nodes visited by ants following the path from Node S to Node D are called Visiting nodes and list of visiting nodes is prepared. Visiting nodes list takes the form of multipath route table Rt.

STEP 2:   Node S is taken as initial node from where the transmission will start and will also initialize neighbor discovery process.

STEP 3:   Node S will initialize and transmit a Fant (Forward Ant- Route Request) to reach node D through via all path nodes at 1-hop distance from Node S. The Fant contains various parameters like address of source node, address of destination node, hop count and network speed.

STEP 4:   On pheromone evaporation, evaluation of 1-hop distance nodes will be performed. Each node 'i' maintains a table called "Pheromone Table", specifying the amount of available pheromone on every link (). This quantity is initialized to constant C.

$$\text{Ph}(i,j) = Ph(i,j) = \frac{[\tau_{i,j}]^{\alpha} \cdot [\eta_{i,j}]^{\beta}}{\sum_{k \in M} [\tau_{i,k}]^{\alpha} \cdot [\eta_{i,k}]^{\beta}} \tag{1}$$

$\tau_{i,j} \rightarrow i_s$ the amount of pheromone on the link.

$\eta_{i,j} \rightarrow$ link visibility.

α and β states the importance of pheromone to determine efficient route paths.

$M \rightarrow$ regarded as the set of nodes Vk, not traversed by ant during packet transmission.

STEP 5:   Calculation of pheromone evaporation of all 2-hop distance sensor nodes in the network.

STEP 6:   The path preference probability value of each path from source S with the help of pheromone evaporation of every node. A node j from a set of adjacent nodes (j, k … n) of i is selected as MPR node such that it covers all the 2-hop distance nodes and its path preference probability is better than others.

STEP 7:   If, path preference probability amount is higher as compared to predefined requirements, the path gets accepted and proceed with memory storage for effective utilization.

STEP 8:   On reaching the destination Fant gets converted to Bant. The Bant will take the same path like Fant in opposite way.

STEP 9:   The path having higher path preference probability will be considered as the optimal path for transmission of data packets from S source node to D destination node.

3.2   IEEMARP Routing Protocol- Algorithm

Input: Feature Matrix
Output: Fitness Value
STEP 1: Initialize Population,
  //Where, x and y - input features of node;   (2)

STEP 2: Initialize path, R = random value for size of feature matrix
STEP 3: Initialize Velocity,

For i=1,
$$V(i) = V + P\ (R(i), R(j));$$
        End loop

For k = 1 to number of cluster
Omega, $O(K+1) = max(omega) - (max(omega) - min(omega). max(R));$
$V\ (k+1) = O(k) * v(k) + *(pb(k) - x(k)) + * random * (Gb(k) - x(k));$ //Where, pb – Path best; gb – Global Best; k- size of feature vector; b –number of updation;   (3)
$Pd = trial\ intensity\ (k)*Pb(path(k));$

STEP 4: Distance Calculation
STEP 5: Update PBest and GBest
STEP 6: Fitness value updating

Detailed step by step work-flow analysis of IEEMARP protocol is demonstrated in Fig. 1.

3.3   IEEMARP Routing Protocol – Phase of Operation

IEEMARP Routing Protocol (Improvised Energy Efficient Multipath Ant Based Routing Protocol) consists of three phases as: Link Knowledge Based Neighbor Discovery, Packet Forwarding/Fault localization and Reliable End-to-End Communication.
Detailed work of each phase in the designed algorithm i.e. IEEMARP Protocol is described as follows

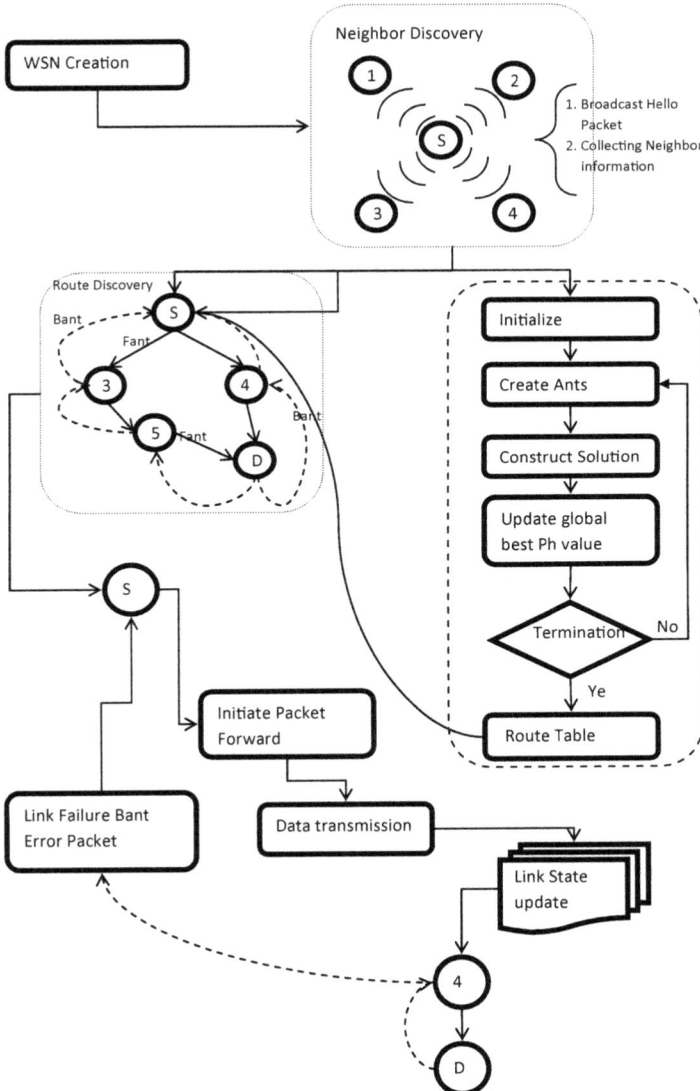

Fig. 1. IEEMARP routing protocol-working

1. Link Knowledge Based Neighbor Discovery

A sensor node sends a Hello message via one-hop broadcast to make its presence known to present nodes in its radio range. Nodes which are in the radio range are called neighbor nodes. A node may go to sleep mode to conserve energy level. When a node wakes up, it sends new hello packet to all the neighbor nodes along with the duration of time it will be in active state in the message. If a node does not wish to be used for packet forwarding, then it need not send a Hello message to its neighbors. Hello message allows the node to track of all its one-hop neighbors that are willing to forward packets and the duration the node is in active or awake state. The protocol doesn't enforce the node to monitor entire one-hop neighbors.

2. Packet Forwarding/Fault Localization

Let the subset of neighbors that the node keeps track be represented as N. Suppose a node s wants to transmit a packet, transmitted by another node, to a destination node d. For each neighbor node n ε N, the node s maintains a metric Rn,d, which represents the end to end reliability of forwarding a packet, going to destination node d through the neighbor node n. Initialization and updation of the Rn,d value are done by exponentially weighted moving average method which is discussed in the later section.

If the destination node cannot be reached directly, then the node forwards the packet to an active and willing neighbor node. This neighbor node to which the data packet is forwarded to will be henceforth referred to as the next-hop node. The next-hop node is chosen among the set of neighbors with highest R value. The data packets are not forwarded to the node from which it received the packet or to the source node which originated the packet. Every node in the network increments the hop-count value present in the header by one. The packet is discarded if the value of the hop-count exceeds a certain value, avoiding infinite loops in the network.

3. Maintaining End-to-End Reliability of Reaching the Destination

The source node solicits an end to end acknowledgement packet known as ACK packet from destination node for packets that it transmits. The packets soliciting acknowledgement are called as ACK Request (ACKR) packets. The source node forwards these ACKR packets in a round robin fashion to all active and willing nodes. However, the ACKR packets are subsequently treated in the same manner as data packets by all the other nodes to forward them to the next- hop node.i.e. the ACKR packets are treated similar to those of the data packets by being forwarded to the node with the highest R value. When the ACKR packet is received, the destination node sends ACK packet to the source node.

For every ACKR packet p a node generates or forwards, it needs to remember the packet's signature, sig(p), consisting of the source node, destination node, sequence number of the packet, the previous node and next hop node. The signature helps the ACK packet to be forwarded to the neighbor node from which it received the ACKR packet. The signature also helps the node to keep track of ACKR packets it received and eliminate any duplicate ACKR packets by discarding them. Every node after regular intervals of time, checks the quantity of signatures and removes signatures only if threshold value increases.

Each ACK packet carries the current value of end-to-end reliability of reaching the destination node d through the neighbor node n along the route taken by the corresponding ACKR packet. The loss of a huge portion of the ACK packets by these transmissions is still acceptable as long as at least one ACK packet reaches the source node within a reasonable amount of time t (e.g. every 10 min). If no ACK packets are received in response to the ACKR packets forwarded to neighbor node n in time interval t.

The ACKR/ACK packets makes use of the highest reliability service that is provided by the MAC layer such as acknowledged transmission.

3.4   IEEMARP Routing Protocol – Properties

Let N be the set of all the nodes in the network and D be the set of all the destination nodes in the network. Let η and Θ denote the cardinality of the sets N and D respectively.

As the node need not keep track of all its one-hop neighbor nodes, η would be the upper limit of the number of neighbor nodes a node keeps track. The following things are required to be stored in node's memory:

- A set N of one-hop neighbors that the node tracks.
- $R_{n, d}$, $\forall$ n ε N and $\forall$ d ε D, will require $O(\eta\Theta)$ memory.
- {sig(p), n}, where sig(p) is the signature of an ACKR packet p forwarded to node n that has not yet reached the destination node and acknowledged.

Each node restricts the number of packet signatures that it can store to some threshold value. Therefore, the total memory requirement of the node to store the packet signatures is $O(\eta)$.

The IEEMARP protocol can have routing loops, but these loops are not persistent. Suppose, we consider a scenario where a node A forwards a packet to another node B. Node B forwards this packet to node C, which in turn forwards this packet back to node A. By imposing the limit on the hop count value ensures that the packet will ultimately be discarded sometime once the hop count exceeds the limit. Also each node keeps track of the signature for the ACKR packet that it has forwarded to its neighbor nodes and has not yet been acknowledged yet. The node uses these signatures to discard any of the duplicate ACKR packets that might be travelling in the loop.

Packets forwarded via broadcast/multicast cannot utilize the MAC-level acknowledgements and they are prone to loss due to collision at MAC-level and PHY-level noise. The IEEMARP protocol avoids broadcast/multicast for data packets forwarding or routing monitoring/discovery.

The protocol does not make use of broadcasting for route discovery and maintenance as it hinders the scalability of the network.

One-hop broadcast is used for route discovery by sending hello packets to neighboring nodes.

4 IEEMARP Simulation

4.1 Parameters of Simulations

See Table 1.

Table 1. Enlists simulation parameters considered for testing IEEMARP protocol

Parameter name	Values
Simulator name and version	ns-allinone-2.35
Base protocol for routing	Ant Colony Optimization (ACO) based routing
Dimension of topology	3000 m x 1000 m
Network type	Wireless
Simulation time	150 s, 300 s, 500 s
Antenna type	Omni antenna
Simulation model	Energy model
Initial energy of nodes	10000 mJ
Number of nodes	100, 150, 200...800 (Max)
Queue length	64
Data rate	Variable
Interface type	Wireless physical interface
Radio range for node	~ 250 m
Mobility speed	1....15 m/s
MAC type	IEEE 802.11
Mobility model	Random way point

4.2 Metrics Used

To determine the novelty of the proposed protocol the following metrics are used:

- Packet Delivery Overhead
  Packet Delivery is regarded as the total number of packets successful transmitted at destination node.

$$\text{Packet Delivery Ratio} = (\text{Total Packets Sent} - \text{Total Packets Lost}) \\ * \ 100/\text{no. of packets sent.}$$

- Throughput
  Throughput, is defined as the quantity of data delivered over physical or logical link at particular amount of time. It is determined in bits per second.

$$\text{Throughput} = \text{Successful transmission of Total Packets}/\text{Total Transmission Time}$$

- Routing Overhead
  Routing overhead is regarded as total number of packets required for communication. It is determined via awk script taking input from trace file and giving the end results.
- Energy Consumption
  Energy consumption is measured in Joules. It is defined as the rate of consuming the power from energy source by sensors during various types of works: Packet Transmission, Clustering etc.
- End to End Delay
  End-To-End delay is the duration taken by the packet to be transferred from source to destination.

$$\text{End-To-End Delay} = \text{Transmission time}(\text{Hop } 1 + \text{Hop } 2 + \ldots + \text{Hop } n).$$

4.3   Simulation Results (Compared with ACO, DSDV and DSR)

Table 2 states performance comparison of protocols: Basic ACO, DSDV, DSR and IEEMARP with respect to various parameters [44–46].

Table 2. ACO V/s DSDV v/s DSR v/s IEEMARP

Parameters	Basic ACO	DSDV	DSR	IEEMARP
Packet Delivery Ratio	94.58	95.96	88.12	97.73
Average End to End Delay	0.21	0.19	0.15	0.58
Average number of hops	1.67	1.092	1.04	8.21
Control packet overhead	9589	4809	5409	6090
Dropped reply messages	44	0	0	1
Throughput (byes/s)	3012	2651	3094	3795

The Results states that IEEMARP Routing Protocol is almost 9–10% efficient in terms of performance as compared to Basic ACO, DSDV, DSR routing protocols.

4.4   Simulation Scenario, Comparison with Other Routing Protocols and Results

Simulation Scenario of IEEMARP routing protocol is demonstrated via NS-2 simulator [47] working and comparison with other routing protocols- ACEAMR, Ant Chain, EMCBR and IACR and results are produced via Data Values and graphs via XGraph.

1. Simulation Scenario
   In Fig. 2, simulation is started demonstrating the updating of neighbors with pheromone values using basic ACO algorithm

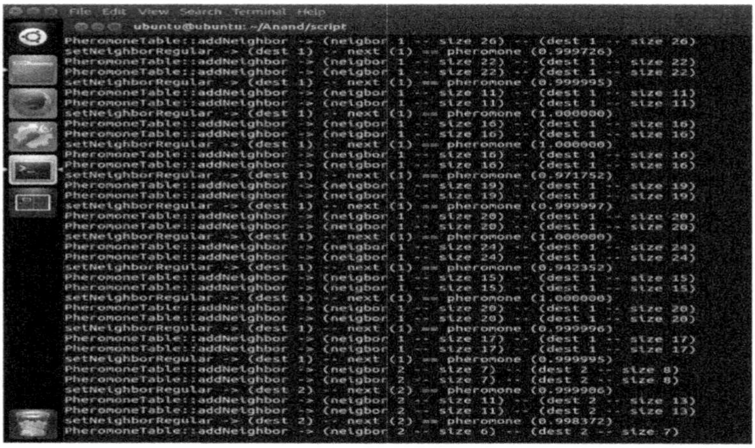

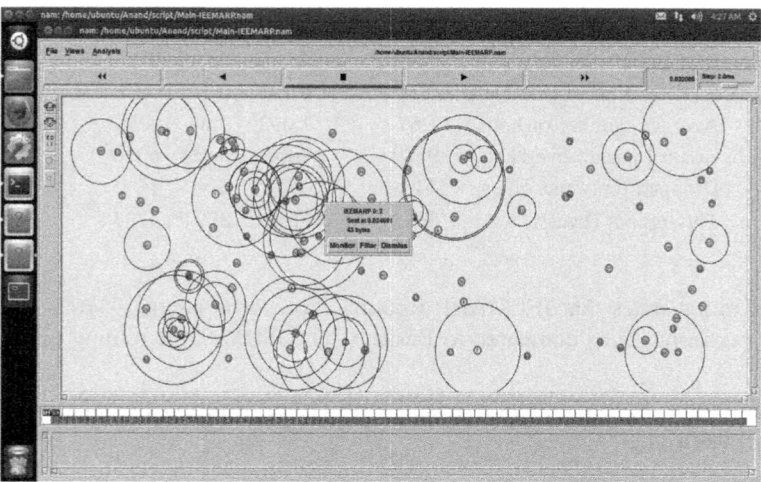

Fig. 2. Simulation scenario started

In Fig. 3, Network Animator window shows the initial stage of IEEMARP routing protocol- Route Discovery in which protocol finds the neighboring sensor node.

Fig. 3. Route discovery by IEEMARP routing protocol

In Fig. 4, after determining the neighbors and best routing paths, the sensor nodes will send the packets to Base Station (Node 0). The TCP protocol is utilized to send packets for reliable end-end communication.

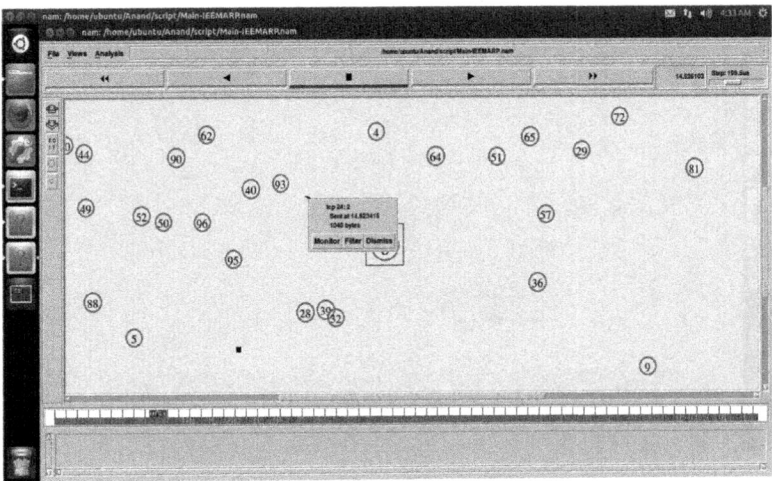

Fig. 4. Packets transmission to base station

In Fig. 5, on the successful receipt of TCP packets from the transmitting node, the base station will send the ACK packet to the sensor nodes confirming the delivery which makes the IEEMARP routing protocol a highly reliable communication protocol.

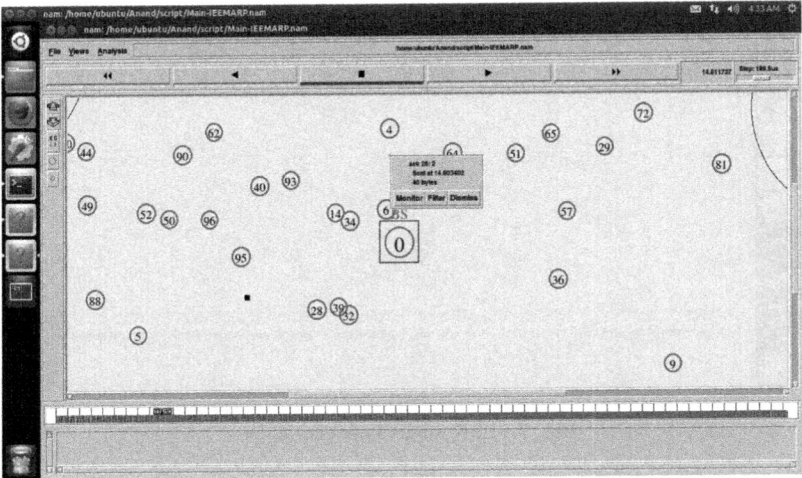

Fig. 5. ACK packet transmission

In Fig. 6, in case of any fault tolerance route discovery process, the packet is dropping due to routing overhead.

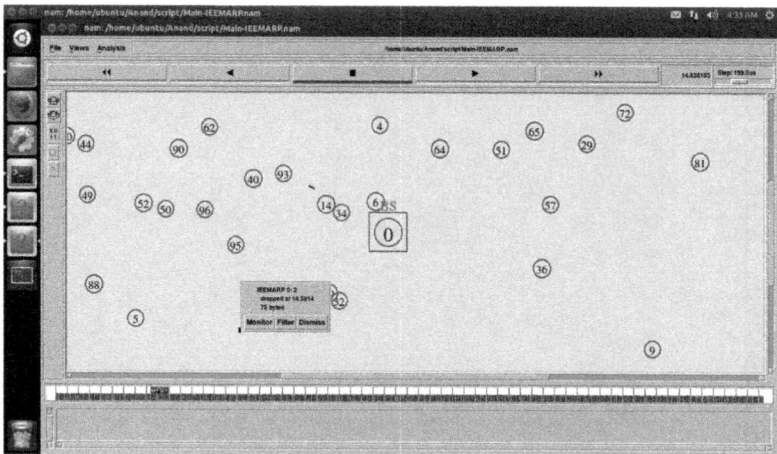

Fig. 6. Packet dropping due to routing overhead

Figure 7, demonstrates the link status between base station 0 and sensor node 3 by 10 Mbits/Sec with delay in 10 s.

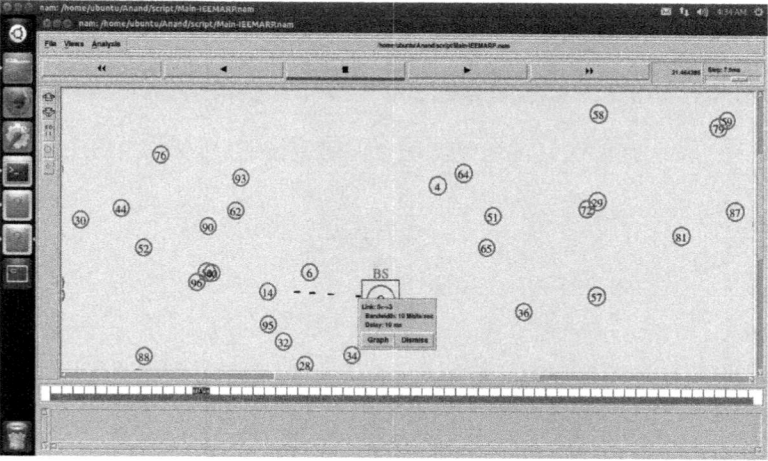

Fig. 7. Link status between nodes

2. Comparison with Other Routing Protocols- ACEAMR, AntChain, EMCBR and IACR

In this part, novel routing Protocol i.e. IEEMARP is compared with other routing protocols (Table 3). In order to prove improvements in Routing protocol, the results are compared with ACEAMR, AntChain, EMCBR and IACR Routing Protocol [47] on varied parameters like: Packet Delivery Ratio, Throughput, Routing Overhead, Energy Consumption, End-to-End Delay.

- Packet Delivery Ratio
  Data values
  Results show that IEEMARP routing protocol is almost 15% more efficient in PACKET DELIVERY as compared to other routing protocols (Fig. 8).

Table 3. Demonstrates Packet Delivery Ratio of routing protocols compared with IEEMARP on varied simulation times.

Packet Delivery Ratio				
Time	ACEAMR	AntChain	EMCBR	IACR	IEEMARP
25	87.76	84.51	90.40	95.03	96.68
50	85.5	86.02	85.30	96.94	97.26
75	82.7	83.31	89.32	98.65	98.36
100	79.87	85.77	83.53	99.13	99.65
125	77.73	87	87.49	92.56	98.65
150	74.97	86.56	84.91	91.26	98.14

- Throughput
  Data Values
  The following Table 4 shows the Throughput of Routing Protocols compared with IEEMARP on varied simulation times.

Table 4. Performance based on Throughput

Throughput (Mbps)				
Time	ACEAMR	AntChain	EMCBR	IACR	IEEMARP
25	198	182	175	190	216
50	223	213	187	182	213
75	217	212	205	207	219
100	189	187	185	213	207
125	193	188	185	184	217
150	178	188	210	204	221

Results show that IEEMARP routing protocol is almost 22% more efficient in THROUGHPUT as compared to other routing protocols (Fig. 9).

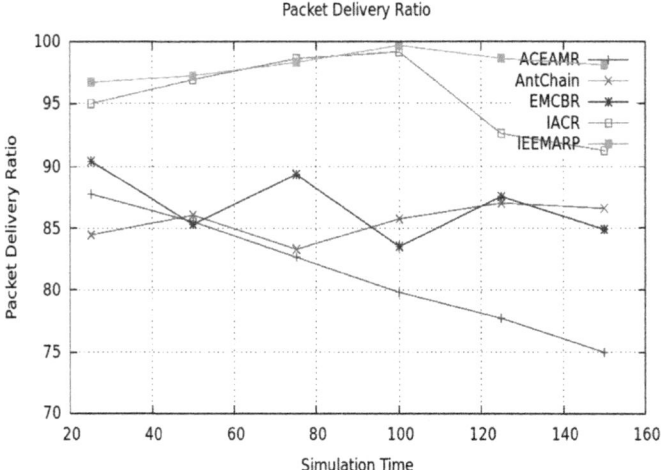

Fig. 8. Xgraph based results demonstrating performance comparison on basis of Packet Delivery Ratio of IEEMARP routing protocol with other routing protocols.

Table 5. Performance based on Routing Overhead

Routing Overhead					
Time	ACEAMR	AntChain	EMCBR	IACR	IEEMARP
25	0.68	0.81	0.62	0.59	0.54
50	0.66	0.78	0.89	0.62	0.52
75	0.65	0.79	0.67	0.62	0.66
100	0.67	0.78	0.67	0.57	0.55
125	0.67	0.79	0.63	0.66	0.56
150	0.63	0.78	0.65	0.63	0.62

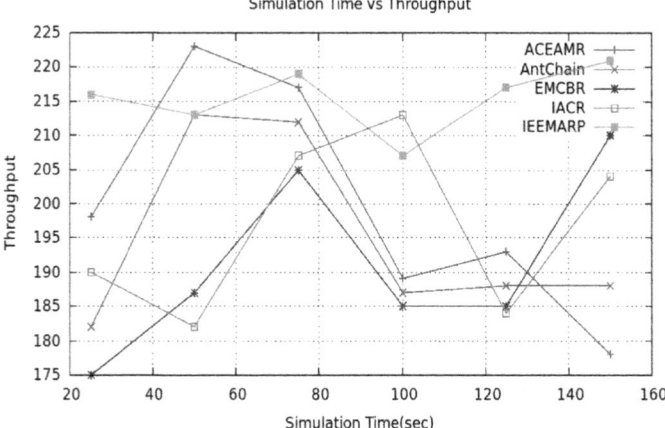

Fig. 9. Xgraph based results demonstrating performance comparison on basis of throughout of IEEMARP routing protocol with other routing protocols.

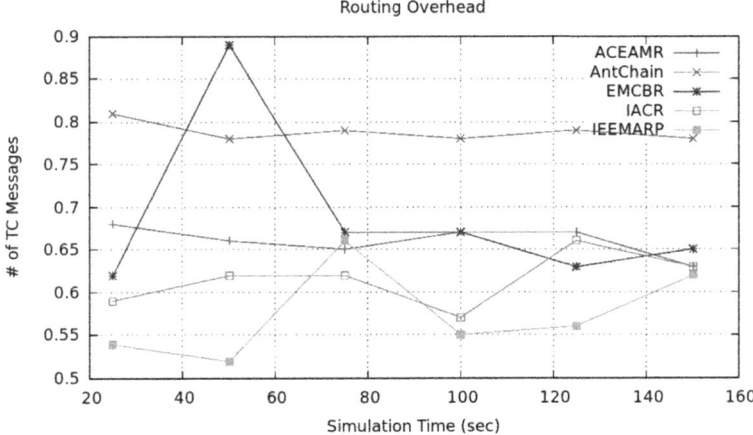

Fig. 10. Xgraph based results demonstrating performance comparison on basis of Routing Overhead of IEEMARP routing protocol with other routing protocols.

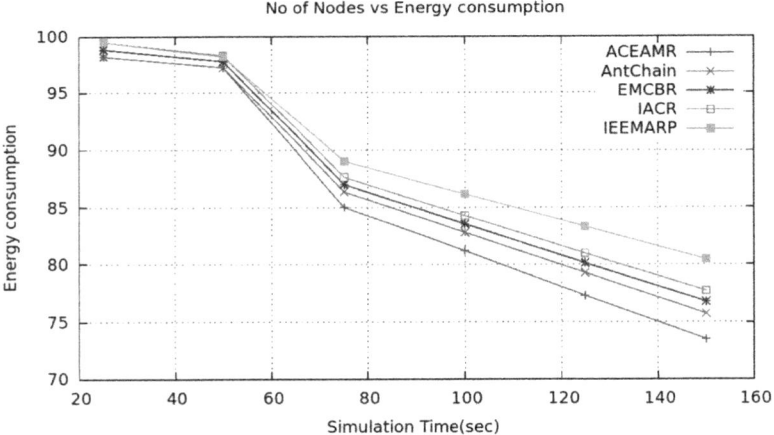

Fig. 11. Xgraph based results demonstrating performance comparison on basis of Energy Consumption of IEEMARP routing protocol.

- Routing Overhead
  Data Values
  The following Table 5 shows the Routing Overhead of Routing Protocols compared with IEEMARP on varied simulation times.
  Results show that IEEMARP routing protocol is almost 13% more efficient in ROUTING OVERHEAD as compared to other routing protocols (Fig. 10).

- Energy Consumption

  Data Values

  Table 6 shows the Energy Efficiency of Routing Protocols compared with IEE-MARP on varied simulation times.

Table 6. Performance Based on Energy Consumption

Energy Consumption (Joules)				
Time	ACEAMR	AntChain	EMCBR	IACR	IEEMARP
25	98.21	98.2	98.81	99.42	99.52
50	97.23	97.25	97.78	98.32	98.21
75	85.05	86.33	86.95	87.59	89.06
100	81.17	82.79	83.54	84.30	86.20
125	77.30	79.26	80.13	81.01	83.33
150	73.43	75.72	76.72	77.72	80.47

IEEMARP routing protocol is almost 8% efficient in ENERGY CONSUMPTION as compared to other protocols (Fig. 11).

- End-To-End Delay

  Data Values

  The following Table 7 shows End-To-End Delay of IEEMARP protocol compared with other protocols on varied simulation times.

Table 7. Performance based on End-To-End Delay

End-To-End Delay (Seconds)				
Time	ACEAMR	AntChain	EMCBR	IACR	IEEMARP
20	67.12	51.99	48.28	50.10	53.97
40	66.89	42.06	57.53	66.47	39.72
60	38.82	67.35	46.39	44.24	29.22
80	44.25	65.30	39.43	42.59	43.41
100	67.55	55.11	41.77	66.52	30.74
120	56.37	60.95	43.03	47.98	37.28
140	64.67	49.13	46.78	67.75	44.34

IEEMARP routing protocol is almost 16% more efficient in END-TO-END DELAY.

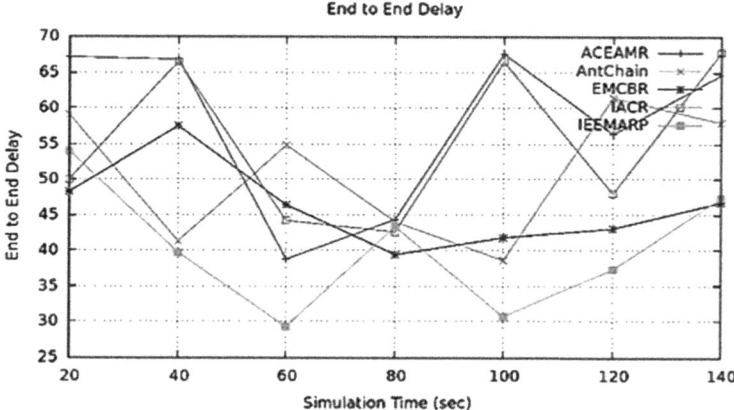

Fig. 12. Xgraph based results demonstrating performance comparison on basis of End to End Delay of IEEMARP routing protocol with other routing protocols.

5   Conclusion and Future Scope

Wireless Sensor Networks are used in real time applications like Environmental Monitoring, Agriculture fields monitoring, battlefields monitoring, industrial and production control based monitoring. Due to topological changes which are highly dynamic in nature, it becomes a challenging task to route the packets efficiency considering varied parameters like Energy, Routing Overhead, End to End delay etc. to final destination in Wireless Sensor Networks. Keeping in view of the same, we proposed a new Novel ACO Based Routing Protocol i.e. IEEMARP (Improvised Energy Efficient Multipath Ant Based Routing Protocol) which considers the real-time Ant based control for movement of packets efficiently from source to destination. In the protocol, the main aim is to search for neighbor and determine optimal shortest paths between transmitting nodes, but also considers multipath links and quality in terms of throughput which makes us the paths. The protocol is properly simulated on NS-2 simulator and compared with various routing protocols like Basic ACO, DSDV, DSR and even other protocols being proposed by other researchers like ACEAMR, Ant Chain, EMCBR and IACR. We have found IEEMARP better in performance i.e. Packet Delivery, Throughput, Energy Efficiency, Routing Overhead and End-to-End delay. The performance is determined via varied simulation scenarios, simulation time and number of nodes and properly analyzed and presented via Graphs in this paper.

Future Scope
We try to compare the proposed routing protocol i.e. IEEMARP with other routing protocols like AntQHSen, FACOR, ANTALG etc. Other features like security enhancement can be considered in near future to make IEEMARP a secure WSN routing protocol.

References

1. Akyildiz, I.F., Su, W., Sankarasubramaniam, Y., Cayirci, E.: Wireless sensor networks: a survey. Comput. Netw. **38**(4), 393–422 (2002)
2. Potdar, V., Sharif, A., Chang, E.: Wireless sensor networks: a survey. In: International Conference on Advanced Information Networking and Applications Workshops, WAINA 2009, pp. 636–641. IEEE, May 2009
3. Yang, K.: Wireless Sensor Networks. Principles, Design and Applications. Springer, Heidelberg (2014). https://doi.org/10.1007/978-1-4471-5505-8
4. Li, M.A., Guoqing, W.A.N.G., Dongchao, M.A., Jianpei, H.E.: Wireless Sensor Networks (2014)
5. Rawat, P., Singh, K.D., Chaouchi, H., Bonnin, J.M.: Wireless sensor networks: a survey on recent developments and potential synergies. J. Supercomput. **68**(1), 1–48 (2014)
6. Dargie, W., Poellabauer, C.: Fundamentals of Wireless Sensor Networks: Theory and Practice. Wiley, Hoboken (2010)
7. Khan, S., Pathan, A.S.K., Alrajeh, N.A. (eds.): Wireless Sensor Networks: Current Status and Future Trends. CRC Press, Boca Raton (2012)
8. Mohan, B.C., Baskaran, R.: A survey: ant colony optimization based recent research and implementation on several engineering domain. Expert Syst. Appl. **39**(4), 4618–4627 (2012)
9. Dorigo, M., Birattari, M., Stutzle, T.: Ant colony optimization. IEEE Comput. Intell. Mag. **1**(4), 28–39 (2006)
10. Stützle, T.: Ant colony optimization. In: Ehrgott, M., Fonseca, C.M., Gandibleux, X., Hao, J.-K., Sevaux, M. (eds.) EMO 2009. LNCS, vol. 5467, p. 2. Springer, Heidelberg (2009). https://doi.org/10.1007/978-3-642-01020-0_2
11. Dorigo, M., Di Caro, G.: Ant colony optimization: a new meta-heuristic. In: Proceedings of the 1999 Congress on Evolutionary Computation, CEC 1999, vol. 2, pp. 1470–1477. IEEE (1999)
12. Dorigo, M., Blum, C.: Ant colony optimization theory: A survey. Theor. Comput. Sci. **344**(2–3), 243–278 (2005)
13. Blum, C.: Ant colony optimization: introduction and recent trends. Phys. Life Rev. **2**(4), 353–373 (2005)
14. Maniezzo, V., Carbonaro, A.: Ant colony optimization: an overview. In: Ribeiro, C.C., Hansen, P. (eds.) Essays and Surveys in Metaheuristics, vol. 15, pp. 469–492. Springer, Boston (2002). https://doi.org/10.1007/978-1-4615-1507-4_21
15. Dorigo, M., Stützle, T.: Ant colony optimization: overview and recent advances. In: Gendreau, M., Potvin, J.Y. (eds.) Handbook of Metaheuristics, pp. 227–263. Springer, Boston (2010). https://doi.org/10.1007/978-1-4419-1665-5_8
16. Nayyar, A., Singh, R.: Ant colony optimization—computational swarm intelligence technique. In: 2016 3rd International Conference on Computing for Sustainable Global Development (INDIACom), pp. 1493–1499. IEEE, March 2016
17. Cauvery, N.K., Viswanatha, K.V.: Enhanced ant colony based algorithm for routing in mobile ad hoc network. World Acad. Sci. Eng. Technol. **46**, 30–35 (2008)
18. Blum, C., Li, X.: Swarm intelligence in optimization. In: Blum, C., Merkle, D. (eds.) Swarm Intelligence, pp. 43–85. Springer, Heidelberg (2008). https://doi.org/10.1007/978-3-540-74089-6_2
19. Kennedy, J.F., Kennedy, J., Eberhart, R.C., Shi, Y.: Swarm Intelligence. Morgan Kaufmann, Burlington (2001)

20. Dorigo, M., Birattari, M., Blum, C., Clerc, M., Stützle, T., Winfield, A.F.T. (eds.): ANTS 2008. LNCS, vol. 5217. Springer, Heidelberg (2008). https://doi.org/10.1007/978-3-540-87527-7
21. Rao, S.S., Singh, V.: Optimization. IEEE Trans. Syst. Man Cybern. **9**(8), 447 (1979)
22. Rao, S.S., Rao, S.S.: Engineering Optimization: Theory and Practice. Wiley, Hoboken (2009)
23. Garnier, S., Gautrais, J., Theraulaz, G.: The biological principles of swarm intelligence. Swarm Intell. **1**(1), 3–31 (2007)
24. Bonabeau, E., Dorigo, M., Theraulaz, G.: Swarm Intelligence: From Natural to Artificial Systems, vol. 1. Oxford university press, Oxford (1999)
25. Engelbrecht, A.P.: Computational Intelligence: An Introduction. Wiley, Hoboken (2007)
26. Dorigo, M., Gambardella, L.M.: Ant colony system: a cooperative learning approach to the traveling salesman problem. IEEE Trans. Evol. Comput. **1**(1), 53–66 (1997)
27. Nayyar, A., Singh, R.: A Comprehensive Review of Ant Colony Optimization (ACO) based Energy-Efficient Routing Protocols for Wireless Sensor Networks (2016)
28. Saleem, M., Di Caro, G.A., Farooq, M.: Swarm intelligence based routing protocol for wireless sensor networks: survey and future directions. Inf. Sci. **181**(20), 4597–4624 (2011)
29. Zungeru, A.M., Ang, L.M., Seng, K.P.: Classical and swarm intelligence based routing protocols for wireless sensor networks: a survey and comparison. J. Netw. Comput. Appl. **35**(5), 1508–1536 (2012)
30. Zengin, A., Tuncel, S.: A survey on swarm intelligence based routing protocols in wireless sensor networks. Int. J. Phys. Sci. **5**(14), 2118–2126 (2010)
31. Ali, Z., Shahzad, W.: Critical analysis of swarm intelligence based routing protocols in adhoc and sensor wireless networks. In: 2011 International Conference on Computer Networks and Information Technology (ICCNIT), pp. 287–292. IEEE, July 2011
32. Okdem, S., Karaboga, D.: Routing in wireless sensor networks using ant colony optimization. In: First NASA/ESA Conference on Adaptive Hardware and Systems, AHS 2006, pp. 401–404. IEEE, June 2006
33. Sim, K.M., Sun, W.H.: Ant colony optimization for routing and load-balancing: survey and new directions. IEEE Trans. Syst. Man Cybern.-Part A: Syst. Hum. **33**(5), 560–572 (2003)
34. Ren, H., Meng, M.Q.H.: Biologically inspired approaches for wireless sensor networks. In: Proceedings of the 2006 IEEE International Conference on Mechatronics and Automation, pp. 762–768. IEEE, June 2006
35. Iyengar, S.S., Wu, H.C., Balakrishnan, N., Chang, S.Y.: Biologically inspired cooperative routing for wireless mobile sensor networks. IEEE Syst. J. **1**(1), 29–37 (2007)
36. Gunes, M., Sorges, U., Bouazizi, I.: ARA-the ant-colony based routing algorithm for MANETs. In: Proceedings of 2002 International Conference on Parallel Processing Workshops, pp. 79–85. IEEE (2002)
37. Shah, R.C., Rabaey, J.M.: Energy aware routing for low energy ad hoc sensor networks. In: 2002 IEEE Wireless Communications and Networking Conference, WCNC2002, vol. 1, pp. 350–355. IEEE, March 2002
38. Hussein, O., Saadawi, T.: Ant routing algorithm for mobile ad-hoc networks (ARAMA). In: Proceedings of the 2003 IEEE International Conference on Performance, Computing, and Communications Conference, pp. 281–290. IEEE, April 2003
39. Di Caro, G., Dorigo, M.: AntNet: distributed stigmergetic control for communications networks. J. Artif. Intell. Res. **9**, 317–365 (1998)
40. Camilo, T., Carreto, C., Silva, J.S., Boavida, F.: An energy-efficient ant-based routing algorithm for wireless sensor networks. In: Dorigo, M., Gambardella, L.M., Birattari, M., Martinoli, A., Poli, R., Stützle, T. (eds.) ANTS 2006. LNCS, vol. 4150, pp. 49–59. Springer, Heidelberg (2006). https://doi.org/10.1007/11839088_5

41. Patel, M., Chandrasekaran, R., Venkatesan, S.: Efficient minimum-cost bandwidth-constrained routing in wireless sensor networks. In: International Conference on Wireless Networks, pp. 447–453, June 2004
42. Xia, S., Wu, S.: Ant colony-based energy-aware multipath routing algorithm for wireless sensor networks. In: 2009 Second International Symposium on Knowledge Acquisition and Modeling, KAM 2009, vol. 3, pp. 198–201. IEEE, November 2009
43. Peng, S., Yang, S.X., Gregori, S., Tian, F.: An adaptive QoS and energy-aware routing algorithm for wireless sensor networks. In: 2008 International Conference on Information and Automation, ICIA 2008, pp. 578–583. IEEE, June 2008
44. Nayyar, A., Singh, R.: Ant colony optimization (ACO) based routing protocols for wireless sensor networks (WSN): a survey. Int. J. Adv. Comput. Sci. Appl. (IJACSA) 8(2), 148–155 (2017)
45. Nayyar, A., Singh, R.: A comprehensive review of simulation tools for wireless sensor networks (WSNs). J. Wirel. Netw. Commun. 5(1), 19–47 (2015)
46. Nayyar, A., Singh, R.: Simulation and performance comparison of ant colony optimization (ACO) routing protocol with AODV, DSDV, DSR routing protocols of wireless sensor networks using NS-2 simulator. Am. J. Intell. Syst. 7(1), 19–30 (2017)
47. Nayyar, A., Singh, R.: Performance analysis of ACO based routing protocols-EMCBR, AntChain, IACR, ACO-EAMRA for wireless sensor networks (WSNs). Br. J. Math. Comput. Sci. 20(6), 1–18 (2017)

Locating Real Time Faults in Modern Metro Train Tracks Using Wireless Sensor Network

Nitya Komalan[✉] and Aarti Chauhan

Computer Engineering Department, Gujarat Technological University,
Ahmedabad, India
niti.dk.1989@gmail.com

Abstract. Track maintenance is the primary concern for metro railways. Currently, tracks are inspected manually which consumes a lot of time, labor and power. Condition monitoring using Wireless Sensor Network can reduce maintenance time through automated monitoring by detecting faults before they escalate. Vibration estimating sensors are laid along the length of tracks which will have a vast amount of data to be communicated where senders and receivers are sensors, trains and sink. Thus, we have used cluster based routing with data aggregation to reduce communication overhead and cluster based fault detection technique to handle cluster head failure as part of network setup and then implemented our proposed track fault detection algorithm in this network. Our proposed track fault detection algorithm provides better results in terms of total energy consumed and total time taken to detect and update train regarding track fault location.

Keywords: Metro railways · Wireless Sensor Network (WSN)
Vibration estimating sensors · Railway track · Track fault location
Cluster based routing · Cluster based data aggregation
Cluster based fault detection

1 Introduction

Metro Railways, also called as "Rapid Transit", are the most widely used mode of public transport in urban areas due to its high speed, capacity and reliability e.g. Delhi Metro, it is the 12th largest metro system in the world for its length and number of stations. It carries average ridership of 2.6 million passengers per day [1]. Figure 1 shows few examples of track damages that are necessary to be detected in time to prevent accidents as risk involved is in terms of human life and infrastructure cost. Thus, track maintenance is the primary concern for railways. Currently in metros, tracks are inspected manually which can be greatly reduced using "Condition Monitoring" as it replaces "Find and Fix" strategy to "Predict and Prevent" [2]. Condition Monitoring using WSN as shown in Fig. 2 can reduce maintenance time through automated monitoring by detecting faults before they escalate. In this way, it can improve safety and reliability of the system. However, to build an efficient track fault detection method using WSN is a challenging task as sensors are power and memory constrained devices [3]. For a denser remote monitoring application like railway, it is

© Springer Nature Singapore Pte Ltd. 2018
P. Bhattacharyya et al. (Eds.): NGCT 2017, CCIS 828, pp. 25–39, 2018.
https://doi.org/10.1007/978-981-10-8660-1_2

very much necessary to preserve energy. Therefore, cluster based routing algorithms are appropriate as it helps to reduce communication overhead, maintenance of routing tables, energy consumption and thus improves network lifetime [4]. Also, in case of node failures, it is very much necessary to recover as quick as possible as it carries relevant information which need to be communicated in time [5]. Cluster-based data aggregation technique will help to collect useful information by eliminating redundant sensor readings. So, using our analysis from surveyed different cluster based routing algorithms [6–12], cluster based data aggregation techniques [13, 14] and cluster based fault detection techniques [15–19], we have built a network set up for our proposed track fault detection algorithm. Unlike existing [29], after sink broadcasting the train location, vibration estimating sensors in our algorithm will communicate their vibration difference to Cluster Head (CH) only when the difference between the current iteration vibration difference and the previous stored normal vibration difference exceeds pre-defined threshold. CH will then forward only the eligible vibration difference to the sink. Sink will check for the series of nodes that gave abnormal vibration difference. If the series exist, then the location of the first node in that series will be provided as track fault location to the train. Our proposed algorithm provides better results in terms of total energy consumed and total time taken to update the track fault location to train by reducing communication overhead.

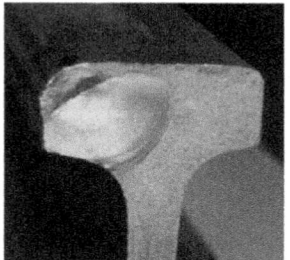
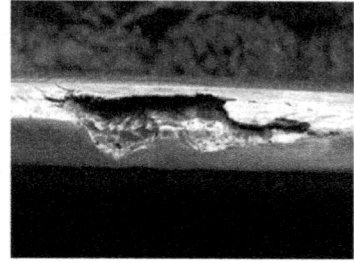

Fig. 1. Typical examples of broken rails and rail damage [20]

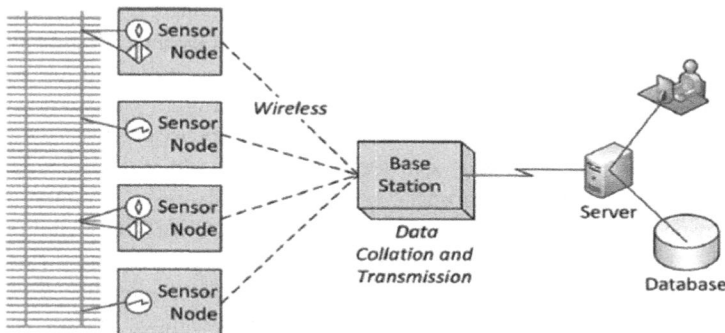

Fig. 2. Typical WSN for railway condition monitoring. Sensors are laid along the length of tracks and will generate a lot of redundant data continuously or periodically. Base Station (BS) will collect these data and sent it to sink. Sink will analyze the received data to identify track faults [2]

This paper presents the analysis on different rail inspection methods [20–29] in Sect. 2. Network set up and proposed track fault detection algorithm is presented in Sect. 3. Section 4 provides our results analysis for both existing and proposed algorithm in terms of parameters like total energy consumption, total energy saving, total time taken and average transmission time taken to detect and update the track fault location to the train. We have further implemented both existing and proposed algorithm by reducing the frequency of sink broadcasting the train location and their results are also presented in this section. Finally, Sect. 5 concludes the paper.

2   Related Work

Traditionally, railways around the world employ signalling system for two important safety functions: (a) Traffic flow regulations and (b) Preventing derailments by detecting broken rails [20]. Track circuit is a simple electrical device used to detect the absence of a train on rail tracks and to inform signallers and control relevant signals [21]. However, this approach is expensive and also it is not able to detect partial rail crack due to electrical continuity. Alternative to track circuits are: Communication Based Train Control (CBTC) [22] and Positive Train Control (PTC) [23] systems which are used for traffic management. These techniques are not usable for detecting broken rails. Visual inspection and Non-Destructive Testing (NDT) [24] based methods offer limited capabilities to conduct global structural damage inspection. The successful implementation of these methods generally requires the regions of the suspected damage to be known before hand and also it should be physically accessible location. As a result, these methods can be time consuming, costly and ineffective for large and complex structural systems such as rail tracks. Very few approaches have been implemented for track breakage detection.

The use of long range ultrasonic testing is proposed in [25] that are suitable for examining inaccessible areas of railway tracks where corrosion occurs. But this approach can give false alarms due to train traffic on other tracks. Also, this approach is slow and tedious when there are thousands of miles of track length to be inspected and the fault location is not known. Sensors and Infra-red rays based fault tolerance technique is proposed in [26] where sensors mounted in train wheels will transmit rays in the track to avoid collision.

The use of fuzzy-logic based data aggregation is proposed in [27] to send useful information from the data received from sensors. It uses multi-layered and multi-path techniques for routing the aggregated packets. However, this approach consumes more energy and time in classification. Also, it provides approximate location of the track fault. A similar approach is proposed in [28] where sensor nodes senses data and send their sensed data to sink. Sink will evaluate the received data based on fuzzy rules and then it will raise an appropriate alarm accordingly.

The use of estimating vibration sensor for track fault detection is proposed in [29]. These vibration sensors will estimate the vibration based on the train location broadcasted by sink. It will then compute the vibration difference between the sensed and the estimated vibration and forward this vibration difference to the sink using multi-hop routing. Sink will then check for the series of nodes in the same direction that gave abnormal vibration difference by comparing the received vibration difference against predefined threshold. If the series exist, then the first node in that series will be provided as track fault location to the train. Based on the distance of the train from the track fault location, the train can either stop or slow down its speed. This approach consumes more energy and time due to communication overhead.

Crack in track is a slow growing process and hence most of the time, it will sense the normal vibration only. Therefore, it is not optimal to send normal vibration difference to the sink every time as it will consume more energy and time. So in order to preserve energy and to improve network lifetime, we have proposed an algorithm that can reduce the total energy consumed and total time taken to update the train regarding the track fault location by reducing communication overhead.

3 Proposed Work

3.1 Sensor Specification and Parameters [29]

ID. A unique ID is assigned to each sensor for identification. Packets from all registered nodes will also forward their IDs.

Geographical Location. All the nodes are GPS enabled to keep track of their locations. ID and the corresponding location of each node are also known to sink.

Direction. Sensor nodes, forwarding nodes and sink are laid in both direction of the track. If network of one direction is down then the other direction network can be used as back up for other track.

Distance From Train. Trains are also GPS enabled. It will register itself to the nearest forwarding node in both directions in the direction of its movement. It will then update their latest location to the sink through these registered forwarding nodes. Sink will then broadcast the received train location to its network.

Estimated Vibration. If (s_x, s_y) is the sensor location and (t_x, t_y) is the train's current location broadcasted by sink, then the estimated vibration is computed as follows:

$$S(i).estimatedVib = 1/sqrt\left(s_x^2 - t_x^2\right) \tag{1}$$

Sensed Vibration. The actual vibration sensed by vibration sensors are called as sensed vibration (S(i).sensedVib). Due to unavailability of actual sensors during the research, we have worked with the assumption that sensors can sense properly and sensed vibration will also follow the same proportionality as estimated vibration but with different constant and dependent on the breakage location.

Vibration Difference. Each sensor node will compute their vibration difference as shown below:

$$S(i).vibDif = |S(i).sensedVib - S(i).estimatedVib| \tag{2}$$

3.2   Network Set Up for Proposed Track Fault Detection Algorithm

Sensors are placed on the track at specific location where they are less susceptible to noise and can sense the vibration intensity flowing through the rails appropriately. These nodes are at level zero of multi-level architecture [29]. All the higher level nodes are forwarding nodes that are used for creating clusters using clustering algorithm [12]. During communication, if the CH have shortage of energy or get crashed, then the second highest residual energy node in the failing CH's cluster will become the new CH. And all the cluster members (CMs) of the failing CH cluster will join the new CH [16]. Multi-hop routing is used for intra-cluster and inter-cluster communication. Each sensor node on the track will first register itself to the nearest forwarding node (next level node) in its range who will act as data collectors for these sensors. At each level, forwarding nodes will collect the data from previous level registered nodes and then send it to the next level node to which it is registered with. This same network is built in both directions of the track.

3.3   Data Aggregation Authority

Sensor nodes at level zero will compute the current vibration difference and then compute the difference between the current vibration difference and the previous stored normal vibration difference as shown below:

$$S(i).\text{Diff} = |S(i).\text{vibDif} - S(i).\text{previousStoredVibDif}| \qquad (3)$$

If this difference exceeds a predefined Threshold_1 (average of normal vibration difference of each sensor), then it will send its current vibration difference by setting its fault flag as 'Y' else it will send an empty packet with its fault flag as 'N' to CH via forwarding nodes. Each forwarding node while forwarding any packet will check for the fault flag of received packets. For all received packets, if the fault flag is 'N' then it will forward an empty packet with its fault flag as 'N' to CH else it will collect vibration difference of those received packets that has fault flag as 'Y' and forward them to CH by setting its fault flag as 'Y'. For all received packets, CH will check for the fault flag. If for all received packets, if the fault flag is 'N' then CH will send an empty packet with its fault flag as 'N' else it will check for vibration difference of those packets whose fault flag is 'Y'. CH will collect all those vibration difference that exceeds Threshold_2 and then forward them by setting its fault flag as 'Y' to the sink using multi-hop routing.

Sink on receiving packets will check for vibration differences of those packets whose fault flag is 'Y'. If there is track breakage, then all the sensor nodes in the same direction will show the same behaviour. Therefore, sink will check for series of nodes that gave abnormal vibration difference. If the series exist, then the location of the first node in that series is provided as track fault location to the train using reverse path to the forwarding node to which it is currently registered with. Train on receiving the track fault location, will compute its distance from the track fault location. If this distance is less than Threshold_3 (2 km) then the train will stop otherwise it will move normally or slow down its speed as per the distance.

3.4 Proposed Track Fault Detection Algorithm

Steps for the proposed track fault detection algorithm are as follows:

1. Sensors collect the sensed vibration.

2. It will receive train's current location $(t_x.t_y)$ broadcasted by sink.

3. For all sensors S(i) where i = 1 to n, do the following:

    a. Compute estimated vibration using (1).

    b. Compute current vibration difference using (2).

    c. Compute the difference (S(i).Diff) using (3).

    d. If S(i).Diff >= Threshold_1

        Frame the packet with its current vibration difference and set its fault flag as 'Y'.

    e. Else,

        Frame an empty packet by setting its fault flag as 'N'.

4. Forward the framed packets to the next level forwarding node to whom these nodes are registered with.

5. Each forwarding nodes will check for all received packet's fault flag.

    a. For all received packets, If the fault flag is 'N' then

        Frame an empty packet with its fault flag as 'N'.

    b. Else,

        Collect vibration difference from all those received packets whose fault flag is 'Y' and frame them into one packet and set its fault flag as 'Y'.

6. Repeat steps (4) and (5) at each level forwarding node till CH is reached.

7. CH will check for the fault flag of all received packets.

    a. For all received packets, if the fault flag is 'N' then

        CH will frame an empty packet with its fault flag as 'N'.

    b. Else,

        CH will check for the vibration difference of those received packets whose fault flag is 'Y'. It will collect all those vibration difference >= Threshold_2 and then frame them into one packet and set its fault flag as 'Y'.

8. Forward the packet to the next hop CH.

9. Next hop CH will check for the fault flag of all received packets.

    a. For all received packets from CH, If fault flag is 'N' then

Frame an empty packet with its fault flag as 'N'.

b. Else,

Frame a packet with only those packets whose fault flag is 'Y' and then set its fault flag as 'Y'.

10. Repeat steps (8) and (9) till sink is reached.

11. Sink on receiving all packets will check for only those packets whose fault flag is 'Y'.

12. It will then check for the series of node that gave abnormal vibration difference and forward the appropriate decision packet to the train.

a. If the series exist, then the first node in the series is provided as track fault location to the train using reverse path by setting its decision packet's susp_break bit on.

b. Else send an empty decision packet with susp_break bit off.

13. Train on receiving the decision packet from sink will check for susp_break bit.

a. If susp_break bit is on then the train will compute its distance from the provided track fault location.

i. If distance < Threshold_3 (2 km)

Train will stop.

ii. Else,

Train will move normal or slow down its speed based on its distance from track fault location.

b. Else the train will move normally.

4 Simulation Results

4.1 Simulation Tool and Parameters

We have implemented both existing and our proposed work in MATLAB R2013a. It is a high performance language for technical computing as it integrates computation, visualization and programming in an easy-to-use environment where problems as solutions can be expressed using mathematical expressions [30]. Table 1 shows simulation parameters for network set up for track fault detection algorithm and Table 2 shows the simulation parameters for transmission which is based on first order radio model.

Table 1. Simulation parameters for network set up [29]

Sr. No.	Parameter	Value
1.	Track length	100 km
2.	Total number of nodes	256
	i. Number of sensors on the track	200
	ii. Number of forwarding nodes	56

Table 2. Simulation parameters for transmission [12]

Sr. No.	Parameter	Value
1.	Initial energy of nodes	0.5 J
2.	Energy consumed by the amplifier to transmit at a short distance	10 pJ/bit/m^2
3.	Energy consumed by the amplifier to transmit at a longer distance	0.0013 pJ/bit/m^4
4.	Energy consumed in the electronics circuit to transmit or receive the signal	50 pJ/bit
5.	Data aggregation energy	5 pJ/bit/report
6.	Data packet	4000 bits
7.	Control packet	100 bits

4.2   Network Architecture

Figure 3 (a) shows the deployment of nodes for track fault detection. There are four levels in this multi-level architecture. Sensor nodes are deployed along the length of tracks at every km which is represented as black dots on the track at Level 0 (L0). Forwarding nodes are at Level 1 (L1) to Level 3 (L3) which is represented as blue circles and sink is at Level 4 (L4) which is represented as green squares. This network is laid on both sides of tracks.

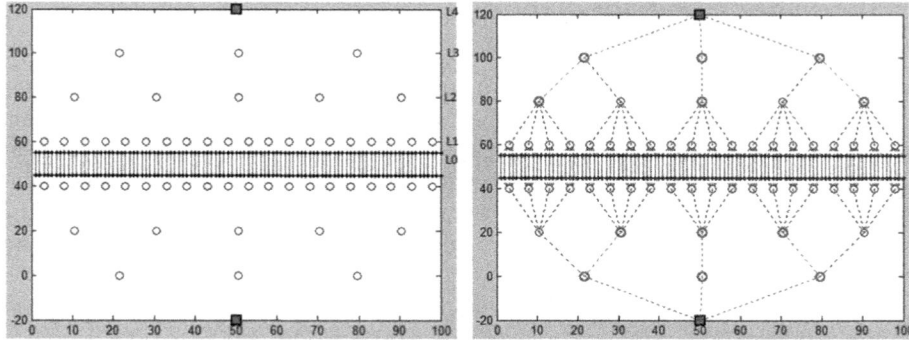

Fig. 3. (a) Deployment of nodes in multi-level architecture (left) and (b) Clustered network set up for proposed track fault detection algorithm (right)

We have implemented existing work in this network set up shown in Fig. 3(a) and (b) shows the network set up for proposed algorithm which is obtained after applying clustering algorithm [12] to multi-level architecture. In this figure, CHs are represented as red highlighted circles. Sensor nodes to forwarding nodes and forwarding nodes (Cluster Members) to CH communication are represented as blue dotted lines. CH to CH and CH to BS communication is represented as red dotted lines.

4.3   Proposed Algorithm Implementation

Moving Train Updating Its Location. Train along its direction of movement, will first register itself to the nearest forwarding node in both directions. It will then keep updating its location to this registered forwarding node who will forward the received train location to the sink which is shown as blue dots in circles in Fig. 4(a) where train is represented as blue star(*) on the track.

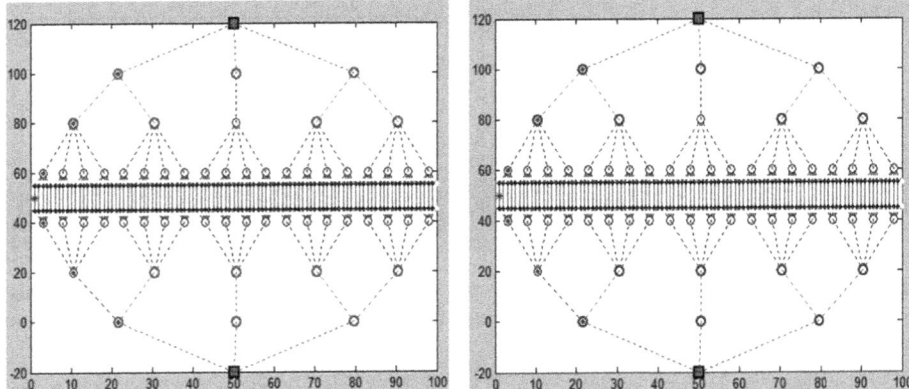

Fig. 4. (a) Train updating its location to the sink (left) and (b) Sink broadcasting the received train location (right)

Sink Broadcasting the Train Location. Sink will broadcast the received train location which is represented as black circles in Fig. 4(b). Sensor nodes on receiving the train location will compute estimated vibration using (1) and then compute current vibration difference using (2). It will then compute the difference using (3) and compare this difference with Threshold_1. If this difference exceeds Threshold_1, then it will send the current vibration difference by setting its fault flag as 'Y' else it will send an empty packet by setting its fault flag as 'N'. Forwarding node at each level will check for fault flag of all received packets. If the fault flag for all received packets are 'N' then it will send an empty packet by setting its fault flag as 'N' to CH via forwarding node otherwise it will aggregate vibration difference from those received packets that has fault flag as 'Y' and send it to CH via a forwarding node by setting its fault flag as 'Y'. CH will check for fault flag for all received packets. If fault flag is 'N' for all received packet then it will send an empty packet by setting its fault flag as 'N' to BS using multi-hop routing else it will check for the vibration difference of all those received packets whose fault flag is 'Y'. It will collect all those vibration difference that exceeds Threshold_2 and send it to sink using multihop routing by setting its fault flag as 'Y'.

Sink Updating the Track Fault Location. Sink will check for vibration difference of all received packets whose fault flag is 'Y'. If the series of nodes in the same direction gave abnormal vibration difference, then the location of the first node in that series is given as track fault location to the train using reverse path to the forwarding node to whom the train is currently registered with as shown in Fig. 5(a) and (b).

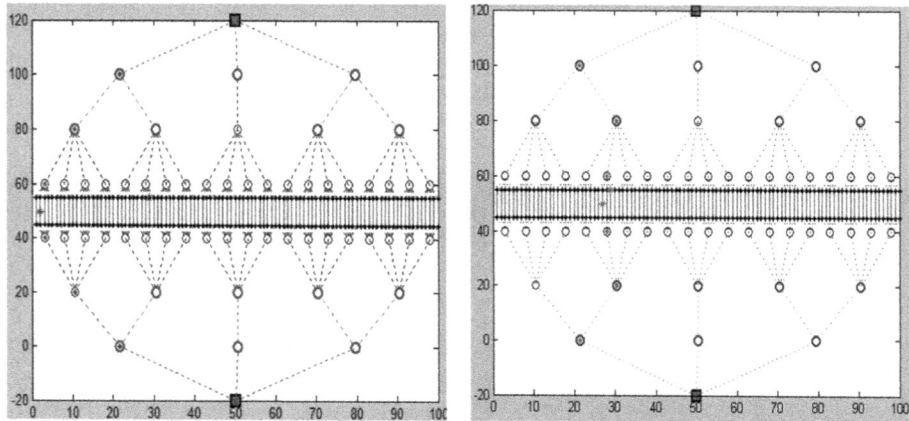

Fig. 5. Sink updating track fault location to the train. (a) Train keeps moving as its distance from track fault location is greater than 2 km (left) and (b) Train stopped as its distance from track fault location is less than 2 km (right)

Decision Making by Train. In Fig. 5(a) and (b), red dot in blue circle shows that there is a fault on the track. Train will then compute its distance from the received track fault location. If the computed distance is greater than 2 kms, then the train will keep moving as shown in Fig. 5(a) and this process repeats for every location update. If the computed distance is less than 2 kms then the train will stop which is shown as red star (*) on the track in Fig. 5(b). Figure 6(a) shows the graph of normalized sensed and estimated vibration of each sensor when the train is at location 19 km and track fault is at location 29 km. It is clearly seen from the graph that normalized sensed vibration started deviating from normalized estimated vibration at 29th km and the corresponding vibration difference is shown in Fig. 6(b). The point from where the normalized sensed vibration started deviating from normalized estimated vibration that point is provided as track fault location to the train by sink.

CH Failure Recovery. We have used [16] for CH failure recovery. During clustering process, the second highest residual energy node in each cluster is selected as Secondary Cluster Head (SCH). During communication, if CH has shortage of energy then it will inform to all its cluster members. If SCH is still highest residual energy node among its cluster members then it will be elected as the new CH else the highest residual node among the cluster members is elected as new CH. All the remaining cluster members will join the new CH as shown in Fig. 7(b).

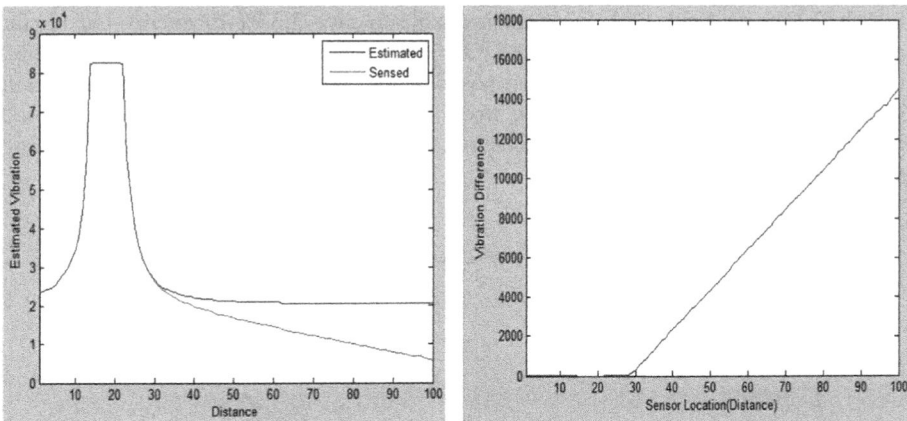

Fig. 6. (a) Normalized sensed vs. estimated vibration (left) and (b) Corresponding vibration difference (right) when train is at 19 km and track fault is at location 29 km.

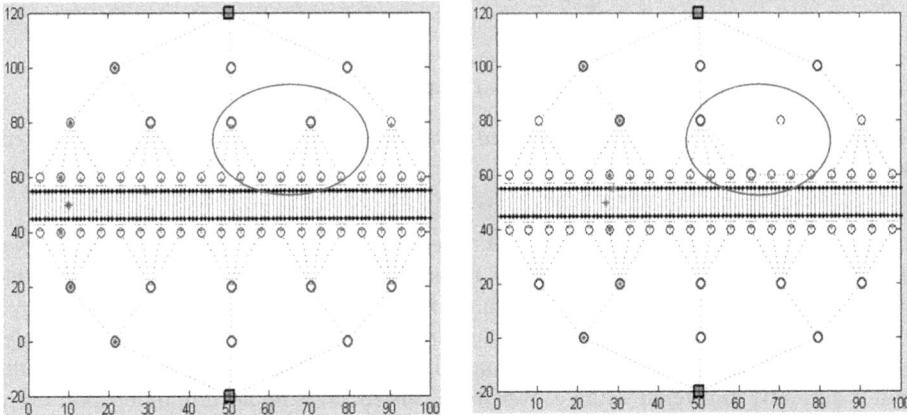

Fig. 7. (a) Initial set up of clustered network (left) and (b) When CH failed, SCH took up the role of CH (right)

4.4   Comparative Results

Existing vs. Proposed. We have implemented existing [29] and proposed track fault detection algorithm for different track fault locations and analysed their results in terms of parameters like total energy consumed, total time taken and average transmission time taken to update train regarding track fault location. Figure 8, Fig. 9(a) and (b) shows total energy consumed, total time taken and average transmission time taken by existing and proposed work to update train regarding track fault at different locations respectively. Figure 8 shows that our proposed algorithm has reduced energy consumption for different track fault locations when compared with existing work. Though for nearer track fault location, it is able to save 3.33% of energy but for far track fault location, it is able to save 88.33% of energy when compared with existing. Figure 9(a) and (b) shows that our proposed work takes less time for far track fault location when compared with existing work. For nearer track fault location, proposed work may take little more time than existing, depending on number of messages being processed.

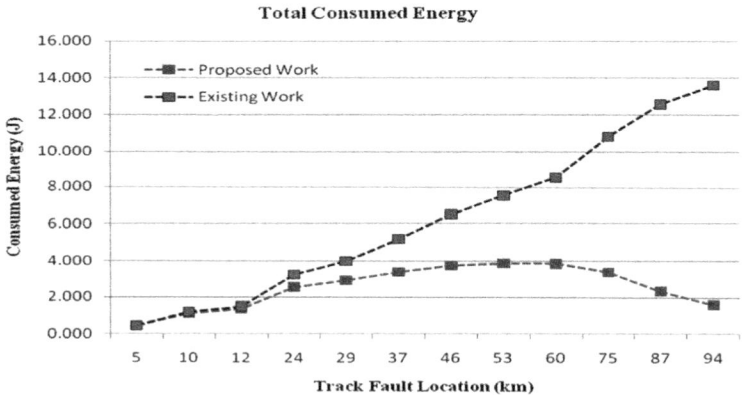

Fig. 8. Comparison of total energy consumed by existing and proposed work for different track fault locations

Existing vs. Proposed with Reduced Frequency Scenario. Till now, we have implemented a scenario where sink will broadcast the updated train location periodically and the track fault location algorithm triggers. To further preserve more energy, we have proposed a scenario in which the sink will broadcast the train location only when it receives the updated train location from the new forwarding node to which the train is currently registered with i.e. When the sink receives updated train location via a forwarding node, it will check if the previous location update is sent by the same forwarding node. If yes, then it will not broadcast the train location else it will broadcast the updated train location to the network. Figure 10(a) and (b) shows the total energy consumed and total time taken to update train regarding track fault at different locations by existing and proposed work in this proposed scenario. In this scenario too, our algorithm provides better results in terms of total energy consumed for updating train regarding track fault at different locations. Though for nearer track fault location, it takes a little more time than existing, it is able to reduce total time taken for far track fault locations when compared with existing work. Considering the fact that

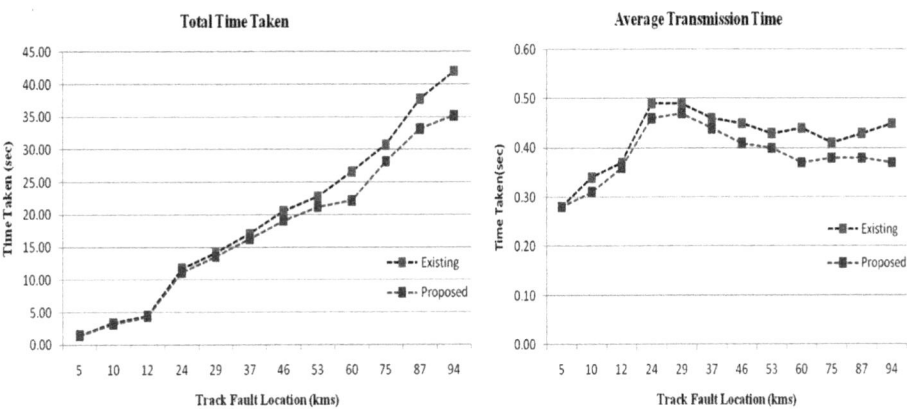

Fig. 9. Comparison of (a) Total time (left) and (b) Average transmission time (right) for existing and proposed work for different track fault locations

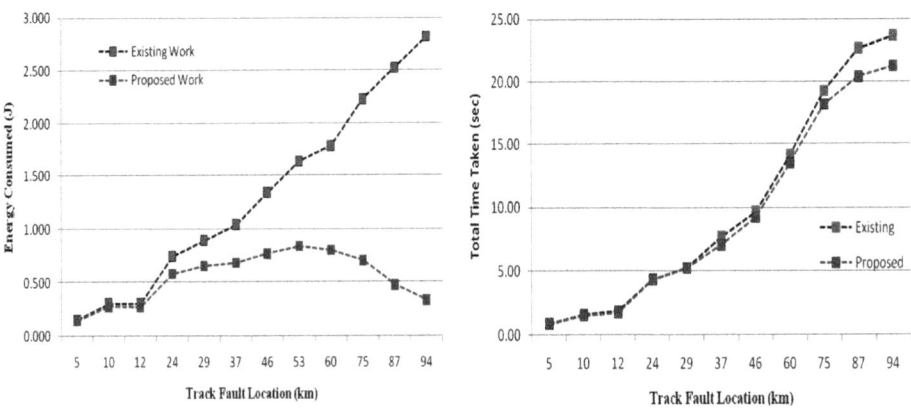

Fig. 10. Comparison of (a) Total energy consumed (left) and (b) Total time taken (right) for different track fault locations by existing and proposed work in reduced frequency scenario

energy is the primary concern for WSN used for remote monitoring, a little increase in time can be traded off when it can save more energy when compared to existing.

5 Conclusion

Manual inspections of metro train tracks are very expensive and tedious. Condition monitoring using WSN can reduce maintenance time through automated monitoring by detecting faults before they escalate. Sensors being a power constrained device, it is very much necessary to preserve their energy. Our proposed algorithm attempts to detect and provide the track fault location to the moving train by reducing the number of messages communicated between the sensors and the sink. Simulation of the network architecture is done with the assumption that vibration signals are successfully captured from vibration sensors. Our proposed algorithm provides better results in terms of total energy consumption and total time taken to detect and update train regarding the track fault location when compared with existing approach. Further, we have proposed a scenario that can help to preserve more energy by reducing the frequency of sink broadcasting the train location. We have implemented both algorithms in this scenario and analysed the received results. In this scenario too, our proposed algorithm proved to be energy efficient. Though, it takes little more time for nearer track fault location, it is able to reduce total time taken for far track fault location when compared with existing algorithm. Also, small increase in time can be traded off when it can result in good energy saving as energy is the primary concern for WSN used in remote monitoring.

References

1. Delhi Metro. https://en.wikipedia.org/wiki/Delhi_Metro. Accessed 27 Aug 2016
2. Hodge, V., Keefe, S., Weeks, M., Moulds, A.: Wireless sensor networks for condition monitoring in the railway industry: a survey. IEEE Trans. Intell. Transp. Syst. **16**(3), 1088–1106 (2015)
3. Yick, J., Mukherjee, B., Ghosal, D.: Wireless sensor network survey. Comput. Netw. **52**(12), 2292–2330 (2008)
4. Singh, S., Sharma, S.: A survey on cluster based routing protocols in wireless sensor networks. In: International Conference on Advanced Computing Technologies and Applications (ICACTA), pp. 687–695. Elsevier (2015)
5. Mahapatro, A., Khilar, M.: Fault diagnosis in wireless sensor networks: a survey. IEEE Commun. Surv. Tutor. **15**(4), 2000–2026 (2013)
6. Kim, J., Park, S., Han, Y., Chung, T.: CHEF: cluster head election mechanism using fuzzy logic in wireless sensor networks. In: IEEE 10th International Conference on Advanced Communication Technology (ICACT), pp. 654–659, February 2008
7. Sharma, T., Kumar, B.: F-MCHEL: fuzzy based master cluster head election leach protocol in wireless sensor network. Int. J. Comput. Sci. Telecommun. **3**(10), 8–13 (2012)
8. Latif, K., Ahmad, A., Javaid, N., Khan, Z., Alrajeh, N.: Divide-and-rule scheme for energy efficient routing in wireless sensor networks. In: The 4th International Conference on Ambient Systems, Networks and Technologies (ANT 2013), vol. 19, pp. 340–347. Elsevier, June 2013
9. Amgoth, T., Jana, P.: Energy-aware routing algorithm for wireless sensor networks. Comput. Electr. Eng. **41**, 357–367 (2015)
10. Park, G., Kim, H., Jeong, H., Youn, H.: A novel cluster head selection method based on K-means algorithm for energy efficient wireless sensor network. In: IEEE 27th International Conference on Advanced Information Networking and Applications Workshops, pp. 910–915, March 2013
11. Wang, N., Zhu, H.: An energy efficient algorithm based on leach protocol. In: IEEE International Conference on Computer Science and Electronics Engineering (ICCSEE), pp. 339–342, March 2012

12. Xu, J., Jin, N., Lou, X., Peng, T., Zhou, Q., Chen, Y.: Improvement of leach protocol for WSN. In: IEEE 9th International Conference on Fuzzy Systems and Knowledge Discovery (FSKD), pp. 2174–2177, May 2012
13. Maraiya, K., Kant, K., Gupta, N.: Wireless sensor network: A review on data aggregation. Int. J. Sci. Eng. Res. **2**(4), 1–6 (2011)
14. Patil, N., Patil, P.: Data aggregation in wireless sensor network. In: IEEE International Conference on Computational Intelligence and Computing Research (2010)
15. Venkataraman, G., Emmanuel, S., Thambipillai, S.: A cluster-based approach to fault detection and recovery in wireless sensor networks. In: IEEE 4th International Symposium on Wireless Communication Systems (ISWCS), pp. 35–39, October 2007
16. Akbari, A., Beikmahdavi, N., Mohammadi, M.: A new algorithm fault management by clustered in wireless sensor network. World Appl. Sci. J. **12**(10), 1784–1790 (2011)
17. Bagheri, T.: DFMC: decentralized fault management mechanism for cluster based wireless sensor networks. In: IEEE Second International Conference on Digital Information and Communication Technology and it's Applications (DICTAP), pp. 67–71, May 2012
18. Chanak, P., Banerjee, I.: Fuzzy rule-based faulty node classification and management scheme for large scale wireless sensor networks. Expert Syst. Appl. **45**, 307–321 (2016)
19. Babaie, S., Rezaie, A.R., Heikalabad, S.R.: DFDM: decentralized fault detection mechanism to improving fault management in wireless sensor networks. In: Cherifi, H., Zain, J.M., El-Qawasmeh, E. (eds.) DICTAP 2011. CCIS, vol. 166, pp. 685–692. Springer, Heidelberg (2011). https://doi.org/10.1007/978-3-642-21984-9_56
20. Bayissa, W.L., Dhanasekar, M.: High speed detection of broken rails, rail cracks and surface faults. In: CRC for Rail Innovation, November 2011
21. Track Circuit. https://en.wikipedia.org/wiki/Track_circuit. Accessed 08 Oct 2016
22. Communcation-based train control. https://en.wikipedia.org/wiki/Communications-based_train_control. Accessed 08 Oct 2016
23. Positive train control. http://www.up.com/media/media_kit/ptc/about-ptc/. Accessed 08 Oct 2016
24. Non Destructive Testing Methods for Rail Inspection. https://en.wikipedia.org/wiki/Rail_inspection. Accessed 08 Oct 2016
25. Castellanos, C., Gharaibeh, Y., Mudge, P., Kappatos, V.: The application of long range ultrasonic testing (LRUT) for examination of hard to access areas on railway tracks. In: IEEE 5th IET Conference on Railway Condition Monitoring and Non-Destructive Testing (RCM 2011), pp. 1–7, November 2011
26. Ramesh, S., Gobinathan, S.: Railway faults tolerance techniques using wireless sensor networks. In: IJECT, vol. 3, no. 1, March 2012
27. Aboelela, E., Edberg, W., Papakonstantinou, C., Vokkarane, V.: Wireless sensor network based model for secure railway operations. In: IEEE International Performance Computing and Communication Conference, pp. 623–628, April 2006
28. Kalimathi, M., Illakya, P., Sathiavathy, E.: Innovative railway track surveying with sensors and controlled by wireless communication. Int. J. Adv. Electr. Electron. Eng. 17–19 (2008)
29. Sharma, K., Maheshwari, S., Solanki, R., Khanna, V.: Railway track breakage detection method using vibration estimating sensor network: a novel approach. In: IEEE International Conference on Advances in Computing, Communication and Informatics (ICACCI), pp. 2355–2362, September 2014
30. MATLAB. http://in.mathworks.com/. Accessed 29 Nov 2016

A Sugeno-Mamdani Fuzzy System Based Soft Computing Approach Towards Sensor Node Localization with Optimization

Abhishek Kumar$^{(\boxtimes)}$ and Bhawana Saini

Faculty- IT, iNurture Education Solutions Private Limited,
Bangalore 560052, India
Abhisheikh.kmr@gmail.com, Kapoorbhawana76@gmail.com

Abstract. Localization implies determining or tracking the position of sensor nodes accurately within the deployment area. Most of the localization approaches involve use of some deployed nodes whose position coordinates are already known to us (using Geographical Positioning System (GPS) or some other method) called landmarks or anchors. As fuzzy systems are apt at handling imprecise and uncertain values, this study attempts to leverage the imprecision and uncertainty handling ability of soft computing techniques such as Fuzzy Logic. An aggregated Mamdani- Sugeno Fuzzy Inference System based localization approach has been proposed using triangular membership functions. One input Received Signal Strength Indicator (RSSI), 5 rules and one output (weight) model has been implemented. The output weight indicated the proximity of a particular anchor to an unknown node. The weight was then used in weighted centroid to compute the estimated position of the unknown sensor node. The solution was optimized using Gauss Newton method. The accuracy of the proposed scheme was 50% to 90% better than centroid, weighted centroid and some other works done using soft computing techniques. A coverage of almost 97–98% can be achieved in least computational time. The average processing time of the proposed technique was approximately 1.5 s. The number of anchors required to localize the nodes is also extremely less. Furthermore, being computationally simple, the algorithm does not require any extra hardware and can be implemented in pure decentralized manner. This study also offers new insights into how optimization techniques such as Gauss Newton method can be used to significantly improve the localization accuracy and to solve the problem of localization in large scale sensor networks where number of sensor nodes are in range of thousands.

Keywords: WSN · Anchors · Range-Free · Sugeno fuzzy inference systems
Mamdani fuzzy inference systems · Localization algorithms
Gauss Newton method

1 Introduction

The usage of sensor nodes has witnessed an exponential uplift in past few years. Wireless Sensor Networks are the autonomous, ad hoc system of tiny sensors in large numbers connected together and communicating with a base station. Trivially, these

© Springer Nature Singapore Pte Ltd. 2018
P. Bhattacharyya et al. (Eds.): NGCT 2017, CCIS 828, pp. 40–55, 2018.
https://doi.org/10.1007/978-981-10-8660-1_3

nodes and the network are subjected to challenges such as limited power, limited coverage region, no existing infrastructure, prone to interferences in communication, channel constraints etc.

Localization refers to the phenomenon of identifying the position of sensor nodes with or without the help of anchors or beacon nodes or also called landmarks. It is obvious to state that all nodes cannot be aware of their locations because of issues or challenges mentioned earlier. Localization of sensor nodes within a deployment region is an imperative task because without it the data collected from sensors and aggregated at base station is of no use.

A sensor node to precisely and accurately accomplish its location computation, communicates with in range anchor nodes. These anchors broadcast their positions in form of beacon signals. With the help of information contained in beacon signals, the unknown sensors locate themselves. Localization process is subjected to various challenges such as: node density, topology, limited resources at the disposal of nodes, presence of obstacles, irregular deployment region and presence of mobility. Each of these factors poses different kind of challenge to localization.

The most traditional method of localization is range based techniques such as: Received Signal Strength Indicator (RSSI), Angle of Arrival (AoA) and Time of Arrival (ToA). RSSI [1] finds the distance between an unknown node and anchor node based upon the attenuation of sent signal. AoA [2] deals with angle subtended by two anchors/landmarks at unknown node and then employing geometry of triangles to compute the position of unknown node. ToA [3, 4] measures the elapsed time between transmission of beacon by anchor and reception of it by unknown node. Among the three techniques, the localization accuracy of AoA and ToA supersedes that of RSSI, but this comes at a cost of rigid computations and need of antenna arrays.

Another category of localization algorithms called range free techniques does not explicitly rely on ranging information. Rather they use connectivity information which is expressed in form of hop count. The hop count reflects how close or far sensor nodes are from each other. The simplest and earliest of range free approaches are: Centroid algorithm [5], A Point In Triangulation (APIT) [6], DV hop [7] and Convex Positioning Estimation (CPE) [8]. CPE has the highest accuracy among all and can find the position of unknown node in presence of obstacles also. But the severe demerit of this algorithm is that it is implemented in centralized manner and thus there exists a single point of failure. DV hop eliminates the need of having at least three anchors to successfully localize an unknown node.

2 Related Work

The work in [9] proposed a probability based fuzzy system in which the authors modeled the localization problem using a probabilistic fuzzy logic approach. It uses if else based fuzzy rules which took RSSI as input and gave Weight as output. The output weight was fed to weighted centroid method to compute the estimated position. Wight reflects the proximity of anchor to the unknown sensor node. The authors used Mamdani Fuzzy inference system. Each of the rule was associated with an output probability vector V. For example, a rule can be defined as

"*IF RSSI is high then Weight is medium with a probability of 0.1 and weight is high with a probability of 0.8 and weight is very high with probability 0.1*".

The authors used one input, five rules and one output fuzzy system. The input has five membership functions namely: very low, low, medium, high, and very high. Therefore the output probability vector for the above rule can be written as

$$V = [0.0\,0.0\,0.1\,0.8\,0.1]$$

Simulations result showed that average localization error for traditional fuzzy based localization system was 2.27 m whereas in case of probabilistic fuzzy approach it was 1.99 m. The latter was more effective in noisy environment and the results were very promising.

In the study done by Kumar et al. in [10], the authors use weighted centroid algorithm by calculating the weights as an output variable from the fuzzy inference system. The FIS takes RSSI as input variable and its range was [0 RSSImax] and the range of output variable was between [0 1]. Five membership functions were defined for each of the input and output variable. The authors study the results of four techniques Sugeno based, Mamdani based, combined Sugeno-Mamdani and ANFIS Sugeno. Combined Sugeno-Mamdani averaged the weights obtained from Sugeno and Mamdani individually. ANFIS was used to refine the membership functions *params* using back propagation method or a hybrid method of back propagation and least square methods. For a simulation environment of 60 unknown sensors and 121 anchors in non-cooperative localization, the average localization error for simple centroid was 1.61 m, for Mamdani FIS was 0.8956 m, for Sugeno was 0.95 m and for combined Sugeno-Mamdani was 0.76 m. The authors also simulated a cooperative localization using 25 anchors, 60 unknown sensors. In this scenario the average error for combined Sugeno-Mamdani was 1.74 m.

The work done by Monfared in his Master's thesis [11], the author explicitly used Sugeno based fuzzy logic to compute the weights which were fed to the weighted centroid algorithm. The fuzzy system used in this study comprised of one input variable: RSSI (logarithm value was taken) with range [−80, 0], one output variable: weight with range [0, 1] and nine if-then rules. Each of the variable has 9 membership functions namely: very very low, very low, low, medium low, medium, medium high, high, very high and very very high. Simulation results of with and without AWGN (Additive White Gaussian Noise with SNR of 10) were studied. The average error for Sugeno FIS without AWGN was 0.26 m and that with AWGN was 0.30. The authors also replicated the results in experimental study to obtain an average error of 0.53 m. The RSSI vs weight surface obtained form FIS was similar to following Fig. 1:

Kumar and Kumar in [12] further improvised their previous work on fuzzy logic based localization. The authors studied a fuzzy logic based weighted centroid scheme in which weight was calculated based on RSSI and Link Quality Indicator (LQI) as input variables. In the first step, unknown sensor finds out the number of anchors it can listen to, based upon the number of beacons received. Next it computes the edge weights using RSSI and LQI where

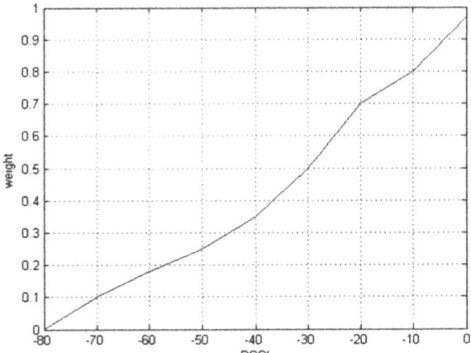

Fig. 1. RSSSI vs weight plot

$$LQI = \frac{255 * (N_{tran} - N_{recvd})}{N_{tran}} \quad 0 < LQI < 255 \quad (1)$$

N_{tran} is the number of bits sent by anchor and N_{recvd} is the number of bits received by unknown sensor with error. The input variables RSSI and LQI each had 3 membership functions: low medium and High, while the output variable edge weight had five membership functions namely: very low, low, medium, high and very high. Total 9 if-then rules were defined. Simulation results showed that in a scenario considering AWGN along with external noise radio frequencies of −30dBm, the mean localization error for Mamdani FIS was 0.89 m, for Sugeno FIS was 0.971 m and for combined Sugeno-Mamdani was 0.781 m.

Indhumathi and Venketasen in [13] propose a deployment model for dynamically deployed nodes to obtain maximum coverage distance using genetic algorithm. Authors used GA to select some best sensor nodes that can be initially deployed in the sensing field. Then in the next step any uncovered or undeployed area is identified. Node distance is the radio range or the coverage of the node. Genetic algorithm involves five steps: Initialization, Selection, Crossover, Mutation and Termination. In the initialization phase, nodes were deployed randomly with each node being represented by 20 bits string gene. Next, the fitness function selects the best nodes using tightness ratio. In the selection phase, tournament procedure is used. Among the two nodes available, the one having the best fitness value is chosen. Then in the crossover phase, gene bit strings are crossed over as the following example:

$$110010000111000|11010 \rightarrow 110010000111000011100$$
$$100110001100011|11100 \rightarrow 100110001100011111010$$

In the mutation phase, a random number was generated and if it was greater than the mutation probability of 0.01, the bit 0 was flipped to 1 and bit 1 to 0 as shown in following example:

$$1100111100000110011 \rightarrow 1100111100000110111$$

Simulation results of 150 total nodes and 100 deployed nodes in a sensing area of 100 * 100 m showed that uncovered area was reduced after the cluster gap was reduced.

In the work done by Gharghan et al. in [14] the authors used Adaptive Neuro Fuzzy Inference System (ANFIS) in which the input was three distinct RSSI values obtained from 3 distinct anchors. For each input, 3, 5 and 7 membership functions (*mf*) were trained. The authors studied and compared the results of two difference kinds of mf_s: *trimf* (triangular *mf*) and *gbellmf* (bell shaped *mf*). Very large samples consisting of 900 RSSI values were used, out of which 70% was used to train the ANFIS, 15% was used to test the ANFIS and remaining 15% was used to validate the ANFIS. The authors studied the result of both indoor and outdoor environment and conclusively found that results of indoor scenario was less accurate and promising because of phenomena such as multipath scattering. The Mean Absolute Error and Root Mean Square Error for indoor scenario was less accurate than that of outdoor scenario for all the three cases. Furthermore the results of *gbellmf* was more promising than that of *trimf*. Also both MAE and RMSE decreased with increase in number of membership functions from three to five and eventually to 7 *mf*.

Morelande and Moran [15] studied application of machine learning methods in sensor networks and proposed a localization technique based on Bayesian probability. Two different kinds of probabilities were used: prior and posterior. Prior probability denotes the probability of a hypothesis when evidence has been observed. The idea was to predict samples that best fit the posterior probabilities or likelihood. This scheme uses very few anchors and worked efficiently for large scale sensor networks where number of deployed nodes are in range of thousands. The algorithm was implemented in centralized mode and was moderately complex.

In the study done by Yang et al. in [16] the authors studied the application of Support Vector Machines (SVM) classifiers to solve the localization problem in wireless sensor networks. A mobility based approach was used in which the movement was tracked by Received Signal Strength Indicator or RF oscillations. A change in value of RSSI denoted that the node has moved to some other location. Large training sets of RSSI were fed to SVM to output the new estimated location. The simulation results showed that the processing time was significantly reduced and so was the computational complexity but, the method was very sensitive to any outliers, incomplete or missing values in the training data set. The technique was less hardware intensive and thus was implemented in distributed manner.

Gu and Hu in [17] attempted to use Gaussian processes to model sensor networks. In this study, the sensors were deployed in the monitoring region through Gaussian distribution process. The mobility was modeled using Distributed Gaussian Process Regression (DGPR) which predicted optimal positions for node movement. Each node implemented the Gaussian Regression locally and independently using collected information from local anchors. Conventional GPR has a complexity of O (N^3), N = sample size, whereas the proposed techniques had a computational complexity significantly low.

Zheng and Dehghani in their work in [18] propose a novel range free connectivity based localization algorithm using Neural Networks i.e. LNNE (Localization using Neural Network Ensembles). The study assumes that there are multiple anchors in the network and unknown sensors node communicate with them directly or indirectly. Every node has fixed radio range R. Further, the authors have used two network ensembles separately for computing X and Y coordinate. Each of the X and Y NNE comprises of 'C' components where, each component represents a 3-tiered feed forward model. The anchor nodes, A_j are logically placed in input layer. The unknown nodes U_i are placed in hidden layer. The input to the NNE is the hop count that is the number of hops and unknown node is away from the anchor. So the input is expresses as $h(U_i, A_j)$. The output from each component is the estimated 'x' coordinate from that particular component $x_{estUi,c}$. To find the estimated location, the authors have used mean.

$$X_{estUi} = \frac{1}{C} \sum_{i=1}^{C} x_{estUi,c} \tag{2}$$

Similar methodology has been used for find the estimated Y coordinate. The authors have also proposed and optimization algorithm for refinement called EMSO ("Enhanced Mass Spring Optimization"). It consists of a cooperative approach, where position data of anchors and unknown nodes are taken into utilization. The authors compared the results vis-a-vis traditional range free approaches: Centroid and DV Hop. The localization accuracy was improved by a factor of 21% approximately. The mean localization error in LNNE with 30 anchors was 2.78 m and that with 70 anchors was 2 m.

Kumar et al. in [19] studied the application of neural network techniques in sensor node localization. In this study, the authors proposed a neural network based localization relying on feed forward model. The authors studied the impact of different anchor ratios and their configuration on localization accuracy. The received Signal Strength Indicator (RSSI) from three anchors comprised the input. The hidden layer was modeled as 12-12-2 structure. The first two layers in the hidden layer used Sigmoid functions as activation function and the third sublayer used "*purelin*" activation function. The output layer had two nodes: one each for the computation of x and y coordinate of unknown node. The authors studies the effect of multiple training models: LM ("Levenberg-Marquardth") and BR ("Bayesian Regularization") and concluded that average localization error in BR was less than that of LM training model. Each of the training model used multi-layer perceptron. The results were further validated in real world scenario using 802.15.4 ZigBee sensors and microcontrollers. The average localization error was 0.295 m.

In the work done by Singh et al. [20] the authors propose a distributed, cooperative localization scheme based upon Biogeographic Based Optimization (BBO) and PSO. The impact of multiple variants of BBO namely Blended BBO (BBBO), Enhanced BBO (EBBO) on localization accuracy has also been studied. BBO is a method that emulates the distribution pattern of plants and organism species over the time and space taking into account their migration behavior. It is an optimization technique similar to Ant Colony Optimization (ACO), Genetic Algorithm (GA) and

Simulated Annealing. The localization methodology is as follows: Some target nodes and anchors were randomly deployed in the deployment region. Each unknown node needed a minimum three anchors to be successfully localized. Initially, the mean of position of anchors in the radio range of unknown node was considered to be estimated position. In the next step, each node runs PSO, BBO, EBBO and BBBO. A fitness function in form of least square problem was formed which represented the error between the measured distance and estimated distance, (here measured distance refers to distance computed using BBO, EBBO, BBBO and PSO). Simulation results showed that the average localization error for BBBO was less than that of PSO, BBO and EBBO but at the expense of more computational complexity.

Monica and Ferrari [21] further studied the swarm optimization techniques. This study proposes a cooperative localization scheme using computational intelligence technique known as Particle Swarm Optimization (PSO). Sensor nodes in the deployment area communicated with each other using UWB (Ultra-Wide Band) signaling. The location estimation has been done by considering Two Stage MLE (Maximum Likelihood Estimation) as an optimization problem to be solved by PSO technique. The algorithm starts with four anchors and for each iteration nodes whose position have been computed becomes anchor in next iteration. The PSO technique has been used in following manner: the candidate solutions of the optimization problem framed as least square problem can be considered as a swarm of size M. Every particle in the swarm has, at any moment 'n', a position associated with it say $x^j(n)$, for all $j = 1,2,......,M$.

Every member of the swarm knows at each step the best position of self (*pbest*) and its neighbor members (*gbest*). In the next iteration, they use this information to estimate their best position. Simulation results showed that Mean Square Error (MSE) of PSO was several factors less than that of TSMLE without PSO.

3 Problem Statement

Given N number of sensor nodes deployed in a particular 2-D area, how can we use fuzzy logic systems as a primitive to Gauss Newton Optimization to find the position coordinates (xi, yi), for $i = 1,2,3,......,N$ with the help of only four anchors deployed at four corners of the deployment area? Furthermore, are the results promising and acceptable vis-à-vis parameters such as cost, accuracy, coverage, running time complexity? The objectives of this paper is to design a joint Sugeno-Mamdani Fuzzy Inference System to compute weight corresponding to RSSI value and to assess the impact of Gauss Newton optimization method on localization accuracy.

4 Preliminaries

4.1 Assumptions and Parameters of Interest

- All the sensor nodes, except the anchors, were deployed randomly.
- There is Line of Sight (LoS) communication.

- The anchors are placed on the corner of deployment area.
- There is no attenuation in signal strength while in transit.
- There is no collision among two or more signals.
- The deployment region has no irregularities or obstacles.

The various factors for consideration and comparison are:

1. **Localization coverage:** It refers the percentage or ratio of nodes correctly localized. This study assumes that the nodes whose estimated position lie outside the deployment region are considered to be non-localized.
2. **Localization error:** The mean absolute error will be computed as: Suppose (x_{cen}, y_{cen}) is the computed position of a node and (x_i, y_i) is the actual position of the node then the mean absolute error can be calculated as

$$\sum_{i=1}^{n} \frac{\sqrt{(x_{cen} - x_i)^2 + (y_{cen} - y_i)^2}}{n} \tag{3}$$

3. **Cost trade off**: We should look for a localization algorithm which uses less number of anchors. More the number of anchors, more the cost burden. Furthermore increasing the number of anchors does not necessarily guarantee better localization coverage or accuracy. So we need to maintain an optimal anchor to nodes ratio. Cost will also depend on power Equation
4. **Algorithmic complexity**: The space and time complexity of centralized algorithm is less than distributed algorithm but this comes at a cost of sustaining the fear of single point of failure in case of centralized algorithms. The intent is to reduce the memory requirement
5. **Anchor placement**: The position where anchor is placed is also important. Some localization algorithm require anchor to be placed at corners of simulation area whereas some require anchor to be placed at Centre and start moving.

4.2   Fuzzy Logic

Fuzzy logic is a logical extension to multivalued logic permitting intermediate values to be defined between continuous evaluations such as yes or no, high or low, true or false etc.

There are numerous advantages of using Fuzzy logic: It is simpler to comprehend and less complex more intuitive; flexibility in terms of inputs and outputs, their range; number and types of membership functions; adjoined with traditional control paradigm.

Fuzzy logic offers an additional edge in solving the localization problem in wireless sensor networks because of following reasons:

- Unlike probabilistic system, fuzzy system is not random. Rather it relies on complete understanding of the available dataset. Such situations come in handy to understand the behavior of sensor network.
- Localization in wireless sensor networks is a nondeterministic problem. Thus modelling the network with certain fuzzification is simpler.

- The nonlinear computations involved in calculating the accuracy or other factors involve some arbitrary computational inefficiency.

In this study, a rule set comprising of 5 rules have been incorporated into the Fuzzy Inference System (FIS). Empirical studies and experiments in some of the literatures suggested that accuracy of localization tends to improve with increase in number of membership functions and rule set. However there is no concrete evidence for this kind of uniform behavior. In other to minimize the memory requirements for additional rules, the number of rules should be kept minimum as possible. The rule set used for this study is as follows:

Rule 1: *IF RSSI is very low, THEN weight is very low*
Rule 2: *IF RSSI is low, THEN weight is low.*
Rule 3: *IF RSSI is medium, THEN weight is medium.*
Rule 4: *IF RSSI value is high, THEN weight is high.*
Rule 5: *IF RSSI value is very high, THEN weight is very high.*

Here, the Received Signal Strength Indicator (RSSI) has been calculated using equation:

$$RSSI[dBm] = RSSI_{src} - 10 * n * \log_{10}\left(\frac{dist}{dist_{src}}\right) \qquad (4)$$

$dist_{src}$ is taken to be 1 m (most of the existing literatures [12, 13] used this value, so we assumed same value for impartial comparison of results obtained), $RSSI_{src}$ is RSSI value at a distance 1 m and is taken to be -30 dB [12], n is variable called path loss exponent and is taken to be 3.25, dist is the Euclidean distance between anchor and unknown sensor node.

4.3 Weighted Centroid

Weighted centroid is an extension to the centroid localization technique mentioned in Sect. 1. Weights denote the proximity or closeness of an unknown sensor node to a particular anchor. Greater the weight, more closely is the unknown sensor to that anchor. The accuracy of weighted centroid depends largely on the choice of weight. In the proposed scheme, the weights are output by the fuzzy system, thus relieving the network designer to manually assign weight to each anchor corresponding to its locations. Using weighted centroid, the position of an unknown node 'M' can be found as:

$$(X_M, Y_M) = \left(\sum_{j=1}^{4} \frac{x_j w_j}{w_j}, \frac{y_j w_j}{w_j}\right) \qquad (5)$$

x_j and y_j are the X and Y coordinates of anchor 'j', w_j is the corresponding weight for that anchor. With a tight upper bound on the approximation in Gauss Newton method and less number of anchors, the summated value of weights can be upper bound to be 1.

4.4   Gauss Newton Method

Gauss Newton optimization is used to solve nonlinear least square problems without having to compute the second differential. It requires the user to provide with the initial guess that is fed as an initialization vector to the optimization process.

Suppose we have 'M' functions f_a (a = 1, 2, 3,......, M) of N variables V (V_1, V_2, ...). The Gauss Newton Optimization (GNO) can be used to compute minimal value of sum of squares.

$$S(V) = \sum_{a=1}^{M} f_a(V) \tag{6}$$

Initial guess: V [0]

$$V[k+1] = V[k] + \delta_k \tag{7}$$

$$\delta_k = -\left(J_f\right)^T * f \tag{8}$$

And J_f is the Jacobean matrix of 'f' with respect to the V[k].

In this study of the proposed scheme, the estimated position obtained from aggregated Sugeno-Mamdani FIS (as explained in Algorithm 1) serves as the initial guess, say, ψ_{di}

$$\psi_i[k] = \psi_{di} \tag{9}$$

$$\psi_i[k+1] = \psi_i[k] + \delta_k \tag{10}$$

Here it must be noted that successive iteration involves computation of Jacobean, so the algorithm fails when singular matrix is obtained. Use of fuzzy logic estimated position as initial guess eliminates the odds of having to obtain a singular matrix.

Time division multiplexing (TDM) technique is used to avoid interference of beacons transmitted by neighboring anchor nodes. The radio transmission range of all nodes is assumed to be identical and perfectly spherical. Here, it can be seen that the positions obtained from fuzzy logic weighted centroid is used as initial inputs for the Gauss Newton Method. Simulation results and their explanation has been mentioned in the subsequent section.

ALGORITHM 1: Pseudo code of proposed algorithm

STEP 1: Choose square deployment area of 10*10m.
STEP 2: Deploy four anchors, one at each corner.
STEP 3: Deploy unknown sensor nodes randomly.
STEP 4: Compute Euclidean distance between unknown sensors with each of the anchor.
STEP 5: Compute RSSI value with path loss exponent value (n) as 3.25 using Equation. 4.
STEP 6: Use RSSI as input to Sugeno FIS.
STEP 7: Use RSSI as input to Mamdani FIS.
STEP 8: Compute average weight as (Weight_Sugeno + Weight_Mamdani) / 2.
STEP 9: Compute estimated position using weighted centroid approach as mentioned in section 4.3
STEP 10: Formulate the least square problem as:

$$f(x, y) = \frac{1}{A}\sum_{i=1}^{A}(\sqrt{(x_{est} - x_i)^2 + (y_{act} - y_i)^2} - \tilde{d_i})$$

(11)
   A= Number of nodes
$\tilde{d_i}$ is distance corresponding to additive noise and standard deviation approximated as distance measurement error of 0.1
STEP 11: Apply Gauss Newton method as mentioned in 4.4 with number of iterations equal to 100, to compute the minimum of the function in Step 10.
STEP 12: Compute the Average Localization Error (ALE) after employing the Gauss Newton method using Equation 3.

5   Result and Discussions

The proposed approach was implemented in MATLAB 2012a using the fuzzy logic tool box. The various setup parameters were: the network area consisted of 10 * 10 m 2-D region where both X and Y axes are 10 m long. The number of unknown sensor nodes was ranging from 50 to 100 and the number of locator nodes or anchors were only 4. Each of the 4 anchor was placed at 4 corners of the network area i.e. the anchors were at (0, 0), (0, 10), (10, 0), (10, 10). The unknown nodes were randomly deployed. Various assumptions and parameters of consideration have already been discussed in Sect. 4.1.

In the fuzzy logic toolbox, we modeled the Sugeno type and the Mamdani type separately and then computed the average of the output weight as depicted in flowchart of research methodology.

In the Mamdani type fuzzy logic designed, the input membership functions are triangular (trimf) and so is the output membership function. 5 rules were created based on the 5 membership functions, as discussed in Sect. 4.2. The input variable i.e. RSSI ranged from −80 to 0, where −80 is the minimum RSSI value and 0 is the maximum. The output i.e. weight value was between [0, 1]. In the Sugeno type logic, the input membership functions were triangular (trimf) and the output membership functions are linear. The range of value was as follows: very low: [0, 0.2], low: [0, 0.4], medium: [0, 0.6], high: [0, 0.8], very high: [0, 1]. As it was inferred from the designed systems that in Sugeno type when RSSI value is −19.8 dBm, the weight is 0.826; and in the Mamdani type when weight is somewhere near to 0.7. Thus both types of Fuzzy Logic behave differently and the output depends on which FL type we are using.

Figure 2 shows the localization before employing the Gauss Newton optimization. This is node localization purely based on the average weight obtained from the Sugeno and Mamdani FL and fed into weighted centroid algorithm as discussed in Sect. 4.3. The mean estimation localization error ranged from 3 to 4 m, as different times simulations were run.

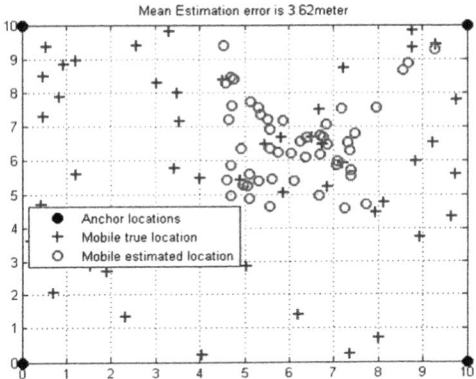

Fig. 2. Localization before Gauss Newton Optimization

Figure 3 depicts the node localization after employing the Gauss Newton optimization. The procedure for the same and mathematical equations have been discussed in Sect. 4.4. GN optimization improved the localization accuracy significantly by reducing the mean estimation error from ~ 3.5 m to range of ~ 0.4 m to 0.45 m. Furthermore, since the least square problem formed contained only two variables, the running time complexity was also low. GN method optimizes a least square problem without having the user to compute the second order derivatives. So the overhead involved is also low as processing time was reduced by a factor of nearly 45–50%.

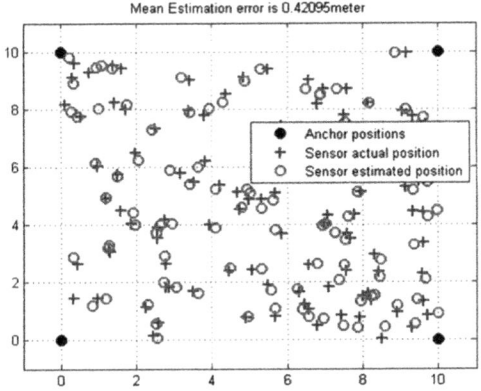

Fig. 3. Localization after Gauss Newton optimization

Figure 4 shows the plot of variation in Mean Estimation error vis-à-vis number of sensor nodes deployed. As it can be seen clearly, the men estimation error increased somewhat linearly from 0.12 to 0.32 as number of nodes increased from 10 to 60. Then there was a sharp increase in error as number of node increase to 60 to 70 and after that it became almost constant. Here it must be noted that this plot was drawn upon the results obtained empirically.

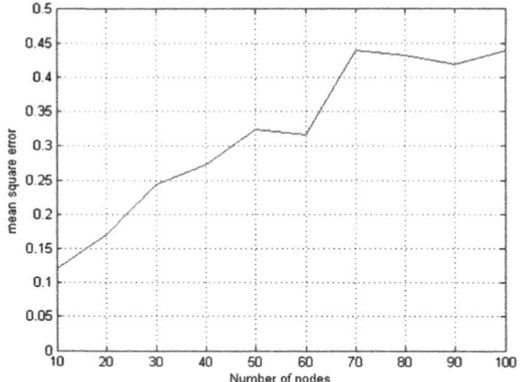

Fig. 4. Localization error vs. number of sensor nodes

Figure 5 shows a bar chart of average localization error comparison of the proposed scheme with the existing works in soft computing based localization. As it can be inferred from the diagram that the mean localization error of simple centroid scheme was 1.61 m and that of individual Mamdani FIS and Sugeno FIS was 0.90 m and 0.95 m respectively. A combined Mamdani and Sugeno approach yielded a localization error of nearly 0.77 m. The mean localization error of proposed scheme is 0.43 m.

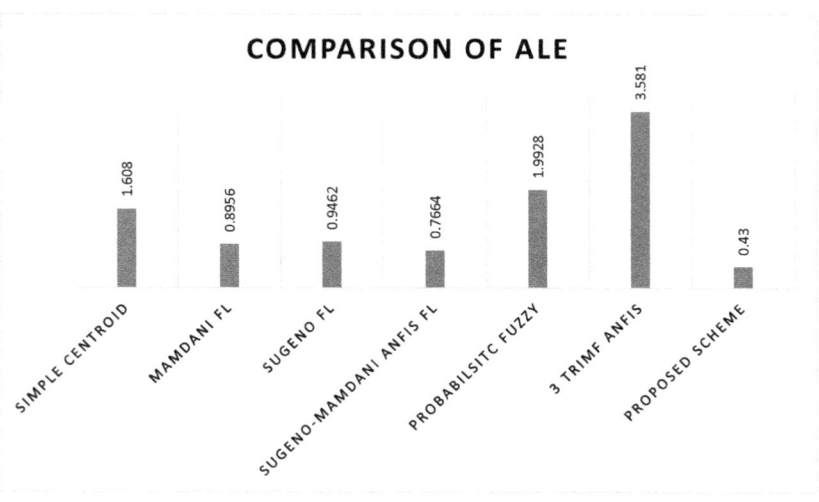

Fig. 5. Comparison of average localization error

Also, here is worth mentioning that the studied existing works used an anchor ratio of at least 66.8% and up to a total of 121 anchors to localize 80 nodes. The proposed scheme used only a total of 4 anchors to achieve the localization of 100 randomly deployed node in an average time duration of within 3–4 s in MATLAB. **Here it must be noted that the simulation parameters such as network area, number of nodes deployed, radio range of nodes and communication mode etc. have been kept same as that of existing literatures to have an impartial comparison of results obtained.** A tabular representation of comparison of existing schemes with proposed one has been depicted in Table 1.

Table 1. Comparison of proposed scheme with existing works

Technique	Mean Estimation Error (in meters)	Number/Ratio of anchors
Simple centroid [5]	1.6080	66.8%
Mamdani fuzzy logic [10]	0.8956	66.8%
Sugeno type FL [11]	0.9462	66.8%
Sugeno-mamdami ANFIS [12]	0.7664	66.8%
Probabilistic fuzzy [9]	1.9928	121
3 *trimf* ANFIS [14]	3.581	—
Proposed scheme	0.4295	4

5.1 Discussion of Other Parameters

Apart from average localization error, the effectiveness of proposed scheme can also be assessed in terms of other parameters such as cost, running time complexity, localization coverage, scalability. Cost in context of localization majorly stems from the number of anchors deployed. The proposed scheme is intrinsically cost effective as it used only 4 anchors to localize 100 nodes. Running time of the proposed scheme is also promising, although the results may vary for different processing capabilities and hardware platforms. The proposed scheme localized on average at least 97 nodes out of 100 deployed to achieve a coverage of 97%. One major issue with the proposed scheme is scalability. The scheme does not scale well with large scale sensor node deployment in its present form. The solution to scalability bottleneck can be to implement this scheme by partitioning the large scale network into a number of clusters of 100 nodes each and implement this scheme for each cluster.

6 Conclusion and Future Work

Soft computing techniques such as fuzzy inference systems, genetic algorithms, particle swarm optimization etc. effectively take into account the uncertainty and randomness in real world problems and handle them accordingly. Wireless sensor networks being non deterministic in nature, can conveniently be modeled using soft computing techniques.

This study proposed a new fuzzy system based soft computing approach to solve the issue of node localization in wireless sensor networks. The position error was then optimized using Gauss Newton method to improve the mean localization error from nearly 3.5 m to 0.42 m. The proposed work is also cost effective since it used only 4 anchors to localize successfully with a promising localization coverage. The limitation of this study is that it works well with the 2-D deployment area, however in order to scale it efficiently to 3-D network deployment region, we need to use more robust optimization techniques which achieves the same level of accuracy and coverage as that of 2-D regions. Another limitation is that it does not incorporates mobility in the sensor nodes, upon which future work can be done.

Future work in this regard can also be done to integrate the fuzzy logic approach towards localization with other optimization techniques such as ant colony optimization. The position information obtained from fuzzy logic can be used as initial input to ACO. Additionally, novel schemes can be designed to incorporate mobility using Random Way Point or Random Direction into Fuzzy based approaches. In area of secure localization, work can be done to add signatures to beacon signals send by anchors to unknown sensor nodes. Furthermore work can be done to achieve better localization results in presence of hurdles or in irregular deployment. The sole purpose is to achieve an accurate position of sensors with minimal cost (in terms of anchor), minimal power consumption, minimum space and time complexity.

References

1. Zheng, P., Ni, L.: Smart Phone and Next Generation Mobile Computing. Elsevier, Amsterdam (2006)
2. Gui, L.: Improvement of range-free localization systems in wireless sensor networks. Univ. Toulouse (2013)
3. Hofmann-Wellenhof, B., Lichtenegger, H., Collins, J.: Global Positioning System Theory and Practice. Springer, Heidelberg (2001). https://doi.org/10.1007/978-3-7091-6199-9
4. Patwari, N., Hero, A.O., Perkins, M., Correal, N.S., O'Dea, R.J.: Relative location estimation in wireless sensor networks. IEEE Trans. Signal Process. **51**(8), 2137–2148 (2003)
5. Bulusu, D.E.N., Heidemann, J.: GPS-less low cost outdoor localization for very small devices. IEEE Pers. Commun. Mag. **7**(5), 28–34 (2000)
6. He, T., Huang, C., Blum, B.M., Stankovic, J.A., Abdelzaher, T.: Range-free localization schemes for large scale sensor networks. In: Proceedings of 9th Annual International Conference on Mobile Computing and Networking, (MobiCom 2003), p. 81 (2003)
7. Mesmoudi, A., Feham, M., Labraoui, N.: Classification of wireless sensor networks localization algorithms: a survey. In: Giis 2013, vol. 52, no. 4, pp. 2419–2436 (2013)
8. Doherty, L., Pister, K.S.J., El Ghaoui, L.: Convex position estimation in wireless sensor networks. In: Proceedings IEEE INFOCOM 2001. Conference on Computer Communications. Twentieth Annual Joint Conference of the IEEE Computer and Communications Society (Cat. No. 01CH37213), vol. 3, pp. 1655–1663 (2001)
9. Kadkhoda, M., Totounchi, M.A., Yaghmaee, M.H., Davarzani, Z.: A probabilistic fuzzy approach for sensor location estimation in wireless sensor networks (2010)

10. Kumar, A., Chand, N., Kumar, V., Kumar, V.: Range free localization schemes for wireless sensor networks. Int. J. Comput. Netw. Commun. **3**(6), 115–129 (2011)
11. Monfared, M.A.: Range free localization of wireless sensor networks based on sugeno fuzzy inference. no. c, pp. 36–41 (2012)
12. Kumar, A., Kumar, V.: Fuzzy Logic based improved range free localization for wireless sensor networks. vol. 177005, no. 5, pp. 534–542 (2013)
13. Indhumathi, S., Venkatesan, D.: Improving coverage deployment for dynamic nodes using genetic algorithm in wireless sensor networks. Indian J. Sci. Technol. **8**(16) (2015)
14. Gharghan, S.K., Nordin, R., Ismail, M.: A wireless sensor network with soft computing localization techniques for track cycling applications. Sensors (Switzerland) **16**(8), 1043 (2016)
15. Morelande, M.B.M., Moran, B.: Bayesian node localization in wireless sensor networks. In: IEEE International Conference on Acoustics, Speech and Signal Processing, pp. 2545–2548 (2008)
16. Yang, B., Yang, J., Xu, J., Yang, D.: Area localization algorithm for mobile nodes in wireless sensor networks based on support vector machines. In: Zhang, H., Olariu, S., Cao, J., Johnson, David B. (eds.) MSN 2007. LNCS, vol. 4864, pp. 561–571. Springer, Heidelberg (2007). https://doi.org/10.1007/978-3-540-77024-4_51
17. Gu, D., Hu, H.: Spatial Gaussian process regression with mobile sensor networks. IEEE Trans. Neural Netw. Learn. Syst. **23**(8), 1279–1290 (2012)
18. Zheng, J., Dehghani, A.: Range-free localization in wireless sensor networks with neural network ensembles. J. Sens. Actuator Netw. **1**(3), 254–271 (2012)
19. Kumar, S., Sharma, R., Vans, E.R.: Localization for wireless sensor networks: a neural network approach. vol. 8, no. 1, pp. 61–71 (2016)
20. Singh, S., Shivangna, S., Mittal, E.: Range based wireless sensor node localization using PSO and BBO and its variants. In: 2013 International Conference Communication Systems and Network Technologies, pp. 309–315 (2013)
21. Monica, S., Ferrari, G.: Particle swarm optimization for auto-localization of nodes in wireless sensor networks. In: Tomassini, M., Antonioni, A., Daolio, F., Buesser, P. (eds.) ICANNGA 2013. LNCS, vol. 7824, pp. 456–465. Springer, Heidelberg (2013). https://doi.org/10.1007/978-3-642-37213-1_47

Interference Aware Adaptive Transmission Power Control Algorithm for Zigbee Wireless Networks

K. Vikram and Sarat Kumar Sahoo$^{(\boxtimes)}$

School of Electrical Engineering, VIT University, Vellore 632014, Tamil Nadu, India
sksahoo@vit.ac.in

Abstract. In Zigbee wireless networks, transmission power control (TPC) is very important for adjusting the transmission power dynamically to minimize the energy consumption. The existing works on Zigbee wireless networks involve high computational and storage overhead. To enhance the Zigbee performance there is a necessity to consider the channel variations, co-channel interference, and transmission failures during TPC. In this paper, interference aware adaptive TPC (IAATPC) algorithm is proposed to perform data communication after considering the communication features like interference level, signal strength, node distance and power level. Then the further transmissions will be performed by analyzing the power level needed in the network to ensure reliable data delivery. Thus, the data transmission is performed under different network conditions by adaptively controlling the transmission power and in turn ensuring network efficiency.

Keywords: Interference · Transmission power control · Personal area networks · Wireless sensor networks · Zigbee

1 Introduction

The Wireless sensor networks (WSNs) draw significant attention from academics, industries, and researchers equally, because of the promising and innovative applications in the perspective of Internet of Things (IoT), automation and advanced monitoring owing to the lower cost of the components, which enables a widespread deployment. The functional scenarios for WSNs can be categorized in three main groups: rural, urban, and indoor [1]. The IEEE 802.15.4 standard was basically developed only for the personal area networks. However, in the course of time, as the characteristics of the wireless sensor networks evolved, the IEEE 802.15.4 standard was used in numerous applications like home area networks (HAN), building automation, IOT applications, smart metering etc. The target of the IEEE 802.15.4 standard is to permit the communication between the wireless devices with minimum battery power and also with moderate bit rate. Zigbee alliance has followed the IEEE 802.15.4 standards and has defined Zigbee communication for applications operating with low power. It is also possible to deploy larger networks using Zigbee [1, 2]. The

© Springer Nature Singapore Pte Ltd. 2018
P. Bhattacharyya et al. (Eds.): NGCT 2017, CCIS 828, pp. 56–69, 2018.
https://doi.org/10.1007/978-981-10-8660-1_4

Zigbee wireless network performs communication at a fixed highest transmission power according to the Z-Stack/Zigbee protocol stack. This logic of communicating at fixed transmitting power even when the distance between communicating nodes are different leads to wastage of energy, which in turn deteriorates the lifetime of the network [3].

TPC is concerned with controlling the transmission power at the transmitter node at the lowest level so as to assure reliable data transfer along with better Quality of Service (QoS). This can be achieved by adapting the transmission power level moderately while designing the network along with considering the network topology. Also, it is possible for the TPC protocol to handle the transmission power in a dynamic manner in order to minimize the energy utilization by the mobile node as well as increase its life span. This in turn reduces the co-channel interference when transmission is being performed in a shared medium [4].

It is essential to estimate the transmission power based on the link quality and also it is very important to adjust the availability of wireless channel in a robust manner. Several TPC algorithms are being designed by keeping the channel capacity in mind. The optimal broadcasting power level is computed on the basis of the link quality indicator (LQI) as well as Received Signal Strength (RSS). Then an adaptive transmission power control algorithm (ATPC) is used to adapt the data transmission in a robust manner as per the network requirement. Normally, the WSN based on Zigbee devices perform data transmission with minimal power consumption when compared with the Bluetooth or WiFi devices. Hence, while designing the TPC algorithm, it is necessary to take into consideration the interference possible from the devices operating at 2.4 GHz [5, 10, 11].

IAATPC algorithm in this paper is proposed by considering factors like:

- Ability to increase the battery lifetime in certain applications
- Ability to actively adjust to ensure device future energy needs
- Facilitates minimizing the transmission power and helps in energy savings.
- Enables co-existence by ensuring interference suppression, spectrum proficiency as well as topology controlling features [3].

2 Related Works

The work in [4] have proposed TPC algorithm designed for industrial applications on the basis of the theoretical and empirical studies. Simulation results have proved that this technique adjusts to changes in the link quality. This algorithm is hardware independent and also is easily deployable for practical purposes. A TPC mechanism was proposed in [6] suitable for IEEE 802.15.6 networks working in a beacon mode by estimating with superframe boundaries. In this work the broadcast power is estimated on a frame basis, as per the run time requirement of the network channels. The power level is estimated regularly through the aid of the beacon frames, offering the reverse channel gain. Also, based on the previous power level changes seen, an opportunistic fade margin is included. Through this technique, it is possible to track the much varying on node to node propagation channel, even without requiring extra probe frame transmission.

The mechanism in [7] is based on adaptive transmission power control for WSN to adapt the energy consumption under various network conditions. This proposed technique aims to achieve power control in WSN even when its resources characteristics are limited and not well defined. Minimizing the power consumption may lead to backfiring effects in the network. Also, the interference effect will be higher due to the usage of the power boosting feature. The proposed work may also need to work on comprehending the conditions wherein the usage of reduced power will benefit by enhancing the spectrum proficiency and also reduce interference. An innovative transmit power control technique in [8] is based on optimization theory for the WSN. In this mechanism, many nodes transmit data directly to a specific access point. An optimal transmit power assignment technique is developed by considering the total network power as a finite and the traffic level is lesser. This technique reduces the packet error rate at the access point. The proposed power control mechanism is developed on the basis of the CSMA/CA MAC protocol modeling using finite state machines and also considers the network adjacency matrix according to the transmit power distribution and then the network connectivity is computed. Through the experimental result obtained confirms about the minimized transmit power allocation issue.

3   Interference Aware Adaptive Transmission Power Control Algorithm (IAATPC)

3.1   Problem Identification and Objectives

In TPC algorithm of [4], Received Signal Strength Indicator (RSSI) and Signal to Interference Noise Ratio (SINR) are checked with the Golden Receive Power Range (GRPR) thresholds. For this, the TPC table has to be built with appropriate power levels. But this method incurs huge storage overhead while building the TPC for all the pair of nodes. Moreover, it does not consider transmission failures. In [7, 9], TPC is conducted on the basis of Packet Reception Rate (PRR) only. However, TPC algorithms based on the PRR may cause large overheads and cannot effectively respond to the link quality variations [5].

Hence the main objective of this work is to design a TPC algorithm for multi-channel networks such that,

- The computation overhead is reduced
- The storage overhead is lessened
- The channel variations and data transmission failures are considered.

In this paper, IAATPC is proposed for multi-channel Zigbee wireless networks. The IAATPC algorithm is applied when multiple channels are discovered between the transmitting node to the receiving node in a WSN. The proposed algorithm is implemented into two phases: Initialization stage and Operational stage. In the Initialization phase, the Transmit Power Matrix (TPM) is generated based on the network node status. In the Operational phase, the packet transmission is initiated based on the TPM values. Then based on the collected transmission status, the transmission power is adapted to ensure reliable data transmission. The TPM depends on factors like distance between the nodes, initial transmission power, SINR and RSSI. Since the proposed algorithm avoids the usage of PRR and considers transmission failures, the overhead will be low and the average packet delivery ratio will be high.

3.2 Initialization Stage

In the initialization stage of algorithm, for each pair of nodes: the source and the destination node; and for each channel, a TPM is constructed with varying distance between the nodes, measured RSSI, measured SINR and suggested initial power level [4]. Then accordingly two threshold SINR values depicting the lower bound and upper bound values are determined. This process is described in algorithm 1. Nomenclature of this phase is as shown in Table 1.

1. For every path between the two nodes N_i and N_j, through a given channel C_k, the distance between the two nodes, D_{ij} is determined.
2. Next, the $RSSI_{ij}$ value at N_i from N_j is estimated on the basis of the Eq. (1) shown below:

$$RSSI_{ij} = 10.q.\log_{10}[D_{ij} + I + N] \tag{1}$$

$$I = \sum I_m \tag{2}$$
$$m = 1 \text{ to M}$$

3. Then the $SINR_{ij}$ at N_i with respect to N_j is computed according to Eq. (3) given below:

$$SINR_{ij} = 10\log_{10}[\frac{D_{ij}}{(I+N)}] \tag{3}$$

4. The P_t^I is estimated according to Eq. (4) as shown below:

$$P_t^I = TP_{x=1} \tag{4}$$

5. Then the TPM is generated for channel, C_k between nodes N_i and N_j as per Eq. (5) given below:

$$TPM = <D_{ij}, RSSI_{ij}, SINR_{ij}, P_t^I> \tag{5}$$

6. Then two threshold values for $SINR$ are maintained as $SINR_{low}$ and $SINR_{high}$.

In this way, the TPM is constructed based on the involved node distance, its measured SINR, measured RSSI and initial transmission power value. Since the

Table 1. Nomenclature: initialization phase

Notation	Meaning
N_i	Sender node i
N_j	Receiver node j
C_k	Channel k
D_{ij}	Distance among node i and node j
$RSSI_{ij}$	Received signal strength indicator between node i to node j
S_{ij}	Signal Power at i from j
I	Total interference power
N	Noise power
I_m	Interference from interferer node m
M	Total number of interferers
m	Interferer node
$SINR_{ij}$	Signal to interference plus noise ratio
P_t^I	Initial transmission power
$TP_{x=1}$	Lowest discrete transmission power level
TPM	Transmit power matrix
$SINR_{Low}$	Low limit of SINR Value
$SINR_{High}$	Higher limit of SINR value

generated metric considers all the critical data transmission features, this helps in building adaptive transmission process.

3.3   Operational Stage

In the operational stage of the algorithm, the sender transmits data stream to the receiver with the initial power estimated from TPM. Based on the received acknowledgment message, the sender node estimates the failed transmission count. Then accordingly average SINR is estimated. Based on the comparison level of average SINR value and average count of failed packet transmission, the transmission level is adapted to enhance the future data stream transmission. This process is described in Algorithm 2. Nomenclature of this phase is as shown in Table 2.

1. After the generation of the *TPM*, the sender node, N_i sends its data stream to the receiver node, N_j with P_t^i

$$N_i \rightarrow \left\{ Data, P_t^i \right\} \rightarrow N_j$$

2. When the N_j receives the data stream correctly from N_i, the N_j sends an *ACK* message to the N_i as a confirmation of message reception.

$$N_i \leftarrow \{ACK\} \leftarrow N_j$$

3. When the N_j receives the data stream incorrectly or when the data stream is not received from N_i, the N_j does not send any *ACK* message to the N_i.
4. The N_i keeps track of all the *ACK* messages received from N_j for each transmitted data stream.
5. Based on the number of missing *ACK* messages and transmitted packet details, the N_i measures P_{col} and P_{err} according to Eqs. (6) and (7) given below:

$$P_{col}(N_i) = 1 - [1 - T_{txn(i)}(G_i + F_i) + \sum T_{txn(j)}(G_j + F_j)^2]$$
$$j \in H(N_i) \quad (6)$$

$$P_{err}(N_i) = BER.P_{size} \quad (7)$$

Then N_i estimates $\beta(N_i)$ according to Eq. (8) given below:

$$\beta(N_i) = P_{col}(N_i) + P_{err}(N_i) \quad (8)$$

6. Next N_i computes N_F according to Eq. (9) given below:

$$N_F(N_i) = \frac{\beta(N_i)}{[1 - \beta(N_i)]} \quad (9)$$

7. The N_j considers a W of G and then computes $SINR_{avg}$ according to Eq. (10) shown below:

$$SINR_{avg} = \int_0^W (\sum_{m=1\ to\ G} SINR_m) \quad (10)$$

8. The estimated $SINR_{avg}$ is compared with the $SINR_{low}$ and $SINR_{high}$ values.
9. If it falls between the optimum range $<SINR_{low}, SINR_{high}>$, then the transmission is considered as normal.
10. If $SINR_{avg} < SINR_{low}$, then the TPC mode is set and N_j sends it as a feedback to N_i.

$$N_i \leftarrow \langle TPC, (SINR_{avg} < SINR_{low}) \rangle \leftarrow N_j$$

11. After getting the feedback message from N_j, the N_i verifies the value of N_f.
12. If $N_f > N_{f,\ min}$, then transmit power P_t is reduced by a factor ΔP_t.
13. If $N_f < N_{f,\ min}$, then P_t is increased by 1, until $N_f > N_{f,\ min}$.
14. If $SINR_{avg} > SINR_{high}$, then the N_j sends feedback to N_i.

$$N_i \leftarrow \langle TPC, (SINR_{avg} > SINR_{low}) \rangle \leftarrow N_j$$

15. On receiving the feedback message from N_j, the N_i increases P_t by ΔP_t.

Table 2. Nomenclature: operational phase

Notation	Meaning
N_i	Sender node i
N_j	Receiver node j
ACK	Acknowledgement message
P_{col}	Collision probability
P_{err}	Packet error probability
$T_{txn(i)}$	Transmission time of a data packet sent by node Ni
G_i	Packet generation rate for node Ni
F_i	Packet forwarding rate by node Ni
$H_{(Ni)}$	Set of neighbour nodes of node Ni
BER	Bit error rate
P_{size}	Packet size
$\beta_{(Ni)}$	Probability of unsuccessful transmission for node Ni
N_F	Average number of failed transmission for a packet
$SINR_{avg}$	Average signal to interference noise ratio
W	Window
G	Group of packets
N_f^{min}	Minimum value for average count of failed packet transmission
P_t	Transmit power
ΔP_t	Smaller value of transmit power

Thus, the transmission power is adaptively controlled by the nodes involved in data transmission to ensure successful and reliable data communication.

4   Experimental Results

4.1   Simulation Parameters

The IAATPC protocol was implemented using ns2.34 software. The Zigbee network is implemented based on IEEE 802.15.4 for the MAC layer settings. The importance of this is, when the node is ready for transmitting the data, the network is informed about the link breakage. The simulation is carried by varying the number of nodes in the network as 21, 41, 61, 81 and 101. The Size of area considered is 50 m × 50 m square region and simulation is carried for 50 to 300 s of simulation time. The simulated traffic is Constant Bit Rate (CBR).

4.2   Performance Metrics

The proposed IAATPC algorithm is compared with the Adaptive Multi-channel Transmission Power Control (AMTPC) algorithm [4]. The performance of the two algorithms is evaluated in terms of end-to-end delay, packet delivery ratio, throughput, average residual energy and overhead. The simulation settings and parameters considered are summarized in Table 3.

Table 3. Simulation parameters

Simulation parameter	Value
Number of nodes	20, 40, 60, 80 and 100
Area size	50 × 50 m
MAC protocol	IEEE 802.15.4
Routing	Zigbee cluster tree
Transmission range	12 m
Simulation time	50 s
Traffic type	Constant Bit Rate (CBR) and Exponential (EXP)
Packet size	512 Bytes
Number of data flows	2 to 10
Antenna	Omni antenna
Propagation	TwoRayGround
Initial energy	10 J
Receive power	0.3 W
Transmit power	0.5 W

4.3 Results and Analysis

The number of nodes and number of data flows are varied to evaluate the performance of these two techniques.

4.4 Varying the Number of Nodes by Keeping the Number of Data Flows Constant

In order to analyze the effect of interference on network size, the number of nodes is varied from 20 to 100 for 6 data flows.

The delay measured is as shown in Fig. 1, for IAATPC and AMTPC when the nodes are varied. From the figure, the delay of IAATPC increases from 14.3 to 21.2 ms, the delay of AMTPC increases from 15.4 to 23.3 ms. Thus, the delay of IAATPC is 12% of less when compared to AMTPC.

The packet delivery ratio is measured between IAATPC and AMTPC when the nodes varied is as shown in Fig. 2. The packet delivery ratio of IAATPC decreases from 0.31 to 0.23 and the packet delivery ratio of AMTPC decreases from 0.24 to 0.14. Thus the Packet delivery ratio of IAATPC is 32% of higher than AMTPC.

Figure 3 shows the overhead considered in packets for IAATPC and AMTPC when the number of nodes is varied. From the figure it can observed as, the overhead of IAATPC increases from 6.07 KB to 10.2 KB and the overhead of AMTPC increases from 8.3 KB to 13.1 KB. Thus overhead of IAATPC is 24% less when compared to AMTPC.

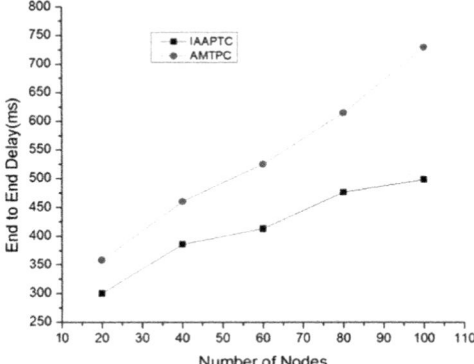

Fig. 1. Comparison of number of nodes to end-end delay (ms)

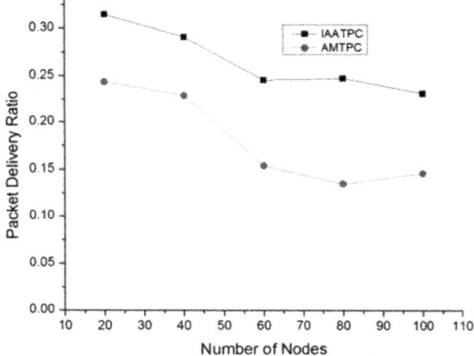

Fig. 2. Comparison of number of nodes to packet delivery ratio

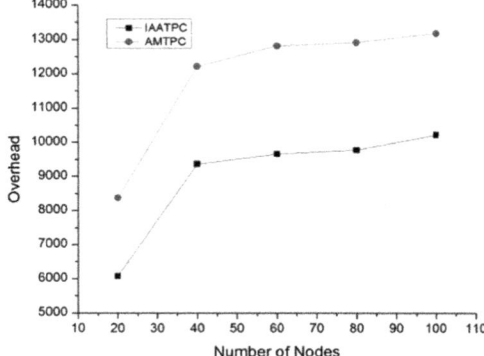

Fig. 3. Comparison of number of nodes to overhead

The throughput measured for IAATPC and AMTPC when the number of nodes is varied is as shown in Fig. 4. The throughput of IAATPC increases from 0.16 to 0.32 Mb/s and the throughput of AMTPC increase from 0.1 to 0.19 Mb/s. The throughput of IAATPC is 26% high when compared to AMTPC.

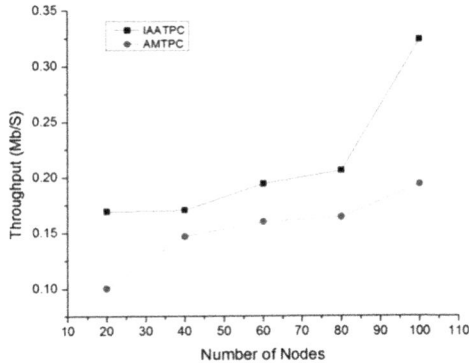

Fig. 4. Comparison of number of nodes to throughput

The Fig. 5 shows the average residual energy measured for IAATPC and AMTPC when the number of nodes is varied. From the results obtained it can be inferred as residual energy of IAATPC is 9.6% higher than AMTPC.

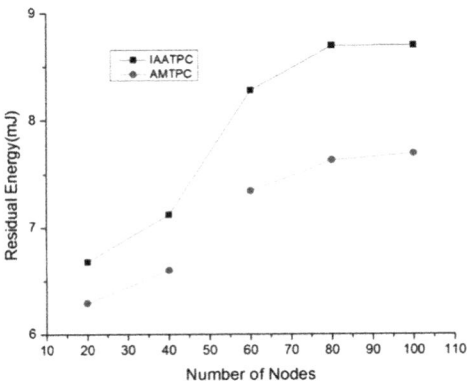

Fig. 5. Comparison of number of nodes to residual energy

4.5   Varying the Number of Data Flows by Keeping Number of Nodes Constant

The parameter number of data flows is varied from 2 to 10 for 100 nodes.

The delay measured for IAATPC and AMTPC when the data flows are varied is as shown in Fig. 6. From the figure it can inferred as the delay of IAATPC increases from 14.6 to 16.7 ms and the delay of AMTPC increases from 16.3 to 23.3 ms. Thus the delay of IAATPC is 23% less when compared to AMTPC.

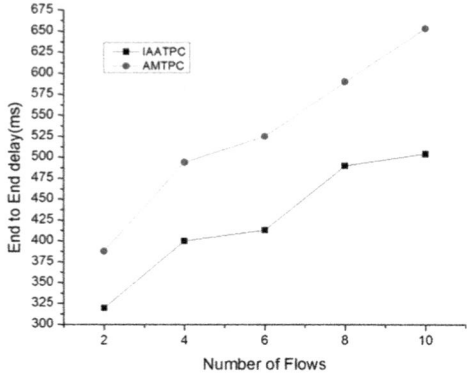

Fig. 6. Comparision of number of flows to end to end delay (ms)

The packet delivery ratio is measured for IAATPC and AMTPC when the number of flows is varied is shown in Fig. 7. The Packet delivery ratio of IAATPC decreases from 0.43 to 0.21 and the packet delivery ratio of AMTPC decreases from 0.30 to 0.15. Thus the packet delivery ratio of IAATPC is 24% higher when compared to AMTPC.

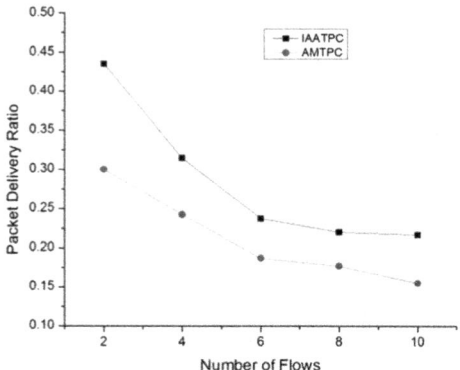

Fig. 7. Comparison of number of flows to packet delivery ratio

The overhead occurred for IAATPC and AMTPC when the data flows are varied is shown in Fig. 8. From the figure it can be observed as, the overhead of IAATPC increases from 5.1 KB to 23.4 KB and the overhead of AMTPC increases from 8.1 KB to 25.2 KB. Thus, the overhead of IAATPC is 16% less when compared to AMTPC.

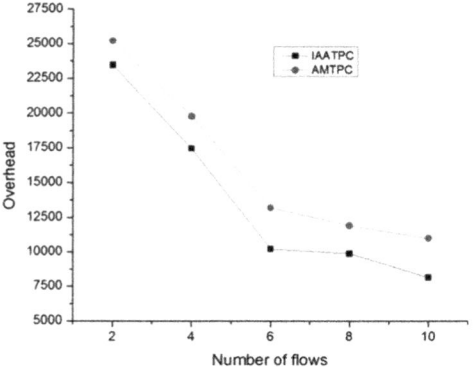

Fig. 8. Comparison of number of flows to overhead

The Fig. 9 shows the throughput measured for IAATPC and AMTPC when the flows are varied. It can be inferred from the figure, the throughput of IAATPC increases from 0.18 to 0.24 Mb/s and the throughput of AMTPC increases from 0.09 to 0.13 Mb/s. Thus the throughput of IAATPC is 49% higher than AMTPC.

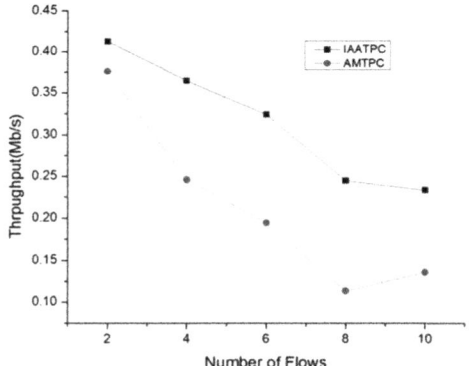

Fig. 9. Comparison of number of flows to throughput

The Fig. 10 shows the average residual energy measured for IAATPC and AMTPC when the flows are varied. From the figure we can observe, that the residual energy of IATPC is 7% of less when compared to AMTPC.

5 Conclusion

In this paper, IAATPC technique for Multi-channel Zigbee Wireless Networks was proposed and implemented. The proposed technique is divided into two stages: Initialization stage and operational stage. In the initialization stage, the characteristics

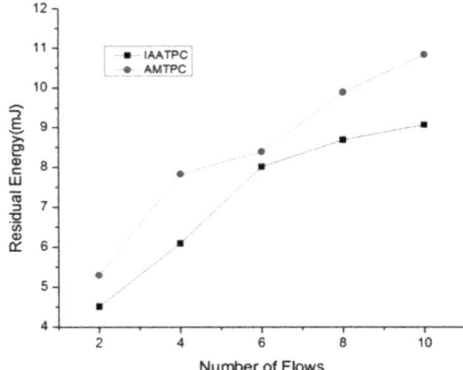

Fig. 10. Comparison of number of flows residual energy (mJ)

which decide the data transmission efficiency such as RSSI, SINR, initial transmit power, etc. are estimated in order to construct the Transmit Power Matrix. Then in the operational phase, the sender node starts transmitting its data stream to the receiver node at the destination. Based on the acknowledgment received, the sender node estimates the average transmission failure rate and keeps monitoring the SINR value at every specified time window. The estimated SINR average value is then compared with lower and upper limit value of SINR, so as to adapt the transmit power for further data transmission. In this way, the transmission power is adaptively controlled with respect to the interference level in the Zigbee network.

References

1. Ouni, S., Ayoub, Z.T.: Predicting communication delay and energy consumption for IEEE 802.15.4/Zigbee wireless sensor networks. Int. J. Comput. Netw. Commun. (IJCNC) **5**(1), 141 (2013)
2. Patel, N., Kathiriya, H., Bavrava, A.: Wireless sensor network using Zigbee. Int. J. Res. Eng. Technol. **02**(06) (2013). ISSN 2319-1163
3. Panxing, L., Tong, W.: A method for adjusting transmit power of ZigBee network node based on RSSI. In: IEEE International Conference on Signal Processing, Communications and Computing (ICSPCC), Ningbo, pp. 1–4 (2015)
4. Ikram, W., Petersen, S., Orten, P., Thornhill, N.F.: Adaptive multi-channel transmission power control for industrial wireless instrumentation. IEEE Trans. Ind. Inf. **10**(2), 978–990 (2014)
5. Kimy, J., Kwon, Y.: Interference-aware transmission power control for wireless sensor networks. In: Emerging Technologies for Practical Ubiquitous and Sensor Networks (2008)
6. Di Franco, F., Tachtatzis, C., Atkinson, R.C., Tinnirello, I., Glover, I.A.: Channel estimation and transmit power control in wireless body area networks. IET Wirel. Sens. Syst. **5**(1), 11–19 (2014)
7. Chincoli, M., Syed, A.A., Exarchakos, G., Liotta, A.: Power control in wireless sensor networks with variable interference. Mob. Inf. Syst. **2016**, 10p. (2016). Hindawi Publishing Corporation, Article ID 3592581

8. Consolini, L., Medagliani, P., Ferrari, G.: Adjacency matrix-based transmit power allocation strategies in wireless sensor networks. Sensors **9**, 5390–5422 (2009)
9. Yang, G., Guan, X.: A non-cooperative game theoretic approach to energy-efficient power control in wireless sensor networks. Int. J. Future Gener. Commun. Netw. **7**(1), 169–180 (2014)
10. Vikram, K., Narayana, K.V.L.: Cross-layer multi channel MAC protocol for wireless sensor networks in 2.4-GHz ISM band. In: 2016 International Conference on Computing, Analytics and Security Trends (CAST), Pune, pp. 312–317 (2016)
11. Vikram, K., Sahoo, S.K., Narayana, K.V.L.: Forward error correction based encoding technique for crosslayer multi channel MAC protocol. Energy Procedia **117**, 847–854 (2017)

Controlled Replication Based Bubble Rap Routing Algorithm in Delay Tolerant Network

Sweta Jain[(⊠)] and Pavan Yadav

Department of Computer Science and Engineering,
Maulana Azad National Institute of Technology,
Bhopal 462051, Madhya Pradesh, India
shweta_j82@yahoo.co.in, yadav85pavan@gmail.com

Abstract. Delay-tolerant or opportunistic networks (DTNs) [1, 2] are special types of networks which allow transmission of data where there may be no end to end connection between source and destination. DTNs may lack continuous network connectivity and there may be very large delay in message delivery because of sparse node density. Thus routing in DTNs is a very challenging task because it must handle very long delays, frequent network partitions and resultant inconsistent network topology. Social-based routing approaches have arouse great interest in the context of DTN, where different social characteristics of DTN nodes are used to make better routing decisions. A controlled replication based scheme has been used to improve the performance of Bubble Rap routing algorithm. The proposed algorithm has been tested in both heterogeneous and real world mobility scenarios.

Keywords: Routing · Social network · Bubble Rap · DTN

1 Introduction

Delay Tolerant Networks are a type of wireless mobile networks which are characterized by intermittent connectivity, long or variable delay, asymmetric data rates and high link error rates [1, 2]. To overcome the problem of intermittent connectivity, DTN nodes use buffer space to store the messages and carry them until new node encounter occurs, hence a message may take very long or variable delay to reach its destination. There are many real applications of DTNs like Pocket Switched Networks (PSNs) [3], Inter Planetary Networks (IPNs) [4], Under Water Sensor Networks (UWSN) [5] etc. In PSNs, the mobile devices are carried by humans; hence social characteristics of the nodes may be exploited to take routing decisions. Some of the common social characteristics of a node depends on the person's daily routine or activities like how often a person can move from one location to another, social groups in which he participates and people whom he meet frequently etc. Many routing algorithms [6, 10, 11] have been developed for DTNs which utilize the social metrics of participating nodes in the network and have performed well in terms of message delivery.

"Bubble Rap" [6] algorithm is one of the most popular social based routing algorithm in this category. It uses two social metrics namely community and centrality to decide the message transmission. The term community is defined as a group of

© Springer Nature Singapore Pte Ltd. 2018
P. Bhattacharyya et al. (Eds.): NGCT 2017, CCIS 828, pp. 70–87, 2018.
https://doi.org/10.1007/978-981-10-8660-1_5

people living together and interacting with each other in a group, whereas the centrality of a node denotes its social importance in the group or network. Bubble Rap algorithm has many limitations problems: firstly it allows a message to replicate in a network until it's Time to Live (TTL) falls to zero and thus there is no bound on the number of copies created of a message in the network. Secondly it does not use any mechanism to delete delivered messages from other node's buffer in the network. The proposed work tackles both these problems by fixing the number of message copies and using ACK IDs [16] to delete delivered messages from other nodes buffers respectively.

The rest of the paper is structured as follows: Sect. 2 describes related work. Section 3 contains detailed description of the proposed algorithm. Section 4 describes simulation setup. Section 5 describes simulation results and analysis of results. Finally Sect. 6 concludes our paper including future work description.

2 Related Work

To design routing algorithms in non-connected and sparse networks is a very challenging task. A wide variety of routing algorithms have been designed for DTNs. Direct delivery [7] is a single copy routing algorithm in which a node keeps a message in its buffer and waits for encountering the destination to directly transmit the message to destination only. It does not require any knowledge about network. However, it results in a very low delivery ratio. In replication based routing algorithm, a node replicates a message copy to every other node it meets and creates many copies of the message. Epidemic [8] is a flooding based routing algorithm in which a node replicates a message copy to every other meeting node, if that node does not already contain the message copy. However this leads to high congestion in the network because of the flooding and performs poorly in DTNs. To overcome this problem, Spray and Wait (SaW) [9] uses controlled replication based scheme in which a fixed number of copies of a message will be replicated in the network, thus it reduce congestion while still achieving comparable delivery ratio [8]. It works in two phases: spray phase and wait phase. In spray phase, a node on encountering a new node transmits half of its copies of a message to encountered node until message count goes to one. After this, it switches to wait phase where it waits for the destination for direct delivery. PROPHET [17] and MaxProp [18] are also replication based routing protocols which utilise forwarding probability of a node, which is calculated based on the history of node encounters, for taking routing decisions.

Social based routing algorithms are a class of routing algorithms which use social properties of node to take forwarding decision [15]. Label Routing [10] was the earliest social based routing algorithm, proposed by Hui and Crowcroft, which uses labels of community in PSNs. Daly and Haahr introduced SimBet routing [11] which uses two social characteristics namely betweennes centrality and similarity. Nodes with high betweenness centralities are those which can be good relays in their neighbourhood, while nodes with high similarities with the destination are more likely to find a common neighbour with the destination which can act as the good forwarder.

Hui *et al.* introduced another social-based forwarding algorithm called Bubble Rap [6] which takes advantage of node popularity for message forwarding. It works in two phases, in first phase messages are transmitted to nodes which are more popular in the global network then in the second phase when a message reaches its destination community, nodes that are more popular in the local community are as message relays. This strategy allows a message to relay to more popular nodes in network which have a higher probability to meet others.

3   Controlled Replication Based Bubble Rap Algorithm

Controlled Replication Based Bubble Rap Algorithm (CR-Bubble Rap) is an improved version of Bubble-Rap routing algorithm which has been designed with the aim of increasing delivery ratio and at the same time reducing overhead ratio of the network. It overcomes two major limitations of Bubble Rap algorithm i.e. creating unlimited number of copies of a message in the network and secondly keeping already delivered messages in node buffers which unnecessarily occupy the limited buffer space of nodes and subsequently result in message drops of other undelivered messages. CR-BubbleRap overcomes both these limitations by two mechanisms as described in Sects. 3.1 and 3.2 respectively.

Assumptions for proposed work:

1. Each message is assigned a message count property which defines the maximum number of copies of a message that can be created in the network.
2. Each node belongs to a community and single node communities are also allowed. The distributed K-Clique community detection algorithm [6] is used for community detection where K is set to 5.
3. A node has two types of centrality measures: first global centrality within the network and second is local centrality within the community. These centralities are calculated by Cumulative-Window centrality [6] approach.

3.1   Controlled Replication Scheme

In order to overcome the unlimited message copy problem of Bubble Rap routing algorithm, CR-Bubble Rap uses a fixed number of message copies to be transmitted in the network just like Spray and Wait routing. But CR-Bubble Rap does not have wait phase. Instead if a message count goes to one it allows a node to continuously forward the message copy to more popular nodes within the network until it reaches the destination community or within the destination community once it reaches there. The forwarding strategy used by CR-Bubble Rap can be described as follows, suppose node A has message m for destination D. When A meets B, A checks if message m has number of message copies (nrOfCopies) greater than zero or not, if so then it decides to forward to node B or not and how many copies to spray to B. Three cases may arise as discussed below.

In first case, if both nodes A and B belong to the same community as destination node D, then A will compare its local centrality (L_A) with the local centrality of node B (L_B) and if it lesser than B, then A will transmit the $B_{M_{nrOfCopies}}$ $number$ of message copies to B:

$$B_{M_{nrOfCopies}} = \left\lceil \left(\frac{L_B}{L_B + L_A} * A_{nrOfCopies} \right) \right\rceil$$

and A keeps following number of copies for itself:

$$A_{M_{nrOfCopies}} = A_{M_{nrOfCopies}} - \left\lceil \left(\frac{L_B}{L_B + L_A} * A_{M_{nrOfCopies}} \right) \right\rceil$$

In this case, the message copies are distributed in proportion to the local centralities of the two nodes. Figure 1 shows the message copy distribution between nodes A and B.

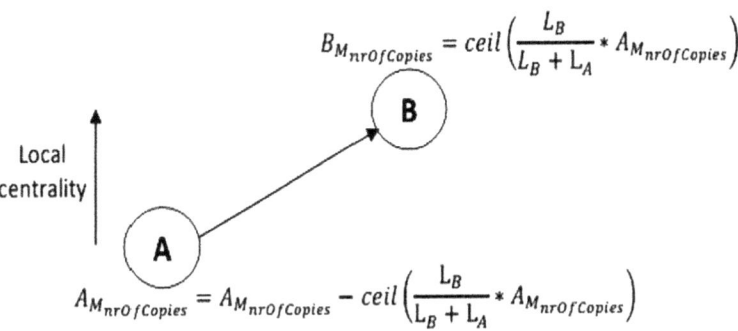

Fig. 1. Message distributions between nodes A and B when both nodes are in destinations community

In the second case, if node B is in the same community as destination node D while A does not belong to the destination community, then A will transmit all of m's remaining nrOfCopies to B, no matter whether A's global/local centrality is higher than B's global/local centrality.

$$B_{M_{nrOfCopies}} = \left(A_{M_{nrOfCopies}} \right)$$

Now A will delete the message from its buffer because once a message reaches its destinations' community then it is considered that it will be delivered to its destination. Figure 2 shows the message distributions between nodes A and B.

In the last case, if both nodes A and B do not belong to the destination community of node D, then node A will compare its global centrality (G_A) with that of node B (G_B) and if it is less than node B, then node A will transmit $B_{M_{nrOfCopies}}$ to B as shown in Fig. 3.

In this case, the message copies are distributed in proportion to the global centralities of the two nodes.

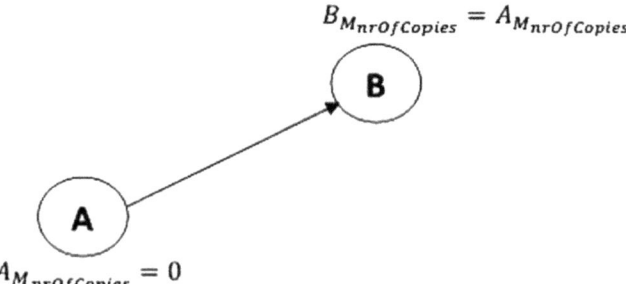

Fig. 2. Message distributions between nodes A and B when only node B is in destinations community

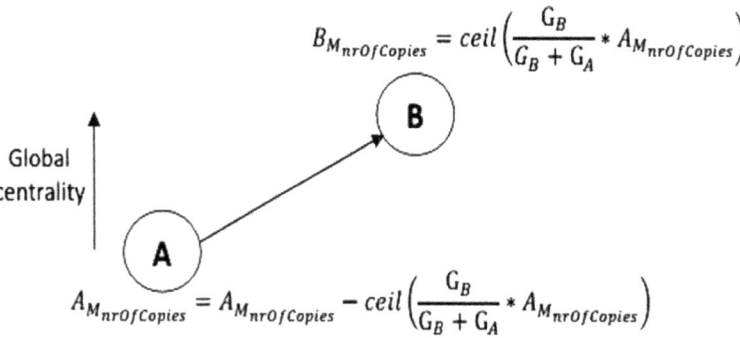

Fig. 3. Message distributions between nodes A and B when both nodes are not in destinations community

$$B_{M_{nrOfCopies}} = \left\lceil \left(\frac{G_B}{G_B + G_A} * A_{nrOfCopies} \right) \right\rceil$$

Now, A will keep following number of copies:

$$A_{M_{nrOfCopies}} = A_{M_{nrOfCopies}} - \left\lceil \left(\frac{G_B}{G_B + G_A} * A_{M_{nrOfCopies}} \right) \right\rceil$$

The idea behind controlled replication is to transmit fixed number of a message copies in the network thus there will be overall more buffer space available for other messages to stay in and get chance for further transmission to more popular nodes in network. This will help in increasing the delivery ratio while also decreasing the overhead ratio.

3.2   Delete Delivered Messages (Exchange ACK IDs)

CR-Bubble Rap uses another mechanism called delete delivered message i.e. when two node meet they exchange ACK IDs (IDs of messages which are already delivered to their destination) [12, 16] to delete messages from there buffers. In PSNs the buffer size is very limited and if the buffer is full, a new message arrives to this node will drop and delivery ratio will go down. Thus, an efficient buffer management scheme plays an important role in PSNs for achieving better delivery ratio. Deleting messages which are delivered, results in good buffer management and better delivery ratio.

4   Simulation Setup

Opportunistic Network Environment (ONE) [13] has been used for evaluation and comparison of CR-Bubble Rap with simple Bubble Rap. ONE is a Java based tool that offers a broad set of DTN protocol simulation capabilities in a single framework. CR-Bubble Rap has been compared with Bubble Rap in both heterogeneous scenario and real life mobility traces scenario like Cambridge, Infocom05.

In heterogeneous scenario city life is simulated with 150 nodes where Helsinki city map is used. 150 nodes are grouped into 8 different groups of people and 9 different groups of vehicles. The settings of this scenario are given in Table 1. External load files are used for generating messages for the simulation.

Table 1. Settings for heterogeneous scenario

Scenario parameters	Values
Simulation time	700 k sec
Transmission speed	250 KBps
Transmission range	10 m
Buffer size	2 M
Message size	1 to 100 KB
No. of nodes	150 nodes
No. of node groups	17 (8 people groups, 9 vehicle groups)
People_group1 to 8	Movement Model = WDM No. of nodes = 16 per group Wait Time = 0 s Speed = 0.8 to 14 m/sec
Vehicle_group1	Movement Model = SPBM No. of nodes = 6 Wait Time = 100–300 s Speed = 7 to 10 m/sec
Vehicle_group2 to 9	Movement Model = BBM No. of nodes = 2 per group Wait Time = 10–30 s Speed = 7 to 10 m/sec

Table 2. Settings for Working Day Movement Model (WDM)

Scenario parameters	Values
No. of offices	50
Working day length	28800 s (equals to 8 h)
Minimum groups size for evening activity	1
Maximum groups size for evening activity	3
Minimum pause time after evening activity	3600 s
Maximum pause time after evening activity	7200 s
Probability that the node owns a car	50%
Probability to do evening activity	50%
No. of meeting spots	10
The coefficient for the Pareto distribution controlling pause time inside office	0.5
Min pause time inside office	10 s
Max pause time inside office	100000 s
Size of the office	100 m
Std. Dev. for the normal distribution controlling differences in schedules nodes	7200

Table 3. Settings for Cambridge traces

Scenario parameters	Values
Simulation time	1036800 s
No. of nodes	36
Buffer size	2 M
Transmit range	10
Transmit speed	250 k
Message size	1to 100 KB

Table 4. Settings for Infocom05 traces

Scenario parameters	Values
Simulation time	1036800 s
No. of nodes	41
Buffer size	2 M
Transmit range	10
Transmit speed	250 k
Message size	1to 100 KB

The settings for Cambridge and Infocom05 are given in Tables 3 and 4 respectively. The Cambridge students were the part of the Haggle project to collect trace data. The students of IEEE conference in Grand Hyatt Miami were the part of Infocom05 trace for 7th to 10th march 2005 [14]. The iMote Bluetooth devices were used for data log information. These two real time scenarios also use external load file to generate messages for simulation (Table 2).

5 Results and Analysis

The simulation results in heterogeneous and real life scenarios for varying number of message copies, and message TTL values are presented in this section. For all the results presented here, the simulation was run five times, with different seed value every time. Average of five is used to evaluate the metrics named delivery ratio, overhead ratio and average latency.

Delivery Ratio (DR): It is the ratio of total number of messages delivered ($NrOfMsg_{delv}$) to the total number of messages created ($NrOfMsg_{creat}$).

Overhead Ratio (OR): It is the ratio of the total number of messages relayed minus the total number of messages delivered to $NrOfMsg_{delv}$.

Latency Average (AL): Average Latency (AL) is the ratio of summation of the latency of number of messages delivered to total number of messages delivered.

5.1 Effect of Varying Message Copies

The effect of varying message copies on different metrics DR, OR and Al are shown below. The TTL value and total number of messages generated in the simulation are set to 48 h and 1000 messages respectively.

5.1.1 Delivery Ratio
The delivery ratio for heterogeneous, Cambridge and Infocom05 scenarios are shown in Figs. 4, 5 and 6 respectively. It is observed that the delivery ratio increases with the increasing number of message copies as the message is distributed to more number of nodes in network. But it is also seen that increasing number of message copies beyond a certain limit does not result in increased DR as there will be more congestion in the network and messages will occupy overall more buffer space. From Figs. 4, 5 and 6 it may be observed that the 20%, 40% and 30% message copies are enough to achieve a high delivery ratio in heterogeneous, Cambridge and Infocom05 scenarios respectively.

5.1.2 Overhead Ratio
The variation of overhead ratios with varying number of message copies is shown in Figs. 7, 8 and 9 respectively. The number of message relays will increase with the increase in number of message copies. Since there is no wait phase in CR-Bubble Rap, the message will replicate to every other node with higher centrality value. Therefore, with the increase in number of message copies the OR also increases in all scenarios.

5.1.3 Average Latency
Figures 10, 11 and 12 show the variation of average latency with varying number of message copies for heterogeneous, Cambridge and Infocom05 traces respectively. Figure 10 illustrates that the AL decreases with increasing number of message copies

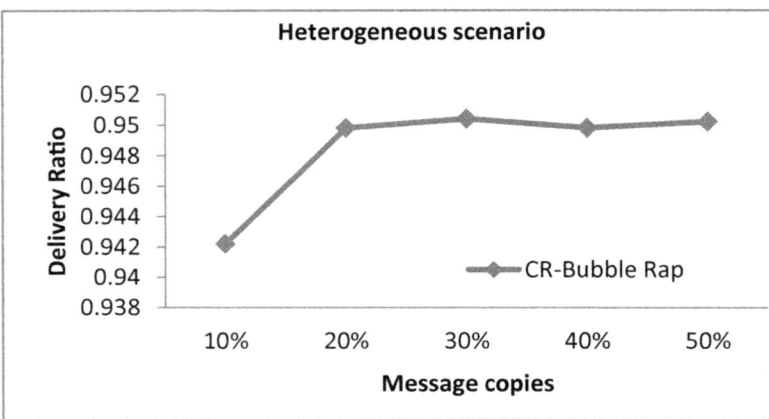

Fig. 4. Delivery ratio of CR-Bubble Rap for varying number of message copies in heterogeneous scenario.

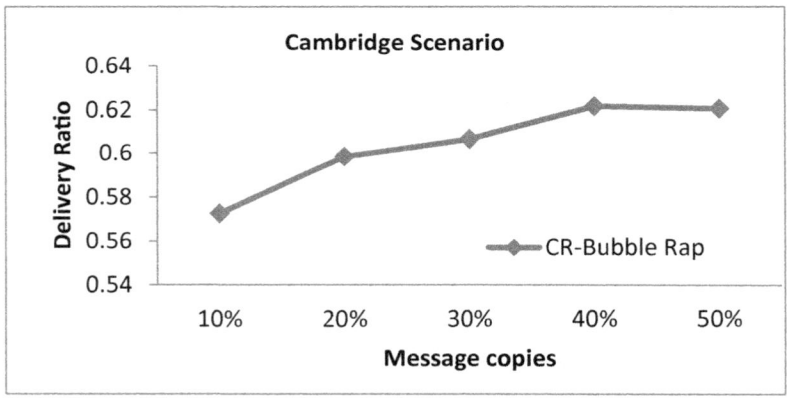

Fig. 5. Delivery ratio of CR-Bubble Rap for varying number of message copies in Cambridge scenario.

in heterogeneous scenario. As the nodes in this scenario have varying nt centrality values implying that message replication will occur for most of the meetings. Hence, with a larger number of message copies, the probability to reach its destination is high.

Figure 11 shows that the AL does not decrease in Cambridge scenario as the centrality of nodes is almost same because the users of the nodes are students and they frequently meet each other. Therefore, the message replication process is very slow. Thus with slow replication process the messages belonging to other communities will take more time to replicate. This is the main reason for high AL in Cambridge scenario.

In Incocom05, a large number of small sized overlapping communities are formed. Thus, it allows message copies to spread among multiple communities' faster as

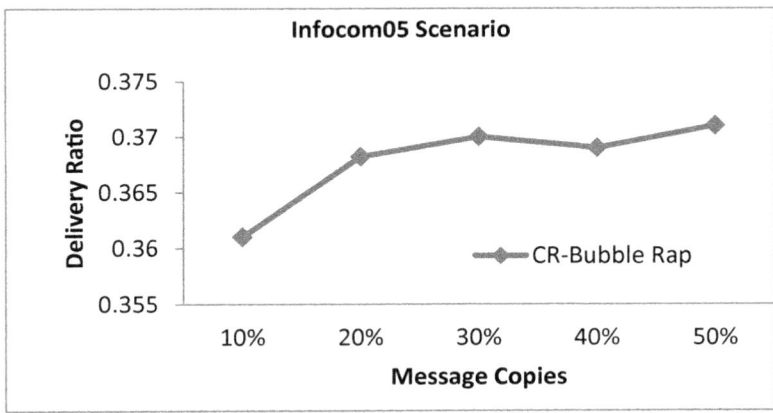

Fig. 6. Delivery ratio of CR-Bubble Rap for varying message copies in Infocom05 scenario.

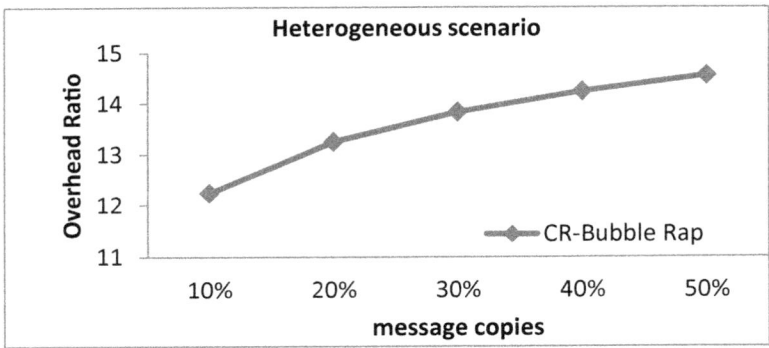

Fig. 7. Overhead ratio of CR-Bubble Rap for varying message copies in heterogeneous scenario.

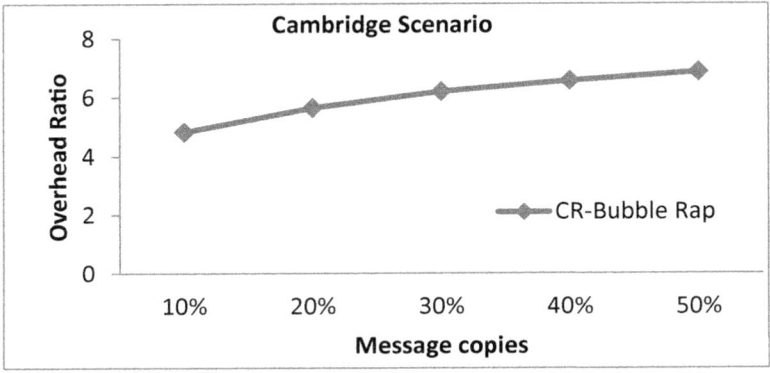

Fig. 8. Overhead ratio of CR-Bubble Rap for varying message copies in Cambridge scenario.

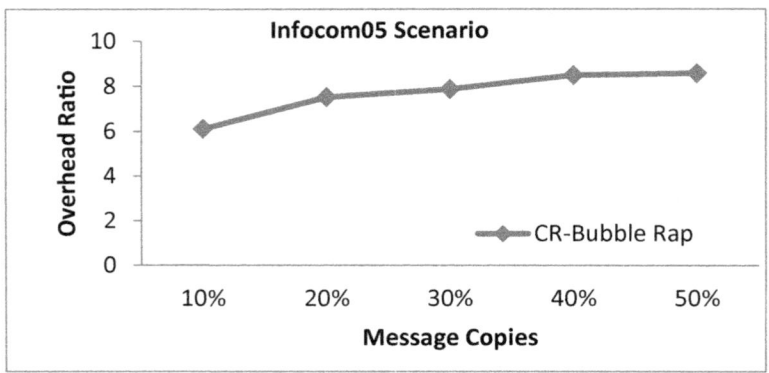

Fig. 9. Overhead ratio of CR-Bubble Rap for varying message copies in Infocom05 scenario

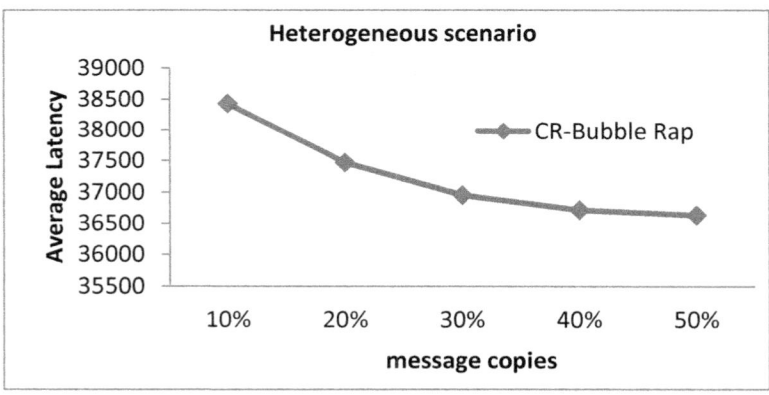

Fig. 10. Average latency for varying message copies in heterogeneous scenario

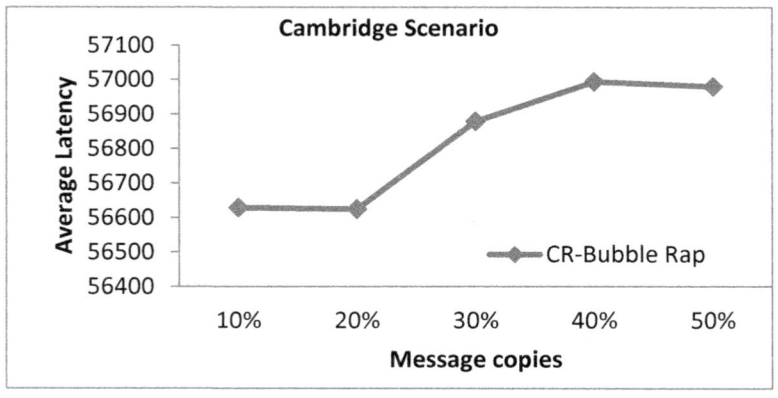

Fig. 11. Average latency for varying message copies in Cambridge scenario

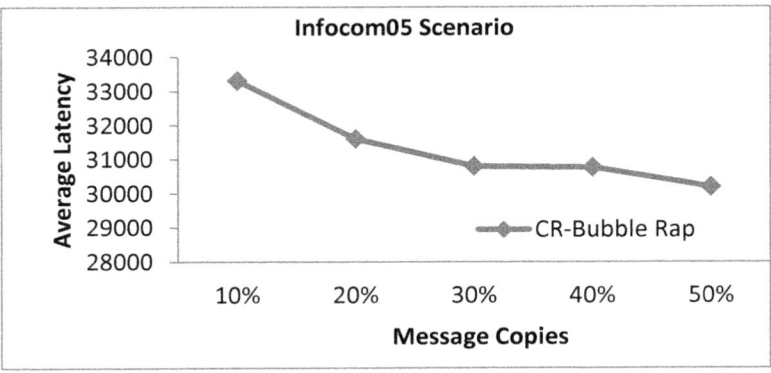

Fig. 12. Average latency for varying message copies in Infocom05 scenario

comparing to Cambridge scenario. Therefore, with more number of message copies the message reaches its destination faster.

5.2   Effect of Varying TTLs

The impact of varying TTL on the performance of both the routing protocols, i.e. CR-Bubble Rap and Bubble Rap is presented in this sub-section. The number of message copies for all scenarios is set to10% and the traffic load (total number of messages generated in the simulation) is set to 1000 messages.

5.2.1   Delivery Ratio
The impact of varying TTL on the delivery ratio of both the routing protocols, CR-Bubble Rap and Bubble Rap in heterogeneous, Cambridge and Infocom05 scenarios are shown in Figs. 13, 14 and 15 respectively. Figure 13 clearly depicts that

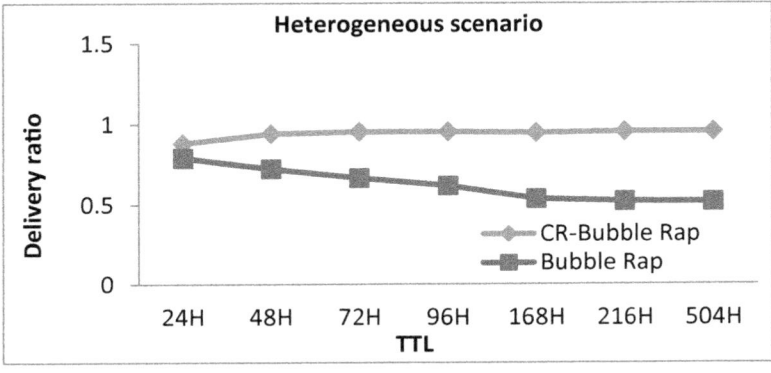

Fig. 13. Delivery ratio for varying message TTL in heterogeneous scenario

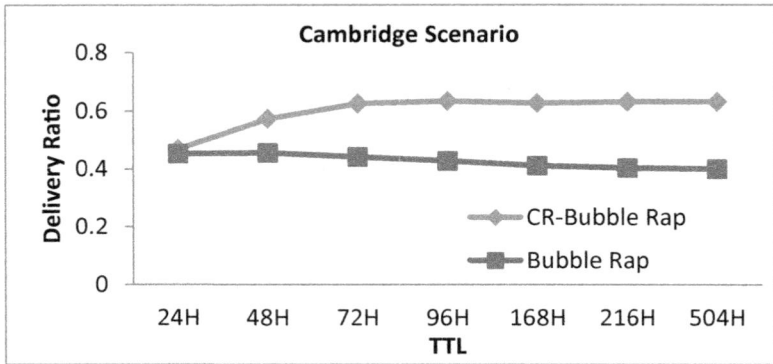

Fig. 14. Delivery ratio for varying message TTL in Cambridge scenario.

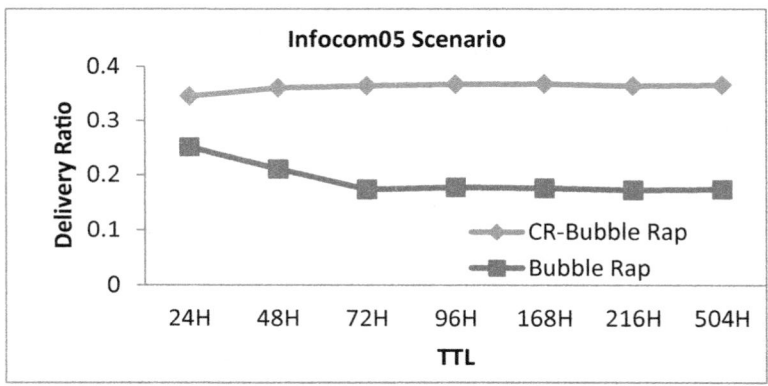

Fig. 15. Delivery ratio for varying message TTL in Infocom05 scenario.

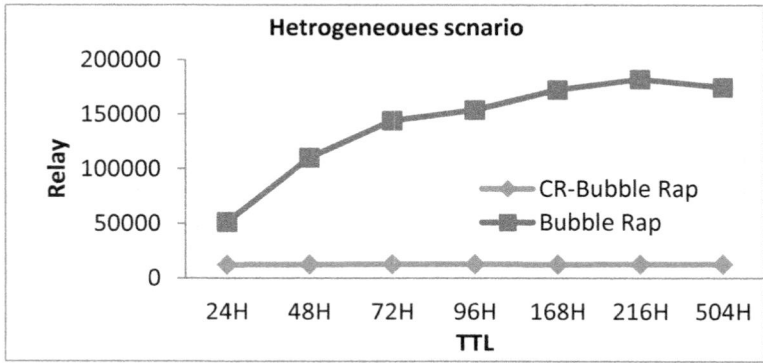

Fig. 16. Number of message relay for varying message TTL in heterogeneous scenario.

CR-Bubble Rap achieves better delivery ratio than Bubble Rap, while Bubble Rap observes a decline in its DR, as TTL increases. A large portion of the nodes are having heterogeneous centralities in the network. Accordingly message transmission will occur for the most of the meetings increasing the number of message copies in the network.

On varying message TTL, the messages stay in node buffer for long time until its TTL expires and occupies overall more buffer space which may lead to high message drop rate ultimately reducing the overall network delivery ratio.

This problem is reduced in CR-Bubble Rap which uses controlled replication scheme to fix the number of message copies to be distributed in network; thus the buffer occupancy of CR-Bubble Rap is comparatively low. CR-Bubble Rap also uses delete delivered mechanism which allows deletion of already delivered messages by exchanging ACK IDs. Thus it saves buffer space and energy preventing unnecessary replication of already delivered messages. Therefore, CR-Bubble Rap overall uses low buffer space efficiently and limits message replication process, both resulting in improvement of delivery ratio.

In both the real mobility traces scenarios as well CR-Bubble Rap demonstrates a better performance as compared to traditional Bubble Rap, as can be seen from Figs. 14 and 15. On increasing TTL of messages, Bubble Rap observes a decrease in the delivery ratio due to reasons already mentioned in Sect. 5.1.1. In Cambridge and Infocom05 scenarios, where replication process is very slow, a good buffer management scheme gives higher delivery ratio. CR-Bubble Rap overcomes this problem by bounding the number of message copies to save overall buffer space. Also, deletion of already delivered messages plays an important role in maintaining the high delivery ratio of CR-Bubble Rap, as TTL increases.

5.2.2 Overhead Ratio

The change in overhead ratios on varying message TTL for different mobility scenarios are shown in Figs. 17, 18 and 19. The simulation results presented in Fig. 17 illustrates that CR-Bubble Rap has an almost constant and small overhead ratio for different values of message TTL which is due to the fact that number of message relays does

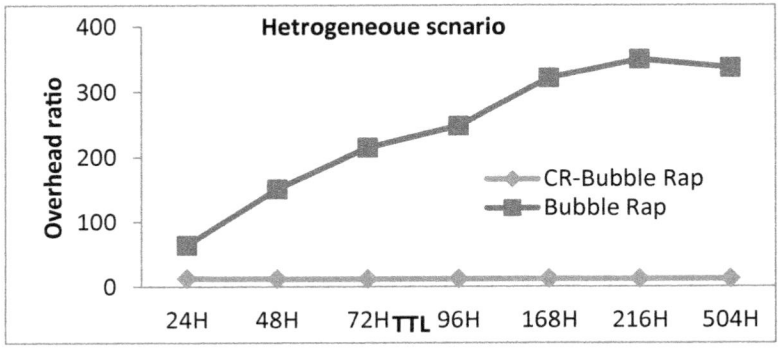

Fig. 17. Overhead ratio for varying message TTL in heterogeneous scenario.

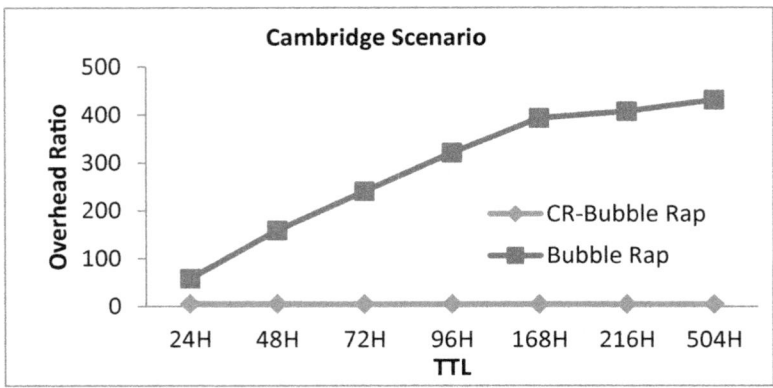

Fig. 18. Overhead ratio for varying message TTL in Cambridge scenario

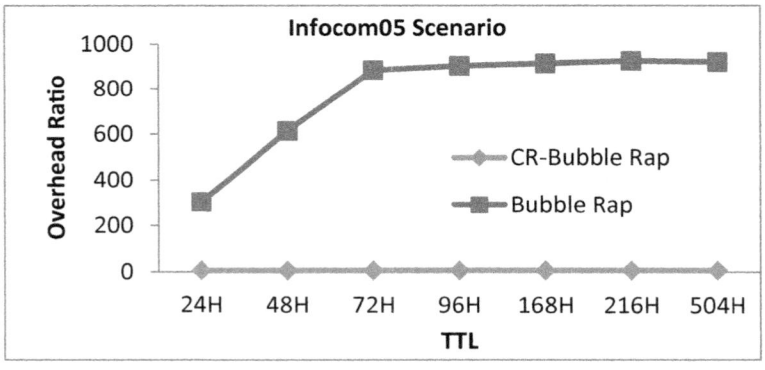

Fig. 19. Overhead ratio for varying message TTL in Infocom05 scenario

change much with the increasing message TTL as visible from Fig. 16. The reason behind this is the fixed number of message copies which restrict a message from further replication, when a node is left with zero message copies. Also, exchange of ACK IDs restricts the messages from unnecessary replication by deleting those messages from a node's buffer that have been delivered to its destination. However in Bubble Rap, it is found that the overhead ratio increases with increasing message TTL. The fundamental reason being: Bubble Rap does not delete the messages delivered to its destination and keep them replicating until their TTL expires, therefore a high value of message TTL implies more replication of messages. The above reasoning can also be accommodated for Cambridge and Infocom05 traces. Although from the graphs shown in Figs. 18 and 20, the overhead ratios of CR-Bubble Rap in Cambridge and Infocom05 scenarios seems to be approximately zero but it is varying between 6.08044 to 6.1728 and 4.47862 to 4.76404 respectively.

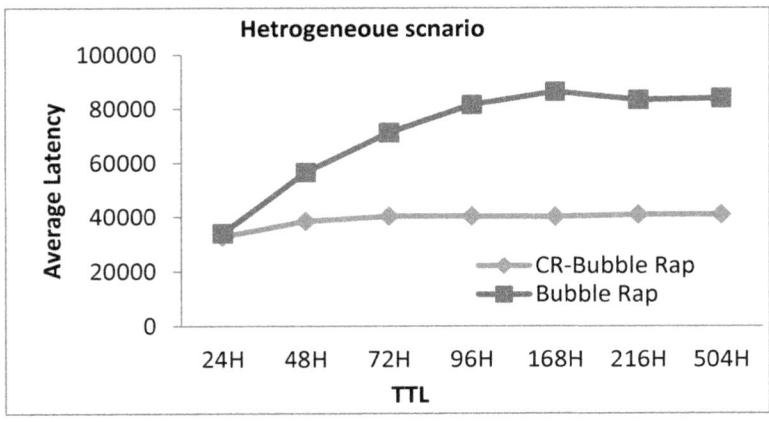

Fig. 20. Average latency for varying message TTL in heterogeneous scenario.

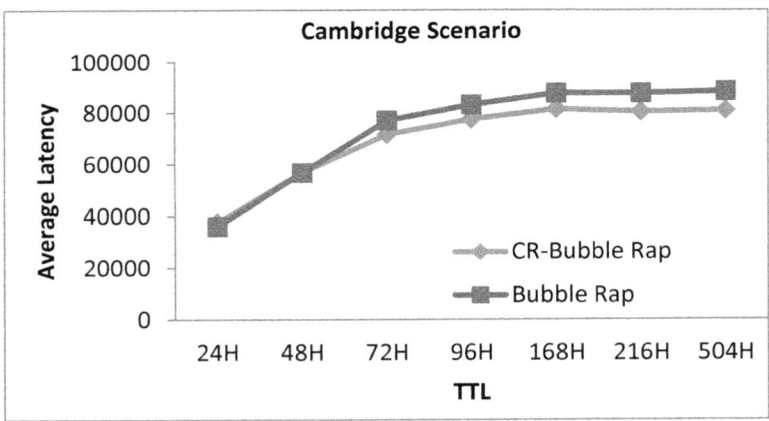

Fig. 21. Average latency for varying message TTL in Cambridge scenario.

5.2.3 Average Latency

Figures 20, 21 and 22 present the simulation results for average latency for hetero-geneous, Cambridge and Infocom05 scenarios respectively with varying message TTL values. In the heterogeneous scenario, CR-Bubble Rap achieves lower average latency than Bubble Rap because of faster delivery of messages to their destinations. In heterogeneous scenario, a large number of the nodes have varying centralities in the network causing messages transmission for the majority of the meetings. Bubble Rap observes an increase in average latency as message TTL increase because messages will be replicated until TTL falls to zero. This leads to more congestion in the network restricting messages from spreading faster in the network. The controlled replication scheme and ACK IDs scheme of CR-Bubble Rap reduce unnecessary congestion and

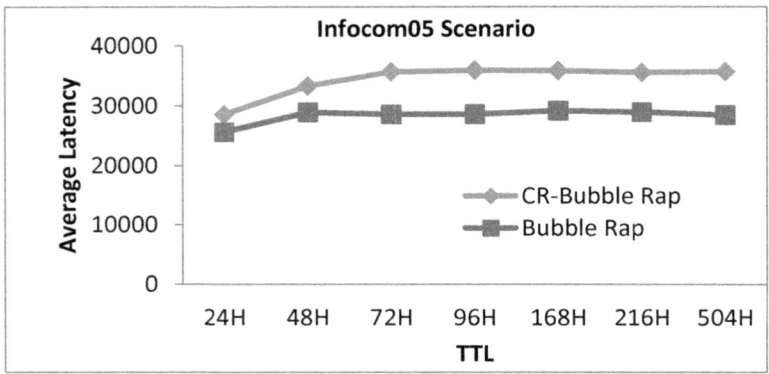

Fig. 22. Average latency for varying message TTL in Infocom05 scenario

buffer consumption, allowing messages to travel fast in the network and reach their destination quicker. However, CR-Bubble Rap observes high latency than Bubble Rap in Infocom05 scenario as observable from Fig. 22, because CR-Bubble Rap uses controlled replication scheme in which number of message copies are fixed. Because of limited number of message copies the possibility of a message to reach fast at its destination is low. Even if CR-bubble Rap reduces congestion in the network but slow replication process causes messages to reach late at its destination.

6 Conclusion and Future Work

In this paper, CR-Bubble Rap routing algorithm is proposed with the objective of achieving improved performance over Bubble Rap routing algorithm which is a popular social based routing algorithm developed for DTNs. The main contribution of CR-Bubble Rap is to decrease congestion and restrict messages from unnecessary replications. CR-Bubble Rap uses different mechanisms like controlled replication scheme to fix the number of message copies and delete delivered messages (ACK IDs) to delete already delivered messages from the buffer of other nodes in the network thereby giving place to other undelivered messages. Thus it restricts messages from unnecessary replication and decreases congestion in network. The simulation results confirm improved performance of CR-Bubble Rap over Bubble Rap in various scenarios like heterogeneous, Cambridge and Infocom05. In future, we would like to extend our work to dynamically fix the number of message copies depending on the number of community formed and number of nodes in the network.

References

1. Fall, K.: A delay-tolerant network architecture for challenged internets. In: Proceedings of ACM Special Interest Group Data Communications Workshop (SIGCOMM 2003) (2003)
2. Warthman, F.: Delay Tolerant Networks (DTNs) A Tutorial. version 1.1, 3 May 2003

3. Hui, P., Chaintreau, A., Scott, J., Gass, R., Crowcroft, J., Diot, C.: Pocket switched networks and the consequences of human mobility in conference environments. In: WDTN 2005: Proceedings of the 2005 ACM SIGCOMM Workshop on Delay-Tolerant Networking (2005)
4. Cerf, V., Burleigh, S., Dust, R.: Interplanetary internet (IPN): architectural definition. Phil. Trans. Roy. Soc. London. **A247**, 529–551 (1955)
5. Dunbabin, M., Corke, P., Vailescu, I., Rus, D.: Data muling over underwater wireless sensor networks using an autonomous underwater vehicle. In: Proceedings of International Conference on Robotics and Automation (ICRA). IEEE (2006)
6. Hui, P., Crowcroft, J., Yoneki, E.: BUBBLE rap: social-based forwarding in delay tolerant networks. In: MobiHoc, pp. 241–250. ACM, China (2008)
7. Grossglauser, M., Tse, D.: Mobility increases the capacity of ad hoc wireless networks. IEEE/ACM Trans. Netw. **10**(4), 477–486 (2002)
8. Vahdat, A., Becker, D.: Epidemic routing for partially connected ad hoc networks. Technical report CS-200006, Duke University, April 2000
9. Spyropoulos, T., Psounis, K., Raghavendra, C.S.: Spray and wait: an efficient routing scheme for intermittently connected mobile networks. In: Proceedings of ACM SIGCOMM Workshop on Delay-Tolerant Networking, pp. 252–259. ACM, Philadelphia (2005)
10. Hui, P., Crowcroft, J.: How small labels create big improvements. In: International Workshop on Intermittently Connected Mobile Ad-hoc Networks in Conjunction with IEEE PerCom 2007 (2007)
11. Daly, E.M., Haahr, M.: Social network analysis for routing in disconnected delay-tolerant MANETs. In: Proceedings of the 8th ACM International Symposium on Mobile Ad Hoc Networking and Computing MobiHoc 2007 (2007)
12. Burgess, J., Gallagher, B., Jensen, D., Levine, B.N.: Max-prop: routing for vehicle-based disruption tolerant networks. In: Proceedings of 25th IEEE International Conference on Computer Communications, pp. 1–11. IEEE (2006)
13. Keränen, A., Ott, J., Kärkkäinen, T.: The ONE simulator for DTN algorithm evaluation. In: SIMUTools 2009: 2nd International Conference on Simulation Tools and Techniques, Rome (2009)
14. Homepage of CRAWDAD archive. http://www.crawdad.org/
15. Zhu, Y., Xu, B., Shi, X., Wang, Y.: A survey of social-based routing in delay tolerant networks: positive and negative social effects. IEEE Commun. Surv. Tutor. **15**(1), 387–401 (2013)
16. Jain, S., Kishore, N., Chawla, M., Soares, V.N.G.J.: Composite mechanisms for improving Bubble Rap in delay tolerant networks. J. Eng. **2014**(1), 1–7 (2014). IET
17. Lindgren, A., Doria, A., Schelen, O.: Probabilistic routing in intermittently connected networks. SIGMOBILE Mob. Comput. Commun. Rev. **7**(3), 19–20 (2003)
18. Burgess, J., Gallagher, B., Jensen, D., Levine, B.N.: Max-prop: routing for vehicle-based disruption tolerant networks. In: Proceedings of 25th IEEE International Conference on Computer Communications, pp. 1–11, April 2006

Plasmonics for THz Applications: Design of Graphene Square Patch Antenna Tested with Different Substrates for THz Applications

Manisha Khulbe[1,2(✉)], Malay Ranjan Tripathy[2],
and Harish Parthasarathy[3]

[1] Ambedkar Institute of Advance Communication Technology and Research,
New Delhi, New Delhi, India
manisha.khulbe@gmail.com
[2] AMITY University, Noida, Uttar Pradesh, India
[3] Netaji Subhash Institute of Technology, New Delhi, India

Abstract. This paper gives a brief description of the mathematical techniques used to define plasmonics. The kinetic theory using Vlasov equation is one that gives the concept of plasma generation. Plasmonic antennas better suited for THz applications has added advantages in terms of bandwidth. Taking Graphene patch antenna, which is one of the plasmonic material, is designed in the THz range. This antenna gives wide bandwidth in GHz and THz range. The Graphene patch is designed and tested with Si, SiO_2 and Al_2O_3 substrates, which gives S11 at different THz frequencies and different bandwidths.

Keywords: Graphene patch antenna · 5G applications · Si
Al_2o_3 and SiO_2 substrates

1 Introduction

As mobile communication in the next decade is going to be 1000 times larger in bandwidth and 100 times more in speed, which is going to be dependent on THz communication. Next generation communication will also be working without the human intervention [1]. In 5G communication we need ultrafast signal transmission in data processing. This is going to be possible with nanoscale using some newly found materials such as Graphene, Carbon Nano tubes [2], Gold and Silver. These materials support plasmonics, which also show strong nonlinear optical behavior. These materials have large potential application in ultrafast communication and switching.

1.1 Plasmonics

In near future, plasmonics will be the only solution in the realization at nanoscale. Some metamaterial also support plasmonics like properties [16]. Negative refraction, super lensing and clocking are such properties which is also defined by plasma. In the frequency region of interest, plasmonics produces losses so we need to explore some new materials, which have low losses. One new materials on which a lot of research is going on is graphene, which can be used in optical frequencies [3]. Properly sized

© Springer Nature Singapore Pte Ltd. 2018
P. Bhattacharyya et al. (Eds.): NGCT 2017, CCIS 828, pp. 88–98, 2018.
https://doi.org/10.1007/978-981-10-8660-1_6

graphene can be used in THz [4]. Graphene shows a broad spectral range with ultrafast response time [5] and dynamic configuration.

In microwave region, graphene antenna does not show a good radiation due to intrinsic impedance losses [17]. In the microwave real part of the conductivity dominates. Plasma frequencies are typically in the visible to ultraviolet range. Miniaturization using graphene leads to antenna dynamic configuration [6] and mechanical flexibility. Its surface conductivity tensor is the main property [7, 8] this conductivity is a function of number of parameters including temperature, scattering rate, forming energy electron velocity transport [17] and its feature is that these antennas can be controlled via static electrical and magnetic field bias which gives them unprecedented dynamic configuration. Graphene plasmonics has also been explained by theoretical physics including quantum description based upon the random phase approximations [6].

1.2 Nonlinear Optical Properties

The nonlinearity is observed at very high frequencies. As Graphene has large photo physical properties have potential applications in fast switching networks and tailoring with modifications to chemical structures [5]. Graphene strong nonlinear properties are third order nonlinearity and four wave mixing. Interband electron transition gives large nonlinear property. Hence the susceptibility of Graphene is eight times large than the same nonlinearity in normal dielectric materials. Thus, this property of large nonlinearity of Grapheme can be used as a tool in imaging.

2 Mathematical Formulation

The kinetic theory in plasma is defined by Lorentz force and Vlasov equations [16]. If we take only elastic interaction in plasma that are given by Maxwell's equations for interaction between ions and neutral particles [8]. The coulomb interactions between charged particle is given by Vlasov Poisson equation defined by

$$\frac{\partial f}{\partial t} + v.\nabla_x f + F(x).\nabla_v f = 0 \tag{1}$$

$$\left[\text{Where } F = -\nabla V, \; V = \frac{e^2}{4\pi r \epsilon_0} * \rho \right] \quad \text{and} \tag{2}$$

$$\rho(t, x) = \int f(t, x, v) dv$$

Where $(r, v) = (x, y, z, v_x, v_y, v_z)$ defines the electron position and velocity in the plasma it is six dimensional space [16]. Volume of small element of velocity space is $dv_x \, dv_y \, dv_z = d^3 v$. $f(x, y, z, v_x v_y v_z, t)$ describes the state of plasma velocity distribution function. Charge density is defined by $\rho = \sum_s q_s n_s$ and current density is defined by J = $\sum_s q_s n_s u$. Where u is bulk velocity of charge defined by u = $\frac{1}{n} \int v f(r, v, t) d^3 v$ [15] where n is the number of electrons.

From here the Boltzmann equation for plasma is written as [16] -

$$\frac{\partial f}{\partial t} + v.\frac{\partial f}{\partial r} + a.\frac{\partial f}{\partial v} = 0 \text{ Where } a = F/m \tag{3}$$

Where F is the force on an electron due to applied electric field, m is mass of an electron. In terms of Lorentz force, we write plasma equation as

$$\frac{\partial f}{\partial t} + v.\frac{\partial f}{\partial r} + \frac{q}{m}.[E + (v \times B)]\frac{\partial f}{\partial v} = 0 \tag{4}$$

This equation with E (electric field) and B (magnetic field) and Vlasov equation represent a complete set for the derivation of plasma generation.

Plasma function can further be explained by the Vlasov–Poisson equations [16] which describes various phenomenon in plasma. This equation is for Collison less plasma such as hot plasma [16]. With collision the basic equation is given by

$$\frac{\partial f}{\partial t} + v.\frac{\partial f}{\partial r} - \frac{e}{m}.E\frac{\partial f}{\partial v} = C[f] \tag{5}$$

∇_x is velocity gradient. C represent the rate of change of f due to collision. The change of energy state is given by the change in Fermi levels, which generates conductivity [9]. In graphene, plasmonic nature of imaginary conductivity allows the Transverse Magnetic (TM) modes. Hence, by controlling the drift of electrons in plasma we can control conductivity, which is the main equation to determine propagation constant K_{SPP}.

2.1   Conventional Methods: Working Principal of Graphene Antennas

Conductivity is because of plasma like behaviors of electrons. Drude model also Derive equation for **TE** and **TM** modes. In order to determine propagation constant K_{SPP} for TM Modes the SPP electric field $\vec{E}$ and magnetic field $\vec{H}$ are governed by the Maxwell's equations

$$\nabla \times \vec{E} = -\mu_x \frac{\partial \vec{H}}{\partial t} \tag{6}$$

$$\nabla \times \vec{H} = \vec{J}\frac{\partial \vec{D}}{\partial t} = \vec{J} + \varepsilon\frac{\partial \vec{E}}{\partial t} \tag{7}$$

(μ_x is the permeability and ε permittivity of the medium). J is the current density. D is divergence.

Modes in the medium is given by [15]

$$\sqrt{\omega^2 - \omega_p^2} = ck \qquad (8)$$

For frequencies $\omega \gg \omega_p$ where ω_p is the plasma frequency. $\frac{\epsilon(\omega)}{\epsilon_o} \approx .\mathbf{1} - \frac{\omega_p^2}{\omega^2}$, where $\omega_p^2 = \frac{NZe^2}{\epsilon_o m}$ is defined as plasma frequency where NZ is given as electron/unit volume. If we take a slab of $L \times W$ dimension then this equation gives the dependence of conductivity on modes (wave vector k) field profile of Plasmon's in graphene when there are two different layers of dielectrics are given by [10].

$$\frac{\varepsilon_{r_1}}{\sqrt{k^2 - \frac{\varepsilon_{r_1}\omega^2}{c^2}}} + \frac{\varepsilon_{r_2}}{\sqrt{k^2 - \frac{\varepsilon_{r_2}\omega^2}{c^2}}} = -\frac{6(\omega,K)i}{\omega\epsilon_o} \qquad (9)$$

2.2 Antenna Length Calculations

Length of patch can be given by [2, 4, 10]

$$L = m\frac{\lambda\, spp}{2} = m\frac{\pi}{Re\{K_{spp}\}} \qquad (10)$$

and

$$\overrightarrow{E_{inc}}(z,t) = E_o e^{i(-k_1 z + \omega t)}\hat{\lambda}, \hat{\lambda} = \hat{x}, \hat{y} \qquad (11)$$

E_o is the field amplitude, K_{spp} is propagation constant, ω is the angular frequency. The inductive nature of Grapheme conductivity gives TM Plasmon's [2, 10]. A Graphene layer supports TM SPP wave with effective mode index defined by [11, 18]

$$\eta_{eff}.(\omega) = \sqrt{1 - 4\frac{\mu_0}{\varepsilon_o}\frac{1}{6(\omega)^2}} \qquad (12)$$

$\overrightarrow{E_{inc}}$ Irradiates the antenna; it excites free electrons on the Graphene Layer. The electronic response of the Graphene layer to an EM field is given by its dynamic complex conductivity 6. The patch behaves as a resonator. The resonance conditions are given by [18] $m\frac{1}{2}\frac{A}{\eta_{eff}} = L + 2\delta L$ where m determine the order of resonance, λ is the wavelength of incident radiations, L is the antenna length, δL is a measure of field penetration outside the Graphene based Nano patch antenna. ω_m Corresponds to m modes of resonator [19].

2.3　Factor Affecting Optical Conductivity, Temperature and Doping

Drude model gives the time between electron collisions, the electron moves under the influence of the field between the collisions and contribute to the current flow. Electrical biasing can better control Graphene conductivity. Real and imaginary part of the conductivity gives a good dynamic control [17]. Graphene can be used for plasmonic Nano antenna [19] the SPP waves in the Graphene can be observed at magnitude below SPP waves in gold and other noble materials [8].

3　Experiments with Graphene in the THz Range

The conventional metallic square patch antenna fed by micro strip line with square wave transformer is designed with 10-micrometer substrate thickness. The Graphene square patch is tested for their different substrates. We observe THz radiation in different frequency range.

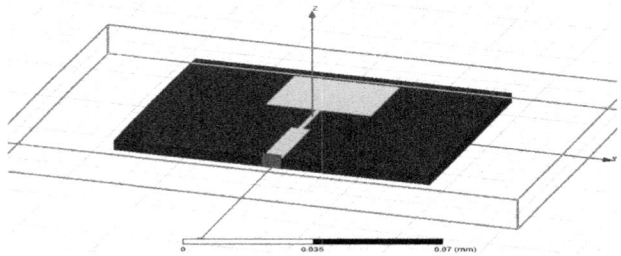

Fig. 1. Graphene patch antenna

3.1　Graphene as a Saturable Absorber

Graphene is used as a saturable absorber in wide optical response [5]. It can cover all telecommunication bandwidths. Graphene can be used in high speed processing. Femtosecond signals can be processed from it. It can absorb wavelength in the infrared and THz range and can turn continuous wave output into a train of ultrafast optical pulse.

Due to absorbing property, Graphene has pulse-shaping ability [5]. The nonlinearity is typically observed at very high light intensities. Thus, it has large potential applications in optical switching. Recently it has been predicted that Graphene shows strong nonlinear behavior in microwave and terahertz frequencies [12]. The material, which show photo physical properties and large optical nonlinearities are used in fast optical communication. Figure 2 shows Graphene saturable absorption property of material where absorption of light decreases with increasing light intensity [1, 5, 17].

In our experiment, square patch (see Fig. 1) of Graphene grown over the SiO_2 substrate shows a strong absorption peak at 5.2 THz. Absorption decreases as frequency increases [see Fig. 2].

3.2   Plasmonics as SPR Sensor

Plasmoics can be used in sensing. SPR sensors are being developed using localized surface plasma resonances (LSPRs) or propagating surface plasma polaritrons (SPPs) [13]. SPR sensors are based on resonant peak shift of power of SPs by the refractive index of the surrounding environment [13]. These SPRs are developed with the help of nanowires. Nanowires have potential applications in Nano photonic circuits. Nanowires Plasmon's are sensitive to the dielectric environment, which makes them a new type of structure for sensing applications.

In our experiment changing the local dielectric surrounding by Al_2O_3 deposition changes have been observed. Graphene layer deposited over Al_2O_3 shows S11 in Fig. 5 (a) and (b) in THz range. Tong *et al.* have experimented graphene NW (Nano wire) coated with Al_2O_3. It shows oscillations in intensity. It works like Fabry Perot (FB) resonator. In our experiment graphene deposited as a patch over Al_2O_3 substrate proves FB resonance in THz range by multiple dips in the s11 in THz range.

The dependence of spectra and near field distributions on dielectric environment provide new approaches to detect thickness and refractive index of the films and hence can be used as sensing element in nanowire circuits also [13].

3.3   High Bandwidth

Graphene with SiO_2/Si substrate and with Gold deposition shows radiation in THz range [14] at 120 GHz. In our experiment Graphene over Si, substrate shows s11 at 12.55 THz and 14.55 THz with bandwidth in THz.

4   Results and Observation

The simulation and design optimization has been performed using high frequency simulator software (HFSS) which is commercially available electromagnetic simulator based on finite element technique.

1. In our experiment with Graphene patch on SiO_2 Substrate show strong absorption peak at 5.2 THz (Fig. 2).
   With SiO_2, substrate in 10 to 15 THz range S11 is shown at −9.3 dB with 1 dB gain (Figs. 3, 4).

2. With Al_2O_3 substrate of same width, Graphene shows different behavior. It gives bands at 18.05 THz, 23 THz, 20.25 THz, and 21.5 THz. The gain is 1 dB. Hence, sweep frequency is kept from 10 to 30 THz. At sweep of 10 to 25 THz, the antenna shows Fabry Parot resonator like resonance giving multiple bands from 1.5 to 18 THz (Fig. 5a, b).

3. With Si substrate graphene shows a sharp dips of S11 at two point one in 12.55 THz and 13.65 THz with huge bandwidth 12.15THz–13.0 THz and 13.6 THz–13.8 THz. It also gives dual band. The gain obtained is 1 dB (Figs. 7, 8, 9 and 10).

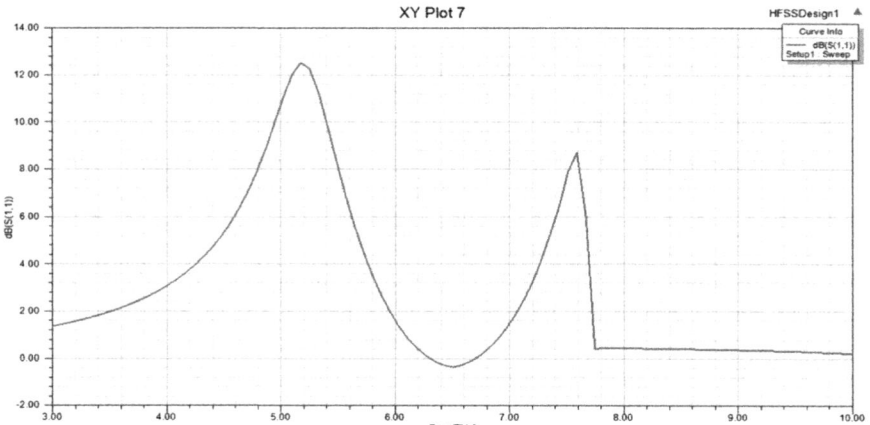

Fig. 2. Absorption peaks shown by the Graphene patch with SiO$_2$ substrate maximum at 5.2 THz

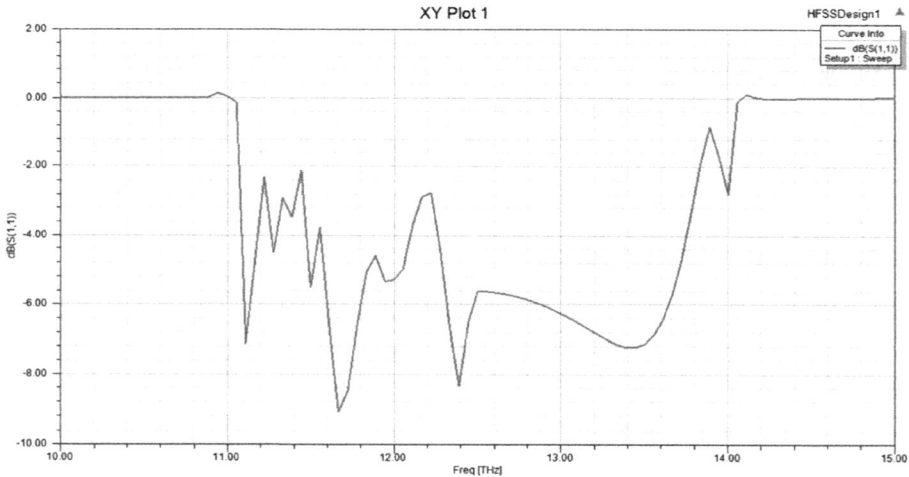

Fig. 3. S11 with SiO$_2$ substrate

Fig. 4. Gain of the single square patch antenna with SiO$_2$ substrate

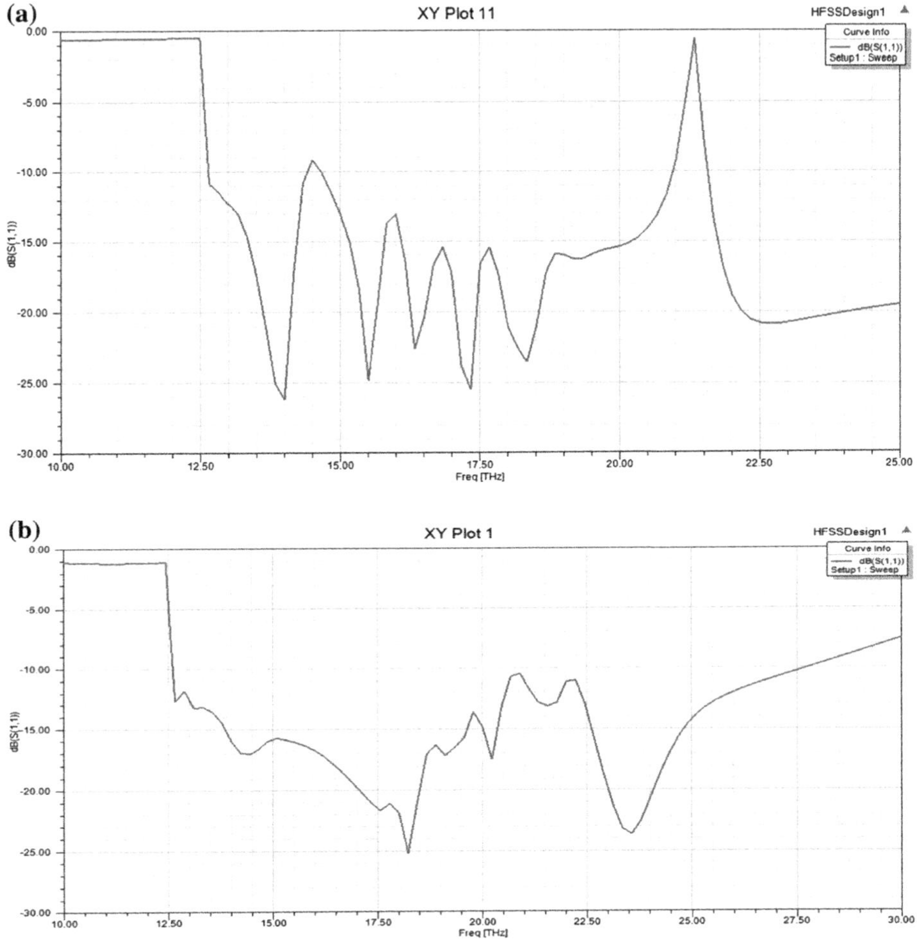

(a)
XY Plot 11
HFSSDesign1
Curve Info
dB(S(1,1))
Setup1 : Sweep
dB(S(1,1))
Freq [THz]
(b)
XY Plot 1
HFSSDesign1
Curve Info
dB(S(1,1))
Setup1 : Sweep
dB(S(1,1))
Freq [THz]

Fig. 5. (a) S11 with Al_2O_3 substrate, (b) S11 with Al_2O_3 substrate

dB(GainTotal)
1.0000E+000
9.3333E-001
8.6667E-001
8.0000E-001
7.3333E-001
6.6667E-001
6.0000E-001
5.3333E-001
4.6667E-001
4.0000E-001
3.3333E-001
2.6667E-001
2.0000E-001
1.3333E-001
6.6667E-002
0.0000E+000
Z
Y
X

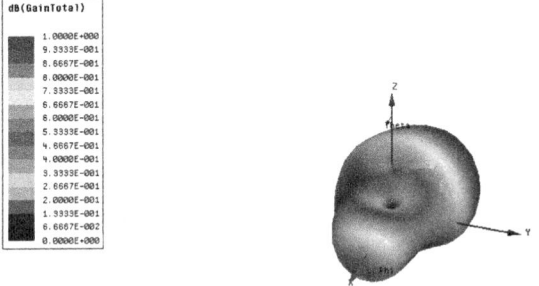

Fig. 6. Gain of the Graphene square patch antenna with Al_2O_3 substrate

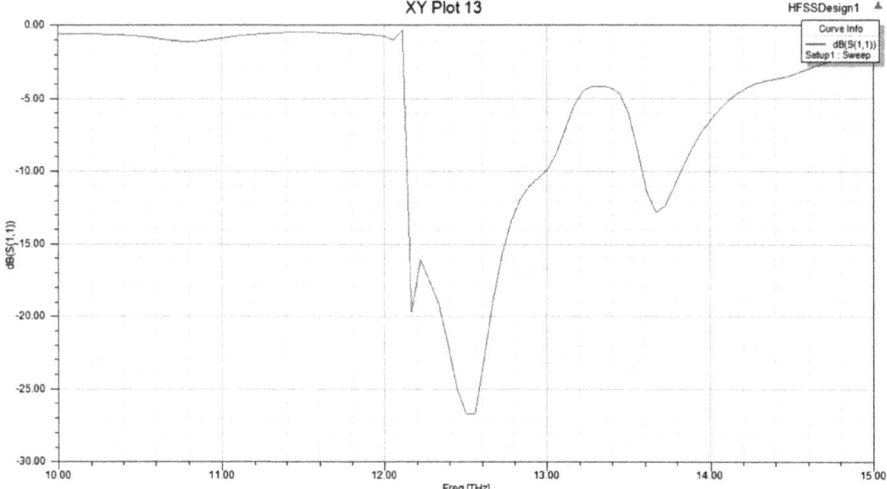

Fig. 7. S11 of Graphene patch antenna with Si substrate

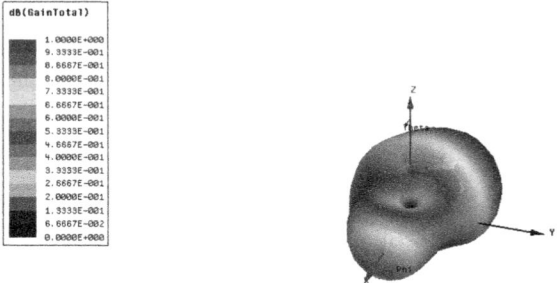

Fig. 8. Gain with Si substrate

Fig. 9. Gain total of square patch antenna with Si substrate

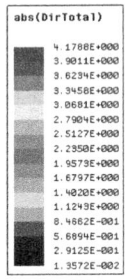
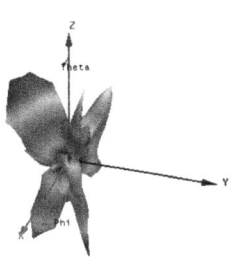

Fig. 10. Total directivity of Graphene patch antenna with Si substrate

5   Conclusion

The basic physics of plasmonics is discussed in this paper. Main application of surface plasma polaritron property is explored using nano technology. Plasmonics sensing is a research field where the physics of Plasmon generation governs the kinetic theory of plasma. In this paper, kinetic theory of plasma is defined and a new material Graphene that shows low losses is tested in THz frequencies with different substrates.

Plasmonics in microwave region produces losses hence we need to work in the nanoscale and explore new materials such as graphene with absorption band in 1 to 10 terahertz with SiO_2 substrate and resonance in Terahertz frequencies with Al_2O_3 substrate. It is useful for the 5G applications as in next generation networks will demand for THz bands. Si substrate will be useful to obtain the high bandwidth.

Applications
As THz, radiation is used for communication in 5G networks. Graphene shows remarkable properties in THz range from low to high terahertz frequencies. It has wide applications in THz imaging, SPR sensing and inverse scattering.

Advantages
Other technologies have important limitation at terahertz; Graphene provides a low loss and simple mean for dynamics reconfiguration. Graphene based Nano antennas and waveguides of um to nm size will be one of the promising applications in wireless applications, networking and SPR sensing.

References

1. Sadon, S.N.H., Kamarudin, M.R., Ahmad, F., Jusoh, M., Majid, H.A.: Graphene array antenna for 5G applications. Appl. Phys. A **123**(2), 118 (2017)
2. Thampy, A.S., Darak, M.S., Dhamodharan, S.K.: Analysis of graphene based optically transparent patch antenna for terahertz communications. J. Phys. Phys. E: Low-dimens. Syst Nanostruct. **66**, 67–73 (2015)

3. Grushin, A.G., Valenzuela, B., Vozmediano, M.A.: Effect of coulomb interaction on the optical properties of doped graphene. Phy. Rev. B **80**, 155417 (2009)
4. Llatser, I., Kremers, C., Cabellos-Aparicio, A., Jornet, J.M., Alarcon, E., Chigrin, D.N.: Graphene-based nano-patch antenna for terahertz radiation. Photon. Nanostruct. Fundam. Appl. **10**, 353–358 (2012)
5. Liu, Z.B., Zhang, X.L., Yan, X.Q., Chen, Y.S., Tian, J.G.: Nonlinear optical properties of graphene-based materials. Chin. Sci. Bull. **57**(23), 2971–2982 (2012). Review Special Issue: Graphene
6. Lin, Y.M., Jenkins, K.A., Valdes-Garcia, A., Small, J.P., Farmer, D.B., Avouris, P.: Operation of graphene transistors at gigahertz frequencies. Nano Lett. A **9**(1), 422–426 (2009)
7. Gusyrin, V.P., Sharapov, S.G., Carbotte, J.P.: Magneto optical conductivity in graphene. J. Phys.: Condens. Matter **19**(2), 02622 (2007)
8. Hanson, G.W.: Dyadic Green's functions for an anisotropic non local model of biased graphene. IEEE Trans. Antennas Propag. **56**(3), 747–757 (2009)
9. Villani, C.: A review of mathematical topics in collisional kinetic theory. Handb. Math. Fluid Dyn. **1**, 71–305 (2002). Elsevier Science
10. Akyildiz, I.F., Jornet, M.: Grapheme based plasmonic nano antenna for terahertz. IEEE J. Sel. Areas Commun. **31**(12), 685–694 (2013)
11. Vakil, A., Engheta, N.: Transformation optics using graphene. Science **332**(6035), 1291–1294 (2011)
12. Dragoman, M., Muller, A.A., Dragoman, D., Coccetti, F., Plana, R.: Terahertz antenna based on graphene. J. Appl. Phys. **107**, 104313 (2010)
13. Tong, L., Wei, H., Zhang, S., Xu, H.: Recent advances in plasmonics sensors. Sensors **14**, 7959–7973 (2014). ISSN 1424-8220
14. Bala, R., Marwaha, A.: Characterization of graphene for performance enhancement of patch antenna in THz region, Elsevier (2014)
15. Jackson, J.: Classical Electrodynamics, 3rd edn. Wiley, India (2010)
16. Gallagher, P.T.: Introduction to plasma physics, lecture 6: Kinetic theory, Astrophysics Research Group, Trinity College Dublin, 25 Sept 2013
17. Paruisseaee, J., Tamagnone, C.M., Gomez- Diaz, J.S., Carrasco, E.: Grapheme antennas: can integration and reconfigurability compensate for loss. In: Microwave Conference (EuMC) (2013)
18. Llatser, I., Kremers, C., Chigrin, D.N., Jornet, J.M., Lemme, M.C., Aparicio, A.C., Alarcon, E.: Characterization of graphene based nano antennas in Terahertz Band. In: EuCAP 2012, Prague (2012)
19. Jornet, J.M., Akyildiz, I.F.: Grapheme based Plasmonic Nano antenna for electromagnetic Nano communication is the Terahertz Band. In: European Conference on Antenna and Propagation, Barcelona (2010)

Sparse Channel Estimation Based on Compressive Sensing with Overcomplete Dictionaries in OFDM Communication Systems

Yi Zhang[✉], Ramachandran Venkatesan, Octavia A. Dobre, and Cheng Li

Memorial University, St. John's, NL A1B 3X5, Canada
{yz7384,venky,odobre,licheng}@mun.ca

Abstract. In this paper, sparse channel estimation in OFDM communication systems is investigated. Particularly, the application of compressive sensing theory into sparse channel estimation is studied. Several existing sparse signal recovery algorithms are compared along with the conventional least-square method. Furthermore, overcomplete dictionaries are considered for sparse representations of the multipath channels. Simulation results show that the oversampled DFT matrices lead to sparser channel coefficients and superior estimation quality when compared to the baseband channel representations, and AS-SaMP provides a better estimation accuracy without requiring excessively higher complexity among the compared recovery algorithms.

Keywords: Sparse channel estimation · Compressive sensing
Sparsity adaptive matching pursuit · Sparse recovery algorithms
Overcomplete dictionary

1 Introduction

Orthogonal frequency division multiplexing (OFDM) has been widely used in broadband wireless systems e.g., fourth generation mobile communication systems, underwater acoustic (UWA) networks, and digital audio and video broadcasting systems thanks to its high spectral efficiency and low complexity of the receivers required to cope with multipath fading [1, 2]. In a coherent receiver, the knowledge of the channel is essential, and needs to be estimated from time to time. Previously, researchers have demonstrated many wireless communication channels have a sparse representation, which means a few significant taps dominate the channel impulse response (CIR) while most of taps are zero or close to zero [3–5]. Conventional approaches for data-aided channel estimation, such as least square (LS) and minimum mean squared error (MMSE) [6] cannot utilize the sparse property of the channels and they often result in excessive spectrum utilization.

© Springer Nature Singapore Pte Ltd. 2018
P. Bhattacharyya et al. (Eds.): NGCT 2017, CCIS 828, pp. 99–111, 2018.
https://doi.org/10.1007/978-981-10-8660-1_7

Recently, several researchers have looked into sparse channel estimation [4, 5, 7, 8]. By exploiting the sparse nature of channels, sparse estimation methods based on the compressive sensing (CS) theory [9–11] have demonstrated better performance compared to the LS method [12–15]. In a nutshell, CS allows an accurate, and sometimes exact, recovery of the target signal which permits sparsely representation on a certain basis, from a lower-dimension random linear projections, and thus it reduces the amount of computation. According to CS, appropriate choices of the sparse signal recovery algorithm, sparse signal representation, and measurement matrix are essential in obtaining a faithful reconstruction.

On one hand, two popular types of recovery algorithms are linear programming (LP) and dynamic programming (DP). As a representative of the LP-type algorithms, the basic pursuit denoising (BPDN) offers a good estimation accuracy. However, the high computational complexity makes it less favoured for implementation in the real applications. Meanwhile, as a representative of the DP algorithms, orthogonal matching pursuit (OMP) is widely used due to its low computational cost [13–18]. Moreover, the recently-reported methods based on the idea of message passing, e.g., the approximate message passing (AMP) algorithm [19] and expectation maximization-Bernoulli Gaussian-AMP (EM-BG-AMP) [20] can reconstruct the target signal with nearly the same accuracy as the LP-type algorithms, but at a lower computation complexity [19]. However, the performance of these algorithms relies on the pre-assumed statistics of the target signal, measurement matrix, and noise.

In [21], the sparsity adaptive matching pursuit (SaMP) was proposed. This MP-based algorithm does not require *a priori* knowledge of the sparsity level. In this algorithm, the number of the recovered entries is gradually increased by a fixed step size over several steps. However, this algorithm requires selection of optimal step size that leads to a good balance between the convergence speed and the estimation accuracy. In [22], an improved SaMP algorithm, namely adaptive step size SaMP (AS-SaMP), is proposed. Here, an adaptive step size is adopted for a better estimate of the sparsity of the target signal. This paper presents a comparative performance analysis of various MP-based recovery algorithms for estimating sparse channels in OFDM systems.

On the other hand, CS theory is concerned about the reconstruction of signals which can be sparsely represented in certain orthonormal basis. However, the sparse representations of signals may not exist in an orthogonal basis (i.e., incoherent dictionary), but in a redundant basis (i.e., overcomplete dictionary) in many practical situations. For example, a sparsifying orthonormal basis may not exist for the signal which is represented using oversampled discrete Fourier Transform (DFT) and curvelets [23, 24] Fortunately, it has been shown not only that CS is viable for signals which have overcomplete sparse representations, but also that accurate recovery is possible with certain conditions on the measurement matrix [24, 25]. In this paper, we consider sparse representation over an overcomplete dictionary, i.e., the oversampled DFT matrices for sparse channel estimation in OFDM systems. Through the numerical simulations, we show that the AS-SaMP algorithm using the oversampled DFT matrices outperforms the other compared algorithms using the standard DFT matrix without increasing the computational complexity significantly.

This paper is organized as follows. Section 2 introduces background on CS and formulates the channel estimation problem. Section 3 presents a comparative study of various OMP-like recovery algorithms. Section 4 compares the performance through the simulation results. Finally, Sect. 5 draws the conclusion.

Notation: Acapital letter represents frequency domain representation, and a bold symbol stands for a vector or a matrix. $(\cdot)^H$ and $(\cdot)^T$ denote the Hermitian form and the transpose form of $(\cdot)$ respectively. $\|(\cdot)\|$ is short for $\|(\cdot)\|_2$, where $\|(\cdot)\|_p$ is the p-norm of $(\cdot)$ which equals to $(\sum |(\cdot)|^p)^{1/p}$.

2 Background and Problem Formulation

2.1 Background on CS

Suppose that we have a discrete-time signal vector denoted as $\mathbf{x} \in \mathbb{R}^N$ and there exists an orthonormal basis $\boldsymbol{\Phi}$ over which $\mathbf{x}$ can be represented as

$$\mathbf{x} = \boldsymbol{\Phi}\boldsymbol{\eta}, \tag{1}$$

where $\boldsymbol{\eta}$ is another representation of $\mathbf{x}$ over the basis $\boldsymbol{\Phi}$. CS is concerns about the sparse signal $\mathbf{x}$ (or $\boldsymbol{\eta}$) in the sense that among the N elements, only K elements in $\mathbf{x}$ (or $\boldsymbol{\eta}$) are significant and $K \ll N$. Assuming that measurements $\mathbf{y} \in \mathbb{R}^M$ is obtained by linear projecting $\mathbf{x}$ onto another set of vectors $\boldsymbol{\Psi} = [\boldsymbol{\varphi}_1 \boldsymbol{\varphi}_2 \cdots \boldsymbol{\varphi}_M]^T$, where the N-by-1 vector $\boldsymbol{\varphi}_j$ denotes the j th column of $\boldsymbol{\Psi}$. Thus, we have

$$\mathbf{y} = \boldsymbol{\Psi}\mathbf{x} + \mathbf{w} = \boldsymbol{\Psi}\boldsymbol{\Phi}\boldsymbol{\eta} + \mathbf{w}, \tag{2}$$

where $\boldsymbol{\Psi}\boldsymbol{\Phi}$ is referred to as the measurement matrix, and $\mathbf{w} \in \mathbb{R}^M$ is a noise vector with bounded energy $\|\mathbf{w}\| < \varepsilon$ [10]. As can be seen, the recovery of $\boldsymbol{\eta}$ from the compressed observations $\mathbf{y}$ is underdetermined as $M < N$. However, CS theory claims that the exact recovery of $\boldsymbol{\eta}$ is possible if M is larger than $\mathcal{O}\left(K \log\left(\frac{N}{K}\right)\right)$ and if the measurement matrix satisfies the restrict isometry property (RIP) [9–11]. RIP can be defined as given below:

Definition 1. *Let us denote the measurement matrix as* $\boldsymbol{\Theta}$. *For an arbitrary* $\delta \in (0, 1)$ *and any index set* $\mathbf{Q} \subset \{0, 1, \ldots, N - 1\}$ *so that the cardinality of* $\mathbf{Q}$ *is smaller than K, there is*

$$1 - \delta \le \frac{\|\boldsymbol{\Theta}_\mathbf{Q}\boldsymbol{\eta}\|}{\|\boldsymbol{\eta}\|} \le 1 + \delta, \tag{3}$$

where $\boldsymbol{\Theta}_\mathbf{Q}$ *is the partial matrix with the corresponding columns of* $\boldsymbol{\Theta}$, *i.e.,* $\mathbf{Q}$ *is composed of the indices of the columns.*

According to [9], one can estimate $\boldsymbol{\eta}$ through solution of a convex optimization problem, i.e., $\hat{\boldsymbol{\eta}} = \text{argmin} \, \|\boldsymbol{\eta}\|_1$, subject to $\|\mathbf{y} - \boldsymbol{\Theta}\boldsymbol{\eta} \leq \varepsilon\|$, for a given $\varepsilon > 0$. This is known as BP optimization problem. However, the high complexity is an issue for efficient implementations. Alternatively, greedy algorithms like OMP have been successfully employed to reconstruct the target signal. In this paper, we focus on the performance comparison of various OMP-based algorithms.

2.2   Problem Formulation

Let P out of the total K subcarriers in an OFDM system represent pilots. Let $X(k)$, $0 \leq k \leq N - 1$ denote the transmitted symbol on the k th subarrier. After an inverse fast Fourier transform (IFFT), the n th OFDM symbol can be obtained as

$$x(n) = \sum_{k=0}^{N-1} X(k)e^{\frac{j2\pi nk}{N}}. \tag{4}$$

Each OFDM symbol is followed by cyclic prefix (CP) to avoid intersymbol interference (ISI). Let us denote α_p and τ_p as the p th path's gain and the delay, respectively, and N_p as the total number of multipaths. The time-invariant impulse response of the multipath channel can be represented as

$$h(\tau) = \sum_{p=0}^{N_p-1} \alpha_p \delta(\tau - \tau_p). \tag{5}$$

After passing through the noisy channel, the FFT output of the k th subcarrier at the receiver side, can be simplified as

$$\mathbf{R} = \mathbf{XDh} + \mathbf{W}, \tag{6}$$

where $\mathbf{X}$ is an N-by-N diagonal matrix with $X(k)$ on its main diagonal, $\mathbf{h}$ is L-by-1 CIR vector, $\mathbf{D}$ is the N-by-L partial DFT matrix, and $\mathbf{W}$ are the N-dimension frequency responses of the additive white Gaussian noise (AWGN). To extract the pilot subcarriers, we calculate

$$\mathbf{R'} = \mathbf{X'D'h} + \mathbf{W'}, \tag{7}$$

where $\mathbf{S}$ is a P-by-N matrix for pilot extraction, $\mathbf{R'} = \mathbf{SR}$, $\mathbf{X'} = \mathbf{SXS}^T$, $\mathbf{D} = \mathbf{SD'}$, and $\mathbf{W} = \mathbf{SR'}$. Define $\mathbf{A} \triangleq \mathbf{X'D'}$ as the measurement matrix in CS theory. To this end, we aim to recover $\mathbf{h}$ from the fewer pilot $\mathbf{R'}$, provided the matrix $\mathbf{A}$ using the CS-based sparse recovery algorithms.

Remark 1. From Eq. (6) the non-zero entries of $\mathbf{h}$ needs to be reconstructed, and the j th element of $\mathbf{h}$ corresponds to the j th path delay τ_j, $0 \leq j \leq L - 1$. However, the actual delay of the multipath may not coincide with the assumed delay points, which is known as the off-grid problem [26]. Hence, a redundant basis (also known as dictionary) generated from a finer-grained delay points leads to a better approximation of the continuous delay, and improves the estimation quality [12].

3   Sparse Recovery Algorithms

To ensure a reliable reconstruction of the target signal, sparse recovery algorithms are essential. As mentioned, this paper concentrates on the OMP algorithm [27] and its variants, which heuristically identify the support set[1] of the target signal. In [28], an OMP variant, namely compressive sampling matching pursuit (CoSaMP) was proposed with the MSE performance close to that of the BP algorithm. Unlike OMP which chooses one column of the measurement matrix that has the strongest correlation with the currently remaining measurements (residual) per iteration (this is referred to as the *maximum correlation test*), CoSaMP, firstly, forms a candidate support set by choosing multiple columns per iteration, and then refines the candidate support set by removing the low-correlated columns through another correlation test (known as the *final test*[2]). However, CoSaMP requires *a priori* information of the sparsity level, which may often not available in practical systems.

Later in [21] SaMP was proposed to address this issue. In SaMP, the estimation process is carried out in stages, with each stage containing multiple iterations. During each stage, a particular number of columns which exhibit the strongest correlation with the current residual are identified. While the number of the identified indices is fixed among the iterations in the same stage, it is increased by a fixed step size s as the algorithm moves to the next stage. Although an exact recovery is guaranteed after a limited number of stages [21] an optimal choice of the step size s, which leads to a trade-off between the accuracy and the convergence speed, needs to be determined. Recently, a variable step size algorithm, abbreviated to VSStAMP, has been proposed in [29]. However, the adjustment of s depends on a specific relationship between the sparsity level of the target signal and the number of measurements, which may not be satisfied in real applications.

Furthermore, [22] proposed an improved algorithm based on SaMP, namely AS-SaMP, which can adaptively adjust s among different stages. It begins with a larger $s(<K)$ to approach the true sparsity rapidly, and adaptively decrease s for a fine tuning as the stage proceeds. As a result, a preset threshold Γ is adopted for the initiation of fine tuning. Particularly, when the energy difference of the recovered signals becomes falls below Γ, s is decreased by a factor of two to avoid overestimation of the sparsity, and therefore the estimation quality is improved [13]. Flow charts of the selected OMP-type algorithms are shown in Fig. 1 where $\mathbf{C}^i$, $\mathbf{F}^i$, $\mathbf{r}^i$, and K denote the candidate support set, the final support set, the residual vector in the i th iteration, and the sparsity level of the target signal, respectively.

---

[1] The support set of a vector $\mathbf{x}$ is defined as the set of indices which correspond to the non-zero elements of $\mathbf{x}$.

[2] The elimination of the low-correlated columns using final test is referred to as backtracking which improves the estimation accuracy of CoSaMP [28].

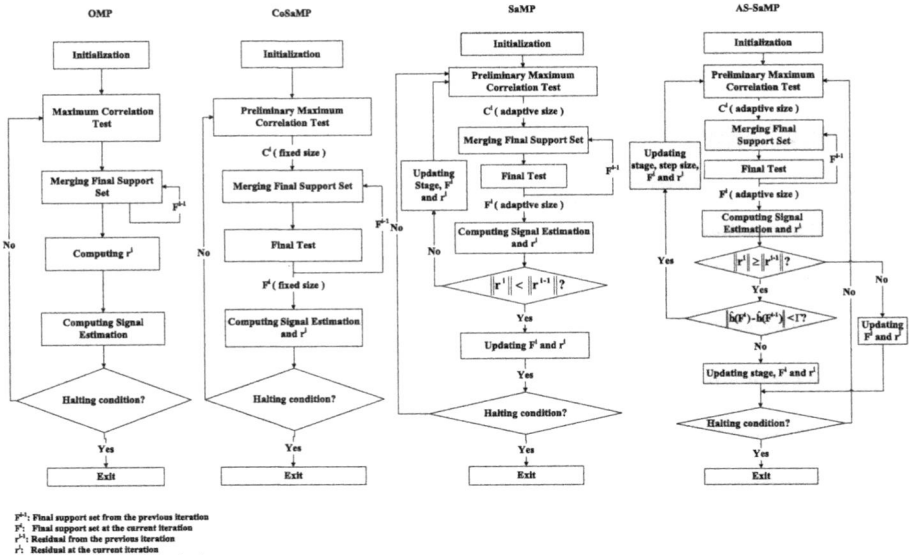

Fig. 1. Flow charts of OMP and its variants.

4   Simulation Results

4.1   Sparse Approximation

To demonstrate the sparse approximation performance using the overcomplete dictionaries, we study the same simple case in [12]. Suppose there are $N_p = 10$ multipaths in Eq. (5). Each path p is associated with a complex amplitude α_p and a delay τ_p. Strictly speaking, τ_p is a random value from a continuous distribution, which means it is impossible to find a sparsifying basis Φ which can represent all possible vectors of α_p. Hence a more redundant Φ will lead to a sparser channel representation, and vice versa. Firstly, let us consider the commonly used baseband model, where the assumed delay points are multiples of the sampling time (or $1/B$, B is the bandwidth). As a result, with the potential delay points $\tau_p \in \{0, 1/B, \ldots, (N-1)/B\}$ and $N = 256$, Φ turns out to be a standard DFT matrix. As the DFT matrix is a unitary transform, the sampled CIR can be obtained by calculating the IDFT of its sampled frequency response, which is usually not sparse.

An example of CIR and its corresponding frequency response $H(f) = \sum_{p=0}^{N_p-1} \alpha_p \cdot e^{-j2\pi\tau_p f}$ are shown in Fig. 2(a) and (b), respectively. It can be observed in Fig. 2(c), the baseband CIR which is determined from the sampled frequency response $H(f_k)$ is not strictly sparse.

As previously mentioned, the off-grid problem happens when one or more of the actual delays do not coincide with the potential delay points, and this can be mitigated by using a redundant basis for sparse signal representation. Therefore, an overcomplete

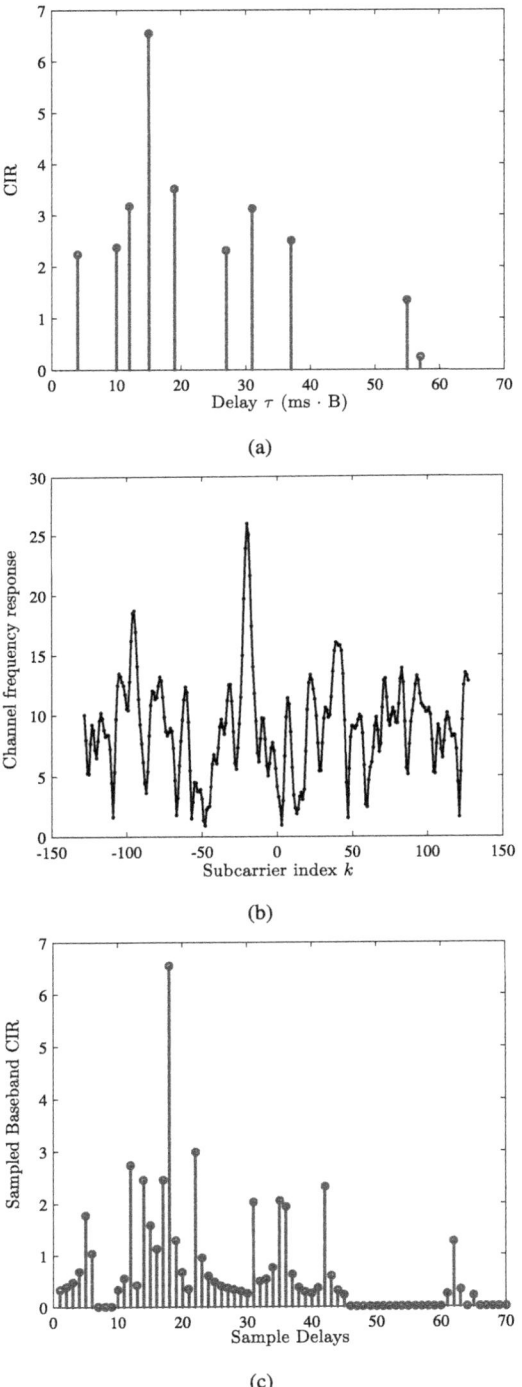

Fig. 2. Sparse approximation using the DFT matrix. In this example, there are 10 multipaths and 256 frequency samples.

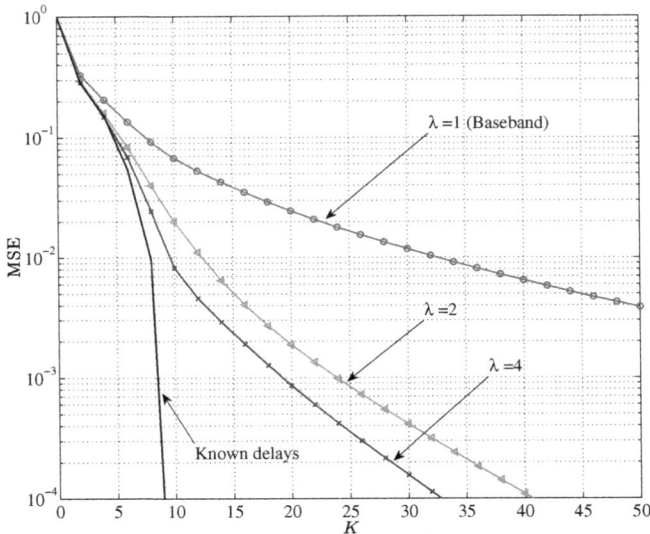

Fig. 3. MSE of the sparse approximation of $H(f_k)$ using oversampled DFT matrices with various λ

DFT generated by sampling the CIR at a finer grained resolution, is considered, and the assumed delay points become $\tau_p \in \{0, 1/\lambda B, \ldots, (N-1)/\lambda B\}$, where λ is the over-sampling factor. Figure 3 shows a MSE comparison of the sparse approximation of $H(f_k)$ using K terms using different basis models.[3] As can be seen, MSE decreases for an increased K. For instance, the MSE becomes zero for $K = N_p$ provided the delays of the multipaths are known. The faster MSE decreases, the sparser the corresponding basis can approximate $H(f)$, thus, significant fewer terms are required for a specific MSE using the overcomplete dictionaries. Moreover, MSE decreases faster for the more highly redundant dictionary, and results in a sparser representation of the multipath channel. This is consistent with the results shown in [12].

4.2   Performance of the Considered Recovery Algorithms

Simulation Setup
We consider an OFDM system with $N = 1024$ subcarriers, $P = 256$ pilot subcarriers, $B = 9.8$ kHz, and symbol period $T_s = 104.86$ ms. The CP duration is approximately 26 ms to avoid ISI, and this corresponds to the CP length $N_{CP} = 256$. It is assumed that 16-QAM modulation is used for both pilot and data symbols.

---

[3] The MSE of the sparse approximation is defined as $\mathrm{E}\left[\sum_{m=1}^{N} |H(m) - \hat{H}_K(m)|^2\right]$, where $\hat{H}_K(m)$ is the mth element of sparse approximation using K terms with the corresponding basis model.

To apply the aforementioned techniques to channel estimation, an appropriate representation of the sparse channel is required. In this paper, the unique properties of the UWA channels is adopted.

The average difference between any two propagation paths is 1.5 meters which corresponds to the delay difference of about 1 ms. This makes the sampled CIR a sparse vector in the sense that most taps are zero or close to zero as the delay difference is much larger than the sampling interval with a 9.8 kHz bandwidth. For each instance of the channel, assuming there are $N_p = 15$ multipaths of which the amplitudes are Rayleigh distributed where the average power exponentially decreases with the delay, and these parameters remain unchanged during one OFDM symbol.

The considered algorithms are LS, the aforementioned OMP-type methods, and an AMP-type method, namely EM-BG-AMP. Table 1 provides the parameters in the OMP-type methods. It should be noted that only CoSaMP requires the sparsity level as *a priori* information among all the considered algorithms. Additionally, to ensure a fair comparison, we use the same stopping criterion for all the considered algorithms, i.e., all algorithms stop when the signal residual falls below the preset threshold ϵ. For EM-BG-AMP, the convergence tolerance for EM is chosen as 10^{-5} and the maximum number of EM iterations as 200 [20]. The performance metrics are the MSE and CPU execution time,[4] and simulations are conducted in MATLAB R2014a using a 2.8 GHz Intel Core i7 CPU with 8 GB of memory.

Table 1. Parameters of the considered MP-type algorithms.

Considered algorithms	Maximum iterations	Sparsity level K	Tolerance ϵ	Step size s	Threshold Γ	Ratio u
CoSaMP	20	15	$\|\mathbf{W}\|$	N/A	N/A	N/A
OMP	20	N/A	$\|\mathbf{W}\|$	N/A	N/A	N/A
SaMP	N/A	N/A	$\|\mathbf{W}\|$	6	N/A	N/A
AS-SaMP	N/A	N/A	$\|\mathbf{W}\|$	Initially 6	1	N/A
VSStAMP	N/A	N/A	$\|\mathbf{W}\|$	Initially 6	N/A	$\leq \frac{1}{4}$

Performance of the Considered Recovery Algorithms

The MSE and the CPU running time for the selected algorithms are compared in Figs. 4 and 5 respectively. For a complete comparison, the lower bound of an ideal channel estimation with known indices of the significant elements in **h** is also included. Clearly, the considered CS-based algorithms provide superior MSE performance when compared to the conventional LS method. Also, the VSStAMP, SaMP and AS-SaMP algorithms outperform the OMP and CoSaMP algorithms which means the former sparsity adaptive algorithms can offer the same estimation quality with fewer pilots.

---

[4] The recovery MSE is defined as $\mathrm{E}\left[\sum_{k=1}^{N} |H(k) - \hat{H}(k)|^2\right]$. Instead of the number of iterations, we use the running time for complexity comparison because of the different computational complexity per iteration for different algorithms [13].

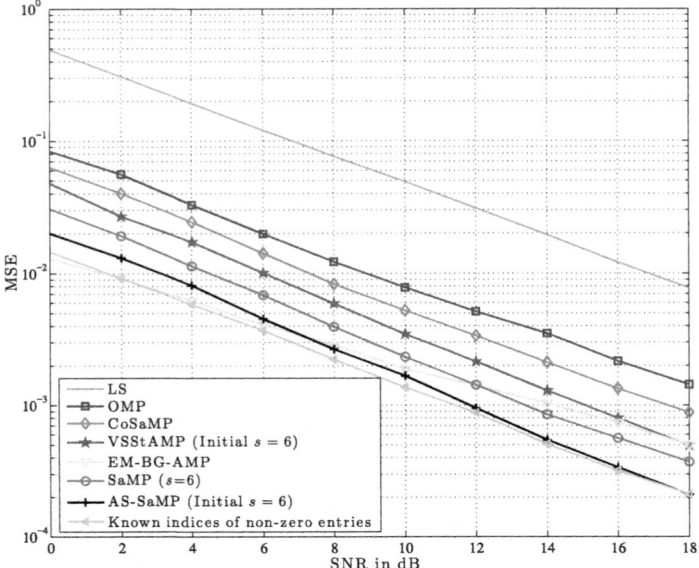

Fig. 4. MSE comparison of the considered algorithms. The lower bound for known indices of the non-zero entries of **h** is also included.

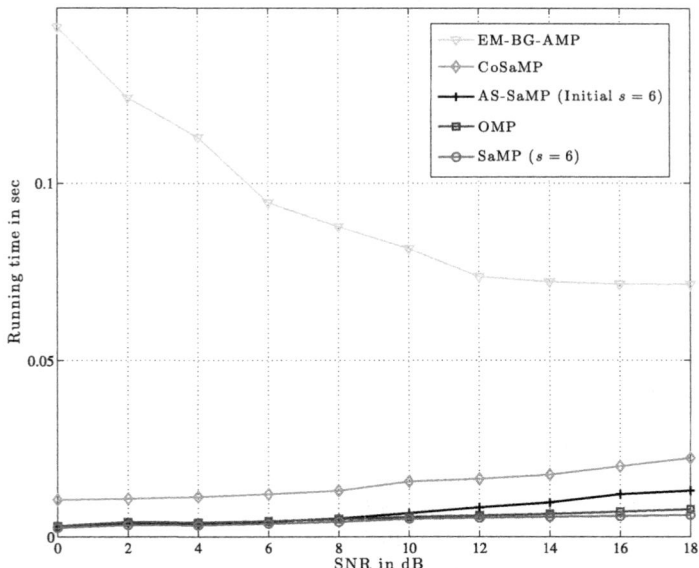

Fig. 5. CPU running time comparison of the selected algorithms.

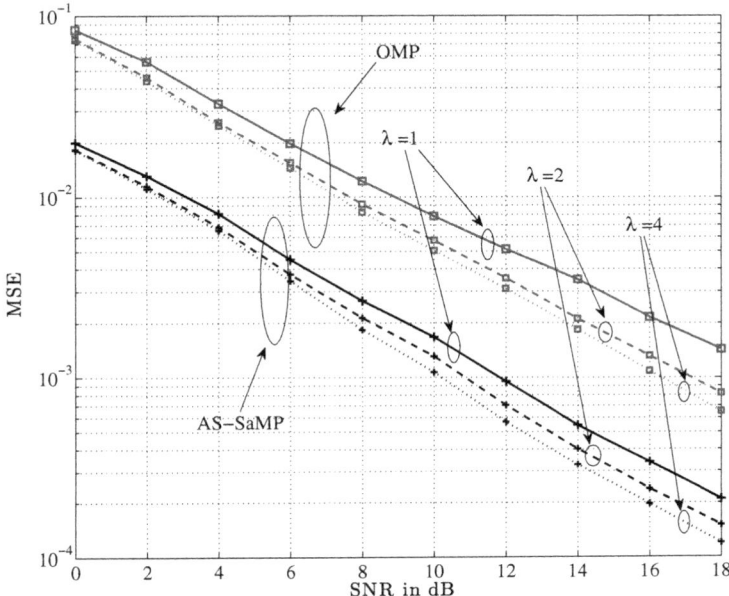

Fig. 6. MSE performance of the selected algorithms with different λ.

Additionally, despite of a slightly better performance offered by EM-BG-AMP when SNR < 8 dB, the AS-SaMP algorithm outperforms the other considered algorithms when SNR ≥ 8 dB. Furthermore, the MSE of AS-SaMP approaches the aforementioned lower bound at higher SNRs e.g., SNR ≥ 14 dB, for a specific sparsity level.

Next, From Fig. 5, the running time of EM-BG-AMP is much larger than those of the other algorithms due to the iterative parameters learning process via EM, and a larger number of iterations is required for EM. Moreover, the running time of the CoSaMP algorithm is the highest among the considered MP-type algorithms as each step per iteration requires a higher running time. Furthermore, the CPU running time of the AS-SaMP algorithm is marginally higher than that of the SaMP for the same initial s due to the reduced step sizes as the stage proceeds in AS-SaMP. We conclude that the AS-SaMP algorithm provides a better estimation accuracy while not requiring excessively high complexity.

Finally, Fig. 6 compares the MSE of the considered algorithms using the overcomplete dictionaries with different λ. It should be noted that only the results for OMP and AS-SaMP are shown for the readability of the figure. Previously, we saw that oversampled DFT matrices lead to sparser multipath channel representations, and thus are expected to have a reduced estimation error when compared with the standard DFT matrix. As shown in Fig. 6, the MSE performance is improved by using the oversampled DFT matrix with an increased λ for both algorithms. Moreover, AS-SaMP using the standard DFT matrix with baseband time resolution still outperforms OMP using the overcomplete dictionary with quadruple time resolution. It may be noted that the gain achieved by using the overcomplete dictionaries is obtained at the cost of increased computational complexity, and such gain diminishes when λ continues to increase.

5   Conclusion

In this paper, various state-of-the-art algorithms for sparse signal recovery are compared with the application to sparse channel estimation in OFDM systems. Among the considered algorithms, the recently-reported AS-SaMP has the merits of not requiring *a priori* knowledge of the sparsity level of the target signal, as well as the adaptively adjusted step size, which improves the recovery quality. Moreover, to mitigate the off-grid problem, the overcomplete dictionaries are considered which lead to sparser multipath representations. Simulation results show that the AS-SaMP algorithm displays a better trade-off between the MSE and running time through the use of overcomplete dictionaries when compared with the other considered recovery algorithms using the baseband representation.

References

1. Prasad, R.: OFDM for Wireless Communication Systems. Artech House, Norwood (2004)
2. Zhou, S., Wang, Z.: OFDM for Underwater Acoustic Communications. Wiley, Hoboken (2014)
3. Mallat, S.G., Zhang, Z.: Matching pursuits with time-frequency dictionaries. IEEE Trans. Sig. Process. **41**(12), 3397–3415 (1993). https://doi.org/10.1109/78.258082
4. Wang, N., Gui, G., Zhang, Z., Zhang, P.: Suboptimal sparse channel estimation for multicarrier underwater acoustic communications. Int. J. Phys. Sci. **6**, 5906–5911 (2011)
5. Bajwa, W.U., Sayeed, A.M., Nowak, R.: Sparse multipath channels: modeling and estimation. In: Proceedings of the 13th IEEE Digital Signal Processing Workshop, Marco Island, FL, pp. 320–325 (2009). https://doi.org/10.1109/dsp.2009.4785942
6. Hanzo, L., Akhtman, J., Jiang, M., Wang, L.: MIMO-OFDM for LTE, WIFI and WIMAX: Coherent Versus Non-coherent and Cooperative Turbo-Transceivers. John Wiley and IEEE Press (2010). https://doi.org/10.1002/9780470711750
7. Cotter, S., Rao, B.: Sparse channel estimation via matching pursuit with application to equalization. IEEE Trans. Commun. **50**(3), 374–377 (2002). https://doi.org/10.1109/26.990897
8. Carbonelli, C., Mitra, U.: A simple sparse channel estimator for underwater acoustic channels. In: Proceedings of OCEANS, pp. 1–6. MTS/IEEE (2007). https://doi.org/10.1109/oceans.2007.4449228
9. Donoho, D.L.: Compressed sensing. IEEE Trans. Inf. Theory **52**, 1289–1306 (2006). https://doi.org/10.1109/TIT.2006.871582
10. Candès, E.J., Romberg, J., Tao, T.: Robust uncertainty principles: exact signal recovery from highly incomplete frequency information. IEEE Trans. Inf. Theory **52**, 489–509 (2006). https://doi.org/10.1109/TIT.2005.862083
11. Candès, E.J., Tao, T.: Near-optimal signal recovery from random projections: universal encoding strategies. IEEE Trans. Inf. Theory **52**, 5406–5425 (2006). https://doi.org/10.1109/TIT.2006.885507
12. Berger, C.R., Wang, Z., Huang, J.-Z., Zhou, S.: Application of compressive sensing to sparse channel estimation. IEEE Commun. Mag. **48**(11), 164–174 (2010). https://doi.org/10.1109/MCOM.2010.5621984
13. Zhang, Y., Venkatesan, R., Dobre, O.A., Li, C.: Novel compressed sensing-based channel estimation algorithm and near optimal pilot placement scheme. IEEE Trans. Wirel. Commun. **15**(4), 2590–2603 (2016). https://doi.org/10.1109/TWC.2015.2505315

14. Berger, C.R., Zhou, S., Preisig, J., Willett, P.: Sparse channel estimation for multicarrier underwater acoustic communication: from subspace methods to compressive sensing. IEEE Trans. Sig. Process. **58**(3), 1708–1721 (2010). https://doi.org/10.1109/TSP.2009.2038424
15. Bajwa, W.U., Haupt, J., Sayeed, A.M., Nowak, R.: Compressive channel sensing: a new approach to estimating sparse multipath channels. Proc. IEEE **98**(6), 1058–1076 (2010). https://doi.org/10.1109/JPROC.2010.2042415
16. Tauböck, G., Hlawatsch, F., Eiwen, D., Rauhut, H.: A compressive sensing technique for OFDM channel estimation in mobile environments: exploiting channel sparsity for reducing pilots. In: IEEE International Conference on Acoustics, Speech, Signal Process, (ICASSP), Las Vegas, pp. 2885–2888 (2008). https://doi.org/10.1109/icassp.2008.4518252
17. Meng, J., Yin, W., Li, Y., Nguyen, N.T., Han, Z.: Compressive sensing based high resolution channel estimation for OFDM system. IEEE J. Sel. Topics Sig. Process. **6**(1), 15–25 (2012). https://doi.org/10.1109/JSTSP.2011.2169649
18. Huang, J.-Z., Berger, C.R., Zhou, S., Huang, J.: Comparison of basis pursuit algorithms for sparse channel estimation in underwater acoustic OFDM. In: Proceedings of OCEANS, pp. 164–174. MTS/IEEE (2010). https://doi.org/10.1109/oceanssyd.2010.5603522
19. Donoho, D.L., Maleki, A., Montanari, A.: Message passing algorithms for compressive sensing. Proc. Nat. Acad. Sci. **106** (2009). https://doi.org/10.1073/pnas.0909892106
20. Vila, J., Schniter, P.: Expectation-maximization Bernoulli-Gaussian approximate message passing. In: Proceedings of Asilomar Conference Signals Systems Computers, Pacific Grove, CA, pp. 799–803 (2011). https://doi.org/10.1109/acssc.2011.6190117
21. Do, T.T., Lu, G., Nam, N., Tran, T.D.: Sparsity adaptive matching pursuit algorithm for practical compressive sensing. In: Proceedings of 42nd Asilomar Conference on Signals Systems Computers, pp. 581–587 (2008). https://doi.org/10.1109/acssc.2008.5074472
22. Zhang, Y., Venkatesan, R., Dobre, O.A., Li, C.: An adaptive matching pursuit algorithm for sparse channel estimation. In: Proceedings of IEEE Wireless Communications and Networking Conference, New Orleans, LA, pp. 626–630 (2015). https://doi.org/10.1109/wcnc.2015.7127542
23. Candès, E.J., Demanet, L.D., Donoho, L., Ying, L.: Fast discrete curvelet transforms. Multiscale Model. Simul. **5**(3), 861–899 (2006)
24. Candès, E.J., Eldar, Y.C., Needell, D., Randall, P.: Compressive sensing with coherent and redundant dictionaries. Appl. Comput. Harmon. Anal. **31**(1), 59–73 (2011). https://doi.org/10.1016/j.acha.2010.10.002
25. Davenport, M.A., Needell, D., Wakin, M.B.: Signal sparse CoSaMP for sparse recovery with redundant dictionaries. IEEE Trans. Inf. Theory **59**(10), 6820–6829 (2013). https://doi.org/10.1109/TIT.2013.2273491
26. Tang, G., Bhaskar, N., Shah, P., Recht, B.: Compressive sensing off the grid. IEEE Trans. Inf. Theory **59**(11), 7465–7490 (2013). https://doi.org/10.1109/Allerton.2012.6483297
27. Tropp, J.A., Gilbert, A.C.: Signal recovery from random measurements via orthogonal matching pursuit. IEEE Trans. Inf. Theory **53**(12), 4655–4666 (2007). https://doi.org/10.1109/TIT.2007.909108
28. Needell, D., Tropp, J.A.: CoSaMP: iterative signal recovery from incomplete and inaccurate samples. Commun. ACM **53**(12), 93–100 (2010). https://doi.org/10.1145/1859204.1859229. California Institute of Technology, Pasadena
29. Bia, X., Chen, X., Zhang, Y.: Variable step size stagewise adaptive matching pursuit algorithm for image compressive sensing. In: Proceedings of IEEE International Conference on Signal Processing, Communication and Computing (ICSPCC), Kunming, China, pp. 1–4 (2013). https://doi.org/10.1109/icspcc.2013.6663917

Gesture Supporting Smart Notice Board Using Augmented Reality

P. Selvi Rajendran$^{(\boxtimes)}$ 🆔

KCG College of Technology, Chennai, India
selvi.cse@kcgcollege.com

Abstract. Generally, notice board is the most important thing in the academic institution and public places. However, conveying various notifications day-to-day is an extremely difficult strategy. This paper focus on advanced notice board called the Smart Notice Board (SNB) follows the novel procedure to obtain the data for the users. The information is generally reached by the authorized person only. Moreover, the approved users only can see the content of the SNB. The user can communicate with Board by free hand using Augmented Reality Interface. The AR Interface is an integrated interface system that links a network of smart devices together, and allows users to communicate with the physical objects using hand gestures. The user wears a smart glass which shows the user interface in an augmented reality view. The Hand signals are identified by the smart glass and after recognizing the correct hand gesture input, the SNB will communicate with the associated smart devices to carry out the designated operations. SNB provides common inter-device operations such as file transfer, printing, zooming and touch screen based operations.

Keywords: Augmeneted reality · Smart board · Gesture support board
Virtual bulletin board

1   Introduction

A Notice Board is an area in which people are able to put down public information. In the context of, to promote items to buy or sell by the people, to convey about events, or to provide the information to people. The common notice boards are generally making cork material. It allows to insert and also elimination of circulars and any paper based notices [1, 2]. Easily, this kind of information may be captured by the electronic gadgets like computers, phones. So people can post the information in the notice board to deliver the information to many persons. In any College, there is a lot of wall notice boards placed on different location whereby people with their announcement type on a sheet of paper and place it on the notice boards for other people to read through while passing through those notice boards. Hence there is plenty of piling up of papers on account of negligence of the person who put them and no one person who is responsible for eliminating it. Furthermore, the announcement may not reach again to the people who are planned. Hence there may be a lot of stress on the person who are handling to post the notices by ensuring that the announcements are put all over the place, all of this comes mainly because the software is not used in this context [2–4].

P. Bhattacharyya et al. (Eds.): NGCT 2017, CCIS 828, pp. 112–123, 2018.
https://doi.org/10.1007/978-981-10-8660-1_8

So, people may place and also remove information for others to read and see. The main aim of this research work to disseminate the information to the public with a paperless method such electronic mode as well as to provide the new mechanism for easy mode of transfer the electronic file to their personal electronic gadgets. This article concerns the implementation of SNB for the university to disseminate the academic information to the students and staffs. Usually, the colleges having the separate notice boards for every department and other common notice board to post the circulars and some administration related information. This work typically proposed a solution to provide the support system for the existing method in which notices have been put up in the SNB and it will function as the web application.

The problems faced by wooden notice board could be well resolved by the implementation of the Smart Notice Board application. With this virtual application, the information which is posted on the notice board can be passed on much easier and efficient way. In this system the authorized user only has a permission to upload the notices of different categories and departments which is recommended and approved by the higher authorities. After getting the approval, notices can be published in the SNB. Respective viewer may access the content virtually and will make best use out of it. If the user wants to know more about the information received, they can open and use the file which is transferred from SNB.

2 Literature Review

The existing notice board system that is used in the institution works on the basis of the manual updating method. An Online Announcement Displaying System (OADS) has been developed by Senzota et al. [5]. In their research work, research instruments such as observation and judgmental techniques were used to get the updates and know what is going on within the environment wherever they are on righty time.

Gurav et al. [3, 6] has developed a wireless Digital Notice Board Using GSM Technology. They implemented the system in such a way that it can display messages from authorized user sends to GSM module which is located on the notice board. The GSM module which is located at Digital notice board receives the message from authorized user and displayed on notice board which is situated at remote locations, at the same time this message will be sent to different users mobile numbers that are stored in microcontroller memory.

Anushree et al. [1, 7, 8] have developed the e-notice board in their research work. To provide the easiest way of accessing the information from the notice board, they designed the online notice board. This kind of notice board can be accessed quickly not only within the college campus also the information can be accessed from anywhere using internet. The major strength of this notice board is, it's working as an online web application and it's fully capable of passing relevant notices and announcements, and keeping the users updated from time to time. The user is kept updated each time the E-Notice Board is uploaded. According the department preferences, the alert will be sent to the users through SMS. The weakness of this method is that it will function only on online.

The Smart Notice Board is an interesting new innovative way to obtain information for the customers, staffs and students. In addition, the information can be accessed by the authorized person only. The user can interact with Board by free hand using AR Interface. The OADS and e-notice board are working in online only. The wireless Digital notice board can't support for online [5, 9]. The proposed SNB will be working in both online and offline modes.

The Augmented Reality Interface (AR) is a built-in interface system that connects a network of smart devices with each other, and it allows the users to communicate with the SNB using hand gestures. The user wears a smart glass which displays the user interface in an augmented reality view. Hand gestures are captured by the smart glass and upon recognizing the correct gesture input, the SNB will communicate with the associated smart devices to complete the specified operations. SNB facilitates popular inter-device operations such as file transfer, printing as well as device pairing.

3 System Design

The Smart Notice Board is an augmented reality application which requires users to work with wearable equipment such as smart glass. The Smart glasses are configured with cameras, processors, network functionality which enables it to show augmented views to the users [9–11]. All of these features are usually necessary for the SNB strategy. Since the user is wearing the smart glass, the camera will capture the scene of the adjacent physical environment. The camera recognizes the smart devices in the environment as well as keeps track of their locations according to the details on the corresponding markers. The camera on the smart glass also understands the user hand gestures which allow the user to communicate with objects by freehand manner. The smart glass also provides users with an augmented reality view, which overlays information and interface neatly over the real world.

Designing a SNB takes the consideration of the following:

  (i)   Physical affordance, which can be accessed from the user's electronic devices.
 (ii)   To introduce the free-hand working virtual interface for the users.
(iii)   To provide the efficient way of communication path for the end users to link the virtual interface and the physical objects.

The Interactive Smart Notice Board (SNB) can be used in two different modes. The modes of operation are,

(1) **Virtual mode:** When the SNB is in virtual mode, which means the user wears the AR glass and attempts to access the contents of SNB through AR Interface. It allows the user to access the contents of the notice board using hand gesture. The SNB uses several types of hand gestures to provide the multiple freehand interactions, which are used for various file transfer operations by the user. Figure 1 shows the Types of hand gestures which are supported interacting with the interface.

(2) **Non Virtual Mode:** The SNB will be acting as an electronic notice board. In this context, the viewer or user is connected to the E-notice board through internet,

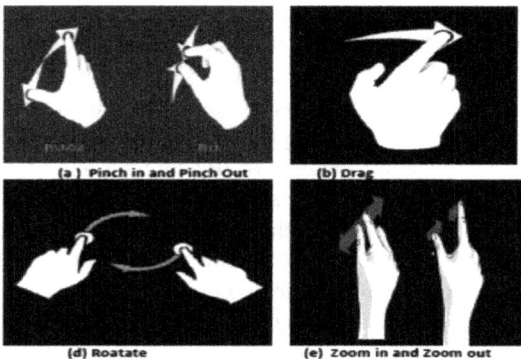

Fig. 1. The supported hand gesture for SNB

and checks for updated notice and also has the privilege to download the updated notices. All the notices are stored in and retrieved from the database.

The following are the various operations which can be recognized from the shape of the position of the hands [12].

Pick Operation: A Pinch gesture is interpreted as pick operation. The select operation needs to be carried out on a menu item, otherwise it will be invalid.

Drop Operation: An un-pinch gesture plays the role of dropping the picked item. A pick operation needs to always end with a drop operation.

Drag Operation: This operation is recognized by combined operation of pick and direction. The selected item is attached and move together with directional gesture when simple drag operation is carried out in the event of file transferring. Every drag interaction ends at any time when a drop operation performs.

Rotate Operation: A pair of pinch operation gestures moves in X and Y direction in that order on screen space. This kind of interaction is used to find the relative distance between them which will be useful to find the rotation angle. The Rotation operation is used for menu implementation. The menu provides various options to perform on the interface. The Rotation operation ends whenever either or both pinch gestures end.

Zoom: The zoom operation is activated when a combination of two drag operations carried out on the same item. The relative movement of the drag operation is used to increase and decrease the item size. The zoom operation ends in the event of one of or both drag operations terminated.

4   Prototype Development

The system Implementation needs technologies from the aspects of object tracking and hand gesture identification. The physical marker-based approach can be used for physical object tracking [12, 15]. A pair of distinct strategies which includes the double-threshold algorithm, and pre-trained SVM with Bag-Of-Words model, is attempted together with assessing for pinch gesture detection.

The system architecture of SNB is shown in Fig. 2. The camera configured with AR Glass takes live videos of the scenarios around users, which are streamed for image analysis of object tracking and hand recognition. The QR code which is pasted on the objects is used to extract object information of IP addresses and object's type. This can be used for recognizing the physical objects and to provide the network communication among the electronic devices which are placed in the surrounding places. The camera which is used in the virtual interface is updated periodically as per the real camera pose to make 3D menus from corresponding viewpoint and creating virtual menus associate with surfaces of physical objects. In this scenario, the menus are designed using the AR overlays and video stream, and then displayed on AR Glass display prism.

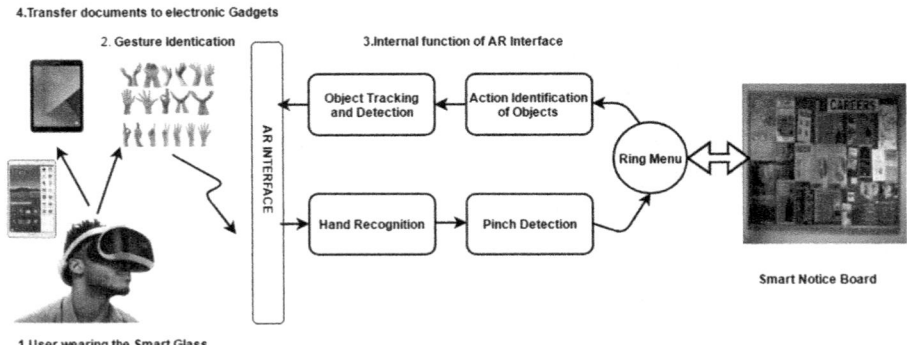

Fig. 2. System architecture of SNB

Hand gestures are taken out of video stream using a modified inexpensive technique according to the method [13, 14]. The contours are then filtered, making use of double thresholds to find out pinch gestures. Users have the ability to communicate with physical objects by way of virtual menus using pinch gestures, which are usually interpreted as socket to carry out communication between physical objects via underlying network.

4.1 Marker Design

The physical markers have used to act as the unique tags to the objects. The information which is used to identify the objects is object type, location of the network and some addition information about objects. This kind of information is hidden in the marker. Using this valuable information the user can interact with the objects. The users can share the files with other users easily.

All the devices are linked to the printed physical marker and it uses the QR code to encode the information which is hidden in the marker [16].

4.2 Object Tracking

The object tracking consists of in identifying objects and also analyzing spatial relationships between objects and users. The marker-based baseline has been applied to do this work, which may be normally more precisely and also a suitable method for image distortion and illumination variation [10, 17]. In this system, the QR codes are being used as fiducial markers to encode added information as object features for physical objects. The fiducial markers are the markers which can be placed on the field of view of the imaging system. The object information which includes IP address and object type is encoded in QR code in advance using the qrcode tool.

4.3 Menu Design

The AR supported menus are designed with attributes of depth, rotation and position. The following specifications have been taken into consideration in designing the menu.

Placement: In this specific context, the object-referenced placement has been used to assign the menus to the physical objects [19]. The visual markers are affixed to the physical objects. It achieves the goal of designing the system to split the centralized interface into a specific interface for the users.

Orientation: Menu alignment is required to provide, the easier view to read the options. The alignment of the menu is performed by marker which is tagged on the surface of the objects [20].

Triggering: According to the active state of the corresponding object in the menu may be able to be seen or unseen. The user can see the menu only in the in the status of the visual marker of the physical object appears in the user's view. Whenever the user applies the pinch operation on the file icon the menu item is triggered and the capture zone is turned on if menu icon is put in the capture zone.

4.4 Hand Gesture Recognition

This approach follows Wilson's vision-based technique to recognize single as well as two-hand pinching gestures, with various enhancements in our technique [13, 21]. The first and foremost process is for identifying the hand gestures from the background image and it is done by segmentation and connected component techniques of computer vision. Generally, the background image id darker then foreground and the system needs the foregrounds image such as hand gestures. So, the foreground hand gestures extract from the background for further processing. The hand skin color is used as the reference color while extracting the images. Contour of hand images is extracted based on the size of the contour. The incorrect contours are filtered according to the size bounds which are specified previously. The bounds ranges are recognized by the acceptance and elimination curve. Any inner contour exceeds the specified bound value are eliminated.

While identification of hand gestures, the space between the thumb and index fingers, decides the type of the operation and it plays the main role in recognizing the pinch gesture, but this method will fail in the condition of whole background space is occupied by the other fingers. The system will not work in the case of hole is unseen to the cameras. For example, sometime thumb and index fingers will be in the position of horizontal. The real time contour method is used for gesture recognition process. It provides accurate results for most of the cases and it can't recognize the gesture while the background is complicated.

In general, the pinch gestures are determined by the posture of the thumb and index fingers touching with each other and it have a hole between the fingers as shown in the Fig. 4a. Here, OpenCV software has been used for separating the unnecessary gestures other than pinch and also eliminate the interruptions.

Pre-sampling: As per the strategy used in [18], the user's skin color of hand has been taken into consideration for pre-sample in order to remove the background. The HSV method is used for skin recognition.

Initially, all the RGB color space frames, which are obtained from the camera image, are converted into HSV color. In this stage, the users' hand's skin color is collected by the camera for sampling. Usually multiple sampling is obtained for each user.

Processing Stage: At this stage, the noise has been eliminated using Gaussian Blur Algorithm. Following that, the hand color, shape has been taken out based on the sample colors in addition to color radius to generate the exact hand shape. Finally, to eliminate the irrelevant colors the medium blur is implemented on the combined shape. In the next stage, contours of hand color sections are extracted based on the threshold value. The threshold value is decided according to the distance between arm length and camera. The convex polygonal features are extracted from the contours to differentiate the pinch and non-pinch gestures. Usually, the ratio for pinch gesture is lower than 2.2 and non pinch gestures are higher than 2.2.

5 Evaluation and Experimentation

There are three experiments have been designed to assess the method from a different perspective. Different level of participants was asked to carry out the experiments in the devices owned by the users. The task completion time and also failed trials in offline and online were calculated and compared. A technology acceptance model (TAM) [9] was one of the main assessment and it followed to assess user practical experience.

To perform the experiment, the participants were equipped with AR glass and mobile or Tab. The messaging software Skype4 and share tool Dropbox 5 have been installed initially into the system for transferring as well as sharing document. Many accounts have been created earlier using the software. Printers and electronic gadgets which are attached to the notice board were running in order that participants could not have to login or turn on devices.

Ex1: The initial task is to copy documents between SNB (in Virtual mode) and Mobile. First Participants needed to copy specified documents from the notice board in manual operation like to take pictures by mobile camera. In SNB, participants were required to carry out pick, drag, and drop operations with their hands to transfer the file from SNB to the electronic gadgets. To access the various items which are folded into the menu, the rotate operation also needed.

Ex2: On the following task, the copying documents between non virtual modes of SNB and Mobile are taking into consideration. The participants were asked to transfer the contents from SNB to mobile using Bluetooth or wifi options.

Ex3: Detection rate and failure rate of gesture identification is taken into consideration for the third task. Here, a shape of the hand plays the major role in gesture reorganization. The shape of the hand section is extracted while copying the document from SNB. The biggest one is the outer contour (i.e. shape of the hand) of the hand section as illustrated in Fig. 4. Mostly it is in dark color. Any inner contour refers an inner hole appeared when we fold the fingers in the hand section. General illumination along with other non-pinch gestures may additionally generate the inner contours and it is shown in Fig. 4e and f.

6   Results and Discussion

Figure 3 Compares the participants' task completion time using SNB(virtual mode) system and other traditional techniques like document copy via USB devices and Skype, document share through Dropbox and using other networking features. The time expense of SNB is significantly a lot less than other traditional methods in every task. Particularly, it is taken 360 ms (Red bar) for move the contents which is nearly 4 to 7 times much faster respectively, when compared to transferring on Skype (Green bar, Non Virtual mode = 3317 ms) and USB flash copy. The manual transfer will be done through observing the content manually or photo image taken by mobile. It takes 7442 ms for processing manually in Ex1.

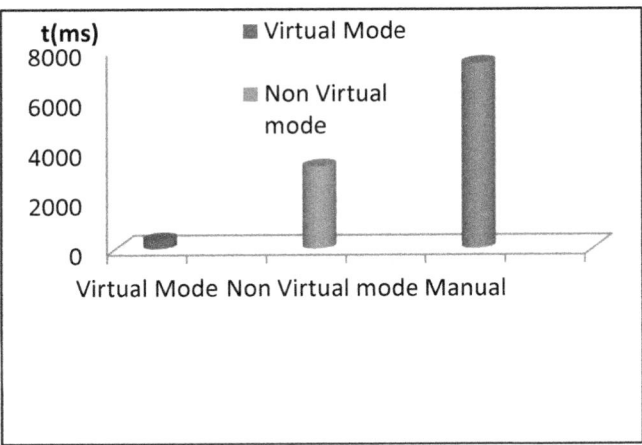

Fig. 3. Comparison of task completion time of experiments using SNB and traditional methods. (Color figure online)

The performance of Wilson's vision approach is compared with an SVM method to recognize single along with two-hand pinching gestures by various categories of people. The evaluation was performed by the Google glass with non virtual to a Tablet (2.6 GHZ Intel Core i5, 16 GB Memory). The Google glass is used to copy the files from SNB to seven users. The users are from different genders and skin color. The environmental setting for evaluation consists of corridor (direct sun light), computer lab and classroom. All the background may have complicated objects in the different environments. The various illumination ranges are shown in Table 1.

Table 1. Amount of lighting used in different scenarios

Scenario	Amount of lighting	Avg value in HSV
Corridor	60–100	60 ± 20
Ground (direct light)	10000	225 ± 30
Class room	320–520	160 ± 30
Computer lab	310–530	160 ± 30

All the users are carried out the pinch and un-pinch gesture to copy the file from SNB to Tablet. During the task, the glass and hands were used frequently. Approximately around 250 frames have been used by one user in one scenario. The frames are interpreted by hands to classify the pinch and un-pinch gestures and then compare the recognition results with another method such as SVM approach. The accuracy of the both methods has been shown in the Table 2. From the values shown in the Table 2 indicates that the Wilson method works well in some of the situations and SVM provides the good result in some situations. The Wilson technique uses the convexity defects and inner contour sizes as constraints to predict the incorrect contour and it will be filtered out. But the SVM technique involves many undefined attributes to recognize the gesture and it can recognize the gesture from different perspectives.

Table 2. Gesture recognition accuracy in different scenario

	Corridor		Ground		Class room		Computer lab	
	Wilson	SVM	Wilson	SVM	Wilson	SVM	Wilson	SVM
User1	77.5	67.3	75.2	65.2	62.7	74.1	60.2	70.7
User2	78.3	63.4	73.5	61.5	63.1	70.5	61.2	78.6
User3	77.1	65.5	74.6	64.5	61.6	76.6	61.2	77.6
User4	80.2	67.8	71.4	67.8	62.1	72.4	60.5	74.2
User5	72.2	69.1	70.5	66.8	61.3	71.5	62.2	71.1
User6	73.3	65.8	72.2	62.3	62.7	72.7	65.1	73.3
User7	71.5	69.2	73.3	61.6	60.1	75.3	61.3	76.2
Average	78.3	63.4	73.5	61.5	63.1	70.5	61.2	78.7

The above Table 2 shows accuracy rate of gesture recognition by different people in different places. It concludes that both methods are performing equally. In open space environments such as corridor and ground, the Wilson method performs well compare with SVM. In low illumination areas like Classroom and computer lab, which are closed portion and it will get lesser amount light. The SVM performance is satisfactory compare with Wilson method. Overall, the performance of both methods has been affected in low illumination areas.

Generally, copying the documents from one device to another device involves plugging in, plugging out and copying documents between devices and mobiles and needed some physical actions of users. But, in the context of SNB, It simplifies the manipulations without direct physical touch and provides the fast secure accessing technique. When the printer is connected with the SNB virtual mode, the SNB takes 380 ms for print the document. It saves the time spending for doing the operations by clicking "\print…" menu item and choosing specified printer from the printer list needed by traditional methods (10242 ms). It was clear that that a few participants to complete the task when by selecting a printer from the configuration panel. In that case, the SNB takes 307 ms and the traditional manual operation takes 8735 ms. It can also be more effective in document sharing in comparison with Dropbox sharing (Manual = 13502 ms, SNB = 1127 ms), as it would not require verifying target user's Dropbox account, that may be normally not the same as target computer's account.

Almost all pinch gestures identification will pass when the threshold is small and the recognition accuracy decreases when the threshold goes up. A lower bound 0.6 and upper bound value 0.8 has been set to achieve over 85% accuracy of both pinch gesture detection and non-pinch gesture removal. The approach will work in both one and two-hand pinch gesture identification as shown in Fig. 4. Actually, it is very difficult to remove other non-pinch gestures. Figure 4 shows two gestures with holes in the

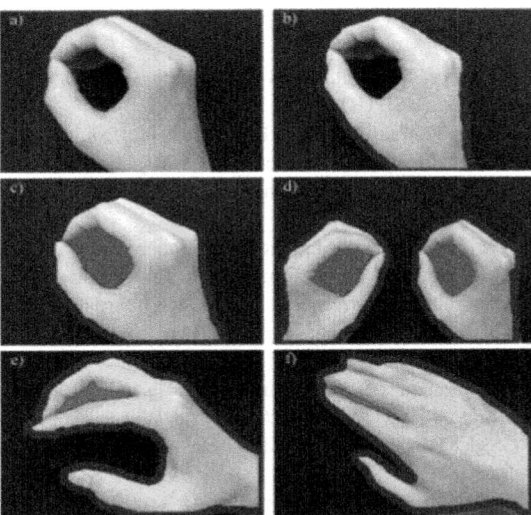

Fig. 4. The pinch gesture detection. (a) a typical pinch gesture; (b) outer contour of hand is extracted; (c) and (d): red closed regions are recognized as pinch holes; (e) and (f): green closed regions are eliminated as non-pinch holes. (Color figure online)

unusual position of the hands, but they are removed by this approach by comparing with the lower bound threshold values. In practice, the larger upper bound consists of the result set of smaller upper bound and it can be applicable to uncheck the upper bound. However, size of pinch hole may vary by person and it is the main constraint in this context.

7 Conclusion

Thus, SNB provides a decentralized user interface system for manipulation between the physical and digital worlds. User interface and communication are carefully designed to manage free-hand user experience. This technique is evaluated from both aspects of technological and user experience. By communicating with objects at a high-level of physical affordance instead of fundamental electronic counterparts, this approach supports users carry out operations in much comfort as well as natural way. It has been shown to be helpful for simple and frequently-performed manipulations with associated digital devices in closed environments.

In our experiments, it was clear that a lot of failures were occurring due to hand gesture detection. The color-based method is selected to relieve computational cost, but it is not correct enough in backgrounds with similar color of hand skin. In future we decided to incorporate depth and visual cameras to enhance the accuracy. Another problem is the limitation of weak computational capability and minimal power capacity of AR Glass. The approach has been verified to improve both real-time performance and runtime sustainability.

References

1. Anushree, S.P., Divyashree, V., et al.: Electronic notice board for professional college. Int. J. Sci. Eng. Technol. Res. (IJSETR) 3(6), 1712–1715 (2014)
2. Jagan Mohan Reddy, N., Venkareshwarlu, G.: Wireless electronic display board using GSM technology. Int. J. Electr. Electron. Data Commun. 1(10), 10–16 (2013)
3. Gurav, R.K., Jagtap, R.: Wireless digital notice board using GSM technology. Int. Res. J. Eng. Technol. 2(9), 57–59 (2015)
4. Swiatkowski, M., Fac, M., et al.: Student notice board based on LED matrix system controlled over TCP/IP protocol. Int. J. Appl. Innov. Eng. Manag. 6(3), 142–146 (2017)
5. Semakuwa, S.K., et al.: Migrant from on wall notice-board to an online announcement displaying system for tanzanian college's. Int. J. Res. Comput. Appl. Robot. 2(9), 88–95 (2014)
6. Mansikkaniemi, T., Keinonen, T., et al.: Wireless family bulletin board, Patent Application Publication, United States, 30 May 2002 (2012)
7. Kumar, P., et al.: GSM based e-notice board: wireless communication. Int. J. Soft Comput. Eng. 2(3), 601–605 (2012)
8. Bansal, V.S., et al.: Digital notice board. Int. J. Tech. Res. Appl. Special Issue 39 (KCCEMSR), 81–83 (2016)

9. Haugstvedt, A.C., Krogstie, J.: Mobile augmented reality for cultural heritage: a technology acceptance study. In: IEEE International Symposium on Mixed and Augmented Reality (ISMAR), pp. 247–255 (2012)

10. Heun, V., Kasahara, S., Maes, P.: Smarter objects: using ar technology to program physical objects and their interactions. In: Proceedings of CHI EA, pp. 2817–2818 (2013)

11. Schmalstieg, D., Wagner, D.: Experiences with handheld augmented reality. In: 6th IEEE and ACM International Symposium on Proceedings of Mixed and Augmented Reality, pp. 3–18 (2007)

12. Huang, Z., Li, W., Hui, P.: Ubii: towards seamless interaction between digital and physical worlds. In: IEEE Transactions on Mobile Computing (2016). https://doi.org/10.1109/tmc.2016.2567378

13. Wilson, D.: Robust computer vision-based detection of pinching for one and two-handed gesture input. In: Proceedings of UIST, pp. 255–258 (2006)

14. Chung, C.O., et al.: Augmented reality navigation system on android. Int. J. Electr. Comput. Eng. 6(1), 406–412 (2016)

15. Brata, K.C., et al.: Location-based augmented reality information for bus route planning system. Int. J. Electr. Comput. Eng. 5(1), 142–149 (2015)

16. Baur, D., Boring, S., Feiner, S.: Virtual projection: exploring optical projection as a metaphor for multi-device interaction. In: Proceedings of CHI, pp. 1693–1702 (2012)

17. Neumann, U., You, S.: Natural feature tracking for augmented reality. IEEE Trans. Multimedia 1(1), 53–64 (1999)

18. Andresen, S.: Hand Tracking and Recognition with OpenCV (2013). http://simena86.github.io/blog/2013/08/12/hand-trackingand

19. Brudy, F.: Interactive menus in augmented reality environments. Technical report, Media Informatics at the University of Munich (2013)

20. Dachselt, R., Hubner, A.: Virtual environments: three-dimensional menus: a survey and taxonomy. Comput. Graph. Arch. 31(1), 53–65 (2007)

21. Ren, G., Neill, E.O.: 3D selection with freehand gesture. Comput. Graph. 37(3), 101–120 (2013)

Non-live Task Migration Approach for Scheduling in Cloud Based Applications

Neelam Panwar[1(⊠)] (ID), Sarita Negi[2] (ID),
and Man Mohan Singh Rauthan[1] (ID)

[1] School of Engineering and Technology, HNB Garhwal University,
Srinagar Garhwal 249161, Uttarakhand, India
neelam.panwar001@gmail.com
[2] Uttarakhand Technical University, Dehradun 248007, Uttarakhand, India

Abstract. Cloud computing is one of the most innovative technologies to present computerized generation. Scheduling plays a major role in it. The connectivity of Virtual Machines (VMs) to schedule the assigned tasks is most attractive field to research. This paper introduces a confined Task Migration based Scheduling Algorithm using enhanced-First Come First Serve (TM-eFCFS) method. This paper focuses on Non-live task migration to transmit partially executed tasks to another VM in order to achieve fastest execution. Objective of this work is to minimize the MakeSpan and to optimize the resource utilization. The proposed work has been simulated in CloudSim toolkit package. The results have been compared with pre-existing scheduling algorithms with same experimental configuration. Important parameters such as MakeSpan and utilization of resources are compared to measure the performance of TM-eFCFS. Extensive simulation results prove that introduced work has better results compared to existing approaches. Results show that 99% resource utilization has been achieved. Plotted graphs and calculated values show that the proposed work is very effective for task scheduling.

Keywords: Cloud computing · Task · Task migration · Virtual machine
Resource utilization

1 Introduction

Cloud computing technology is emerging as standard advanced computer technology where the network functioning knowledge is no longer needed for the user. This computing paradigm contributes delivering application based services and resources over the web-shared pool as per the user demand. The cloud computing characteristics include: On–demand services, broad network access, resources pooling, measured service, reliability *etc.* The user utilizes different cloud service models *i.e.,* Infrastructure as a Service (IaaS), Platform as a Service (PaaS) and Software as a Service (SaaS). IaaS especially provides the storage resources (*e.g.,* Amazon Elastic Compute Cloud, GoGrid, Nimbula *etc.*) whereas PaaS allows users to develop the application in the cloud (*e.g.,* Google App Engine, Github, Gigaspaces *etc.*) and lastly, SaaS enhances user services by providing complete software application (*e.g.,* Google App, Facebook,

© Springer Nature Singapore Pte Ltd. 2018
P. Bhattacharyya et al. (Eds.): NGCT 2017, CCIS 828, pp. 124–137, 2018.
https://doi.org/10.1007/978-981-10-8660-1_9

Linkedin, slideshare *etc.*). To deploy these cloud services, cloud computing categorizes deployment models into: Public, Private, Hybrid and Community cloud. Deployment models handover the cloud services to the multi-user, single-user and specific-user. The major components of cloud are: Application, Client, Infrastructure, Platform, Service, Storage and Processing Power. The popularity of cloud computing enhances by taking care of better Resource utilization, Average cost, Load balancing factor, Completion time, Execution time, Average Power Consumption, Network Latency, Bandwidth, Average Energy Consumption, MakeSpan and Response Time *etc.* Apart from the various outperform services delivered by cloud technology, Virtualization; Load Balancing; Fault Tolerance; Security and Scheduling (VM and Tasks) are the major issues to be addressed. There are two main areas to be scheduled, *i.e.,* allocation of processor to VM, which is done by VM scheduler and submission of task to VM, which is done by task scheduler. Scheduling of tasks is one of the major challenges in cloud technology to achieve highly efficient computations among the machines [1–3].

Study has images that to maintain the work efficiency of VMs having lengthy tasks, a migration scheme has potential to achieve such issues. The concept includes task migration where tasks are transmitted from one VM to another. The different types of task migration are categorized as:

- Live Migration: In this process, the tasks are transmitted from source VM to destination VM while the execution of task is in progress at source VM. It does not require stopping task execution before transmission.
- Non-live Migration: This type of migration stops task execution on source VM before transmission. After the information is transmitted to destination VM, the execution is resumed.

This research work adds up non-live migration approach to formulate the task scheduling. The VM having highest capacity executes its assigned tasks early and hence a task which is partially executed or waiting for execution on slower VM can be migrated to the faster VM in pre-emptive way. Framework of task migration on cloud environment is shown in Fig. 1.

In this work, a new task scheduling method is introduced and its performance has been compared with some pre-existing scheduling algorithms (FCFS and RR). This paper demonstrates the task scheduling by using a method called task migration. The Non-live migration of task concept has been used for first time. The primary objectives of this paper are as follows:

(i) Formulation of a method to schedule the tasks in cloud environment to reduce the MakeSpan (overall time of execution) and increase the resource utilization.

(ii) Design of TM-eFCFS algorithm (Enhanced- First Come First Serve with Task Migration) which is a task scheduling based on task migration method.

The entire work can be described as, a new scheduling algorithm TM-eFCFS which comprises of a concept called "Task Migration". Previously proposed scheduling algorithms were totally based on the type of tasks assigned to the VMs. However, this work focuses on the migration of independent task which is assigned to every VM where the VM which executes its assigned tasks earlier can take to the next partially executed task which is assigned to the slower VM in pre-emptive way.

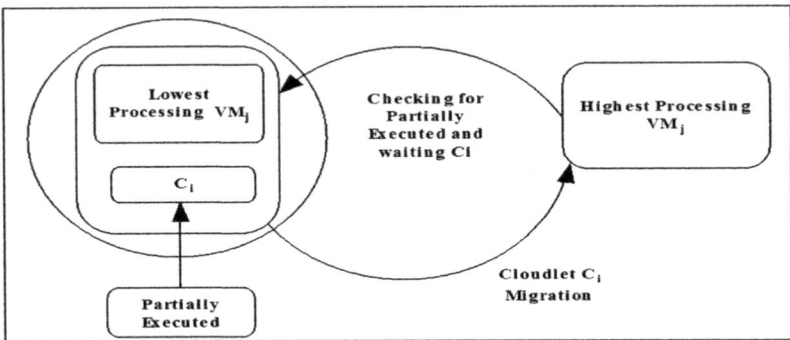

Fig. 1. Task migration

This paper is systematized as follows. Section 2 explores literature review related to the proposed work. Section 3 includes brief description of CloudSim. Section 4 describes proposed approach. Research implementation and simulation results are discussed in Sect. 5. Lastly, Sect. 6 concludes the research work and discusses new era for future work.

2 Literature Review

In cloud, scheduling plays a significant role to increase reliability, efficiency and flexibility of the system. In a decade, there has been an increasing interest in task scheduling over cloud computing. It has been analyzed that the scheduling algorithms can be categorized on the basis of objective functions. Objective functions can be either application centric or resource centric. In application centric, an algorithm beneficial for user is designed to minimize the execution and cost. In case of resource centric, an algorithm beneficial for service provider is designed to maximize resource utilization and profit. Several other cloud based task scheduling schemes have been proposed and such related schemes are reviewed in this section. The performances of each algorithm measured with the specified metrics to describe the processing unit in the resource system are *MakeSpan, Cost, Execution time, Completion time, Resource Utilization*.

From the decades the basic task scheduling algorithms: First Come First Serve (FCFS), Shortest Job First (SJF) and Round Robin (RR) have been focused to enhance the advancement of scheduling. FCFS works on the first come first serve principle, where the task that arrives first will be assigned to VM first. Although, the algorithm is simple to implement but not appropriate for heavy tasks as it leads to higher MakeSpan. SJF takes up the tasks with shortest length first and assigns it to VM. SJF may lead to starvation for lengthy tasks. RR focuses on assigning tasks to each VM equally. Using this algorithm; the scheduler allocates one task to a VM in a cyclic manner. RR works on time slice manner so it uses Time-Shared Task Scheduler. The introduced work has overcome the problems and shortcomings of these basic algorithms.

Tawfeek *et al.* [3] and Dorigo and Blum [6] introduced Ant Colony Optimization based algorithm (ACO) that exhibits food searching behavior of ant colonies. An army of ants uses pheromone chemical to communicate while searching for food. The ACO algorithm initializes pheromone, chooses VM for next task and updates pheromone. The scheduling problem symbolized using a graph $G = (N, E)$, where N denotes VMs and tasks and E denotes the connections between the number of tasks and VMs. It was assumed that tasks were independent of each other, *i.e.*, the execution of one task has no effect on the execution of other tasks. Also, tasks were considered non-pre-emptive and non-interruptible.

Lin *et al.* [11] introduced Bandwidth Aware Divisible Task Scheduling (BATS). Under the bounded multi-port model [12] a nonlinear programming model was introduced. The model obtains enhanced allocation scheme to define appropriate set of tasks allocated to each resource. On the ground of the enhanced scheme of allocation, BATS algorithm was proposed. The algorithm allocates the suitable number of tasks to all resources according to their CPU capacity, memory, network bandwidth and space.

Santhosh and Manjaiah [13] worked to introduce Improved Max-Min based algorithm. In the algorithm, an exceptional variation to the improved Max-min [14] algorithm was performed, where a task is selected whose CPU time is larger than average execution time. The task allocated to the resource which completes the task in minimum time. The algorithm overcomes some limitations of Max-Min. The foremost drawback of the Max-Min was the execution of the smaller jobs was delayed and postponed indefinitely, which has been taken care in proposed algorithm.

Priyadarsini and Arockiam [20] introduced Min-Min Algorithm, in which least possible completion time is evaluated for all tasks on each resource. The task with least possible completion time is picked and assigned to resource that provides it. The recently mapped task is detached from task-list and this procedure is repeated till entire task list is mapped to resources. Min-Min is unsophisticated and speedy algorithm which accomplished good performance. Min-Min schedules "best case" tasks first producing good schedules, but allocating small task first is its disadvantage. Min-Min computes least possible completion time for the tasks which are not yet scheduled, and then allocates tasks with least possible completion time to a resource which provides it.

Chen *et al.* [21] proposed an effective algorithm which reduces the scheduling span by using the budget level (MSLBL) in order to select resources which minimize the budget constraint and the scheduling span of an application. Scheduling problem is categorized into two sub-problems *i.e.*, satisfying the budget constraint and minimizing the scheduling span. To solve the first problem budget constraint of the application is transmitted to each task and in order to solve the second problem heuristic algorithm is used, where each task is executed with low-time complexity.

Awad *et al.* [22] introduced a mathematical model which is based on Load Balancing Mutation and Particle Swarm Optimization (LBMPSO) scheduling. The scheduling takes care of MakeSpan, execution time, transmission time, round trip time, reliability, transmission cost and load balancing between VM and tasks. LBMPSO considers the resource availability and reschedules tasks that fail to allocate, hence it plays major role in accomplishing reliability.

Ali *et al.* [23] worked to introduce the Grouped Tasks Scheduling (GTS) algorithm that applies quality of service to schedule the tasks in cloud computing environment in order to fulfill user's requirement. GTS algorithm categorizes tasks into five groups; each group has tasks having similar characteristics (task type, length of task, latency and user type). By adding tasks to the accurate group, it starts scheduling these tasks into available resources. Scheduling is performed in two stages: in first stage it is decided which group will be scheduled first. This decision depends on the task characteristics that belong to each group so the group that has tasks with high value of characteristics will be scheduled first. Which task inside the chosen group will be scheduled, is decided in second stage and depends on the task size.

3   CloudSim

The cloud computing technology provides better framework *i.e.,* CloudSim (Cloud Simulator) to simulate the research work. CloudSim first introduced by GRIDS laboratory Melbourne, Australia [18]. CloudSim provides various simulation models to experiment cloud computing terminologies. CloudSim is the most popular open source cloud simulator that comprises of various java packages which further extend to multiple classes (object oriented properties). Further, CloudSim enables better designing of cloud computing infrastructure. Figure 2 shows the Framework of CloudSim Environment.

3.1   CloudSim Simulation Environment

The CloudSim comprises of set of virtual machines $(VM_1, VM_2....VM_j)$ in each host of a datacenter. Number of tasks (cloudlets: $C1, C_2......C_{ij}$) is assigned to each VM respectively to perform their execution. Each VM runs on its own resources in parallel or independently.

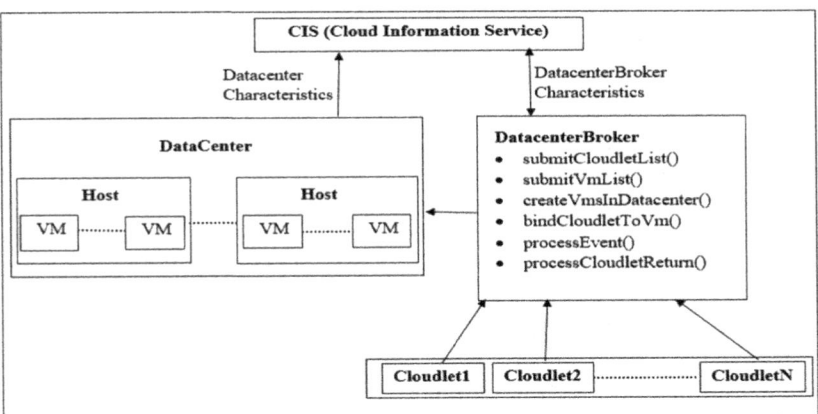

Fig. 2. Framework of CloudSim environment

The simulation work has been performed under CloudSim tool which includes various cloud environment configurations such as:

- *Cloudlet:* User tasks are known as cloudlet in cloud computing. The task can be dependent or independent to each other. Cloudlet stores information and the id of VM running it. Characteristics of cloudlet are length, input file size, output file size, number of required processing elements, utilization model.
- *Datacenter:* Datacenter class is a cloud-resource which has virtualized hosts which can be either homogeneous or heterogeneous. It handles VMs and provides infrastructure delivered by service providers. It can model servers having same or diverse RAM, storage and bandwidth requirements.
- *Datacenter Broker:* It acts on behalf of user and abstracts the part of VM management *i.e.,* submission of cloudlet to VM, creation of VM and deletion of VM.
- *Host:* It takes the responsibility to execute actions correlated to VM management. It is associated to the datacenter and can host VMs. Its characteristics are RAM, bandwidth, storage, number of processing elements and MIPS (million instructions per second).
- *Virtual Machine:* It is associated to a host and shares list of hosts with other VMs. Tasks are assigned to VMs through cloudlet scheduler for their execution. Characteristics of VMs include RAM, bandwidth, storage and number of processing elements.
- *VM Scheduler:* It is responsible to divide the hosts into VMs. It has two policies for allocating processor cores to VM as Time-shared scheduler and Space-shared scheduler.
- *Cloudlet Scheduler*: It acts as an abstract class that handles the scheduling policy performed by VM.

The CloudSim toolkit has been used to simulate the proposed scheduling algorithm. The overview of cloud setup configuration for four numbers of VM is shown in Table 1.

Table 1. Cloud setup configuration details

Tool configuration	No. of VM = 4
System architecture	X86
Operating system	Linux
VMM	Xen
Host description	
RAM	2048 (MB)
Storage	1000000
Bandwidth	10000
No. of PE	4
VM description	
RAM	512
Size (amount of storage)	10000 (MB)
MIPS	1000
	1100
	700
	600

4 Proposed Work

4.1 Algorithm for Proposed Approach

The work comprises of two algorithms, one for TM-eFCFS scheduler and another for Task Migration. Figure 3 shows the basic working mechanism of the algorithm. All the cloudlets are kept in CloudletList as they enter the system. Then cloudlets are assigned to VMs on the basis of earliest completion time. Various notations used in the paper are described in Table 2 along with their meaning.

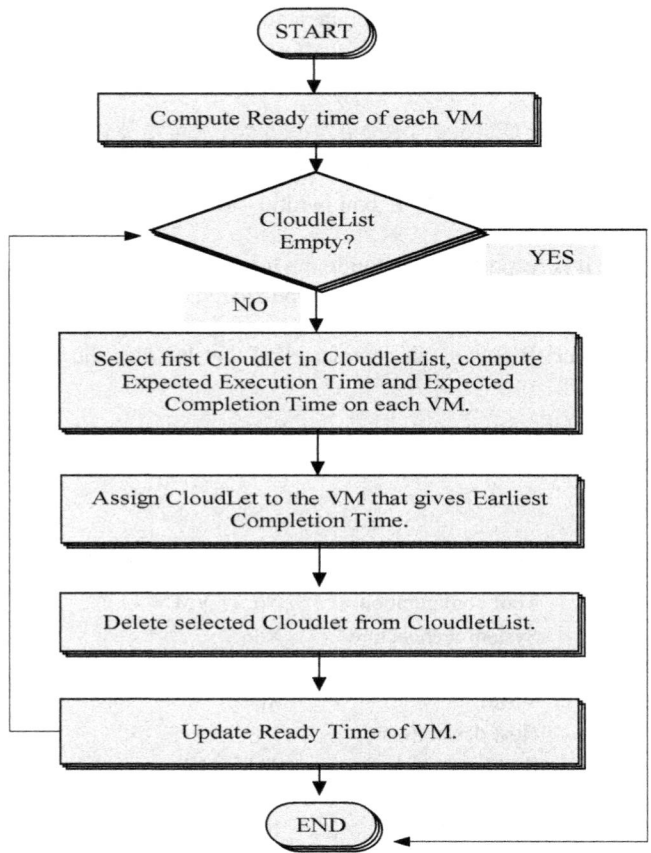

Fig. 3. Flow diagram of TM-eFCFS

Tasks are assigned to VMs in the same order as they arrive in the system by comparing ECT_{ij} of C_i on each VM_j. The ECT_{ij} is calculated using RT_j which depends on the clock time of system (initially $CLK_{sys} = 0.1$) and EET_{ij}. All VMs share the clock of the host on which they were created and destroyed. Equations (1), (2) and (3) formulated as RT_j, EET_{ij} and ECT_{ij} respectively [20],

Table 2. Notations and their meaning

Nomenclatures	
C_i	i^{th} number of Cloudlet
ECT_{ij}	Expected completion time of C_i on VM_j
ECT_m	Expected completion time of cloudlet after migration to fastest VM
EET_{ij}	Expected execution time of C_i on VM_j
$ERCT_i$	Earliest completion time of C_i
L_{ci}	Total length of C_i
$MIPS_j$	Processing speed of V_j (million instructions per second)
PE_j	Number of processing elements allocated to VMj
RL_m	Remaining length to be executed of cloudlet
RT_j	Ready time of VM_j
VM_{ie}	Virtual machine that gives $ERCTi$

$$RT_j = CLK_{sys} \tag{1}$$

$$EET_{ij} = L_{ci}/(PE_j * MIPS_j) \tag{2}$$

$$ECT_{ij} = RT_j + EET_{ij} \tag{3}$$

Where $j = (1, 2, 3, \ldots n)$ and $i = (1, 2, 3, \ldots n)$ symbolized the number of VMs and number of tasks respectively. The matrix representation of EET_{ij} is shown in Table 3 where each task with subsequent length ranges from 2000 to 5000 (Million Instructions) is represented. Matrix shows the expected execution time of each task on different VM. This matrix is used to compute the expected completion time of C_i in order to achieve earliest completion time of C_i ($ERCT_i$). $ERCT_i$ is calculated using Eq. (4).

$$ERCT_i = Min[ECT_{i1}, ECT_{i2}, ECT_{i3}......ECT_{ij}] \tag{4}$$

Where, $ERCT_i$ takes the minimum expected completion time of C_i on VM_j. Now, C_i is assigned to VM that gives $ERCT_i$ (VM_{ie}) and ready time of VM_{ie} is updated using Eq. (5).

$$RT_{VM_{ie}} = ERCT_i \tag{5}$$

This procedure is repeated until all the tasks are mapped to VMs, then all VMs start processing tasks. The VM which processes its assigned task early can make any partially executed or unprocessed task to be migrated which is assigned to the slower VM in pre-emptive way.

Table 3. Matrix representation of EET_{ij}

EET_{ij}					
	Length (MI)	VM_1	VM_2	VM_3	VM_4
C_1	5000	5.00	4.54	7.14	8.33
C_2	2000	2.00	1.82	2.86	3.33
C_3	3000	3.00	2.73	4.29	5.00
C_4	2400	2.40	2.18	3.43	4.00

ALGORITHM 1: TM-eFCFS scheduler.

(1) Identify the Ready Time of VMs, when cloudlets are submitted to broker for mapping.
    (a) For j from 0 by 1 to getVmsCreatedList.Size-1
       do{
           Set ReadyTimeofVm[j] = CloudSim.Clock
           }

(2) Identify the Earliest Completion time of each Cloudlet by calculating the Expected Execution Time and Expected Completion Time of Cloudlets on each VM. Assign Cloudlet to VM which gives Earliest Completion time.
    For i from 0 by 1 to getCloudletList.Size-1
    do   {
        For j from 1 by 1 to getVmsCreatedList.Size-1
        do   {
        (a) Set ExpectedExecutionTimeofC$_i$onVM$_j$ = LengthofC$_i$/ CapacityOfVM$_j$
        (b) Set ExpectedCompletionTimeofC$_i$onVM$_j$= ReadyTimeofVm[j] + ExpectedExecutionTimeofC$_i$onVM$_j$
        (c) To find EarliestCompletionTimeofC$_i$:
           Set EarliestCompletionTimeofC$_i$ = 0
           If (j equals 1)
               Set   EarliestCompletionTimeofC$_i$ = ExpectedCompletionTimeofC$_i$onVM$_1$
           EndIf
           If (ExpectedCompletionTimeofC$_i$onVM$_j$less than EarliestCompletionTimeofC$_i$)
               Set   EarliestCompletionTimeofC$_i$=   ExpectedCompletionTimeofC$_i$onVM$_j$
               Set vmid = j
        EndIf
           }
    Set vm = getVmsCreatedList.get (vmid)
    Set Cloudlet.setVmId (vm.getId)
    SendNow(getVmsToDatacentersMap.get(vm.getId),CloudSimTags.
    CLOUDLET_SUBMIT,Cloudlet)/*Assign Cloudlet to the VM that gives Earliest Completion Time for that Cloudlet*/
    Increase cloudletsSubmittedList by 1
        Update ReadyTimeofVm[vmid] = EarliestCompletionTimeofC$_i$
    }
(3) Remove all the assigned Cloudlets from the cloudletList.

4.2 Task Migration

The tasks are assigned to the number of VMs. The VM having highest capacity executes its assigned tasks early and hence a task which is partially executed or waiting for execution on any slower VM can be migrated to the faster VM in pre-emptive way. The Expected completion time of task after migration can be evaluated by Eq. (6).

$$ECT_m = CLK_{sys} + RL_m/(Capacity * PE_j) \tag{6}$$

where, CLK_{sys} is the current time of the system, RL_m is the remaining length to be executed of the task which has to be migrated. Capacity is the number of processing elements to MIPS of a PE [19].

ALGORITHM 2: Task Migration

(1) Identify the VM which has highest capacity.
    (a) Set highestCapacity$_{vm}$ = getVmList.get(0).getMips
    (b) Set vmIndex = 0
    (c) For vmNumber from 1 by 1 to totalNumberOfVMs
       do {
           If (getVmList.get (vmNumber).getMips greater than highestCapacityvm)
           Set highestCapacity$_{vm}$ = getVmList.get (vmNumber).getMips
           Set vmIndex = j
       EndIf
       }
    (d) Set VmfastestVM = getVmList.get(VmIndex)

(2) Identify, if VM with highest capacity has executed all the Cloudlets assigned to it.
    If (fastestVM.getCloudletScheduler.runningCloudlets equals 0)
    {
    Find Cloudlet to be migrated and store related data in an array.
    (a) Set cloudletToMigrate = 0
    (b) For Cloudlet cloudlet in getCloudletSubmittedList
       do {
           If (cloudlet.getCloudletStatus equals (QUEUED or INEXEC)
           and cloudletToMigrate equals 0)
               Set oldVmId = cloudlet.getVmId
           EndIf
       }
    (c) Set cloudletToMigrate = cloudlet.getCloudletId
    (d) Set UserId = cloudlet.getUserId
    (e) Set intarr[] = new int[5]
    (f) Set arr[0] = cloudletToMigrate
    (g) Set arr[1] = UserId
    (h) Set arr[2] = oldVmId
    (i) Set arr[3] = fastestVM.getId
    (j) Set arr[4] = datacenterId
    Endif
    }

(3) Migration of Cloudlet to new VM.
    (a) SendNow (datacenterId, CloudSimTags.CLOUDLET_MOVE, arr)

(4) Start Cloudlet execution on new VM with highest capacity.

4.3 MakeSpan

The complete time that elapsed from the starting of the scheduling process till the end is called MakeSpan and it is calculated by Eq. (7).

$$\text{MakeSpan} = \max(\text{CT}_j) \qquad j \in \text{VMs} \tag{7}$$

4.4 Resource Utilization

One of the major challenges in cloud environment is to achieve high resource utilization. The average utilization of an algorithm can be evaluated as [26]:

$$\textbf{Average Utilization} = \sum\nolimits_{j \in \textbf{VMs}} \textbf{CT}_j / \textbf{MakeSpan} * \textbf{NumberofVMs} \tag{8}$$

5 Implementation

5.1 Result

This section elaborates the comparison of TM-eFCFS with other scheduling algorithms. The comparative analysis has been done with two pre-existing task scheduling algorithms under the same cloud computing system configuration. The two pre-existing scheduling algorithms are FCFS and RR. With the purpose of analyzing the performance of the proposed algorithm, the simulation work performed over two vital parameters *i.e.,* MakeSpan and Resource Utilization. The following section limelight's the implementation result by comparing with experimental parameters (MakeSpan and Resource Utilization).

Comparison of MakeSpan
In this scenario four VMs are taken and comparisons are performed between 600 to 1000 numbers of tasks. The MakeSpan is calculated using Eq. (7). Figure 4 illustrates the MakeSpan of algorithms having four VMs with different range of task length. The size of each task is randomly generated. Table 4 depicts the total MakeSpan for FCFS, RR and TM-eFCFS. The comparison of results illustrates that with increased number of tasks TM-eFCFS achieves less MakeSpan.

Comparison of Resource Utilization
The utilization of resources must be maximized so that maximum number of users can be served in a better way. The average utilization of resources is calculated using Eq. (8). Figure 5 depicts that TM-eFCFS maintains a 99% utilization of the resources whereas RR and FCFS utilizes 75% and 76% respectively. Hence, with these simulation results it is concluded that TM-eFCFS is performing better than other algorithms.

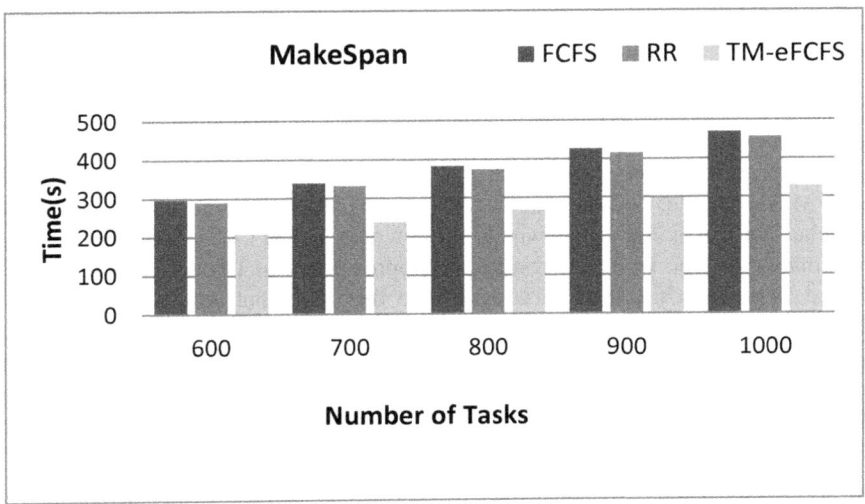

Fig. 4. Calculated MakeSpan for different algorithms.

Table 4. MakeSpan table for algorithms

No. of VM	No. of tasks	FCFS	RR	TM-eFCFS
4	600	296.48	289.99	207.05
	700	339.24	331.65	236.76
	800	382.57	373.31	267.49
	900	425.76	414.97	297.25
	1000	469.09	456.58	327.93

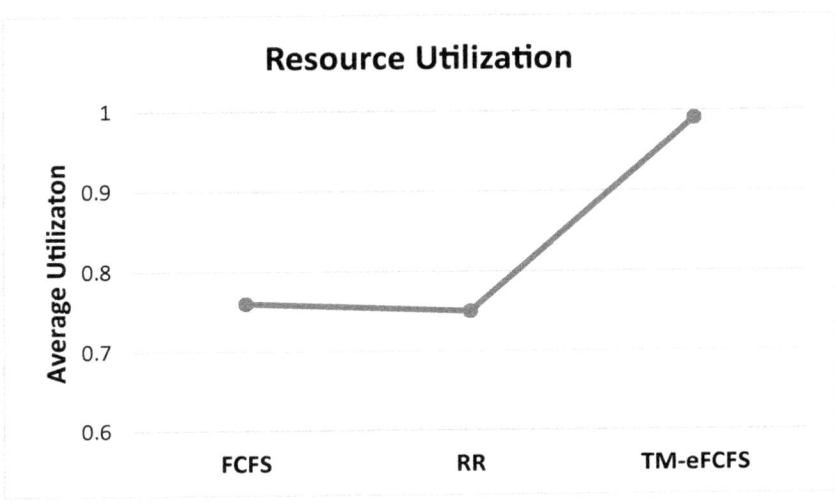

Fig. 5. Illustration of calculated resource utilization by different algorithms.

6 Conclusion

This paper proposed and formulated a new approach of task scheduling. The work focuses on Non-live task migration to transmit partially executed task to another VM in order to achieve faster execution. Tasks are arranged and assigned to VMs depending on their expected completion time and also migrated from one VM to another in case a better VM is available. The calculation of expected completion time and task migration approaches for a new algorithm which is known as TM-eFCFS and the results have been remarkable. The work has resulted in improvement of Execution time (MakeSpan) and Resource Utilization as compared to the traditional scheduling algorithms. The results make TM-eFCFS as one of the finest algorithm to be used in cloud computing. 99% resource utilization has been achieved which makes introduced approach well suited for cloud computing. In future, we will experiment for more performance parameters with large number of VMs and tasks to achieve better results.

References

1. Li, Q., Hao, Q., Xiao, L., Li, Z.: Adaptive management of virtualized resources in cloud computing using feedback control. In: First International Conference on Information Science and Engineering, Nanjing, China, pp. 99–102. IEEE (2009)
2. Parikh, K., Hawanna, N., Haleema, P.K., Jayasubalakshmi, R., Iyengar, N.: Virtual machine allocation policy in cloud computing using CloudSim in Java. Int. J. Grid Distrib. Comput. **8**(1), 145–158 (2015)
3. Tawfeek, M., El-Sisi, A., Keshk, A., Torkey, F.: Cloud task scheduling based on ant colony optimization. Int. Arab J. Inf. Technol. **12**(2), 129–137 (2015)
4. Gao, K., Wang, Q., Xi, L.: Reduct algorithm based execution times prediction in knowledge discovery cloud computing environment. Int. Arab J. Inf. Technol. **11**(3), 268–275 (2014)
5. Pop, F., Dobre, C., Cristea, V., Bessis, N.: Scheduling of sporadic tasks with deadline constrains in cloud environments. In: 27th International Conference on Advanced Information Networking and Applications, Barcelona, Spain, pp. 764–771. IEEE (2013)
6. Dorigo, M., Blum, C.: Ant colony optimization theory: a survey. Theor. Comput. Sci. **344**, 243–278 (2005)
7. Guo, L., Zhao, S., Shen, S., Jiang, C.: Task scheduling optimization in cloud computing based on heuristic algorithm. J. Netw. **7**(3), 547–553 (2012)
8. Kennedy, J., Eberhart, R.: Particle swarm optimization. In: Proceedings of the IEEE International Conference on Neural Networks, Washington, USA, pp. 1942–1948 (1995)
9. Cope, J.M., Trebon, N., Tufo, H.M., Beckman, P.: Robust data placement in urgent computing environments. Paper Presented at the 23rd IEEE International Symposium on Parallel and Distributed Processing, IPDPS, Rome, Italy, 23–29 May 2009 (2009)
10. Saaty, T.L.: Decision making with the analytic hierarchy process. Int. J. Serv. Sci. (IJSS) **1**(1), 83–98 (2008)
11. Lin, W., Liang, C., Wang, J.Z., Buyya, R.: Bandwidth-aware divisible task scheduling for cloud computing. Softw.-Pract. Exp. **44**(2), 163–174 (2014)
12. Hong, B., Prasanna, V.K.: Distributed adaptive task allocation in heterogeneous computing environments to maximize throughput. In: Proceedings of the 18th International Parallel and Distributed Processing Symposium (IPDPS 2004), Santa Fe, USA, pp. 52–60. IEEE (2004)

13. Santhosh, B., Manjaiah, D.H.: An improved task scheduling algorithm based on max-min for cloud computing. Int. J. Innov. Res. Comput. Commun. Eng. **2**(2), 84–88 (2014)
14. Elzeki, O.M., Reshad, M.Z., Elsoud, M.A.: Improved max-min algorithm in cloud computing. Int. J. Comput. Appl. **50**(12), 22–27 (2012)
15. Chawla, Y., Bhonsle, M.: Dynamically optimized cost based task scheduling in cloud computing. Int. J. Emerg. Trends Technol. Comput. Sci. (IJETTCS) **2**(3), 38–42 (2013)
16. Chen, H., Wang, F., Helian, N., Akanmu, G.: User-priority guided min-min scheduling algorithm for load balancing in cloud computing. In: National Conference on Parallel Computing Technologies, Bengaluru, India, pp. 1–8. IEEE (2013)
17. Yu, X., Yu, X.: A new grid computation-based min-min algorithm. In: IEEE 6th International Conference on Fuzzy Systems and Knowledge Discovery, Tianjin, China, pp. 43–45 (2009)
18. Buyya, R., Ranjan, R., Calheiros, R.N.: Modeling and simulation of scalable cloud computing environments and the CloudSim toolkit: challenges and opportunities. In: Proceedings of the 7th High Performance Computing and Simulation Conference, Leipzig, Germany, pp. 1–11 (2009)
19. Radulescu, A., Gemund, A.: Fast and effective task scheduling in heterogeneous systems. In: Proceedings of the 9th Heterogeneous Computing Workshop (HCW 2000), Cancun, Mexico, pp. 229–238 (2000)
20. Priyadarsini, R.J., Arockiam, L.: Performance evaluation of min-min and max-min algorithms for job scheduling in federated cloud. Int. J. Comput. Appl. **99**(18), 47–54 (2014)
21. Chen, W., Xie, G., Li, R., Bai, Y., Fan, C., Li, K.: Efficient task scheduling for budget constrained parallel applications on heterogeneous cloud computing systems. Future Gen. Comput. Syst. **74**, 1–11 (2017)
22. Awad, A.I., El-Hefnawy, N.A., Abdel_kader, H.M.: Enhanced particle swarm optimization for task scheduling in cloud computing environments. Procedia Comput. Sci. **65**, 920–929 (2015)
23. Ali, H.G., Saroit, I.A., Kotb, A.M.: Grouped tasks scheduling algorithm based on QoS in cloud computing network. Egypt. Inf. J. **18**, 11–19 (2017)
24. Xiong, F., Yeliang, C., Lipeng, Z., Bin, H., Song, D., Dong, W.: Deadline based scheduling for data-intensive applications in clouds. J. China Univ. Posts Telecommun. **23**(6), 8–15 (2016)
25. Wu, X., Deng, M., Zhang, R., Zeng, B., Zhou, S.: A task scheduling algorithm based on QoS-driven in cloud computing. Procedia Comput. Sci. **17**, 1162–1169 (2013)
26. Chitra, D., Uthariaraj, Y.R.: Load balancing in cloud computing environment using improved weighted round robin algorithm for non-preemptive dependent tasks. Sci. World J. Hindawi **2016**, 1–14 (2016)
27. Tian, W., Xu, M., Chen, A., Li, G., Wang, X., Chen, Y.: Open-source simulators for cloud computing: comparative study and challenging issues. Simul. Model. Pract. Theory **58**, 239–254 (2015)

Enhanced Secure Transmission of Data in Wireless Body Area Network for Health Care Applications

Sumit Kumar$^{(\boxtimes)}$, Anurag Singh Tomar, and Sandip K. Chaurasiya

School of Computer Science and Engineering, College of Engineering Studies,
University of Petroleum and Energy Studies, Dehradun, India
Sumitaggarwal001@gmail.com,
anuragtomar3105@gmail.com, sandipchaurasiya@gmail.com

Abstract. The advent of new technologies like cloud computing, Internet of Things and Wireless Body Area Networks (WBAN) have largely promoted the e-healthcare management. E-healthcare eases the life of patients in society and provides them freedom from going to hospital physically on regular intervals. Presently, E-healthcare is facing the challenges including authenticity and privacy of information during transmission. To maintain secrecy of messages knapsack cryptosystem have been applied in WBAN. For authentication of data transmitted in WBAN, we have recommended a modified and improved recovery based digital signature scheme with batch verification of messages that improve the performance of underlying algorithm in terms of computation. Proposed algorithm does not require computing one way hash for digital signature generation. Security analysis of proposed work has been presented to validate the privacy and security of message against various attacks. The results demonstrate performance improvement in digital signature verification scheme.

Keywords: Wireless Body Area Network · Batch verification
Recovery based digital signature · Knapsack crypto system · Security
Privacy and authentication

1 Introduction

Wireless Body Area Network (WBAN) is a new era of research that provides the mechanism to monitor the patient remotely by using wearable sensors. As sensitive data is transmitted through the public network and due to reveal of data, patient may lose his job, humiliation in society, insurance problem etc. Therefore by looking into these problems, security and privacy become the major concern in WBAN. WBAN security works for two scenarios that are; when patient is inside the hospital and when patient is outside the hospital. In both the cases different level of security is required. The cryptographic solutions are discussed in the subsequent sections which include knapsack cryptography and digital signature scheme.

Knapsack crypto system is based on knapsack problem. In knapsack problem there are a number of integers and a given weight k. We need to find integers, if possible; whose sum is equal to k. Knapsack problem is NP-complete. In knapsack cryptosystem

© Springer Nature Singapore Pte Ltd. 2018
P. Bhattacharyya et al. (Eds.): NGCT 2017, CCIS 828, pp. 138–145, 2018.
https://doi.org/10.1007/978-981-10-8660-1_10

a super-increasing vector is used that encrypt the message. In order to decrypt the message, the intruder does not know private parameters of receiver so it will be difficult to decrypt message. On the other hand legal receiver can easily decrypt the message as shown in proposed scheme section. This scheme applied in WBAN when patient is inside the hospital to ensure confidentiality of messages. Authentication is not required in this scenario as base station and hospital server are both within the hospital.

When the patient is outside the hospital then it require more secure algorithms with high performance in terms of computation requirement. In this paper we have analyzed various digital signature schemes with message recovery. In recovery based digital signature schemes the message is assorted into the signature and does not need to transmit separately. The receiver first recovers the message from signature and then validates it using sender's public key. Conventional message recovery based digital signature schemes verify each signature independently. It causes the increase in computation time as each packet validated separately. Hence we need to construct a batch verifying digital signature scheme based upon these recovery based schemes without increasing the communication overhead and without causing additional latency. The design objective of the scheme is to eliminate the correlation among messages. Thus the proposed scheme will provide perfect resilience to packet loss as it will be used in wireless networks where packet loss is inevitable. The proposed algorithm used in combination with knapsack cryptosystem in WBAN to ensure authentication and confidentiality of messages when patient is outside the hospital.

2 Literature Review

Wireless Body Area Network allows patients to be remotely monitored by hospital staff. Although several security issues like Authentication, confidentiality, network availability etc. are the major issues in security of WBAN. Architecture of WBAN [1] contains the three separate levels that are Tier-1, Tier-2 and Tier-3. Tier-1 contains patients and implanted sensors; Tier-2 contains relay nodes and internet connectivity while Tier-3 contains hospital cloud and a server. Several security threats [2] like unauthorized access, disclosure of message, message modification, routing attack are likely to arise in this network. Current security measure in WBAN includes biometric authentication, hardware encryption, Bluetooth security, Tinysec, wireless security protocols. Secure Key management algorithm [13, 14] are also used to establish the secret key between the communication entities in WBAN, cryptographic based key management like ECC, RSA as well as patient's psychological parameter based key can established. In this paper we have applied public key cryptography on WBAN to ensure confidentiality, authentication and avoidance of other attacks.

Knapsack crypto system [15] is based upon knapsack problem. The algorithm is used in public key cryptography. It provide confidentiality to sensitive information transferred from sender to receiver using sender's public key and only receiver can decrypt the cipher text using its private key. In this paper we have applied knapsack crypto system when the patient is inside the hospital where complex public key crypto systems are not necessarily required.

The scheme proposed in [3] is a recovery based digital signature scheme suitable for resource constraint devices and as secure as RSA algorithm. It does not have hash function to compute the digital signature. The sender implant the message within digital signature during signature generation phase. Then receiver first recovers the message from digital signature and then validates it using public key of the sender. The original scheme does not protect against reveal of message, as any user can recover the message using transmitted parameters and public key of the sender. Security of scheme relies on difficulty of calculating discrete logarithms over finite fields. A number of attacks have been proposed on the scheme in [4–7] based upon forgery attack, cryptanalysis and impersonation. Later Kang and Tang [8] proposed a new scheme which resist against all known attacks. But the scheme ideally works on the basic concept of signing and verifying one message independently. Therefore verification cost of messages at receiver end is still expensive. In order to reduce the verification cost various schemes have been proposed [9, 10] to verify a number of messages in less computation than independent message verification. But these schemes generally generate digital signature on a block of messages at the expense of increased communication overhead or susceptibility to packet loss which is inevitable in wireless networks. So, if a message lost during transmission then the digital signature will not be verified for the whole block. Some schemes are resistant to packet loss [11] up to certain level as hash of a message are concatenated with multiple messages. There exist a tradeoff between packet loss during transmission and redundancy of hashes which leads to communication overhead. Later a variant of RSA algorithm called batch RSA [12] have been proposed which is not having dependency among messages and also there is no communication overhead. But the scheme does not protect against repudiation attack [10].

The proposed scheme in the paper, when patient is outside the hospital, is an improvement of Kang's scheme because instead of verifying each message independently, multiple signatures are verified in single step. The proposed scheme does not generate any communication overhead and also perfectly resilient to packet loss during transmission as there is no correlation among packets. The proposed scheme takes nearly constant time to verify multiple messages as modular exponential operation is replaced by modular addition. Therefore the proposed scheme is suitable for hospital applications.

3 Proposed Work

In this section we are proposing approaches for secure transmission of data in WBAN that will work for two different scenarios as follows:

Scenario 1: When the Patient is Inside the Hospital
Initially patient will be diagnosed by the doctor and after that a number of sensors have been attached with the body of patient. As the patient is within the premises of hospital, data will be routed within local area network instead of internet; therefore complex and time consuming strong encryption systems are not necessary. In this scenario the sensors will not receive any data as the patient will be diagnosed physically on the basis

of information received by doctor in the hospital from those sensors. The proposed scheme contains the following phases:

1. Registration phase: In this phase the sensor IDs along with patient details, will be stored in the hospital database by the authorized person. These IDs will be used by the hospital for authentication of sensor.
2. Encryption phase: The encryption system used in the scenario is knapsack based cryptosystem. Initially the hospital server will perform the following tasks:
   a. It will generate the super increasing knapsack vector of arbitrary length denoted by $A = \{a_1, a_2, a_3, \ldots, a_n\}$, such that $a_j = \sum_{i=1}^{j-1} a_i$.
   b. Select a number Z such that the summation of all elements of A is less than Z. And a positive integer T such that GCD (T, Z) is 1.
   c. Now the device will compute a vector $B = \{b_1, b_2, \ldots, b_n\}$ using the following formula:
      $b_i = (T * a_i, \bmod Z)$ for $i = 1, 2, \ldots, n$. The operation indicates B results from A using strong modular multiplication with respect to Z and T.
   d. Parameters Z, T and A will be kept private by hospital server and B will be made public to all sensors.
   e. Sensors will perform the encryption on any message, to be transmitted to hospital server in the following manner:
      i. The message m along with sensor ID and time stamp will be split into blocks of n-bit size (equal to number of elements in B vector).
      ii. Add the elements of B where corresponding binary value of message is 1 which will result to a number β.
      iii. The sensor will then transmit this β to hospital server.
3. Decryption phase: The hospital server will compute the message by using following steps:
      i. Calculate $u = T^{-1} \bmod Z$
      ii. Compute $\alpha = (u\beta, \bmod Z)$
      iii. Now server will solve the instance (A, α) using knapsack algorithm to get the message and authenticate recovered sensor ID with its database entry. The timestamp will be used to avoid replay of message.

Scenario 2: When the Patient is Outside the Premises of Hospital
In this scenario sensors will transmit the messages to a base station that is located nearby sensors. Further the base station will transmit messages through the public network from to hospital server and vice versa. Therefore we need more secure algorithm as comparison to knapsack cryptosystem and also it must be efficient for devices such as base station, which need to perform numerous computation throughout the day. Knapsack algorithm also does not provide the message authentication therefore we need to incorporate an improved recovery based batch verification algorithm. As discussed in literature review section, in recovery based digital signature algorithm, the message assorted within the digital signature. Therefore receiver first recovers the message from digital signature and then verifies its authenticity. Here we proposed batch verification digital signature scheme which is the improved version of Kang et al. scheme [8]. In the proposed scheme multiple messages will be verified in a single step

without affecting the security strength of underlying algorithm. The proposed batch verification scheme will be secure as long as its underlying algorithm is secured. The proposed scheme contains the following steps which will be performed by base station and hospital server separately:

1 Initialization step: Suppose P be a large prime number and g is a primitive element in Z_P. Base station and hospital server selects its private key X ranges between 0 to (P−1) such that GCD(X, P−1) is 1. Then they will calculate their public key by using the following equation:

$$Y = (g)^X \bmod P$$

It must be relative prime to P. When the sender i.e. either base station or hospital server need to sign a message M $\in$ GF(P), it perform the following steps.

2 Digital signature generation step: The algorithm assorts the message (m) and timestamp, into its digital signature in the form of three parameters s, r and t. M denotes the concatenation of message with timestamp. These parameters are computed as follows:

a. $s \equiv Y^M \bmod P$

b. Select a random number q between 1 to (P−1) and compute
$r \equiv [s + M * (g)^{-q}] \bmod P]$

c. Calculate value of t by solving the following equation
$$(s+t) \equiv \left[(X)^{-1} * (q-r) \right] \bmod (P-1)$$

The digital signature for the message is (s, r, t). These parameters will be encrypted by using knapsack cryptosystem using public parameter B of receiver. The resultant number β will be transferred to the receiver.

3 Message recovery and batch digital signature verification step: Initially the receiver will decrypt β to get actual (s, r, t) from the number. The process will be same as defined in the case when patient is inside the hospital. After that, for n messages received by receiver from single sender, ideally receiver will recover and verify each message exclusively in Kang's scheme. In the proposed scheme the messages will be recovered separately from digital signatures and then verified using single equation. For n messages having digital signature (s_i, r_i, t_i) where i ranges from 1 to n, the messages will be recovered using the following equation:

a. $M'_i \equiv \left\{ (r_i - s_i) * (Y)^{s_i + t_i} * g^{r_i} \right\} \bmod P$

Proof of this equation has been given in [8].

b. After recovery of all messages, the proposed scheme improves the performance of digital signature verification by using batch verification of number of messages. These messages will be verified using a single equation which is:

$$\prod_{i=1}^{n} Si \equiv (Y)^{\sum_{i=1}^{n} Mi \bmod (P-1)} \bmod P$$

If the above equation holds true then all the messages are authenticated that these messages came from a single source. Time stamp of messages will be used to avoid replay attack.

Proof:

If P is a prime number and a is a positive number such that GCD(a, P) is 1 then: $a^{p-1} \equiv 1 \pmod{p}$ holds according to Fermat's theorem. Therefore,

$$a^{n*(p-1)} \equiv 1 \pmod{p}$$

Thus,

$$a^{(r+n(p-1))} \equiv a^{r} \pmod{p}$$

For n messages:

$$\prod_{i=1}^{n} Si \bmod P \equiv \left\{ Y^{m1} \bmod P * Y^{m2} \bmod P * \ldots \ldots * Y^{mn} \bmod P \right\} \bmod P$$

$$\equiv \left\{ Y^{m1+m2+\ldots mn} \right\} \bmod P$$

By using equation (1)

$$\equiv \left\{ Y^{(m1+m2+\ldots mn)\bmod(P-1)} \right\} \bmod P$$

$$\equiv (Y)^{\sum_{i=1}^{n} Mi \bmod (P-1)} \bmod P$$

Mathematical Justification of Performance Improvement

The mathematical comparison between kang's scheme and our proposed scheme is as follows (Table 1):

Table 1. Computation comparison between Kang's and proposed scheme

Algorithms	Sender computation (per message)	Receiver computation (per n messages)
Kang's algorithm	2nE + 2 nM	3nE + 2 nM
Proposed algorithm	2nE + 2 nM	(2n + 1)E + (3n − 1)M

Where, M, E and n denote modular multiplication operation, modular exponentiation operation and number of messages respectively.

4   Security Analysis

In this section security strength of our proposed work has been analyzed on the basis of following attacks:

(a) **Replay attack**

As the base station is transmitting β. It will be decrypted using knapsack crypto system to recover s, r and t. The message will be recovered and verified by receiver by using these recovered parameters. Therefore if an attacker capture the transmitted parameter and later retransmitting the same parameter then receiver can identify the replay attack by computing the message M that contains the original message and timestamp. So now receiver can verify the received timestamp with current timestamp, if it matches then accept it otherwise its replay attack.

(b) **Impersonation attack**

User's private key is assumed to be secure as it is has not been shared with others and user utilizes its own private key to generate the parameters r, s and t which are combined into β. So intruder cannot generate the authentic parameter on an arbitrary message, hence proposed work resist the Impersonation attack.

(c) **Man in Middle attack**

In the proposed scheme if any attacker intercepts the transmitted message between base station and hospital server, he will not be able to recover the value of r, s, t due to Knapsack algorithm as well as he cannot compute the forged r, s, t due to use of private key during parameters generation. So the proposed security algorithm is secure against the Man in Middle attack.

(d) **Secrecy of Message**

Base station is computing the parameters after that we apply the knapsack over these parameters to generate the value of β, and then β is transmitted from base station to hospital server. Hence attacker cannot recover the original message due to lack of private parameters used in knapsack cryptography and secrecy of message is maintained.

(e) **Recovery of user's private key using publically known parameters**

Attacker tries to find the private key of user by using the public key $Y = (g)^X$ mod P to transmit the information in behalf of user. But due to discrete logarithm in the equation, attacker can't find the private key and secrecy of private key is maintained.

5 Conclusion

Security and privacy are major concern in Wireless Body Area Network (WBAN). Proposed schemes works in two scenarios, one is for patients inside and other is for patients outside the hospital network. When patient is inside the hospital and the communication occurs between sensors and hospital server, knapsack crypto system based algorithm have been applied and analyzed to maintain confidentiality of messages. For patient outside hospital premises, improved recovery based digital signature algorithm with knapsack cryptography has been applied to ensure authentication, confidentiality and performance improvement. The proposed scheme withstands to attacks discussed in security analysis section. This study has focused on authentication and confidentiality in WBAN. In future research can be done to provide quality of service (QoS) along with security in WBAN.

References

1. Al-Janabi, S., Al-Shourbaji, I., Shojafar, M., Shamshirband, S.: Survey of main challenges (security and privacy) in wireless body area networks for healthcare applications. Egypt. Inf. J. **18**(2), 113–122 (2017)
2. Sangari, S., Manickam, J.M.L.: Public key cryptosystem based security in wireless body area network. In: International Conference on Circuits, Power and Computing Technologies (ICCPCT 2014), Nagercoil, pp. 1609–1612 (2014)
3. Shieh, S.P., Lin, C.T., Yang, W.B., Sun, H.M.: Digital multisignature schemes for authenticating delegates in mobile code systems. IEEE Trans. Veh. Technol. **49**, 1464–1473 (2000)
4. Chang, C.C., Lu, E.-H., Pon, S.-F., Lee, J.-Y.: Applying Harn-Kiesler multisignature scheme to electronic document systems. In: Proceedings of National Information Security Conference, pp. 35–38 (1995)
5. Zhang, F.G.: Cryptanalysis of Chang et al'.s signature scheme with message recovery. IEEE Commun. Lett. **9**(4), 358–359 (2005)
6. Chien, H.Y.: Forgery attacks on digital signature schemes without sing one-way hash and message redundancy. IEEE Commun. Lett. **10**(5), 324–325 (2006)
7. Chang, C.-C., Chang, Y.-F.: Signing a digital signature without using one-way hash functions and message redundancy schemes. IEEE Commun. Lett. **8**(8), 485–487 (2004)
8. Kang, L., Tang, X.H.: Digital signature scheme without hash functions and message redundancy. J. Commun. **27**(5), 18–20 (2006). (in Chinese)
9. Wong, C.K., Lam, S.S.: Digital signatures for flows and multicasts. In: Proceedings of the Sixth International Conference on Network Protocols (ICNP 1998), pp. 198–209 (1998)
10. Zhu, W.T.: A comment on "MABS: multicast authentication based on batch signature". IEEE Trans. Mob. Comput. **11**(11), 1775–1776 (2012)
11. Park, J.M., Chong, E.K.P., Siegel, H.J.: Efficient multicast packet authentication using signature amortization. In: Proceedings of IEEE Symposium on Security and Privacy (SP 2002), pp. 227–240 (2002)
12. Bellare, M., Garay, J.A., Rabin, T.: Fast batch verification for modular exponentiation and digital signatures. In: Nyberg, K. (ed.) EUROCRYPT 1998. LNCS, vol. 1403, pp. 236–250. Springer, Heidelberg (1998). https://doi.org/10.1007/BFb0054130
13. He, D., Zeadally, S., Kumar, N., Lee, J.-H.: Anonymous authentication for wireless body area networks with provable security. IEEE Syst. J. **11**(4), 2590–2601 (2017)
14. Li, X., Ibrahim, M.H., Kumari, S., Sangaiah, A.K., Gupta, V., Choo, K.-K.R.: Anonymous mutual authentication and key agreement scheme for wearable sensors in wireless body area networks. Comput. Netw. **129**, 429–443 (2017)
15. Goodman, R.M.F., McAuley, A.J.: New trapdoor-knapsack public-key cryptosystem. IEE Proc. E – Comput. Digit. Tech. **132**(6), 289–292 (1985)

Reliable Vertical Handoff Technique Based on Probabilistic Classification Model

C. S. Jayasheela[1(✉)] and Gowrishankar[2]

[1] Department of ISE, BIT, Bangalore, India
sheeladhan1@gmail.com
[2] Department of CSE, BMSCE, Bangalore, India

Abstract. The Next Generation wireless network framework has introduced *cooperative communication* philosophy to provide better service to the clients. *Vertical Handoff* is one such cooperative technique, which switches the client's network from the current to another in-order to continue providing requested Quality of Service (QoS). There are multiple parameters that need to be considered for achieving vertical handoff such as-service cost, data rate, mobile device speed, network latency, interference ratio, device battery level, Received Signal Strength Information (RSSI) etc.

Until now, vertical hand off schemes have targeted to achieve effective selection of suitable alternate networks in providing required connection transfer. Many classification schemes based on Neural Networks, Support Vector Machine were utilized in designing vertical handoff techniques. These techniques do a good job in choosing suitable alternate networks, but, once the handoff is made, there is no guarantee that, the new network will continuously provide the requested QoS. The client might require new handoff if the recently migrated network is not able to deliver the specified QoS. Frequent handoff's can be expensive and inefficient for the client. Ideally, when making the first handoff, it is important to consider the reliability of new networks in continuously providing the requested QoS. In the existing literature, this problem has not been properly addressed.

In this work, new vertical handoff scheme is proposed, which addresses the reliability issue. This proposed vertical handoff scheme is built over probabilistic classification model. Empirical results obtained through simulation, reveal the excellent effectiveness of the proposed vertical handoff scheme.

1 Introduction

The demand on wireless services has been increasing, and to meet this demand, cooperation between different wireless networks such as-wireless local area networks, wireless cellular network, wireless wide area networks are being established. The mobile device users have QoS requirements in variety of applications

© Springer Nature Singapore Pte Ltd. 2018
P. Bhattacharyya et al. (Eds.): NGCT 2017, CCIS 828, pp. 146–154, 2018.
https://doi.org/10.1007/978-981-10-8660-1_11

such as–video conferencing, voice transfer, video transfer, messaging service etc. Many users want the requested QoS with good quality and minimal cost. The Next Generation wireless network aims to build better cooperation among different wireless networks to meet the growing mobile user demands. To effectively build cooperative wireless network mechanism, the mobile nodes should be aware of heterogeneous structure, and should be able to seamlessly perform network switching. Cognitive radio aids in connecting different wireless networks to form an efficient heterogeneous network structure.

The process of migrating a mobile user from the existing wireless network to another wireless network is called as vertical handoff. Currently, many handoff techniques have been proposed [1–20] which aim to perform effective vertical handoff, such that, the alternate network which is selected provides the requested QoS and with low cost. Many classification schemes such as Neural Networks, Support Vector Machines etc have been employed to achieve effective vertical handoff. Different parameters such as–monetary cost, data rate, RSSI etc have been utilized to achieve the handoff goal.

One of the persistent and important issues in vertical handoff is the reliability of the handoff decision. Consider a situation, where, a mobile client is being serviced through a wireless network w_i. The client has constraints specified for QoS parameters such as–minimum bandwidth, RSSI and monetary expenditure. At some point of time, assume that, w_i is unable to meet some of the QoS constraints, mainly due to the current traffic load. Then, a handoff procedure is invoked by w_i to decide on the alternate wireless networks available to service the client by satisfying the client's QoS constraints. Suppose, the wireless network w_j is selected for handoff. Even though, w_j initially satisfies the client QoS constraints, after some time gap, due to exceeding traffic conditions, w_j may not be able to satisfy QoS constraints, in this case, w_j will again invoke handoff procedure, and this time, the options available may not be suitable for the client, especially, wrt monetary constraints. In this case, the client is forced to agree for higher cost options. These kinds of situations, when occur frequently can lead to poor effectiveness in the overall wireless communication service to the client. Hence, it is extremely important to make handoff decisions based on the reliability of the wireless network. Until now, the reliability issue for vertical handoff has not been effectively addressed in the literature.

The following contributions are made in this work:

1. A new vertical handoff scheme is proposed which specifically aims to achieve reliability in handoff decisions. This new scheme is built over Bayesian classification model. This model does not require extensive computational effort, and can be easily implemented in real world scenarios.
2. The proposed vertical handoff scheme is implemented in Network Simulator 3. The predicted reliability of the handoff scheme is compared against actual reliability values obtained through simulation. The proposed handoff scheme demonstrates its reliability advantage by providing tight correlation between predicted reliability values and simulated reliability values.

This paper is organized as follows: Sect. 2 describes the related work in this area. Section 3 describes the Bayesian classification model. Section 4 presents the proposed vertical handoff scheme, which is built over the Bayesian classification model. Section 5 presents the simulated empirical results of the proposed approach. Finally, this work is concluded with future directions in Sect. 6.

2   Related Work

Artificial Intelligence based vertical handoff techniques are extensively found in the literature. In [1], handoff parameters such as-bandwidth, RSSI and monetary cost were used, and fuzzy logic based approach was utilized in designing the handoff scheme. The weight of QoS metrics were varied as the network conditions changed.

A vertical handoff approach which utilized GPRS, GSM and WLAN was proposed in [2]. QoS parameters such as-coverage area, bandwidth, power consumption and sojourn time were included. The handoff scheme was built through fuzzy framework.

The vertical handoff scheme proposed in [3] used UMTS and WLAN. QoS parameters such as-mobile speed, bandwidth and number of user values were utilized. The handoff scheme was also built through fuzzy framework.

The vertical handoff scheme which utilizes both Neural Networks and fuzzy logic was proposed in [4]. This approach utilized multi-criteria decision making model. Bit error rate, signal to interference ratio and data transmission rate were considered as QoS parameters.

Combination of genetic algorithm and fuzzy logic was utilized to perform vertical handoff in [5]. WiMAX and UMTS networks were utilized in applying this handoff scheme. QoS parameters such as-RSS and monetary cost were included.

Neural Network based handoff scheme was proposed in [6]. The handoff decision is made through parameters such as-RSS information and traffic intensity.

Another Neural Network based handoff scheme was proposed in [7], which utilized network security, cost, network transmission range and network capacity as QoS parameters.

In [20], a vertical handoff scheme which reduces the handoff latency was proposed. This scheme utilized Artificial Neural Network to achieve the said goal.

3   Probabilistic Classification Model

Consider a classification problem, which has K defined classes indicated by $[C_1, C_2, ...C_K](1 \leq k \leq K)$. Let, $\mathbf{x}$ be the data point, which is a $(d \times 1)$ random vector. The data point $\mathbf{x}$ is assigned to that class k which has the highest class probability indicated by $P(C_k|\mathbf{x})$. The class conditional probability is represented in Eq. 1, which is derived through Bayes theorem. It is assumed that, class conditional probability is having the distribution represented in Eq. 2. The parameter a_k is defined in Eq. 3.

$$P(C_k|\mathbf{x}) = \frac{P(\mathbf{x}|C_k)P(C_k)}{\sum_j P(\mathbf{x}|C_j)P(C_j)} \tag{1}$$

$$\boxed{P(C_k|\mathbf{x}) = \frac{exp(a_k)}{\sum_j exp(a_j)}} \tag{2}$$

$$a_k = \log(P(\mathbf{x}|C_k)P(C_k)) \tag{3}$$

The posterior probability $P(\mathbf{x}|C_k)$ is represented through Eq. 4.

$$P(\mathbf{x}|C_k) = \frac{1}{2\pi^{\frac{d}{2}}|\mathbf{\Sigma}|^{\frac{1}{2}}} exp(\frac{-1}{2}(\mathbf{x}-\mu_k)^T \mathbf{\Sigma}^{-1}(\mathbf{x}-\mu_k)) \tag{4}$$

Based on the result in Eq. 4, the parameter $a_k(\mathbf{x})$ can be represented through Eq. 5.

$$a_k(\mathbf{x}) = \mathbf{w_k^T}\mathbf{x} + w_{k0} \tag{5}$$

The parameters $\mathbf{w_k}$ and w_{k0} are represented in Eqs. 6 and 7 respectively.

$$\mathbf{w_k} = \mathbf{\Sigma}^{-1}\mu_\mathbf{k} \tag{6}$$

$$w_{k0} = -\frac{1}{2}\mu_\mathbf{k}^\mathbf{T}\mathbf{\Sigma}^{-1}\mu_\mathbf{k} + \log P(C_k) \tag{7}$$

The parameter $\mu_\mathbf{k}$ indicates the mean of kth class, which is represented in Eq. 8. Here, $\mathbf{x_1^k}, \mathbf{x_2^k}, ... \mathbf{x_{n_k}^k}$ indicates the data points of the training set which belong to the kth class.

$$\mu_\mathbf{k} \approx \frac{\sum_{i=1}^{n_k} \mathbf{x_i^k}}{n_k} \tag{8}$$

The parameter $\mathbf{\Sigma}$ indicates the covariance of kth class, which is represented in Eq. 9, and each class is assumed to have the same covariance matrix.

$$\mathbf{\Sigma} \approx \frac{1}{n_k - 1} \sum_{i=1}^{n_k} (\mathbf{x_i^k} - \mu_\mathbf{k})(\mathbf{x_i^k} - \mu_\mathbf{k})^T \tag{9}$$

The prior probability $P(C_k)$ is assigned through Eq. 10.

$$P(C_k) = \frac{1}{K} \tag{10}$$

The data point $\mathbf{x}$ is assigned to that class which has the highest class probability represented in Eq. 2.

4   Reliability Oriented Vertical Handoff Scheme

Every wireless network will be defined through 3 QoS parameters to perform vertical handoff namely:

1. *Bit rate(br)*–it indicates the bit rate provided by the wireless network.
2. *Cost(co)*–it indicates the monetary cost to transmit p data packets.
3. *RSSI(rssi)*–it indicates the received signal strength, which decides the quality of received data.

The feature vector shown in Eq. 11 represents the wireless network $\mathbf{x}$ through the above mentioned 3 QoS parameters.

$$\mathbf{x} = \begin{bmatrix} br \\ co \\ rssi \end{bmatrix} \tag{11}$$

Each wireless network will be defined through a reliability index, which indicates the reliability of the wireless network in providing the said QoS parameters. The reliability index values are indicated by $(0, 1, 2, ...9)$. Here, 9 indicates the lowest reliability and 0 indicates the highest reliability. Each index can be considered as a class indicated by $C_1, C_2, ...C_K$. Here, $K = 10$. The reliability index for the training set feature vector is calculated through the Eqs. 12 and 13. Here, the function $reliability(\mathbf{x_j})$ calculates the reliability index of training set wireless network $\mathbf{x_j}$, $case_i(\mathbf{x_j})$ is defined over a particular time interval in which the network $\mathbf{x_j}$ was observed to obtain handoff statistics. The time interval for all the cases will be equal and mutual independent, $nhandoff(case_i, \mathbf{x_j})$ indicates the number of handoff's designated to the network $\mathbf{x_j}$ during the time interval corresponding to $case_i$, $n\hat{h}andoff(case_i, \mathbf{x_j})$ indicates the number of handoff's which were designated to the network $\mathbf{x_j}$ during the time interval corresponding to $case_i$, but, which had to be provided with new handoff due to traffic congestion in $\mathbf{x_j}$, and m are the number of cases considered.

$$\boxed{reliability(\mathbf{x_j}) = (\frac{\sum_{i=1}^{m} case_i(\mathbf{x_j})}{m}) \mod K} \tag{12}$$

$$case_i(\mathbf{x_j}) = \frac{n\hat{h}andoff(case_i, \mathbf{x_j})}{nhandoff(case_i, \mathbf{x_j})} \times 100 \tag{13}$$

The proposed vertical handoff scheme is described in Algorithm 1. The training set is prepared by creating reliability labels for all the wireless feature vectors in the training set. The Eq. 12 is used to achieve this labeling task. The reliability class parameters are calculated through Eqs. 8 and 9.

The mobile device user who requires vertical handoff specifies the required values for QoS parameters, which is represented in Eq. 14. Here, $\mathbf{u}$ represents the feature vector for the uth user.

$$\mathbf{u} = \begin{bmatrix} br_u \\ co_u \\ rssi_u \end{bmatrix} \tag{14}$$

Among all the available wireless networks which user u can access, only those networks which at-least satisfy the user QoS requirements represented in Eq. 14 wrt *Bit rate* and *RSSI*, and the *Cost* within co_u are selected. This selected wireless network set is denoted as $handoff\_set$. The class probability for all the $K = 10$ classes are calculated using Eq. 2 for every wireless network $\mathbf{x} \in handoff\_set$. The wireless network $\mathbf{x}$ is labeled with the reliability index from that class which has the highest class probability. Finally, $\mathbf{u}$ is subjected to vertical handoff by selecting that wireless network $\in handoff\_set$ which has the lowest reliability index.

Algorithm 1. Vertical Handoff Scheme

Prepare the training set by using the formulation presented in Equation 12.
Calculate the parameters $\mu_{\mathbf{k}}$ and Σ from the training set feature vectors by using Equations 8 and 9.
Let, $(br_u, co_u, rssi_u)$ be the specified QoS parameters of the mobile device user u who requires handoff.
Select the available wireless networks around u which at-least satisfy *Bit rate* and *RSSI* parameters of the user, and the *Cost* within the user specified cost.
This selected wireless network set be denoted as $handoff\_set$.
for each wireless network $\mathbf{x} \in handoff\_set$ **do**
    for each class C_k **do**
        Calculate the class probability $P(C_k|\mathbf{x})$ by using Equation 2.
    end for
    Assign $\mathbf{x}$ to that class $C_j(1 \leq j \leq K)$, which has the highest probability, and $\mathbf{x}$ is labeled with the reliability index j.
end for
Perform handoff for u to that wireless network $\mathbf{x_r} \in handoff\_set$ which has the lowest reliability index.

---

5   Results and Discussions

5.1   Simulation Settings

The proposed vertical handoff scheme is implemented in Network Simulator 3. Four different types of wireless networks were used in the simulation namely– GSM, UMTS, WiFi and WiMAX. Totally, 40 wireless networks were used in the simulation study, and each wireless network type had 10 instances.

The training set included totally 100 wireless networks, which were selected from the four wireless networks described above. Each wireless network was given different simulation parameters. The traffic was randomly generated for each wireless network. The *message size* varied between 10 Kb/s to 100 Kb/s. The data rate varied between 1 Mb/s to 5 Mb/s. The frequency band for WiFi was set to 2400 MHz, GSM was set to 900 MHz, UMTS was set to 2000 MHz and WiMAX was set to 3000 MHz. The monetary cost was set between 1.0 and 5.0. The RSSI value was set between -20 and 0.

5.2   Empirical Analysis

The reliability value for a network predicted by the proposed handoff scheme is compared against the actual reliability values obtained in the simulation. The results of this experimental analysis are shown in Figs. 1, 2 and 3. In Fig. 1, the handoff reliability result is exhibited, when user specified bit rate parameter br_u is varied. Similarly, in Fig. 2, the handoff reliability result is exhibited when user specified monetary cost parameter co_u is varied. Finally, in Fig. 3, the handoff reliability result is exhibited when user specified RSSI parameter $rssi_u$ is varied. It is evident that, the predicted reliability index for a network by the proposed vertical handoff scheme almost agrees with the actual reliability obtained in the simulation.

The same experiment described above is analyzed for the execution time of the proposed vertical handoff scheme. The results of this analysis are presented in Figs. 4, 5 and 6. It is clear that, the proposed vertical handoff scheme mechanism requires limited computational effort.

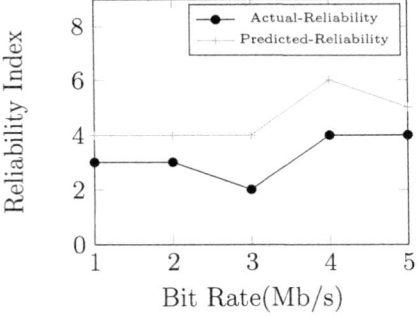

Fig. 1. Reliability vs br_u

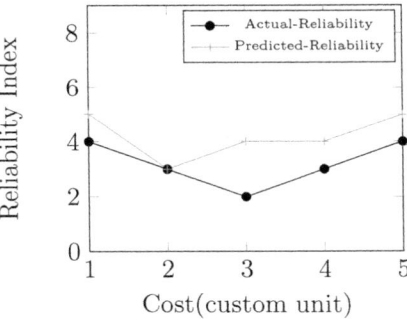

Fig. 2. Reliability vs co_u

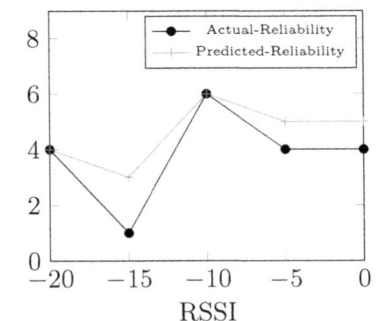

Fig. 3. Reliability vs $rssi_u$

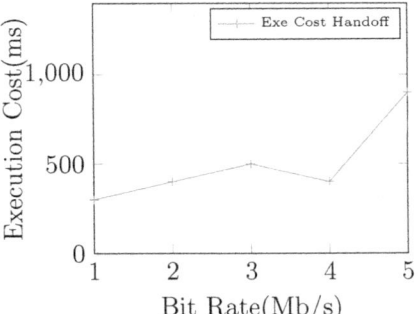

Fig. 4. Execution cost vs br_u

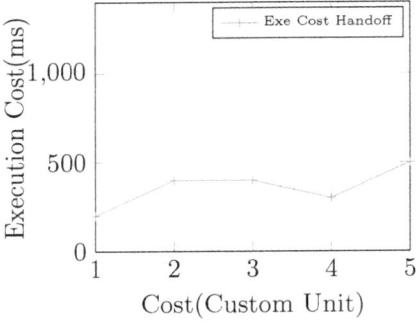

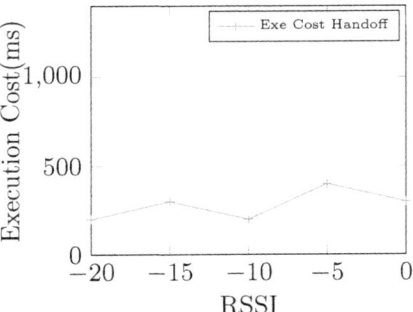

Fig. 5. Execution cost vs co_u **Fig. 6.** Execution cost vs $rssi_u$

6   Conclusion

A new vertical handoff scheme for wireless networks, which targeted the reliability aspect of the handoff decision was proposed in this work. This proposed scheme was built over the probabilistic classification scheme. The empirical analysis exhibited the tight correlation between predicted reliability values and the actual reliability values obtained through simulation. Also, the proposed handoff scheme is computationally light, and thus provides an attractive option to be integrated in future design of heterogeneous wireless networks.

In future, it would be exciting to analyze other probabilistic classification models to perform vertical handoff. In this work, a defined probability distribution function was utilized, but, in future, adaptation of empirical distribution function to build the probabilistic classification model may yield better results.

References

1. Xia, L., Ling-ge, J., Chen, H., Hong-wei, L.: An intelligent vertical handoff algorithm in heterogeneous wireless networks. In: Neural Networks and Signal Processing, International Conference, pp. 550–555 (2008)
2. Ling, Y., Yi, B., Zhu, Q.: An improved vertical handoff decision algorithm for heterogeneous wireless networks. In: Wireless Communications, Networking and Mobile Computing, WiCOM 2008, pp. 1–3 (2008)
3. Guo, Q., Zhu, J., Xu, X.: An adaptive multi-criteria vertical handoff decision algorithm for radio heterogeneous network. In: IEEE International Conference on Communications, ICC 2005, pp. 2769–2773 (2005)
4. Stoyanova, M., Mahonen, P.: Algorithmic approaches for vertical handoff in heterogeneous wireless environment. In: Wireless Communications and Networking Conference, WCNC, pp. 3780–3785 (2007)
5. Nkansah-Gyekye, Y., Agbinya, J.I.: A vertical handoff decision algorithm for next generation wireless networks. In: Third International Conference on Broadband Communications, Information Technology and Biomedical Applications, pp. 358–364 (2008)

6. Bhattacharya, P.P.: Application of artificial neural network in cellular handoff management. In: Conference on Computational Intelligence and Multimedia Applications, International Conference, vol. 1, pp. 237–241 (2007). https://doi.org/10.1109/ICCIMA.2007.252.1232414

7. Nasser, N., Guizani, S., Al-Masri, E.: Middleware vertical handoff manager: a neural network-based solution. In: IEEE International Conference on Communications, ICC 2007, pp. 5671–5676 (2007). https://doi.org/10.1109/ICC.2007.940

8. Onel, T., Ersoy, C., Cayırcı, E., Parr, G.: A multi criteria handoff decision scheme for the next generation tactical communications systems. Comput. Netw. **46**(5), 695–708 (2004)

9. Çalhan, A., Çeken, C.: An optimum vertical handoff decision algorithm based on adaptive fuzzy logic and genetic algorithm. Wirel. Pers. Commun. (2010). https://doi.org/10.1007/s11277-010-0210-6

10. Horrich, S., Ben Jamaa, S., Godlewski, P.: Neural networks for adaptive vertical handover decision. In: 5th International Symposium on Modeling and Optimization in Mobile, Ad Hoc and Wireless Networks and Workshops 2007, WiOpt 2007, pp. 1–7 (2007). https://doi.org/10.1109/WIOPT.2007.4480068

11. Zayani, R., Bouallegue, R., Roviras, D.: Levenberg-marquardt learning neural network for adaptive pre-distortion for time-varying HPA with memory in OFDM systems. In: 16th European Signal Processing Conference on EUSIPCO 2008 (2008)

12. Rumelhart, D.E., Hinton, G.E., Williams, R.J.: Learning representations by back-propagation errors. Nature **323**, 533–536 (1986)

13. Hagan, M.T., Menhaj, M.B.: Training feed forward network with the Marquardt algorithm. IEEE Trans. Neural Netw. **5**(6), 989–993 (1994)

14. Levenberg, K.: A method for the solution of certain nonlinear problems in least squares. Q. Appl. Math. **2**, 164–168 (1944)

15. Marquardt, D.W.: An algorithm for least-squares estimation of nonlinear parameters. J. Soc. Ind. Appl. Math. **11**, 431–441 (1963)

16. Ceken, C., Arslan, H.: An adaptive fuzzy logic based vertical handoff decision algorithm for wireless heterogeneous networks. In: Wireless and Microwave Technology (WAMI) Conference (WAMICON 2009), pp. 1–9 (2009)

17. Çalhan, A., Çeken, C.: Case study on handoff strategies for wireless overlay networks. Comput. Stan. Interfaces (2012). https://doi.org/10.1016/j.csi.2012.06.002

18. Çalhan, A., Çeken, C.: An adaptive neuro-fuzzy based vertical handoff decision algorithm for wireless heterogeneous networks. In: The 21th Personal, Indoor and Mobile Radio Conference, pp. 2271–2276 (2010)

19. Tripathi, N.D., Reed, J.H., Van Landingham, H.F.: Radio Resource Management in Cellularsystems. Kluwer, Dordrecht (2001)

20. Calhan, A., Ceken, C.: Artificial neural network based vertical handoff algorithm for reducing handoff latency. In: Wireless Personal Communication (2013). https://doi.org/10.1007/s112277-012-0944-4

Optical Wireless Systems with DPSK and Manchester Coding

Jagana Bihari Padhy$^{(\boxtimes)}$ and Bijayananda Patnaik

Department of Electronics and Telecommunication Engineering,
IIIT Bhubaneswar, Bhubaneswar, India
jaganpadhy@gmail.com, bijayananda@iiit-bh.ac.in

Abstract. Free-space optical (FSO) communication is an alternative method of allocating high bandwidth links in short to medium range over RF communication systems. It is observed as a growing increase in research and development activities over the past few years due to the innumerous advantages. The advantages of FSO communication include a much larger data rate, lower power consumption, more compact equipment, greater security against eavesdropping, better protection against electromagnetic interference and license free data transmission. However, the performance of the FSO system is greatly influenced by atmospheric temperature, pressure, humidity etc. To overcome these challenges various techniques have been proposed in the literature. Generally, the average bit error rate (BER) and quality factor (Q-factor) are prime parameters to measure the performance of the FSO systems. In this paper, a comparative study and mathematical modeling have been done using differential phase shift keying (DPSK) modulation technique with Manchester coding to conventional DPSK modulation technique for different FSO configurations. Manchester encoding synchronizes the signal itself; hence, it minimizes the error rate and optimizes the reliability of the system. For analyzing, the low to high turbulence level of atmosphere Gamma-Gamma type channel model is preferred.

Keywords: DPSK · Scintillation · OWC · Diffused channel
Manchester coding

1 Introduction

In the past three decades, the demand for high-speed communications has increased drastically, which is accomplished by fiber optic communications for majority of data transmission networks with data rate of up to 100 Gbps. However, due to the infrastructure development difficulty, time-consuming for installation, complexity in installation and relatively expensive of fiber technology in shorter to medium range transmission another alternate optical technology came to picture. The free space optical (FSO) technologies have led to a rebirth of optical broadband access as an attractive alternative for ultra high-speed networking. FSO systems (in space and in terrestrial regions) have evolved in counter to a growing need for high-speed and bug free information transmission and reception systems [1]. The last-mile applications like communication involving deep-space link establishment, terrestrial stations links, unmanned aerial vehicles (UAVs), high altitude platforms (HAPs), inter-satellite communications, airline

© Springer Nature Singapore Pte Ltd. 2018
P. Bhattacharyya et al. (Eds.): NGCT 2017, CCIS 828, pp. 155–167, 2018.
https://doi.org/10.1007/978-981-10-8660-1_12

and other nomadic communication systems can be used in integrated systems of military and civilian contexts [1]. Because of its unregulated spectrum range, huge data transmission potential, relative low power prerequisite, low bit error rate (BER) and simplicity of redeployment, wireless communications have attracted the researchers for the evolution of short distance ultrahigh bit rate mobile applications [2]. In spite of various advantages, the performance of the FSO system is influenced by the atmospheric turbulence, which costs distortion of transmitted signal along the path of propagation. Thus it is exposed to beam wandering, intensity fluctuation (scintillation) and beam broadening at the receiver, which is leading to significant decrease of coupling efficiency at the receiving terminal [3]. Due to the above atmospheric effects the optical links suffer from random variation in index-of-refraction turbulence (IRT), as a result image blurring effect will occur by the obscuration such as clouds, snow and rain etc. [4]. To mitigate the above mentioned challenges, various researches are being carried out not only in the physical layer but also in the transport layer. The innovative techniques such as orthogonal frequency division multiplexing (OFDM), multiple-input multiple-output (MIMO) communication systems, cooperative diversity and adaptive transmission system which was implemented in RF technology can also be applied for FSO for better spectral efficiency [3]. In past literature, to withstand data transmission in low to high turbulence regime different advanced modulation techniques are used. Generally the modulation technique like on-off keying (OOK), differential phase shift keying (DPSK), binary phase shift keying (BPSK), pulse amplitude modulation (PAM), quadrature phase shift keying (QPSK) and pulse position modulation (PPM) are used in FSO technology [4]. To analyze the transmission efficiency at different turbulence level, choice of appropriate channel model is very crucial for system design [5]. In past literature various types of stochastic channel models has been proposed such as Log-normal, negative exponential, K-distribution, Rayleigh distribution, I-K distribution and Gamma–Gamma etc. Out of all these models, the Gamma-Gamma model is double stochastic model, which can be implemented for weak turbulence channel to high turbulence channel and is widely accepted in current literature [5]. The system performance can be increased by incorporating error control coding in addition with advanced modulation techniques. There are several coding techniques such as non-return-to-zero (NRZ), 8B/10B, forward error correction (FEC) which are already implemented in past literatures in optical fiber communication systems [3]. In this paper, for the 1st time, we have used the Manchester coding with DPSK modulation over different wireless optical configurations like FSO channel, optical wireless channel (OWC), diffused wireless channel (DWC) and the results are compared with conventional DPSK modulation technique. Mathematical modeling has also been incorporated.

2 Modulation and Coding

Modulation techniques are playing a major role in all wired as well as wireless communication systems. Hence for better data transmission performance choosing of right modulation technique is highly necessary. In the optical communication system, the carrier is being modulated by message signal in its frequency, amplitude, phase and polarization [4, 6].

2.1 On-Off Keying (OOK)

Mostly on-off keying (OOK) signaling format with fixed threshold level is implemented in FSO, because of its simplicity in design. Intensity modulation is a scheme, where the optical source (carrier) is turned on to transmit logic "high" and turned off to transmit a logic "low". For better transmission sensitivity, this modulation scheme is also incorporated with some line coding techniques such as non-return-to-zero (NRZ)-OOK or return-to-zero (RZ)-OOK coding [4]. The system capability is also additionally exaggerated by utilization of multiplexing and multi-carrier transmission. But OOK demands dynamic threshold for optimum detection in high turbulent atmospheric condition [2]. Thus in literature DPSK modulation is proposed because of its power efficiency compared to OOK technique [7].

2.2 Binary Phase Shift Keying (BPSK)

The optical PSK was used extensively for coherent photonic transmission systems. For instance, the phase of the coherent laser light is switched between two states in binary phase shift keying (BPSK) modulation. Coherent detectors synchronizes the received light with the light of a local oscillator, thus the coherent receivers are very much sensitive (around one to 2 orders) in magnitude compared to OOK systems [6]. The coherent detection system face challenges such as broad linewidth and chirping problems of the laser source. It requires manipulation of the absolute phase of the lightwave carrier, thus precise alignment of the transmitter and demodulator center frequencies for the coherent detection is required [8].

2.3 Differential Phase Shift Keyed (DPSK)

The presence of local oscillator makes the receiver circuit complex, hence self-homodyne is preferred which is present in differential phase shift keying (DPSK) systems. Due to the homodyne detection scheme in DPSK, there is an improvement in sensitivity by 3 dB compare to OOK technique [8]. The DPSK optically-modulated signals can be detected incoherently. Here the coherence light wave carrier is used for one bit period and hence froth comparing with the differentially coded phase of the adjacent bit. Here the transmitted bits can be encoded in a way like XOR operation. But the main challenge in DPSK is the bit synchronization at the demodulator circuit [7]. Wang et al. [4] showed that the numerical analysis for BER performance of DPSK is better than OOK formats not only in the moderate but also in the strong turbulent channel. Popoola et al. [7] verified the BER performance of DPSK modulated system and they have shown that the DPSK system is better than higher order QAM systems as well as BPSK modulation systems. Also DPSK requires least amount of power compare to OOK modulation (both RZ and NRZ signaling) technique.

2.4 Pulse Position Modulation (PPM)

In this modulation scheme, each pulse of a laser can be used to represent one or more bits of information by its position in time relative to the start of a symbol whose duration is identical to that of information bits it contains. The elimination of decision threshold dependence on the input power is a great advantage of PPM scheme [8].

In case of NRZ and RZ, loss of clock synchronization is observed, if long strings of ones or zeros are transmitted. This problem may be avoided with Manchester coding, in which, it is possible to recover the clock of the digital signaling. Manchester coding is also known as bi-phase coding. Due to the features such as simple clock extraction operation and differential detection scheme, this allows a high level intensity fluctuation tolerance. For this reason it is used in high speed brust mode transmission link [8–11].

3 FSO Configurations

Optical communication channel can be categorized into two types: guided and unguided. All guided optical communication systems currently use optical fibers; the commonly used term for them is fiber-optic communication system. In the case of unguided optical communication systems, the optical beam emitted by the transmitter propagated through space, known as optical wireless channel (OWC), free-space optical channel (FSO) and diffused free space optical wireless channel (DFWC) [7]. Generally optical wireless communication can be classified as indoor optical wireless system and outdoor optical wireless system. Indoor OWC is subdivided into four generic system channel configurations i.e., diffused, tracked, and directed line-of-sight (LOS) and non-directed LOS. Similarly the outdoor OWC can be of terrestrial link or deep space link. In terrestrial link data transmission can be carried out by either FSO channel for short range or OWC channel for long range transmission [3]. For understanding the behavior of the channel in low to high turbulence level and to verify the impact of atmospheric turbulence on the FSO systems, accurate modeling of channel is highly necessary. There are various statistical channel models such as lognormal, negative exponential, K-distribution and Gamma–Gamma etc. have been proposed in past literatures [5]. The Gamma–Gamma distribution which is also verified with experimental data is suitable model for wide range of turbulence conditions (from weak to strong turbulence) [7]. In past literature it has been verified, the scintillation index is proportional to the Rytov variance given by [7],

$$\sigma^2 = 1.23 C_n^2 K^{7/6} L^{11/6} \tag{1}$$

where C_n^2 is the scintillation index or strength of turbulence, K (the optical wave number) is $2\pi/\lambda$, L is the link distance, λ is the operating wavelength. The value of C_n^2 is constant in horizontal link upto a several kilometer, but in vertical link C_n^2 can be dependent on height according to Hufnagel-Valley model [5].

4 Mathematical Modeling and Proposed Setup

The BER of the optical signal transmitted in Gamma –Gamma distribution channel from low to high turbulence can be computed as given below. The average BER of an FSO modulated system over strong atmospheric turbulence channel can be computed as [4],

$$P_{eMOD} = \int_{0}^{\infty} p_{ec}(h)F_h(I)dh \tag{2}$$

where P_{eMOD} is the average BER of an FSO modulated system, $p_{ec}(h)$ is the probability of conditional BER, h is the channel state, $F_h(I)$ is the probability distribution function of Gamma-Gamma type channel model, which is given by [7],

$$F_h(I) = \frac{2(\alpha\beta)^{\frac{\alpha+\beta}{2}}}{\Gamma(\alpha)\Gamma(\beta)} I^{\frac{\alpha+\beta}{2}-1} K_{\alpha-\beta}\left(2\sqrt{\alpha\beta I}\right), I > 0 \tag{3}$$

where, α, β are the parameters of pdf function, which physically represents the small signal and large scale eddies of turbulent atmosphere as given below, I is the received signal intensity, $K_{(\alpha-\beta)}$ is the modified Bessel's function of second order.

$$\alpha = [exp^{0.49\sigma^2/(1+1.11\sigma^{12/5})^{7/6}} - 1]^{-1} \tag{4}$$

$$\beta = [exp^{0.51\sigma^2/(1+1.11\sigma^{12/5})^{5/6}} - 1]^{-1} \tag{5}$$

where, σ^2 is the Rytov variance as given by Eq. (1). The probability of conditional BER of OOK modulation is given by [12],

$$[p_{ec}(h)]_{OOK} = Q\left(\frac{RP_t h}{\sigma_n}\right) \tag{6}$$

Where, Q (.) is the Gaussian Q function, which is $Q(x) = 1/2 erfc(x/\sqrt{2})$, erfc(x) is the complementary error function, R is the responsivity of photo detector, P_t is the signal power at transmitter, σ_n is the noise standard deviation. The probability of conditional BER of DPSK modulation is given by [13],

$$[p_{ec}(h)]_{DPSK} = 0.5 \times exp^{[-\frac{\eta ATh}{Pv}]} \tag{7}$$

where, η is the quantum efficiency of the detector, A is the detector area in m^2, T is the DPSK symbol duration in seconds, P is the plank's constant and v is the frequency of the received signal in Hz. Similarly, the probability of conditional BER of M-array PPM modulation is given by [13],

$$[p_{ec}(h)]_{M-PPM} = \frac{M}{4} \times erfc\left(\gamma P\left(\frac{\eta A}{\lambda L}\right)^2 \frac{\sqrt{MLog_2M}}{2\sigma_n} h\right) \tag{8}$$

In PPM, each symbol interval of duration $T = Log_2 \frac{M}{R_b}$ is partitioned into M sub-interval of length $\frac{T}{M}$, and the transmitter sends an optical pulse during one and only one of these chips. For any L greater than 2, PPM requires less optical power than OOK [13]. The main problem in PPM is its low bandwidth efficiency. The loss of clock synchronization problem in DPSK system may be avoided with Manchester coding [10], in which, it is possible to recover the clock of the digital signaling. Manchester coding is also known as bi-phase coding due to the features such as simple clock extraction operation and differential detection scheme, thus allows a high level of intensity fluctuation tolerance. For this reason it is used in high speed burst mode transmission link. The error performance of this coding is given by [14],

$$P_{eCODING} = \frac{1}{2} \times erf(\sqrt{\frac{E_b}{N_0}}) \tag{9}$$

$P_{eCODDING}$ is the BER of Manchester coded signal. The overall error performance of the DPSK system with Manchester coding can be calculated as [8],

$$P_{OVERAL} = P_{eMOD} \cdot P_{eCODING} \tag{10}$$

From the above analysis, we can conclude that the overall error performance can be improved in the proposed system, which is as shown in Fig. 1. It consists of three major sections 1. transmitter; 2. channel; 3. receiver. The transmitter transmits the encoded modulated data through the channel. The input data is generated by a bit sequence generator at a rate of 40 Gbps. The Manchester encoder shown in Fig. 2(a) encodes the bit stream into Manchester encoded form [10]. The DPSK transmitter modulates a CW laser with linewidth of 0.1 MHz and operated at frequency of 193.1 THz which generates the carrier light with power of 10 dBm with the encoded data stream from the encoder. The modulated signal then propagated through the channel. Here, we have used 3 different type of free space channel for data transmission, a. FSO channel; b. OWC channel; c. DFWC channel. The receiver contains the DPSK demodulator, Manchester decoder, low pass filter and the visualizer for checking the result. The demodulator consists of the photo detector, which receives the distorted light signal form channel. Here, we have used PIN photo detector having responsivity of 1 A/w and the dark current of 10 nA. The received modulated signal is demodulated at DPSK demodulator. Then the demodulated data is fed to the Manchester decoder [9, 10] as shown in Fig. 2(b). The decoded data is passed through a low pass filter (LPF) having cut off frequency of 75% of the bit rate. The final output is verified in the BER analyzer for the parameters Q-factor and BER for specific link distance.

5   Simulation and Result Discussion

The proposed system of DPSK modulation formats over different wireless optical configurations with Manchester coding, given in Fig. 1 is designed and simulated in Optisystem 14.2 environment. The details regarding the simulation parameters used for the system are given in Appendix. The input power level applied to laser is 10 dBm for wavelength 1550 nm. After successful transmission of the optical signal through the different free space configurations with different turbulent conditions (Rytov variance), the following conclusions has been observed as shown in Table 1 for data rate of 40 Gbps.

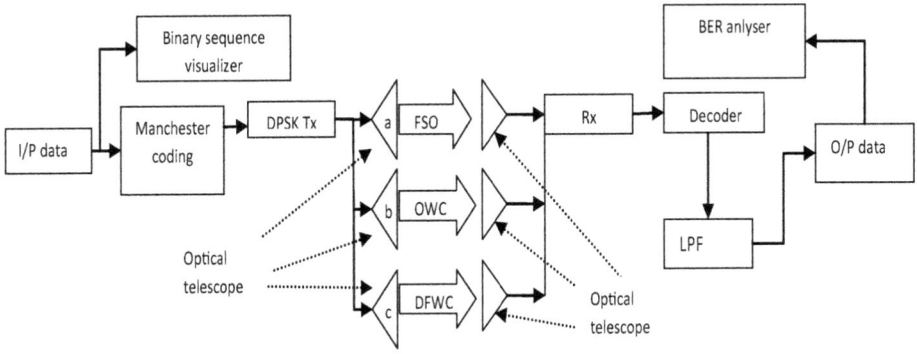

Fig. 1. Proposed model with (a) FSO channel (b) OWC channel (c) DWOC channel

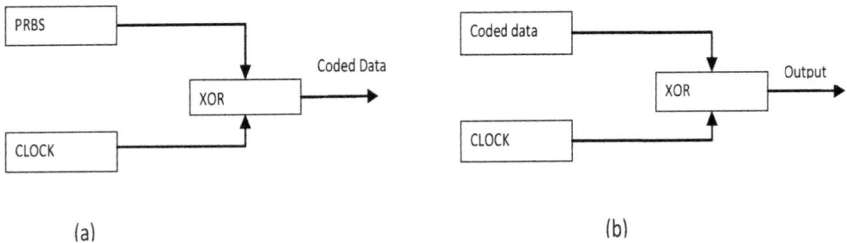

(a)   (b)

Fig. 2. (a) Manchester encoder (b) Manchester decoder

Table 1. Q-factor and BER for different free space channels

Channel	Q-factor without Manchester coding	Q-factor with Manchester coding	BER without Manchester coding	BER with Manchester coding	Link distance
FSO	5.56	7.09	10^{-8}	10^{-13}	497 m.
OWC	4.3098	7.1075	10^{-5}	10^{-13}	1.5 km
DFWC	4.70	7.001	10^{-6}	10^{-12}	6.5 m

The proposed system is simulated for the three types of wireless optical configurations such as FSO; OWC; DWFC. By varying the link distance of each system, it has been observed that with Manchester coding the link distance is found to be increase comparing to without Manchester coding technique. The analysis of the three configurations has been done in detail as given below.

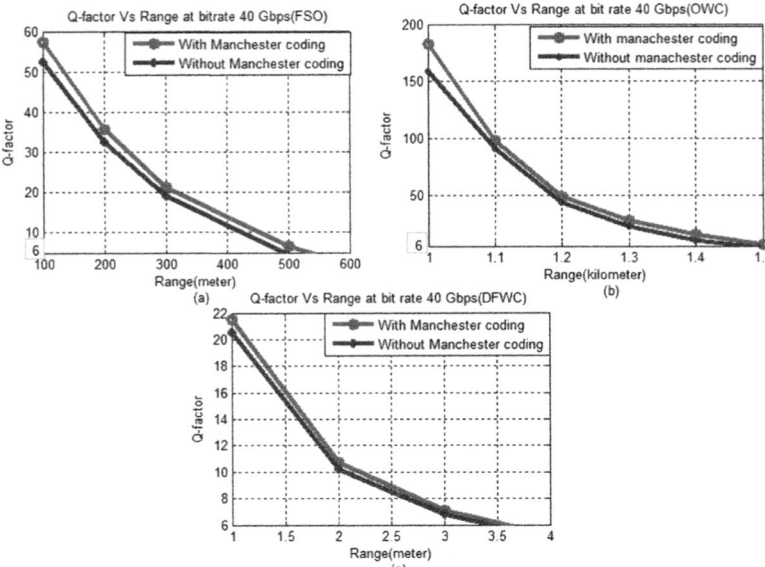

Fig. 3. (a), (b), (c) Q-factor Vs range at bit rate 40 Gbps for FSO channel, OWC channel, DWFC channel.

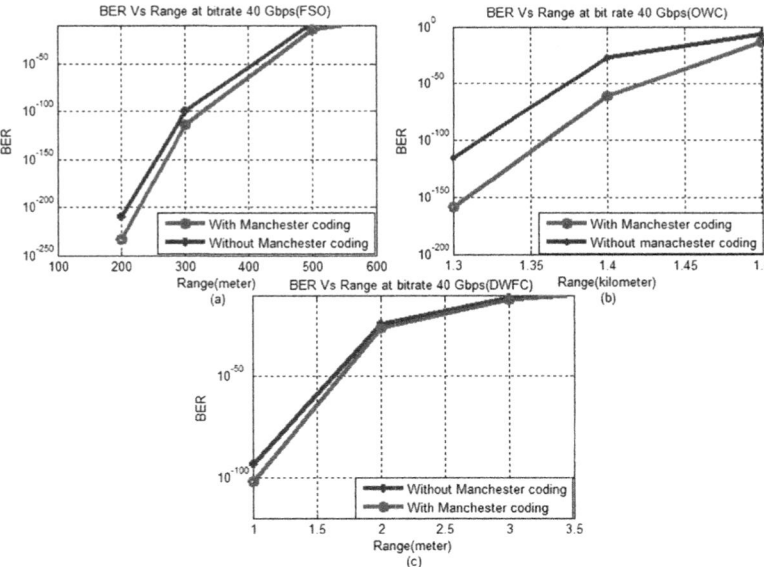

Fig. 4. (a), (b), (c) BER Vs range at bit rate 40 Gbps for FSO channel, OWC channel, DWFC channel.

1 For FSO system by varying the range from 100 m to 700 m in presence of high
   turbulence with refractive index structure value C_n^2 of 10^{-14} m$^{-2/3}$ and atmospheric
   attenuation of 25 dB/km, the Q-factor Vs range and the BER Vs range has been
   plotted as shown in Figs. 3(a) and 4(a). From the results, we can conclude that, the
   system performance is improved in the DPSK modulated system due to Manchester
   coding for a fixed bit rate of 40 Gbps. The proposed system is also simulated for
   various bitrates standardized by ITU-T [3] at fixed link distance as shown in Fig. 5

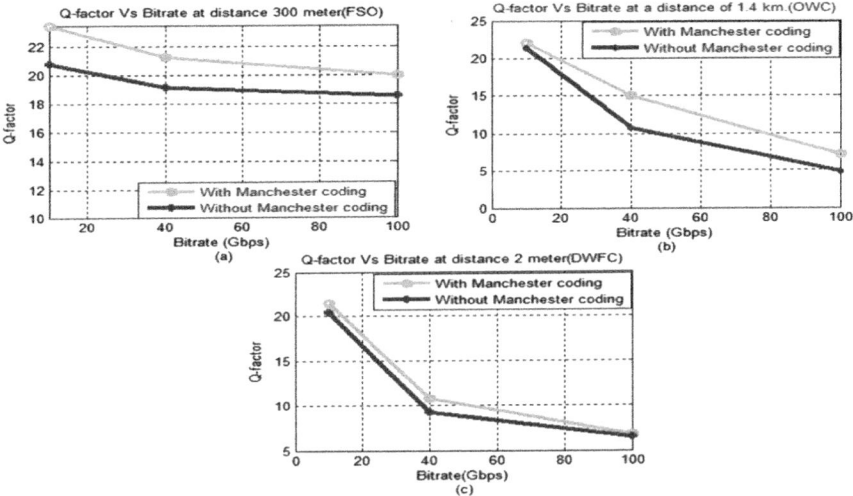

Fig. 5. (a), (b), (c) Q-factor Vs bit rate for FSO channel, OWC channel, DWFC channel.

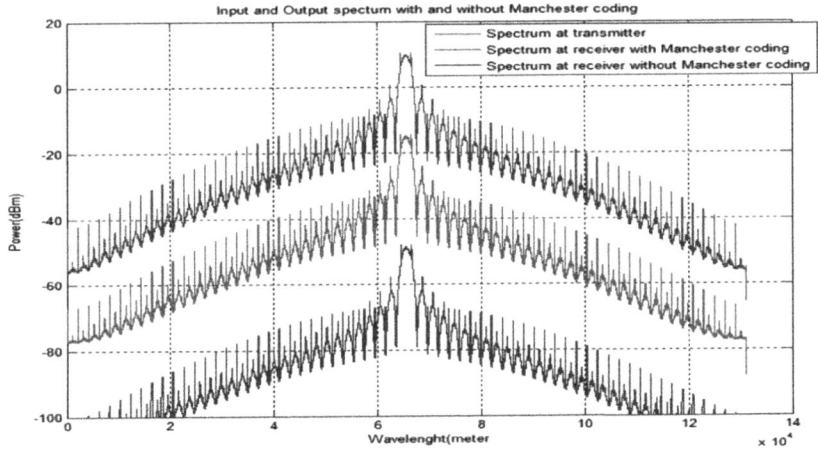

Fig. 6. Outputs spectrum analyzer for OWC channel

(a)

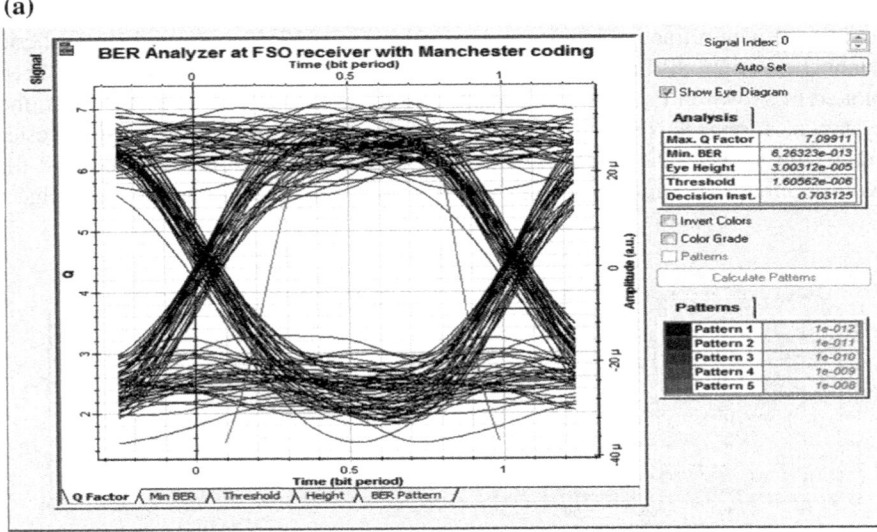

(b)

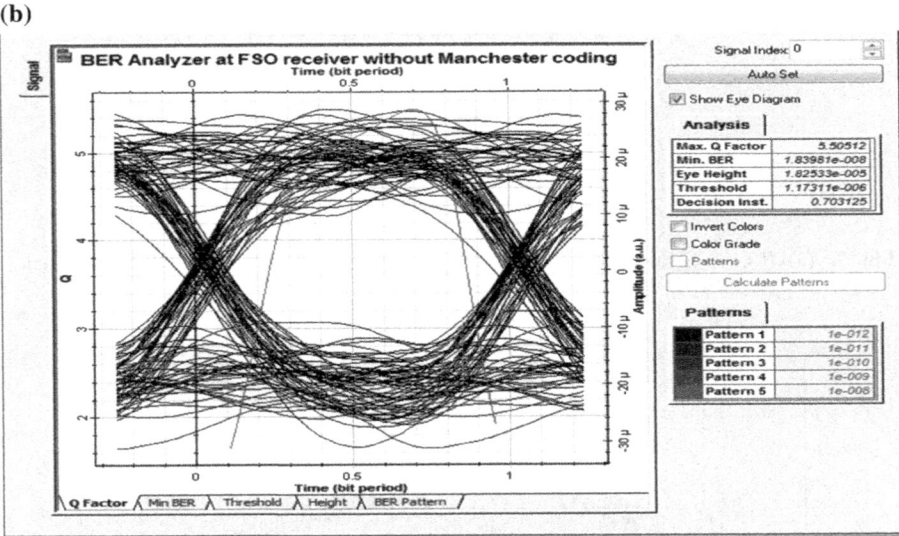

Fig. 7. (a) Eye diagram at receiver with Manchester coding for FSO channel (b) Eye diagram at receiver without Manchester coding for FSO channel.

(a), the result shows that the system with Manchester coding shows high reliability to bit error rate. Due to the self synchronization property of Manchester coding, the bit errors can be controlled. As a result, there is improving of Q-factor which can be verified in Fig. 7(a), (b). Hence the link distance may be increased with susceptible bit error rate.

2 The OWC system is simulated by varying the range from 1 km to 1.5 km in presence of high turbulence with refractive index structure value (C_n^2) of 10^{-14} m$^{-2/3}$. Here for the terrestrial OWC the atmospheric attenuation of 25 dB/km is considered. The Q-factor Vs range and the BER Vs range have been plotted as shown in Figs. 3(b), 4(b). From the simulated curve, we can conclude that the system performance is improved in the DPSK modulated system due to Manchester coding for a fixed bit rate of 40 Gbps. The proposed system is also simulated for various bitrates standardized by ITU-T [3] at fixed link distance of 1.4 km as shown in Fig. 5(b). Here, we can conclude that, the system with Manchester coding shows high credibility to bit error rate in not only in low data rate but also in high data rate for long range terrestrial optical communication systems. At the output of the spectrum analyzer connected to the receiver, it has been observed that due to zero dc content on individual input pulse the power level can be improved as shown in Fig. 6.

3 The system is also simulated by varying the range from 1 m to 6 m in diffused wireless channel in presence of high turbulence with refractive index structure value (C_n^2) of 10^{-14} m$^{-2/3}$. The Q-factor Vs range and BER Vs range have been plotted as shown in Figs. 3(c) and 4(c) respectively . From the simulated curve, we can conclude that, the system performance is improved in the DPSK modulated system due to Manchester coding for a fixed bit rate of 10 Gbps. The proposed system is also simulated for various bitrates standardized by ITU-T [3] at fixed link distance of 2 m as shown in Fig. 5(c). It can be concluded that, the system with Manchester coding shows high trustworthiness to bit error rate in indoor wireless optical communication systems.

6 Conclusion

A free space optic system with DPSK modulation formats over different wireless optical configurations with Manchester coding is proposed. For analysing the proper bit error performance Gamma-Gamma channel model is considered, which is preferable in low to high turbulence atmospheric conditions. A comparative analysis has been done with mathematical modelling on different free space optic channels in low to high atmospheric turbulence conditions. The observed results are compared with and without Manchester coding for each channel configurations such as FSO; OWC; DFWC. With Manchester coding the performance is found to be better comparing to without Manchester coding because of self synchrinization of transmitted bits. The system may further be analyzed for more number of input output channels, other advanced modulation and coding techniques.

Appendix

Bit-rate (Gbps)	40 Gbps
Transmitted laser power (dBm)	10dBm
Distance	
i. FSO(meter)	100-600
ii. OWC (kilometer)	1 − 1.5
iii. DFWC (meter)	1 − 6
Symbol rate (Gbps)	20 Gbps
Wave length (nm)	1550
Frequency (THz)	193.1
1. FSO channel	
i. Attenuation(dB/km)	25
ii. Transmitter aperture diametr (cm)	5
iii. Receiver aperture diameter (cm)	20
iv. Beam divergence(mrad)	2
2. OWC channel	
i. Attenuation(dB/km)	25
ii. Transmitter aperture diameter (cm)	10
iii. Receiver aperture diameter (cm)	20
3. DFWC channel	
i. Detection surface area (mm^2)	100
ii. Optical concentration factor	30
Additional losses (dB)	1
Optical Bandwidth (GHz)	60
Electrical Bandwidth (GHz)	40
C_n^2 (m$^{-2/3}$)	$10^{-17} − 10^{-13}$
σ^2 (Rytov variance)	$0.029 − 1.99$
Sequence length	2048

References

1. Seeds, A., Shams, H., Fice, M., Renaud, C.: TeraHertz photonics for wireless communications. J. Lightwave Technol. **33**, 579–587 (2015)
2. Kumar, N., Rana, A.K.: Impact of various parameters on the performance of free space optics communication system. Optik (Stuttg.) **124**, 5774–5776 (2013). https://doi.org/10. 1016/j.ijleo.2013.04.062
3. Khalighi, M.A., Uysal, M.: Survey on free space optical communication: a communication theory perspective. IEEE Commun. Surv. Tutor. **16**, 2231–2258 (2014). https://doi.org/10. 1109/COMST.2014.2329501
4. Wang, Z., Zhong, W.D., Fu, S., Lin, C.: Performance comparison of different modulation formats over free-space optical (FSO) turbulence links with space diversity reception technique. IEEE Photonics J. **1**, 277–285 (2009). https://doi.org/10.1109/JPHOT.2009. 2039015
5. Popoola, W., Ghassemlooy, Z., Leitgeb, E.: BER and outage probability of DPSK subcarrier intensity modulated free space optics in fully developed speckle. J. Commun. **4**, 546–554 (2009)
6. Agrawal, G.P.: Fiber-Optic Communications Systems, 3rd edn. (2002)
7. Majumdar, A.K.: Free-space laser communication performance in the atmospheric channel. J. Opt. Fiber Commun. Rep. **2**, 345–396 (2005). https://doi.org/10.1007/s10297-005-0054-0
8. Binh, L.N.: Digital Optical Communications. CRC Press, London, New York (2008)
9. Forouzan, A.B.: Data Communications and Networking. McGraw-Hill, New York (2007)
10. Zhang, J.Z.J., Chi, N.C.N., Holm-Nielsen, P.V., Peucheret, C., Jeppesen, P.: Method for high-speed Manchester encoded optical signal generation. In: Optical Fiber Communication Conference 2004, OFC 2004, vol. 1, p. 2800 (2004). https://doi.org/10.1109/ofc.2004. 1359241
11. Chi, N., Huang, D.: Improved label property of orthogonal ASK/DPSK labeling by using a 40 Gb/s Manchester coded payload. In: OFC/NFOEC 2007 - Optical Fiber Communication and the National Fiber Optic Engineers Conference, pp. 6–8 (2007). https://doi.org/10.1109/ ofc.2007.4348769
12. Patnaik, B., Sahu, P.K.: Inter-satellite optical wireless communication system design and simulation. IET Commun. **6**, 2561–2567 (2012). https://doi.org/10.1049/iet-com.2012.0044
13. Prabu, K., Kumar, D.S., Srinivas, T.: Performance analysis of FSO links under strong atmospheric turbulence conditions using various modulation schemes. Optik (Stuttg.) **125**, 5573–5581 (2014). https://doi.org/10.1016/j.ijleo.2014.07.028
14. Illinois, J.L.L., Patel, B.P.: Line coding. In: Mobile Communications Handbook. CRC Press (1999)

CAMQU: A Cloudlet Allocation Strategy Using Multilevel Queue and User Factor

Vinayak Bajoria[(✉)] and Avita Katal[(✉)]

UPES, Dehradun, Uttrakhand, India
bajoriavinayak@gmail.com, akatal@ddn.upes.ac.in

Abstract. Cloud computing has developed as a prevailing and transformational worldview in Information innovation space throughout the most recent couple of years. It has influenced a huge number of ventures, for example, government, broadcast communications etc. The Quality of Service (QoS) of a cloud specialist organization is a vital research field which envelops distinctive basic issues, for example, effective load adjusting, reaction time enhancement, culmination time change and diminishment in wastage of data transfer. This paper highlights cloudlet scheduling policy. The proposed policy CAMQU reduces the execution time of the cloudlet(s). The term UserFactor proposed within the policy gives power to user to make the process cost or time efficient on the basis of his needs whereas the term cost quantum a static value can be set by CSP to determine the cost of execution of the instructions of the cloudlets. The policy increases the Quality of Service (QoS) for both User and Cloud Service Provider.

Keywords: Cloud computing · Cloud Service Provider (CSP)
Virtual Machine (VM) · Data Center (DC) · User factor

1 Introduction

Cloud Computing is on demand delivery of compute power, database storage, applications and other IT resources through a cloud service platform via the internet with pay as you go pricing. Whether you are running application that share photos of millions of mobile users or performing some critical operations for your business, a cloud service platform provides a rapid access to the flexible and low cost IT resources. With Cloud Computing you don't need to make upfront huge investment in hardware. Cloud Computing provides a simple way to access servers, storage and databases and other broad set of application services over the internet. Cloud computing has three main types which are commonly referred as Infrastructure as a Service (IaaS), Platform as a Service(PaaS) and Software as a Service (SaaS).

This paper focuses on improving Cloud services provided under SaaS. Software as a Service provides us with completed product that is run and managed by the service provider. In most cases people referring to software as a service are end users applicants. Every request for a software service is a task which when submitted to CIS is known as cloudlet, processed upon the Virtual Machines. With millions of user accessing services at a moment these cloudlets have to be processed faster and

© Springer Nature Singapore Pte Ltd. 2018
P. Bhattacharyya et al. (Eds.): NGCT 2017, CCIS 828, pp. 168–182, 2018.
https://doi.org/10.1007/978-981-10-8660-1_13

economically by the VM's, to ensure benefits both to user and Cloud Service provider. This is where the requirement of scheduling the cloudlets strategically to maximize the benefits and use the hardware effectively with short response time for the services requested arises. The proposed Cloudlet Scheduling policy CAMQU maintains multiple queues with decreasing priority from which the Cloudlets are extracted and executed upon the most suitable VM for a specified time quantum. If the Cloudlet is still left for execution it is moved to a lower priority queue.

2   Related Work

In this paper, few existing allocation policies are taken into account to analyze and compare the advantages of the proposed allocation policy. They are described as follows.

2.1   Min-Min

Initially a matrix is taken for all unassigned cloudlets. The whole assignment process is divided into two phases. In the first phase the set of minimum computation time for each cloudlet in the matrix is calculated and found. In the second phase, the cloudlet with the overall minimum expected computation time is chosen from the matrix and assigned to the corresponding VM. Then the assigned cloudlet is removed from the matrix and the entries of the matrix are modified accordingly. This process of Min-Min is repeated until there is no cloudlet left in the matrix, that is, all cloudlets in the matrix are mapped. This algorithm takes $O(mn^2)$ time where m is the number of VMs and n is the number of cloudlets [6].

2.2   Max-Min

This algorithm is almost similar to Min-Min, but there is a distinctive difference in the second phase. Max-Min first chooses the cloudlet with maximum computation time from the matrix and assigns it to the VM on which the chosen cloudlet gives minimum time to compute. This algorithm also takes $O(mn^2)$ time where m is the number of VMs and n is the number of cloudlets [6].

2.3   Rasa

This algorithm actually combines the advantages of both Min-Min and Max-min. If the number of available VMs is odd, the Min-Min algorithm is applied to allocate the first cloudlet, otherwise the Max-min algorithm is applied. The whole process can be divided into a number of rounds where in each round two cloudlets are allocated to appropriate VMs by one of the two strategies, alternatively. The rule is, if the first cloudlet of the current round is allocated to a VM by the Min-Min strategy, the next cloudlet will be allocated by the Max-min strategy. In the next round, the cloudlet allocation begins with an algorithm different from the last round. For example if the first round begins with the Max-min algorithm, the second round will begin with the

Min–min algorithm. Experimental results show that if the numbers of available resources are odd then starting with applying the Min–min algorithm in the first round gives the better result. Otherwise, it is better to apply the Max-Min strategy at first. Min–min and Max-Min are exchanged alternatively to result in consecutive execution of small and large cloudlets on different VMs and therefore, the waiting time of the small cloudlets in Max-Min algorithm and the waiting time of the large cloudlets in Min–min algorithm are ignored. As RASA doesn't consist of any time consuming instruction, the time complexity of RASA is $O(mn^2)$ where m is the number of VMs and n is the number of cloudlets [6].

2.4 Round Robin Allocation (RRA)

Consider there are four cloudlets (C_0, C_1, C_2, C_3, and C_4) and three VMs (VM0,VM1, VM2,VM3). It allocates the cloudlet to first available VM. For example, Table 1 illustrates the allocation fashion. According to this policy, cloudlet C_0 is allocated to VM_0, C_1 allocated to VM_1, C_2 allocated to VM_2, C_3 allocated to the VM_3 and C_4 allocated to VM_0. The RRA policy is much dynamic and easy to implement but large cloudlets are often allocated to VM with lower MIPS thus increasing waiting time and response time [6].

Table 1. Round Robin Allocation policy of the cloudlets

Cloudlets	Virtual Machine
C0	VM0
C1	VM1
C2	VM2
C3	VM3
C4	VM0

2.5 First Come First Serve (FCFS)

In this the cloudlets are taken from the global queue and allocated to the first available Virtual Machine. It's a non-pre-emptive scheduling algorithm. It is poor in performance as the waiting time for the cloudlets is large. It leads to starvation of the cloudlets the end of the queue. Smaller length cloudlets are allocated to high processing power Virtual machines while opposite happens with smaller processing power VM which leads to poor resource utilization [7].

2.6 Shortest Job First (SJF)

In this the global cloudlet queue is firstly sorted on the basis of the cloudlet length generally ascending order then FCFS is applied. It also leads to large waiting time and poor resource utilization. It's only better in case that it doesn't lead to starvation of cloudlets of shorter length [7].

In this paper a new cloudlet allocation policy CAMQU, has been proposed which decreases the execution time of the cloudlets using a priority based multilevel feedback queue and also increases the Quality of Service (QoS) for both user and CSP.

3 Proposed Work

This work highlights a new cloudlet allocation strategy which will improve the completion time of the cloudlets. It will make the service more user interactive by letting the user specify if he wants the processing of his tasks to be cost efficient or time efficient. The Cloud Service Provider can also set the cost of execution of instructions for the VM by using the static value Qs. The policy CAMQU supports a finite number of queues n and a finite no of cloudlets N. Each task requires arrival time A and Burst time B and user Factor P (which helps us to prioritize tasks that will require faster execution).

Let

$Q = \{Q_1, Q_2, Q_3, \ldots Q_n\}$ be the set of n queues

$T = \{T_1, T_2, T_3 \ldots T_N\}$ be the set of N cloudlets.

Then $\{A_i \mid i = 1 \ldots N\}$ represents the Arrival time

$\{B_i \mid i = 1 \ldots N\}$ represents the Burst time

$\{M_i \mid i = 1 \ldots N\}$ represents the cloudlet Length

$\{P_i \mid i = 1 \ldots N\}$ represents the user factor of the ith cloudlet respectively which is an input given by CSP on the demand of the User whether he wants the tasks to be cost or time efficient.

The total Virtual machines (VM) created are m then $VM = \{VM_1, VM_2, VM_3, \ldots, VM_m\}$.

The policy divides the global cloudlet list into finite number of queues based on requirements.

3.1 Data Base

The Burst time of each cloudlet is calculated on the basis of formulae below.

$$B_i = (M_i/VM_{avg}) \text{ (in seconds)} \tag{1}$$

where

$$VM_{avg} = (VM_1 + VM_2 + VM_3 + \ldots \ldots VM_m)/m \text{ (in MIPS)} \tag{2}$$

$$M_{avg} = (M_1 + M_2 + M_3 \ldots \ldots M_N)/N \text{ (in MI)} \tag{3}$$

$$M_{max} = \max\{M_1 + M_2 + M_3 \ldots \ldots M_N\} \text{ (in MI)} \tag{4}$$

$$M_{min} = \min\{M_1 + M_2 + M_3\ldots\ldots\ldots M_N\} \quad \text{(in MI)} \tag{5}$$

$$Q_s = CostPerSec + CostPerMem + CostPerStorage + CostPerBandwidth \tag{6}$$

Where
CostPerSec-   cost incurred per second in executing instructions,
CostPerMem-   cost incurred per byte of RAM memory usage,
CostPerStorage-   cost incurred per byte of disk space usage,
CostPerBandwidth-   cost incurred per byte of Bandwidth usage.

3.2   Inference System

Our algorithm has the ability to learn from itself, it learns from the current behaviour of the active cloudlets and based on the ability it converts the inputs to desired outputs making it user interactive too. Here the aim is to generate an optimum value for time quantum. Hence the algorithm takes cloudlet length and number of cloudlets as inputs and maps these inputs into an optimum size of time quantum. It has 3 modules:

3.2.1   Logic Module
Convert the inputs into the respective vague values to handle the dependability of the tasks in universe of disclosure [0,1]. These vague values are defined with true membership function (tq) and false membership function (fq). It takes two parameters Cloudlet length (M) and number of tasks (N) as inputs from database. Based on these inputs the tq and fq are calculated as below:

$$t_q = (M_{avg})/(M_{avg} + M_{max} + N) \tag{7}$$

$$f_q = (M_{avg})/(M_{avg} + M_{max} + N) \tag{8}$$

It handles the uncertainty and impreciseness by considering the in between dependability of different attributes of cloudlets during its decision making. It results in formation of these two membership functions on which the decision of our scheduler depends.

3.2.2   Grade Module
It defines the degree of accuracy of the vague values. It takes the two membership functions as inputs and by adding those two functions it returns the accuracy among the vague values as given below:

$$S_q = t_q + f_q \tag{9}$$

3.2.3 Inference Module

This returns the optimum value of time quantum. It fetches the value of Qs from the database and the degree of accuracy from the grade module. Finally, on the basis of the given rules it returns the size of time quantum Qd.

If (for $i = 1......N \mid A_i = = 0$) then

$$Q_d = S_q * Q_s \qquad (10)$$

else

$$Q_d = Q_s \qquad (11)$$

Where Qs is a Cost Quantum whose value is assigned by the Cloud Service Provider.

3.3 Virtual Machine Selection Algorithm

The total number of VMs created is 'm'. Now the first priority is to choose a suitable VM of certain MIPS for the arriving cloudlet according to the cloudlet length. Initially we have defined a cloudlet length acceptance range for each VM. The distribution of different ranges is calculated in the manner described.

Cmin, Cmax are minimum and maximum cloudlet length (in MI). MIPSi is the processing speed of VMi so the total of the processing speed of the VM's is

$$MIPS_{total} = (MIPS_1 + MIPS_2 + ...MIPS_m)/m \qquad (12)$$

x is defined as:

$$X = (C_{max} - C_{min})/MIPS_{total} \qquad (13)$$

fi denotes the MIPS of the VMi and since the VM's are arranged in order of the increasing order of the processing speed so $MIPS_{i+1} > MIPS_i$. The cloudlet acceptability ranges are depicted in Table 2. After the arrival of a cloudlet; it finds the suitable VM considering the cloudlet's length. The VM chosen in this phase is termed as targeted VM.

Table 2. Formulae to calculate upper and lower limits of the Virtual Machines [1]

VM id	VM lower limit (in MIPS)	VM upper limit (in MIPS)
VM_1	C_{min}	$C_{min} + f_{1x}$
VM_2	$C_{min} + f_{1x} + 1$	$C_{min} + f_{1x} + f_{2x}$
VM_3	$C_{min} + f_{1x} + f_{2x} + 1$	$C_{min} + f_{1x} + f_{2x} + f_{3x}$
VM_m	$C_{min} + f_{1x} + f_{2x} + f_{3x}......f_{m-1x} + 1$	$C_{min} + f_{1x} + f_{2x} + f_{3x}......f_{mx}$

3.4   Algorithm

Begin
Qs= static cost quantity assigned by the Cloud Service Provider
N= number of cloudlets
Initialize all the variables (inputs)
B= Burst time of the cloudlet
A= Arrival time of the Cloudlet
M= cloudlet length
P= User factor
RBT= B// initial value of remaining burst time
Do Loop 1...........N
Assign all cloudlets to Q1
Calculate Qd for Q1
End loop
Do Loop 1......N
Calculate the Response Ratio(RR) using equation:
RR= ((waiting time*P) + Burst Time)/Burst Time   (14)
End Loop
Sort the Queue in descending order of RR
Do Loop 1.......N
Schedule the cloudlet to targeted VM using the 3.3 VM Selection Algorithm
$M_i = M_i -$ (Targeted VM * Q_d)   (15)
$B_i = B_i - Q_d$ (16)
End Loop
Do loop 1.......N
If(M_i==0)
Cloudlet instructions are completely executed
(output: complete time of execution)
Else
Cloudlet moves to the lower queue Q_i where $2 \le i \le n$
End if
End loop
Calculate the dynamic time quantum for lower level queues Q_2 to Q_n using eq below
$Q_d = S_q(Q_d + N)$ (17)
Go to Begin until N==0
End

3.5   Working of the Algorithm

The workflow of the algorithm is as follows-

- Tasks are submitted to the Cloud Information Service (CIS) no sooner than they have arrived. These tasks are known as Cloudlets here.
- These set of cloudlets are constantly retrieved by the Broker (created by the CIS) who is responsible to submit them to data center.
- Within the Data center (DC) these cloudlets are assigned to a particular Host which has multiple Virtual Machines to execute these upon.
- The cloudlets are assigned to the VM's on the basis of the proposed CAMQU policy.
- The cloudlets have predefined User Factor value assigned by the CSP, the value is higher if the cloudlet has to time efficient and lower if cost efficient.
- A queue Q1 is created by assigning all the cloudlets to this Queue. Inference System (Sect. 3.2) is used to calculate the time quantum Q_d for Q1. It is the amount of time for which all the cloudlets in Q1 are executed on the assigned VM.
- Q1 is now sorted in descending order on the basis of Response Ratio calculated as per the Eq. 14 and each cloudlets target VM is found using the VM selection Algorithm 3.3
- Cloudlets are now executed on their respective target VM for exact time quantum Q_d of that queue thus eliminating the need of a Load Balancing and resolving problem of starvation
- Cloudlets when executed for time Q_d are pre-empted, if they cloudlet length is not zero then they are moved to lower Queue Q2(a new lower priority queue) whereas if cloudlet length is zero then the task has been completed.
- Once the higher priority Queue Q1 is completely executed the lower priority Queue Q2's execution begins with above 4 steps repeated for it.
- The incomplete cloudlets are again shifted to a lower priority queue Q3 and so on until all the cloudlets are completely executed.

4   Experiment

The proposed algorithm CAMQU has been described and analyzed with help of a suitable example. Due to space constraint, ten cloudlets and three Virtual Machines in a host within a data center has been considered in these experiments. The proposed algorithm is simulated under a Java Environment.

Table 2 Sect. 3.3 Virtual Machine Selection Algorithm represents the formulae for calculating the upper and lower limits of the Virtual Machines specifying the range of cloudlets they can accept.

From Table 3; $M_{max} = 100$, $M_{min} = 10$, Therefore $M_{avg} = 450/10 = 45$, $VM_{avg} = (1 + 2 + 3)/3 = 2$ And $t_q = 45/(45 + 100 + 10) = 0.29$.

Table 3. Reference cloudlet

	C0	C1	C2	C3	C4	C5	C6	C7	C8	C9
Arrival time	0	0	0	0	0	0	0	0	0	0
Size (MI)	100	10	50	30	90	20	20	40	80	10
UserFactor (P)	1	1	1	1	1	1	1	0	1	1

Table 4. Reference VM

	VM0	VM1	VM2
Processing speed (MIPS)	1	2	3

$$f_q = 45/(45 + 10 + 10) = 0.69 \text{ and } S_q = 0.29 + 0.69 = 0.98 \ Q_s = 3.051$$

$$C_{max} = 100, \ C_{min} = 10, \ \text{MIPS}_{total} = 6 \text{ x} = (100 - 10)/6 = 15$$

The cloudlets with cloudlet size not equal to zero are moved on into the lower queue, Queue2. Now a new Queue, Queue2 is formed which has the following details (Tables 5, 6, 7, 8, 9, 10, 11 and 12).

Table 5. Queue 1 with various factors before execution

Cloudlet Id	Burst Time	Remaining burst time	Length	Target VM	Remaining Length	Waiting time	Response ratio	Executed time
C0	50	-	100	VM2	-	-	-	-
C1	5	-	10	VM0	-	-	-	-
C2	25	-	50	VM1	-	-	-	-
C3	15	-	30	VM1	-	-	-	-
C4	45	-	90	VM2	-	-	-	-
C5	10	-	20	VM0	-	-	-	-
C6	10	-	20	VM0	-	-	-	-
C7	20	-	40	VM1	-	-	-	-
C8	40	-	80	VM2	-	-	-	-
C9	5	-	10	VM0	-	-	-	-

$Q_d = 0.98 * 3.051 = 2.99$ (the time quantum for Queue 1)

$$C_{max} = 91.03, \ C_{min} = 7.01, \ \text{MIPS}_{total} = 6 \text{ x} = (91.03 - 7.01)/6 = 14$$

The cloudlets with cloudlet size not equal to zero are moved on into the lower queue, Queue3. Cloudlets shown 0 cloudlet length left are completely executed. Queue2 is sorted on the basis of response ratio in descending order to form queue.

Table 6. Cloudlet length acceptability ranges of the VMs

VM	Lower Limit	Upper Limit
VM0	10	10 + 1*15 = 25
VM1	26	25 + 2*15 = 55
VM2	56	55 + 3*15 = 100

Table 7. Queue 1 with various factors after execution

Cloudlet id	Burst Time	Remaining burst time	Length	Target VM	New length	Waiting time	Response ratio	Executed time
C0	50	47.01	100	VM2	91.03	0	1.0	2.99
C1	5	2.01	10	VM0	7.01	0	1.0	2.99
C2	25	22.01	50	VM1	44.02	0	1.0	2.99
C3	15	12.01	30	VM1	24.02	2.99	1.24	2.99
C4	45	42.01	90	VM2	81.03	2.99	1.07	2.99
C5	10	7.01	20	VM0	17.01	2.99	1.42	2.99
C6	10	7.01	20	VM0	17.01	5.98	1.85	2.99
C7	20	17.01	40	VM1	34.02	5.98	1.35	2.99
C8	40	37.01	80	VM2	71.03	5.98	1.16	2.99
C9	5	2.01	10	VM0	7.01	8.97	5.46	2.99

Table 8. Queue2 with various factors before execution

Cloudlet id	Burst Time	Remaining burst time	Length	Target VM	Remaining length	Waiting time	Response ratio	Executed time
C9	2.01	-	7.01	VM0	-	-	-	2.99
C6	7.01	-	17.01	VM0	-	-	-	2.99
C5	7.01	-	17.01	VM0	-	-	-	2.99
C7	17.01	-	34.02	VM1	-	-	-	2.99
C3	12.01	-	24.02	VM1	-	-	-	2.99
C8	37.01	-	71.03	VM2	-	-	-	2.99
C4	42.01	-	81.03	VM2	-	-	-	2.99
C0	47.01	-	91.03	VM2	-	-	-	2.99
C2	22.01	-	7.01	VM1	-	-	-	2.99
C1	2.01	-	44.02	VM0	-	-	-	2.99

$Q_d = 0.98 * (2.99 + 10) = 12.73$(the time quantum for Queue 2)

Cmax = 52.84, Cmin = 4.28   MIPStotal = 6 x = $(52.84 - 4.28)/6 = 8.1$

Table 13 represents the Queue3 state after execution with various factors, the cloudlets with cloudlet size not equal to zero are moved on into the lower queue, Queue4.

Thus all the cloudlets have been executed completely.

Table 9. Cloudlet length acceptability ranges of the VMs

VM	Lower limit	Upper limit
VM0	7.01	7.01 + 1*14 = 21.01
VM1	22.01	21.01 + 2*14 = 49.01
VM2	50.01	91.01

Table 10. Queue2 with various factors after execution

Cloudlet id	Burst Time	Remaining burst time	Length	Target VM	Remaining length	Waiting time	Response ratio	Executed time
C9	2.01	−5.0	7.01	VM0	0	0.0	-	10.0
C6	7.01	−5.72	17.01	VM0	4.28	7.01	−0.22	15.72
C5	7.01	−5.72	17.01	VM0	4.28	19.74	−2.45	15.72
C7	17.01	4.28	34.02	VM1	8.56	0.0	1.0	15.72
C3	12.01	0	24.02	VM1	0	12.73	-	15.0
C8	37.01	24.28	71.03	VM2	32.84	0.0	1.0	15.72
C4	42.01	29.28	81.03	VM2	42.84	12.73	1.43	15.72
C0	47.01	34.28	91.03	VM2	52.84	25.46	4.74	15.72
C2	22.01	9.28	44.02	VM1	18.56	25.46	3.74	15.72
C1	2.01	−5.0	7.01	VM0	0	32.47	-	10.0

Table 11. Queue 3 with various factors before execution

Cloudlet id	Burst Time	Remaining burst time	Length	Target VM	Remaining length	Waiting time	Response ratio	Executed time
C2	9.28	-	18.56	VM1	-	-	-	15.72
C0	34.28	-	52.84	VM2	-	-	-	15.72
C4	29.28	-	42.84	VM2	-	-	-	15.72
C8	24.28	-	32.84	VM2	-	-	-	15.72
C7	4.28	-	8.56	VM0	-	-	-	15.72
C6	−5.72	-	4.28	VM0	-	-	-	15.72
C5	−5.72	-	4.28	VM0	-	-	-	15.72

$Q_d = 0.98 * (12.73 + 7) = 19.34$ (the time quantum for Queue 3)

Table 12. Cloudlet length acceptability ranges of the VMs

VM	Lower Limit	Upper Limit
VM0	4.28	12.38
VM1	13.38	28.58
VM2	29.58	52.84

Table 13. Queue3 with various factors after execution

Cloudlet id	Burst Time	Remaining burst time	Length	Target VM	Remaining length	Waiting time	Response ratio	Executed time
C2	9.28	0	18.56	VM1	0	0	-	25.0
C0	34.28	16.67	52.84	VM2	0	0	-	33.34
C4	29.28	15	42.84	VM2	0	17.61	-	30.0
C8	24.28	13.34	32.84	VM2	0	28.55	-	26.67
C7	4.28	−4.28	8.56	VM0	0	0	-	24.28
C6	−5.72	−10.0	4.28	VM0	0	8.56	-	20.0
C5	−5.72	−10.0	4.28	VM0	0	12.84	-	20.0

5 Results and Analysis

The performance of the proposed algorithm is compared and analyzed with three existing algorithms i.e. Round Robin Allocation (RRA), First Come First Serve (FCFS) and Shortest Job First (SJF). The simulated results are evaluated and analyzed in terms of completion time. The performance is measured by setting up different simulation environments with varying number of cloudlets and the Virtual Machines. The results are as:

5.1 Completion Time

The Table 14 and Fig. 1 represents the execution time required by various cloudlets when loaded with ten cloudlets and three Virtual Machines given in the Tables 3 and 4.

Table 14. Execution time of various cloudlets via proposed algorithm

Cloudlet id(on X axis)	Execution time of cloudlets via proposed algorithm(on Y axis)(in seconds)
C0	33.34
C1	10.0
C2	25.0
C3	15.0
C4	30.0
C5	20.0
C6	20.0
C7	24.28
C8	26.67
C9	10.0

The completion time as visible from the result have largely decreased for the large cloudlets and also lessened for the smaller cloudlets. Also the algorithm is user interactive and removes the problem of starvation as seen in the other algorithms. The

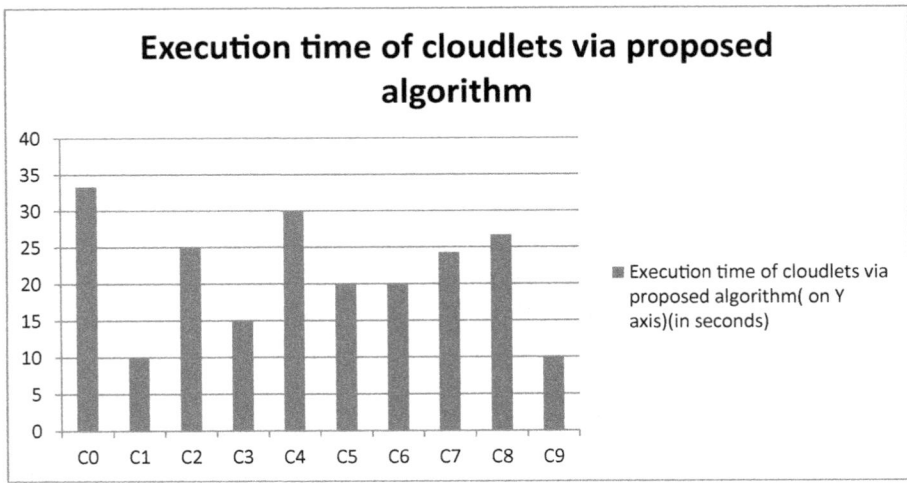

Fig. 1. Graph depicting completion time of cloudlets using proposed algorithm

Fig. 2 is a clear depiction that as the size of the cloudlets increases the algorithm gives better results. It is a nature of realistic approach (Table 15).

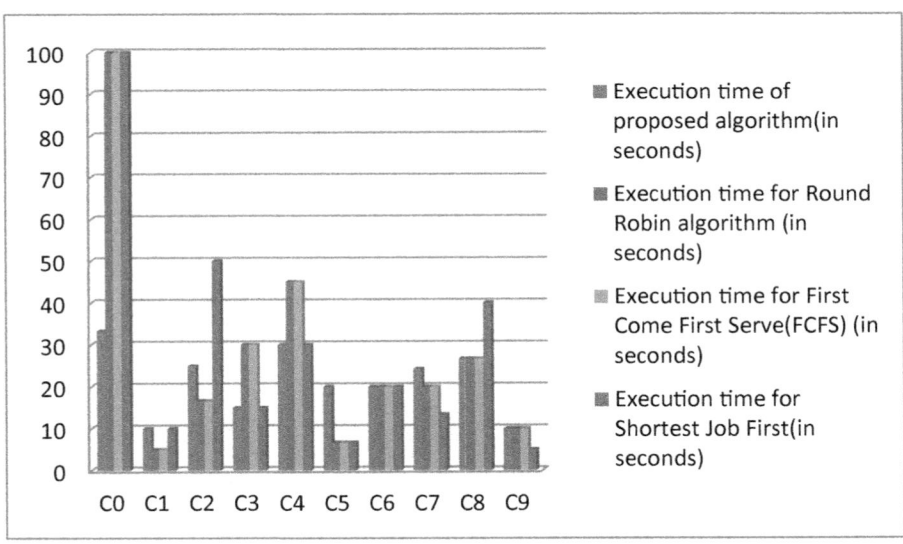

Fig. 2. Using bar graph to compare proposed algorithm with RRA, FCFS & SJF

Table 15. Comparison of various algorithms with proposed algorithm CAMQU

Cloudlet id	Execution time of proposed algorithm (in seconds)	Execution time for Round Robin algorithm (in seconds)	Execution time for First Come First Serve (FCFS) (in seconds)	Execution time for Shortest Job First (in seconds)
C0	33.34	100.0	100.0	100.0
C1	10.0	5.0	5.0	10.0
C2	25.0	16.67	16.67	50.0
C3	15.0	30.0	30.0	15.0
C4	30.0	45.0	45.0	30.0
C5	20.0	6.67	6.67	6.67
C6	20.0	20.0	20.0	20.0
C7	24.28	20.0	20.0	13.34
C8	26.67	26.67	26.67	40.0
C9	10.0	10.0	10.0	5.0

6   Conclusion and Future Scope

This work highlights a new cloudlet allocation policy which provides better completion time for the cloudlets and also makes the process more interactive for both the client and the Cloud Service Provider. Hence the Quality of Service (QoS) and the resource utilization of the overall system have been improved in comparison to the existing cloudlet allocation policies. The completion time of longer cloudlets decreases as they are assigned to VM's with higher MIPS whereas the problem of starvation of shorter cloudlets is removed. In terms of Quality of Service the CSP is able to set costs using the constant Qs and user can decide if it wants the processing to be time or cost efficient.

In our future study, we shall focus on taking this to a new dimension of green cloud computing by controlling and decreasing the power consumption in the execution of the cloudlets.

References

1. Banerjee, S., Adhikari, M., Chaudhary, K.R., Biswas, U.: Development and analysis of a new cloudlet allocation strategy for QoS improvement in cloud. Arab. J. Sci. Eng. **40**(5), 1409–1425 (2015). ISSN 1319-8025
2. Raheja, S., Dadhich, R., Rajpal, S.: Designing of vague logic based multilevel feedback queue scheduler. Egypt. Inform. J. **17**, 125–137 (2016)
3. Bhatia, W., Buyya, R., Ranjan, R.: CloudAnalyst: a CloudSim based visual modeller for analysing cloud computing environments and applications. In: 24th IEEE International Conference on Advanced Information Networking and Applications, pp. 446–452
4. Calheiros, R.N., Ranjan, R., De Rose, C.A.F., Buyya, R.: CloudSim: a novel framework for modelling and simulation of cloud computing infrastructures and services

5. Calheiros, R.N., Ranjan, R. De Rose, C.A.F., Buyya, R.: CloudSim: A Toolkit for Modelling and Simulation of Cloud Computing Environments and Evaluation of Resource Provisioning Algorithms. Wiley Online Library wileyonlinelibrary.com

6. Parsa, S., Entezari-Maleki, R.: RASA: a new grid cloudlet scheduling algorithm. World Appl. Sci. J. 7, 152–160. (Special Issue of Computer & IT)

7. Liu, X., Chen, B., Qiu, X., Cai, Y., Huang, K.: Scheduling parallel jobs using migration & consolidation in the cloud. In: Hindwai Publications of Mathematical Problems in Engineering, July 2012

8. Pop, F.: Communication model for decentralized meta-scheduler in grid environments. In: Proceedings of The Second International Conference on Complex, Intelligent and Software Intensive System, Second International Workshop on P2P, Parallel, Grid and Internet computing – 3PGIC-2008 (CISIS 2008). Barcelona, Spain, pp. 315–320. IEEE Computer Society (2008). ISBN 0-7695-3109-1

9. Livny, M., Melman, M.: Load balancing in homogenous broadcast distributed systems. In: Proceedings of the ACM Computer Network: Performance Symposium, pp. 47–55 (2011)

10. Amalarethinam, D.I.G., Muthulakshmi, P.: An overview of the scheduling policies and algorithms in grid computing. Int J. Res. Rev. Comput. Sci. 2(2), 280–294 (2011)

Performance Analysis of Hybrid CPU Scheduling Algorithm in Multi-tasking Environment

Harvinder Singh[✉], Sachin Kumar Sarin, Arushi Patel, and Supriya Sen

Department of Informatics, School of Computer Science Engineering,
University of Petroleum and Energy Studies, Dehradun, India
hsingh@ddn.upes.ac.in,
{kumar.sarinsachin14,arushipatel14,sen.supriya14}@stu.upes.ac.in

Abstract. High performance computing systems consists of many computer resources like servers, storage memory, application softwares, processors and networks etc. When a user submits a job, he specify the type of resources he need like nodes from clusters or large memory nodes. Job schedulers allocates a priority to every job waiting in the queue. The elevated priority job sits at the peak of the queue waiting for computer resources to become obtainable. The jobs are then executed again and adjustments are made to the queue based on certain parameters and respective priority levels of jobs after fixed quantum of time. In spite of various researches in the area of scheduling and optimization, still most of algorithms suffers from problems like convoy effect, indefinite blocking or starvation. In this research paper, hybrid algorithms, namely Round Robin with Shortest Job First (RRSJF), Round Robin with First Come First Serve (RRFCFS) and Round Robin with Priority (RRPR) has been proposed to overcome such problems. Considering average waiting time and average turnaround time, a simulation based analysis of proposed algorithms was performed using C programming language. The improvement in average waiting time is more relevant with increasing the number of tasks in case of Round Robin with Shortest Job First algorithm (RRSJF). It is proved and validated by comparative analysis among proposed hybrid algorithms in results and discussion section of the research paper.

Keywords: Task · Resources · Scheduling · Time quantum
Convoy effect · Starvation · Hybrid algorithms · Average waiting time
Average turnaround time

1 Introduction

In computing, scheduling is the technique by which task defined by users is assigned to resources that executes the tasks [1]. Scheduling of CPU is a methodology that permits one task to make utilization of the CPU while the execution

© Springer Nature Singapore Pte Ltd. 2018
P. Bhattacharyya et al. (Eds.): NGCT 2017, CCIS 828, pp. 183–197, 2018.
https://doi.org/10.1007/978-981-10-8660-1_14

of another task is on hold i.e. in waiting state due to scarcity of any resource like I/O etc., so that full utilization of CPU can be made [2]. The goal of CPU scheduling is to make the system efficient, swift and equitable [3]. It is the duty of CPU scheduler to capture another process from the ready queue to run next, at any moment the CPU becomes idle. Heterogeneous processes are scheduled by the process scheduler and allocated to CPU deployed on some scheduling algorithms. The following scheduling algorithms are classified as non-preemptive or preemptive [4,5]. Non-preemptive scheduling algorithms are build for a task that enters the executing state, cannot be preempted or occupied till the time it finishes its assigned duration, but the preemptive scheduling algorithms relies on priority of the processes and here the scheduler will acquire lower priority processes anytime when a process that is having high priority gets enrolls into a ready state queue. The traditional scheduling algorithms are [6]:

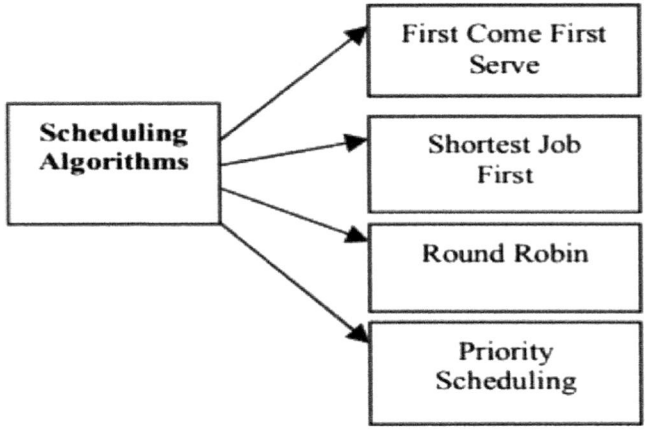

Fig. 1. Different scheduling algorithms [5]

First come first serve: In FCFS, on the basis of first come and first serve, the jobs are executed. It is also termed as Non-preemptive algorithm. The FCFS has simple implementation as well [7,8]. The implementation of this algorithm is based on FIFO queue. It has less efficiency in performance as the average waiting time is quite large (called, convoy effect) [9].

Shortest job first: The Shortest Job first scheduling algorithm is a non preemptive scheduling algorithm. It chooses among the best way possible to minimize waiting time. In batch systems, the implementation of shortest job first is quite easy where it is required to know CPU time in advance. The implementation of SJF is quite impossible in systems that has interactive nature, where required CPU time is not known in advance. The processor should have an idea earlier that how much amount of time a process will require for its execution [7].

Priority scheduling: The Priority scheduling algorithm is also termed as non-preemptive algorithm. This scheduling algorithm is the most common scheduling algorithms in batch systems. Here, every task is allocated a priority. Those tasks that have the highest priority are implemented first [7]. Those tasks that has equal priority are implemented on the basis of first come first serve. The priority could be assigned to processes according to their memory needs, time needs or any different resources requirements.

Shortest remaining time first: Shortest remaining time first (SRTF) scheduling algorithm is the pre-emptive model of the Shortest Job First algorithm [7]. Here job is allocated to the processor that is near to completion but it can be preempted by a current ready job with much shorter completion time [6]. The implementation of SRTF is impossible in those systems that are interactive in nature, where CPU time is not known earlier, that is required. It is used in batch environments many a times where the jobs are short in nature, needs high priority.

Round robin scheduling: Round Robin algorithm is pre-emptive in nature [7,10]. In Round robin each process is given a time slot, which is fix in nature, called Time Quantum. For a specific time interval, when a process is executed so it is preempted and rest of the remaining processes are executed for the specified time period [11]. Context switching technique is used here to save states of preempted processes.

2   Literature Review

To make out the finest use of CPU and not to misuse any CPU cycle, CPU would be running most of the time (Ideally 100% of the time) [12–14]. Considering a real system, the consumption of CPU should extent from around 40% i.e. lightly loaded to 90% i.e. heavily loaded. A scheduling structure allows one process to utilize the CPU while the next process is waiting for I/O, and making full utilization of lost or misplaced CPU cycles [15]. The scheduler is a module of an operating system that decides the next jobs that are allowed into the system and the another processes to execute. The Operating systems are classified into three distinct scheduler types: a long-term scheduler, a mid-term or medium-term scheduler, and a short-term scheduler [16]. The motive of scheduling algorithm is to lessen resource starvation [17] and to ensure equality among the processes deploying the resources.

The term Scheduling tackles with the complexities of deciding which of the requests is to be allocated resources. Scheduling algorithms are of different types. Scheduling decisions of CPU may took place when a process [2,18]:

(i)   Performs switching from running state to waiting state,
(ii) Performs switching from running state to ready state,
(iii) Performs switching from waiting state to ready,
(iv) Performs termination

Scheduling technique that resides under points 1 and 4 are entitled as non-preemptive scheduling techniques whereas the remaining scheduling techniques are entitled as preemptive scheduling techniques [6].

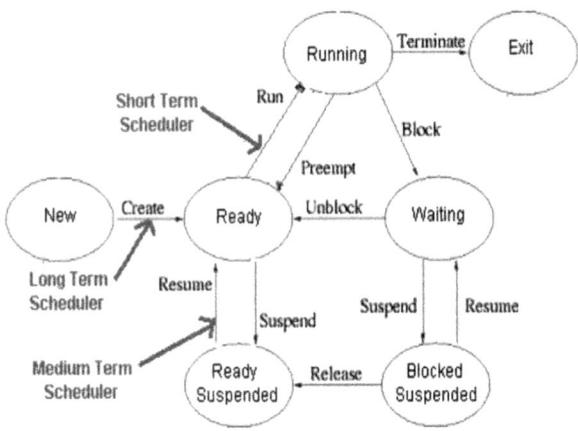

Fig. 2. Process life cycle [16]

2.1   Related Work

The main aim of concurrent execution is enhancing the performance of CPU by means of some process executing everytime in the Central Processing Unit. During the time of execution in the operating system, a task or a process changes its position that possibly be in one of the states i.e. new, ready, waiting, running, terminate. The scheduler's job is to select processes from the state queues. There is a crucial factor that influences the performance of the computer system is, scheduling of processor. The computer system's efficiency is increased when all the processes are allocated by distinct scheduling algorithms, to a processor in a specific manner. Assigning processes to be executed by the processor is the main objective of CPU scheduler. In this research paper, the author has proposed a new hybrid algorithm that contains both features of pre-emptive [4] and nonpre-emptive algorithm to find a solution for CPU Scheduling. The proposed algorithm is based on the technique of Novel algorithm. The main objective of proposed hybrid algorithm is to optimize average waiting time and average turnaround time for the specified number of tasks and enhances the novel algorithm [10,19]. In concurrent executing systems i.e. in systems where various processes reside in memory, organization of processes is very significant so that CPU always has one to execute. Scheduling of CPU is the foundation of concurrent executing operating systems. CPU executes one process at a point and switches between processes to enhance CPU utilization. CPU scheduling approach helps in selecting the next process to be executed by the CPU. The methodology of CPU scheduling is one of the most remarkable activities accomplished by the operating system which helps in increasing the throughput of the computer system therefore if the implementation of scheduling will improve then their computer system will become more productive [20]. The approach which is used for increasing the speed up factor is 'Pipelining'. The Pipelining technique can be implemented to any CPU scheduling algorithm to optimize its performance. The analysis presents that the proposed algorithm is more appropriate than the traditional scheduling algorithms. The performance is improved by 40% to 50% [21, 22]. In concurrent executing system, the distribution computes time among program is managed by a clock cycles in CPU, which obstructs program execution more often and initiates a monitor program. The system stores the registers of the obstructed program and assigns the next session of computing time to another program. Swapping from one program to another is also carry whenever a program waits for the completion of I/O. Thus although the system is only able to execute one instruction at a certain time of interval, concurrent execution creates the vision that programs are being executed simultaneously, mainly because peripherals alloted to different programs indeed operate in concurrently [13]. A few transmission scheduling algorithms are throughput efficient and rest of them are equality efficient. In this research paper, a new transmission scheduling algorithm has been proposed to improve outcome with acceptable equality. The procedure used here targets to take the benefit of two scheduling algorithms that are already existing. The results of merged algorithm shows that the proposed scheduler provides much better throughput as compared to the proportional fair scheduler with reasonable fairness [3]. The methodology of scheduling is used for managing the order of process. It is done to be performed by a CPU of a computer. A few of the popular traditional CPU scheduling algorithms are First Come First Served (FCFS), Shortest Job First (SJF), Priority Scheduling, Round Robin (RR) and Shortest Remaining Time First (SRTF). Many of the traditional CPU scheduling algorithms focuses on maximizing CPU utilization and throughput and minimizing turnaround time, response time, waiting time, and number of context switches for a set of requests. In this paper, an enhanced Round Robin Scheduling Algorithm has been proposed with the simulated results [22].

3   Proposed Approach

Scheduling of CPU is the methodology by which tasks or data are given access to system compatible resources. It is usually perform to load balance or load equilibrium and share system compatible resources efficiently to gain an objective quality of service. The requirement arises for a scheduling algorithm from the need for most up to date systems of today, to perform multitasking and multiplexing. The main challenge is to fulfill the requirement of an efficient scheduling algorithm. This necessity gave birth to hybrid algorithm which will be created by combining any two or more basic scheduling algorithms. The goal of this research paper is to design and develop a hybrid scheduling algorithm and compare it with existing algorithms on the basis of certain parameters.

3.1   Notations

The provocation is to make the comprehensive body of system as "efficient" and "fair" as possible, of concern to diversifying and often dynamic circumstances, and where "efficien" and "fair" are rather subjective expressions, often concerned to shifting priority policies. Notations and variable definitions used in the proposed algorithm are defined in Table 1 as follows:

Table 1. Notations

Symbol	Meaning
p	Process number
n	Variable to store the process number till the limit user enters
g	Reference variable
at	Arrival time
bt	Burst time
ct	Completion time
wt	Waiting time
rt	Reference variable to store sorted array
pr	Priority
tq	Time quantum
tat	Turn around time
pos	Refers to position
avgwt	Average waiting time
avgtat	Average turnaround time
remain	Reference variable
temp	Reference variable
counter	Counter variable to count the occurrence

4   Design and Implementation of Proposed Algorithms

In this research paper, the Traditional Scheduling Algorithms are merged in such a way that they can become more optimized and efficient by the combination and designing of the modified ones.

4.1   Round Robin with First Come First Serve Algorithm

Use Cases refers to the diagrams required to build any software project. They are fed into the design phase to define the technical road map. Use case diagrams answer what will the system do? Use Cases are tools for defining user interaction requirements. They are introduced as a method for defining the software solutions using a diagrammatic representation. In this research paper, there are three Use case diagrams that define the working of hybrid algorithms over traditional Scheduling Algorithms. Use Case Diagram of Round Robin with First Come First Serve Hybrid Algorithm is shown in Fig. 1.

Use case diagram of Round Robin with First come first serve begins initially with the sorting of algorithms using selection sort technique, then execution of tasks and then finally calculating the optimized average waiting and turnaround time.

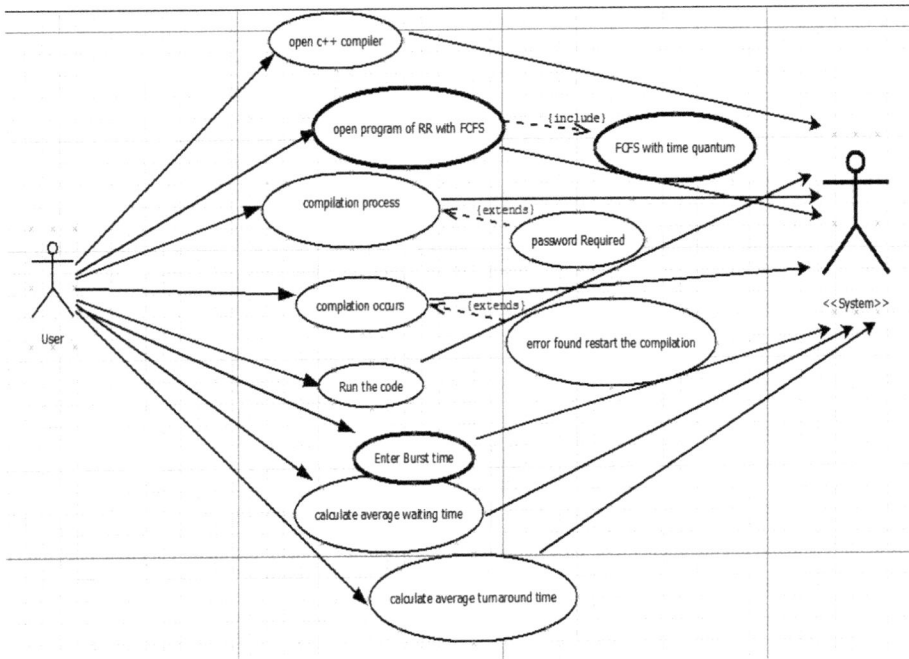

Fig. 3. Use case diagram for Round Robin with First Come First Serve

Pseudocode of Round Robin with First Come First Serve Hybrid Algorithm
Data: p, bt, at
Result: avgwt and avgtat
Start initialization;
tat=0, wt=0, total=0, flag=0;
Read p, bt, at;
for *i= 1 to n* **do**
| Display p, bt and at;
end
;
Sort the p, bt, at in ascending order using selection sort;
Read time quantum, tq from the user;
Display p, at, bt;
compute turnaround time, tat=ct*at;
compute waiting time, wt=tat*bt;
compute average waiting time, avgwt=wt*1.0/n;
compute average turnaround time, avgtat=tat*1.0/n;
Display avgwt and avgtat;
Stop

Algorithm 1. RRFCFS Algorithm

Algorithm 1 shows the pseudo code of Round Robin with First Come First Serve Hybrid Algorithm. The algorithms are sorted initially using the selection sort technique and then they are executed according to their arrival, so as to calculate the average turnaround time and average waiting time.

4.2   Round Robin with Shortest Job First Algorithm

Use Case Diagram of Round Robin with Shortest Job First Hybrid Algorithm is shown in Fig. 2. It begins initially with the sorting of processes using quick sort technique, then execution of processes and then finally calculating the optimized average waiting and turnaround time.

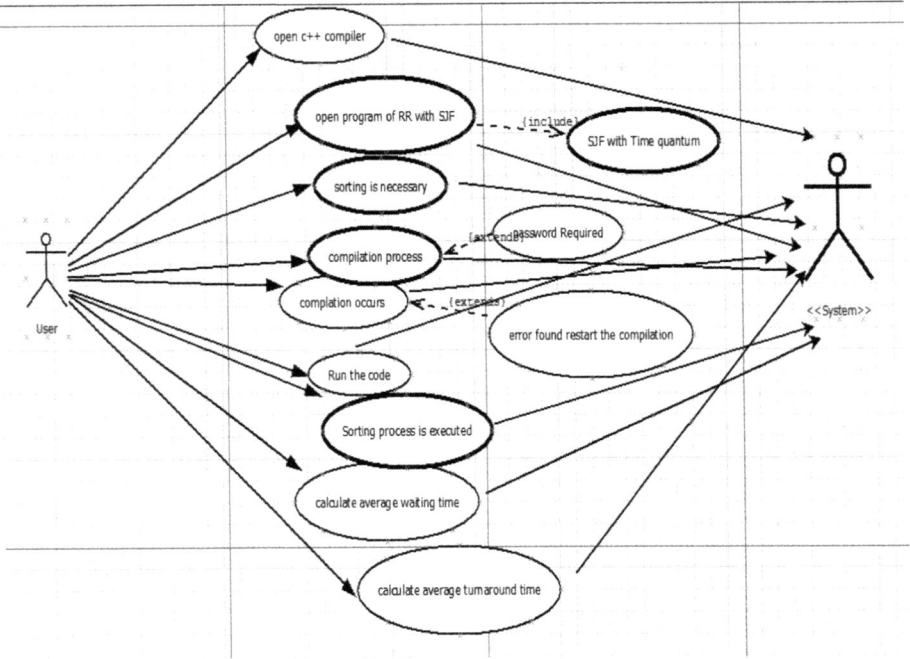

Fig. 4. Use case diagram for Round Robin with Shortest Job First

Pseudocode of Round Robin with Shortest Job First Hybrid Algorithm:

Algorithm 2 shows the pseudo code of Round Robin with Shortest Job First Hybrid Algorithm. The processes are sorted initially using the quick sort technique and then they are executed according to the respective time quantum, so as to calculate the average turnaround time and average waiting time.

Data: p, bt, at
Result: avgwt and avgtat
Start initialization;
tat=0, wt=0, total=0, flag=0;
Read p, bt, at;
quicksort(rt,0,n-1);
for *i= 1 to n* **do**

> Read time quantum from user;
> Display p, bt, gt and at;
> compute turnaround time, tat=ct*at;
> compute waiting time, wt=tat*bt;
> compute average waiting time, avgwt=wt*1.0/n;
> compute average turnaround time, avgtat=tat*1.0/n;

end
Display avgwt and avgtat;
Stop

Algorithm 2. RRSJF Algorithm

4.3   Round Robin with Priority Scheduling Algorithm

Use Case Diagram of Round Robin with Priority Scheduling Hybrid Algorithm is shown in Fig. 3. It begins initially with the sorting of processes using selection sort technique, then execution of processes and then finally calculating the optimized average waiting and turnaround time.

Pseudocode of Round Robin with Priority Scheduling Hybrid Algorithm:

Data: p, bt, at
Result: avgwt and avgtat
Start initialization;
tat=0, wt=0, total=0, flag=0;
Read p, bt, at, pr;
for *i= 0 to n* **do**

> Read bt and at from user;

end
;
Sort the p, bt, pr in ascending order using selection sort;
Read time quantum, tq from the user;
Display p, at, bt;
compute turnaround time, tat=ct*at;
compute waiting time, wt=tat*bt;
compute average waiting time, avgwt=wt*1.0/n;
compute average turnaround time, avgtat=tat*1.0/n;
Display avgwt and avgtat;
Stop

Algorithm 3. RRPR Algorithm

Algorithm 3 shows the pseudo code of Round Robin with Priority Scheduling Hybrid Algorithm. The processes are sorted initially using the selection sort

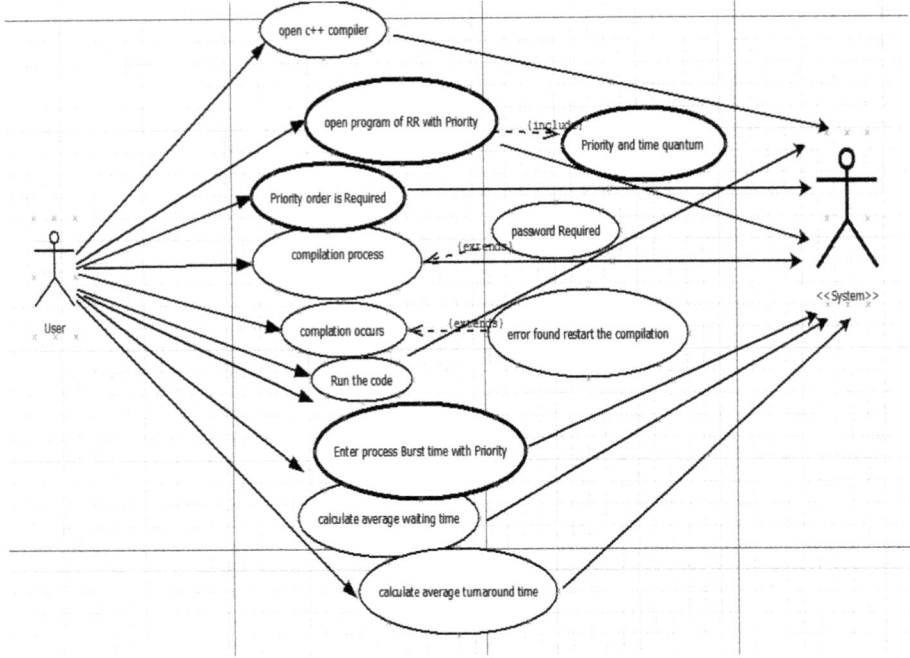

Fig. 5. Use case diagram for Round Robin with Priority Scheduling Algorithm

technique and then they are executed according to the respective priority, so as to calculate the average turnaround time and average waiting time.

5   Results and Discussions

As graph is the method of representing pictorial way of relationships between measurable quantities in nature and a graph is used to show how one quantity changes with respect to another quantity. In this research paper, graphs represent the relationship between number of processes with respect to average waiting time and average turnaround time, so as to measure the finite optimization of various hybrid algorithms.

Figure 4 shows the graphical representation of the turn around time w.r.t to number of processes for various hybrid algorithms like Round Robin with Shortest job first, Round Robin with Priority and Round Robin with First Come First Serve. Here x axis represents number of processes and y axis represents Turnaround Time.

Figure 5 shows the average turnaround time of the different hybrid algorithms i.e. Round Robin with Shortest job first, Round Robin with Priority and Round Robin with First Come First Serve. This graph defines the efficiency

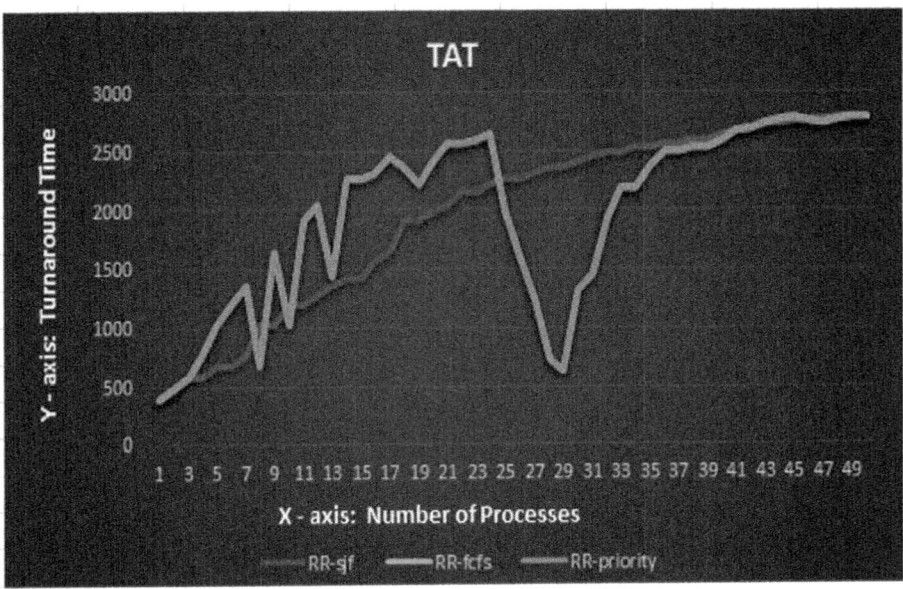

Fig. 6. Turn around time

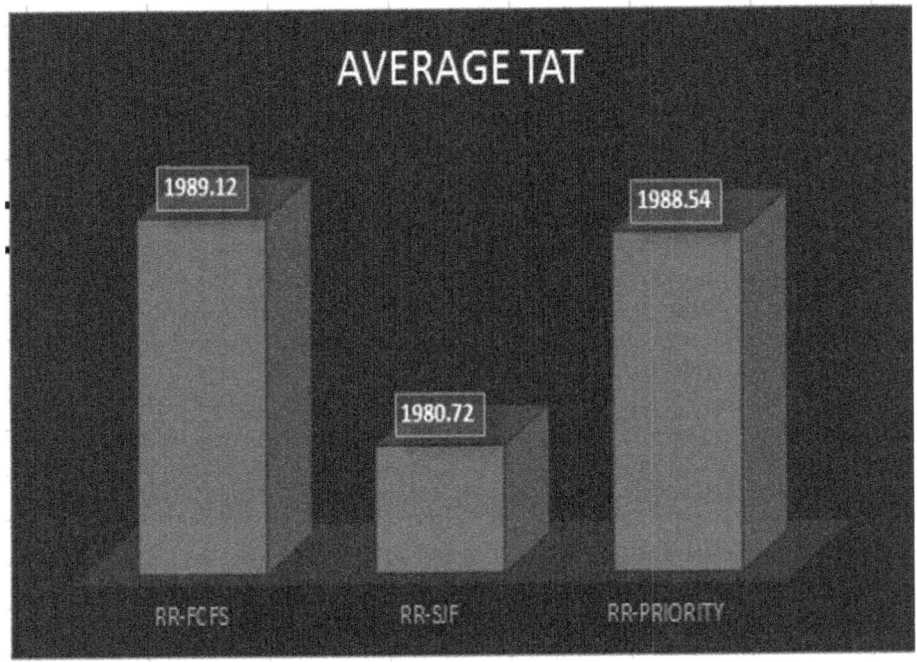

Fig. 7. Average turn around time

and throughput based on the turnaround time parameter of the various hybrid scheduling algorithms.

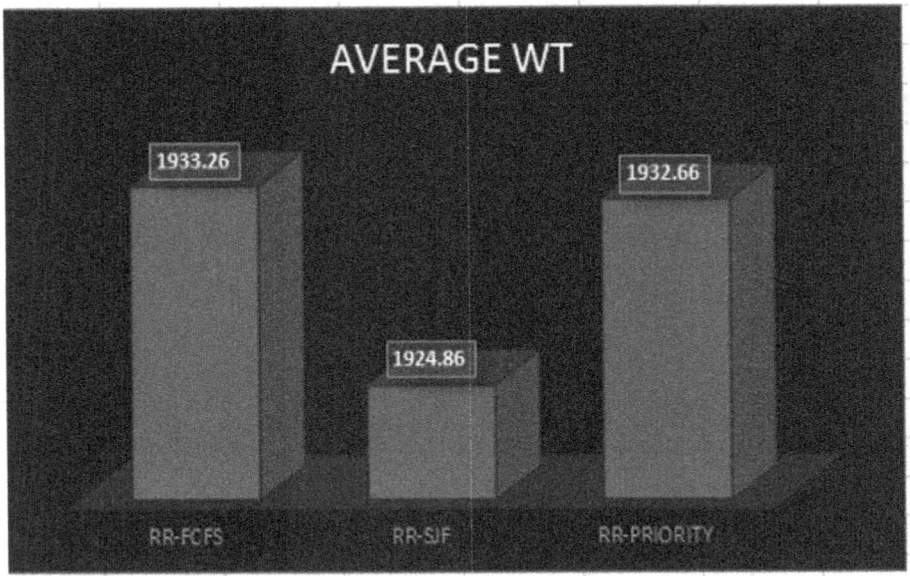

Fig. 8. Average waiting time

The average waiting time of different hybrid algorithms i.e. Round Robin with Shortest job first, Round Robin with Priority and Round Robin with First Come First Serve is shown in Fig. 6. This graph defines the efficiency and throughput based on the waiting time parameter of the various hybrid scheduling algorithms.

The waiting time of various hybrid algorithms i.e. Round Robin with Shortest job first, Round Robin with Priority and Round Robin with First Come First Serve is shown in Fig. 7. In this graph, x-axis represents number of processes and y-axis represents Waiting Time.

Table 2 shows quantitative analysis of RR FCFS, RR SJF and RR PR hybrid algorithms that has been taken for 10 processes defines the turnaround time and waiting time for the respective hybrid algorithms. This experimental analysis depicts that RR SJF is the optimal algorithm among the other hybrid algorithms (Fig. 8).

Table 3 shows quantitative analysis of RR FCFS, RR SJF and RR PR hybrid algorithms that has been taken for 20 processes defines the turnaround time and waiting time for the respective hybrid algorithms. This experimental analysis shows that the RR SJF is the optimal algorithm among the other hybrid algorithms, also if taken for more number of processes (Fig. 9).

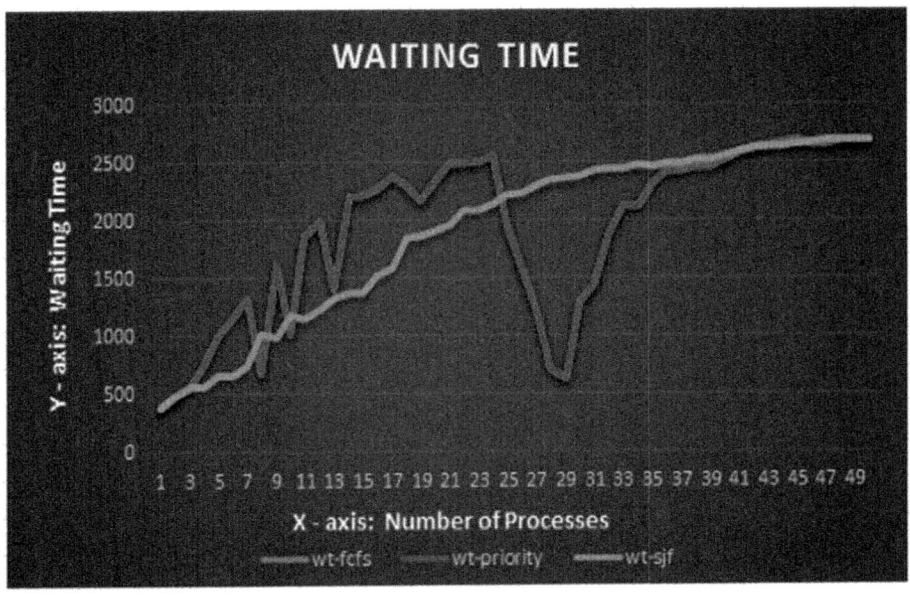

Fig. 9. Waiting time

Table 2. Analysis for 10 processes

RR FCFS (TQ = 2)			RR SJF (TQ = 2)			RR PR (TQ = 2)		
Process no.	TAT	WT	Process no.	TAT	WT	Process no.	TAT	WT
P[5]	188	169	P[1]	180	158	P[5]	188	169
P[1]	200	178	P[2]	200	172	P[1]	200	178
P[2]	250	222	P[3]	250	219	P[2]	250	222
P[3]	279	248	P[4]	279	220	P[3]	279	248
P[6]	307	271	P[5]	305	286	P[6]	307	271
P[7]	368	321	P[6]	366	330	P[7]	368	321
P[8]	393	340	P[7]	391	344	P[8]	393	340
P[9]	400	345	P[8]	398	345	P[9]	400	345
P[4]	407	348	P[9]	407	352	P[4]	407	348
P[10]	409	349	P[10]	409	349	P[10]	409	349

Table 3. Analysis for 20 processes

RR FCFS (TQ = 2)			RR SJF (TQ = 2)			RR PR (TQ = 2)		
Process no.	TAT	WT	Process no.	TAT	WT	Process no.	TAT	WT
P[3]	325	307	P[1]	321	287	P[3]	325	307
P[17]	619	587	P[2]	589	536	P[17]	619	587
P[1]	627	593	P[3]	627	609	P[1]	627	593
P[7]	637	603	P[4]	629	586	P[7]	637	603
P[4]	792	749	P[5]	790	736	P[4]	792	749
P[19]	817	774	P[6]	791	714	P[19]	817	774
P[20]	874	827	P[7]	848	814	P[20]	874	827
P[2]	927	874	P[8]	927	849	P[2]	927	874
P[5]	929	875	P[9]	928	839	P[5]	929	875
P[10]	936	883	P[10]	930	877	P[10]	936	883
P[16]	948	894	P[11]	932	833	P[16]	948	894
P[14]	1071	1004	P[12]	1059	964	P[14]	1071	1004
P[6]	1140	1063	P[13]	1140	1048	P[6]	1140	1063
P[8]	1142	1064	P[14]	1142	1075	P[8]	1142	1064
P[15]	1200	1114	P[15]	1192	1106	P[15]	1200	1114
P[9]	1213	1124	P[16]	1213	1159	P[9]	1213	1124
P[13]	1227	1135	P[17]	1223	1191	P[13]	1227	1135
P[12]	1238	1143	P[18]	1236	1138	P[12]	1238	1143
P[18]	1244	1146	P[19]	1242	1199	P[18]	1244	1146
P[11]	1245	1146	P[20]	1245	1198	P[11]	1245	1146

6 Conclusion

The purpose of scheduling is to keep CPU busy all the time so that maximum CPU utilization can be achieved. This research paper provides an analytical overview of a merging of scheduling algorithms. Three of these algorithms were designed and merged in a structural programming language. These are the First-Come First-Served (FCFS) with the Round-Robin (RR), Shortest Job First (SJF) with Round Robin (RR), and Priority Algorithm with Round Robin (RR). After implementation and testing according to various testing parameters, the most efficient hybrid scheduling algorithm turned out to be the Shortest Job First with RR algorithm, and it has to be utilized with quite a small time slice. The longest and most time-consuming is Priority algorithm with Round Robin algorithm, because all the data structures and associated functionality has to be set up from scratch. The intermediate solution can be obtained from FCFS with Round Robin Algorithm and it has easy and straightforward design as compared to other two algorithms.

References

1. Sangwan, S., Sangwan, S.: An effective approach on scheduling algorithm in cloud computing. Int. J. Comput. Sci. Mob. Comput. **3**(6), 19–23 (2014)
2. Nasir, S., Shah, M., Zakaria, M.N.B., Kamil, A., Mahmood, B., Pal, A.J., Haron, N.: Agent based priority heuristic for job scheduling on computational grids. Procedia - Procedia Comput. Sci. **9**, 479–488 (2012)
3. Altubaishi, E.S.: An efficient hybrid scheduling algorithm for high speed cellular networks, no. 1, pp. 1–4 (2014)
4. Kishor, L., Goyal, D.: Comparative analysis of various scheduling algorithms. Int. J. Adv. Res. Comput. Eng. Technol. **2**(4), 1488–1491 (2013)
5. Qureshi, I.: CPU scheduling algorithms: a survey. Int. J. Adv. Netw. Appl. **5**, 1968–1973 (2014)
6. Patel, J., Solanki, A.K.: Performance enhancement of CPU scheduling by hybrid algorithms using genetic approach. Int. J. Adv. Res. Comput. Eng. Technol. **1**(4), 142–144 (2012)
7. Sukumar Babu, B., Neelima Priyanka, N., Sunil Kumar, B.: Efficient Round Robin CPU scheduling algorithm. Int. J. Eng. Res. Dev. **4**(9), 36–42 (2012)
8. Mishra, M.K.: An improved FCFS (IFCFS) disk scheduling algorithm. Int. J. Comput. Appl. **47**(13), 20–24 (2012)
9. Behzad, S., Fotohi, R., Effatparvar, M.: Queue based Job scheduling algorithm for cloud computing. Int. Res. J. Appl. Basic Sci. **4**(12), 3785–3790 (2013)
10. Hyytiä, E., Aalto, S.: On Round-Robin routing with FCFS and LCFS scheduling. Perform. Eval. **97**, 83–103 (2016)
11. Hwang, L.-C., Hsu, S.J., Wang, S.-Y., Huang, Y.-H.: A hybrid scheduling algorithm with low complexity: jumping virtual clock Round Robin, no. 1, pp. 1–6 (2005)
12. Giaccone, P., Prabhakar, B., Shah, D.: Randomized scheduling algorithms for high-aggregate bandwidth switches. IEEE J. Sel. Areas Commun. **21**(4), 546–559 (2003)
13. Harkut, D.G.: Comparison of different task scheduling algorithms in RTOS: a survey. Int. J. Adv. Res. Comput. Sci. Softw. Eng. **4**(7), 1236–1240 (2014)
14. Srivastav, M.K., Pandey, S., Gahoi, I., Namdev, N.K.: Fair priority Round Robin with dynamic time quantum: FPRRDQ. Int. J. Mod. Eng. Res. **2**(3), 876–881 (2012)
15. Yashvir, P.S., Prakash, O.: Selection of scheduling Algorithm. Int. J. Adv. Res. Comput. Sci. **1**(2), 1–9 (2012)
16. Gupta, A.K.: Hybrid CPU scheduling algorithm. Int. J. Comput. Sci. Inf. Technol. **6**(2), 1569–1572 (2015)
17. Akhtar, M., Hamid, B., Humayun, M.: An optimized shortest job first scheduling algorithm for CPU scheduling. J. Appl. Environ. Biol. Sci. **5**(12), 42–46 (2015)
18. Somani, J.S., Chhatwani, P.K.: Comparative study of different CPU. Int. J. Comput. Sci. Mob. Comput. **2**, 310–318 (2013)
19. Jain, S., Jain, S.: A review study on the CPU scheduling algorithms. Int. J. Adv. Res. Comput. Commun. Eng. **5**(8), 22–31 (2016)
20. Microprocessing, N.-H., Leonardo, R.: vol. 28, pp. 211–216 (1989)
21. Rosemarry, P., Singh, R., Singhal, P., Sisodia, D.: Grouping based job scheduling algorithm using priority queue and hybrid algorithm in grid computing. Int. J. Grid Comput. Appl. **3**(4), 55–65 (2012)
22. Shyam, R., Kumar, P.: Improved Round Robin with shortest job first scheduling. Int. J. Adv. Res. Comput. Sci. Softw. Eng. **5**(3), 156–162 (2015)

Location and Energy Based Hierarchical Dynamic Key Management Protocol for Wireless Sensor Networks

S. Christalin Nelson$^{(\boxtimes)}$ and J. Dhiviya Rose

University of Petroleum and Energy Studies, Dehradun, India
christalinnelson@gmail.com

Abstract. In wireless sensor networks (WSN), the multi-level dynamic key management scheme may result in high storage overhead. Also considering the residual battery power alone for dynamic key generation may not be accurate and secured. Hence, in the paper we had proposed to design a grid location and energy based hierarchical dynamic key management protocol in WSN. In this technique, the sensor nodes in the network are grouped into clusters with unique ID provided by the base station and assigned a primary encryption key. The network then selects the cluster heads based on their physical locations. Each cluster is in-turn divided into virtual grids so that each cluster head can have more grids. The process of dynamic key generation is initiated after formation of virtual grids to reduce the energy consumption in the network. By simulation results, we show the proposed technique reduces the energy consumption and enhances security.

Keywords: Wireless sensor networks · Key management · Clusters

1 Introduction

1.1 WSN

Wireless Sensor Network (WSN) is a group of sensor nodes where each node is embedded with a sensor to detect physical changes such as light, heat, pressure, etc. These resource constrained sensor nodes form a network and communicate with each other through the wireless medium. In recent days, the cost of sensor nodes had become cheap. Moreover, as these nodes are self-manageable and flexible for deployment the implementations of the task becomes much easier, but due to set backs including restricted battery, restricted processing power, and restricted memory, applications of WSNs has become a more renowned research area [1].

The applications of WSNs include target identification and surveillance in military, medical applications and various scientific investigation in civilian procedures. The data collected by various sensor nodes in the network is forwarded to the Base Station (BS) using a wireless channel [2]. Because of the small nature in size the sensors can be scattered ultimately forming an ad-hoc network, which ultimately leads in identification of a good cryptosystem that establishes a secure and communal trust in the wireless

© Springer Nature Singapore Pte Ltd. 2018
P. Bhattacharyya et al. (Eds.): NGCT 2017, CCIS 828, pp. 198–211, 2018.
https://doi.org/10.1007/978-981-10-8660-1_15

communication. Key Management is one of the main important issues of a secure cryptosystem in their operation with respect to the issues dealt with the management of keys [3].

1.2   Need for Key Management in WSN

In WSN, Key management protocols plays an important role in secure communication between individual sensor nodes (also realized as unicast), between groups of sensor nodes (also realized as multicast) and between nodes and base-station (also realized as broadcast). Key management comes as a package of components that helps in sharing secret keys between the communicating parties during the key establishment phase. There are three main categories of key management systems identified as symmetric, asymmetric and hybrid [1].

The main objective of key management techniques is to protect the data from being tampered by maintaining its integrity and accuracy. In order to achieve this, the key management protocol is mostly dependent on key sharing, key discovery, path key connections, key-revocation, re-keying and incremental inclusion of sensor nodes. Once generated, each key has a fixed lifetime. This is often termed as the life cycle of the key management process. The life cycle starts from key generation sub-process, key circulation, usage, storage, backup, recovery and finally ends-up in key destruction.

The hacker who physically captured some of the nodes in the network hampers the entire network by impersonating the nodes to send wrong information in an uniden- tified way giving a breach to the security. To efficiently protect data, dynamic key management has been introduced [4].

1.3   Dynamic Key Management in WSN

The promising key management techniques termed as Dynamic key management consist of set of operations which performs rekeying periodically or when the need for demand arises in the network. In this keying process due to the revocation of keys in the compromised nodes, dynamic key management protocol considerably boosts the survivability and network flexibility of the network. Usage of dynamic keys in the place of pre-deployed keys has proved in efficiency towards memory optimization by minimizing the number of keys stored by nodes. The frequent updating of keys decreases the adversaries to determine the network's key is a unique feature of this approach.

This technique of key management protects the network during the deployment phase and in the runtime phase. Depending upon the use of a central key controller or a distributer key controller the architecture can be classified as centralized or distributed. Rekeying is a process of achieving network survivability by replacing the set of key in a specified period manner. This rekeying process provides better support during the network capture by adding new nodes, thereby providing a security, if the network size changes. An efficient and organized rekeying mechanism is the major challenge in security [5, 6].

Energy Issues: Some of the energy issues in this key management include poor network scalability, energy consumption, communication overhead, number of message transmission, high computation, repetition of nodes and battery life.

Security Issues: Few notable issues in security includes, Physical tampering, Compromised node, Multi-hop transmission, Fake packets injection, Data availability, Scalability [7, 8].

1.4   Problem Identification

Due to the recent developments and invention of equipment in the field of wireless communication key distribution plays a significant role in WSN design. Hence providing key management in an efficient way is one of the essential things to be considered.

When the keys are managed dynamically through multi-level schemes [13], each node should collect the public key of its neighbor node from the agent called the Mobile Certification Authority (MCA). This process further adds to the overhead in communication and storage.

In one of the novel dynamic key management system suggested [15], the clusters are separated virtually to form virtual grids and energy consumption is achieved by making only one virtual grid active. The key management is dynamic and a polynomial and random number based pair-wise key is used. In this technique, neighboring cluster heads communicate using the distributed pre-key. Security and scalability are the two-main parameters achieved by this system. However, the formation of cluster and cluster heads (CH) is not vividly stated in this scheme and the dynamic key generation formula is ineffective.

VEBEK [16], considers only residual battery power alone for dynamic key generation, which may not be accurate and secured.

This study has facilitated to propose our new design of dynamic key management protocol in WSN using the variation in the grid location considering the energy based hierarchical approach.

2   Literature Review

The Energy Aware Group Diffie-Hellman key management (EAGDH) protocol for mobile wireless sensor networks proposed by He et al. [9] have reduced the computational burden on the low energy level sensor nodes. The proposed key management protocol provides significant improvement in maximizing the lifetime of networks. However, there occurs computation and communication overhead.

The system proposed by Zhang et al. [10] has a splay tree-based rekeying approach, which have proved to increase the network security especially in the security protocol LEACH. Based on the splay tree architecture the real-time rekey mechanism was triggered initially. The process of key change was done during the transfer of messages which provided its security against eavesdropping. The on-off cluster key mechanism is a challenging face in the runtime phase of the rekeying mechanism leads to increase in the energy consumption.

Bai [11] has proposed a technique of secret key sharing wherein he has merged the tiered structure of WSN with various dynamic keying scheme. His work has witnessed the increase in the security over captured attack and has reduced communication overhead. However, it has led increase in the storage overhead.

Lightweight key management approach proposed by Shen and Shi [12] has the efficient security engine embedded in the wireless sensor system which can identify if a node has its energy or it is compromised. This system can yield to cluster key storage burden and communication load.

Multi-level dynamic key management system proposed by Sahingoz [13] has proposed his system with embedded Unmanned Aerial Vehicle (UAV). This vehicle is responsible for key distribution and establishment of coordination between asymmetric keys. Later the nearby nodes communicate and creates the symmetric key which is used for achieving data encryption and mutual authentication. Apart from the storage issues the system is more scalable.

The various keying mechanism of securing inter and in clusters with the key refreshing on demand added with the mechanism of managing network scalability was proposed by Jeong et al. [14]. It has resulted with higher connectivity against impersonating when compared to most other systems. However, there occurs communication overhead in all the keying phases.

The construction of virtual grid from the cluster of nodes proposed by Haijun Liang has reduced energy consumption. The key management is implemented by adopting polynomial expressions and random number generation. The mathematical formula used is based on random number for each active node and head polynomial for the distribution of pre-key between active node and head leading to better performance on security and scalability.

The overall count of the transmission messages for rekeying process is reduced tremendously in the system proposed by Uluagac et al. [16] for WSNs. This also resulted in elimination of stale keys in the network. While monitoring the wireless system its observed the primitive properly expected for military applications is minimized usage of energy in the node by reducing transmission. In his proposed framework, the data a permutation code with the help of RC4 encryption. By increasing the size of the packet, the number of message communication is optimized resulted in an energy efficient solution in the network. However, the loss will be huge if there is no proper communication channel in case of packet loss.

Resource constrained scheme proposed by Zhang et al. [17] for deterministic key management focuses on usage of pairwise keys and the local cluster keys for establishment and maintenance, which has helped to fix some problems in the existing systems. The digital elliptic curve signature algorithm the merging of mobile sensor node and the new ones occur in a protected way. The dependency with the base station is removed to achieve higher flexibility with the variation of few centralized rekeying systems, which provide low computation and communication overhead.

3 Proposed System

3.1 Overview

An energy aware and grid location based hierarchical dynamic key management protocol used for WSN. An unique ID and a main encryption key was provided by the base station to the cluster formed by grouping few sensor nodes. The network then selects the cluster heads based on their physical locations. Each cluster is further divided into virtual grids so that each cluster head can have more grids. Then an efficient dynamic key is generated to reduce the energy consumption in virtual grid environment.

3.2 Estimating Energy Level of the Node

The energy consumed for/during data transmission is given using following Eq. (1)

$$Etx\,(n, d) = Eelec * n * \gamma_a * n * d * d \qquad (1)$$

where,

n = data packet
Eelec = energy consumed by sender and receiver node
γ_a = amplification energy
d = distance

The energy consumption during the data capturing is given using following equation

$$Erx\,(n) = Eelec * n \qquad (2)$$

The residual energy of the node is given using following Eq. (3)

$$Eres\,(i) = Ei - (Etx\,(n,\, d) + Erx\,(n)) \qquad (3)$$

3.3 Exclusion Basis System (EBS) Structure

Each cluster member can hold only log2 (Y) keys to update the cluster. Here Y represents the number of cluster members in the group and group need to hold $2^{\log_2 N - 1}$ keys. In case the number of cluster member is increased, storage capacity also needs to be increased. This is accomplished using EBS group key algorithm.

The set of members grouped to form the subsets is termed as EBS. Each subset holds a key and each node relate to a subset that holds the key. Let F be the dimension of EBS, $F \in (Y, K, P)$.

The secure group created has Y members numbered from 1 through Y, and key server (KS) holding a unique key for each subset. For a subset Qi exists in EBS, the key Ki is known to all the members whose number is available in the subset Qi.

In addition, for individual time $t \in [1, Y]$, there will be P elements in EBS with union $[1, N] - \{t\}$. This is done by removing key by the key server for the member t, re-key and establishes the replacement key details to the remaining members through multicasting technique. The generated new key is encrypted along with its predecessor for security.

When BS constructs EBS (Y, K, P) model, more management key can be generated using Y, K, and P parameters to utilize it during new nodes addition.

3.4 Formation of Clusters

The algorithm by which the clusters are forms is as follows:

1. The physical location is intimated to the base stations by the nodes when they get deployed in the network. The network then initiates the cluster head (CH) selection.
2. Once the node believes that it can serve as CH, it broadcasts the HELLO packet encrypted with initial key Ki.

$$Ni \rightarrow {}^*E\,(Ki, HELLO)$$

3. When any neighbor node (Neighi) receives hello message, it sends a cluster declaration message (CD_mes) that includes its ID and acknowledgement (ACK) message.

$$Neighi \rightarrow Ni : E\,(Ki, ID\,(Neighi) \| ACK)$$

4. The IDs are assigned to all nodes who joins the cluster and accept to transfer the information to BS.
5. BS constructs EBS structure for the cluster and produces the cluster key and associated management key. It also assigns the cluster ID for the EBS structure.
6. Within the cluster the shared main key (Kshare) is used by BS to encrypt the data transferred with the CH and Ni. All encrypted data are then transmitted to CH.
7. CH holds the required partial data and transmits the remaining data portion to other nodes.
8. After clustering process completion, all Ni's discards the Ki from its memory.

$$Ni \rightarrow BS : E\,(Kshare\,(Ni), ID\,(Neighi) \| ID\,(Neighj)$$

3.5 Cluster Head Update

After time t, the system re-selects the CH using the security broadcasting agreement of the protocol μ TESLA. It involves the following steps:

1. The new CH sends a key request (K_REQ) to BS through its current CH for the keys of adjacent clusters.

$$\text{CHnew} \rightarrow \text{CH2} \rightarrow \text{BS} : \text{REQ}\,[\text{E}\,(\text{Kshare}\,(\text{CHnew})]$$

2. When BS receives the K_REQ message, it evaluates the reachability of the new CH with other three nearby clusters with respect to the location of the new CH. So that it transmits the keys of the three nearby clusters to the new CH.

$$\text{BS} \rightarrow \text{CH2} \rightarrow \text{CHnew} : \text{E}\,(\text{Kshare}\,(\text{CHnew}),\, \text{Kc1}\,\|\,\text{Kc2}\|\text{Kc3})$$

3. On encryption of the HELLO packet sent by the CH with the received keys it broadcasts the packet to the nearby three clusters.

$$\text{CHnew} \rightarrow {}^*\text{E}\,(\text{Kc1},\,\text{HELLO})\,\|\,\text{E}\,(\text{Kc2},\,\text{HELLO})\|\text{E}\,(\text{Kc3},\,\text{HELLO})$$

4. The cluster member (CMj) reports to BS through their CH that they are ready to join the cluster.

$$\text{CMj} \rightarrow \text{CHj} \rightarrow \text{BS} : \text{E}\,(\text{Kshare}\,(\text{CMj})$$
$$\text{ID}\,(\text{CMj})\|\text{ACK}$$

5. The cluster and management keys are transmitted to the CHs and nmoves to their nodes after constructing the EBS for the new cluster generated with the gathered data.

$$\text{BS} \rightarrow \text{CHj} \rightarrow \text{CMj} : \text{E}\,(\text{Kshare}\,(\text{CMj})$$
$$\text{ID}\,(\text{CLnew})\|\text{Kcl}\,(\text{CLnew})\|\text{Kebs\_new}\ldots)$$

6. The node IDs of the new cluster, key and management keys are transferred by the BS to CHnew.

$$\text{BS} \rightarrow \text{CH2} \rightarrow \text{CHnew} : \text{E}\,(\text{Kshare}\,(\text{CHnew})$$
$$\text{ID}((\text{CMj})1\|\,\text{ID}\,((\text{CMj})2\ldots\|\text{Kcl}\,(\text{CHnew})\,\text{Kebs\_new}$$

3.6   Virtual Grid Formation

Once the clusters are formed, it is divided into virtual grids, such that each CH contains more grids. Each cluster member (CMi) is assigned with unique location ID (Xid) which comprises the cluster member, grid location in (x, y) form and the node ID. For example, Consider Fig. 1 (For a node N1 in cluster (C2) with grid index (1, 3), X will be 2131).

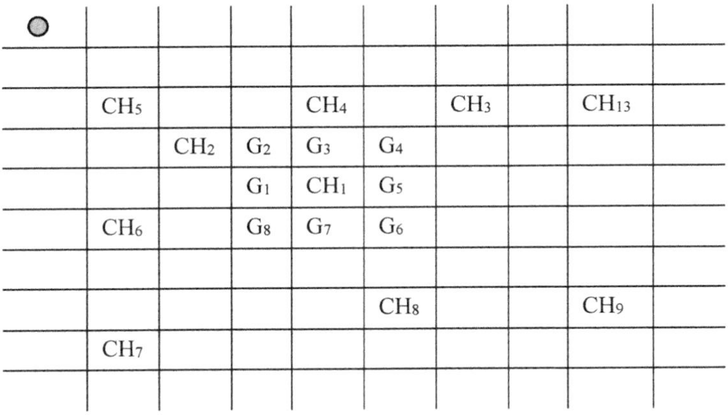

CH_5			CH_4			CH_3		CH_{13}	
	CH_2	G_2	G_3	G_4					
		G_1	CH_1	G_5					
CH_6		G_8	G_7	G_6					
				CH_8			CH_9		
CH_7									

Fig. 1. Virtual grid

3.7   Dynamic Key Generation

During node deployment, sink nodes first randomly selects a following polynomial:

$$f(z) = \sum_{i=0}^{i=t-1} g_i z (\bmod w) \tag{4}$$

where,

w = large prime
t = C × (C1, N1), where (C1, N1) represents the virtual grid
gi = random integer

BS then broadcasts the polynomial value to all CHs. Each CH randomly selects n parameters from the polynomial and form itself sub-polynomial

$$fCHi(z) = \sum_{j=0}^{j=n-1} v_i z^j (\bmod w) \tag{5}$$

where, $vj \in \{u_0, u_1, \ldots, u_{t-1}\}, n \in [t/2, t]$
Each CH generates a random integer z and estimates the dynamic key using following equation

$$KCHj = fch(xch) + El + Xid * rj \tag{6}$$

where,

xch – random integer generated by the CH
fch(xch) – the polynomial sent by the sink node to all cluster heads through broadcasting,

El – energy level of each node after performing each operation

Xid – Location id of each node

rj – random integer generated from CH by node

To assure the proper working and extended lifetime of the network a sleeping node of the virtual grid is made active at a time in the place of the exhausted node or disabled node to conserve energy.

3.8 Dynamic Key Update

The WSN nodes are often vulnerable to physical damage or capture attacks. To update or withdraw the dynamic key, it is required to remove the damaged nodes outside the network or add new nodes on requirement.

1. Adding New Nodes: In general, the active nodes and cluster head holds the key. At the time of node insertion, it is added to one cluster and one virtual grid. However, the relevant virtual grid holds the active node and the new node is in sleep mode. Hence, the key among the active node and cluster head is not renewed.

2. Updating Active Node Key: Event monitoring within the grid and transmission of the data to CH is the primary role of an active node. It computes the residual energy Eres (i). If Eres (i) < threshold value (Eth), the active node goes to sleeping mode. On the other hand, if the Eres (i) is more than threshold value (Eth), then the active node transmits its ID and random number to CH and CH computes the Eq. (5) and transmits it to new active node key.

3. Updating Pair-wise key: When Eres (i) is less than threshold value (Eth), the current CH utilizes the dynamic clustering algorithm to construct a new CH and transmits its stored key to new CH. The new CH estimates the new pair-wise key K' CHi_CHj with its neighbor CH and stored in its table, while the new CH broadcasts information to all active nodes in cluster. Each active node generates a random number and transmits back to new CH. Then new CH estimates the key used to communicate with active node and transmits back to each active node.

4 Simulation Results

4.1 Simulation Model and Parameters

The proposed system is simulated and checked using Network Simulator (NS2) [18]. A 1000 sq.m region area the time range of 50 s was simulation and tested. The environment is set for 250 m as the transmission range for all the nodes and Constant Bit Rate traffic. The packet size is fixed as 512 with the rate as 50 kb for the simulation time 50 s. 200 nodes were created with initial energy as 10.1 J, receiving power as 0.395 W and transmission power as 0.660.

4.2   Performance Metric

Location and Energy based Hierarchical Dynamic Key Management Protocol (LEHDKM) the proposed system is compared with the DKMPC [15] and various secure key generation based on Frequency-Selective Channels SKGFSC methods. The various performance metrics evaluated to prove the efficiency of the system are as follow,

- **Packet Delivery Ratio:** Calculated by the proposition of the received packets vs sent packets.
- **Packet Drop:** Calculated with the average transmitted packet loss.
- **Residual Energy:** Left out energy of the sensor nodes after the transmission.
- **Time Delay:** The time calculated between the transmission and reception of data packets.

4.3   Results

Depending on Number of Sensor Nodes: The experiment was tested with varying the number of sensor nodes and results were obtained for time delay, delivery ratio and packet drop.

In Fig. 2 given below the time delay of LEHDKM, DKMPC and SKGFSC techniques for 50,100,150 and 200 number of nodes was shown. The result has concluded with the metric, time delay in which LEHDKM system has 13% lesser than DKMPC and 25% lesser than SKGFSC approach. The packet delivery ratio shown in Fig. 3 for LEHDKM, DKMPC and SKGFSC techniques with varying the number of nodes. With respect to the metric, our proposed LEHDKM system has concluded 18% higher with DKMPC and 38% higher with SKGFSC approach. The experiment conducted for the total number of packet drop metric with different number of nodes our LEHDKM system has 62% less compared with DKMPC and 77% less of packet loss than SKGFSC approach (Fig. 4).

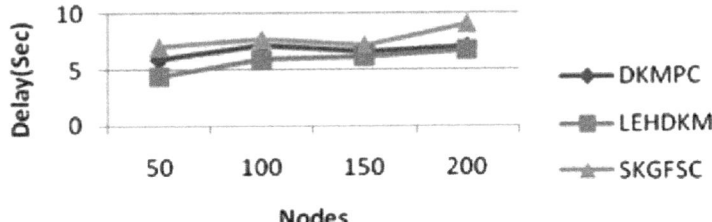

Fig. 2. Nodes vs delay

As depicted in the results shown in Fig. 5 the residual energy of LEHDKM, DKMPC and SKGFSC has been concluded by our LEHDKM approach has 8% of higher with DKMPC and 12% higher than approach SKGFSC systems.

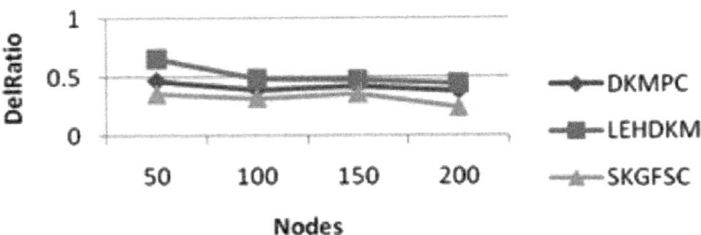

Fig. 3. Nodes vs delivery ratio

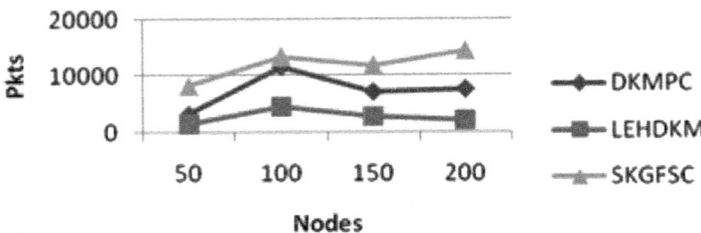

Fig. 4. Nodes vs drop

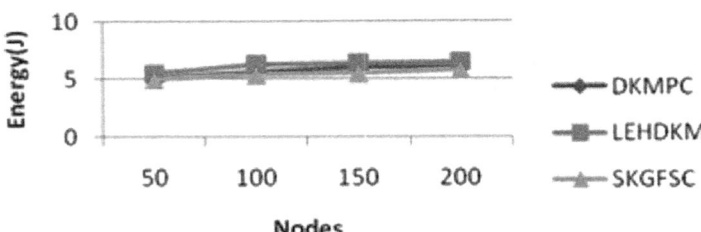

Fig. 5. Nodes vs residual energy

Depending on Security: The experiment was conducted by adding the count of intruder count as 10, 15, 20, 25 and 30 against time delay, delivery ratio and packet drop.

The comparison of metrics with the distinct number of attackers 10, 15, 20, 25, and 30 performed is shown in Fig. 6 for the various techniques LEHDKM, DKMPC and SKGFSC. The time delay of our LEHDKM approach proved 10% lesser than DKMPC and 15% lesser than the SKGFSC approach. In Fig. 7 the packet delivery ratio of LEHDKM, DKMPC and SKGFSC reports that the ratio of packet delivery for LEHDKM technique is 38% and 60% more when compared with DKMPC and SKGFSC approaches respectively.

The percentage of drop of packets is vivid in Fig. 8 for the various LEHDKM, DKMPC and SKGFSC systems with reference to the number of attackers as 10, 15, 20, 25, and 30. It is clear that the packet drop of LEHDKM approach is 49% lesser than

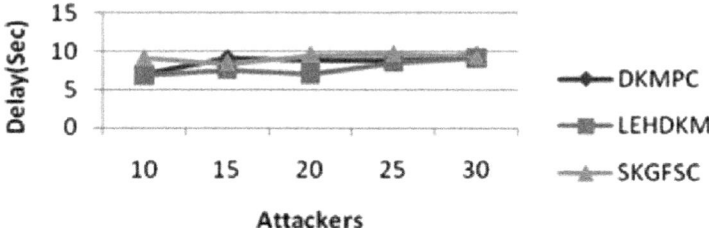

Fig. 6. Attackers vs delay

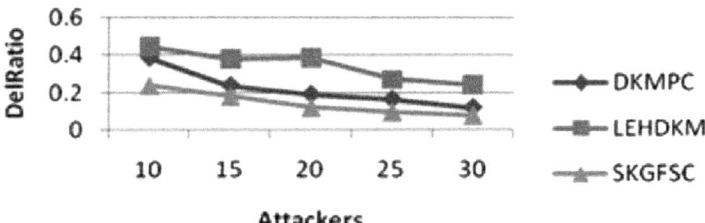

Fig. 7. Attackers vs delivery ratio

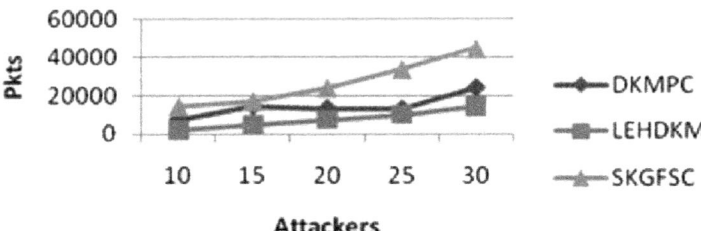

Fig. 8. Attackers vs drop

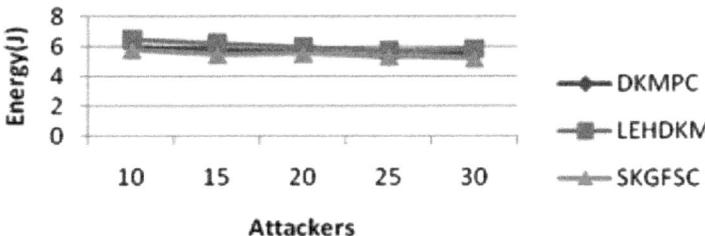

Fig. 9. Attackers vs residual energy

DKMPC and 72% lesser than SKGFSC approach. Moreover, the residual energy LEHDKM, DKMPC and SKGFSC techniques shown in Fig. 9 concludes that our LEHDKM approach has 7% higher energy than DKMPC and 10% higher residual energy than SKGFSC approach.

5   Conclusions

Location and Energy based Hierarchical Dynamic Key Management Protocol for Wireless Sensor Networks is proposed in this paper. In the system design the sensor nodes with high energy constraint are grouped into clusters and a unique ID and main encryption key is provided by the base station. Based on the physical location the cluster heads are identified. Virtual grids are constructed from the clusters so that each cluster head has control over more virtual grids. Based on the algorithm discussed an efficient dynamic key is generated to reduce the energy consumption in virtual grid environment. To update or withdraw the dynamic key, the damaged nodes outside the network are removed or new nodes are added on requirement as per the algorithm. The performance results for energy consumption and enhanced security is shown in the simulation results performed by varying the number of nodes and attackers against time delay, packet delivery ration, packet drop and residential energy.

References

1. Bala, S., Sharma, G., Verma, A.K.: Classification of symmetric key management schemes for wireless sensor networks. Int. J. Secur. Appl. **7**(2), 117–138 (2013)
2. Kim, J.-M., Cho, J.-S., Jung, S.-M., Chung, T.-M.: An energy-efficient dynamic key management in wireless sensor networks. In: 9th International Conference on Advanced Communication Technology, vol. 3. IEEE (2007)
3. Chen, C.-L., Tsai, Y.-T., Castiglione, A., Palmier, F.: Using bivariate polynomial to design a dynamic key management scheme for wireless sensor networks. Comput. Sci. Inf. Syst. **10**, 589–609 (2013)
4. Gupta, N., Jain, A., Singh, H.K.: An efficient key strategy for prolonging network lifetime in wireless network. In: Fourth International Conference on Computing, Communications and Networking Technologies (2013)
5. Goyal, P., Kumar, M., Sharma, R.: A novel and efficient dynamic key management technique in wireless sensor network. Int. J. Adv. Netw. Appl. **4**(1), 1462–1466 (2012)
6. Landstra, T., Zawodniok, M., Jagannathan, S.: Energy-efficient hybrid key management protocol for wireless sensor networks. In: 32nd IEEE Conference on IEEE Local Computer Networks (2007)
7. Singh, K., Sharma, L.: Hierarchical group key management using threshold cryptography in wireless sensor networks. Int. J. Comput. Appl. **63**(4) (2013). ISSN 0975-8887
8. He, X., Niedermeier, M., de Meer, H.: Dynamic key management in wireless sensor networks: a survey. J. Netw. Comput. Appl. **36**, 611–622 (2013)
9. He, X., Szalachowski, P., Kotulski, Z., Fotiou, N., Marias, G.F., Polyzos, G.C., de Meer, H.: Energy-aware key management in mobile wireless sensor networks. Ann. UMCS, Informatica **12**(4), 83–96 (2012)

10. Zhang, Y., Li, X., Yang, J., Liu, Y., Xiong, N., Vasilakos, A.V.: A real-time dynamic key management for hierarchical wireless multimedia sensor network. Multimed. Tools Appl. **67**(1), 97–117 (2013)
11. Bai, E., Jiang, X.: A dynamic key management scheme based on secret sharing for hierarchical wireless sensor networks. TELKOMNIKA **11**(3), 1514–1523 (2013)
12. Shen, L., Shi, X.: A dynamic cluster-based key management protocol in wireless sensor networks. Int. J. Intell. Control Syst. **13**(2), 146–151 (2008)
13. Sahingoz, O.K.: Large scale wireless sensor networks with multi-level dynamic key management scheme. J. Syst. Architect. **59**, 801–807 (2013)
14. Jeong, G., Seo, Y.-H., Yang, H.S.: Impersonating-resilient dynamic key management for large-scale wireless sensor networks. Int. J. Distrib. Sens. Netw. (2013)
15. Liang, H., Wang, C.: An energy efficient dynamic key management scheme based on polynomial and cluster in wireless sensor networks. J. Converg. Inf. Technol. **6**(5), 321–328 (2011)
16. Uluagac, A.S., Beyah, R.A., Li, Y., Copeland, J.A.: VEBEK: virtual energy-based encryption and keying for wireless sensor networks. IEEE Trans. Mob. Comput. **9**(7), 994–1007 (2010)
17. Zhang, X., He, J., Wei, Q.: EDDK: energy-efficient distributed deterministic key management for wireless sensor networks. EURASIP J. Wirel. Commun. Netw. **2011**, 765143 (2011)
18. Wilhelm, M., Martinovic, I., Schmitt, J.B.: Secure key generation in sensor networks based on frequency-selective channels. IEEE J. Sel. Areas Commun. **31**(9), 1779–1790 (2013)

Performance Evaluation of RPL Routing Protocol for IoT Based Power Distribution Network

Rijo Jackson Tom[(✉)] and Suresh Sankaranarayanan

SRM University, Chennai 603203, India
rijojackson@gmail.com, suresh.sa@ktr.srmuniv.ac.in

Abstract. Power distribution automation plays an important role in the smart grid world. With the development of Internet of Things (IoT) technology and fog computing capability, real time streaming analytics and efficient monitoring of the grid is possible. So towards this an IoT based Power Distribution system integrated with Fog been proposed. 6LoWPAN which is IPv6 over Low Power Personal Area network been integrated into smart meters, pole transformer Intelligent Electronic Devices (IEDs) and distribution line sensors of the IoT based system for transmitting data wirelessly using 6LoWPAN communication network to fog which acts as a 6LoWPAN gateway.

Now for efficient transmission of data from 6LoWPAN devices to fog for analysis, there is a need to look into efficient routing protocol for efficient power distribution. Routing Protocol for Low power Lossy Networks (RPL) is the most standard routing protocol been used in 6LoWPAN network.

So now for efficient distribution of power using IoT Technologies employing 6LoWPAN network, we here have evaluated the RPL routing protocol for a small area in a town with fog router as the 6LoWPAN gateway in real time. The system been evaluated for a real time situation of power distribution network for varying transmission range and number of nodes. Also the system been evaluated by changing the position of fog router to a center point of the area where maximum network efficiency is achieved. These been simulated using Cooja Network simulator running on Contiki OS.

Keywords: Power distribution · Automation · Smart grids · Fog computing
Sensors · Wireless sensor networks

1 Introduction

The power distribution part which starts from 33 kV substation till the 230/440 V end users is the major part in smart grid. As the power that is generated is based on the end user needs, proper metering, maintenance and power quality check are important features that smart grid requires.

So towards Power Distribution Automation which covers a large geographical area, the current Supervisory Control and Data Acquisition (SCADA) system in the distribution substation is not good enough in monitoring the large geographical area for proper monitoring and control. So with the advent of IoT along with developments in

P. Bhattacharyya et al. (Eds.): NGCT 2017, CCIS 828, pp. 212–226, 2018.
https://doi.org/10.1007/978-981-10-8660-1_16

Fog and Cloud computing has paved way in bringing the Power Distribution Automation (DA) to a reality. Fog computing acts as a bridge between Cloud and the end devices thereby reducing the traffic that goes to the cloud.

So accordingly an IoT based SCADA integrated with Fog for Power Distribution Automation been developed where Smart Meters, IEDs of pole transformer, distribution line sensors which forms the Automatic Metering Infrastructure (AMI) are connected to fog router by means of 6LoWPAN communication [1]. The fog router act as the 6LoWPAN gateway, where the data from smart meters, line sensors, IEDs are collected in real time by means of 6LoWPAN communication for analytics and use 3G/4G Backbone network for communicating to Cloud. The Neighborhood area Network (NAN) [2] is formed by metering devices and fog router.

Now for the IoT based Power Distribution System to efficiently route the data emanating from smart meters, line sensors and IEDs of pole transformer which are 6LoWPAN based to fog router for timely analysis with response, there is need for proper routing protocol. Routing over Low-Power Lossy Network (ROLL) work group has come up with a routing protocol specifically designed for IoT based applications called RPL [3]. This is an IPv6 based routing protocol specifically designed for battery operated embedded devices, which are used in homes and offices. The RPL works for different traffic patterns like, point-to-point, multipoint-to-point and multipoint-to-multipoint communication. They form a Directed Acyclic Graph (DAG) and form tree based architecture. The fog router acts as the Low-Power Border Router (LBR), thus forming a Destination Oriented DAG (DODAG).

Since the standardization of the RPL by ROLL, quite amount of research been carried out towards performance evaluation of protocol in simulation as well as in real time. In one of the research [4], authors have done critical evaluation of RPL in both simulation as well as in real time wireless sensor network test bed. Also authors [5] have developed a self-organizing algorithm for smart meters to automatically discover congestion and recover from connectivity loss. Researchers also have developed an energy efficient region based RPL for energy efficient delivery where the protocol been compared with RPL and P2P RPL with results.

Research also been carried out in 6LoWPAN network with multiple gateways towards reduction in packet loss. Researchers have also evaluated Contiki RPL in Cooja too. RPL been developed for Power Line Communication (PLC) where the routing on medium voltage PLC for smart grid been studied and accordingly the system performed well for light traffic. Also the researchers have studied the effect of TCP over RPL in LLN. RPL been studied specific to smart grids where robustness of protocol for AMI been validated towards reliability. There is room for more improvements in the routing protocol.

The literatures so far have evaluated RPL routing protocol for 6LoWPAN, Power line communication and AMI. The IoT based power distribution network here consists of smart meters, IEDs and fog border router which is the 6LoWPAN gateway. But there has been no research which effectively evaluates RPL for Power Distribution Automation in IoT integrated with Fog. So accordingly we here have evaluated the RPL routing for our IoT based Power distribution system integrated with fog for a small area in a town in real time towards efficient power analysis which is novel. The performance evaluation and analysis of RPL been done for IoT based system for varying number of nodes and transmission range in terms of end to end delay, Throughput, hop count against distance. Also RPL routing protocol been evaluated by changing the position of fog router to a center point of an area in a town which is an important criteria for getting maximum network efficiency with efficient power analysis and distribution for varying transmission range. The entire evaluation been carried out using Cooja Network simulator in Contiki OS. The rest of the paper is organized as follows Sect. 2 gives a complete literature review pertaining to RPL based routing in LLNs Sect. 3 talks about the proposed evaluation architecture. Section 4 talks about the results and analysis Sect. 5 gives conclusion and the future work that has to be carried out.

2 Literature Review

So before going into the evaluation of RPL routing protocol in IoT based Power distribution system integrated with Fog, quite amount of research has been done in regards to the performance evaluation of routing protocol in simulation as well as in real time mode. This section provides a brief account on the works done so far with RPL.

RFC 6550 provides a detailed documentation for RPL. RFC 5548, RFC 5673 and RFC 5826 provides the requirements in Low-Power Lossy networks towards routing for urban, industry and home automation respectively [6, 7].

RFC 8036 [8] provides information regarding the applicability of RPL for AMI applications. This gives an account on the traffic pattern for the power distribution.

In [9] the critical evaluation of RPL been carried out by the researcher in both simulation as well as in real time wireless sensor network test bed. They explained the under specification of the RPL and also evaluated the trickle convergence issues that occur in real time. They found a difference in convergence in theory and in simulation.

The authors in [10] proposed a self-organizing algorithm for the smart meters to automatically discover congestion and recover from the loss of connectivity. They also studied the impact of these algorithms on latency discovery and Packet Delivery Ratio (PDR).

Researchers also have developed an energy efficient region based RPL (ER-RPL) for energy efficient data delivery. They compared the protocol with, RPL and P2P RPL with promising results.

Researchers [11] also provided a survey on the IoT protocols RPL and Constraint Application Protocol (CoAP) in regards to multihop nature of IoT devices.

Researchers also proposed a fundamental formula [18] for representing the interaction of power distribution and communication network where the DA system act as a protection system [12].

Research was also carried out in 6LoWPAN network with multiple gateways and an algorithm was proposed to reduce the packet loss [13]. The simulation was carried out in ns2. Research [14] was also carried out towards evaluation of the ContikiRPL in Cooja but not specific to any particular application.

RFC 6550 which is RPL Routing protocol been proposed to work over Power Line communication. So accordingly routing on medium voltage PLC for smart grid applications been studied which showed that the system performed well for light traffic conditions. Another author studied the effect of TCP over RPL in LLN [15] with multihop environment.

In [16] authors proposed an enhanced RPL to overcome the limitations on the storage capabilities of the parent nodes. In [17] they studied the influence of RPL parameters in IEEE 802.15.4 multihop network. In [18–20] the author studied the performance of RPL in terms of data delivery.

Specific to smart grids, few authors have studied the robustness of RPL in AMI [21, 22], thus showing that RPL is reliable but improvements are still to be made in the routing protocol.

So based on literature review pertaining to RPL Routing protocol, we here have evaluated RPL Routing protocol for IoT based Power Distribution System integrated with Fog which is novel. These are explained in the forthcoming sections.

3   RPL Routing Protocol in IoT Based Power Distribution System

The current electrical grid which is 50 years old is being transformed into smart grid and in that power distribution is a very key element. SCADA system which is well established inside the substation has very less monitoring done on the distribution side due to the geographical distribution. SCADA systems provide no real time information on power distribution for any action. So accordingly with the advent of IoT which enables much effective and beneficial power distribution and automation, an IoT based SCADA integrated with Fog for Power Distribution Automation system has been proposed as shown in Fig. 1 which takes care of the consumer utilization, outage management, power quality control and pole transformer health. Pole mounted fog router are placed in such a way that pole transformer's IEDs use single hop to reach fog router for better efficiency. All the smart meters, IEDs of pole transformers and line sensors use 6LoWPAN communication method which is nothing but IPv6 over IEEE 802.15.4 for transmission of data for analysis by fog router before reaching the cloud.

Now for such an IoT system towards analyzing the data collected by the fog router for timely analysis and quick action, there is need to look into proper routing protocol with minimal delay, minimal packet loss and effective throughput. Also the placement of fog router needs to be carefully chosen for better network efficiency which would result in timely analysis and action.

RPL routing protocol developed by ROLL working Group is the most standardized routing protocol for an IoT System. Lot of work been carried out in the past in employing RPL routing protocol for AMI, Power Line Communication in smart grid. But no research been reported so far in evaluating the RPL Routing protocol for an IoT based system integrated with fog particularly in relevance to power distribution which is novel. The evaluation of routing protocol is very much necessary to analyze the efficiency of an IoT network which requires time critical analysis and quick action.

The evaluation of routing protocol for an IoT system been carried out in terms of end to end delay, throughput and hop count for varying number of nodes i.e. 10, 20 and 50 against distance of fog router with two different transmission ranges which are 30

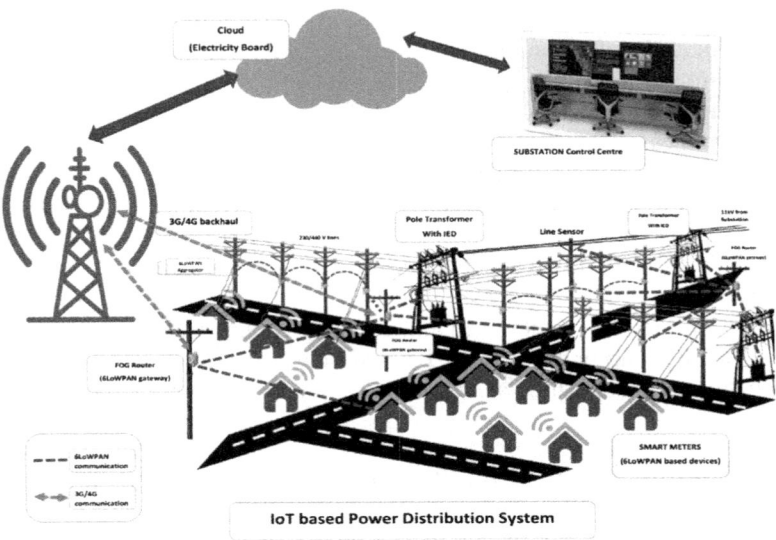

Fig. 1. IoT based SCADA integrated with Fog for Power Distribution

and 50 m. In addition to the above evaluation, placement of fog router also changed to an intermediate position rather than close to pole transformer which is far from nodes and accordingly system evaluated for the same number of nodes and transmission range. The smart meters and pole transformer IEDs are 6LoWPAN nodes in the network.

Fog router here is nothing but 6LoWPAN Border Router or gateway. Figure 2 shows the actual sensor map of a small area in a town for which the simulation parameters were set and analyzed for our IoT based network integrated with fog for power distribution. The network architecture was designed with the image of the actual physical infrastructure in mind. This evaluation would be very much necessary in deploying an effective IoT system for power distribution automation integrated with proper placement of fog router.

4   Simulation Results

IoT based system integrated with Fog been simulated in Contiki which is open Source Operating System for IoT. Figure 2 which shows the actual sensor map of a small area in a town been simulated in Cooja Network Simulator which runs on Contiki OS. The network nodes here refer to smart meters and pole transformer IED.

The node density generally varies from place to place. Rural areas have sparse density and urban places have hundreds of nodes in close proximity. Simulation was carried out with 10, 20 and 50 nodes which are all connected to a 6LoWPAN border router which is fog router. Figures 3, 4 and 5 shows the 10, 20 and 50 nodes network topology of IoT Network with Fog Router. The simulation was conducted with

Fig. 2. Sensor map for small area in network.

transmission and reception range of 30 m and 50 m. The fog router is placed at the end of the street and near to the pole transformer IED. This is done with the view that pole transformer parameters are more critical and are to be analyzed and action to be taken without delay or near real time. Fog routers form clusters and can pass on the data to the cloud. This simulation was carried out to find the performance of the RPL routing protocol in terms of throughput and end to end delay for timely delivery of data for analysis.

4.1 Simulation Result Analysis

The network been simulated for 10, 20 and 50 nodes for two different transmission range which is 30 and 50 m. The throughput been evaluated for network against distance of fog router from 6LoWPAN nodes for varying number of network size which is 10, 20 and 50 nodes. From the simulation it is clear that as the number of nodes increases, the throughout drastically drops against distance which is clear from Fig. 6. The simulation parameters are shown in Table 1.

When the number of nodes is less say 10, throughput of the network is still 90% and 80% for a maximum distance of 200 m for 30 and 50 m transmission range. But when the number of nodes is increased from 10 to 20 nodes, it is seen that throughout of 5% and 15% been achieved for a maximum distance of 143 m only from fog router to nodes with 30 m and 50 m transmission range. Now for a maximum number of nodes of 50, the throughput been achieved is 0% and 20% for distance of 140 m only for 30 m and 50 m transmission range. That shows that no packets been received for a maximum distance of 140 m for 50 number of nodes for 30 m transmission range. But for 50 m transmission there is a throughout of 20% which means maximum packets been lost.

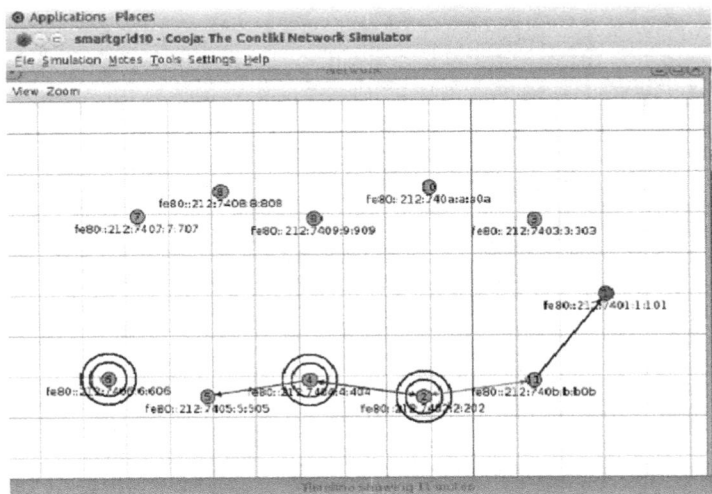

Fig. 3. 6LoWPAN network for 10 nodes

So it can be concluded that throughput is maximum when number of nodes are less. But as nodes increases, throughput drops drastically with distance. That means data transmitted from consumer's smart meters are not received successfully by fog router for analysis when number of nodes increases with network becoming larger and also distance from the fog router is more.

Table 1. Simulation parameters for the network to be set in Cooja

Settings	Values
Radio medium model	Unit Disk Graph Medium (UGDM) distance loss
Area	200 m x 150 m
Range of nodes	Rx, Tx: 30 m, 50 m; Interference: 100 m
PHY and MAC	IEEE 802.15.4
Duty cycle	Contiki MAC
Sensor mote	Tmote Sky
Transport layer	UDP
Network layer	uIPv6, 6LoWPAN
Objective function	ETX

Now similar to throughput, hop count also been analysed against distance for varying number of nodes which are 10, 20 and 50 nodes for 30 and 50 m transmission ranges. Hop count is an important criteria in routing the data to reach the destination node which is fog router in our case for analysis. The network topology is designed such that each smart meter can communicate to the fog router by multihop. From simulation results, it is clear that hop count reduces for 50 m transmission range compared to 30 m against distance of fog router for different nodes.

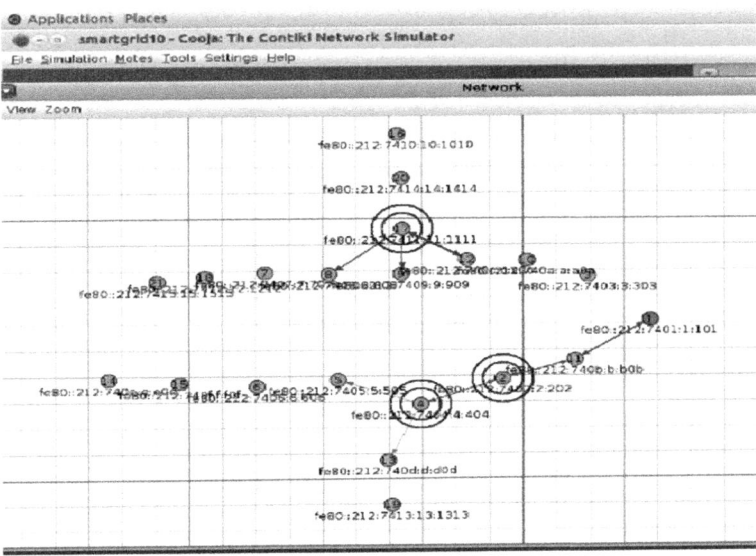

Fig. 4. 6LoWPAN network for 20 nodes

The results show that 50 m transmission range helps in reducing the number of hops in the network. This helps in data to be received by the fog router in time with less number of hops rather than traversing the network with more hops that would take more time to reach fog router for analysis. Network with more hops would result in data being received very late which can result in analysis becoming obsolete

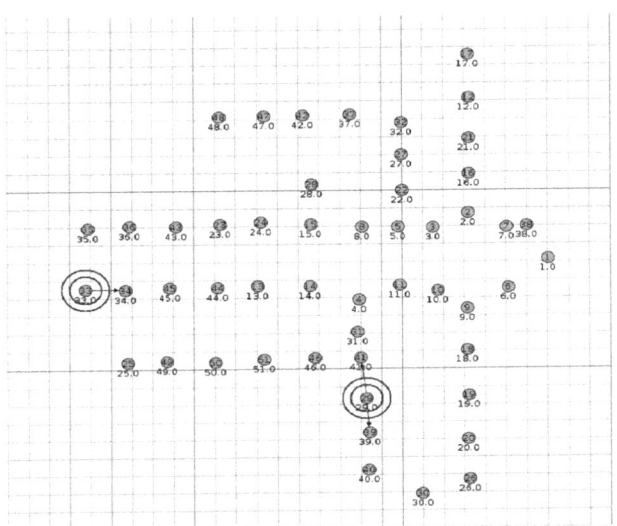

Fig. 5. 6LoWPAN network for 50 nodes

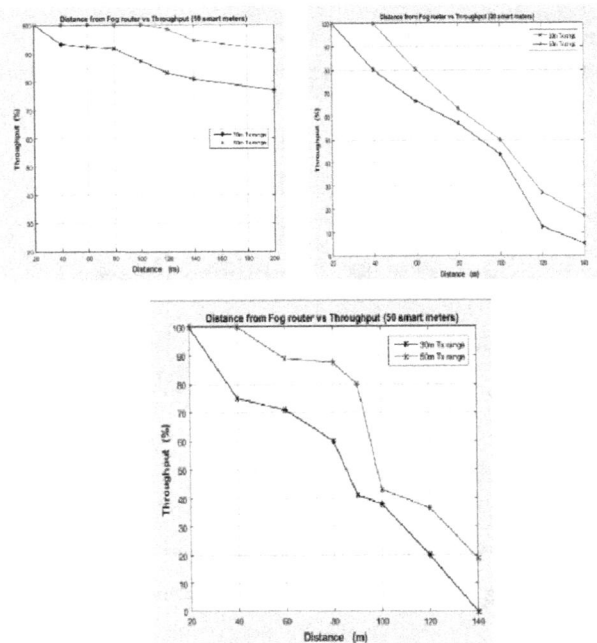

Fig. 6. Distance from fog router vs throughput – 10, 20 and 50 nodes

particularly in such time critical analysis. As the number of hops reduces, the power consumption of the nodes decreases. These been shown in Fig. 7.

Having seen the analysis of throughput and hop count against distance for varying number of nodes for 30 m and 50 m transmission range, we have also analyzed the end to end delay for the network. Delay is an important criterion in a network which gives a complete picture as how much of delay is incurred by the network in receiving the data sent by nodes.

It is clear from the simulation results that the end to end delay is 230 ms and 200 ms for 30 m and 50 m transmission range for 10 nodes against distance of fog router from nodes. Similarly for 20 nodes, the end to end delay is 320 ms and 280 ms for 30 m and 50 m transmission range against distance of fog router from different nodes. Also end to end delay for 50 nodes been simulated too which resulted in 480 ms and 350 ms for 30 m and 50 m transmission range against distance of fog router from nodes.

So in summary it is clear that end to end delay increases with varying number of nodes against the distance of fog router from nodes. As the network size increases with more number of nodes, time taken for fog router to receive the data from nodes increases which again result in data being received very late and accordingly the analysis would have no meaning for taking quick action. Also in applications like power distribution where time critical analysis is important, end to end delay should be kept as minimal as possible for timely analysis and action. These been shown in Fig. 8.

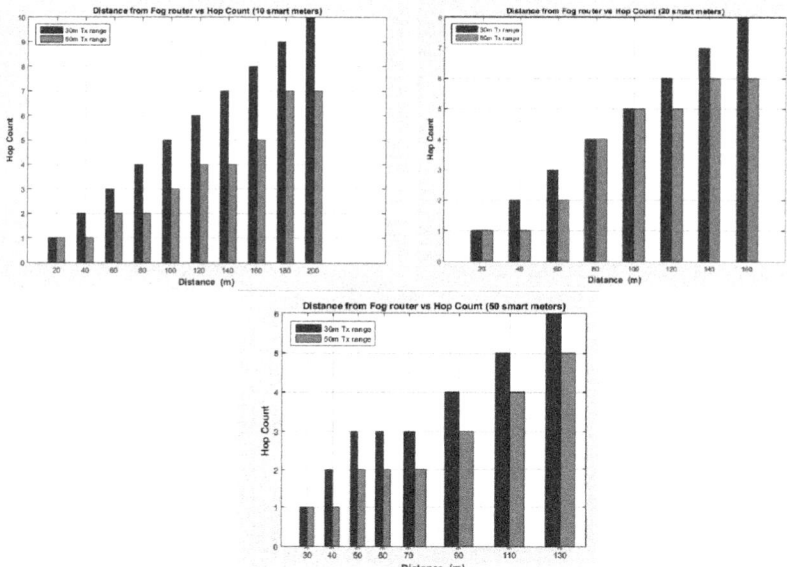

Fig. 7. Distance from fog router vs Hop count- 10, 20, 50 nodes

So from simulation analysis results of throughput, hop count and end to end delay, it is clear that network should be designed in such a way the data being delivered with less number of hops and lesser delay which would result in maximum packets being delivered at the fog router for analysis resulting in maximum throughput irrespective with varying number of nodes. So this is based on modified topology where placement of fog router would play an important role in getting the maximum network efficiency for timely analysis by fog router which is been explained in the forthcoming section.

4.2 Modified Topology Analysis

The topology so far been deployed based on physical infrastructural design of small area in a town is such that fog router is kept close to the pole transformer. That is the pole mounted fog router are placed in such a way that pole transformer's IEDs use single hop to reach fog router for better efficiency.

But during simulation, it has been found that network throughput and end to end delay been heavily affected due to fog router placed near the pole transformer's IED.

That is due to large distance, most of the data from 6LoWPAN nodes which are smart meters do not reach to fog router for analysis or they reach the fog router with more delay making it obsolete for analysis.

So for better network efficiency with timely analysis and action, proper placement of fog router is necessary where analysis of parameters from all devices are important which includes Pole Transformer IEDs, Smart Meters and Line sensors. So accordingly we have moved the pole mounted fog router to an intermediate position where maximum

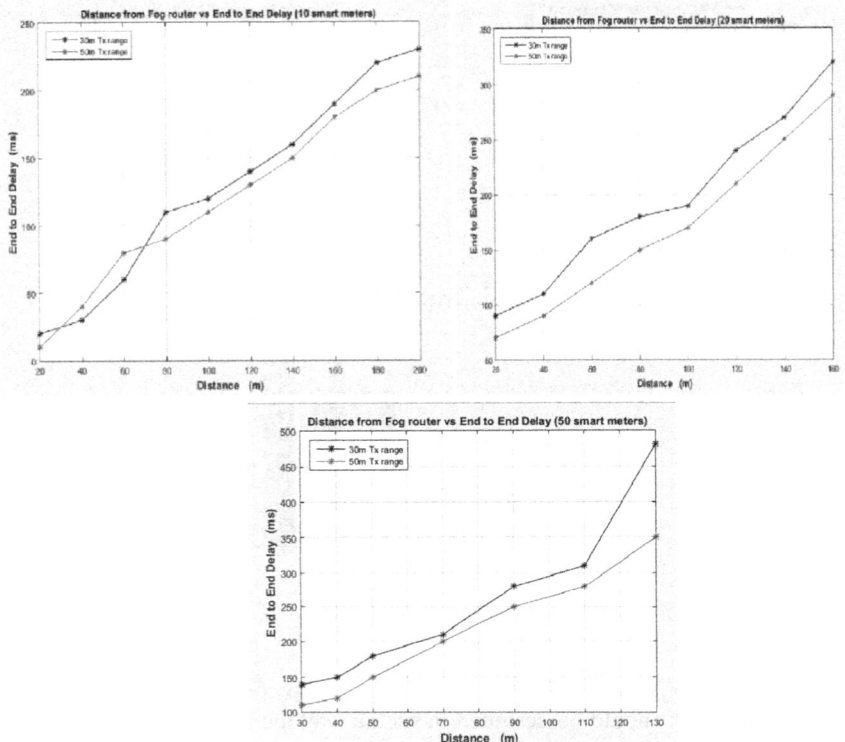

Fig. 8. Distance from fog router vs end to end delay (10, 20, 50 nodes)

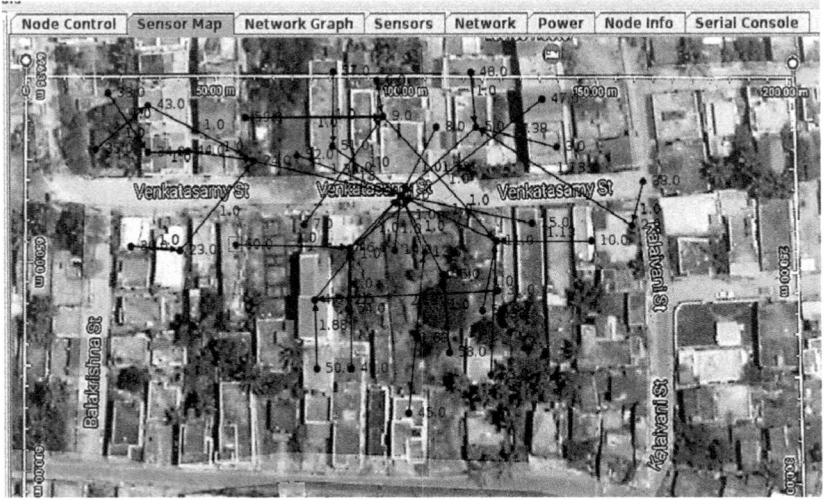

Fig. 9. Fog router position modified network topology

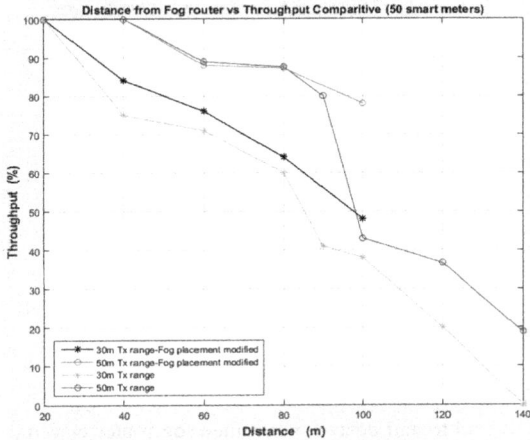

Fig. 10. Throughput for modified fog router position comparative plots

concentration of nodes is sought resulting in a better network efficiency compared to previous scenarios. This is shown in Fig. 9 in real time scenario. The simulation with modified fog router placement been done only for 50 node networks for throughput, hop count and end to end delay. These are shown in Figs. 10, 11 and 12.

It is clear from simulation results that data been captured from the simulator for a maximum distance of 100 m which is around 0.1 to 0.4 km. This is fairly a small area in a town comprising few streets. So from the analysis it is clear that maximum throughout efficiency 80% been achieved for maximum distance of 100 m which is 0.1 km for 50 m transmission range for modified fog router placement. That is maximum number of packets been received with minimal placket loss of 20%.

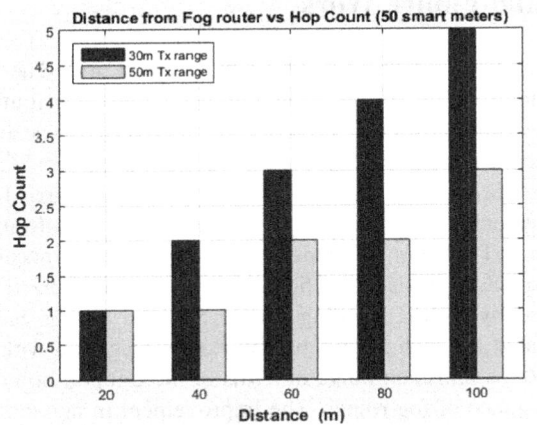

Fig. 11. Hop count for modified fog router placement

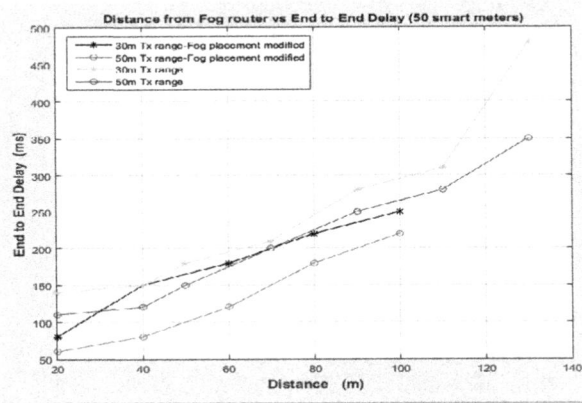

Fig. 12. End to end delay for modified fog router placement

Hop count also been reduced still more to 3 for 50 m transmission range against maximum distance of 100 m which result in data being delivered quickly in time with less power consumption by nodes. Also end to end delay of network have shown great improvement of 220 ms for 50 m transmission range for modified fog router placement against maximum distance of 100 m nodes i.e. 0.1 km. So it is clear that with less number of hops and reduced end to end delay, maximum throughput been achieved for 50 m transmission range which proves that maximum amount of consumer data, transformer data been transmitted to fog router with minimal packet loss, end to end delay and less number of hops for timely analysis and action against maximum distance of 100 m nodes i.e. 0.1 km from fog router comprising a small area in a town. The analysis has proved to be better with modified fog router placement for 50 nodes covering a maximum distance of 100 m nodes.

5 Conclusion and Future Work

Power Distribution and Automation is a key area in smart grid. The current SCADA system is not suitable or well equipped to monitor the power distribution area of large geographical region resulting in poor monitoring and control. So accordingly with the upcoming of IoT technologies and Fog computing, an IoT based SCADA integrated with Fog been developed where all real time analysis been carried out at the pole mounted fog router which is kept one single hop from pole transformer.

But for such an IoT system, a proper routing protocol is necessary for timely delivery of data for quick analysis and action. RPL is the standardized routing protocol for IoT as developed by ROLL working group. So with that as basis RPL routing protocol been evaluated for such an IoT based system integrated with fog for varying number of nodes and transmission range in terms of throughput, hop count and end to end delay against distance of fog router. The improvement in network efficiency been achieved by moving the fog router position to intermediate position where maximum concentration of nodes achieved and accordingly network efficiency improved drastically in terms of throughput, hop count and end to end delay. These been simulated and shown graphically taking a real time situation of a small area in a town for analysis.

This modified fog router topology is not a complete solution for achieving maximum network efficiency as the network size becomes larger covering more number of nodes. This might result in more fog router deployment and also changing the fog router frequently which becomes challenging. In Future, an improvement of existing RPL routing protocol need to be developed for providing better network efficiency rather than moving the fog router position with the increasing number of nodes each time covering a larger area. In addition Fog router be placed in a perfect position in an area irrespective of increasing number of nodes for timely delivery for analysis.

References

1. Tom, R.J., Sankaranarayanan, S.: IoT based SCADA integrated with fog for power distribution automation. In: 12th Iberian Conference Information Systems Technologies, Lisbon, Portugal, pp. 1772–1775 (2017)
2. Garcia-Hernandez, J.: Recent progress in the implementation of AMI projects: standards and communications technologies. In: Proceedings of 2015 International Conference Mechatronics, Electron Automotive Engineering, ICMEAE 2015, pp. 251–256 (2016). https://doi.org/10.1109/icmeae.2015.43
3. Winter, T., Thubert, P., Kelsey, R.: IPv6 Routing Protocol for Low-Power and Lossy Networks [RFC 6550] (2012)
4. Saad, L., Chauvenet, C., Tourancheau, B.: Simulation of the RPL routing protocol for IPv6 sensor networks: two cases studies. In: Fifth International Conference Sensor Technologies Applications, pp. 128–133 (2011)
5. Elkadeem, M.R., Azmy, A.M.: Optimal automation level for reliability improvement and self-healing MV distribution networks (2016)
6. Watteyne, T., Berkeley, U.C., Winter, T., Barthel, D.: Routing Requirements for Urban Low-Power and Lossy Networks, RFC 5548, pp. 1–21 (2009)
7. Buron, J., Brandt, A., Porcu, G.: Rfc 5826: Home Automation Routing Requirements in Low-Power and Lossy Networks, pp. 1–17 (2010)
8. Popa, D., Monden, K., Toutain, L., Hui, J., Gillmore, M., Ruben, R.: Applicability Statement for the Routing Protocol for Low Power and Lossy Networks (RPL) in AMI Networks, pp. 1–25 (2017). Draft-Ietf-Roll-Applicability-Ami-09
9. Clausen, T., Herberg, U., Philipp, M.: A critical evaluation of the IPv6 routing protocol for low power and lossy networks (RPL). In: International Conference Wireless Mobile Computing Networking Communications, pp. 365–372 (2011). https://doi.org/10.1109/wimob.2011.6085374
10. Kulkarni, P., Gormus, S., Fan, Z., Ramos, F.: AMI mesh networks—a practical solution and its performance evaluation. IEEE Trans. Smart Grid 3, 1469–1481 (2012). https://doi.org/10.1109/TSG.2012.2205023
11. Sheng, Z., Yang, S., Yu, Y., Vasilakos, A., McCann, J., Leung, K.: A survey on the IETF protocol suite for the internet of things: standards, challenges, and opportunities. IEEE Wirel. Commun. 20, 91–98 (2013). https://doi.org/10.1109/MWC.2013.6704479
12. Bush, S.F.: Network theory and smart grid distribution automation. IEEE J. Sel. Areas Commun. 32, 1451–1459 (2014). https://doi.org/10.1109/JSAC.2014.2332132

13. Ha, M., Kwon, K., Kim, D., Kong, P.Y.: Dynamic and distributed load balancing scheme in multi-gateway based 6LoWPAN. In: Proceedings of 2014 IEEE International Conference Internet Things, iThings 2014, 2014 IEEE International Conference Green Comput Communications GreenCom 2014, 2014 IEEE International Conference Cyber-Physical-Social Computing CPS 20, pp. 87–94 (2014). https://doi.org/10.1109/ithings.2014.22

14. Zhang, T., Li, X.: Evaluating and analyzing the performance of RPL in contiki. In: Proceedings of First International Workshop Mobile Sensing, Computing Communication, pp. 19–24 (2014). https://doi.org/10.1145/2633675.2633678

15. Kim, H.S., Im, H., Lee, M.S., Paek, J., Bahk, S.: A measurement study of TCP over RPL in low-power and lossy networks. J. Commun. Netw. 17, 647–655 (2015). https://doi.org/10.1109/JCN.2015.000111

16. Ghaleb, B., Al-dubai, A., Ekonomou, E., Wadhaj, I.: A new enhanced RPL based routing for internet of things. In: ICC2017 WS06-Convergent Internet Things- Synergy IoT Systems, pp. 1–6 (2017)

17. Kermajani, H., Gomez, C.: On the network convergence process in RPL over IEEE 802.15.4 multihop networks: improvement and trade-offs. Sens. (Switz.) 14, 11993–12022 (2014). https://doi.org/10.3390/s140711993

18. Kiraly, C., Istomin, T., Iova, O., Picco, G.P.: D-RPL: overcoming memory limitations in RPL point-to-multipoint routing. In: Proceedings of Conference Local Computer Networks, LCN, 26–29 October 2015, pp. 157–160 (2015). https://doi.org/10.1109/lcn.2015.7366295

19. Han, D., Gnawali, O.: Performance of RPL under wireless interference. IEEE Commun. Mag. 51, 137–143 (2013). https://doi.org/10.1109/MCOM.2013.6685769

20. Ancillotti, E., Bruno, R., Conti, M.: Reliable data delivery with the IETF routing protocol for low-power and lossy networks. IEEE Trans. Ind. Inform. 10, 1864–1877 (2014). https://doi.org/10.1109/TII.2014.2332117

21. Wang, D., Tao, Z., Zhang, J., Abouzeid, A.A.: RPL based routing for advanced metering infrastructure in smart grid. In: 2010 IEEE International Conference Communications Workshops, pp. 1–6 (2010). https://doi.org/10.1109/iccw.2010.5503924

22. Ho, Q.D., Gao, Y., Rajalingham, G., Le-Ngoc, T.: Robustness of the routing protocol for low-power and lossy networks (RPL) in smart grid's neighbor-area networks. In: IEEE International Conference Communications, September 2015, pp. 826–831 (2015). https://doi.org/10.1109/icc.2015.7248424

Throughput and Energy Efficiency Analysis of the IEEE 802.11ah Restricted Access Window Mechanism

Miriyala Mahesh$^{(\boxtimes)}$ and V. P. Harigovindan

Department of Electronics and Communication Engineering,
National Institute of Technology Puducherry,
Karaikal, Union Territory of Puducherry, India
miriyalamahesh4u@gmail.com, hari@nitpy.ac.in

Abstract. Internet of Things (IoT) is an emerging technology, which enables the interconnection of computing devices through Internet. IEEE 802.11ah is introduced as an amendment to IEEE 802.11 standard to provide ubiquitous connectivity, scalability and to reduce the energy consumption in dense networks like IoT. IEEE 802.11ah implements Restricted Access Window (RAW) mechanism to reduce packet collisions and improve energy efficiency. RAW reduces contention among the devices by dividing them into several groups and channel time into various slots. In this article, we have developed an analytical model to evaluate the performance of RAW mechanism in terms of throughput and energy efficiency in a dense IoT network. We have also analyzed the performance of RAW mechanism for different Modulation and Coding Schemes (MCS) proposed in the draft standard. The analytical model has been validated through the simulation studies. The results show that, the RAW mechanism outperforms the legacy DCF in a dense IoT scenario.

Keywords: Internet of Things (IoT)
Restricted Access Window (RAW) · IEEE 802.11ah

1 Introduction

Internet of Things (IoT) has integrated the entire world under a common platform to make Human-Machine interaction much simpler. The vision of IoT is to equip everyday objects with sensing, networking, and processing capabilities that allow them to talk with one another over Internet [7]. This paradigm has applications in various domains such as medical aids, Intelligent Transportation System (ITS), smart grids, health care, industrial automation, agriculture monitoring and many others [14]. Analyst forecast that there may be 50 billion devices connected to Internet by 2020 [6].

For ubiquitous connectivity and superior performance in dense networks, IoT needs a low power, wide range, and scalable wireless networking technology.

© Springer Nature Singapore Pte Ltd. 2018
P. Bhattacharyya et al. (Eds.): NGCT 2017, CCIS 828, pp. 227–237, 2018.
https://doi.org/10.1007/978-981-10-8660-1_17

Technologies like RFID, Wireless Personal Area Network (WPAN) (for example Bluetooth, ZigBee) and Low Power Wireless Local Area Network (LPWAN) (for example SigFox, LoRa) are suggested networking technologies because of their good throughput, simple association, and ease of deployment. But these technologies are not suitable in large networks because of their limited coverage, data rates, and number of associated devices. On the other hand, though the technologies like WiMax, LTE have longer range and data rates, they consume more energy, hence making them inappropriate for IoT [8].

To overcome these drawbacks in wireless networking technologies, IEEE 802 LAN/MAN Standards Committee (LMSC) has formed IEEE 802.11ah Task group to support IoT [11]. Even though IEEE 802.11 is a popular WLAN standard, it suffers severe contention and hidden terminal problem in a dense network. IEEE 802.11ah operates at Sub 1 GHz (S1G) ISM frequency band. Due to superior low-frequency propagation characteristics, it can provide a coverage up to 1 Km with a data rates from 100 Kbps to 78 Mbps. It also consumes less energy and can be associated up to 8000 devices [5].

IEEE 802.11ah implements a novel channel access scheme called Restricted Access Window (RAW) to reduce channel contention and to decrease collision probability. RAW divides the total devices into smaller groups and channel time into RAW slots. It allocates each RAW slot to a group of devices to spread their channel access time for a longer duration to reduce the contention among them [12]. Besides, 802.11ah also introduces Traffic Indication Map (TIM) segmentation, Target Wakeup Time (TWT), Access Point (AP) power management, short headers, Null Data Packets (NDP) MAC frames and short beacons to reduce energy consumption in the network [13]. Detailed overview of the 802.11ah protocol is provided in Sect. 2.

An analytical model is presented in [15] to evaluate the Group Synchronized Distributed Coordination Function (GS-DCF) using centralized and decentralized grouping schemes. Duration of RAW is an important factor to analyze the network performance. Park *et al.* in [9] proposed a new algorithm to find the optimal size of RAW. They have used the success probability to find the relation between number of devices and size of RAW. In [2], authors proposed a novel method to estimate the RAW size based on traffic load and also provide relay node support for devices. To support large number of devices, RAW divides the devices into groups and allocates time slot to each group. A novel grouping scheme is discussed in [1]. The scheme divides the total devices into groups and choose a group head for contending to reduce the channel contention.

In this article, we present a simple yet accurate analytical model to evaluate the performance of IEEE 802.11ah and its RAW mechanism. The model employed for the analysis is developed from Bianchi's model [3] and similar to that of [4]. The paper outlines the performance of IEEE 802.11ah and its RAW mechanism for different Modulation and Coding Schemes (MCS), proposed in the draft standard. The performance of RAW mechanism in high density network is evaluated and compared with legacy DCF. Using the analytical model developed, we have also evaluated the performance of different Modulation and Coding Schemes (MCS) proposed for IEEE 802.11ah. Throughput

Table 1. Data rates of different MCS for 2 MHz Channel

MCS	Mod.	CR	Bits per OFDM symbol	Data rate Mbps
MCS0	BPSK	1/2	52	0.65
MCS1	QPSK	1/2	104	1.30
MCS2	QPSK	3/4	104	1.95
MCS3	16QAM	1/2	208	2.60
MCS4	16QAM	3/4	208	3.90
MCS5	64QAM	2/3	312	5.20
MCS6	64QAM	3/4	312	5.85
MCS7	64QAM	5/6	312	6.50
MCS8	256QAM	3/4	416	7.80

and energy consumption per group are evaluated using analytical models and validated through simulations.

The rest of the paper is organized as follows: Sect. 2 gives a brief description of the protocol, Sect. 3 discusses a mathematical model to evaluate the performance of the RAW, Sect. 4 deals with the simulation results and finally the paper is concluded in Sect. 5.

2   Overview of IEEE 802.11ah

IEEE 802.11ah is an amendment of the legacy 802.11 standard to provide better coverage and high scalability for IoT devices. This section highlights the salient features of the IEEE 802.11ah standard. Detailed description of the protocol can be found in [5].

2.1   Physical Layer

The IEEE 802.11ah PHY layer is inherited from the 802.11ac standard. The protocol operates at Sub 1 GHz (S1G) ISM band with five different channels (1, 2, 4, 8 and 16 MHz). The ISM bands available for S1G communications are different for each country. For example, US uses 902–928 MHz, 863–868.6 MHz is used in Europe and Japan uses 916.5–927.5 MHz frequency spectrum. IEEE 802.11ah standard uses Orthogonal Frequency Division Multiplexing (OFDM), Multiple Input Multiple Output (MIMO) and Downlink Multi-User MIMO (DL MU-MIMO). Ten different Modulation and Coding Schemes (MCS0-MCS9) are inherited from 802.11ac with different transmission rates. Out of these, MCS0 with 1 MHz and 2 MHz channel is the most robust coding scheme and provides large coverage. It is shown that the coverage of 802.11ah is around 850 m using MCS0 [11], which is higher range over the conventional Wi-Fi. The data rate of various MCSs for 2 MHz channel is shown in Table 1.

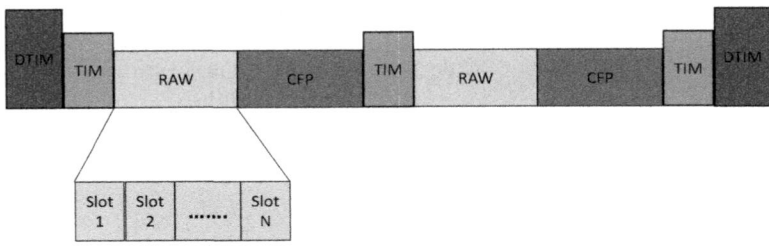

Fig. 1. Structure of RAW

2.2   MAC Layer

The Access Point (AP) increases the scalability of the network by assigning a unique 13-bit Association Identifier (AID) for every device.The first two bits of AID organize the total devices into four pages. The next five bits divide each page into 32 blocks. The following three bits divide each block into eight sub-blocks. Finally, the last three bits are used to find the device index.

Figure 1 shows that the standard splits the Traffic Indication Map (TIM) into TIM segments and transmits separately. The AP informs all the devices about the TIM segment in which they have data, by using Delivery Traffic Indication Map (DTIM) broadcast. In between two consecutive TIM there are several RAW periods and Contention Free Periods (CFP). Each RAW period has several RAW slots. RAW is introduced in this new standard to reduce collisions among the devices by dividing them into groups and the channel time into RAW slots. Then each device or a group of devices are assigned a RAW slot and spreading their channel access times over a longer period of time.

All the devices wake up at Target Beacon Transmission Time (TBTT). AP broadcasts RAW Parameters Set (RPS) element to all the devices. The RPS element contains information about the RAW start time, duration of RAW, AID's of the devices. During a RAW period, a device chooses a RAW slot using the following Eq. (1).

$$\chi_{slot} = (AID_N + N_{offset}) \ mod \ R_{slot} \tag{1}$$

χ_{slot} is the slot chosen by a device N with Association Identifier (AID_N), N_{offset} is used to improve fairness among the devices and R_{slot} is the total number of RAW slots [5,11]. All the devices access the channel using Enhanced Distributed Channel Access (EDCA) in each RAW slot. As shown in Fig. 2, the AP allocates each RAW slot to a group of devices. All the devices who have uplink data, contend for the channel to transmit PS_Poll frames with Uplink Data Identification (UDI) set to 1 in their respective RAW slots. The device which is acknowledged after SIFS time by the AP, waits for a SIFS duration and sends the data packet. After SIFS time, the device will be acknowledged for its successful transmission of data by the AP.

IEEE 802.11ah conserves energy by reducing the MAC overhead using short headers, Null Data Packet (NDP) MAC frames, and short beacons. Further,

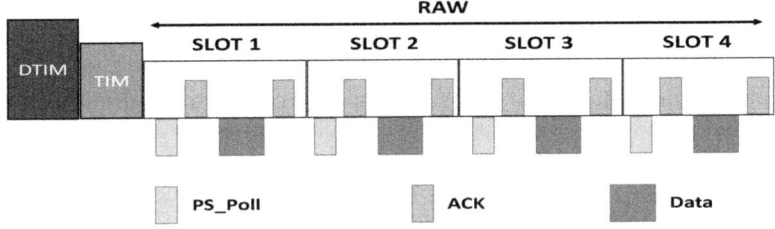

Fig. 2. RAW channel access mechanism for uplink transmission

devices are divided into TIM and Non-TIM devices. TIM devices wake up periodically and listen to TIM beacons. Non-TIM devices do not wake up periodically [16]. In TWT mode, the wakeup times of all the devices are scheduled and is informed to AP.

3   Performance Analysis

We assume that all the devices present in the network are fully connected and every device has at least one packet to transmit all the time. The channel is error-free and is divided into mini-slots with duration σ. We evaluate the uplink performance of the devices. Let us consider N devices, divided into K groups with each group of size, $g = N/K$. T_R is the duration of RAW and $T_{s,j}$ is the duration of jth RAW slot. As there are K groups and corresponding K RAW slots, $\sum_{j=1}^{K} T_{s,j} = T_R$. All the devices in a group access the channel using conventional Distributed Coordination Function (DCF). DCF implements binary exponential backoff algorithm. A device in the jth group during the allocated RAW slot, takes a backoff for random amount of time before sensing the channel. After DIFS time, if the channel is sensed idle, then the device starts transmitting a packet, else it will initialize a random backoff counter. At each packet transmission, the backoff time is uniformly chosen in the range $[0, W-1]$ where W is the contention window (CW). At the first transmission, CW is set to minimum Contention Window (CW_{min}). After each unsuccessful transmission, W is doubled upto maximum Contention Window (CW_{max}). Let W_0 represent the minimum Contention Window. The contention window for the ith retry/retransmission is given by,

$$W_i = \begin{cases} 2^i \times W_0 & i = 0, 1, ..., m-1 \\ 2^m \times W_0 & m \leq i \leq R \end{cases} \tag{2}$$

where m is the retransmission attempt and R is the retry limit of a packet transmission before being discarded[1]. When the backoff counter is decreased to

---

[1] According to the 802.11ah draft [6] the default value of m and R are chosen as 5 and 7 and $CW_{min} = 32$.

zero then the device is allowed to transmit a packet. In between two consecutive transmissions, a device takes a backoff followed by DIFS time [15].

In this section, we propose an analytical model which is developed from [3,4] to evaluate the performance of RAW scheme in terms of throughput and energy efficiency. Let τ_j be the probability that a device transmits a packet during the allocated j^{th} RAW slot and $p_{c,j}$ is the probability that the transmitted packet encounter a collision. The probability that a packet transmission takes place in a jth RAW slot is given by,

$$
\tau_j = \frac{2(1 - p_{c,j}^{R+1})(1 - 2p_{c,j})}{\left(\begin{array}{l} (1 - 2p_{c,j}) \left(1 - p_{c,j}^{R+1}\right) \\ + W_0(1 - (2p_{c,j})^{m+1})(1 - p_{c,j}) \\ + W_0 2^m p_{c,j}^{m+1}(1 - 2p_{c,j})(1 - p_{c,j}^{R-m}) \end{array} \right)} \tag{3}
$$

Let there are g devices contending for the channel access in the jth RAW slot. Then the collision probability is given by Eq. (4),

$$
p_{c,j} = 1 - (1 - \tau_j)^{g-1} \tag{4}
$$

Equations (3) and (4) form a system of non linear equations with two unknowns that can be solved using numerical methods. Let $P_{tr,j}$ be the probability that there is at least one transmission in a given j^{th} RAW slot.

$$
P_{tr,j} = 1 - (1 - \tau_j)^g \tag{5}
$$

$P_{s,j}$ is the probability that the packet is successfully transmitted i.e., there is exactly one device transmitting and $g - 1$ devices differ the transmission conditioned that there is at least one transmission in a given j^{th} RAW slot.

$$
P_{s,j} = \frac{g\tau_j (1 - \tau_j)^{g-1}}{1 - (1 - \tau_j)^g} \tag{6}
$$

Saturation Throughput. The saturation throughput can be expressed as the ratio of average information transmitted in a time slot to the average length of the time slot. The saturation throughput of the jth RAW slot is given by,

$$
S_j = \frac{\left(\begin{array}{c} \text{Average payload information} \\ \text{transmitted in a time slot} \end{array} \right)}{\text{Average length of a slot time}} \tag{7}
$$

We define $E[L]$ as the average size of packet, $P_{tr,j}P_{s,j}$ is the probability of successful transmission in a jth RAW slot, $(1 - P_{tr,j})$ is the probability of the channel being idle and $P_{tr,j}(1 - P_{s,j})$ is the probability of collision in a jth RAW slot. Therefore the throughput is given by,

$$
S_j = \frac{P_{tr,j}P_{s,j}E[L]}{(1 - P_{tr,j})\sigma + P_{tr,j}P_{s,j}T_s + P_{tr,j}(1 - P_{s,j})T_c} \tag{8}
$$

Here, T_s is the average time the channel is sensed busy because of a successful transmission, T_c is the average time the channel is sensed busy because of a collision and σ is the duration of empty time slot.

$$T_s = T_{PS\_Poll} + T_{E[L]} + 2T_{ACK} + 3SIFS + DIFS + 3\delta$$
$$T_c = T_{PS\_Poll} + DIFS + \delta \tag{9}$$

Transmission time of the payload $E[L]$ can be calculated by using Eq. 10 and $T_{E[L]}$ will vary with the data rate corresponding to the MCS used. The transmission time of the control frames (PS_poll, ACK) can be calculated by using Eq. (11). Payload can be sent using any MCS with different data rate mentioned in Table 1. It should be noted that the PHY header and the control frames must be sent using the most robust modulation scheme MCS0, which is referred as *basic_datarate*. $L_{sym}^{basic\_datarate}$ is the bits per OFDM symbol when basic data rate is used.

$$T_{E[L]}(Rate) = ceil \left(\frac{8 \times (Payload + MAC)}{\frac{Rate}{basic\_datarate} \times L_{sym}^{basic\_datarate}} \right) \times T_{sym} + PHY \tag{10}$$

$$T_{control} = ceil \left(\frac{8 \times ControlFrame}{L_{sym}^{basic\_datarate}} \right) \times T_{sym} + PHY \tag{11}$$

Energy Efficiency. The energy consumed during a successful transmission of a packet [10] is given by

$$E_s = P_{Tx}(T_{PS\_Poll} + T_{E[L]}) + P_{Rx}(T_s - T_{PS\_Poll} + T_{E[L]}) \tag{12}$$

The energy consumed due to collision is given by

$$E_c = P_{Tx}(T_{PS\_Poll}) + P_{Rx}(T_c - T_{PS\_Poll}) \tag{13}$$

The total energy consumed to successfully transmit a packet in the jth RAW slot is given by

$$E_T \simeq (1 - P_{tr,j})\sigma P_{idle} + P_{tr,j} P_{s,j} E_s + P_{tr,j}(1 - P_{s,j})E_c \tag{14}$$

We define the energy consumption per bit η_{T_j} as the energy required to successfully transmit one bit of data. It is given by

$$\eta_{T_j} \approx \frac{E_T}{P_{tr,j} P_{s,j} E[L]} \tag{15}$$

4   Simulation and Analysis

In this section, we present analytical and simulation results. Analytical results corresponding to the mathematical model, presented in the previous section are obtained using MATLAB. Simulations are carried out to validate the

Table 2. Protocol parameters

Payload	1024 Bytes
MAC header	14 Bytes
PHY header	156 bits
Ps_Poll	20 Bytes
ACK	14 Bytes
$basic\_datarate$	650 Kbps
T_{sym}	40 μs
σ	52 μs
SIFS	160 μs
DIFS	264 μs
P_{Tx}	255 mW
P_{Rx}	135 mW
P_{idle}	1.3 mW

performance characteristics of IEEE 802.11ah in a dense network using a discrete event simulator implemented in C++. In this paper, we considered $N = 256$ devices which are divided into K groups. Here we consider different groups of size 8, 16, 32, 64, 128 and 256. For example if the group size is equal to 64, it means that all the 256 devices are divided into 4 groups with each group consists of 64 devices. The RAW mechanism is evaluated in terms of throughput and energy consumption of a network using different MCSs. The RAW duration is considered as 500 ms. The IEEE 802.11ah protocol parameters used for obtaining the results are given in Table 2.

Figures 3 and 4 show the performance of RAW for different group size and also for different MCSs. The results are also compared with the legacy DCF. The default parameters used to evaluate the performance of legacy DCF can be seen in [3]. The performance is evaluated for $N = 256$ devices which are divided into groups of size 8, 16, 32, 64, 128 and 256 respectively. Among all the MCS, with increase in number of groups, the throughput increases and the energy consumption per bit decreases. On the other hand DCF consumes more energy and degrades the throughput due to increased contention among the large number of devices. As RAW implements grouping, the contention in the network is evenly distributed into various RAW slots, thus improving its performance.

Finally, Table 3 gives a performance comparison between RAW access scheme and legacy DCF in a dense IoT network. We evaluate the performance of RAW mechanism with number of devices (N upto 8000 devices). In the RAW mechanism these devices are divided into two groups ($K = 2$). In a dense IoT network, when legacy DCF is used, large number of devices contend for the channel. This high contention increases the collisions between them. Due to increased collisions, the throughput is degraded and more energy will be consumed. As RAW divides the devices and spread their access in defined slots, it outperforms the legacy DCF in a dense network, in terms of its energy efficiency and throughput.

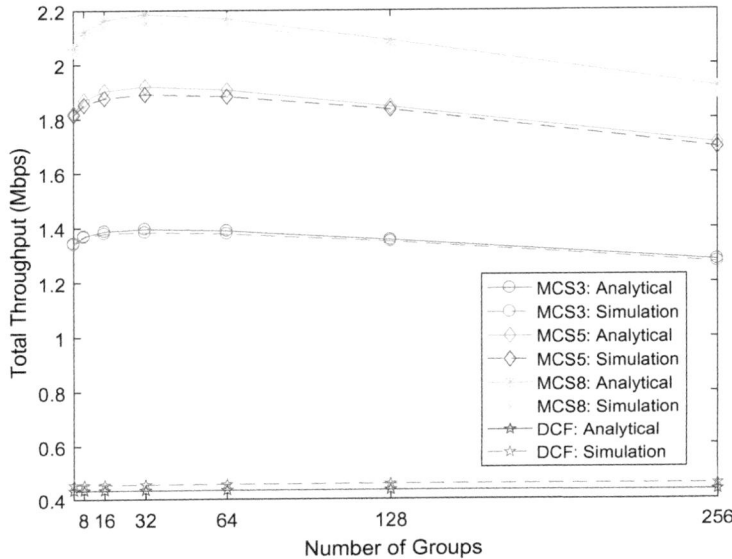

Fig. 3. Throughput versus group size

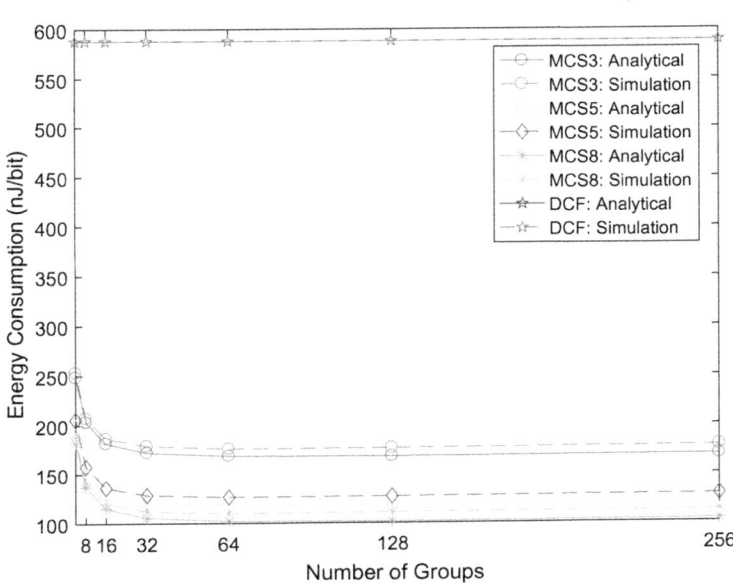

Fig. 4. Energy efficiency versus group size

Table 3. Comparison between RAW and legacy DCF in a dense IoT network for MCS0

Number of devices	Throughput (Mbps)		Energy consumption (nJ/bit)	
	RAW	DCF	RAW	DCF
1000	0.5046	0.2998	495	852
2000	0.4874	0.1802	518	1460
3000	0.4685	0.1064	563	2580
4000	0.4431	0.0491	607	4680
5000	0.4079	0.0303	677	10700
6000	0.3929	0.0139	786	22600
7000	0.3153	0.0073	987	55500
8000	0.2555	0.004	1240	814000

5   Conclusion

In this paper, a simple analytical model developed from Bianchi's model, is presented to evaluate the performance of RAW mechanism in IEEE 802.11ah in terms of throughput and energy efficiency. The performance of RAW mechanism is extremely better than the legacy DCF in a dense IoT network. We have evaluated the performance of the RAW mechanism for different MCSs. We have observed that the RAW mechanism results in improving the throughput as well as reducing the per bit energy consumption in a dense IoT network. This makes IEEE 802.11ah standard a good candidate for super dense IoT network.

References

1. Abichar, Z., Chang, J.M.: Group-based medium access control for IEEE 802.11n wireless LANs. IEEE Trans. Mob. Comput. **12**(2), 304–317 (2013)
2. Ahmed, N., Hussain, M.I.: Relay-based IEEE 802.11ah network: a smart city solution. In: 2016 Cloudification of the Internet of Things (CIoT), pp. 1–6, November 2016
3. Bianchi, G.: Performance analysis of the IEEE 802.11 distributed coordination function. IEEE J. Sel. Areas Commun. **18**(3), 535–547 (2000)
4. Chatzimisios, P., Boucouvalas, A.C., Vitsas, V.: IEEE 802.11 packet delay-a finite retry limit analysis. In: Global Telecommunications Conference, GLOBECOM 2003, vol. 2, pp. 950–954. IEEE, December 2003
5. Khorov, E., Lyakhov, A., Krotov, A., Guschin, A.: A survey on IEEE 802.11ah: an enabling networking technology for smart cities. Comput. Commun. **58**, 53–69 (2015). http://www.sciencedirect.com/science/article/pii/S0140366414002989. Special Issue on Networking and Communications for Smart Cities
6. LAN/MAN Standards Committee of the IEEE Computer Society: IEEE Standard 802.11ac-2013: Part 11: Wireless LAN Medium Access Control (MAC) and Physical Layer (PHY) Specifications, Amendment 4 Enhancements for Very High Throughput for Operation in Bands below 6 GHz (2013)

7. Miorandi, D., Sicari, S., Pellegrini, F.D., Chlamtac, I.: Internet of things: vision, applications and research challenges. Ad Hoc Netw. **10**(7), 1497–1516 (2012). http://www.sciencedirect.com/science/article/pii/S1570870512000674

8. Palattella, M.R., Accettura, N., Vilajosana, X., Watteyne, T., Grieco, L.A., Boggia, G., Dohler, M.: Standardized protocol stack for the internet of (important) things. IEEE Commun. Surv. Tutor. **15**(3), 1389–1406 (2013)

9. Park, C.W., Hwang, D., Lee, T.J.: Enhancement of IEEE 802.11ah MAC for M2M communications. IEEE Commun. Lett. **18**(7), 1151–1154 (2014)

10. Raeesi, O., Pirskanen, J., Hazmi, A., Talvitie, J., Valkama, M.: Performance enhancement and evaluation of IEEE 802.11ah multi-access point network using restricted access window mechanism. In: 2014 IEEE International Conference on Distributed Computing in Sensor Systems, pp. 287–293, May 2014

11. Sun, W., Choi, M., Choi, S.: IEEE 802.11ah: a long range 802.11 WLAN at sub 1 GHz. J. ICT Stand. **1**, 1–26 (2013). http://riverpublishers.com/journal_read_html_article.php?j=JICTS/1/1/5

12. Tian, L., Famaey, J., Latr, S.: Evaluation of the IEEE 802.11ah restricted access window mechanism for dense IoT networks. In: 2016 IEEE 17th International Symposium on A World of Wireless, Mobile and Multimedia Networks (WoWMoM), pp. 1–9, June 2016

13. Wang, Y., Li, Y., Chai, K.K., Chen, Y., Schormans, J.: Energy-aware adaptive restricted access window for IEEE 802.11ah based smart grid networks. In: 2015 IEEE International Conference on Smart Grid Communications (SmartGridComm), pp. 581–586, November 2015

14. Zanella, A., Bui, N., Castellani, A., Vangelista, L., Zorzi, M.: Internet of things for smart cities. IEEE Internet Things J. **1**(1), 22–32 (2014)

15. Zheng, L., Ni, M., Cai, L., Pan, J., Ghosh, C., Doppler, K.: Performance analysis of group-synchronized DCF for dense IEEE 802.11 networks. IEEE Trans. Wirel. Commun. **13**(11), 6180–6192 (2014)

16. Zheng, S., Lei, Z.: TIM encoding for IEEE 802.11ah based WLAN. In: 2014 IEEE International Conference on Communication Systems, pp. 559–563, November 2014

Underwater Navigation Systems
for Autonomous Underwater Vehicle

Sachi Choudhary[(⊠)], Rashmi Sharma, Amit Kumar Mondal,
and Vindhya Devalla

University of Petroleum and Energy Studies, Dehradun, Uttarakhand, India
sachi.choudhary1617@gmail.com

Abstract. Over the past few decades, researchers, navy of different countries
and different organizations related to maritime archaeology, underwater mines &
pipelines etc. had paid considerable attention towards underwater surveying &
inspection by autonomous robot or vehicle. Considerable improvements for
better AUV navigation have seen in different sensors in recent years. The
sensors are available with not only improved performance but lesser cost and
reduced size as well. In addition to these developments, huge improvements in
path planning of AUVs have also seen with advanced navigation techniques &
algorithm such as SLAM. This paper presents a survey on some important
navigation systems for AUV. These techniques can be used to calculate the
current position or to localize the robot/vehicle underwater.

Keywords: Autonomous Underwater Vehicle (AUV) · Inertial navigation
Acoustic navigation · Geophysical navigation

1 Introduction

Underwater divers & archaeologist have to dive underwater for information collection
previously. As human body is not physiologically and anatomically well adapted to the
underwater environmental, divers have to face lots of challenges like immersion,
exposure, breath hold limitation, ambient pressure change etc. To overcome the
problems of underwater divers lots of equipment have been developed which also helps
in increasing depth range as well as time. Again diving activities are restricted to depths
range even after wearing atmospheric suits and to conditions which are not extremely
risky.

So to explore the underwater area, development & enhancement of unmanned
underwater vehicles (UUV) have been a major area of research from past few decades.
UUVs are classified into two categories as mentioned in Sect. 2 of this paper. This
paper more focuses on AUV navigation & localization.

AUV navigation & self-localization is a challenging task due to penetration of radio
waves & GPS signals underwater [6]. Radio waves can be used for communication at
shallow depth. Acoustic based sensors perform better for underwater communication.
The traditional sensors for navigation are magnetic compass, pressure depth sensors,
acoustic navigation systems etc. From last few decades there is a huge development in

© Springer Nature Singapore Pte Ltd. 2018
P. Bhattacharyya et al. (Eds.): NGCT 2017, CCIS 828, pp. 238–245, 2018.
https://doi.org/10.1007/978-981-10-8660-1_18

the navigation sensors such as Doppler sonars, optical gyrocompasses, and inertial measurement units (IMUs) etc. [2].

Navigating autonomously is the biggest challenge for any AUV, as opposed to a ROV whose location can be measured accurately relative to the surface vessel that is connected to it.

2 Unmanned Underwater Vehicles

Unmanned Underwater Vehicle (UUV) or underwater drone is any vehicle that can operate underwater without any human occupant. UUVs were developed to perform Intelligence, Surveillance and Reconnaissance, Mine Countermeasures, Anti-Submarine Warfare, Underwater Inspection/Identification, Oceanography/Hydrography, Communication/Navigation Network Nodes, Underwater Archaeologies etc. Unmanned Underwater vehicles are broadly categorized as Autonomous Underwater Vehicle (AUV) & Remotely Operated Underwater Vehicles (ROV).

Autonomous Underwater Vehicle (AUV) is UUVs without any human or remote interference. They are preprogrammed vehicles and operate autonomously. AUVs can be used to perform underwater inspection missions such as detecting and mapping submerged crashes, rocks, and obstructions that pose a hazard to navigation for commercial and recreational vessels. When a mission is complete, the AUV will return to a pre-programmed location to transfer the collected data during surveillance.

Remotely Operated Vehicle (ROV) is controlled by a remote human operator at sea/water surface. The main application areas of ROVs are in deep water industries such as offshore hydrocarbon extraction. They are linked to a surface vessel or host ship by a neutrally buoyant cable or, often when working in rough conditions or in deeper water, a load-carrying umbilical cable is used along with a tether management system (TMS).

3 Challenges with Underwater Autonomous Vehicles

3.1 Unstructured Environment

Underwater surveillance is more complex than surface or land surveillance using mobile robot or autonomous vehicles. The navigation & obstacle avoidance in unstructured underwater environment is very difficult due to low visibility & more penetration of light. It is challenging for autonomous vehicles to explore & navigate without any knowledge of environment, geophysical landmarks, obstacles & environmental factors like turbidity, water current, tide level, etc.

3.2 Unavailability of Satellite Based Navigation or GPS

GPS is a space based radio frequency signal used for navigation at surface. GPS is unavailable after a certain range as radio frequency cannot penetrate sea water. Very low frequency radio waves i.e. 3–30 kHz can penetrate sea water but not more than range of 20 m. So for underwater navigation, vehicles have to depend on different acoustic based sensors. Section 4 of this paper focuses on different techniques that can be used to locate the vehicle's current position underwater.

3.3 Underwater Communication

Communication among the underwater vehicles or in between underwater vehicle & surface vehicle is still a broad area of research. As radio waves can't be used underwater, vehicles have to depend on acoustic signals. In case of ROV, communication is possible because vehicle is tide to surface vehicle via a cord. In this case the noise level may be high due to physical disturbance transmitted along the cable to surface (Fig. 1).

4 Underwater Navigation Systems

To solve the navigation problem different sensors can be used which can locate the AUVs current position. The different AUV navigation techniques/methods can be classified into three categories [5, 6]:

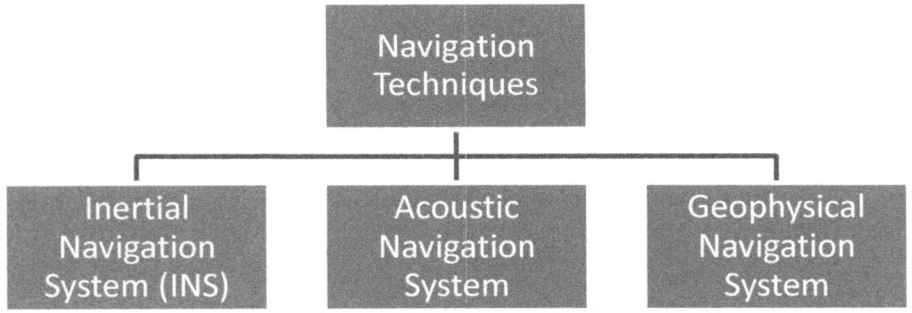

Fig. 1. Underwater navigation techniques

4.1 Inertial Navigation System (INS)

AUV can estimate its position at sea by estimating the distance & direction travelled called as **Dead reckoning.** Dead reckoning (DR) is the method of calculating AUV's positon at sea autonomously without help of any positioning support or landmarks.

In DR AUV can estimates its position based upon its previous orientation & velocity or acceleration vector.

INS uses onboard sensors & no other external resources for positioning. The initial position of AUV is set by GPS or any other positioning system. The position of AUVs get updated underwater using on-board sensors. To update the position of AUV on-board sensor are used along with previously stored position. On-board sensors measure acceleration, change in velocity along with time.

DR is the oldest & low cost method of navigation. DR uses inertial sensors such as gyroscopic sensor or gyrocompass and an accelerometer, to estimate the orientation and distance traveled by the AUV with respect to a reference coordinate system. The disadvantage of DR is the measurement error due to noise from gyroscopes which affect navigation [11]. The source of error also includes inaccurate knowledge of start position & time varying effects of on-board sensors. The AUV's motion is affected by ocean waves. A neural network based DR method (DR-N) was proposed in [11] to overcome these problems.

INS uses gyroscopic and/or accelerometers to calculate the current position of AUV. It can be used with Doppler Velocity Log (DVL) feature and Acoustic Doppler Current Profiler (ADCP) [5]. INS can be combined with DVL to use bottom tracking feature for better navigation. The current position of AUV can be calculated by combining velocity of vehicle with previous position & data from accelerometer. Kalman filter (KF) is used to reduce the uncertainty of the position estimated [5]. Extended Kalman Filter (EKF) can be used for state estimation.

An acoustic Doppler current profiler (ADCP) is a hydro acoustic current meter, uses Doppler Effect of sound waves. It can measure velocity of water current. ADCP can measure water current over ranges of about 1000 m.

4.2 Acoustic Navigation System

Acoustic navigation system works with the help of acoustic beacons placed in navigation area. It is used to improve the efficiency of navigation of large mission. The main approaches of acoustic navigation are Long baseline (LBL), Short baseline (SBL) & Ultra short baseline (USBL) [5, 12] (Table 1).

Table 1. Acoustic baseline is the distance between active sensors.

Acoustic system	Acoustic baseline length
LBL	100 m–10 km
SBL	20 m–50 m
USBL	<10 cm

In classical Long-Baseline (LBL) transponders are placed in sea floor or sea bed separated by a long distance that is why it is called Long baseline [12]. The other LBL system available is Mobile LBL which has beacons (GIBs) at water surface & transponders submerged in the water at a specified depth. It is not portable (Fig. 2).

The SBL has acoustic baseline of range 20 m–50 m. SBL uses single beacon at AUV & multiple acoustic transponders on the ship (the accuracy can be increased by increasing distance between the transponders) [12]. The position of AUV is calculated by acoustic signals travel time from different transponders placed on ship to AUV. It is not used because of low accuracy (Fig. 3).

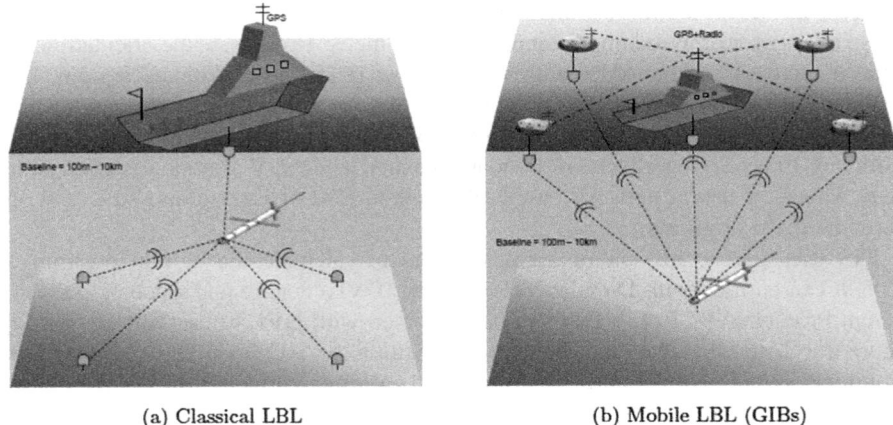

(a) Classical LBL   (b) Mobile LBL (GIBs)

Fig. 2. Long baseline (LBL) navigation system

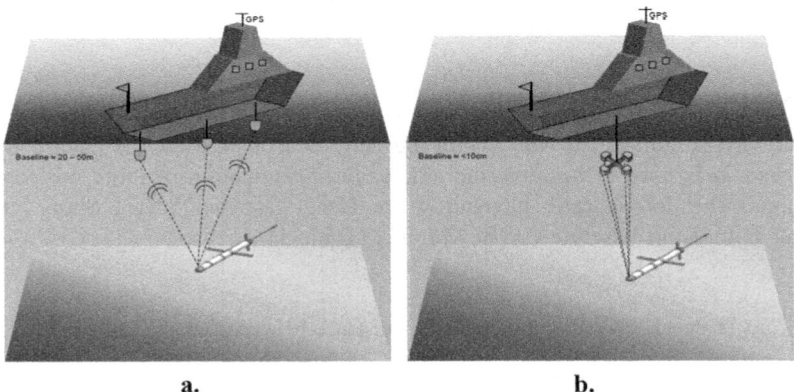

a.   b.

Fig. 3. (a) Short baseline (SBL) navigation system (b) Ultrashort baseline (USBL) navigation system

The third is ultra-short baseline (USBL) positioning have a single multi-element transducers or transducer array (minimum 3 transducer in an array) called trans-receiver on AUV and a single beacon at sea bottom [12]. The distance between transducer in array is <10 cm i.e. ultra-baseline. The transducers in AUV pings the trans-receiver by acoustic signal & receive the response. The round trip time along with angle & direction are used to calculate the position of AUV in an inertial frame. USBL is easy to deploy than above mention acoustic navigation systems, that is why it is most widely used. But USBL is less accurate than other two as the baseline is small.

Source of error in acoustic navigation system are:

I. Deployment of transponders on the sea bed & beacons at AUV [2].
II. Information of sound velocity as sound velocity is dependent on water temperature & density [2].

4.3   Geophysical Navigation

DR cannot be used for long mission & cost of INS & acoustic baseline system is high for multipurpose AUVs. Therefore researches have more focus on cost effective systems which can use AUVs surrounding data to position it without help of GPS and any other external system [9]. It is based on the physical features captured/observed by onboard sensors like sonar & optical sensors [5]. The difficulties faced by AUVs using geophysical navigations are to identify & process gathered features/data.

Different Geophysical Navigation Systems are:

4.3.1   Optical

Optical navigation system uses camera images to find the position of robot. The cameras used for this type of navigations are either monocular or stereo cameras [6].

A **monocular camera** passes light through a series of lenses or primes to magnify the images of distant objects. Stereo cameras have full six degree-of-freedom transformations between consecutive image pairs [6]. The optical navigation is dependent on the available features, so it can be used for small maps.

4.3.2   Sonar

Sonar system uses sound propagation to navigate underwater. Sonar emits sound energy and analyses the echo from underwater object or sea floor. The Sonar is categorized as passive & active sonar. Passive sonar relies on sound made by vessels while active sonar emits pulses of noise & then listen for echoes. Sonar is designed to work at specific frequency depending on the required range & resolution [6]. This section contains a brief description of (a) imaging sonar and (b) ranging sonar [6] (Tables 2 and 3).

Table 2. Sonar imaging devices used for underwater navigation

Sonar	Description
Side-scan Sonar	Sonar towed in surface vessel emits sounds energy in conical or fan-shaped pulses towards sea bed continuously & analyses the return echo to create a picture of sea floor or underwater object. The sound frequencies used in side-scan sonar usually range from 100 to 500 kHz; higher frequencies yield better resolution but less range. The side scan sonar can be used with single beam & multi-beam sonar system for better results [6]
Forward look sonar	The working is similar to side scan sonar only beams are in forward direction of vessel [6]
Synthetic aperture sonar	It uses multiple pulses to create a large synthetic array (or aperture). It has more resolution than advanced side scan sonar i.e. hundreds of meters. It combines multiple echoes to form an image
Mechanical scanned imaging sonar	It scans 2D horizontal plane by rotating a mechanically actuated transducer head at pre-set angle [13]

Table 3. Sonar imaging devices used for underwater navigation

Sonar	Description
Echo sounder	It measures depth by emitting sound pulses into water. The calculation depends on difference between time of emission, echo arrival and speed of sound
Profiler	It gives cross sectional profile of seabed or object. Profilers operate by rotating a transducer attached to a stepper motor through a number of angular ping positions within a defined scan width
Multi beam	Similar to other sonar it also uses sound pulses except it uses beamforming by which it can find the information of direction from returning echoes

5 Conclusion

Different underwater navigation techniques have been reviewed. The navigation techniques for autonomous underwater vehicles are inertial navigation system (INS), acoustic navigation & geophysical navigation system. Along with navigation techniques the different state estimation techniques such as Kalman Filter (KF), Extended Kalman Filter (EKF), Unscented Kalman Filter (UKF), Extended Information Filter (EIF), Particle Filter (PF) ect can be combined for better estimation & accurate results. To improve the efficiency of different techniques, localization techniques can be used such as SLAM.

SLAM (Simultaneous localization & mapping) is a robot mapping technique used by autonomous vehicle to construct & update map of unknown environment and it maintains the track of vehicle's current location.

References

1. Wynn, R.B., et al.: Autonomous underwater vehicles (AUVs): their past, present and future contributions to the advancement of marine geoscience. Mar. Geol. **352**, 451–468 (2014)
2. Kinsey, J.C., Eustice, R.M., Whitcomb, L.L.: A survey of underwater vehicle navigation: recent advances and new challenges. In: Proceedings of the Conference of Maneuvering Control Marine Craft, pp. 1–12 (2006)
3. Bingham, B.: Navigating autonomous underwater vehicles. In: Inartzev, A. (ed.) Underwater Vehicles, p. 582. I-Tech, Vienna, Austria (2009). ISBN 978-953-7619-49-7
4. Ribas, D., Ridao, P., Tardós, J.D., Neira, J.: Underwater SLAM in man-made structured environments. J. Field Robot. **25**, 898–921 (2008)
5. Stutters, L., Liu, H., Tiltman, C., Brown, D.J.: Navigation technologies for autonomous underwater vehicles. IEEE Trans. Syst. Man Cybern.C. Appl. Rev. **38**(4), 581–589 (2008)
6. Paull, L., Saeedi, S., Seto, M., Li, H.: AUV navigation and localization: a review. IEEE J. Oceanic Eng. **39**, 131–149 (2014)
7. Teixeira, F. Pascoal., A.: Geophysical navigation of autonomous underwater vehicles. In: IFAC Conference on Control Applications in Marine Systems - CAMS 2007, Bol, Croatia (2007)
8. Olson, E., Leonard, J.J., Teller, S.: Robust range-only beacon localization. IEEE J. Oceanic Eng. **31**(4), 949–958 (2006)

9. Teixeira, F.C., Pascoal, A.M.: Geophysical navigation of autonomous underwater vehicles using geomagnetic information*. In: IFAC Proceedings Elsevier, vol. 41(1), pp. 178–183 (2008)
10. Miller, P.A., Farrell, J.A., Zhao, Y., Djapic, V.: Autonomous underwater vehicle navigation. IEEE J. Oceanic Eng. **35**(3), 663–678 (2010)
11. Xie, Y., Liu J., Hu, C., Cui, J. Xu, H., AUV Dead-Reckoning Navigation Based On Neural Network Using a Single Accelerometer. In: WUWNet-16 Proceedings of the 11th ACM International Conference on Underwater Networks and Systems, p. 44 (2016)
12. Austin, T., Hosom, D. Kuchta, D.: Long baseline acoustic navigation - a flexible approach to custom applications. In: IEEE OCEANS 1984, Washington, DC, USA, pp. 69–74 (1984)
13. Ribas, D., Ridao, P., Neira, J.: Understanding mechanically scanned imaging sonars. In: Underwater SLAM for Structured Environments Using an Imaging Sonar. STAR, vol 65. Springer, Heidelberg (2010). https://doi.org/10.1007/978-3-642-14040-2_4

Fast and Efficient Data Acquisition in Radiation Affected Large WSN by Predicting Transfaulty Nodes

Manish Pandey$^{(\boxtimes)}$, Sachin Dhanoriya, and Amit Bhagat

Maulana Azad National Institute of Technology, Bhopal 462003, India
contactmanishpandey@yahoo.co.in,
sachindhanoriya@outlook.com, am.bhagat@gmail.com

Abstract. Wireless Sensor Network is a collection of spatially distributed sensor nodes/motes those are connected wirelessly to form network topology. However, despite their great usefulness they are also vulnerable to misbehaviours. One such misbehaviour is Transfaultyness in which a sensor node is unable to transmit the data correctly under the effect of radiation, and it is called as Transfaulty node. Sensor node affected by radiation becomes isolated from the network, thus a dynamic hole is formed in the network. Formation of these dynamic holes in the wireless sensor network leads to data loss. To handle loss of data due to transfaulty nodes in WSN few algorithms have been proposed but none of them is efficient in large network having few thousands of sensor nodes. In our method, we have considered a large wireless sensor network having more than 1000 sensor nodes. We have used sensor nodes with dual mode of communication i.e. (1) Radio Frequency (RF) mode of communication and (2) Acoustic (AC) mode of communication. The nodes inside dynamic hole communicate using acoustic mode, nodes at the boundary of holes communicate using both RF and acoustic mode and all other nodes communicate using RF mode. Determination of transmission failure nodes is also predicted based on its previous observations. Simulation results show that our proposed algorithm achieves better throughput, energy efficiency, running time as compared to other proposed algorithms.

Keywords: Wireless sensor network · Radio frequency communication
Acoustic communication · Data Acquisition · Dempster Shafer Theory
Hypothesis testing · K-means clustering · Transfaulty nodes

1 Introduction

Recent advancements in low power wireless sensing devices which are able to communicate with same device over a small range had led the invention and development of Wireless Sensor Network (WSN) [1, 2]. These sensing devices are known as sensor motes or sensor nodes. Generally, they are deployed randomly or in a pre-planned fashion over a geographical area to form a network topology which covers the area optimally [3, 4]. These tiny nodes are capable of sensing important information and interesting events in their vicinity i.e. sensing range and transmit the sensed

© Springer Nature Singapore Pte Ltd. 2018
P. Bhattacharyya et al. (Eds.): NGCT 2017, CCIS 828, pp. 246–262, 2018.
https://doi.org/10.1007/978-981-10-8660-1_19

information to sink/base station via single-hop or multi-hop. Sensor nodes are connected to other nodes wirelessly in their transmission range. A typical WSN is composed of several hundred nodes and scales up to a few thousand nodes. WSN follows IEEE 802.11 specifications for wireless LAN (WLAN) protocols. Sensor nodes detect, sense and then transmit sensed information to other nodes and/or sink node/base station wirelessly. Generally, sensor nodes are battery powered devices, though there are sensors which require continuous power source other than battery [5].

Sensor Nodes detect and sense various physical and chemical phenomenon like pressure, smoke, temperature, humidity, presence of certain chemicals, etc. The various application areas of WSNs are forest fire detection, weather forecast, air pollution monitoring, environmental sensing, industrial application, military application, etc. [5]

In out proposed scheme, Efficient Data Acquisition in Radiation Affected WSN by Predicting Transfaulty Nodes, we try to handle data loss due to the presence of trans-faulty nodes in WSN. A node is said to be transfaulty node when it is not able to transmit the information it has sensed, because of the presence of environmental radiation, electromagnetic radiation or nuclear radiation. A transfaulty node may sense the physical phenomenon correctly but is unable to transmit the sensed information. A detailed study of effects of radiation on wireless nodes is given in literature [6, 7]. This leads to data loss and also creates dynamic holes in the network. These holes are dynamic in nature as these holes are created, courtesy to the presence of electromagnetic or nuclear radiation which is present for a temporary amount of time. Since, nature of radiation here is temporary, transfaultyness of radiation affected nodes is also temporary. Sensor nodes start to communicate and sense normally after radiation effect is gone.

Duration of a wave of radiation effect sometimes remains for indeterministic time and sometimes for very short duration time. Either way normal of working of WSN is affected which is undesirable for sensor networks deployed for crucial applications, those require continuous and uninterrupted working of WSN. Removal of trans-faulty nodes from sensor network and replacing them with new ones is not a solution. As this practice incurs very high maintenance cost and does not even solves the real problem. To solve this problem ReDAST proposes a method in which special kind of sensing nodes are used which are capable of communicating with other nodes using radio frequency communication mode (RF) and acoustic communication mode [8]. ReDAST uses Dempster Shafer Theory [9] and Hypothesis Testing [10] to determine communication failure nodes and nodes on the boundary of radiation. To gather approximately accurate information from radiation affected area K-means clustering algorithm [11] is used to determine cluster(s) of wireless sensory nodes in radiation affected area. Applying dampster-shafer theory and hypothesis testing for determining communication failure node are costly operations. So, observing the behaviour of communication failure nodes we predict a set of nodes to be transfaulty node(s).

1.1 Motivation

Wireless sensors are generally deployed in the area where they work autonomously, remain unattended for longer time and are more energy constrained. WSNs with huge no. of node are more prone to misbehaviours and faults. To enhance lifetime and energy utilization of WSN, one need to devise faster energy efficient and fault tolerant algorithm.

Transfaultyness of wireless sensory nodes is one such misbehaviour which adversely affects performance and efficiency of wireless sensor network. Removal and replacing of trans-faulty nodes is not a solution as WSN is huge and it will incur huge cost to make those changes. Hence there is great need of reconstruction of network topology.

1.2   Contribution

Information loss due to transfaulty behaviour shown by nodes is matter of great concern as, data lost due to transfaulty behaviour may be very important and critical data. Method proposed in ReDAST to overcome the problem associated with transfaulty nodes provides a descent solution to the concerned problem. Although, determining transfaulty nodes and boundary nodes is costly process, and as the network size scales up performance of ReDAST begins to cripples. Therefore, in our proposed scheme we are proposing a faster algorithm to observe and predict a set of nodes(s) to be transfaulty. Hence, improving overall performance of ReDAST making the algorithm significantly faster and help improving lifetime and energy efficiency of WSNs.

Outline of overall contribution of our work:

- We have discussed various issues in WSN due to the presence of radiation.
- We have analysed performance hit of ReDAST in large WSN.
- Discussing proposed method and algorithm.
- Performance evaluation based on various performance constraints through simulation.

1.3   Organization

Remaining paper is organized into four sections as follows. In Sect. 2, we have discussed related work that has been done in this field. Section 3, describes proposed methodology and algorithm. In Sect. 4, we have discussed simulation results. And in Sect. 5, we conclude our proposed scheme and provides direction to further extend our work in future.

2   Related Work

Cooperation and collaboration among wireless nodes are two important factors that affects operations of multihop WSN. Misbehaviour and faults in WSN are major concerns that affects proper co-operation and collaboration between nodes. There has been lot of work going on in wireless sensor network's field to enhance it and rectify faults and misbehaviours. Kar and Misra [8] focuses on faults and misbehaviours that are temporary in nature e.g. adverse effects of radiation on transmission and sensing of node. Rajasegrar et al. [12] proposed a non-parametric, distributed anomaly detection algorithm. Their algorithm identifies anomalous behaviour at nodes using clustering of data. Abid and Huangshui et al. [13] discuss various fault management frameworks those are specifically developed for WSN. They analysed two classes of problems, responsible for faulty functioning of nodes. First, nodes show abnormal behaviour in the presence of malicious attacks, interference and environmental noise. Second is physical damage to nodes leading to depletion of energy to be the reason behind the improper behaviour of wireless nodes. Kamhoua et al. [14] discussed routing misbehaviour issue in the presence of selfish nodes in the using evolutionary game theory. Their proposed work is a distributed algorithm that forces a selfish node to co-operate and forward data packets. Soltanmohammadi et al. [15] proposed a distributed scheme to detect various classes of misbehaving wireless nodes by using binary hypothesis testing.

Khan et al. [16] have proposed bridge protection algorithms (BPA) to prevent the network from getting bridged fragmented due to catastrophic. Munir et al. [17] investigated faults in WSN using various fault detection algorithms. They have proposed a duplex fault tolerant WSN model which consists of one active sensory node and one inactive spare sensory node.

Vladimirova et al. [18] experimentally observed effects of electro-magnetic interference on wireless jennic nodes. Shea [7] and Dargie and Poellabauer [19] investigated space effects of radiation on MEMS. They observed that due to effects of radiations on nodes, their sensing capability is affected.

Dini et al. [20] proposed a method for repairing a split network. They used mobile nodes to repair split WSN. Senal et al. [21] proposed a spider web based scheme which uses minimum cost spanning tree algorithm to reconnect the partitioned WSN because of damage done to sensor nodes.

3 Proposed Work

In Sect. 2. Related Work, we have briefly discussed about various works that have been done in the field of WSNs that improve performance and efficiency of WSN or rectifies various classes of faults and misbehaviours. It has been observed that, nearly all of the work that focuses on permanent and/or persistent faults and misbehaviours in small-medium sized networks. Very less work has been done to rectify faults and misbehaviours that are temporary in nature for large networks.

3.1 Problem Description

In our work, radiation affects normal working of sensor nodes which results in dual behaviour of sensor node, first is normally behaving sensor node and second is transfaulty behaving sensor node. Sensor nodes under normal working conditions are known as normal sensor nodes and sensor nodes under the effect of radiation are considered as transfaulty sensor nodes (Fig. 1).

Let, node's initial communication range be R_c. And $r_c(t)$ be the communication range of a node at any instant of time t. Therefore, $r_c(t) \leq R_c$. And d_{min} be the distance of a node from its nearest neighbour. Therefore, we have

$$d_{min} = \min\left(r_c^{ne}\right) \quad \forall ne \tag{1}$$

Where, ne is nearest active neighbour and r_c^{ne} is communication range of a node up to nearest active neighbour.

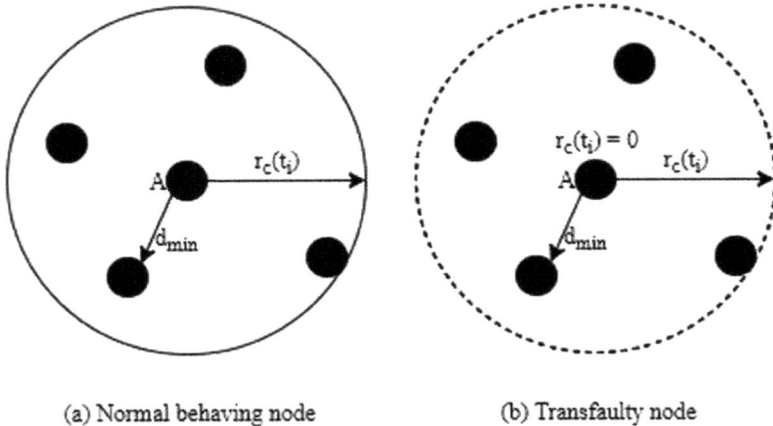

(a) Normal behaving node   (b) Transfaulty node

Fig. 1. Variation in communication range of a sensor node

$$d_{min} \leq r_c(t_i) \leq R_c \tag{2}$$

All the sensory nodes must satisfy above property so as to ensure normal working of WSN. Due to effect of radiation on a proper subset of nodes, they are unable to communicate properly, hence they become transfaulty node. Thus, at any instant of time t_j during radiation effect communication range becomes zero i.e. $r_c(t_j) = 0$. After sometime when radiation effect is over, favourable conditions for normal working of affected wireless sensory nodes are resumed and affected nodes start to communicate normally. This behaviour of wireless sensory nodes is termed as transfaulty behaviour of wireless nodes under radiation effect.

Normal behaving sensor nodes can also be defined as: A sensor node which can sense interesting and important event in its surrounding correctly and is able to communicate with other normal behaving sensor nodes.

$$\psi_n = \begin{cases} 1, & (0 < d_{min} \leq r_c(t_i) \leq R_c) \quad \forall t_i \\ 0, & otherwise \end{cases} \tag{3}$$

Transfaulty behaving sensor nodes can be defined as: A sensor node which is under the effect of radiation, may be able to sense the data correctly and is not able to communicate with other sensor nodes is known as transfaulty node.

$$\psi_t = \begin{cases} 1, & \{(0 < d_{min} \leq r_c(t_i) \leq R_c) \\ & \quad \cap (r_c(t_j))\} \quad \forall t_i, t_i, t_i \neq t_j \\ 0, & otherwise \end{cases} \tag{4}$$

where, ψ_n and ψ_t are denoting normal behaving node and transfaulty behaving node respectively (Table 1).

Table 1. Table of notations

Notation	Description
R_c	Initial communication range
ψ_n	Normal behaving node
ψ_t	Transfaulty behaving node
d_{min}	Distance between a node and its nearest neighbour
r_c^{ne}	Communication range of a node to its nearest neighbour ne
ne	Neighbour node
$r_c(t)$	Communication range of a node at any time instant t
r_k^n	Reward point assigned to n^{th} node by its kth neighbour
p_k^n	Penalty point assigned to n^{th} node by its kth neighbour
$m(B)^n$	Mass belief of nth node
$m(D)^n$	Mass disbelief of nth node
$m(U)^n$	Mass uncertainty of nth node

Conventional network topology of a WSN under the influence of radiation is shown below.

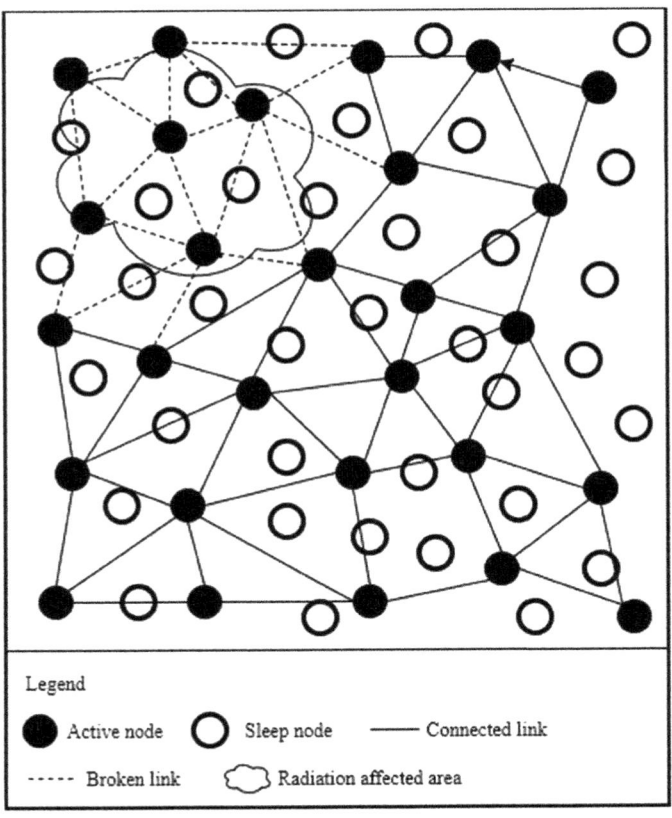

Fig. 2. A typical WSN under the influence of radiation

In the above Fig. 2 shows a traditional WSN is shown which is affected by environmental, electromagnetic or nuclear radiation effect. Likewise, a larger network may consist of a few thousands of nodes. After deployment of sensor network a subset of wireless nodes are activated to span entire area under consideration optimally. After activating a subset of nodes, remaining nodes are set to sleep mode. Switching between active nodes and sleep nodes follow some schedule. Generally, there is high concentration of sleep nodes in vicinity of an active node to provide for fault tolerance. Sensing nodes which are under the prominence of radiation are not able to communicate with other nodes via radio frequency communication mode. This is because of the fact that radiation effect, be it electromagnetic radiation, nuclear radiation or environmental radiation etc. interfere with radio transmission frequency transceiver of affected nodes.

Sensor nodes those are under prominence of radiation can identify themselves to be under prominence of radiation by checking their signal-to-noise ratio (SNIR). If SNIR of a node is higher than communication threshold then a node identifies itself to be under prominence of radiation and switches to acoustic communication mode, then send *ACTIVATION* packet to its sleep neighbours. These newly activated nodes, instantly identifies themselves to be under prominence of radiation and hence, switches to acoustic communication. Newly activated sensors nodes and activating sensor node will now sense redundant data and will send redundant data to sink for data aggregation. Although, nodes under prominence of radiation are now capable of communication via acoustic communication mode, but are not totally immune to radiation. There will still be noise in the data sensed and transmitted by radiation affected nodes, that is why there is need to sense redundant data and transmit redundant data from radiation prominent area and then aggregate redundant data received from affected nodes. Architecture of wireless sensornode with dual communication mode is given below (Fig. 3).

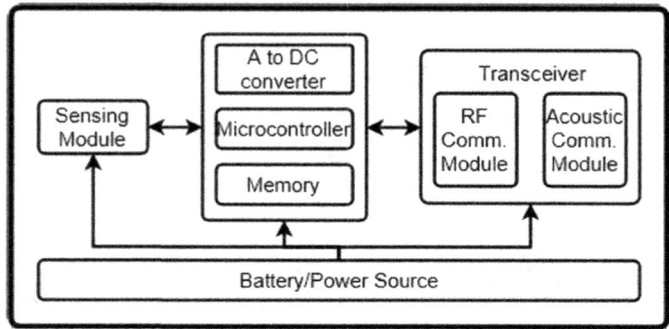

Fig. 3. Architecture of sensor node with dual communication mode

ReDAST proposed a method to deal with radiation by using wireless nodes which are having dual mode of communication [8]. ReDAST uses dampster-shafer theory and hypothesis testing to detect transfaulty node, and k-means clustering algorithm to determine clusters having transfaulty nodes. ReDAST works well for small-medium WSN, but takes huge performance hit in large WSN.

3.2 System Model

We have deployed homogeneous nodes which are having GPS, so that every node could know its own geographical position. Sensor nodes used are having dual mode of communication i.e. RF mode of communication and acoustic mode of communication. Deployed WSN follows standard networking protocols to elect sink node, route data packets, route control packets and all other networking operations. Each node maintains their *neighbour_list*, which it updates on receiving of *HELLO* packet from its neighbours and timely send its updated neighbours list to sink. Sink maintains *NET_INFO* table which have tuple <*node_id, initial_neighbour_list, current_neighbour_list*> corresponding to every node in the network. On receiving *neighbours_list* from a node, sink updates its *NET_INFO* table. Sensor nodes identifying themselves to transfaulty, immediately switches their communication mode to acoustic mode of communication. When radiation effect is gone, transfaulty nodes identifies it based on their SNIR value and switch back to RF mode of communication and sends *SLEEP* packets to its neighbours those were newly activated by it and whole network starts to work normally. Sink Determines boundary nodes at dynamic radiation hole, and summons boundary nodes to switch their communication mode to dual communication mode by sending them *SETMODE* control packet. Boundary nodes send data and receive data via both RF and acoustic mode of communication.

3.3 Prediction Algorithm

In our proposed work, we have incorporated transfaulty node prediction logic which will predict that if a node is transfaulty or not. Sink have *NET_INFO* table which contain tuple <*node_id, initial_neighbour_list, current_neighbour_list*> corresponding to every wireless node in the WSN. Tuples which have less number of entries in *current_neighbour_list* than in *initial_neighbour_list* are interesting to sink. Sink looks for tuples in which *initial_neighbour_list > current_neighbour_list*, and node corresponding to this tuple is a boundary node. Sink tells this boundary node to switch to dual communication mode. Sensor nodes corresponding to tuples in which *current_neighbour_list* is empty are candidates for transfaulty node. ReDAST employs dampster-shafer theory and hypothesis testing to determine communication failure nodes. ReDAST algorithm is a two-phase algorithm:

i. Detection of transfaulty and boundary nodes.
ii. Clustering of nodes using k-means clustering and extracting approximate accurate information

Determination of a transfaulty node is costly process, as it is required to check whether *HELLO* packet of node under consideration has been received by its neighbours or not. If a neighbour has received *HELLO* packet of node under consideration then it will assign a *reward* point to that node and if it has not received *HELLO* packet then it will assign *penalty* point to that node. For example, let us take node 1 as the node under consideration and node 2, node 3 and node 4 are neighbours of node 1. Node 2 and node 3 has received *HELLO* packet from node 1, and node 4 doesn't then node 2 and 3 will assign 1 *reward* point to node 1 each, and node 4 will assign 1 *penalty* point to node 1. Checking of reception of *HELLO* packets by neighbours of node 1 i.e. node 2, 3, 4 takes $O(3^2)$ time. Thus, for n number of nodes, each having m number of neighbours takes $O(n \times m^2)$ time. Thus, for large WSN which is having 1000–3500 nodes, performance hit is significant resulting in throughput crippling.

Thus, in our proposed scheme we are giving a prediction algorithm which will predict a node to be transfaulty based on previous observations of it getting transfaulty. If probability of a node of being transfaulty is higher than working threshold value then we can directly declare that node as transfaulty again. But to predict that, if a node is transfaulty we have to observe the behaviour of all the nodes for Δt time, e.g. if probability of a node being transfaulty is 0.9 then that node is likely to become transfaulty again in 9/10 times. Hence, we can safely declare that node to be transfaulty again.

To predict transfaulty behaviour, first need sink to learn behaviour of all the nodes for Δt_{obs} *(observation time)* time. After learning, in the upcoming rounds sink will can predict a node for transfaulty behaviour based on its observations from previous rounds. Probability of a node being transfaulty is given below.

$$P_i(transfaulty) = \frac{no.\ of\ times\ node\ becomes\ transfaulty}{total\ no\ of\ observations} \forall i \in N \tag{5}$$

For upcoming r_{pre} number of rounds sink will check every node whose *current_neighbour_list* is empty for transfaulty behavior. Number of rounds r_{pre} for which sink will apply prediction algorithm for predicting transfaulty nodes is 10 times the value of maximum probability of nodes becoming transfaulty.

$$r_{pre} = 10 \times \max(P_i(transfaulty)) \quad \forall i \in N \tag{6}$$

A trade-off is also associated with application of prediction algorithm, say after k number of observations we get to know that certain number of nodes are becoming transfaulty with P_i *(transfaulty)* > x. We can conclude that these nodes are likely to be transfaulty again. But this may not be the case forever. As radiation source may be removed or is automatically rectified after some time then there is no need to employ prediction algorithm because radiation source is not present and there no more need to predict transfaultyness. Thus, to deal with this problem we will predict Transfaultyness of nodes only for certain no. of r_{pre} rounds. After r_{pre} rounds, observation phase is restarted to record latest behaviour of sensing nodes. In case radiation source does not persist any more, probability of all the nodes of becoming transfaulty decreases and drops below the working threshold. Then in next probabilistic prediction none of the nodes are found to be transfaulty nodes. The two phases, observation and prediction, are executed in sort of round robin manner to maintain accuracy of prediction. Determining whether a node is transfaulty is given by formula given below.

$$N_i = \begin{cases} node\ is\ transfaulty, & P_i(transfaulty) \geq tc \\ node\ is\ not\ transfaulty, & P_i(transfaulty) < tc \end{cases} \quad \forall i \in N \qquad (7)$$

Observation and prediction phases will run in sort of round robin manner, where optimal no. of rounds of observations r_{obs} are defined before deployment of WSN and number of rounds of prediction r_{pre} is the function of probabilities of nodes recorded in observation phase.

$$r_{pre} = f(10 \times \max(P_i(transfaulty))) \quad \forall i \in N \qquad (8)$$

Deciding no. of rounds of observation r_{obs} depends on various factors, like environment, cause of radiation, source of radiation, type of nodes, nature of observation, etc. If radiation source is immobile, then no. of rounds of observation can be kept as low as 20 and if radiation source is mobile then observation rounds can be as high as 500. Deeper analysis of sources of radiation should be carried out along with survey of deployment area. Based on analysis of sources of radiation nodes should be programmed accordingly. Mathematical modelling of execution of two phases, observation and prediction is discussed below.

Observation Phase:

$$t_1 = t_0 + r_{obs} \times t^r_{obs} \qquad (9)$$

Prediction Phase:

$$t_2 = t_1 + r_{pre} \times t^r_{pre} \qquad (10)$$

Observation Phase:

$$t_3 = t_2 + r_{obs} \times t^r_{obs} \qquad (11)$$

Prediction Phase:

$$t_4 = t_3 + r'_{pre} \times t^r_{pre} \qquad (12)$$

Observation Phase:

$$t_5 = t_4 + r_{obs} \times t^r_{obs} \qquad (13)$$

Prediction Phase:

$$t_6 = t_5 + r''_{pre} \times t^r_{pre} \qquad (14)$$

$$\vdots$$
$$\vdots$$

where,

t_{obs}^r -   *time required to run 1 round of observation phase*

t_{pre}^r -   *average time required to run 1 round of prediction phase.*

Algorithm 1. Algorithm 1: Prediction algorithm

Input:
N ← Active nodes list
POS ← Position of active nodes list
K ← Number of rounds of observation

Output:
Predict transfaultyness of sensor nodes.

```
1  : Begin
2  : Pᵢ ← Probabilities of sensor nodes of being transfaulty
3  : if (observation count ≥ K)
4  :        prediction count ← prediction count + 1
5  :     for i = 1 to N
6  :           if (current_neighbour_list of iᵗʰ node is null)
7  :                if (Pᵢ ≥ working threshold)
8  :                     iᵗʰ node is transfaulty node,
                          switch its communication mode
                          to acoustic mode
9  :                     isPredicted[i] ← true
10 :                end if
11 :           end if
12 :        end for
13 :        if (prediction count > max(Pⱼ))   ∀ j∈N
14 :             observation count ← 0
15 :             prediction count ← 0
16 :        end if
17 :     end if
18 :  End
```

4   Performance Evaluation

4.1   Simulation Setup

In this section, we present performance evaluation of our proposed scheme. Simulation based study is used to evaluate performance of our proposed scheme. We have used Network Simulator 2 v2.35 (NS2) to simulate, evaluate and compare our proposed scheme on WSN. NS2 make use of *AODV* routing protocol for packet routing in network and follows IEEE 802.11 standard for WLAN. To simulate WSN and using

AODV protocol in NS2 TCL scripting language is used in front end, and linking of C++ file in back end respectively.

We considered simulation area of *2500* m × *2500* m and 1000–3500 sensor nodes are deployed randomly over the simulation area optimally. Sensor network follows *AODV* routing and networking protocols. Sink node is also placed randomly, and every node knows its geographical position. After network setup phase every node updates it *neighbour_list*, and sink updates *NET_INFO* table based on information it gets about the network. Sensor network deployed is a homogeneous WSN and all nodes are identical. All the nodes are equipped with dual communication mode module i.e. RF and acoustic communication mode. Sensor nodes switch between both communication modes as required. Sensing range of sensors is considered as 30 m. Transmission range of RF communication mode is considered as 90 m and that of acoustic communication mode is considered as 70 m due to the fact that acoustic communication is more vulnerable to noise and have higher attenuation and propagation delay. Propagation speed of RF signal is taken as 3×10^8 m/s i.e. speed of light and that of ultrasonic acoustic signal is 330 m/s i.e. speed of sound in air. Packet size of *SETMODE*, *HELLO*, *SLEEP* and *ACTIVATION* packets are taken as 6, 10, 6, 6 bytes respectively. Various parameters of simulation are listed in table below (Table 2).

Table 2. Simulation parameters

Parameter	Value
Number of nodes	1000–3500
Simulation area	2500 m × 2500 m
Area affected by radiation	Up to 22500 m^2
Sensor sensing range	30 m
RF mode communication range	90 m
Acoustic mode communication range	70 m
Radio signal propagation speed	3×10^8 m/s
Ultrasonic sound propagation speed	330 m/s
Transmission and reception energy	20 nJ/bit
Battery	6100 mAh, 0.5 v output
Initial residual energy	1.5–2.0 J

4.2 Performance Evaluation Results

We analyse performance and simulation results of proposed scheme in this section. We also compare performance of proposed scheme with ReDAST based on various parameters.

Figure 4 shows execution times of proposed scheme and ReDAST with respect to no. of nodes deployed. It can be derived from the plots that proposed scheme is up to 25% faster than ReDAST. With simulation having 1000 nodes performance increase is just over 23%. With increase in no. of nodes deployed performance difference becomes significant.

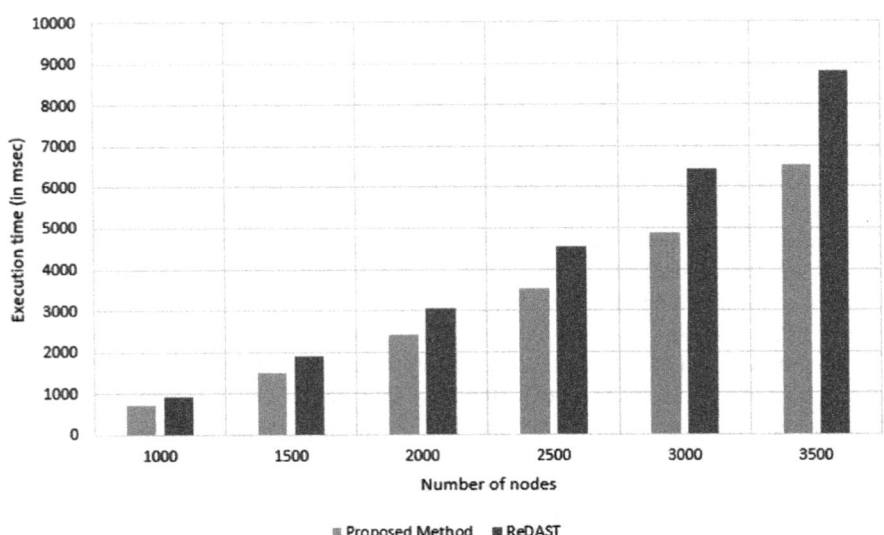

Fig. 4. Execution time performance w.r.t. no. of nodes

Figure 5 depicts execution times w.r.t. increase in no. of transfaulty nodes. It can be referenced that for a network with 1000 nodes proposed scheme has up to 23% performance improvements over ReDAST.

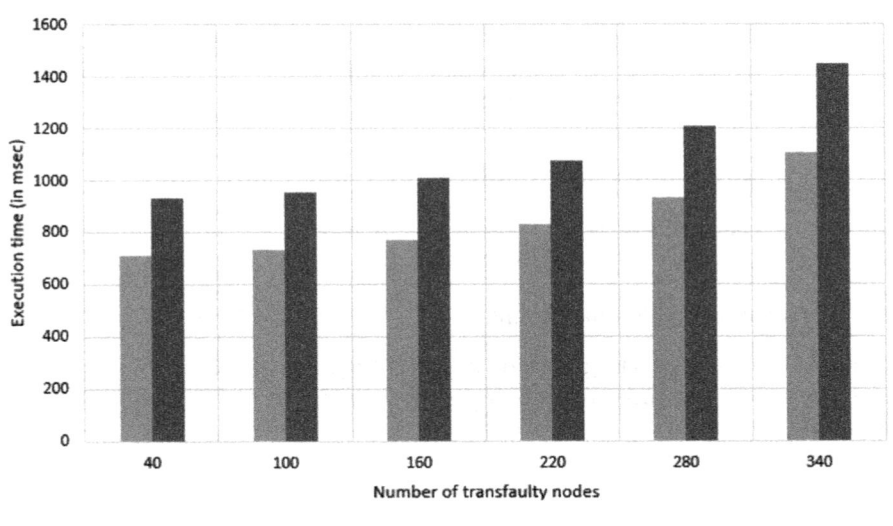

Fig. 5. Execution time performance w.r.t. number of trans-faulty nodes

Figure 6 shows throughput of proposed method w.r.t. no. of active node. Proposed method gives up to 23% more throughput than ReDAST. It can be observed that, as no. of nodes increases ReDAST throughput decreases. This is not the case with our proposed scheme.

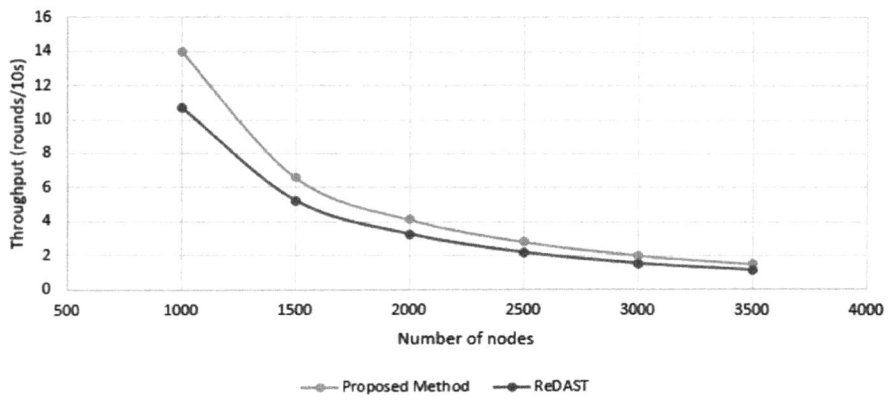

Fig. 6. Throughput of proposed scheme w.r.t. no. of nodes

Figure 7 depicts throughput of proposed method and ReDAST with respect to number of trans-faulty nodes. It can be referenced from Fig. 7 that proposed method outperforms ReDAST on increase in no. of transfaulty nodes by 23%.

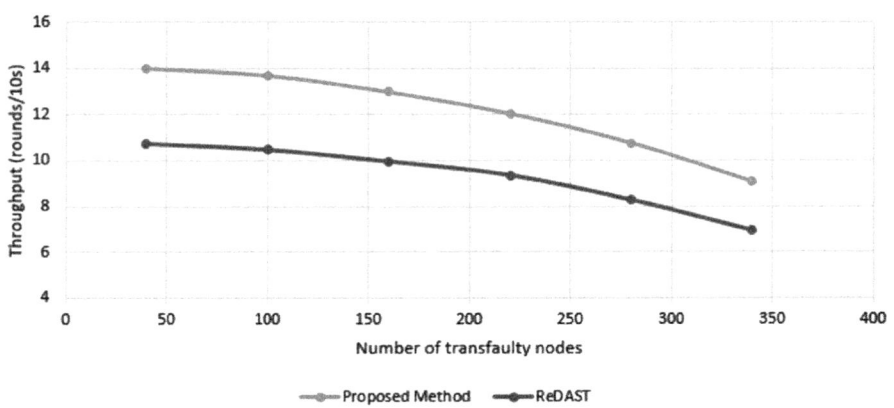

Fig. 7. Throughput of proposed scheme w.r.t. number of trans-faulty nodes

Figure 8 shows how many comp-add and transfer of control instructions are performed on increase of number of trans-faulty nodes. Proposed method executes

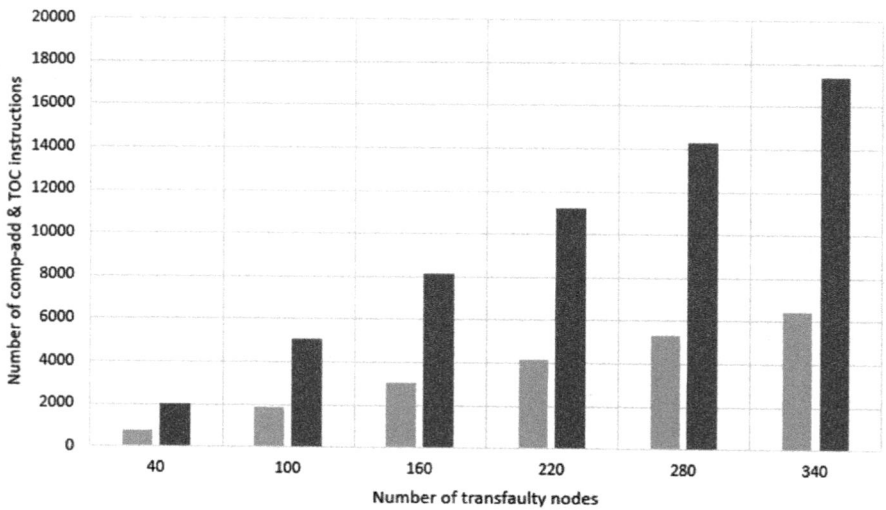

Fig. 8. Number of comp-add and transfer of control instructions w.r.t. number of trans-faulty nodes

significantly less number of comp-add and transfer of control operation as it is predicting trans-faulty nodes.

Figure 9 shows consumption of energy by sink node with increase radiation affected area. It is inferenced from results that sink consumes significantly less energy in processing than that of ReDAST. On increase in number of transfaulty nodes,

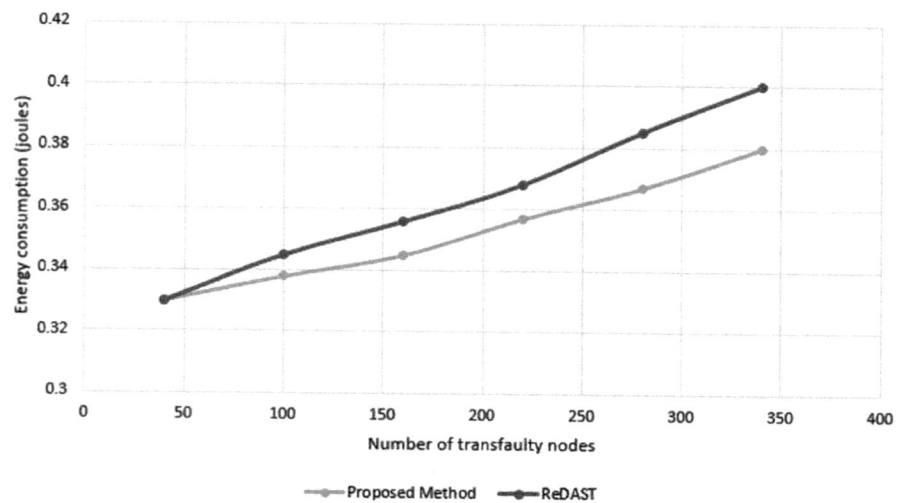

Fig. 9. Energy consumption w.r.t. increase in radiation prominent area

proposed algorithm consumes less energy, courtesy to prediction logic which significantly decrease comp-add and transfer of control instructions.

5 Conclusion

Sensor nodes shows transfaulty behaviour under the prominence of radiation due to the fact that radiation interferes with radio transmissions between nodes. To overcome this problem nodes having dual communication mode are used i.e. RF and acoustic communication mode. Although, ReDAST provides solution to problem associated with radiation effect on WSN but is also a computational costly algorithm. As nodes are having limited resources be it processing, memory or power, it is highly recommended to devise algorithms which are efficient in utilising resources and are optimized for underlying hardware.

In our work, we propose an algorithm which employs prediction logic to predict if a node is transfaulty or not. Executing prediction logic is computationally light. Proposed algorithm runs faster than ReDAST, have better energy efficiency, computationally light algorithm and is as accurate as ReDAST.

In future, our proposed work can make use of machine learning techniques and make nodes to learn to switch communication mode to RF, acoustic or dual communication mode. Running in dual communication mode also consumes lot of energy. Our work can also be continued to efficiently utilize energy of boundary nodes.

References

1. Rehmani, H.M., Shadaram, M., Zeadally, S., Bellavista, P.: Special issue on recent developments in cognitive radio sensor networks. Pervasive Mob. Comput. **22**, 1–2 (2015)
2. Akyildiz, I.F., Weilian, S., Sankarasubramaniam, Y., Cayirci, E.: A survey on sensor networks. Commun. Mag. **40**(8), 102–114 (2002)
3. McCusker, K., Connor, N.E.O.: Low-energy symmetric key distribution in wireless sensor networks. IEEE Trans. Depend. Secur. Comput. **8**(3), 363–376 (2011)
4. Alippi, C., Anastasi, G., Francesco, M.D., Roveri, M.: An adaptive sampling algorithm for effective energy management in wireless sensor networks with energy-hungry sensors. IEEE Trans. Instrum. Meas. **59**(2), 335–344 (2010)
5. Akyildiz, I.F., Su, W., Sankarasubramaniam, Y., Cayirci, E.: Wireless sensor networks: a survey. Comput. Netw. **38**(4), 393–422 (2002)
6. McClure, S.S., et al.: Radiation effects in micro-electromechanical systems (MEMS): RF relays. IEEE Trans. Nucl. Sci. **49**(6), 3197–3202 (2002)
7. Shea, H.R.: Radiation sensitivity of microelectromechanical system devices. J. Micro/Nanolithogr. MEMS MOEMS **8**(3), 1–11 (2009)
8. Kar, P., Misra, S.: Reliable and efficient data acquisition in wireless sensor networks in the presence of transfaulty nodes. IEEE Trans. Netw. Serv. Manag. **13**(1), 99–112 (2016)
9. Ahmed, M., Huang, X., Sharma, D., Shutao, L.: Wireless sensor network internal attacker identification with multiple evidence by Dempster-Shafer theory. In: Xiang, Y., Stojmenovic, I., Apduhan, B.O., Wang, G., Nakano, K., Zomaya, A. (eds.) ICA3PP 2012. LNCS, vol. 7440, pp. 255–263. Springer, Heidelberg (2012). https://doi.org/10.1007/978-3-642-33065-0_27

10. Wilcox, R.R.: Introduction to Robust Estimation and Hypothesis Testing, 3rd edn. Elsevier, Amsterdam (2012). ISBN 978-0-12-386983-8
11. Kanungo, T., Mount, D.M., Netanyahu, N.S., Piatko, C.D., Silverman, R., Wu, A.Y.: An efficient k-means clustering algorithm: analysis and implementation. IEEE Trans. Pattern Anal. Mach. Intell. **24**(7), 881–892 (2002)
12. Rajasegarar, S., Leckie, C., Palaniswam, M.: Hyperspherical cluster based distributed anomaly detection in wireless sensor networks. J. Parallel Distrib. Comput. **74**(1), 1833–1847 (2014)
13. Huangshui, H., Guihe, Q.: Fault management frameworks in wireless sensor networks. In: Proceedings od the Intelligent Computation Technology and Automation, Guangdong, China, vol. 2, pp. 1093–1096, March 2011
14. Kamhoua, C.A., Pissinou, N., Miller, J., Makki, S.K.: Mitigating routing misbehavior in multi-hop networks using evolutionary game theory. In: Proceedings of GLOBECOM Workshops Advanced Communication Networks, pp. 1957–1962 (2010)
15. Soltanmohammadi, E., Orooji, M., Naraghi-Pour, M.: Decentralized hypothesis testing in wireless sensor networks in the presence of misbehaving nodes. IEEE Trans. Inf. Forensics Secur. **8**(1), 205–215 (2013)
16. Khan, S., Turgut, D., Boloni, L.: Bridge protection algorithms–a technique for fault-tolerance in sensor networks. Ad Hoc Netw. **24**, 186–199 (2015)
17. Munir, A., Antoon, J., Gordon, A.R.: Modeling and analysis of fault detection and fault tolerance in wireless sensor networks. ACM Trans. Embed. Comput. Syst. **14**(1), 1–42 (2015)
18. Vladimirova, T., et al.: Characterising wireless sensor motes for space applications. In: Proceedings of 2nd NASA/ESA Conference on Adaptive Hardware and Systems, Edinburgh, UK, August 2007, pp. 43–50 (2007)
19. Dargie, W., Poellabauer, C.: Fundametals of Wireless Sensor Networks. Wiley, Hoboken (2010). Shen, X., Pan, Y. (eds.)
20. Dini, G., Pelagatti, M., Savino, I.M.: An algorithm for reconnecting wireless sensor network partitions. In: Verdone, R. (ed.) EWSN 2008. LNCS, vol. 4913, pp. 253–267. Springer, Heidelberg (2008). https://doi.org/10.1007/978-3-540-77690-1_16
21. Senel, F., Younis, M.F., Akkaya, K.: Bio-inspired relay node placement heuristics for repairing damaged wireless sensor networks. IEEE Trans. Veh. Technol. **60**(4), 1835–1848 (2011)

An Energy Efficient Clustering Algorithm for Increasing Lifespan of Heterogeneous Wireless Sensor Networks

Manish Pandey[✉], Lalit Kumar Vishwakarma, and Amit Bhagat

Maulana Azad National Institute of Technology, Bhopal 462003, India
contactmanishpandey@yahoo.co.in,
lalit.vishwakarma123@gmail.com, am.bhagat@gmail.com

Abstract. Wireless Sensor Network is a network of sensor nodes that are deployed in some geographical area or concerned entities for monitoring of physical conditions. Environmental sensing, health care monitoring, border surveillance, forest monitoring is some of the application areas of wireless sensor networks. Sensory nodes sense relevant data which will be forwarded to base station. Wireless sensor nodes are remotely deployed therefore they may remain unattended for long. The energy utilization is thus a key challenge in wireless sensor network. Various algorithms have been proposed for efficient energy utilization in wireless sensor network. Most of them are clustering based algorithms that provides solution for energy efficiency and hot-spot problem. This paper introduces a clustering algorithm which is energy efficient and increases lifetime of Heterogeneous WSN. In our proposed algorithm cluster-heads are selected in an effective way and size of the clusters is variable and is calculated on the basis of energy and distance. Then the data is transmitted using chaining. Simulation study shows that our proposed algorithm is performing better than DEEC and LEACH protocols. Our proposed algorithm is increasing the overall network's lifespan and transmitting more packets of data to base-station than LEACH and DEEC algorithm.

Keywords: Clustering algorithms · Wireless sensor network · Load balancing
Energy efficiency · Increasing lifetime of WSN

1 Introduction

A network of sensing devices which are able to sense environment and communicate with each other wirelessly are deployed in area randomly is as called Wireless Sensor Network (WSN). Sensor nodes work autonomously in WSN. Every sensor, senses the environmental and physical area and gather important information. Multi-hop or Single-hop transmission are used for transmitting the information gathered by sensory nodes. In a single-hop transmission, data is directly forward to base-station but in multi-hop transmission, data forwarding is done via other sensor nodes. Observed information is gathered at the base-station and analyzed. The WSNs are used in numerous fields like health care, military surveillances, environment sensing, fire detection in forest, disaster prevention etc. An architecture of a sensory node/mote is shown below:

© Springer Nature Singapore Pte Ltd. 2018
P. Bhattacharyya et al. (Eds.): NGCT 2017, CCIS 828, pp. 263–277, 2018.
https://doi.org/10.1007/978-981-10-8660-1_20

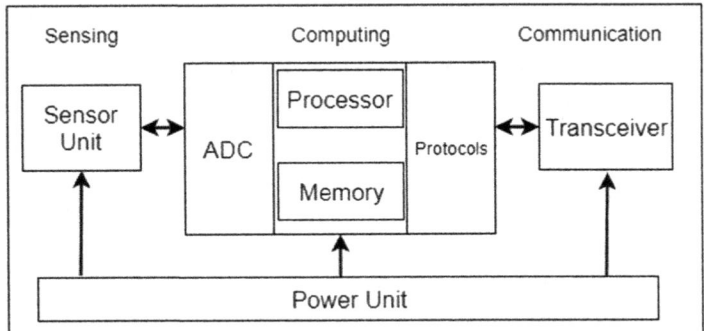

Fig. 1. Architecture of a sensor node/mote Node of WSN [Source: internet]

Sensing module sense interesting events. This sensed information is sensed in the form of analog signals that are converted in digital signals. A memory module and microcontroller is used to process and store intermediate information. Transceiver is responsible for communication between sensory nodes (Fig. 1).

The major challenge's in WSN are energy efficiency and hot-spot problem and load balancing.

1. Energy efficiency problem: In WSN, nodes placed in area where human intervention is not frequently possible to replace the batteries of sensor. The better utilization of battery power by sensors is required.
2. Hot-spot problem: Sensor nodes forward the gathered and grasped information to station. Then there may be possibility that sensor node's energy of particular area depletes quicker than other nodes is called as hot-spot problem.
3. Load balancing: Load balancing is distribution of the work-load of sensory nodes among other sensory nodes for balancing energy consumed by sensor devices in network.

For increasing lifetime various algorithms are introduced which uses clustering techniques in WSN. Clustering is a technique which divides the total WSN in sub-networks. The sub-networks are called clusters. In past decades, many algorithms are introduced for enhancing the energy utilization in WSN like LEACH, HEED, T-LEACH. In these algorithms, the WSN is partitions into clusters, where every cluster elects a leader among nodes called cluster-head. Remaining sensory nodes of cluster are called cluster-members. Leader of a cluster receive sensed data from cluster members. Information received at cluster-head is forward to base-station. Aggregation of gathered information is done by CH, it fuses collected data and forward that data to base-station.

WSN is broadly categorized into Homogeneous WSN and Heterogeneous WSN. In homogeneous WSN, all nodes are indistinguishable to each other. In homogeneous WSN every node contains same of energy but in heterogeneous WSN nodes differ in energy and h/w capabilities. There are 2-level of heterogeneous WSN, 3-level of heterogeneous WSN and multi-level of heterogeneous WSN exists. The 2-level of heterogeneous WSN is the network of 2 varieties of sensory nodes, advances nodes (AN) and normal nodes(NN). The AN have more initial energy relative to NN. The AN node contains α fraction of energy more compared to NN.

The parameters which are used to selecting cluster-head and forming clusters for energy efficiency are:

1. Energy consumption: It is average dissipation of energy of WSN in every round in clustering algorithm.
2. Residual Energy: It is remaining energy contain by sensory nodes. The sensory node whose residual energy is high, has more chances to become cluster-head in next round.
3. Degree of node: total nodes in range of sensory node is called the degree of that node. The node, which have highest degree has greater priority of becoming cluster-head.

2 Literature Review

In WSN, for efficiently utilizing node's energy and increasing lifetime of network, many algorithms are introduced. That are based on probability, fuzzy logic, swarm optimization and tree basis. The Heinzelman have given a very first and popular clustering protocol known LEACH which is totally based on probability. In LEACH, each cluster node will get opportunity of becoming clusterhead in every r round. The probability for becoming cluster-head is by calculating threshold value as:

$$T(N) = \begin{cases} \frac{x}{1-x\left(r\,mod\frac{1}{x}\right)}, & if\ n \in G \\ 0, & othewise \end{cases} \qquad (1)$$

Where, p is the inceptive percentage of cluster-heads, G is set of sensors from last $\frac{1}{x}$ rounds which haven't become cluster-head while r is current round. Random no. generated by each node in between 0 to 1. If random no. is below the threshold then only node will become leader. This algorithm run in 2 phases. In leader selection phase, CH's are selected. In second phase, cluster-head gets data from member nodes using TDMA. The cluster-head sends received data to base-station. PEGASIS is an advancement to the LEACH algorithm. This algorithms states that lifetime of WSN can increase without using clustering which is the overhead. In this algorithm, a chain is formed from farthest sensor to nearest sensory node to base-station. Each sensory node sense some data and merge it with received data and forward it to its neighbor. The neighbor sensor node who receives data is nearer to base-station. Finally, the sensory node nearest to the base-station will send that processed information to base-station. TEEN uses 2-level hierarchy of sensor nodes. CH's do not forward information directly to base-station, they first forward it to cluster-heads which are nearer to the base-station for increasing lifetime of WSN. TEEN used to sense data when an event is happened. The APTEEN algorithm is time driven algorithm and it is improvement of TEEN algorithm. APTEEN capture the information periodically when and also at event occurrence.

In HEED, member nodes send data to cluster-head using single and multi-hop communication, further cluster-heads sends the same date to base-station via single and multi-hop communication [4]. HEED chooses the cluster-heads based on communication and remaining energy cost. Remaining energy is a parameter used in HEED to choose cluster-heads. In HEED, each sensory node is part of only 1 cluster and it can directly interact to cluster-head. Initially each node generates a number b/w zero and one called C_{prob}. Each sensory node calculate probability for becoming cluster-head, CH_{prob}, as follows:

$$CH_{prob} = C_{prob} \times \frac{E_{remaining}}{E_{initial}} \qquad (2)$$

Where $E_{remaining}$ is remaining energy, and $E_{initial}$ is initial energy of nodes. The T-LEACH [5] is extension of LEACH protocol. This algorithm is for cluster-head replacement in optimum way. It decides a threshold level for cluster-head replacement. Until the energy-level of the clusterhead not fall below the threshold value, cluster-head will not get replaced and re-clustering will not be performed. T-LEACH provides better energy utilization than LEACH algorithm because it is reducing the overhead for replacement of cluster-head for a while. BLEACH select the cluster-heads on basis of alive nods in WSN. In BLEACH, a face-value is calculated for nodes and find an ideal node that could be cluster-head. In NEECP A grouping component presented with customizable detecting range for cluster-heads determination presented in [9] for homogeneous WSN. The EECP and MEECP [15] algorithms select the leader on weighted probability. The weight depends on average and remaining energies of WSN. In EECP, energy consumed by nodes which are far from BS is more compare with other nodes. This problem solved in MEECP.

DEEC is a heterogeneous WSN protocol. Based on is ratio of energy remaining and avg energy in rounds cluster-head is selected [14]. It is two- level heterogeneous WSN's model. In DEEC Complete operation is done in rounds. When new round begins every node calculate its average probability. The average probability used for calculating probability become cluster-head. That calculated probability is used find the threshold value, will be used for choosing cluster-head.

The DEEC algorithm is an improvement in LEACH for HWSN. DEEC-2 algorithms work on two-level of HWSN. The ESDEEC [14] algorithm is provided for 4-level HWSN where normal, advanced, super and sonic nodes are used HWSN. The SEP [11] provide the well efficient and distributed consumption of energy nodes. The stability of WSN is increased. The IBLEACH provide optimum clustering so energy dissipation is balanced in cluster.

The above Heterogeneous WSN algorithms does not consider adjustable detecting range for balancing energy dissipation. In this algorithm, we are re-forming the clusters by considering energy of sensory nodes in respective cluster w.r.t. avg. energy of the WSN. Chain formation approach used for forwarding data in inter and intra-cluster communication for balancing the load in WSN.

3   Proposed Algorithm

3.1   Radio Model

The radio model is used for calculating energy dissipation for sending K-bit packet of data to d distance when the noise affecting data transmission. Total energy dissipation in transmitting K-bit packet of data to d distance is:

$$E_{Tr}(\text{K, d}) = \begin{cases} K * E_{elec} + K * \varepsilon_{fs} * d^2, & d \le d_0 \\ K * E_{elec} + K * \varepsilon_{mp} * d^4, & d > d_0 \end{cases} \quad (3)$$

Where E_{elec} is energy dissipation for transmitting or receiving 1-bit data. The E_{elec} depends on modulation, digital coding and spreading signal. ε_{fs} and ε_{mp} depend on amplifier model used. Here both, free-space and multi-path fading models used for transmission of the data. The distance d is b/w sending and receiving sensor nodes. If $d \ge d_0$ then data will transmit using free-space model is used else multi-path transmission model for transmission will be used.

3.2   Network Model

For the heterogeneity of the network, 2 kinds of nodes are used. Nodes differ in energies level that they are having. There are N nodes in WSN. The m fraction of total nodes is advanced nodes (AN) which contains α fraction more energy than normal nodes. Nodes are deployed in M × M physical region randomly. Number of normal nodes are $(1 - m)N$. Initial energy of the NN is E_0. Total number of AN are m × N, which contains $(1 + \alpha)E_0$ energy each. Total energy normal nodes is $(1 - m) * N * E_0$. Total energy of Advanced nodes is $m * N * (1 + \alpha)E_0$. Total energy of WSN is:

$$E_{total} = (1 - m) * N * E_0 + m * N(1 + \alpha)E_0 = N * E_0(1 + \alpha m) \quad (4)$$

Assumption - All nodes in the area deployed are in unplanned manner and BS is in the center of the region.

LEACH clustering algorithm uses probability uniformly for cluster-head selection. The total cluster in the WSN is $p_{opt} * N$. In this every node will get chance to become CH once in every r rounds. A node will become CH in every $r_i = \frac{1}{p_{opt}}$.

In WSN, data sensed by every node and transmit it to the CH then cluster-head collects and aggregates data then sends to base-station. The consumption of energy in a round is given as:

$$E_{round} = K * \left(2NE_{elec} + NE_{DA} + number\ of\ cluster * \varepsilon_{mp}d^4 + N\varepsilon_{fs}d^2\right) \quad (5)$$

The total rounds that can possible calculated as:

$$R = \frac{E_{total}}{E_{round}} \quad (6)$$

In r_{th} round for a sensory node average energy is calculated as:

$$\overline{E}(i) = \frac{1}{N}E_{total}\left(1 - \frac{r}{R}\right) = \frac{1}{N}\sum_{i=1}^{N} E(i) \quad (7)$$

the average probability of node for becoming cluster-head is:

$$p_i = p_{opt} \frac{E_i(r)}{\overline{E}(r)} \tag{8}$$

The node having high remaining energy have the greater probability for becoming cluster-head. Total energy of WSN is increase by $(1 + \alpha m)$. Logically there are $(1 + \alpha m)$ more normal nodes total nodes in WSN. For maintaining probability, we need to add this factor for balance the probability. Each AN becomes can cluster-head $(1 + \alpha)$ times more than NN.

The avg. probability of a node i to become the cluster-head in r_{th} round of NN and AN is:

$$p_i = \begin{cases} \frac{p_{opt}*E_i(r)}{(1+\alpha m)\overline{E}(r)}, & \textit{for normal nodes} \\ \frac{(1+\alpha)p_{opt}*E_i(r)}{(1+\alpha m)\overline{E}(r)}, & \textit{for advaced nodes} \end{cases} \tag{9}$$

3.3   Cluster-Head Selection

This protocol is works on 2-level hierarchy. In first level of hierarchy every member forwards their data to cluster-head using chaining. In the second-level of hierarchy, cluster-heads forward their data to cluster-head which is near to base-station relative to it. Then next CH will forward data to next CH. Above process continues till data reached to BS.

For cluster-head selection we are considering exhaustion of energy, remaining energy, degree of nodes. By using these parameters, the election of CH will optimum.

The sensor whose unconsumed energy is more compared to other nodes will have greater probability for becoming cluster-head. Ratio of unconsumed energy and inceptive energy of the nodes is used for further optimizing the threshold value. The nodes whose remaining energy is preeminent relative to other nodes thus, ratio of residual energy and initial energy is preeminent than other nodes. Then probability of such nodes for becoming CH is greater.

The nodes whose degree is comparatively higher relative to other sensory nodes should have greater probability of becoming cluster-head. The nodes whose degree is higher as to other nodes thus, the ratio of total no. of neighbor nodes (degree) and total no. of nodes in WSN is higher as to other nodes. Then, probability of such nodes of becoming cluster-head is greater.

Every node calculates its threshold value in each round. We are using the parameters, the avg. probability of a node of becoming the cluster-head in each round, the ration of residual and initial energy and the ratio of degree of the node and total no. of motes in WSN for calculating the threshold. By using these parameters in consideration, the threshold value calculated by the sensors will be optimum of becoming the cluster-head.

$$T(i) = \begin{cases} \dfrac{p_i}{1-p_i\left(r\,mod\frac{1}{p_i}\right)} * \dfrac{E_{residual}(i)}{E_{initial}} * \dfrac{D_i}{N}, & i \in G' \\[3ex] \dfrac{p_i}{1-p_i\left(r\,mod\frac{1}{p_i}\right)} * \dfrac{E_{residual}(i)}{E_{initial}} * \dfrac{D_i}{N}, & i \in G'' \end{cases} \qquad (10)$$

Where energy left of node i is $E_{residual}$, E_{total} is the energy at start $(E_{initial})$ of sensory nodes, D_i is degree of node i and N is no. of nodes in the WSN. The NN which are not became the CH from last (1/r) rounds is belongs to set G'. The AN which are not became the CH from last (1/r) rounds is belongs to set G''.

3.4   Cluster Formation

In cluster-head selection phase, nodes are selected for CH then we are forming the clusters using sensing range of cluster-heads. The sensing range is calculated as:

$$R_{Cluster-head} = \left(1 - \left(\dfrac{d_{max} - d(BS, S_i)}{d_{max} - d_{min}}\right)\right)R_n \qquad (11)$$

Where, d_{max} is distance b/w base-station and farthest node from BS. d_{min} is the distance b/w BS and closest node to base-station. $d(BS, S_i)$ is distance b/w cluster-head and BS. R_n is the actual grasping range of the CH as in NEECP. The size of clusters which are nearer to base-station will be small, so the communication cost inside the cluster will be less for the cluster-heads and will consume more chunk of energy in communication b/w cluster-heads. Because the CH's which are closer to base-station will deliver the data of another clusters to BS. this will solve the hot-spot problem. Every CH will calculate their adjustable detecting range. The nodes which lies in the grasping range of CH will become cluster members of that cluster-head. After forming clusters some nodes will left outside from clusters. The nodes, which left outside will join cluster whose cluster-head is nearest (Fig. 2).

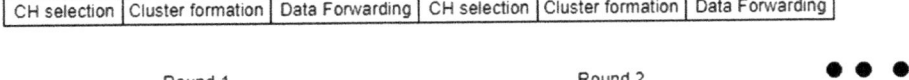

Fig. 2. Proposed algorithm, rounds and phases

3.5   Re-formation of Clusters

In the heterogeneous WSN, variable sized clusters will be created. The large sized clusters are far from base station and small sized clusters will be near to base station. There may be chance that the sensory nodes of the small clusters contains more energy than the sensory nodes of large size clusters. The sensory nodes which are the near to base station and form a small size cluster and contain more energy than other sensory nodes. The sensory nodes which are far from the base station and form large size cluster and contain less energies than other sensory nodes. Thus, the energy exhaustion in small cluster will less and in large clusters will be more. The energy exhaustion of the sensory nodes of small clusters will be less and the energy exhaustion of sensory nodes of large clusters will be more compared to other sensory nodes.

The clusters which are near to base station and the sensory nodes of that clusters contain more energy than other nodes. The size of these clusters should be large. The clusters which are far from base station and the sensory nodes of that clusters contain less energy than other nodes. The size of these clusters should be small.

There is the need for balancing the energy dissipation of sensory nodes. Then re-formation of the clusters is needed on the basis of energies of the sensory nodes. The range of the clusters is calculated by considering the average energies of sensory nodes with respect to the average energy of the all sensory nodes as:

$$R'_{cluster-head}(i) = R_{Cluster-head}(i) \times \frac{E_{average}(cluster(i))}{E_{average}} \tag{12}$$

Where, $R'_{cluster-head}(i)$ is the re-formation radius of the cluster- head of i_{th} cluster and $R_{Cluster-head}(i)$ is the adjustable detecting range of i_{th} cluster. $E_{average}(cluster(i))$ is avg. energy of the i_{th} cluster and $E_{average}$ is the avg. energy of whole network.

If the avg. energy of the cluster which is near to base-station is greater than the avg. energy of WSN. Then the ratio of avg. energy of the cluster and avg. energy of WSN will be greater than one. Then multiplying this value to adjustable detecting radius of the cluster-head will increase the size of the radius and increase the size of cluster. If the avg. energy of the cluster which is far from base-station is less than the avg. energy of the network. Then the ratio of avg. energy of the cluster and avg. energy of WSN will be less than one. Then multiplying this value to adjustable detecting radius of the cluster-head will decrease the size of the radius and decrease the size of cluster. This will balance the energy exhaustion in the WSN.

3.6   Data Transmission and Chain Construction Approach

In WSN, it is possible that same phenomena observed by more than one sensory nodes. Thus, packets of data of sensory nodes may be replicated. This algorithm will remove data replication at each sensory node except boundary sensory nodes in the chaining. Thus, only the meaningful information will be transmitted to BS.

In this algorithm, the cluster members forward their data to CH using chaining approach. Each boundary node of cluster will dispatch its data to sensor which is nearest to it and nearer to base-station as relative to it. Then that node will aggregate its own sensed and received data. If data packets are same then it will forward only one data packet and discard another packet. Then that node will forward aggregated and fused data packet to sensor which is closer to it and near to CH as compared to it. This process will continue till data reached to CH. The cluster-head will forward data received to anther CH which is close to it and near to base-station as relative to it. This process will repeat till data is reached to base-station.

In chaining approach whenever a sensory node is failed or unavailable then the node, who is forwarding data to failed node will again find a node for chaining and dispatching the data by bypassing the failure node.

Proposed Algorithm

```
1  :- Begin
2  :- Initialize the network and set values to parameters
3  :- while average energy > 0
4  :-     for (i = 1 to n)
5  :-         calculate threshold value T(i)
6  :-         generate random no. between 0 and 1
7  :-         if (random no. < T(i))
8  :-             declare node as CH
9  :-         end if
10 :-     end for
11 :-     for (i = 1 to m)
12 :-         calculate adjustable detection range  i.e. adj[n]
13 :-         for (j = 1 to n)
14 :-             if (dist(i, j) ≤ adj [i])
15 :-                 node j is cluster member of  CHᵢ
16 :-             end if
17 :-             else
18 :-                 for (k = 1 to C)
19 :-                     if (dist(i, j) < dist(iₖ, jₖ))
20 :-                         node k is cluster member
                             CHₖ
21 :-                     end if
22 :-                 end for
23 :-             end else
24 :-         end for
25 :-     end for
26 :-     for (i = 1 to m)
27 :-         calculate Re-clustering detection range. i.e. re-a[n]
28 :-         for (j = 1 to n)
29 :-             if (dist(i, j) ≤ re-a [i])
30 :-                 node j is cluster member of  CHᵢ
31 :-             end if
32 :-             else
33 :-                 for (k = 1 to C)
34 :-                     if (dist(i, j) < dist(iₖ, jₖ))
35 :-                         node k is cluster member
                             CHₖ
36 :-                     end if
37 :-                 end for
38 :-             end else
39 :-         end for
40 :-     end for
41 :-     for (i = 1 to m)
42 :-         find farthest node in cluster a
```

43 :-   find nearest node *b* from *a*
44 :-   *a* will send data to *b*
45 :-   *b* finds nearest node *c* in cluster from itself
46 :-   *b* will forward data to *c*
47 :-   repeat 22 & 23 until data is reached to CH
48 :-   **end for**
49 :-   CH will find nearest CH and forward data to it
50 :-   repeat 26 until data is reached to BS
51 :- **end while**
52 : -**End**

4   Illustration

Proposed algorithm is simulated on ns-2 simulator. For simulating the algorithm, we have simulated the WSN in tcl language. In which we have initial the network parameters wireless channel, physical layer, MAC layer data link layer and used 802.11 as mac layer protocol. Transmission range of sensory nodes is 25 m. Data is transmitted using UDP application layer protocol. AODV protocol is used for wireless communication b/w the sensory nodes in WSN. For cluster-head selection and cluster formation c++ program is developed using AODV.cc file.

5   Simulation Results and Analysis

In this algorithm, we have focused on efficient energy utilization for increasing lifespan of WSN and in the WSN. This algorithm is proposed for heterogeneous WSN which is giving better results compared to DEEC algorithm and LEACH algorithm. The simulation code is developed and compared with DEEC and LEACH algorithms in ns-2.

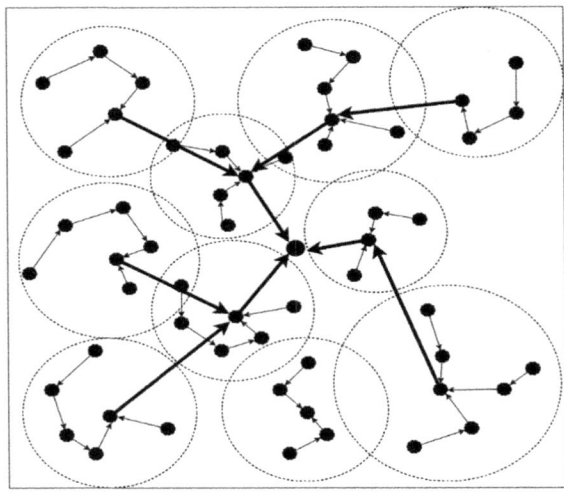

Fig. 3. Chain construction and data aggregation

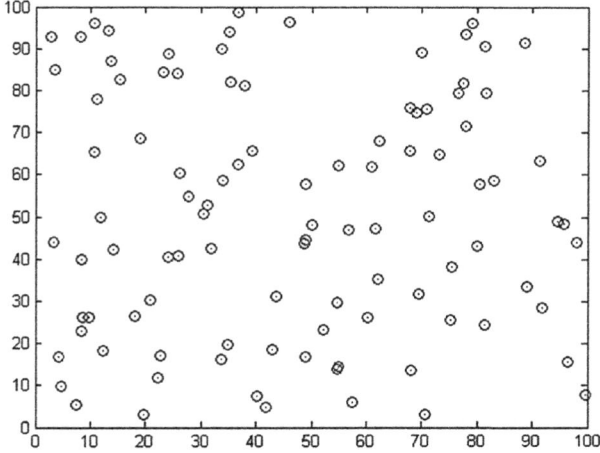

Fig. 4. Random deployment of sensory nodes in physical area

In simulation, we have compared algorithms w.r.t. no. alive nodes and dead nodes in r rounds in WSN. We have run the simulation up to 5000 rounds. We have deployed 100 sensory nodes in 100 m × 100 m area. Sensor nodes were deployed randomly as represented in Fig. 3. Initial energy (E_0) of sensory nodes is 0.5 J. The length of packet of data is 4000 bits. There are 50% of total nodes are advances nodes, remaining nodes are NN as in Table 1. The energies of AN's is double than normal nodes (NN). We have computed the performance on based on lifetime of WSN, when the first and last node of the WSN died and the total packet delivered to base-station (Table 2).

Table 1. Simulation parameters

Parameter	Value
Network grid	100 m × 100 m
Sink	(50, 50)
Initial energy (E_0)	0.5 J
Total nodes	100
E_{elec}	50 nJ/bit
ε_{fs}	10 pJ/bit/m^2
ε_{mp}	0.0013 pJ/bit/m^4
m	0.5
α	1
Packet size	4000 bits

Table 2. Node dead w.r.t. rounds

Algorithms	First node dead at	Tenth node dead at	Last node dead at
LEACH	994	1246	2325
DEEC	1521	1724	3189
Proposed algorithm	2015	2257	4213

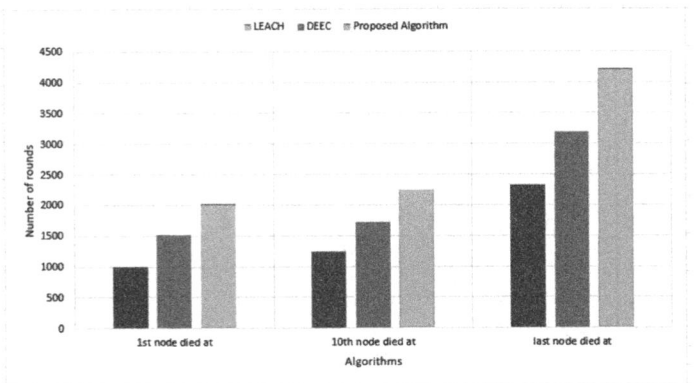

Fig. 5. First and last dead sensory node in proposed algorithms

5.1   Network Lifetime

Lifetime of WSN is calculated up to how many rounds in the network are alive. The whole network will die when last node will be dead. In proposed algorithm, last node dead at round number 4213. The lifetime increased by 32% from DEEC and 70% from the LEACH algorithm of WSN as in Fig. 4.

5.2   Data Packet Forwarded to BS

In the simulation, we have considered the packets of data sent to base-station by algorithms as performance evaluation parameter. In the proposed algorithm, the packets of data sent to base-station is 1.6×100000 which is 55% more than DCCE and 10 more than LEACH. Which shows that proposed algorithm sent more packets than HEED or LEACH using the same energy used by LEACH and HEED as in Fig. 5 (Figs. 6 and 7).

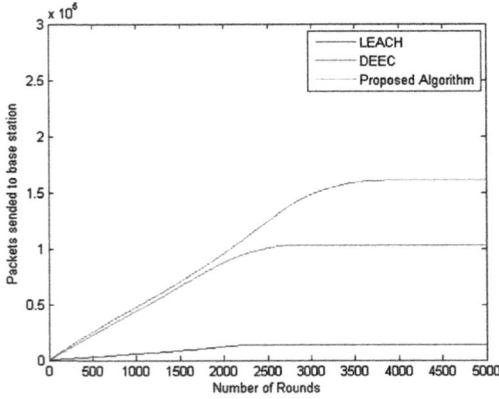

Fig. 6. Data packet delivered to base-station w.r.t. rounds

5.3   Energy Consumption

The lifetime of WSN is depends on total energy consumed in rounds. The parameters that affect the lifetime is amount of consumed energy and amount of left energies of nodes. We have calculated the energy degradation in every round of data transmission. In proposed algorithm, the energy consumption rate is less compared to LEACH algorithm and DEEC algorithm as in the Fig. 8 (Fig. 9).

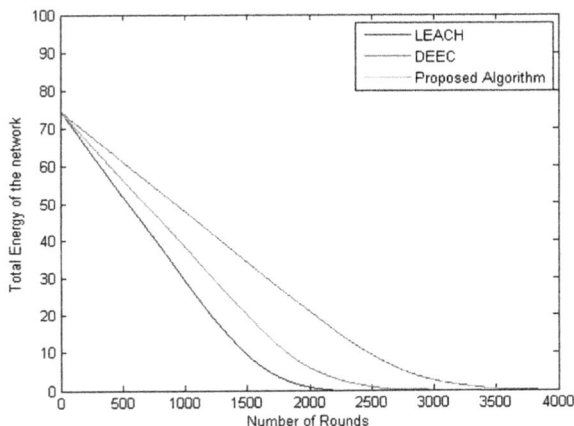

Fig. 7. Total remaining energy w.r.t. to rounds

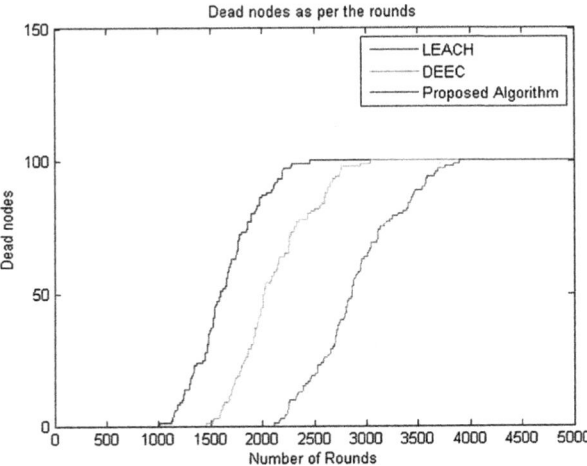

Fig. 8. Number of dead nodes w.r.t. to rounds

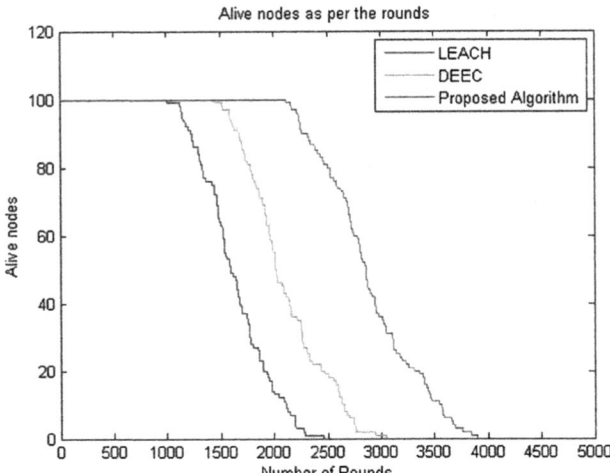

Fig. 9. Alive nodes w.r.t. rounds

6 Conclusion

A clustering algorithm for making energy efficient in heterogeneous WSN and increasing the lifespan is proposed. This algorithm is selecting cluster-heads in efficient way by considering energy consumption, residual energy and degree of nodes. Then for cluster formation this protocol is using adjustable detecting range for uniform consumption of energy in WSN. It is using the chaining approach for gathering and data forwarding. Simulation results show that, our proposed algorithm is performing better then LEACH and HEED clustering algorithms on the basis of lifetime and packets of data transmitted to base-station. In future, many different algorithms can be hybrid together for further enhancing life of WSN.

References

1. Culer, D., Estrin, D., Srivastava, M.: Overview of sensory networks. In: IEEE Computer, USA, vol 37, pp. 41–49, August 2004
2. Yadav, L., Sunitha, C.: Low energy adaptive clustering hierarchy in wireless sensory networks (LEACH). IJCST **5**(3), 466–4664 (2014)
3. Lindsey, S., Raghavenda, C.S.: PEGASIS: power efficient gathering in sensory information systems. In: Proceeding of IEEE Aerospace Conference, Montana, USA, vol. 3, pp. 1125–1130 (2002)
4. Younis, O., Fahmy, S.: HEED: a hybrid, energy- efficient, distributed clustering protocol for ad hoc sensory networks. IEEE Trans. Mob. Comput. **3**(4), 366–379 (2004)
5. Hong, J., Kook, J., Lee, S., et al.: T-LEACH: the method of threshold-based CH replacement for wireless sensory networks. Inf. Syst. Front. **11**(5), 513–521 (2009)
6. Nayak, P., Shree, P.: Comparison of routing protocols in WSN using NetSim simulator: LEACH Vs LEACH-C. Int. J. Comput. Appl. **106**, 1–6 (2014)

7. Martincic, F., Schwiebert, L.: Introduction to Wireless Sensory Networking, pp. 1–26. Wiley, New York (2005)
8. Goyal, S., Jain, B.: Location based-balanced clustering algorithm for wireless sensory network – BLEACH (2016)
9. Singh, S., Chand, S., Kumar, R., Malik, A., Kumar, B.: NEECP: novel energy-efficient clustering protocol for prolonging lifetime of WSNs. IET Wirel. Sens. Syst. **5**, 151–157 (2016)
10. Ok, C., Lee, S., Mitra, P., Kumara, S.: Distributed routing in wireless sensory networks using energy welfare metric. Inf. Sci. **180**(9), 1656–1670 (2010)
11. Farouk, F., Rizk, R., Zaki, F.W.: Multi-level stable and energy- efficient clustering protocol in heterogeneous wireless sensory networks. IET Wirel. Sens. Syst. **4**(4), 159–169 (2014)
12. Bsoul, M., Al-Khasawneh, A., Abdallah, A.E., et al.: An energy-efficient threshold-based clustering protocol for wireless sensory networks. Wirel. Pers. Commun. **70**(1), 99–112 (2013)
13. Jin, Y., Wang, L., Kim, Y., et al.: EEMC: an energy-efficient multi-level clustering algorithm for large-scale wireless sensory networks. Comput. Netw. **52**, 542–562 (2008)
14. Singh, S., Malik, A., Kumar, R.: Energy efficient heterogeneous DEEC protocol for enhancing lifetime in WSNs. Eng. Sci. Technol. Int. J. **20**, 345–353 (2017)
15. Sinha, A., Paulus, R., Jaiswal, A.K., Ashok, E.A.: E-SDEEC: enhanced sonic distributed energy efficient clustering scheme for heterogeneous WSN. Int. J. Innov. Technol. Res. **4**(4), 3161–3164 (2016). ISSN 2320 –5547
16. Smaragdakis, G., Matta, I., Bestavros, A.: SEP: a stable election protocol for clustered heterogeneous wireless sensory set of connections. In: Second International Workshop on Sensory and Actor Set of connection Protocols and Applications (SANPA 2004) (2004)

Analysis of Heterogeneity Characteristics for Heterogeneous WSNs

Sukhwinder Sharma[1,2(✉)] (iD), Rakesh Kumar Bansal[3,4] (iD),
and Savina Bansal[3,4] (iD)

[1] IKG Punjab Technical University, Kapurthala, India
[2] BBSB Engineering College, Fatehgarh Sahib, India
sukhwinder.sharma@bbsbec.ac.in
[3] GZSCCET, Bathinda, India
drrakeshkbansal@gmail.com, savina.bansal@gmail.com
[4] MRS Punjab Technical University, Bathinda, India

Abstract. Heterogeneity aims to prolong the effective lifetime of WSNs. A network becomes energy heterogeneous when nodes with dissimilar initial energy are deployed. Energy heterogeneity of a WSN is represented by two heterogeneity characteristics- fraction of heterogeneous nodes and additional energy factor between nodes at different energy levels. This paper aims to analyze the impact of energy heterogeneity on WSNs to draw relationship between heterogeneity characteristics and stability period. Well known clustering techniques specially designed for heterogeneous WSNs like SEP, DEEC, DDEEC and HEC are evaluated and analyzed for different values of heterogeneity characteristic parameters. Results clearly indicate the need of having more number of advanced nodes with lesser additional energy as compared to lesser number of advanced nodes having higher additional energy for the network having same total energy. It will certainly bring attention of researchers towards importance of heterogeneity characteristics while designing clustering techniques for WSNs.

Keywords: Clustering · Energy · Heterogeneity · Stability period
Wireless sensor network

1 Introduction

Wireless sensor network (WSN) is a collection of nodes having capabilities to sense the surrounding environment and transmit the sensed data to another node or sink in wireless manner. The lifetime and reliability of a WSN is influenced by its network energy. The sensor nodes are equipped with limited capacity batteries enabling a limited lifetime for the WSN [2, 9]. The lifetime of WSN can be prolonged by deploying additional sensor nodes, design of energy-efficient mechanisms for utilization of available energy and/or introduction of heterogeneity [1, 3, 11]. Deployment of additional sensor nodes is very costly because the cost of sensor is much higher than the cost of battery. Further, many energy-efficient mechanisms are proposed by researchers that improve network lifetime but only up to certain extent. Heterogeneity

© Springer Nature Singapore Pte Ltd. 2018
P. Bhattacharyya et al. (Eds.): NGCT 2017, CCIS 828, pp. 278–290, 2018.
https://doi.org/10.1007/978-981-10-8660-1_21

is a low cost solution to prolong the limited lifetime of WSNs through deployment of nodes having dissimilar computational power, link level and/or initial energy [7, 13].

Energy heterogeneity is considered much important as computational power and link level heterogeneity finally get manifested in the form of energy heterogeneity [10]. This work primarily focuses on heterogeneous WSN having energy heterogeneity. WSNs having nodes with dissimilar initial energies are known as Heterogeneous WSNs (HWSNs) while WSNs having nodes with similar initial energies are known as Homogeneous WSNs. Heterogeneous WSNs may be divided into three categories-two-level, multi-level and random HWSNs. In two-level HWSNs, two energy levels are assigned to different nodes- some nodes are equipped with level-1 initial energy while others are equipped with level-2 initial energy. In multi-level HWSNs, more than two levels of initial energy are assigned to different nodes i.e. level-1, level-2, level-3 and so on. Nodes having level-1, level-2 and level-3 initial energy are known as normal nodes, advanced nodes and super nodes respectively. In random HWSNs, the nodes are equipped with random initial energy from a given range. Homogeneous WSNs become random HWSNs in their lifetime due to different amount of energy depletion for different nodes.

Heterogeneity characteristics- fraction of heterogeneous nodes and additional energy factor between nodes at different energy levels are used to calculate the number of nodes and their initial energy at different levels. The total energy of network increases with the increase in value of heterogeneity characteristic parameters that results in increased effective lifetime of the network. Energy-efficient techniques designed for homogeneous WSNs failed to effectively utilize the energy of heteroge-neous nodes that gave rise to development of energy-efficient techniques specially designed for heterogeneous WSNs [6, 10, 12].

Stability period is the effective lifetime of the network i.e. it is the time when the network starts operation till the death of first node in the network. Effective utilization of increased total network energy of WSN due to energy heterogeneity is desirable to prolong the stability period. This paper aims to analyze the impact of energy hetero-geneity on WSNs to draw relationship between heterogeneity characteristics and sta-bility period, and decide the factors to be considered while designing an HWSN. Well known clustering techniques specially designed for energy heterogeneous WSNs like SEP, DEEC, DDEEC and HEC are evaluated and analyzed for different values of heterogeneity characteristic parameters. This section gives brief introduction to the topic followed by related work in Sect. 2, Problem formulation in Sect. 3, Hetero-geneity in HWSNs in Sect. 4, performance evaluation and analysis in Sect. 5, and conclusions in Sect. 6.

2   Related Work

Development of energy-efficient clustering techniques is a prominent area of research for different authors working in the field of WSNs. Initially, techniques were designed keeping in mind the homogeneous nature of sensor nodes i.e. all nodes were having equal computational power, link levels and energy. With the introduction of hetero-geneity, new techniques are designed having special attention for heterogeneity induced

in WSNs. Some of the well known techniques designed for homogeneous and heterogeneous WSNs are discussed here. Heinzelman et al. [5] proposed Low-Energy
Adaptive Clustering Hierarchy (LEACH) protocol for homogeneous WSNs where all
nodes in the network have identical initial energy. All nodes having equal probability
participate in the cluster head selection process based upon a threshold value. It could
improve network lifetime as compared to conventional direct transmission protocols.
Mhatre and Rosenberg [7] presented a cost based comparative analysis of homogeneous
and heterogeneous networks. They discussed the need of heterogeneity and efficient
clustering techniques for heterogeneous WSNs. Smaragdakis et al. [12] extended the
work for HWSNs by introducing few high energy advanced nodes having high probability to become cluster head than normal nodes and proposed Stable Election Protocol
(SEP). It gives increased stability period in comparison to LEACH by 26%. Qing et al.
[8] proposed Distributed Energy-efficient Clustering (DEEC) for HWSNs considering
residual energy of each node and average energy of the network as the major criteria for
cluster head selection. The nodes with high initial and residual energy have more
chances to become cluster heads than the low-energy nodes. It gives 15% increased
stability period as compared to SEP. Elbhiri et al. [4] proposed Developed Distributed
Energy-Efficient Clustering (DDEEC) to balance the cluster head selection over all
network nodes following their residual energy. Advanced nodes are given high priority
to be selected as cluster heads for the first transmission rounds, and when their energy
decrease sensibly, these nodes are treated with same cluster head election probability as
the normal nodes. It improved the stability period of the network as compared to DEEC
technique by 15%. Sharma et al. [10] introduced the concept of network lifecycle phases
to effectively utilize the energy heterogeneity. The network lifetime is divided into three
phases- initial, active and dying out. They proposed Heterogeneity-aware Energy-
efficient Clustering (HEC) technique to effectively utilize the additional energy of
advanced nodes through autonomous cluster head selection process for each lifecycle
phase rather than single selection process for the complete lifetime. Simulation results
observed improvement for stability period over LEACH, FAIR and SEP techniques by
65%, 15% and 30% respectively. They assessed the impact of heterogeneity characteristic parameters on the proposed technique and revealed the need to further explore
their significance on energy-efficient clustering techniques.

3   Problem Formulation

Clustering techniques aim to prolong the network lifetime, stability period and reliability of WSNs. Stability period represents the effective lifetime of the network. Stability period starts when the network becomes operational till the first node dies. It
gives the duration for which the network can work without any loss of connection or
communication. While network lifetime may be prolonged due to lifetime of nearest
neighbor of sink, stability period gives real picture of the network effectiveness.
Clustering consists of cluster formation, cluster head selection and data communication
from sensing nodes to sink(s) through cluster heads. The network is divided into
clusters having cluster heads responsible to sense data, receive data from sensor nodes
within cluster, aggregate the sensed and received data, and forwarding of processed

data to the sink or base station. Clustering Techniques designed for homogeneous WSNs remain unable to take advantage of energy heterogeneity when applied to energy heterogeneous WSNs. Energy heterogeneous WSNs require efficient clustering techniques to effectively utilize the increased network energy due to energy heterogeneity. It needs understanding of energy heterogeneity characteristics and their impact on the network lifetime and reliability. Further, increasing the energy levels also increase the total network energy that needs thorough investigation to ascertain whether the lifetime and reliability improvement is due to the increased network energy or the clustering technique itself. Various well known clustering techniques designed for two-level and multi-level energy heterogeneity are evaluated and analyzed for possible directions in the field of energy heterogeneous WSNs.

4   Heterogeneity in HWSNs

Consider a HWSN having T_n number of total nodes, with identical computational power and link levels, uniformly randomly distributed across a $X * Y$ region. For two-level HWSN, T_n is a combination of N_n number of normal nodes with energy E_0 and A_n number of advanced nodes with enhanced energy E_a. Further, two heterogeneity characteristics- fraction of advanced nodes (m) and additional energy factor between advanced and normal nodes (α) are used to calculate the number of advanced nodes and their initial energy. The total energy of the network E_{total} is represented as

$$E_{total} = N_n \cdot E_0 + A_n \cdot E_a \tag{1}$$

where

$$N_n = (1 - m).T_n \tag{2}$$

$$A_n = m \cdot T_n \tag{3}$$

and

$$E_a = (1 + \alpha) \cdot E_0 \tag{4}$$

Hence,

$$E_{total} = (1 - m).T_n.E_0 + m \cdot T_n(1 + \alpha) \cdot E_0 = T_n(1 + \alpha.m).E_0 \tag{5}$$

The total energy of network increases with the increase in value of heterogeneity characteristic parameters.

Following are the steps to introduce energy heterogeneity in HWSNs:

1. Decide the total number of nodes, T_n to be deployed in the network.
2. Decide the number of energy levels for the network nodes. For two-level HWSNs, there will be two energy levels while multiple energy levels will be used for multi-level HWSNs.

3. Depending upon the energy levels, decide the heterogeneity parameters: $(m : m1, m2, m3, \ldots)$, the fraction of advanced nodes and $(\alpha : \alpha1, \alpha2, \alpha3, \ldots)$, the additional energy factor between advanced and normal nodes.
4. Calculate the total number of normal nodes (N_n) and advanced nodes $(A_n : A_{n1}, A_{n2}, A_{n3}, \ldots)$:
For 2-level energy heterogeneity (using Eqs. 2 and 3):

$$N_n = (1 - m) \cdot T_n \tag{6}$$

$$A_n = m \cdot T_n \tag{7}$$

For 3-level energy heterogeneity:

$$N_n = (1 - m1) \cdot T_n \tag{8}$$

$$A_{n1} = (1 - m2).m1 \cdot T_n \tag{9}$$

$$A_{n2} = m2.m1 \cdot T_n \tag{10}$$

Similarly the network can be extended for more than three levels of energy heterogeneity.
5. Decide the initial energy of normal nodes, E_0. Calculate the initial energy of advanced nodes, $(E_a : E_{a1}, E_{a2}, E_{a3}, \ldots)$ and total network energy, E_{total}
For 2-level energy heterogeneity (using Eqs. 4 and 5):

$$E_a = (1 + \alpha) \cdot E_0 \tag{11}$$

$$E_{total} = T_n \cdot E_0(1 + \alpha.m) \tag{12}$$

For 3-level energy heterogeneity:

$$E_{a1} = (1 + \alpha1) \cdot E_0 \tag{13}$$

$$E_{a2} = (1 + \alpha2) \cdot E_0 \tag{14}$$

$$E_{total} = T_n \cdot E_0(1 + m1(\alpha1 + m2.\alpha2)) \tag{15}$$

Similarly the network can be extended for more than three levels energy heterogeneity.
6. Deploy the network nodes with their corresponding energies.

Above discussed steps to introduce energy heterogeneity in WSNs are shown below in the form of flow chart (Fig. 1).

Different naming conventions are used by researchers to represent the nodes. While two-level HWSN nodes are named as normal and advanced nodes, 3-level HWSN nodes are termed as normal, advanced and super nodes. This gives better understanding of heterogeneous nodes having dissimilar initial energy i.e. super nodes have highest initial energy while advanced nodes have α times higher initial energy than normal nodes.

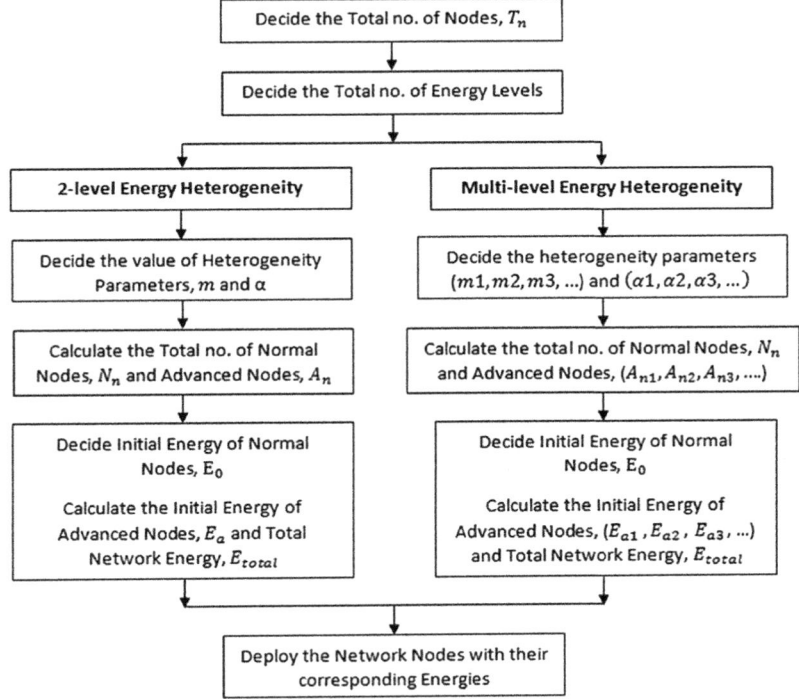

Fig. 1. Steps to introduce energy heterogeneity in WSN.

5   Performance Evaluation

In this section, well-known clustering techniques- SEP, DEEC, DDEEC and HEC specially designed for HWSNs are evaluated. The performance in terms of stability period for different values of energy heterogeneity characteristic parameters is considered for evaluation. Stability period is the time for which the network is stable i.e. all nodes are alive in this period. Period starts when the network becomes operational till the first node dies. This is the effective lifetime of the network. Heterogeneity characteristics m and α represents the fraction of advanced nodes and additional energy factor between advanced and normal nodes. The radio energy consumption model used in this work is shown in Fig. 2.

According to the radio energy consumption model, for transmitting a L-bit packet over a distance d such that Signal-to-Noise Ratio (SNR) is minimum; the energy expended by the radio is given by:

$$E_{Tx}(L, d) = \begin{cases} L * E_{elec} + L * E_{fs} * d^2 & \text{if } d < d_0 \\ L * E_{elec} + L * E_{mp} * d^4 & \text{if } d \geq d_0 \end{cases} \tag{16}$$

$$E_{Rx}(L) = L * E_{elec} \tag{17}$$

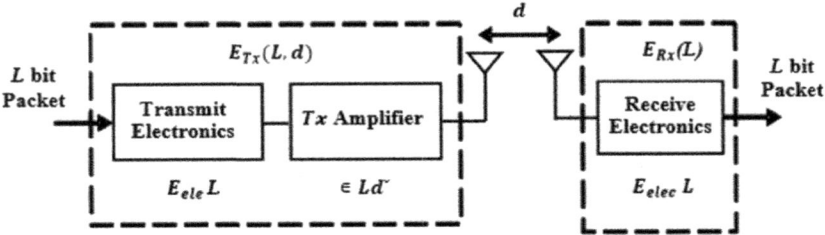

Fig. 2. Radio energy consumption model.

Where E_{Tx} is energy required for transmission, E_{Rx} is energy required for reception, E_{elec} is the energy dissipated per bit to run the transmitter or the receiver circuit, E_{fs} and E_{mp} depend on the transmitter amplifier model we use, and d is the distance between the sender and the receiver and maximum distance of any node to the sink is $\leq d_0$.

Tables 1 and 2 represent the simulation parameters and radio characteristics used for performance analysis.

Table 1. Simulation parameters

Simulation parameters	Values
Total no. of nodes (T_n)	100
Field size $(X * Y)$	100 m*100 m
Initial energy of normal node (E_0)	0.5 Joules
Fraction of advanced nodes (m)	0.1,0.2,0.3,0.4,0.5
Additional energy factor between advanced and normal nodes (α)	1,2,3,4,5
Message size	4000 bits
P_{opt}	0.1
No. of iterations	10

Table 2. Radio characteristics used in simulation

Operation	Energy dissipated
Transmitter/receiver electronics	$E_{elec} = 50\,\text{nJ/bit}$
Data aggregation	$E_{DA} = 5\,\text{nJ/bit/signal}$
Transmit amplifier if $d_{maxtoBS} \leq d_0$	$E_{fs} = 10\,\text{pJ/bit/m}^2$
Transmit amplifier, if $d_{maxtoBS} \geq d_0$	$E_{mp} = 0.0013\,\text{pJ/bit/m}^4$

The wireless sensor network is simulated using MATLAB having field dimensions of $100\,\text{m} * 100\,\text{m}$ with 100 nodes. The field size and total number of nodes are kept constant to make the analysis focused and simple. Nodes are uniformly randomly distributed in the network field. The sink is deployed at the center of the field. Figures 3 and 4 show the node deployment and cluster formation in the sensing field.

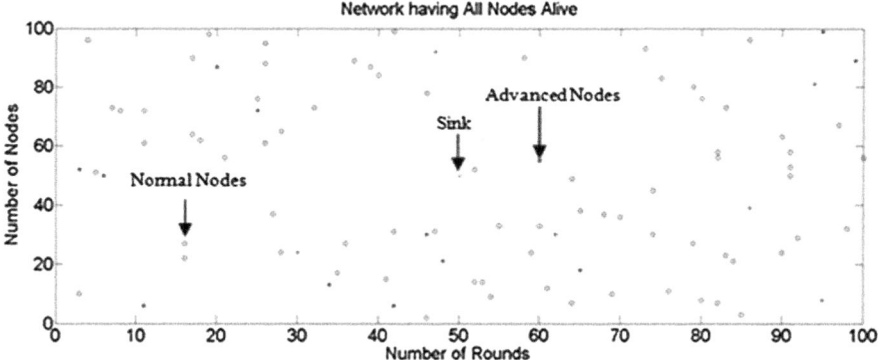

Fig. 3. WSN node deployment.

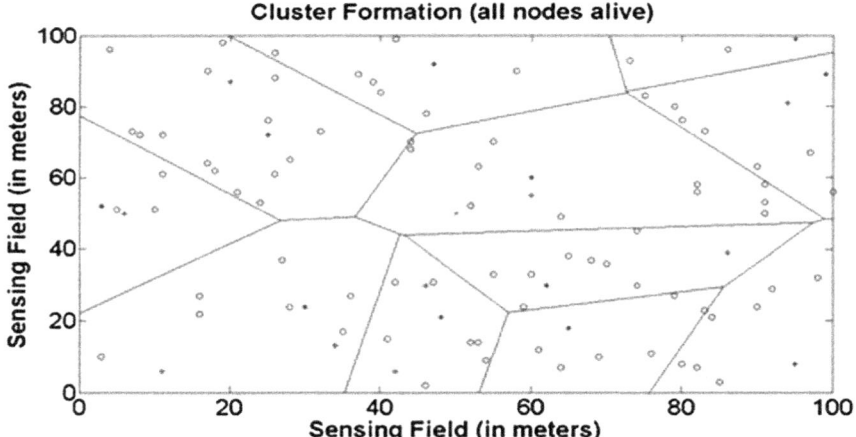

Fig. 4. Cluster formation in WSN.

To analyze the relationship between heterogeneity characteristics and stability period, two categories of input are considered- Category 1 and Category 2. Category 1 represents network having more number of advanced nodes with lesser initial energy while Category 2 represents network having less number of advanced nodes with higher initial energy. Category 1 consists of inputs having High m and Low α while Category 2 consists of inputs having Low m and High α, where total network energy is identical. Table 3 shows the stability period of the network for different values of m and α.

A network having 100 nodes with (m = 0.2, α = 1) will have same total network energy (= 60 Joules) as for the same network with (m = 0.1, α = 2). Similar will be the case with (m = 0.3, α = 2) and (m = 0.2, α = 3). The results of (m = 0.2, α = 1) and (m = 0.3, α = 2) will be kept under Category 1 while results of (m = 0.1, α = 2) and (m = 0.2, α = 3) will be kept under Category 2. Figures 5, 6, 7 and 8 show the

Category-wise stability period of clustering techniques- SEP, DEEC, DDEEC and HEC respectively for different values of heterogeneity characteristic parameters m and α.

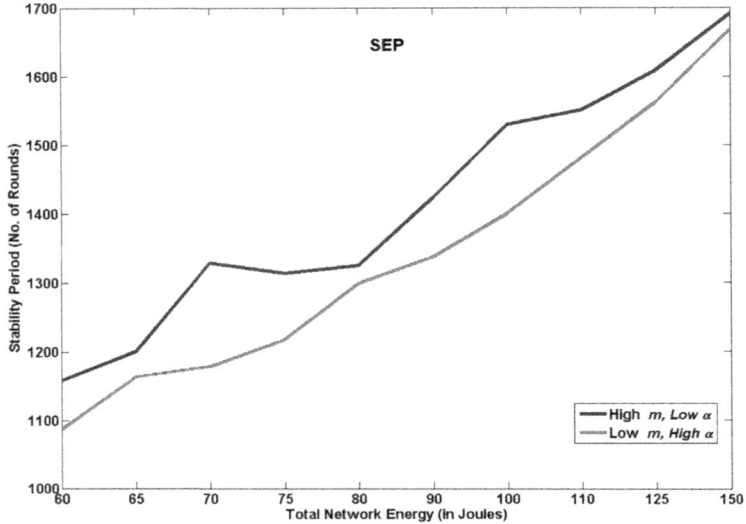

Fig. 5. SEP protocol: stability period v/s total network energy.

SEP gives increased stability period with increase in total network energy while DEEC gives almost similar results for different values of total network energy. This may be due to their cluster formation and cluster head selection process. While SEP gives high probability to advanced nodes during cluster formation and cluster head selection process, DEEC decides cluster heads based upon initial and residual energy. SEP and DEEC gives better results for Category 1 inputs as compared to Category 2 inputs.

It indicates the need of having more number of advanced nodes with lesser additional energy than lesser number of advanced nodes having higher additional energy for stability period improvement.

DDEEC gives similar but slightly better results than DEEC, while HEC outperforms all the techniques. For all the techniques, the results indicate that the Category 1 having High m and Low α gives better stability period than the Category 2 having Low m and High α for same amount of total network energy. This may be due to the reason that clustering techniques can better utilize the additional advanced nodes during cluster formation and cluster head selection process. The burden of existing advanced nodes is reduced with introduction of additional advanced nodes. As limited initial energy of normal nodes is the bottleneck for HWSNs, additional energy to existing advanced nodes remains unable to improve the stability period. It clearly indicates to have more number of advanced nodes with lesser additional energy than lesser number of advanced nodes having higher additional energy.

Table 3. Stability period for category 1 and category 2 inputs of different techniques

Total network energy (E_total) in Joules	Category 1 (High m, Low α)						Category 2 (Low m, High α)						Change in stability Period from category 1 to category 2 (no. of rounds)			
	m	α	Stability period (no. of rounds)				m	α	Stability period (no. of rounds)				SEP	DEEC	DDEEC	HEC
			SEP	DEEC	DDEEC	HEC			SEP	DEEC	DDEEC	HEC				
60	0.2	1	1159	1340	1316	1106	0.1	2	1088	1301	1309	1011	71	39	7	95
65	0.3	1	1201	1384	1373	1272	0.1	3	1164	1355	1278	1075	37	29	95	197
70	0.4	1	1329	1396	1423	1494	0.1	4	1179	1372	1299	1092	150	24	124	402
75	0.5	1	1314	1398	1396	1658	0.1	5	1218	1325	1357	1071	96	73	39	587
80	0.3	2	1325	1360	1356	1747	0.2	3	1299	1330	1280	1713	26	30	76	34
90	0.4	2	1423	1339	1371	2031	0.2	4	1337	1276	1330	1946	86	63	41	85
100	0.5	2	1529	1353	1340	2069	0.2	5	1400	1321	1299	2004	129	32	41	65
110	0.4	3	1551	1349	1347	2123	0.3	4	1481	1279	1297	2060	70	70	50	63
125	0.5	3	1609	1300	1366	2095	0.3	5	1562	1291	1331	2063	47	9	35	32
150	0.5	4	1691	1322	1375	2096	0.4	5	1668	1283	1310	2071	23	39	65	25

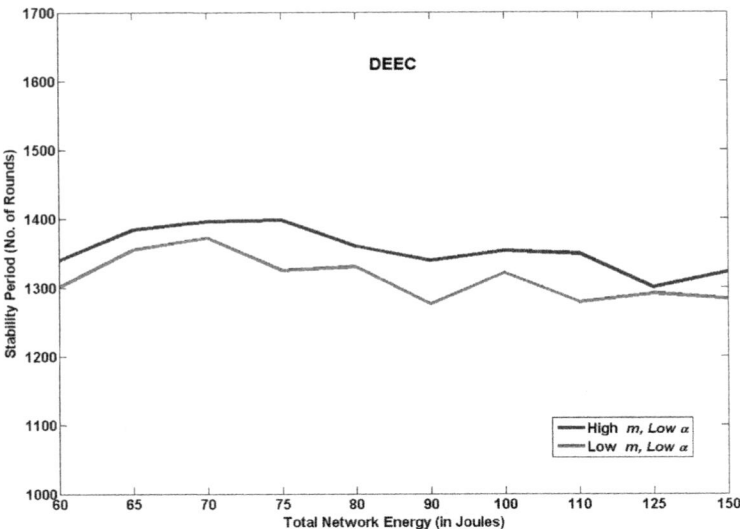

Fig. 6. DEEC protocol: stability period v/s total network energy.

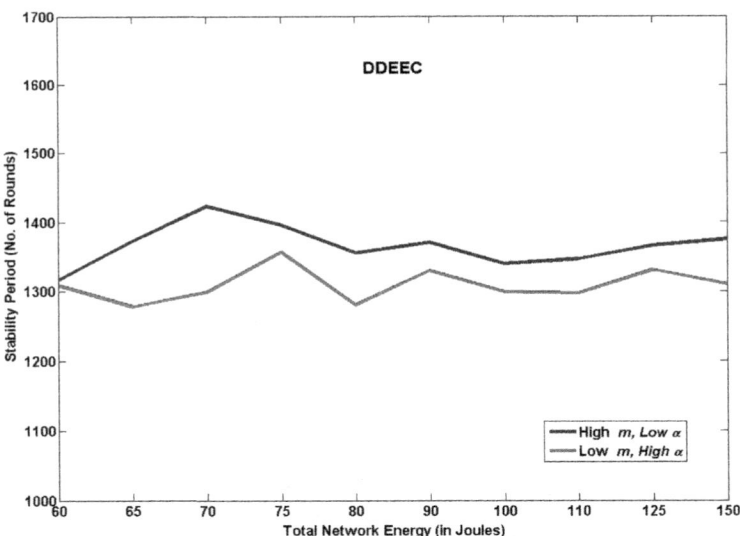

Fig. 7. DDEEC protocol: stability period v/s total network energy.

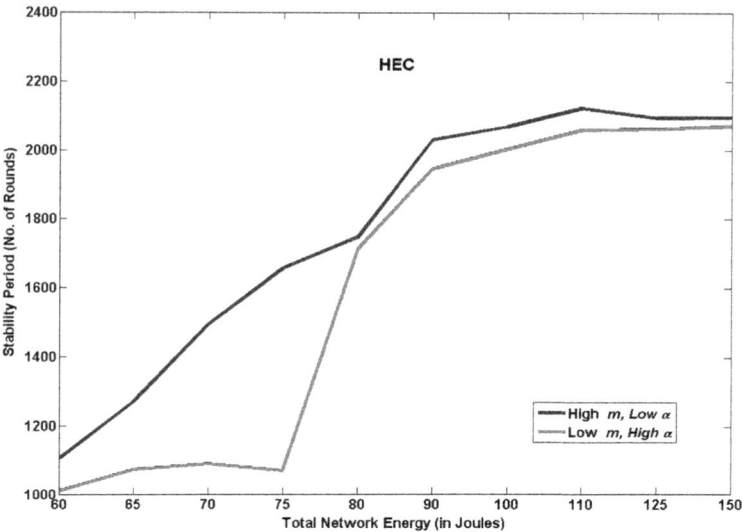

Fig. 8. HEC protocol: stability period v/s total network energy.

6 Conclusions

Clustering techniques- SEP, DEEC, DDEEC and HEC designed for energy hetero-geneous wireless sensor networks are evaluated for different values of heterogeneity characteristic parameters. Simulation results indicate that the increase in value of heterogeneity parameters increases the overall energy of network that contributes to increased stability period. Results obtained for higher number of advanced nodes are better than the higher amount of additional energy which indicates the need of having more number of advanced nodes with lesser additional energy as compared to less number of advanced nodes having higher additional energy for the network having same total energy. It will result in increased effective lifetime of future WSNs.

References

1. Akkaya, K., Younis, M.: A survey on routing protocols for wireless sensor networks. Ad Hoc Netw. **3**(3), 325–349 (2005). https://doi.org/10.1016/j.adhoc.2003.09.010
2. Akyildiz, F., Su, W., Sankarasubramaniam, Y., Cayirci, E.: A survey on sensor networks. IEEE Commun. Mag. **40**(8), 102–114 (2002). https://doi.org/10.1109/MCOM.2002.1024422
3. Anastasi, G., Conti, M., Francesco, M.D., Passarella, A.: Energy conservation in wireless sensor networks: a survey. Ad Hoc Netw. **7**(3), 537–568 (2009). https://doi.org/10.1016/j. adhoc.2008.06.003
4. Elbhiri, B., Saadane, R., El-Fkihi, S., Aboutajdine, D.: Developed distributed energy-efficient clustering (DDEEC) for heterogeneous wireless sensor networks. In: 5th International Symposium on I/V Communications and Mobile Network Proceedings, 2, pp. 1–4. Rabat, Morocco (2010). https://doi.org/10.1109/isvc.2010.5656252

5. Heinzelman, W.B., Chandrakasan, A.P., Balakrishnan, H.: An application-specific protocol architecture for wireless microsensor networks. IEEE Trans. Wirel. Commun. **1**(4), 660–670 (2002). https://doi.org/10.1109/TWC.2002.804190

6. Kumar, D., Aseri, T.C., Patel, R.B.: EEHC: energy efficient heterogeneous clustered scheme for wireless sensor networks. Comput. Commun. **32**(4), 662–667 (2009). https://doi.org/10.1016/j.comcom.2008.11.025

7. Mhatre, V., Rosenberg, C.: Homogeneous vs Heterogeneous clustered sensor networks: a comparative study. In: 2004 IEEE International Conference on Communications Proceedings, vol. 6, pp. 3646–3651. Paris, France (2004). https://doi.org/10.1109/icc.2004.1313223

8. Qing, L., Zhu, Q., Wang, M.: Design of a distributed energy-efficient clustering algorithm for heterogeneous wireless sensor networks. Comput. Commun. **29**, 2230–2237 (2006). https://doi.org/10.1016/j.comcom.2006.02.017

9. Sharma, S., Bansal, R.K., Bansal, S.: Issues and challenges in wireless sensor networks. In: IEEE International Conference on Machine Intelligence Research and Advancement Proceedings, pp. 58–62. Katra, India (2013). https://doi.org/10.1109/icmira.2013.18

10. Sharma, S., Bansal, R.K., Bansal, S.: Heterogeneity-aware energy-efficient clustering (HEC) technique for WSNs. KSII Trans. Internet Inf Syst. **11**(4), 1866–1888 (2017). https://doi.org/10.1201/b20085-16

11. Sharma, S., Bansal, R.K., Bansal, S.: Energy-efficient data collection techniques in wireless sensor networks. In: Emerging Communication Technologies Based on Wireless Sensor Networks: Current Research and Future Applications. CRC Press/Taylor & Francis, Boca Raton/Abington (2016). https://doi.org/10.1201/b20085-16

12. Smaragdakis, G., Matta, I., Bestavros, A.: SEP: a stable election protocol for clustered heterogeneous wireless sensor networks. In: 2nd International Workshop on Sensor and Actor Network Protocols and Applications Proceedings, pp. 251–261, Boston, Massachusetts (2004)

13. Yarvis, M., Kushalnagar, N., Singh, H., Rangarajan, A. Liu, Y. Singh, S.: Exploiting heterogeneity in sensor networks. In: INFOCOM Proceedings, vol. 2, pp. 878–890. Miami, FL, US (2005). https://doi.org/10.1109/infcom.2005.1498318

Performance Evaluation of Adaptive Telemetry Acoustic Modem for Underwater Wireless Sensor Networks

Hareesh Kumar[1,2]([✉]), Y. N. Nirmala[3], and M. N. Sreerangaraju[4]([✉])

[1] BIT Research Centre, Department of ECE, Bangalore Institute of Technology,
Bangalore 560004, Karnataka, India
hareevlsi@gmail.com
[2] Department of ECE, Dayananda Sagar Academy of Technology
and Management, Bangalore 560082, Karnataka, India
[3] Department of ECE, Dr. Ambedakar Institute of Technology,
Bangalore 560056, Karnataka, India
[4] Department of ECE, Bangalore Institute of Technology,
Bangalore 560004, Karnataka, India
mnsrr@rediffmail.com

Abstract. Underwater acoustic communication is generally slow when contrasted with radio system. The medium is moderate as well as there are difficulties with the transmission because of signal absorption, multipath delay, channel can shift significantly between various transmitter and receiver pairs. So we should pick modem parameters in view of channel conditions. Oceanographers utilize acoustic signal to control submerged instruments and secure the information they gather remotely. This innovation can likewise be utilized to control anonymous submarines, called self-ruling submerged ocean vehicles (AUV's) and get information once again from them in real time. There are a few techniques for transmitting information acoustically (i.e. modulation) used in Underwater communication. In this paper we proposed an Adaptive acoustic modem which adopts the suitable modulation technique between Quadrature Amplitude Modulation (QAM) and Frequency Shift Keying (FSK) on the basis of channel parameters i.e. Signal to Noise Ratio (SNR), Doppler shift, Bit error rate (BER), based on these parameters, the best modulation technique will be selected for communication purpose. The analysis of these parameters is done using MATLAB SIMULINK which is a graphical representation of simulation systems in real time environment.

Keywords: QAM · FSK · SNR · BER · Matlab-simulink · Doppler shift
Adaptive acoustic modem

1 Introduction

Underwater sensor arrangement is a system of self-ruling sensor hubs, which are spatially distributed and submerged to detect the water-related properties, for example, quality, temperature and pressure utilizing acoustic channels. Sensor nodes and

© Springer Nature Singapore Pte Ltd. 2018
P. Bhattacharyya et al. (Eds.): NGCT 2017, CCIS 828, pp. 291–304, 2018.
https://doi.org/10.1007/978-981-10-8660-1_22

vehicles must have self-plan limits, i.e., they ought to have the ability to encourage their operation by trading arrangement, zone and improvement information, and to hand-off checked data. This innovation can be utilized to control anonymous submarines, called self-ruling submerged ocean vehicles (AUV's) [3] and get information from them continuously. For reliable communication, we should pick modem parameters for most optimistic scenario channel conditions, it has isolate modem for both the modulation strategies [1]. The applications require long haul, the battery lifetime of systems like shallow-water acoustic channel qualities, for example, low data transmission, multipath and propagation delays, limiting the power is difficult. The underwater wireless communication network system is shown in Fig. 1.The major drawback of acoustic communication is due to extensive and variable multipath Doppler spread [14]. Acoustic channel can shift impressively between various transmitters and collector pairs, the transmitter was intended to work with a range from 0–100 kHz, due to this reason FSK was used. In order to transmit more bits per symbol (deliver more data) higher order constellation is required which is obtained by using QAM. Even in the presence of multipath fading, the better demodulation results are obtained due to flexibility in the design of underwater equipment. We propose a submerged acoustic modem that adjusts its information rate and modulation scheme to channel conditions.

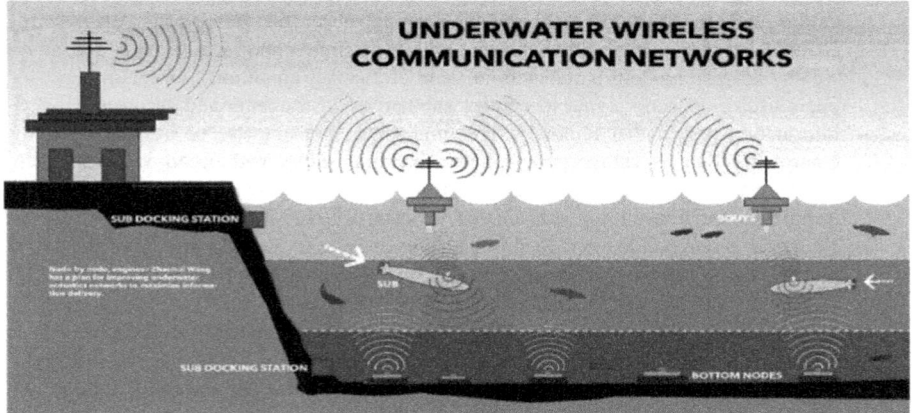

Fig. 1. Underwater wireless communication networks

The QAM is both digital and analog modulation technique. It passes two analog message or two digital bit streams by evolving (balancing) the amplitudes of two carrier waves by utilizing the amplitude shift keying (ASK) digital modulation technique or amplitude balance (AM) analog modulation technique. The two carrier waves of a similar frequencies are generally sinusoidals are out of phase with each other by 90° is called quadrature carrier or quadrature segments. There are two levels of amplitudes for each phase i.e. d1 level and d2 level, fc carrier frequency.

$$s(t) = d_1(t)\cos(2 * pi * f_c * t) + d_2(t)\sin(2 * pi * f_c * t) \tag{1}$$

Frequency-shift keying (FSK) is a frequency modulation technique in which digital data is transmitted via discrete frequency changes of a carrier signal. The technology is utilized for communication applications like amateur radio, caller ID and emergency broadcasts. The easiest FSK is Binary FSK (BFSK). BFSK utilizes a couple of discrete frequencies to transmit parallel (1's) data. With this scheme, the "1" is called the mark frequency and the "0" is called the space frequency. Binary 1 is represented by high frequency 'f1' and binary 0 is represented by low frequency 'f2', s (t) is transmitted signal, A is Amplitude.

$$s_1(t) = A \cos(2\pi f_1 t) \quad for \ Binary(1) \tag{2}$$

$$s_2(t) = A \cos(2\pi f_2 t) \quad for \ Binary(0) \tag{3}$$

In this work, the two modulation systems QAM and FSK are analyzed and gives an ADAPTIVE MODEM which delivers the best outcome. We have compared parameters such as SNR, Doppler Spread and BER between both the techniques to achieve Adaptive results. Our proposed work can be utilized for submerged telemetry, AUV control, submerged vehicle checking. Our proposed work can be used to send and get information in the underwater communication. It also has various applications such as Seismic activity detection, Submarine tracking, Military & homeland security.

1.1 Challenges for Efficient Communication

Standard acoustic transducers can't transmit and receive at the same time. Submerged systems communication are quite often half-duplex. AUVs are frequently confined to utilize higher center frequencies for the most part over 10 kHz. Another problem for the AUVs [12] to transmit at high information rates however harder for them to retrieve back at high rates. Underwater sensors are involved in three-dimensional (3-D) application situations, which is significantly more difficult to break down contrasted with 2-D arrangement areas [13]. Acoustic system has some draw back due to variable multipath fading, multipath delay and doppler spread. All the above challenges is due to the layers of water density and the nature of environment, because of this reason we are designing an Adaptive Acoustic Modem for underwater Sensor Network.

1.1.1 Fading and Doppler Shift

Fading or loss of signals is a vital role that identified in the wireless communications Field. The distortion of signals is due to multipath is known as fading. Fading is caused by various physical effects, like Doppler Shift that the identified frequency increases when objects moving towards each other and decreases when the source moves away from each other. This Phenomenon is known as Doppler Effect [3].

$$f' = \frac{(v \pm v_0)}{v} f \quad \text{(Observer at rest)} \tag{4}$$

$$f' = \frac{v}{(v \pm v_s)}f \quad \text{(Stationary Source)} \tag{5}$$

Where v_s Velocity of the Source, v_0 Velocity of the Observer, v Velocity of sound in medium, f Real frequency, f' Apparent frequency.

There are two types of fading with respect to the doppler Spread which as follows:

(a) Slow fading means when the coherence time of the channel is huge in respect to the delay limitation of the channel, then slow fading will arise. The amplitude and phase change introduced by the channel can be constant over the time of use.

(b) Quick fading means when the coherence time of the channel is little in respect to the delay limitation of the channel causes the quick fading. The amplitude and phase change introduced by the channel can be varies over the time of use.

1.1.2 Relationship Between BER and SNR in Under Water Communication

Unlike the communication in terrestrial and underground applications, for underwater wave propagation, the challenges are quitesdifferent. The water itself as becomes the main source for the signal interference. The type of water (fresh water/sea water), depth pressure, dissolved impurities, water composition and temperature affect the sound propagation. Common terrestrial phenomena like scattering, reflection, refraction also occur in underwater communication. The BER characteristics for an underwater wireless communication channel is directly related to the various networking parameters. Hence a thorough analysis of BER characteristics proves to be useful while designing an efficient underwater communication channel. The BER of a communication channel for underwater environment primarily depend on the channel model, the signal modulation method and SNR for the channel. The depth at which the sensing device are deployed significantly affect the path loss which intern result in fluctuation in the BER values. Depending up on the sensors nodes are positioned, the higher fluctuation rate in BER value. For sensor nodes deployed deep into the water, the BER is stabilized.

2 Modem Design

Underwater acoustic modems consist of three fundamental components as shown in Fig. 2. A transmitter, a switching network and a receiver for signal processing. We provide details about major parts of the communication modem which has been performed using Simulink which provides a practical aspects of underwater communication. The functional block of Adaptive modem subsystem is shown in Fig. 3.

2.1 Modulation

There are various types of modulation technique used in underwater system. These include FSK [2], QAM, PSK [2, 6], OFDM [9], and DSSS [1, 10]. In our work, the adaptive modem can switch between FSK and QAM. There are many advantages of using

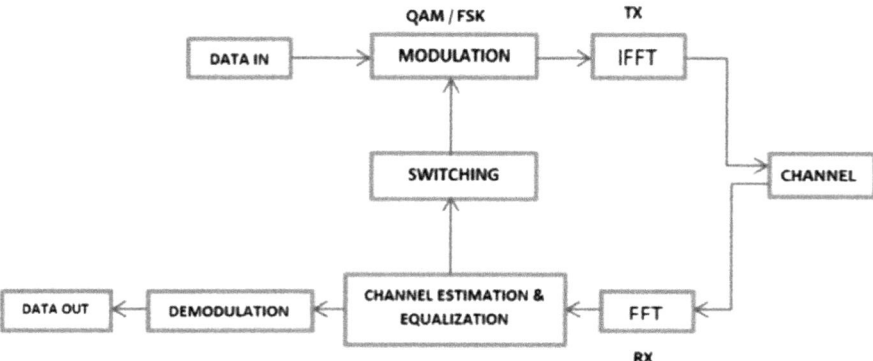

Fig. 2. Designed block diagram of Adaptive modem

FSK such as resilient to noise, resilient to signal strength variations, it is still widely used for many broadcast and acoustic communications applications. QAM appears to increase efficiency of transmission by utilizing both phase and amplitude variations and effective use of bandwidth which in turn carries more bits of information per symbol.

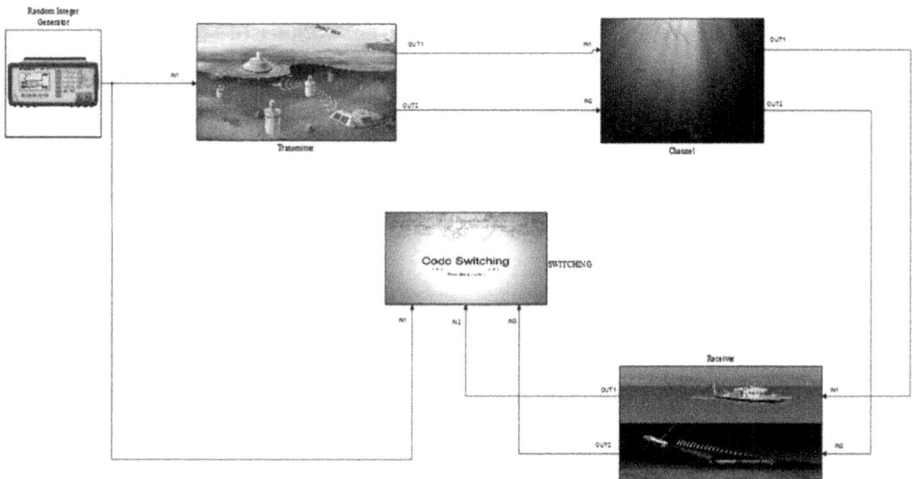

Fig. 3. Adaptive modem subsystem of all blocks

2.2   Channel Estimation

Channel Estimation is a decision making circuit which checks the parameters of SNR [1], Doppler shift, BER and switch to a suitable modulation technique. Doppler Effect is caused due sound or light waves with respect to frequency, but there is a constant relative motion between the source and the observer, causing the observed frequency to change.

SNR is the ratio of the received signal quality over the noise quality in the frequency range of the operation. It is a vital parameter of the physical layer of Local Area Wireless Network (LAWN). BER is inversely related to SNR, that is high BER causes low SNR. High BER causes increase in packet loss, delay and decreases the throughput. S/N is the signal-to-noise ratio (SNR) in decibels.

$$SNR = \frac{E_b * R_b}{N_0 * B} \tag{6}$$

Where, B is the Bandwidth of unit noise and SNR will be more than Eb/N0 by a factor of Rb (if Rb > 1 bit/second) else SNR and Eb/No are same.

$$SNR = \frac{E_b * R_b}{N_0} \tag{7}$$

$$SNR(dB) = \frac{E_b}{N_0}(dB) + 10 \log_{10} \frac{R_b}{B} \tag{8}$$

Where, Rb = bit rate in bits/second, Eb = Energy per bit in Joules/bit, S = Total Signal power in Watts, B = noise bandwidth (B = 1), N_0 = Noise spectral density in joules

The bit error rate (BER) is defined as the ratio of Number of error bits to the total number of bits sent, BER is a unit less performance measure, often expressed as a percentage.

$$Bit\ Error\ Rate\ (BER) = \frac{Number\ of\ error\ bits}{Total\ number\ of\ bits\ sent} \tag{9}$$

$$C = B \log_2 \left(1 + \frac{S}{N}\right) \tag{10}$$

Where C = channel capacity in bits per second, B = bandwidth of the channel in hertz.

2.3   Switching

While transmission it should check for the parameters and satisfies the following three criteria. Based on the best criteria it will switch between FSK and QAM which leads to Adaptive technique, using this technique comparison can be done easily. For comparison, we have used the maximum and minimum functional block which is available in matlab Simulink library.

(a) BER should be low.
(b) SNR should be high.
(c) Doppler shift should be low.

The Output coming from both the techniques QAM and FSK is given to a minimum functional block available in the Simulink library which will switch to the minimum most result obtained for BER and Doppler shift and to maximum functional block for SNR to get maximum result [4].

2.4 Equalization

Equalization is the way toward adjusting the time fluctuating properties of the communication channel, where Decision Feedback Equalization (DFE) technique is preferred. Long multipath spreads in the submerged channel to make channel balance altogether and more difficult than radio channels, thus play a vital role in the modem [8].

2.5 Demodulation

Demodulation is the process of retrieving original message signal by using suitable modulation technique. The output of FFT is taken and given as an input to the FSK and QAM Demodulator block. It is very difficult to determine the incoming data correctly at the front end of the receiver.

3 Implementation of Adaptive Acoustic Modem Using Matlab Simulink

Functional block of underwater acoustic modems as many major blocks as shown in Fig. 4 such as Random Integer, QAM, IFFT, FFT, FSK, BER, SNR, Doppler Spread, Channel, and Demodulation. Random Integer block generates random uniformly distributed integers signal in the range [0, M-1], where M is the M-array number. Where M = 8 hence it generates data from 0 to 7. We have used two modulation techniques QAM and FSK.

3.1 QAM (Quadrature Amplitude Modulation)

Modulate the input signal fed by random integer generator by using the QAM method. This block accepts a scalar or column vector as input signal.

$$\textbf{\textit{Signal constellation}} \; = \; \left[\textbf{exp} \left(\textbf{2} \; * \; \textbf{\textit{pi}} \; * \; \textbf{\textit{i}} \; * \; \frac{\textbf{[0 : 7]}}{\textbf{8}} \right) \right] \tag{11}$$

The QAM modulated signal is fed to the impose carrier, this IFFT algorithm is used to carrier signal from one place to another. In channel, functional blocks are programed to add white Gaussian noise [15] and Rayleigh noise to create a real world scenario while transmission. The received signal from channel is then fed to FFT algorithm block to retrieve the original signal and removing carrier from it, due to this signal can be analyzed. To compute IFFT and FFT, we have to set the 'IFFT' and 'FFT' parameter to 'Radix-2', the FFT length is power of two. We transmitted the various

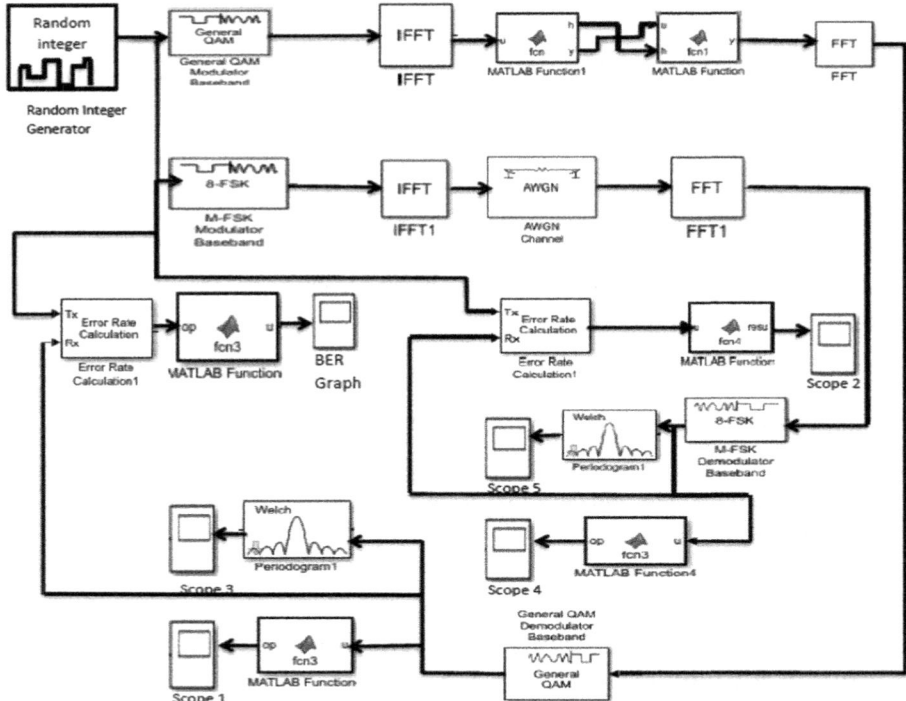

Fig. 4. Adaptive modem schematic diagram

data rates, at each data rate, 20 packets containing 2040 symbols were transmitted. Each packet contains 102 bits [5].

Demodulate the input signal using the quadrature amplitude modulation method. When 'Output type' is set to 'Integer', the block performs hard decision demodulation. When 'Output type' is set to 'Bit', the size of signal constellation is an integer power of 2 and the output width is multiple of the number of bits per symbol [11]. The Data were collected at a distance of 265 m from transmitter.

3.2   FSK (Frequency Shift Keying)

The FSK is the second modulation method which is similar to QAM, we have depicted this technique and received the signal on the receiver. For comparison we are checking three parameters BER, SNR and Doppler shift. After receiving data signal from transmitter, BER is checked and it is the ratio of loss of data packets to fully transmitted packets. To compute the error rate of the obtained data by comparing it with a deferred version of the transmitted information. To calculate SNR we have used period gram watch block which is available in matlab simulink library.

The Output block is a three-component vector comprising of error rate, the number of error recognized and the total number of symbols matched. The input to the transmitter and receiver ports must be scalars or column vectors. The 'Stop simulation' option stops the simulation upon detecting a target number of errors or symbols, whichever comes first.

4   Flow Chart

The Data is fed into the Modulation block it consists of two techniques QAM and FSK. After modulation the data is transmitted over an Acoustic channel. The flow chart is shown in Fig. 5. The data fetched at the receiver end, the received data is channel estimated using switching technique is performed based on the parameters. On the basis of the best result of the parameter, the demodulation is performed [5]. The software modem allows the user to select a desired modulation technique [7].

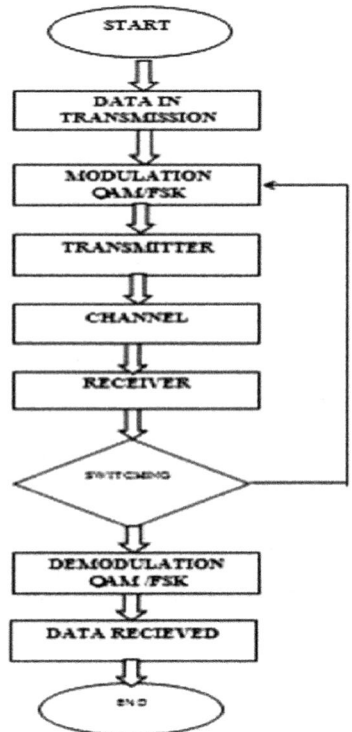

Fig. 5. Flowchart of Adaptive modem

5 Simulation Results

In our proposed modem, the data is transmitted using digital modulation techniques (FSK and QAM). Suppose if the modem performs FSK modulation technique, performance parameters are stored and then QAM is performed, performance parameters of both modulation techniques are compared and it switches to best modulation technique.

5.1 Bit Error Rate of QAM, FSK and Adaptive Modem

As we can observe in Fig. 6, result obtained for BER of QAM shows that the number of bit error for energy level 7 dB is $10 * 10^{-3}$ and for energy level 10 dB the BER reduces to $9 * 10^{-3}$. And for 14 dB the BER reduces to $7 * 10^{-3}$. As we keep increases the energy levels, the BER will get reduces and it get saturated from some point. And for BER of FSK shows that the bit error reduces to $10 * 10^{-3}$ for energy level 4 dB and for energy level 6 dB the BER reduces to $8.3 * 10^{-3}$. In the Adaptive BER graph the best result is shown by comparing both QAM and FSK, as we can for energy level 4 dB the bit error reduces to $10 * 10^{-3}$ and it saturates from some point. The Adaptive modem takes the FSK for BER.

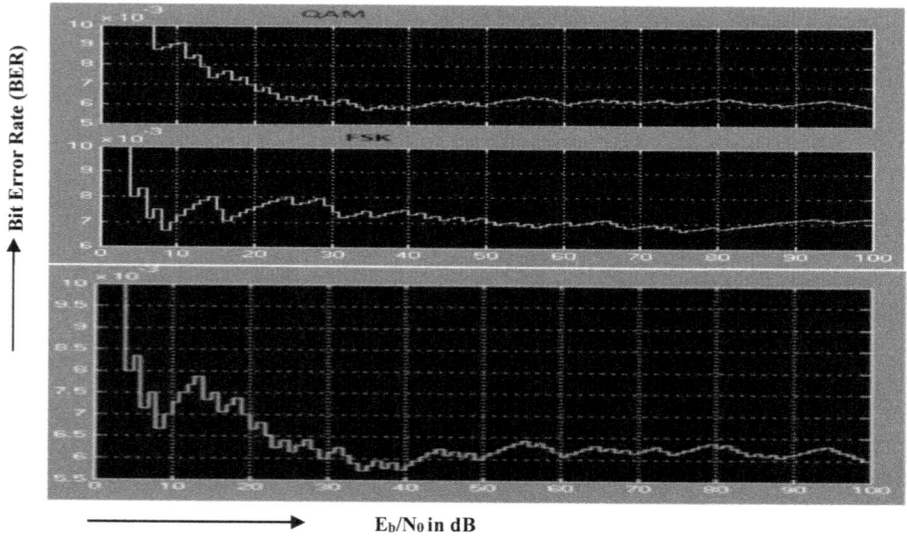

Fig. 6. BER of QAM, FSK and Adaptive modem

In our proposed Adaptive system BER reduces when SNR increases and data rate also increases, as the SNR and data rate keep on increasing then the BER is constant after certain point. The results also indicate that packets transmitted at 400 bps have a slightly lower BER Then compared to the packets transmitted at 200 bps. This difference in BER is most likely attributed to alignment resolution. This characteristic translates to faster bit rates having a higher alignment resolution when compared with slower bit rates. Since 400 bps is twice faster than 200 bps, it will have two times the alignment resolution, resulting in a potentially more accurate alignment and a higher probability of having a lower BER when compared with packets transmitted at 200 bps. In our proposed Adaptive model is expressed in units of 10^{-3} and existing system [5] is expressed in units of 10^{-2}, this shows that our proposed system gives the best result with respect to existing system of DSSS & FSK. Also BER reduces considerably as shown in the Table 1.

Table 1. BER OF FSK, QAM & Adaptive modem

Parameters		Proposed system (10^{-3})			Existing system (10^{-2})	
SNR (dB)	Data Rate	BER of FSK (%)	BER of QAM (%)	BER of Adaptive modem (%)	BER of FSK (%)	BER of DSSS (%)
1	100	1	1	1	19.33	1.47
3	200	1	1	1	12.58	1.53
5	300	0.83	1	0.83	21.86	0.78
6	400	0.72	0.88	0.72	21.67	3.56
12	500	0.76	0.84	0.76	35.26	16.97
19	600	0.75	0.70	0.70	–	–
24	700	0.72	0.64	0.64	–	–
30	800	0.62	0.65	0.62	–	–
40	900	0.75	0.60	0.60	–	–

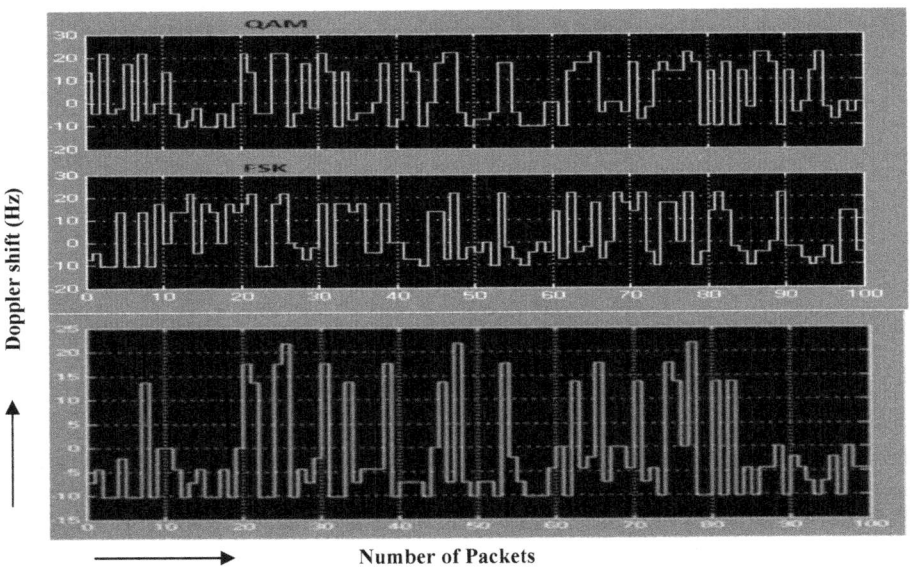

Fig. 7. Doppler spread QAM, FSK and Adaptive modem

5.2   Doppler Spread of QAM, FSK and Adaptive Modem

The Fig. 7 shows the Doppler spread, the x- axis is number of packets and the y-axis is Doppler shift (Hz), the result obtained for Doppler spread of QAM shows that the packet 1 arriving at 13 means it is arriving late, the packet supposed to arrive at 0 and the packet 19 arriving at −10 it is arriving early, All the packets supposed to arrive at 0. For FSK the packet 1 is arriving at −8 and packet 25 arriving at 20. In the Adaptive Doppler spread graph the best result is shown by comparing both QAM and FSK. We see that the packet 1arriving at −8 and the packet 10 arriving at 0.

With reference to the Fig. 8, Here when Doppler shift moves towards the positive axis, then transmits the signal at a shorter distance. When Doppler shift moves towards the negative axis, and then transmits the signal at a longer distance. Therefore the Doppler shift always should be less than or equal to zero for reliable communication (transmission of the signal to a longer distance). The Fig. 8 shows the proposed Doppler shift with respect to simulation results along with existing Doppler shift [5].

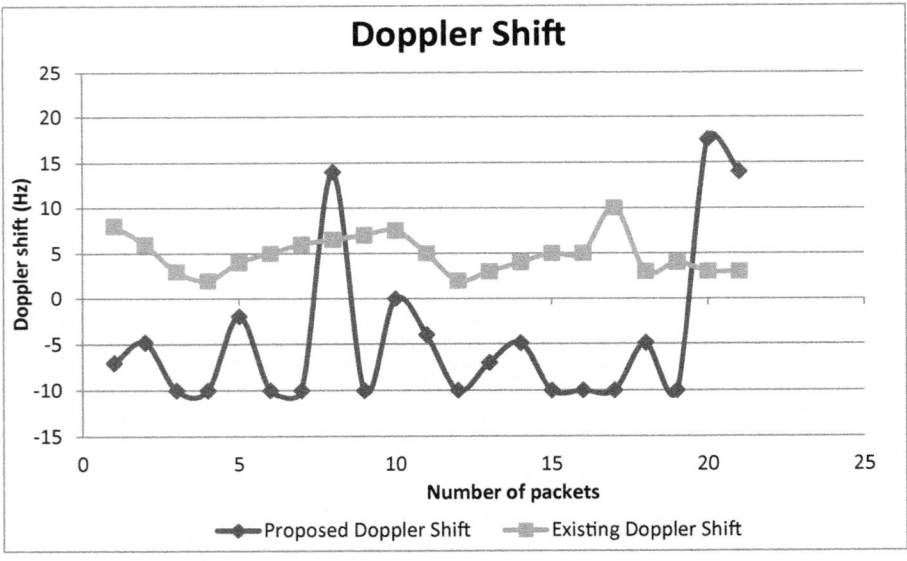

Fig. 8. Doppler spread of Adaptive modem

5.3   Signal to Noise Ratio of QAM, FSK and Adaptive Modem

The Fig. 9 shows the Signal to noise ratio of the Adaptive modem block, x- axis shows the frequency in kHz and the y-axis shows SNR in dB, the result obtained for Signal to noise ratio of QAM the Frequency 7 kHz is at 22 dB, the 21 kHz is at 18 dB and for FSK the 7 kHz is at 17 dB, the 21 kHz is at 24 dB and frequency which is arriving at 72 kHz at 40 dB is best signal to noise ratio

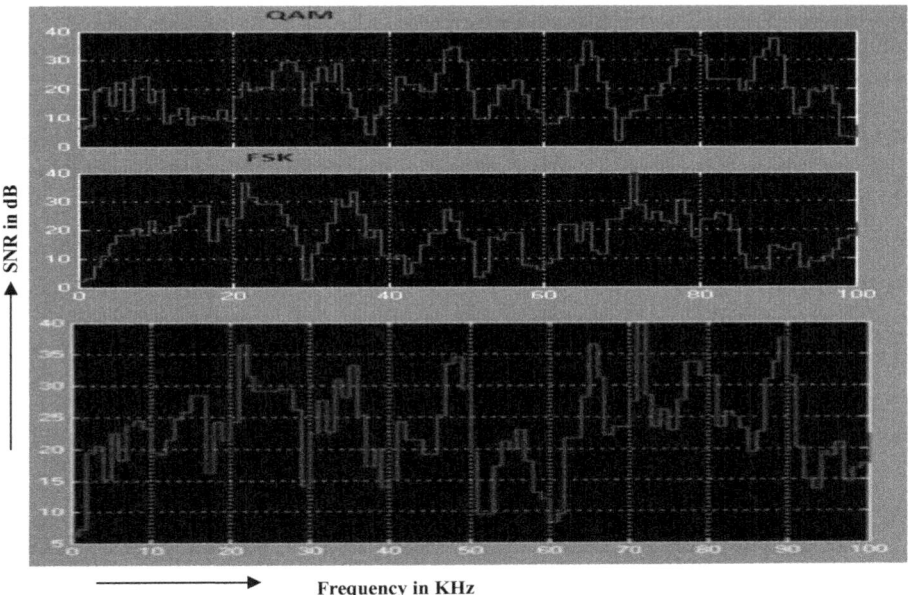

Fig. 9. SNR of QAM, FSK and Adaptive modem

In the Adaptive modem for Signal to noise ratio, the best signal to noise ratio is arriving at 72 kHz at 40 dB is best signal to noise ratio. The Adaptive modem compares both QAM and FSK, and it takes the best result by comparing both techniques. Therefore here the channel efficiency or data rate increases, when the Bandwidth is increase as shown in the Table 2.

Table 2. Bandwidth, data rate & SNR in dB of Adaptive modem

SNR in dB	Bandwidth in KHz	Channel efficiency or data rate
24	10	046.43 Kbps
35	21	107.00 Kbps
23	30	135.70 Kbps
29	50	245.34 Kbps
40	72	385.74 Kbps
38	90	472.31 Kbps
24	100	464.38 Kbps

6   Conclusion

The proposed Adaptive acoustic modem in underwater sensor network performs a adaptive technique which combines both QAM and FSK for the underwater transmission which adapts the best technique depending upon the channel estimation parameters such as BER, SNR, and Doppler shift. We have described the potential benefits of the adaptive acoustic modem, and also we have performed a set of simulations that quantify the benefits of different modulation techniques. The Doppler shift is analyzed and plotted with respect to existing system and also the Bit error rate, signal to noise ratio are tabulated. All these tested simulation results have been obtained on MATLAB Simulink. In spite of much improvement here in underwater wireless communication, there is yet a massive degree of more research in some portion of the sea base still unexplored.

References

1. Tao, Y., Zhu, P., Xu, X.: Dual-mode modulation based research of underwater acoustic modem. In: Proceedings of IEEE International Conference WiCOM, Chengdu, China, pp. 1–3 (2010)
2. Gallimore, E., Partan, J., Vaughn, I., Singh, S., Shusta, J., Freitag, L.: The WHOI Micromodem-2: a scalable system for acoustic communications and networking. In: Proceedings of Oceans, Seattle, WA, pp. 1–7 (2010)
3. Radosevic, A., Duman, T.M., Proakis, T.M., Stojanovic, M.: Channel prediction for adaptive modulation in underwater acoustic communications In: Proceedings of Oceans, Santander, Spain, pp. 1–5 (2011)
4. Li, Y., Zhang, X., Benson, B., Kastner, R.: Hardware implementation of symbol synchronization for underwater FSK. In: Proceedings of IEEE International Conference SUTC, Newport Beach, CA, pp. 82–88 (2010)
5. Wu, L., Trezzo, J., Mirza, D., Roberts, P., Jaffe, J., Wang, Y., Kastner R.: Designing an Adaptive Acoustic Modem for Underwater Sensor Networks. In: IEEE Embedded Systems Letters, vol. 4, no. 1, March 2012
6. Freitag, L., Singh, S.: Performance of micro-modem PSK signaling under variable conditions during the 2008 RACE and SPACE experiments. In: Proceedings of Oceans, Biloxi, MS, pp. 1–8 (2009)
7. Borowski, B. Duchamp, D.: The software modem-A software modem for underwater acoustic communication. In: Proceedings of Wuwnet 2009, Berkeley, CA, November 2009
8. Chitre, M., Shahabodeen, S., Stojanovic, M.: Underwater acoustic communications and networking: recent advances and future challenges. Mar. Technol. Soc. J. 42(1), 103–116 (2008)
9. Yan, H., Zhou, S., Shi, Z., Li, B.: A DSP implementation of OFDM acoustic modem. In: Proceedings of Wuwnet 2007, Montreal, QC, Canada, pp. 89–92, September 2007
10. Iltis, R.A., Lee, H., Kastner, R., Doonan, D., Fu, T., Moore, R., Chin, M.: An underwater acoustic telemetry modem for eco-sensing. In: Proceedings of Oceans, Washington, DC, pp. 1844–1850 (2005)
11. Benson, B., Li, Y., Kastner, R., Faunce, B., Domond, K., Kimball, D., Schurgers, C.: Design of a low-cost underwater acoustic modem for short-range sensor networks In: Proceedings of Oceans, Sydney, Australia, pp. 1–9 (2010)
12. Jaffe, J., Schurgers, C.: Sensor networks of freely drifting autonomous underwater explorers. In: Proceedings of Wuwnet 2006, Los Angeles, CA, pp. 93–96 September 2006
13. Akyildiz, I.F., Pompili, D., Melodia, T.: Challenges for efficient communication in underwater acoustic sensor networks. ACM Sigbed Rev. 1(2), 3–8 (2004)
14. Sozer, E.M., Stojanovic, M., Proakis, J.G.: Underwater acoustic networks. IEEE J. Ocean. Eng. 25(1), 72–83 (2000)
15. Patil, H.N., Ohatkar. S.N.: Design and Simulation of Software Defined Radio Using Matlab Simulink. E & TC Dept, Cummins College of Engineering, Pune, India. IEEE (2014)

Chain Assisted Tree Based Self-healing Protocol for Topology Managed WSNs

Shivangi Katiyar[1(✉)] and Devendra Prasad[2]

[1] Information and Technology Department,
MM University, Mullana, Ambala, India
katiyar.shivangi91@ieee.org
[2] Chandigarh Engineering College, Landran, Punjab, India
devendraacad@gmail.com

Abstract. The sensor node in a wireless sensor network is prone to failure if they have to survive in a harsh environment. In such environment link failure is also a very common problem, and that failure can be temporary or may be permanent. These failures may be left the network with an orphan node or disconnected branches and thus sometimes make the network useless. Till now many research has been proposed in the field of topology management most of them worked on sleep and wakeup scheme. Here we presented a scheme for Energy-Efficient data aggregation in Chain Assisted Tree based structure (CAT). We are introducing agent with sensor networks to collect data from the sensor nodes in tree fashion while repair links by forming a chain of disconnected nodes. The proposed scheme especially worked on link repair and put best efforts to reconnect orphan nodes or disconnected branches with the tree network. This CAT protocol ensure a very minimal amount of data loss while keeping network connected throughout the lifetime. Simulation results depict the improved lifetime of the network.

Keywords: Topology · Energy · Node degree

1 Introduction

A wireless sensor network is a collection of nodes into a cooperative network whereas each node consists of Programmable microprocessor, memory, Hardware defined-unit for sensor usage, power sensor and communication components with wireless connectivity technologies as shown in Fig. 1 which is depicting Internal architecture of wireless sensor node. WSN is an innovative area within the broad spectrum of wireless networks that specifically designed to measure small amounts of data and often that is related to sensor data. Here we can think of temperature sensors or an open-closed sensor that detects if a door is open or closed these little pieces of information are extremely valuable to companies because it provides insights into events that might happen in their business processes. It can perform certain operations such as they can monitor an event like an explosion or some-thing's being stolen. In general terms we can say it is the combination of check, track and trace capabilities, with check it mean wireless monitoring so the ability to sense what's going on in the world, track this

© Springer Nature Singapore Pte Ltd. 2018
P. Bhattacharyya et al. (Eds.): NGCT 2017, CCIS 828, pp. 305–320, 2018.
https://doi.org/10.1007/978-981-10-8660-1_23

means that we can also locate objects where they are, for example in a hospital or in a warehouse we know the location of physical assets third trace this is the ability for sensors which we call smart points to log the history of their sensor measurements.

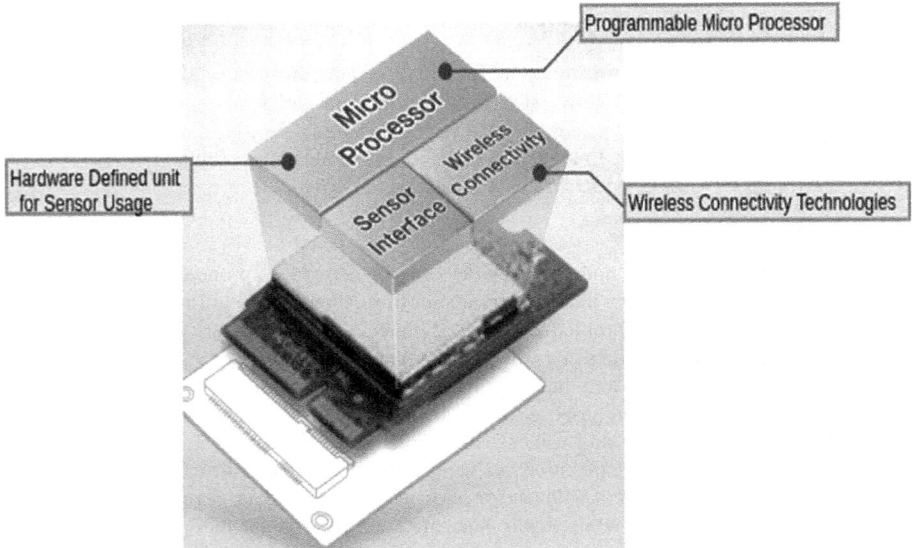

Fig. 1. Sensor node architecture

For Example, the smart city where some of the application offered by sensor networks, are forest fire detection, smartphone detection, streetlight management and much more. In architecture point of view WSNs consists i.e. Coverage area, collection of sensor nodes, Base Station or sometimes called as Gateway (Sink) as well as external network that will help to establish connection with Users as depicted in Fig. 2 where each sensor node communicate with each other using various protocols finally the message arrives at the sink and the same transmit the message to the user. Wireless sensor nodes that supportively sense and may govern the surrounding environment, in fact, to identify any activity along with data processing and delivery to the right address, generates the requirement of layered design typically demanding a suitable combination of processing, controlling and routing protocols because renewable of energy in these nodes is not possible which is the major challenge of WSNs. In such networks, if we look into sensitive facts then we found that some factors are majorly responsible for uncertain sensor network's life and these are limited energy, the delicate temperament of sensor nodes and sometimes stern environment. Like defense and health-care based sensor applications are more sensitive areas which can't tolerate sudden network failure or disconnection. For such types of critical areas, WSNs demands a suitable combination of energy-efficient protocol along with topology managed scheme which should assure network connectivity throughout the life. In such lossy and bandwidth restricted wireless network it is very difficult to achieve perfection with connectivity. In this paper, we have presented an energy-efficient framework to manage topology with the help of exploiting agent capabilities for small-scale firstly. Topology control and Topology management we can't use these terms interchangeably whereas both are different in responsibilities.

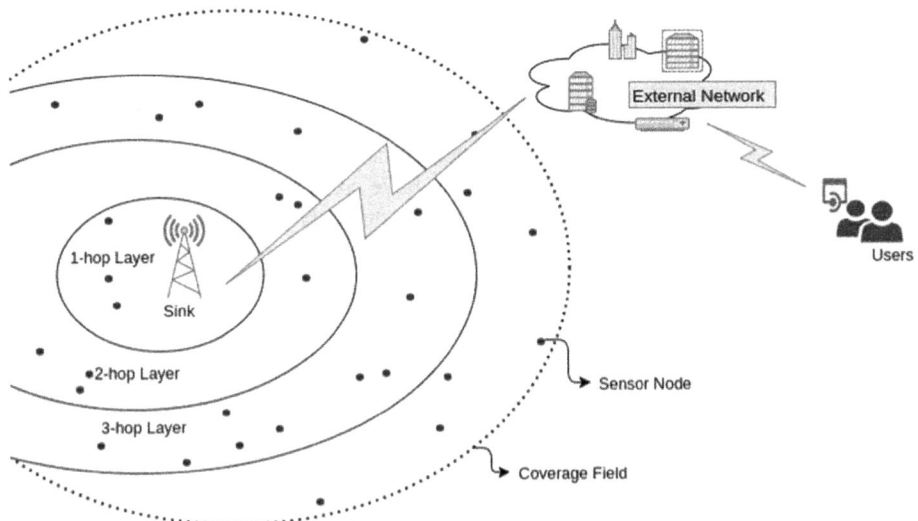

Fig. 2. Wireless sensor network architecture

So for the purpose of clear problem formulation, both terms are discussed below:

1.1 Topology Control

As per literature, topology control techniques can be classified into two categories i.e. network coverage and network connectivity [1]. Coverage describes basically how much the target field has been covered along with quickness of response, whereas connectivity describes the quality of node to node reachability as well as how to fetch and deliver a message.

1.2 Topology Management

Topology management can be described as how fast a network can recover from any failure for the purpose of keep maintaining connectivity throughout the network life. Current topology management techniques/algorithms for WSNs can be categorized on the basis of few parameters like Node discovery, sleep cycle management, power control, and movement control etc. [2].

From the very beginning, the most considered way for topology management was, to sustain energy by periodically placing nodes to sleep [3]. Some popular solutions are STEM [4, 5], GAF [6], and Naps [7]. These all strategies are sharing a common plan i.e. to put radios off for utilizing redundancy in order to sustain power. For managing topology just in case of unexpected node failure [Hardware problems, Disaster etc.] till now many researchers have been proposed that cope soundly with the dynamic modification in topology but on the other hand, the fact can't be neglected that these protocols either needs human intervention or compensatory node to fill the hole of the network [8–11]. It is well understood that such type of resolution in wsn is incredibly troublesome to attain reason being is, most of the time deployment area for wsn remains harsh, battlefield or not simply approachable for human [2], perceiving the challenges and the requirements of the wsn, we have presented this paper, with offering solutions for such issues. The proposed topology not only provides a communication abstraction but also assures connectivity up to some extent. The performance of the proposed topology is compared with other topologies with respect to energy consumption and the lifetime of the network.

The rest of this paper is organized as follows: in Sect. 2, Research motivation of the work has been discussed. In Sect. 3, a survey of the previous developments for topology management in wireless sensor networks is presented. In Sect. 4, an algorithm for topology managed transmission with optimized node degree is proposed to attain efficient reachability in a wireless sensor network topology. In Sect. 5, to verify the performance of the proposed algorithm, a series of simulations are designed and conducted to examine the impact factors including energy depletion, network lifetime and frequency of node's death. Section 6 summarize the work whereas Sect. 7, Discussed Future scope.

2 Motivation

The link fix probability for an orphan node or disconnected branch node will depend on such factors like surrounding environment, the distance between the victim and their next hop neighbor node, energy, and transmission range. It has been illustrated from few past research [12, 13] they either worked on direct data send to sink node in case of link break or not considering range and distance as a serious factor for the sake of energy saving which seems impractical. But according to literature, transmission range and distance between source and destination has a major impact on sensor node's energy as well as signal quality. In [14, 15] it has been suggested that increasing transmission value after some extent will tend the network to decreased lifetime. [16] this paper mentioned that greater range requires more power for transmission. [17] also opposing to use long-range communication to keep maintain signal quality as well as saving energy in long distance data transmission. One more important factor has been mentioned in [18], extra expended transmission range could increase the chances of no routing capacity of a router. So keeping suggestions in mind we provided a range based scheme which works either under fixed range fashion or in well-calculated range criteria. In this section, we presented an empirical analysis for examining impact of proposed scheme which is assuring link fix issue for tree type structure by forming a chain of all disconnected candidate nodes and linking this chain with already connected tree nodes. The results have been validated by comparing presented work with Multi-chain Pegasis and MAIDA protocols [19].

3   Related Work

Many research has been conducted for sensor networks in topology control field. Some previous research summarizes and proposed a classification for topology control scheme. This paper categorizes topology control in two sections, network coverage, and network connectivity. As per explanation they further divide network coverage issues into three parts i.e. Barrier coverage, blanket coverage and sweep coverage. And network connectivity issues also in three parts i.e. temporal control and spatial control. Here they provided a taxonomy for network control scheme based on existing research and provided well justified brief descriptions for the same without any fail. The other some approaches to employ power control are [20–22] in such cases, each node dynamically adjusts its transmission power to control the number of the neighboring node. Since the physical degree of a node strongly influences the utilization of available bandwidth and energy consumption. [23] developed an energy efficient zone routing algorithm, called EZone, which helps to tactically control the network topology with the assurance of full-service period of all the participated node along with longer network life. EZone algorithm provides an opportunity to extend tactical WSN service life at the same time maintaining tactical control of the network in both single and multi-gateway configurations. Paper [24] worked for fragmented WSNs by exploiting capabilities of mobile agents. As per its assumption here mobile agents are self-sufficient with rich resources also they assumed mobility factor for mobile relays. They guaranteed that proposed model perfectly evaluates fragment to fragment and fragment to sink delay. And as per result analysis, it is recommended that movement policy may have better performance impact instead of being placed some extra relays. Other than that for achieving connectivity in wireless sensor networks in [25] author presented relay placement technique. This work has taken advantage of the feasibility of finding the optimal solution for the case of three terminals. And presented a novel relay node placement heuristics approach i.e. Incremental Optimization based on Delaunay Triangulation (IO-DT). Paper [26] works for offering pre-failure solutions for wireless networks by searching spare node in the network and replacing them with the failed one. Concepts may work effectively but for some specific applications.

4 Working Model

This section shows a short description of the network model that is adapted to the proposed scheme. Target deployment field is a large and dense area. Sensor network has been assumed to work in a proactive mode which considers that each node will send data periodically to the Sink in a multi-hop way. Nodes are energy constrained and stationary. The energy model we adopted is First order energy model presented in [27].

4.1 The Logical Topology Construction

The topology management minimizes the problems evolved from a redundant variety of nodes and their dense preparation i.e. interference, use of maximum power to speak to distant nodes directly. The topology management preserves property with the utilization of minimal power. The sensing element node should realize its own position, the position of the neighboring nodes and base station during network topology construction section. In the very initial phase of topology construction already presented algorithm i.e. MAIDA constructs tree structure logical network. As per assumptions: The presence of GPS in sensor nodes so that node can realize own position and make aware about it to sink also. Sink node initiates topology construction by broadcasting a "HELLO" message. Once the sink receives "ACK" successfully from all the active nodes, it will move forward for further data processing phases. After that Sink node creates an "ACTOR" packet which has hidden software code termed as Agent and forwards it to one hop neighbor so that to initiates topology construction phase as shown in Fig. 3a. Apart from that this "ACTOR" message contains node ID, Level L, energy level Eo, buffer status Bf, its hop-count (hc) to reach to BS, its Parent ID, and last but not the least Distance form BS (Dist). Initially, The "ACTOR" message contains hc = 0 (Zero). The nodes that receive this "ACTOR" message further transmit that message to carry on the logical topology construction process. The sensor node that hears the ACTOR message transmitted from BS sets its hc and level value as one, then transmits that message. Further next the node that receives this message sets its hc and level as two and so on. A software agent that is hidden inside this ACTOR packet will let know about best parent ID with respect to each node and stay on that node only. The selection of best parent has been covered in our previous work that is MAIDA. This process continues till all the nodes are included in the hierarchy or the time for logical topology construction is over. Now nodes are ready to send data to the sink. As depicted in Fig. 3b, each parent will be responsible for aggregating the data which is received by their children. In such way, the data aggregation takes place from the leaf node to sink. Further data aggregation processing will remain same as [19].

Topology Construct Algorithm:

Sink initiate: Topology Construct Run MAIDA algorithm	6. *parent= nbr(parent);* ← *i.e. now all v_i of E(row,2) become parent one by one.*
Step-1 **Input:**	7. *for each parent* a. *repeat step 3-6*
V, L: *a sensor network V with L links*	8. *end*
Notations:	9. *if (nbr(parent)) ≠ nil*
v_i: *a node of V*	a. *goto step 7*
nbr(v_i): neighbor nodes of v_i	b. *else*
r: communication range of each node v_i	c. *stop* 10.*endif*
BS: base station or sink	
E← a matrix	**Step-2**
Output:	**Input:** *Matrix E*
N: Network, updated E matrix	**Output:**
Working steps:	*T: data aggregation Tree*
1. *parent= BS;*	**Working steps:**
2. *dist← distance from parent node to other nodes*	*for each nbr(parent) in E* 1. *Count(v_i)*
3. *for each v_i in V*	2. *If count(v_i) >1*
a. *if(dist<r)*	a. *For each vi*
b. *E(row,1)=parent;*	b. *Compare_dist(parent,vi)*
c. *E(row,2)=nbr(parent);*	c. *Select min(dist)*
d. *E(row,3)=dist(nbr(parent))* ← *i.e. distance between parent to nbr(parent);*	d. *Connect_min_dist* *(v_i , parent) ←i.e. connect vi to the parent having minimum distance*
e. *row= row+1;*	3. *end*
f. *endif*	4. *else*
4. *end*	a. *Connect(v_i, parent)*
5. *V=V-nbr(parent);*	5. *endif* 6. *end*

4.2 Agent

As per assumption here we are trying to introduce agent in the sensor nodes while these nodes already have very limited strength in terms of energy, memory, and processing. That's why the assumed agent is a very small software code to perform any specific task. As an extension, we can track such agents on GUI also currently it is not considered in present work. The best part is they can continue their work even if the node is disconnected. An agent can survive till the end of node's life until unless any hardware or system failure does not occur within the node. They can perform lots of work on behalf of the node like it can trigger an alarm, can take decisions as per the direction of the code and can generate a warning if any.

4.3 Link Failure

In Tree Structure of topology, if any node or link fails, it is possible for the graph/tree to become disconnected. A disjoint graph in some domains can be fatal. There are two possible solutions in context with a disconnected graph. One is connection repair has been performing at tree end node i.e. via parent end or other is if repairing has been initiated at orphan node end. In our case, we have chosen the second option that is to fix link failure from orphan end not via parent end, the reason being is periodic node discovery may consume considerable amount of energy for a parent while it is totally unsure like whether the lost node is able to contribute or not. So as shown in Fig. 3c, node H, and K suddenly get failed because of that some nodes i.e. L, O, Q and a branch of parent M get disconnected from the tree.

4.4 Range Selection

If link break occurs then the node which realizes this breakage will increase their range according to the given formula,

$$R = \left[\frac{(\alpha * \beta)}{(\pi * N)}\right] * \left(\frac{\upsilon}{\omega}\right)$$

R = Range
N = Number of nodes
υ = Degree of the node initially
ω = Degree of the node after link break
$\alpha * \beta$ = Area of the network

Node Degree (υ)-The degree of a node can be calculated as total number of the available child for that node.

4.5 Failure Recovery/Self Healing

In case of any link breakdown, this is obvious that any two nodes are going to be affected assumed A, B. As presented scheme worked in a Tree structure, in that case with each node there can be two possible values in terms of node degree, either its value will be 1 or >1. if we combine these two statements then we found four possible situations as shown in Table 1. In case 1, both nodes have degree 1 which indicates if such link breaks then both node will be left as an orphan node. One more point to notice here is, if such link exists in the network then any one of them should be sink node otherwise it will be considered as the already disconnected link of the network. In case 2, if the link breaks then node B will be orphan node because of its current degree values is 1, i.e. no more connected link.

In case 3, the parent will be left as an orphan node and another one will be a disconnected branch. One other thing is here the parent will be sink itself. In case 4, This is basically link break down between two branches itself. This can be relaxed situation because here recovery possibility is more because of higher node degree at both ends as compared to other situations.

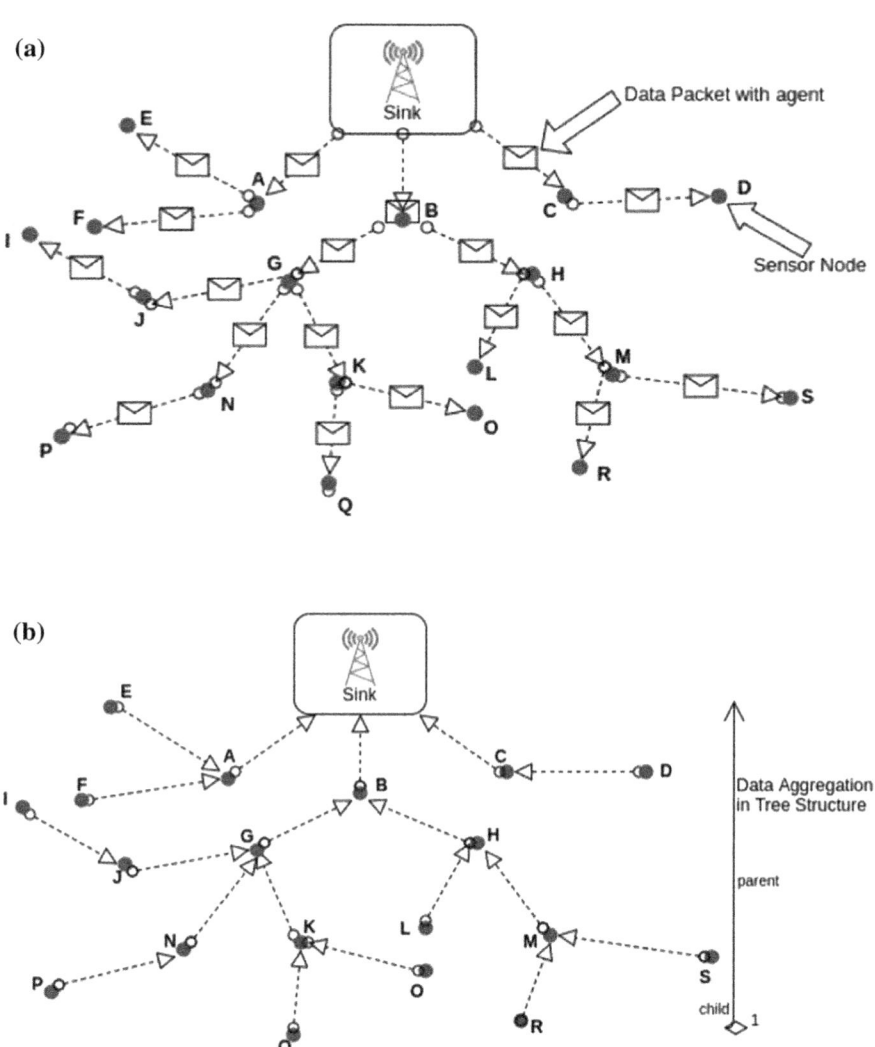

Fig. 3. a. Dispatch of agent with topology construction from sink, b. Data aggregation in tree structure, c. Sudden death of node H, K, d. Chain formation of disconnected nodes

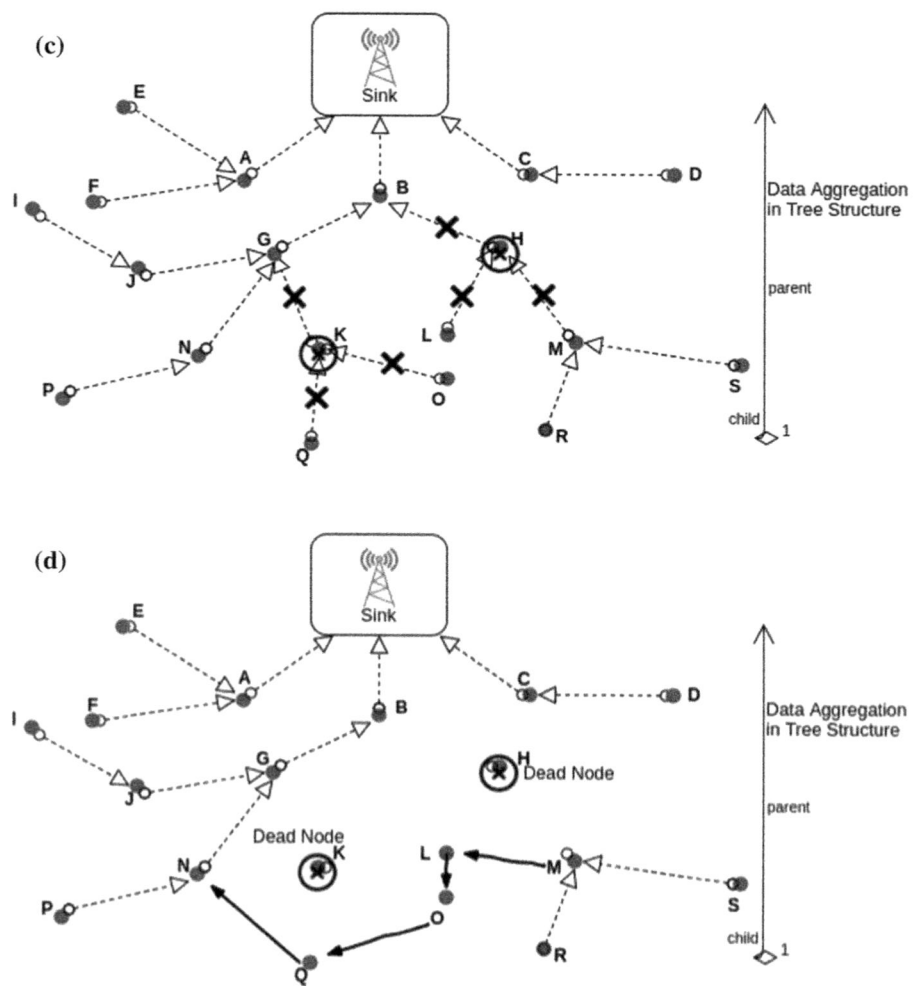

Fig. 3. (*continued*)

Table 1. Possible cases if any node fails in tree network.

Case number	Node A	Node B	Orphan node
1	1	1	A, B
2	>1	1	B
3	1	>1	A
4	>1	>1	Branch disconnection

4.6   Chain Formation

If node gets disconnected from the network due to sudden parent death or because of any hurdle, then it will try beyond the already set range which is initially programmed by the sink. If it finds any neighbor t_{new} then send data to t_{new} node, now responsibility goes to t_{new} node for transmitting that data to the sink node, if this node is also a disconnected node then it will also increase own range and try to find the a neighbor. In such way all these disconnected node forms a chain and this process remains continue until this chain find a leader node who can either be the member of the connected tree or sink itself. So that it can transfer the aggregated data to the sink. As depicted in Fig. 3d, a successful chain has been formed i.e. M, L, O, Q with N.

Link Repair algorithm:

Node t_b detects link failure

Link_Repair (Actual Node degree v , Node degree after link break w, Aggregation Tree T_{da})
      Wait random time t_i chosen uniformly from [0, T)
      If Connection_fail then
Update node t_b Range r ← R, {where as R will be calculated via $R = \left[\frac{(\alpha*\beta)}{(\pi*N)}\right] * \left(\frac{v}{\omega}\right)$}
Found_new_node t_{new}
Establish link t_b and t_{new}
   if t_{new} ∈ T_{da}
      Network repaired : update T_{da}
   else
      send do_repair message to next child if any
   or
      R←λ*r [while 0<λ< avg(a,b)]
Link_Repair until t_b, t_{new} ∈ T_{da}

5   Simulation and Result Analysis

For the performance appraisal of the proposed scheme, in this section, we have used a simulation tool MATLAB to conduct various experiments.

5.1   Simulation Parameters

Table 2. Describing all simulation parameters that has been considered at the time of implementation.

Table 2. Simulation parameters.

Sr. no.	Parameters	Value
1	Network size	100 m * 100 m
2	Number of nodes	100
3	Packet size	2000 bits
4	Agent size	200 bits
5	Rounds	6000
6	Initial energy of nodes	0.5 J
7	Range	30 m
8	E_{elec}	50 nJ/bit
9	E_{fs}	10 pJ/bit/m^2
10	E_{mp}	0.0013 pJ/bit/m^4
11	E_{DA}	5 nJ/bit
12	DA (Data aggregation factor)	0.6

5.2   Result Analysis

Here the simulation results and performance matrices prove the reliability of proposed scheme. For analyzing the performance of the proposed scheme we have conducted the simulation for three protocols i.e. proposed scheme CAT, earlier mentioned MAIDA and Multi-chain Pegasis. Figure 4 shows the energy graph for all three schemes and depicting that CAT protocol consuming energy in better proportion than other schemes.

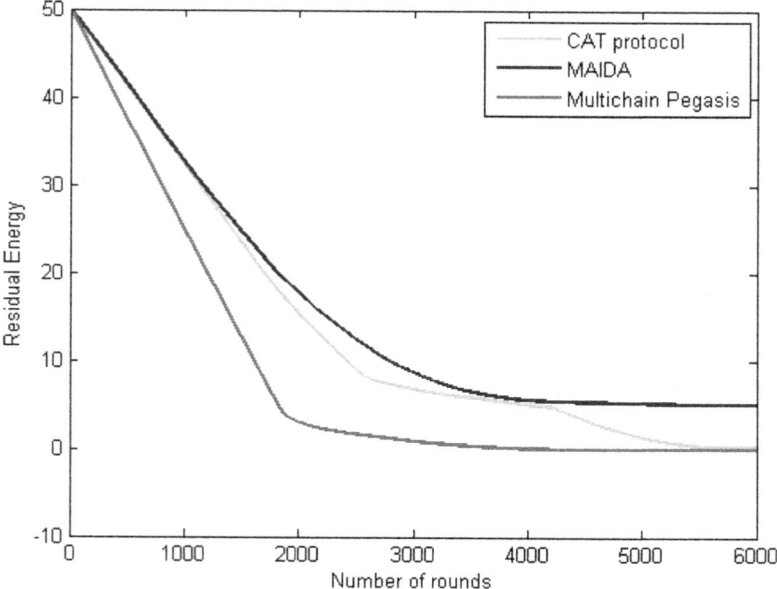

Fig. 4. Energy consumption graph for proposed and existing scheme.

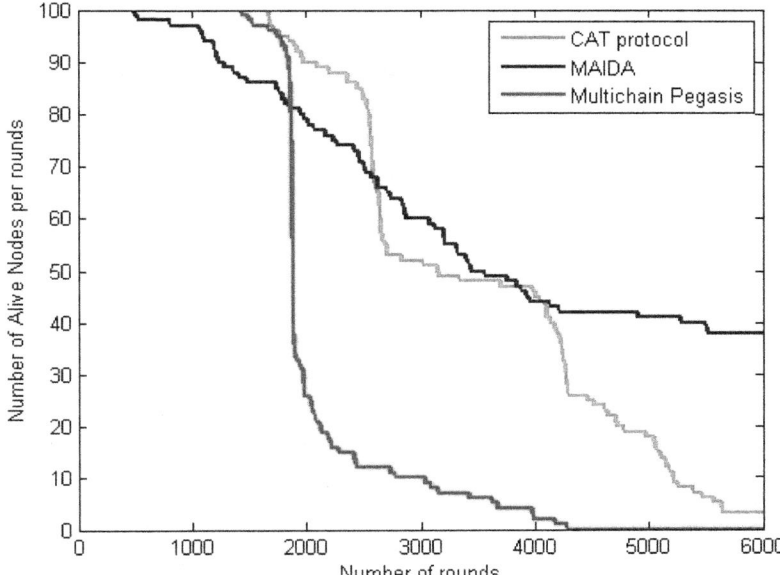

Fig. 5. Alive node graph for CAT and existing schemes.

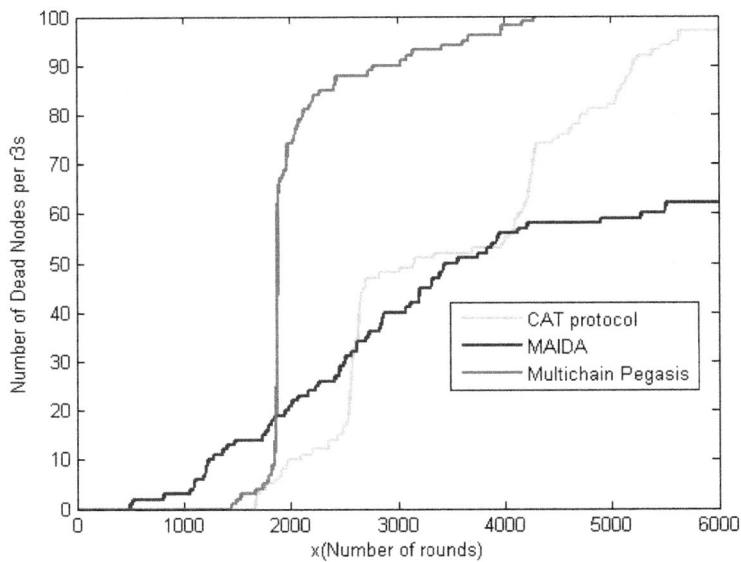

Fig. 6. Dead node graph for CAT and existing schemes.

Also we can analyses from the results the improved lifetime of the network. Whereas MAIDA unable to utilize orphan nodes energy and Multichain Pegasis even exhausted around 4300 life round only. Figures 5 and 6 Depicting death and alive node graph for above three techniques. And it is shown in the graph that MAIDA protocol exhausted before 5000 round, and left the network with orphan nodes which are unable to connect with the network.

6 Conclusion

In this paper, we presented a Chain Assisted Tree based protocol which can handle the failure of any node in a connected WSN. As well as it provides technique for all disconnected nodes to connect them in the form of chain for the purpose of successful data delivery. Basically, if a node finds out itself disconnected from the network then agent instruct that node to recover from this disconnection, in this way the failure recovery is performed by the node itself rather than a parent. Given protocol works in optimal range and transfer data over tree but if network found any orphan node or broken link then runs Link repair algorithm (CAT). Simulation results confirmed that CAT performed very well in terms of topology management as well as efficiently utilizing orphan nodes energy which ultimately increases network lifetime.

7 Future Scope

For the future scope to fully introduce Agent into sensor node can be a revolution in WSN technology, because it has the capability to work at a very large scale which can help to fulfill the demand of new sensor era. Through uniting existing WSN applications as part of the intelligent networking and communication system, possibly fresh applications can be recognized and expand to meet upcoming trends and technologies. For example, WSN technology applications for underwater, fully automate healthcare and smart transportation systems generate immense amounts of data, and this information can serve several objectives. Nowadays IoT is a very well known sector of Wireless technology, that was parallelly developed with WSNs. Till now IoT does not assume any particular communication technique which added an extra layer of responsibility in the area of research. That's why this is the recent interest of market, researchers, and developers, which shifts to this new era of WSNs in the IoT. As per future requirements, many research trends and techniques will reach over time. In such phase, most challenging problems can be concurrency control and interaction between diverse protocols and standards. Here Agent technology can play a major role to add flexibility and intelligence as it is self-sufficient to perform actions and make decisions.

References

1. Li, M., Li, Z., Vasilakos, A.V.: A survey on topology control in wireless sensor networks: taxonomy, comparative study, and open issues. Proc. IEEE **101**(12), 2538–2557 (2013)
2. Younis, M., Senturk, I.F., Akkaya, K., Lee, S., Senel, F.: Topology management techniques for tolerating node failures in wireless sensor networks: a survey. Comput. Netw. **58**, 254–283 (2014). ISSN 1389-1286
3. Frye, L., Cheng, L., Du, S., Bigrigg, M.W.: Topology maintenance of wireless sensor networks in node failure-prone environments. In: IEEE International Conference on Networking, Sensing and Control (2006)
4. Schurgers, C., Tsiatsis, V., Ganeriwal, S., Srivastava, M.: Optimizing sensor networks in the energy-latency-density design space. IEEE Trans. Mob. Comput. **1**(1), 70–80 (2002)
5. Schurgers, C., Tsiatsis, V., Ganeriwal, S., Srivastava, M.: Topology management for sensor networks: exploiting latency and density. In: MOBIHOC 2002, 9–11 June 2002. ACM, Lausanne (2002)
6. Xu, Y., Bien, S., Mori, Y., Heidemann, J., Estrin, D.: Topology control protocols to conserve energy in wireless ad hoc networks. Technical report 6, Center for Embedded Networked Computing, University of California, Los Angeles, January 2003
7. Godfrey, B.P., Ratajczak, D.: Naps: scalable, robust topology management in wireless ad hoc networks. In: ISPN 2004, 26–27 April 2004. ACM, Berkeley (2004)
8. Younis, M., Akkaya, K.: Strategies and techniques for node placement in wireless sensor networks: a survey. Ad Hoc Netw. **6**(4), 621–655 (2008)
9. Bendigeri, K.Y., Mallapur, J.D.: Multiple node placement strategy for efficient routing in wireless sensor networks. Wirel. Sens. Netw. **7**, 101–112 (2015)
10. Coskun, V.: Relocating sensor nodes to maximize cumulative connected coverage in wireless sensor networks. Sensors (Basel) **8**(4), 2792–2817 (2008)
11. Cinque, M., Cotroneo, D., De Caro, G., Pelella, M.: Reliability requirements of wireless sensor networks for dynamic structural monitoring. In International Workshop on Applied Software Reliability, WASR, pp. 8–13, June 2006
12. Lindsey, S., Raghavendra, C.S.: PEGASIS: power-efficient gathering in sensor information systems. In: 2002 IEEE Aerospace Conference Proceedings, vol. 3. IEEE (2002)
13. Jafri, M.R., et al.: Maximizing the lifetime of multi-chain pegasis using sink mobility. arXiv preprint arXiv:1303.4347 (2013)
14. Gandham, S.R., et al.: Energy efficient schemes for wireless sensor networks with multiple mobile base stations. In: 2003 IEEE Global Telecommunications Conference, GLOBECOM 2003, vol. 1. IEEE (2003)
15. Kaurav, J., Ghosh, K.: Effect of transmitting radius, coverage area and node density on the lifetime of a wireless sensor network (2012)
16. Ye, M., et al.: EECS: an energy efficient clustering scheme in wireless sensor networks. In: 2005 24th IEEE International Performance, Computing, and Communications Conference, IPCCC 2005. IEEE (2005)
17. Pottie, G.J., Kaiser, W.J.: Wireless integrated network sensors. Commun. ACM **43**(5), 51–58 (2000)
18. Tsai, C.H., Tseng, Y.C.: A path-connected-cluster wireless sensor network and its formation, addressing, and routing protocols. IEEE Sens. J. **12**(6), 2135–2144 (2012)
19. Katiyar, S., Prasad, D.: Mobile agent initiated energy efficient data aggregation in WSNs: MAEDA. Int. J. Comput. Appl. (IJCA) **140**, 10–15 (2016)

20. Blough, D.M., Leoncini, M., Resta, G., Santi, P.: The k-neighbors approach to interference bounded and symmetric topology control in ad hoc networks. IEEE Trans. Mob. Comput. **5** (9), 1267–1282 (2006)
21. Santi, P.: Topology control in wireless ad hoc and sensor networks. ACM Comput. Surv. **37** (2), 164–194 (2005)
22. Li, N., Hou, J.C., Sha, L.: Design and analysis of an MST-based topology control algorithm. In: IEEE INFOCOM (2003)
23. Thulasiraman, P., White, K.A.: Topology control of tactical wireless sensor networks using energy efficient zone routing. Digit. Commun. Netw. **2**(1), 1–14 (2016)
24. Almasaeid, H.M.: Data delivery in fragmented wireless sensor networks using mobile agents. Iowa State University (2007)
25. Senel, F., Younis, M.: Optimized relay node placement for establishing connectivity in sensor networks. In: 2012 IEEE Global Communications Conference (GLOBECOM). IEEE (2012)
26. Vaidya, K., Younis, M.: Efficient failure recovery in wireless sensor networks through active, spare designation. In: 2010 6th IEEE International Conference on Distributed Computing in Sensor Systems Workshops (DCOSSW). IEEE (2010)
27. Heinzelman, W., Chandrakasan, A., Balakrishnan, H.: Energy-efficient communication protocols for wireless microsensor networks. In: Proceedings of the 33rd Hawaaian International Conference on Systems Science (HICSS), January 2000

Smart and Innovative Trends in Security and Privacy

Isotropic Pore Detection Algorithm for Level 3 Feature Extraction

Subiya Zaidi[✉], Shrish Kumar Singh, and Sandhya Tarar

IEC College of Engineering and Technology, Greater Noida, UP, India
subiyazaidi.cs@ieccollege.com

Abstract. Level 3 features on fingerprints have gained popularity because of their characteristic ability to provide discriminative properties. Sweat pores on fingerprints are one such level 3 features which can be spotted as white blobs in a high resolution image of size >500 dpi. Earlier studies in this area show that pores are fine details that are not easily visible. Level 2 features like minutiae are a popular choice in a forensic for recognition system because they are not limited to the quality of the image. The effectiveness is proved through the commercially available software like Verifinger while no such software is available for matching through pores. The paper proposes a new method to extract pores in an image of 1000 dpi resolution. The proposed algorithm has numerous positives over the methods in the previous work, such as increased computational efficiency and higher sensitivity. This research work provides an objective assessment of the algorithm used for the extraction of features. The results indicate the superiority of the proposed method over the existing methods like "Difference of Gaussian" approach. Experimental analysis is done by computing sensitivity and specificity on the fragment of an image. The next generation of AFIS can avail the proposed method to make the process of identification more accurate.

Keywords: High resolution fingerprint image · Isotropic model
Pore extraction

1 Introduction

The authentication of the user based on biometric features has gained attention over the past decade. The purpose of building such an authentication system is to ensure reliability, so that the service is accessible to the legitimate user.

Traditionally accepted methods for designing an identification system included the use of passwords which were knowledge based security, use of token based security included ID cards. However these systems were not very successful in limiting unauthorized access since, the passwords could be easily guessed by following a pattern of words through hit and trial method and the tokens could be stolen by imposters [2]. It was thus required to make the system more robust by introducing biometric features for identification.

© Springer Nature Singapore Pte Ltd. 2018
P. Bhattacharyya et al. (Eds.): NGCT 2017, CCIS 828, pp. 323–334, 2018.
https://doi.org/10.1007/978-981-10-8660-1_24

Level 1 Features in Finger Prints

They represent the flow of ridges (thin lines on a finger print) and how they associate to form a pattern.

Loops   Whorls   Arches

Fig. 1. Level 1 features

Level 2 Features in Finger Prints

There has been a considerable research work that has taken place for the extraction of level 2 features, minutia. For a given fingerprint, minutiae are represented by the ridge endings and ridge bifurcations. Over 100 minutiae can be extracted in a given fingerprint [3] (Fig. 2).

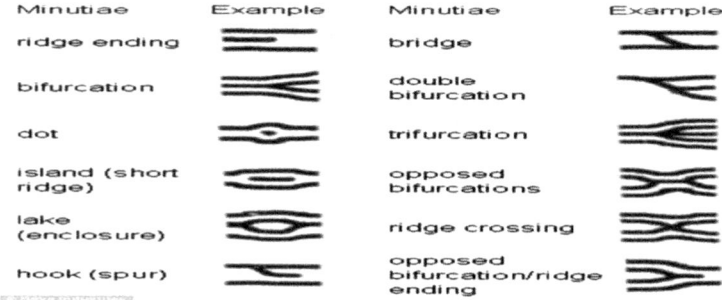

Fig. 2. Level 2 features

With the progress in research work it was observed that the matching of a full finger print image, which is stored in the database with a partial image, does not give accurate results. This happens because of the following reasons: (i) in a given fragment, the number of minutiae reduces with the reduction in the size of the template (ii) the impression might have not been acquired effectively due to environmental factors (iii) human skin tendency alters elasticity which disorients the impression (iv) singularity points like core and delta are lost and require fool proof matching algorithm [4]. All these constraints degrade the efficiency of a recognition system.

Therefore, to overcome such limitations, the extended feature set (EFS) can be employed. EFS are level 3 features that under research for some time. These include pores, line shapes, incipient ridges, creases, warts and scars. Level 3 features can be identified in a high resolution image of 1000 dpi.

Level 3 Features in Finger Prints
In this paper, we have worked on the sweat pores on database acquired from IIITD Delhi [18]. The paper is organised with detailed emphasis on the fragmentation of 1000 resolution image for feature extraction. Section 2 details the related work that is carried out on features of level 2 and level 3. Section 3 proposes a methodology for conducting experiments and Sect. 4 gives a performance evaluation on the experimental result. Section 5 describes the application areas for the pores extracted and the concluding comments (Fig. 3).

Fig. 3. Pores as level 3 features in finger prints

2 Related Work

The research work in biometrics has been extensive and one of its major applications is that of forensic science. Prabhakar *et al.* [6], in their article has described the current state-of-art and the advancements that have taken in the field of biometric recognition. The article was an introduction to a special issue to invite papers on the change in technology and how effective algorithms and approaches were being developed for improving the recognition potential of a system. The issue received tremendous response and categorized papers into two models; one that measured performance and the other that measured the quality of the biometrics. Among the popular techniques were the Bayesian inference technique, Random effects model, differential processing techniques; sample replacement, algorithm selection, threshold adaptation and so on.

Grother *et al.* [5], presented an approach to measure the quality of the biometrics. The need for evaluating the quality emerged because the samples quality suffered severe degradation in terms of quality attributes which made recognition process difficult. The author used FNMR and FAR to evaluate the error rate. The experimental analysis showed that false non-match rate should be chosen as the indicator for performance evaluation.

Jea and Govindaraju [4] observed that the sensors with silicon chips captured only a part of the fingerprint. Thus when low quality partial images and latent fingerprints were used for matching, it was noticed that the process was not satisfactory. It was observed that there was a gap between the full sized templates stored in the database to the partial fingerprint that was acquired. The paper proposed a model to extract minutiae from a fragment of the fingerprint and later this was aligned to match with the database. It was noticed that the incomplete fingerprint had to be modified so that the tradeoff between the reduced set of minutiae and increase in the number of matches was accomplished. A neural network was trained to enhance the distance ratios and produce a matching score that was accurate.

Pores have been identified as one of the features in a fingerprint that can be used for matching without or with minutiae. Malathi *et al.* [15], used the watershed marker control segmentation to extract the pores and later utilize this for matching. This method had no relation with the level 2 features and it did not take much time as per experimental results.

Zhao *et al.* [12], in the paper titled, High resolution partial fingerprint alignment using pore- valley descriptor, have utilised the partial fingerprint image for extraction of distinguishing features. The paper states that in a partial fingerprint it is often not easy to extract high number of minutiae, thus the recognition rate drops. However, in a high resolution image it is considerably easier to spot pores and ridges which are present in abundance. Pores are extracted using the Difference of Gaussian approach and Pore Valley Descriptor (PVD) is proposed. The pores are aligned after the orientation is calculated. The experimental results verify that unlike the minutiae based methods; the PVD method identifies more features and gives sound result.

Zhao *et al.* [13], in their paper, Adaptive Fingerprint pore modelling and extraction, have discussed the how the traditional method of pore extraction from a given image is static isotropic in nature and hence the output is not always accurate. To overcome this, a dynamic anisotropic method is proposed. The given image is first divided into partial blocks and based on the dominant frequency, its orientation is calculated. This data is used to extract pores after applying filtering. The experimental results prove the proposed method is highly effective in detecting pores.

Kryszczuk *et al.* [17] in their work propose a new strategy and implementation of a series of techniques for automatic level 2 and level 3 feature extraction in fragmentary fingerprint comparison. According to their study, the main challenge in achieving a better dependability on a recognition system was that a partial segment of the fingerprint might not contain enough minutiae to detect identity, but the uniqueness of the pore configurations provides a powerful means to compensate for this insufficiency. A pilot study performed to test the presented approach confirms that the usage of pores improves the results when compared to the traditionally used minutiae in fragmentary fingerprint comparison.

3   Level 3 Features

Minutiae (level 2 features) are just a small set of features that identify the individual. A considerable amount of work is being done to make the process of identification more robust. One such work is to identify features that can be spotted in abundance. These are called the **extended feature set (EFS)** and mainly include the incipient ridges, dots, ridge edge and pores (Fig. 4).

Pores are present on the ridges and can be seen in two forms either open or closed, depending on their location on the ridge. A pore that is closed lies in between the ridges, totally covered. An open pore appears as hooks between the ridges. An example is given below where open pores are in white and closed pores are in black [16]:

One of the traditional approaches of pore extraction is DoG (Difference Of Guassian) [13]. Referring to Fig. 1, the images of the fingerprint highlight two regions. The prominent ones are either the dark lines or the lighter ones that are called valleys

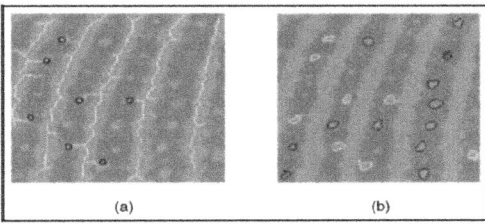

Fig. 4. Pores

and ridges respectively. While if you observe closely than the white dots that are easily visible on the dark ridges are called pores or blobs. These appear effectively in images of high resolution captured through optical sensors.

The pores on the basis of their location on the dark ridges are classified as either open or closed. The open pores are completely surrounded by the ridges and the closed pores appear as hooks lined on the outer boundaries of the ridges. For a fingerprint image, the pores can be closed or open depending on the pressure applied while taking these prints. The space distribution of the pores resembles the 2-D Gaussian functions.

The valleys which are the lighter lines in the fingerprints are 1-D Gaussian functions and their scales when compared with the pores are bigger. The pores in the Difference of Gaussian approach are calculated by applying the Gaussian filters twice with different scales on the same fingerprint. The scales are chosen at opposite ranges, one at high and one at low, both to improve the image. The output of applying both the filters is subtracted from each other and the resultant image highlights the pores as white circle like structures.

However the limitation of this procedure is that of estimating scales. The Difference of Gaussian approach is found to involve considerable effort in deducing the high and low scale to enhance the image.

4 Proposed Work

Our proposed methodology continues from where the DoG approach left. In order to detect sweat pores, first binarizing the original gray scale image is used to set a threshold. The method works on a local threshold where a value is taken which separates the foreground and the background.

The method works on the concept of thresholding to detect the presence of an object and extract it from the background. This is achieved by reducing the inter class variance. A threshold value T is assigned to each pixel. The intensity of the pixels differentiates the pixels of the background from that of the object point. In our approach we are dealing with closed pores. Closed pores appear as white blobs which are often not in a definite shape. They are lie completely within the ridges which are dark and thick lines spreading across the image.

Thus the idea is to take into account the white coloured pixels engulfed by the black colour pixels. When local thresholding is performed on the image, it is noticed that noise and other artifacts appear as pores. Therefore, it is important to define a range.

In the post processing stage, two values are decided. These values refine the searching of pores. A value range can be shown by P_{low} and P_{high}, where P_{low} is used to set the lowest intensity pixel. Pixels that are less than P_{low} are considered as noise which takes place during the acquisition process. P_{high} is used for the upper limit, all objects which have pixel value beyond this specified intensity are discarded. The values of P_{low} and P_{high} are empirically chosen based on the experiments conducted (Fig. 5)

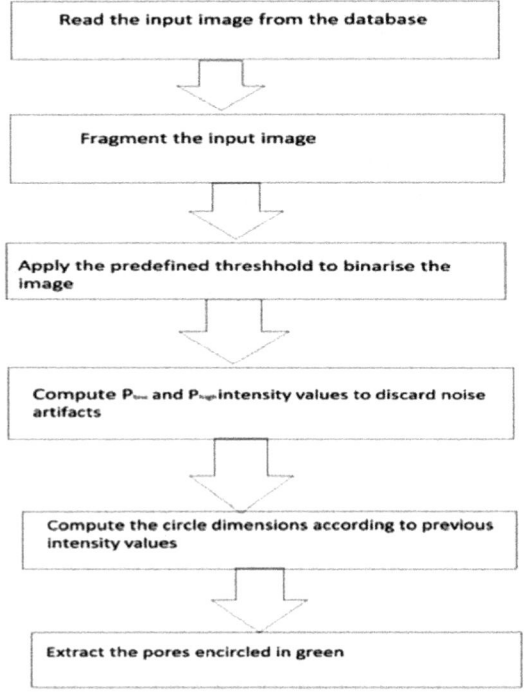

Fig. 5. Proposed algorithm

5 Performance Evaluation

A. Datasets: FVC Database

The Fingerprint Verification Competition (FVC) is internationally approved standard for verifying any technique to extract and match fingerprints [11]. Till date four research groups have worked on the same and presented FVC 200-FVC2006. These groups are as follows:

1. Biometric System Laboratory, University of Bologna, Italy [11]
2. Pattern Recognition and Image Processing Laboratory, Michigan State University, USA [11]
3. Biometric Test Center, San Jose State University, USA [11]
4. Biometric Recognition Group – ATVS, Universidad Autonoma de Madrid, (Spain) [11]

Various types of sensor technologies are used to acquire the fingerprints. These include thermal sensors, optical sensors and capacitive sensors. on the basis of capturing, four databases mainly DB1, DB2, DB3 and DB4. The distinctiveness of the DB4 database lies in the fact that it is developed through Synthetic Fingerprint Generator (SFinGe). Sample images taken from these databases are shown below (Fig. 6):

Fig. 6. Examples of fingerprint images from FVC 2002

DB2 used live scans to capture the prints. Unlike the previous method of using card for scanning, this technology is different. These databases are verified by biometric experts as hence their utility lies in testing the effectiveness of the proposed technology. FVC however lacks some advanced features and hence its use is limited. These are:

1. The resolution of the captured images is 500 DPI which is similar to already available NIST database.
2. The finer details especially pore are not visible in the images.
3. The database is limited to only fingerprint extraction and matching and not to other biometrics.

B. IIITD 1000 dpi Database
The 1000 DPI database has been taken from the IIITD. The database is developed by capturing images using SecuGen Hamster IV. The fine details like pores are easily visible as white blobs in the images. The database also provides latent fingerprints for testing of feature extraction and matching algorithms. In the entire database provide considerable images, where 10 fingers of 15 subjects have been taken from various sources. The database is freely available to the public for research work [18]. The foreground and background are illuminated accordingly to improve the quality of the images. A sample of the images acquired is shown below (Fig. 7):

Fig. 7. Examples of fingerprint images of 1000 dpi from IIITD Database

C. Detection of Pores

The pores are detected using proposed algorithm; the Sensitivity (SEN) and Specificity (SPE) are measured over the database. The SEN and SPE indicate the ability of the algorithm to detect the true pores and reject false pores respectively [19].

$$Sensitivity(SEN) = 1 - \frac{Missedpores}{Groundtruthno.ofpores}$$

$$Specificity(SPE) = 1 - \frac{Falsepores}{Groundtruthno.ofpores}$$

To calculate the ground truth, the pores are counted manually since there is no commercially available pore extractor. The fixed threshold of the input image is set. There is a change in the number of pores that are missed during the extraction and a change in the falsely detected pores can also be observed. This experiment is performed on ten images to see the effect and is represented in a tabular form. P represents the values against the proposed method and E represents the values against one of the existing methods for pore extraction.

The values of SEN and SPE acquired through the proposed algorithm are checked against the existing Difference of Gaussian approach. As is evident, there is considerable difference in the output, thus making the proposed approach a better choice for extracting pores (Fig. 8).

D. Experimental Results and Discussions

The following screenshots show how the number of missed pores and false pores change with the change in the algorithm. The pores circled with blue color represent the ground truth i.e. the number of actual pores counted manually and the ones represented in red show the false pores extracted and the dark red shows the pores extracted through the algorithm. As shown in the table the SEN and SPE show that the proposed algorithm extracts more pores without having to worry about the scale to be considered for finding the difference between the images to extract pores (Fig. 9).

Table 1. Computation of SEN and SPE for the existing and the proposed algorithm

Image ID	Ground truth	False pores(F)		Missed pores(M)		Sensitivity% (SEN)		Specificity% (SPE)	
		P	E	P	E	P	E	P	E
1	49	4	9	11	7	77.5	69.3	91.8	81.6
2	35	4	10	6	8	82.8	74.2	88.5	71.4
3	27	0	10	5	7	81.4	74.0	100.0	62.9
4	33	10	14	1	8	96.0	75.0	69.6	57.5
5	22	2	12	3	9	86.3	59.2	90.9	45.4
6	21	0	10	9	10	57.1	52.3	100.0	52.3
7	11	1	7	2	4	81.8	63.6	90.1	36.6
8	55	6	6	6	11	89.0	80.1	89.0	89.0
9	21	7	4	2	11	90.4	47.5	66.2	80.2
10	38	16	14	1	4	97.3	89.2	57.8	63.7

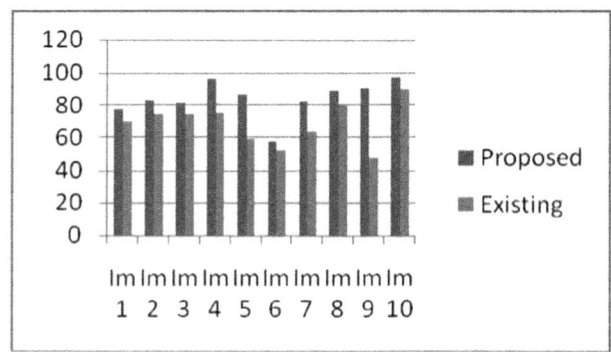

Fig. 8. Graph displaying higher sensitivity (SEN) of the proposed algorithm

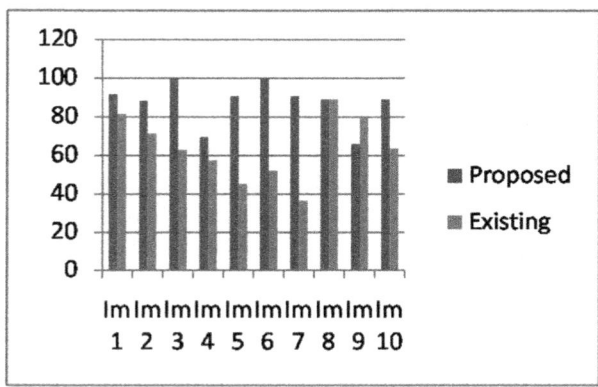

Fig. 9. Graph displaying higher specificity (SPE) of the proposed algorithm

T=49, M=7, F=11=> SEN=69.3, SPE=77.5%

T=21,M=10,F=10 => SEN=52.3%,SPE=52.3%

T=27, M=7, F=10 => SEN=74%, SPE=47.6%

T=35, M=6, F=4 =>SEN=82.8%, SPE=88.5

The above screenshots display the result of performing experiments using the Difference of Gaussian method in column 1 and the proposed algorithm in column 2. T represents the actual pores that are counted manually, M represents the missed pores, F represents the false pores detected by the method and based on these values sensitivity and specificity are calculated. As is evident, the performance metrics SEN and SPE show considerable rate of change and prove why the proposed method is better than the existing one (Table 1).

6 Conclusion

Sweat pores are easily visible through an image of high resolution. For this research work, I have used images of 1000 dpi.

It was noticed through the research that pores have gained popularity for building biometric research systems because they are found in abundance. Several methodologies have been implemented for the extraction of features. One such technique was the Difference of Gaussian approach. However, the limitation of the approach was that it demanded fixing the scale for difference in every input image. This technique not only slowed the system but was also expensive in terms of computation.

Taking cue from the DoG method, in my research work, I have proposed an algorithm which can extract pores that lie within the boundary of the ridges. The performance of the algorithm is validated by comparing it with the existing DoG method. The performance metrics like Sensitivity (SEN) and Specificity (SPE) show that the proposed algorithm provides better performance.

The limitation of the level 3 feature is that they demand images with high resolution which are >500 dpi. In forensic science which deals with nabbing culprits through latent fingerprints, it is not feasible to acquire high resolution images from the site of the crime scene. However it is believed with change in technology, the clarity can be improved to extract pores for identification.

References

1. Uchida, K.: Detection and recognition technology fingerprint identification. NEC J. Adv. Technol. **2**, 806–811 (2008)
2. Bolle, R., Connell, J., Chandra, S., Ratha, N., Seine, A.: Guide to Biometrics. Springer, New York (2003). https://doi.org/10.1007/978-1-4757-4036-3
3. Jaggerband, M., Moran, K.S.: J. Anc. Fingerpr. (2007)
4. Jea, T.-Y., Govindaraju, V.: A minutia-based partial fingerprint recognition system. J. Pattern Recogn. Soc. **38**, 1672–1684 (2005)
5. Grother, P., et al.: Performance of biometric quality measures. IEEE Trans. Pattern Anal. Mach. Intell. **29**(4), 531–543 (2007)
6. Prabhakar, S., et al.: Introduction to the special issue on biometrics: progress and direction. IEEE Trans. Pattern Anal. Mach. Intell. **29**(4), 513–516 (2007)
7. Wang, Y., et al.: A fingerprint orientation model based on 2D fourier expansion (FOMFE) and its application to singular point detection and fingerprint indexing. IEEE Trans. Pattern Anal. Mach. Intell. **29**(4), 573–585 (2007)
8. Poh, N., et al.: Benchmarking quality-dependent and cost-sensitive score-level multimodal biometric fusion algorithms. IEEE Trans. Inf. Forensics Secur. **4**(4), 849–866 (2009)
9. Farina, A., et al.: Fingerprint minutiae extraction from skeletonized binary images. J. Pattern Recogn. Soc. **32**, 877–889 (1999)
10. Tan, X., Bhanu, B.: Fingerprint matching by genetic algorithms. J. Pattern Recogn. Soc. **39**, 465–477 (2006)
11. Cappelli, R., et al.: Performance evaluation of fingerprint verification systems. IEEE Trans. Pattern Anal. Mach. Intell. **28**(1), 3–18 (2006)

12. Zhao, Q., Zhang, D., et al.: High resolution partial fingerprint alignment using pore-valley descriptors. Pattern Recogn. Lett. **43**, 1050–1106 (2010)
13. Zhao, Q., Zhang, D., et al.: Adaptive fingerprint pore modelling and extraction. Pattern Recogn. Lett. **43**, 2833–2844 (2010)
14. Malathi, S., Meena, C.: A novel approach for fingerprint recognition based on pores. IJCSR Int. J. Comput. Sci. Res. **1**(1), 10–14 (2010)
15. Vatsa, M., Singh, R., Noore, A., Singh, S.K.: Quality induced fingerprint identification using extended feature set
16. Chen, Y., Jain, A.: Dots and incipients: extended features for partial fingerprint matching. In: Proceedings of Biometric Symposium, Biometric Consortium Conference (2007)
17. Kryszczuk, K., Drygajlo, A., Morier, P.: Extraction of level 2 and level 3 features for fragmentary finger print comparison. In: Speech Processing and Biometrics Group Signal Processing Institute, Swiss Federal Institute of Technology Lausanne, Switzerland (2004)
18. Sankaran, A., Dhamecha, T.I., Vatsa, M., Singh, R.: On matching latent to latent fingerprints. In: Proceedings of International Joint Conference on Biometrics (2011)
19. Sherlock, B.G., Monro, D.M., Millard, K.: Fingerprint enhancement by directional fourier filtering. Visual Image Sig. Process. **141**, 87–94 (1994)

An SQL Injection Defensive Mechanism Using Reverse Insertion Technique

Shaji N. Raj[1(✉)] ⓘD and Elizabeth Sherly[2]

[1] Mahathma Gandhi University, Kottayam, Kerala, India
ammashajinraj@gmail.com
[2] IIITM-K, Techopark, Kazhakkoottam, Kerala, India
sherly@iiitmk.ac.in

Abstract. One of the top 10, 2017 attacks in the world is SQL injection. Though there are a number of different approaches available to prevent the SQL injection attack, it's considered as a serious security threat to Web applications, even today. SQL injection employs a code injection technique of hacking login credentials or other information that destroys your database. In this paper, we presented a new reversed insertion algorithm using a simple technique which prevents almost all types of SQL injection. This proposed model is implemented and tested by developing a prototype using SQL map. The proposed model shows a high level of security with an accuracy of 92%.

Keywords: SQL injection · Security · Vulnerabilities
Reverse insertion algorithm · Tautology · Piggybacked · Union-query

1 Introduction

SQL injection attacks are one of the most vulnerable web hacking method, which allows intruder to exploit the access to databases. It is most affected by database driven web applications as it injects malicious code in SQL statements, via web page input. The security of database driven application is highly challenged as SQL injection attacks affect the confidentiality and integrity of data. The attacker's inject data can trick the interpreter into executing unintended commands without proper authorization [17]. Statistics show that about 33% of websites are vulnerable to SQL injection due to poor security design [2]. There are a number of defensive mechanisms in place to prevent SQL injection attacks (SQLIA), but due to severity of attacks, many fail to defend the full scope of the vulnerability [8]. Attackers bypass most of the defensive techniques such as proxy firewall, coding practices, Intrusion detection systems and SQL injection attacks, therefore all these are still remain as a daunting problem for researchers.

In SQLIA, attackers use specially crafted SQL queries by inserting new SQL keywords or operators that bypass the validation of login credentials. There are different injection mechanism such as an injection through user input, cookies,server variables,second order injection etc. [3]. In this paper, we present a SQL injection prevention method named reverse insertion algorithm (RIA) for a user input injection mechanism. User input injection is very common in SQLIA, through which login

© Springer Nature Singapore Pte Ltd. 2018
P. Bhattacharyya et al. (Eds.): NGCT 2017, CCIS 828, pp. 335–346, 2018.
https://doi.org/10.1007/978-981-10-8660-1_25

credentials are retrieved, and the entire database information can be severely exploited. The proposed RIA algorithm prevents user input injection to login page, which helps to defend various types of SQL injection methods.

The paper is stuctured as follows: After introducing the background information on SQLIAs and related concepts, Literature review follows. Section 3 presents the proposed methodology and new algorithm. The implementation is describes in Sects. 4 and 5 presents the results and evaluation. The paper end with Sect. 6, with future work.

1.1 Basics of SQLIA

Different input mechanism can be performed to make a web application vulnerability by using malicious SQL statements. SQL injection generates malicious SQL statements to databases by inserting new SQL keywords that can tamper with the original query. One easy way to detect SQL injection is to insert a meta character into an input that you know, use to craft a database access statement [4]. For example, if the username is "abc" and the password is "123", to verify the credentials the web application sends an SQL query as shown below.

```
SELECT * FROM Users WHERE name = 'abc'AND password = '123'
```

Suppose a hacker enter username as 1' OR '1' = '1 instead of the actual username and 'sss' as a password instead of actual password. Then the SQL query become,

```
SELECT* FROM Users WHERE name = 1OR1 = 1AND password = 'sss'
```

This SQL statement will always return a true value. The database returned a true value, the attacker was able to a logged in session without the need to guess the credentials. There are various types of SQL injection methods used by the attackers named tautology, blind SQL, union query, piggy - backed queries, logically incorrect queries, queries for stored procedures, etc. These attacks can perform in isolation or together, depending on attacker's intention.

A tautology is a simple way of attack in which it bypass validation and extract the data. In a union-query, a vulnerable parameter is injected that can change the data in the table. As a result, the intended data from the table will not be retrieved. In Piggy-backed queries,the attacker inject additional queries into the original query which may add or modify data. This is an extremely harmful attack.

2 Literature Review

Efficient method for preventing SQL injection attack on web application using encryption and tokenization (2014) Anjugam and Murugan [7] presented a lightweight method to prevent SQL injection attack by using tokenization techniques to convert SQL queries into token and encrypted using AES algorithm. This includes a. Encryption and decryption (b) Query tokenization (c) Comparison of dynamic table. The tokenization is applied to the input query by detecting single quotes, double quotes, etc. These tokens are stored in a dynamic table at client side. The table name, field name and data are encrypted. Then both are directed to the server machine. The server machine, input query is decrypted and turn into tokens and stored in a dynamic table. If both the dynamic tables are same, it prevents from SQL injection. However, this algorithm will not prevent blind SQL injection.

SQL Injection Attack Prevention Based on Decision Tree Classification-2015 Hanmanthu et al. [10]. In this model an attack class and non attack class are classified using decision tree classification model. The client URL request to the server to filter based on the classifier and only safe data will be sent to the database.

Runtime monitoring technique to handle tautology based SQL injection attack (SQLIA) (2012) Dharam and Shiva [16], proposed a framework called Runtime monitoring framework which performs runtime monitoring of web application and prevent SQLIA. It use two testing techniues basic data flow and runtime monitors. The basis data flow to identify all valid execution paths of application and Runtime monitors are used for runtime monitoring of applications. All valid execution paths are located by the use of a mixture of basis path and data flow testing technique.

The evolution of web security mechanisms using vulnerability & attack injection (2014) Fonseca et al. [17], proposed a tool to evaluate the application security mechanism. The idea behind this method is that, attacking the website automatically by injecting vulnerabilities. The entire process is automated using VAIT TOOL. This method focuses on SQLIA and cross site scripting. The injection attacks can be done using HTTP communication and other for database communication.

A novel method for SQL injection attack detection based on removing SQL query attribute values (2012) LEE et al. [13], proposed a method to remove SQL query attribute of web pages comparing with predefined one. In this method SQL injection can be detected by comparing static SQL queries with dynamically generated queries.

An authentication Mechanism to Prevent SQL Injection Attacks (2011) (Balasundaram and Ramraj [12]). This scheme uses Advanced Encryption Standard (AES) for preventing SQL injection attack. Here the server database maintains three parameters for every user such as username, password and secret key. This model has three phases named 1. Registration phase 2. Login phase and 3. Verification phase. In the registration phase, the server maintains an user account table with the three parameters and send the user secret key to the user. In login phase the username and password is encrypted by using AES algorithm by using user secret key. In th last phase the server has received the login query and verifies the corresponding users' secret key. If the match is found login is performed.

Random 4: An Application Specific Randomized Encryption Algorithm to Prevent SQL Injection (2012) (Avireddy et al.) [14]. In this method to convert the input data into a coded form the randomization algorithm is used. The concept of cryptographic salt is used for this conversion. The input from the user is encrypted based on randomization. This can be stored in a database on server side. The main disadvantages of this approach is that it doesn't prevent all types of SQL injection and requires a lookup table.

3 Reverse Insertion Algorithm (RIA)

The proposed reverse insertion algorithm called RIA is designed for user input injection attacks, which prevents SQL injection in a very simple manner without programming effort. The basic principle of this method is to filter the SQL command and store the data in a coded format. All the user input data are first reversed and form a group of two characters. Minimum characters required is two(example OR). A special character is then inserted in between each group of two letters and stored in a table. For example, the given user data are reversed and form a group of two characters. At the end of each group, a special character is inserted that stored in the table.The length of the first filed input data is also computed. Table 1 shows the original data and the stored data. Table 2 shows the structure of table with sample data.

Table 1. Login data storage after reversed insertion

User name	Password	Stored username	Stored password
abc	pqr	cb#a	rq#p
123	asd	32#1	ds#a

Table 2. Structure of table with sample data

User name	Password	Key value	Length of user name
cb#a	rq#p	abc#pqr	3

The first part of RIA algorithm is to store the coded input data in a table, which works in login register phase of a web page is given below.

Algorithm 1. RIA Algorithm- Registration Phase

1: Input Data -username and password
2: Find the length of the field
3: Combine the username and password
4: Insert a special character in between them
5: Reverse the user input(username and password)
6: Split the data into group of two
7: Insert special symbol in between each group
8: Insert all the data into the table

Code Segment for Algorithm 1

1: $username = $ _POST['use'];
2: $password = $_ POST['pas'];
3: $length = strlen($_ POST['use']);
4: $finalkey = $username:"#":$password;
5: $userreverse = strrev($username);
6: $passreverse = strrev($password);
7: $usersplit = str split($userreverse; 2);
8: $passsplit = str split($passreverse; 2);
9: $finaluser = implode("#"; $usersplit);
10: $finalpass = implode("#"; $passsplit);
11: $sq = "insertintomultivalues('$finaluser';
'$finalpass';' $finalkey';' $length')";

The **login phase** has three levels of validation to be performed. **Level 1:** When a registered user enters the data, first reverse the user input and split into the group of two characters and insert the special character. Then compare with data stored in the server. **Level 2:** In this level, these data are combined and insert a special character, then compare it with the value in the table. **Level 3:** At this level, length of the data was computed and compare it with original length already stored in the table.

Algorithm 2. RIA Algorithm- Login Phase

1: Collect data from the form
2: Reverse the user input(username and password)
3: Split the data into group of two
4: Insert special symbol in between each group
5: Compare the reversed grouped data with data in the table.
6: Combine the username and password
7: Insert a special character in between them and form a key value
8: Compare the key value with key data in the table
9: Find the length of the username field
10: Compare the length of data with actual length
11: If all the comparisons are successfully log into the page.

If an attacker try to retrieve data from the database, it is not possible due to these three levels of validation. The PHP code used for this purpose is given below.

```
Code Segment for Algorithm 2

$userreverse = strrev($username);
$passreverse = strrev($password);
$usersplit = str split($userreverse; 2);
$passsplit = str split($passreverse; 2);
$finaluser = implode("#"; $usersplit);
$finalpass = implode("#"; $passsplit);
$length = strlen($_GET['use']);
$finalkey = $username:"#":$password;
$se = "select from multi where(USERNAME ='
Finaluser'andPASSWORD =' $finalpass')";
$sd = mysql query($se);
while($r = mysql fetch array($sd))if (($r['KEY V ']
= $finalkey)and($r['length'] = $length))
```

4 Implementation

The proposed algorithm is implemented using a live environment by creating a website www.learnlive.co.in. In the login page, we experimentally inserted 100 data during the registration and login phase. This application is tested by the standard of Open Web Application Security Project(OWASP). In this paper, SQL injection methods such as tautology, union query, piggybacked queries, blind SQL injection, logically incorrect queries and queries for stored procedure have been tested separately and verified.

4.1 Tautology

This attack intent to bypass the authentication, exploiting the login details by injecting specially crafted values, that affect the WHERE conditional of the SQL query. When the user enters 1 'or'1'='1 in the username with any password (here abc), the query generated changes the conditions, that return all the rows or a single row from the table. The SQL query looks like,

```
SELECT* FROM Users WHERE name = 1OR1 = 1ANDpassword='abc'
```

By implementing RIA algorithm, the values will be reversed and the query execution will be performed as shown in Fig. 1., which prevents the database to extract the login details without displaying the list.

Input(username) : 1'or'1'='1
Input(password) : 1'or'1'='1

Query : $se="select * from
multi where (USERNAME=' 1'#='#1' #ro#'1'
and PASSWORD='1'#='#1'#ro#'1')

Fig. 1. Tautology attack prevention using RIA

4.2   Union Query

This is also bypassing authentication by injecting UNION statement. This query can retrieve the table name and all information from the table. As a result, the records displayed will be the union of original and injected query. The proposed algorithm effectively prevents the union attack. Fig. 2 shows the converted query, while applying RIA algorithm.

Input(username) : 123

Input(password) : 123 union   select all from multi

Query : $se="select * from multi where (USERNAME=' 32#1'
and PASSWORD='it#lu#mm#or#fl#la#tc#el#es#no#in#u3#21')

Fig. 2. Union query attacks prevention using RIA

4.3   Piggybacked SQL Injection

In Piggybacked SQL injection, the attacker injects additional queries into the original query to extract data. The new query will act as a piggyback on the original query, and both the queries will be executed one by one. i.e. *Normal SQL statement +";" + Injected Sql command.* . For example,

```
$se="select * from multi where (USERNAME='32#
1'and PASSWORD='12# 3';drop table multi)
```

The RIA algorithm prevents this attack by reversing the input fields in the SQL statement. The query after the delimiter; is the injected query as shown in Fig. 3.

Input(username) :admin
Input(password) : pass1;drop   table multi
Query   :Select * from multi where
USERNAME ='ni#md#a' and
PASSWORD ='it#lu # me# lb#at#po#rd#;1#ss#ap';

Fig. 3. Piggybacked attack Prevention using RIA

4.4   Logically Incorrect Queries

In this technique a hacker retrieves valuable information of the back-end database. This is done by injecting illegal or logically incorrect SQL syntax to the database. This vulnerability resulted an error message that reveals injectable paramters to the attacker. The inject statement can cause syntax or logical error in the database, that can enable attackers to bring out the meta data. For example, A syntax error, a quotation mark at the end of the user input some time return a error message with some valuable information. Our proposed method enables to prevent such type of logically incorrect SQL injection. For example, Fig. 4 show how the proposed method prevent these types of attack.

Input(username) : user'
Input(password) : pass1

Query   : $se=" select * from multi
where (USERNAME ="r#es#u'
and PASSWORD ='1s#sa#p')

Fig. 4. Logically incorrect attack prevention using RIA

4.5   Blind SQL Injection

In this attack, by asking the database a series of true or false questions, attacker collect data. It is 'blind' because the results are not visible. The database information will be pulled out by a series of query and retrieve the data. After implementing our algorithm, if we change the URL by inserting values with a valuable user name and password, it will return the same page, no error message is displayed. When we change the URL by inserting 1 = 2 and 1 = 1, the same SQL query will be executed. An example is given in Fig. 5.

```
Correct Url:http://www.learnlive.co.in/ multilogin.php?
use = user & pas= pass1 & serch =login

Output:Original page

Url1:http://www.learnlive.co.in/multilogin.php?
use= user& pas=pas1&1=2& serch = login

Output:Original page(no error)

Url2:http://www.learnlive.co.in/multilogin.php?
use =user & pas= pas 1&1=1 &serch =login %27

Output:Original page(no error)

Query:select * from multi where
(USERNAME='re#su' and PASSWORD='1s#sa#p')
```

Fig. 5. Blind SQL attack prevention using RIA

4.6   Stored Procedure Injection

It is often believed that stored procedures are safe to SQL injection attacks, but it is also vulnerable. It depends on how safely you write the code in stored procedure. More often, injection into stored procedures is possible when dynamic SQL is being used in the procedure. The proposed RIA algorithm prevents certain attacks as it sends the user data to the procedure after reversing and inserting the special characters. For example the procedure look like,

```
CREATE PROCEDURE Check
user varchar(20),
pass varchar(20)
AS BEGIN
Select * from multi where USERNAME = user
and PASSWORD = pass;
END
```

When a user sends username as 'user' and password as 'pass1; drop table multi', the query result is shown in Fig. 6. However, the proposed model partially prevents attacks in Stored procedures.

5   Evaluation and Results

The evaluation has been carried out by checking various attacks like tautology, logically incorrect queries, piggy backed „union query, blind SQL injection and stored procedures and the result obtained in shown in Table 3 and its graph is shown in Fig. 7.

Input(username) : user
Input(password) : pass1;drop   table multi
Query   :Select * from multi where
USERNAME ='re#su' and
PASSWORD ='it#lu # me# lb#at#po#rd#;1#ss#ap';

Fig. 6. Stored procedure attack prevention uses RIA

Table 3. Evaluation of result

Attack	Tautology	Union	Stored procedure	Logically incorrect	Blind	Piggybacked
Total	100	100	100	100	100	100
Failure	0	0	40	0	0	0
Success	100	100	100	100	100	100

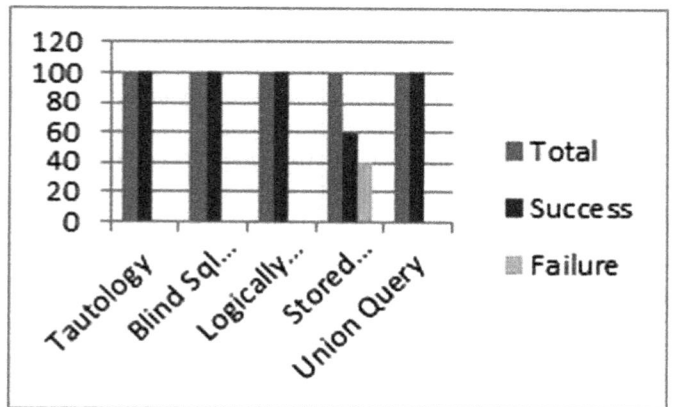

Fig. 7. Graphical representation of success and failure of attack

The Table 4 gives a comparison of a set of SQL injection prevention techniques along with the proposed reverse insertion algorithm techniques. The overall accuracy obtained in our algorithm is 92%.

6   Conclusions and Future Works

The proposed algorithm is implemented in different SQL injection methods and evaluated using a website www.learnlive.co.in. Most of the attacks in SQL injection in user input mechanism are prevented successfully with an overall accuracy of 92%. The

Table 4. Comparison different technique with proposed model

Method	Tautology	Union	Stored procedure	Logically incorrect	Blind	Piggybacked
AMNESIA	Y[1]	Y	N[2]	Y	Y	Y
SQLRand	Y	Y	N	N	Y	Y
CANDID	Y	N	N	N	N	N
SQLIDS	Y	Y	Y	Y	Y	Y
SQLIPA	Y	N	N	N	N	N
RIA (Proposed)	Y	Y	P[3]	Y	Y	Y

[1]Prevented
[2]Not prevented
[3]Partially prevented

main advantage of this algorithm is that without any development effort it detects the vulnerabilities and protect the web from SQL injection attacks.

Future Works: The proposed algorithm is now tested in HTML web pages and PHP only with input mechanism. The other injection mechanisms like injection through cookies and second order injection has to be checked, evaluated and prevented by modifying the proposed algorithm. The work can be extended to URL level detection and prevention for SQL injection.

References

1. Avresky, D., Arlat, J., Laprie, J.C., Crouzet, Y.: Fault injection for tolerance. IEEE Trans. Reliab. **45**(3), 443–455 (1994)
2. Gudipati, V.K., Venna, T., Subburaj, S., Abuzaghleh, O.: Advanced automated SQL injection attacks and defensive mechanisms. In: IEEE Transactions on Security (2016)
3. Halfond, W.G.J., Viegas, J., Orso, A.: A classification of SQL injection attacks and countermeasures. In: Proceedings of the International Symposium on Secure Software Engineering, March 2006
4. Chellamal, P., Vilasini, V.: Eliminate SQL injection using LINQ. IJARCST **2**(1), 361 (2014)
5. Atoum, J.O., Qaralleh, A.J.: A hybrid techniques for SQL injection attacks detection and prevention. IJDMS **6**(1), 21 (2014)
6. Stallings, W.: Network Security Essentials Applications and Standards, 3rd edn. Prentice Hall, Upper Saddle River (2011). ISBN 13: 978-0-13-706792-3
7. Anjugam, S., Murugan, A.: Preventing SQL injection attacks. Int. J. Adv. Softw. Eng. **4**(4), 174–177 (2014)
8. Halfond, W.G.J., Orso, A.: Preventing SQL injection attacks. In: IEEE/ACM International Conference on Automated Software Engineering, pp. 174–183 (2005)
9. Powell, D., Stroud, R.: Conceptual Model and Architecture. Deliverable D21 Edition (2003)
10. Hanmanthu, B., Raghu Ram, B., Niranjan, P.: SQL injection prevention based on decision tree classification. In: IEEE International Conference on Intelligent System and Control (2015)

11. Kaur, H., Dhingra, S.: A Practical approach for SQL injection prevention attacks using IPS. Int. J. Adv. Res. Comput. Commun. Eng. **3**(10), 8118–8122 (2014)
12. Balasundaram, I., Ramraj, E.: An authentication mechanism to prevent SQL injection attacks. Int. J. Comput. Appl. **19**(1), 30–33 (2011)
13. Lee, I., Jeong, S., Yeo, S., Moon, J.: A novel method for SQL injection attack detection based on removing SQL query attribute value. Math. Comput. Model. **55**(1–2), 58–68 (2012)
14. Avireddy, S., Perumal, V. et al.: Random 4: an application specific randomized encryption algorithm to prevent SQL injection. In: 12th IEEE International Conference on Trust, Security and Privacy in Computing and Communications, pp. 1327–1333, June 2012
15. Anjugam, S., Murugan, A.: Efficient methods for preventing SQL injection attack on web application using encryption and tokenization. Int. J. Adv. Res. Comput. Sci. Softw. Eng. **4**(4), 173–177 (2014)
16. Dharam, R., Shiva, S.G.: Runtime monitoring technique to handle tautology based SQL injection attacks. Int. J. Cyber-Secur. Digit. Forensics (IJCSDF) **1**, 189–203 (2012). ISSN: 2305-0012
17. Fonseca, J., Vieira, M., Madeira, H.: The evaluation of web security mechanisms using vulnerability & attack injection. IEEE Trans. Dependable Secur. Comput. **11**(5), 440–453 (2014)
18. https://www.w3schools.com/sql/sqlinjection.asp
19. https://www.owasp.org/index.php/Category

Study and Proposal of Probabilistic Model for SIP Server Overload Control

Atul Mishra[(⊠)]

SOET, BML Munjal University, Gurgaon, India
atul.mishra@bml.edu.in

Abstract. We introduced a new mathematical model named AIPC (Additive increase with probabilistic changes). In our mathematical model, there will be a probabilistic change in the sending rate during the overload condition. The probabilistic change can be sender or receiver based or both together synchronized. In this paper, AIPC is sender synchronized. We show that mechanism is stable, counter-active, reliable and fair. Sender will change its sending rate in accordance with the receiver's capacity. AIPC work towards equalizing the behavior of SIP Server during an overload condition and prevent the services from complete collapse. Test cases are based on performance metrics. Simulation is used to analyze the factors viz. effectiveness, efficiency, fairness and stability.

Keywords: SIP · AIPC · AIMD · VoIP · SIP Server · Probability of rejection

1 Introduction

SIP server's plays significant role in signaling, processing and enhancing the services such VoIP and voice mail etc. The servers constitute the core components and are responsible for the quality of services [1]. SIP is also the foundation for various other communication oriented services including web and video conferencing [12].

Generally, phone call over Internet uses the Internet for connecting phone calls, especially for consumers. But in most cases, businesses prefer private networks for using IP telephony because it ensures better quality of service and security. VoIP works on Session Initiation Protocol. SIP works in various phases of call such as Availability, Localization, negotiation, Analyzing recipient profile and resources & communication parameters.

In this paper, we are trying to develop a new mechanism for controlling the rate of transmission during an overload condition. There may be several reasons for overload occurrence in SIP server viz. network latency, Attacks (DoS or flooding) or component failure. Primary emphasis is always given, how to reduce the sending rate at sender side or the receiving window on the receiver side. Our AIPC mechanism in this paper focuses on sender side mechanism and it tries to reduce the rate of transmission based on probabilistic factor.

SIP is independent of the session. This employs that it is not a media transport neither protocol nor a conference control protocol. Also, it is not a resource allocation protocol. Hence it can be used with UDP, TCP, and ATM etc. But it does not offer

© Springer Nature Singapore Pte Ltd. 2018
P. Bhattacharyya et al. (Eds.): NGCT 2017, CCIS 828, pp. 347–360, 2018.
https://doi.org/10.1007/978-981-10-8660-1_26

sufficient mechanism for transmission of large amount of data, hence the preferred with User Datagram protocol (UDP)

2 Ease of Use

2.1 Overview

Session Initiation Protocol is a transaction oriented protocol. Transactions are of two types viz. the INVITE and NON-INVITE transactions. INVITE transactions includes INVITE request while the NON-INVITE transaction includes requests other than INVITE or ACK. Transaction is initiated when a client sent a request to server responding that request. Transaction is thus most important as it is instigating strategies related to request-response, timeout handling and retransmission (Fig. 1).

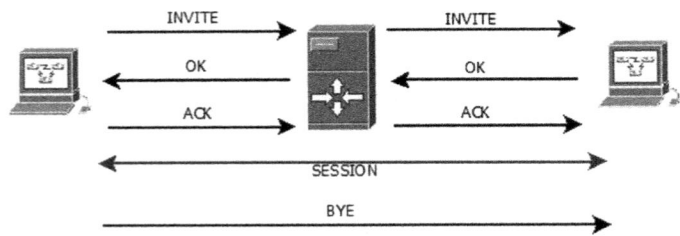

Fig. 1. SIP call session

SIP is proposed and developed by IETF. The architecture includes following protocols [4]:

- RTP: It is used for transmission of audio, video and other time-bound data.
- RTSP: It is used for establishing and controlling the on-demand media streams.
- MGCP: It is used for controlling media gateways.
- SDP: It is used for describing media sessions.
- SAP: It is used for announcing the multicast sessions.

2.2 Causes of SIP Server Overlaod

SIP architecture, does not suggest adequate mechanisms to handle the overload conditions. SIP defines several retransmission strategies amplified with messages loss inducing substantial drop in the throughput. This leads to lower call throughput and are often regarded as Congestion failure (Fig. 2).

SIP Server experiences overload condition whenever the number of received SIP messages exceeds the number of messages it can process. Hence it is required to have sufficient resources to process the incoming requests or Messages. These resources may include the Processing unit, memory devices, input/output devices, or storage resources.

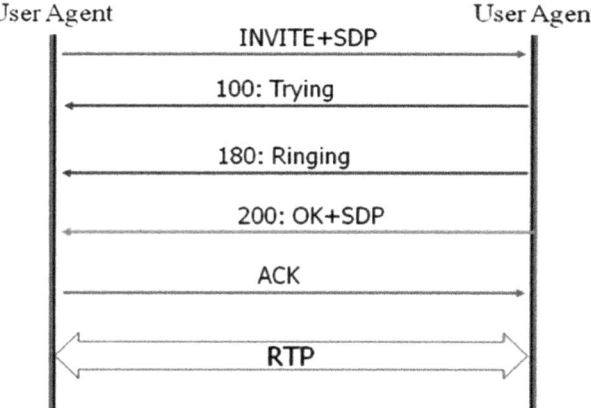

Fig. 2. SIP user agent session

Retransmission behavior of Session Initiation protocol is a foremost contributor to SIP Congestion Failure [5]. It follow retransmission strategies while running over an unreliable User Datagram Protocol and thereby imposes additional load to the Server. These retransmission strategies are due to the messages that are dropped or delayed by a server in certain time frames. This leads to server overload and message rejection.

Overload condition can also occur due to increase in remarkable volume of traffic. Process discussed by Rosenberg [5] put forward that overload condition reduces the performance of a VoIP server and lead to impasse the VoIP services. To oppose all of a sudden increase in traffic, SIP Server and Proxies must offer overload control mechanisms that reduces the work load of these servers and prevent over-utilization of their resources.

Overload is usually offered by substantial User Agents or UAS or Forward Servers, sending individual messages. When taken together, the traffic can overload a SIP Server. Supervising the rate of Transmission is therefore, is a threat from the sources. Implementing the mechanisms on individual User Agent Servers or Forward Servers may not be effective for minimizing the overload. Non SIP mechanism are also available to counter the incoming load and can operate independently or in conjunction with the existing mechanism.

2.3 Parameters for Analysis

Throughput analysis is one of the Performance indicator for SIP server under overload condition. Other important indicators are Responsiveness, Delay and stability. We have considered parameters described and defined in IETF draft for all the measurements [8]. The parameter measurement is based on sender and receiver ends. Hence we use hardware utilization parameters as well, in order to monitor the performance of memory and resources of the proxies.

Call statistics and duration of calls during the message exchange is monitored at the Sender end. Real-time Transport protocol samples are taken into consideration as well. The complete list of measured parameters includes:

- Number of Successful calls
- Number of Unsuccessful calls
- Probability of Rejection.

2.4 Types of SIP Server Overload

Two prominent tiers of SIP Server overload are Server-Server overload and Client-Server overload. In this paper we have adopted the former category i.e. Server Level overload. If Server on attaining the capacity continues to handle requests, it may lead to diminution of application performance and stability.

Server-Server Overload
It occurs when upstream server starts sending substantial amount of traffic (Engineered Traffic E) to the SIP server, pushing it towards overload. We have adopted this scenario for our research in this paper.

Client-Server Overload
It occurs when a sizable clients make a simultaneous request that are not handled by the forward server, thereby, putting the server into overload.

3   Related Work

To override an overload condition of a server, where all its resources are rejecting sessions, Hilt et al. [3] outlined a SIP overload control mechanism based on Feedback control. In this, feedback is communicated from one server to another. The feedback information can be in form of a transmission rate or a load limiting window size. The main idea of feedback based overload control is to deploy the transmission of a 503 (Service Unavailable) response to the posterior server.

Bansal et al. [2] examined the functioning of SIP Server and VoIP calls during a Denial of Services attack. It has been observed that there is substantial reduction in the quality of Call during the attack along with negligible packet loss. A sudden decrease in delay increases with the increase in flooding and stress on SIP server increases. A mild deviation in the latency on a packet flow between two servers is checked with the increase in load on server.

Gu et al. [7] suggested that a new class of AIMD algorithm works well during overload condition. Additive increment is decreasing functions of the current sending rate. The congestion control algorithm is globally asymptotically stable and will converge to equilibrium. Mechanism uses a decreasing function of the increase factor and a constant decrease factor. A special case of DAIMD algorithm is considered for various grid based applications.

Hilt and Widjaja [6] proposed the mechanism which aims at stabilizing the proxy behavior during the overload condition. It prevents the server from being completely used up during a collision collapse. Mechanism consider both elements of overload and cause of overload together. Dropping and rejecting the incoming request are realized by sending back a 5xx response. AIPC mechanism adopted the probabilistic factor obtained as a change factor between sender and receiver in synchronized manner. Sender depicts the probabilistic change during an overload condition.

Kusching [10] illustrates that Multiplicative decrease step of AIMD algorithm reduces the receiving window (and the corresponding throughput) in case of the packet loss drastically, before the Additive increase step is initiated and tries to increase the window again. This can lead to remarkable variation of the throughput in networks with large RTTs.

4 AIPC Mechanism

4.1 Statement

The goal of any overload control scheme is to reduce the load on engaged resources. Reducing the load has their costs in terms of CPU and Memory Utilization as well (Fig. 3).

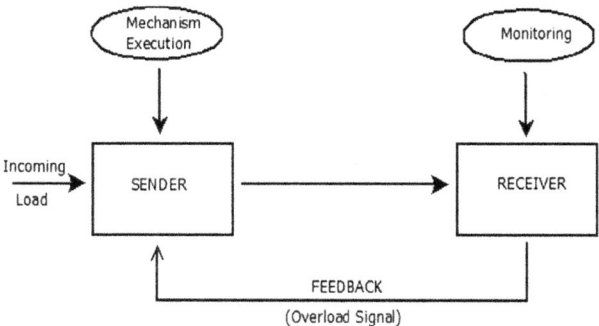

Fig. 3. AIPC mechanism overview

4.2 Proposed Mechanism

- The mechanism would synchronize both the sender and the receiver. Mechanism focus on downsizing the incoming traffic at receiver end based on a Probabilistic factor thereby dropping the traffic or rejecting the traffic. While at the sender end, the sender would adjust its transmission strategies in accordance with the Receivers capacity. Receiver would increase the rate of transmission until the notice of overload occurrence and would decrease it substantially as soon as overload is noticed. In this way, both the sender and the receiver share their status to get synchronized and decrease the rate of rejection which will surely enhance the CPU utilization and corresponding Proxy Throughput.

- Overload condition of a SIP Server is recorded when at least one of its resource surpasses a value more than a specified limit. In our mechanism, we set this limit as R_{LOW}. It is a point beyond which a server starts overloading to some extent. And beyond R_{UP} (upper limit), a SIP Server is declared overloaded. Above R_{UP}, the system is considered as Overloaded and it cannot handle any more requests and it starts rejecting the entire request until the Rate of Transmission falls between the R_{LOW} and R_{UP}. One can observe a decrease in the load on the SIP proxy by either dropping incoming requests or rejecting them, e.g., sending back a 5xx reply. Therefore, dropping incoming requests [4], consumes slightly less CPU utilization at the SIP proxy than rejecting them.
- In order to reduce the possibility of an overload situation at the receiver side, the senders of the SIP traffic should adapt their transmission rates to the capabilities of the receivers. That is, if a SIP proxy that is currently sending traffic to another proxy notices that the receiving proxy is overloaded; the sending proxy should reduce its transmission rate so as to avoid overloading the receiving one.
- In order to avoid the sudden changes, we should take the average of Probability of rejection
- AIPC combines linear growth of the transmission rate with the Probabilistic change during an overload condition.

4.3   Mathematical Model

AIPC defines two threshold points (for CPU and memory): lower (RLOW) and Upper Threshold (RUP). AIPC work in a way that the number of rejection during the overload condition is minimized.

- There will be a probabilistic change size of receiving window when the rate of receiving incoming requests lies between the Upper and Lower thresholds
-

$$\text{PoR (I)} = \frac{Rtrans - Rlow}{Rup - Rlow} \text{R}_{\text{TRANS}} > \; = \text{R}_{\text{LOW}}\} \tag{1}$$

- Parameter obtained in Eq. (1) is the Probability of rejection calculated at fixed time intervals (say T) where R_{TRANS} is the load status on SIP Server [3]. In order to avoid sudden change and to obtain a smooth graph, Average of PoR is taken in Eq. (1) over the time. When:
  - *PoRAVG $\leq$ 0.05* system is not considered as Overload and there will be no dropping or rejection of incoming request is initiated.
  - *1 $\geq$ PoR $\geq$ 0.05*, SIP Sever is considered as Overloaded. Counteractive measures are required to Sop is from being overloaded. Hence, the incoming successful INVITE messages are rejected with the parameter used in Eq. (1).
  - *PoR = 1*, SIP Server is considered as complete overloaded and no incoming request is entertained viz. requests are rejected.

At Sender Side.

AIPC enables SIP Server to estimates the overload status at its neighboring servers and adopt the change in transmission accordingly. AIPC mechanism allows a faster reaction to a substantial overload condition and careful preventive reaction during the under load phases (Fig. 4).

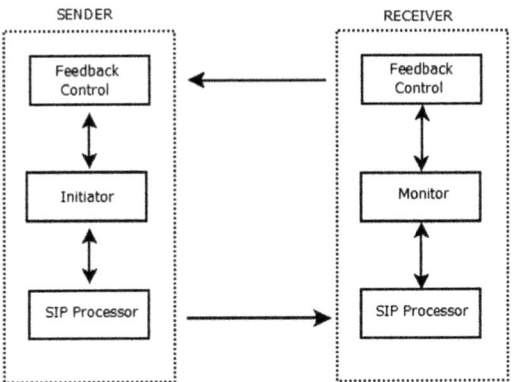

Fig. 4. Feedback based control strategy

- At starting or under normal condition, when no overload status is received and no retransmission occurs, the sender adjusts its sending rate in an increasing manner. It follows additive increase behavior probing to usable bandwidth until the loss occurs. AIPC increases the sending by a fixed amount every round trip time.

$$R_{TRANS+1} = R_{TRANS} + \delta \{\delta = \text{Linear increase}\} \tag{2}$$

- In order to accommodate different types of servers, I can be determined as using following parameters:

$$I_{n+1} = (1 - R_{TRANS}/R_{UP}) \tag{3}$$

Here I_{n+1} transitive factor to accommodate different servers of different capabilities. Using Eq. (3), I can be calculated as

$$I = 1 - e^{-(I_n+1)} \tag{4}$$

- Upon receiving an Overload Status (i.e. 5xx reply) AIPC uses Probabilistic parameter used in Eq. (1) for reducing the rate of transmission. It is observed that overload status is received when the transmission rate exceeds the Lower threshold value. The sender will adjust its rate of transmission accordingly. When:

- $R_{TRANS} \geq R_{LOW}$, corresponding value of I lies between 0.5 to 0.9 and the rate of transmission is illustrated as

$$R_{TRANS+1} = R_{TRANS}(1 - I) \tag{5}$$

The transmission rate will be adjusted in the manner of PoR at the receiver side.
- $R_{TRANS} \geq R_{UP}$, corresponding value of I will be 1 and the receiver side is regarded as complete or severely overloaded. The rate of transmission will be illustrated as

$$R_{TRANS+1} = R_{TRANS} \times I \tag{6}$$

Note that the working of the Eqs. (5) and (6) is somewhat similar. The blocking probability is lower when the transmission rate lies between lower and upper bound while it is max during the complete or severe overload condition.

4.4   AIPC Constraints

- The overloaded server sends explicit congestion information to the proxy or neighboring server, the sender side (receiving this information) needs to entirely adjust its transmission rate accordingly. The complication lies here not in the rate adjustment but in determining the appropriate overload information at the overloaded server. Hence, in our approach, we will restrict the analysis to the conditions in which the overloaded servers send only implicit congestion information, e.g., rejecting or dropping traffic. These mechanisms are already part of the SIP specifications and do not require any additional logic at the receiving SIP proxies server.
- We assume the overload notification is solely based on closed loop feedback: Detection, Signaling and Reaction. Detection phase will monitors the buffer utilization at Overload point and collects data. Signaling phase will generate proper message response (5xx) and gives feedback. The Reaction phase will refine the changes in the sending rate according to the receiver failure message (Fig. 5).
- Routines used for sending should be asynchronous and non-blocking whereas the receive routines can be either blocking or non-blocking.

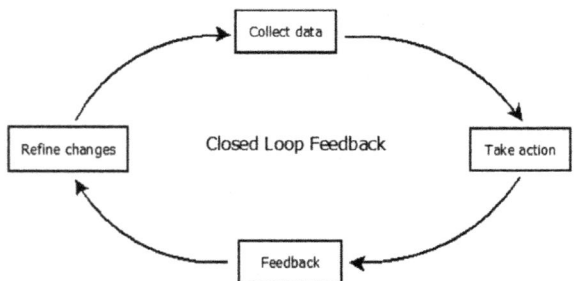

Fig. 5. Closed loop feedback for handling the congestion

- Actions are taken on the sending receiving end through the message response buffer.
- The value of probabilistic factor can be negotiated among the Servers at service level, for adjusting its transmission rate at sender side.
- Since media and signaling follow separate path in SIP, hence, RTP stream does flow through the SIP server and will not represent any load for it [9].

4.5 AIPC Analysis Tools

For evaluation of our mechanism, we have used following tools for conducting the experiment:

1. *Asterisk Server* [13, 14]: It is a complete PBX in software. Its runs on various platforms viz. Linux, windows, MAC OS etc. It supports three way calling, caller ID services, ADS1, IAX, SIP, H.32x, MACP and SSCP.
2. *Star Trinity SIP tester* [16]: It is a VoIP load testing tool which enables you to test VoIP network, SIP Software and hardware. It can simulate thousands of incoming and outgoing SIP calls with RTP streams. It can also analyze call and real time reports.
3. *SIPp tool* [15]: *SIPp* is a free Open Source test *tool*/traffic generator for the *SIP* protocol. Features include dynamic display of statistics about running tests (call rate, round trip delay, and message statistics) and dynamically adjustable call rates.
4. MATLAB: MATLAB® is a high-level language and interactive environment for numerical computation, visualization, and programming. Using MATLAB, you can analyze data, develop algorithms, and create models and applications.

4.6 Experimental Test BED

In this section, we describe our experimental setup used for the performance analysis of AIPC mechanism under several load conditions. The test setup consists of sender and a receiver emulated using a SIP tester. Main components of the test setup are:

SIP Server
ASTERISK is used as a SIP server. It is an open source PBX machine in software [11].

Evaluation Machine
To analyze the throughput, we have used *Star Trinity SIP tester*. SIP tester acts like a stress call generator. It has a timer which triggers execution of call using the XML script. Scripting makes a delay, accepts or rejects a call, plays a WAV file and aborts the call within specified period of time.

5 Performance Evaluation

For analyzing the scenario to an extent, SIP requests (INVITE) are sent to a proxy server. Successful INVITE requests are followed by another two requests viz. ACK & BYE. Rejecting INVITE requests, thereby, will save the resources required for processing the INVITE request and corresponding in-dialog request as well.

The goal of our experiment is to evaluate the ability of Sip Server to handle the number of simultaneous requests during an overload condition. We evaluated the performance of AIPC during several scenarios.

5.1 TOOL Based Simulation

Due to the limitation of the traffic generator tool i.e. it's simple and single threaded architecture design, which prevents it from using the multiple cores at a time. Thus, to increase the call capacity, it is required to run the processes of SIPp on multiple machines.

During the simulation, we observed that a single SIPp process on a machine can generate 250 simultaneous requests. Hence we adopted four machines to generate 1000 simultaneous requests. The upper threshold beyond which the server gets overloaded is 1000. Ultimately the lower threshold is assumed to be 500 simultaneous requests. Since the media stream and signaling follow separate path in SIP, hence on the load on media stream will not affect the signaling stream.

For evaluating the blocking probability, we used the Star Trinity SIP tester. The Simulation includes both single and load variance approach. AIPC aims at reducing the number of rejections during an overload condition according to the capability of the server to handle the simultaneous request (Fig. 6).

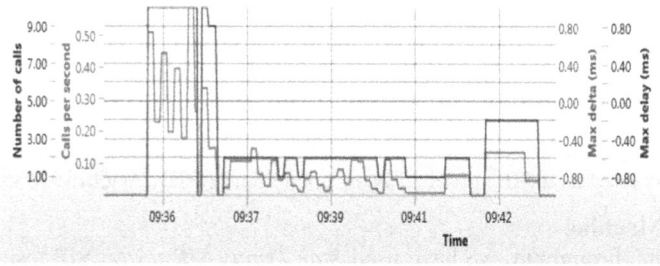

Fig. 6. Experimental result: number of calls vs. number of rejections (source star trinity SIP tester [16])

5.2 MATLAB Simulation

The matlab simulation will include the simulation of mathematical model viz. Eqs. (5) and (6). The code used is described below:

Matlab Code:
```
x = 0:0.1:1;
y = 500:50:1000;
Bar(x, y)
Figure, plot(x, y)
```

In this section, we are trying to verify the truth of our mathematical model by exporting the model the Matlab. The result is illustrated in Fig. 7. The result is almost identical to that outlined by mathematical function.

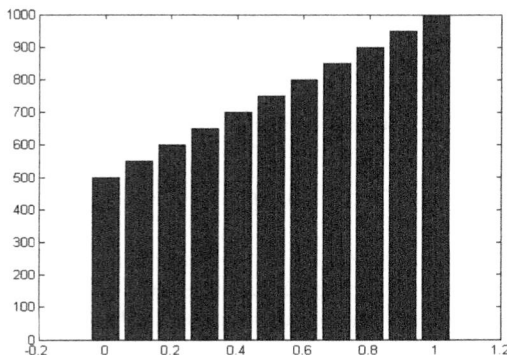

Fig. 7. MATLAB result: number of calls and probability of rejection

6 Result and Conclusion

For evaluation of AIPC mechanism, different test cases are implemented on sender side, with and without Overload scenarios. During no overload condition, there will no probability of rejection.

The AIPC will starts as the number of incoming request exceeds the Lower threshold. Figures 8 and 9 illustrates the effect of Probability of rejection on number of incoming requests. There is slight increase in the projection of rejection with the increase in the incoming request.

Figure 8 also illustrates the percentage reduction in the number of requests with the probability of rejection with variable difference of 0.1. The slope in the figure represents the variance in the reduction of incoming requests with the probability of rejection.

Sender side will reduce the rate of transmission or simply the number of request sent to the overloaded server as the Lower threshold is exceeded. The transmission rate is thus adjusted in accordance with the Table 1. No request will be entertained beyond the upper threshold. Table 1 represent the effect of probabilistic factor I on the outgoing request.

For smooth working of the AIPC mechanism, the triggering policies are based on the response messages i.e. the AIPC is revoked on sender side till the overload response

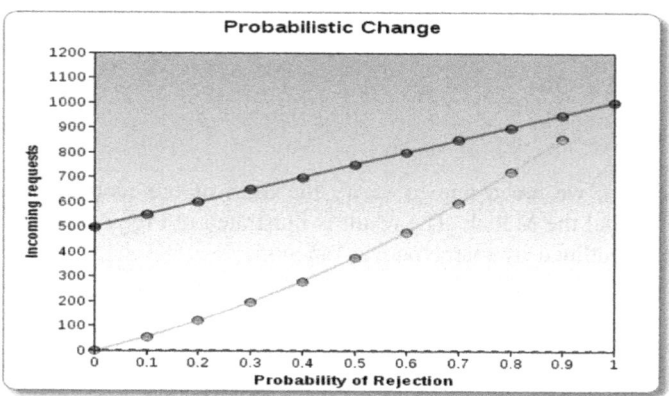

Fig. 8. Probabilistic change: incoming calls vs. probability of rejection

is received on the sender side. It will automatically start increasing the rate of transmission linearly thereafter.

Figure 9 illustrates the effect of AIPC mechanism on the rate of transmission at
sender side. It clear stated from the figure that the sending rate is inversely proportional
to the probabilistic factor. Only the initials requests i.e. INVITE messages are dropped
by the AIPC mechanism at the sender side. This will not only reduce the load on the
overloaded server but also reduce the number of resources required to process theses
requests. It is because of the fact that a successful INVITE message is followed by two
more consecutive in-dialog messages viz. ACK and BYE.

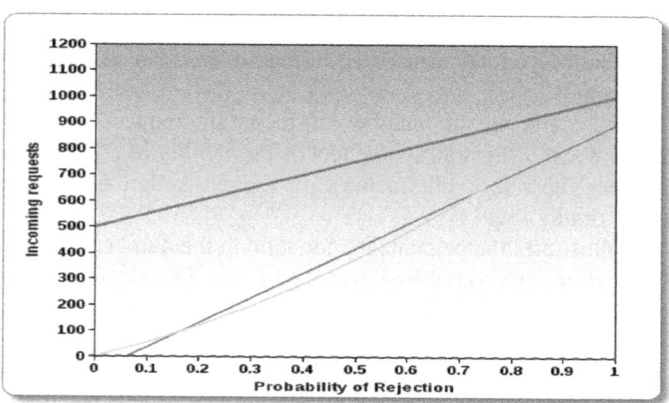

Fig. 9. Probability of rejection

Tables

The table represents the effect of PoR on the outgoing request at sender side.

Table 1. PoR-outgoing-rejected- request response

Prob. of rejection	Outgoing requests	Rejected requests
0	500	0
0.2	600	120
0.4	700	280
0.6	800	480
0.8	900	720
1	1000	1000

6.1 Conclusion

We observed, in our findings, that dropping the INVITE requests at sender side, not only save the resources required for handling the requests but also reduce the extra load on the Server as well. During an interoperability event, we measured the performance of our server using a professional performance measurement tool and our server was able to fully saturate the tool.

Hence, we conclude that:

- INVITE requests are followed by another two requests viz. ACK & BYE. Rejecting them before processing will save resources required to handle these request.
- Initial request are rejected at sender side. Server side perform monitoring task.
- The mathematical model proposed, gives identical outcomes with that of Matlab results.

The curve analysis shows that AIPC mechanism performs better during the overload condition. The analysis is based on comparison between the previous and current simulation along with the mathematical model.

6.2 Future Work

Our future can extend to analyze the working of AIPC mechanism in various types of attacks. Also, there is need to define appropriate triggering policies for enhancement tuning and to obtain customized result.

References

1. Dacosta, I., Balasubramaniyan, V., Ahamad, M., Traynor, P.: Improving authentication performance of distributed SIP proxies. IEEE Trans. Parallel Distrib. Syst. **22**(11), 1804–1812 (2011)
2. Bansal, A., Kulkarni, P., Pais, A.R.: Effectiveness of SIP messages on SIP server. In: IEEE Conference on Information & Communication Technologies (ICT) (2013)

3. Hilt, V., Widjaja, I., Malas, D., Schulzrinne, H.: Session Initiation Protocol (SIP) Overload Control. Internet draft, February 2008. Work in progress
4. Schulzrine, H., Rosenberg, J.: The session initiation protocol: internet-centric signalling. IEEE Commun. Mag. **38**, 134–141 (2000)
5. Rosenberg, J.: Requirements for Management of Overload in the Session Initiation Protocol. RFC 5390, December 2008
6. Hilt, V., Widjaja, I.: Controlling overload in networks of SIP servers. In: IEEE International Conference on Network Protocols, ICNP 2008. IEEE (2008)
7. Gu, Y., Hong, X., Grossman, R.: An analysis of AIMD algorithms with decreasing increases. In: Proceedings of GridNets 2004 (2004)
8. Poretsky, S., Gurbani, V., Davids, C.: Terminology for Benchmarking Session Initiation Protocol (SIP) Networking Devices. Wiley, Hoboken (2009). Dorgham Sisalem, John Floroiu, Ulrich Abend, Henning Schulzrinne
9. Voznak, M., Rozhon, J.: SIP end to end performance metrics. Int. J. Math. Comput. Simul. **6**, 315–323 (2012)
10. Kuschnig, R., Kofler, I., Hellwagner, H.: Improving internet video streaming performance by parallel TCP-based request-response streams. In: 2010 7th IEEE Consumer Communications and Networking Conference (CCNC) (2010)
11. Manda, R.N., Auguste, R.A.: Proposed mathematical model for a SIP call. IEEE (2012)
12. Rohricht, M., Bless, R.: Advanced quality-of-service signalling for the session initiation protocol (SIP). In: Workshop on Telecommunications: From Research to Standards. IEEE (2012)
13. http://www.boray.se/software/averagecpu/
14. http://www.asteriskwin32.com/
15. http://sipp.sourceforge.net/
16. http://startrinity.com/VoIP/SipTester/SipTester.as

A Novel Approach to Detect and Mitigate Cache Side Channel Attack in Cloud Environment

Bharati S. Ainapure[1(✉)], Deven Shah[2], and A. Ananda Rao[1]

[1] JNTU, Anantapur, Andra Pradesh, India
ainapuressa@gmail.com, akepogu@gmail.com
[2] Thakur College of Engineering, Mumbai, Maharashtra, India
sir.deven@gmail.com

Abstract. Multiple instances of virtual machines can run on a single physical host sharing hardware and software resources in cloud computing. One of the resources that is shared among multiple Virtual Machines (VM) in the cloud is Cache. Such Virtual machines are targeted for an abnormal activity like side channel attack. Cache-based side channel attack is one of the side channel attack in cloud environment which leaks the private information of the client. The proposed approach includes the detection and mitigation of cache-based side channel attack in cloud infrastructure. The proposed approach comprises of three components: a collection of virtual machine status, the Fuzzy controller to detect attack and mitigation. The fuzzy rule-based controller is incorporated in this approach to identify the cache-attack on the log file. This system works dynamically to prevent cache attacks on the cloud environment and will incur very small overhead in performance.

Keywords: Fuzzy controller · Cloud computing · Cache
Cache side channel attack · Virtual machine · Hypervisor

1 Introduction

Cloud computing facilitates the multiple clients to share physical resources over the internet. Such clients in a cloud environment are called multi-tenant clients. Multi-tenant clients run in a cloud environment with the help of Virtualization. Virtualization is accomplished in a cloud environment with the help of Hypervisor. It is software that helps the cloud provider to run multiple clients on the single physical machine. When we create and run multiple virtual machines (VM) in a cloud environment, it is called as multi-tenancy. The multi-tenancy, where sharing of resources is provided, leads to the security problem [17]. Cache memory is one of resource which is shared among multiple users. This resource adds new surface attack called cache-based side channel in the cloud. It is challenging task to prevent such attacks in the cloud because cloud runs on resource sharing concept.

Cache memory one of the components present in the computer. It the smallest and fastest memory compared to another memory component present in the computer. Cache memory is present between the primary memory and processor. Whenever the

© Springer Nature Singapore Pte Ltd. 2018
P. Bhattacharyya et al. (Eds.): NGCT 2017, CCIS 828, pp. 361–370, 2018.
https://doi.org/10.1007/978-981-10-8660-1_27

data need to be processed, the processor first checks into the cache memory for data, because it is time-consuming to get the data from main memory. The main memory access is very slow compared to the processor speed. Therefore the cache memory is introduced. Depending upon the architecture of the processor, the cache memory is present in multiple levels. Figure 1 shows the three levels of cache memory. These are named as L1, L2, and L3. L3 is the last level cache which is shared among all the cores present in that processor.

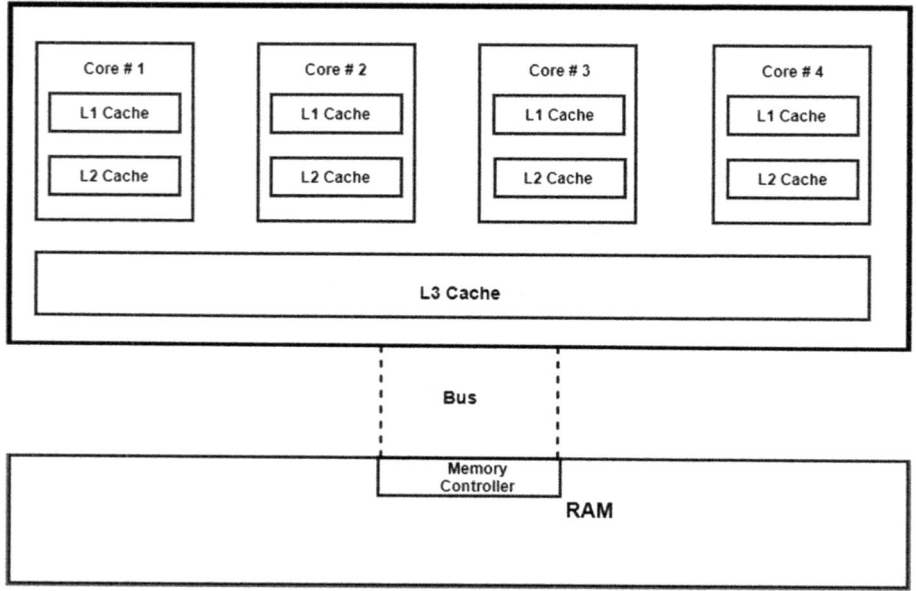

Fig. 1. Cache memory hierarchy

Two effects are going occur when CPU tries to access the data or instruction from cache: cache hit or cache miss. As depicted in Fig. 1, CPU will first check into the L1 level cache for data, if a data is found CPU experiences cache hit and it will proceed for processing otherwise cache miss will occur, and the CPU checks for next level of cache that is L2. The cache miss is experienced in L2 by CPU then it searches for next level that L3. If the cache miss continued in L3 also which is the last level, then CPU refers the data from the main memory which will cause the delay to load the data into all level of cache and to process. The delay caused by cache miss will invite the adversaries to guess what is happening and to perform cache attack.

The cache-based attack is performed in a cloud environment by placing the attacker VM on the same core where the target VM is running, so that cache is shared between these two. Figure 1 shows the configuration at cloud provider's end, where multiple VMs are allowed to run in same core sharing the cache. In this situation, if attacker machine is placed with the target then, an attacker can easily perform the attack. For the first time, in 2000, J. Kelsey & etl., in their publication mentioned about the cache based side channel attack based on the cache hit ratio [1]. In general CPU cache is shared in two different ways: sequentially or parallelly. In sequential access, two VMs must access cache one after the other [2] and in parallel two VMs are allowed access the cache simultaneously.

As mentioned above, the CPU accesses data from the cache, if the required data is not found in the cache, then a cache miss occurs [16]. The cache miss causes the delay to load the data from memory into cache. This delay gives scope to the attacker to attack the cache. The occurrence and frequency of cache misses are measured by attackers to perform the cache-based attacks. This technique of measuring the delay due to a cache miss is called as cache-based side channel attack.

The remaining sections of this paper are organized as follows. The literature review is mentioned in Sect. 2. System overview and four different inputs for the fuzzy controller are explained in Sect. 3. Section 4 presents the cache-attack detection and mitigation using the fuzzy system. Experimental results and comparative analysis of the existing system and the outcome of the proposed approach is explained in Sect. 5. Lastly, in Sect. 6 conclusion of this paper presented.

2 Literature Review

This section discusses researcher's approach and different techniques used to perform the cache-attack and their mitigation.

Twofold cache-based side channel attack mitigation strategies at the server side are proposed, in which one focused on an algorithm which handles sequential occurrences of side channels it also minimized the overhead. The other defense focused on coloring technique on parallel side-channels to prevent the occurrence of side channel's and also enhances the cache efficiency. Here, the cache was flushed between the prime and trigger. Thus, the implemented defenses could prevent the side-channel attacks. However, the process of flushing is time-consuming [2].

The authors had presented a technique that influenced dynamic cache coloring to prove that stealing cryptographic information in the cloud could be a risk by finding a cache-based side-channel attack against an encryption process. Dynamic cache coloring referred to a technique, where the VMM was informed of changing the related data to a cache line which is a safe one. This approach had reduced cache-based side-channel but introduced the performance overhead. The performance reduces in cache isolation while returning pages when the protection system is stopped [3].

CSDA was proposed, to detect cache-based side channel attacks and, thereby, reduce the security threat in the cloud based on the side channel effects in resource utilization. The technique was proposed in two modes: first is host detection and second is fast detection, which combined two tests, shape, and regularity tests to mine the features that attack from hosts and guests. In this proposed method the malicious VMs from the original VMs are differentiated using pattern reorganization algorithm. However, the test based detection techniques degrade the performance [4].

The above mentioned all proposed research include hardware based or software based solution to mitigate the cache-based side channel attacks. However, it is challenging to propose a new preventive measure which will not involve any of the overhead and without altering any hardware component. So, the proposed approach deals with the cache side channel in a cloud environment, which collects system calls in the form of logs from virtual machines running on the same hypervisor. These system calls are used to record the Input/Output operation carried out by virtual machines. This system call collector is supposed to run at the hypervisor level. There are many suitable, system call tracer tools which are available to run at cloud environment. Few of such tools are explained as below.

Nitro is virtual machine introspection (VMI) tool based on hardware System Call Tracing [5]. It is integrated with KVM hypervisor to monitor the VMs. for Virtual Machines. It is hardware-based system call tracing and monitoring tool. Intel x86 architecture provided three different types of system calls are traced by this tool. During monitoring of VM, this tool collects the information of systems calls. The information collected is raw bits, and then this tool converts these raw bits into human readable form to detect the root kit attacks on VM. The advantage of this tool is that it is able to collect system calls from 64-bit and 32-bit Window and Linux based VMs running on hypervisor [18].

Ether [6] is VMI tool used to detect the malware in the system. It detects malware using system call internally. The configuration of Intel VT technology with this tool detects the malware present in the VMs. Ether runs on XEN hypervisor. It includes three functionalities like tracing of instruction, memory writes, and system calls to detect the malware [18].

LibVMI is the virtual machine introspection tool which is open source. API (application programming interface) present in LibVMI [7] performs the introspection of the virtual machine at a low level. This API makes use of the library which is created using python bindings and C library. All activities of the VM are observed by this tool. It captures the information about registers, hardware events, guest memory and does the analysis. Open source hypervisors like KVM and XEN are used integrate the LibVMI [18].

3   System Overview

The proposed approach incorporates a novel method of identifying the cache based side channel threat criticality over VMs. The prime motive of the undertaken method is to identify the vulnerable VMs considering that Cloud Service Provider is harmless. The system consists of four major components: 1. A malicious user, 2. The target, 3. System calls collector Nitro [5], and 4. Method of detection and mitigation of cache-based side channel attacks, the Fuzzy Controller. To perform cache-based side channel attack, the malicious user has to be placed as co-resident with the target machine [8]. After placing VM as co-resident, the attacker has to establish a side channel with target VM. Then make the cache based side channel attack on the target VM [15]. The system call collector at hypervisor need to collect all system calls as logs, at the time of the system call trap.

The VM running in the cloud environment needs to generate a system call to the hypervisor as shown in Fig. 2. This VM is running in userspace, which does not have any permission to the kernel space commands like input/output (I/O). In this case, if the VM is generating such system calls, then this generates a trap to the hypervisor. So VM exit will occur from user space to kernel space. Then hypervisor records the calls generated by vm exit and VM are allowed to perform I/O in kernel space. Once I/O is executed, then again VM entry is performed, which will return the call back to the user space of VM through the hypervisor.

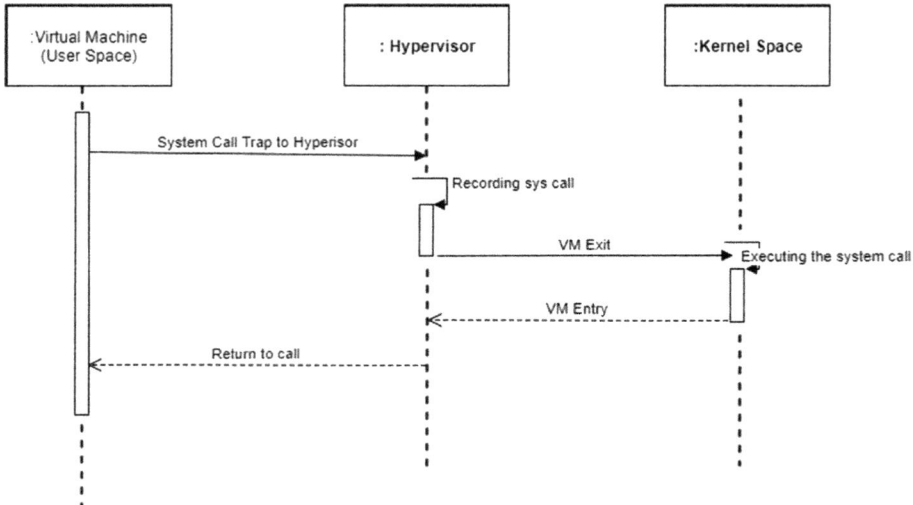

Fig. 2. System call tracking

Detection of cache-based side channel attack can be made by measuring the loads on the cache. The load on the cache is detected using cache access during I/O operations performed by VMs running in the cloud environment. These I/O accessed data are collected by the system call collector which is running on a hypervisor that is outside the VM to protect it from attacks. This system call collector will collect cache load variation in VM. This load variation on cache data collected by system call can be concluded using following three parameters:

Cache data Access (CDA): This feature is used to know the amount cache resource utilized by a user during the data access. If utilization is more means more cache miss which may predict about the attacker, because the attacker's purpose is to let the victim to do more cache misses.

Size of cache data access (SCDA): This feature specifies the amount or space of cache utilized by user. The user one who utilizes large amounts of cache may be identified as an attacker in cloud environment which increases the cache miss rate for legitimate users, as the user tries to consume a large-sized cache.

Cache miss rate: This is one of well know feature to detect cache side-channel attacks. To know the cache contents attacker will continuously read and write cache memory with the help prime and probe operation. This makes cache memory to become evicted frequently resulting into more and more cache misses throughout the attack.

In the next section we will see how we can make use of the above-mentioned parameters to detect the cache-attack in the cloud.

4 Detection and Mitigation of Cache Attack on Cloud

Once the log is collected at the hypervisor level, then this log is used to detect the cache attack using a fuzzy controller as shown in Fig. 3. The fuzzy system consists of fuzzifier, inference engine, defuzzification, and knowledge base rules [14]. The fuzzifier consists of fuzzy sets as follows:

1. Cache data access denoted by CDA
2. The size of cache data access denoted by SCDA
3. Cache Miss is denoted by CM

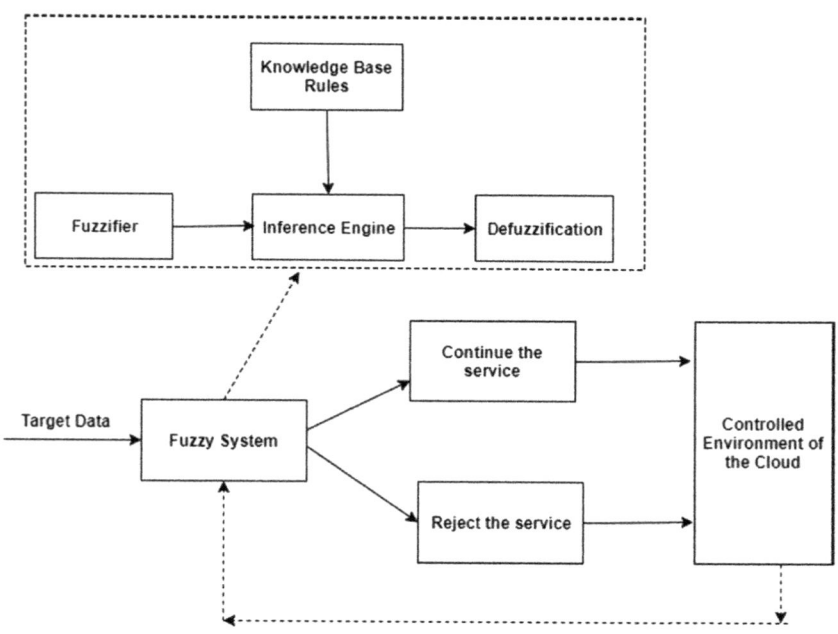

Fig. 3. Fuzzy controller

Each fuzzy set contains members and each member in the fuzzy set is identified with some degree of membership functions. These functions act as input variable and are shown as below:

(i) $CDA = \{Y\}$
(ii) $SCDA = \{S, L\}$
(iii) $CM = \{S, L\}$

Where, Y denotes Yes, S and L denotes Small and Large, respectively, and degree of membership function varies from [0,1]. Depending on the analysis, the variables and the labels can be combined to create rules know as knowledge base rules as given below:

Rule 1: If CDA is Y, $SCDA$ is S, and CM is S, then Continue with a service.
Rule 2: If CDA is Y $SCDA$ is L, and CM is S, then REJECT.
Rule 3: If CDA is Y $SCDA$ is S, and CM is L, then REJECT.
Rule 4: If CDA is Y $SCDA$ is L, and CM is L, then REJECT.

The mathematical representation of Rule 1 consists of AND operation, so {min} value of the membership function values of both the fuzzy sets should be considered for decision. Therefore the following equation holds:

$$\mu(\overline{cda} \cap \overline{scda} \cap \overline{cm}(x)) = min\left(\mu_{\overline{cda}}(x), \mu_{\overline{scda}}(x), \mu_{\overline{cm}}(x)\right), \forall x \in \quad (1)$$

Mathematical representation of Rule 2,3 and four consists of OR operation, so {max} value of the membership values of both the fuzzy sets should be taken into consideration. Therefore the following equations apply.

$$\mu(\overline{cda} \cup \overline{scda} \cup \overline{cm}(x)) = max\left(\mu_{\overline{cda}}(x), \mu_{\overline{scda}}(x), \mu_{\overline{cm}}(x)\right), \forall \in X \quad (2)$$

$$\mu(\overline{cda} \cup \overline{scda} \cup \overline{cm}(x)) = max\left(\mu_{\overline{cda}}(x), \mu_{\overline{scda}}(x), \mu_{\overline{cm}}(x)\right), \forall x \in X \quad (3)$$

$$\mu(\overline{cda} \cup \overline{scda} \cup \overline{cm}(x)) = max\left(\mu_{\bar{a}}(x), \mu_{\overline{scda}}(x), \mu_{\overline{cm}}(x)\right), \forall x \in X \quad (4)$$

Where 'x' is the value for the membership function of the fuzzy sets.

This knowledge base rules can be defined as a matrix form as follows:

The first rule states that if CDA is Yes, is Small and CM is small, the fuzzy system decides that the user is a genuine user. Hence, the system continues with the process. The statement in rule 2, 3, and 4 suggests that, when CDA is Yes, $SCDA$ is Large and CM is LArge, the one who accesses the cloud is an attacker, as the user tries to consume a large-sized cache and more cache miss. Therefore, the fuzzy system rejects the process of communication (Table 1).

Table 1. Fuzzy rule matrix

Rule no.	CDA	SCDA	CM	Decision reject/continue
1	Y	S	S	Continue
2	Y	L	S	Reject
3	Y	S	L	Reject
4	Y	L	L	Reject

The fuzzy logic system will produce output in the form of defuzzification which is crisp set. This crisp set is used to mitigate the cache-attack by continuing the service of the process by providing data access to the cloud user or reject the process.

5 Experimental Results and Discussion

The results of the proposed work are simulated using a simulator tool, cloudsim. Cloudsim is executed in a system operated with 64-bit Windows 8 operating system and Intel processor running inside, with 4 GB of RAM. The well-known parameter accuracy is used to calculate the degree of performance of the proposed work. It defines the closeness of a value measured to a standard value as,

$$Accuracy = \frac{TP + TN}{TP + TN + FP + FN}$$

Where, True Positive, TP identifies the correct cache attacker, TN is True Negative, used to identify the genuine users as attackers, FP is False Positive, which is falsely identified as the attacker, and FN is False Negative, which identifies the falsely genuine users as attackers.

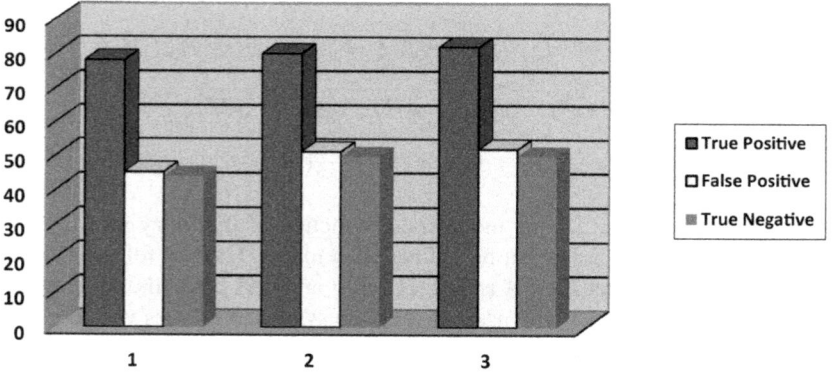

Fig. 4. Accuracy graph

Figure 4 show the accuracy of the proposed methodology measured for time instants 10, 20, and 30 secs. The maximum true positive accuracy is achieved at the time interval of 30 secs. with 82.16% of actual attackers in a cloud environment.

Table 2 shows a comparison of true positive detection of attack with two existing techniques [2, 4]. The proposed solution is independent of any operating system and no need to make any changes to the hardware. Overall comparisons show that the proposed approach is more efficient and effective offering better results for cache-based security.

Table 2. Performance analysis

Techniques	Detection accuracy
Michael Godfrey, etl.	73%
Si Yu, etl.	62%
Proposed approach	82.16%

6 Conclusion

Multi-tenancy property of the cloud has proved many side channel attacks in cloud environment. The side channel attacks are not new, but these are proved long back only, but due to sharing of resources in cloud environment, these attacks have gained more attention. The proposed approach identifies the cache based side channel attack and its mitigation on a cloud using a fuzzy controller. This proposed fuzzy controller makes decisions whether the user is an attacker or a legitimate user. Four different fuzzy rules used to categorize the attackers and genuine user. These rules are formed in the fuzzy controller using the input values of cache data access, the size of the cache data access, and cache miss ratio. The experimental results prove that we can reduce the true positive and false positive ratio to identify the true attacker and genuine user. The proposed approach could attain a maximum of 75.33% genuine user details, 76.19% attacker details, and 75.18% of accuracy. However, n future we are planning to add more fuzzy based rules to prevent all levels of cache attacks as this work is handling only last level cache attacks.

References

1. Kelsey, J., Schneier, B., Wagner, D., Hall, C.: Side channel cryptanalysis of product ciphers. J. Comput. Secur. **8**(2–3), 141–158 (2000)
2. Godfrey, M., Zulkernine, M.: Preventing cache-based side-channel attacks in a cloud environment. IEEE Trans. Cloud Comput. **2**(4), 395–408 (2015)
3. Shi, J., Song, X., Chen, H., Zang, B.: Limiting cache-based side-channel in the multi-tenant cloud using the dynamic page coloring. In: Proceedings of International Conference on Dependable Systems and Network shops, pp. 194–199 (2011)
4. Yu, S., Gui, X., Lin, J.: An approach with two-stage mode to detect cache-based side channel attacks. In: Proceedings of International Conference on Information Networking, pp. 186–191 (2013)
5. Pfoh, J., Schneider, C., Eckert, C.: Nitro: hardware-based system call tracing for virtual machines. In: Iwata, T., Nishigaki, M. (eds.) IWSEC 2011. LNCS, vol. 7038, pp. 96–112. Springer, Heidelberg (2011). https://doi.org/10.1007/978-3-642-25141-2_7
6. Dinaburg, A., Royal, P., Sharif, M., Lee, W.: Ether: malware analysis via hardware virtualization extensions. In: Proceedings of the 15th ACM Conference on Computer and communications security, pp. 51–62. ACM, New York (2008)
7. Payne, B.D.: Simplifying Virtual Machine Introspection Using LibVMI. Sandia National Laboratories No. SAND 2012–7818 (2012)
8. Ristenpart, T., Tromer, E., Shacham, H., Savage, S.: Hey, you, get off of my cloud: exploring information leakage in third-party compute clouds. In: CCS, pp. 199–212 (2009)

9. Acıiçmez, O., Brumley, B.B., Grabher, P.: New results on instruction cache attacks. In: Mangard, S., Standaert, F.-X. (eds.) CHES 2010. LNCS, vol. 6225, pp. 110–124. Springer, Heidelberg (2010). https://doi.org/10.1007/978-3-642-15031-9_8

10. Aciiçmez, O., Koç, Ç., Seifert, J.: On the power of simple branch prediction analysis. In: Proceedings of the 2nd ACM Symposium on Information, Computer and Communications Security, ASIACCS 2007 (2007)

11. Yarom, Y., Falkner, K.: FLUSH + RELOAD: a high resolution low noise, l3 cache side-channel attack. In: 23rd USENIX Security Symposium (USENIX Security 2014), pp. 719–732. USENIX Association, San Diego, August 2014

12. Osvik, D.A., Shamir, A., Tromer, E.: Cache attacks and countermeasures: the case of AES. In: Pointcheval, D. (ed.) CT-RSA 2006. LNCS, vol. 3860, pp. 1–20. Springer, Heidelberg (2006). https://doi.org/10.1007/11605805_1

13. Liu, F., Lee, R.B.: Security testing of a secure cache design. In: Proceedings of the 2nd International Workshop on Hardware and Architectural Support for Security and Privacy - HASP 2013, New York (2013)

14. Zimmermann, H.J.: Introduction to fuzzy sets. In: Zimmermann, H.J. (ed.) Fuzzy Set Theory —and Its Applications. Springer, Dordrecht (1991). https://doi.org/10.1007/978-94-015-7949-0_1

15. Wu, Z., Xu, Z., Wang, H.: Whispers in the hyper-space: high-speed covert channel attacks in the cloud. In: USENIX Security, p. 9 (2012)

16. Canteaut, A., Lauradoux, C., Seznec, A.: Understanding cache attacks. Technical report, April 2006. ftp://ftp.inria.fr/INRIA/publication/publi-pdf/RR/RR-5881.pdf

17. Ainapure, B.S., Shah, D., Rao, A.A.: Understanding perception of cache-based side-channel attack on cloud environment. In: Sa, P.K., Sahoo, M.N., Murugappan, M., Wu, Y., Majhi, B. (eds.) Progress in Intelligent Computing Techniques: Theory, Practice, and Applications. AISC, vol. 519, pp. 9–21. Springer, Singapore (2018). https://doi.org/10.1007/978-981-10-3376-6_2

18. Ainapure, B.S., Shah, D., Rao, A.A.: Performance analysis of virtual machine introspection tools in cloud environment. In: Proceedings of the International Conference on Informatics and Analytics, ICIA 2016, Article No. 27. ACM digital library (2016)

Normalized Scores for Routes in MANET to Analyze and Detect Collaborative Blackhole Attack

Abhishek Bajpai and Shivangi Nigam[(✉)]

SRM University, Barabanki 225003, India
abhishek.srmu@gmail.com, shivi.nigam15@gmail.com

Abstract. The divergent Ad-hoc network environs are exposed to various intrusions and threats like Black hole and Gray hole. These intrusions are hard to detect as the intruders attract the traffic of the network behaving as a legitimate node of the network. The traditional AODV protocol is unable to provide security from such attacks. This research work attempts to add security aspects to the traditional AODV by providing aid to the source node in route selection for an efficient communication. A route normalization scheme (NRS-RH) is proposed which helps in appropriate route selection by providing rank to various routes. The research study has reduced computational overhead as compared to various schemes with a significant increase in packet delivery ratio and throughput.

Keywords: Black hole attack · Gray hole attack · Malicious · Routing
Ad-hoc On Demand Distance Vector

1 Introduction

Mobile Ad-hoc network (MANET) is a meshwork of mobile entities with heterogeneous capabilities communicating in a highly dynamic topology. The mobility of the nodes continuously is the reason for these dynamic changes in topology. This comes with lots of challenges to be considered for an effective and secure communication among these mobile entities. The infrastructureless network makes decentralization the major challenge in deploying this network. The routing protocols have been proposed to make the most out of the least characteristics of MANET as low powered mobile entities and less processing capabilities. Still they are not up to the mark regarding the network parameters as Packet Delivery ratio, Throughput, End-to-End delay etc. There are many security breaches in the standard protocols for MANET as they do not take the dynamic network attacks into consideration. Some of the major attacks as Blackhole attack, Grayhole attack, Wormhole attack and DoS attacks are the major intrusions [1]. All these intrusions attract the traffic of the network and perform various malicious activities as the denial of service (DoS). The most widely used routing algorithm Ad-hoc On Demand Distance Vector (AODV) also doesn't secure the network from these intrusions when they get inside the network.

© Springer Nature Singapore Pte Ltd. 2018
P. Bhattacharyya et al. (Eds.): NGCT 2017, CCIS 828, pp. 371–380, 2018.
https://doi.org/10.1007/978-981-10-8660-1_28

1.1 AODV Overview

The AODV protocol was proposed for MANET to discover the route from the source to destination at the instant the source wants to communicate with it [2, 3]. The source node (SN) maintains the route information of the previous communications. It checks it information for the destined route and sends a Route Request (RREQ) to all its neighbors. The route discovery process starts when none of the neighbors have a route to the destination mentioned in the RREQ. The RREQ packet is send with Source IP, Destination IP, and Sequence Number (latest sequence number saved with source for this destination). The intermediate nodes (IN) check for the route to the destination node (DN) and if the route is found an Route Reply (RREP) packet is sent with the route information and the sequence number (SQN) for that route. RREP packet comprise of Source IP, Destination IP, Hop Count and destination Sequence Number. If no route found with IN, it sends the request to its neighbors and gradually it reaches the destination. When the destination receives the RREQ packet it increments its sequence number and replies with the RREP packet with updated information. The RREP follows the same route the respective RREQ came from and the hop count is incremented at every intermediate node up to the SN. The SN then search for the route with the highest SQN and minimum Hop count.

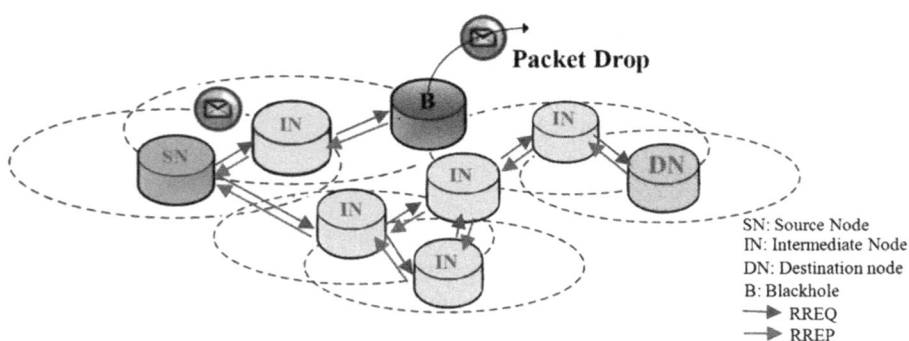

Fig. 1. Blackhole attack in MANET

1.2 Black Hole Attack in MANET

The assumptions of AODV that all the communicating entities are well-mannered and no malicious activity is there in MANET make it vulnerable to security threats. The major threat Black hole attack is a DoS variant where the services from source to destination are affected due to the falsification of Identity [4–8]. The black hole node pretends as the destined node of communication and thus falsely attracts the data packets from the source node. The black hole sends the RREP with a fake IP address that may or may not exist in the network. It sends a randomly chosen high SQN so that the SN considers the route as the fresh one. It sits closer to the SN so that the hop count is minimum for the route and thus maliciously behaves as a false DN. The SN chooses this node for further communication and it drops all the packets it receives. The black hole when performing as independent is called Single Black hole. It more worse when the black holes are more in numbers and they cooperate to perform Collaborative Black hole attack. A variant of this attack is Gray hole attack which performs similarly. The variation is that the gray hole transfers only some of the traffic and discarding the rest. The Fig. 1 illustrates the instance of MANET under Black hole attack.

2 Research Work

The study in [1] presents a significant scrutiny of the research towards Black hole attack detection. It presents various aspects of the schemes in terms of Network Synchronization models as Synchronous and asynchronous networks, Communication models for the communication among the mobile agents meant to analyze the network and perform related computations. The models of communication as used in various studies for black hole attack detection are Whiteboard Model, Pure token model, Enhanced token model and Face to Face model. The research examines the network parameters such as topology, size and direction with respect to the agent requirement for efficient black hole detection. There has been no use of the Whiteboard Model, Enhanced token model for the BH detection in Synchronous networks but the Face to Face model and Pure token model solutions have been explored.

The research in [2] considers routing attacks and other security concerns in MANET. The authors also present the concerning aspects of various recent approaches in the field. The security issues considered are as Wormhole attack, black hole attack, DoS attacks, Spoofing Attacks.

Other Review studies regarding the AODV protocol for BH detection is presented in [3, 4]. These present a structured review of the various existing schemes and also present an analysis over the comparison with other routing protocols such as DSR. The analysis reveals that although the AODV is much more prone to the BH attack than DSR, AODV has better adaptation to the dynamic network parameters. Kumar et al. 2016 modifies the AODV in MANET with a swarm optimization for BH detection.

The author [5] categorizes the various approaches to solve black hole attack into 3 categories as Fidelity, Data Routing information and Trust based schemes. The effects of various schemes have also been listed out. The proposed scheme uses the previous data about the black hole nodes. The scheme proposed takes as input the Average Destination Sequence Number (ADSN) and the Black Hole list prepared previously. The scheme proposed has a reduced overhead as compared to the existing solutions.

The research study in [6] percept the black hole attack to be reactive and proactive on the basis of weather the Blackhole node receives the RREP messages or it generates them behaving as the legitimate intermediate node. The proactive BH attack can detected just by performing a check at every node to see if the RREP message was actually send by the host in the message. The study does extensive simulations to study the effect of SQN to the percentage of win by the BH nodes. Then Cumulative Sum (CUSUM) test provide information about any significant changes in the SQN.

The scheme results in high accuracy regarding the BH detection with low computations.

Praveen et al., [7] in his study presents a comparison among the AODV and OLSR protocols in MANET with and without a Black hole attack. The network behaviour is observed under two parameters as Packet delivery ratio and Throughput of the network. The simulations results show that OLSR have better PDR in case of no attack but AODV outperforms the throughput in case of a BH attack.

The study in [8] provides a GA based security solution for all the dynamic network attacks as black hole attack etc. The Solution is inspired by the behaviour of the E.coli bacteria which performs 2 behaviors as Swim and Tumble. Where swim (Node navigating the network for acquiring network information) requires Low power low security (LPLS), Tumble (node not performing up to the mark) requires High power High security (HPHS) as it may be a normal node or a BH node outperforming its duties. The proposed work adds up the security in GA by encrypting the messages by Three Pass Protocol (TPP) which reduces the communication overhead of the key exchange among the nodes in communication. The GABFO TPP is compared to existing methods as IPv4, SecIPv4, IPv6 and IPv6 for a wide variety of nodes as from Wireless sensors to the mobile nodes. Security is measured by Hackman tool where Genetic Algorithm based Bacterial Forage Optimization - Three Pass Protocol GABFO TPP outperforms the security and power consumption test for wide variants of dynamic attacks.

The scheme [9] here considers two parameters of AODV routing for communication among nodes as Response sequence (ResS) and Code Sequence (CodS). The ResS is sent in reply to the CodS request from the source of intermediate node for establishing the connection. The scheme discards the request packets with very high CodS by analyzing the CodS from various neighbors received.

The research [10] modifies the current AODV protocol for Routing in MANET for reducing the black hole attacks in MANET. Similar to above approach it analyze the received sequence numbers but here the source waits only for a predefined period of time. The simulations results report a drop of 60% on the black hole attacks and also a significant increase in throughput.

Other BH detecting techniques modifying AODV routing protocol are as studied recently. Arora and Monga [11] provide a combined solution for black hole and worm hole attack by keeping track of the Round Trip Time (RTT) of the packets in communication. Another approach by Rani and Kaur [12] propose the use of counter variables one for RREP send and for RREC receive. The unequal comparison of these values indicates a BH node. An indexing scheme for the nodes in MANET for BH detection is proposed by [13]. There is threshold value for the index computed for every node as the number of packets transmitted successfully. The index value decreases on packet drop. The invalid nodes are detected on a negative index value. A study by [14] provide single BH attack detection by using extra details with the RREQ packet to denote the identity of the node thus identifying if any Black hole. Similar to this approach, the research in [15] the extra detail of the nodes is maintained as Data routing information (DRI) table for further cross checking. It provide efficient detection scheme for Collaborative BH detection. Table 1 provides an overview of various approaches.

These schemes did not provide solutions for the gray hole attack which is considered by [16] although Cooperative Gray hole attacks still not considered. The node

Table 1. Relevant recent research works for Blackhole detection in MANET

Research Method	Intrusion Schemes	Research Observation/Defects
Comparison of existing schemes	Wormhole, Blackhole, DoS, Spoofing Attacks.	• Static tables kept by the networks can be accessed by malicious nodes. • Shared keys and Time stamping, Node Signatures can prevent spoofing attack but are still prone to Wormhole attack. • Neighbour node authentication may prevent many attacks from malicious node but still can have DoS attacks. • With strong cryptographic features also the network may be prone to tunnelling and wormhole attacks but make the Blackhole attacks as impossible.

Comparison of existing schemes	Black hole attack	• The problem of multiple black hole detection found to be unsolvable and NP Hard under various aspects. The solutions found are always under some restrictions.
		• In a synchronous network,
		  ▪ Complexity of the problem as presented by various significant studies under Face to Face model and Pure token model is discussed.
		  ▪ Under the Pure token model, Movable tokens found to be more cost effective than unmovable token.
		• In an asynchronous network
		  ▪ Co-located agents with network map in pure token models may positively detect BH attack with a ping-pong technique.
		  ▪ Enhanced token model have greater cost in unknown network cases.
		  ▪ Considering the restriction imposed on other model, Whiteboard model still mostly opted for asynchronous networks.

D-MBH	Single and collaborative black hole	• Not useful for a new network setup. It uses apriori data. • Does not consider black nodes sending the DSN below ADSN. • The scheme has risk of black hole attacks at initial levels. • Storage Overhead.
CUM SUM	Single and collaborative black hole	• The study excludes the intensive BH attacks as just detecting the SQN may not be fruitful as the attacker may be aware of the underlying scheme and can act smartly.
AODV Vs. OLSR RP	Single black hole	• The study has a very narrow domain of the Black hole perspective. • It does not take network parameters into consideration.
GABFO TPP	Dynamic Attacks	• No specific solution for black hole attack detection. • Network parameters as PDR, End to End delay and throughput not considered. • Overhead of encryption with private key cryptography.
Analyzing SQN	Gray hole and BH attack	• The scheme assumes that the malicious nodes are the first one to reply. May not be always true. • Storage overhead for storing all the CodS and Computation overhead of performing analysis. • The scheme presents a straitened solution to the problem of BH detection disregarding the discrepancies of dynamic network parameters as PDR, End-to-End delay and throughput.
Analyzing SQN	Black hole attacks	• Storage and computation overhead. • The scheme pre assumes some significant parameters which are dynamic in a real scenario.

when receiving an unknown IP address sends artificial packets to the destination and the neighboring node observe the communication.

Different variants of cryptographic solutions have been proposed but these methodologies have its cons of computational overhead. The study in [17] gives a RSA based solution for observing SQN and detecting single BH attack.

The research as reviewed in this section reveals that finding a generic solution to the problem of Collaborative Black hole attack as well as the Gray hole attack is a NP problem. All the above solutions have some restrained boundaries for the desired out-turns. This research study proposes a solution for collaborative black hole attacks and gray hole attack by minimizing the inhibitions imposed. The further sections discuss the proposed scheme and analyze the approach for the desired objectives of the research.

3   Proposed Work

The prerequisites of a diverse MANET necessitate a dynamic security provision to cover varied dimensions of the network. The Black hole and Gray hole attack exploit these dynamic traits to attract the data packets from a source node towards itself to perform its malicious activities. The proposed provision provide security from these intrusions by computing the rank of destination nodes by Normalized Rank Scheme NRS ($\check{D}$: SQNDes,) which takes as input the Destination Vector $\check{D}$ and their respective Sequence numbers SQN_{Des}. A threshold value is defined for checking the legitimacy of nodes in communication [18]. The NoR values outside this threshold limit are considered as the dubious nodes. The NoR of the destination nodes are received by the source nodes which in turn are used to Compute Route Honesty RoH of various routes discovered by the AODV paradigm. The RoH parameters are forwarded to the neighbor nodes to update their routing tables. Since these nodes are not in the list of Black hole nodes, it's given a chance to prove if it's a legitimate node. To perform this check a spurious message is send to the nodes and the communication is observed for various network parameters as packet drop, end to end delay and throughput of the network. On positive observation results, the node is marked for latter observations otherwise it is listed as a Blackhole and is then discarded from the nodes involved in the Route Discovery Process.

3.1   Normalized Rank Based Route Honesty Computation

The proposed scheme redefines the route selection process in the AODV routing protocol. The source node (SN) performs route discovery process by sending the Route request (RREQ) packets with the destination ID to all the neighboring nodes which then further sends the packets after checking if the packet was intended for the current node. Multiple RREQ packets reach the destination. The destination replies all requests as a RREP with the Sequence number (SQN_{Des}) and Hop Count (HopC) as 0. Each intermediate nodes increment the HopC by one until it reaches the source node. Now the SN starts the Route selection process on the set of varied SQN_{Des} received from a DN. The RoH for every route is incremented by one (For any new routes, RoH initializes as zero). The scheme assumes multiple Blackhole in the network thus considering the Collaborative Blackhole attack. All the SQN_{Des} received comprise a single destination vector $\check{D}$ for the current SN – DN communication. The NRS starts with computing the Expected value E (SQN_{Des}) for destination vector $\check{D}$. The difference of the SQN_{Des} and its respective E (SQN_{Des}) divided by the error probability gives the NoR. The SN selects the node with NoR 3.5 and HopC minimum. It also increments RoH by one. All the routes with NoH > 3.5 are considered Dubious. The SN sends a spurious packet to the dubious nodes and its RoH reduced by two. If the packet transfer is successful the RoH is incremented by one. These nodes are considered under observation for the next communication. When the RoH of nodes equals zero or is negative the nodes are listed as Blackhole and are discarded from future communications.

3.2   Algorithm for NRS-RHC

Components of NRS-RHC
    SN: Source Node
    DN: Destination node
    RREQ; Route request
    RREP: Route Reply
    HopC: Hop Count
    SQN_{Des}: Sequence Number of Destination
    Ď: Destination Vector
    NoR: Normalised Rank
    RoH: Route Honesty
    σ: Standard Deviation
    ϓ: Probable Error
    $E(SQN_{Des})$: Expected SQN_{Des}
    PRO-C: Proportionality constant (0.6745)

Algorithm NRS-RHC

Route Discovery Process:
1.   SN sends RREQ (D, SQN_{Des}=0) to neighbouring nodes and further until Destination.
2.   DN replies with RREP (HopC, SQN_{Des}) via various RREQ routes.
3.   SN maintains the newly received *(Ď:SQN_{Des},)* and calls *NRS(Ď:SQN_{Des},)*.
4.   Initialize RoH for all routes: RoH := 1.

   Normalized Rank Scheme NRS(Ď:SQN_{Des},)
5.   Loop i:☐ SQN_{Des} in Ď
6. $E(SQN_{Des})_i$:= median| SQN_{Des} |
7. $σ_i(SQN_{Des})$:= $\sqrt{V(SQNDes}$
8. $ϓ_i$:= PRO-C . $σ_i(SQN_{Des})$
9.   NoR := $\frac{|SQNDes - E(SQNDes)i|}{ϓi}$

   Route Honesty Computation RHC(Ď: NoR)
10.   Loop i:☐ SQN_{Des} in Ď
11.   if (NoR ≥ 3.5):
12.   RoH= RoH-2
13.   Node listed as Dubious
14.   else:
15.   RoH= RoH+1
16.   Select DN with min(HopC)
17.   if (RoH ≤ 0)
18.   Node listed as Blackhole

---

4 Implementation and Analysis

The analysis of the proposed work is checked on the parameters Packet Delivery Ratio (PDR), End-to-End Delay and throughput. The proposed scheme analyses the collaborative black hole attack by analyzing the Route honesty of the various routes resulted as the NRS-RHC. The scheme detects any significant variation in the SQN generated by the black hole. It maintains two list of malicious nodes Black hole and dubious node List. The scheme provides multilayer security provision by detecting any malicious activity as dubious node and then observing the route for PDR. The negative results found over some iterations mark the node as Black hole. The two parameters of the scheme as NoR and RoH alarm the occurrence of any malicious activity. Though the activity may not be actually malicious for instance the packets drop may be due to the power failure. This situation is considered by the proposed approach as it does not at the first mark it as black hole. This multilayer approach is fruitful to detect gray hole attacks though this research is not focused on detecting the black hole attack.

Table 2 represents the details of simulation performed with NS3 and packets are analyzed through Wireshark. The results of extensive simulations are presented in the Fig. 2 which depicts the packet delivery ratio of the simulation under various circumstances. The PDR is compared between a normal AODV routing scheme with the other two schemes having multiple black holes. The NRS-RHC shows an improved PDR with respect to the simple AODV. The proposed algorithm inspects the PDR and depicts that this techniques introduces very little computational overhead with respect to other schemes and outperforms the recent schemes for detecting collaborative black hole attack. The overhead increases up to a lower limit after which the computational complexity is constant and thus provides better throughput.

Table 2. Simulation of NRS-RHC

Parameter	Values
Number of nodes	100 (Max)
Radio range	0–100 m
Mobility type	Random Waypoint
Packet size	512 B
Channel capacity	2 Mbps

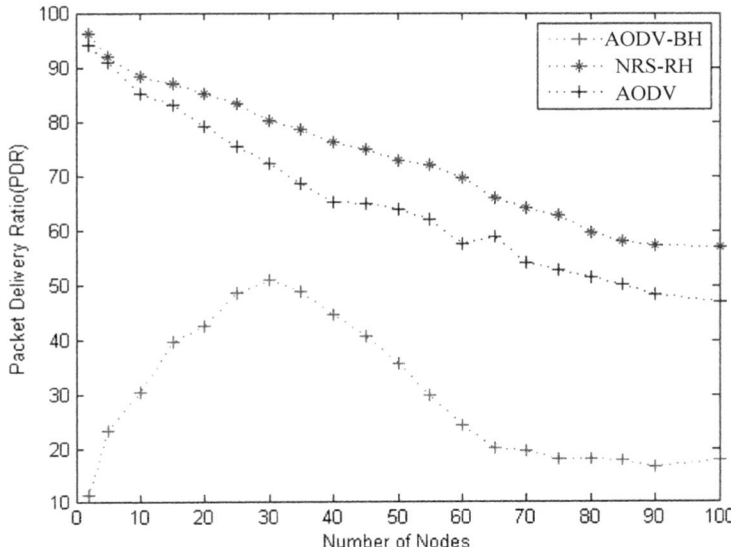

Fig. 2. Packet delivery ratio (PDR) with and without Black holes

5 Future Research and Conclusion

A generic approach for black hole attack detection for this diverse MANET environment is a NP problem. The proposed work is intended to cover a large domain of the problem but with some error assumptions. The scheme has a constant computational overhead and routing overhead is only what is due to the AODV. The future research in this respect will consider improving the proposed work for considering the Gray hole and Worm-hole attacks.

References

1. Peng, M., Shi, W., Corriveau, J.P., Pazzi, R., Wang, Y.: Black hole search in computer networks: state-of-the-art, challenges and future directions. J. Parallel Distrib. Comput. **88**, 1–15 (2016)
2. Aluvala, S., Sekhar, K.R., Vodnala, D.: An empirical study of routing attacks in mobile ad-hoc networks. Procedia Comput. Sci. **92**, 554–561 (2016)
3. Kumar, K., Aulakh, T.S.: Black hole attack in MANETs preventions and advancements: a review. Int. J. Comput. Appl. (0975–8887). International Conference on Advances in Emerging Technology (ICAET 2016) (2016)
4. Brar, S., Angurala, M.: Cooperative Black Hole Attack Prevention by Particle Swarm Optimization with Multiple Swarms (2017)
5. Arathy, K.S., Sminesh, C.N.: A novel approach for detection of single and collaborative black hole attacks in MANET. Procedia Technol. **25**, 264–271 (2016)

6. Panos, C., Ntantogianb, C., Malliarosb, S., Xenakisb, C.: Analyzing, quantifying, and detecting the blackhole attack in infrastructure-less networks. Comput. Netw. **113**, 94–110 (2017)
7. Praveen, K.S., Gururaj, H.L., Ramesh, B.: Comparative Analysis of Black Hole Attack in Ad Hoc Network Using AODV and OLSR Protocols. Procedia Comput. Sci. **85**, 325–330 (2016)
8. Nithya, S., Meena, K.: Genetic algorithm based bacterial foraging optimization with three-pass protocol concept for heterogeneous network security enhancement. J. Comput. Sci. **21**, 275–282 (2017)
9. Dhaka, A., Nandal, A., Dhaka, R.S.: Gray and black hole attack identification using control packets in MANETs. Procedia Comput. Sci. **54**, 83–91 (2015)
10. Choudhury, D.R., Ragha, L., Marathe, N.: Implementing and improving the performance of AODV by receive reply method and securing it from black hole at-tack. Procedia Comput. Sci. **45**, 564–570 (2015)
11. Arora, S.K., Monga, H.: Combined approach for the analysis of black hole and worm hole attack in MANET. Indian J. Sci. Technol. **9**(20), May 2016. https://doi.org/10.17485/ijst/2016/v9i20/90391
12. Rani, R., Kaur, G.: Black hole attack detection using counters for AODV in MANET. Int. J. **8**(5), 402–406 (2017)
13. Shivhare, M., Gautam, P.K.: Prevention of black hole attack in MANET using indexing algorithm. Int. J. Eng. Sci. **12603**, 12603–12606 (2017)
14. Sharma, R., Sharma, M.: A technique to establish shortest route in manet by detecting multiple cooperative black hole attack. In: Proceedings of IRF International Conference, Bangalore (2014). ISBN 978-93-82702-68-9
15. Wahane, G., Lonare, S.: Technique for detection of cooperative black hole attack in MANET. In: 2013 Fourth International Conference on Computing, Communications and Networking Technologies (ICCCNT), pp. 1–8. IEEE, July 2013
16. Dahiya, V., Dureja, A.: Detection of black hole & gray hole in MANET. Int. J. Comput. Sci. Mob. Comput. **3**(7), 466–473 (2014). ISSN 2320– 088X
17. Vennila, G., Arivazhagan, D., Manickasankari, N.: Prevention of co-operative black hole attack in manet on DSR protocol using cryptographic algorithm. Int. J. Eng. Technol. (IJET) **6**(5), 2401 (2014)
18. Iglewicz, B., Hoaglin, D.C.: How to Detect and Handle Outliers, vol. 16. Asq Press (1993)

Light Weight Two-Factor Authentication Using Hybrid PUF and FSM for SOC FPGA

J. Kokila[✉], Manjith Baby Chellam, Arjun Murali Das,
and N. Ramasubramanian

Department of Computer Science and Engineering,
National Institute of Technology, Trichy, Tiruchirappalli, India
jk.cse09@gmail.com

Abstract. SoC FPGA are shrinking is size with advancement in the technologies. Miniaturization alone may not be sufficient to meet user requirements and hence security challenges remain unsolved. Existing approaches have their own limitations in terms of area and power. A model for two factor authentication is proposed with low- power, area and highly automative. It consists of a hybrid Physical unclonable functions (PUFs), which is used to abstract the unique ID of a chip and finite state machine (FSM) to verify that the Intellectual property (IP) is authentic or not. Recent hardware security applications such as IP protection, IC metering, hardware signature and obfuscation are mostly using PUF. Though most of these applications require a database to store the random outputs and complex security algorithms. This in turn increases the area, power, cost and energy consumption. A lightweight hybrid PUF model consisting of arbitrary and butterfly PUF along with the two-level FSM is projected for such security breaches which can be used for many IOT applications. Experimental results show that the area and power consumed is 5% and 9% respectively, for authenticating 26 IP in 13.25 s which is less than that of the conventional design.

Keywords: Two-factor authentication · SoC design
Physical unclonable function · Finite state machine · Hardware security

1 Introduction

As embedded devices expand in our everyday life and their cost gets lower, there is more demand of having a lightweight authentication method that can be implemented on a prevalent device with little cost. The authentication method should be resistant against interference as the attacker has full physical contact to the device most of the time [1]. The existing authentication methods will have a computational delay and reduction in performance, which is not suitable for any high speed and sensitive applications. SOC is incorporating the entire modern computer system on to a distinct die. It usually contains a high speed CPU like ARM along with GPU, memory (DDR), USB controller, WIFI, power

© Springer Nature Singapore Pte Ltd. 2018
P. Bhattacharyya et al. (Eds.): NGCT 2017, CCIS 828, pp. 381–395, 2018.
https://doi.org/10.1007/978-981-10-8660-1_29

management circuits, and wireless radios and so on. As embedded system is the parental technology for SoC, all the features are included and extra features are added to meet today's expectations [2]. A recent advancement without embedded system is like a book without any future reference. The embedded system is implanted in every human being like primary needs. The SoC is the multidisciplinary technology, which is used in smart phone and consumer devices that plays its vital role in agriculture, medical, academic, research, engineering and technology.

All secure and sensitive information's are greatly relied on the integrated circuits (ICs), and people are much more addicted to electronics devices as they are global and interconnected. The field programmable gate array (FPGA) is more adorable then Application-specific Integrated Circuits (ASICs), because it is extra flexible, low cost and fewer time-to-market. The major applications such as end-user electronics, self-propelled electronics and aerospace equipment made FPGA a standard design platform [3]. Latest FPGAs along with the high speed CPUs are combined into a single core to form SoC FPGA, hence they provide higher integration, lower power, smaller board size and high bandwidth communication. The Intellectual property (IPs) are mostly used in this SOC FPGA-based design platform, due to technical and non-technical merits. The SoC, FPGA, SoC FPGA, and many more are relaying on the reusable IPs for flexible and time-to -market design platform. This creates a high importance for IP protection and anti-counterfeiting in the IC markets [4]. The major concerns of using the soft and hard IPs are: IP leakage, computation and cost is high and license is limited only for specific FPGAs. The existing IP protection are based on the following mechanisms they are generating patent, copyright form, trademark and encrypting secrete key. Hence all this mechanism will strictly use encryption and secure database to store secrete key. The hard IP protection techniques have the disadvantage over the existing methods they are: (a) strong and high cost encryption algorithm for individual IP core configuration in FPGA. (b) No pay-per licensing scheme for large and single IP cores and (c) Perpetual Key storage and organization need protection against security attacks [5].

The IC design complexity is increasing tremendously due to less design cycle, increasing functionality, time-to -market and indefinite targets. In practical application if any reusable IP core is satisfying the user needed with less process technology and integrated into a complex design suit then it can be executed and verified in any major core. The SoC IP are of three types they are hard, soft and firmware. To use any one of these IP in complex design, IP provider have to give license so that we can complete integration, testing and verification phases and decide to use this reusable IPs for other complex design space. The reverse engineering is the future thread to IP cores, where someone can buy IPs and copy its RTL and modify it to suitable for upcoming technologies and at last claim the ownership of it and earn money from it [6]. Hence IP Protection is very much essential for SOC FPGA. The beginning phase of IP protection is authenticating different IPs, followed by authorization, maintenance and making vulnerable to hardware attacks for IOT applications. The traditionally used a password-based and knowledge-based authentication (KBA) are more susceptible than the systems which requires several independent methods. One of the approaches of hardware authentication is using a widely distributed public key to encrypt sensitive data and program a secret key into non-volatile memory, such as EEPROM, and then uses cryptographic procedures such as a digital signature to authenticate a device [7]. There are several problems with this approach. First, with symmetric key applications, universal devices need to store sensitive information which might be compromised with security attacks. Second, each time an authentication occurs, there is a large number of logical blocks that need to engage in the process of authentication, which makes this procedure vulnerable to side channel attacks as it empties lots of power out of the device. Third, programming device-specific secrets in memory are very expensive since the designer has to keep a record of the specific private keys generated for each device. To address the problems of the secret key-based approach, researchers have proposed physical unclonable function (PUF) as a powerful hardware authentication mechanism [8].

2   Related Works

The requirement of security and reliability in SOC is very much essential and that is the main base for PUFs [12]. In order to authenticate heterogeneous IPs and to balance weak and strong PUFs different articles have been studied. The protection of IPs and its feature for SoC design is the main confront, which is existing with many solution still future direction is need due to complication in the design and integration. The different types of PUFs have been analyzed and selected for our work. The device authentication is playing a major role in network, real-time multimedia, IOTs, mobile services and many more [13]. Hence the endpoint authentication using two PUFs along with FSM for heterogeneous IP cores is the main core of this proposal.

Physical unclonable functions (PUF) can produce random outputs which can be incorporated in many cryptographic applications like key generation and chip authentication. Intellectual Property (IP) protection has become an important challenge for the next decade. This paper talks about designing a two level FSM to address this problem. Challenge Response pairs (CRP) of a PUF are used to generate chip unique signatures for an authentication system [14]. PUFs are noisy in nature which are due to temperature changes, voltage drifts and aging effects. One solution to this problem is to incorporate error correcting codes like BCH codes. It should be area efficient to make the entire system to use in lightweight hardware devices. This paper presents a two level Finite State Machine (FSM) architecture which can be used to authenticate a chip or IP inside a chip. They propose a two level FSM architecture which is capable of authenticating IPs and correct certain number of PUF response bit errors caused due to environmental variations. This significantly lower cost than the error correcting methods that are previously used for PUF based authentication. In this proposal the PUFs is used for low-cost authentication of chip and to generate secret keys for cryptographic operations. The Suh and Devadas [15] introduced a new ring oscillators PUF circuit design, which has benefits in the ease of implementation and reliability over previously proposed designs. The PUF circuits can also be used as hardware random number generators. The main focuses is on device authentication and key generation. A technique has been suggested for the piracy and licensing challenges. This proposal uses a binding mechanism which is appropriate for protecting reusable IPs to the approved FPGA devices. This article also consists of PUF circuit for security premises and FSM for RTL design purpose with non-encryption based scheme. The architecture focus on low hardware cost and pay-per-device licensing mechanism.

This paper talks about a new approach based on Physical Unclonable Functions (PUF) for IP protection on FPGAs. Earlier SRAM based PUF were in existence. This had a drawback that not all FPGAs supported uninitialized SRAM memory. So a new PUF structure called Butterfly PUF was proposed which can be used in all FPGAs. Later it was classified as a weak PUF. A cross coupled combinational loop using latches is used, which is difficult to implement in FPGAs. Experimental results show that it is very stable to environmental and other FPGA operating parameter variations. A two-way real time multimedia authentication scheme has been proposed that covers both device and multimedia content authentications [16]. The main aim of this proposal is to employ ring oscillators PUF for authentication in security premises. In surveillance video streaming to authenticate multimedia and device a protocol called multimedia authentication protocol is designed with RO PUF and used. The RO-based design which is considered in this work is the ease of implementation on FPGAs. Dynamic partial reconfiguration (DPR) enabled FPGAs is used to define an IoT architecture by modifying the hardware component dynamically [17]. They had proposed and demonstrated the feasibility of implementation of two different low overhead secure DPR architectures targeted for IoT applications. They analyzed possible threats that can emanate from the availability of DPR at IoT nodes, and propose possible solution techniques based on the Physically Unclonable Function (PUF) circuits to prevent such threats. The physically authenticated SoC platform (PASC) [18] is an run-time authentication system which uses both the hardware and software approach of SoC. The hardware system is employing the PUF architecture, which can produce the unique ID at real-time with the help of processor clock frequence. The ID is extracted at run time and all post processing is done in software. Hence the elasticity is combined with the uniqueness of hardware to achieve a excellent authentication systems. The local authentication of the device using PUF and FSM is the base in which many future directions for two factor authentication and hardware signature is also specified. Same concept for pay-per- license is also suggested in one more transaction. Device authentication and secret generation is the main application of PUF which is elaborated with analysis and complexity. The implementation of Butterfly and Arbitrary PUF is also studied. In real time how this PUF can be used with runtime and partial reconfiguration concept is also projected and which helped us for determining the next phase of our work.

3 Motivation

The reliability and security are the vital issue in SOC design [19]. The PUF is a random number generator and its unique for each chip set. This feature have been attracted and selected to solve the security problem in chip designing. The major advantage of using FSM is that it is not removed from the synthesized design. If an adversary wants to extract or change the FSM with RTL knowledge of IPs, then majority of the stages has to be redesigned. The combination of both strong and weak PUF are hard to implement and analyzing the result to make it suitable for device and IP authentication in SOC FPGA is very much difficult. The proposal uses two level FSM to authenticate various IPs by balancing the weak with strong PUF. The Butterfly PUF is chosen for weak, which have many drawbacks like less number of responses and implementation in FPGA may lead may false negative values. The Butterfly PUF promises to be a significantly secure way to protect IP with no additional costs in manufacturing and not affected by environmental changes. The Arbiter PUFs is selected as strong, which are essentially linear classifiers of challenges and responses in n-dimensional. Arbiter PUFs are vulnerable to machine learning attacks. Even an adversary possessing trusted hardware can use the features authentic Device. To authenticate and protect IP in different Chip set requires challenging mechanisms. The Existing method relies on PUF, crpto system for key security, FSM, Dynamic and partial reconfiguration to authenticate and protect IP in real time applications. All this mechanism needs a database and high computation cost and time. This motivated us to design a low power authentication system which uses hybrid PUF along with the FSM with less effort and without a database.

4 Preliminaries

4.1 Physical Unclonabe Function (PUF)

Physical unclonable function (PUF) is a emerging security and reliability feature, which is recently used for IC authentication and cryptographic application [9]. Storing and managing secrets in digital memory are more challenging tasks, but PUFs are called as innovative primitives for deriving secrets from complex physical structures. The random variation of an IC fabrication phase is used to extract the PUFs which is really hard to predict. The secrets can be generated by the unique characteristics of the physical hardware like material, transistors, wires, glitches, location and fabrication etc.

Types of PUFs. The PUF are classified based on the randomness generated for different devices or ICs. The randomness may be due to external or internal. The external PUfs depends on the materials used for manufacturing that device such as optical and coating PUFs. The internal PUFs depend on the internal behavior of the circuit which is concern with the design part of the IC or device such as delay PUF, SRAM PUF, butterfly PUF, Digital PUF, Magnetic PUF and so on.

4.2   Weak PUFs

Weak PUFs are a special case of saving keys to non-volatile memory [8]. It has only a small number of challenges. The response of a weak PUF is used to derive a cryptographic embedded system and, therefore, the output available to the outside world is an indirect response to the original challenge given to the PUF. Examples of weak PUF include SRAM PUF, Butterfly PUF [10], and Coating PUF. One of the advantages of the weak PUF is that it is harder for an adversary to obtain CRPs. Also, the error correction process is done internally with the error correcting helper data stored in non-volatile memory, which ensures security. On the other hand, strong PUFs have the error-correction process handled by external blocks, which have access to the responses.

4.3   Strong PUFs

Strong PUFs are those that have numerous CRPs, so each time the authentication procedure can require new CRPs that have not been used before [11]. As a result, a potential attacker cannot perform a replay attack by recording and applying the CRPs already used in previous authentications. Although it can prevent replay attacks, the strong PUF is still vulnerable to modelling attacks where the attackers attempt to collect a large number of CRPs and build a software model to emulate the PUF behaviour. Typically there is no built-in protection mechanism to restrict the access to responses created by strong PUFs. Also, most electrical strong PUFs operate at low frequencies and, consequently, even short time access to the system enables reading a large number of CRPs.

4.4   Finite State Machine (FSM)

In Verilog the sequential, combinational and output logic all together is defined as state machine. The term finite refers to the number of finite state the machine needed to operate. A clock signal is used to trigger the FSM, so that there will be a transition from one state to another. To construct an FSM the following have to be considered: (a) Countable states encoding each state from initial state to final states separately. (b) Keep track of current state. (c) Mark the state transition and trigger edge (d) note the output change and current state.

5   Proposed Model

The proposed model is for authenticating the IP cores in SOC-FPGA. The introduction has depicted the feature and use of IP and PUF which forms the basic block for the design. The Fig. 1 illustrates the PUF-based authentication process, which uses the hybrid PUF model. The authentication system consists of three basic hardware modules.

1. Integrating Various IP cores
2. Hybrid Pufs
3. Two-level finite state machine.

An IP core is a ready-made function that can be instantiated in your design as a black box. Designing heterogeneous core for single SoC is more complicated. The complexity of the cores can range in the following way that is it may be a simple arithmetic functions, or DSP blocks like filter, transformer etc or it may high level specialized processor or combinations of all.

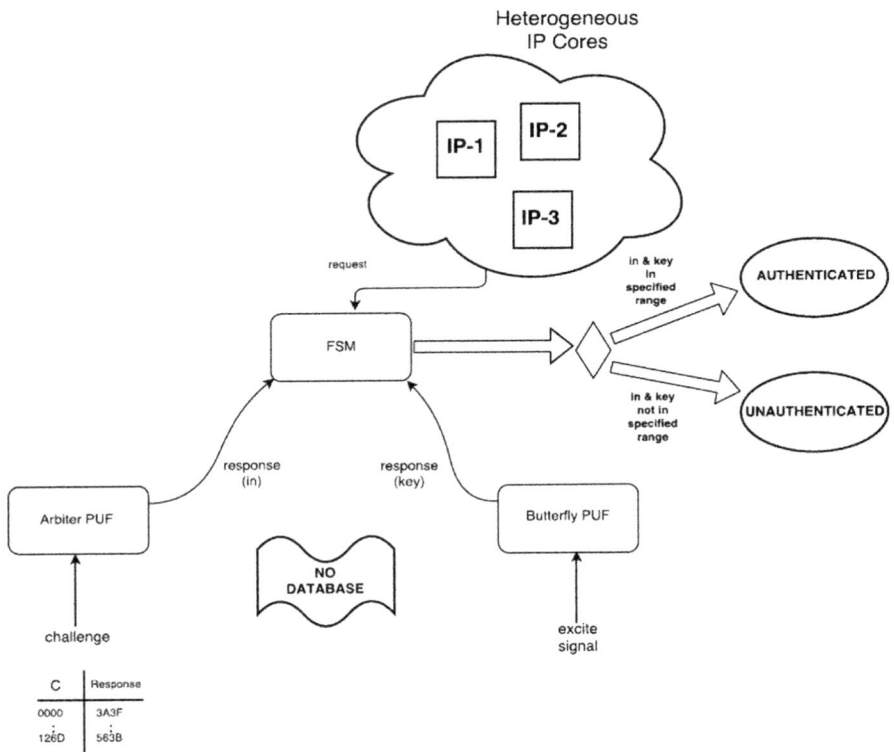

Fig. 1. Block diagram of proposed model

5.1   Integrating Various IP Cores

Various IP cores are widely used in system-on-chip devices such as tablets, smartphones, other mobile devices, and video game consoles for performing different tasks. The 28 nm is a deeper process nodes, which permit device convergence and hence more cores are included in the SoC along with added subsystems for hardware acceleration. These designs can include well over 100 IP cores combined with multiple subsystems connected across multiple supply voltages and dozens of switched power domains, in addition to 6–12 clock domains and a multitude of switched clock domains. The SoC possess difference IP cores such as processor IP cores, Memory based, GPU, programmable etc. with different integration techniques.

5.2 Hybrid PUF

APUF and BPUF from the hybrid model. The BPUF does not need any input which is triggered n by excite signal while APUF has an input which is termed as 'challenge' denoted as 'C' in the diagram. The output of BPUF is the 'key' which is one of the inputs to the FSM. This key is unique to each design and it varies for different chips. Other input is the response (in) of APUF. The response is very difficult to predict and it also varies for each challenge pairs, design and chip. IPs are authenticated when in and key are in the desired range. It is to be noted that the response of APUF is not taken directly instead hamming distance between challenge and response pair is fed as input to the FSM. This makes the design and analysis easier and harder for attackers. The advantage of this design is that there is no need for a database. Hence an attacker cannot find the key and in easily. The experimental analysis for weak and strong PUFs are made and the performance of each is recorded based on uniqueness, randomness and reliability [20,21].

5.3 FSM Model

Figure 2 describes the two-level finite state machine (FSM). The FMS is defined has a five tuple entity with set of initial state, input symbols, transition function, output symbols and final states. S0 is the initial state. The next state is determined by the response from the BPUF which is input symbols for first level. For second level the input symbols are the hamming distance (hd) of ABUF CRP.

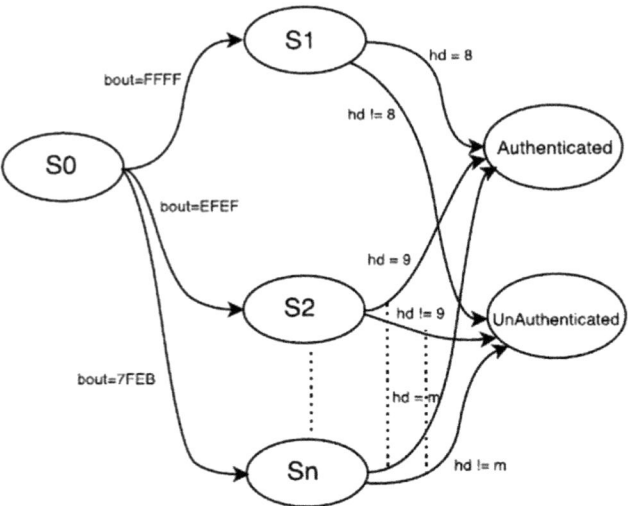

Fig. 2. Two-level finite state machine

The transition from first level to second level is based on this hd which is determined each time to check the condition and reaches the final state which is the authenticated or unauthenticated state. For example if it is FFFF, the next state becomes S1. If it is EFEF the next state becomes S2. We can say that it a two level FSM. S1, S2 Sn forms the first level of the FSM. It further proceeds to Authenticated or Unauthenticated state based on the hamming distance values. These values are fixed after some preliminary analysis which is described in the later section. Hamming distance can be a range or a definite value in the FSM which is upto the designer. Here we are using fixed hamming distances. For example if hd = 9 and bout = FFFF next state is 'thenticated'. If the hd is not equal to 9 it is Unauthenticated.

5.4 Vivado Block Design

Figure 3 shows the block diagram of implemented design. APUF, BPUF and FSM is connected to the ZYNQ. Internal FPGA clock of 126 MHz is used for all elements. AXI GPIO block is also attached to the ZYNQ which is used to observe the state transitions. Each IP blocks are connected through S-AXI bus of the Zedboard. The status of the LEDs change according to the output of the FSM. LED1 shows unauthenticated state while LED8 shows Authenticated state of IP1. In my design the scenario of authenticating IP with 16 bit BPUF response pair of is explained. This can be further extended to more number if IPs, CRP and responses.

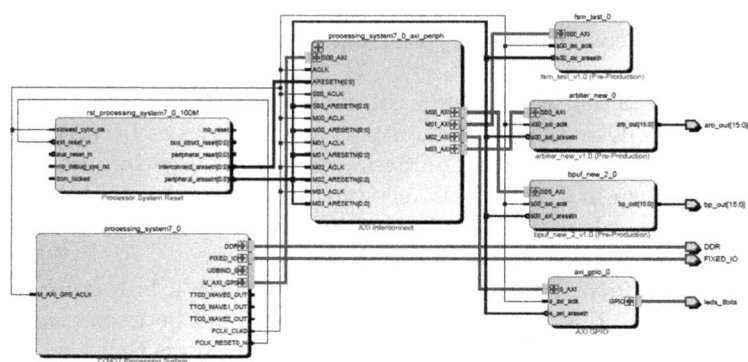

Fig. 3. Vivado block diagram

6 Experimental Setup and Results

Table 1 list the experimental details for the proposed design. Since Zedboard is a low cost, area and power based SOC FPGA which is used to implement the proposed design. Xilinx Vivado 2016.2 is used to design the various IP blocks.

Xilinx SDK is used to control the IPs and to test the design. Serial Terminal called PuTTy is used to observe the outputs and results are analyzed. Internal FPGA clock of frequency 126 MHz is used. In Xilinx SDK a C code is written to repeat the process of response generation 100 times. It takes approximately 13.25 sec to complete the execution. Status leds in zedboard shows the transition of states. Operating temperature range of zedboard is from 35 to 55 °C.

Table 1. Experimental details

Operating system	Ubuntu 14.04 LTS
Development board used	Zedboard
Languages used	Verilog, C
For hardware part of zedboard	Xilinx Vivado 2016.2
For software part of zedboard	Xilinx SDK 2016.2

Figure 4 shows the implemented design in zedboard. The entire design is implemented as logic cells as shown in yellow color marking. The design comprises of weak and supporting strong PUFs with a decision making FSM. The utilization graph Fig. 5 is also provided. The utilization results, consume nearly 4% of the overall logic cells in, the board which is comparatively very minimum. Power consumptions along with junction temperature is also given below in Fig. 6, which states that PUF is not affected by the external environment. The power consumed is also less compared to that of the design involving database and high computing encryption algorithms as we are storing the details implicitly.

It is to be noted that IO Resource consumes nearly 20% of the total resource but we are using IO to observe the outputs which may not be necessary while practically implementing the design. Serial terminal is used to observe the random outputs shown in Fig. 7. It also shows the challenge fed to APUF and the hamming distance calculated between challenge and response bits of APUF. The status of led is also shown.

In Figs. 8 and 9 the hamming distance is plotted as a histogram for different iterations. Here the hamming distance is calculated between challenge and response of APUF for 10 different CRP. Observation shows that each CRP will lead to a varying HD and it is depending on the BPUF keys. Each histogram represents hamming distance starting from 6 up to 14 and it vary for different CRP. We can observe that the probability of occurrence is more for hd = 9 and bpuf = FFFF. This can be used as the parameters in FSM. All the above data is taken for 100 iterations, each 10 times is tested for different Keys and HD. The results may change when we increase the number of iterations, CRP and Key. Tables 2 and 3 is showing the relation between BPUF Keys and APUF HD along with time and performance. The performance is analyzed for 10 CRP for 100

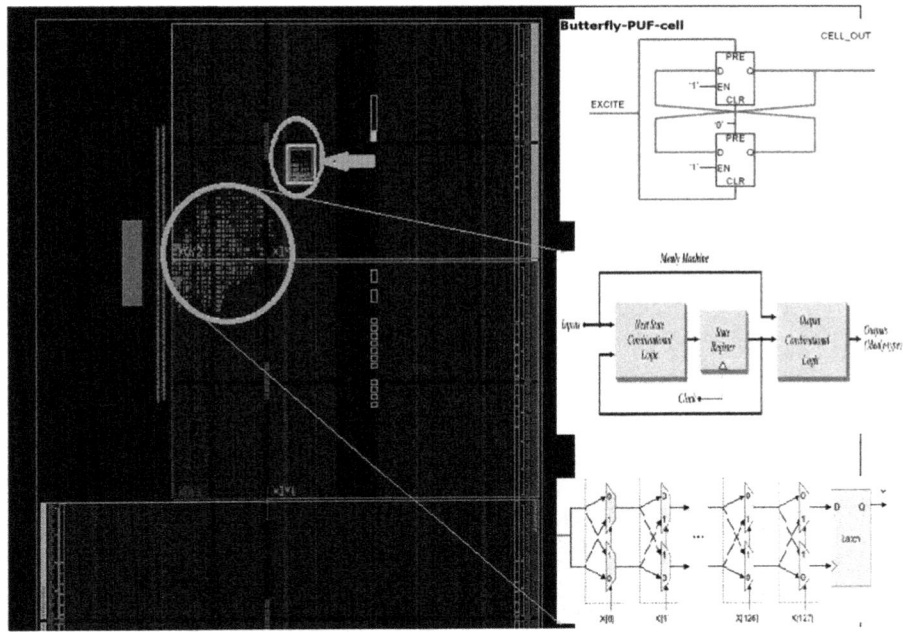

Fig. 4. Implementation design

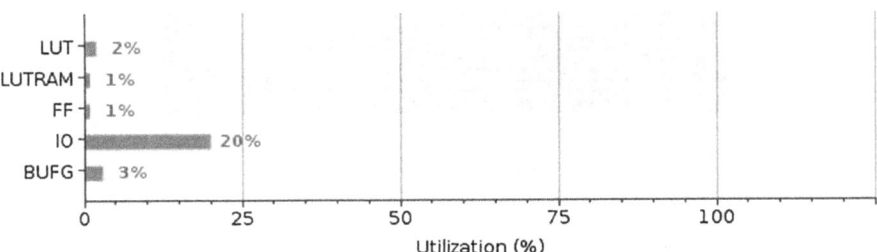

Fig. 5. Utilization graph

iteration by fixing HD between 6 and 14 for different keys so that no attackers can guess the CRP or Key and no need of any database. The time taken for authenticating each IP is also measured.

In Fig. 10 the number of IP which can be authenticated using an existing CRP pair is shown. The highest IPs which can be authenticated is under CRP8, which depends on APUF and BPUF response pair. Hence the design is called two factor authentication.

Power analysis from Implemented netlist. Activity derived from constraints files, simulation files or vectorless analysis.

Total On-Chip Power:	**1.785 W**
Junction Temperature:	**45.6 °C**
Thermal Margin:	39.4 °C (3.3 W)
Effective θJA:	11.5 °C/W
Power supplied to off-chip devices:	0 W
Confidence level:	Medium

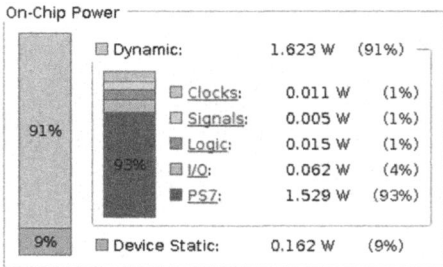

Fig. 6. On-Chip power

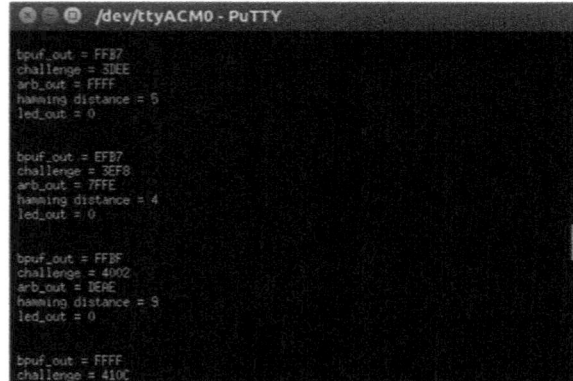

Fig. 7. Putty output terminal

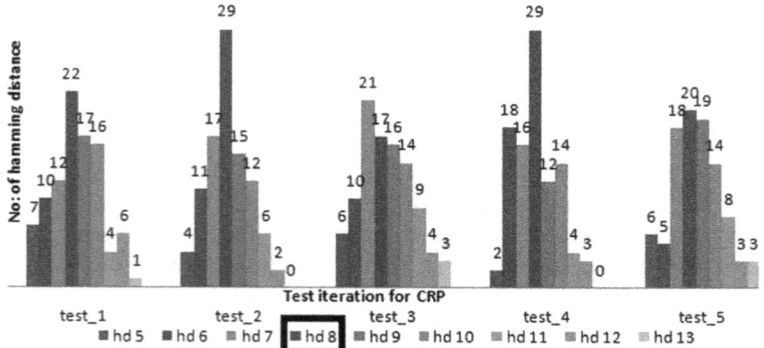

Fig. 8. Hamming distance for CRP-1

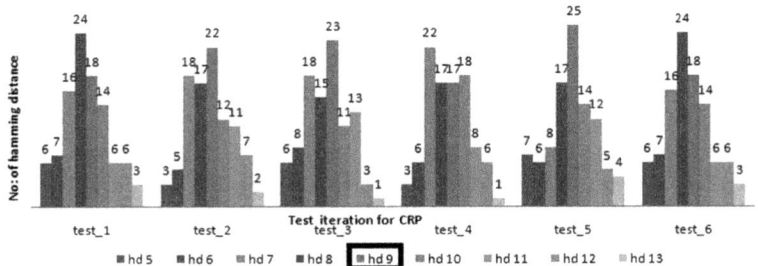

Fig. 9. Hamming distance for CRP-2

Table 2. Performance measure for BPUF key and CRP-1 APUF HD

BPUF response	APUF HD	Time (sec)	Performance percentage (%)
ID1	12	13.1	99
ID2	11	11.9	90
ID3	9	11.5	87
ID4	3	11.8	89
ID5	10	12.2	92
ID6	8	10.5	79
ID7	7	12	91
ID8	10	10.9	82
ID9	9	10.5	79
ID10	9	13	98

Table 3. Performance measure for BPUF key and CRP-2 APUF HD

BPUF response	APUF HD	Time (sec)	Performance percentage (%)
ID1	10	13.1	98
ID2	12	11.9	89
ID3	10	12.8	96
ID4	13	12	90
ID5	7	12.4	93
ID6	12	12.8	96
ID7	8	12.2	91
ID8	14	11.8	88
ID9	13	10.6	79
ID10	8	11.7	87

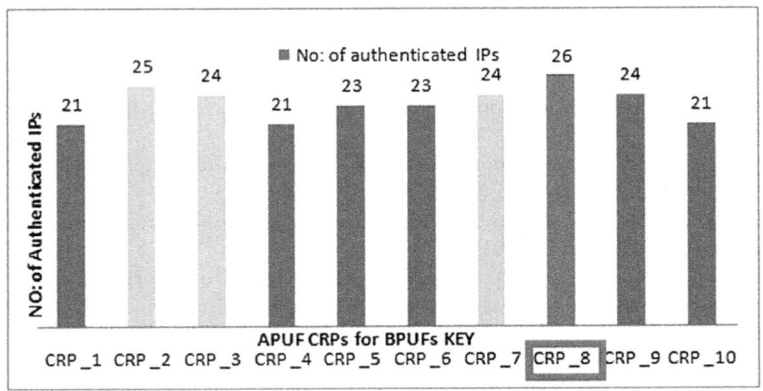

Fig. 10. Number of IP authenticated by CRP

7   Conclusion

Physical Unclonable Function (PUF) is a physical entity that is embodied in a physical structure and is easy to evaluate but hard to predict. The implemented of two types of PUF is used in this model which comprises of a strong PUF and a weak PUF. The responses are analyzed and a hybrid model using these PUFs are proposed for SoC based authentication applications. Zedboard is used for implementing the design and serial terminal (PuTTy) is used to record the outputs. In the conventional model, a database is used along with the PUF to store the random outputs which are used to compare with the output generated at runtime to decide whether a device is authenticated or not. This has a drawback of increasing the area and power consumption which in turn makes the design complex. This is overcome by using an FSM along with the PUF to make decisions. The results obtained are promising that it can be used in hardware signature applications and IC metering applications for (internet of things) IOTs.

References

1. Wang, D., et al.: Anonymous two-factor authentication in distributed systems: certain goals are beyond attainment. IEEE Trans. Dependable Secure Comput. **12**(4), 428–442 (2015)
2. Baklouti, M., et al.: FPGA-based many-core System-on-Chip design. Microprocess. Microsyst. **39**(4), 302–312 (2015)
3. Trimberger, S.M., Moore, J.J.: FPGA security: motivations, features, and applications. Proc. IEEE **102**(8), 1248–1265 (2014)
4. Yan, W., Tehranipoor, F., Chandy, J.A.: A novel way to authenticate untrusted integrated circuits, pp. 89–94 (2014)
5. Zhang, J., et al.: A PUF-FSM binding scheme for FPGA IP protection and pay-per-device licensing. IEEE Trans. Inf. Forensics Secur. **10**(6), 1137–1150 (2015)
6. Narasimhan, S., Chakraborty, R.S., Chakraborty, S.: Hardware IP protection during evaluation using embedded sequential trojan. IEEE Des. Test Comput. **29**(3), 70–79 (2012)
7. Aysu, A., Schaumont, P.: Hardware/software co-design of physical unclonable function based authentications on FPGAs. Microprocess. Microsyst. **39**(7), 589–597 (2015)
8. Zaker Shahrak, M.: Secure and lightweight hardware authentication using isolated physical unclonable function (2016)
9. Herder, C., et al.: Physical unclonable functions and applications: a tutorial. Proc. IEEE **102**(8), 1126–1141 (2014)
10. Kumar, S.S., et al.: The butterfly PUF protecting IP on every FPGA. In: IEEE International Workshop on Hardware-Oriented Security and Trust, HOST 2008. IEEE (2014)
11. Zhang, J., et al.: Design and implementation of a delay-based PUF for FPGA IP protection. In: 2013 International Conference on Computer-Aided Design and Computer Graphics (CAD/Graphics). IEEE (2013)

12. Kokila, J., Ramasubramanian, N., Indrajeet, S.: A survey of hardware and software co-design issues for system on chip design. In: Choudhary, R.K., Mandal, J.K., Auluck, N., Nagarajaram, H.A. (eds.) Advanced Computing and Communication Technologies. AISC, vol. 452, pp. 41–49. Springer, Singapore (2016). https://doi.org/10.1007/978-981-10-1023-1_4

13. Frikken, K.B., Blanton, M., Atallah, M.J.: Robust authentication using physically unclonable functions. In: Samarati, P., Yung, M., Martinelli, F., Ardagna, C.A. (eds.) ISC 2009. LNCS, vol. 5735, pp. 262–277. Springer, Heidelberg (2009). https://doi.org/10.1007/978-3-642-04474-8_22

14. Lao, Y., et al.: Reliable PUF-based local authentication with self-correction. IEEE Trans. Comput.-Aided Des. Integr. Circ. Syst. 36(2) 201–213 (2017)

15. Suh, G.E., Devadas, S.: Physical unclonable functions for device authentication and secret key generation. In: Proceedings of the 44th Annual Design Automation Conference. ACM (2007)

16. Shahrak, M., et al.: Two-way real time multimedia stream authentication using physical unclonable functions. In: IEEE 18th International Workshop on Multimedia Signal Processing (MMSP). IEEE (2016)

17. Johnson, A.P., Chakraborty, R.S., Mukhopadhyay, D.: A PUF-enabled secure architecture for FPGA-based IoT applications. IEEE Trans. Multi-Scale Comput. Syst. 1(2), 110–122 (2015)

18. Aysu, A., Schaumont, P.: PASC: physically authenticated stable-clocked SoC platform on low-cost FPGAs. In: 2013 International Conference on Reconfigurable Computing and FPGAs (ReConFig). IEEE (2013)

19. Sutar, S., Raha, A., Raghunathan, V.: D-PUF: an intrinsically reconfigurable DRAM PUF for device authentication in embedded systems. In: 2016 International Conference on Compliers, Architectures, and Sythesis of Embedded Systems (CASES). IEEE (2016)

20. Wang, X., et al.: IIPS: Infrastructure IP for secure SoC design. IEEE Trans. Comput. 64(8), 2226–2238 (2015)

21. Maiti, A., Gunreddy, V., Schaumont, P.: A systematic method to evaluate and compare the performance of physical unclonable functions. In: Athanas, P., Pnevmatikatos, D., Sklavos, N. (eds.) Embedded Systems Design with FPGAs, pp. 245–267. Springer, New York (2013). https://doi.org/10.1007/978-1-4614-1362-2_11

A Simple, Secure and Time Efficient Multi-way Rotational Permutation and Diffusion Based Image Encryption by Using Multiple 1-D Chaotic Maps

K. Abhimanyu Kumar Patro$^{(\boxtimes)}$ ⓘ, Ayushi Banerjee,
and Bibhudendra Acharya

Department of Electronics and Telecommunication,
National Institute of Technology, Raipur, Chhattisgarh 492010, India
abhimanyu.patro@gmail.com,
ayushi96banerjee@gmail.com, bacharya.etc@nitrr.ac.in

Abstract. Nowadays, the security of transmitting and receiving multimedia data basically digital images through internet has become a challenge to all internet users. This paper proposes a secure, simple and time efficient digital image encryption scheme which takes up a combination of 1-D chaotic maps to perform multi-way rotation based permutation operations and different stages of diffusion operations. The proposed algorithm performs three sectional ways of operations: First the image matrix is divided into blocks of various sizes and then multi- way rotation operations are performed on them. Followed by which the row and column rotation based permutation operations takes place by using multiple 1-D chaotic maps. At the end of operation, row, column and then block diffusion are performed by using multiple 1-D chaotic maps. The proposed algorithm is very much simple and secure because in this algorithm some simple rotation based permutation operations are performed by using 1-D chaotic maps. The proposed algorithm is also time efficient because only 0.208 s is required for implementing the whole program. Apart from that, multi-way rotation based permutation operations and different stages of diffusion operations more confuse the attacker for attacking the proposed cryptosystem. The SHA-256 hashing is used in this algorithm to resist against known-plaintext attack and chosen-plaintext attack. The simulation results and security analysis indicates that the proposed algorithm has good encryption effect, large secret-key space, high key and plaintext sensitivity, and enough resistance against various common attacks.

Keywords: Security · Image encryption · Time efficient · 1-D chaotic maps
Secure Hash Algorithm SHA-256

1 Introduction

With the rapid growth in internet and other public source networks, there is increasing interest in transmissions of digital information; however, security has become a major issue while transmitting that digital information. The transfer of digital information basically the digital images are prone to various attacks with hacker trying to gain the

© Springer Nature Singapore Pte Ltd. 2018
P. Bhattacharyya et al. (Eds.): NGCT 2017, CCIS 828, pp. 396–418, 2018.
https://doi.org/10.1007/978-981-10-8660-1_30

restricted access. Though cryptographic measures like DES [1], 3DES, AES [2], RSA encryption techniques were present but they were highly unfitting for encrypting digital images because of some intrinsic features of digital images like bulky data capacity, high correlation among adjacent pixels, high redundancy, etc. [3–6].

From past few years image encryption has been done using the chaos-based map for scrambling the information matrix so as to represent the data in an uncorrelated form. The chaotic maps were used due to its random behavior and properties like ergodicity, non-periodicity, sensitivity to the initial values and system parameters, etc. [7, 8]. These chaotic behaviors make the cryptosystem more secure and stronger and also more efficient. Chaotic map based encryption technique is first proposed by Matthews [9], in 1989, since then, many researchers followed chaotic map based encryption techniques to design various secure cryptosystems. In chaotic map based encryption systems, basically, two groups of chaotic maps that have been used, one is one-dimensional chaotic map and other one is high-dimensional chaotic map (especially, hyper-chaotic map) [10]. Out of that, one-dimensional chaotic maps are suitable to use in encryption because one-dimensional chaotic maps are structurally simpler, highly efficient, limited requirement of hardware resources but it suffer the problem of smaller key space, on the other hand, high-dimensional chaotic maps provide larger key space but it suffer the problem of complex structure and large number of hardware resources are required which will increases the cost of the product [11]. So to overcome the problem of smaller key space in one-dimensional chaotic maps, this paper uses multiple one-dimensional chaotic maps which in combine provide larger key space. Lots of researches have been done by using multiple one-dimensional chaotic maps. In 2012, Abd El-Latif et al. [12] proposed an image encryption scheme by using multiple one-dimensional chaotic maps such as Logistic map, Sine map, Cubic map, and Tent map. In 2017, Ahmad et al. [13] proposed a multiple chaotic map based simple and secure hash function scheme which to generate hash functions of variable sizes.

In these days, DNA cryptography, the rapid emerging technology, is used in image encryption for obtaining higher security. DNA cryptography has several prominent characteristics such as ultra low-power consumption, huge data storage capacity, massive parallelism, etc. Many researchers have been used DNA techniques in image encryption [8, 14–17] but the drawbacks of DNA make them inefficient in image encryption. Some of the drawbacks of DNA are no universal property of solving problems, large numbers of steps required for processing DNA operations, requires human reprocessing, difficult to increase the key size, too much cost is required in real-time applications, etc. [18]. Hence, most of the researchers used only chaos in image encryption. This paper uses only 1-D chaotic maps such as Beta map, Logistic-Sine System (LSS), Logistic-Tent System (LTS), Tent-Sine System (TSS), and Piece-wise Linear Chaotic Map (PWLCM) to perform image encryption.

The main contribution includes in this paper are as follows:

- Multiple ways of rotation based permutation operations and multiple stages of diffusion operations are presented to confuse the attackers and basically, rotation based permutation operations are presented to reduce the total execution time.
- Multiple 1-D chaotic maps are utilized to obtain the large secret key space.

- The Secure Hash Algorithm SHA-256 is used in this algorithm to resist against known-plaintext attack and chosen-plaintext attack.
- The 1-D chaotic maps such as Beta map, LSS, LTS, TSS, and PWLCM are used to obtain better security in the proposed cryptosystem.

The rest of the paper is organized in the following way. Section 2 discusses the multiple 1-D chaotic maps which are used in this algorithm. The proposed image encryption and decryption algorithm is elaborated in Sect. 3. The simulation results and the security analysis are presented in Sect. 4. Section 5 concludes the paper.

2 Multiple 1-D Chaotic Maps

2.1 Beta Map

The Beta chaotic Map [19] is based on the Beta function given as follows,

$$Beta(x; \alpha, \beta, x_1, x_2) \begin{cases} \left(\frac{x-x_1}{x_0-x_1}\right)^{\alpha} \left(\frac{x_2-x}{x_2-x_0}\right)^{\beta} & if \ x \in \,]x1, x2[\\ \qquad\qquad 0 & else \end{cases} \tag{1}$$

where $\alpha, \beta, x_1 \ and \ x_2 \in R, x_1 < x_2 \ and \ x_0,$

$$x_0 = \frac{(\alpha x_2 + \beta x_1)}{(\alpha + \beta)} \tag{2}$$

Mathematically, the Beta chaotic map is implemented in the following way:

$$x_{n+1} = k \times Beta(x_n; x_1, x_2, \alpha, \beta) \tag{3}$$

where

$$\alpha = p_1 + q_1 \times r \tag{4}$$

and

$$\beta = p_2 + q_2 \times r \tag{5}$$

In Eqs. (4) and (5), p_1, q_1, p_2, q_2 are defined as constants and r is denoted as the bifurcation parameter. In Eq. (3), k is the control parameter to control the amplitude of the Beta map.

As defined in [19], the equations for Beta chaotic map are very much simple and produce different chaotic maps by simply varying their parameters. This shows that the key parameters used in Beta chaotic map are highly sensitive. Apart from that, it has large number of parameters which will increase the key space of the proposed algorithm. And also it has better pseudo random chaotic sequences that will increases the chaotic behavior so as to increase the level of security. At last, the Beta chaotic map has large range of bifurcation parameter.

2.2 Logistic-Sine System (LSS)

The Logistic-Sine system proposed in [20] is the new chaotic system composed of traditional chaotic maps-Logistic map and Sine map. It is defined by the equation:

$$x_{n+1} = (k \times x_n(1 - x_n) + (4 - k) \sin(\pi x_n)/4) \bmod 1 \tag{6}$$

where k is in the range of (0, 4]. Advantage of LSS over its conventional maps is that its chaotic property exists over entire range [20].

2.3 Tent-Sine System (TSS)

By using the conventional maps – Tent map and Sine map, the new chaotic system generated is Tent-Sine system [20]. Equation describing its behavior is:

$$x_{n+1} = \begin{cases} \left(\frac{kx_n}{2} + (4 - k)\sin(\pi x_n)/4\right) \bmod 1 & x_n < 0.5 \\ \left(\frac{k(1-x_n)}{2} + (4 - k)\sin(\pi x_n)/4\right) \bmod 1 & x_n \geq 0.5 \end{cases} \tag{7}$$

where k belongs to the range (0, 4]. It also has the advantages of broader chaotic range and uniformity in distribution [20].

2.4 Logistic-Tent System (LTS)

With seed maps as Logistic and Tent map, Logistic-Tent chaotic system is obtained consisting advantages of supreme chaotic properties similar to LSS and TSS [20]. It can be described by the equation:

$$x_{n+1} = \begin{cases} \left(kx_n(1 - x_n) + \frac{(4-k)x_n}{2}\right) \bmod 1 & x_n < 0.5 \\ \left(kx_n(1 - x_n) + \frac{(4-k)(1-x_n)}{2}\right) \bmod 1 & x_n \geq 0.5 \end{cases} \tag{8}$$

where $k \in (0, 4]$.

2.5 Piece-Wise Linear Chaotic Map (PWLCM)

The PWLCM system is recently widely used in the encryption algorithms due to its less sensitivity towards external perturbation than conventional Logistic map [21]. A chaotic sequence in PWLCM is generated by using the equation:

$$x_{n+1} = \begin{cases} \frac{x_n}{\mu} & if\ 0 \leq x_n < \mu \\ \frac{x_n - \mu}{0.5 - \mu} & if\ \mu \leq x_n < 0.5 \\ (1 - x_n) & if\ 0.5 \leq x_n < 1 \end{cases} \tag{9}$$

where μ lies in the range (0, 0.5). This map is extensively used for chaotic sequence generation due to its perfect properties such as uniform invariant density function;

exactness, mixing and ergodicity; exponentially decaying correlation function and simple realization in both hardware and software [22].

3 Proposed Methodology

3.1 Generation of Secret Keys

In this proposed algorithm, the initial values and system parameters (represented as secret keys) of chaotic maps are updated by the combinations of original initial values and system parameters of the above 1-D chaotic maps and the 256-bit hash values of the original image. The steps for generating the updated secret keys are as follows:

Step-1: Take an original gray scale image, I.
Step-2: Then, apply SHA-256 hashing on this gray scale image, I. This generates a 256-bit hash values which then expressed into 64-hex values (4-bits of each). This will be expressed as follows:

$$hash = h_1, h_2, h_3, \cdots \cdots, h_{63}, h_{64} \tag{10}$$

Step-3: Next, the updated initial values and system parameters of Beta map, LSS map, LTS map, TSS map, and PWLCM system can be calculated in the following way:

The initial values and system parameters of Beta map can be calculated as

$$\begin{cases} x(1) = xx(1) - tan\left(\frac{\pi * sum(h1:h4)}{10^5}\right) - 0.0956 * tan(sum(h1:h4)) \\ k = kk - tan\left(\frac{\pi * sum(h5:h8)}{10^5}\right) + 0.0956 * sin(sum(h5:h8)) \\ x1 = xx1 - tan\left(\frac{\pi * sum(h9:h12)}{10^5}\right) + 0.0656 * sin(sum(h9:h12)) \\ x2 = xx2 - tan\left(\frac{\pi * sum(h13:h16)}{10^5}\right) + 0.0956 * sin(sum(h13:h16)) \\ p1 = pp1 + tan\left(\frac{\pi * sum(h17:h20)}{10^5}\right) + 0.0956 * sin(sum(h17:h20)) \\ p2 = pp2 + tan\left(\frac{\pi * sum(h21:h24)}{10^5}\right) + 0.0956 * sin(sum(h21:h24)) \\ q1 = qq1 + tan\left(\frac{\pi * sum(h25:h28)}{10^5}\right) + 0.0956 * sin(sum(h25:h28)) \\ q2 = qq2 - tan\left(\frac{\pi * sum(h29:h32)}{10^5}\right) + 0.0956 * sin(sum(h29:h32)) \\ r = rr - tan\left(\frac{\pi * sum(h33:h36)}{10^5}\right) + 0.0956 * sin(sum(h33:h36)) \end{cases} \tag{11}$$

In the above Eq. (11), $xx(1)$ is the original initial value and $x(1)$ is the updated initial value of Beta map, $kk, xx1, xx2, pp1, pp2, qq1, qq2, rr$ are the original system parameters and $k, x1, x2, p1, p2, q1, q2, r$ are the updated system parameters of Beta map.

The initial values and system parameters of LSS map can be calculated as,

$$\begin{cases} y(1) = yy(1) + tan\left(\frac{\pi * sum(h37:h40)}{10^4}\right) + 0.0992sin(sum(h37:h40)) \\ r1 = rs1 + tan\left(\frac{\pi * sum(h41:h44)}{10^5}\right) - 0.0998sin(sum(h41:h44)) \end{cases} \quad (12)$$

In the above Eq. (12), $yy(1)$ is the original initial value and $y(1)$ is the updated initial value of LSS map, $rs1$ is the original system parameter and $r1$ is the updated system parameter of LSS map.

The initial values and system parameters of LTS map can be calculated as,

$$\begin{cases} z(1) = zz(1) + tan\left(\frac{\pi * sum(h45:h48)}{10^5}\right) + 0.00998 * sin(sum(h45:h48)) \\ r2 = rs2 + tan\left(\frac{\pi * sum(h49:h52)}{10^5}\right) - 0.0998 * sin(sum(h49:h52)) \end{cases} \quad (13)$$

In the above Eq. (13), $zz(1)$ is the original initial value and $z(1)$ is the updated initial value of LTS map, $rs2$ is the original system parameter and $r2$ is the updated system parameter of LTS map.

The initial values and system parameters of TSS map can be calculated as,

$$\begin{cases} w(1) = ww(1) + tan\left(\frac{\pi * sum(h53:h56)}{10^5}\right) + 0.0998 * sin(sum(h53:h56)) \\ r3 = rs3 + tan\left(\frac{\pi * sum(h57:h60)}{10^5}\right) - 0.000998 * sin(sum(h57:h60)) \end{cases} \quad (14)$$

In the above Eq. (14), $ww(1)$ is the original initial value and $w(1)$ is the updated initial value of TSS map, $rs3$ is the original system parameter and $r3$ is the updated system parameter of TSS map.

The initial values and system parameters of PWLCM system can be calculated as,

$$\begin{cases} mue = mue1 + tan\left(\frac{\pi * sum(h61:h62)}{10^5}\right) - 0.0098 * sin(sum(h61:h62)) \\ e(1) = ee(1) + tan\left(\frac{\pi * sum(h63:h64)}{10^5}\right) - 0.0098 * sin(sum(h63:h64)) \end{cases} \quad (15)$$

In the above Eq. (15), $ee(1)$ is the original initial value and $e(1)$ is the updated initial value of PWLCM system, $mue1$ is the original system parameter and mue is the updated system parameter of PWLCM system.

3.2 Proposed Encryption Algorithm

This section presents the proposed encryption algorithm for encrypting gray scale images. Figure 1 shows the detailed block diagrammatic representation of the proposed encryption algorithm and the step-by-step descriptions of each of the blocks are as follows:

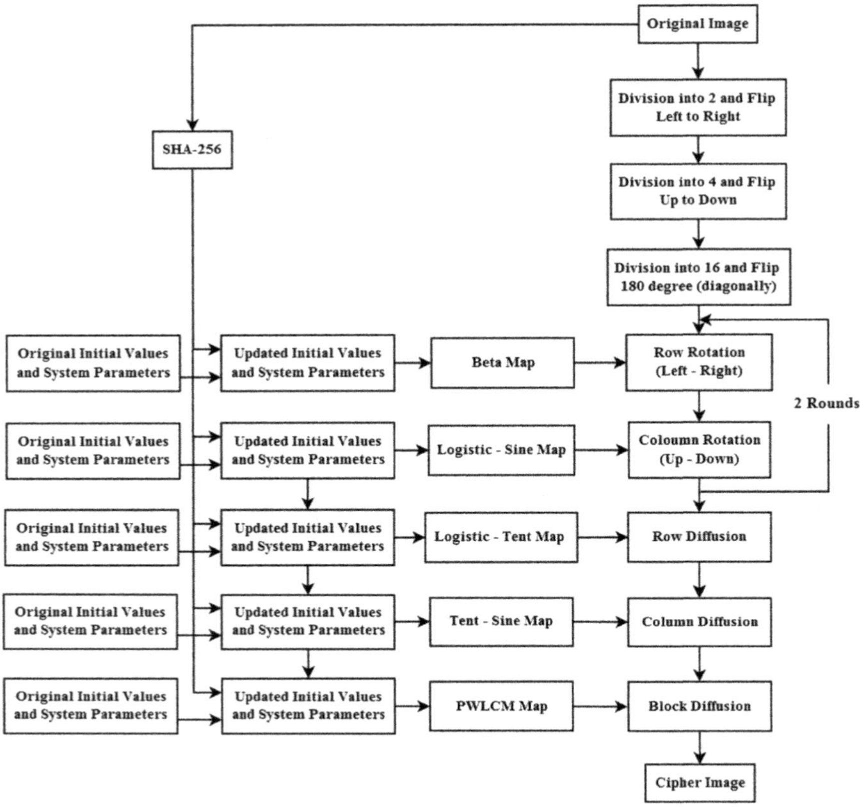

```
                                              ┌─────────────────┐
                                              │ Original Image  │
                                              └────────┬────────┘
                                                       │
                                              ┌────────▼────────┐
                                              │ Division into 2 and Flip │
                                              │   Left to Right  │
              ┌──────────┐                    └────────┬────────┘
              │ SHA-256  │                             │
              └──────────┘                    ┌────────▼────────┐
                                              │ Division into 4 and Flip │
                                              │   Up to Down    │
                                              └────────┬────────┘
                                                       │
                                              ┌────────▼────────┐
                                              │ Division into 16 and Flip │
                                              │ 180 degree (diagonally) │
                                              └────────┬────────┘
```

Original Initial Values and System Parameters	Updated Initial Values and System Parameters	Beta Map	Row Rotation (Left - Right)
Original Initial Values and System Parameters	Updated Initial Values and System Parameters	Logistic - Sine Map	Coloumn Rotation (Up - Down)
Original Initial Values and System Parameters	Updated Initial Values and System Parameters	Logistic - Tent Map	Row Diffusion
Original Initial Values and System Parameters	Updated Initial Values and System Parameters	Tent - Sine Map	Column Diffusion
Original Initial Values and System Parameters	Updated Initial Values and System Parameters	PWLCM Map	Block Diffusion

2 Rounds

Cipher Image

Fig. 1. Encryption block diagram of the proposed cryptosystem.

Step-1: Take an original gray scale image, I of size $M \times N$.

Step-2: Horizontally divide the whole gray scale image, I into two parts, I_1 and I_2. Then perform left rotation on I_1 and right rotation on I_2. This will be done in the following way,

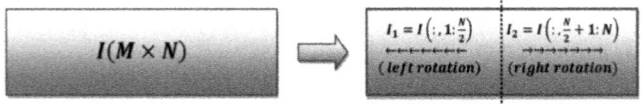

After performing rotation operation, combine I_1 and I_2 to generate a scrambled image, I'.

Step-3: Horizontally and vertically divide the whole image, I' into four parts, $I_3, I_4, I_5,$ and I_6. Then perform up rotation on I_3 and I_4, down rotation on I_5 and I_6. This will be done in the following way,

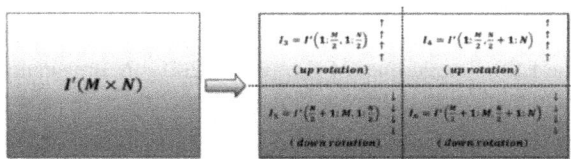

After performing rotation operation, combine $I_3, I_4, I_5,$ *and* I_6 to generate another scrambled image, I''.

Step-4: Again, horizontally and vertically divide the whole image, I'' into 16 (sixteen) parts, $I_7, I_8, I_9, I_{10}, I_{11}, I_{12}, I_{13}, I_{14}, I_{15}, I_{16}, I_{17}, I_{18}, I_{19}, I_{20}, I_{21},$ *and* I_{22}. Then perform $180°$ rotation on each of the parts by using the MATLAB function *"imrotate"*. The process for division is in the following way,

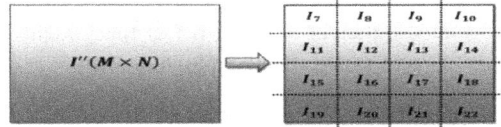

After performing rotation operation, combine all the parts $I_7, I_8, I_9, I_{10}, I_{11}, I_{12},$ $I_{13}, I_{14}, I_{15}, I_{16}, I_{17}, I_{18}, I_{19}, I_{20}, I_{21},$ *and* I_{22} to get another scrambled image, I'''.

Step-5: According to Sect. 3.1, generate the initial value $x(1)$ and system parameters $k, x1, x2, p1, p2, q1, q2, r$ of Beta map.

Step-6: By using the newly generated initial value and system parameters of Beta map (Step-5), iterate the Beta chaotic map of Eq. (3) for $200 + M$ times and then discard the first 200 iterations to avoid transit effects. This generates the Beta map chaotic sequence as

$$x = (x(1), x(2), x(3), \cdots\cdots\cdots, x(M)) \tag{16}$$

Next, the Beta chaotic sequence is sorted in ascending order by using the function

$$[xsort, xindex] = sort(x) \tag{17}$$

where *xsort* is the sorting order chaotic sequence of x and *xindex* is the corresponding index value of *xsort* only.

Step-7: Now, according to the index value *xindex*, the rows of the scrambled image, I''' are rotated either in left or right of that much of index valued. The row rotation process is performed in the following way:

$$\begin{cases} xindex\,(even) \longrightarrow\longrightarrow Right\ rotation\ of\ rows \\ xindex\,(odd) \longrightarrow\longrightarrow Left\ rotation\ of\ rows \end{cases} \tag{18}$$

This generates the row scrambled image, I_scr_row.

Step-8: According to Sect. 3.1, generate the initial value $y(1)$ and system parameter $r1$ of LSS map.

Step-9: By using the newly generated initial value and system parameter of LSS map (Step-8), iterate the LSS chaotic map of Eq. (6) for $200 + N$ times and then discard the first 200 iterations to avoid transit effects. This generates the LSS map chaotic sequence as

$$y = (y(1), y(2), y(3), \cdots\cdots\cdots\cdots, y(N)) \tag{19}$$

Next, the LSS chaotic sequence is sorted in ascending order by using the function

$$[ysort, yindex] = sort(y) \tag{20}$$

where *ysort* is the sorting order chaotic sequence of y and *yindex* is the corresponding index value of *ysort* only.

Step-10: Now, according to the index value *yindex*, the columns of the scrambled image I_scr_row are rotated either in up or down of that much of index valued. The column rotation process is performed in the following way:

$$\begin{cases} yindex\,(even) \longrightarrow\longrightarrow Up\,rotation\,of\,columns \\ yindex\,(odd) \longrightarrow\longrightarrow Down\,rotation\,of\,columns \end{cases} \tag{21}$$

This generates the column scrambled image, I_scr_col.

Step-11: Repeat Step-7 then Step-10 by using the same initial conditions and system parameters of Beta map and LSS map generated in Step-5 and Step-8. After repeating Step-7, let the scrambled image be $I1\_scr\_row$. Similarly, after repeating Step-10, let the scrambled image be $I1\_scr\_col$.

Step-12: According to Sect. 3.1, generate the initial value $z(1)$ and system parameter $r2$ of LTS map.

Step-13: By using the newly generated initial value and system parameter of LTS map (Step-12), iterate the LTS chaotic map of Eq. (8) for $200 + N$ times and then discard the first 200 iterations to avoid transit effects. This generates the LTS map chaotic sequence as

$$z = (z(1), z(2), z(3), \cdots\cdots\cdots\cdots, z(N)) \tag{22}$$

Next, the LTS chaotic sequence is sorted in ascending order by using the function

$$[zsort, zindex] = sort(z) \tag{23}$$

where *zsort* is the sorting order chaotic sequence of z and *zindex* is the corresponding index value of *zsort* only. The generated *zindex* sequence of Eq. (23) is as follows:

$$zindex = (zindex(1), zindex(2), zindex(3), \cdots\cdots\cdots, zindex(N)) \tag{24}$$

Step-14: Then perform bit-XOR operation between the index value generated in *zindex* and the first row of the scrambled image, $I1\_scr\_col$. This output is then bit-XORed with the second row of $I1\_scr\_col$, till all the rows of $I1\_scr\_col$ are bit-XORed. Let the output of the row diffused image is denoted as $diffu\_row$.

Step-15: According to Sect. 3.1, generate the initial value $w(1)$ and system parameter $r3$ of TSS map.

Step-16: By using the newly generated initial value and system parameter of TSS map (Step-15), iterate the TSS chaotic map of Eq. (7) for $200 + M$ times and then discard the first 200 iterations to avoid transit effects. This generates the TSS map chaotic sequence as

$$w = (w(1), w(2), w(3), \cdots\cdots\cdots\cdots, w(M)) \tag{25}$$

Next, the TSS chaotic sequence is sorted in ascending order by using the function

$$[wsort, windex] = sort(w) \tag{26}$$

where $wsort$ is the sorting order chaotic sequence of w and $windex$ is the corresponding index value of $wsort$ only. The generated $windex$ sequence of Eq. (26) is as follows:

$$windex = (windex(1), windex(2), windex(3), \cdots\cdots\cdots, windex(M)) \tag{27}$$

Step-17: Then perform bit-XOR operation between the index value generated in $windex$ and the first column of the row diffused image, $diffu\_row$. This output is then bit-XORed with the second column of $diffu\_row$, till all the columns of $diffu\_row$ are bit-XORed. Let the output of the column diffused image is denoted as $diffu\_column$.

Step-18: According to Sect. 3.1, generate the initial value $e(1)$ and system parameter mue of PWLCM system.

Step-19: By using the newly generated initial value and system parameter of PWLCM system (Step-18), iterate the PWLCM system of Eq. (9) for $200 + (8 \times (4 \times 4))$ times and then discard the first 200 iterations to avoid transit effects. This generates the PWLCM sequence as

$$e = (e(1), e(2), e(3), \cdots\cdots, e(128)) \tag{28}$$

By using the sequence e, generate a block of size 4×4. The generation of 4×4 sized block by using the sequence e is as follows:

```
for i = 1: 128
    if e(i) > 0.25
        e(i) = 1;
    else
        e(i) = 0;
    end
end
for j = 0: 15
    diffu_block(j + 1) = bin2dec (int2str(e(8 * j + 1: 8 * j + 8)));
end
    diff_block = reshape(uint8(diff_block), [4 4]);
```

The above function generates a block of size 4×4 by using the PWLCM system.

Step-20: Divide the column diffused image *diffu_column* into blocks of size 4×4.

Step-21: Then perform bit-XOR operation between the first block of column diffused image *diffu_column* and the block generated from PWLCM system. This output is then bit-XORed with the second block of *diffu_column*, till all the blocks of *diffu_column* are bit-XORed. Let the output of the block diffused image is denoted as *diffu_block*. The block diffused image *diffu_block* is the final encrypted image.

3.3 Decryption Algorithm

The decryption algorithm is performed in the reserve manner of encryption algorithm. The steps for decryption are as follows:

Step-1: In the receiver side, receiver receives the encrypted image and also receives the 256-bit hash values of original image. Simultaneously, receiver obtain the original initial values and system parameters of Beta map, LSS map, LTS map, TSS map, and PWLCM system from the transmitter side.

Step-2: In the receiver side, receiver generate the updated initial values and system parameters of 1-D chaotic maps by using the original initial values and system parameters of 1-D chaotic maps and the 256-bit hash value of the original image.

Step-3: Generate a 4×4 sized block by using PWLCM system as generated in the transmitter side (Step-19 of Sect. 3.2).

Step-4: Then, divide the encrypted image matrix into blocks of size 4×4 each.

Step-5: Now, perform bit-XOR operation between the PWLCM generated block and the blocks generated from encrypted image, as performed in the transmitter side (Step-21of Sect. 3.2). But here, the bit-XOR operation is performed in the reverse order, that is, last block is bit-XORed with the second last block, then the second last block is bit-XORed with the third last block and so on till the first block is bit-XORed with the PWLCM generated block.

Step-6: By using the index values generated from the sequence of TSS chaotic map, perform column diffusion operation with the output image matrix of Step-5 in reverse order as like of block diffusion operation is performed in Step-5.

Step-7: By using the index values generated from the sequence of LTS chaotic map, perform row diffusion operation with the output image matrix of Step-6 in reverse order as like of block diffusion operation is performed in Step-5 and column diffusion operation is performed in Step-6.

Step-8: Now, by using the index values generated from the chaotic sequence of LSS map, the columns of the output matrix of Step-7 are rotated either in up or down of that much of index valued. The column rotation process is performed in the reverse way of the column rotation operation of Step-10 of Sect. 3.2 which is as follows:

$$\begin{cases} index\,value\,of\,chaotic\,sequence\,of\,LSS\,map\,(even) \rightarrow\rightarrow Down\,rotation\,of\,columns \\ index\,value\,of\,chaotic\,sequence\,of\,LSS\,map\,(odd) \rightarrow\rightarrow Up\,rotation\,of\,columns \end{cases} \quad (29)$$

Step-9: Then, by using the index values generated from the chaotic sequence of Beta map, the rows of the output matrix of Step-8 are rotated either in left or right of that much of index valued. The row rotation process is performed in the reverse way of the row rotation operation of Step-7 of Sect. 3.2 which is as follows:

$$\begin{cases} index\ value\ of\ chaotic\ sequence\ of\ Beta\ map\ (even) \longrightarrow \longrightarrow Left\ rotation\ of\ rows \\ index\ value\ of\ chaotic\ sequence\ of\ Beta\ map(odd) \longrightarrow \longrightarrow Right\ rotation\ of\ rows \end{cases} \quad (30)$$

Step-10: Repeat Step-8 then Step-9 by using the same initial values and system parameters of LSS map and Beta map.

Step-11: Horizontally and vertically divide the output of the whole image matrix of Step-10 into 16 (sixteen) parts. Then perform 180° rotation on reverse way of using 180° rotation in Step-4 of Sect. 3.2. Then combine all the 16 parts.

Step-12: Horizontally and vertically divide the output of the whole image matrix of Step-11 into 4 (four) parts. Then perform up rotation and down rotation on reverse way of using up rotation and down rotation in Step-3 of Sect. 3.2. That means the up rotation in encryption algorithm (Step-3 of Sect. 3.2) is down rotation in decryption algorithm (Step-12 of Sect. 3.3) and down rotation in encryption algorithm (Step-3 of Sect. 3.2) is up rotation in decryption algorithm (Step-12 of Sect. 3.3). Then combine all the 4 parts.

Step-13: Horizontally divide the output of the whole image matrix of Step-12 into 2 (two) parts. Then perform left rotation and right rotation on reverse way of using left rotation and right rotation in Step-2 of Sect. 3.2. That means the left rotation in encryption algorithm (Step-2 of Sect. 3.2) is right rotation in decryption algorithm (Step-13 of Sect. 3.3) and right rotation in encryption algorithm (Step-2 of Sect. 3.2) is left rotation in decryption algorithm (Step-13 of Sect. 3.3). Then combine the 2 parts. This generates the decrypted image which is same as the original image.

4 Simulation Results and Security Analysis

This section presents the simulation results and the security analysis of the proposed image encryption and decryption algorithm. For the purpose of simulating the proposed algorithm, in this paper, three standard gray scale images "Cameraman", "Lena", and "Baboon" of size 256×256 each are used. The simulation and the security analysis is performed in MATLAB R2012a in system with INTEL CORE i7 3.40 GHz processor with 4 GB RAM and hard disk of 500 GB with Windows 10 operating system. The original initial values and system parameters of 1-D chaotic maps are taken as, $xx(1) = -0.2, kk = 0.9, xx1 = -0.7, xx2 = 1, pp1 = 8, pp2 = 3, qq1 = 1, qq2 = -1, rr = -0.2$ for Beta map; $yy(1) = 0.5, rs1 = 3.60$ for LSS map; $zz(1) = 0.5, rs2 = 4.0$ for LTS map; $ww(1) = 0.5, rs3 = 3.78$ for TSS map; $ee(1) = 0.2, mue1 = 0.3$ for PWLCM system and the threshold value required in PWLCM system is 0.25. The simulation results of the proposed encryption scheme are shown in Fig. 2. By observing the original images and their corresponding encrypted images in Fig. 2, we found that the encrypted images are totally different than the original images and there is no relationship in between them. In the same way of observing the original images, their corresponding encrypted images and corresponding decrypted images, we found that the encrypted images are properly decrypted by using the right secret keys. This concludes that the proposed algorithm is very much effective for encrypting gray scale images. The security analysis of the proposed encryption algorithm is explained as below.

4.1   Key Space Analysis

Key space is one of the most important measurements for analyzing the security. Key space can be defined as set of different possible keys that can be used in the encryption algorithm [29]. Key size of any encryption algorithm should be greater than 2^{128} to withstand brute-force attack [23]. The secret keys used in this proposed algorithm are:

a. The initial values and system parameters of Beta map, LSS map, LTS map, TSS map, PWLCM system.
b. The threshold value used in PWLCM system
c. The 256-bit hash value.

This paper uses 64-bit double precision format for initializing and updating the initial values and system parameters of 1-D chaotic maps. For 64-bit double precision format, a precision value of 10^{-15} is suggested by IEEE floating point standard [24]. So, in this algorithm, a precision of 10^{-15} is used to define the secret keys of 1-D chaotic maps and a precision of 10^{-2} is used to define the threshold of PWLCM system. Furthermore, the security of resisting the best attack in SHA-256 hash function is 2^{128}. Therefore, the total key space is calculated as $(10^{15} \times 10^{15} \times 10^{15} \times 10^{15} \times 10^{15} \times 10^{15} \times 10^{15} \times 10^{15} \times 10^{15}) \times (10^{15} \times 10^{15}) \times (10^{15} \times 10^{15}) \times (10^{15} \times 10^{15}) \times (10^{15} \times 10^{15} \times 10^{2}) \times 2^{128} = 10^{257} \times 2^{128} = 1.665 \times 2^{853} \times 2^{128} = 1.665 \times 2^{981}$ which is very much larger than 2^{128}.

The computational load is calculated as follows, let us consider, in 1 s, 2^{80} computations are performed by a fastest computer [25]. In 1 year, $2^{80} \times 365(\text{days}) \times 24(\text{hours}) \times 60(\text{minutes}) \times 60(\text{seconds})$ computations are performed by a fastest computer. Therefore, to compute 1.665×2^{981} computations, a total of $\frac{1.665 \times 2^{981}}{2^{80} \times 365 \times 24 \times 60 \times 60} = 8.92552 \times 10^{263}$ years required. This much of computation load is very much big enough. This proves that the proposed algorithm is very much strong enough for protecting brute-force attack.

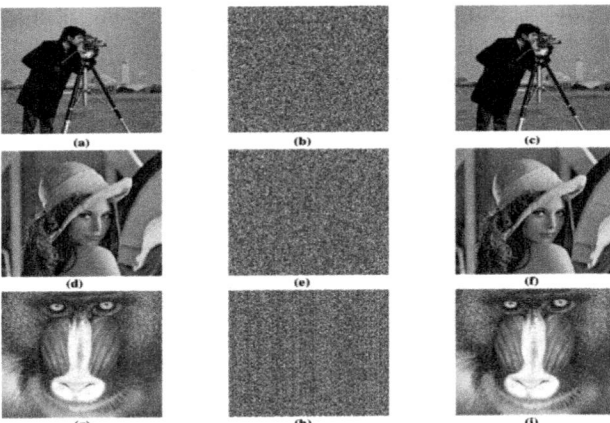

Fig. 2. Simulation results: (a), (d), and (g) Original "Cameraman", "Lena", and "Baboon" images, respectively; (b), (e), and (h) Corresponding encrypted images of (a), (d), and (g), respectively; (c), (f), and (i) Corresponding decrypted images of (b), (e), and (h), respectively.

4.2 Statistical Attack Analysis

Statistical attack analysis is an important analysis for analyzing the statistical attack. The power of statistical attack is like that, any encryption algorithm can be easily broken, without resisting to statistical attack [25]. Histogram analysis and correlation analysis are the two important measures which are basically used for analyzing the statistical attack, which are as follows.

Histogram Analysis. Histogram is the graph between the tonal values of the image on the x-axis and number of pixels for each tonal value is on the y-axis. To resist against statistical attack, two criteria should be satisfied for histogram images, one is that, the histogram of encrypted images should be entirely different than the histogram of original images, and other one is that, the histogram of encrypted images should be uniformly distributed over the entire range of gray scale values [26]. Figure 3 shows the histogram images of original, encrypted, and decrypted "Cameraman", "Lena", and "Baboon" images. By observing the histograms of original images and their corresponding encrypted images in Fig. 3, we found that the histograms of encrypted images are totally different than the histograms of original images and also by observing the histograms of encrypted images in Fig. 3, we found that the histograms of encrypted images are uniformly distributed over the entire range of gray scale values hence even if hacker decrypts a certain portion, decrypting the entire information will still be difficult task to do. In the same way of observing the histograms of original images and decrypted images in Fig. 3, we found that both the images are same which confirms that there is no loss of information while transmission. Hence, histogram analysis shows the proposed algorithm withstands statistical attacks as well as shows integrity in transmission.

Correlation Analysis. Correlation coefficient gives amount of linear correlation among the adjacent pixels in an image. Meaningful images contain a high correlation between a pixel and its neighboring pixels in vertical, horizontal and diagonal directions. The aim of the encryption algorithm is to break such the correlation between the adjacent pixels along all the three directions so as to arrive at the image with maximum randomness and zero or little correlation. To test the correlation between the two adjacent pixels the following formula is used:

$$r_{xy} = \frac{covariance(x,y)}{\sqrt{D(x)D(y)}} \tag{31}$$

where

$$covariance(x,y) = \frac{1}{N}\sum_{i=1}^{N}(x_i - E(x))(y_i - E(y)) \tag{32}$$

$$D(x) = \frac{1}{N}\sum_{i=1}^{N}(x_i - E(x))^2 \text{ and } D(y) = \frac{1}{N}\sum_{i=1}^{N}(y_i - E(y))^2 \tag{33}$$

$$E(x) = \frac{1}{N}\sum_{i=1}^{N}x_i, E(y) = \frac{1}{N}\sum_{i=1}^{N}y_i \tag{34}$$

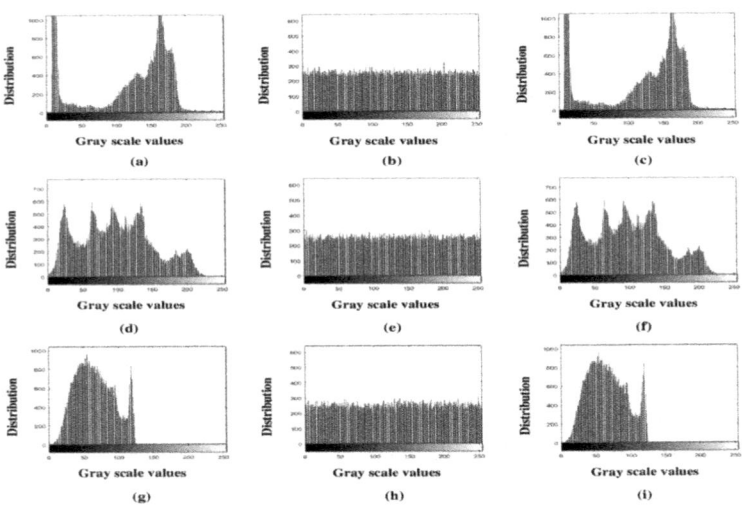

Fig. 3. Histogram analysis results: (a), (d), (g) Histograms of original "Cameraman", "Lena", and "Baboon" images, respectively; (b), (e), (h) Corresponding histograms of encrypted images, respectively; (c), (f), (i) Corresponding histograms of decrypted images, respectively.

The value for correlation coefficient is in between -1 to 1. Value of correlation coefficient greater than 0 (zero) indicates positive correlation; value of correlation coefficient less than 0 (zero) indicates negative correlation; and value of correlation coefficient equal to 0 (zero) indicates zero correlation or non-correlation of adjacent pixels [27]. For an original image, the correlation coefficient value either reaches to $+1$ or -1, but for a good encryption algorithm, to withstand statistical effects, the correlation coefficient value for encrypted images should be very close to 0 [28]. In this paper, 10,000 pairs of two adjacent pixels are randomly selected along horizontal, vertical, and diagonal directions to measure the correlation coefficient value in between these pairs of two adjacent pixels. Table 1 shows the correlation coefficient values of original images and their corresponding encrypted images along all the three directions by using the proposed encryption scheme. As observable from Table 1, the correlation coefficient values of two adjacent pixels of original images along horizontal, vertical, and diagonal directions for all images are nearly equal to 1, however, the correlation coefficient values of two adjacent pixels of encrypted images along all the three directions for all the images are almost equal to 0. This concludes that the proposed encryption algorithm successfully breaks the correlation of two adjacent pixels in original images. Hence the proposed algorithm successfully resists statistical attack.

Figure 4 shows the correlation plot between 10,000 pairs of adjacent pixels selected randomly for "Lena" image. Figure 4 shows that the adjacent pixels along horizontal, vertical, and diagonal directions in original images are highly correlated whereas the adjacent pixels along all the three directions in encrypted images are weekly correlated. This concludes that the proposed algorithm strongly resists statistical attack.

Table 1. Correlation coefficient values of different images with proposed encryption scheme.

Images	Correlation in original images			Correlation in encrypted images		
	Horizontal	Vertical	Diagonal	Horizontal	Vertical	Diagonal
Cameraman (256×256)	0.9371	0.9642	0.9217	-0.0029	-0.0042	-0.0040
Lena (256×256)	0.9374	0.9711	0.9279	-0.0022	-0.0023	-0.0039
Lena (512×512)	0.9609	0.9846	0.9569	0.0024	0.0029	-0.0039
Baboon (256×256)	0.8655	0.8238	0.8047	0.0042	-0.0011	0.0035

4.3 Differential Attack Analysis

NPCR (Number of Pixel Changing Rate) and UACI (Unified Average Changing Intensity) are the two most common quantities used to evaluate the strength of the encryption algorithm against the differential attack. NPCR measures the difference in pixels between the two encrypted images. The first encrypted image, C_1 is produced by directly applying the proposed encryption algorithm on the original image. The second encrypted image, C_2 is produced by changing any one random pixel value of that original image and then encrypting the changed original image. $C_1(i,j)$ and $C_2(i,j)$ are the corresponding elements of the encrypted image matrix of ith row and j^{th} column. Therefore, the NPCR is calculated as:

$$NPCR = \frac{\sum_{i,j} D(i,j)}{M \times N} \times 100 \tag{35}$$

where $M \times N$ is the size of the image matrix and $D(i,j)$ is given by

$$D(i,j) = \begin{cases} 0 & if \ C_1(i,j) = C_2(i,j) \\ 1 & if \ C_1(i,j) \neq C_2(i,j) \end{cases} \tag{36}$$

For a 256-gray scale image, the expected value of NPCR is around to be 99.6094% [5].

UACI is the average changing intensity between the two encrypted images $C_1(i,j)$ and $C_2(i,j)$. The UACI is calculated via the formula

$$UACI = \frac{1}{N} \left[\sum_{i,j} \frac{|C_1(i,j) - C_2(i,j)|}{2^l - 1} \right] \tag{37}$$

where l stand for number of bits to represent the gray scale pixel values in an image. In this proposed algorithm, 256-gray scale pixel values are used, hence the value for $l = 8$; therefore $2^l - 1 = 255$. For a 256-gray scale image, the expected value of UACI is around to be 33.4635% [5]. The NPCR and UACI values of various images by using the proposed encrypted algorithm are shown in Table 2. The values listed in Table 2 are the average value taken over 100 different ciphered images by changing one pixel values by using the same encryption algorithm.

4.4   Information Entropy

Information entropy measures the degree of uncertainty and randomness of distribution of pixels in an encrypted image. It is calculate by using the function,

$$H_e = - \sum_{k=0}^{G-1} P(k) log_2(P(k)) \tag{38}$$

where H_e is the entropy, G is the gray value of the input image $(0, 1, 2, \cdots\cdots\cdots, 255)$. $P(k)$ determines the probability of occurrence of symbol k. For a secure encryption algorithm, the entropy falls near to 8. The entropy of various images by using the proposed encryption algorithm is as shown in Table 3. Table 3 shows that the entropy of "Lena" image of size 512×512 is 7.9993 which is very much close to 8 and the entropy of other images having sizes 256×256 are also closes to 8. This concludes that the proposed algorithm provides desired degree of randomness.

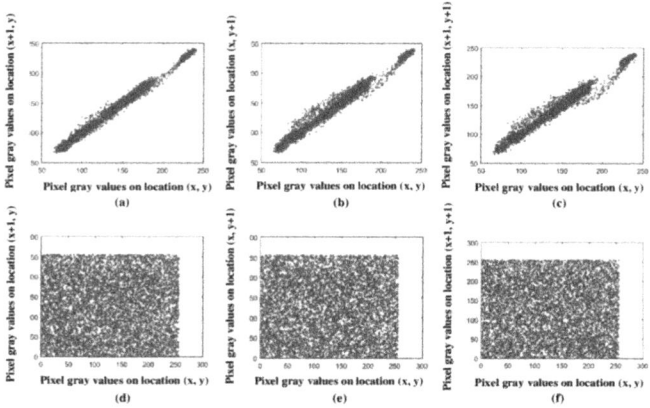

Fig. 4. Correlation distribution results of "Lena" image: (a), (b), (c) Horizontal, vertical and diagonal distribution of original "Lena" image, respectively; (d), (e), (f) Horizontal, vertical and diagonal distribution of corresponding encrypted "Lena" image, respectively.

Table 2. Avg. NPCR and UACI results of different images with proposed encryption scheme.

Images	Average NPCR (%)	Average UACI (%)
Cameraman (256 × 256)	99.6108	33.4587
Lena (256 × 256)	99.6037	33.4653
Lena (512 × 512)	99.6121	33.4711
Baboon (256 × 256)	99.6014	33.4124

Table 3. Information entropy results of different images with proposed encryption scheme.

Images	Information entropy	
	Original images	Encrypted images
Cameraman (256 × 256)	7.0097	7.9947
Lena (256 × 256)	7.5813	7.9977
Lena (512 × 512)	6.6966	7.9969
Baboon (256 × 256)	7.4455	7.9993

4.5   Key Sensitivity Analysis

Key sensitivity defines how a secret key is sensitive in an algorithm. For a good and secure encryption algorithm, the secret keys which are used in that algorithm should be sensitive so that a small change in a secret key will produce large change in an output [30]. Figure 5 shows the key sensitivity results of "Lena" image by using the proposed encryption scheme. By observing the difference images in Fig. 5, we found that there is a large difference in between the original encrypted image and the changed encrypted images and also by observing the decrypted images in Fig. 5, we found that the changed encrypted images are not decrypted by using the right secret keys. Likewise the sensitivity test will be applied to other secret keys. From the sensitivity analysis tests of Fig. 5, we concluded that the proposed algorithm is sensitive to the secret keys.

4.6   Plaintext Sensitivity Analysis

The plaintext sensitivity is analyzed by changing pixel values at different positions randomly in the original images while keeping other pixel position values remains constant. Then apply the proposed encryption algorithm on the changed original image to get changed encrypted images. Finally, examine the difference images of original encrypted images and changed encrypted images. In this paper, we have randomly changed pixel values at positions (64, 64), (128, 128) and (256, 256) in the original image (Fig. 2(e)). Figure 6 shows the plaintext sensitivity results of "Lena" image. The difference images of Fig. 6 clearly show that even changing one pixel alters the encrypted image to a great extent. Hence, the proposed algorithm is highly sensitive to the plaintext.

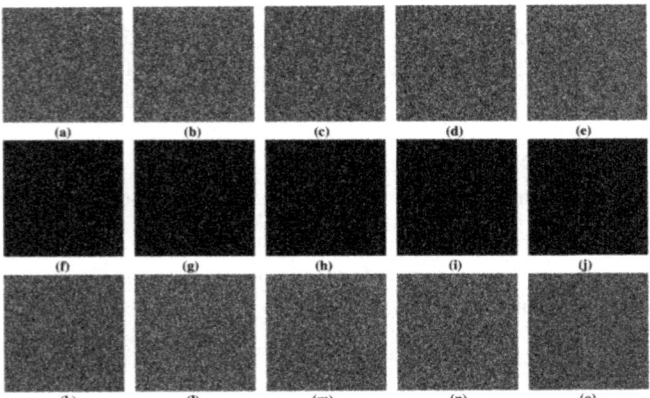

Fig. 5. Key sensitivity results of "Lena" image: (a), (b), (c), (d), (e) shows encrypted images with $xx(1)\,to\,xx(1) + 10^{-15}$, $yy(1)\,to\,yy(1) + 10^{-15}$, $zz(1)\,to\,zz(1) + 10^{-15}$, $ww(1)\,to\,ww(1) + 10^{-15}$, and $ee(1)\,to\,ee(1) + 10^{-15}$, respectively; (f), (g), (h), (i), (j) shows difference images of Figs. 2(e) and 5(a), (b), (c), (d), (e), respectively; (k), (l), (m), (n), (o) shows decrypted images of (a), (b), (c), (d), (e), respectively by using the right secret keys.

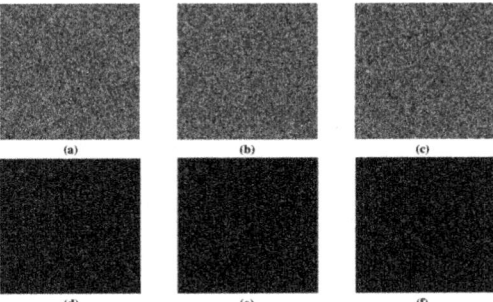

Fig. 6. Plaintext sensitivity results of "Lena" image: (a), (b), (c) are the encrypted images with changed pixel value at position (64, 64), (128, 128) and (256, 256), respectively; (d), (e), (f) are the difference images of Figs. 2(e) and 6(a), (b), (c), respectively.

4.7   Known-Plaintext and Chosen-Plaintext Attacks Analysis

In this algorithm, the secret keys that mean the initial values and system parameters of Beta map, LSS map, LTS map, TSS map, and PWLCM system are generated from the original initial values and system parameters of the above maps and the 256-bit hash value of the original image. So all the secret keys are dependent on the hash value of the original image, hence a small change in the original image, will get different initial values and system parameters and generate different encrypted image. This shows that the proposed algorithm is highly image – dependent and capable of effectively repel known-plaintext and chosen-plaintext attacks.

4.8   Comparison Analysis

In this paper, the performance of the proposed encryption scheme is compared with the performance of some other encryption schemes [29, 30]. The comparison is done by using "Lena" image of size 256 × 256. Table 4 shows the comparison of the proposed encryption scheme with some other encryption schemes by using different measuring criteria such as correlation coefficient, NPCR and UACI, entropy. The proposed algorithm only uses 2 (two) rounds of row rotation and column rotation operations whereas Ref. [30] uses 7 (seven) rounds of all operations. From Table 4, we can see that the entropy of the proposed image encryption algorithm is very much close to 8 and also better than the other existing works [29, 30]. By observing the NPCR and UACI values in Table 4, we can see that the NPCR and UACI values of the proposed image encryption algorithm are very much close to the expected NPCR and UACI values as compare to the other existing works [29, 30]. Finally by observing the correlation coefficient values along all the three directions, we realize that all have correlation coefficient values very much close to zero. From the comparison analysis, we concluded that the proposed image encryption algorithm is better secure and simple as compared to the existing works [29, 30].

Table 4. Comparison of different criteria of proposed scheme and other existing schemes for "Lena" image of size 256×256

Algorithms	Correlation coefficients			NPCR (%)	UACI (%)	Entropy
	Horizontal	Vertical	Diagonal			
Ours (2 rounds)	−0.0022	−0.0023	−0.0039	99.6037	33.4653	7.9977
Ref. [29]	−0.0230	0.0019	−0.0034	99.6200	33.5100	7.9974
Ref. [30] (7 rounds)	0.0019	0.0038	−0.0019	99.6566	33.4782	7.9970

4.9   Encryption Speed

The total time elapsed for executing the proposed algorithm is 0.208 s for a 256×256 sized image. This much of execution time is very much less which is all about $1/5^{th}$ of 1 s. Hence the proposed algorithm is very much efficient to apply in real-time applications.

4.10   Future Scope

This paper gives an idea of simple, secure, and time efficient image encryption technique and the proposed idea is implemented on gray scale images. The proposed idea can be implemented for color images.

5   Conclusion

This paper proposed a simple, secure, and time efficient multi-way rotational permutation operation and multiple diffusion operation based image encryption scheme by using 1-D chaotic maps and the Secure Hash Algorithm SHA-256. From the above discussion, first, the image is divided into number of blocks and then applying rotational operations on them to permute the pixels, second, row rotational and column rotational permutation operations are performed by using 1-D chaotic maps. The row rotational and column rotational permutation operations are performed 2 times to get good results. Finally, multi-way diffusion operations are performed to get the final encrypted image. The proposed algorithm produces better encryption results and also produces better security as comparison to the other existing works used in this paper. The better security is in the sense of higher secret key space, higher entropy, etc. The proposed algorithm is also time efficient that mean very much less time is required for implementing the proposed algorithm. Since the rotational based permutation operations are used in this algorithm hence the proposed algorithm is very much simple, also the new 1-D chaotic maps are used and the security analysis wilds the proposed algorithm is secure. All these features show that the proposed algorithm is secure and very much suitable for digital image encryption.

Acknowledgments. This research work is supported by Information Security Education Awareness (ISEA) project phase – II, Department of Electronics and Information Technology (DeitY), Govt. of India.

References

1. Coppersmith, D.: The Data Encryption Standard (DES) and its strengths against attacks. IBM J. Res. Dev. **38**(3), 243–250 (1994)
2. Pub NF. 197: Advanced encryption standard (AES). Federal Information Processing Standards Publication 197, 441-0311 (2001)
3. Gao, H., Zhang, Y., Liang, S., Li, D.: A new chaotic algorithm for image encryption. Chaos, Solitons Fractals **29**(2), 393–399 (2006)
4. Samhita, P., Prasad, P., Patro, K.A.K., Acharya, B.: A secure chaos-based image encryption and decryption using crossover and mutation operator. Int. J. Control Theory Appl. **9**(34), 17–28 (2016)
5. Gupta, A., Thawait, R., Patro, K.A.K., Acharya, B.: A novel image encryption based on bit-shuffled improved tent map. Int. J. Control Theory Appl. **9**(34), 1–16 (2016)
6. Shadangi, V., Choudhary, S.K., Patro, K.A.K., Acharya, B.: Novel arnold scrambling based CBC-AES image encryption. Int. J. Control Theory Appl. **10**(15), 93–105 (2017)
7. Guesmi, R., Farah, M.A.B., Kachouri, A., Samet, M.: Hash key-based image encryption using crossover operator and chaos. Multimed. Tools Appl. **75**(8), 4753–4769 (2016)
8. Guesmi, R., Farah, M.A.B., Kachouri, A., Samet, M.: A novel chaos-based image encryption using DNA sequence operation and Secure Hash Algorithm SHA-2. Nonlinear Dyn. **83**(3), 1123–1136 (2016)
9. Matthews, R.: On the derivation of a "chaotic" encryption algorithm. Cryptologia **13**(1), 29–42 (1989)
10. Liu, W., Sun, K., Zhu, C.: A fast image encryption algorithm based on chaotic map. Opt. Lasers Eng. **84**, 26–36 (2016)
11. Wang, X., Wang, S., Zhang, Y., Guo, K.: A novel image encryption algorithm based on chaotic shuffling method. Inf. Secur. J.: Glob. Perspect. **26**(1), 7–16 (2017)
12. Abd El-Latif, A.A., Li, L., Zhang, T., Wang, N., Song, X., Niu, X.: Digital image encryption scheme based on multiple chaotic systems. Sens. Imaging: Int. J. **13**(2), 67–88 (2012)
13. Ahmad, M., Khurana, S., Singh, S., AlSharari, H.D.: A simple secure hash function scheme using multiple chaotic maps. 3D Res. **8**(2), 13 (2017)
14. Zhang, Q., Guo, L., Wei, X.: Image encryption using DNA addition combining with chaotic maps. Math. Comput. Model. **52**(11), 2028–2035 (2010)
15. Enayatifar, R., Abdullah, A.H., Isnin, I.F.: Chaos-based image encryption using a hybrid genetic algorithm and a DNA sequence. Opt. Lasers Eng. **56**, 83–93 (2014)
16. Wang, X.Y., Zhang, Y.Q., Bao, X.M.: A novel chaotic image encryption scheme using DNA sequence operations. Opt. Lasers Eng. **73**, 53–61 (2015)
17. Zhang, Q., Guo, L., Wei, X.: A novel image fusion encryption algorithm based on DNA sequence operation and hyper-chaotic system. Optik-Int. J. Light Electron Opt. **124**(18), 3596–3600 (2013)
18. Yin, Z., Pan, L., Fang, X.: Proceedings of The Eighth International Conference on Bio-Inspired Computing: Theories and Applications (BIC-TA), vol. 212. Springer, Heidelberg (2013). https://doi.org/10.1007/978-3-642-37502-6
19. Zahmoul, R., Ejbali, R., Zaied, M.: Image encryption based on new Beta chaotic maps. Opt. Lasers Eng. **96**, 39–49 (2017)
20. Zhou, Y., Bao, L., Chen, C.P.: A new 1D chaotic system for image encryption. Sig. Process. **97**, 172–182 (2014)
21. Wang, X.Y., Yang, L.: Design of pseudo-random bit generator based on chaotic maps. Int. J. Mod. Phys. B **26**(32), 1250208 (2012)

22. Li, S., Chen, G., Mou, X.: On the dynamical degradation of digital piecewise linear chaotic maps. Int. J. Bifurcat. Chaos **15**(10), 3119–3151 (2005)
23. Kulsoom, A., Xiao, D., Abbas, S.A.: An efficient and noise resistive selective image encryption scheme for gray images based on chaotic maps and DNA complementary rules. Multimed. Tools Appl. **75**(1), 1–23 (2016)
24. Floating-Point Working Group: IEEE Standard for Binary Floating-Point Arithmetic. ANSI. IEEE Std. 754-1985 (1985)
25. Brindha, M., Gounden, N.A.: A chaos based image encryption and lossless compression algorithm using hash table and Chinese Remainder Theorem. Appl. Soft Comput. **40**, 379–390 (2016)
26. Wang, X., Zhang, H.L.: A novel image encryption algorithm based on genetic recombination and hyper-chaotic systems. Nonlinear Dyn. **83**(1–2), 333–346 (2016)
27. Zhang, J., Fang, D., Ren, H.: Image encryption algorithm based on DNA encoding and chaotic maps. Math. Prob. Eng. **2014** (2014)
28. Hu, T., Liu, Y., Gong, L.H., Ouyang, C.J.: An image encryption scheme combining chaos with cycle operation for DNA sequences. Nonlinear Dyn. **87**(1), 51–66 (2017)
29. Xu, L., Li, Z., Li, J., Hua, W.: A novel bit-level image encryption algorithm based on chaotic maps. Opt. Lasers Eng. **78**, 17–25 (2016)
30. Wang, X., Liu, L., Zhang, Y.: A novel chaotic block image encryption algorithm based on dynamic random growth technique. Opt. Lasers Eng. **66**, 10–18 (2015)

Design and Development of a Cloud Assisted Robot

Rajesh Singh[1(✉)], Anita Gehlot[1], Mamta Mittal[2], Rohit Samkaria[1],
Devendra Singh[3], and Prakash Chandra[4]

[1] University of Petroleum and Energy Studies, Dehradun, India
rsingh@ddn.upes.ac.in
[2] G. B. Pant Engineering College, New Delhi, India
[3] Uttranchal University, Dehradun, India
[4] REMTECH, Shamli, India

Abstract. In this paper cloud assisted robot is designed and developed. (IoT) Internet of things has been recognized to be the next revolutionary technology which connects all the systems together and make them smart. In the typical cases the IoT based smart robot are becoming the most popular systems. The previous tradition network are changing due to the advent of the Internet of things which include various Android operated Smart phone connected with service oriented robot and are using wireless protocol to communicate. The robot is controlled through the Android app or through the web page designed with html and various task of robot and motion is realized. The results achieved shows the approach is efficient in terms of connectivity and convergence

Keywords: IoT · Zigbee · Robot · Node MCU

1 Introduction

Progressing transformation about (IoT) Internet of things, together with the developing dispersion for robots on a significant number exercises about consistently life; makes IoT-aided mechanical technology requisitions a substantial truth from claiming the approaching future. Accordingly, new propelled services, In view of those transaction the middle of robots and more "things", would constantly considered previously supporting people [1]. Internet of Things permits the interconnection of savvy objects for example versatile robots, remote sensors, and by utilizing distinctive communication conventions by building up a dynamic multi-modular heterogeneous system [2]. The virtualization and cloud handling perspective makes a fused framework that appears to customers to be a brought together framework. Here figuring and correspondence resources are not in the client PCs yet rather in a planned system that is accessible wherever and at whatever time. The Internet of Things increases the cloud idea past enlisting and correspondence to fuse everything, particularly, the contraptions [3]. The Internet of Things (IoT) idea draws in impressive enthusiasm from the scholarly world and industry. In view of such IoT uses, which go for continuous

© Springer Nature Singapore Pte Ltd. 2018
P. Bhattacharyya et al. (Eds.): NGCT 2017, CCIS 828, pp. 419–429, 2018.
https://doi.org/10.1007/978-981-10-8660-1_31

information along the assembling forms that empowers a responsive generation administration and upkeep, including vitality utilization and water use observing at each phase of a creation cycle [4]. There is a RSi Research Cloud (RSi-Cloud), which empowers joining of robot administrations with web administrations. As of recently, we have reconnaissance benefit utilizing robot cameras on the cloud condition, and have acknowledged web association from robots actualized with RSNP (Robot Service Network Protocol). The plan after effect of Robot Service HTML interface (RSHi), which is a component to treat robot applications conveyed in RSi-Cloud by an indistinguishable path from RSNP robot customers. RSHi makes it conceivable to convey RSNP benefit applications inside firewall frameworks and therefore a robot benefit extension can be exacted [5]. IoT's framework empowers associations between various elements (living or non-living), utilizing distinctive yet interoperable correspondence conventions. Along these lines in the IoT, a robot can be associated as a thing and set up associations with Internet or as a wellspring of data or potentially as a customer. The joining of robots inside the IoT can offer extraordinary points of interest in many fields. The recently created IoT stages conquer any hindrance between the genuine and the virtual world [6]. Work presented a network controlled four wheel robot assembled on a chassis powered up with the NodeMCU open source platform building blocks which provides an extensible base for various application emerging mixing robotics with Internet of things [7]. The developing an intelligent and reliable robotics system which are used to enable remote operation of unmanned robot requires innovative and various novel technical solutions [8]. The Internet of Things approach is based on the computation of the algebraic connectivity and algorithm used is virtual environment [9]. The benefits of IoT would be very useful in robotic domain with the Cloud robotics and its various roles of the robotics aiding in sensing the function of sensors and their manipulation [10]. The advent of cloud robotics and its role in aiding robot functions like sensing, manipulation, and mobility [11]. A smart robotics assistant helps the human being in a multiple way, which accepts voice data by human through cloud and respond corresponding to the instruction [12]. Around the world there only 1% things which are interconnected with each other like refrigerator, Car, TV, washing machine, garage, should all be connected with each other but are not. For all these things the internet is the living entity which is evolving and changing the world at a rapid rate. The broadband technology is becoming cheap and more powerful. The proliferation of number of devices becoming connected with each other and is leading to a new paradigm: Internet of Things [13] (Fig. 1).

The Fig. 2 shows the cloud assisted mini robot. The control algorithm of the designed system is written in the Arduino open source environment. The algorithm is based on the embedded C language and html. The controlling action is done with the Arduino Uno in serial interface with the Node MCU. The mobile app is linked with the network data to the cloud. The mini robot having the Node MCU which need to be connected with the internet and having a SSID and Password [14]. The mobile app is required the same SSID and Password. The communication protocol is served by the ESP module which is embed on the Node MCU which is 32 bit ARM microprocessor

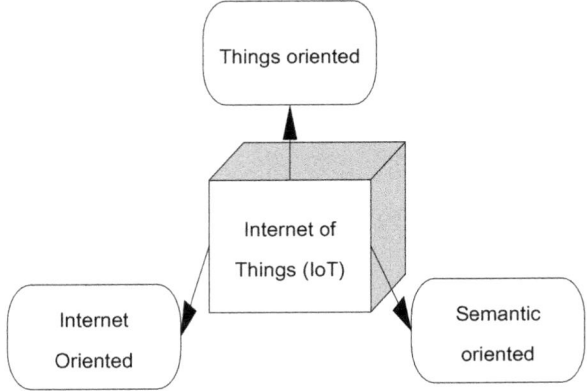

Fig. 1. Different visions for the convergence of Internet of Things

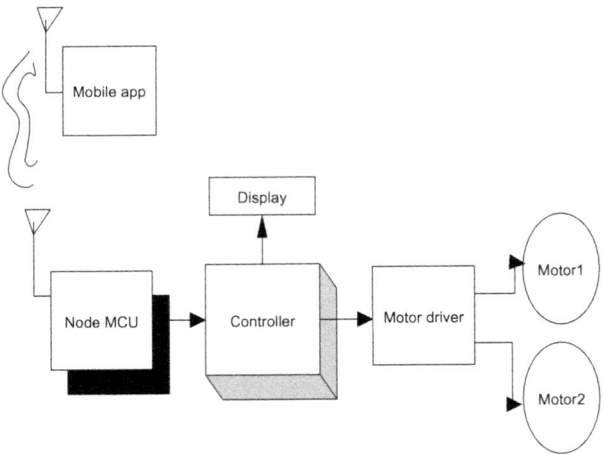

Fig. 2. Block diagram for the cloud assisted mini robot

with full support of WiFi network. This architecture allows it to be programmed independently. Building of a chain of other integrated components to make it required. Several boards have been developed which includes ESP8266, NodeLHC, ESP201, Wemos D1, Adafruit HUZZAH ESP8266 etc. NodeMCU has a complete hardware environment and software for prototyping IoT [15].

2 Function for ESP8266

```
#include <ESP8266WiFi.h>

const char* ssid = "R@Samkaria";

const char* password = "qwerty123";

WiFiServer server(80);

// int ledPin = D7; // GPIO13

//int ledPin1=D6;//GPIO12

//int ledPin2=D5;//GPIO12


void setup() {

Serialbegin(115200);

 delay(10);

 PinMode(ledPin, OUTPUT);

 DigitalWrite(ledPin, LOW);

 PinMode(ledPin1, OUTPUT);

 DigitalWrite(ledPin1, LOW);

 PinMode(ledPin2, OUTPUT);

 DigitalWrite(ledPin2, LOW);

 // Connect to WiFi network

 Serialprintln();

 Serialprintln();
Serialprint("Connecting to ");

 Serialprintln(ssid);

 WiFi.begin(ssid, password);
```

```
while (WiFi.status() != WL_CONNECTED) {

delay(500);

Serialprint(".");

  }

  Serialprintln("");

  Serialprintln("WiFi connected");

  // Start the server

  serverbegin();

  Serialprintln("Server started");

  // Print the IP address

  Serialprint("Use this URL to connect: ");

  Serialprint("http://");

  Serialprint(WiFi.localIP());

  Serialprintln("/");

  }
```

Function to Control Data Pin for Robot

```
int ledPin = D7;  // GPIO13

int ledPin1=D6; //GPIO12

int ledPin2=D5; //GPIO12
PinMode(ledPin, OUTPUT);

DigitalWrite(ledPin, LOW);

PinMode(ledPin1, OUTPUT);
```

```
DigitalWrite(ledPin1, LOW);

PinMode(ledPin2, OUTPUT);

DigitalWrite(ledPin2, LOW);

 if (request.indexOf("/DATA1=100") != -1)  {

  DigitalWrite(ledPin, HIGH);

  value = HIGH;

  DigitalWrite(ledPin1, LOW);

   DigitalWrite(ledPin2, LOW);

 }

 if (request.indexOf("/DATA2=200") != -1)  {

  DigitalWrite(ledPin, LOW);

  value = LOW;

  DigitalWrite(ledPin1, HIGH);

  DigitalWrite(ledPin2, LOW);

 }

  if (request.indexOf("/DATA3=300") != -1)  {

  DigitalWrite(ledPin, LOW);

  value = LOW;

  DigitalWrite(ledPin1, LOW);

  DigitalWrite(ledPin2, HIGH);

   }

 if (request.indexOf("/DATA3=400") != -1)  {

   DigitalWrite(ledPin, LOW);

   value = LOW;
```

```
   DigitalWrite(ledPin1, LOW);

   DigitalWrite(ledPin2, HIGH);

  }
```

Function for Webserver Display

```
clientprintln("HTTP/1.1 200 OK");

  clientprintln("Content-Type: text/html");

  clientprintln(""); //  do not forget this one

  clientprintln("<!DOCTYPE HTML>");

  clientprintln("<html>");

  clientprint("Cloud Control minirobot : ");

  if(value == HIGH) {

   clientprint("On");

  } else {

   clientprint("Off");

  }

  clientprintln("<br><br>");

  clientprintln("<a href=\"/DATA1=100\"\"><button>FORWARD </button></a>");

  clientprintln("<a href=\"/DATA2=200\"\"><button>REVERSE </button></a>");

  clientprintln("<a href=\"/DATA3=300\"\"><button>RIGHT </button></a>");

  clientprintln("<a href=\"/DATA4=400\"\"><button>LEFT </button></a><br />");

 clientprintln("</html>");

delay(1);

 Serialprintln("Client disonnected");

 Serialprintln("");

 }
```

3   Proteus Simulation Model

The Fig. 3 shows the design developed with the Proteus simulation. The various virtual components placed on workbench, interconnected with each other and Arduino hex uploaded to the system.

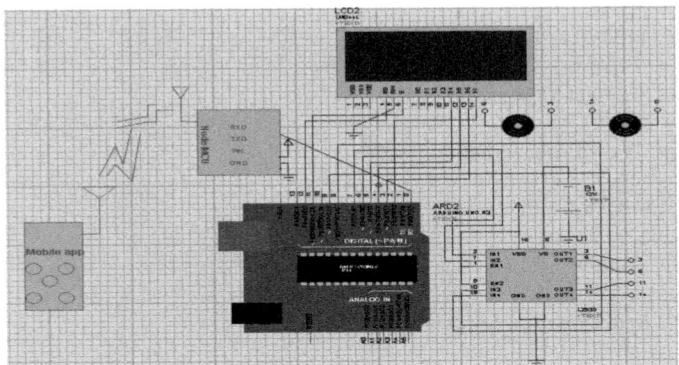

Fig. 3. Proteus simulation of the model

4   Software Development of the System

In the software development the hierarchy based algorithm is designed. The Fig. 4 shows the flow chart of the various conditions. The four different buttons provided with the Mobile app, which is having the different value for the different button. Once the

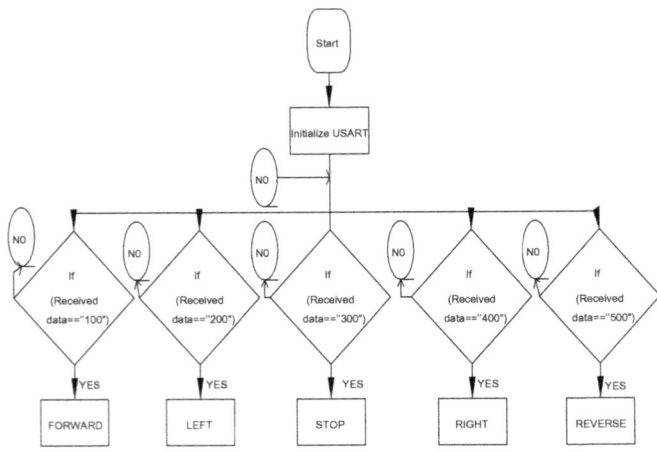

Fig. 4. Flow chart for the algorithm

button is pressed it transmits the desired integer value and in the receiving side if the desired value meets the conditions then corresponds to the action taken (Figs. 5 and 6).

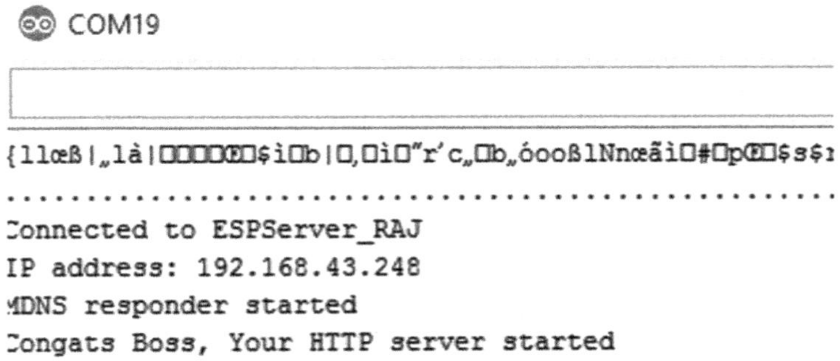

⊙ COM19

{11œß|„là|□□□□œ□\$i□b|□,□ì□"r'c„□b„óooß1Nnœãì□#□pœ□\$s\$ɪ

....

Connected to ESPServer_RAJ
IP address: 192.168.43.248
MDNS responder started
Congats Boss, Your HTTP server started

Fig. 5. COM port showing the IP address

ESP8266 Web Server n

TEMP METER TEMPERATURE (oC)

MOTOR1-STATUS ON OFF

MOTOR2-STATUS ON OFF

MOTOR2-STATUS ON OFF

MOTOR2-STATUS ON OFF

Fig. 6. Mobile app to control robot

5   Conclusion

Due to the advancement of technology, nowadays the availability of the internet is everywhere. So the systems can be controlled with IoT enabled devices and these devices can be operated from anywhere in world. In the developed system the mini robot is accessed through the IP address. The developed robot is accessible by any mobile or the web browser with access to the IP and controlled via any mobile phone (Fig. 7).

Fig. 7. Snapshot of the developed mini robot

In future this type of minirobot system can be used to retrieve the useful information throughout the glob without any restriction to the distance or line of sight. The system developed is very convenient to retrieve the data on the multiple systems without restriction of number of user to access the data. However still there are a number of challenges to implement the internet of Things.

References

1. Metev, S.M., Veiko, V.P.: Laser Assisted Microtechnology, 2nd edn. Springer, Berlin (1998). https://doi.org/10.1007/978-3-642-87271-6. Ed. by R.M. Osgood Jr.
2. Breckling, J. (ed.): The Analysis of Directional Time Series: Applications to Wind Speed and Direction. Lecture Notes in Statistics, vol. 61. Springer, Berlin (1989). https://doi.org/10.1007/978-1-4612-3688-7
3. Zhang, S., Zhu, C., Sin, J.K.O., Mok, P.K.T.: A novel ultrathin elevated channel low-temperature poly-Si TFT. IEEE Electron Device Lett. **20**, 569–571 (1999)

4. Wegmuller, M., von der Weid, J.P., Oberson, P., Gisin, N.: High resolution fiber distributed measurements with coherent OFDR. In: Proceedings of ECOC 2000, paper 11.3.4, p. 109 (2000)
5. Sorace, R.E., Reinhardt, V.S., Vaughn, S.A.: High-speed digital-to-RF converter. U.S. Patent 5 668 842, 16 September 1997
6. The IEEE website (2002). http://www.ieee.org/
7. Shell, M.: IEEEtran homepage on CTAN (2002). http://www.ctan.org/tex-archive/macros/latex/contrib/supported/IEEEtran/
8. FLEXChip Signal Processor (MC68175/D), Motorola (1996)
9. PDCA12-70 data sheet. Opto Speed SA, Mezzovico, Switzerland
10. Karnik, A.: Performance of TCP congestion control with rate feedback: TCP/ABR and rate adaptive TCP/IP. M. Eng. thesis, Indian Institute of Science, Bangalore, India, January 1999
11. Padhye, J., Firoiu, V., Towsley, D.: A stochastic model of TCP Reno congestion avoidance and control. Univ. of Massachusetts, Amherst, MA, CMPSCI Technical report 99-02 (1999)
12. Wireless LAN Medium Access Control (MAC) and Physical Layer (PHY) Specification, IEEE Std. 802.11 (1997)

Adaptive Dynamic Partial Reconfigurable Security System

B. C. Manjith$^{(\boxtimes)}$, J. Kokila, and Ramasubramanian Natarajan

Department of Computer Science and Engineering,
National Institute of Technology, Tiruchirappalli, Tamil Nadu, India
406114001@nitt.edu

Abstract. FPGAs plays a major role in areas like cloud, aerospace, defense etc. due to hardware acceleration and reprogrammable feature. Adaptive hardware which can change the hardware design after production on site is finding more application. Through partial reconfiguration, an adaptive hardware can change the design itself based on current requirements or other environmental conditions. The article proposes an adaptive security system where encryption and hash code generation hardware accelerators can be dynamically created on FPGA according to the application need using partial reconfiguration. The system can swap in and swap out the corresponding hardware accelerator during run time, which in turn reduces the area and power. Two reconfigurable partitions are created for encryption and hash code generation algorithm. Each can swap in and out two algorithms depending on application requirement are presented here. Using the proposed method, the partial reconfigurable design reduces the amount of resource requirement to 35.63% than a static design.

Keywords: Dynamic partial reconfiguration · Hardware accelerator
Reconfigurable computing · Reconfigurable partition · Reconfigurable module
Adaptive hardware

1 Introduction

The development of Field Programmable Gate Arrays (FPGAs) in last two decades results in upgrading its usage from prototyping to hardware accelerators ranging from highly complex system to low end devices like home network equipment, flat screen display etc.

Because of the reconfigurable nature of FPGA, a new field called reconfigurable computing that can change the circuit configuration after hardware production came into existence. Usage of reconfigurable computing for self-adaptive hardware allows hardware to adapt to different environmental conditions and different needs by swapping or loading different computational modules. Adaptive hardware can efficiently configure hardware circuit to partially load and run in places where area is less (like small devices) and at the same time, same hardware can be made to run for efficient speed where area is more. Another use of adaptive hardware is that it allows dynamic change of parameters in hardware algorithms. Currently adaptive hardware is being used in many fields like fault tolerant networks, in DSP (Digital Signal Processing)

© Springer Nature Singapore Pte Ltd. 2018
P. Bhattacharyya et al. (Eds.): NGCT 2017, CCIS 828, pp. 430–439, 2018.
https://doi.org/10.1007/978-981-10-8660-1_32

where change of parameters in filters occur dynamically, in cryptography where swapping in and out sequentially required accelerators etc. Adaptive hardware is implemented through Partial Reconfiguration (PR) [1].

The proposed work focuses on doing encryption and hash code generation functions by loading the necessary encryption accelerator and hash code generation accelerator at run time. Depending on application or need, either Data Encryption Standard (DES) or Advanced Encryption Standard (AES) accelerator can be loaded for encryption and either Secure Hash Algorithm (SHA) or MD5 [2, 3] accelerator can be loaded for hash code generation.

2 Background and Related Works

When the user data and applications found its limitation to push the processor to achieve more and more performance, dedicated hardware came into existence in the form of ASIC. The disadvantage of being useful only for a single application of ASIC is removed by FPGAs which was using to create prototype for building hardware. FPGAs are reconfigurable devices that allows to run multiple applications on the same device. The flexibility of FPGAs as reconfigurable devices allows it to be useful in many fields of computing from large scale computations like in defense, aerospace and cloud to small scale computation like home automation, mobile phones etc. [4]. Partial reconfiguration means configuring only a part of FPGA without disturbing the rest of the circuit. It can be done either when the rest of the circuit is idle or running.

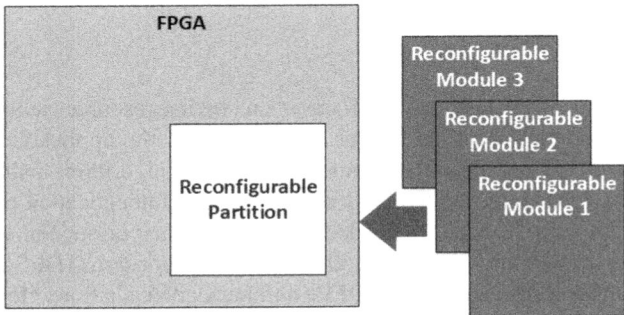

Fig. 1. Overview of partial reconfiguration idea.

Partial reconfiguration allows to save space (resource), performance and power. Resource sharing is done by sharing reconfigurable space (called Reconfigurable Partition or RP) among more than one Reconfigurable Modules (RMs). When a particular RM is needed, it is loaded to the corresponding RP. An existing RM should be swapped out from a RP if a new RM is to be loaded to the same partition as shown in Fig. 1. Likewise, any number of RMs can be swapped in and out of a RP. The process allows to save space. While coming to performance, more resources can be allocated for a certain accelerator. As a result, high level of parallelism and faster processing can be achieved compared to a static system. In short, PR allows tradeoff between space and time. Electronic devices consumes a lot of static power. This causes need of more cooling effort and more power loss in small devices like mobile phones. Implementation of PR allows reduction of static power to a large extend since modules are loaded only when they are needed [1].

Raikovich and Fehér [5] shown the importance of dynamic partial reconfiguration for image processing applications. The works shows that filters for image processing can be partially reconfigured at run time which reduces the configuration time than reconfiguring full system. Authors in [6] compares the dynamic partial reconfiguration and evolvable hardware which is built as a virtual reconfigurable circuit on the top of FPGA. Both methods are tested for 2D image processing in terms of performance and time. Lifa et al. [7] shows that some features of application changes over time that needs the hardware to be changed which are not predicted at compile time. Such cases can use dynamic partial reconfiguration to change the hardware design at run time. They proposes a hardware prefetching mechanism for image processing application that gives 32% more performance that fetch on demand and 20% more than static prefetching. A prototype of controller which can be dynamically modified depending on the need is presented in [8]. The system is initialized based on an UML description and can be dynamically reconfigure any part of controller as needed. Authors in [9] uses Dynamic Partial Reconfiguration (DPR) for loading median filter in image processing is presented. Krill et al. [10] proposed an adaptive system for image processing and signal processing application using three IP cores. Partial reconfiguration is done to load algorithm based on requirement.

3 Proposed Work

The proposed adaptive security system focuses on sharing resources among encryption algorithms and authentication algorithms. Depending on the application and security level, different encryption algorithms and authentication algorithms will be used. The proposed system loads only the required encryption and authentication accelerator at a time. The system uses DES and AES accelerators for encryption. For authentication, SHA and MD5 accelerators are used. Both encryption algorithms (DES and AES) and authentication algorithms (SHA and MD5) won't be needed at a time. Hence in order to save space and power, only one encryption algorithm and one authentication algorithm will be loaded to FPGA depending on the application requirement.

One RP will be created for RMs - DES and AES. Another RP that shares RMs-SHA and MD5 will also be created as shown in Fig. 2. Light blue portion indicates the static region and white region indicates the reconfigurable region on FPGA. The proposed system consists of two RPs, each RP has two RMs. First RP is for encryption which contains AES and DES accelerators as RMs. Second RP is for authentication and consists of MD5 and SHA accelerators as RMs. Depending on the request, either DES or AES will be loaded in the first RP and either SHA or MD5 will be loaded in the second RP dynamically (refer Fig. 1). Using dynamic partial reconfiguration, both area and power consumption can be reduced.

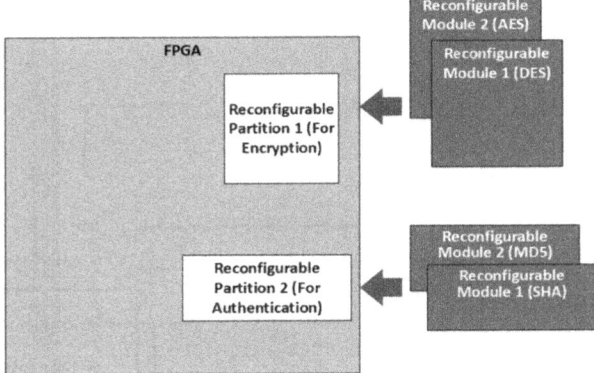

Fig. 2. Proposed partial reconfiguration view with two RPs. (Color figure online)

Figure 3 shows the basic model for the proposed system for two RPs with two RMs for each. With sharing of resources among different modules, the idea is multiplexing the modules which are to be loaded. Bistreams are loaded by internal configuration module that writes the configuration to any of its configuration port. As different modules are required at different time, resources can be shared between the modules and hence FPGA appears bigger. The multiplexer can select the encryption algorithm

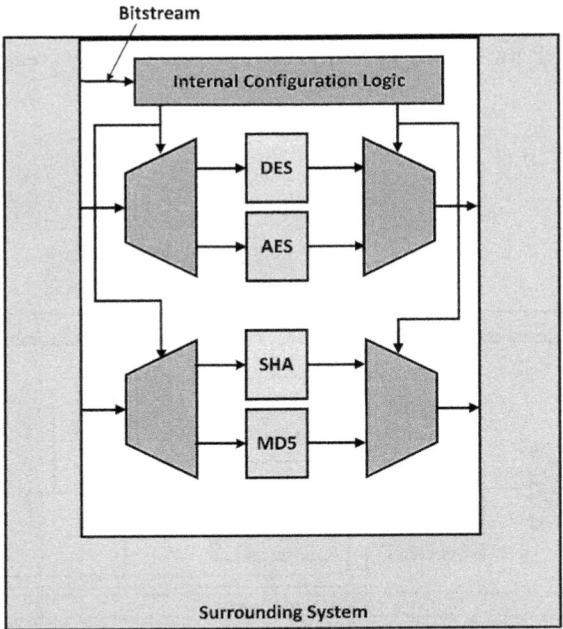

Fig. 3. Basic model for the proposed reconfigurable system.

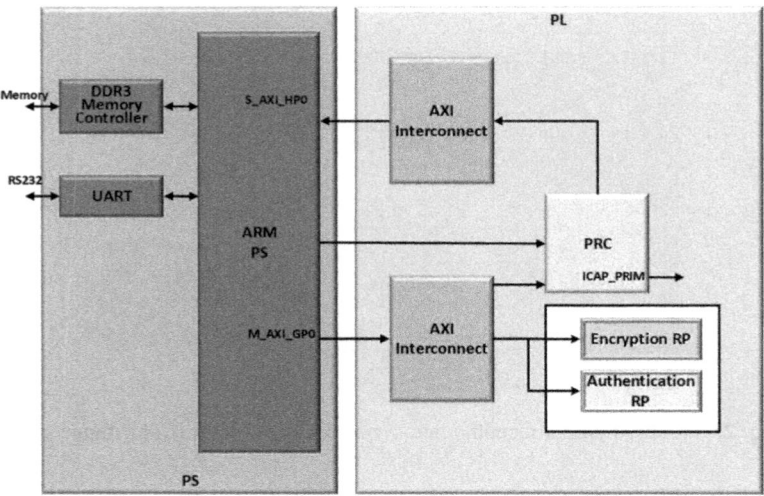

Fig. 4. Proposed system in PL part of FPGA.

and authentication algorithm for a particular application. Then using internal configuration port, it can load the corresponding partial bitstream for RM to the RP.

Figure 4 shows the internal connections of the proposed work. Partial Reconfiguration Controller (PRC) is used to reconfigure the RP with two RMs depending on the trigger it receives during run time. It can be configured to receive both software and hardware triggers. In the proposed system, the PRC is configured to receive software triggers for both RP for loading the RMs. PRC is configured by creating virtual socket

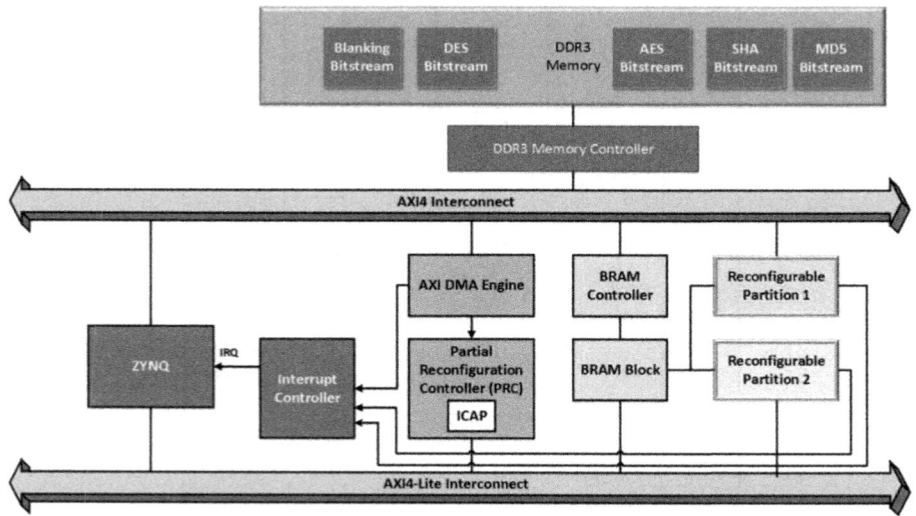

Fig. 5. Detailed view of the system connections.

manager for each RP and creating RMs for each RP. The partial bitstream address and length of bitstream has to be provided for each RM in PRC.

The more detailed view of the system connection is shown in Fig. 5. The ZYNQ and other peripheral communicate through AXI4 and AXI4-Lite interfaces [11–13]. ZYNQ is connected to RMs using AXI4-Lite interface through which it gives control signals and input/output. BRAM blocks are used to save program data and intermediate results. It is connected to ZYNQ through BRAM controller. PRC is connected through high performance port of ZYNQ through DMA. The partial and blanking bitstreams are initially loaded to DDR3 memory. From there, it will be loaded to RPs at run time depending on demand.

4 Implementation and Results

The proposed design is simulated, synthesized, placed and routed using Xilinx HLx system edition and tested in zedboard [11–13].

IPs for encryption and hashing algorithms are created in vivado HLS and imported to design. Bottom-up synthesis (synthesis by module) is used in PR. Both RPs are made as black boxes. After synthesis of static and reconfigurable modules, Design Check Points (DCPs) are saved. For starting the RMs by using software triggers, Partial Reconfiguration Controller (PRC) is configured accordingly. Two virtual socket manager with two reconfigurable modules for each are created. Only software trigger is enabled to receive in PRC. After the static design and one RM for each RP are loaded, floor planning can be done. Reconfigurable regions must be fully contained in a single Super Logic Region (SLR). The static part should be same for all RMs. After floor planning, placement and routing can be done for each RP separately. Blanking configuration is created without including RPs. After generating configurations, PR verification has to be done. Full bitstream and partial bitstreams for all RMs are done. The design is tested by creating a boot image which consists of blanking bit file and an application which gives input to the RMs and triggers the RM which has to be loaded [14]. The entire process is shown in Fig. 6. Figure 7 shows the system layout after placement and routing.

Partial reconfiguration feature allows to reduce the total number of slices used.

Table 1 shows the resource requirement of each module separately. When all the modules are executed in parallel, the modules takes this much of resources. But using partial reconfiguration, when the modules are executed serially, the resource utilization will be less. Only the blanking module will be loaded initially which reduces the static power consumption. When the need for any of the module arises, only the particular module will be loaded. When another module in the same RP is needed, already loaded module will be swapped out and loads the new module. This will reduce the area requirement of the RP. The difference in resource utilization of static module design and dynamic partial reconfiguration design is shown in Fig. 8.

Using static design, both encryption algorithms (AES and DES) will be loaded concurrently and takes a total of 775 number of slices, while using DPR, only 445 slices will be used. DPR shares 445 between AES and DES. Similarly, for finding hash code using SHA or MD5, static design takes 1145 slices and DPR takes 791 slices. The

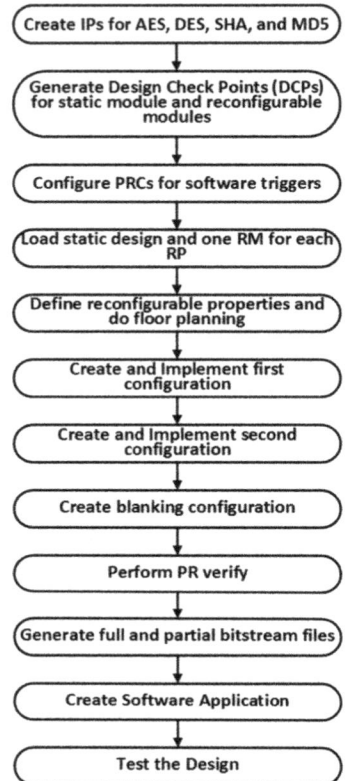

Fig. 6. Design and implementation flow of the proposed system.

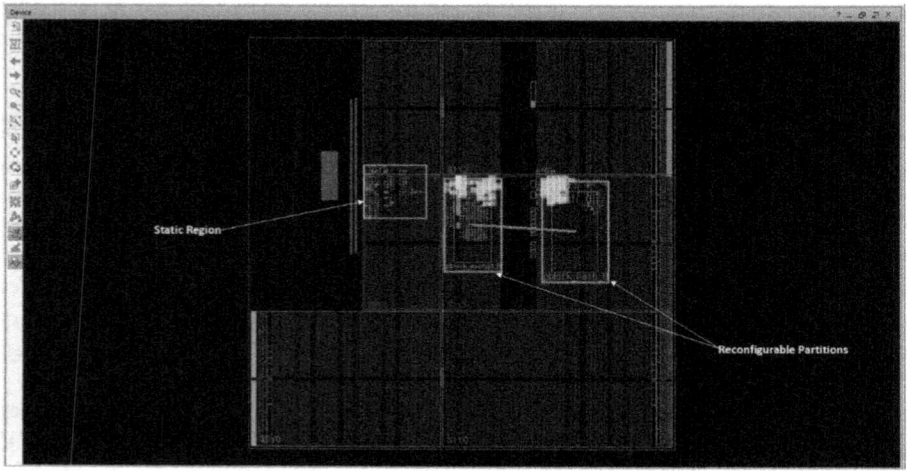

Fig. 7. Chip layout for the proposed system on xc7z020clg484-1 device.

Table 1. Resource utilization of individual RMs.

RPs	RMs	No. of Slices
RP1	DES	173
	AES	445
RP2	SHA	791
	MD5	242

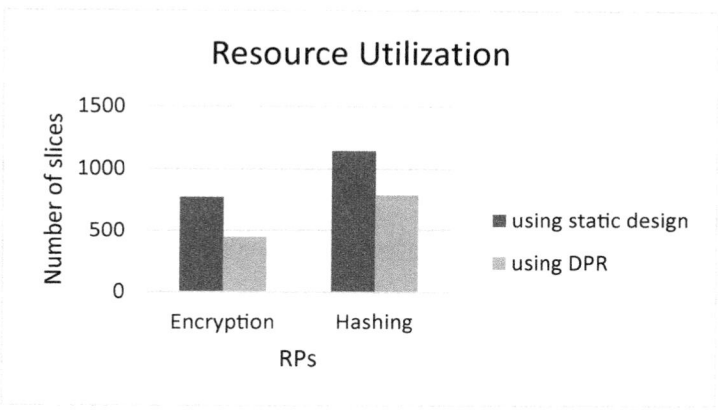

Fig. 8. Comparison of resource utilization between static design and reconfigurable design.

overall percentage of reduction in resource utilization of both RPs and the entire system is shown in Fig. 9. Using DPR, 42.58% and 30.92% resources for encryption and hash code generation respectively will be saved.

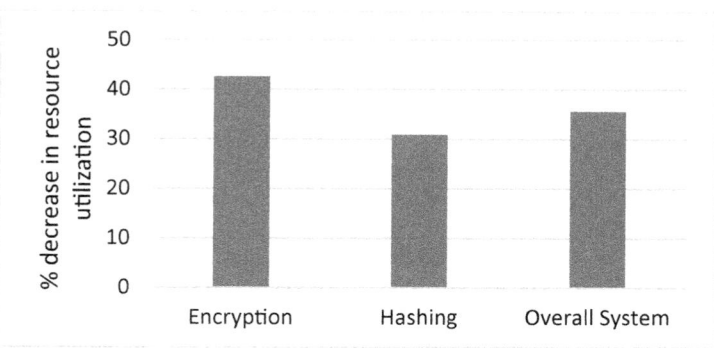

Fig. 9. Percentage decrease in resource utilization for the system based on reconfigurable design with static design.

5 Conclusion

The article presented a self-adaptive hardware which reconfigure itself with necessary accelerator using dynamic partial reconfiguration. The proposed design utilized the resources more efficiently by sharing resources among different reconfigurable modules. The need for sharing resources and thereby reduction in resource utilization is shown. Comparison shows that the resource utilization in partial reconfiguration decreased to 42.58% for encryption 30.92% for hash code generation than a static design. It resulted in an overall reduction in system resource utilization to 35.63%.

References

1. Dirk, K.: Partial Reconfiguration on FPGAs: Architectures, Tools and Applications, vol. 153. Springer Science & Business Media, New York (2012). https://doi.org/10.1007/978-1-4614-1225-0
2. Stallings, W., Tahiliani, M.P.: Cryptography and Network Security: Principles and Practice, vol. 6. Pearson, London (2014)
3. Stallings, W.: Network Security Essentials: Applications and Standards. Pearson Education India, Delhi (2007)
4. Hauck, S., Andre, D.: Reconfigurable Computing: The Theory and Practice of FPGA-based Computation, vol. 1. Morgan Kaufmann, Burlington (2010)
5. Raikovich, T., Fehér, B.: Application of partial reconfiguration of FPGAs in image processing. In: 2010 Conference on Ph. D. Research in Microelectronics and Electronics (PRIME), 18 July 2010, pp. 1–4. IEEE (2010)
6. Salvador, R., Otero, A., Mora, J., de la Torre, E., Riesgo, T., Sekanina, L.: Implementation techniques for evolvable HW systems: virtual vs. dynamic reconfiguration. In: 2012 22nd International Conference on Field Programmable Logic and Applications (FPL), 29 August 2012, pp. 547–550. IEEE (2012)
7. Lifa, A., Eles, P., Peng, Z.: A reconfigurable framework for performance enhancement with dynamic FPGA configuration prefetching. IEEE Trans. Comput.-Aided Design Integr. Circuits Syst. **35**(1), 100–113 (2016)
8. Wisniewski, R., Bazydlo, G., Gomes, L., Costa, A.: Dynamic partial reconfiguration of concurrent control systems implemented in FPGA devices. IEEE Trans. Ind. Inform. **13**, 1734–1741 (2017)
9. Rani, L.U., Jagajothi, G., Selvan, P.T.: Digital filter for real-time impulse noise suppression in video processing using Dynamic Partial Reconfiguration technique. In: 2015 International Conference on Control Communication & Computing, India, (ICCC), 19 November 2015, pp. 433–436. IEEE (2015)
10. Krill, B., Ahmad, A., Amira, A., Rabah, H.: An efficient FPGA-based dynamic partial reconfiguration design flow and environment for image and signal processing IP cores. Sig. Process. Image Commun. **25**(5), 377–387 (2010)
11. Vivado Design Suite Tutorial: High-Level Synthesis (UG871) – Xilinx. https://www.xilinx.com/support/documentation/sw_manuals/xilinx2014_1/ug871-vivado-high-level-synthesis-tutorial.pdf
12. Vivado Design Suite User Guide: Design Flows Overview – Xilinx. https://www.xilinx.com/support/documentation/sw_manuals/xilinx2013_3/ug892-vivado-design-flows-overview.pdf

13. Vivado Design Suite User Guide: Using Constraints (UG903) – Xilinx. https://www.xilinx.com/support/documentation/sw_manuals/xilinx2013_1/ug903-vivado-using-constraints.pdf
14. Vivado Design Suite User Guide Partial Reconfiguration, UG909 (v2016.1) 6 April 2016. https://www.xilinx.com/support/documentation/sw_manuals/xilinx2015_4/ug909-vivado-partial-reconfiguration.pdf

Fuzzy Entropy Based Feature Selection for Website User Classification in EDoS Defense

Sukhada Bhingarkar[1]([✉]) [ID] and Deven Shah[2]

[1] MIT College of Engineering, Pune, Pune, India
sukhada.bhingarkar@gmail.com
[2] Thakur College of Engineering and Technology, Mumbai, India

Abstract. Economic Denial of Sustainability (EDoS) attack is one of the major web security attacks performed on cloud hosted websites that exploits cloud's utility model by fraudulently consuming metered resources such as network bandwidth. In such attack, the malicious traffic imitates to be legitimate and hence goes undetected. A way to defend against such attack is to analyze the browsing behavior of the users and classify them. A training dataset to be used for this classification includes some features that are fuzzy which may lead to incorrect results. Hence, there is a need of feature selection mechanism that selects only important features from the feature set and discards the irrelevant one. This paper proposes to use fuzzy entropy based feature selection for classification of website users in EDoS defense. To evaluate the performance, the classification is done with and without doing feature selection. The classification accuracy shows that the proposed approach is capable of producing more accurate results with fewer features than original feature space.

Keywords: Classification · EDoS · Data mining · Feature selection
Fuzzy entropy

1 Introduction

In today's world, many essential services such as online shopping, banking, transportation are offered through web based applications and such applications are cloud-based as it offers trustworthy, easily scalable hosting. However, this inherent property of cloud architecture provides opportunities to perform various attacks such as Distributed Denial of Service (DDoS) and Economic Denial of Sustainability (EDoS) [1]. EDoS attack stretches elasticity of metered services employed by service provider e.g. cloud based web server and results into increasing the billing and decreasing the profit. This also makes it economically unfeasible for service provider to sustain with further demands of legitimate users. In EDoS attack, attacker generates anomalous requests which cause a heavy workload effect on metered services. The workload can be on any of the resources like bandwidth, processing, memory etc. To meet the SLA for the availability of the service for the customer, the service provider activates more and more resources that eventually add extra billing cost. In order to defend this attack,

© Springer Nature Singapore Pte Ltd. 2018
P. Bhattacharyya et al. (Eds.): NGCT 2017, CCIS 828, pp. 440–449, 2018.
https://doi.org/10.1007/978-981-10-8660-1_33

the website users need to be classified as attacker or legitimate user by analyzing the browsing behavior of the users. Given the fact that such attack resembles legitimate traffic, it becomes quite challenging to effectively classify the website visitors. The web server logs reveal the browsing and utilization behavior of the users. Thus, the various features calculated from the log like the number of data bytes sent from the destination to the source, the number of failed login attempts, the percentage of connections to the same service, the percentage of connections to different services, total number of purchases, average difference in purchase recency, recency of last purchase, frequency of order, total number of products viewed, average depth of page and number of sessions form the feature dataset and can be used to classify the user as an attacker or legitimate user. But, some of these features are fuzzy. E.g. the features like total number of purchases, average difference in purchase recency, recency of last purchase, frequency of order etc. may not precisely tell that the user is attacker or normal user. This is because some of the users might have a habit of window-shopping and they only surf the application without buying intention. If such fuzzy data is used as training dataset for classification purpose, it may lead to incorrect results. Hence, there is a need of feature selection mechanism which will select only important and significant features having good discrimination ability from a given feature space and will discard irrelevant features. Feature selection has many advantages such as improving the accuracy of the model, reducing over-fitting and making the training faster.

Feature selection methods are generally classified into filter and wrapper models [2]. In filter models, each feature's correlation with output variable is evaluated through various statistical tests such as ANOVA, Chi-Square, Pearson's Correlation etc. and the features are selected depending on their scores in such tests. This model is independent of any machine learning algorithm. In wrapper model, feature subset is generated to train the model. Depending upon the inferences drawn from previous model, the features are added or removed from the subset for next iteration. Some common examples of such model are forward feature selection, backward feature elimination, recursive feature elimination, etc. These models are computationally very expensive. This paper proposes to use filter based feature subset selection using fuzzy entropy measure [3] for classification of website users. Entropy is an amount of the information obtained when the outcome of random experiment X is observed. Entropy is a function of distribution of X. The entropy does not depend on the actual values taken by X, but on the probabilities. The Shannon's entropy [4] is based on probability of occurring elements. The paper utilizes fuzzy entropy which is an extension of Shannon's entropy. The fuzzy entropy reflects more information in the actual distribution of patterns in the pattern space and determines match degree which is measured via membership values of occurring elements. The proposed method is evaluated using three different classification algorithms for the given dataset.

The rest of the paper is organized as follows: Sect. 2 discusses related work about usage of fuzzy entropy in various domains. Section 3 describes the methodology of using fuzzy entropy for feature selection in web user classification for EDoS defense. Section 4 gives experimental results. Finally, the paper concludes in Sect. 5.

2 Related Work

Fuzzy entropy approach for feature selection was introduced in [3]. This paper has compared Shannon's entropy and fuzzy entropy and has proposed fuzzy entropy based fuzzy classifier that partitions pattern space into nonoverlapping fuzzy decision regions. Since the fuzzy entropy is able to discriminate pattern distribution better, it is used to evaluate the separability of each feature. The lower the fuzzy entropy of a feature is, the higher the feature's discriminating ability is. It has utilized K-Means clustering algorithm to determine membership function of each feature. After the fuzzy entropy is calculated for each feature, the features are selected by forward selection or backward elimination. The classification performance is evaluated over Iris and Wisconsin breast cancer database.

Jaganathan and Kuppuchamy [5] have proposed to use fuzzy entropy measure for feature selection in classification of medical database. The membership function is calculated for every input feature and based upon the results similar features are clustered together. Fuzzy C-Means (FCM) algorithm is used for feature selection and the performance is tested with Radial Basis Function Network Classifier.

Jeyarani and Pethalakshmi have also employed fuzzy entropy for high dimensional data [6] against four different datasets such as WILT, ORL, LC and CTG with four different threshold values.

Pal [7] has proposed a fuzzy entropy based feature selection approach to reduce the dimensionality of Digital Airborne Imaging Spectrometer (DAIS) image hyper spectral data. Four feature selection methods such as entropy, fuzzy entropy, signal to noise ratio and relief are employed to compare classification accuracy. A support vector machine is used as a classification algorithm. The fuzzy entropy measure uses triangle fuzzy neighbourhood. The value of the radius of the fuzzy neighbourhood impacts the number of selected features which in turns affects the classification accuracy of the classifier. It is been observed that the classification accuracy achieved by fuzzy entropy is better as compared to other approaches.

Mac Parthaláin et al. [8] have proposed to use fuzzy entropy in fuzzy rough approach which operates on real valued and/or noisy data. Here, two fuzzy sets are defined as fuzzy lower and upper approximations. The elements have been assigned membership degree in the range of [0, 1]. The elements of lower approximation (i.e. having membership degree = 1) are of absolute certainty. The elements of upper approximation (i.e. membership degree < 1) possibly belong to that set. This paper proposes FREQUICKREDUCT algorithm that begins with an empty set and adds individual feature to the set in each iteration. The fuzzy entropy value is calculated for each subset in each iteration and compared with the entropy value computed for last subset in previous iteration. If the entropy value of current subset is lower, the feature added in the set is retained.

Maji and Pal [9] have developed fuzzy rough set based feature selection in which Shannon's entropy is calculated and is represented in the form of fuzzy equivalence partition matrix. The features having maximum relevance and minimum redundancy are retained in the set. The relevance and redundancy of the features suitable for real valued data sets is measured by f-information measure. F-information measure is a measure of dependence that calculates the distance between a given joint probability/frequency and joint probability/frequency when the variables are independent.

Thus, it can be observed from the work done till now that fuzzy entropy is applicable for fuzzified data and it can handle uncertainty effectively.

The next section of the paper elaborates the usage of fuzzy entropy methodology for feature selection in website user classification.

3 Methodology

To classify website users, web server log file is important as it consists of details of service request and utilization behavior of each user. Let L denotes the log file that consists of different fields, such as, IP address of the user, user id, date and time at which service is requested, the page requested by the user, return status from the web server, size of the response, number of bytes sent from source to destination and the date and time at which the request is serviced.

$$L = [U^{IP}, U^{ID}, DT^{REQ}, P, S, B^R, B^S, DT^{RES}] \tag{1}$$

where,

U^{IP} is the IP address of the user

U^{ID} is the user ID requesting for a service

DT^{REQ} is date and time at which service is requested

P is the page requested by the user

S is the return status from the web server

B^R is the size of the response.

B^S is the number of bytes sent from source to destination

DT^{RES} is the date and time at which the request is serviced.

The feature dataset D is created from a given log file L wherein following features are calculated for each unique user/visitor:

$$D = \{f_1, f_2, \ldots, f_j\}, 1 \leq j \leq 12 \tag{2}$$

where,

f_1:   The number of data bytes sent from the source to the destination,

f_2:   The number of data bytes sent from the destination to the source,

f_3:   The number of failed login attempts,

f_4:   The percentage of connections to the same service

f_5:   The percentage of connections to different services

f_6:   Total number of purchases,

f_7:   Average difference in purchase recency

f_8:   Recency of last purchase

f_9:   Frequency of order

f_{10}:   Total no. of products viewed

f_{11}:   Average depth of page
f_{12}:   No. of sessions.

Now, fuzzy entropy measure is used to select the relevant and significant features from above feature dataset for classification purpose.

The Classical Shannon's Entropy is an average amount of information from an event. This event is modeled as a random variable and the amount of information gathered is the negative of the logarithm of the probability distribution of the event. Thus, Shannon's entropy tackles probabilistic uncertainties/randomness. Fuzzy entropy is an extension of Shannon's entropy which is non-probabilistic and is measured by calculating membership values of occurring elements [10].

The objective of fuzzy entropy in classification process is to select the features without losing useful information. Here, fuzzy entropy is calculated for each feature dimension and the features having minimum fuzzy entropy value are shortlisted for classification. The process of fuzzy entropy calculation is defined as follows:

1. Consider, $V = \{V_1, V_2, \ldots\ldots, V_h\}$, $1 \leq k \leq h$ as a universal set of elementary values v_h in the feature dataset.
2. Let $C = \{C_A, C_N\}$, where C_A and C_N represent two classes as "attacker" and "normal user". Each unique feature in the data is separated into these two classes.
3. Let $SC_i(V_h)$ denotes a set of elements of class i on the universal set V.
4. The fuzzy set uses match degree to classify the features. Thus, match degree P_q of class q is calculated as:

$$P_q = \frac{\sum_{h \in SC_{i(V_h)}} \mu_{f_i}(h)}{\sum_{h \in V} \mu_{f_i}(h)} \tag{3}$$

Where, $\mu_{f_i}(h)$ is mapped membership degree of the element V_h with the set $SC_i(V_h)$
5. Now, the fuzzy entropy belonging to the class q is represented as:

$$FE_{C_q}(f_i) = -P_q \log P_q \tag{4}$$

6. The total fuzzy entropy of feature dimension f_i is the summation of fuzzy entropy values of both the classes and is calculated as:

$$FE(f_i) = \sum_{q=1}^{m} FE_{C_q}(f_i) \tag{5}$$

Where, m = 2, representing the two classes described above.

The above process of fuzzy entropy calculation is illustrated below with the help of an example.

Consider feature f_1 (the number of data bytes sent from the source to the destination) calculated for each unique user of the log file as shown in Table 1. The class represents the category of the user where A = Attacker and N = Normal User.

Table 1. Feature f_1 values per unique user

User	Value of f_1	Class (A/N)
A_1	1241	A
B_1	217	A
C_1	1241	N
D_1	216	N

Step 1: The membership function of a fuzzy set is a generalization of the indicator function in classical sets. In fuzzy logic, it represents the degree of truth as an extension of valuation. Assume there are two triangular membership functions $\bar{A}$ and $\bar{B}$ for above given data with overlapped regions. Each membership function is represented by a triangle (a, b, c) as shown in below Fig. 1:

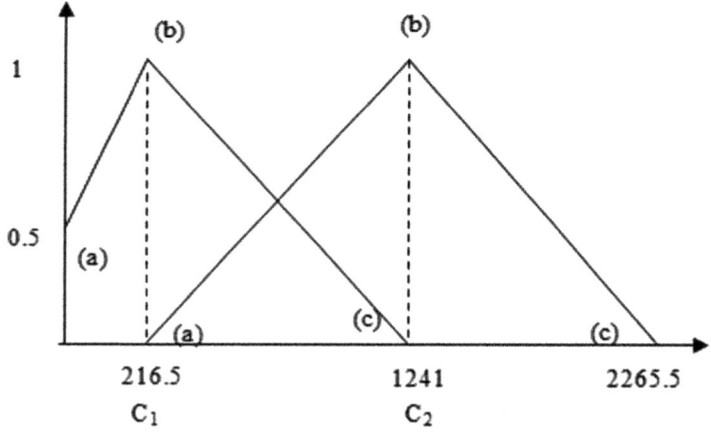

Fig. 1. Triangular membership function

The number of intervals on each feature dimension is to be determined. Initially, the no. of intervals I = 2 and the two centers C_1 and C_2 are calculated by K-Means Clustering algorithm where K = 2 as 216.5, and 1241 respectively.

For $\bar{A}$, the values of a, b and c are set to a = 0.5, b = 216.5 and c = 1241.

For $\bar{B}$, the values of a, b and c are set to a = 216.5, b = 1241 and c = 2265.5.

Step 2: Now, the membership function is evaluated on each interval for both classes to determine the membership degree of the elements. The membership degree of an element within an interval is the degree of this element belonging to this interval. When x = 0, the membership degree is set to 0.5 as shown in Fig. 1. The membership degree of class q is given by following equation:

$$\mu_{C_q} = \begin{cases} 0, & z \le a \\ \frac{z-a}{b-a} & a < z \le b \\ \frac{c-z}{c-b} & b < z \le c \\ 0 & z > c \end{cases} \tag{6}$$

Where, z is the value of the feature dimension for each user.

For Membership function $\bar{A}$,
a = 0.5, b = 216.5, c = 1241
Class A:
For User $A_1(z = 1241)$, $\mu_{C_A} = 0$
For User $B_1(z = 217)$, $\mu_{C_A} = 0.99$
Class N:
For User $C_1(z = 1241)$, $\mu_{C_N} = 0$
For User $D_1(z = 216)$, $\mu_{C_N} = 1.0$
Membership degree of Class A: $\mu_{C_A} = 0 + 0.99 = 0.99$
Membership degree of Class N: $\mu_{C_N} = 0 + 1.0 = 1.0$

For Membership function $\bar{B}$,
a = 216.5, b = 1241, c = 2265.5
Class A:
For User $A_1(z = 1241)$, $\mu_{C_A} = 1.0$
For User $B_1(z = 217)$, $\mu_{C_A} = 0$
Class N:
For User $C_1(z = 1241)$, $\mu_{C_N} = 1.0$
For User $D_1(z = 216)$, $\mu_{C_N} = 0$
Membership degree of Class A: $\mu_{C_A} = 1.0 + 0 = 1.0$
Membership degree of Class N: $\mu_{C_N} = 1.0 + 0 = 1.0$

Step 3: Calculate match degree P_q of class q according to Eq. (3).

For Membership function $\bar{A}$,
Match degree of class A: $P_A = \frac{0.99}{0.99 + 1.0} = 0.497$
Match degree of class N: $P_N = \frac{1.0}{0.99 + 1.0} = 0.502$
For Membership function $\bar{B}$,
Match degree of class A: $P_A = \frac{1.0}{1.0 + 1.0} = 0.5$
Match degree of class N: $P_N = \frac{1.0}{1.0 + 1.0} = 0.5$

Step 4: Calculate fuzzy entropy for each class of each membership function according to Eq. (4)

For Membership function $\bar{A}$,

$$FE_{C_A}(\bar{A}) = -0.497 * \log(0.497) = 0.15$$
$$FE_{C_N}(\bar{A}) = -0.502 * \log(0.502) = 0.15$$

Fuzzy entropy for membership function $\bar{A}$ is:

$$FE(\bar{A}) = 0.15 + 0.15 = 0.3$$

For Membership function $\bar{B}$,

$$FE_{C_A}(\bar{B}) = -0.5 * \log(0.5) = 0.15$$
$$FE_{C_N}(\bar{A}) = -0.5 * \log(0.5) = 0.15$$

Fuzzy entropy for membership function $\bar{B}$ is:

$$FE(\bar{B}) = 0.15 + 0.15 = 0.3$$

Step 5: Calculate total fuzzy entropy for feature dimension f_1 according to Eq. (5)

$$FE(f_1) = 0.3 + 0.3 = 0.6$$

Step 6: Now, assume k = 3, apply K-Means clustering and find fuzzy entropy as per the steps discussed above.

Step 7: Repeat the process until fuzzy entropy decreases.

4   Experimental Results

In this section, we have evaluated the performance of fuzzy entropy based feature selection for website user classification. We have calculated fuzzy entropy values according to above discussed method for 12 features as discussed in Sect. 3. The values calculated were as follows:

The feature having minimum fuzzy entropy value is considered to be most relevant feature. Hence, the features are sorted in decreasing order of fuzzy entropy values and the first three features having maximum entropy are eliminated.

According to Table 2, the features f_5, f_7 and f_9 have maximum fuzzy entropy value and hence these features are excluded from the feature database. Thus the dimensionality of feature database is reduced to 9. This reduced feature dataset is given as input to classification algorithm for classifying website users. We have evaluated the performance of 3 classification algorithms under two situations: without feature selection (using all 12 features) and with feature selection (using selected 9 features). These algorithms are Naïve Bayes (NB), Neural Network + Back Propagation (NN + BP) and Neural Network + Levenberg-Marquardt (NN + LM) algorithm. Table 3 shows the results of classification accuracy of all 3 classification algorithms mentioned above for both situations.

Table 2. Fuzzy entropy values

Features	Fuzzy entropy value
f_1: The number of data bytes sent from the source to the destination	0.2502
f_2: The number of data bytes sent from the destination to the source	0.2527
f_3: The number of failed login attempts	0.2130
f_4: The percentage of connections to the same service	0.0013
f_5: The percentage of connections to different services	0.5991
f_6: Total number of purchases	0.2702
f_7: Average difference in purchase recency	0.6020
f_8: Recency of last purchase	0.2051
f_9: Frequency of order	0.6020
f_{10}: Total no. of products viewed	0.2185
f_{11}: Average depth of page	0.2201
f_{12}: No. of sessions	0.2997

Table 3. Classification accuracy

Algorithm	Without feature selection	With feature selection
Naïve Bayes	73.17%	77.6%
Neural network with back propagation	79.58%	81.4%
Neural network with Levenberg-Marquardt	83.47%	85.6%

Figure 2 below shows the classification accuracy graph for all 3 classification algorithms.

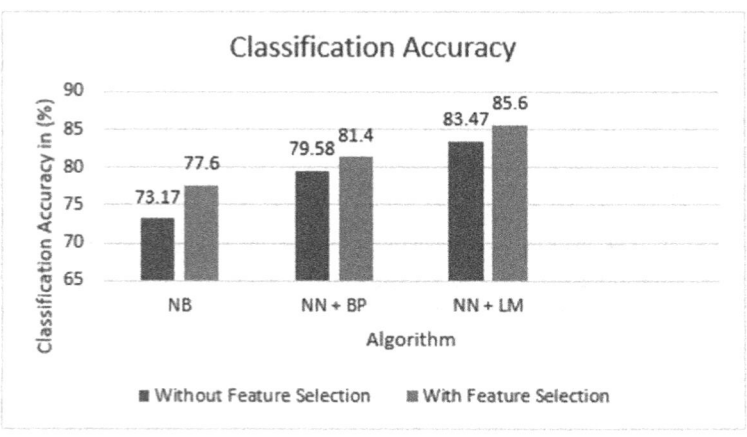

Fig. 2. Classification accuracy

The above results show that the feature selection improves classification performance of all 3 classification algorithms mentioned above.

5   Conclusion

EDoS is one of the web security attacks in cloud environment that seeks to disrupt long-term financial viability of operating in cloud by exploiting utility pricing model. In this kind of attack, the attacker sends malicious traffic to the web application. The Cloud Service Provider (CSP) scales the architecture automatically to service those requests for which cloud consumer is charged. Thus the intention of attacker is not to disrupt the service but to put financial burden on cloud consumer.

The remedy over this attack is effective classification of web application users. This classification is based on browsing behavior attributes of the user that are derived from web server log file. This dataset is very huge having multiple attributes some of which are fuzzy in nature as explained earlier and hence not relevant for classification task. Keeping such irrelevant attributes may result into unfavorable results. Hence, it is required to use a feature selection method. Fuzzy entropy measure has good discrimination ability. After calculating fuzzy entropy for each feature dimension, the features having minimum entropy are selected for classification. The experimental results show that fuzzy entropy based feature selection not only selects relevant features but also increases accuracy of classification algorithm by discarding unimportant features.

References

1. Yu, S., Tian, Y., Guo, S., Wu, D.: Can we beat DDoS attacks in clouds? (Supplementary Material). Nsp.Org.Au, vol. 25, no. 9, pp. 1–4 (2000)
2. Chandrashekar, G., Sahin, F.: A survey on feature selection methods. Comput. Electr. Eng. **40**(1), 16–28 (2014)
3. Lee, H.M., Chen, C.M., Chen, J.M., Jou, Y.L.: An efficient fuzzy classifier with feature selection based on fuzzy entropy. IEEE Trans. Syst. Man Cybern. Part B Cybern. **31**(3), 426–432 (2001)
4. Colin Green: Shannon Entropy. http://heliosphan.org/shannon-entropy.html. Accessed 17 July 2017
5. Jaganathan, P., Kuppuchamy, R.: A threshold fuzzy entropy based feature selection for medical database classification. Comput. Biol. Med. **43**(12), 2222–2229 (2013)
6. Jeyarani, D.S., Pethalakshmi, A.: An efficient fuzzy entropy based feature selection algorithm for high dimensional data. Int. J. Adv. Res. Comput. Sci. [S.l.] **6**(6) (2017). ISSN 0976–5697
7. Pal, M.: Fuzzy entropy based feature selection for classification of hyperspectral data. Geospatial World Forum, January 2011
8. Mac Parthaláin, N., Jensen, R., Shen, Q.: Fuzzy entropy-assisted fuzzy-rough feature selection. In: IEEE International Conference on Fuzzy Systems, Canada, 16–21 July 2006
9. Maji, P., Pal, S.K.: Feature selection using f-information measures in fuzzy approximation spaces. IEEE Trans. Knowl. Data Eng. **22**(6), 854–867 (2010)
10. Azhagusundari, B., Thanamani, A.S.: Feature selection based on fuzzy entropy. Int. J. Emerg. Trends Technol. Comput. Sci. **2**(2), 30–34 (2013)

Spark Based ANFIS Approach for Anomaly Detection Using Big Data

Thakur Santosh and Dharavath Ramesh[(✉)]

Department of Computer Science and Engineering, Indian Institute
of Technology (ISM), Dhanbad, Dhanbad 826004, Jharkhand, India
santosh.t68@gmail.com, ramesh.d.in@ieee.org

Abstract. Business intelligence is one of the applications that can benefit from various techniques and methodologies to patronize the unlablled big data anomalies. To address this issue, in this paper, we present a model to identify anomalies in spark environment using related big data. To optimize this instance, we use an open source software framework named Spark for analyzing the big data. Spark contains powerful APIS for machine learning and soft computing algorithms. To handle and detect the anomaly instances in the perspective of big data, Apache spark is installed on the top of the Hadoop and Adaptive Neuro Fuzzy Interface System (ANFIS) is implemented in spark. The variant of Hadoop HDFS is used as a data source through resilient distributed data sets (RDDs) data which is fetched in the spark. Experimental results show that the proposed method outperforms in a fault tolerant manner and also records accurate instances in the distributed environment.

Keywords: Apache spark · Hadoop · ANFIS · Big data · Anomaly detection

1 Introduction

Anomaly detection means finding the abnormal patterns which are not in normal nature. These abnormal patterns are considered as anomaly instances that must be patronized to perform operational tasks. Anomaly detection is extensively used in different application domains such as credit card fraud, health care, insurance fraud, and cyber security, etc. To illustrate this precisely, let's consider an anomaly in credit card transactions considered as credit card fraud. The anomaly in a CT scan of the head is considered as tumor [1]. The anomaly in network traffic is considered as malicious activity [2]. There are three types of anomalies pointed towards any application; Point anomaly, Contextual anomaly, a Collective anomaly. In the literature, several anomaly detection methods have been proposed, where each method has its own importance in different applications. With the technological advancements in internet technologies and mobile devices, big data attracts many researchers to exemplify the suitable data [3]. It includes the modern distributed file systems and efficient processing entities. Big data are considered to be a huge volume, which is difficult to handle with existing tools [4]. Big data can be mostly handled in a distributed environment. Hadoop is an open source software framework, which is preferred as a distributed environment for storing and processing the data [5]. Hadoop is presented in a MapReduce framework for data

© Springer Nature Singapore Pte Ltd. 2018
P. Bhattacharyya et al. (Eds.): NGCT 2017, CCIS 828, pp. 450–458, 2018.
https://doi.org/10.1007/978-981-10-8660-1_34

processing in a distributed environment [6]. The performance of MapReduce framework is poor when compared with Apache Spark [7]. To address some related issues and to perform anomaly detection through big data technologies, we propose a model based on adaptive neuro fuzzy approach. This approach works based on spark integrated technologies to perform anomaly detection using big data.

1.1 Preliminaries

Big Data: As the data is increasing in exponential rate day-by-day, performing anomaly detection with respect the growth of data is one of the biggest challenges. On the other hand, patronizing the unstructured big data which is collected from various internet sources will also increase the difficulty. This data contain following properties such as Volume, Velocity, Variety, and Veracity [8]. Current anomaly detection methods need to be more efficient and scalable in order to manage a large amount of data. To accommodate these problematic instances, Big Data technology's is the best solution [9]. In the past time, many big data technologies were proposed to store and process the data. In 2004, MapReduce framework was proposed [10] to process the data in a parallel and distribute manner. Hadoop is implemented on MapReduce with distributed file system for storing and processing the large scale data [11]. On the other hand, on iterative computing, Hadoop has low performance when compared to Spark [12]. Compared to Spark, performing iterative programming sequences in Hadoop MapReduce is somewhat difficult. Except for pig and Hive, Hadoop does not hold any iterative process, where as spark holds iterative process with online streaming data modification. In spark, main memory is used for caching the distributed workloads for fastest execution while Hadoop has latency as long as it uses disk storage [13]. Hadoop has an advantage with its file system HDFS and this file system can be integrated with Spark. Because Spark doesn't exist with its own file system. The Spark must be integrated with some other file systems to manage its files. To accumulate this, in this paper, we integrate spark and the Hadoop file system with adaptive neuro fuzzy interface system for anomaly detection.

Spark: Apache Spark is a data processing framework for large scale applications. It has a number of benefits over Hadoop MapReduce, in terms of in-memory execution, mainly in distributed environment when multiple processes are made over the same data such as MapReduce data processing. For complex or unstructured large data processing, Spark provides related APIs which also includes different matching learning libraries. With resilient distributed data set (RDD), Spark fetches the data from the distributed environment as its storage. The spark streaming library includes spark streaming for batch processing operations [14]. There are different APIs are designated for the spark engine, which can process machine learning related strategies. Meng et al. presented a related open-source distributed machine learning library named *MLLib* to integrate the machine related approaches with Spark [15]. MLLib deals a high-level of API which makes spark powerful environment for machine learning. Bharill et al. proposed a clustering algorithm with Optimization of Fuzzy c-Means in spark using MLLib to handle big data problems [16].

ANFIS: Fuzzy Logic and Artificial Neural Network are two of the main components of soft computing [17]. Artificial neural networks have the capability of learning by training, whereas the fuzzy logic is a rule centered model. In 1990's, Dr. Roger Jang proposed a hybrid model called adaptive neuro fuzzy inference system by combining the best features of Artificial neural networks and fuzzy systems [18]. Due to higher reasoning ability, ANFIS can learn and predict the events with higher accuracy [19]. ANFIS plays important role in training of rules from observation. The following sections will annotate its overview.

Fuzzy Sets: Fuzzy logic has derived from the fuzzy set theory with membership functions [20]. In Fuzzy logic, linguistic language such as words are used instead of numbers. A fuzzy set is a class of objects with a range of grades of membership function. The range of membership function is limited between zero and one.

Membership Function: Membership function defines boundaries of language variables. In this, zero to one range is defined as smooth boundaries instead of crisp boundaries. Depending on the problem requirement, a range of different membership functions is selected. In spite of the availability of different functions most commonly used membership functions are trapezoidal function and triangular function. Spark based ANFIS model uses the Gaussian function. At the fuzzy interface level, the input and output mapping are done using fuzzy logic. The fuzzy rules are called knowledge base, where on this basis of this base, the fuzzy interface system works. For the fuzzy inference system advancement, the generated fuzzy rules play an important role in maximizing the sequenced boundaries. To develop these rules knowledge base experts are required, hence, human based domain experts can formulate the rules. On the other hand, in the absence of a domain, an expert system can be modeled with prior knowledge. This prior knowledge is used to train the ANFIS. With this knowledge, ANFIS can learn the behavior of the system.

2   Related Study

Extensive work has been done in the field of anomaly detection. Each work has its way of interpretation on the specific application. Son et al. proposed Moving average model to detect the anomalies in Hadoop envoronment. In this model Ganglia monitoring system is used to store log data on HDFS [21]. Sulaiman et al. proposed adaptive neuro fuzzy interface method to detect anomalies in smart meter data on mat lab [22]. Hayes et al. proposed a multivariate cluster based anomaly detection in big sensor data. In this model, contextual anomalies were detected using similar group profiles and it is performed in R tool [23]. Hill and Minsker proposed a data-driven modeling method to recognize point anomalies in such a way that different predictions are expected based on historical data [24]. This method uses a Bayesian algorithm for anomaly detection for single sensor or multiple sensors [25]. But these methods depend on the sequential sensor data. Xie et al. proposed an anomaly detection method based on histograms within the sensor networks. In this work, the authors use histograms to focus on the content instead of multivariate data [26]. Kittler et al. tried to identify anomalies in machine perception by framing system architecture. In specific, they suggest a set of classifications to describe the roles and certain limits within the architecture. Their work is featured with a Bayesian probabilistic predictor which is improved by notions such as outlier, noise, distribution point, and rare incidents [27]. In recent times, a number of Big Data frameworks have been proposed that report the scalability problems [28]. On the other hand, they perform batch processing on distributed frameworks that process streaming data.

3 Proposed Approach: Spark Based ANFIS

In this section, we describe our proposed methodology to perform anomaly detection occurrences using big data. Proposed method consists of a multilayer neural network with five layers (shown in Fig. 1). As shown in Fig. 1, layer$_1$ is an input data layer, where it has an adaptive node.

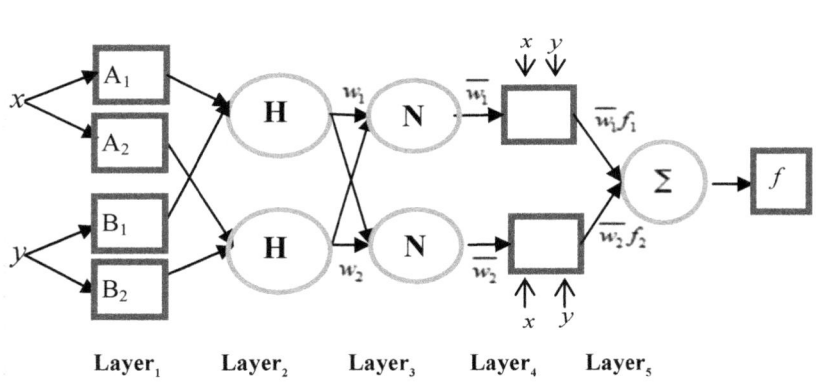

Fig. 1. Adaptive neuro fuzzy interface system

Layer$_2$ multiplies input signals and computed as rule node. Layer$_3$ normalizes the computed rule node. Layer$_4$ computes the rules for an output. Layer$_5$ contains a single node which computes the overall output and corresponds towards the result. The expansion, in terms of computation of ANFIS is described in the following manner.

$$f = \frac{w_1}{w_1 + w_2}f_1 + \frac{w_2}{w_1 + w_2}f_2 \tag{1}$$

Where, A_1 as x and B_1 as y then, $f_1 = p_1 x + q_1 y + r_1$ and A_2 as x and B_2 as y then $f_2 = p_2 x + q_2 y + r_2$. Where A_1, A_2 and B_1, B_2 are the membership functions of each input x and y respectively. The symbols, p_1, q_1, r_1 and p_2, q_2, r_2 are the parameters set.

In layer one, each node i is an adaptive node with the function $Q_i^1 = \mu_{Ai}(x)$, where x is the input node I and A_i is the variable associated with node and μ_{Ai} is membership function. The functionality of $\mu_{Ai}(x)$ is computed as;

$$\mu_{Ai}(x) = e^{\frac{-(x-c)^2}{bi^2}} \tag{2}$$

Layer two calculates the firing strength of rule w_i and the output of each node is represented as;

$$Q_i^2 = w_i = uA_i(x) + uB_i(y), \ i = 1,2 \tag{3}$$

At layer three, the sum of rules firing strength is calculated at I^{th} node and the output of Ith node is normalizes as;

$$Q_i^3 = \overline{w_i} = \frac{w_i}{w_1 + w_2}, i = 1,2 \tag{4}$$

At layer four, the function is represented as $Q_i^4 = \overline{w_i}f_i = w_i(p_ix + q_iy + r_i)$,where as $\overline{w_i}$ in the output of layer three and $p_ix + q_iy + r_i$ are the papramaters.

Layer five combines the input and calculates the overall output with;

$$Q_i^5 = \sum_i \overline{w_i}f_i = \frac{\sum_i w_if_i}{\sum_i w_i} \tag{5}$$

3.1   Training and Testing

In order to shape the fuzzy inference system, the ANFIS model is trained with the test data system and its membership function is adjusted later with back propagation algorithm. Usually, the data are divided into two groups; training data and test data. The proposed model is trained with 80% of the available data and remaining 20% of data is used for testing to calculate the performance of the proposed model. The membership function parameters, can be adjusted to produce the fuzzy rules of ANFIS model.

3.2   Experimental Setup

To evaluate the proposed model, we used a three cluster node setup. Each node is configured with the following hardware: Intel(R) Xeon(R) E5645 CPU, 2.40 GHz with 16 GB RAM for master node. Intel i7 CPU, 2.00 GHz with 8 GB RAM as two slave nodes. The softwares installed for this configuration are: UBUNTU 4.0.1 as an operating system and Apache on the top of Hadoop with SCIKIT Learn and MLLIB library. To perform the experiments, credit card data sets are used for Anomaly detection. This experiment is performed on synthetic credit card data sets which are retrieved from [29]. Due to limited access to genuine credit card data sets, we have used synthetic data sets [30]. This data set contains ten million samples with seven features. The features are: *customer-ID, state, gender, credit limit, number of transactions, the number of international transactions*, and *balance*. The credit card data sets are stored in various nodes of clusters in HDFS as a data source with 64 MB block size.

4 Result Analysis

In this section, we elaborate our results in a concise manner. Initially, we draw the correlations to observe the variable strength which affects the outcome. From the observed correlation part, we exclude the variables which are not important for considering analysis. The observed correlation strength of different variables is represented in a heat map. This illustrated in Fig. 2.

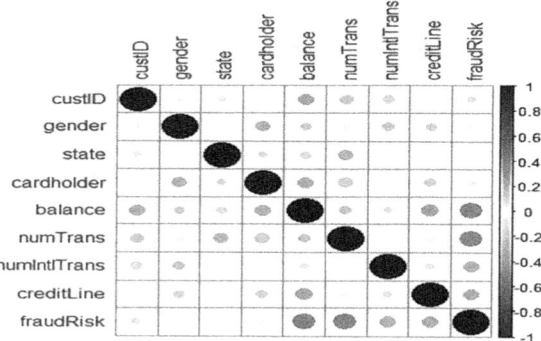

Fig. 2. Generated correlations through heat map

As a credit limit, numbers of normal and international transactions and balance are shown as a high correlation. Hence, remaining variables do not correlate strongly therefore, we ignore these variables. With these occurrences, we detect the number of normal and fraud transactions in four phases, which are depicted in Fig. 3.

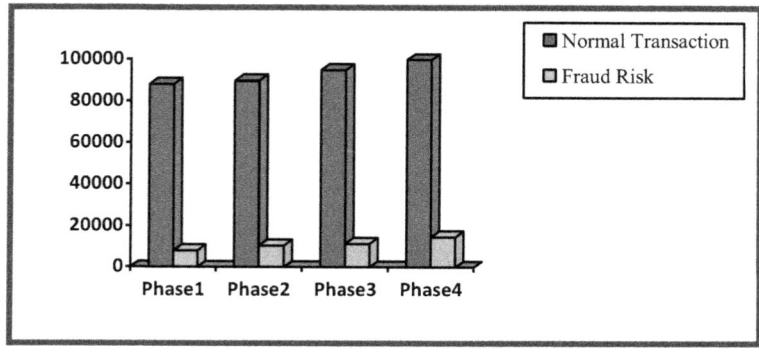

Fig. 3. Occurrence of fraud and normal transactions

With the illustration of the methodology described in Sect. 3, the proposed model outperforms in terms of accuracy and its execution time. The instance of accuracy and response time is represented in Figs. 4 and 5. Figure 4 shows the execution time of the proposed model in comparison of other models. Figure 5 shows the comparison of different methods in terms of accuracy of detecting the anomalies. Proposed method records 95% accuracy, when it was compared with the original data.

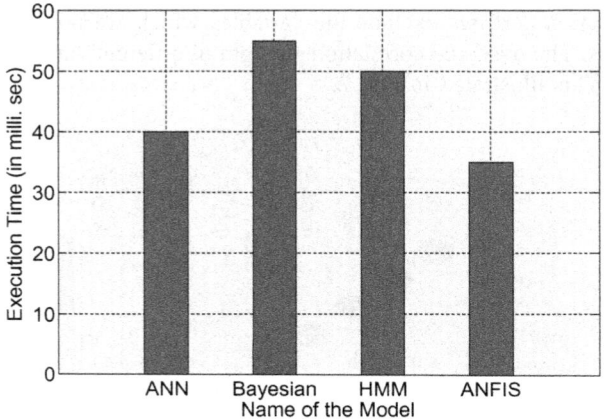

Fig. 4. Execcution comparison with other approaches

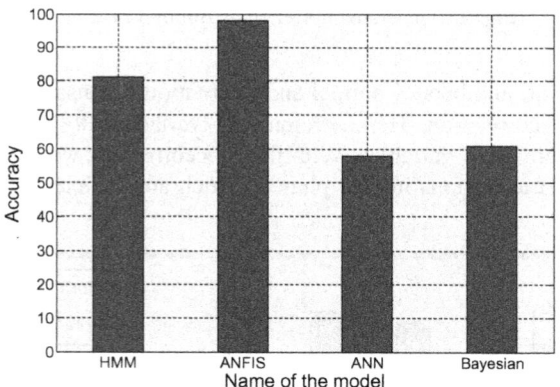

Fig. 5. Accuracy comparison with other approaches

5   Conclusion and Future Work

This paper aims to describe how the anomaly detection can be done using a spark based Adaptive Neuro Fuzzy Interface System (ANFIS). To perform the related operations, in this study, Spark is presented with adaptive neuro fuzzy interface system to detect the anomalies in big data. We present the anomalies with credit card data sets in which, the model identifies whether the transaction is a fraud or normal transaction. Initially, we have collected the data and stored in Hadoop HDFS and we perform a correlation to see the strength of variables for ANFIS model construction. This model proves to be more efficient when compared with other models which are mentioned in the literature. As a future work, we come up with different application areas to increase the effectiveness of the proposed models.

Acknowledgments. This work is partially supported by Indian Institute of Technology (ISM), Govt. of India. The authors wish to express their gratitude and thanks to the Department of Computer Science & Engineering, Indian Institute of Technology (ISM), Dhanbad, India for providing their support in arranging necessary computing facilities.

References

1. Chandola, V., Banerjee, A., Kumar, V.: Anomaly detection: a survey. ACM Comput. Surv. (CSUR) **41**(3), 15 (2009)
2. Savage, D., Zhang, X., Yu, X., Chou, P., Wang, Q.: Anomaly detection in online social networks. Soc. Netw. **39**, 62–70 (2014)
3. Drosou, M., Jagadish, H.V., Pitoura, E., Stoyanovich, J.: Diversity in big data: a review. Big Data **5**(2), 73–84 (2017)
4. Erl, T., Khattak, W., Buhler, P.: Big Data Fundamentals: Concepts. Drivers & Techniques. Prentice Hall Press, Upper Saddle River (2016)
5. Holmes, A.: Hadoop in Practice. Manning Publications Co, Shelter Island (2012)
6. Grolinger, K., Hayes, M., Higashino, W.A., L'Heureux, A., Allison, D.S., Capretz, M.A.: Challenges for MapReduce in big data. In: 2014 IEEE World Congress on Services (SERVICES), pp. 182–189. IEEE, June 2014
7. Dittrich, J., Quiané-Ruiz, J.A.: Efficient big data processing in Hadoop MapReduce. Proc. VLDB Endow. **5**(12), 2014–2015 (2012)
8. Sri, P.A., Anusha, M.: Big data-survey. Indones. J. Electr. Eng. Inform. (IJEEI) **4**(1), 74–80 (2016)
9. García, S., Ramírez-Gallego, S., Luengo, J., Benítez, J.M., Herrera, F.: Big data preprocessing: methods and prospects. Big Data Anal. **1**(1), 9 (2016)
10. Dean, J., Ghemawat, S.: MapReduce: simplified data processing on large clusters. Commun. ACM **51**(1), 107–113 (2008)
11. Jach, T., Magiera, E., Froelich, W.: Application of HADOOP to store and process big data gathered from an urban water distribution system. Procedia Eng. **119**, 1375–1380 (2015)
12. Gunarathne, T., Zhang, B., Wu, T.L., Qiu, J.: Scalable parallel computing on clouds using Twister4Azure iterative MapReduce. Future Gener. Comput. Syst. **29**(4), 1035–1048 (2013)
13. Chowdhury, M., Zaharia, M., Stoica, I.: Performance and scalability of broadcast in Spark (2014). http://www.cs.berkeley.edu/~agearh/cs267.sp10/files/mosharaf-spark-bc-report-spring10.pdf. Accessed 08 Oct 2014
14. Shanahan, J.G., Dai, L.: Large scale distributed data science using apache spark. In: Proceedings of 21th ACM SIGKDD International Conference on Knowledge Discovery and Data Mining, pp. 2323–2324. ACM, August 2015
15. Meng, X., Bradley, J., Yavuz, B., Sparks, E., Venkataraman, S., Liu, D., Freeman, J., Tsai, D.B., Amde, M., Owen, S., Xin, D.: Mllib: machine learning in apache spark. J. Mach. Learn. Res. **17**(1), 1235–1241 (2016)

16. Bharill, N., Tiwari, A., Malviya, A.: Fuzzy based clustering algorithms to handle big data with implementation on Apache Spark. In: 2016 IEEE Second International Conference on Big Data Computing Service and Applications (BigDataService), pp. 95–104. IEEE, March 2016

17. Chen, L., Wang, F., Deng, H., Ji, K.: A survey on hand gesture recognition. In: 2013 International Conference on Computer Sciences and Applications (CSA), pp. 313–316. IEEE, December 2013

18. Chang, F.J., Chang, Y.T.: Adaptive neuro-fuzzy inference system for prediction of water level in reservoir. Adv. Water Resour. 29(1), 1–10 (2006)

19. Polat, K., Güneş, S.: An expert system approach based on principal component analysis and adaptive neuro-fuzzy inference system to diagnosis of diabetes disease. Digit. Sig. Process. 17(4), 702–710 (2007)

20. Klir, G., Yuan, B.: Fuzzy Sets and Fuzzy Logic, vol. 4. Prentice Hall, Upper Saddle River (1995)

21. Son, S., Gil, M.S., Moon, Y.S.: Anomaly detection for big log data using a Hadoop ecosystem. In: 2017 IEEE International Conference on Big Data and Smart Computing (BigComp), pp. 377–380. IEEE, February 2017

22. Sulaiman, S.M., Jeyanthy, P.A., Devaraj, D.: Big data analytics of smart meter data using Adaptive Neuro Fuzzy Inference System (ANFIS). In: International Conference on Emerging Technological Trends (ICETT), pp. 1–5. IEEE, October 2016

23. Hayes, M.A., Capretz, M.A.: Contextual anomaly detection framework for big sensor data. J. Big Data 2(1), 2 (2015)

24. Hill, D.J., Minsker, B.S.: Anomaly detection in streaming environmental sensor data: a data-driven modeling approach. Environ. Model Softw. 25(9), 1014–1022 (2010)

25. Berger, J.O.: Statistical decision theory and Bayesian analysis. Springer Science & Business Media, New York (2013)

26. Xie, M., Hu, J., Tian, B.: Histogram-based online anomaly detection in hierarchical wireless sensor networks. In: 2012 IEEE 11th International Conference on Trust, Security and Privacy in Computing and Communications (TrustCom), pp. 751–759. IEEE, June 2012

27. Kittler, J., Christmas, W., De Campos, T., Windridge, D., Yan, F., Illingworth, J., Osman, M.: Domain anomaly detection in machine perception: a system architecture and taxonomy. IEEE Trans. Pattern Anal. Mach. Intell. 36(5), 845–859 (2014)

28. Solaimani, M., Iftekhar, M., Khan, L., Thuraisingham, B., Ingram, J.B.: Spark-based anomaly detection over multi-source VMware performance data in real-time. In: 2014 IEEE Symposium on Computational Intelligence in Cyber Security (CICS), pp. 1–8. IEEE, December 2014

29. ccFraud Dataset, August 2017. http://packages.revolutionanalytics.com/datasets/. Accessed 12 July 2017

30. Kamaruddin, S., Ravi, V.: Credit card fraud detection using big data analytics: use of PSOAANN based one-class classification. In: Proceedings of International Conference on Informatics and Analytics, p. 33. ACM, August 2016

Data Privacy in Hadoop Using Anonymization and T-Closeness

Praveen Kaushik[✉] and Varsha Dipak Tayde

Maulana Azad National Institute of Technology, Bhopal 462003, India
praveenkaushikmanit@gmail.com, vtayde4@gmail.com

Abstract. As everyone uses internet today, modern technology generates huge amount of data every fraction of second. Data gets generated from social sites, private and government organization, hospitals and educational institutes. As everyone wants to remain in touch with their companion and other people, they prefer to have their account on many of social sites and that's result in generation of huge data. In addition, there are organizations, which has huge number employees, the personal data of employees is very important and it should be secured from any kind of misuse. Similarly in hospitals, patient's data is very important to do patient analysis for future use. There is need to provide privacy and security to all such data. Hadoop is there for storing and analyzing such huge data. There are various tools which work on the top of Hadoop stack to provide privacy and security to data. One of existing method which contains slicing with l-diversity to provide protection to data from attribute disclosure, but it can't avoid skewness attack. This paper proposed an algorithm for avoiding skewness attack.

Keywords: Bigdata · Hadoop · HDFS · MapReduce

1 Introduction

Hadoop is used to store large quantity data and processing it. Hadoop has two parts: Hadoop Distributed File System (HDFS) and MapReduce [1]. HDFS is related to storing process of data. It can store employee datasets or patient data set etc. MapReduce is another phase of Hadoop which is used to process huge data. Following Fig. 1 shows Hadoop cluster architecture.

1.1 Security Aspects in Hadoop

Hadoop is use to store and process the data. It does not consider data security and privacy. Various security aspects which are required for data protection are as follows [2]:

Availability: Data should available to authenticated user whenever they require.

Integrity: It means after storing data, it should maintain accuracy. Similarly consistency of data shouldn't be lost.

Confidentiality: It means data can seen by only those people who are actually supposed to see

© Springer Nature Singapore Pte Ltd. 2018
P. Bhattacharyya et al. (Eds.): NGCT 2017, CCIS 828, pp. 459–468, 2018.
https://doi.org/10.1007/978-981-10-8660-1_35

Security: Data stored in databases should be protected; it cannot be access by unauthorized person.

Privacy: It means controlling spreading of information to unauthenticated person.

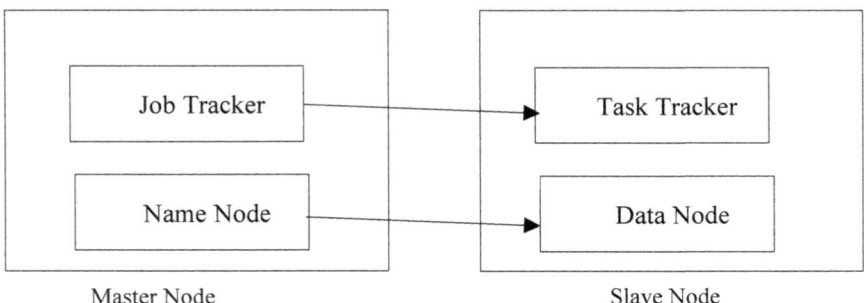

Fig. 1. Architecture of hadoop

Some of above aspects and challenges can be overcome as follows: Hadoop store huge data and on Hadoop anyone can access data. This data may be important for user. So we can apply authorization to provide security to data. Authorization is a process in which accessing privileges are given to selected user. Similarly, we can use authentication which identify legitimate user for accessing particular data. Kerberos is an authentication protocol which can use in hadoop. Encryption - decryption is another way to protect data. Anonymization is a process of making generalize data and converting the data into unreadable format so that unwanted person cannot access original data.

2 Related Work

Different algorithms are there in data mining to provide protection to data and provide privacy to data. Some of them are as follows:

Table 1. Original data

Emp ID	EmpName	Designation	Salary
1011	Akash	Developer	12K
1022	Vikas	Developer	14K
1033	Sanjay	Developer	15K
1034	Richa	Manager	21K
1056	Shila	Tester	16K
1066	Shila	Tester	18K
1067	Meena	Peon	13K
1068	Meena	Tester	19K
1069	Usha	Tester	22K

We used employee database which contains Employee ID, Employee name, designation and salary for showing different behavior of different privacy methods [10].

2.1 Differential Privacy

Data store on Hadoop can be access by any user from HDFS. There is a privacy algorithm called Differential privacy. It added noise to data at certain threshold and maximizes the accuracy of queries from databases while minimizing disclosure of identity [7]. There is sensitive function which calculates difference between data blocks P1 and P2. Then noise get added to function sensitivity that is called laplace distribution. Requested data and laplace distribution gives differential privacy to data. It assure that the probability of output doesn't depend on any individual tuple in data. There is Apache Airvat is a privacy tool which works on top of Hadoop stack. It uses differential privacy in MapReduce phase to provide protection to data.

$$Dp = f(x) + Lap(\Delta(f))$$
$$\Delta f = max|f(P1) - f(P2)|$$
Where,

Dp — Differential Privacy

$F(x)$ — requested data

Lap — Laplace distribution

$\Delta(f)$ — Function sensitivity

$P1$ — data block1

$P2$ — data block2

2.2 K-Anonymity

Data Stored on Hadoop may be structured or unstructured format. Any Hadoop user can access data of other user. Let's consider Table 1, there is one Hadoop user Nic who wants to know information of one employee Akash, so he can easily fetch Akash's data. This is nothing but identity disclosure. K-anonymity tries to protects identity disclosure of datasets. If data contains unique values for each person then identification of single person gets more easy. So it is necessary to mix up such data so identification of individual will become complex. A process in which dataset attributes are making generalize until a tuple is similar to K-1 other tuples. This process is nothing but K anonymity. In this method, when value of k high, chance for re-identification is less [8].

2.3 L-Diversity

Structured data store on Hadoop may contains some sensitive attributes like Disease or salary. This sensitive attributes contains limited different values. So by using this attribute knowledge one can easily gets information about other. Let's consider in a table, there are first 4 tuples having same value for Salary column. If attacker knows name and salary of employee, he can get information by firing query on HDFS. To prevent this, there is L-diversity. In this process, data diverted into different group such that each group contains L different values for that group, this process is L-diversity [9] (Table 2).

Table 2. Comparison among privacy methods

Sr. no	Method	Datacomplexity	Data utility	Information loss
1	Differential privacy	Low	High	Low
2	K-anonymity	High	Medium	Medium
3	L-diversity	Medium	High	Low
4	Slicing	High	Medium	Low

Table 3. Generalized data

Emp ID	EmpName	Designation	Salary
10**	Akash	Developer	12K
10**	Vikas	Developer	14K
10**	Sanjay	Developer	15K
10**	Richa	Manager	21K
10**	Shila	Tester	16K
10**	Shila	Tester	18K
10**	Meena	Peon	13K
10**	Meena	Tester	19K
10**	Usha	Tester	22K

Table 4. Bucketized data

Emp ID	EmpName	Designation	Salary
10**	Akash	Developer	12K
10**	Vikas	Developer	14K
10**	Sanjay	Developer	15K
10**	Richa	Manager	21K
10**	Shila	Tester	16K
10**	Shila	Tester	18K
10**	Meena	Peon	13K
10**	Meena	Tester	19K
10**	Usha	Tester	22K

There are different anonymization techniques like Bucketization and Generalization [5, 6]. Generalization makes generalize data for data sets. It hides different data and makes similar N tuples so it is complex to detect single person from data sets. It loses some data. There is Bucketization, in which N tuples are grouped into single group. It makes N groups of data in which each group treated as separate sub table. These methods are there for providing protection to data from identity disclosure efficiently. Tables 3 and 4 shows generalized and Bucketized data.

2.4 Existing Privacy Module on Hadoop

One of privacy and security model on hadoop contains generalization, bucketization, slicing and L-diversity to get secured data. Figure 2 explain working architecture of slicing with l-diversity. It extracts data from dataset. Anonymization divides records into two and interchange sensitive values. Slice the data and divide the table into small sub tables and perform l-diversity to protect attribute disclosure. Displaying attributes those are collective and secure data [3].

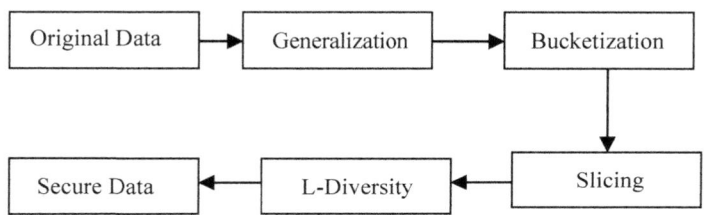

Fig. 2. Slicing with l-diversity architecture on hadoop

2.5 Drawback of Existing System

Existing system contains K-Anonymity methods generalization and bucketization. These methods can protect data from identity revelation but these methods get fail to protect attribute disclosure. For that existing system used slicing method. In slicing, each slice of data is considered as separate sub table. It protects from attribute disclosure. Consider Table 1, as shown in table, if one person know that Vikas's record is in first three rows. One more person know that Vikas's salary in between 3K to 5K then they both can identify Vikas's record from datasets. This is nothing but skewness attack. Slicing with L-diversity can't provide protection from skewness attack.

3 Proposed Method

This paper propose a method to overcomes the drawbacks of slicing with L-diversity. Existing method on hadoop uses generalization, bucketization, l-diversity and slicing to protect data from various attacks. Existing method prevents from identity attack and attribute revelation attack but it can't protect from skewness attack. Proposed method prevents data from skewness attack. Proposed methods merge three methods together to protect data from various attacks. On original data, we used bucketization which protects data from identity revelation. After applying bucketization there will be distribution of tuples according to calculated threshold value. A process in which calculating distance between buckets of a sensitive attribute and same attributes in whole table not more the threshold value. Distance can be calculated using various distance formulas. Proposed algorithm uses multiset-based generalization after applying t-closeness. Multiset-based generalization is extension to k-anonymity to avoid attribute disclosure. By following this method, we provide protection to data from identity disclosure, attribute disclosure and skewness attack. Architecture of proposed system is as follows (Fig. 3):

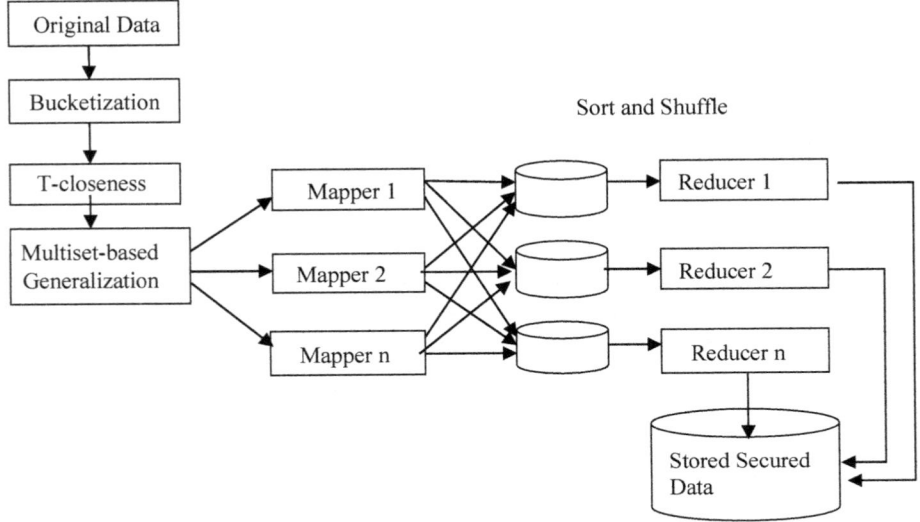

Fig. 3. Architecture of proposed method

For applying T-closeness, we have to use Earth Mover Distance's equation given below [9] by which we will calculate distance between B and T. Let, B = (b1, b2, b3....), T = (t1, t2, t3.....), xi = bi − ti, then distance can be calculated as:

$$D[B, T] = \frac{1}{n-1}(|x_1| + |x_2| + |x_3| + \ldots |x_{n-1}|)$$

After bucketizing the data of original datasets as shown in Table 3, we will apply T-closeness on that data sets as follows:

T = {12k, 13k, 14k, 15k, 16k, 18k, 19k, 21k, 22k}
B1 = {12k, 14k, 15k}
B2 = {16k, 18k, 21k}
B3 = {13k, 19k, 22k}

Distance of bucket B1 from T is: (12k → 13k), (12k → 14k), (14k → 15k), (14k → 16k), (14k → 18k), (15k → 19k), (15k → 21k), (15k → 22k). Cost of this is 1/9 × (1 + 2 + 1 + 2 + 4 + 4 + 6 + 7)/8 = 27/72 = 0.375. Distance of bucket B1 from T is as follows: (16k → 12k), (16k → 13k), (16k → 14k), (18k → 15k), (18k → 16k), (21k → 19k), (21k → 22k). Cost of this is 1/9 × (4 + 3 + 2 + 3 + 2 + 2 + 1)/8 = 17/72 = 0.236. Distance of bucket B1 from T is as follows:

(13k → 12k),   (13k → 14k),   (19k → 15k),   (19k → 16k),   (19k → 18k), (22k → 19k),   (22k → 21k).   Cost   of   this   is $1/9 \times (1 + 1 + 4 + 3 + 1 + 3 + 1)/$ $8 = 14/72 = 0.195$. D[B1, T] is 0.375, D[B2, T] has a distance of 0.236 and D[B3, T] has a distance of 0.195. Therefore, B3 reveals less private data. So threshold is 0.195. We have to rearrange all tuples in such way that distance of each bucket is not more than threshold 0.195 as follows (Tables 5 and 6):

Table 5. T-closeness (Threshold = 0.195)

Emp ID	EmpName	Designation	Salary
1011	Akash	Developer	12K
1068	Meena	Tester	19K
1033	Sanjay	Developer	15K
1034	Richa	Manager	21K
1056	Shila	Tester	16K
1067	Meena	Peon	13K
1022	Vikas	Developer	14K
1066	Shila	Tester	18K
1069	Usha	Tester	22K

Table 6. Multiset-based generalization

Emp ID	Employee name	Designation	Salary
1011:1, 1068:1, 1033:1	Akash: 1, Meena: 1, Sanjay: 1	Developer: 2, Tester: 1	12K:1, 19K:1, 15K:1
1034:1, 1056:1, 1067:1	Richa: 1, Shila:1, Meena: 1	Manager: 1, Tester: 1, Peon: 1	21K:1, 16K:1, 13K:1
1022:1, 1066:1, 1069:1	Vikas: 1, Shila: 1, Usha: 1	Developer: 1, Tester: 2	14K:1, 18K:1, 22K:1

4   Results and Analysis

The working environment comprises of Ubuntu 16.X. The end user can use any OS as Java is platform independent. Intel Idea with Java SE Development Kit, the end-user needs to have Java SE Runtime Environment installed. Apache's Hadoop Framework - Hadoop 2.X is required which provides HDFS capabilities and is used to run MapReduce paradigm and YARN resource manager. The hardware configuration required consists of Intel core i5 CPU processor, 8 GB RAM and maximum of 10 GB storage space. As data is very important for user, it is necessary to apply security and privacy on data to protect data from vulnerabilities. After applying privacy methods on data structure of original data gets change. Although structure of data gets change but actual information gaining from data should not change. Privacy algorithm should not affect the performance of data. We can analyse the performance by using different performance measures such as total information loss, total data utility, how much data gets complex after applying privacy algorithms. We used different performance metrics to test the effectiveness of proposed work.

4.1   Data Complexity and Utility

After executing privacy algorithms on original data such as generalization makes original data more generalize and data complexity gets increase. We used bucketization so data become less complex. T-closeness distributes tuple over table according to threshold but it doesn't increase data complexity. Data utility is nothing but finding accuracy of results after applying privacy on data. Data utility can be calculated using three factors, they are: generalization height, average group size and discernibility. Generalization height is nothing but total numbers of operations are needed to make data generalize. Here Table 1 contains 9 tuples. It requires 15 operations to perform bucketization and multiset-based generalization. As we increase data size, generalization height gets increase. Average group size is nothing but total number of buckets gets generated during generalization. Discernibility is a process which makes data indistinguishable. Here data discernibility is high as data transform into more generalize form. Figure 4 shows data utility in the form of generalization height, group average size and discernibility. Here Y axis represents total number of operations to represents generalization height, total bucket size to represents group average size and total number of indistinguishable tuples to represents discernibility. X axis represents total number of tuples in datasets.

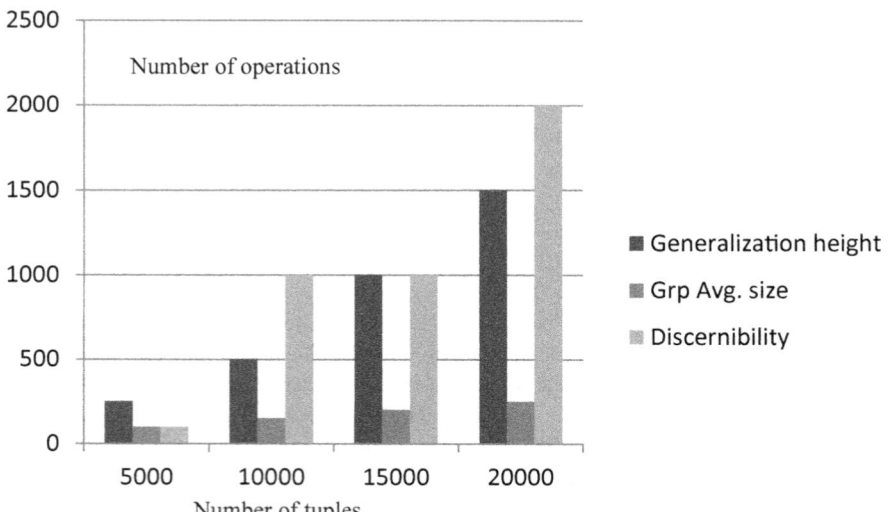

Fig. 4. Data utility according to generalization height, group average size and discernibility

4.2   Execution Time

The graph as shown in Fig. 5 uses time v/s data size, with X-Coordinate representing Data Size and Y-Coordinate representing Overall Time. Time is taken in nano seconds. Total of 5000 instances has been taken of employee database. Experiment performed started with 5000 instances and took 8 ns for execution. Further when we increased number of instances to 10,000, the time taken can be seen to increase. Whereas, when instances increase from 15,000 to 20,000, time taken increases for executing t-closeness as shown in Fig. 4 but for multiset-based generalization it is near about same for dataset of 5000 to 20000 instances. Performing t-closeness on data sets takes more time to execute as data gets increases. But multiset-based generalization takes less time to execute.

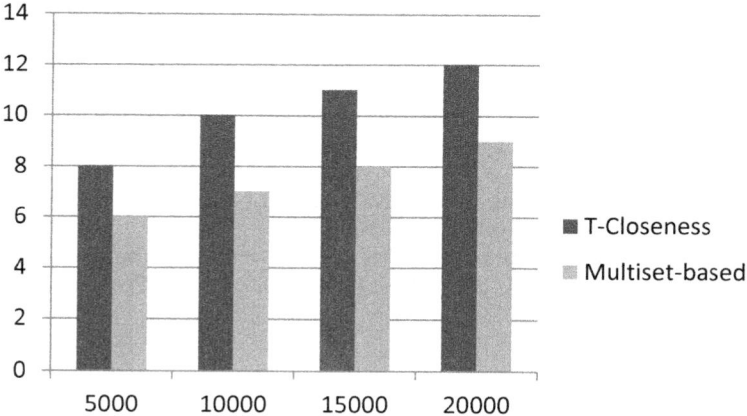

Fig. 5. Time required by t-closeness and multiset-based generalization for executing different size of datasets

5   Conclusion

Hadoop is use by different commercial organizations. So it's important to provide proper privacy and security to the data. As anyone can access the data which is stored on hadoop, protection of data plays important role. Proposed work trying to avoid different attacks on datasets such as identity attack, attribute attack and overcome drawbacks of existing method. This method protects data from skewness attack. Proposed algorithm provides better privacy as compared to existing slicing algorithm on hadoop which is able to fulfil industrial needs.

References

1. Shvachko, K., Kuang, H., Radia, S., Chansler, R.: The hadoop distributed file system. mass storage systems and technologies. In: IEEE/NASA Goddard Conference (2012). https://doi.org/10.1109/msst.2010.5496972
2. Derbeko, P., Dolev, S., et al.: Security and privacy aspects in MapReduce on clouds: a survey. Comput. Sci. Rev. **20**, 1–28 (2016). Elsevier
3. Kishor1, A.V., Balasaheb, D.P., Balasaheb, S.: Privacy preservation for high dimensional data using slicing method in data mining. IJMTER **02** (2015). ISSN 2349–9745
4. Mohanapriya, D., Meyyappan, T.: Slicing: a efficient method for privacy preservation in data publishing. Int. J. Eng. Res. Appl. (IJERA) **3**(4), 1463–1468 (2013)
5. Singh, A.K., Keer, N.P., Motwani, A.: A review of privacy preservation technique. Int. J. Comput. Appl. **90**(3) (2014). ISSN 0975–8887
6. Thanamani, A.S.: Comparison and analysis of anonymization techniques for preserving privacy in big data. Adv. Comput. Sci. Technol. **10**(2), 247–253 (2017). ISSN 0973-6107
7. Dwork, C.: Differential privacy. In: Bugliesi, M., Preneel, B., Sassone, V., Wegener, I. (eds.) ICALP 2006. LNCS, vol. 4052, pp. 1–12. Springer, Heidelberg (2006). https://doi.org/10.1007/11787006_1
8. Aristodimou, A., Antoniades, A., Pattichis, C.S.: Privacy preserving data publishing of categorical data through k-anonymity and feature selection. **3**(1), 3 (2016). IEEE. https://doi.org/10.1049/htl.2015.0050
9. Gehrke, A.M.J., Kifer, D.: L-diversity: privacy beyond k-anonymity. In: 2006 IEEE ICDE (2006). IEEE https://doi.org/10.1109/icde.2006.1
10. Veena, D.: Data anonymization approaches for data sets using map reduce on cloud: a survey. Int. J. Sci. Res. (IJSR) **3**(4) (2014). ISSN (Online): 2319-7064

An Eagle-Eye View of Recent Digital Image Forgery Detection Methods

Savita Walia$^{(\boxtimes)}$ⓘ and Krishan Kumar

University Institute of Engineering and Technology, Panjab University,
Chandigarh, India
savita_walia@rediffmail.com, k.salujauiet@gmail.com

Abstract. In today's modern era, digital images have noteworthy significance because they have become a leading source of information dissemination. However, the images are being manipulated and tampered. The image manipulation is as old as images itself. The history of modifying images dates back to the 1860s', though it has become very popular in recent times due to the availability of various open source software available freely over the internet. Such software is responsible for eroding our trust on the integrity of the visual imagery. In this paper, a comprehensive survey of various image forgeries, its types and the currently used techniques to detect such forgeries is presented. The review delivers the downsides of various controversial forgeries that have happened in the history. It provides the taxonomy of various forgeries in digital images and a redefined the classification of forgery detection methods. It also highlights the pros and cons of forgery detection methods currently in use and directs path towards challenges for further research.

Keywords: Image manipulation · Digital image forgery · Image forensics

1 Introduction

Nowadays, digital data is everywhere. Images obviously are one of the most important categories among the available data. Image and audio data is increasing and will continue to increase in near future. Digital images are being used in our daily lives. Digital photographs are everywhere; one can see them on the covers of magazines, in newspapers, in courtrooms, social networking websites and all over the Internet. Everyone is exposed to them throughout the day and most of the time. Digital imaging has demonstrated its worth in various fields like education, medicine, military, media, scientific purpose, glamour, forensics, industrial purpose etc. So the integrity of images used in these fields is paramount.

It is essential for us to be observant that seeing does not always infer believing. With the advent of the internet, the image manipulations have become very easy as there are various photo editing tools available. The available software ranges from professional tools to basic image editing software for normal users such as GIMP, Adobe Photoshop, etc.

© Springer Nature Singapore Pte Ltd. 2018
P. Bhattacharyya et al. (Eds.): NGCT 2017, CCIS 828, pp. 469–487, 2018.
https://doi.org/10.1007/978-981-10-8660-1_36

There are various ethical issues concerned with image manipulations [1]. The photo manipulations are being used to betray the viewers. Learning when a manipulation has been done on the image is absolutely important because even delicate and minor changes in the image can make an immense difference on the way image is judged and understood. As with the arrival of technology, people have easy access to freeware software which makes them edit the digital images. In journalism, people used to think that whatever is published is true. The readers embark on the moral principles of the publications which sometimes results in the clashes. There was a time when images were considered as a truthful media of communication. But this is no longer true. Image forgery is the term used to refer to the act of making changes or alterations in a digital image. There are many cases of digital image forgery [2] seen in history which are discussed in next section.

As such forgeries are increasing with the advent of internet and technology; it has become a need of the hour to detect such forgeries in order to check the authenticity of the image [3]. Numerous researchers are working towards detecting image forgeries. It has been observed that a number of research papers are being published in the field digital image forensics by authors from around the world. It has been analysed by submitting a query "Image forgery detection" on IEEE (ieeexplore.org) and Elsevier (sciencedirect.com) which shows the increase in the number of publications per year (see Fig. 1) in image forensics from year 2000 to 2017 on these two libraries.

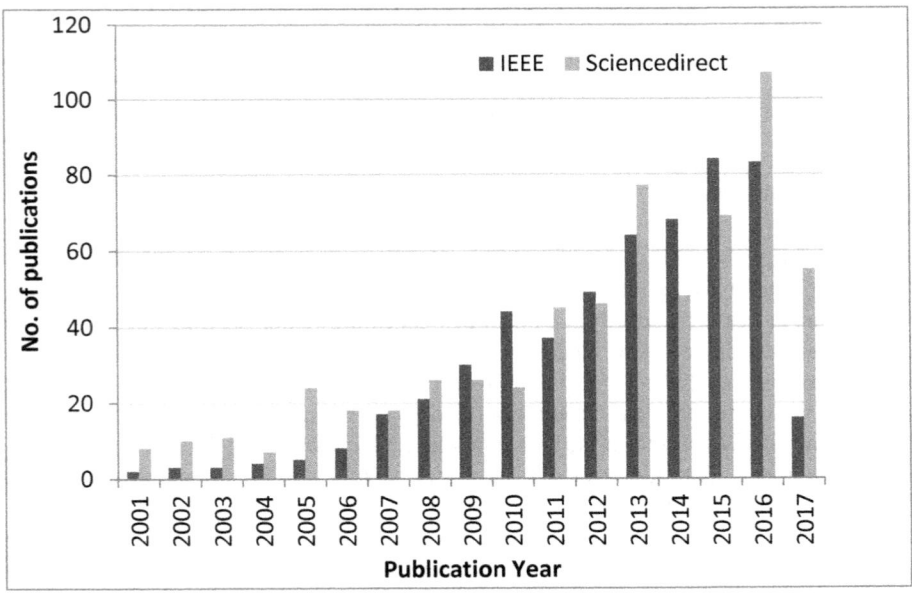

Fig. 1. Increasing number of publications over past 17 years on "image forgery detection" in IEEE (ieeexplore.org) and Elsevier (Sciencedirect.com)

Now, the major goal of image forensics is to detect such attacks in order to confirm the authenticity of an image. Various methods are used which focus either on a single type of forgery or they target multiple forgeries. The ideal approach to be followed by researchers should be to target multiple approaches as well as to identify post-processing operations performed on images in order to conceal the traces of forgeries.

Image forgery detection has attracted many researchers to contribute in the field of image forensics due to its significance. Numerous survey articles are available on various libraries. By far, the survey articles [4, 5] are two of the best articles which provided the most influential and extensive reviews of the forgery methods available. Even with availability of various review articles, still most of the digital image forgery detection methods stand unfamiliar. The basic idea behind the review presented here is to enlighten the researchers about the various kinds of forgeries a forger can attempt to create and to briefly enlist the recently developed techniques, their advantages, disadvantages and future challenges that the researchers have faced till now. Major contributions of this paper can be stated as follows:

1. To report the various image manipulation incidents throughout the history.
2. To deliver a detailed taxonomy of various forgeries in a digital image.
3. To provide improved classification of digital image forgery detection methods.
4. To critically review various recent forgery detection methods and offering future directions for researchers.

The whole paper is organized as follows: Sect. 2 provides a brief evaluation on the history of photo manipulations. Section 3 provides the taxonomy of various digital image forgeries. Section 4 provides an improved classification of methods and their critical review. Along with that, Sect. 4.3 covers the drawbacks of various methods In Sect. 5, the conclusions are drawn and future challenges are identified.

2 History of Photo Manipulations

In this section, various image manipulations throughout the history are discussed. The major purpose of exposing the image forgery incidents is that the researchers can read the mind of the forgers by knowing about the kind of forgeries attempted in history. Once it is known that what can be different ways of attempting forgeries, it can provide a way to detect them. Knowing only that the forgery has been attempted on an image would not be helpful for recognition of forgery. To accurately recognize and localize a forgery region in an image, the researcher should have entire knowledge about the kind of forgeries happened in history and the recent trend followed by forgers to modify an image

The first photograph was created in 1814 by Niepce and just after a few decades, photographs were being altered. Photo manipulation has been ever-existent since the 1860s. The U.S. President Abraham Lincoln's portrait was forged (see Fig. 2) by simply stitching Lincoln's head to the Southern politician John Calhoun's body [6].

Fig. 2. Lincoln's head over Southern politician John Calhoun's body

During 1910s, the composites of photographs were commercialized by photographic studios. Portraits of families were constructed by stitching together multiple individual images into a single frame, thus bringing families together, so to say. In Fig. 3, just the woman on the right was originally in the picture. Family members were taken off from other pictures and pasted on top to produce a composite image.

Fig. 3. Photographic composites of family members

In 1937, Joseph Goebbels, a propaganda minister under Adolf Hitler, was seen in a picture with a bunch of other people. Adolf Hitler ordered to remove Joseph Goebbels from the original. The reason, as to why the image was doctored, remains unclear (see Fig. 4).

Fig. 4. Jospeh Goebbel removed from the original photograph

In a 1982 cover of National Geographic magazine, photographer Gordon Gahen, who had taken a horizontal image of the Great Pyramids of Giza, had to squeeze the image inwards so as to accommodate both pyramids into the vertical format of the magazine [7]. The doctored cover picture (see Fig. 5) was criticized by Tom Kennedy who was the Director of Photography at National Geographic. Later, he insured that the technology to manipulate elements in an image is no longer employed and regarded the manipulation a mistake not to be repeated.

Fig. 5. Squeezed image of Great pyramids of Giza to fit it on cover story.

In 1989, similar to the Abe Lincoln portrait in 1860 (the very first doctored image), the popular talk-show host Oprah Winfrey had her head morphed over actress Ann-Margret's body for the cover of TV Guide (see Fig. 6). The picture of Ann-Margret was taken from a decade older publicity shoot and was used without the consent of either Oprah Winfrey or Ann-Margret. Ann-Margret's fashion designer recognized the dress and that's how this forgery came into light.

Fig. 6. Forged image of talk-show host Oprah Winfrey

Due to the emergence of high-resolution digital cameras in the 1990s, along with powerful personal computers, the manipulation of images has become overly common. Also, sophisticated photo-editing software has made it difficult to detect fakes.

Fig. 7. Bobbi McCaughey's edited teeth on the cover of the Time magazine

In year 1997, Bobbi McCaughey gave birth to septuplets and appeared on the cover of both Time and Newsweek magazine with her husband Kenny McCaughey. This time, Newsweek magazine altered the image by digitally straightening [8] Bobbi's teeth whereas Time magazine used an unaltered image. As a result, Newsweek was suspected of trying to make Bobbi "more attractive" (see Fig. 7).

In 2000, the brochure for the University of Wisconsin at Madison showcased an image inserting an African-American student in a crowd of football fans in order to diversify student enrollment. The original image was taken at a football game in 1993 whereas the doctored image showed an additional student, senior Diallo Shabazz, to show the diversity of students at the University. Consequently, the University officials confessed and said they were unable to find a picture that would show the school's diversity but couldn't find one, hence the image manipulation (see Fig. 8).

Fig. 8. An African-American student inserted in the brochure of a University in order to diversify the enrollments

As Senator John Kerry was campaigning for the Democratic nomination during the 2004 Presidential primaries, a picture of him sharing the stage with Jane Fonda at an anti-war rally surfaced shown in Fig. 9. It turned out that the image was doctored and the original picture showed John Kerry preparing for speech for Peace Rally which took place in Mineola, New York, in June 1971. Whereas, Jane Fonda was photographed by Owen Franken as she was speaking at a political gathering in 1972 [9].

Heath Ledger, who died in 2008, was photographed for his film "Brokeback Mountain" in 2005. In 2009, an article published by Vanity Fair paid tribute to a series of acclaimed Actor-Director pairings. This article showed the Heath Ledger image from "Brokeback Mountain" with Christopher Nolan digitally inserted into it (see Fig. 10).

Fig. 9. Spliced image of Senator John Kerry and Jane Fonda

Fig. 10. Doctored image of Heath Ledger

Other Recent Forgeries: In today's world, forgeries are making people dumber and dumber. In 2013, Discovery telecasted two-hour special called "Megalodon: The Monster Shark Lives" which convinced 70% of the viewers that the giant prehistoric shark to be existent even as annoyed experts claimed that the show was illogical and practically completely fabricated. An image is shown in Fig. 11 from "Megalodon" [10].

A photo of Indian Prime Minister Narendra Modi was posted by Press Information Bureau on its website purportedly showing him in a helicopter during an aerial survey of flood-hit Chennai (Fig. 12). The image was removed after questions were raised in social media about its authenticity.

Fig. 11. Discovery: Megalodon lives evidence

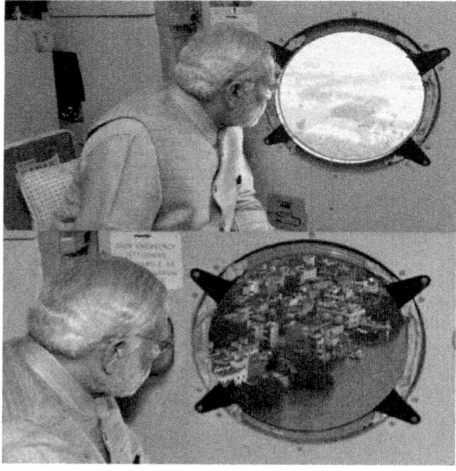

Fig. 12. Indian Prime Minister's faked photo during Chennai floods in Nov 2015

There are numerous forgery cases which made it to the news but it is not possible to put all of them into a single article because the number is too large. Such forgeries pose a major threat as they erode our trust from digital images due to the free availability of photo manipulation software. It has been observed that such forgeries are done by forgers for their financial, social or political benefits.

3 Taxonomy of Digital Image Forgeries

Image forgery is the term used to define any alteration in the original image. Such alterations are categorized (see Fig. 13) into four major groups, namely; Copy-move Forgery, Image Splicing, Image Resampling and Image Retouching. They are briefly defined as under:

3.1 Image Retouching

Retouching refers to the refining of the surface of an image after the acquisition process. Before the time of digital image editing, retouching was performed manually. There are several methods of the manual-retouching. Digital retouching, on the other hand, undertook a recent but speedy expansion in the last few years, and is now crucial in modern media. Image retouching is used mostly in fashion photography (see Fig. 14).

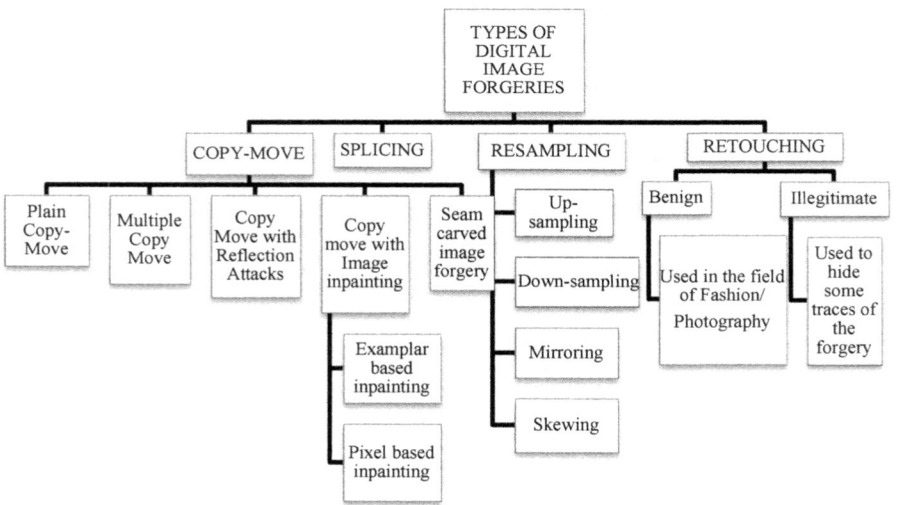

Fig. 13. Various types of digital image forgeries

3.2 Image Splicing

Splicing is another most commonly used technique to tamper the images. Image splicing [11] is a technique of creating an image by combining two different images. In splicing a majority part of one image is used. An example of image splicing has been shown in Fig. 15 in which the bird is copied from some other image. The image is taken from CASIA v1.0 dataset.

Fig. 14. An example showing image retouching (before and after)

Fig. 15. Example of image splicing showing the bird copied from another image.

3.3 Copy-Move Attack

In copy-move type of forgery, a part of the image is generally copied and pasted onto another part of the image to hide some object or some detail in the image. It is similar to splicing, the only difference is that in copy-move a region is copied and pasted into the same image [12]. Copy-move forgery can be further categorised as plain copy-move, multiple copy move forgery (MCMF), copy-move using seam carving and image inpainting based forgery. Figure 16 shows an example of copy move forgery in which the middle lion is original while the lions on both sides are copied from the middle one. The image is taken from CASIA v1.0 dataset.

Fig. 16. An example showing copy-move forgery

3.4   Image Resampling

Image Resampling is the process in which the images are transformed geometrically. It can be performed as a monotonic operation or in combination to other operations. Resampling can be of various types; down-sampling, up-sampling, etc. It is basically performed in order to change the size of the image. It is considered as forgery because it can change the way the objects appear in an image.

To hide the hints of above forgery operations, various pre and post processing operations are used by forgers. There can be multiple operations on a single image which makes the detection even more complex. Such operations can be of various

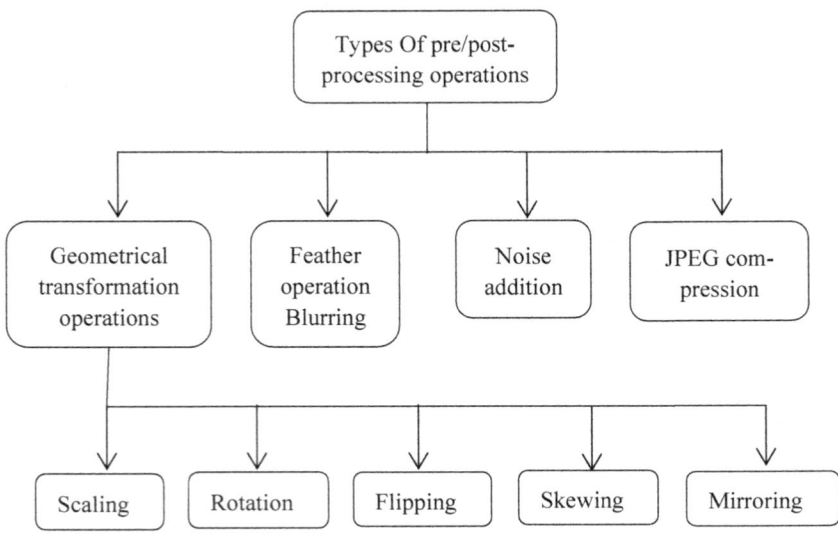

Fig. 17. Various types of pre/post-processing operations

types (see Fig. 17). Geometrical transformations are used when an object is copied from the image and it needs to pasted in order to create forgery, then sometimes the object is first rotated, scaled or skewed so that the viewer may not identify the forgery attempted.

4 Recent Digital Image Forgery Detection Methods

In this section, various methods for detection of digital image forgeries are discussed and an improved classification of methods is provided in Sects. 4.1. In Sect. 4.2, various recent methods for detection of image manipulations are critically reviewed. In the end of this section, common weaknesses of existing detection methods are stated.

4.1 Classification of Forgery Detection Methods

Image forgery detection techniques (see Fig. 18) are mainly classified into two major categories; Active methods and Passive methods of forgery detection. Active methods [13] are the methods which require some priori information regarding the image to validate its authenticity. They are further of two categories; Digital Signatures and Digital Watermarking. In active methods, a digital signature or watermark [14] is inserted into the original image by the sender. On the receiver side, the digital signature or the watermark is matched with the one received in the image. As these methods are only applicable when there is a priori knowledge about the image, thus its advantages

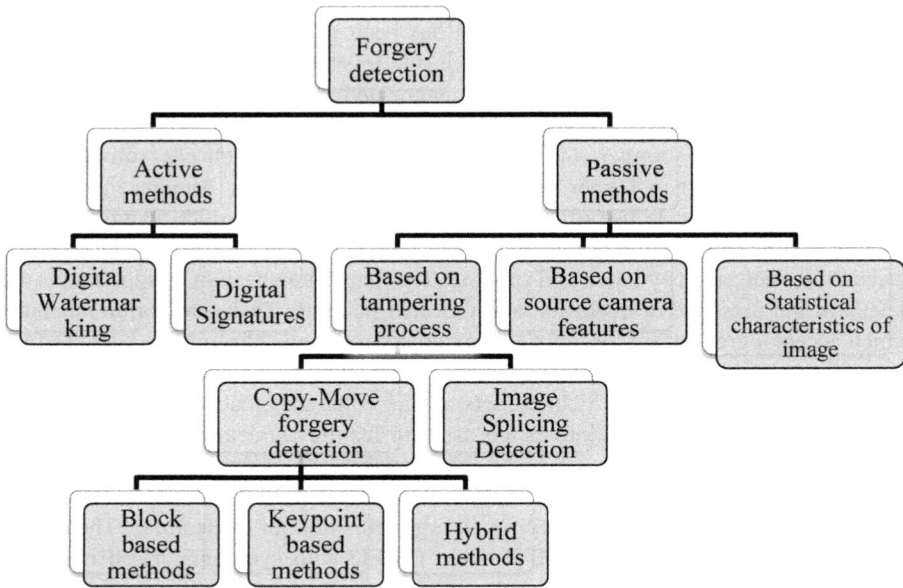

Fig. 18. Various types of digital image forgery detection methods

are limited to a certain extent. These methods cannot be rewarding when there is only a single image available and we need to tell whether it is forged or authentic. In order to overcome the drawbacks of active methods, passive methods [15] are developed. In contrast to active methods, passive or blind methods of image forgery detection take the advantage of the traces left by the processing steps in different phases of acquisition and storage of digital images. These traces can be treated as a fingerprint of the image source device. Passive methods work in the absence of protecting techniques. They do not use any pre-image distribution information inserted into the digital image. Passive methods [16] use only the image function and the fact that specific changes in the digital image could be detected when that image had tampered. They work by analyzing the binary information of the digital image in order to detect forgery traces if any.

Most common among all the possible forgeries are copy-move and splicing. The researchers focus on these two types as these forgeries are performed in combination with other forgery operations like resampling, retouching and various post-processing operations. In following sections, methods to detect common forgeries are discussed.

4.2 Review of Present-Day Forgery Detection Methods

In this section, recent methodologies that are being used in image forensics are analyzed so that the researchers can get some future directions to pursue their research in this domain. The works discussed in this section are mostly from 2015 to 2017. Numerous methods are available for detection of copy-move forgeries. Various review papers [17–20] are also available in literature. But the recent works are not covered in available articles. One of the aims of this paper is to cover the works which are not discussed in other literary articles.

Recently, a very significant work [21] has been proposed in which two existing methods are improved and their results are fused together tampering possibility maps. Various fusion rules are described and implemented in order to integrate the results from both the methods. The major advantage of this method is in cases when one method fails due to stronger rotation/scaling but other approach can still detect the region because it triggers higher responses in its respective map. Another method [22] is proposed which made use of two different approaches to extract features. In this, DCT and DWT are applied for feature extraction and feature reduction. The method successfully detects copy move and splicing. The major drawback of this method is that it fails in the presence of occlusion and repeated patterns. There are various methods which accept a grey-image for input as they do not work on color images whereas most of the forgery images are colored. In order to overcome this, the color information is taken into account in [23] which extracts all the color information from the blocked image and then the Markov features are used for feature extraction in QDCT domain. Another novel method [24] is proposed which makes use of two features, KAZE and SIFT. Both the features are combined together to make a hybrid feature for detection of copy-move forgery. The method utilizes the strengths of both the features. The authors in [25] creatively combines the SIFT based CMFD with symmetry based matching. The method is invariant to reflection attacks and any combination of reflection attacks with geometrical transforms. In [26], the fusion of forgery detection methods based on

Table 1. Present-day image forgery detection methods

Method	Types of forgery targeted	Features	Dataset	Classifier/model	Performance
Li [21]	Copy-move, splicing	SCRM feature set	IFS-TC image forensic challenge dataset	Ensemble classifier with LDA	F1-score = 0.4925
Hayat [22]	Copy-move	DCT	No standard dataset used	Feature matching using Correlation coefficients between feature vectors	Accuracy = 73.62%
Li [23]	Splicing	Markov features	CASIA v1.0, CASIA v2.0	PrimalSVM	Accuracy = 96.435% (CASIA v1) = 92.668% (CASIA v2)
Yang [24]	Copy-move	SIFT and KAZE	Benchmark database for CMFD [32]	RANSAC algorithm with SLIC segmentation	Precision = 90.27% recall = 78.61% F1 = 0.8704
Warif [25]	Copy- move	SIFT	NB-CASIA created from CASIA v2.0	Symmetry matching	F-score = 0.898
Hadigheh [26]	Splicing	DWT, GLCM, N-Run length	Columbia data set	SVM and neuro-fuzzy interface system	Sensitivity = 72.37% Specificity = 91.33%
Zheng [27]	Copy-move	SIFT, Zernike	Benchmark database for CMFD [32]	RANSAC algorithm	Precision = 88.51 Recall = 86.48% F1 score = 0.8717
Bayar [28]	Multiple forgeries	—	Created own dataset	CNN	Accuracy = 99.10%
Fei [29]	Copy-move	SIFT	Benchmark database for CMFD [32]	Swarm intelligent optimization	FNR = 6.25% FPR = 31.25%
Wo [30]	Copy-move	PCET	IMD, Kodak true color suite	Feature matching	F1-score = 83.4%
Rao [31]	Copy-move, splicing	Residual maps in SRM	CASIAv1.0, v2.0, Columbia DVMM	SVM	Accuracy = 97.42%

Fuzzy inference rules is addressed. A neuro-fuzzy inference system (NFIS) is developed for forgery detection for better time complexity. Another fusion based method [27] is proposed in which block based method using Zernike moments and keypoint-based method using SIFT keypoints are fused together in order to use the advantages of both the techniques. The method works well even in smooth regions and is robust against noise addition and JPEG compression. Another method [28] is proposed in which the features are automatically selected to detect manipulations without relying on pre-selected features or pre-processing. Selection of features is one of the major part of the forgery detection as there is no specific criteria as to which feature to be used for particular forgery detection. The method makes use of Convolutional Neural Networks (CNN) for automatic feature selection.

A brief comparison of the methods is given in the Table 1. The table shows few parameters which are significant for any forgery detection method. The most important parameter of any method is the number of forgeries it targets. The performance of all the methods can be noticeably matched with each other from the given table.

Most of the above methods fail in detecting the smooth regions in an image. Directing at this problem, a method [29] has been proposed which makes use of image segmentation and swarm optimization to detect small and smooth regions. Another problem in forgery detection mainly in case of copy-move forgery is large scaling and rotations. To target this, an effective approach [30] is proposed in which multi-radius PCET features are used in order to make the features rotation invariant and multi-scale invariant. To improve the execution time, acceleration with Graphic processing unit is used. The method is also robust against JPEG compression.

As various problems are arising in digital image forensics, the researchers are focusing on implementing the approaches with the help of deep learning methods. One of the most commonly used among them is CNNs. Few CNN based methods are also discussed above. CNNs provide automatic selection of features and extraction based on the intrinsic characteristics of the input image. A CNN based method [31] is designed specifically for splicing and copy-move detection in which residual maps of Spatial rich models (SRM) are used to capture the delicate artefacts introduced by tampering processes. By reviewing the literature, it has been established that the most commonly used features are SIFT and Zernike moments in case of copy-move forgery. The reason for opting SIFT features and Zernike moments by researchers is that SIFT features are computational more simple and efficient whereas Zernike moments are invariant against some of the geometrical transforms which yield good performance.

4.3   Drawbacks of Existing Approaches

There are various drawbacks of existing methods which can motivate the researchers to further continue research in this field in order to improve and develop better and reliable methods. Few of the major drawbacks are:

1. Many methods require manual intervention which can produce errors and can affect the results.
2. The detection approaches fail when the post processing operations are involved in forgery creation. Even if there are methods which can detect such post processing operations, they fail to detect the forged region when their magnitude is larger.
3. Another drawback of existing methods is the high computational complexity and longer execution times. Implemented feature extraction methods in most of the approaches are not invariant to all geometrical transformations and the procedures are complex which increases the time complexity.

5 Conclusion

In this paper, a light has been drawn on the importance of forgery detection. Digital image forgery is as old as the images itself. Various forgeries happened in history serve as an evidence to justify this statement. Taxonomy of digital image forgeries and forgery detection methods is provided and newly arrived methods have been discussed in order to recognize the key challenges in this area. It has been concluded that still a lot needs to be done in the field of image forensics. Though there are numerous approaches available in literature but every other approach suffers from some drawbacks. Based on the weaknesses of various methods, research gaps can be formulated which will give a direction to the researchers.

The drawbacks established from the available literature will help the researchers to motivate for future research in this field. It has been concluded that the performance of the detection methods may be improved by combining existing techniques by employing suitable fusion methods. Forgery localization is another challenge that needs to be focused for images with stronger post processing operations. There is a vital need to develop reliable and invariant feature extraction methods which can decrease the time and computational complexity. This can be achieved with the help of deep learning methods which can learn the relevant features automatically.

Hybrid features can be used to take the advantage of multiple features in order to make them invariant against all the geometrical transforms.

We examined the recent trends in digital image forgery detection and found out that researchers are moving towards implementing their works using deep learning methods. Deep learning methods such as Convolutional Neural Networks proved to be reliable for various image processing tasks and hence, they have the ability to prove their worth in digital image forensics also. Deep learning methods have the ability to provide promising results in digital image forensics with better reliability and accuracy.

References

1. Luo, W., Qu, Z., Pan, F., Huang, J.: A survey of passive technology for digital image forensics. Front. Comput. Sci. China **1**(2), 166–179 (2007)
2. Farid, H.: Digital doctoring: how to tell the real from the fake. Significance **3**(4), 162–166 (2006)
3. Farid, H.: Image forgery detection. IEEE Sig. Process. Mag. **26**(2), 16–25 (2009)
4. Birajdar, G.K., Mankar, V.H.: Digital image forgery detection using passive techniques: a survey. Digit. Investig. **10**(3), 226–245 (2013)
5. Qureshi, M.A., Deriche, M.: A bibliography of pixel-based blind image forgery detection techniques. Sig. Process. Image Commun. **39**, 46–74 (2015)
6. Mhiripiri, N.A., Chari, T.: Media Law, Ethics and Policy in the Digital Age. Information Science Reference IGI, Hershey (2017)
7. History of Photo Manipulations. Fourandsix Technologies Inc. http://pth.izitru.com/. Accessed 30 July 2017
8. Jones, M., Heyes, C.J.: Cosmetic Surgery: A Feminist Primer. Ashgate, Aldershot (2009)
9. Anderson, K.V., Sheeler, K.H.: Woman President: Confronting Postfeminist Political Culture, vol. 22. Texas A&M University Press, College Station (2013)

10. Winsor, B.: Discovery is becoming more and more ridiculous with its fake documentaries. In: Business Insider (2014)
11. Zhang, Z., Zhou, Y., Kang, J., Ren, Y.: Study of image splicing detection. In: Huang, D.-S., Wunsch, Donald C., Levine, Daniel S., Jo, K.-H. (eds.) ICIC 2008. LNCS, vol. 5226, pp. 1103–1110. Springer, Heidelberg (2008). https://doi.org/10.1007/978-3-540-87442-3_136
12. Shih, F., Yuan, Y.: A comparison study on copy-cover image forgery detection. Open Artif. Intell. J. **4**, 49–54 (2010)
13. Yeung, M.M.: Digital watermarking. Commun. ACM **41**(7), 30–33 (1998)
14. Rey, C., Dugelay, J.L.: A survey of watermarking algorithms for image authentication. EURASIP J. Appl. Sig. Process. Special issue on Image Anal. Multimed. Interact. Serv. **2002**, 613–621 (2002)
15. Mahdian, B., Saic, S.: Blind methods for detecting image fakery. IEEE Aerosp. Electron. Syst. Mag. **25**(4), 18–24 (2010)
16. Ranty, R.E.J., Aditya, T.S., Madhu, S.S.: Survey on passive methods of image tampering detection. In: International Conference on Communication and Computational Intelligence (INCOCCI), pp. 431–436 (2010)
17. Warbhe, A.D., Dharaskar, R., Thakare, V.: A survey on keypoint based copy-paste forgery detection techniques. Procedia Comput. Sci. **78**, 61–67 (2016)
18. Qazi, T., Lin, W., Khan, S., Yow, K., Madani, S., Xu, C., Kołodziej, J., Khan, I., Li, H., Hayat, K.: Survey on blind image forgery detection. IET Image Proc. **7**(7), 660–670 (2013)
19. Mahdian, B., Saic, S.: A bibliography on blind methods for identifying image forgery. Sig. Process. Image Commun. **25**(6), 389–399 (2010)
20. Mahmood, T.: A survey on block based copy move image forgery detection techniques. In: International Conference on Emerging Technologies (ICET) (2015)
21. Li, H., Luo, W., Qiu, X., Huang, J.: Image forgery localization via integrating tampering possibility maps. IEEE Trans. Inf. Forensics Secur. **12**(5), 1240–1252 (2017)
22. Hayat, K., Qazi, T.: Forgery detection in digital images via discrete wavelet and discrete cosine transforms. Comput. Electr. Eng. **62**, 1–11 (2017)
23. Li, C., Ma, Q., Xiao, L., Li, M., Zhang, A.: Image splicing detection based on Markov features in QDCT domain. Neurocomputing **228**, 29–36 (2017)
24. Yang, F., Li, J., Lu, W., Weng, J.: Copy-move forgery detection based on hybrid features. Eng. Appl. Artif. Intell. **59**, 73–83 (2017)
25. Warif, N.B., Wahab, A.W., Idris, M.Y., Salleh, R., Othman, F.: SIFT-symmetry: a robust detection method for copy-move forgery with reflection attack. J. Vis. Commun. Image Represent. **46**, 219–232 (2017)
26. Hadigheh, H.G.: Feature base fusion for splicing forgery detection based on neuro fuzzy. arXiv:1701.08374 (2017)
27. Zheng, J., Liu, Y., Ren, J., Zhu, T., Yan, Y., Yang, H.: Fusion of block and keypoints based approaches for effective copy-move image forgery detection. Multidimens. Syst. Sig. Process. **27**, 989–1005 (2016)
28. Bayar, B., Stamm, M.C.: A deep learning approach to universal image manipulation detection using a new convolutional layer. In: Proceedings of 4th ACM Workshop Information Hiding Multimedia Security, pp. 5–10 (2016)
29. Fei, Z., Wenchang, S., Bo, Q., Bin, L.: Image forgery detection using segmentation and swarm intelligent algorithm. Wuhan Univ. J. Nat. Sci. **22**(2), 141–148 (2017)
30. Wo, Y., Yang, K., Han, G., Chen, H., Wu, W.: Copy – move forgery detection based on multi-radius PCET. IET Image Process. **11**(2), 99–108 (2017)

31. Rao, Y., Ni, J.: A deep learning approach to detection of splicing and copy-move forgeries in images. In: IEEE International Workshop on Information Forensics and Security (WIFS) (2016)
32. Christlein, V., Riess, C., Jordan, J., Riess, C., Angelopoulou, E.: An evaluation of popular copy-move forgery detection approaches. IEEE Trans. Inf. Forensics Secur. **7**(6), 1841–1854 (2012)

Quantum IDS for Mitigation of DDoS Attacks by Mirai Botnets

Yagnesh Balasubramanian[✉], Durga Shankar Baggam[✉],
Swaminathan Venkatraman, and V. Ramaswamy

Department of Computer Science and Engineering, Srinivasa Ramanujan Centre,
SASTRA University, Kumbakonam, India
{yagnesh,durgashankar}@src.sastra.edu

Abstract. The exponential growth and development of IoT has created
several issues which will have to be tackled to ensure network security.
Currently available intrusion detection systems not fully capable of protecting systems against sophisticated attacks. Our work explores Quantum Algorithms applied to Intrusion Detection Systems. We propose
Quantum Intrusion Detection System which is a fusion of classical and
quantum techniques. We do hope our methodology will be in a position
to safeguard systems against any sophisticated attacks. We also fore-
see improvement in accuracy and precision rate and reduction in the
false positive rate besides protecting data integrity, confidentiality and
availability. We also discuss DDoS attacks launched by Mirai botnets for
evaluating the system.

Keywords: IoT · DDoS · Mirai · Botnets · Quantum computing
Grover search algorithm

1 Introduction

Internet of things is becoming popular with every passing day. It is estimated
that by 2020 there will be around 24 billion IoT devices [18]. This has transformed the way people carry out their day to day activities transforming the
world. Enterprises are becoming smart and innovative with IoT. At the same
time, threat perceptions are also increasing the threat level of botnets on IoT
were largely ignored until internet went down one fine day. Bot is a computer
or a device infected with malware and controlled by central command and control server used to carry out DDoS attacks [19]. There are few attacks of this
kind namely Lizzard Stresser, Mirari and Leet. Botnets that consist of lots of
IoT devices such as home routers, CCTV cameras and DVRs are not new. IoT
botnets were initially found in year 2015 followed by Mirai Botnets in IoT in
2016 which was exposed to DDoS attack. These botnets consisted of hundreds
of infected IoT devices and launched attacks upwards of 600 Gbps [17]. The
main purpose of our work is to find infected devices in the IoT infrastructure
effectively and efficiently. However, the model we adopt here is also analysed

© Springer Nature Singapore Pte Ltd. 2018
P. Bhattacharyya et al. (Eds.): NGCT 2017, CCIS 828, pp. 488–501, 2018.
https://doi.org/10.1007/978-981-10-8660-1_37

with post quantum computing using Grover approach. This work is expected to help in understanding how quantum algorithms can be made full use of and its advantages over classical algorithms to overcome DDoS attacks.

2 Challenges for IDS

Intrusion Detection System (IDS) products have been found to be wanting in advancement in keeping up with the rapid advancement in switching and bandwidth growth and increased sophisticated attacks that need to be handled today. Current IDS products often operate in a monitoring mode only. For example, Sniffers can detect attacks but cannot effectively and reliably block malicious traffic before the damage is done.

The 8 Challenges [6] *are:*

1. Inaccurate detection
2. Incomplete attack coverage
3. More detection, less prevention
4. Designed primarily for sub-100 Mbps network
5. Performance challenged
6. Scalability issues
7. Security policy enforcement related issues
8. Require significant information technology.

3 Motivation

Intrusion Detection is gaining importance both in industries and academia. Due to various types of attacks that are taking place in cyberspace today, it is of utmost importance to device systems which can provide security in the cyberspace. Improvements to Intrusion Detection can be achieved by making use of a more comprehensive approach which involves monitoring security events from many different heterogeneous sources. The application of Quantum based techniques has been found to be useful in real-time intrusion detection systems. Besides reducing detection classification times, they also improve classification accuracy. At the same time, care must be taken while applying quantum techniques. It is important to understand where and how it can be applied effectively, especially while dealing with unstable Intrusion Detection data sets. More specifically, it is important to understand how these techniques can play a role in security event data that is constantly evolving with new characteristics because of new techniques as well as new cyber attacks. Thus, the stability of feature sets is very significant in the cyber security domain where the landscape is extremely dynamic as opposed to some other domains such as bioinformatics where hybrid technique can also be applied. Quantum based intrusion detection system could play a very prominent role while analyzing diverse heterogeneous sources. The achievement of zero-day attacks coupled with reduction in search space are sufficient motivations for developing a Quantum intrusion detection system which is capable of faster detection.

4   DDoS Attack and Mirai

In DDoS attack, services become unavailable for legitimate users [12]. These attacks are targeted towards banks, business organizations, video streaming services etc. The ultimate aim is to throw a challenge to people who would like to access important information. The common strategy is to build a network of infected computers and launch an attack on targets. Following are some of the DDoS attacks.

TCP Connection Attacks: These kinds of attacks occupy the connections that are available to other devices. The devices that can maintain states are also susceptible to these attacks.

Volumetric Attacks: The bandwidth is consumed within the network or between the network and internet.

Fragmentation Attacks: A particular target is flooded with TCP or UDP packets so as to reduce the performance.

Application Attacks: Targets a specific service or application. These attacks are effective and non-detectable because of low traffic.

Mirai is a malware that turns IoT devices into a botnet. This botnet army are capable of launching DDoS attacks targeting servers and flooding with malicious traffic. In a matter of few weeks mirai had almost infected 900,000 devices [16]. Evidence shows that around 80 models of Sony cameras are vulnerable to mirai. The malware infects the vulnerable IoT devices with factory username and passwords using a table. The main agenda in targeting IoT devices is to bypass the anti-DoS software. Other reason is to avoid trace.

Characteristics of Mirai

1. The command and control centre is coded with Go while its botnets are programmed using C.
2. IP scanning is performed to identify potential targets except IANA, US postal services and Department of Defence.
3. On successful infection mirai launches HTTP flooding and Layer 3/4 (OSI) attacks.
4. GRE Flooding, SYN Flooding, DNS floods, UDP floods and STOMP floods are also possible.
5. Mirai destroys other malware with its killer scripts.

5   Quantum Information Theory

Richard Feynman in 1981 proposed that it would be impossible to simulate quantum mechanical systems on a classical computer. This contentions that a quantum computer will obey and built on the principle on quantum mechanical laws [3]. Classical computers cannot simulate these system due to the exponential growth of the amount of data required to represent a quantum system. Quantum computers make use of unique non-classical properties of quantum laws which allow them to process large amount of information in polynomial time. The most known development in quantum information theory is Shor's quantum algorithm [9], which performs prime factorization of integers in polynomial time. Apart from Shor's algorithm, a wide variety of other interesting algorithms have been developed for quantum computers.

The algorithm that is employed in this paper is Lov Grover's quantum database search [5]. The algorithm searches for a specific entry in an unordered database. A technique called amplitude amplification is used to achieve polynomial speedup. Grover's algorithm is optimal for any quantum algorithm for performing such a search [11]. The searching for a specific element in an unordered set can be generalized to apply to a wide variety of problems. Even though this algorithm does not provide an extreme increase in efficiency still it performs well with large input.

5.1   Complexity Theory

Let us compare the computational power of quantum computers with their classical counterparts. The problems in P are decision problems which can be solved in polynomial time by a deterministic Turing machine. The equivalent for space efficiency is referred to as PSPACE. NP problems require nondeterministic Turing machines to solve efficiently. NP-complete (NPC) are the hardest problems in NP. Every problem in NP can be reduced to a problem in NPC. If one NPC problem is found to be in P, then all the problems would also be in P. This may have resulted in proving $P = NP$. Bounded-error Probabilistic Polynomial time (BPP) are decision problems that can be solved by using a probabilistic Turing machine in polynomial time. Though there are problems solvable in BPP that are not in P, the number of such problems are decreasing after the introduction of BPP in the 1970's. It is also not known whether $P = BPP$, but there is a conjecture. Bounded-error Quantum Polynomial time (BQP) is the quantum extension of BPP. It is suspected that $P = BQP$ [14], which means quantum computers are capable of solving some problems in polynomial time that cannot be solved using classical Turing machines!

5.2   The Quantum Search Algorithm

Let us begin with the search algorithm in terms of an oracle which allows to present a very general description of the search procedure, and see how it performs.

The Oracle - Quantum Black Box. We would like to search through a space of $N = 2n$ elements. The instance can be represented by a function f, which takes an input y between 0 and $N - 1$. $f(y) = 1$ if y is a solution, and $f(y) = 0$ if y is not a solution. Suppose we have a quantum oracle which is a black box with the ability to recognize solutions to the search problem. This recognition can be signaled with the help of an oracle qubit. Oracle is a Unitary operator which can be represented as:

$$|y\rangle|k\rangle \rightarrow |y\rangle|k \bigoplus f(y)\rangle$$

The Algorithm Procedure. The search algorithm works as shown in Fig. 1. It makes use of a single n qubit register. Internal workings of the oracle are not important to the description of the algorithm. The goal is to find a solution with less applications of the oracle.

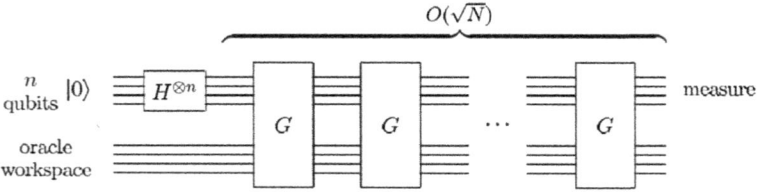

Fig. 1. Schematic circuit for search algorithm

The algorithm consists of repeated application of a quantum subroutine called the Grover iteration as shown in Fig. 2.

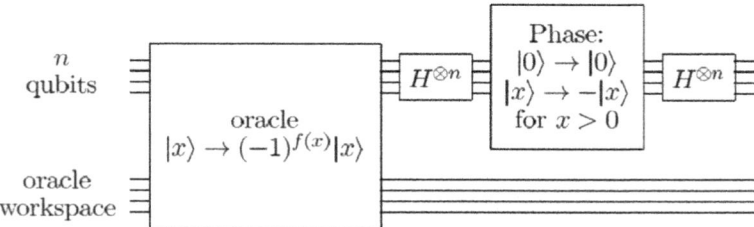

Fig. 2. Grover iteration circuit

1. Apply oracle O.
2. Apply Hadamard transform.
3. Perform a conditional phase shift on the computer with every computational basis state except $|0\rangle$ receiving a phase shift of -1.
4. Apply Hadamard transform.

Algorithm 1. Quantum Search

Input:(1) a black box oracle O: $O|y\rangle = |y\rangle|k \oplus f(y)\rangle$
(2) $n + 1$ qubits in the state $|0\rangle$.
Runtime: $O(\sqrt{2^n})$ **operations. Succeeds with probability** $O(1)$.

1: **procedure**
2:　　$|0\rangle^{\oplus n}|0\rangle$
3:　　$\rightarrow \dfrac{1}{\sqrt{2^n}} \sum\limits_{y=0}^{2^n-1} |y\rangle \left[\dfrac{|0\rangle - |1\rangle}{\sqrt{2}} \right]$
4:　　$\rightarrow [(2|\psi\rangle\langle\psi| - I)\,O]^R \dfrac{1}{\sqrt{2^n}} \sum\limits_{y=0}^{2^n-1} |y\rangle \left[\dfrac{|0\rangle - |1\rangle}{\sqrt{2}} \right]$
5:　　$\approx |y_0\rangle \left[\dfrac{|0\rangle - |1\rangle}{\sqrt{2}} \right]$
6:　　$\rightarrow y_0$.
　　　　Output: y_0.

6   Proposed Mechanism

The architecture of a typical IoT network with a QIDS (Quantum Intrusion Detection System) installed as a dedicated machine is represented in Fig. 3. The switch which contains Modified SNORT Packet Scanner (MSPS) constantly monitors the attributes of network packets. Consider a scenario were an attacker scans for vulnerable devices in the network. Identified device is injected with a malware and attacks are launched. The packets have to be forwarded via MSPS. The malicious behavior of the packet flips the MSPS to suspicious mode. In this mode, it queries QIDS for conformation. QIDS has an in built table with signatures for various attacks. Since QIDS is a quantum computer, signatures are initialized to super position. Using grover algorithm, the signature is searched for a match with the query. The signatures are represented internally as states. Each state has an associated probability in the final stage of measurement. The state which matches with the solution will have highest probability. QIDS will return 1 if the signature matches. MSPS is then informed that the packet is infected. MSPS sets the device to black list and alarms the administrator.

6.1   SYN Flooding

This is one of the most popular network attacks. DOS (Denial of Service) and DDOS (Distributed Denial of Service) attacks are very often based on massive SYN Flooding [12]. SYN flooding works by exploiting the weakness in three-way handshake.

The Handshake Process. The three-way handshake is a method that TCP uses to synchronize sequence numbers is necessary for its proper functioning. There are three steps for synchronizing sequence numbers.

1. Host initiates the connection and sends a TCP packet with SYN flag.

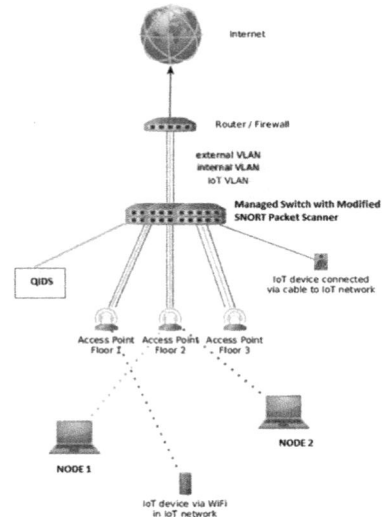

Fig. 3. Architecture of the proposed system

2. Server replies with a SYN/ACK packet.
3. Host replies with an ACK packet.

1. Server sends SYN/ACK packet and waits for response.
2. This wait state is registered in memory.
3. The registered state in the memory is removed after a time-out.
4. SYN flooding causes more number of half-opened connections and exhausts server's memory.

1. The affected node will start sending SYN packets to the server in order to cause SYN flooding thereby draining resources of the server.
2. The packets have to pass through MSPS.
3. In this case SYN flooding will trigger the suspicious mode of MSPS which will send the attributes for QIDS machine in the network.
4. QIDS uses grover to search the tables in $\sqrt{N}$ times.
5. If a particular signature is matched and has a high probability, the infection is confirmed and the corresponding message is passed to MSPS.
6. MSPS blacklists the node using its MAC address and drops all its further communication to the server.
7. Immediately the information is passed to administrator's console for further action.

The following table shows the attribute signature of SYN flooding designed for QIDS

Qubit1	Qubit2	State
0	0	Good
0	1	Not valid
1	0	Not valid
1	1	Infected

6.2   HTTP Flooding

HTTP flood attack is a type of Layer 7 application attack. It utilizes valid
GET/POST requests to flood the victim. This is a volumetric attack hence, it
does not use malformed packets, spoofing or reflection techniques. Following are
the characteristics of HTTP flooding

1. URL does not contain valid user agents.
2. There will be dynamic referrers with same packet size.
3. The volume of GET/POST will be high.
4. Some attacks will use rotating IP addresses.

Thus from the above characteristics we were able to construct a quantum signature table.

Qubit1	Qubit2	Qubit3	Qubit4	State
0	0	0	0	Good
0	0	0	1	Infected
0	0	1	0	Infected
0	0	1	1	Infected
0	1	0	0	Infected
0	1	0	1	Infected
0	1	1	0	Infected
0	1	1	1	Infected
1	0	0	0	Not valid
1	0	0	1	Infected
1	0	1	0	Infected
1	0	1	1	Infected
1	1	0	0	Infected
1	1	0	1	Infected
1	1	1	0	Infected
1	1	1	1	Infected

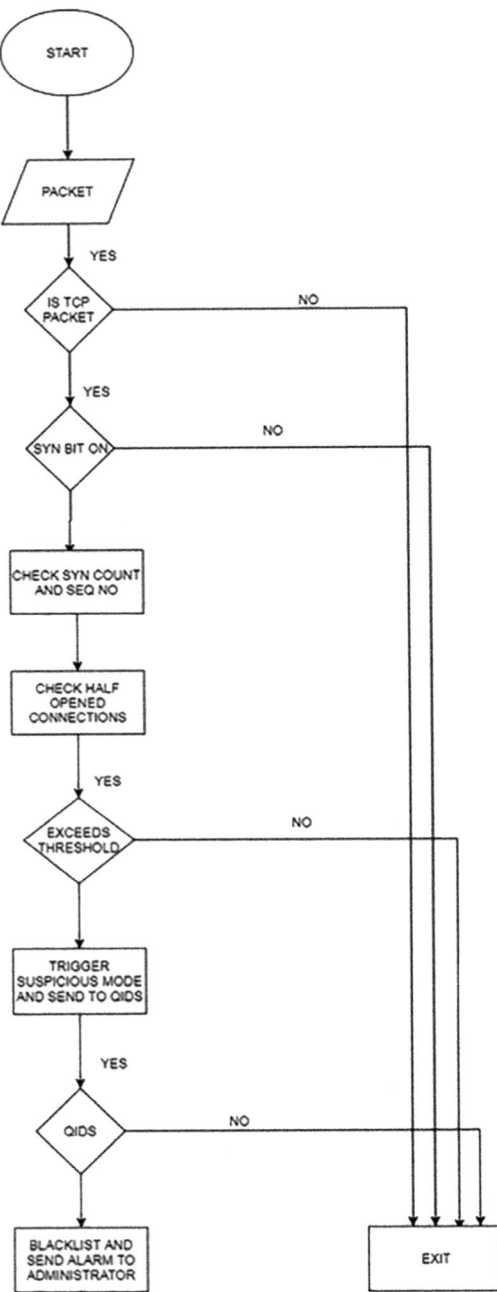

7   Results and Discussion

Simulation for SYN Flooding and HTTP flooding identification using QIDS are illustrated in this section.

7.1   SYN Flooding Infected State

Step 1: Initial State

$\text{noq} = 2;$
$$|s\rangle = \frac{1}{\sqrt{2^{\text{noq}}}} \sum_{j=0}^{2^{\text{noq}}-1} |j\rangle_{\text{noq}}$$

$\frac{1}{2}(|00\rangle + |01\rangle + |10\rangle + |11\rangle)$

Step 2: Operators U_s and U_ω

$\frac{1}{2}|00\rangle\langle00| + \frac{1}{2}|01\rangle\langle00| + \frac{1}{2}|10\rangle\langle00| + \frac{1}{2}|11\rangle\langle00| + \frac{1}{2}|00\rangle\langle01| + \frac{1}{2}|01\rangle\langle01| + \frac{1}{2}|10\rangle\langle01| +$
$\frac{1}{2}|11\rangle\langle01| + \frac{1}{2}|00\rangle\langle10| + \frac{1}{2}|01\rangle\langle10| + \frac{1}{2}|10\rangle\langle10| + \frac{1}{2}|11\rangle\langle10| + \frac{1}{2}|00\rangle\langle11| + \frac{1}{2}|01\rangle\langle11| +$
$\frac{1}{2}|10\rangle\langle11| + \frac{1}{2}|11\rangle\langle11| - 1$

Step 3: Algorithm Iterations
$$No. of Steps = \frac{\pi}{4 ArcSin\left(\frac{1}{\sqrt{2}(noq)}\right)}$$
$|11\rangle$

Final Stage: Measurement

Probability	Measurement	State
1.	$(1_1\ 1_2)$	$|1\rangle \otimes |1\rangle$
Probability	Measurement	State

7.2   HTTP Layer 7 Flooding Infected State

Step 1:Initial State

$\text{noq} = 4;$
$$|s\rangle = \frac{1}{\sqrt{2^{\text{noq}}}} \sum_{j=0}^{2^{\text{noq}}-1} |j\rangle_{\text{noq}}$$

$\frac{1}{4}(|0000\rangle + |0001\rangle + |0010\rangle + |0011\rangle +$
$|0100\rangle + |0101\rangle + |0110\rangle + |0111\rangle + |1000\rangle +$
$|1001\rangle + |1010\rangle + |1011\rangle + |1100\rangle + |1101\rangle$
$+|1110\rangle + |1111\rangle)$

Operators U_s and U_ω

$\frac{1}{8}|0000\rangle\langle 0000| + \frac{1}{8}|0001\rangle\langle 0000| + \frac{1}{8}|0010\rangle\langle 0000| + \frac{1}{8}|0011\rangle\langle 0000| + \frac{1}{8}|0100\rangle\langle 0000|+$
$\frac{1}{8}|0101\rangle\langle 0000| + \frac{1}{8}|0110\rangle\langle 0000| + \frac{1}{8}|0111\rangle\langle 0000| + \frac{1}{8}|1000\rangle\langle 0000| + \frac{1}{8}|1001\rangle\langle 0000|+$
$\frac{1}{8}|1010\rangle\langle 0000| + \frac{1}{8}|1011\rangle\langle 0000| + \frac{1}{8}|1100\rangle\langle 0000| + \frac{1}{8}|1101\rangle\langle 0000| + \frac{1}{8}|1110\rangle\langle 0000|+$
$\frac{1}{8}|1111\rangle\langle 0000| + \frac{1}{8}|0000\rangle\langle 0001| + \frac{1}{8}|0001\rangle\langle 0001| + \frac{1}{8}|0010\rangle\langle 0001| + \frac{1}{8}|0011\rangle\langle 0001|+$
$\frac{1}{8}|0100\rangle\langle 0001| + \frac{1}{8}|0101\rangle\langle 0001| + \frac{1}{8}|0110\rangle\langle 0001| + \frac{1}{8}|0111\rangle\langle 0001| + \frac{1}{8}|1000\rangle\langle 0001|+$

. . . .

. . . .

$\frac{1}{8}|1111\rangle\langle 1111| - 1$

Step 3: Algorithm Iterations
$No.of\,Steps = \dfrac{\pi}{4 ArcSin\left(\frac{1}{\sqrt{2}^{(noq)}}\right)}$

$-\frac{13}{256}|0000\rangle - \frac{13}{256}|0001\rangle - \frac{13}{256}|0010\rangle - \frac{13}{256}|0011\rangle - \frac{13}{256}|0100\rangle - \frac{13}{256}$
$|0101\rangle - \frac{13}{256}|0110\rangle - \frac{13}{256}|0111\rangle - \frac{13}{256}|1000\rangle - \frac{13}{256}$
$|1001\rangle + \frac{251}{256}|1010\rangle - \frac{13}{256}|1011\rangle - \frac{13}{256}|1100\rangle - \frac{13}{256}$
$|1101\rangle - \frac{13}{256}|1110\rangle - \frac{13}{256}|1111\rangle$

Final Stage: Measurement

Probability	Measurement	State
0.00257874	$\left(0_1\, 0_2\, 0_3\, 0_4\right)$	$|0\rangle \otimes |0\rangle \otimes |0\rangle \otimes (-1.|0\rangle)$
0.00257874	$\left(0_1\, 0_2\, 0_3\, 1_4\right)$	$|0\rangle \otimes |0\rangle \otimes |0\rangle \otimes (-1.|1\rangle)$
0.00257874	$\left(0_1\, 0_2\, 1_3\, 0_4\right)$	$|0\rangle \otimes |0\rangle \otimes |1\rangle \otimes (-1.|0\rangle)$
0.00257874	$\left(0_1\, 0_2\, 1_3\, 1_4\right)$	$|0\rangle \otimes |0\rangle \otimes |1\rangle \otimes (-1.|1\rangle)$
0.00257874	$\left(0_1\, 1_2\, 0_3\, 0_4\right)$	$|0\rangle \otimes |1\rangle \otimes |0\rangle \otimes (-1.|0\rangle)$
0.00257874	$\left(0_1\, 1_2\, 0_3\, 1_4\right)$	$|0\rangle \otimes |1\rangle \otimes |0\rangle \otimes (-1.|1\rangle)$
0.00257874	$\left(0_1\, 1_2\, 1_3\, 0_4\right)$	$|0\rangle \otimes |1\rangle \otimes |1\rangle \otimes (-1.|0\rangle)$
0.00257874	$\left(0_1\, 1_2\, 1_3\, 1_4\right)$	$|0\rangle \otimes |1\rangle \otimes |1\rangle \otimes (-1.|1\rangle)$
0.00257874	$\left(1_1\, 0_2\, 0_3\, 0_4\right)$	$|1\rangle \otimes |0\rangle \otimes |0\rangle \otimes (-1.|0\rangle)$
0.00257874	$\left(1_1\, 0_2\, 0_3\, 1_4\right)$	$|1\rangle \otimes |0\rangle \otimes |0\rangle \otimes (-1.|1\rangle)$
0.961319	$\left(1_1\, 0_2\, 1_3\, 0_4\right)$	$|1\rangle \otimes |0\rangle \otimes |1\rangle \otimes |0\rangle$
0.00257874	$\left(1_1\, 0_2\, 1_3\, 1_4\right)$	$|1\rangle \otimes |0\rangle \otimes |1\rangle \otimes (-1.|1\rangle)$
0.00257874	$\left(1_1\, 1_2\, 0_3\, 0_4\right)$	$|1\rangle \otimes |1\rangle \otimes |0\rangle \otimes (-1.|0\rangle)$
0.00257874	$\left(1_1\, 1_2\, 0_3\, 1_4\right)$	$|1\rangle \otimes |1\rangle \otimes |0\rangle \otimes (-1.|1\rangle)$
0.00257874	$\left(1_1\, 1_2\, 1_3\, 0_4\right)$	$|1\rangle \otimes |1\rangle \otimes |1\rangle \otimes (-1.|0\rangle)$
0.00257874	$\left(1_1\, 1_2\, 1_3\, 1_4\right)$	$|1\rangle \otimes |1\rangle \otimes |1\rangle \otimes (-1.|1\rangle)$
Probability	Measurement	State

7.3   SYN Flooding Non Infected State

Step 1: Initial State **noq = 2;**
$|s\rangle = \frac{1}{\sqrt{2^{noq}}} \sum_{j=0}^{2^{noq}-1} |j\rangle_{noq}$

$\frac{1}{2}(|00\rangle + |01\rangle + |10\rangle + |11\rangle)$

Operators U_s and U_ω $\frac{1}{2}|00\rangle\langle00| + \frac{1}{2}|01\rangle\langle00| + \frac{1}{2}|10\rangle\langle00| + \frac{1}{2}|11\rangle\langle00| + \frac{1}{2}|00\rangle\langle01| + \frac{1}{2}|01\rangle\langle01| + \frac{1}{2}|10\rangle\langle01| + \frac{1}{2}|11\rangle\langle01| + \frac{1}{2}|00\rangle\langle10| + \frac{1}{2}|01\rangle\langle10| + \frac{1}{2}|10\rangle\langle10| + \frac{1}{2}|11\rangle\langle10| + \frac{1}{2}|00\rangle\langle11| + \frac{1}{2}|01\rangle\langle11| + \frac{1}{2}|10\rangle\langle11| + \frac{1}{2}|11\rangle\langle11| - 1$

Step 3: Algorithm Iterations
$$No.\,of\,Steps = \frac{\pi}{4ArcSin\left(\frac{1}{\sqrt{2}^{(noq)}}\right)}$$
$|01\rangle$

Final Stage: Measurement

Probability	Measurement	State
1.	$(0_1\,1_2)$	$|0\rangle \otimes |1\rangle$
Probability	Measurement	State

7.4   HTTP Layer 7 Flooding Non Infected State

Step1: Initial State

noq = 4;
$|s\rangle = \frac{1}{\sqrt{2^{noq}}} \sum_{j=0}^{2^{noq}-1} |j\rangle_{noq}$

$\frac{1}{4}(|0000\rangle + |0001\rangle + |0010\rangle + |0011\rangle + |0100\rangle + |0101\rangle + |0110\rangle + |0111\rangle + |1000\rangle + |1001\rangle + |1010\rangle + |1011\rangle + |1100\rangle + |1101\rangle + |1110\rangle + |1111\rangle)$

Step 2: Operators U_s and U_ω

$\frac{1}{8}|0000\rangle\langle0000| + \frac{1}{8}|0001\rangle\langle0000| + \frac{1}{8}|0010\rangle\langle0000| + \frac{1}{8}|0011\rangle\langle0000| + \frac{1}{8}|0100\rangle\langle0000| +$

. . . .

. . . .

$\frac{1}{8}|1010\rangle\langle1111| + \frac{1}{8}|1011\rangle\langle1111| + \frac{1}{8}|1100\rangle\langle1111| + \frac{1}{8}|1101\rangle\langle1111| + \frac{1}{8}|1110\rangle\langle1111| + \frac{1}{8}|1111\rangle\langle1111| - 1$

Step 3: Algorithm Iterations
$$No.\,of\,Steps = \frac{\pi}{4ArcSin\left(\frac{1}{\sqrt{2}^{(noq)}}\right)}$$
$|01\rangle$

$\frac{251}{256}|0000\rangle - \frac{13}{256}|0001\rangle - \frac{13}{256}|0010\rangle - \frac{13}{256}|0011\rangle - \frac{13}{256}|0100\rangle - \frac{13}{256}|0101\rangle - \frac{13}{256}|0110\rangle - \frac{13}{256}|0111\rangle - \frac{13}{256}|1000\rangle - \frac{13}{256}|1001\rangle - \frac{13}{256}|1010\rangle - \frac{13}{256}|1011\rangle - \frac{13}{256}|1100\rangle - \frac{13}{256}|1101\rangle - \frac{13}{256}|1110\rangle - \frac{13}{256}|1111\rangle$

Final Stage: Measurement

Probability	Measurement	State
0.961319	$(0_1\ 0_2\ 0_3\ 0_4)$	$\lvert 0\rangle \otimes \lvert 0\rangle \otimes \lvert 0\rangle \otimes \lvert 0\rangle$
0.00257874	$(0_1\ 0_2\ 0_3\ 1_4)$	$\lvert 0\rangle \otimes \lvert 0\rangle \otimes \lvert 0\rangle \otimes (-1.\lvert 1\rangle)$
0.00257874	$(0_1\ 0_2\ 1_3\ 0_4)$	$\lvert 0\rangle \otimes \lvert 0\rangle \otimes \lvert 1\rangle \otimes (-1.\lvert 0\rangle)$
0.00257874	$(0_1\ 0_2\ 1_3\ 1_4)$	$\lvert 0\rangle \otimes \lvert 0\rangle \otimes \lvert 1\rangle \otimes (-1.\lvert 1\rangle)$
0.00257874	$(0_1\ 1_2\ 0_3\ 0_4)$	$\lvert 0\rangle \otimes \lvert 1\rangle \otimes \lvert 0\rangle \otimes (-1.\lvert 0\rangle)$
0.00257874	$(0_1\ 1_2\ 0_3\ 1_4)$	$\lvert 0\rangle \otimes \lvert 1\rangle \otimes \lvert 0\rangle \otimes (-1.\lvert 1\rangle)$
0.00257874	$(0_1\ 1_2\ 1_3\ 0_4)$	$\lvert 0\rangle \otimes \lvert 1\rangle \otimes \lvert 1\rangle \otimes (-1.\lvert 0\rangle)$
0.00257874	$(0_1\ 1_2\ 1_3\ 1_4)$	$\lvert 0\rangle \otimes \lvert 1\rangle \otimes \lvert 1\rangle \otimes (-1.\lvert 1\rangle)$
0.00257874	$(1_1\ 0_2\ 0_3\ 0_4)$	$\lvert 1\rangle \otimes \lvert 0\rangle \otimes \lvert 0\rangle \otimes (-1.\lvert 0\rangle)$
0.00257874	$(1_1\ 0_2\ 0_3\ 1_4)$	$\lvert 1\rangle \otimes \lvert 0\rangle \otimes \lvert 0\rangle \otimes (-1.\lvert 1\rangle)$
0.00257874	$(1_1\ 0_2\ 1_3\ 0_4)$	$\lvert 1\rangle \otimes \lvert 0\rangle \otimes \lvert 1\rangle \otimes (-1.\lvert 0\rangle)$
0.00257874	$(1_1\ 0_2\ 1_3\ 1_4)$	$\lvert 1\rangle \otimes \lvert 0\rangle \otimes \lvert 1\rangle \otimes (-1.\lvert 1\rangle)$
0.00257874	$(1_1\ 1_2\ 0_3\ 0_4)$	$\lvert 1\rangle \otimes \lvert 1\rangle \otimes \lvert 0\rangle \otimes (-1.\lvert 0\rangle)$
0.00257874	$(1_1\ 1_2\ 0_3\ 1_4)$	$\lvert 1\rangle \otimes \lvert 1\rangle \otimes \lvert 0\rangle \otimes (-1.\lvert 1\rangle)$
0.00257874	$(1_1\ 1_2\ 1_3\ 0_4)$	$\lvert 1\rangle \otimes \lvert 1\rangle \otimes \lvert 1\rangle \otimes (-1.\lvert 0\rangle)$
0.00257874	$(1_1\ 1_2\ 1_3\ 1_4)$	$\lvert 1\rangle \otimes \lvert 1\rangle \otimes \lvert 1\rangle \otimes (-1.\lvert 1\rangle)$
Probability	Measurement	State

8   Conclusion

This work has illustrated the design of a quantum search based IDS. To the best of our knowledge, the mitigation of Mirai based DDoS attacks in IoT using quantum approach has been well addressed. Our architecture provides faster results as well as higher accuracy as compared to classical counter parts. The present system is designed for detection; in future we will incorporate intelligence in order to learn itself in analysing the traffic log.

References

1. Diao, Z., Zubairya, M.S., Chenb, G.: A quantum circuit design for Grover's algorithm. Zeitschrift für Naturforschung A **57**, 701–708 (2002)
2. Dirac, P.A.M.: A new notation for quantum mechanics. In: Mathematical Proceedings of the Cambridge Philosophical Society, vol. 35, no. 3, pp. 416–418 (1939)
3. Feynman, R.P., Leighton, R.B., Sands, M.: A new notation for quantum mechanics. In: The Feynman Lectures on Physics, vol. III. Addison-Wesley, Boston (1965). ISBN 0-201-02115-3
4. Grover, L.K.: A fast quantum mechanical algorithm for database search. In: 28th Annual ACM Symposium on the Theory of Computing, p. 212 (1996)
5. Grover, L.K.: From Schrödinger's equation to quantum search algorithm. J. Phys. **69**(7), 769–777 (2001)
6. Bashir, U., Chachoo, M.: Intrusion detection and prevention system: challenges and opportunities. In: International Conference on Computing for Sustainable Global Development. IEEEXplore (2014)

7. Monowar, H.B., Bhattacharyya, D.K., Kalita, J.K.: Network anomaly detection: methods, systems and tools. IEEE Commun. Surv. Tutor. **16**(1), 303–336 (2015). First Quarter
8. Ju, Y.-L., Tsai, I.-M., Kuo, S.-Y.: Quantum circuit design and analysis for database search applications. IEEE Trans. Circuits Syst.-I: Regul. Papers **54**(11), 2552–2563 (2007)
9. Nielsen, M.A., Chuang, I.L.: Quantum Computation and Quantum Information, p. 13. Cambridge University Press, Cambridge (2010). ISBN 978-1-107-00217-3
10. Zeilinger, A.: Dance of the Photons: From Einstein to Quantum Teleportation, pp. 189–192. Farrar, Straus and Giroux, New York (2010). ISBN 0374239665
11. Jiayu, Z., Junsuo, Z., Fanjiang, X., Haiying, H., Peng, Q.: Analysis and simulation of grover's search algorithm. Int. J. Mach. Learn. Comput. **4**(1), 21 (2014)
12. Zargar, S.T., Joshi, J., Tipper, D.: A survey of defense mechanisms against distributed denial of service (DDoS) flooding attacks. IEEE Commun. Surv. Tutor. **15**(4), 2046–2069 (2013). Fourth Quarter
13. Rai, A., Challa, R.K.: Survey on recent DDoS mitigation techniques and comparative analysis. In: Second International Conference on Computational Intelligence and Communication Technology. IEEEXplore (2016). ISBN 978-1-5090-0210-8/16
14. Watrous, J.: PSPACE has 2-round quantum. Interact. Proof Syst. arXive eprint, cs/9901015 (1999)
15. Menon, P.S., Ritwik, M.: A comprehensive but not complicated survey on quantum computing. In: International Conference on Future Information Engineering, IERI Procedia, vol. 10, pp. 144–152 (2014)
16. John, B.: Hackers release source code for a powerful DDoS app called Mirai. TechCrunch, Krebs Brian (2016)
17. Brian Krebs: Krebs on Security Hit with Record DDoS (2016)
18. Gubbi, J., Buyya, R., Marusic, S., Palaniswami, M.: A vision, architectural elements, and future directions. Future Gener. Comput. Syst. **29**(7), 1645–1660 (2013)
19. Cao, L., Qiu, X.: Defence against botnets: a formaldefinition and a general framework. In: IEEE Eighth International Conference on Networking, Architecture and Storage (2013)

Smishing-Classifier: A Novel Framework for Detection of Smishing Attack in Mobile Environment

Diksha Goel and Ankit Kumar Jain[(✉)]

Computer Engineering Department, National Institute of Technology,
Kurukshetra, Haryana, India
dikshagoel.kkr@gmail.com, ankitjain@nitkkr.ac.in

Abstract. Smishing is SMS Phishing in which an attacker tricks the user by sending a text message aiming to steal sensitive information of the user for financial gain by pretending to be a trustworthy source. The trust level of users on their smart devices has attracted attackers for performing various mobile security attacks like Smishing attack. Various reports evidently indicate that Smishing attacks have dramatically increased over the last few years. In this paper, we propose a novel framework for Smishing attack detection. This model uses Naïve Bayesian classifier to filter text messages. Moreover, proposed model analyses the content of the text message and extracts the words commonly used in Smishing messages. Since the SMS text messages are very short and generally written in Lingo language, we have used text normalization to convert them into standard form to obtain better features.

Keywords: Smishing · Short messaging service · Mobile phishing
Machine learning

1 Introduction

Nowadays, smartphones have become very popular due to their compact size, portability, and longer battery life. Smartphones popularization has led to the increase in usage of SMS and instant messaging as a medium for communication. SMS is the most popular and widely used text-based telecommunication service. According to a Portio report, mobile messaging revenue was USD 128 billion worldwide in 2012, and it is expected to be USD 227 billion by 2017 [1]. Increase in the usage of SMS based services among the mobile users and unlimited messaging plans has resulted in an upsurge in unsolicited messages by the attacker to the mobile users without worrying about the cost.

Smishing is phishing through SMS in which an attacker tricks the user by sending a text message aiming to steal user's confidential information for financial gain by pretending to be a trustworthy source. Through Smishing, malicious code can enter in the mobile devices. Attackers have now shifted their focus to mobile users due to several reasons. The first is - extensive use of smartphones, second is - increase in dependency of users on smartphone applications for performing various tasks. The

P. Bhattacharyya et al. (Eds.): NGCT 2017, CCIS 828, pp. 502–512, 2018.
https://doi.org/10.1007/978-981-10-8660-1_38

third is - user believe that with two-factor authentication method, only trusted messages will be delivered to their devices [2]. Many solutions have been proposed to detect Smishing attacks, but attackers find the vulnerability in existing solutions and have developed methods which can bypass the security. Therefore, it is essential to come up with a solution that can efficiently detect Smishing attacks.

In this paper, we propose a novel security model 'Smishing-Classifier' which is effectively able to distinguish between Smishing messages and the Normal ones. The proposed model analyses the content of the text message and extracts the words commonly used in Smishing messages. The text normalization technique is utilized to convert the message into standard form.

The paper is structured as follow. In Sect. 2, we have discussed the background of Smishing attacks that includes statistics, smishing attack procedure, and various classification techniques. Section 3 discusses some related work of Smishing attacks. In Sect. 4, we present a novel security model Smishing-Classifier, its architecture and flowchart. Section 5 contains a comparative analysis of our proposed framework with already existing smishing detection techniques. Finally, Sect. 6 concludes the paper and discusses future work.

2   Background

2.1   Statistics

Phishing attack targeting the mobile users through SMS are increasing day by day. Attackers are preferring SMS over e-mail as a communication medium to fool users. There are around 7 billion mobile subscriptions but only 2.5 billion email users worldwide [3]. Moreover, there is 98% of SMS open rate and 45% response rate while only 20% open rate and 6% response rate for e-mail which reduces the attacker's success rate [3]. According to a report, 33% of mobile users have received a Smishing message which offers various deals and discounts to attract them [4]. SMS phishing generally contains a message along with a link to a fake login page. Studies have shown that 42% of the mobile users click on the malicious link [5].

Cloudmark annual threat report [2] states that one out of four unwanted messages tries to steal personal information of user. MEF report [6] reveals that 28% of SMS users receive unwanted messages daily, 58% receive at least once in a week. On the other hand, when we look at messaging apps, the threat is somewhat less severe. 26% of messaging app users get unsolicited messages every day while 49% receive at least once in a week. Even when the number unsolicited messages are increasing on mobile phones then also users trust SMS more than the other messaging applications. Figure 1 shows User's trust level on various messaging platforms. 35% of the users believe SMS to be the most reliable channel, 28% of the users trust messaging applications like WhatsApp, 18% trust Facebook, Skype and Yahoo [6]. On the other hand, countries like Brazil and China trust messaging apps more than the SMSes and the trust level of these countries on the messaging applications is 50% and 38% respectively [6]. In 2016, a customer of UK bank Santander lost 22,700 lb in SMS phishing scam [7]. Due to lack of SMS filtering mechanisms, attackers have identified that sending SMSes can be beneficial for them by fooling the user into giving their credentials [5].

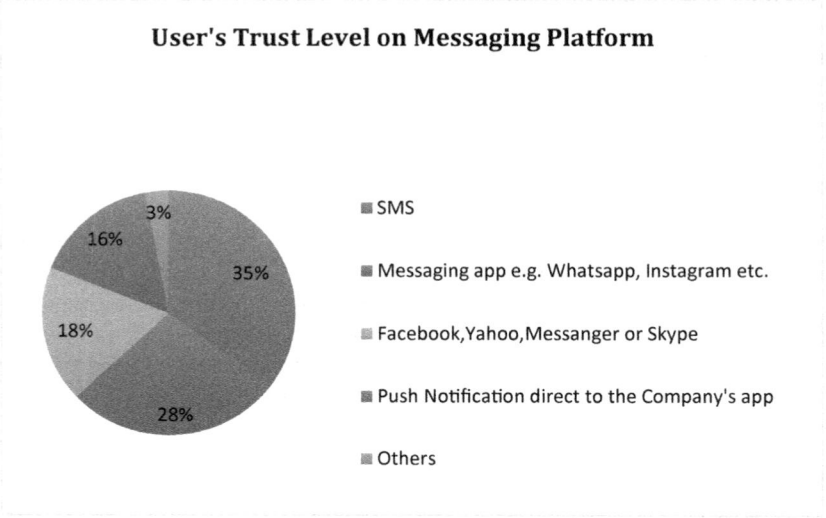

Fig. 1. Statistics of trust level of user on different messaging platforms.

2.2 Smishing Attack Procedure

Smishing is regarded as carrying out phishing through SMS [10]. It is an act of tricking users over the mobile phones into accessing a malicious URL in the message by masquerading as a trustable person, firm or any government organization. Attacker may install a malware that will control user's smartphone device. A lot of personal information is stored on mobile phones like financial information, personal information which can be stolen if malware gets installed in it [11]. Smishing attack is based on social engineering, and users are readily attacked by it. Blacklist technique was used to detect malicious URLs in the SMS but URLs included in the Smishing message are changed very fast which makes it difficult to find whether they are harmful or not. Smishing message generally includes offers, discount coupons, and lottery. The following steps are used in Smishing attack (Fig. 2).

Step 1: Attacker designs a malicious application or a phishing web page having a Login page.

Step 2: Attacker sends an SMS containing URL to the targeted users.

Step 3: On receiving the message, the user opens the SMS, reads it and clicks on the link that directs the user to a malicious login page or to a page having malicious application.

Step 4: User either submits the credentials to the fake login page or a malicious application gets downloaded.

Step 5: User installs the malicious application which sends user's sensitive information to the attacker. Attacker makes use of this information for financial gain or other motives.

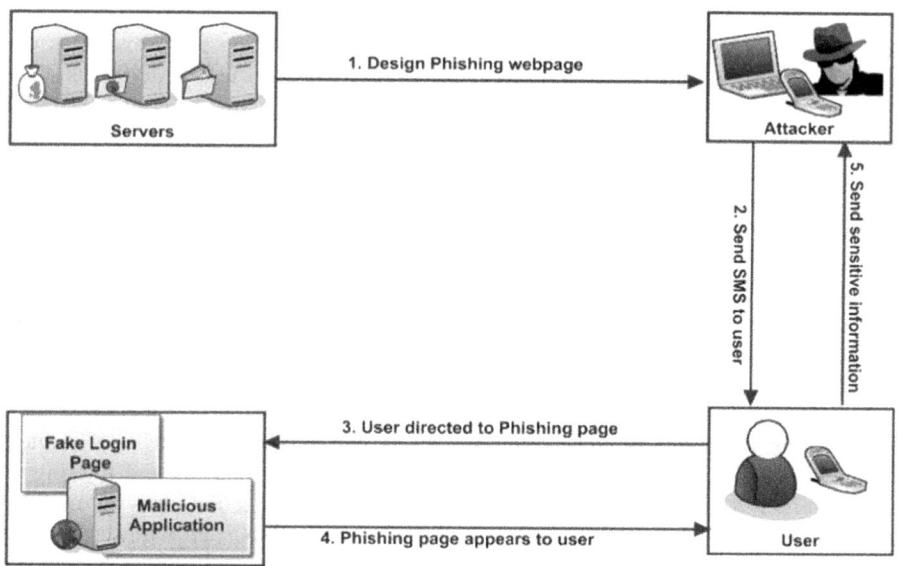

Fig. 2. Smishing attack procedure

3   Related Work

Joo et al. [8] proposed a model 'S-Detector' for detecting Smishing attack. S-Detector consists of SMS monitor, SMS analyzer, SMS determinant, and Database. It analyzes the URL and content of the text message. They used Naïve Bayesian Classifier in their system to distinguish Smishing messages from the legitimate messages by finding the words used more often in Smishing messages.

Yadav et al. [9] designed 'SMSAssassin' a mobile spam filtering application based on Bayesian learning and blacklisting the sender's mechanism. To achieve higher accuracy, Support Vector Machine (SVM) is used along with Bayesian classifier. Since the patterns and keywords in the spam messages are changed frequently, so crowd sourcing is used to keep it updated. The application requires a feedback from the user to correct the error made by the classifier so that filter can learn new spam keywords. Mobile phones having SMSAssassin application can share their reported spam list and can update their Spam Keyword Frequency (SpamKeywordsFreq) list for better filtering.

El-Alfy and AlHasan [12] proposed a framework for filtering multimodal text messages like short messages and emails. Developed framework is based on Dendritic

Cell Algorithm (DCA). This information fusion model is inspired from the human immune system and hybrid methodologies of machine learning. The system includes pre-processing, feature extraction, and DCA based classification. In order to enhance the performance of the system, two machine learning algorithms are used to analyze various features that were obtained from the received messages. Some spam filtering techniques are discussed in [13–15].

Almeida et al. [16] proposed an approach for normalizing and expanding short, messy and noisy text messages in order to improve classification performance as well as to obtain better attributes. It makes use of two dictionaries, lexicographic and semantic dictionaries with state of the art techniques for disambiguity, semantic analysis, and context detection. Authors concluded that with the help of text processing, classification performance can be enhanced by avoiding usual text representation problems. In another paper, Silva et al. [17, 18] proposed an approach for filtering undesired short messages based on minimum description length principle.

Hauri Inc. developed an application "Smishing defender" that blocks smishing messages in Android smartphones. The application monitors the SMSes and informs the user in real time whenever a smishing message is received. With the help of report function, suspicious message can be sent to hauri which further extract and analyze them [19].

Lee et al. [20] proposed an approach for detecting smishing text messages using cloud virtual environment. The approach takes decision on the basis of content, application source, and server's location. Program interface analysis and filtering are used in order to increase the probability of Smishing detection and to minimize incorrect detection. When a message is received, the risk associated with the message can be computed by the user in the virtual environment. In this approach complete processing is done on the cloud. On the completion of the process, screenshot and report are sent to the user with the help of which user can decide either it is a smishing message or general one.

Wu et al. [21] proposed an anti-phishing scheme "MobiFish" that defends users from phishing attack on mobile applications, and mobile web pages. System analyses the URL, IP address, HTML source code to determine the legitimacy of the webpage. OCR tool is also used to convert screen shot of the webpage into text for further analysis.

4 The Proposed Framework: Smishing-Classifier

In this section, we discuss the architecture and flowchart of the proposed framework. Smishing-Classifier is a security model that protects the user from the phishing SMSes by blocking these messages and delivering only Normal ones to the user. Smishing-Classifier analyses the content of the message and uses Naïve Bayesian algorithm to classify the messages. We inspect the URL and for better classification, we normalize the text into standard form with the help of dictionaries.

4.1 Architecture of Smishing-Classifier

The proposed framework Smishing-Classifier consist of three phases SMS analysis phase, SMS normalization phase, and SMS classification phase (Fig. 3).

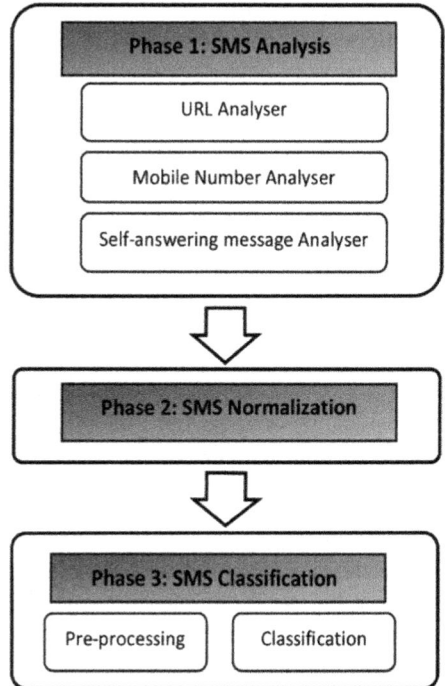

Fig. 3. Architecture of Smishing-Classifier

Phase 1: SMS Analysis Phase. In this phase, URL analyzer checks for the presence of URL in the text message since attackers can trick users by sending a URL link in the text message which when opened either direct the user to a malicious login page or a malware is downloaded in the user's mobile phone. If URL is found in the text message, then it is checked whether blacklist contains this URL or not. If the URL is not present in the Blacklist, it is invoked to check if an APK file is downloaded or a login page appears. Downloaded APK file may be a malicious application or malware which may further forward sensitive information of the user to the attacker.

Mobile number analyzer will analyze the mobile number from which SMS is received to check if this mobile number is already listed in the blacklist. Some smartphones have the feature that if any mobile number is blacklisted in them then only incoming calls will be blocked but not the SMSes. Mobile number analyzer overcomes this vulnerability. Self-answering message analyzer checks for messages which ask for a reply "yes" to subscribe for a service.

Phase 2: SMS Normalization Phase. In this phase, obfuscated noisy text is normalized and replaced by its standard form. English dictionary and Lingo dictionary are used for this purpose. To check for an English word, English dictionary is used and it normalizes each word into its root form. For example, "eating" is normalized to "eat". Language used on the Internet for conversation or chatting is known as Lingo language and this language is also commonly used in SMS text messages. So to convert Lingo words to English words, Lingo dictionary is used [14]. The output of this phase is normalized and unambiguous text that makes further processing of the text easier for the upcoming phases.

Phase 3: SMS Classification Phase. SMS classification phase consists of preprocessing and classification modules. Preprocessing is accompanied by the identification of sentence's boundaries, conversion of text into lowercase characters, and division of message into tokens. In the classification module, Naïve Bayesian classifier is used to classify the messages as Smishing or Normal. Tokens identified during the preprocessing stage are given as input to the Naïve Bayesian classifier. Naïve Bayesian classifier is based on Bayes theorem. The theorem computes the spaminess probability of each word in the message, and then the spaminess probability for the whole message. This computed probability is then compared with the predefined threshold value. Based on this, classifier classifies the messages as Smishing or Normal and blocks the Smishing messages and deliver the rest to the user.

4.2 Flowchart of Smishing-Classifier

In this section, we describe the working of Smishing-Classifier. The flow chart of Smishing-Classifier is shown in Fig. 4. The proposed framework inspect URL, analyze content, use blacklisting, text normalization, Bayesian classification techniques in order to separate smishing messages from the normal ones.

Step 1: When a SMS is received, first it is checked for the presence of URL. If URL is present in the SMS, then check if the blacklist contains this URL. If URL is present in the blacklist, then it is Smishing message.

Step 2: If URL is not present in blacklist, then system access this URL to check whether it downloads an APK file or not. If yes, the message is regarded as Smishing message.

Step 3: If neither URL is blacklisted nor an APK file is downloaded then check if the URL takes the user to a login page and ask for sensitive information. If yes, then it is Smishing message.

Step 4: Check whether the sender of the SMS is already included in the blacklisted database in order to determine if SMS message is Smishing or Normal.

Step 5: If SMS is self-answering message, then it is regarded as Smishing message else content of the text message is processed and analyzed.

Step 6: After this, text normalization takes place in which text is normalized with the help of two dictionaries – English and Lingo. Text normalization helps to obtain better features which further helps in better classification.

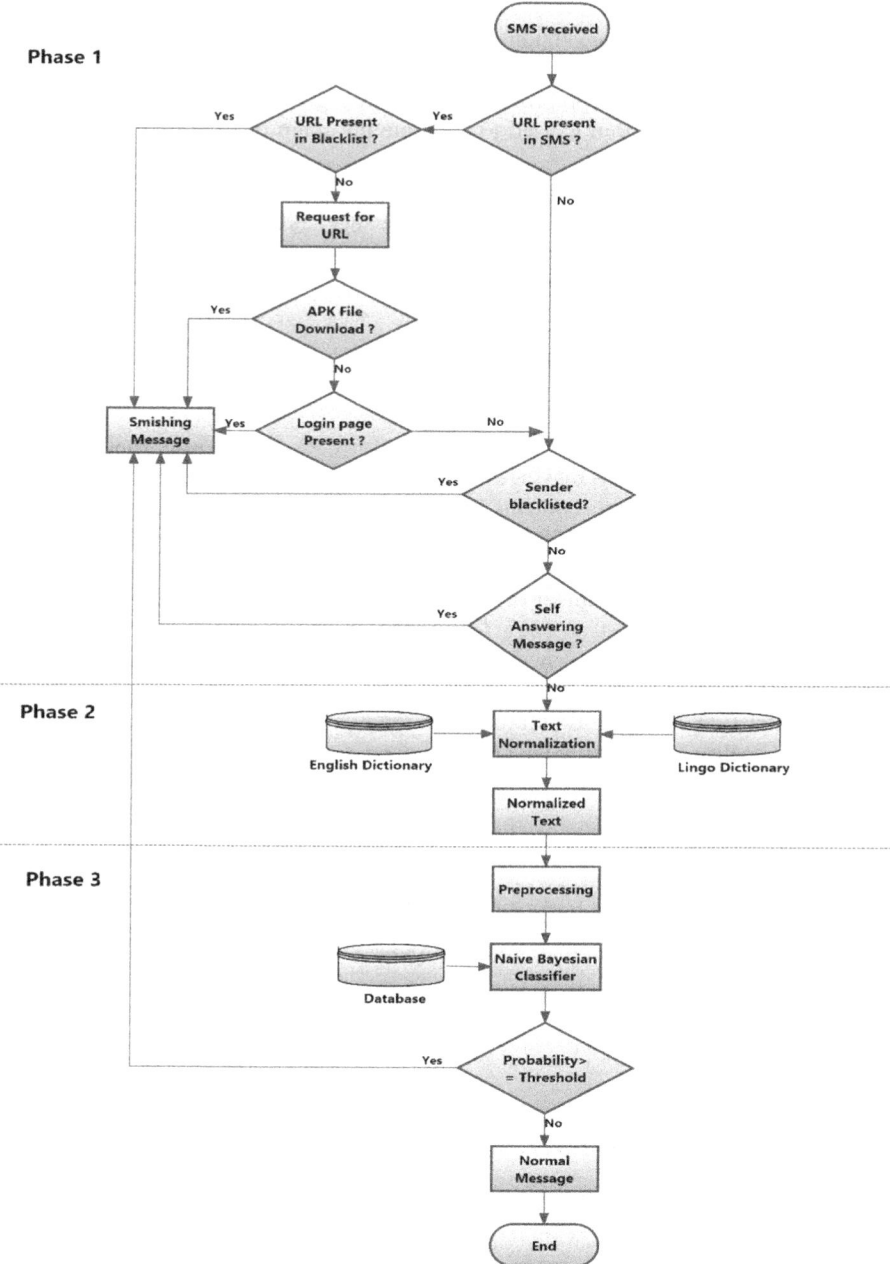

Fig. 4. Flowchart of Smishing-Classifier

Step 7: The normalized text message obtained is preprocessed for identification of sentence's boundaries, conversion of text into lowercase characters, or division of strings into tokens.

Step 8: The normalized and preprocessed terms are given as input to Naïve Bayes classifier. Bayes algorithm is used to compute the spam probability of the SMS on the basis of trained dataset.

Step 9: If the spam probability of the SMS is greater than some predefined threshold value, message is categorized as Smishing message and is blocked else regarded as Normal message.

5   Comparative Analysis

The proposed framework SMS-Classifier checks for URL, login page, mobile number of the sender, self-answering messages, and download of APK file. It normalizes the text message and perform content based analysis. Various smishing detection approaches have been proposed. Most of these approaches analyze URL, if it downloads an APK file or not but do not check if the user is directed to phishing login page. Detection using the mobile number of the sender is not used in the approaches given by Yadav et al. [9] and Wu et al. [21]. Our approach use blacklist to detect smishing message. Checking for self-answering message is not supported by any of the researchers till now. It greatly helps to reduce the spam messages on mobile phone. Text normalization is done to improve the quality of text message which in turn improve the quality of the attributes obtained. Comparative analysis of SMS-Classifier with other existing techniques is shown in Table 1.

Table 1. Comparison of our proposed system with the existing smishing detection systems.

Security	Joo et al. [8]	Yadav et al. [9]	Lee et al. [20]	Wu et al. [21]	Smishing defender [19]	Proposed framework
Check for presence of URL	✓	x	✓	✓	✓	✓
Check for APK download	✓	x	✓	✓	✓	✓
Check for login page	x	x	x	✓	x	✓
Check for sender's mobile number	✓	x	✓	x	✓	✓
Check for self-answering messages	x	x	x	x	x	✓
Text normalization	x	x	x	x	x	✓
Content based analysis	✓	✓	x	x	✓	✓

6 Conclusion and Future Work

With the increasing use of smart devices, security threats related to these devices are also increasing. The process of designing a system which can accurately detect Smishing attacks is still a big challenge. There are two concerns that make this task difficult. Firstly, most of the messages contain abbreviations and idioms which makes it difficult for the system to extract correct features. Secondly, due to shorter lengths of text messages, very few features can be extracted from them. To fill these gaps, we presented a novel framework 'Smishing-Classifier' for detecting Smishing attacks. Text normalization is done to replace abbreviations and idioms into their standard form. Naïve Bayesian Classifier is used to differentiate between Smishing messages and the Normal messages. The URL and sender's mobile number included in the message is checked first and then analyzed. Commonly used Smishing words included in the message are extracted by Bayesian Classifier. We have compared our framework with the other existing system and our system covers more aspects as compared to other techniques. This model is likely to provide better security against security threats.

There is always a possibility that an attacker would find new ways to carry out smishing attacks. So we aim to extend our proposed techniques to defend users against those attacks. We also aim to implement our technique on cloud environment for its use in real time. Also, user's perspective for the same SMS may vary from person to person. Hence, we can involve user to maintain a list of ham or spam words and while performing classification, this list will be given more weightage as compared to other features in order to get better classification accuracy. Our aim is to provide more security to prevent data leakage and security threats.

References

1. Worldwide A2P SMS Markets 2014–2017. http://www.xconnect.net/wp-content/uploads/worldwide-sms-markets-portio-strikeiron.pdf. Accessed 21 June 2017
2. The Social Engineering Framework. https://www.social-engineer.org/framework/attack-vectors/smishing/. Accessed 02 July 2017
3. Daily SMS Mobile Usage Statistics. https://www.smseagle.eu/2017/03/06/sms-mobile-statistics-2/. Accessed 07 June 2017
4. Phishingpro. http://www.phishingpro.com/. Accessed 01 July 2017
5. The Human Factor 2017. https://proofpoint.com/us. Accessed 16 June 2017
6. MEF Mobile Messaging Fraud Report 2016. https://mobileecosystemforum.com//wp-content/uploads/2016/09/Fraud_Report_2016.pdf. Accessed 10 June 2017
7. Smishing. http://resources.infosecinstitute.com/category/enterprise/phishing/phishing-variations/phishing-variations-smishing/. Accessed 05 July 2017
8. Joo, J.W., Moon, S.Y., Singh, S., Park, J.H.: S-Detector: an enhanced security model for detecting Smishing attack for mobile computing. Telecomm. Syst. **66**(1), 29–38 (2017)
9. Yadav, K., Kumaraguru, P., Goyal, A., Gupta, A., Naik, V.: Smsassassin: crowdsourcing driven mobile-based system for SMS spam filtering. In: 12th Workshop on Mobile Computing Systems and Applications, pp. 1–6. ACM, New York (2011)

10. Choudhary, N., Jain, A.K.: Comparative analysis of mobile phishing detection and prevention approaches. In: Satapathy, S.C., Joshi, A. (eds.) ICTIS 2017. SIST, vol. 83, pp. 349–356. Springer, Cham (2018). https://doi.org/10.1007/978-3-319-63673-3_43

11. Tewari, A., Jain, A.K., Gupta, B.B.: Recent survey of various defense mechanisms against phishing attacks. J. Inf. Priv. Secur. 12(1), 3–13 (2016)

12. El-Alfy, E.S.M., AlHasan, A.A.: Spam filtering framework for multimodal mobile communication based on dendritic cell algorithm. Future Gener. Comput. Syst. 64, 98–107 (2016)

13. Chan, P.P., Yang, C., Yeung, D.S., Ng, W.W.: Spam filtering for short messages in adversarial environment. Neurocomputing 155, 167–176 (2015)

14. Arifin, D.D., Bijaksana, M.A.: Enhancing spam detection on mobile phone Short Message Service (SMS) performance using FP-growth and Naive Bayes classifier. In: Asia Pacific Conference on Wireless and Mobile (APWiMob), pp. 80–84. IEEE, Indonesia (2016)

15. Nagwani, N.K., Sharaff, A.: SMS spam filtering and thread identification using bi-level text classification and clustering techniques. J. Inf. Sci. 43(1), 75–87 (2017)

16. Almeida, T.A., Silva, T.P., Santos, I., Hidalgo, J.M.G.: Text normalization and semantic indexing to enhance instant messaging and SMS spam filtering. Knowl.-Based Syst. 108, 25–32 (2016)

17. Silva, R.M., Alberto, T.C., Almeida, T.A., Yamakami, A.: Towards filtering undesired short text messages using an online learning approach with semantic indexing. Expert Syst. Appl. 83, 314–325 (2017)

18. Silva, R.M., Almeida, T.A., Yamakami, A.: MDLtext: an efficient and lightweight text classifier. Knowl.-Based Syst. 118, 152–164 (2017)

19. Smishing Defender. http://www.hauri.co.kr/support/hauriNews_view.html?intSeq=303&page=7&keyfield=&key. Accessed 19 Sept 2017

20. Lee, A., Kim, K., Lee, H., Jun, M.: A study on realtime detecting Smishing on cloud computing environments. In: Park, J.J., Chao, H.-C., Arabnia, H., Yen, N.Y. (eds.) Advanced Multimedia and Ubiquitous Engineering. LNEE, vol. 354, pp. 495–501. Springer, Heidelberg (2016). https://doi.org/10.1007/978-3-662-47895-0_60

21. Wu, L., Du, X., Wu, J.: MobiFish: a lightweight anti-phishing scheme for mobile phones. In: Computer Communication and Networks (ICCCN), pp. 1–8. IEEE (2014)

Cluster Based Mechanism for Avoidance of Duplicate Tag Data in RFID Networks

S. Bagirathi$^{(\boxtimes)}$, Sharmila Sankar, and Sandhya

B.S Abdur Rahman University, Chennai, India
rathi.bagi@gmail.com,
{sharmilasankar,sandhya}@bsauniv.ac.in

Abstract. Radio Frequency Identification (RFID) is a wireless technology that is used to determine the objects that has been lost or that has to be tracked through the use of radio waves. These objects contain electronically stored information and each tag has a unique identification number to distinguish one from another. RFID is used for automatic information monitoring and management during the tracking process in many fields. Clustering is the technique of dividing the set of data into groups (i.e.) data segregation. The objective of clustering is to reduce the amount of data by grouping similar data items together. Readers read the same tag data during each cycle of tag detection. To avoid this problem and to enhance the energy efficiency of the system, the Duplicate data avoidance algorithm is proposed in this paper. To filter the duplicate data in the network local cluster head node and inter cluster head nodes are used. The proposed work shows improved performance in duplicate data filtering and in terms of energy efficiency which increases the throughput of the system. Also the collisions among tag are also reduced as the same tag need not reply to the readers again and again.

Keywords: RFID · Clustering · Inter cluster head node · K means clustering

1 Introduction

Radio Frequency Identification (RFID) is a wireless technology that is used to determine the objects that has been lost or that has to be tracked through the use of radio waves. An RFID system is an advancement of Barcode technology which uses horizontal and vertical lines with the gaps in between. The disadvantage of the barcode is that if there is any damage on the lines of the barcode the object could not be detected. This disadvantage could be overcome by RFID. RFID systems contain tags, readers and antenna as its basic components. Each and every object contains the tags embedded within it that has to be tracked. Readers are used to detect the tags that fall under its coverage area. Antenna is used by the reader to send the radio waves to identify the tags. Thus Radio Frequency Identification Device (RFID) is the name given to the wireless, radio wave technology that allows for a small RFID chip to be embedded in any physical object and uniquely identified by an RFID reader. Tags contain unique id that distinguishes one from another as shown in Fig. 1. Tags are of three types: active, passive and semi passive. Passive tags use the radio waves generated by the reader to

© Springer Nature Singapore Pte Ltd. 2018
P. Bhattacharyya et al. (Eds.): NGCT 2017, CCIS 828, pp. 513–525, 2018.
https://doi.org/10.1007/978-981-10-8660-1_39

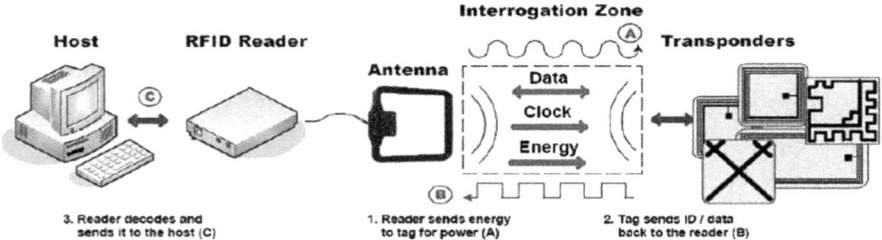

Fig. 1. RFID system components.

transmit the data to the reader. Active tags do not depend on the power from the reader but instead has its own battery to power up the circuit. Semi passive tags is an intermediate between active and passive tags. It possesses a battery and also uses the energy from the reader to transmit the data. Readers are of two types: fixed readers and mobile readers. RFID is considered as a non specific short range device. It can use frequency bands without a license. Nevertheless, RFID has to be compliant with local regulations (ETSI, FCC etc.) Reader queries the tags on different frequencies which depend on the type of application that is to be executed and the tags deployed in the RFID environment. Tags will be present in the overlapping regions of the two readers. So during detection process these overlapping tags will be read by both the readers which cause redundant tag data in the reader. To avoid this duplication and to increase the energy efficiency of the system, clustering technique is used in this paper.

Clustering is the technique of segregating the given set of data (i.e.) data grouping based on a specific property. The objective of clustering is to minimize the given set of data by the principle of grouping similar data together. The two important clustering methods are hierarchical clustering and partitional clustering. Hierarchical clustering as in Fig. 2 aims to divide a large group into small clusters or to merge two or more

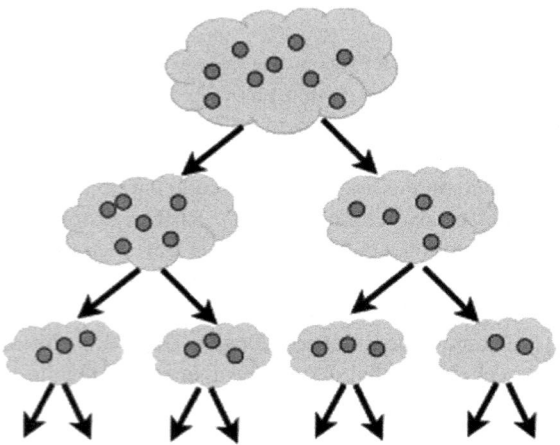

Fig. 2. Hierarchical clustering technique

clusters which are smaller into a single cluster such that each group forms a disjoint set of data. This is done by agglomerative and divisive methods. Agglomerative method proceeds to cluster data from bottom towards the top where small datas are merged together to form a cluster. In diffusive technique top down approach is followed where verge large group of data is divided recursively to form a smaller cluster. In partitional clustering as in Fig. 3 the given data is divided into small clusters of disjoint data. In this paper we use K means algorithm for cluster formation that deploys the minimization of an objective function and calculation of centroid values for grouping the data.

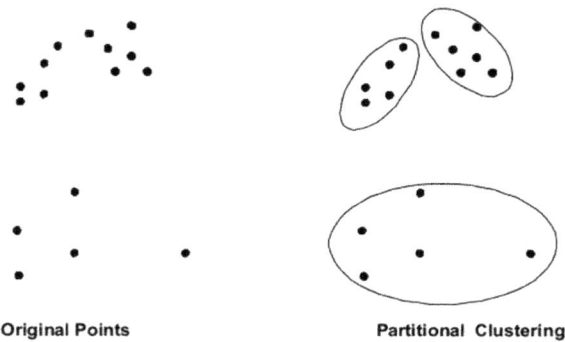

Original Points   **Partitional Clustering**

Fig. 3. Partitional clustering technique

2 Related Work

Number of protocols was proposed for tag detection and duplicate tag data elimination. Bashir et al. [1] proposed an RFID data filtering scheme that efficiently filters the duplicate data at the sink. Cluster heads are deployed in the network to filter duplicate data at the base station. Also the proposed method facilitates energy minimization and enhances the throughput of the system.

Ferreira Chaves et al. [2] uses the principle of clustering to develop RPCV algorithm for finding location of misplaced items in retail. RPCV algorithm works by representing a tag item as two dimensional vectors and then clusters the data based on the product type. Each antenna captures all the tags based on a planogram. Realistic scenarios were based on RFID-equipped goods and smart shelves.

Wu et al. [3] proposed a cloud based technique of RFID Trajectory Clustering Algorithm which is less sensitive to noise. RFID data is affected by various factors such as hardware flaws, transmission faults and environment instability. To overcome this a cloud based approach is implemented to manage the RFID data to improve the scalability and efficiency.

Tanbo et al. [4] implemented a hierarchical clustering algorithm based on RSSI values. It determines the distance between the pair of tags from RSSI series to form the clusters. The lost objects could be located more efficiently and the algorithm outstands in terms of financial and installation cost. The proposed algorithm is validated based on pairs of four distance functions and four clustering algorithms.

Soltani et al. [5] proposed Cluster-based movable RFID Tag Localization technique using artificial neural networks and virtual reference tags using handheld readers and applying K nearest neighbour algorithm. A multidimensional clustering technique between target and reference tags is determined and interpolation technique is deployed for grid formation within the cluster of reference tags. An artificial neural network is used to position the target tags.

3 Proposed System Model

In this paper, we consider a RFID heterogeneous sensor network with 'n' number of tags, 'n' number of readers and 'n' number of cluster nodes. Both passive tags and active tags are deployed in the network. RFID active readers ate used for tag detection. These cluster nodes are distinguished as local cluster node and inter cluster node. The local head cluster nodes are located within the clusters to communicate with the reader and the inter head cluster nodes are set in the overlapping regions of the two coverage areas of the readers. In order to have a balance in the energy consumption among nodes, the local cluster heads and inter cluster heads will be shifted on a probability basis but this is not within the scope of the work.

3.1 Cluster Formation

The first step in the tag determination process is the cluster formation. The most commonly used clustering technique is K means algorithm which partitions the n tags into m clusters so that each tag belongs to one cluster. Consider that the RFID network consists of X tags and K readers. K means algorithm aims to partition these X tags to the K readers using the objective function:

$$\mathbf{F} = \sum_{j=1}^{k} \sum_{x_i \in S_j} \|x_i - \mu_j\|^2 \tag{1}$$

The aim of k means algorithm is to minimize the objective function given in Eq. (1). The clusters of tags to reader are formed by the following steps:

1. Select X tags and assign each tag to the nearest reader randomly
2. μ_j is the geometric centroid of the tags. Calculate the centroid value and assign the tags to the nearby reader.
3. Step 2 is repeated until there is no change in the tag assignment to the cluster.

3.2 Assignment of Cluster Nodes

Once the tags have been grouped under the readers based on K means clustering algorithm the assignment of cluster nodes is done. In the proposed system model two cluster nodes are included viz the local cluster head node and the inter cluster head node. Local cluster head nodes are the ones that is within the coverage area of the reader. These cluster nodes contain the data of the tags detected by the reader. Inter cluster head nodes are set in the overlapping region of the two readers which collects the data from the local cluster head nodes and forward it to the base station. The local cluster head nodes and the inter head cluster nodes are differentiated by an ID value. The system model is shown in Fig. 4.

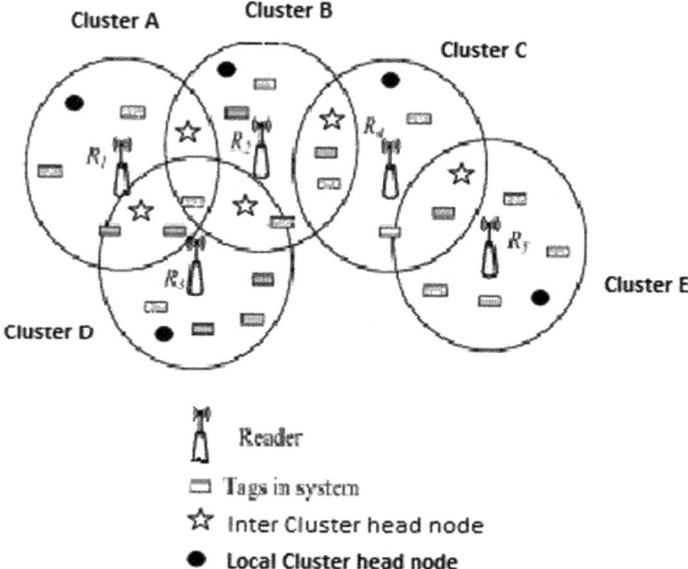

Fig. 4. System model diagram which shows local cluster head node and inter cluster head node

In the above proposed system model A, B,C, D and E are the five clusters which contains the tags grouped as per the k means algorithm. The overlapping region between the two readers contains the inter cluster head node and the local cluster head node is present within the coverage area of the reader. Readers use slotted aloha protocol for tag determination. The reader broadcasts a frame size and a random number to the tags. The tags use the random number and its ID in the hash function to fix a slot in the frame transmitted by the reader. After each cycle of tag detection the collected data is sent to the local cluster head node. The clusters are executed one by one. Also the local cluster head node and inter cluster head node consists of a routing table to store the data from the reader and the local cluster head respectively. The routing table format for local cluster head node and inter cluster head node are shown below in Fig. 5:

Routing table of intra cluster head node

Local cluster head ID	Tag ID	Reader ID	Timestamp

Routing table of Local Cluster head node

Tag ID	Reader ID	Timestamp

Fig. 5. Routing table format of Intra cluster head node and local cluster head node

3.3 Data Duplication Avoidance (DDA) Algorithm

The RFID network should filter data to avoid redundancy and also for minimizing the energy efficiency of the system. The clusters are executed on a sequential basis. Consider the following two assumptions done in the algorithm. First is that all the inter cluster head nodes and local cluster head nodes are assigned node ID. Second, the local cluster head nodes contain node id of nearby inter cluster head node stored in it. Consider the Fig. 4. Cluster A is first executed and the reader 1 sends the collected data of the tags to the local cluster head node of Cluster A. The local cluster head node stores the data sent by the reader in its routing table and forwards it to the nearby inter cluster head node which in turn forwards the data to next reader which is yet to start the tag detection process. Tags which are present in the overlapping region of two clusters will be detected by next reader also. Data duplication avoidance algorithm is used here and the reader will not read the data which is already detected by the previous reader. This filtration process is enhanced by means of the routing table data sent by the inter cluster head node. If an incoming tag ID is already present in the routing table the reader will simply avoid detecting those tags and filter it from being stored in its database. Thus this filtration process continues for all the readers in the remaining clusters and the inter cluster head node contains only non duplicate tag information.

Finally all the inter cluster head nodes will contain only unique tag data and not the duplicate tag data. Each and every inter cluster head nodes route the collected data to the base station. Also an important feature of this algorithm is that if a tag is determined to be missed by a reader under its coverage area it could be traced out through the routing table information that is maintained by the inter cluster head node. Thus localization of tag information could be updated by means of cluster nodes. The collision among the tags will also be avoided as the duplicate tags will not participate in the tag detection process. Below is the pseudo code for data duplication filtering.

```
Function Data_Duplicate_filtering()
```

//Assumption 1: Assign node ID to local cluster head node and inter cluster node ID.

//Assumption 2: Assign nearby inter cluster node ID to the local cluster head node of all clusters.

// K means clustering

Let {x1, x2,....xn } be the set tags and K be the number of readers

// Cluster Formation

1. For Clusters A, to N ←-------select random tags

   [(x1,x2,...xn) ,K]

2. Compute the objective function

$$\mathbf{F} = \sum_{j=1}^{k} \sum_{x_i \in S_j} \|x_i - \mu_j\|^2 \qquad (1)$$

3. Determine the centroid to minimize the objective function

4. Assign {x1, x2,....xn } to the nearby reader

5. Repeat steps 3 and 4 until stable clusters are reached

6. Let N be the number of clusters generated as per K means algorithm

7. for clusters 1 to N do

8. Execute the slotted aloha algorithm at the reader

9. Local cluster head node ←--- {set of tags detected}

10. update routing table of Local cluster head node

11. Broadcast the routing table data to Inter cluster head node

12. Repeat step 8 for next cluster execution

// duplicate data filtration

13. update the reader database with routing table of inter cluster head node

14. check the incoming tag_data with the reader database

13. If tag data not duplicate update the reader database with the new tag ID

14. else

15. drop the data

16. end if

17. Repeat steps 8 to 16 for remaining clusters

18. Transmit the data from all the inter cluster head node to sink.

Rayleigh fading is a statistical model that is used by the wireless devices to monitor the effect of radio signal propagation. The main concept of this application model is that the signals may fade or vary randomly due to many objects in the environment that are present in the path between the transmitter and the receiver. If noise is higher, then the Rayleigh fading model is given by the following probability density function using a random variable r and Ω is the average power during tag detection for a threshold value R

$$p_R(r) = \frac{2r}{\Omega} e^{\frac{-r^2}{\Omega}}, \; r \geq 0$$

Where,

$$\Omega = E(R^2).$$

The block diagram that depicts the duplicate data filtration process in the RFID network is shown in Fig. 6 below:

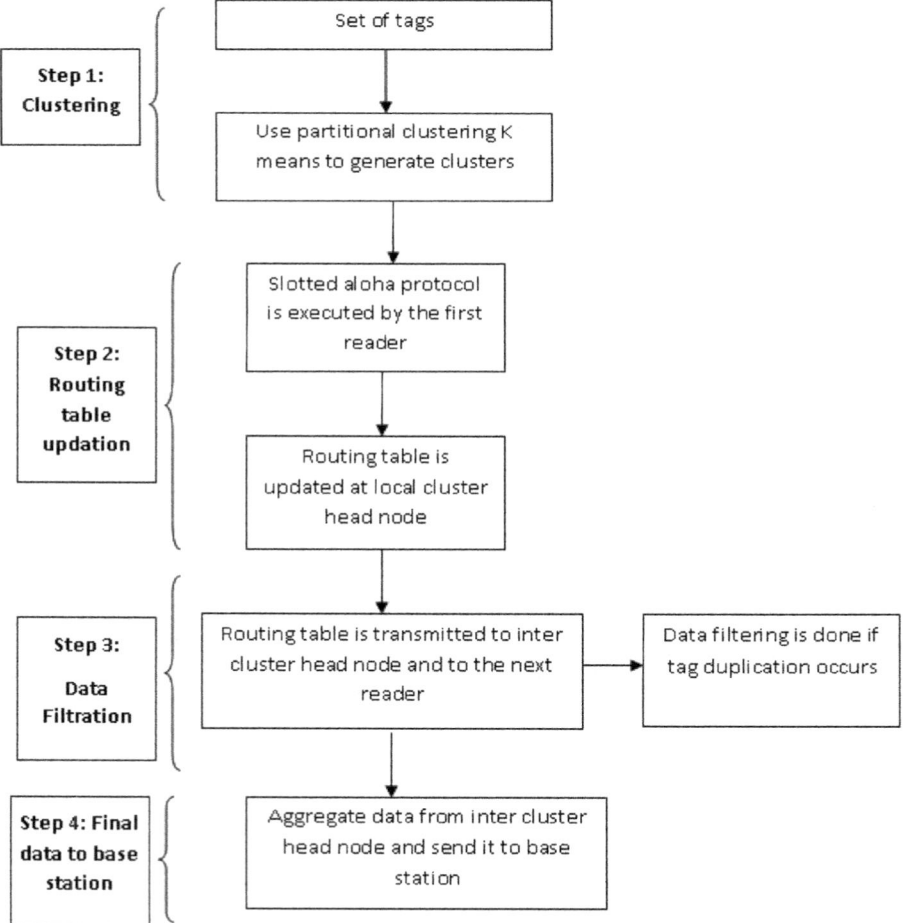

Fig. 6. Flow diagram that depicts the duplicate data filtering process

4 Simulation Results

Data duplication filtering algorithm performs better in both inter cluster and intra cluster regions of RFID network. Simulation was performed using both active tags and passive tags. The results obtained were compared with CLIF [15] algorithm which divides duplication in the inter cluster and intra cluster regions. In CLIF algorithm filtering all the data in intra cluster regions increases the overhead and communication cost. But in the proposed DDA algorithm clusters are executed sequentially and when the readers find the already detected tag data in the frame slot it avoids reading the same data again. The inter cluster head node will contain only unique tag data and not duplicate data. Thus the proposed method improves the throughput the system and increases the scalability and efficiency of the RFID network. The experimental setup values that were assigned during the implementation of the proposed protocol is shown in Table 1.

Table 1. Experimental set up values

Parameter	Values
Field area	$100 \times 100 \text{ m}^2$
Number of tags	400
Number of readers	20
Number of clusters	20
Number of local cluster head nodes	20
Number of inter cluster head node	8
Reading range	5 m
Transmission range	10 m
Number of slots in a read cycle	15

Table 2 shows the results obtained in duplicate data determination when executed in both CLIF algorithm and DDA algorithm. In the graph given in Fig. 7 the percentage of duplicate data that is filtered during the execution is shown. The result is compared with that of CLIF algorithm and the results show that that DDA algorithm performs better than CLIF algorithm.

Table 2. % of filtered data vs number of tags

Number of tags	% of filtered data	
	CLIF algorithm	DDA algorithm
50	9	10
100	12	18
150	14	19
250	31	28
300	45	54
400	68	74

Table 3 shows the energy efficiency comparison when executed in both CLIF algorithm and DDA algorithm. The graph shown in Fig. 8 the percentage of energy efficiency of the system. Since the duplicate tags are filtered by the reader through the inter cluster head nodes the tags in the overlapping region of two readers are not read and thus the energy efficiency of active tags is increased when compared to that of CLIF algorithm which detects the tags and then filters in the coverage area.

Table 3. % energy efficiency vs number of tags

Number of tags	% energy efficiency	
	CLIF algorithm	DDA algorithm
50	5	6
100	10	14
150	12	16
250	17	18
300	21	27
400	28	32

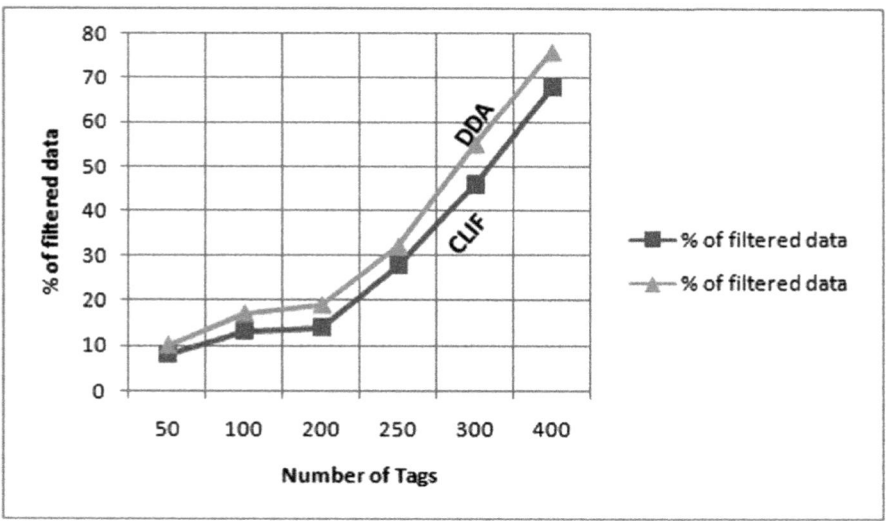

Fig. 7. % of duplicate data vs number of tags

In the simulations, RFID Tags experiences various noises. In each frame the reader initiates the communication by sending commands to the tags and waits for tag's response. The server is capable of obtaining all the information from the reader. The tag data experience noise effects during transmission in the propagation path to the reader. All presented results are obtained by averaging over 150 runs. Applying Rayleigh effect on the clustering protocol the following graph in Fig. 9 is obtained.

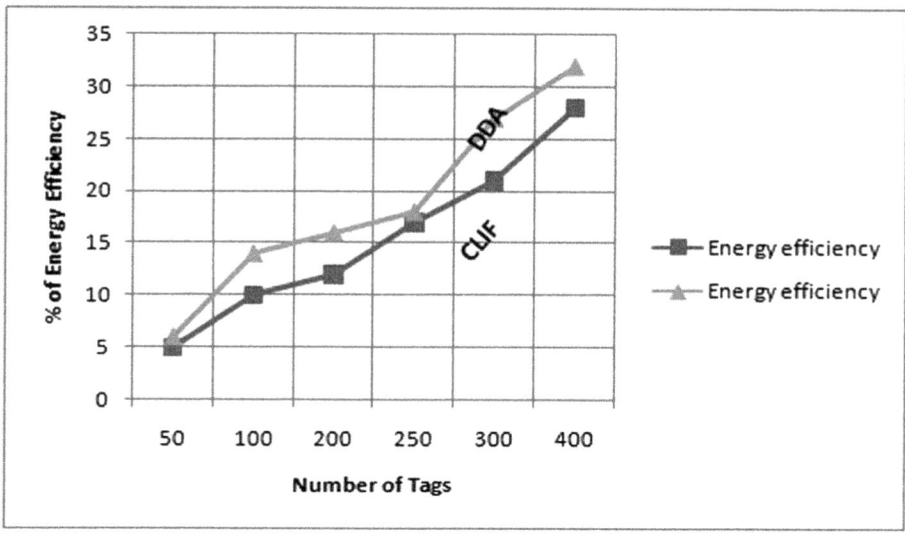

Fig. 8. % energy efficiency vs number of tags

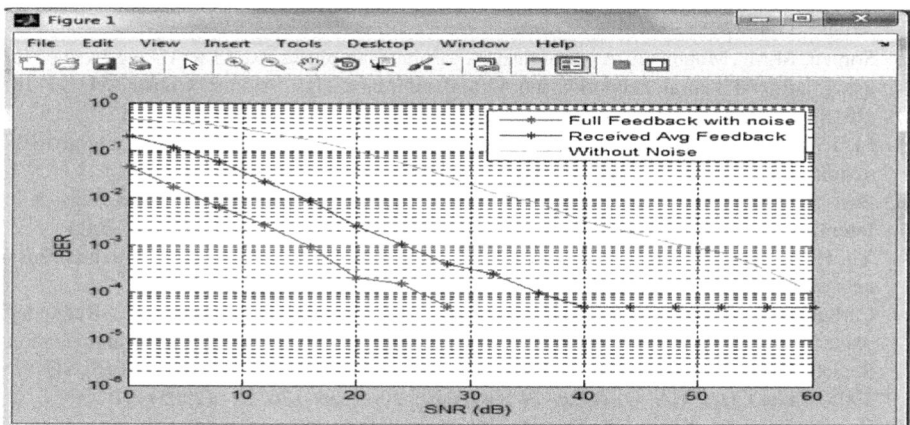

Fig. 9. Rayleigh effect on the feedback comparison of clustering protocol

Since the propagation range of both RFID readers and RFID tags are limited, many large-scale applications deploy multiple readers to enhance the coverage for a large number of tags in the interrogation region. In such scenarios, duplicate readings of the same object are very common since tags might overlap in interrogation region and its response might be overheard by multiple readers. But in data duplication avoidance algorithm tags are being clustered from reader perspective by using centroid through k-means clustering algorithm. Hence so, duplication or loss of data in server is evaded.

5 Conclusion

Duplicate data filtration algorithm is executed and the results were compared with that of CLIF algorithm. The proposed work shows improved performance in duplicate data filtering and in terms of energy efficiency which increases the throughput of the system. Also the collisions among tag are also reduced as the same tag need not reply to the reader again and again. The inter cluster head node plays an important role in data filtration by sending the data to the readers before execution. Thus the lifetime of the network is also increased.

References

1. Bashir, A.K., Lim, S.-J., Hussain, C.S., Park, M.-S.: Energy efficient in-network RFID data filtering scheme in wireless sensor networks. Sensors **11**, 7004–7021 (2011). https://doi.org/10.3390/s110707004
2. Ferreira Chaves, L.W., Buchmann, E., Böhm, K.: Finding misplaced items in retail by clustering RFID data. https://openproceedings.org/2010/conf/edbt/ChavesBB10.pdf
3. Wu, Y., Shen, H., Sheng, Q.Z.: A cloud-friendly RFID trajectory clustering algorithm in uncertain environments. IEEE Trans. Parallel Distrib. Syst. **26**(8), 2075–2088 (2015)
4. Tanbo, M., Nojiri, R., Kawakita, Y., Ichikawa, H.: Active RFID attached object clustering method with new evaluation criterion for finding lost objects. Mob. Inf. Syst. **2017** (2017). Article ID 3637814
5. Soltani, M.M., Motamedi, A., Hammad, A.: Enhancing cluster-based RFID tag localization using artificial neural networks and virtual reference tags. Autom. Constr. **54**, 93–105 (2015). Elsevier
6. Li, T., Chen, S., Ling, Y.: Efficient protocols for identifying the missing tags in a large RFID system. IEEE/ACM Trans. Netw. **1**(35) (2013)
7. Bai, Y., Wang, F., Peiya, L.: Efficiently filtering RFID data streams. In: Proceedings of 1st International VLDB Workshop on Clean Databases, Seoul, Korea, September 2006
8. Yu, H.B., Zeng, P., Wang, Z.F., Liang, Y., Shang, Z.J.: Study on distributed wireless sensor networks communication protocols. J. Commun. **25**, 102–110 (2004)
9. Carbunar, B., Ramanathan, M.K., Koyuturk, M., Hoffmann, C., Grama, A.: Redundant reader elimination in RFID systems. In: Proceedings of 2nd Annual IEEE Communications Society Conference on Sensor and Ad Hoc Communications and Networks, IEEE SECON 2005, Santa Clara, CA, USA, 26–29 September 2005, pp. 176–184 (2005)
10. Dai, D., Xia, F., Wang, Z., Sun, Y.: A survey of intelligent information processing in wireless sensor network. In: Proceedings of International Conference on Mobile Ad-Hoc and Sensor Networks (MSN), Wuhan, China, 13–15 December 2005, pp. 123–132 (2005)
11. Halermek, I., Ramesh, G., Deborah, E.: Directed diffusion: a scalable and robust communication paradigm for sensor networks. In: Proceedings of 6th Annual International Conference on Mobile Computing and Networking (MOBICOM 2000), Boston, MA, USA, August 2000, pp. 56–67 (2000)
12. Srinivasa Rao, S., Rajan, E.G., Lalkishore, K.: ASAF ALOHA protocol for dense RFID systems. Wirel. Commun. **66**, 667–681 (2012). Springer
13. Fyhn, K.: Fast capture - recapture approach for mitigating the problem of missing RFID tags. IEEE Trans. Mob. Comput. **11**(3), 518–528 (2012)

14. Schneegans, S., Vorst, P., Zell, A.: Using the RFID snapshots for mobile robot self-localization. In: Proceedings of European Conference on Mobile Robots (ECMR), Freiburg, Germany (2007)
15. Kim, D.-S., Kashif, A., Ming, X., Kim, J.-H., Park, M.-S.: Energy efficient in-network phase RFID data filtering scheme. In: Sandnes, F.E., Zhang, Y., Rong, C., Yang, L.T., Ma, J. (eds.) UIC 2008. LNCS, vol. 5061, pp. 311–322. Springer, Heidelberg (2008). https://doi.org/10.1007/978-3-540-69293-5_25

A Secure and Flexible One Way Hash Function for Data Integrity Verification in Cloud Computing Environment

Meena Kumari[✉] and Rajender Nath

Department of Computer Science and Applications, Kurukshetra University,
Kurukshetra, Haryana, India
sanger.meena@gmail.com, rnath@kuk.ac.in

Abstract. Cloud Computing (CC) migrates the application software's and databases to the huge data hubs, where the administration of data along with services is done by the cloud provider. However, this characteristic, presents various security concerns which have not been well comprehended. Information authentication and its integrity verification are main challenges which are faced by CC today. Recently, many authors proposed hash algorithms for data integrity verification using a one way hash function. However, there are some security limitations of these existing algorithms like high time complexity and lack of proper framework. In this paper, an attempt is made to implement a secure and flexible one way hash function to eliminate these drawbacks. Furthermore, This paper present the security analysis and computation of the proposed algorithm, which shows that the proposed data integrity verification algorithm is more secure and efficient in its implementation and fulfills the performance requisites of a robust hash function.

Keywords: Cloud computing · Integrity · Hash · Digest · Invertible matrix

1 Introduction

The significance of CC is growing and is attaining a rising consideration in the fields of science and technology. Stability, flexibility, rapid provisioning, scalability and reliability [13] are some advantages of CC over traditional IT implementations. The user can liberate or rent any service from cloud provider site as and when required. Though, this new processing concept generates evident security issues also. In CC, services, information does not necessarily reside in locally confined locations. It can be managed in cloud provider site or in an isolated server, which brings about probable safety issues. CC security is a continuously evolving concept in the field of IT industry. CC security refers to the set of procedures, tools, and techniques utilized for protection of data, applications, and the infrastructure accompanied with CC.

The leading concern associated with CC storage security is that of verification of integrity of data at remote sites. Data integrity means maintenance and assurance of correctness and consistency of data throughout its whole life cycle. It is a crucial part of any secure system. Even a slight unintended change to data during storage, retrieval or

© Springer Nature Singapore Pte Ltd. 2018
P. Bhattacharyya et al. (Eds.): NGCT 2017, CCIS 828, pp. 526–535, 2018.
https://doi.org/10.1007/978-981-10-8660-1_40

processing operation results in failure of data integrity. There should be some measures to verify accuracy and consistency of data. To address the challenge of integrity verification, there are numerous methods are proposed in the literature. One of such schemes is hash functions.

Hash functions have a substantial role in judgement of authenticity and accuracy of data in remote cloud data centers. A hash function produces a digest which in turn assists an analyst to recognize malicious alterations in data. A Cloud user stores data file at remote data centers along with digest associated with that file for further reference. One of the essential characteristics of a hash function is One-way hash property. This property states that it is computationally infeasible to estimate input string from a given digest. The existing one way hash algorithms involves a substantial execution time for calculation of hash value. Moreover, as the file size increases, the hash generation time also increases proportionately. To address these issues, a secure and flexible One-way hash functions is proposed [15]. This have been proved experimentally that the proposed hash algorithm provide more secure and efficient measures for data integrity verification in CC environment.

The rest of the paper is organized as follows: Sect. 2 presents the summary of related work. Section 3 deals with the concept of problem formulation along with the detailed review of existing one way hash functions and Sect. 4 discusses the proposed one way hash algorithm and Sect. 5 describes experimental study, computation and performance evaluation of proposed scheme. Section 6 delivers the concluding remarks along with potential research perspectives.

2 Related Work

Berisha et al. [1] has suggested a class of non-invertible matrices in GF (2). The generated matrices were permutation matrices having '1' entry in every row and column and other entries are filled with '0'. The proposed method could be used for small sized data, which infers that it could be used for user certification and message authentication code generation only. For file size less than 6.2 KB it outperforms SHA-2 but as the file size increases hash generation time rises exponentially.

Abutaha et al. [2] has offered a method for generation of a one way hash algorithm by means of non-invertible matrix. Authors also presented an algorithm for the purpose of conversion of an invertible matrix into noninvertible one. The proposed algorithm is also compared with MD5, SHA1, SHA-512 on the basis of selected parameters of data size and matrix size and digest generation time. The experimental results shows that the proposed algorithm performs better and is very close to the performance of MD5 algorithm.

Kavuri et al. [3] has proposed a message integrity verification process based on hash functions. Authors encouraged the need of TPA by generating hash value of 512 bits for a file by third party auditor. User has to register before using data and only authenticated user can retrieve the requested files. They also made a comparison between their proposed work and existing models on the basis of file size, time and security attacks.

Zheng [5] et al. had put forward a hash algorithm named HAVAL. HAVAL works by compression of a message of random size into a digest of 128, 160, 192, 224 or 256 bits. Moreover, HAVAL has a check to govern how many times 1024 bits message is processed. The algorithm can be processed in 3, 4 or 5 passes. According to level of secrecy needed, they presented 15 choices for realistic usage by uniting digest size with passes. Analytical tests exhibited that HAVAL performs faster when compared to MD5.

Acharya et al. [4] had recommended a few techniques for generation of self-invertible matrices for application in Hill Cipher algorithm.

Abutaha et al. [6] has offered a hashing technique employing non-invertible matrix. They also presented experimental analysis to verify that their proposed algorithm satisfy required characteristics of a secure hash function.

Srikantaswamy [7] had presented a hash function by using exclusive OR function along with matrix multiplication. Their method of hash generation includes checksum generation as well as padding of original message.

Hamamreh [8] had suggested an improvement in Hill Cipher algorithm. Since hill cipher incorporates the concept of matrix multiplication, it is susceptible to known plaintext attack. Authors addressed this issue in their paper by generating public key without exploiting linear algebra. Furthermore authors suggested a means of sharing key for the very first use.

Kumar [9] had recommended a signature scheme for data integrity verification by incorporating conventional network security measures. Rashmi et al. [12] had fabricated an sophisticated verification mechanism using access rights. Their designed procedure includes striking characteristics of public verifiability and availability.

Li [14] had proposed a hash algorithm founded on chaotic maps by means of variable constraints. The two important features of the proposed algorithm were message expansion and parallel processing and. The algorithm involves the translation of preprocessed plaintext blocks into their respective ASCII code values and multiple repetitions of the chaotic asymmetric tent map. Final digest of size 128 bits is generated by using logical Exclusive OR operation.

3 Problem Formulation

Existing one-way hash algorithms encompass the exploitation of a singular matrix. These involve the concept of matrix multiplication of user's data represented in matrix form with a singular key matrix for generation of digest. Algorithms in [1, 2, 11] differ the way the singular key matrix is generated. It is generated by addition of two permutation matrices having each element from GF(2) in [1] and it is generated randomly by checking if its determinant is zero or not in [2] whereas concept of linear combination of rows or columns is used in [11]. Afterwards, this matrix is multiplied with users data represented in number of blocks of fixed size one by one. Intermediate hashes produced during each multiplication step is XOR'ed with next block multiplication operation to produce final hash. The main limitation for these algorithms is that they involves a substantially high execution time for calculation of hash value. As the file size increases, the hash generation time also increases exponentially. Moreover, the time period involved in multiplication operation only is taken into consideration in [1]. Although, a considerable amount of time is spent on former steps of preprocessing of data files. In [11], authors generates only intermediate hashes i.e. method to generate final hash is not clearly specified.

In [7], compression technique is applied on final hash which is generated in similar fashion as stated above. Subsequently resultant hash is truncated to get digest of size 1 KB which is very large. The truncation of hash value ultimately results in data loss. From truncated hash one cannot obtain complete data back.

4   Proposed Algorithm Based on One Way Hash Property

In order to alleviate the drawbacks of [1, 2, 7, 11], this paper proposes a one-way hash algorithm consisting of the following major three phases: (a) File Preprocessing phase, (b) Singular key matrix generation phase and (c) Final Hash generation phase.

4.1   Phase 1: File Preprocessing

Some preprocessing steps are performed in this stage on user's file. The user's file with random size message is initially padded with a number of bits, in such a way that the size of padded message turn out to be a multiple of the block size. Block size may vary from 4 to 64 bytes depending upon singular key matrix dimension which is to be generated in second phase. The plaintext user's file that is expressed in blocks Bi, i = 1 to n where n is the number of blocks and then each block Bi is transformed into m*m matrices Bijk. Then each value in matrix Bijk is converted into ASCII character having each element size of 8 bits.

4.2   Phase 2: Singular Key Matrix Generation

For the purpose of realizing the One-way property of a hash function, a singular key matrix is used. A matrix is said to be singular, if its determinant |d| is 0. When a singular matrix is multiplied with another matrix 'A', then original matrix cannot be obtained by any other mechanism. In this way one-way hash function property is realized.

During this phase, a square matrix R having the same dimension as of block matrix, is generated randomly. Then the matrix R is transformed into singular matrix by using the concept of linear dependency among rows or columns of a matrix [10]. Because of this linear dependency determinant 'd' of the key matrix 'R', d = |R| would always come out to be zero.

4.3   Phase 3: Hash Generation

Subsequently, each block matrices Bijk are multiplied individually with the singular key matrix R to generate intermediate hash matrices Hijk's. Ultimately, final Hash value Hjk is generated by applying XOR operation on the resultant Hijk's. The whole process is shown in Fig. 1.

$$H_{jk} = H_{jk}^1 \oplus H_{jk2}^2 \oplus \ldots\ldots\ldots\ldots.H_{jk}^n \tag{1}$$

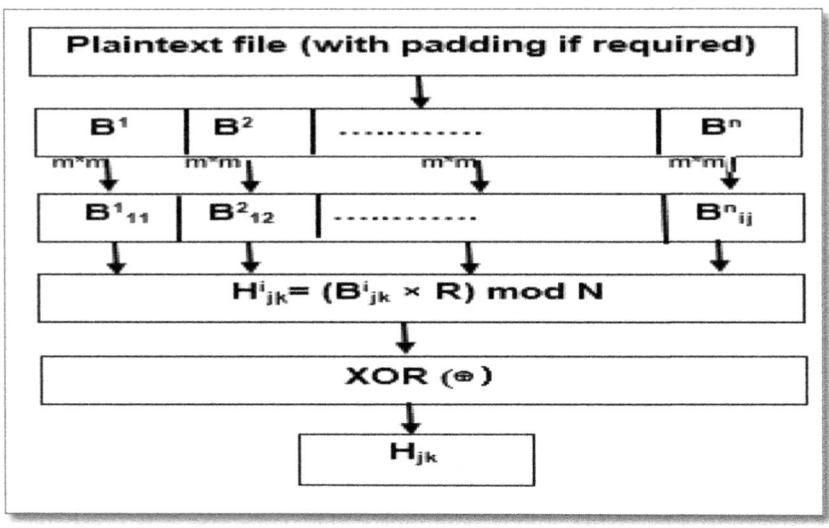

Fig. 1. Structure of proposed hash algorithm

Algorithm: Hash Generation

Begin
1. Generate R, a 2 dimensional matrix initialized with random values.
2. Convert R into a singular matrix.
3. Padding of file F (whose hash is to be generated) with zeros in order to make its size divisible by block size.
4. Split the file F into n number of blocks B^i and convert them into m*m square matrices B_{jk}^i in row order.
5. Take N as some prime number.
6. Generate intermediate hashes using $H_{jk}^i = (B_{jk}^i \times R) \bmod N$.
7. Generate   final   hash   using H_{jk} $=$ $H_{jk}{}^i$ $\oplus$ $H_{jk}{}^{i+1}$
End

Table 1. Comparative hash generation time (in ms)

Algorithm	File size						
	8 KB	16 KB	32 KB	64 KB	128 KB	256 KB	512 KB
Proposed	2.52	3	4.94	6.44	9.5	16.42	30.56
Existing	169.309	271.741	556.486	1089.793	2128.705	4247.966	8750.417
Tiger160	2.9	4.14	5.7	9.78	16.46	16.42	21.84
Whirlpool2003	23.5	17.86	18.3	20.84	21.28	35.68	42.58

5   Experimental Evaluation and Discussion

5.1   Evaluation of the Proposed Algorithm Against Existing Algorithms

The proposed algorithm and the existing one-way hash algorithms [1, 2, 11], Tiger160 and whirlpool2003 were implemented in Java on NetBeans IDE 7.3 platform. Seven distinct data files of different file sizes were taken as dataset.

For experiment purpose, all algorithms were executed ten times and readings of hash generation time were obtained for each. Table 1 shows the average results of hash generation time for individual algorithms conforming to dataset. Figure 2 clearly shows that the hash generation time for the proposed algorithm is much less as compared to the existing algorithms. It is also evident that when file size increases then hash generation time for the proposed algorithm increases nominally while for the existing algorithms it becomes exponential.

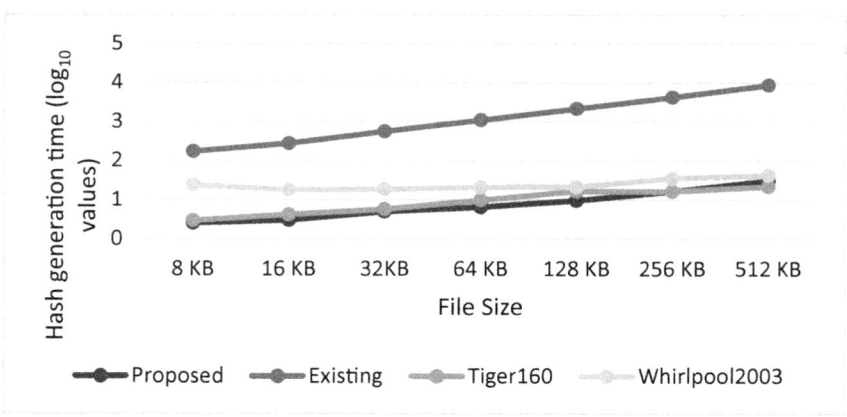

Fig. 2. Hash generation time (logarithmic values) of proposed algorithm with existing algorithms

Proposed algorithm outperforms Whirlpool2003 and Tiger160 at file sizes 8 KB to 256 KB. On file size of 512 KB, Tiger160 performs better than proposed algorithm for the reason that proposed algorithm is based on the concept of matrix multiplication and as the file size increases the number of multiplication operations also increases.

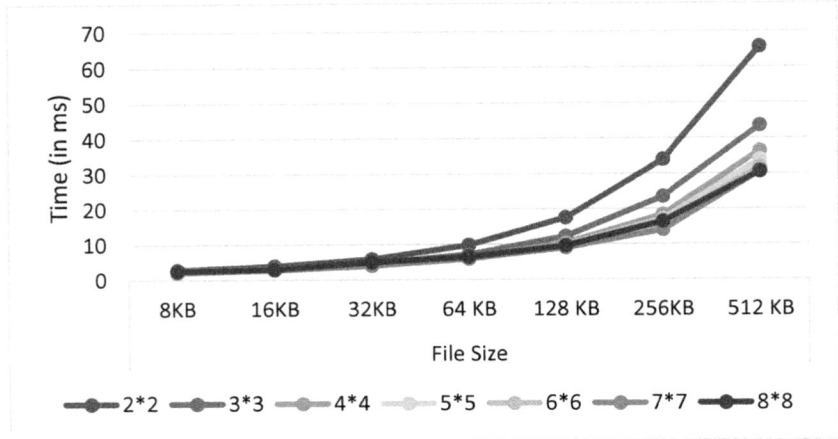

Fig. 3. Hash generation time (in ms) for different key dimensions.

The proposed algorithm is flexible in the sense that it can produce hash value of varying size subject to key matrix dimension. Currently prevailing algorithms like MD5, SHA, Tiger, Whirlpool deficit in this aspect. These algorithms generate hash of preset size regardless of the key size. The matrix size may vary from 2×2 to 8×8. The matrix dimension of 7×7 is most optimal in terms of hash generation time complexity as compared to other dimensions. Results obtained from using matrix dimension 4×4 and 8×8 are comparatively similar (from Fig. 3.). Moreover, while considering hash size, matrix dimension of 8×8 produces final hash of 64 bytes which is quite susceptible to collision attack as it is always assumed that large hash size lessen the chances of collision. Hence, this paper uses the results of 8×8 key matrix for further experimental evaluation.

5.2   Distribution of Hash Value

A secure hash function should uniformly distribute hash values [14]. For the purpose of verification of this property, the proposed hash function is tested on following paragraph:

> *"The current cloud computing systems pose serious limitation to protecting user's data confidentiality. Since user's sensitive data is presented in unencrypted forms to re-mote machines owned and operated by third party service providers, the risks of unauthorized disclosure of the user's sensitive data by service providers may be quite high, there are many techniques for protecting user's data from outside attackers. An approach is presented to protecting the confidentiality of user's data from service providers, and ensures service providers cannot collect user's confidential data while the data is processed and stored in cloud computing systems. Cloud computing systems provide various Internet based data storage and services."*

Graphs are elicited to show the variations in original paragraph and corresponding hash value. Figure 4(a) shows the distribution of ASCII values of the original message while Fig. 4(b) shows distribution of hash values generated by the proposed algorithm.

ASCII values vary from 32 to 127, the corresponding message characters are confined in a limited zone, whereas the hexadecimal representation of hash value spans irregularly in a large area.

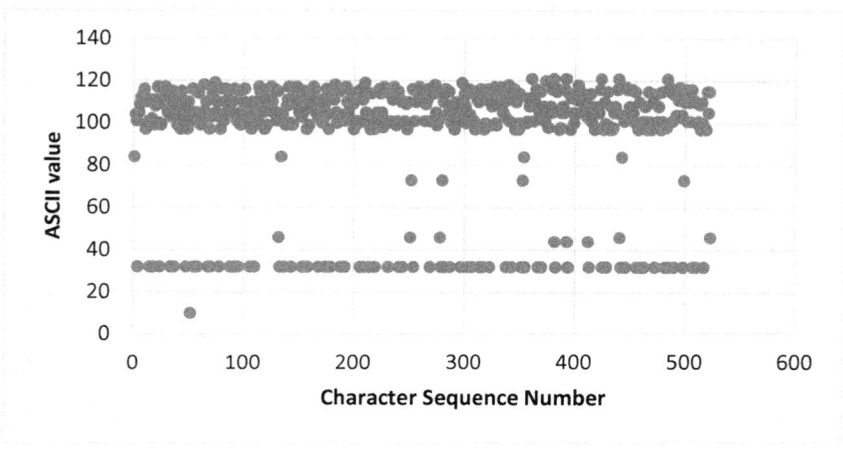

(a) Distribution of message in ASCII format

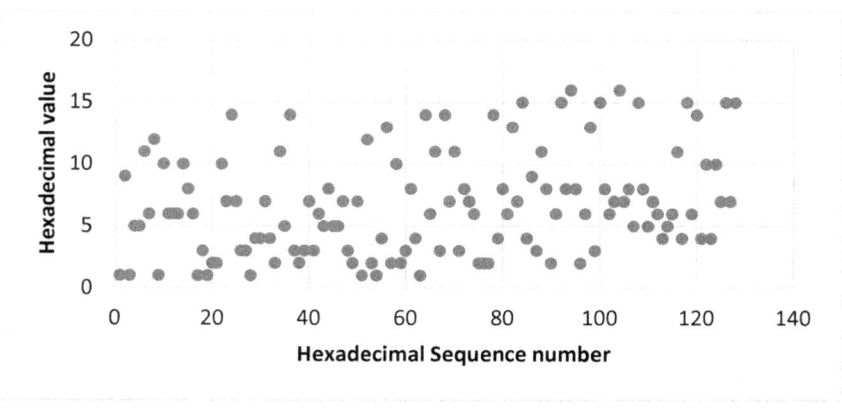

(b) Hexadecimal representation of hash value

Fig. 4. (a) Distribution of message in ASCII format, (b) hexadecimal representation of hash value

5.3 Sensitivity of Hash Value with Original Message

So as to assess the sensitivity of hash value to the original paragraph, algorithm testing have been performed under the following specifications:

H1: The original paragraph with no change.

H2: Switch the first expression 'The' in the original paragraph to 'THE'.

H3: Switch the word "limitation" in the original paragraph to "shortcoming".
H4: Append a blank space at the end of the original paragraph.
H5: Replace the statement "The current cloud computing systems pose serious lim
itation " with "provide various Internet based data storage and services."

Figure 5 shows the graphical representation of binary sequences of first 128 bits of
hash values when changes in the original text are made corresponding to H1, H2, H3,
H4, H5. The results signifies that the proposed algorithm is very sensitive to alteration
in the message.

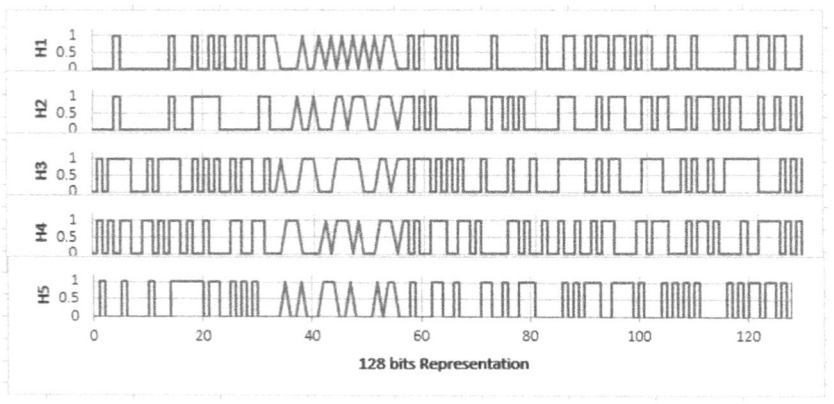

Fig. 5. Binary sequences of hash values

6   Conclusion and Future Research Directions

This paper has presented a secure and flexible One-way hash algorithm for integrity
verification of data in CC environment. The proposed algorithm has been tested by
implementing it in Java NetBeans IDE 7.3 platform. The experimental results have
shown that the proposed algorithm is more efficient and flexible as compared to its
existing counterparts. Existing algorithms hash generation time increases exponentially
with increase in file size in contrast to proposed algorithm. The proposed algorithm also
satisfies the essential characteristics of a hash function like distribution of hash value
and sensitivity to modification in data.

For future research perspectives, proposed algorithm might be tested against collision. A secure CC framework could be constructed to guarantee the integrity and
confidentiality of user's data over cloud storage.

References

1. Berisha, A., et al.: A class of non invertible matrices in GF (2) for practical one way hash algorithm. Int. J. Comput. Appl. **54**(18), 15–20 (2012)
2. Abutaha, M., et al.: New one way hash algorithm using non-invertible matrix. In: Proceedings of International Conference on Computer Medical Applications (ICCMA). IEEE (2013)
3. Kavuri, S., et al.: Data authentication and integrity verification techniques for trusted/untrusted cloud servers. In: Proceedings of International Conference on Advances in Computing, Communications and Informatics (ICACCI), pp. 2590–2596, 24–27 September 2014
4. Acharya, B., et al.: Novel methods of generating self-invertible matrix for Hill cipher algorithm. Int. J. Secur. **1**(1), 14–21 (2007)
5. Zheng, Y., Pieprzyk, J., Seberry, J.: HAVAL — a one-way hashing algorithm with variable length of output (extended abstract). In: Seberry, J., Zheng, Y. (eds.) AUSCRYPT 1992. LNCS, vol. 718, pp. 81–104. Springer, Heidelberg (1993). https://doi.org/10.1007/3-540-57220-1_54
6. Abutaha, M., et al.: A practical one way hash algorithm based on matrix multiplication. Int. J. Comput. Appl. **23**(2), 34–38 (2011)
7. Srikantaswamy, S.G., et al.: Hash function design using matrix multiplication, ex-or, checksum generation and compression technique approach. Int. J. Comput. Sci. Inf. Technol. Secur. **3**(1), 115–119 (2013)
8. Hamamreh, A.R, et al.: Design of a robust cryptosystem algorithm for non-invertible matrices based on Hill cipher. IJCSNS Int. J. Comput. Sci. Netw. Secur. **9**(5), 11–16 (2009)
9. Kumar, N.G., et al.: Hash based approach for providing privacy and integrity in cloud data storage using digital signatures. Int. J. Comput. Sci. Inf. Technol. **5**(6), 8074–8078 (2014)
10. Tom, P.: Properties of matrices. p. 4 (2015). https://www.tomzap.com/notes/MatricesM340L/Matrices.pdf
11. Hamamreh, R.A., et al.: Hash algorithm for data integrity based on matrix combination. In: Proceedings of International Arab Conference on Information Technology (2013)
12. Jogdand, R.M., et al.: Enabling public verifiability and availability for secure data storage in cloud computing. Evolving Syst. **6**, 55–65 (2013). Springer
13. Mell, P., Grance, T.: The NIST Definition of Cloud Computing (ver. 15). National Institute of Standards and Technology, Information Technology Laboratory, 7 October 2009
14. Li, Y., et al.: Parallel hash function construction based on chaotic maps with changeable parameters. Neural Comput. Appl. **20**, 1305–1312 (2011). Springer
15. Kumari, M., et al.: One-way hash algorithms in cloud computing security - a systematic review. Int. J. Sci. Eng. Res. (UGC Approved Journal) **7**(12), 187–191 (2016)

Analyzing Threats of IoT Networks Using SDN Based Intrusion Detection System (SDIoT-IDS)

Azka Wani[✉] and S. Revathi

Crescent B. S. Abdur Rahman University, Vandalur, Chennai 600048, India
graceazka@gmail.com

Abstract. Internet of things (IoT) is developing and has become popular among individuals as well as industry. The IoT has revolutionized the technological aspect by making ordinary mundane devices smart and automatic. However, it is susceptible to various security threats. This paper highlights major security threats of IoT and uses a Software Defined Networking (SDN) based Intrusion Detection System (IDS) as a countermeasure towards such threats. Software Define Network (SDN) decouples the data and control planes resulting in programmable network architecture with centralized control. SDN based Intrusion Detection System (IDS) for IoT can rectify abnormal activity in an IoT network by examining network traffic in real time. The programmability feature of SDN makes IDS flexible and does not burden the forwarding devices. The SDN based IDS mechanism is run on a simulated IoT network. The experimental results exhibit 99% accuracy and can efficiently detect various attacks in an IoT environment.

Keywords: Internet of things · Software Defined Networks
Intrusion Detection System

1 Introduction

The Internet of Things (IoT) is a heterogeneous network consisting of sensor nodes, smart phones, switches/routers, servers, and software. IoT has been designed in a way that activities or movements are sensed and processed in real-time. IoT constitutes a means of communication between internet and physical world of ordinary things. The concept of IoT has led to improvement in production, processing and consumption of data.

The number of devices connected through internet has already exceeded the world population and is estimated to increase by large in a decade [1]. Since devices with very limited resources are participating in IoT, hence threats and vulnerabilities have amplified significantly. The proper analysis of the recorded data, over a period of time, in IoT environment can help to predict threats and detect them at an early stage. IDS are able to rectify malicious behavior in a network by analyzing the IoT traffic in real-time. On detecting an attack IDS takes the measures to protect the system from damage. SDN is a naïve way of networking that decouples the control plane and packet forwarding plane. SDN allows centralized control and a global view of the network.

© Springer Nature Singapore Pte Ltd. 2018
P. Bhattacharyya et al. (Eds.): NGCT 2017, CCIS 828, pp. 536–542, 2018.
https://doi.org/10.1007/978-981-10-8660-1_41

A lot of research has been done regarding intrusion detection systems in traditional networks, and limited research focuses on detection of malicious behavior in IoT. The concept of intrusion detection system based on software define network technology is new particularly in the area of IoT. This paper discusses major security threats of the IoT and presents a brief survey of various research efforts put towards the development of intrusion detection system in IoT. Section 1 provides a brief introduction, Sect. 2 introduces the various threats in IoT network, Sect. 3 gives an overview of the SDN technology, Sect. 4 the discusses various types of IDS so far introduced in the area of IoT. The proposed SDN-based solution for IoT is discussed in Sect. 5. Finally, conclusions and future work are presented in Sect. 6.

2 Major Threats to the IoT

With limited resources it is difficult to provide a complete security mechanism in IoT devices and hence the attacks on Internet are on a rise; IoT attacks can be classified into following four types [2]:

(1) Distributed Denial of Service (DDoS) – This makes resources unavailable to user by keeping network busy with meaningless traffic. The volume of DDoS attacks has increased with more and more IoT devices participating in Internet.
(2) Botnets – Network of systems which are run by botnet operators. Such networks are joined for distributing malware and controlling network devices. Increasing number of networking objects and devices has led to formation of thingbots (botnet containing independent connected things).
(3) Virus or Malware – Some malicious code is executed to infect the devices on the IoT network. Such code can be used to steal sensitive information, or gain unauthorized access to the devices. The attacker can also control the devices after executing malware and can uses those devices to launch attacks.
(4) Data Theft – Confidential and crucial information is retrieved from the network because of poorly protected IoT devices. Spoofing or Phishing can be used to retrieve such information.

3 Overview of Software Defined Network (SDN)

In traditional networks the control mechanism and data forwarding capability is present in network devices i.e. switches or routers. The concept of Software Defined Network (SDN) makes networks programmable; it decouples the data and control planes. The switches or routers are just forwarding devices while as the control mechanism is shifted to a centralized controller. Software Define Network (SDN) manages the network with abstraction of lower level functionality and maintains an Application Programmable Interface (API) for delegating control to the lower level devices.

SDN controllers have a global view of the network and hence configuration of network has become an easy task. Moreover if there are any changes to be incorporated in a network, the programmability feature of SDN makes that quite simple. The security mechanism or other additional features can also be programmed via API and implemented in the network through flow rules. The flow rules are governed by OpenFlow protocol. The programmability feature makes networks more flexible, if any changes are to be made in the network; those are to be included in the control plane instead of reconfiguring each network device [3] separately. A simple logical representation of SDN architecture is shown in figure (Fig. 1).

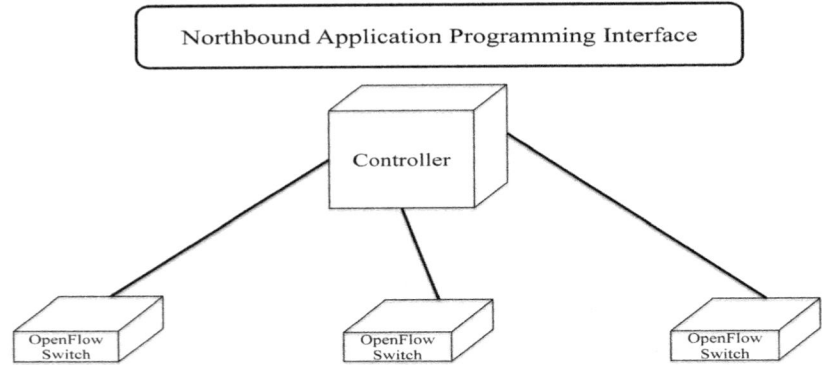

Fig. 1. Separation of data and control planes in SDN

Network control or logic is shifted to centralized SDN controllers for better management of the networks and infrastructure contains mere forwarding devices. The medium between the network infrastructure and the controller is known as southbound interface while as the API and controller communicate through northbound interface.

4   Related Work

In order to improve the security in IoT a lot of research work has been conducted. This section discusses various intrusion detection systems which have been proposed for improvement of security in IoT [4].

Thanigaivelan et al. [5] proposed IDS for internal anomaly detection in IoT. The system records the normal behavior of the network by analyzing the traffic. It looks for abnormalities by monitoring the packet length and frequency of packets for the nodes which are at a distance of one hop.

Pongle and Chavan [6] proposed IDS for wormhole attacks in IoT devices. It is simulated on Contiki OS using Cooja simulator. Using the symptoms of wormhole attack, for example, increase in control packets, anomalies are detected in IoT. The authors have used three algorithms for detection and achieved a better true positive rate for attack detection. Power and memory consumption for the proposed system are lesser and hence suitable for constrained environment of IoT.

Raza et al. [7] presented an intrusion detection system in IoT called as SVELTE which is implemented on Contiki OS and is a real-time mechanism to identify threats in

IoT. The system comprises of three major components kept at 6LoWPAN Border Router. The first component is called Mapper and it gathers information about the RPL protocol. The second component detects the intrusion by monitoring the information gathered by Mapper. The third element is filters the abnormal traffic.

Sforzin et al. [8] proposed an IDS architecture called RPIDS which is a portable device, with an inbuilt IDS. The setup of the proposed system contains a Raspberry Pi equipped with Snort which is a complete IDS mechanism. The devices perform intrusion detection locally or request traffic data from nearby devices in order to carry out intrusion detection more effectively.

Kasinathan et al. [9] presented an IDS for detection of DoS attacks. The proposed mechanism is designed to analyze 6LoWPAN traffic and the architecture is built on ebbits network framework. The major module of the system handles the DoS protection manager which raises alarm upon sensing some abnormality in network.

5   SDN Based Intrusion Detection System for IoT (SDIoT-IDS)

The paper proposes a system SDIoT-IDS to detect security attacks against IoT devices and starts a mitigation mechanism to defend such attacks. In this proposed system, SDN technology is used to provide security services and protect smart things in an IoT from top level. The traditional security features cannot be included in smart things individually since these are constrained. The proposed system is incorporated in SDN controller for better delegation of security policies and more control over the activities of network. The traffic is routed into an IoT network via SDN gateway. The gateway redirects new messages to the controller which generates flow rules based on the type of traffic it encounters. The working of SDIoT-IDS is depicted in following figure (Fig. 2).

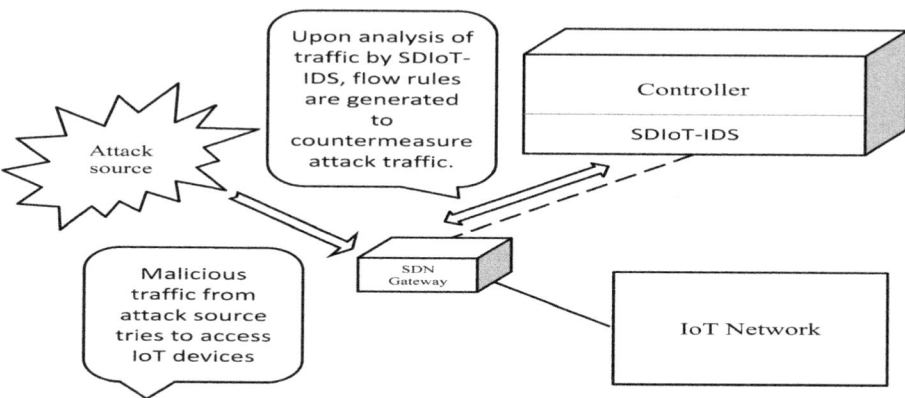

Fig. 2. Working of SDIoT-IDS

SDIoT-IDS consists of following major components:

Activity Monitor: This component monitors the traffic through IoT domain. It is primarily used to collect data for extracting flow statistics which helps in detecting the suspicious behavior. Activity monitor is placed at the IoT gateway which is an Openflow switch. It keeps record of sent and received packets through the IoT network.

Activity Analyzer: The Activity Analyzer is one of the major components of SDIoT-IDS. Here a machine learning algorithm is used to detect the specific type of network attack. Back propagation neural network (BPNN) has been used for detection purpose in this component of the system. First the BPNN is trained to detect different kinds of attacks. The back-propagation neural network used in this work has three layers of nodes (input, hidden, and output). All nodes from the input and hidden layers are connected to each of the nodes in the output layer. Each node from hidden layer is directed to one output. Then output O from the node in consideration can be calculated as below (f is an activation function such as sigmoid) [10] (Fig. 3):

$$O = f(a1 * w1 + a2 * w2 + a3 * w3)$$

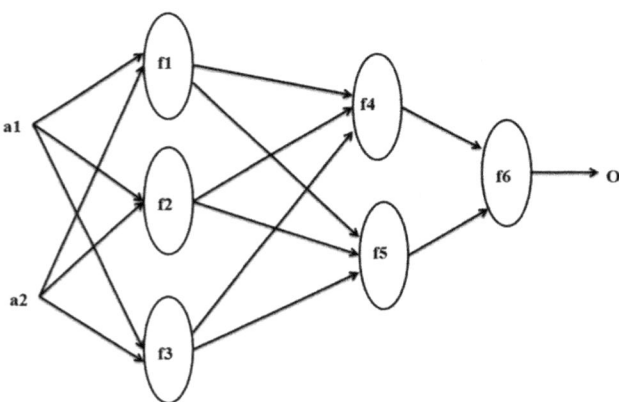

Fig. 3. Feed-forward mechanism in BPNN

Where a1, a2, a3 are inputs at various levels, w1, w2, w3 are the weights and f () is the activation function. The training is performed using NSL-KDD dataset [11]. The signature analysis is also carried out to understand the possible nature of known IoT attacks, before supplying the data to classifier. The accuracy of detection by algorithm is evaluated and improved [12].

Classifier and Alert Mechanism: This component classifies the data or information from the activity monitor as malicious or benign. It also identifies the specific attack that is might hit the network. Once the classification of information is done and it detects any attack, the alert is raised and control is shifted towards mitigation strategy.

The proposed mechanism is implemented using Mininet2.0. The controller used for the set up is the RYU controller, customized to incorporate SDIoT-IDS. The experimentation setup has used attacks like TCP flood and ICMP based attacks. The attacks simulations show ability of system against various attacks.

A flood attack from the attacker to the IoT Device was launched with 2.5 Mps rate and benign traffic was sent at a rate of 1 Mbps (the capacity of the link). As seen from the figure (Fig. 4) the attack which started at 7 s was successfully controlled by SDIoT-IDS by blocking the flood traffic at 11 s. The benign traffic which had been halted during the traffic is resumed after mitigation of attack.

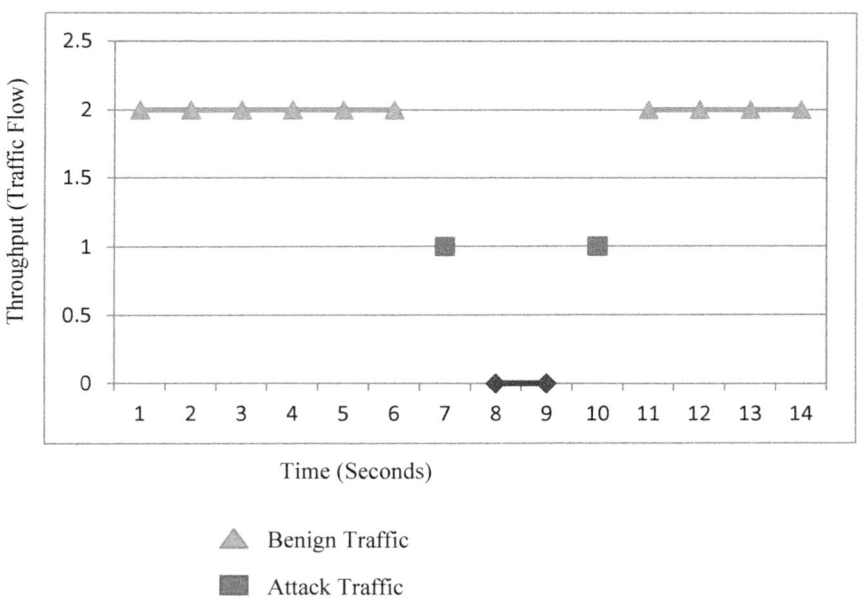

Fig. 4. Flood attack mitigation by SDIoT-IDS

6 Conclusion and Future Work

This paper introduces a new intrusion detection solution for IoT which is based on SDN. SDIoT-IDS can rectify attacks of several types unlike other security mechanism which focus on a single attack. The analysis portion of the system is developed in a way that it can identify several attacks threatening IoT networks currently. As future work, the proposed solution can be enhanced to countermeasure more IoT based attacks, and improve upon the detection capacity. The proposed solution can then be experimented on a real IoT scenario.

References

1. Kolias, C., Stavrou, A., Voas, J., Bojanova, I., Kuhn, R.: Learning internet-of-things Security "hands-on". IEEE Secur. Priv. 2–11 (2016). https://doi.org/10.1109/msp.2016.4
2. Wani, A., Revathi, S.: Protocols for secure internet of things. Int. J. Educ. Manag. Eng. (IJEME) 7(2), 20–29 (2017). https://doi.org/10.5815/ijeme.2017.02.03
3. Wani, A., Revathi, S., Geetha, A.: A survey of applications and security issues in software defined networking. Int. J. Comput. Netw. Inf. Secur. (IJCNIS) 3, 21–28 (2017). https://doi.org/10.5815/ijcnis.2017.03.03
4. Zarpelãoa, B.B., Mianib, R.S., Kawakania, C.T., de Alvarenga, S.C.: A survey of intrusion detection in internet of things. J. Netw. Comput. Appl. 17, 1–46 (2017)
5. Thanigaivelan, N.K., Nigussie, E., Kanth, R.K., Virtanen, S., Isoaho, J.: Distributed internal anomaly detection system for internet-of-things. In: 13th IEEE Annual Consumer Communications Networking Conference (CCNC), pp. 319–320 (2016)
6. Pongle, P., Chavan, G.: Real time intrusion and wormhole attack detection in Internet of Things. Int. J. Comput. Appl. 121(9), 1–9 (2015)
7. Raza, S., Wallgren, L., Voigt, T.: SVELTE: real-time intrusion detection in the internet of things. Ad Hoc Netw. 11, 2661–2674 (2013)
8. Sforzin, A., Conti, M., Marmol, F.G., Bohli, J.-M.: RPiDS: raspberry Pi IDS a fruitful intrusion detection system for IoT. In: International IEEE Conferences on Ubiquitous Intelligence & Computing, Advanced and Trusted Computing, Scalable Computing and Communications, Cloud and Big Data Computing, Internet of People, and Smart World Congress, pp. 440–448 (2016)
9. Kasinathan, P., Costamagna, G., Khaleel, H., Pastrone, C., Spirito, M.A.: DEMO: an IDS framework for internet of things empowered by 6LoWPAN, pp. 1337–1339 (2013)
10. http://home.agh.edu.pl/∼vlsi/AI/backp_t_en/backprop.html
11. http://www.unb.ca/cic/research/datasets/nsl.html
12. Van, N.T.T., Thinh, T.N.: Accelerating anomaly-based IDS using neural network on GPU. In: International Conference on Advanced Computing and Applications (ACOMP), pp. 67–74 (2015)

An Enhanced and Secured RSA Public Key Cryptosystem Algorithm Using Chinese Remainder Theorem

Vinod Kumar[1]([⊠]), Rajendra Kumar[2], and S. K. Pandey[3]

[1] Department of I.T, Centre for Development of Advanced Computing,
Noida, India
vinodmtech2010@gmail.com
[2] Department of Computer Science, Jamia Millia Islamia, New Delhi, India
[3] Department of Electronics and Information Technology, Ministry
of Communication and Information Technology, New Delhi, India

Abstract. The public key cryptosystems are mainly used to provide two cryptographic services called confidentiality and authentication. The RSA is one well known and widely used public key cryptosystem that uses two large and distinct integers to generate the keys. In this paper, we proposed an enhanced and secured RSA public key cryptosystem (ESRPKC) algorithm using Chinese remainder theorem. To increase the complexity of the system the proposed ESRPKC uses four prime numbers instead of two primes to generate the public/private key pairs. To generate the public/private key pairs, the proposed ESRPKC uses similar method as that of traditional RSA. In order to enhance the security level, the encryption and decryption functions are modified in proposed ESRPKC. The encryption function uses one extra key parameter called encryption key which is generated by using Chinese remainder theorem. The decryption function also uses one extra parameter to decrypt the message. The complexity of encryption and decryption functions is also acceptable. The proposed algorithm requires only one extra multiplication to perform encryption and decryption operations as compare to traditional RSA cryptosystem. The proposed scheme is highly secured because the encryption and decryption functions uses one extra key parameter and are not only dependent on the public and private key pairs respectively. The security and performance analysis ensures that the proposed ESRPKC algorithm is highly secure and efficient as compare to existing schemes.

Keywords: RSA public key cryptosystem · Eeuler totient function
Public key generation · Public key · Encryption · Private key generation
Private key · Decryption

1 Introduction

Information security is the technique of preventing unauthorized access, use, disclosure, modification and inspection of information. The confidentiality, integrity and availability are three main information security goals [1]. The confidentiality means that the information is not made available or disclosed to unauthorized entities.

© Springer Nature Singapore Pte Ltd. 2018
P. Bhattacharyya et al. (Eds.): NGCT 2017, CCIS 828, pp. 543–554, 2018.
https://doi.org/10.1007/978-981-10-8660-1_42

Integrity means that information cannot be modified in an unauthorized manner. Availability means the information must be available when it is needed. The cryptography is most widely used technique to implement above mentioned security goals. The cryptography is an art of designing the secure cryptosystem. According to the method and keys used for encryption and decryption of message, the cryptosystems are divided into two main category, symmetric key cryptosystems and asymmetric key cryptosystems. In symmetric key cryptosystems a common shared secret key is used for both encryption and decryption whereas in asymmetric key cryptosystems the public key and private key are used for encryption and decryption respectively. In asymmetric key cryptosystems both public and private keys are mathematically related to each other so that encrypted message can be decrypted correctly [15–20].

The asymmetric key cryptosystems mainly consist of six components, plain-text, public key, private key, encryption method, cipher-text and decryption method [2]. In today's internet era, the security is a major issue in the transmission of secret information from sender to receiver. The asymmetric key cryptosystems are mainly used for key exchange, to transmit secret message and to generate digital signatures. Many of the asymmetric key cryptosystems are available in the literature among which RSA is a most popular and widely used cryptosystem which was developed by Rivest et al. in 1978 at MIT [2]. The RSA cryptosystem mainly consist of three functions, key generation, message encryption and message decryption. In RSA cryptosystem, for message encryption and decryption two keys namely public key and private key are used. The public key pair (e, n) is publically available for everyone while private key pair (d, n) is known only to intended receiver. The RSA cryptosystem uses two distinct and large prime numbers to generate the public and private key pairs. To provide the better security, the size of each prime number should be at least 512 bits (154 decimal digits).

The security of RSA is depends on the difficulty of factoring the modulus $'n'$. Therefore, the modulus $'n'$ should be too large so that for an adversary it is infeasible to factor $'n'$ in a reasonable amount of time. If the modulus $'n'$ is not sufficiently large than in order to compute private key $'d'$ an adversary $\mathcal{A}$ can uses Wiener's attack [4] and he/she can obtain it in polynomial time $O(\log n)$. An encryption exponent attack is possible on RSA if the public exponent $'e'$ is not sufficiently large. In order to thwart this kind of attack the value of $e = 2^{16} + 1$ is recommended to be used. A low decryption exponent attack is also possible on RSA if $q < p < 2q$ and $d < 1/3n^{1/4}$. In order to prevent this kind of attack the value of $d \geq 1/3n^{1/4}$ is recommended to be used. In order to enhance the security level of RSA, many modified RSA cryptosystems have been proposed by the researchers. In many of the modified RSA cryptosystems $'n'$ prime numbers instead of two primes are used for key generation. Al-Hamami and Aldariseh [5] used three prime numbers to generate the public/private key and to encrypt/decrypt the message. Ivy et al. [7] used $'n'$ prime numbers to enhance the security level of traditional RSA cryptosystem. In order to thwart the factorization attack the Chhabra and Mathur [9] eliminate the publically announcement of $'n'$ In order to prevent the Wiener's attack [4] the Segar and Vijayaragavan [12] used Pell's equation to generate the public/private key pairs.

In order to overcome above mentioned weakness of traditional and recently modified RSA cryptosystem, we have proposed an enhanced and secured RSA public key cryptosystem (ESRPKC) algorithm using Chinese remainder theorem. Our modified RSA cryptosystem uses four prime numbers instead of two primes to generate the public/private key pair. To generate the keys, the proposed ESRPKC uses similar method as that of traditional RSA. The encryption and decryption functions are modified in proposed ESRPKC algorithm. The encryption function uses one extra parameter 'μ' called encryption key which is generated by using secret parameters k_1 & k_2. Similarly the decryption function uses one extra parameter either k_1 or k_2 to decrypt the message. The proposed ESRPKC required only one extra multiplication to perform encryption and decryption operations as compare to traditional RSA cryptosystem. The proposed scheme is highly secured because the encryption and decryption functions are not only dependent on the public key pair (e, n) and private key pair (d, n) respectively.

The rest of the paper is organized as follows: Sect. 2 gives the brief survey of recently proposed many modified RSA cryptosystem algorithms and the weakness of those schemes. The Proposed ESRPKC algorithm is presented in Sect. 3. The mathematical proof of ESRPKC algorithm is presented in Sect. 4. Section 4 presents ESRPKC example. In Sect. 5, the security analysis of proposed scheme is done to show that the ESRPKC algorithm is not easily breakable. In Sect. 6, the performance analysis of proposed ESRPKC and other existing schemes is done to show that the proposed scheme is superior as compare to other existing schemes. Finally, the paper ends up with conclusion in Sect. 7.

2 A Brief Survey of Related Work

Many modified RSA key generation schemes for secure communication are available in the literature [1–14]. The security and complexity of encryption and decryption functions are the major issue in most of existing modified RSA schemes. In order to deal with these issues, it is necessary to analyze the various approaches available in the literature. The review of some recently proposed major modifications in traditional RSA cryptosystem is presented in the following paragraphs.

Thangavel et al. [1] proposed a modified RSA key generation scheme and claimed that the scheme is not easily breakable. In the proposed scheme the encryption and decryption functions are performed by using n, where n is multiplication of two prime numbers and the encryption and decryption keys are generated with help of parameter $\mathcal{N}$, where $\mathcal{N}$ is the multiplication of four prime numbers and a multiple of n. The authors claimed that even if an adversary factorizes n, he/she needs to perform brute force attack to obtain the other two primes in order to compute the private key. However, in order to break the system an adversary may use alternative private key which can be generated by using the factors of n. Therefore, to obtain the alternative private key an adversary needs to perform factorization attack and there is no need to perform the brute force attack to obtain the other two prime numbers. Hence, the security level of proposed scheme has not increased and the system is easily breakable if an adversary has factorized the value of n. Al-Hamami and Aldariseh [5] proposed an enhanced method for RSA cryptosystem using additional third prime number. In this algorithm the parameter 'n' is the multiplication of large three prime numbers and the public/private keys are computed using this 'n'. The public/private key generation process and encryption/decryption functions are similar to traditional RSA cryptosystem. In the proposed scheme the complexity of factoring the variable 'n' is increased. However, the security of proposed system is depends only on the factorization of $'n'$ because no any extra parameters are used in the encryption/decryption functions. Further, the factorization is possible by using existing Ali and Salami [6] method. Subsequently, the private key can easily be computed which makes the system insecure.

Ivy et al. [7] proposed $'n'$ prime numbers based modified RSA cryptosystem which provides high security for confidential data over network. To provide the maximum security the proposed cryptosystem uses $'n'$ prime numbers. In the system the encryption and decryption functions are similar to the traditional RSA. The system is not easily breakable because the multiplication of $'n'$ prime numbers is not easily decomposable. The proposed algorithm increases the security of the RSA cryptosystem because the time required to get four prime numbers by factoring the multiplication of them is greater than the time taken to discover two prime numbers in RSA cryptosystem. However, the factorization is possible by using existing Ali and Salami [6] method. Subsequently, the private key can easily be computed which makes the system insecure. Jamgekar and Joshi [8] present a modified RSA public key cryptosystem for secure transmission of files. In this proposed cryptosystem the four prime numbers are used and the key generation process is similar to the traditional RSA cryptosystem. In this algorithm the complexity was enhanced in the encryption and decryption part. Therefore, the proposed cryptosystem is more secure because like RSA, the encryption and decryption functions are not only dependent on (e, n) and (d, n) respectively but also on some other parameters computed. However, the complexity of encryption and decryption functions is very high. Moreover, the overhead of the system is increased because without justification several new parameters are introduced.

Chhabra and Mathur [9] proposed a modified RSA algorithm which eliminates the need of publically announcement of multiplication of chosen prime numbers with public key. So it is not possible to compute the prime numbers which are used in the system with the help of factorization attack by an adversary. However, an adversary can easily attack on the proposed cryptosystem with the help of known values of k_p and d. Mahajan and Easo [10] proposed a new cryptosystem which replace Euler's totient function in RSA by Jordan-totient function. The proposed algorithm uses Jordan-totient function rather than Euler's totient function like in RSA to compute the public/private keys. In this scheme the encryption and decryption functions are similar to traditional RSA cryptosystem. The authors claimed that the proposed scheme gives high security as compare to traditional RSA. However, the security of the scheme only depends on the factorization of $'n'$. Therefore, the security level of the system can't be enhanced if Jordan-totient function rather than Euler's totient function is used.

Minni et al. [11] proposed an algorithm to enhanced the security level of RSA by eliminating the distribution of parameter $'n'$. In this proposed scheme the parameter $'n'$ is replaced by another new parameter $'x'$ which is calculated with the help of $'n'$ and factors of $'n'$. The authors claimed that the proposed scheme is highly secured as compare to traditional RSA. However, in the proposed scheme the private key $'k_2'$ is computed with the help of public key $'k_1'$ and the parameter $'x'$ such that $k_1 \times k_2 \equiv 1 \bmod x$. Therefore, an adversary can easily compute the private key $'k_2'$ with the help of only public key pair (k_1, x). Hence, the proposed cryptosystem is proven insecure. Segar and Vijayaragavan [12] proposed a new variant of RSA in which key generation process is different from the traditional RSA cryptosystem. In this work the authors discuss pell's RSA key generation method and its security over RSA. The authors claimed that the proposed cryptosystem prevents Wiener's attack [4] and the system is highly secured. However, in the proposed scheme an adversary can generate alternative private key $'d'$ with the help of public key parameter $'S'$ and factors of $'n'$.

The proposed scheme is efficient in many ways; first, it requires only one extra multiplication to perform encryption and decryption operations as compare to traditional RSA cryptosystem. The public/private key generation process is based on four prime numbers and similar to traditional RSA cryptosystem. The complexity of encryption and decryption functions is acceptable. Second, In order to provide the high security it requires to computes only one extra parameter 'μ'. The proposed scheme is highly secured because the encryption and decryption functions are not only dependent on the public and private key parameter respectively. The encryption function is dependent on public key pair (e, n) and parameter 'μ'. Similarly the decryption function is dependent on private key pair (d, n) and parameters k_1 or k_2. The security level of the proposed scheme is enhanced because if an adversary $\mathcal{A}$ is able to compute the private key $'d'$ then in order to decrypt the message, he/she is requires to know the value of secret parameters k_1 or k_2. In order to obtain the secret parameters k_1 or k_2 an adversary $\mathcal{A}$ needs to perform brute force attack.

3   Proposed ESRPKC Algorithm

The proposed ESRPKC algorithm mainly focuses on removing the security issues of various modified RSA cryptosystems which have been recently proposed in the literature for secure data transmission. Most of the modified RSA cryptosystems are not secured and easily breakable because the encryption and decryption functions are only dependent on public and private key pair respectively. In existing modified RSA cryptosystems the public and private key generation is based on $'n'$. The value of $'n'$ is the product of only two prime numbers. This $'n'$ can be easily be factor by using Wiener's attack [4] and an adversary $\mathcal{A}$ can easily obtain the private key $'d'$ in polynomial time $O(\log n)$. Therefore, most of the existing modified RSA cryptosystems are easily breakable. The detail explanation of proposed ESRPKC algorithm with major modifications is as follows.

3.1   ESRPKC Key Generation

The proposed ESRPKC algorithm uses four prime numbers instead of two primes to generate the public/private key pair. The encryption and decryption functions are modified in the proposed ESRPKC algorithm. The encryption function uses one extra parameter 'μ' called encryption key to encrypt the message and the decryption function uses one extra parameter either k_1 or k_2 to decrypt the message. In the proposed ESRPKC algorithm the encryption function is dependent on public key pair (e, n) and parameter 'μ' and the decryption function is dependent on private key pair (d, n) and parameter either k_1 or k_2. The use of extra parameters 'μ' and either k_1 or k_2 increases the complexity of proposed ESRPKC algorithm. For security purposes, the size of each prime number is chosen similar to that of the size of primes in traditional RSA cryptosystem. The proposed ESRPKC algorithm involves several computational steps for generating the keys which are described as follows:

Step 1:   First, randomly choose four distinct and large primes' p, q, r and s and computes $n = p \times q$ and $m = r \times s$. Next, compute $N = n \times m$. Also Compute Euler's totient function of n, m and N such that $\varphi(n) = (p-1) \times (q-1)$, $\varphi(m) = (r-1) \times (s-1)$ and $\varphi(N) = \varphi(n) \times \varphi(m)$.

Step 2:   Select a large prime number 'e' as a public exponent which satisfies $2 < e < \varphi(N)$ and $gcd(e, \varphi(N)) = 1$. $\left(i.e., e \in \mathbb{Z}^*_{\varphi(N)}\right)$

Step 3:   Next, compute private key parameter d such that $(e \times d) - 1 = 0 \ mod \ \varphi(N)$, using Extended Euclidean algorithm.

Step 4:   Next, compute n_1 and m_1 such that $n_1 = \frac{N}{n}$ and $m_1 = \frac{N}{m}$. Also compute n_1^{-1} and m_1^{-1} such that $n_1 \times n_1^{-1} \equiv 1 \ mod \ n$ and $m_1 \times m_1^{-1} \equiv 1 \ mod \ m$. Next, choose two distinct and large prime numbers k_1 and k_2 and compute, k_1^{-1} and k_2^{-1} such that $k_1 \times k_1^{-1} \equiv 1 \ mod \ n$ and $k_2 \times k_2^{-1} \equiv 1 \ mod \ m$. And compute message encryption key μ, such that $\mu = (k_1 \times n_1 \times n_1^{-1} + k_2 \times m_1 \times m_1^{-1}) \ mod \ N$.

Step5:   Finally, the public/private key pairs are $(\mu, e, N) \in \mathbb{Z} \times \mathbb{Z}^*_{\varphi(N)}$ and (k_1^{-1}, d, n) or $(k_2^{-1}, d, m) \in \mathbb{Z} \times \mathbb{Z}^*_{\varphi(N)}$ respectively.

3.2   ESRPKC Message Encryption

Let M be a plain text message which satisfies $M < n$ & m. The message encryption is done by using public key pair (μ, e, N). The encryption function $\mathcal{E}_k: \mathbb{Z}_n/\mathbb{Z}_m \to \mathbb{Z}_N$ is defined by the following equation.

$$\mathcal{E}_k(M) : CT = \mu \times M^e \ mod \ N \tag{1}$$

3.3   ESRPKC Message Decryption

The message decryption is done by using the private key pair (k_1^{-1}, d, n) or $(k_2^{-1}, d, m) \in \mathbb{Z} \times \mathbb{Z}^*_{\varphi(N)}$. The decryption function $\mathcal{D}_k: \mathbb{Z}_N \to \mathbb{Z}_n/\mathbb{Z}_m$ is defined by the following equations.

$$\mathcal{D}_k(M): \ M = \left(\left((CT \times k_1^{-1} mod \ n) \ mod \ n \right)^d\right) mod \ n \tag{2}$$

Or

$$\mathcal{D}_k(M): \ M = \left(\left((CT \times k_2^{-1} mod \ m) \ mod \ m \right)^d\right) mod \ m \tag{3}$$

4   Mathematical Proof of ESRPKC

In this section we describe the mathematical proof of proposed ESRPKC algorithm. In the proposed algorithm the encryption of message is done by using Eq. (1) as

$$\mathcal{E}_k(\mathcal{M}) : CT = \mu \times \mathcal{M}^e \, mod \, N$$

The generated cipher text CT is send to receiver. After receiving the cipher text the receiver perform the decryption operation to get the original message by using either Eq. (2) or Eq. (3) as

$$\mathcal{D}_k(\mathcal{M}): \; \mathcal{M} = \left(\left((CT \times k_1^{-1} mod \, n) \, mod \, n \right)^d\right) mod \, n$$

Or

$$\mathcal{D}_k(\mathcal{M}): \; \mathcal{M} = \left(\left((CT \times k_2^{-1} mod \, m) \, mod \, m \right)^d\right) mod \, m$$

$$\mathcal{M} = \left(\left((CT \times k_1^{-1} mod \, n) \, mod \, n \right)^d\right) mod \, n$$

$$= \left(\left(((\mu \times \mathcal{M}^e \, mod \, N) \times k_1^{-1} mod \, n) \, mod \, n \right)^d\right) mod \, n \; ; \qquad \text{From eqn. (1)}$$

$$= \left(\left(((\mu \times \mathcal{M}^e \, mod \, n) \times (k_1^{-1} mod \, n)) \, mod \, n \right)^d\right) mod \, n$$

$$= \left(\left(((\mathcal{M}^e \, mod \, n) \times (\mu \times k_1^{-1} mod \, n)) \, mod \, n \right)^d\right) mod \, n$$

$$= \left(\left(((\mathcal{M}^e \, mod \, n) \times (((k_1 \times n_1 \times n_1^{-1} + k_2 \times m_1 \times m_1^{-1}) \, mod \, N) \times$$

$$k_1^{-1} mod \, n)) \, mod \, n \right)^d\right) mod \, n$$

$$=$$

$$\left(\left(((\mathcal{M}^e \, mod \, n) \times\right.\right.$$

$$\left((((k_1 \times n_1 \times n_1^{-1}) mod N + (k_2 \times m_1 \times m_1^{-1}) mod \, N) mod \, N\right) \times$$

$$\left. k_1^{-1} mod \, n)) \, mod \, n \right)^d\right) mod \, n$$

$$= \left(\left(((\mathcal{M}^e \, mod \, n) \times (((k_1 \times n_1 \times n_1^{-1}) mod \, n + (k_2 \times m_1 \times\right.\right.$$

$$\left. m_1^{-1}) mod \, n) \, mod \, n\right) \times k_1^{-1} mod \, n)) \, mod \, n \right)^d\right) mod \, n$$

$$= \left(\mathcal{M}^e \, mod \, n \times ((k_1 \times k_1^{-1} mod \, n) mod \, n)\right)^d mod \, n$$

Since, $(n_1 \times n_1^{-1}) \equiv 1 \, mod \, n$ and $(m_1 \times m_1^{-1}) \equiv 0 \, mod \, n$

$= (\mathcal{M}^e \, mod \, n)^d mod \, n$ $\qquad$ Since, $k_1 \times k_1^{-1} \equiv 1 \, mod \, n$

$= (\mathcal{M})^{e \times d} mod \, n$

$= (\mathcal{M})^{(k \times (p-1) \times (q-1) \times (r-1) \times (s-1)) + 1} mod \, n$

Since $(e \times d) \, \text{-}1 = 0 \, mod \, \varphi(N)$, therefore $(e \times d) = \left(k \times (p-1) \times (q-1) \times (r-1) \times (s-1)\right) + 1$

$= (\mathcal{M})^1 mod \, n$ $\qquad$ By Euler theorem

$= \mathcal{M} \; ; \qquad$ Since $\mathcal{M} < n$

5   ESRPKC Example

Select four large prime numbers $p = 151, q = 193, r = 211$ and $s = 307$. First Compute, $n = p \times q$ and $m = r \times s$, $n = 29143$ and $m = 64777$. Next compute, $N = n \times m$. $N = 1887796111$. Also Compute Euler's totient function of n, m and N such that $\varphi(n) = (p - 1) \times (q - 1)$, $\varphi(m) = (r - 1) \times (s - 1)$ and $\varphi(N) = \varphi(n) \times \varphi(m)$. $\varphi(n) = 28800$, $\varphi(m) = 64260$ and $\varphi(N) = 1850688000$.

Select a large prime number e, satisfying $2 < e < \varphi(N)$ and $gcd(e, \varphi(N)) = 1$. $e = 103$. Now compute, private key d, such that $d = e^{-1} mod(\varphi(N))$. $d = 952295767$.

Next compute $n_1 = \frac{N}{n}$ and $m_1 = \frac{N}{m}$. $n_1 = 64777$ and $m_1 = 29143$ Also compute, n_1^{-1} and m_1^{-1} such that $n_1 \times n_1^{-1} \equiv 1 \bmod n$ and $m_1 \times m_1^{-1} \equiv 1 \bmod m$ $n_1^{-1} = 8984$ and $m_1^{-1} = 44808$. Next select two distinct and large prime numbers C such that $k_1 = 79$ and $k_2 = 89$. Now compute, k_1^{-1} and k_2^{-1} such that $k_1 \times k_1^{-1} \equiv 1 \bmod n$ and $k_2 \times k_2^{-1} \equiv 1 \bmod m$ $k_1^{-1} = 3689$ and $k_2^{-1} = 4367$. Compute, $\mu = (k_1 \times n_1 \times n_1^{-1} + k_2 \times m_1 \times m_1^{-1}) \bmod N$ $\mu = 47038725517$

Let message $M = 1024$.
Message encryption, $CT = \mu \times M^e \bmod N$. Therefore, $CT = 855954332$
Message decryption, $M = \left(\left((CT \times k_1^{-1}) \bmod n\right)^d\right) \bmod n$
$$= \left(\left((855954332 \times 3689) \bmod 29143\right)^{952295767}\right) \bmod 29143$$
$= 1024$

The message can also be decrypted by using following equation
$$M = \left(\left((CT \times k_2^{-1}) \bmod m\right)^d\right) \bmod m$$
$$= \left(\left((855954332 \times 4367) \bmod 64777\right)^{952295767}\right) \bmod 64777$$
$$= 1024$$

6   Security Analysis

This section provides security analysis of proposed ESRPKC algorithm and shows that our algorithm is not easily breakable. In the proposed ESRPKC algorithm the key generation process uses four distinct and large prime numbers. The encryption and decryption functions uses extra parameters 'μ' and 'k_1'/ 'k_2' respectively. The parameter 'μ' is securely generated by using Chinese remainder theorem. In order to break our cryptosystem an adversary A needs to compute the private key d and one secret parameter either 'k_1' or 'k_2'. The total time required to break the system is consist of two parts. First, the time taken to compute the private key 'd', Second, the time taken to compute the parameter either $'k_1'$ or $'k_2'$. The total time required to break our cryptosystem by and adversary $\mathcal{A}$ is given by the Eq. (4).

$$\tau_{cryptosystem} = \tau_d + \tau_{k_1 \, or \, k_2} \tag{4}$$

where,

$\tau_{cryptosystem}$ = total time required to break the cryptosystem
τ_d = time required to obtain the private key d
$\tau_{k_1 \, or \, k_2}$ = Time taken to obtain the parameter either k_1 or k_2 by using brute force attack.

In order to compute the private key d an adversary $\mathcal{A}$ can perform any existing attacks. The private key d can be computed by an adversary in polynomial time $O(\log N)$. Even after computing the d, finding either k_1 or k_2 is very difficult because these parameters are kept secret. To obtain k_1 or k_2, an adversary $\mathcal{A}$ uses brute force attack. In the proposed ESRPKC scheme the size of k_1 or k_2 considered for experimental analysis is 1024 bits and 2048 bits. Suppose by using brute force attack, the time required to perform one attempt is 1 ηs, then to compute k_1 or k_2, the total time required will be 2^{b-1} ηs where b is the bit size of k_1 or k_2. Therefore, this feature makes the situation impractical for an adversary $\mathcal{A}$ to obtain the secret parameter either k_1 or k_2.

7 Performance Analysis

The proposed ESRPKC algorithm is implemented in JAVA and tested on the computer machine with configuration Intel Pentium Dual core processor, 2 GB RAM, 200 GB HDD, windows-7 OS. The computation time is compared with the existing Ivy et al. [7] and Jamgekar and Joshi [8] to perform the encryption and decryption operations for the different size of p, q, r and s varying from 64 bits to 2048 bits. For handling the large positive integers in experiment, the BigInteger class is used. The experimental results of various algorithms are given in Table 1 which compare the message encryption and decryption time in milliseconds (ms).

From Table 1, it has been observed that the message encryption time of proposed ESRPKC algorithm is slightly larger than that of Ivy et al. [7] algorithm but it is less than Jamgekar and Joshi [8] algorithm. The increased message encryption time of ESRPKC algorithm can be justified by fact that it uses one extra parameter to increase the complexity of encryption function.

The graphical results shown in following figures compare the message encryption and message decryption time of the proposed ESRPKC algorithm with the existing Ivy et al. [7] and Jamgekar and Joshi [8] algorithms. Figure 1, shows that when the size of input prime numbers p, q, r and s is 1024 bits and 2048 bits the message encryption time for proposed ESRPKC is found to be 418 ms and 5293 ms respectively which are slightly larger than that of Ivy et al. algorithm but very less in comparison with Jamgekar and Joshi [8] algorithm. The increased encryption time is tolerable because the security level of proposed ESRPKC algorithm is enhanced to a great extent.

Table 1. Message encryption and decryption time of various algorithms.

Size of p, q, r and s (in bits)	Ivy PU et al.[7]		Jamgekar RS et al.[8]		ESRPKC (Proposed)	
	Encryption time (ms)	Decryption time (ms)	Encryption time (ms)	Decryption time (ms)	Encryption time (ms)	Decryption time (ms)
64 bits	0.2547	0.2748	0.7067	0.6063	0.1965	0.2590
128 bits	2.6659	1.8557	4.9612	2.0773	1.1356	1.2241
256 bits	6.9166	8.6715	29.5015	17.3232	6.8812	7.4482
512 bits	51.5344	53.0373	217.2546	137.0443	53.2567	51.9952
1024 bits	408.9258	445.1866	1702.1842	1001.4214	418.0262	403.2600
2048 bits	4861.7923	4367.1732	9613.1939	7633.7930	5293.2176	4194.5677

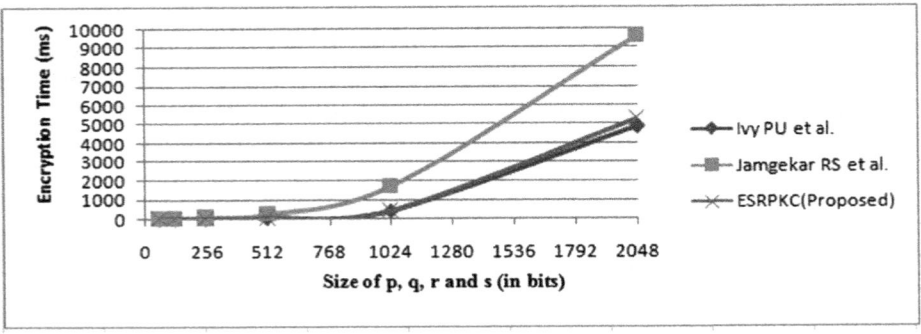

Fig. 1. Comparison of encryption time

From Fig. 2, it is observed that, when the size of input primes is 1024 bits and 2048 bits the message decryption time for proposed ESRPKC is found to be 403 ms and 4194 ms respectively which are slightly smaller than that of Ivy et al. [7] algorithm but very less in comparison with Jamgekar and Joshi [8] algorithm.

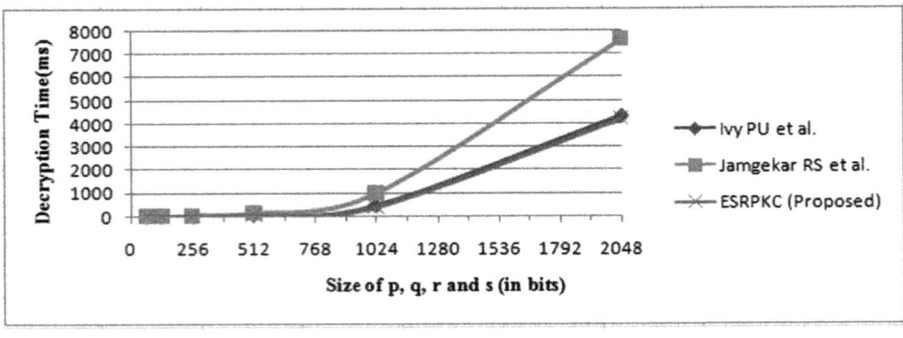

Fig. 2. Comparison of decryption time

8 Conclusion

In this paper, we proposed an enhanced and secured RSA public key cryptosystem algorithm using Chinese remainder theorem. Our modified RSA cryptosystem uses four prime numbers instead of two primes to generate the public/private key pair. In order to provide the high security the encryption function uses one extra parameter 'μ' called encryption key. Similarly the decryption function uses one extra parameter either k_1 or k_2 to decrypt the message. The proposed ESRPKC scheme is highly secured because the encryption and decryption functions are not only dependent on the public key pair (e, n) and private key pair (d, n) respectively. The encryption function is dependent on public key pair (e, n) and parameter 'μ'. Similarly the decryption function is dependent on private key pair (d, n) and parameter either k_1 or k_2. The security level of the proposed scheme is enhanced because if an adversary A is able to compute the private key 'd' then in order to decrypt the message, he/she is requires to know the value of secret parameters k_1 or k_2. In order to obtain the secret parameters k_1 or k_2 an adversary A needs to perform brute force attack. The complexity of encryption and decryption functions is also acceptable. It requires only one extra multiplication to perform encryption and decryption operations as compare to traditional RSA cryptosystem.

References

1. Thangavel, M., et al.: An Enhanced and Secured RSA Key Generation Scheme (ESRKGS). J. Inf. Secur. Appl. **20**, 3–10 (2015)
2. Rivest, R.L., Shamir, A., Adleman, L.: A method for obtaining digital signatures and public-key cryptosystems. Commun. ACM **21**(2), 120–126 (1978)
3. Blömer, J., May, A.: A generalized wiener attack on RSA. In: Bao, F., Deng, R., Zhou, J. (eds.) PKC 2004. LNCS, vol. 2947, pp. 1–13. Springer, Heidelberg (2004). https://doi.org/10.1007/978-3-540-24632-9_1
4. Wiener, M.: Cryptanalysis of short RSA secret exponents. IEEE Trans. Inf. Theory **36**(3), 553–558 (1990)
5. Al-Hamami, A.H., Aldariseh, I.A.: Enhanced method for RSA cryptosystem algorithm. In: International Conference on Advanced Computer Science Applications and Technologies, Kuala Lumpur, pp. 402–408 (2012)
6. Ali, H., Al-Salami, M.: Timing attack prospect for RSA cryptanalysis using genetic algorithm technique. Int. Arab J. Inf. Technol. **1**(1), 80–85 (2004)
7. Ivy, P.U., Mandiwa, P., Kumar, M.: A modified RSA cryptosystem based on 'n' prime numbers. Int. J. Eng. Comput. Sci. **1**(2), 63–66 (2012)
8. Jamgekar, R.S., Joshi, G.S.: File encryption and decryption using secure RSA. Int. J. Emerg. Sci. Eng. (IJESE) **1**(4), 11–14 (2013)
9. Chhabra, A., Mathur, S.: Modified RSA algorithm: a secure approach. In: International Conference on Computational Intelligence and Communication Networks, Gwalior, pp. 545–548 (2011)
10. Mahajan, S., Easo, S.: Performance evolution of RSA and new cryptosystem. Int. J. Emerg. Technol. Adv. Eng. **2**(3), 279–283 (2012)

11. Minni, R., Sultania, K., Mishra, S., Vincent, D.R.: An algorithm to enhance security in RSA. In: Fourth International Conference on Computing, Communications and Networking Technologies (ICCCNT), Tiruchengode, pp. 1–4 (2013)
12. Segar, T.C., Vijayaragavan, R.: Pell's RSA key generation and its security analysis. In: Fourth International Conference on Computing, Communications and Networking Technologies (ICCCNT), Tiruchengode, pp. 1–5 (2013)
13. Sharma, S., Sharma, P., Dhakar, R.S.: RSA algorithm using modified subset sum cryptosystem. In: International Conference on Computer & Communication Technology (ICCCT), Allahabad, pp. 457–61 (2011)
14. Wu, C.H., Hong, J.H., Wu, C.W.: RSA cryptosystem design based on the Chinese remainder theorem. In: Design Automation Conference, Proceedings of the ASP-DAC, Yokohama, pp. 391–395 (2001)
15. Schneier, B.: Applied Cryptography, 2nd edn. Wiley, New Delhi (2012)
16. Kahate, A.: Cryptography and Network Security, 2nd edn. Tata McGraw-Hill, New Delhi (2005)
17. Stallings, W.: Cryptography and Network Security, 4th edn. Pentice-Hall of India, New Delhi (2007)
18. Whitman, M.E., Mattord, H.J.: Principles of Information Security, 5th edn. Cengage Learning, Boston (2015)
19. Pachghare, V.K.: Cryptography and Information Security, 2nd edn. PHI Learning Private Limited, Delhi (2015)
20. Forouzan, B.A., Mukhopadhyay, D.: Cryptography and Network Security, 2nd edn. Tata McGraw Hill Education Private Limited, New Delhi (2016)

A Comparative Analysis of Various Segmentation Techniques on Dental Images

Prerna Singh[1(✉)] and Priti Sehgal[2]

[1] Department of Computer Science, University of Delhi, Delhi, India
prerna.singh@jimsindia.org
[2] Department of Computer Science, Keshav Mahavidyala,
University of Delhi, Delhi, India

Abstract. Image Segmentation has a very important role in medical imaging. It is a process of dividing the image into multiple parts, which are used for identifying objects and other relevant information. Image segmentation bridges a gap between the low-level image details and high-level image components. The role of segmentation is crucial for the tasks that require image analysis. The goal of this paper is to review the image segmentation techniques on dental images. An exhaustive survey of four widely used segmentation techniques has been carried out and the performance comparison of each method within Edge detection, Thresholding, Deformable model and Clustering segmentation technique is provided. The segmentation techniques are Edge Detection, Thresholding, Deformable Model and Clustering. The accuracy of the segmentation process determines the success or failure of the final analysis process. With the help of image quality metrics such as root mean square error, mean square error, average difference, peak signal to noise ratio, normalized cross section, structural content and normalized absolute error, we compare the methods of Edge Detection, Thresholding, Deformable Model and Clustering techniques on dental images.

Keywords: Image segmentation · Medical imaging · Clustering
Thresholding · Edge detection · Deformable model · Dental images

1 Introduction

Image Segmentation is partitioning a digital image into multiple segments and it is often used to locate objects and boundaries. It is the process of assigning a label to every pixel so that every pixel with the same label has common characteristics. SenthilKumaran and Rajesh [3] carried out the survey of edge detection techniques based on Genetic Algorithm, Fuzzy Logic and Neural Network. It was found that different edge detection algorithms work better under different circumstances. Zhang et al. [4] reviewed the different image segmentation techniques applied on remote sensing images. One of the applications of Image segmentation is medical imaging [2]. Medical Image Segmentation can be applied for the detection and localization of fractures, tissue classification, matching of images for human identification, early diagnosis of diseases/ailments while ensuring that the patients receive the most effective treatment

© Springer Nature Singapore Pte Ltd. 2018
P. Bhattacharyya et al. (Eds.): NGCT 2017, CCIS 828, pp. 555–576, 2018.
https://doi.org/10.1007/978-981-10-8660-1_43

or detection of the cancerous cell [1]. It helps to provide information about human body structure that helps the radiologists make a prediction about the diseases [7, 8]. The success of the entire system depends on the accuracy of image segmentation. Sharif et al. [9] discussed the various approaches to medical image segmentation. Ahirwar explained the various segmentation methods for region classification of Brain MRI [5].

In the Dental Image perspective, segmentation is used to extract the tooth in the x-ray image or parts of the tooth such as crown and root of the tooth. According to Gayathri et al., the main concern of dental image segmentation in the research is to separate infected and normal tooth root which is can be extracted using edge segmentation [19]. The various image segmentation techniques on dental radiographs was proposed by Subramanyam et al. They compared various techniques and found out thresholding based technique better than other three techniques [12]. Simon and Felix Joseph [15] discussed the Canny's edge detection algorithm for the teeth segmentation. Rad et al. [16] presented a method for segmentation and feature extraction of dental images. The level set method was used for image segmentation on dental images. After segmentation feature extraction is done and extracted data can be used for dental diagnosis system. Jain and Chen [17] proposed a tooth segmentation method using Naïve Bayes rule and internal projection. Zhou and Abdel-Mottaleb [23] presented segmentation by performing image enhancement, the region of interest localization and finally applying Snake method on the dental x-ray image. Nomir and Abdel-Mottaleb [26] used iterative thresholding and adaptive thresholding for developing the fully automated approach for dental x-ray image segmentation. In this paper, we will consider dental x-ray image for image segmentation. The digital images are the most important medium for carrying the information in the field of image mining.

The Dental x-ray can be divided into three types [6]:

- Bitewing x-ray
  These are the x-ray that shows the upper and lower teeth in one area of the mouth.
- Periapical x-ray
  This x-ray includes whole the tooth from crown to beyond the root, all teeth in one portion of either the upper or lower jaw.
- Panoramic x-ray
  This x-ray includes the broader view of entire dentition. It shows entire teeth, sinus, upper and lower jaw bone.

We will be working on all the three types of dental images. Figure 2 shows the panoramic x-ray dental image. Figure 6 shows the bitewing dental image and Fig. 9 shows the periapical x-ray dental image.

The paper is divided into different sections including Introduction in Sect. 1. Section 2 explains the classification of the image segmentation technique in dental images, Sect. 3 is focused on showing different evaluation metrics for comparison of the various methods within image segmentation techniques in dental images. Section 4 presents the conclusion.

2 Classification of Image Segmentation Techniques

There are numerous techniques for image segmentation. Every technique has its own importance. The different technique can yield a different result when applied to the same image. The technique applied to the image depends on the type of segmentation required. Figure 1 shows the classification of the image segmentation techniques and methods within each segmentation techniques are compared using various quality metrics on the panoramic, periapical and bitewing dental x-ray images.

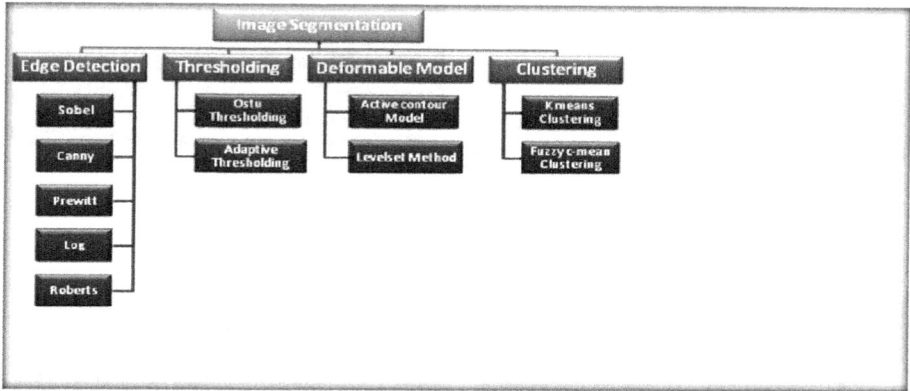

Fig. 1. Classification of image segmentation techniques.

2.1 Edge Detection

A process of locating an edge of an image is edge detection. With the help of edge detection, we can understand image features. Edges contain very important features and meaningful information. Edge detection is the most common approach for detecting meaningful discontinuities in grey level. An edge is a boundary between two regions with relatively distinct grey level properties [9, 10]. Object recognition and recognition of much other application can be done with the help of edge detection. Edge detection is an active area of research and it facilitates higher level image analysis. Various researchers have developed a large number of edge detectors based on a single derivative. Edge Detection is used to detect the discontinuities in grey level. The transition between two regions can be determined on the basis of grey level discontinuities [11]. Edge Detection Techniques are used in [20, 21]. Figures 3, 4 and 5 shows the Sobel Operator, Prewitt operator, Canny operator for panoramic dental image respectively. Figures 7 and 8 shows the Sobel Operator and Log Operator of periapical dental image respectively. Figures 10 and 11 shows the Canny Operator and Log Operator of bitewing dental images.

Different Operators used for edge detection are the following [13, 14, 18]:

- Sobel Operator.
- Prewitt Operator.

- Canny Operator.
- Robert Operator.
- Log Operator.

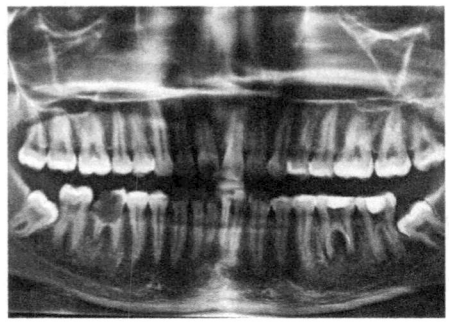

Fig. 2. Panoramic dental x-ray image

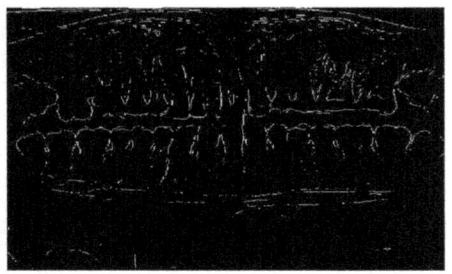

Fig. 3. Sobel operator

Fig. 4. Prewitt operator

Fig. 5. Canny operator

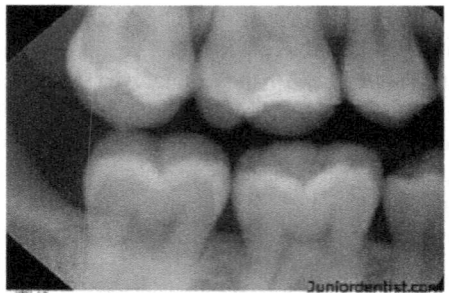

Fig. 6. Bitewing dental xray image

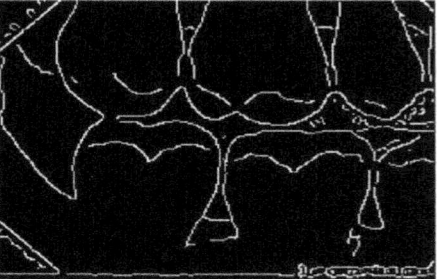

Fig. 7. Canny operator

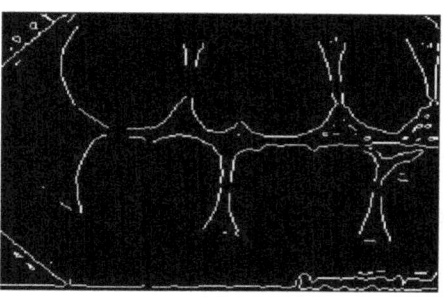

Fig. 8. Log operator

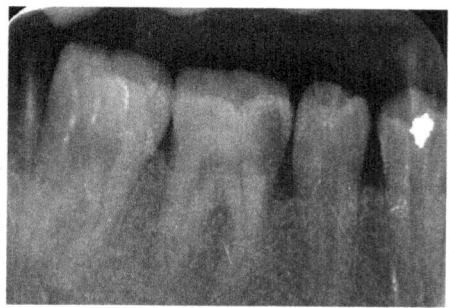

Fig. 9. Periapical dental xray image

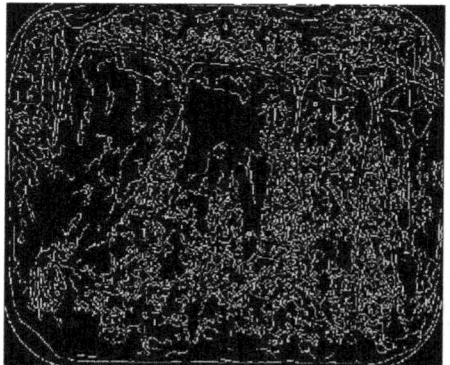

Fig. 10. Canny operator

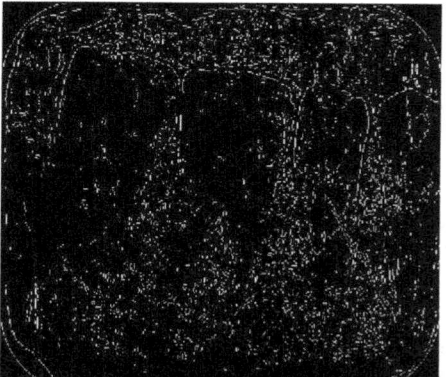

Fig. 11. Log operator

2.2 Thresholding Techniques

In thresholding method, the histogram is partitioned into two areas, foreground and background. After partitioning, a single threshold "T" is assigned to both foreground and background. The image is classified as foreground and background depending on the value of the pixel in the grey level. If the value of a pixel is greater than T then the object belongs to the foreground and if the value of the pixel is less than T then the object belongs to the background. The foreground pixel to white colour and background pixel to black colour. Foreground pixel is denoted by 1 and the background pixel is denoted by 0 [22].

The thresholding techniques are the following:

- Ostu Thresholding
- Adaptive Thresholding

Ostu Thresholding

Ostu method is used as an automatic thresholding method. It is used to find the maximum interclass variance between the two classes of the pixel (Eq. 1).

It is defined as follows

$$\sigma^2(t) = \omega_0(t)\sigma_0^2(t) + \omega_1(t)\sigma_1^2(t) \tag{1}$$

where ω_0 and ω_1 are probabilities of the two classes separated by threshold t and σ_0^2 and σ_1^2 are the variance of the two classes. Figure 12 shows the image segmentation using ostu thresholding for panoramic dental image.

Adaptive Thresholding

Global thresholding is not suitable for segmentation of the image due to the varied background and non-uniformed brightness. In order to change the thresholding dynamically over an image, adaptive thresholding is used. Consider an image to have n * n neighborhood around it. From this, the mean value and pixel is calculated and set to black and white depending on the value of the local threshold. Figure 13 shows the image segmentation using Adaptive Thresholding for panoramic dental image.

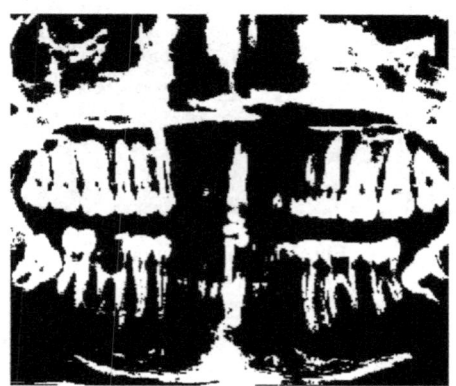   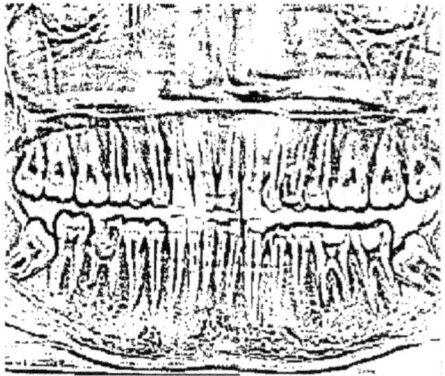

Fig. 12. Ostu thresholding.   **Fig. 13.** Adaptive thresholding

2.3   Deformable Model

The deformable model is a dynamic model, which works under the influence of external and internal forces.

Tripathi et al. publication made deformable model very popular model for image segmentation.

The deformable models are of various types:

- Active Contour Models (ACM)
- Level Set Methods

Active Contour Model (ACM)

For Active Contour Model is also called as Snake method. Here the user has to specify a point on the image contour which can move from internal and external forces to the boundaries of the desired objects. The forces inside the curve are called internal forces and the forces outside curve are called external forces [25]. The snake method uses an energy minimization scheme defined by external constraint forces and influenced by internal and external forces. The internal and external energies constitute the energy function (Eq. 2).

$$E_{snake} = E_{internal} + E_{external} \qquad (2)$$

To keep the continuity and regularity of the surface the internal energy is used. To attract the contour points to appropriate image features [28] external energy is used. There is a need to define the internal energy which increases with its length. The starting point of the snake is the user-defined controlled points. The internal energy function (Eq. 3) can be annotated as the sum of the square of the distance between adjacent control points which obey Hooke's Law. Constant K is multiplied by the sum.

$$E_{internal} = E_{elastic} = K \sum_{i=1}^{N} (d_i, \; 1 - 1) \qquad (3)$$

where i is the index of the control point with coordinates (x_i, y_i). Since the snake is a loop, control point 0 is similar to control point N. At the ith control point, the corresponding forces are obtained by differentiating the energy function given in Eq. 4.

$$F_i(x) = 2k((x_{i+1} - x_i) - (x_i - x_{i-1}))$$
$$F_i(y) = 2k((y_{i+1} - y_i) - (y_i - y_{i-1})) \qquad (4)$$

The forces act on each control point. The control point is moved by the amount proportional to the force. The equations are given by Eq. 5.

$$X_i = CF_i \rightarrow x_i$$
$$Y_i = CF_i \rightarrow y_i \qquad (5)$$

Levelset Methods

Malladi et al. applied level set segmentation for "shape modeling with front propagation. [27]. In level set segmentation [29–31] curve within a surface is enclosed. To detect image characteristics such as corner and edges level set segmentation is used extensively. The contour level is zero and the segmentation body is defined as a part of the surface. Suppose φ be defined as the surface such that

$$\varphi(X, t) = \pm d \qquad (6)$$

In Eq. 6 X is the position of the domain, t is the time and d is the distance between the position x and the zero level set. If X is outside the zero level set then the sign in front of d is positive and if X is within the zero level set then the sign is negative.

$$\varphi(x, y, 0) = -d(x, y, Y) \quad \text{if } (x, y) \text{ are inside the front.}$$
$$0 \tag{7}$$
$$d(x, y, Y) \quad \text{if } (x, y) \text{ are outside the front.}$$

The algorithm for level set segmentation is as follows [32]:

- Initialize the front Y(0).
- Compute $\varphi(x, y, 0)$
- Iterate:

$$\varphi(x, y, t+1) = \varphi(x, y, t) + \Delta \varphi(x, y, t)$$

- Mark the front Y(tend).

Figure 14 shows the result of level set segmentation method for panoramic dental image.

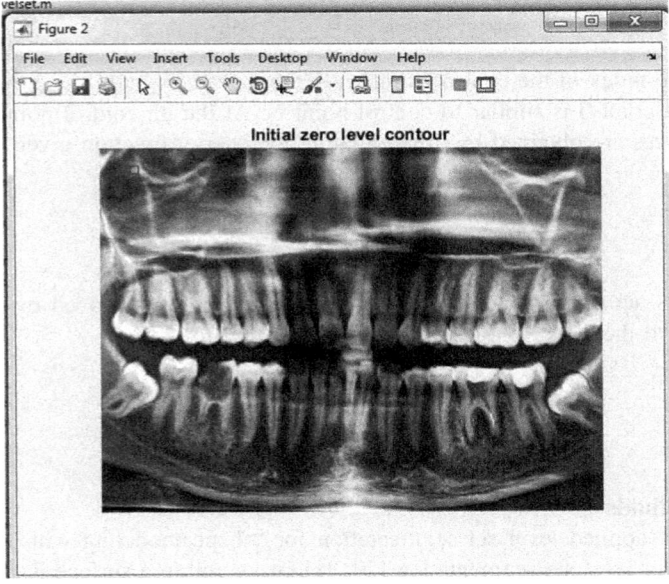

Fig. 14. Level set method

2.4 Clustering

Clustering or cluster analysis can also be used for image segmentation in dental images and it is an unsupervised method. A set of objects which have similar features are grouped in to one cluster and dissimilar object belongs to different cluster [33]. The clustering techniques discussed in this research paper are:

- K-means clustering
- Fuzzy c-mean clustering

K-means Clustering

K-mean is also known as hard clustering since it divides the image into K cluster or groups by adding points p, to the clusters. It defines the K centres, where one center is for one cluster. These centres should be placed far away from each other. Each point is taken from a given dataset and associated with the nearest centre.

The squared error function ($J(v)$) is given by Eq. 8

$$J(v) = \sum_{i=1}^{c} \sum_{j=1}^{c} (||x_i - y_i||)^2 \tag{8}$$

where $x_i - y_i$ is the Euclidean distance between x_i and y_j. c_i is the number of data points in the ith cluster c is the number of the cluster centre.

The algorithm for K-mean clustering was proposed by Lloyd [34] and is as follows:

- Given the number of cluster K, find c_k the centroid for each cluster randomly.
- Calculate the Euclidean distance. If it is 1 then x_i is closest to the cluster k otherwise the Euclidean distance is 0.
- Recalculate cluster centroid from the Euclidean distance.
- Repeat step 2 and 3 until all cluster centroid are unchanged since the last iteration.

Fuzzy c-mean Clustering

Fuzzy c-mean (FCM) is the clustering method [35] which allows one piece of data to belong to two or more clusters. It is frequently used in pattern recognition.

The algorithm for Fuzzy c-mean is as follows [36]:

1. Initialize $U = [u_{ij}]$ matrix, $U^{(0)}$
2. At k-step: calculate the centers vectors $C^{(k)} = [c_j]$ with $U^{(k)}$
3. Update $U^{(k)}$, $U^{(k+1)}$
4. If $|| U^{(k+1)} - U^{(k)}|| <$ then STOP; otherwise return to step 2.

The figures for K-Mean clustering and fuzzy clustering based methods are in Figs. 15 and 17 for panoramic dental image respectively. Figure 16 shows K-means clustering for periapical dental images. Figures 18 and 19 shows fuzzy clustering for periapical dental image and bitewing dental images respectively.

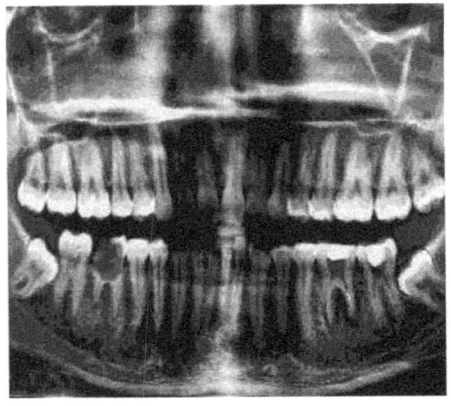

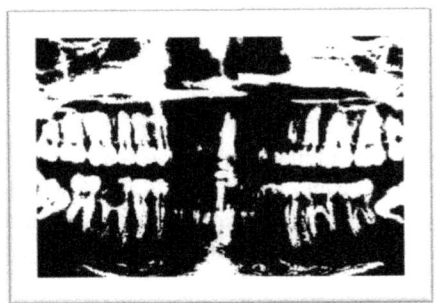

Fig. 15. K-means clustering (panoramic x-ray)

Fig. 16. Fuzzy means clustering (panoramic x-ray)

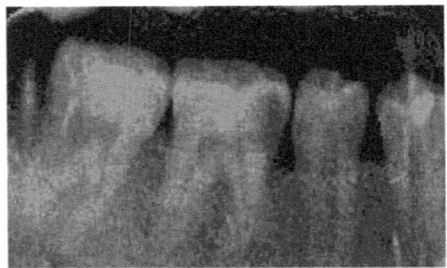

Fig. 17. K-means clustering (periapical x-ray)

Fig. 18. Fuzzy c-mean clustering (periapical x-ray)

Fig. 19. Fuzzy c-mean clustering (bitewing x-ray)

3 Experimental Results

In this section, various Image segmentation techniques for dental images are compared based on the following metrics:

- Root Mean Square Error
- Mean Square Error
- Peak Signal to Noise Ratio
- Normalized Cross Section
- Average Difference
- Structural Content
- Maximum Difference
- Normalized Absolute Error

The result of each technique of image segmentation is explained in Tables 1, 2, and 3 respectively.

Each of the metrics is explained in detail in the following sections.

3.1 Root Mean Square Error

Root mean square error [37] is also known as the root mean square deviation. It is used to calculate the average magnitude of the error. It is the good measure of accuracy. The original image is represented as $f(x,y)$ and the segmented image as $f''(x, y)$ and the error are represented as $e(x,y)$ (Eq. 9).

$$e(x, y) = f''(x, y) - f(x, y) \qquad (9)$$

The root mean square error between original and segmented image is given by Eq. 10.

$$rms = 1/\left[\sum_{x=0}^{m-1} \sum_{y=0}^{n-1} \left[f(''x,y) - f(x,y) \right]^2 \right]^{1/2} \qquad (10)$$

3.2 Mean Square Error

Mean Square error is also called as the mean square deviation. It is used to measure the average of the square of the error [38]. It is the risk function. It is always non-negative. The original image is represented as $f(x, y)$ and the segmented image as $f''(x, y)$ and the error is represented as $e(x, y)$ Eq. 11.

$$e(x, y) = f''(x, y) - f(x, y) \qquad (11)$$

The mean square error between original and segmented image is given by Eq. 12.

$$mse = 1/[\sum_{x=0}^{m-1} \sum_{y=0}^{n-1} [f''(x,y) - f(x,y)]^2 \tag{12}$$

3.3 Peak Signal to Noise Ratio

Peak Signal to noise ratio (Eq. 13) between the maximum possible power of a signal and the power of distorting noise that affect the quality of its representation [39]. MAX is defines as the maximum signal value of the original image and MSE is the mean square error.

$$PSNR = 10 \log_{10}(MAX/\sqrt{MSE}) \tag{13}$$

3.4 Normalized Cross-Correlation

The normalized cross correlation (Eq. 14) of two sequences, $x(n)$ and $y(n)$, of length N. Then the sum is taken from 1 till N. [40, 41] mean(x) is the mean of x. var(x) is the variance of x. sqrt is square root

$$Normalized_{CrossCorr} = 1/N * sum\{[x(n) - mean(x)] * [y(n) - mean(y)]\}/ (sqrt(var(x) * var(y)) \tag{14}$$

3.5 Average Difference

AD (Eq. 15) is simply the average of difference between the reference signal and test image [42].

$$AD = 1/MN(x\,i,j - y\,i,j) \tag{15}$$

3.6 Structural Content

SC (Eq. 16) is also correlation based measure and measures the similarity between two images. Structural Content (SC) is given by the equation [42].

$$SC = \sum_{i=1}^{M} \sum_{j=1}^{N} (y(i,j))^2 / \sum_{i=1}^{M} \sum_{j=1}^{N} (x(i,j))^2 \tag{16}$$

where $x(i, j)$ represents the original (reference) image and $y(i, j)$ represents the distorted (modified) image.

3.7 Normalized Absolute Error

The large value of Normalized Absolute Error means that the image is of poor quality [42].

NAE is defined by Eq. 17.

$$NAE = \sum_{x=0}^{m-1} \sum_{y=0}^{n-1} [f''(x,y) - f(x,y)]/f(x,y) \tag{17}$$

In Table 1 values of various quality metrics for edge detection methods of periapical dental images are given. Table 2 explains the value of various quality metrics for edge detection methods of bitewing dental images and Table 3 gives the value of various quality metrics for edge detection methods of panoramic dental image.

Table 1. Values of quality metrics for edge detection methods of periapical x-ray dental image.

Periapical x-ray dental image								
Edge detection methods	MSE	RMSE	PSNR	N cross section	AD	SC	MD	NAE
Log	3.20E +04	178.9 +02	3.0752	2.80E−04	171.0536	5.90E +05	255	1.00E +00
Canny	3.20E +04	178.905	3.0784	6.46E−04	170.9829	2.56E +05	255	9.99E −01
Prewitt	3.20E +04	179.0134	3.0731	3.87E−05	171.0992	3.64E +06	255	1.00E +00
Sobel	3.20E +04	179.0134	3.0731	3.83E−05	171.0992	3.67E +06	255	1.00E +00
Roberts	3.20E +04	179.015	3.073	2.94E−05	171.1013	4.78E +06	255	1.00E +00

Table 2. Values of quality metrics for edge detection methods of bitewing x-ray dental image.

Bitewing x-ray dental image								
Edge detection methods	MSE	RMSE	PSNR	N cross section	AD	SC	MD	NAE
Log	4.69E +04	216.4998	1.4217	1.29E−04	210.9878	1.49E +06	255	1.00E +00
Canny	4.69E +04	216.48	1.422	2.13E−04	210.96	8.68E +05	255	1.00E +00
Prewitt	4.69E +04	216.516	1.421	5.39E−05	211.0008	2.54E +06	255	1.00E +00
Sobel	4.69E +04	216.517	1.421	4.92E−05	211.0014	2.63E +06	255	1.00E +00
Roberts	4.6882 +04	216.522	1.4207	2.37E−05	211.0067	3.73E +06	255	1.00E +00

Table 3. Values of quality metrics for edge detection methods of panoramic x-ray dental image.

Panoramic x-ray dental image

Edge detection methods	MSE	RMSE	PSNR	N cross section	AD	SC	MD	NAE
Log	36535	191.1401	2.5038	2.80E−04	186.4423	6.68E+05	255	1.00E+00
Canny	36520	191.1028	2.5055	4.75E−04	186.401	3.82E+05	255	1.00E+00
Prewitt	36547	191.1735	2.5023	1.05E−04	186.474	1.65E+06	255	1.00E+00
Sobel	36549	191.1735	2.5023	1.06E−04	186.4746	1.63E+06	255	1.00E+00
Roberts	36549	191.1766	2.5021	8.28E−05	186.4795	2.09E+06	255	1.00E+00

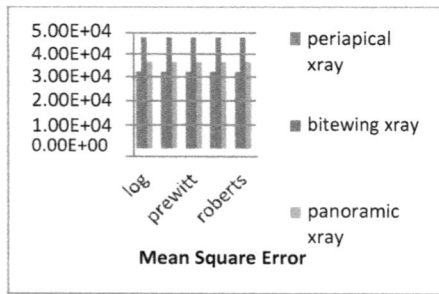

Fig. 20. MSE for three types of dental images   **Fig. 21.** RMSE for three types of dental images

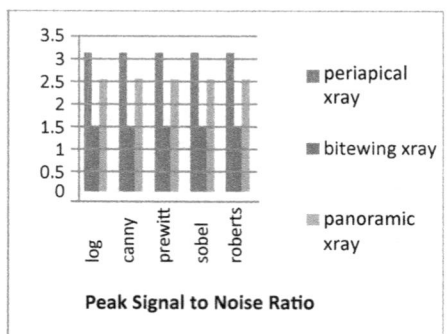
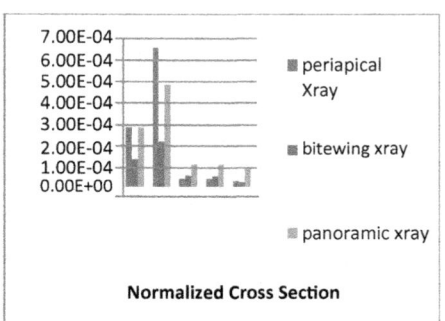

Fig. 22. PSNR for three types of dental images   **Fig. 23.** NCS for three types of dental images

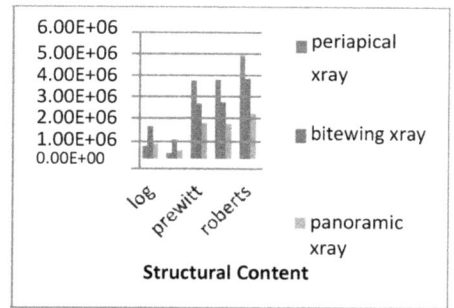

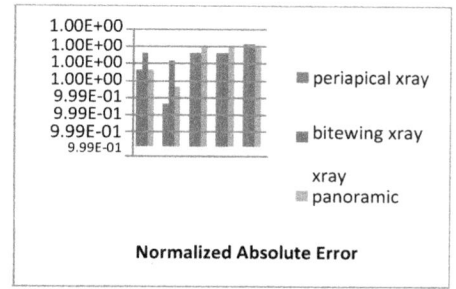

Fig. 24. SC for three types of dental images

Fig. 25. NAE for three types of dental images.

Table 4. Values of quality metrics clustering methods of periapical x-ray dental image.

Periapical x-ray dental image								
Clustering	MSE	RMSE	PSNR	N cross section	AD	SC	MD	NAE
K-means	1.7946E +04	133.9640	5.591	3.50E−03	124.5126	8.14E +04	254.3009	9.97E −01
Fuzzy c means	5.3398E +03	73.0738	10.8556	8.21E−01	42.7294	1.26E +00	180	2.54E −01

Table 5. Values of quality metrics clustering methods of bitewing x-ray dental image

Bitewing x-ray dental image								
Clustering	MSE	RMSE	PSNR	N cross section	AD	SC	MD	NAE
K-means	2.4246E +04	155.7106	4.2844	3.50E−03	143.9979	8.1554E +04	254.0798	9.97E −01
Fuzzy c means	9.219E +03	95.5089	8.5299	7.06E−01	68.788	1.65E +00	213	3.26E −01

Table 6. Values of quality metrics clustering methods of panoramic x-ray dental image.

Panoramic x-ray dental image								
Clustering	MSE	RMSE	PSNR	N cross section	AD	SC	MD	NAE
K-means	2.1071E +04	145.1571	4.894	3.60E−03	132.0545	7.5687E +04	254.1	9.96E −01
Fuzzy c means	1.29E+04	113.5899	7.024	6.85E−01	73.4976	1.34E +00	189	5.36E −01

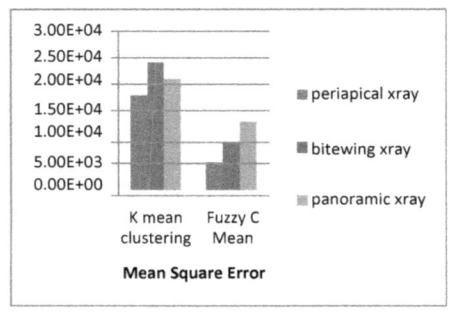

Fig. 26. MSE for different types of dental images.

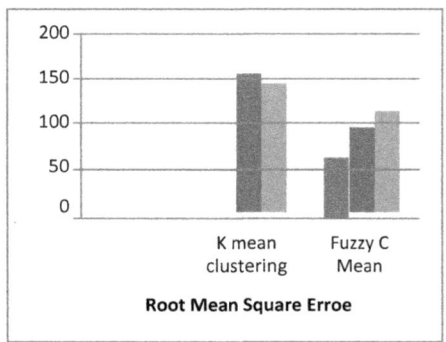

Fig. 27. RMSE for different type of dental images.

Table 7. Values of quality metrics for thresholding methods of periapical x-ray dental image.

Periapical x-ray dental image								
Thresholding	MSE	RMSE	PSNR	N cross section	AD	SC	MD	NAE
Ostu thresholding	1.45E +04	120.5412	6.5081	4.15E−05	111.629	2.95E +06	255	1.00E +00
Adaptive thresholding	2.86E +04	150.6288	4.4458	4.70E−03	170.87	4.76E +04	255	9.97E −01

Table 8. Values of quality metrics for thresholding methods of bitewing x-ray dental image.

Bitewing x-ray dental image								
Clustering	MSE	RMSE	PSNR	N cross section	AD	SC	MD	NAE
Ostu thresholding	4.67E +04	216.008	1.4414	2.40E−03	210.4859	8.32E +09	254.46	9.98E −01
Adaptive thresholding	1.21E +04	110.567	7.529	7.50E−03	117.67	1.80E +04	254	9.99E −01

Table 9. Values of quality metrics for thresholding methods of panoramic x-ray dental image.

Panoramic x-ray dental images								
Thresholding techniques	MSE	RMSE	PSNR	N cross section	AD	SC	MD	NAE
Ostu thresholding	36324	190.58	2.529	3.20E−03	185.96	6.91E +08	254	0.9972
Adaptive thresholding	18109	134.56	5.55	5.40E−03	120.68	2.76E +04	254	0.9945

Figure 20 shows the mean square error graph comparing the three types of dental images. Figure 21 shows the Root Mean Square Error graph for three types of dental images. Figure 22 shows the Peak Signal to Noise ratio graph for comparing three types of dental images. Figure 23 shows the Normalized Cross Section graph for three types of dental images. Figure 24 shows the Structural Content graph for three types of dental images. Figure 25 shows the Normalized Absolute Error graph for three types of dental images.

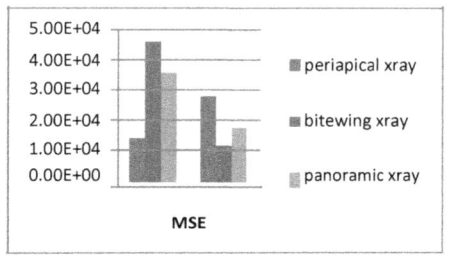

Fig. 28. MSE for different types of dental x-ray image.

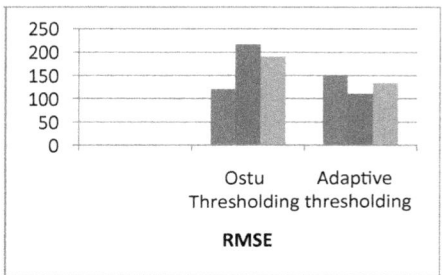

Fig. 29. RMSE for different types of dental x-ray image.

Table 10. Values of quality metrics for deformable methods of periapical x-ray dental image.

Peripical xray dental image								
Deformable model	Mean sq. error	RMSE	PSNR	N cross section	A.D	SC	MD	NAE
Level set	6.78E+04	203.56	5.345	6.57E−01	192.4	8.09E+04	254.6	0.9998
Active contour	5.35E+04	213.43	5.674	4.52E−01	188.3	9.88E+04	255	0.9999

Table 11. Values of quality metrics for deformable methods of bitewing x-ray dental image.

Bitewing xray dental image								
Deformable model	Mean sq. error	RMSE	PSNR	N cross section	A.D	SC	MD	NAE
Level set	7.00E+04	210.56	6.478	5.63E−01	195.6	9.99E+04	255	0.9998
Active contour	5.79E+04	215.43	5.848	5.42E−01	190.3	1.00E+05	255	0.9999

The values of various edge detection techniques from Tables 1, 2 and 3 clearly state that Canny Edge Detection is one of the most suitable methods of segmentation of periapical, bitewing and panoramic x-ray dental images. The results are also plotted in

Table 12. Values of quality metrics for deformable methods of panoramic x-ray dental image.

Panoramic x-ray dental image

Deformable model	Mean sq. error	RMSE	PSNR	N cross section	A.D	SC	MD	NAE
Level set	6.21E+04	*178.45*	*7.825*	7.27E−01	*190.2*	*7.80E+04*	*255*	*0.9976*
Active contour	5.13E+03	200.45	6.113	6.29E−01	180.2	8.62E+04	255	0.9875

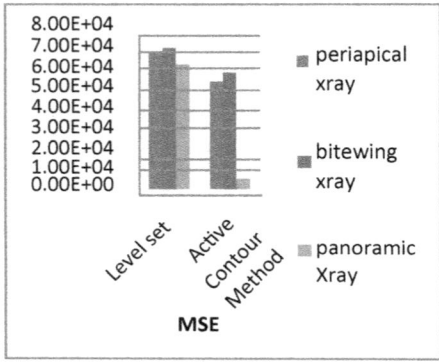

Fig. 30. MSE for type of dental images

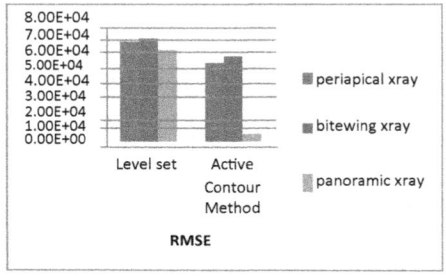

Fig. 31. RMSE for different types of dental x-ray images

the graph Figs. 20, 21, 22, 23, 24 and 25 which clearly distinguished the canny edge detector from the other techniques of the edge detectors. If we compare the values of Mean Square Error, Root Mean Square Error, Structural Content, Normalized Absolute Error (Figs. 20, 22, 24 and 25) the greater value of these metrics means poor quality images and smaller value of the metrics mean good quality images. Since canny edge detector has the least value so it is a good technique as compared to the other. Laplacian Edge Detector is another technique after canny edge detector which has small values as compared to the other techniques. Comparing the values of peak signal to noise ratio and Normalized Cross Section (Figs. 22 and 23), greater values of the metrics means good quality and smaller values of the metrics mean poor quality, hence Canny edge detector has the greatest value of peak signal to noise ratio and normalized cross section which clearly makes it one of the best techniques of edge detection for dental image segmentation. Comparing the three types of dental x-ray images we found that periapical x-ray dental images gives a better result as compared to bitewing and panoramic x-ray images.

Table 4 shows the value of quality metrics for clustering methods of periapical dental x-ray image. Table 5 shows the value of quality metrics for clustering methods of bitewing dental x-ray image. Table 6 shows the value of quality metrics for clustering methods of panoramic dental x-ray image. Figure 26 shows the mean square error graph for different methods of clustering technique comparing the three types of dental x-ray images. Figure 27 shows the root mean square error graph for different methods of clustering techniques comparing three different types of dental images.

The values of various methods of clustering techniques from Tables 4, 5 and 6 clearly state that Fuzzy c-mean clustering is one of the most suitable methods of segmentation of periapical, bitewing and panoramic x-ray dental images. The results are also plotted in the graphs shown in Figs. 26 and 27 which clearly distinguished the fuzzy c-mean clustering from the K mean clustering. Fuzzy c-mean has the least value of Mean Square Error, Root Mean Square Error, Structural Content, Normalized Absolute Error so it is a good technique as compared to the other. Fuzzy c-mean has the greater value of peak signal to noise ratio and normalized cross section which clearly makes it one of the best techniques of clustering for dental image segmentation. Comparing the three types of dental x-ray images we found that periapical x-ray dental images give the better result as compared to bitewing and panoramic x-ray images.

Table 7 shows the value of quality metrics for thresholding methods of periapical dental x-ray image. Table 8 shows the value of quality metrics for thresholding methods of bitewing dental x-ray image. Table 9 shows the value of quality metrics for thresholding methods of panoramic dental x-ray image. Figure 28 shows the mean square error graph for different methods of thresholding technique comparing the three types of dental x-ray images. Figure 29 shows the root mean square error graph for different methods of thresholding techniques comparing three different types of dental images.

The values of various thresholding techniques from Tables 7, 8, 9 clearly state that Adaptive thresholding is one of the most suitable methods of segmentation of panoramic, periapical and bitewing dental images. The results are also plotted in the graphs as shown in Figs. 28 and 29 which clearly distinguished the Adaptive Thresholding from the Ostu thresholding techniques. Adaptive Thresholding has the least value of Mean Square Error, Root Mean Square Error, Structural Content, Normalized Absolute Error so it is a good technique as compared to the other. Adaptive Thesholding has the greater value of peak signal to noise ratio and normalized cross section which clearly makes it one of the best techniques of Thresholding for dental image segmentation. On comparing all the techniques it is clear that bitewing xray dental images give more accurate result by adaptive threshold segmentation technique followed by panoramic xray dental image and lastly periapical xray dental image.

Table 10 shows the value of quality metrics for Deformable methods of periapical dental x-ray image. Table 11 shows the value of quality metrics for deformable methods of bitewing dental x-ray image. Table 12 shows the value of quality metrics for deformable methods of panoramic dental x-ray image. Figure 30 shows the mean square error graph for different methods of deformable technique comparing the three types of dental x-ray images. Figure 31 shows the root mean square error graph for different methods of deformable techniques comparing three different types of dental images.

The values of various Deformable model techniques from Table 10, 11 and 12 clearly state that Level set method is one of the most suitable methods of segmentation of dental images. Level set has the least value of Mean Square Error, Root Mean Square Error, Structural Content, Normalized Absolute Error so it is a good technique as compared to the other. Level Set method has the greatest value of peak signal to noise ratio and normalized cross section which clearly makes it one of the best techniques of Deformable Model for dental image segmentation. On comparing all the type of dental x-ray segmentation, the panoramic x-ray dental image has the highest accuracy as compared to bitewing and periapical x-ray dental images.

4 Conclusion and Future Work

We have compared methods of Image segmentation techniques on dental images on basis of various metrics such as mean square error, peak signal to noise ratio, structural content, average difference. After the image segmentation by various techniques, we have found out that canny edge detector is the best technique for edge detection in dental panoramic images. Adaptive Thresholding is more suitable than Ostu Thresholding and gives more accurate result in image segmentation. The suitable clustering technique for Dental image segmentation is Fuzzy C means. On comparing the Active contour and level set method, the level set method is more accurate for the image segmentation. We have taken three types of tooth images i.e. bitewing, periapical and panoramic x-ray dental images. After comparing variously suitable for methods of the segmentation techniques we found out that edge detection and clustering is most the suitable for periapical xray dental image, Thresholding technique is most suitable for bitewing and Deformable model is most suitable for panoramic x-ray dental image.

References

1. Subramanyam, R.B., Prasad, K.P., Anuradha, B.: Different image segmentation techniques for dental image extraction. J. Eng. Res. Appl. **4**(7), 173–177 (2014)
2. Despotovic, I., Goossens, B., Philips, W.: MRI segmentation of the human brain: challenges, methods, and applications. Comput. Math. Methods Med. **23** (2015). Article ID 450341
3. Senthil Kumaran, N., Rajesh, R.: Edge detection techniques for image segmentation - a survey of soft computing approaches. Int. J. Recent Trends Eng. **1**(2), 250–254 (2009)
4. Dey, V., Zhang, Y., Zhong, M.: A review of image segmentation techniques with remote sensing perspective. In: Proceedings of International Society for Photogrammetry and Remote Sensing Symposium (ISPRC 10), vol. XXXVIII(Part 7A), Austria, 5–7 July 2010
5. Ahirwar, A.: Study of techniques used for medical image segmentation and computation of statistical test for region classification of brain MRI. Inf. Technol. Comput. Sci. **5**, 44–53 (2013)
6. Oliveria, J.P.R., Proenca, H.: Caries detection in panoramic dental images. Comput. Vis. Med. Image Process. **19**, 175–190 (2010)
7. Grau, V., Mewes, A.U.J., Alcaniz, M., Kikinis, R., Warfield, S.K.: Improved watershed transform for medical image segmentation using prior information. IEEE Trans. Med. Imaging **23**(4), 447–458 (2004)
8. Greenspan, H., Ruf, A., Goldberger, J.: Constrained Gaussian mixture model framework for automatic segmentation of MR brain images. IEEE Trans. Med. Imaging **25**(9), 1233–1245 (2006)
9. Massod, S., Sharif, M., Massod, A., Yasim, M., Raza, M.: A survey on medical image segmentation. Curr. Med. Imaging Rev. **11**(1), 3–14 (2015)

10. Dass, R., Priyanka Devi, S.: Image segmentation techniques. Int. J. Electron. Commun. Technol. **3**(1) (2012)
11. Savant, S.: A review on Edge detection techniques for image segmentation. Int. J. Comput. Sci. Inf. Technol. **5**(4), 5898–5900 (2014)
12. Subramanyam, R.B., Prasad, K.P., Anuradha, B.: Different image segmentation technique for dental image extraction. Int. J. Eng. Res. Appl. **4**(7), 173–177 (2014). (Version 4)
13. Vincent, O.R., Florunso, O.: A descriptive algorithm for Sobel image edge segmentation. In: Proceedings of Informing Science & IT Education Conference (2009)
14. Vijayarani, S., Vinupriya, M.: Performance analysis of Canny and Sobel edge detection algorithms in image mining. Int. J. Innov. Res. Comput. Commun. Eng. **1**(8), 1760–1767 (2013)
15. Simon, S.G., Joseph, X.F.: A survey on dental x-ray image segmentation with various techniques. Int. J. Appl. Eng. Res. **10**(59) (2015)
16. Rad, A.E., Rahim, M.S.M., Norouzi, A.: Digital dental x-ray image segmentation and feature extraction. Telkommka **11**(6), 3109–3114 (2014)
17. Jain, A.K., Chen, H.: Matching of dental x-ray for human identification. Pattern Recogn. **37**, 1319–1532 (2004)
18. Adlakha, D., Adlakha, D., Tanwar, R.: Analytical comparison between Sobel and Prewitt detection techniques. Int. J. Sci. Eng. Res. **7**(1) (2016)
19. Gayathri, V., Menon, H.P.: Challenges in edge extraction of dental x-ray images using image processing algorithms - a review. Int. J. Comput. Sci. Inf. Technol. **5**(4) (2014)
20. Yang, G., Fengchang, X.: Research and analysis of image edge detection algorithm based on MATLAB. Procedia Eng. **15**, 1313–1318 (2011)
21. Tirodkar, A.A.: A multi-stage algorithm for enhanced xray image segmentation. Int. J. Eng. Sci. Res. **3**(9), 7056–7065 (2011)
22. Annangi, P., Thiruvenkadam, S., Raja, A., Xu, H., Sun, X.W., Mao, L.: A region based active contour method for x-ray lung segmentation using prior shape and low level features. In: Proceedings of the International Symposium on Biomedical Imaging, pp. 892–895 (2010)
23. Zhou, J., Abdel-Mottaleb, M.: A content-based system for human identification based on bitewing dental x-ray Images. Pattern Recogn. **38**, 2132–2142 (2005)
24. Tripathi, A.K., Mukhopadhyay, S.: A probabilistic approach for detection and removal of rain from videos. IETE Tech. Rev. **57**(1), 82–91 (2011)
25. Airouche, M., Bentabet, L., Zelmat, M.: Image segmentation using active contour model and level set method applied to detect oil spills. In: Proceedings of World Congress on Engineering, vol. I (2009)
26. Nomir, O., Abdel-Mottaleb, M.: A system for human identification from x-ray dental radiographs. Pattern Recogn. **38**, 1295–1305 (2005)
27. Malladi, R., Sethian, J.A., Vemuri, B.: Shape modeling with front propagation: a level set approach. IEEE Trans. Pattern Anal. Mach. Intell. **17**(2), 158–175 (1995)
28. Kun, W., Li, G.: Research of active contour model in aerial image. In: International Conference on Medical Physics and Biomedical Engineering, pp. 542–547 (2012)
29. Deng, J., Tsui, H.T.: A fast level set method for segmentation of low contrast noisy biomedical images. Pattern Recogn. Lett. **23**(1–3), 161–169 (2002)
30. Nilsson, B., Heyden, A.: A fast algorithm for level set-like active contours. Pattern Recogn. Lett. **24**(9–10), 1331–1337 (2003)
31. Jeon, M., Alexandar, M., Pedrycz, W., Pizzi, N.: Unsupervised hierarchical image segmentation with level set and additive operator splitting. Pattern Recogn. Lett. **26**(10), 1461–1469 (2005)

32. Qu, Y., Wong, T.T., Heng, P.A.: Image segmentation using the level set method. In: Qu, Y., Wong, T.T., Heng, P.A. (eds.) Deformable Models, Theory and Biomaterial Applications, pp. 95–122. Springer, New York (2007). https://doi.org/10.1007/978-0-387-68343-0_4
33. Clausi, D.A.: K-means Iterative Fisher (KIF) unsupervised clustering algorithm applied to image texture segmentation. Pattern Recogn. **35**(9), 1959–1972 (2002)
34. Lloyd, S.P.: Least squares quantization in PCM. IEEE Trans. Inf. Theory **28**(2), 129–137 (1982)
35. Yoon, O.K., Kwak, D.M., Kim, D.W., Park, K.H.: MR brain image segmentation using fuzzy clustering. In: IEEE International Fuzzy Systems Conference Proceedings, vol. 2, pp. 853–857 (1999)
36. Aggarwal, S., Kaur, G.: Improving the efficiency of weighted page content rank algorithm using clustering method. Int. J. Comput. Sci. Commun. Netw. **3**(4), 231–239 (2013)
37. Avcıbas, I., Sankur, B., Sayood, K.: Statistical evaluation of image quality measures. J. Electron. Imaging **11**(2), 206–223 (2002)
38. Nisha, S.K.: Image quality assessment techniques. Int. J. Adv. Res. Comput. Sci. Softw. Eng. **3**(7) (2013)
39. Algazi, V.R., Avadhanam, N., Estes, R.R.: Quality measurement and use of pre-processing in image compression. Sig. Process. **70**(3), 215–229 (1998)
40. Wang, Z., Bovik, A.C., Sheik, H.R., Simoncelli, E.P.: Image quality assessment: from error visibility to structural similarity. IEEE Trans. Image Process. **13**(4), 600–612 (2004)
41. Wang, Z., Bovik, A.: A universal image quality index. IEEE Sig. Process. Lett. **9**(3), 81–84 (2002)
42. Kumar, R., Rattan, M.: Analysis of various quality metrics for medical image processing. Int. J. Adv. Res. Comput. Sci. Softw. Eng. **2**(11) (2012)

Inferring Trust from Message Features Using Linear Regression and Support Vector Machines

Shifaa Basharat and Manzoor Ahmad[✉]

University of Kashmir, Hazratbal, Srinagar, India
fazilishifaa@gmail.com,
manzoor@kashmiruniversity.ac.in

Abstract. With the proliferation of social media like Facebook and Twitter more and more people have started depending on it for all sorts of news. Social media (such as Facebook, twitter), topical forums, wikis etc. enable a community of end users to interact or cooperate towards a common goal. However, the effectiveness of disseminating information through social media lacks in quality as a result of less fact checking, low barriers to entry, more biases, and several rumors thereby making social media not only the source of genuine news but also fake news. Thus, in this paper we are dealing with the problem of classifying information on the basis of its reliability using freely available user generated data like tweets on twitter using machine learning algorithms. A variety of machine learning algorithms like linear regression, logistic regression, Naïve Bayes etc. are used to determine the trust carried by the tweets. In addition to basic machine learning algorithms we present a learning model that is based on the combination of naïve Bayes and logistic regression and also naïve Bayes and linear regression. Also a technique has been discussed to determine a threshold parameter which is used for the classification of data in case of SMO and linear regression algorithm in order to increase their accuracy which is achieved for modified linear regression algorithm in most of the cases. The modified linear regression algorithm when used in combination with naïve Bayes achieves a better accuracy than all the other algorithms used in this paper. Also hybrid classification works better than the individual algorithms.

Keywords: NB - naive Bayes · ML - machine learning
MLAs - machine learning algorithms · SMO - sequential minimal optimization

1 Introduction

With the evolution of online social networking and micro-blogging mediums, two major changes have occurred in the landscape of the Internet usage - firstly, the Internet is replacing traditional media like television and print media as a source for obtaining news and information about current events [15]; secondly, the Internet has provided a platform for common people to share information and express their opinions [7]. Quick response time and fast dissemination of information has encouraged more and more users to use social media services like Facebook, twitter, YouTube etc. to obtain news.

© Springer Nature Singapore Pte Ltd. 2018
P. Bhattacharyya et al. (Eds.): NGCT 2017, CCIS 828, pp. 577–598, 2018.
https://doi.org/10.1007/978-981-10-8660-1_44

This paper primarily focusses on twitter; Twitter—a microblogging service that enables users to post messages ("tweets") of up to 140 characters—supports a variety of communicative practices; participants use Twitter to converse with individuals, groups, and the public at large, so when conversations emerge, they are often experienced by broader audiences than just the interlocutors. Twitter facilitates real-time propagation of information to a large group of users. This makes it an ideal environment for the dissemination of breaking-news directly from the news source and/or geographical location of events [7]. However, the news that is propagated cannot always be true. Fake news and rumors are part of genuine news. Indeed, in [17] we observed that immediately after the 2010 earthquake in Chile, when information from official sources was scarce, several rumors posted and re-posted on Twitter contributed to increase the sense of chaos and insecurity in the local population [7]. However, this drawback doesn't make social media any less important or only the source of fake news run by trolls and pranksters because had that been the case, we would have given up on it long ago. The main aim of this paper is to determine the reliability of information spread through twitter. Reliability is defined as the quality of being believed or trusted i.e. whether a message propagated through a tweet can be relied upon or not. The main objective here is to find a way to determine the reliability of a tweet automatically using tweet metadata which includes various user based and message/tweet based features.

2   Literature Review

Though Twitter acts as a real-time news source with people acting as sensors and sending event updates from all over the world, rumors spread via Twitter have been noted to cause considerable damage [10]. Gupta et al. [8] in her paper has quoted some major events of misinformation in social media which include the 2010 earthquake in Chile [17], the Hurricane Sandy in 2012 [9] and the Boston Marathon blasts in 2013 [9]. From a survey on issues and challenges among Malaysian social media users, apart from authenticity,credibility is a major issue either in terms of message/content and source [13]. According to Hilligoss and Rieh [12], the challenge that most people face is to judge which information is more credible. Increased popularity of microblogs in recent years brings about a need for better mechanisms to extract credible or otherwise useful information from noisy and large data [24]. Morris et al. [19] underlines the importance of analyzing a tweet given the fact that the quality of news posted on Twitter is not uniform which may include spam [20, 23, 25], surreptitious advertising [5, 6], false rumors [3, 5, 6, 17], and imposter accounts [22]. However, Kang [24] underlines the complexity in analyzing the reliability in online environments compared to traditional media due to "the multiplicity of sources embedded in the numerous layers of online dissemination of content" [26]. In the context of social media trust, Castillo et al. [2] defines it as the aspect of information credibility that can be assessed using only the information available in a social media platform. Saikaew and Noyunsan have discussed two different classes of credibility computation in social media namely Web-page-independent and Webpage-dependent where Web-page-independent uses messages in social media for computing reliability by comparing the messages with trusted news sources which if similar then the reliability score of the message is high and web-page dependent approaches use features of each social media for computing reliability such as like, comment, and re-tweet. In this paper we have focused on web page dependent approaches.

3 Different Classification Approaches Used

3.1 Naïve Bayes

Naive Bayes, a generative classifier learns a model of joint probability, p(x, y) of the inputs x and the label y, and make their predictions by using Bayes rule to calculate p (y|x), and then picking the most likely label y [14].This means that given a feature vector table, the algorithm computes the posterior probability that the document belongs to different classes and assigns it to the class with the highest posterior probability, assuming that the features are conditionally independent, given the class [28]. In this paper we are working on a binary classification problem with continuous data, were the information to be processed can either be reliable or unreliable. When dealing with continuous data, a typical assumption is that the continuous values associated with each class are distributed according to a Gaussian distribution [21]. In the Gaussian distribution, for every continuous attribute in the training data, we compute the mean and variance of the attribute in each class. Then probability density of any value given a class can be calculated by the following equation [1]

$$p(x = v|c) = \frac{1}{\sqrt{2\pi\sigma_c^2}} e^{\frac{-(v-\mu_c)^2}{2\sigma_c^2}}$$

(1)

where,

x is a continuous attribute
v is any value of x associated with class c
σ_c^2 is the variance of the values in x associated with class c
μ_c the mean of the values in x associated with class c.

Once the probability densities are obtained, we calculate the prior probability of each class using the following formula:

$$Prior_{class} = \frac{Number\ of\ observations\ of\ a\ particular\ class}{Total\ number\ of\ observations}$$

(2)

Using the prior probabilities and probability densities for each attribute in each class, we determine the posterior probability as shown:

$$posterior_{class} = Prior_{class} * pd_1 * pd_2 * \cdots * pd_n$$

(3)

After the posterior probabilities for different classes are obtained, we place the observation in a class with higher probability.

3.2   Batch Gradient Descent Linear Regression

Linear regression, one of the most common statistical techniques is used to determine the value of the dependent variable from a set of independent variables. If Y denotes the dependent variable and xi denotes the ith independent variable then the following equation represents the linear regression model [18]:

$$Y' = b_0 + b_1x_1 + b_2x_2 + b_3x_3 + \ldots + b_nx_n \tag{4}$$

where,

Y' is the expected or predicted value of Y
b_0 is the intercept
b_i is known as the slope or the estimated regression coefficient
x_i represents the independent variable.

For a total of k observations with n independent variables, the regression weights b1 through bn are calculated in a way that minimizes the sum of squared deviations as shown below [18]:

$$\sum_{i=1}^{n} (Y_i - Y'_i)^2 \tag{5}$$

Although linear regression is used in situations where the dependent variable is continuous, we are using it for a dichotomous classification problem in the following manner:

Case 1 (linear regression):

$$Y'_i \begin{cases} Reliable & if\ Y'_i \geq 0 \\ Unreliable & if\ Y_i < 0 \end{cases} \tag{6}$$

Case 2 (modified linear regression):
The following steps are to be followed for modified linear regression implementation (as shown in Fig. 1).

- Divide the training set into two parts depending upon the class (reliable/unreliable) to which they belong.
- Predict the value of the dependent variable for all the observations in each class.
- Calculate the threshold (i.e. the maximum and minimum value for the dependent variable in each class) for both the classes.

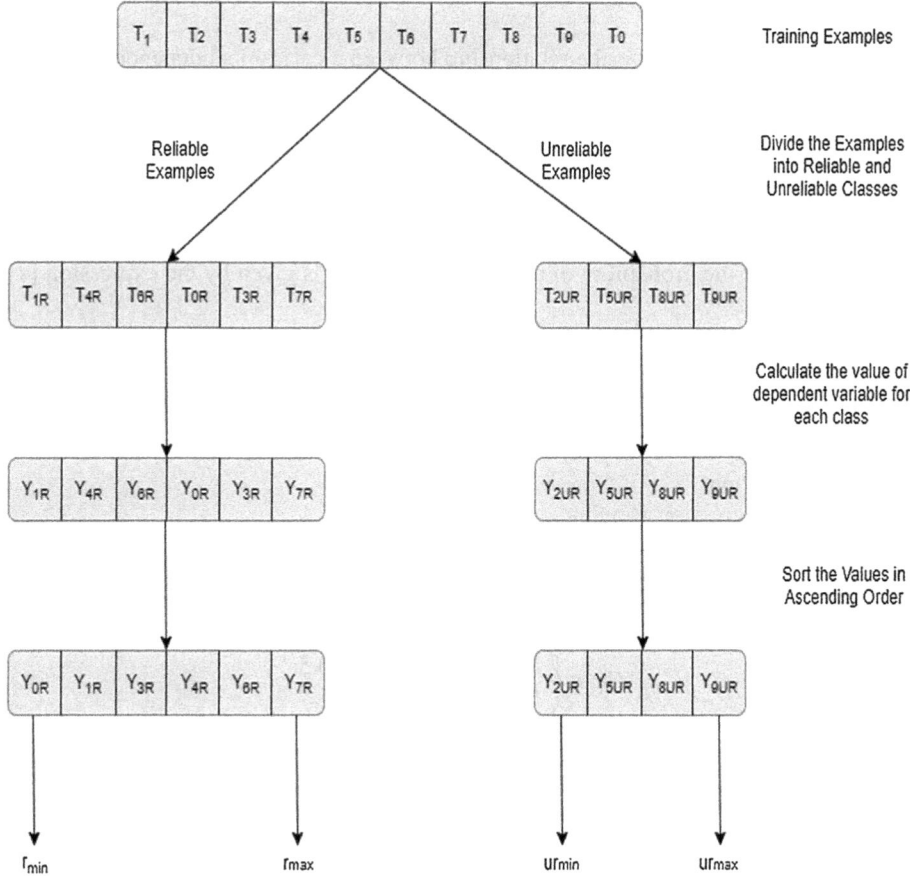

Fig. 1. Calculating threshold value for classification

Now, the dependent variable can be used to determine the class in the following way:

$$Y_i' \begin{cases} Reliable & if\ r_{\min} \leq Y_i' \leq r_{\max} \\ Unreliable & if\ ur_{\min} \leq Y_i' \leq ur_{\max} \end{cases} \tag{7}$$

where,

$r_{\min}$ is the minimum value of the predicted variable in the reliable class
$r_{\max}$ is the maximum value of the predicted variable in the reliable class
$ur_{\min}$ is the minimum value of the predicted variable in the unreliable class
$ur_{\max}$ is the maximum value of the predicted variable in the unreliable class.

3.3 Logistic Regression

Logistic regression measures the relationship between a categorical dependent variable and one or more independent variables (not necessarily continuous), by using probability scores as the predicted values of the dependent variable [16]. It is a special case of linear regression where the dependent variable unlike its generalized counterpart is either binomial (dichotomous) or multinomial (dependent variable can take more than two values). However, in this paper we are focusing only on two aspects of the information namely reliable/unreliable which means we will be using binary logistic regression where the probability of a dependent variable is given by the expression [4]:

$$P = \frac{1}{1 + e^{-(\beta_0 + \sum \beta_i x_i)}} \tag{8}$$

where,

β_0 refers to slope.
β_i refers to regression weights.
x_i represents the independent variable.
e represents the base of a natural algorithm whose value equals 2.71828.
P represents probability.

$$Class \begin{cases} Reliable & if\ P \geq 0.5 \\ Unreliable & if\ P < 0.5 \end{cases} \tag{9}$$

3.4 SVM-SMO

SVM are a class of learning models used for classification problems. In this paper we are focusing on a dichotomous classification problem for which we will be using binary SVM, which discriminates between two classes with a hyperplane. Many different hyperplanes provide a distinction between two classes but SVM selects the one that maximizes the margin, margin being the sum of the shortest distance between the hyperplane and the data points on either side of the plane [29]. The hyperplane is defined by an intercept b and normal vector w which is perpendicular to the hyperplane. Thus, the classification function for the classifier is given by:

$$F(\vec{x}) = sign(\vec{w}^T \vec{x} + b) \tag{10}$$

$$class \begin{cases} Reliable & if\ F(\vec{x}) \geq 0 \\ Unreliable & if\ F(\vec{x}) < 0 \end{cases} \tag{11}$$

The standard formulation of SVM as a maximization problem is [27]:

$$maxmize: \quad Q(a) = \sum_i a_i - \frac{1}{2} \sum_i \sum_j \alpha_i \alpha_j y_i y_j x_i x_j \tag{12}$$

$$subject \ to: \quad \sum_i \alpha_i y_i = 0 \ And \quad \alpha > 0$$

where,

y_i is the class label
x_i is the training data
α_i is the Lagrange multiplier.

The solution is then of the form [27]:

$$\overrightarrow{w} = \sum \alpha_i y_i \overrightarrow{x_i} \tag{13}$$

$$b = y_k - \overrightarrow{w}^T \overrightarrow{x_k} \quad (for \ any \ \overrightarrow{x_k} \ such \ that \ \alpha_k \neq 0) \tag{14}$$

The classification function can then be written as:

$$F(\overrightarrow{x}) = sign(\sum \alpha_i y_i \overrightarrow{x}_i^T \overrightarrow{x} + b) \tag{15}$$

3.5   SMO Modified

Once the value of the dependent variable is calculated for all instances of the test data using the SMO algorithm [11], rather than using it directly for classification, we calculate the upper and lower distinction parameter for both the positive as well as negative instances of the training data which can later be used for comparison with the dependent variable value already calculated for the test data. The procedure for calculating the distinction parameter is shown in Fig. 1.

The distinction parameters obtained are used to determine the class for test data examples in the following manner:

$$Y_i' \begin{cases} Reliable & if \ r_{min} \leq Y_i' \leq r_{max} \\ Unreliable & if \ ur_{min} \leq Y_i' \leq ur_{max} \end{cases} \tag{16}$$

3.6   Linear Discriminant Analysis (LDA)

LDA, a technique proposed by R. consists of finding the projection hyperplane that minimizes the interclass variance and maximizes the distance between the projected means of classes [30]. One major advantage of LDA is that the solution can be obtained by solving a generalized eigenvalue system which allows for fast and massive processing of data samples [30]. Since the problem considered in this paper is based on the classification of tweets as reliable or unreliable, it can be achieved by calculating the discriminant function value for both the reliable and unreliable classes, using the following equations:

$$f_{reliable} = \mu_{reliable} \bullet C^{-1} \bullet x_k^T - \frac{1}{2}\mu_{reliable} \bullet C^{-1} \bullet \mu_{reliable}^T + \ln(P_{reliable}) \qquad (17)$$

$$f_{unreliable} = \mu_{unreliable} \bullet C^{-1} \bullet x_k^T - \frac{1}{2}\mu_{unreliable} \bullet C^{-1} \bullet \mu_{unreliable}^T + \ln(P_{unreliable}) \qquad (18)$$

where,

μ is lxn column matrix representing the mean of the features of a particular class
c^{-1} is the inverse of covariance matrix of a particular class
x_k is the kth observation in the training data
P is the prior probability vector for a particular class.

Any particular data observation is placed in the class with greater value of the discriminant function.

3.7 Hybrid Approach

As mentioned in [1], no classifier can perform well in all situations, so it is better to switch to hybrid configuration where each classifier contributes to other classifier to achieve a high level of accuracy. In this paper we have used two hybrid configurations each with a chain length of 2.

NBlinear
This algorithm combines the features of naive Bayes and linear regression to increase the classification accuracy. Training examples that are wrongly classified by naïve Bayes are fed into linear regression and modified linear regression algorithm which can correctly classify them thereby resulting in the combined accuracy better than both the naive Bayes and linear regression.

NBlogistic
This algorithm combines the features of naive Bayes and logistic regression to increase the classification accuracy. Training examples that are wrongly classified by naïve Bayes are fed into logistic regression algorithm which can correctly classify them thereby resulting in the combined accuracy better than both the naive Bayes and logistic regression in all the cases.

4 Experiment

The architecture used in this paper has been shown in Fig. 2.

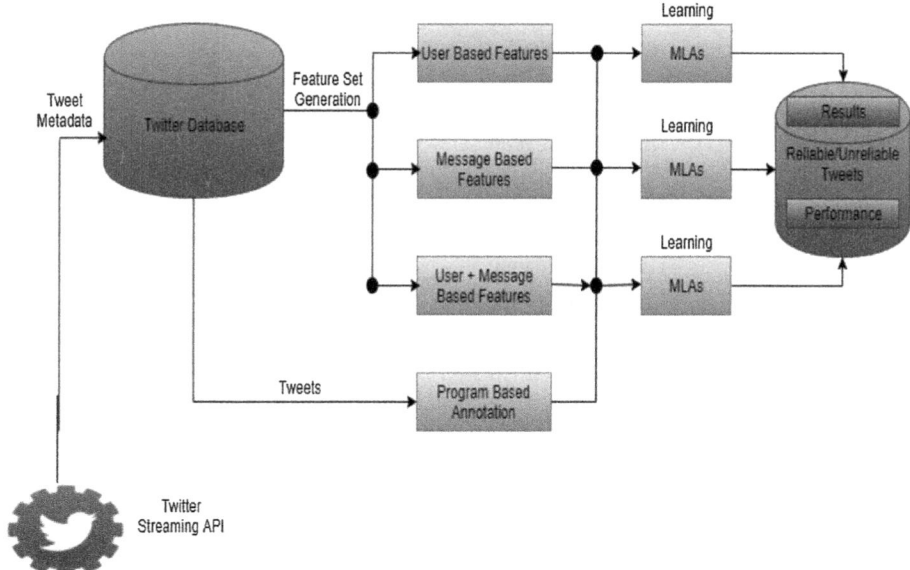

Fig. 2. Describes methodology used in this paper

4.1   Data

To evaluate the effectiveness of various MLAs in determining the reliability of information, we collected data from twitter by using twitters streaming API. Several constraints were placed on the selection of these instances from a huge twitter database. Apart from some random tweets, we also used tweets that were related to two main events that took place in 2016. The details of data used are given in Table 1. The tweets along with the metadata constitute a large number of attributes from which only 16 attributes have been used in this paper, the details of which are given in Table 2: Column 1 refers to the name of the attribute in the data set, column 2 gives the type of attribute and column 3 refers to the details of a particular attribute.

Table 1. Data description

Type of data	Number of tweets	Number of reliable tweets	Number of unreliable tweets
Paris attacks	1048	767	281
India vs WI	1395	978	417
Random tweets	853	490	363
Combined data123	3296	2235	1061

Table 2. Attributes used to determine reliability

Attribute name	Attribute type	Description
Friends_count	User based feature	Number of users this account is following
Listed_count	User based feature	The number of public lists that this user is a member of
Verified	User based feature	When true indicates the user has a verified account
Status_count	User based feature	The number of tweets issued by the User
Followers	User based feature	The number of followers this account has
Default_profile_image	User based feature	When true indicates that the user has used the default egg avatar instead of a profile image
Favorite_count	User based feature	Indicates how many times this tweet has been liked by twitter user
Registration age	User based feature	Time since the user is on twitter
Character_count	Message based feature	Number of characters in a tweet
Word_count	Message based feature	Number of words in a tweet
Special symbols	Message based feature	Number of special symbols (#, @, $, !, ?) in a tweet
Personal Pronoun Count	Message based feature	Number of personal pronouns used in the tweet
url count	Message based feature	Number of Urls in the tweet
Is a retweet?	Message based feature	Whether the tweet is a retweet or not
Swear word count	Message based feature	Number of swear words in a tweet
Sentiment score	Message based feature	Sentiment of a tweet

Training Data

To prepare training data we had the option of either using human based annotation or program based annotation for the tweets. In this paper we have used program based annotation were a java program annotates each tweet as reliable/unreliable based on features selected through literature review. Morris et al. [19] in their paper presented a collection of 26 features to some people and asked them to indicate whether they typically pay attention to each feature when reading a tweet. For each feature respondents were also asked to assess how a particular feature impacts credibility on a 5-point Likert scale. The features like default_user_image, many followers, verification seal, URL in description, many following were found to have high impact on credibility. Castillo et al. [2] specified that credible news/tweets can be indicated by the number of tweets of an author and the amount of retweets. Table 2 shows the features that were used for annotation. A score greater than 0 indicates a credible tweet (Table 3).

Table 3. Features used for annotation

Attribute name	Impact on credibility score
Satus_count	Status_count > 100 and Status_count < 1000, score++ Status_count > 1000 and Status_count < 10000, score+2 Status_count > 10000, score+3
Favorite_count	favorite_count > 0, score++
Verified?	Verified = 0, score− Verified = 1, score++
Default_profile_image?	Default_profile_image = 0, score++ Default_profile_image = 1, score−
Registration age	Registration age >= 5, score++ Registration age < 1, score−
Follower/friend	Follower/friend > 0 and follower/friend < 1, score− Follower/friend > 1 and follower/friend < 10, score++ Follower/friend > 10 and follower/friend < 100, score+2 Follower/friend > 100, score+3
Listed_count	Listed_count > 0 and listed_count < 100, score ++ Listed_count > 100, score+2
Retweet_count	Retweet_count >= 5, score++

4.2 Experimental Procedure

We implement the MLAs discussed in Sect. 2 of this paper on different parts of the data. All the tweets have been divided in a number of ways to see the effect of algorithms on unbalanced training and test data or balanced training and test data, considering only user based features or message based features or both and so on. The following cases have been taken into consideration (Table 4):

- Unbalanced training and test data (only user based features)
- Unbalanced training and test data (only message based features)

Table 4. Different cases of data decomposition

Type of data	Unbalanced training & test data		Balanced training & test data		Balanced training & unbalanced test data		Unbalanced training & balanced test data	
	Training data	Test data	Training data	Test Data	Training data	Test data	Training data	Test data
Paris attacks	383R 142UR	384R 139UR	141R 141UR	140R 140UR	181R 181UR	586R 100UR	627R 141UR	140R 140UR
India vs WI	489R 208UR	489R 209UR	208R 208UR	209R 209UR	208R 208UR	770R 209UR	769R 208UR	209R 209UR
Random data	299R 200UR	290R 163UR	200R 200UR	163R 163UR	200R 200UR	290R 163UR	299R 200UR	163R 163UR
Combined data123	1117R 530UR	1118R 531UR	530R 530UR	531R 531UR	730R 730UR	1505R 331UR	2004R 830UR	231R 231UR

- Unbalanced training and test data (user and message based features)
- Unbalanced training and balanced test data (only user based features)
- Unbalanced training and balanced test data (only message based features)
- Unbalanced training and balanced test data (user and message based features)
- Balanced training and test data (only user based features)
- Balanced training and test data (only message based features)
- Balanced training and test data (user and message based features).

4.3   Results

The various algorithms and data decomposition have been compared in terms of accuracy and results have been depicted using bar charts. A total of 12 cases arise for four different sets of data each of which is tested separately for user based, message based and a combination of user and message based features. In all the 12 cases the hybrid combinations perform better than single algorithms and out of the hybrid combinations it is the Nblinear(threshold) that outperforms the other hybrid configurations in 9 out of 12 cases as shown in the bar charts(Figs. 3, 4, 5, 6, 7, 8, 9, 10, 11, 12, 13 and 14). The output of the algorithms is also used to determine the different class of twitter features that are best suited to analyze the credibility of a tweet. The results which are depicted using line charts (Figs. 15, 16, 17 and 18) show that the user based features play an important part in ascertaining the credibility of a tweet rather than message based features. The results also show that different types of data decomposition be it unbalanced training and test data or balanced training and test data do not affect the accuracy of the algorithms.

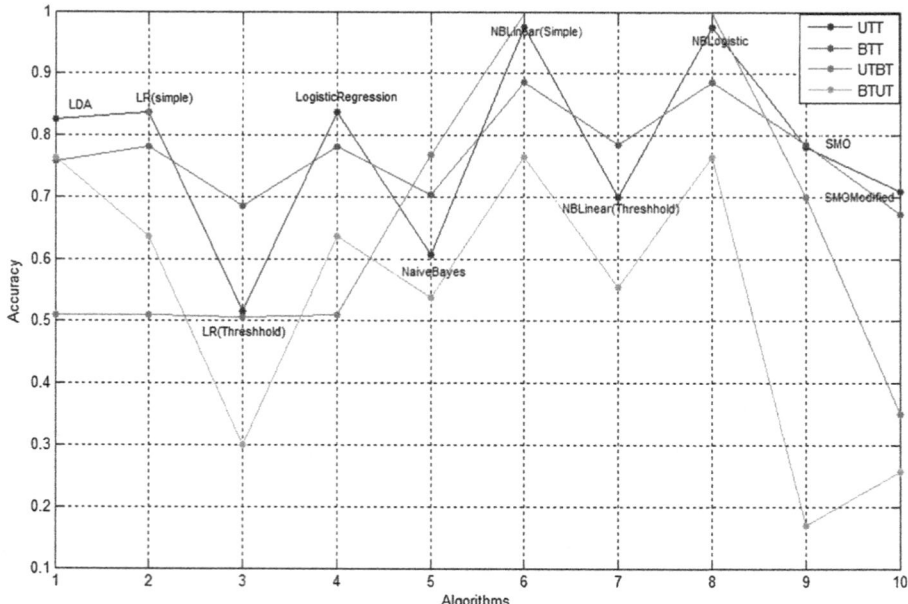

Fig. 3. Paris attacks data (User based features)

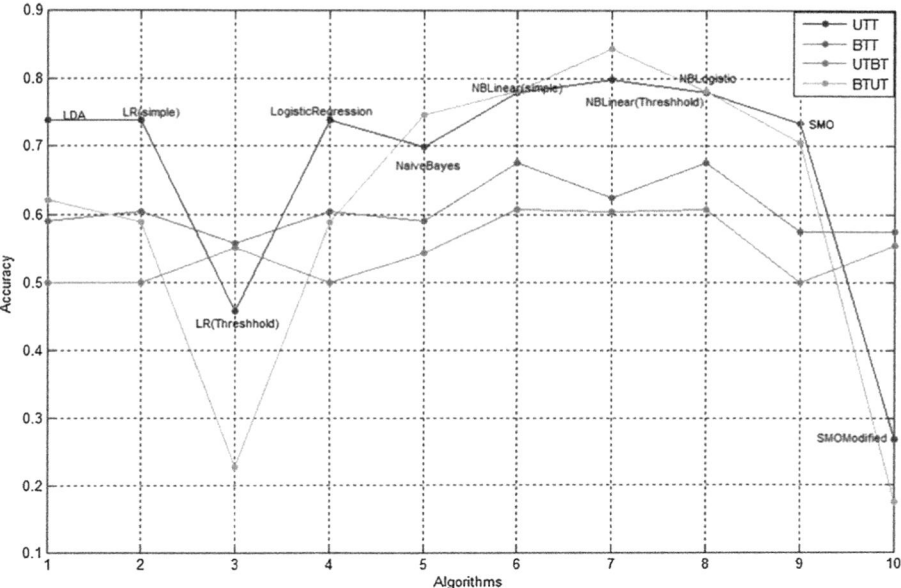

Fig. 4. Paris attacks data (Message based features)

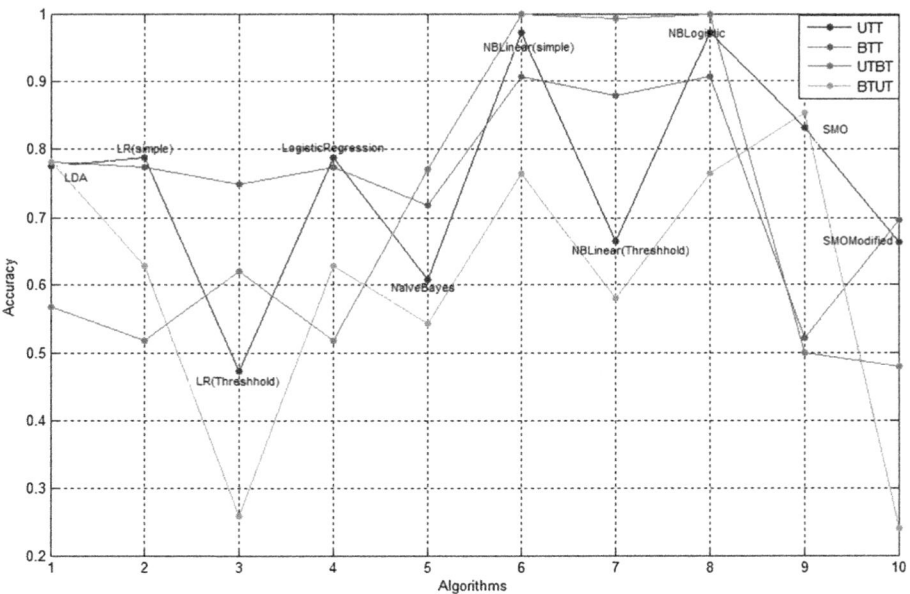

Fig. 5. Paris attacks data (User + Message based features)

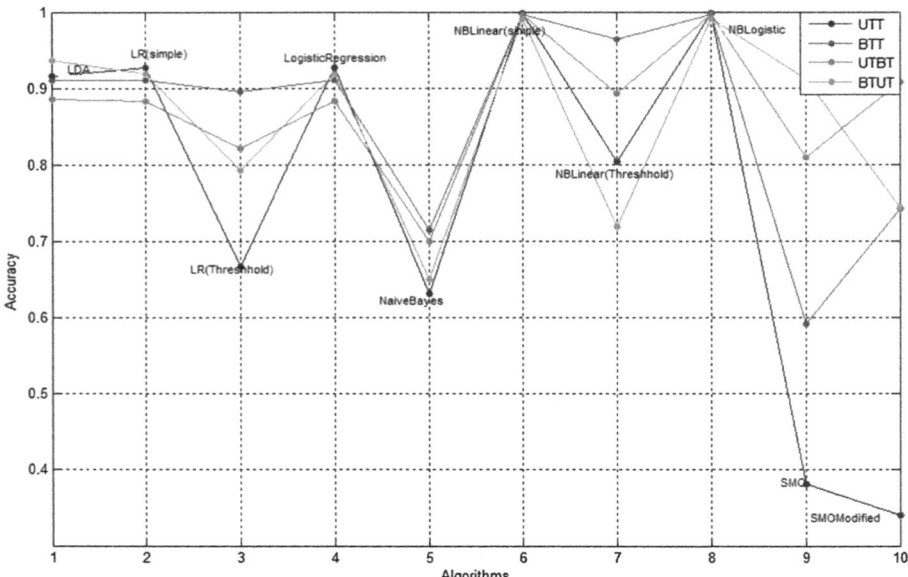

Fig. 6. Random data (User based features)

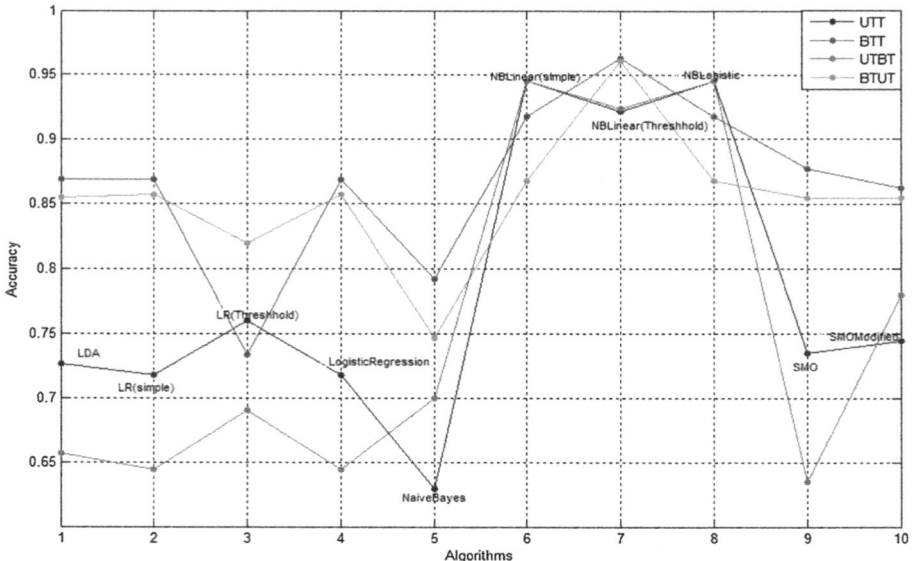

Fig. 7. Random data (Message based features)

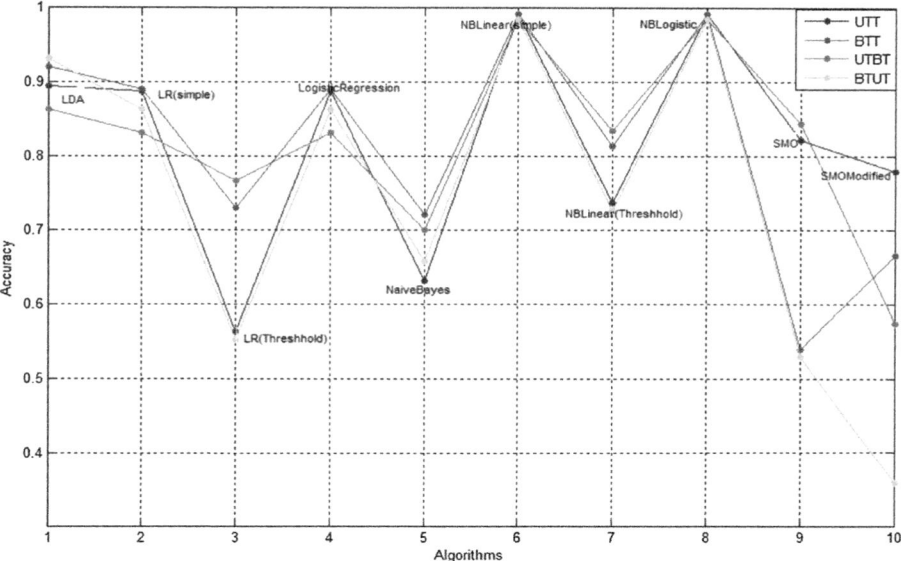

Fig. 8. Random data (User + Message based features)

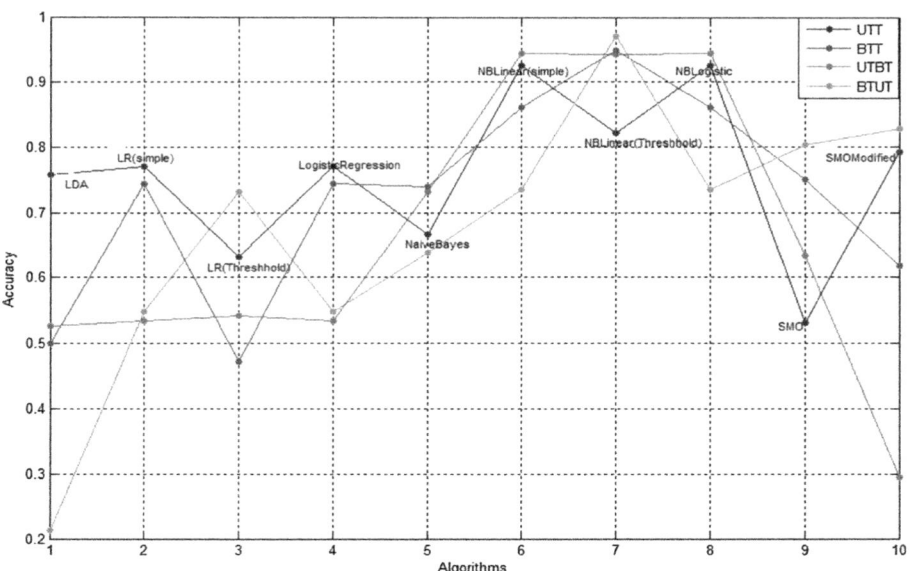

Fig. 9. Ind vs WI data (User based features)

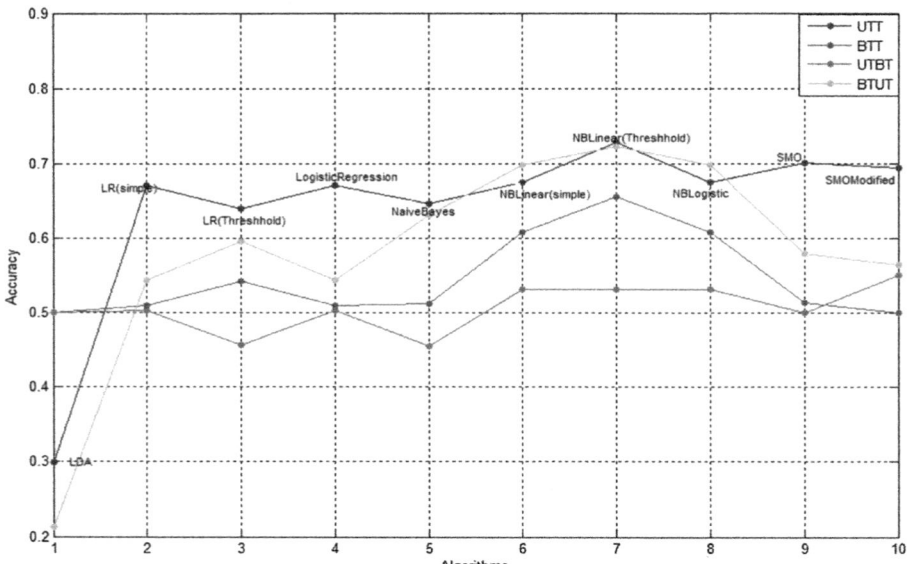

Fig. 10. India vs WI data (Message based features)

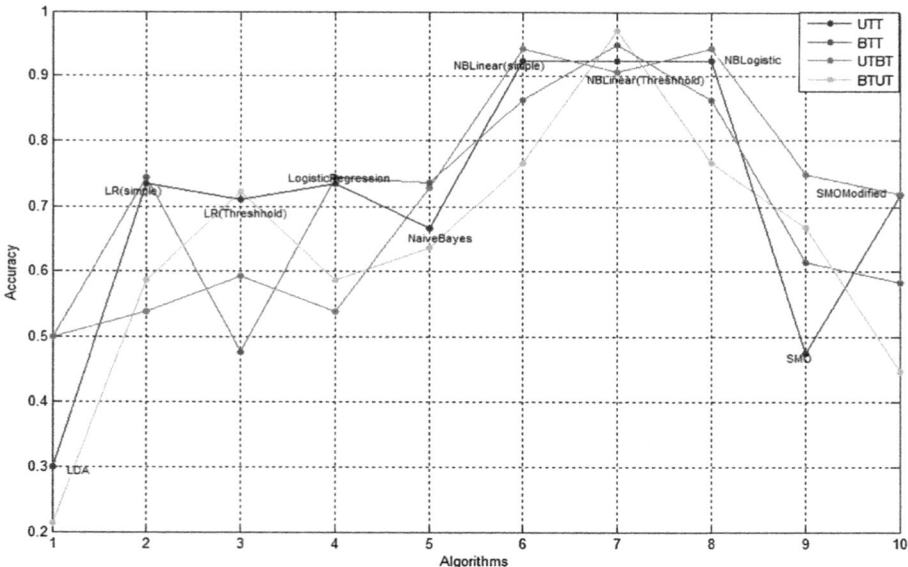

Fig. 11. India vs WI data (User + Message based features)

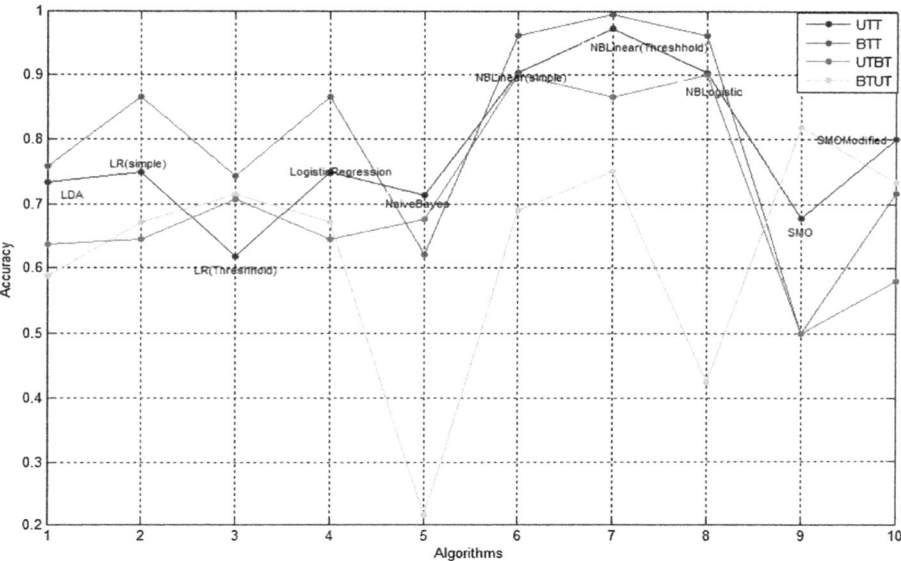

Fig. 12. Combined data123 (User based features)

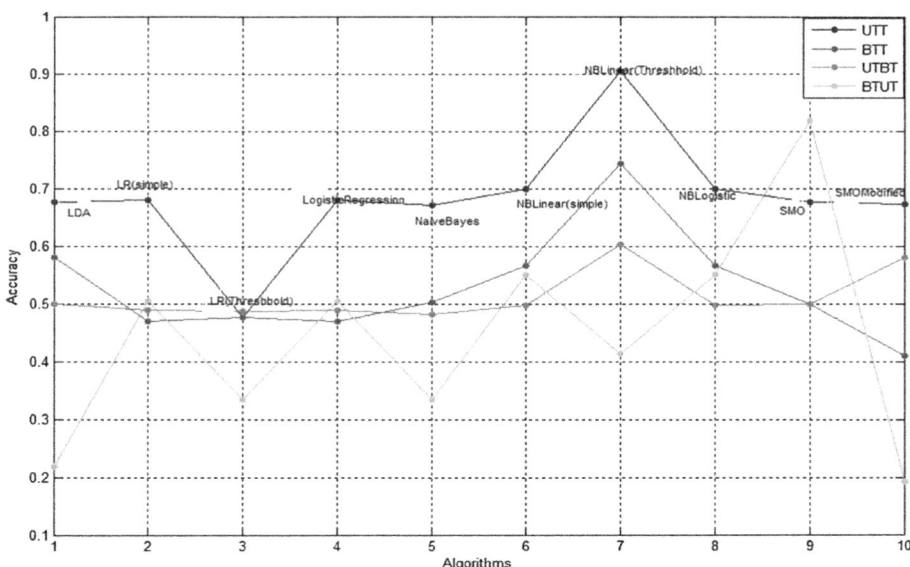

Fig. 13. Combined data123 (Message based features)

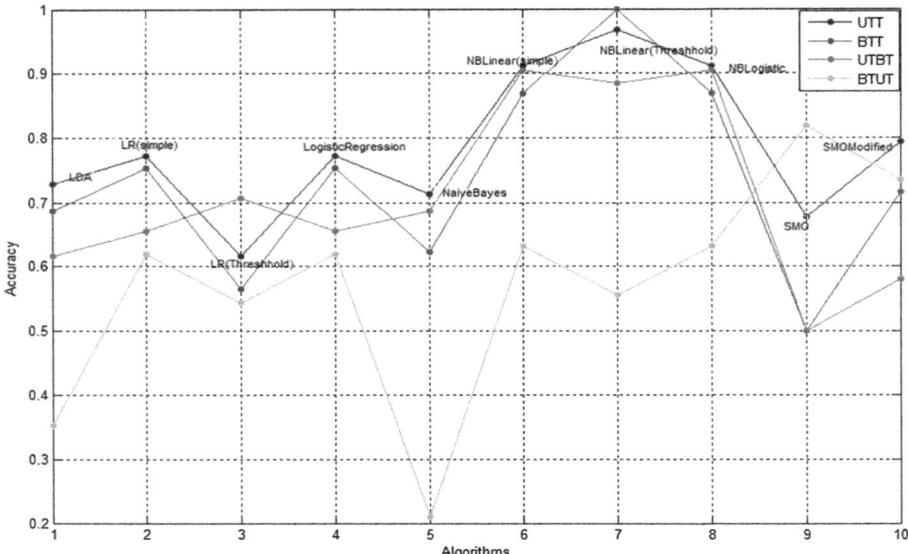

Fig. 14. Combined data123 (User + Message based features)

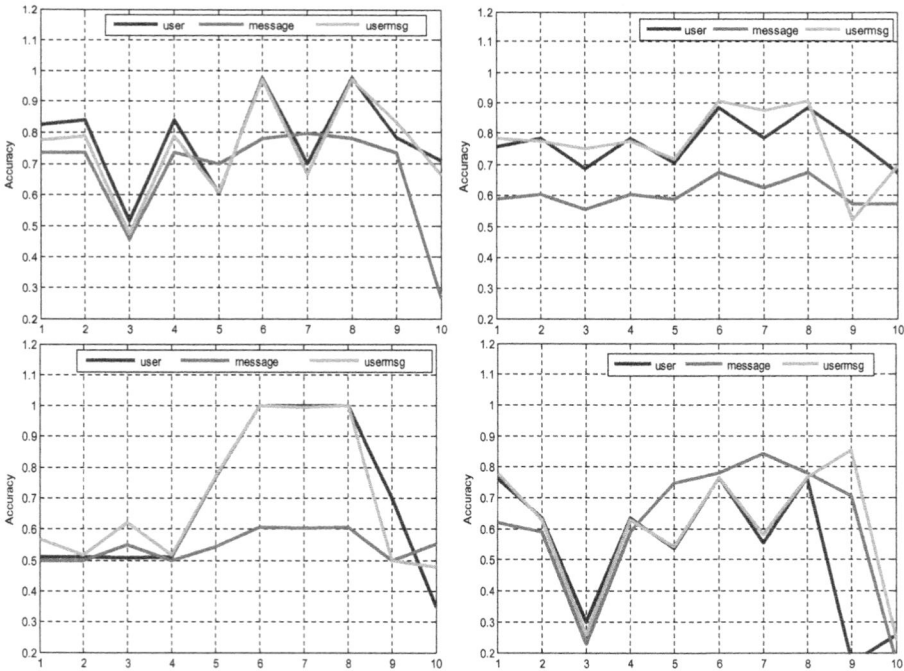

Fig. 15. Comparing algorithm output for Paris attacks data for different class of twitter features

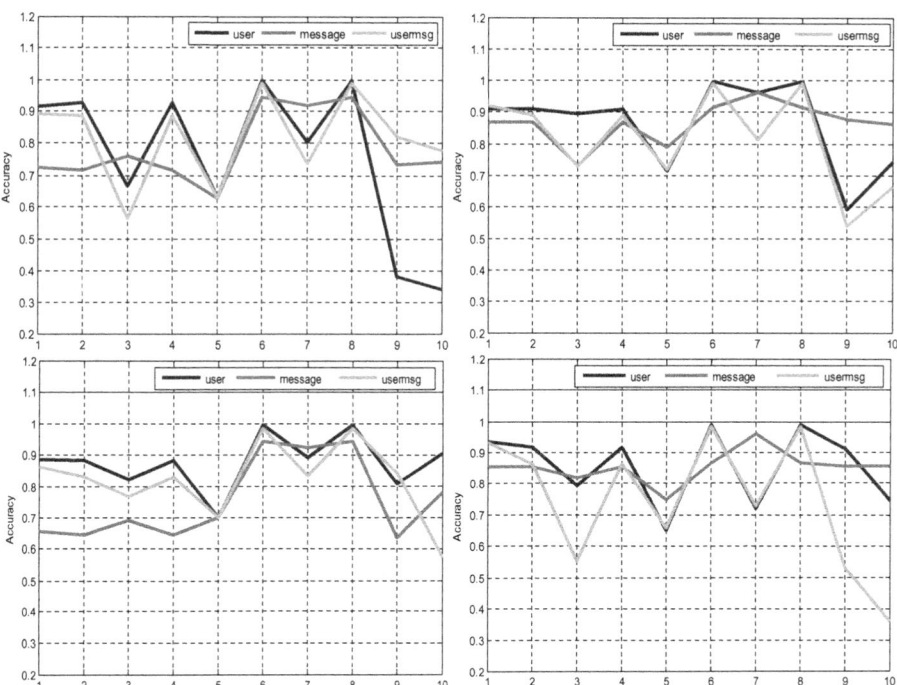

Fig. 16. Comparing algorithm output for Random data for different class of twitter features

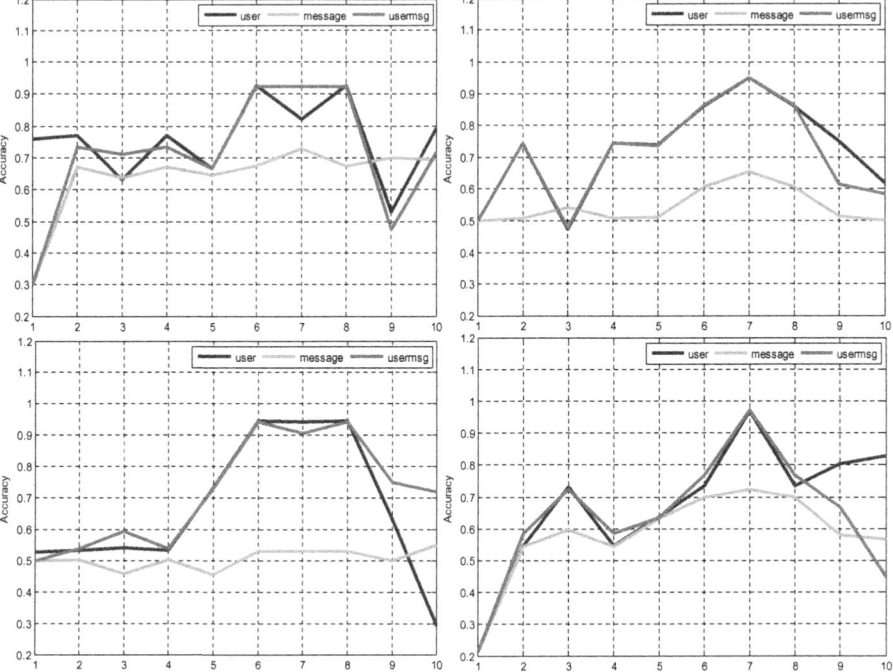

Fig. 17. Comparing algorithm output for Ind vs WI data for different class of twitter features

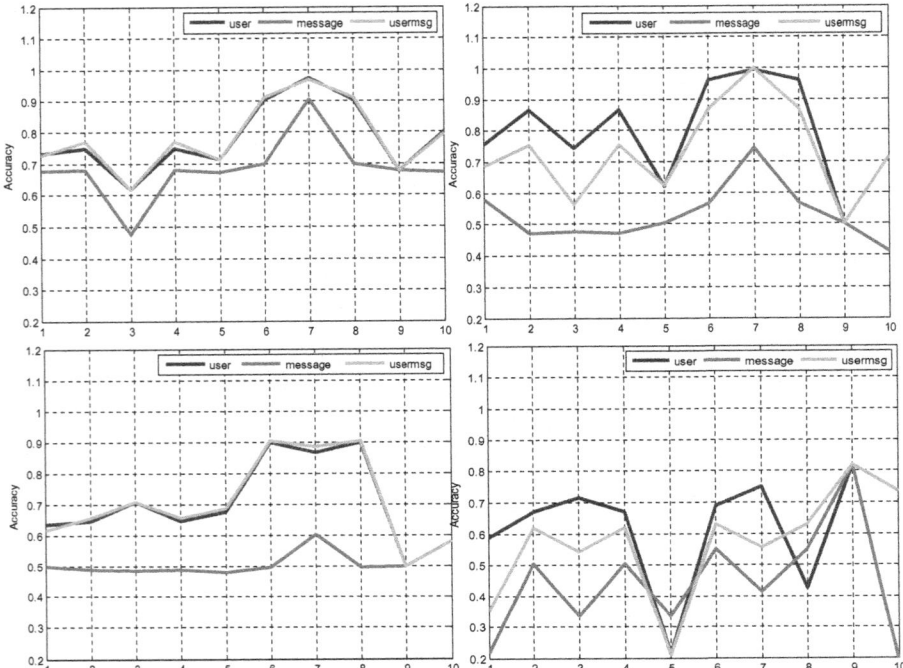

Fig. 18. Comparing algorithm output for combined data for different class of twitter features

5   Conclusion and Future Scope

People who depend on online sources as a news source don't have enough clues to assess its reliability and can therefore be misled by unreliable or fake information. Typically internet and social media are replacing traditional sources of news as more and more people are switching to online medium not only for news but also for sharing their views and opinions. Such circumstances make it necessary to provide tools that can determine the reliability of information available online. In this paper we have shown that information available on a very popular online social media, Twitter, can be automatically checked for reliability by using the twitter features available in the twitter metadata and supervised machine learning algorithms.

As part of future work we plan to incorporate the methodology for larger datasets and include more features from twitter metadata.

References

1. Basharat, S., Chachoo, M.: On linear vs hybrid configuration: an empirical study. In: International Conference on Advances in Computers, Communication and Electronic Engineering, Commune, Srinagar, pp. 180–184 (2015)
2. Castillo, C., Mendoza, M., Poblete, B.: Information credibility on Twitter. In: Proceedings of the 20th International Conference on World Wide Web, pp. 675–684. ACM, March 2011
3. Corcoran, M.: Death by cliff plunge, with a push from twitter. The New York Times (2009)
4. Kleinbaum, D.G., Klein, M.: Logistic Regression. A Self-Learning Text. SBH. Springer, New York (2010). https://doi.org/10.1007/978-1-4419-1742-3
5. Esfandiari, G.: The Twitter devolution. Foreign Policy, 7 June 2010
6. Grover, R.: Ad. ly: The Art of Advertising on Twitter. Businessweek, 6 January 2011
7. Gupta, A., Kumaraguru, P.: Credibility ranking of tweets during high impact events. In: Proceedings of the 1st Workshop on Privacy and Security in Online Social Media, p. 2. ACM, April 2012
8. Gupta, A., Kumaraguru, P., Castillo, C., Meier, P.: TweetCred: real-time credibility assessment of content on Twitter. In: Aiello, L.M., McFarland, D. (eds.) SocInfo 2014. LNCS, vol. 8851, pp. 228–243. Springer, Cham (2014). https://doi.org/10.1007/978-3-319-13734-6_16
9. Gupta, A., Lamba, H., Kumaraguru, P.: $1.00 per rt# bostonmarathon# prayforboston: analyzing fake content on Twitter. In: eCrime Researchers Summit (eCRS), 2013, pp. 1–12. IEEE, September 2013a
10. Gupta, M., Zhao, P., Han, J.: Evaluating event credibility on Twitter. In: SDM, pp. 153–164, January 2012
11. Harrington, P.: Machine Learning in Action, vol. 5. Manning, Greenwich (2012)
12. Hilligoss, B., Rieh, S.Y.: Developing a unifying framework of credibility assessment: construct, heuristics, and interaction in context. Inf. Process. Manag. **44**(4), 1467–1484 (2008)
13. Ismail, S., Latif, R.A.: Authenticity issues of social media: credibility, quality and reality. In: Proceedings of World Academy of Science, Engineering and Technology, no. 74, p. 265. World Academy of Science, Engineering and Technology (WASET), February 2013
14. Ng, A.Y., Jordan, M.I.: On discriminative vs. generative classifiers: a comparison of logistic regression and naive bayes. Adv. Neural. Inf. Process. Syst. **14**, 841 (2002)
15. Kwak, H., Lee, C., Park, H., Moon, S.: What is Twitter, a social network or a news media? In: Proceedings of the 19th International Conference on World Wide Web, pp. 591–600. ACM, April 2010
16. Logistic Regression: Wikipedia (2014). http://en.wikipedia.org/w/index.php?title=Logistic_Regression. Accessed 15 Nov 2014
17. Mendoza, M., Poblete, B., Castillo, C.: Twitter under crisis: can we trust what we RT? In: Proceedings of the First Workshop on Social Media Analytics, pp. 71–79. ACM, July 2010
18. Montgomery, D.C., Peck, E.A., Vining, G.G.: Introduction to Linear Regression Analysis. Wiley, Hoboken (2015)
19. Morris, M.R., Counts, S., Roseway, A., Hoff, A., Schwarz, J.: Tweeting is believing?: understanding microblog credibility perceptions. In: Proceedings of the ACM 2012 Conference on Computer Supported Cooperative Work, pp. 441–450. ACM, February 2012
20. Mustafaraj, E., Metaxas, P.T.: From obscurity to prominence in minutes: political speech and real-time search (2010)
21. Naive Bayes Classifier: Wikipedia (2014). http://en.wikipedia.org/w/index.php?title=Naive_Bayes_classifier. Accessed 15 Nov 2014

22. Owens, S.: How Celebrity Imposters Hurt Twitter's Credibility. Mediashift, 20 February 2009
23. Ratkiewicz, J., Conover, M., Meiss, M., Gonçalves, B., Patil, S., Flammini, A., Menczer, F.: Truthy: mapping the spread of astroturf in microblog streams. In: Proceedings of the 20th International Conference Companion on World Wide Web, pp. 249–252. ACM, March 2011
24. Sikdar, S., Kang, B., ODonovan, J., Höllerer, T., Adah, S.: Understanding information credibility on twitter. In: 2013 International Conference on Social Computing (SocialCom), pp. 19–24. IEEE, September 2013
25. Sullivan, D.: Twitter's Real Time Spam Problem. Search Engine Land (2009)
26. Sundar, S.S.: The MAIN model: a heuristic approach to understanding technology effects on credibility. In: Digital Media, Youth, and Credibility, vol. 73100 (2008)
27. Support vector machines: The linearly separable case, Nlp.stanford.edu (2008). http://nlp.stanford.edu/IR-book/html/htmledition/support-vector-machines-the-linearly-separable-case-1.html
28. Varela, P.L., Martins, A.F., Aguiar, P.M., Figueiredo, M.A.: An empirical study of feature selection for sentiment analysis. In: 9th Conference on Telecommunications, Conftele, Castelo Branco, May 2013
29. Yu, H., Kim, S.: SVM tutorial—classification, regression and ranking. In: Rozenberg, G., Bäck, T., Kok, J.N. (eds.) Handbook of Natural computing, pp. 479–506. Springer, Heidelberg (2012). https://doi.org/10.1007/978-3-540-92910-9_15
30. Xanthopoulos, P., Pardalos, P.M., Trafalis, T.B.: Linear discriminant analysis. Robust Data Mining. BRIEFSOPTI, pp. 27–33. Springer, New York (2013). https://doi.org/10.1007/978-1-4419-9878-1_4

Smart and Innovative Trends in Image Processing and Machine Vision

Improved Reversible Data Embedding in Medical Images Using I-IWT and Pairwise Pixel Difference Expansion

R. Geetha[1][(✉)] and S. Geetha[2]

[1] SENSE, VIT University, Chennai Campus, Chennai, India
geetha.r2014phd1168@vit.ac.in
[2] SCSE, VIT University, Chennai Campus, Chennai, India

Abstract. Reversible Data Hiding is a tactic of conveying secret message by embedding the same in any of the multimedia content and after extracting the hidden information, original cover can be recovered without any deformation to it. In this paper an unique way of embedding the secret data reversibly by applying pairwise prediction error expansion on Integer-Integer Wavelet transformed (I-IWT) image points is proposed for medical images. Considering the statistics of the medical images the neighboring points are considered to be similar and hence the prediction errors are perceived to be close to zero/minimum. The proposed scheme employs I-IWT which is applied to the sub bands of cover image and secret bits are embedded into all sub bands. Experimental analysis is carried out on various test medical images and compared with other recent reversible data hiding schemes. Superior image quality for considerable payload determines the efficiency of the proposed approach.

Keywords: Reversible data hiding · Integer-Integer wavelet transform
Pairwise difference error

1 Introduction

One of the major issues in medical field is to store the medical imaging data for a long period of time. Due to the growth in medical imaging procedures like increase in study size, digitization of data, advanced imaging procedures, image data volumes keep increasing drastically resulting in data explosion. Moreover, there are few perilous security and privacy factors that could alleviate its recognition. Due to the importance of the sensitivity in medical images, the third-party servers could be the main targets of various unlikely behavior which may result in the alteration of the original image data. In order to safe guard the privacy and integrity of the medical images it is better to have some nominal security techniques which could go with the trusted servers.

The technology of data hiding by reversible means is growing rapidly in recent times. Information security is one of the top most priority in this digital world. Data hiding/steganography is the means of covert communication between the sender and the receiver. Steganographic techniques are much more effective in covert communication where there after recovering the secret message, the cover media is of no means.

© Springer Nature Singapore Pte Ltd. 2018
P. Bhattacharyya et al. (Eds.): NGCT 2017, CCIS 828, pp. 601–611, 2018.
https://doi.org/10.1007/978-981-10-8660-1_45

In certain fields like military, medical imaging, law enforcement etc.... preserving the original/cover media is of major concern. A better reversible steganographic scheme need to be lossless, should be imperceptible to visual system, robust in nature, ensure high payload (hiding capacity) and minimum overhead information for recovering the secret message and the cover media. The priority of this paper is to present a simple and efficient reversible data hiding method for medical images. The proposed scheme uses pixel pair prediction error in Integer-Integer wavelet transform domain. The paper is ordered as follows: Sect. 2 - Literature survey, Sect. 3 - Overview about I-IWT and Pairwise Prediction Error approach, Sect. 4 - Proposed method, Sect. 5 - Experimental results, Sect. 6 - Conclusion.

2   Literature Survey

Existing reversible data hiding techniques are broadly classified under four categories: 1. Histogram shifting based schemes 2. Difference Expansion based schemes 3. Prediction Error Expansion based schemes 4. Interpolation based schemes. Major works carried out in each categories are discussed and summarized as follows:

2.1   Histogram Shifting

Histogram shifting is one of the popular and most easiest method of reversible data hiding techniques. The capacity of the histogram shifting based techniques can be increased by cleverly choosing the embedding points in the image. Ni et al. [1] proposed the first histogram modification system by choosing maximum occurring and minimum occuring points in the image and by slight modification embedded the secret data in those points. Lin et al. [2] proposed a scheme in which multilayered difference histogram modification was performed. Tai et al. [3] proposed a new diversity in histogram shifting by forming a binary tree structured format. Kim et al. [4] came up with different methodology by applying histogram shifting in sub sampled images. Yang et al. [5] proposed another system by interleaving the maximum/minimum difference histogram shifting technique which resulted in slight deviation in the image points with high payload of 1.12 bpp and 30 dB PSNR. Histogram based multilevel modification RDH scheme is proposed by Zhao et al. [18]. In that scheme the embedding capacity is enhanced by two factors: Embedding Level (EL) and the histogram bins around zero.

2.2   Difference Error Expansion

Difference Expansion is one of the most oldest techniques that has been introduced in reversible data hiding. Neighboring Image points are grouped together as non-overlapping pairs and a secret bit is hidden along with the difference between paired picture points provided that there is no overflow/underflow. Tian [6] proved that his work could achieve 0.5 bpp capacity. Later Alattar [7] improved the performance of Tian by applying the difference expansion logic on vectors instead of pixel pairs.

Weng et al. [8] proposed a reversible data hiding scheme that made use of the pair-wise pixel adjustment (PDA) and the sum of pixel pairs. It resulted in a recommendable picture quality since the pixel pairs were slightly modified. In another paper Yang et al. [9] proposed a method that subjugated the coefficient preference for hiding the data. In that scheme both spatial and frequency domains were used for data hiding which obviously showed good robustness property.

2.3 Prediction Error Expansion (PEE)

Thodi and Rodríguez [10] first came up with PEE scheme which also used histogram shifting technique. The proposed scheme also proved that the embedding capacity can be increased considerably when compared to histogram shifting and difference expansion schemes. Tsai et al. [11] proposed another scheme which used predicted encoding and histogram shifting. This scheme uses residual histogram based on prediction errors that is obtained by getting the difference between neighboring pixel points. Hu et al. [12] proposed a scheme based on difference value expansion prediction which resulted in very high payload capacity than the previous schemes. This scheme became very popular since it need not require any location map for extracting the secret message. Bo et al. [19] proposed a method which is a slight modification to conventional PEE. In this approach a refined pixel selection is employed and the distortion while embedding is lessened by discarding the prediction error pairs which deviates more.

2.4 Interpolation

Interpolation is a means by which a cover image is down sampled and again resized by interpolating rows and columns in the cover media. Better will be the RDH scheme using the interpolation technique when the approximated/interpolated points have low prediction error when compared to the original cover image points. Jung and Yoo [13] proposed a system by means of Neighbor Mean Interpolation(NMI) which offered low time complexity and high performance. Another method based on interpolation was suggested by Luo et al. [14] which embeds secret data in the interpolated points with almost slight modification. Lee and Huang [15] made a slight modification to Jung and Yoo's scheme by Interpolating Neighbor Pixel (INP) and also the embedding technique which gives slight improvement in the picture quality and the embedding capacity. Another LSB substitution scheme was proposed Jung and Yoo [16] which gives a very high payload. Multilevel embedding technique was proposed in [17] which almost reached Jung and Yoo [16] capacity with low time complexity. Interpolation schemes are hooked upon the quality of the interpolated image. Approximating the interpolated points just by considering the neighboring pixels is a major challenge in interpolation based schemes.

3   Related Theory

This section focus on the concepts related to the proposed approach:

3.1   Integer-Integer Wavelet Transform (I-IWT)

Wavelet transform is generally considered as a significant means for multiple resolutions in digital image processing field. The integer luminance points in spatial domain are transformed into decimal coefficients which are again modified/truncated while data hiding. It is not practicable to represent the transformed coefficients up to its full accuracy. There will be loss of information when reconstructing the original image. Hence original wavelet transform is not suitable for reversible data hiding. To overcome this issue an integer to integer wavelet transform is used in this approach. In I-IWT integers are mapped to integers and so there is no loss of information.

Forward transform for 1-D I-IWT can be defined as follows:

$$
\begin{aligned}
s_{1,n} &= s_{0,2n} - \lfloor 1/4(d_{1,n-1} + d_{1,n}) + 1/2 \rfloor \\
d_{1,n} &= s_{0,2n+1} - \lfloor 1/2(s_{0,2n} + s_{0,2n+2}) + 1/2 \rfloor
\end{aligned}
\tag{1}
$$

In Eq. (1) $s_{i,n}$: n^{th} low frequency wavelet coefficients at the ith level and $d_{i,n}$: n^{th} high frequency wavelet coefficients at the ith level. The floor function($\lfloor \rfloor$) rounds it to the nearest integer value towards minus infinity. Unlike ordinary wavelet transform, even in I-IWT, decomposed low and high frequency wavelet coefficients can be further decomposed into low and high frequency components for multi-resolution. 2D transform for the same can be obtained by applying Eq. (1) in both horizontal and vertical directions.

Inverse transform for 1-D I-IWT can be defined as follows:

$$
\begin{aligned}
s_{0,2n} &= s_{1,n} - \lfloor 1/4(d_{1,n-1} + d_{1,n}) + 1/2 \rfloor \\
s_{0,2n+1} &= d_{1,n} - \lfloor 1/2(s_{0,2n} + s_{0,2n+2}) + 1/2 \rfloor
\end{aligned}
\tag{2}
$$

3.2   Pairwise Pixel Difference Expansion (PPDE)

To exploit the correlation between prediction errors and to achieve an improved performance in reversible data hiding PPEE scheme is proposed. In 2D Pixel Difference Histogram (PDH) the difference sequence $D = (d_1, d_2, \ldots d_M)$ is framed by considering every two adjacent pixel difference. This sequence is transformed into two new sequence D_{odd}, D_{even}.

The pixel difference sequence is calculated using the formula given below:

$$
d_{(i)} = \begin{cases} p_1 & \text{if } i = 1 \\ p_{(i-1)} - p_i & \text{if } 2 < i < \left(\frac{M}{2}\right) * \left(\frac{N}{2}\right) \end{cases}
\tag{3}
$$

$$D_{odd}, D_{even} = \left(d_1, d_2, \ldots d_{M/2}\right)$$
$$\text{Where } d_k = (d_{2k-1}, d_{2k}) \tag{4}$$

$$c(i_1, i_2) = \#\{1 \leq k \leq M/2 : d_{2k-1} = i_1, d_{2k} = i_2\} \tag{5}$$

Equation (4) gives the associated 2D PEH. It is assumed that

$$H(D) = H(D_{odd}) = H(D_{even}) \tag{6}$$

and function H calculates the entropy of the pixel difference sequence D.

In PPDE the bins are either expanded or shifted in a less distorted way. For example mapping $(0, 0)$ to $(1, 1)$ need to be discarded and pairs $\{(0, 0), (0, -1), (-1, 0), (-1, -1)$ is embedded with $\log_2 3$ bits rather than 2 bits in ordinary PEE. Mapping between $(0, 0) \rightarrow (1, 1)$, $(0, -1) \rightarrow (1, -2)$, $(-1, 0) \rightarrow (-2, 1)$ and $(-1, -1) \rightarrow (-2, -2)$ are discarded.

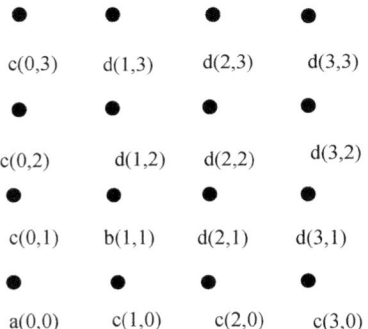

Fig. 1. Ordering of 2D bins in first quadrant of 2D PDH

Figure 1 shows the first quadrant of 2D PDH using PPDE. Remaining three quarters are similar to the first quadrant. Table 1 shows the transformation of 2D bins for all four quadrants. In the above table bold transformations result in embedding and remaining blocks results in shifting.

4   Proposed Method

In the proposed method embedding and extraction procedures are described through flow chart in Fig. 2.

4.1   Embedding Procedure

1. The input image undergoes Integer-Integer Wavelet Transformation which results in four sub-bands LL, LH, HH, HL.

2. In each block determine the pixel difference pair sequence $(d_1, d_2, \ldots d_M)$ by means of prediction.
3. Find the embedding capacity in each block by constructing the histogram of adjacent pixel difference values.
4. Determine the smallest integer ∂ in such a way that you get enough number of pairs to embed the data in the given sub-band.
5. Adjust the pixel value by 1 to avoid overflow/underflow, note down the locations of the modified pixels and compress the location map(LM) losslessly, embed it as part of payload.
6. By means of LSB replacement, embed the value of ∂, size of LM and size of the message bits.
7. Apply inverse I-IWT and combine all the sub-bands to form the marked image.

Step 2 to 6 is performed for all the sub-bands to embed the data.

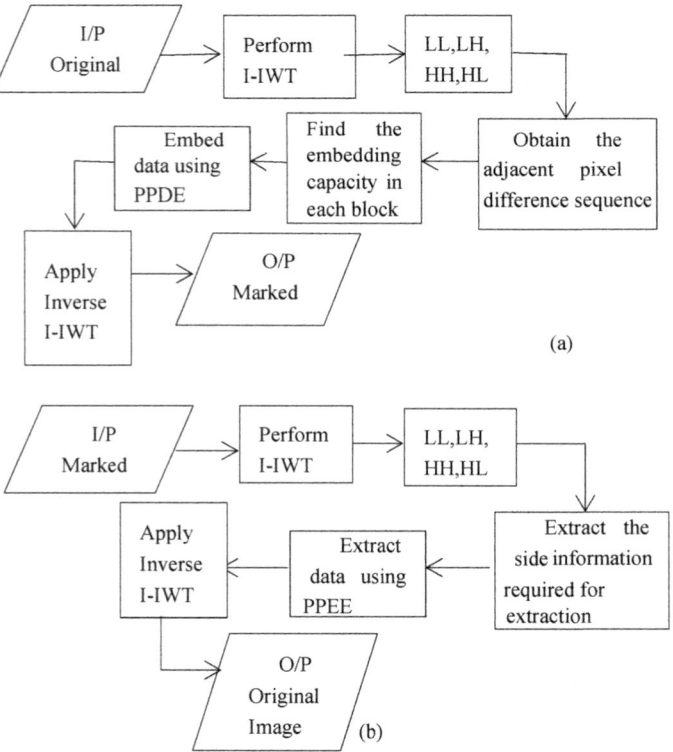

Fig. 2. Flow chart for (a) Embedding (b) Extraction

4.2   Extraction Procedure

1. The marked image as input undergoes I-IWT and the four sub-bands LL, LH, HH, HL are obtained.
2. By means of LSB extraction obtain the value of ∂, size of LM and the size of the message data.
3. Obtain the adjacent pixel difference sequence $(d_1, d_2, ...d_M)$ of each sub-band.
4. Using inverse mapping of PPDE method extract the embedded bits from each embeddable pair of pixel difference value.
5. After extracting the secret message, apply inverse I-IWT to all the sub-bands and combine them to form the original image.

Step 2 to 4 needs to be performed for all sub-bands to extract the secret message.

Our main aim is to expand or to shift the bins in such a way that the distortion is minimum. In conventional PEE for the pair $(0,0)$ is embedded with 2 bits $(0,0),(0,1),(1,0)$ or $(1,1)$ having a distortion of 0, 1, 1, 2 respectively. Mapping $(0,0)$ to $(1,1)$ will cause a distortion of 2. In order to reduce this distortion, mapping of $(0,0)$ to $(1,1)$ should be avoided. In new mapping each pair in $\{(0,-1),(-1,0),(-1,-1),(0,0)\}$ is embedded with $\log_2 3$ bits instead of 2 bits. The above mentioned four pairs are mapped to $(1,-2), (-2,1), (-2,-2)$ and $(1,1)$ respectively with 1 bit being embedded in each pair instead of being shifted in conventional PEE.

5   Experimental Analysis and Results

The proposed scheme is demonstrated and compared over other existing schemes. For experimental purpose six medical images are taken for analysis. Figure 3 shows the selected grayscale medical test images of size 512×512 pixels having smooth and

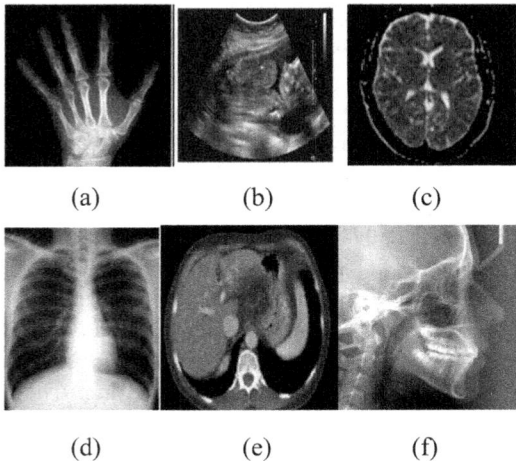

(a)   (b)   (c)

(d)   (e)   (f)

Fig. 3. (a) Palm X-Ray Image (b) Ultra Scan Fetus Image (c) Brain MRI Scan Image (d) Thorax X-Ray Image (e) Brain CT Scan Image (f) Cephalogram Dental Image

rough variations. The proposed method is programmed using MATLAB and pseudo random bit generator function is used for generation of message bits.

In the proposed pairwise pixel difference embedding approach each pixel is modified by 1 that limits the embedding capacity. So for performance comparison only the low capacity cases are considered. It can be determined that a better reversible data hiding scheme can be attained by scheming an image dependent pairwise difference expansion. Higher capacities can be achieved in this scheme by introducing new mapping and discarding mappings with larger distortion.

The performance analysis of the proposed method is measured in terms of PSNR (dB), capacity in bits per pixel(bpp). Equations governing all the above three measures are given below:

$$PSNR = 10log_{10}(255^2/MSE)dB \tag{7}$$

Where MSE is the mean square error and is calculated between the cover image C and marked image C' of size $a \times b$.

$$MSE = \frac{1}{axb}X\sum\nolimits_{i=1}^{a}\sum\nolimits_{j=1}^{b}(C(i,j) - C^{'}(i,j))^2 \tag{8}$$

The graphs shown in Fig. 4 depicts the histogram bins obtained for all the test images after finding the pixel difference values.

Our results are compared with six other schemes listed in Table 1. The outer histogram bin curves (blue color) in Fig. 4 is for Zhao et al. scheme [18] and the inner curves (red color) is for the proposed scheme. Both the schemes are based on pixel differencing but Zhao's scheme is done on spatial domain while the proposed scheme is performed in frequency domain. Even though both the schemes make room for embedding on the basis of pixel differencing, the embedding strategy is different in Zhao's scheme [18] and the proposed scheme. In Zhao's scheme embedding of bit is done based on pixel difference expansion strategy while in the proposed method it is done by pairwise pixel difference expansion.

The tabulated results shows that the performance improvement achieved by our proposed scheme is validated. Since our scheme is based on a pixel-wise differential mechanism embedded using minimum distortion basis in integer to integer wavelet transform, the visual quality of marked images are improved simultaneously and are proved in the following experimental results.

Our scheme is compared with five other existing methods proposed by Luo et al. [14], Kim et al. [4], Tsai et al. [11], Li et al. [12], and Zhao et al. [18]. The performance parameters are compared with [18] since both the schemes adopt histogram modification. Even though the difference value histogram method is the same in both while a pixel pair difference histogram modification on integer to integer wavelet transform coefficients strategy is used in our system. Hence the improvement in performance achieved by our novel method is validated. However, since our scheme is based on a pixel pair difference mechanism done in integer to integer wavelet transform, the hiding capacity and the visual quality of marked images are improved simultaneously and are tabulated in the experimental results.

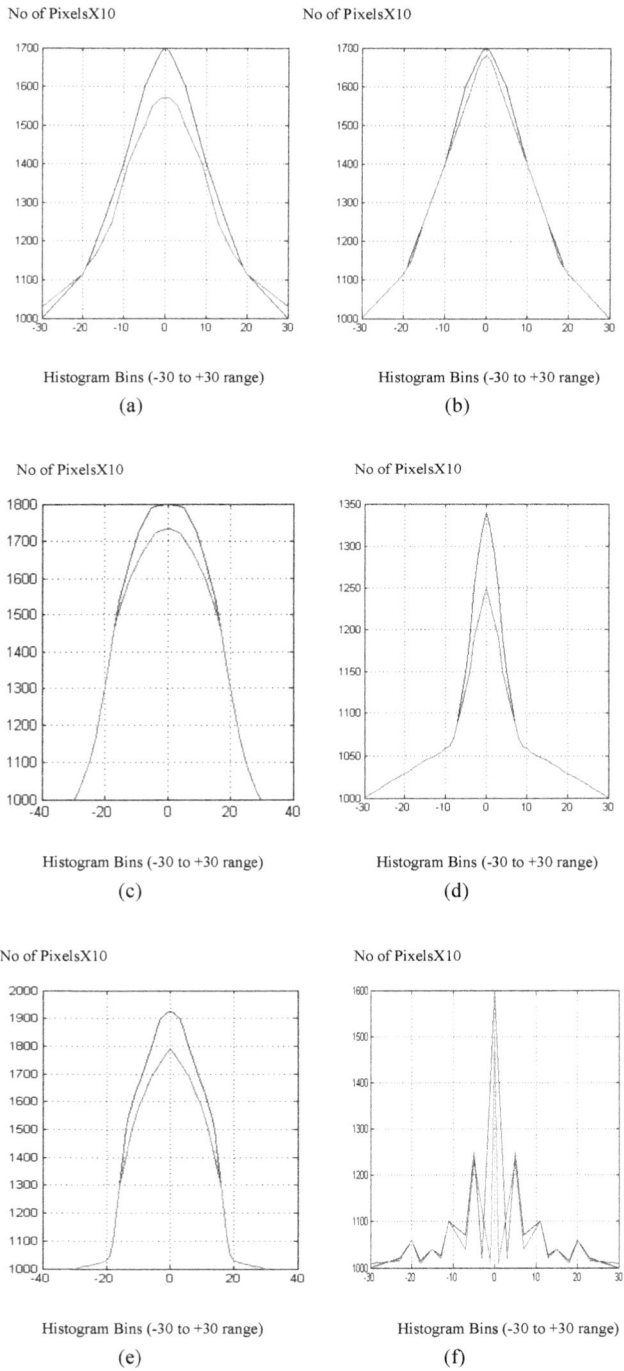

Fig. 4. Histogram bins of (b(−30), b(30)) obtained by Zhao et al.'s scheme [18] (marked as red) and our scheme (blue) on (a) Palm X-Ray image (b) Ultra scan Fetus image (c) Brain MRI Scan image (d) Brain CT Scan image (e) Thorax X-Ray image (f) Cephalogram dental image. (Color figure online)

Table 1. Performance Comparison of proposed scheme and existing scheme

Scheme	Luo [14]	Kim [4]	Tsai [11]	Li [12]	Zhao [18]	Proposed Scheme
Palm Xray image bpp/dB	29813/46.68	59832/44.2	51112/49.1	54326/46.9	52428/47.4	75285/52.6
Ultra Scan Fetus image bpp/dB	44786/48.83	78173/44.55	64996/49.24	77295/48.75	79898/48.88	84398/52.3
Brain MRI image bpp/dB	9522/46.5	20965/42.63	15820/46.73	23946/46.33	20592/47.1	27540/49.8
Brain CT Scanbpp/dB	28271/48.67	59707/44.16	45496/49.03	62255/48.63	64227/47.75	74756/50.7
Thorax X-Ray image bpp/dB	27372/48.65	63399/44.2	48608/49.06	54460/48.6	69635/48.76	78560/51.4
Cephalo - gram bpp/dB	17555/47.52	38289/42.85	29398/47.86	33890/47.42	50383/47.59	55670/50.4

Table 1 shows the experimental analysis performance values of maximum number of embeddable bits (bpp) and PSNR (dB) for the test images of proposed method and other schemes. As said, there may be many two dimensional mappings, and the proposed ones are several in effect attempts for lower capacities. We state that, finding the optimal 2D mapping for a given capacity and giving a way to mappings for different capacities would be a future valuable effort.

6 Conclusion

An improved and efficient RDH method based on pairwise pixel difference expansion using integer-integer wavelet transform is proposed. The pairwise difference expansion embedding is a novel reversible mapping that makes use of the correlations among adjacent pixel difference values. Using this correlation, the distortion of the pixel values can be controlled at a minimum level, neglecting the higher level distortions. So the proposed scheme works well on medical images than some of the existing state-of-the-art RDH schemes. The system offers a high quality stego image than the existing schemes at low capacity embedding. This scheme can be employed efficiently and effectively in hiding data like authentication information, information about the patient in their respective medical images.

References

1. Ni, Z., Shi, Y.-Q., Ansari, N., Su, W.: Reversible data hiding. IEEE Trans. Circuits Syst. Video Technol. **16**(3), 354–361 (2006)
2. Lin, C.C., Tai, W.L., Chang, C.C.: Multilevel reversible data hiding based on histogram modification of difference images. J. Pattern Recogn. **41**(1), 3582–3591 (2008)

3. Tai, W.L., Yeh, C.M., Chang, C.C.: Reversible data hiding based on histogram modification of pixel differences. IEEE Trans. Circuits Syst. Video Technol. **19**(6), 906–910 (2009)
4. Kim, K.S., Lee, M.J., Lee, H.Y., Lee, H.K.: Reversible data hiding exploiting spatial correlation between sub-sampled images. J. Pattern Recogn. **42**(1), 3083–3096 (2009)
5. Nicole, R.: Title of paper with only first word capitalized. J. Name Stand. Abbrev. **2**, 740–741 (1987). in Press
6. Tian, J.: Reversible data embedding using a difference expansion. IEEE Trans. Circuits Syst. Video Technol. **13**(8), 890–896 (2003)
7. Alattar, A.M.: Reversible watermark using the difference expansion of a generalized integer transform. IEEE Trans. Image Process. **13**(8), 1147–1156 (2004)
8. Weng, S., Zhao, Y., Pan, J.-S., Ni, R.: A novel high-capacity reversible water-marking scheme. In: Proceedings of IEEE International Conference on Multimedia and Expo (ICME 2007), pp. 631–634 (2007)
9. Yang, B., Schmucker, M., Niu, X., Busch, C., Sun, S.: Reversible image watermarking by histogram modification for integer DCT coefficients. In: Proceedings of the 6th Workshop on Multimedia Signal Processing (MMSP 2004), pp. 143–146 (2004)
10. Thodi, D.M., Rodríguez, J.J.: Prediction-error based reversible watermarking. In: Proceedings of International Conference on Image Processing (ICIP 2004), vol. 3, pp. 1549–1552 (2004)
11. Tsai, P.Y., Hu, Y.C., Yeh, H.L.: Reversible image hiding scheme using predictive coding and histogram shifting. Sig. Process. **89**(6), 1129–1143 (2009)
12. Hu, Y., Lee, H.K., Li, J.: DE-based reversible data hiding with improved overflow location map. IEEE Trans. Circuits Syst. Video Technol. **19**(2), 250–260 (2009)
13. Jung, K.H., Yoo, K.Y.: Data hiding method using image interpolation. J. Comput. Stand. Interfaces **31**(1), 465–470 (2009)
14. Luo, L., Chen, Z., Chen, M., Zeng, Q., Xiong, Z.: Reversible image watermarking using interpolation technique. IEEE Trans. Inf. Forensics Secur. **5**(1), 187–193 (2010)
15. Lee, C.-F., Huang, Y.-L.: An efficient image interpolation increasing payload in reversible data hiding. Expert Syst. Appl. **39**, 6712–6719 (2012)
16. Jung, K.H., Yoo, K.Y.: Steganographic method based on interpolation and LSB substitution of digitaal image interpolation. Multimed. Tools Appl. **74**, 2143–2155 (2015)
17. Geetha, R., Geetha, S.: Multilevel RDH scheme using image interpolation. In: 2016 International Conference on Advances in Computing, Communications and Informatics (ICACCI), Jaipur, pp. 1952–1956 (2016)
18. Zhao, Z., Luo, H., Lu, Z.M., Pan, J.S.: Reversible data hiding based on multilevel histogram modification and sequential recovery. Int. J. Electr. Commun. (AEÜ) **65**(10), 814–826 (2011)
19. Bo, O., Li, X., Zhao, Y.: Pairwise prediction-error expansion for efficient reversible data hiding. IEEE Trans. Image Process. **22**(12), 5010–5021 (2013)

Fusion Based Image Retrieval Using Local and Global Descriptor

Akshata V. Shendre[1(✉)], Lalit B. Damahe[1(✉)],
and Nileshsingh V. Thakur[2(✉)]

[1] Department of Computer Technology,
Yeshwantrao Chavan College of Engineering, Nagpur, India
akshatashendre99@gmail.com, damahe_l@rediffmail.com
[2] Prof Ram Meghe College of Engineering and Management,
Badnera-Amravati, India
thakurnisvis@rediffmail.com

Abstract. In the Content Based Image Retrieval, accurate image retrieval using different methods and descriptors is an important task. The single descriptor, local or global, gives different results for the same query image, as the local descriptor works on a part of an image and global descriptor works on whole image and to overcome this issue of single descriptor, the fusion technique is introduced. The fusion technique combines the local and global descriptor to improve the performance and it extracts multi-features which are more informative about local and global features for the query image. The proposed method, reduces and manages multi-features for relevant output. The experimentation is done on sample of Holidays dataset and the comparison between fusion, local and global descriptor method is presented. The proposed method outperforms, in terms of precision and recall rate.

Keywords: Content Based Image Retrieval (CBIR) · Fusion · Local descriptor
Global descriptor · Multi-features

1 Introduction

In Content Based Image Retrieval (CBIR), it extracts the visual contents of the image like shape, texture, and color of the query image and matches the similarity with large image database on the basis of desired features. The process of extracting the image contents according to the user's interest by applying different descriptor is called as feature extraction. The processing of input image may have large and redundant data which can be converted into the reduced set of features (feature vector) which contains desired relevant information for the entire data. The redundant features are reduced by using various methods like Principal Component Analysis (PCA), Bag of Words (BoG), K-means Clustering, Hierarchical vocabulary trees, Vector of locally aggregated descriptor (VLAD) which can be applied on the extracted multi-features to reduce the memory complexity. The feature extracted can be stored as an Inverted index, Graphs, Hash codes, Bag of Words, Codebook, Tree structure, Histogram, Distance vector etc. and the concept of graph storage helps in relevant storage of

© Springer Nature Singapore Pte Ltd. 2018
P. Bhattacharyya et al. (Eds.): NGCT 2017, CCIS 828, pp. 612–627, 2018.
https://doi.org/10.1007/978-981-10-8660-1_46

features and makes the matching process easy and simple as the direct node to node matching takes place. In Hash codes generation, features are assigned hash values according to the weights which may vary and decrease the performance with dynamic weights and the histogram based features storage helps in the global descriptor. The descriptors processes and encode an image so that it can be compared and matched to other images. The Feature descriptors may be local or global.

1.1 Local Descriptor

Local descriptor extracts feature using a part or region of an image and thus it is robust to small changes in images. There are many local descriptors which work differently according to the feature contents. Local features are a compact vector representations of a local neighbourhood pixels and the building blocks of many computer vision algorithms. The local features extract blobs, corners, texture, and edge etc. There are various local descriptors like LBP [32] descriptor which is used for texture feature extraction, SIFT and SURF extract interest points and are used for object detection, tracking.

1.2 Global Descriptor

The Global Descriptor feature uses the visual content of the whole image and thus it is not robust because a change in part of the image will lead to failure. The Global features include shape, color, texture features and contour representations. There is a lack of spatial feature distribution information in global features which fails to capture enough semantic information due to limited descriptive power. There is various global descriptor like HSV, GIST, HOG. The HSV descriptor is used to extract color features as shown in Fig. 1(a).

In some cases local descriptor retrieves relevant output than global descriptor and vice-versa as shown in Fig. 1. The global descriptor in Fig. 1(a) does not retrieve relevant output as the HSV descriptor work on color features. The local descriptor in (b) in Fig. 1 gives relevant output as the SURF descriptor work on interest point detection. In Fig. 1, the Red boxes show irrelevant images retrieved and the Black box shows relevant images retrieved.

Fig. 1. (a) Shows irrelevant images using HSV global descriptor and (b) gives relevant output using SURF local descriptor (Color figure online)

1.3 Fusion Descriptor

The information provided by a single descriptor can be limited as the image features is based on one descriptor and thus have limited accuracy, to overcome this issue fusion based technique is used. Fusion method is the combination of features from the query images which may vary in feature content acquired from different descriptors in which the multi-features can be more informative and distinct about feature contents which help in the proper image classification on the basis of extracted features and its relativity with images. In fusion based techniques, weights can be assigned to the features to combine multi-features, Score level fusion is also used in which scores are assigned according to top N images retrieved and various different methods can be used to combine the features. The fusion can be categorized as pixel level, feature level and decision level.

- Pixel level/data level- The original pixel values of an image are directly fused and combines the raw data from multiple images into a single image.
- Feature level fusion- The features are extracted using descriptor and then they are merged. The features are first extracted using descriptors and then the extracted features are combined and stored.
- Decision level fusion- In this, the fusion depends on the features extracted and accordingly the decision to apply weights, classical inference, Bayesian inference etc. can be made.

The Fusion can be performed in many ways like combining both global and local descriptor, by combining only local or global descriptors, image and textual features and by combining the images which can be compared with the database images to match the similarity and improve the accuracy. Similarly the fusion can be early or late fusion for the extracted features, which can be useful to improve the accuracy of retrieval.

- Early fusion: It combines the features of an image into a single form before the learning or comparison. In this type of fusion, feature vectors are concatenated into one single feature vector which is represented as a unique feature vector. In this, decision rule is applied on all feature vector uniformly and could be used without applying any weights to the features such that they can be concatenated on the normalized feature spaces of the visual and textual features.
- Late fusion: It combines the image features at the last stage after the learning or comparison about individual features. In this type of fusion, extracted features are classified according to the decision rule and then the features are fused.

The remaining portion of paper is organised in the following sections: Sect. 2 consists of related work, Sect. 3 describes the proposed methodology, Sect. 4 consists of results and discussion and finally it is concluded with Future scope.

2   Related Work

Many Researchers have contributed in the field of image processing and computer vision and proposing, techniques on feature extraction, storage of multi-features, fusion based methods, and suggested different evaluating parameters to improve the retrieval process. The existing work done by the reserchers for image fusion can be classified according to the approaches they have used for the retrieval process.

2.1   Unsupervised Learning Methods

In the paper the author Zhang *et al.* [1] aim was to improve the retrieval precision by using the unsupervised learning fusion methods. The output of the fusion is stored graphically using weighted maximum density subgraph and page rank algorithm. The proposed approach by Zheng *et al.* [4] describes unsupervised score level Late fusion method based on L shape score curve to make the method query adaptive. The score value for the graph is normalized using $l1$ normalization technique and then the graph is fused. The Cumulative Match Characteristic (CMC) curve method eliminates the negative impact of worst features and the computational complexity increases for sensitive parameters and assigning global weights to features is sensitive to changes with the query image. The review by authors Shendre and Damahe describes various methods [29] used for fusion method. It gives us information about the various unsupervised learning methods, different approaches to handling the fusion complexity, issues and the summary table of different papers on the fusion methods.

2.2   Weight Based Fusion

The author Yuan *et al.* [19] uses fusion matrix and entropy analysis using Multiple Attribute Decision Making (MADM) method, and the weights to the query image are assigned using correlation analysis on each feature. The approach used by author Wenfei *et al.* in the paper [7] uses the fusion method by applying weights for multi-features. In this method, for the multi-features of fusion method, fixed weights are assigned based on the feature and for the single features, it dynamically adjusts the weights. In this paper [16] Liu *et al.* describes the ranking of images on the basis of assigned weights is done. For each query image, bitwise query adaptive weights are assigned using the hash table and the fused output is stored as the multi-hash table.

2.3   Multi-index Fusion

The proposed method [8] by Bhowmik *et al.* stores different multidimensional features as inverted multi-index. The PCA [35] method which is applied to the extracted features is used for dimension reduction and PLS [34] method used, limits the computational complexity. The codebook is generated which is associated with inverted indices. The main objective of the paper [10] described by the author Zheng *et al.* is to improve the recall rate by applying multiple assignments and to overcome the issue of illumination changes using the Coupled Multi-index (c-MI) method which is applied at the index level. The fusion method uses packing and padding system. The packing steps consist of the fusion of descriptor as one dimension of coupled multi-index. The padding steps include techniques to increase the retrieval performance. Further by using the three parameters image ID, TF (Term-Frequency) data and metadata of each index feature an Inverted Index is calculated and stored. The paper [12] by Shi *et al.* is based on the fusion using the mFFMI framework which works by associating feature tuple with visual words. To improve the accuracy of the method, the extracted features are stored in the form of inverted multi-index. In this paper [11], the author Bai and Bai used Sparse Contextual Activation (SCA) method for local features encoding of an image. The image features are stored as an inverted index having two parameters image ID and membership grade.

2.4   Online and Offline Fusion

The contribution made by the authors Wang *et al.* [18] on online and offline stages separately for the improvement in the fusion method and used the concept of re-ranking. The task of assigning keywords to the query image and storing them as a semantic signature is done on the offline stage and the similarity matching and re-ranking using the reference classes is done on the online stage. The main objective of the author Alghamdi *et al.* in the paper [6] is to do the fusion by extracting the visual and textual information of the image. The method uses association rules mining and clustering algorithm the two data mining techniques, for image retrieval. The offline phase in this method uses the semantic association rule mining algorithm to combine the visual and textual features of the image and the main retrieval procedure and comparison takes place in the online phase using clustering. The fusion method by Kavitha and Sudhamani [21] combines the global and local features. The offline phase works on the feature extraction from the image and the online phase works on fusion and similarity matching. In this paper [9] the author introduced Yang *et al.* the Markov model for the Fusion of Multiple features and stored as graphs. The Vector of Locally Aggregated Descriptor (VLAD) is used for aggregating multi-features and weights assigned to images are query specific and calculated using data-driven learning method. The noise is minimized by using the diffusion method which is applied after the fusion method and to get better retrieval performance. The diffusion is done in the online phase and feature extraction is done in offline phase. The proposed method [27] used by the author Xu *et al.* states the local features extracted are arranged semantically in the online phase and the indexing and feature fusion is done on the offline phase. The hyper-graph method is used to obtain the relations between low-level visual features and their additional information regarding its location. The method [28] by Gao *et al.* used Democratic Diffusion method(DDA). In the offline phase fusion is done and in the online phase, the re-weighting of the feature vectors takes place which is later aggregated to contract the image.

2.5   Feedback Based Fusion

The authors Wang and Zhu used feedback based multi-feature fusion method [2] for extracting the shape features using moment invariants, the color features using the color histogram, and the texture features using gray co-occurrence matrix. The performance is evaluated by the precision rate which increases by using the weighted regulation algorithm. In this paper [20] the author Bagheri *et al.* used the feedback based Borda count fusion method based on Support Vector Machine (SVM) and short term learning (STL) algorithms.

2.6   General Fusion

The various image features are extracted and fused to obtained the desired output with respect to the query image and due to modification in the query image [31] matching affected. The various operators of edge detection can be better alternative to match the images with respect to query and it also affect when the edge pixels are weak and to deal with weak edge detection in all color spaces Sidhu [25] proposes good extensions. The image feature fusion demand for the most of the application areas such as remote sensing, logo matching [37] and better image classification. The paper [17] Kekre et al. using the fusion of Gabor filter and Modified Block truncation coding (MBTC). The RGB color is separated by an Inter Band Average Image (IBAI) created by using modified BTC. In paper [13] of Kabbai et al. introduced the HLG-SIFT, in which the histogram of global and local features using Upper-Lower LBP (UL-LBP) and SIFT is used respectively. The segmentation of image is also suitable technique to reduce the no of dimensions of the image and hence it is suitable for the feature extraction. The approach presented [24] by the authors Sural *et al.* has explained the HSV descriptor and the calculation of the Hue, Saturation, and value on the basis of pixel intensity of the image and color histogram and segmentation is generated. The K-means clustering is used for the segmentation of colors by combining it with the pixel having the similar colors. The author Daga used Spectral clustering method [26] to overcome the issues of inappropriate segmentation. The spectral clustering algorithm is applied to cluster the region of interest. The graphical representation allows to match the retrieved images based on exact and partial matching of graph and re-ranking can be performed based on the retrieved output. The approach in the paper [3] by author Wang *et al.* is based on multi-modal graph based learning for web image search. The author differentiated between two ranked lists by using squared loss method and re-ranking is done using normalized graph Laplacian. The SURF descriptor is one of the good alternative for the retrieval of similar images but the optimisation of this descriptor minimise the size of the significantly. The author Pancham *et al.* [14] provides the solution to the storage problem and computational complexity in the fusion method based on local descriptor SURF-PCA. The PCA is the dimension reduction technique and SURF which can work for 64D and 128D is used for motion tracking, object detection, image registration, and classification.

The Feature Fusion is challenging task in CBIR and undergoes different processing, representation, segmentation, feature extraction, combinations and similarity matching. Table 1 provides, various existing local, global descriptor, and fusion methods. There are also some issues for fusion based technique discussed in Table 2.

Table 1. Summary local, global and fusion descriptors

Ref	Local descriptors	Ref	Global descriptors	Ref	Fusion method
[1, 4, 5, 8, 10, 11, 33]	Scale Invariant Feature Transform (SIFT)	[1]	Hue, Saturation, Value (HSV)	[1]	Graphical
[8]	Speeded Up Robust Features (SURF)	[1]	GIST	[11]	Sparse Contextual Activation
[15, 32]	Local Binary Patterns (LBP)	[10]	Color Names	[10]	Co-Regularized Multi-Graph, Coupled Multi-index
[30]	BRISK, MSER, FREAK, FAST, Harris, Hessian	[23]	Histogram Oriented Gradients (HOG), Wavelet moments, Shape matrices [23]	[6]	Multimodal Fusion method based on Association rules mining
		[7]	Hu moments, Zernike moments, generic Fourier descriptor (GFD), angular radial transform (ART), Gray level co-occurence matrix	[9]	Score level Fusion, Vector of locally Aggregated descriptor, Markov model
				[22, 30]	Feature level Fusion

Table 2. Issues for fusion methods

Sr. no	Issues	Description
1	Memory complexity	Multiple features are extracted from both global and local descriptors which increase memory space to store features
2	Time complexity	Increase in time for similarity matching due to multi-features
3	Computational complexity	Sensitive to small changes in neighborhood pixels and feature weights which decrease performances and increases computational complexity
4	Selection of descriptors	To make the image query adaptive
5	Learning methods	Supervised and Unsupervised learning methods affects the retrieval process

3 Proposed Work

In our proposed work we are focusing to improve the performance of image retrieval using fusion technique which combines the local and global features. The SURF and HSV descriptor is used as it complement each other. The SURF descriptor extracts blob features from the part of an image according to the strong interest point and the PCA (Principal component analysis) is applied on SURF to reduce the number of features. The HSV is used as global descriptor which only extracts color features which cannot retain semantic information after certain degree [24]. The proposed method of fusion method is shown in Fig. 2.

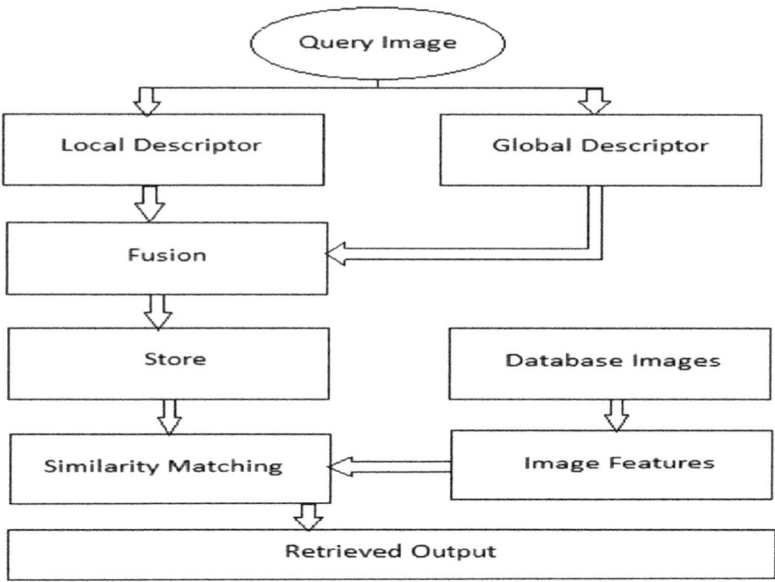

Fig. 2. Proposed work for fusion technique

3.1 SURF Descriptor

1. The query image features are extracted using SURF [14, 35] descriptor. SURF descriptor is used due to its properties of scale and rotation invariant and used for image registration, object recognition, 3D reconstruction or classification and it performs better than SIFT descriptor [35].
2. The blob features extracted from the query image is reduced using Principal component analysis(PCA) [14, 35] to minimize the overall computational time.
3. Further, the reduced image features are stored as adjacency matrix M1.

3.2 HSV Descriptor

The HSV descriptor extracts the color features of the whole image which gives information about the Hue, Saturation, and Value (HSV). Hue represents the color values as an angle in the range of [0–360°] with Red at angle 0°, green at 120°, blue at 240° and red again at 0°. Saturation gives the amount of grayness in the color in the range of 0 to 1 and value represents the brightness in the range of 0 to 1.

The HSV descriptor is used because we are focusing on the color features of the image and it is device independent [24], while in most of the global descriptor the image is converted to gray scale image which limits the color information.

1. The color features are extracted from the same query image using HSV [24] descriptor.
2. A Large number of color features from global descriptor is segmented in the Hue, Saturation, and value and forming individual histogram [7, 22].

3. The average of highest and lowest value of the individual histogram is calculated and a threshold value is set. All the features between these values are extracted.
4. Adjacency matrix M2 for HSV features is also made.

3.3   Fusion Method

1. For the fusion of the features extracted from both descriptor, M * M matrix of both descriptors should be same.
2. Fusion of the local descriptor using SURF and global descriptor using HSV both adjacency matrix is done by taking the intersection of both adjacency matrix.

$$M = M1 \cap M2 \tag{1}$$

where M- Fusion adjacency matrix, M1- SURF adjacency matrix, M2- HSV adjacency matrix

3. Adjacency matrix gives information about the dependencies of edges and nodes. The final fusion matrix made from the intersection of two matrix reduces the dependencies in the fusion method which reduces the memory space for storage and computational complexity for similarity matching.

3.4   Similarity Matching

The similarity of the query image is matched with the database images in the CBIR process to retrieve relevant images from the database. Jaccard similarity is calculated for similarity matching for the proposed fusion method.

$$J(X, Y) = \frac{\sum \min(X, Y)}{\sum \max(X, Y)} \tag{2}$$

where J(X, Y)- Jaccard Similarity, X- (x1, x2, ….. xn) image matrix for SURF, Y- (y1, y2, …. yn) image matrix for HSV.

3.5   Image Retrieval

The retrieved images should be exact or relevant to the query image. The image is retrieved on the basis of Jaccard Similarity matching between the extracted image and the database images. The experimentation is done on 20 sample images from the Holidays dataset [36] shown in Fig. 3. The sample dataset has various different images from different categories like flowers, man, buildings, water, natural images which are rotated, some images which are taken from far view, some are taken from close view etc.

The Image retrieval for one sample image for Fusion method, local descriptor SURF and global descriptor HSV is done as shown in Figs. 4, 5 and 6 respectively. The top six relevant images are retrieved from the database which is similar to the query image.

Fig. 3. Sample images from Holiday database

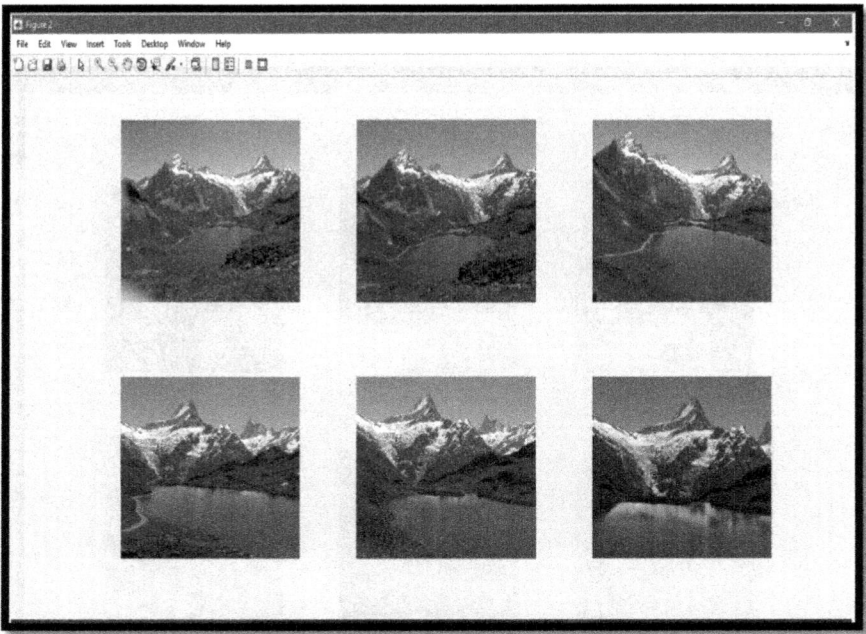

Fig. 4. Image retrieval using fusion technique

Fig. 5. Image retrieval using SURF descriptor

Fig. 6. Image retrieval using HSV descriptor

4   Results and Discussions

4.1   Results

The experimentation is done on MATLAB 2014b on Windows 10, core i7, 64 bit OS, 8 GB RAM for 20 sample images from Holidays dataset as shown in Fig. 3. The overall performance of the methods used in the process of CBIR is measured using performance metric.

- Precision rate- It is used for measuring the accuracy of the system.

$$\text{Precision} = \frac{\text{Count of Relevant Images Retrieved}}{\text{Total Image Retrieved}} \tag{3}$$

- Recall Rate- It measures the Robustness of the system.

$$\text{Recall Rate} = \frac{\text{Count of Relevant Images Retrieve}}{\text{Total Relevant Images in Database}} \tag{4}$$

The performance evaluation parameter, Precision Rate and Recall rate is calculated for 20 images and compared for Fusion method, SURF descriptor, and HSV descriptor. The precision rate for fusion method is 77.497%, for local descriptor SURF it is 53.33% and for global descriptor HSV it is 32.496% as shown in Fig. 7 and the recall rate for fusion method is 74.85%, for local descriptor SURF it is 71.85% and for global descriptor HSV it is 70.91% shown in Fig. 8.

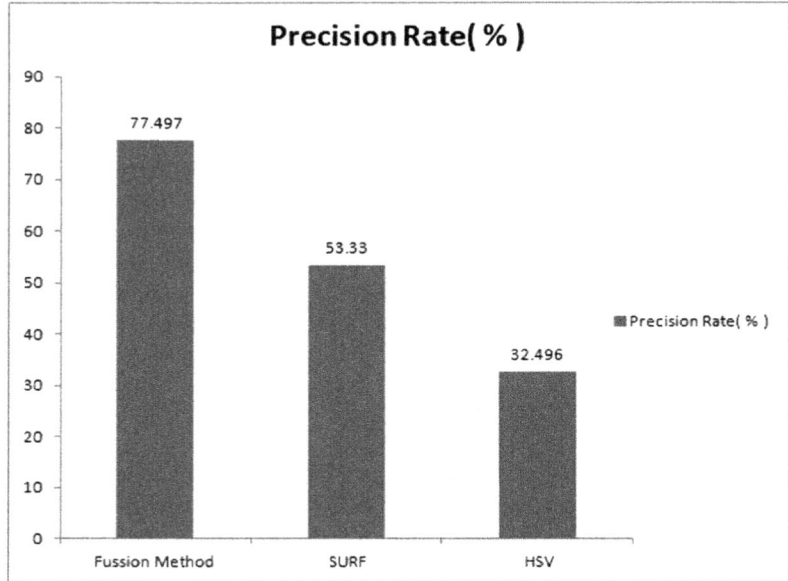

Fig. 7. Precision rate for fusion method, local descriptor SURF and global descriptor HSV

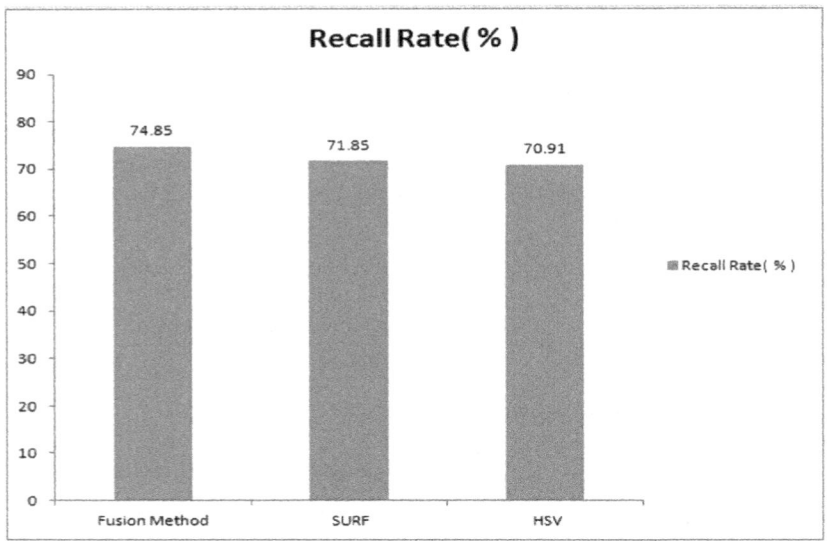

Fig. 8. Recall rate for fusion method, local descriptor SURF and global descriptor HSV

4.2 Discussions

Selecting descriptors for fusion method like HSV global descriptor and SURF as the local descriptor which is scale and rotation invariant makes the image query adaptive as the global descriptor is sensitive to small changes whereas local descriptor is not sensitive to small changes which compliment eachother and also decreases the computational complexity. The multi-features and redundant features extracted from the descriptors are reduced using PCA for the blob features and the matrix representation of features helps to reduce the memory complexity. The computational complexity decreases as weights are not assigned to the features in the fusion method. The comparison of image retrieval for Fusion method gives better results than SURF and HSV descriptor. In fusion method, sometimes the query image is not the topmost retrieved image which decreases the performance. Combining the color features and blob features, the performance evaluating parameters precision rate and recall rate of fusion method is more than SURF and HSV descriptor as it extracts single features blob and color respectively which limits the performance of image retrieval.

5 Conclusion and Future Scope

The Fusion method combines the local descriptor SURF and global descriptor HSV for the same query image which extracts features for both descriptors and further, the extracted features are reduced using PCA for the local descriptor. The extracted reduced features for both descriptors are stored as adjacency matrix and fusion is done and a fusion matrix is obtained. The image retrieval for Fusion method, SURF descriptor and HSV descriptor for one sample image shows Fusion method extract relevant images as compared to SURF and HSV descriptor. The experimentation is done on 20 samples from the Holidays database and the comparison is done between the proposed fusion method and the local descriptor, global descriptor on the basis of performance evaluating parameters precision rate and recall rate. The performance of Fusion method is better than the local and global descriptor. Various Fusion issues are handled using the proposed method. In future, experimentation can be done on a large number of images from the Holidays database. The supervised learning method in Fusion technique can be done as a future work to improve the image retrieval process.

References

1. Zhang, S., Yang, M., Cour, T., Yu, K., Metaxas, D.N.: Query specific rank fusion for image retrieval. IEEE Trans. Pattern Anal. Mach. Intell. **37**(4), 803–815 (2015)
2. Wang, J.-Y., Zhu, Z.: Image retrieval system based on multi-feature fusion and relevance feedback. In: Proceedings of International Conference on Machine Learning and Cybernetics, vol. 4, pp. 2053–2058 (2010)
3. Wang, M., Li, H., Tao, D., Ke, L., Xindong, W.: Multimodal graph-based reranking for web image search. IEEE Trans. Image Process. **21**(11), 4649–4661 (2012)
4. Zheng, L., Wang, S., Tian, L., He, F., Liu, Z., Tian, Q.: Query-adaptive late fusion for image search and person re-identification. In: Proceedings of International Conference on Computer Vision and Pattern Recognition, pp. 1741–1750 (2015)
5. Deng, C., Ji, R., Liu, W., Tao, D., Gao, X.: Visual reranking through weakly supervised multi-graph learning. In: Proceedings of International Conference on Computer Vision, pp. 2600–2607 (2013)
6. Alghamdi, R.A., Taileb, M., Ameen, M.: A new multimodal fusion method based on association rules mining for image retrieval. In: Proceedings of Mediterranean Electrotechnical Conference (MELECON), pp. 493–499 (2014)
7. Wenfei, D., Shuchun, Y., Songyu, L., Zhiqiang, Z., Wenbo, G.: Image retrieval based on multi-feature fusion. In: Proceedings of International Conference on Instrumentation and Measurement, Computer, Communications and Control, pp. 240–243 (2014)
8. Bhowmik, N., González, R., Gouet-Brunet, V., Pedrini, H., Bloch, G.: Efficient fusion of multidimensional descriptors for image retrieval. In: Proceedings of International Conference on Image Processing (ICIP), pp. 5766–5770 (2014)
9. Yang, F., Matei, B., Davis, L.S.: Re-ranking by multi-feature fusion with diffusion for image retrieval. In: Proceedings of Winter Conference on Applications of Computer Vision, pp. 572–579 (2015)
10. Zheng, L., Wang, S., Liu, Z., Tian, Q.: Packing and padding: coupled multi-index for accurate image retrieval. In: Proceedings of International Conference on Computer Vision and Pattern Recognition, pp. 1947–1954 (2014)
11. Bai, S., Bai, X.: Sparse contextual activation for efficient visual re-ranking. IEEE Trans. Image Process. **25**(3), 1056–1069 (2016)
12. Shi, X., Guo, Z., Zhang, D., Fang, X.: Multiple features fusion based inverted multi-index for image retrieval. In: International Conference on Virtual Reality and Visualization (ICVRV), pp. 148–153 (2015)

13. Kabbai, L., Abdellaoui, M., Douik, A.: Content based image retrieval using local and global features descriptor. In: Proceedings of International Conference on Advanced Technologies for Signal and Image Processing (ATSIP), pp. 151–154 (2016)

14. Pancham, A., Withey, D., Bright, G.: Tracking image features with PCA-SURF descriptors. In: Proceedings of International Conference on Machine Vision Applications (MVA), pp. 365–368 (2015)

15. Banerji, S., Sinha, A., Liu, C.: A new bag of words LBP (BoWL) descriptor for scene image classification. In: Wilson, R., Hancock, E., Bors, A., Smith, W. (eds.) CAIP 2013. LNCS, vol. 8047, pp. 490–497. Springer, Heidelberg (2013). https://doi.org/10.1007/978-3-642-40261-6_59

16. Liu, X., Huang, L., Deng, C., Lang, B., Tao, D.: Query-adaptive hash code ranking for large-scale multi-view visual search. IEEE Trans. Image Process. 25(10), 4514–4524 (2016)

17. Kekre, H.B., Bharadi, V.A., Thepade, S.D., Mishra, B.K., Ghosalkar, S.E., Sawant, S.M.: Content based image retrieval using fusion of gabor magnitude and modified block truncation coding. In: Proceedings of International Conference on Emerging Trends in Engineering and Technology (ICETET), pp. 140–145 (2010)

18. Wang, X., Liu, K., Tang, X.: Query-specific visual semantic spaces for web image re-ranking. In: Proceedings of International Conference on Computer Vision and Pattern Recognition (CVPR), pp. 857–864 (2011)

19. Yuan, H., Ye, L., Du, L.: A novel method for image feature fusion based on MADM. In: Proceedings of International Conference on Multimedia Technology (ICMT), pp. 2877–2879 (2011)

20. Bagheri, B., Pourmahyabadi, M., Nezamabadi-pour, H.: A novel content based image retrieval approach by fusion of short term learning methods. In: Proceedings of International Conference on Information and Knowledge Technology (IKT), pp. 355–358 (2013)

21. Kavitha, K., Sudhamani, M.V.: Object based image retrieval from database using combined features. In: Proceedings International Conference on Signal and Image Processing, pp. 161–165 (2014)

22. Rahman, M.M., Desai, B.C., Bhattacharya, P.: A feature level fusion in similarity matching to content-based image retrieval. In: Proceedings of International Conference in Information Fusion, pp. 1–6 (2006)

23. Guan, H., Antani, S., Long, L.R., Thoma, G.R.: Comparative study of shape retrieval using feature fusion approaches. In: IEEE International Symposium on Computer Based Medical System (CBMS), pp. 226–231 (2010)

24. Sural, S., Qian, G., Pramanik, S.: Segmentation and histogram generation using the HSV color space for Image retrieval. In: Proceedings of International Conference on Image Processing, vol. 2, pp. 589–592 (2002)

25. Sidhu, R.K.: Improved canny edge detector in various color spaces. In: Proceedings of International Conference on Reliability, Infocom Technologies and Optimization (ICRITO), pp. 1–6 (2014)

26. Daga, P., Dewangan, R.K.: Segmentation singpectral clustering based on texture features. Int. J. Res. Eng. Appl. Sci. 2(2), 37–40 (2014)

27. Xu, Z., Du, J., Ye, L.: Multi-feature Indexing for image retrieval based on hypergraph. In: Proceedings of International Conference on Cloud Computing and Intelligence Systems (CCIS), pp. 494–500 (2016)

28. Gao, Z., Xue, J., Zhou, W., Pnag, S., Tian, Q.: Democratic diffusion aggregation for image retrieval. IEEE Trans. Multimed. 18(8), 1661–1674 (2016)

29. Shendre, A.V., Damahe, L.B.: A review: image retrieval using fusion based technique. In: Proceedings of 2nd International Conference on Sustainable Computing Techniques in Engineering, Science and Management (SCESM), vol. 9, no. 41, pp. 945–955 (2016)

30. Mistry, Y., Ingole, D.T., Ingole, M.D.: Efficient content based image retrieval using transform and spatial feature level fusion. In: Proceedings of International Conference on Control, Automation and Robotics (ICCAR), pp. 299–303 (2016)
31. Sharma, R.D., Damahe, L.B.: A review: modified query based image retrieval. In: Proceedings of 2nd International Conference on Sustainable Computing Techniques in Engineering, Science and Management (SCESM), vol. 9, no. 41, pp. 957–968 (2016)
32. Vadhana, R., Venugopal, N., Kavitha, S.: Optimized rotation invariant content based image retrieval with local binary pattern. In: Proceedings of International Conference on Computing and Communications Technologies (ICCCT), pp. 306–311 (2015)
33. Ying, Z., Jun, Z.: An image sorting algorithm based on SIFT feature matching. In: proceedings of International Conference on Computer and Computational Sciences (ICCCS), pp. 275–278 (2015)
34. Rosipal, R., Krämer, N.: Overview and recent advances in partial least squares. In: Saunders, C., Grobelnik, M., Gunn, S., Shawe-Taylor, J. (eds.) SLSFS 2005. LNCS, vol. 3940, pp. 34–51. Springer, Heidelberg (2006). https://doi.org/10.1007/11752790_2
35. Valenzuela, R.E.G., Schwartz, W.R., Pedrini, H.: Dimensionality reduction through PCA over SIFT and SURF descriptors. In: Proceedings of IEEE Conference on Cybernetics Intelligent Systems, pp. 58–63 (2012)
36. Holidays Dataset. https://lear.inrialpes.fr/∼jegou/data.php
37. Sontakke, R.R., Damahe, L.B.: Logo matching and recognition: a concise review. In: Proceedings of World Conference on Futuristic Trends in Research and Innovation for Social Welfare, pp. 1–6 (2016)

V-HOG: Towards Modified Query Based Image Retrieval

Ruchi D. Sharma[1(✉)], Lalit B. Damahe[1(✉)],
and Nileshsingh V. Thakur[2(✉)]

[1] Department of Computer Technology,
Yeshwantrao Chavan College of Engineering, Nagpur, India
ruchidsharma2@gmail.com, damahe_l@rediffmail.com
[2] Prof Ram Meghe College of Engineering and Management,
Badnera-Amravati, India
thakurnisvis@rediffmail.com

Abstract. Nowadays image editing tools lead to the modification of the original images with ease which includes different operation such as applying various filters, adding additional clipart, partial deletion of image that alters image in terms of shape, color and texture information making it complicated to be retrieved by using existing image mining systems. In this paper, experimentation have been done by creating variants of global Histogram of Oriented Gradients descriptor to extract the features from modified query image which are artificially modified using image editing tools. Experimentation is done on Holidays Dataset, results show that proposed descriptor having 1176 features is better in terms of accuracy and time required for retrieval.

Keywords: Content based image retrieval · Modified images
Feature extraction · Partially-duplicate image · Histogram of oriented gradients

1 Introduction

Recently, the use of digital images has increased a lot for purpose of sharing information, thus large amount of images are continuously generating every day leaving us with large amount of image-based data. In such scenario task of searching for a particular image depending upon the content of image, becomes complicated as we are working with millions of images. A fundamental aspect of content-based image retrieval (CBIR) is mainly focused on the extraction and the representation of extracted visual feature which is an effective discriminative component among pairs of images, trending image sharing feature of social networking sites is leading to modification of images using easily available image editing tools. Thus corpus of the researchers working on CBIR is focusing on techniques of retrieving such artificially modified images, although lot of work has been done but existing work does show good results while working with modified images, thus a lot of scope of work is still remaining.

Modified images are those which are edited by using some image editing applications and task of retrieval of such image is to retrieve the image from the database which matches with all or some of the contents of query image. Some of the examples

© Springer Nature Singapore Pte Ltd. 2018
P. Bhattacharyya et al. (Eds.): NGCT 2017, CCIS 828, pp. 628–639, 2018.
https://doi.org/10.1007/978-981-10-8660-1_47

of artificially modified images to be used as query taken from HOLIDAYS dataset are shown in Fig. 1. The output of retrieval may possibly be the image before modification of the query image followed by the similar versions of the query image. All the images which contain partial duplication of image, filters, flipping or rotating images, adding text, changes in color, texture of image and various types of other transformation are modified images.

Fig. 1. Examples of artificially modified images used as query.

Content-based image retrieval (CBIR) which is also known as query by image content or content-based visual information retrieval (CBVIR) is the technique of searching for relevant images in large databases application by using a query as image. CBIR technique includes few steps, firstly, image pre-processing is done which involves operation on image at lowest level of abstraction whose aim is to improve image data that reduces noise and enhances some image features for better retrieval of images. Some techniques can be sensitive to noise present in image so it is essential to preprocess the images and enhance it for further processes. Image preprocessing may include gray scale conversion, resizing, Gaussian smoothing, etc. Secondly, feature extraction is done where, features can be shape, texture, color, etc. used to denote contents of an image. They specify some quantifiable property of an object, and it is computed in such a way that it quantifies some important characteristics of the object. Features of image are extracted by feature descriptors, depending upon the type of features need to be extracted feature descriptors are used. Feature extraction process is the most important phase of CBIR, the powerful extracted features are better the accuracy of the system will be. The example of such descriptor includes HOG [18], SIFT, ORB [20] SURF [16]. Then, appropriate similarity matching techniques are used to match the features extracted from the query image with the extracted features of the images in database which should compute scoring fast and accurate. Different types of similarity matching techniques include Manhattan distance, Euclidean distance, *etc.*

2 Related Work

In various research on Content-based image retrieval (CBIR) matching visual similar images have been considered as a prominent problem, various local descriptor had successfully resolved to this problem to a certain extent like SIFT [13] but while working with modified images local descriptors become less efficient as the extent to which the modification is done is uncertain. Various researchers worked on this visual similarity problem, Frome et al. [3], addresses the problem of visual category recognition by using the distance function between images. Shrivastava et al. [23], also proposed a method based on visually similar images. Proposed technique performs better on multi-domain visually similar operations such as matching images taken from camera to images tuned into paintings or sketches. Local features from images consisting architectural scenes are extracted in the method proposed by Hauagge and Snavely [4]. To match internal self-similarity between visual entities of images Shechtman and Iran 2007 presented a method [21].

Work on Partially Duplicate images motivated for research on query as modified image, The problem of searching an image before its modification is addressed by the Zhang and Akashi [5]. To extract the features they used variant of HOG as the descriptor. They extract HOG feature in compressed way thus reducing the dimension. Also, Pan et al. [22] proposed an image retrieval algorithm using improved HOG descriptor. They extracted the features using HOG and by using principle component analysis reduced the dimension of features extracted. Zhang et al. [14], proposed a technique to retrieve partial duplicate image by using tree partition voting min hash (TmH) which partitions point of interest in image based on photometric or geometric properties. Spatial partition tree data structure are used to find partial duplicate image by using partition method [19].

Wu et al. [1], proposed a technique by bundling image features into local groups, thus making each group more discriminative than SIFT features. Two groups of SIFT features can be partially matched providing robustness to transformations like photometric and geometric changes. Jiang et al. [9], proposed a method which captures the internal geometric layout called as Local Self Similarity Descriptor which are rotation invariant. They combined Local Self Similarity descriptor with SIFT developing multi descriptor for better retrieval of image. Zhang et al. [12], proposed a descriptor called as Edge-SIFT descriptor which is a local descriptor. Edge-SIFT is based on edge maps patches of local image which have information about both orientation and location of edges making it different from histogram of gradient based descriptor. They also proposed inverted file based indexing technique. Pourreza et al. [2] proposed a technique for partial duplicate image retrieval which extracts the features based on proposed color-based SIFT features eliminating false positive matches, rather than SIFT which only considers the local gradient distribution without including color information.

Li et al. [17], proposed a method for improving the accuracy of Bag of word model by verifying the global geometric consistency of subset of features. The proposed method show improved accuracy and it is robust for the retrieval of some specific partial-near duplicate image.

Harmanci et al. [6], presents a high performance method for near-duplicate image searching. The proposed algorithm uses local features to detect resized, cropped, re-encoded images, modified images and its parts by using content adaptive hash lookups to search.

Wu et al. [7], presents an improved method of bundling the local visual words into groups by bundled feature with an added affine invariant geometric constraint providing good results with transformations such as flipping or rotation of image. Shenjie [11] presented an image retrieval technique which is based on saliency analysis for extraction of region. In addition to that, method [7] was improvised by restricting visual words detection in the region. The discriminative power was increased by improving the bundled features using an elaborate contour. Sluzek [15], proposed a technique for partial near duplicate image retrieval addressing the issue of matching images based on individual keypoints only, the proposed representation supports wide variety of distortion.

Shirke et al. [10], presented a review based on the problems while understanding of an image of natural scene, captured images consist of some ambiguity preserved so it is a challenging task to classify an image while preserving the ambiguity. By using Fuzzy classifier this problem of classification can be solved by considering fuzzy membership function with non-mutually exclusive classes used as categories. Sontakke et al. [8] also presented a concise review based on the logo matching techniques. To overcome the drawbacks of edge detectors and shape detectors they have introduced various methods of previous and recent work which used various descriptors such as SIFT, HOG, SURF and hybrid descriptors like ORB. Shendre et al. [25] presented a review on methods and issues in CBIR for fusing local descriptor and local descriptor so that multiple features can be extracted. Multiple features provides better representation of image contents like color, shape, texture providing better accuracy. Sharma et al. [26] presented a review on retrieval of partially duplicate image retrieval and various issues encountered during retrieval of modified images.

3 Proposed Methodology

The general flow of our proposed method is given in Fig. 2. Proposed method contain three major phases which are explained in detail below.

3.1 Preprocessing

Before calculating the feature vector preprocessing is carried out which includes Gamma correction to optimize the usage of bits, Gaussian smoothing to reduce the noise present in image, resizing of images to size 256×224, conversion of RGB image to gray scale so as to reduce the number of bits required to represent an image.

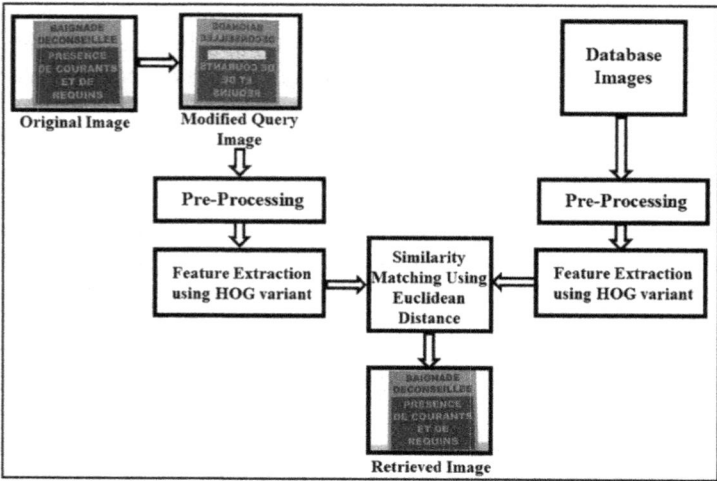

Fig. 2. General framework of CBIR using query as modified image.

3.2   Feature Extraction

Features are extracted from pre-processed images using variant of Histogram of Oriented Gradient (HOG), as it works on Gradients it is invariant to illumination changes or flipping transformation which makes it powerful for using in modified image retrieval. The images are segmented into cells and blocks, where 4 cells make a block and each block consist of 50% overlapping, each cell is of size 32×32, the number of bins are set to 7. The visualization of feature extracted using Variant of HOG is given in Fig. 3. The number of blocks and the dimension of the feature vector is calculated as follows,

Fig. 3. (a) Original unprocessed image (b) Visualization of variant of HOG features extracted.

$$\text{Number of Blocks} = [((\text{Width of Window})/(\text{Block stride in X direction})) - 1]$$
$$\times\ [((\text{Height of Window})/(\text{Block stride in Y direction})) - 1]$$
$$= [(224/32) - 1]\ \times\ [(256/32) - 1] \tag{1}$$
$$= (7 - 1) \times (8 - 1) = 6\ \times\ 7\ =\ 42$$

$$\text{Size of HOG Feature Vector} =\ (\text{Number of blocks} \times \text{Cells per Block}$$
$$\times\ \text{Number of bins per Histogram})\ =\ 42\ \times\ 4\ \times\ 7\ =\ 1176 \tag{2}$$

3.3 Similarity Scoring

The feature vector of query image is compared with the feature vector of images in the database using Euclidean distance measure, it is fast and simple method to calculate the distance measure.

$$\text{Euclidean Distance } d(x,y) = \sqrt{\sum\nolimits_{i=1}^{n} (x_i - y_i)^2} \tag{3}$$

Where x denote the vector $(x_1, x_2, ...x_n)$ which represent the query image and y denote the vector $(y_1, y_2, ...y_n)$ representing an image from the database.

4 Experimentation

Experimentation of proposed method was done on HOLIDAYS dataset [24] which consist of huge variety of images containing water, man-made, natural, fire effects and some personal photographs taken in high resolution on holidays. Some images are added purposely to analyze the robustness of the system under different modifications like rotation, illumination changes, etc. Query Test images are modified artificially using image editing tools which are shown in Fig. 4, they contain various modifications like change in illumination, adding cliparts, cropping, blurring, partial deletion of images, etc.

Different variants of HOG descriptor were developed and experimented using modified query test images based on evaluation parameter such as recall, precision and time taken for retrieval by testing over different query image. We considered Original HOG having 3870 features and developed different variants of HOG having features 1296, 1176, 672 and performed a comparison of recall, precision and time taken for retrieval for query test images shown. The variant of HOG having 672 feature dimension is developed by resizing image to 160×240, the images are segmented into cells and blocks, where 4 cells make a block and each block consist of 50% overlapping,, total number of blocks are 24, each cell is of size 32×32, the number of bins are set to 7 and another variant of HOG having 1296 feature dimension is developed by resizing image to 320×240, the images are segmented into cells and blocks, where 4 cells make a block and each block consist of 50% overlapping, total number of blocks are 54, each cell is of size 32×32, the number of bins are set to 6 and descriptor with 3780 features is developed by resizing images to 64×128, each

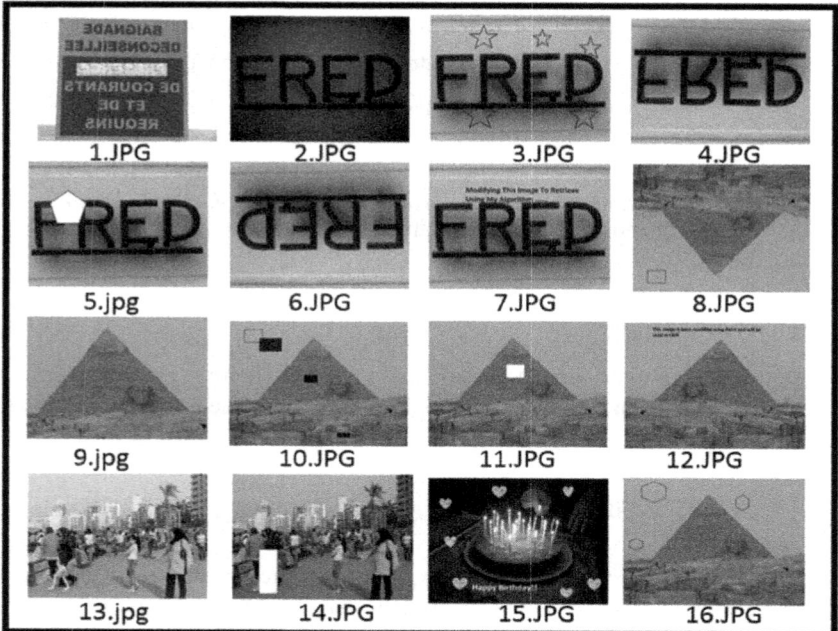

Fig. 4. Artificially modified query test images used in experimentation.

cell is of size 8 × 8, block size set to 16 × 16, bins are set to 9 and total number of blocks are 105. Figure 5 shows the variation of Recall for different modified test images. It can be concluded from the observation of recall that the variant of HOG descriptor with 1176 features shows better recall for some images where other variants show poor results.

Figure 6 shows the variation of precision for different modified test images. It can be seen from the results of precision that the variant of HOG descriptor with 1176 features shows better precision followed by the variant of HOG descriptor having 672 features for some images.

The time required for retrieval by using original HOG descriptor and proposed variants of HOG descriptors are shown in Fig. 7. We can see that proposed method having 1176 features takes usually less time for retrieval as less number of features are to be compared using proposed method making it a compressed descriptor, thus faster retrieval is possible.

The comparison of four descriptors over parameters which are retrieval time, recall and precision of the system is shown in Table 1. Consider image 16.JPG, we can see that retrieval time taken by proposed method is less and also precision and recall is better by using proposed method having 1176 features.

The output of retrieval are shown in Fig. 8 by using proposed method and existing method which is executed using MATLAB version R2014b. Figure 8(a) shows the output retrieved using the variant having 1296 features where query image is the

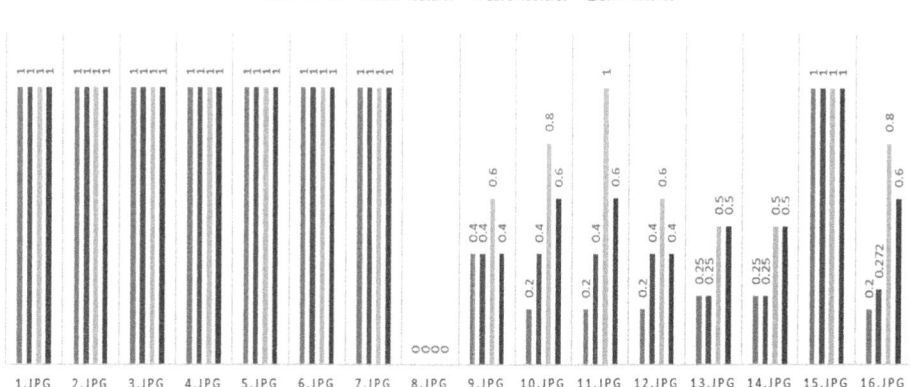

Fig. 5. Experimental results on HOLIDAYS dataset compared by recall.

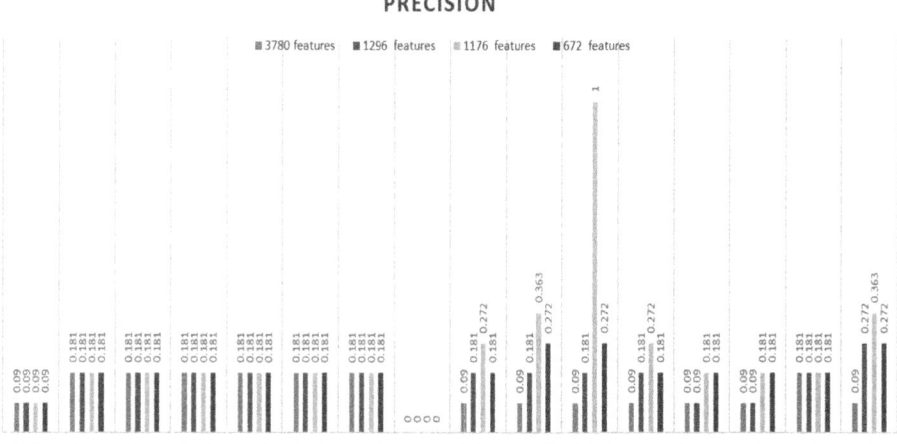

Fig. 6. Experimental results on HOLIDAYS dataset comparing by precision.

modified using editing tool, which is given as the query to the method and the first image is the most similar image to the query image and the numbers above the image denotes the Euclidean distance with the query image, least the distance most similar the image is, here top two similar images have been retrieved. The output retrieved using the HOG having 3780 features, where query image is the modified image, the first image is the most similar image from the database but the other similar image present in the database have not been retrieved which is not the desired output. The output retrieved using the variant having 672 features, where query image is the modified

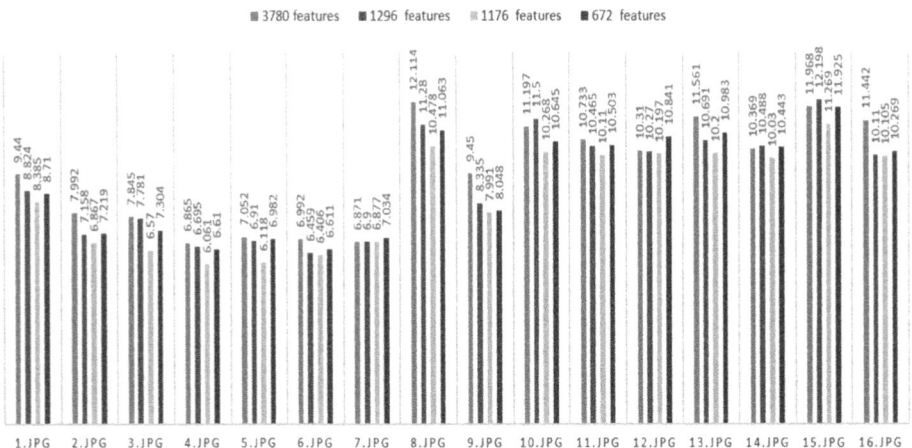

Fig. 7. Retrieval time taken by original HOG descriptor and proposed method.

Table 1. Comparative table showing retrieval time, recall and precision

Sr. no.	Image name	Retrieval time in seconds				Recall				Precision			
		No. of features				No. of features				No. of features			
		3780	1296	1176	672	3780	1296	1176	672	3780	1296	1176	672
1	1.JPG	9.44	8.824	8.385	8.71	1	1	1	1	0.090	0.090	0.090	0.090
2	2.JPG	7.992	7.158	6.867	7.219	1	1	1	1	0.181	0.181	0.181	0.181
3	3.JPG	7.845	7.781	6.57	7.304	1	1	1	1	0.181	0.181	0.181	0.181
4	4.JPG	6.865	6.695	6.061	6.61	1	1	1	1	0.181	0.181	0.181	0.181
5	5.JPG	7.052	6.91	6.118	6.982	1	1	1	1	0.181	0.181	0.181	0.181
6	6.JPG	6.992	6.459	6.406	6.611	1	1	1	1	0.181	0.181	0.181	0.181
7	7.JPG	6.871	6.9	6.877	7.034	1	1	1	1	0.181	0.181	0.181	0.181
8	8.JPG	12.114	11.28	10.478	11.063	0	0	0	0	0	0	0	0
9	9.JPG	9.45	8.335	7.991	8.048	0.4	0.4	0.6	0.4	0.090	0.181	0.272	0.181
10	10.JPG	11.197	11.5	10.268	10.645	0.2	0.4	0.8	0.6	0.090	0.181	0.363	0.272
11	11.JPG	10.733	10.456	10.11	10.503	0.2	0.4	1	0.6	0.090	0.181	1	0.272
12	12.JPG	10.31	10.27	10.197	10.841	0.2	0.4	0.6	0.4	0.090	0.181	0.272	0.181
13	13.JPG	11.561	10.691	10.2	10.983	0.25	0.25	0.5	0.5	0.090	0.090	0.181	0.181
14	14.JPG	10.369	10.488	10.03	10.443	0.25	0.25	0.5	0.5	0.090	0.090	0.181	0.181
15	15.JPG	11.968	12.198	11.269	11.925	1	1	1	1	0.181	0.181	0.181	0.181
16	16.JPG	11.442	10.11	10.105	10.269	0.2	0.272	0.8	0.6	0.090	0.272	0.363	0.272

image, the top three images are the most similar images. The output retrieved using the variant having 1176 features, where query image is the modified image, in this example the top three images are the most similar retrieved which is the desired output which is shown in Fig. 8(d).

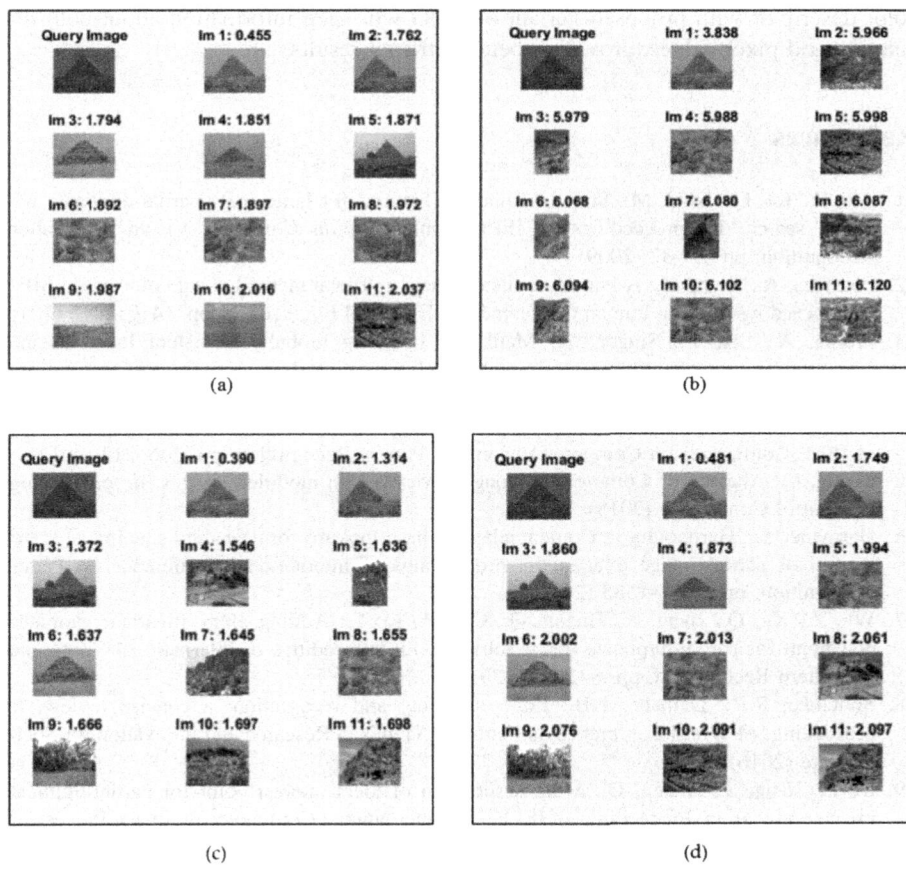

Fig. 8. (a) Shows the retrieved output by using variant having 1296 features (b) Shows the retrieved output by using 3780 features (c) Shows the retrieved output by using variant having 672 features (d) Shows the retrieved output by using variant having 1176 features.

5   Conclusion

The method for retrieval of modified images given as query using Variant of Histogram of Oriented Gradient (HOG) has been introduced. HOG descriptor is mainly designed for human detection as it works on localized cells it is robust to the modification done. HOG features are invariant to various transformations such as flipping image, changes in illumination, thus they provide better results for modified images as new features are also robust to changes. Experimentation on proposed method shows better accuracy and faster retrieval time.

   In future, investigation can be done on proposed method with various compression mechanism. By compressing the large size feature vector to small size while preserving the accuracy of system can further improve the retrieval time of the system. Fusion of color descriptor with proposed variant of HOG will keep information about both orientation and pixel values, providing better retrieval results.

References

1. Wu, Z., Ke, Q., Isard, M., Sun, J.: Bundling features for large scale partial-duplicate web image search. In: proceedings of IEEE Conference on Computer Vision and Pattern Recognition, pp. 25–32 (2009)
2. Pourreza, A., Kiani, K.: A Partial-duplicate image retrieval method using color-based SIFT. In: proceedings of 24th Iranian Conference on Electrical Engineering, pp. 1410–1415 (2016)
3. Frome, A., Sha, F., Singer, Y., Malik, J.: Learning globally-consistent local distance functions for shape-based image retrieval and classification. In: proceedings of International Conference on Computer Vision (2007)
4. Hauagge, D.C., Snavely, N.: Image matching using local symmetry features. In: proceedings of IEEE Conference on Computer Vision and Pattern Recognition, pp. 206–213 (2012)
5. Zhang, C., Akashi, T.: Compressive image retrieval with modified images. In: proceedings of Control Conference (2015)
6. Harmanci, O., Haritaoglu, I.: Content adaptive hash lookups for near-duplicate image search by full or partial image queries. In: proceedings of International Conference on Pattern Recognition, pp. 1582–1585 (2010)
7. Wu, Z., Xu, Q., Jiang, S., Huang, Q., Cui, P., Li, L.: Adding affine invariant geometric constraint for partial-duplicate image retrieval. In: proceedings of International Conference on Pattern Recognition, pp. 842–845 (2010)
8. Sontakke, R.R., Damahe, L.B.: Logo matching and recognition: a concise review. In: proceedings of World Conference on Futuristic Trends in Research and Innovation for Social Welfare (2016)
9. Li, L., Jiang, S., Huang, Q.: Multi-description of local interest point for partial-duplicate image retrieval. In: Proceedings of IEEE 17th International Conference on Image Processing, pp. 2361–2364 (2010)
10. Shirke, J., Shahane, N.: A review of the methods for qualitative understanding of a scene image. J. Res. Eng. Appl. Sci. **01**(01), 37–41 (2016)
11. Shengjie, H.: Region-based partial-duplicate image retrieval. In: proceedings of International Conference on Industrial Control and Electronics Engineering, pp. 1521–1524 (2012)
12. Zhang, S., Tian, Q., Lu, K., Huang, Q.: Edge-SIFT: discriminative binary descriptor for scalable partial-duplicate mobile search. IEEE Trans. Image Process. **22**(7), 2889–2902 (2013)
13. Wang, Z., Wang, Z., Liu, H., Huo, Z.: Scale-invariant feature matching based on pairs of feature points. IET Comput. Vis. **9**(6), 789–796 (2015)
14. Zhang, Q., Fu, H., Qiu, G.: Tree partition voting min-hash for partial duplicate image discovery. In: Proceedings of IEEE International Conference on Multimedia and Expo (2013)
15. Sluzek, A.: Affine-invariant description of keypoint bundles for detecting partial near-duplicates in random images. In: Proceedings of IEEE 20th International Conference Electronics, Circuits and Systems, pp. 269–272 (2013)
16. Bay, H., Tuytelaars, T., Van Gool, L.: SURF: speeded up robust features. In: Leonardis, A., Bischof, H., Pinz, A. (eds.) ECCV 2006. LNCS, vol. 3951, pp. 404–417. Springer, Heidelberg (2006). https://doi.org/10.1007/11744023_32

17. Omari, M., OuledJaafri, S., Karour, N.: Image compression based on exploiting similarities in a group of pictures. In: Proceedings of International Conference on Industrial Informatics and Computer Systems (2016)
18. Dalal, N., Triggs, B.: Histograms of oriented gradients for human detection. In: Proceedings of IEEE Computer Society Conference on Computer Vision and Pattern Recognition (2005)
19. Lee, D.C., Ke, Q., Isard, M.: Partition min-hash for partial duplicate image discovery. In: Daniilidis, K., Maragos, P., Paragios, N. (eds.) ECCV 2010. LNCS, vol. 6311, pp. 648–662. Springer, Heidelberg (2010). https://doi.org/10.1007/978-3-642-15549-9_47
20. Rublee, E., Rabaud, V., Konolige, K., Bradski, G.: ORB: an efficient alternative to sift or surf. In: Proceedings of International Conference on Computer Vision, pp. 2564–2571 (2011)
21. Shechtman, E., Iran, M.: Matching local self-similarities across images and videos. In: Proceedings of IEEE Conference on Computer Vision and Pattern Recognition, pp. 1–8 (2007)
22. Pan, S., Sun, S., Yang, L., Duan, F., Guan, A.: Content retrieval algorithm based on improved HOG. In: Proceedings of 2nd International Conference on Computational Science and Intelligence, pp. 438–441 (2015)
23. Shrivastava, A., Malisiewicz, T., Gupta, A., Efros, A.A.: Data driven visual similarity for cross-domain image matching. ACM Trans. Graph. 30(6), 1–10 (2011)
24. Holidays Dataset. http://lear.inrialpes.fr/people/jegou/data.php#holidays. Accessed 10 Oct 2016
25. Shendre, A., Damahe, L.: A review: image retrieval using fusion based technique. Int. J. Control Theory Appl. 9(41), 945–955 (2017)
26. Sharma, R., Damahe, L.: A review: modified query based image retrieval. Int. J. Control Theory Appl. 9(41), 957–968 (2017)

A Hybrid Feature Extraction Approach for Finding Local Discriminative Coordinates for Face Recognition

Abhisek Gour[✉] [ORCID]

Jai Narain Vyas University, Jodhpur, India
abhisek.gour@gmail.com

Abstract. Several techniques have been proposed for face recognition that use global and local approaches for finding most eligible features for classification. Generally, methods based on localized feature selection techniques are found to be more robust towards illumination, pose and expression variations. In this paper, author has proposed an architecture that uses wavelet decomposition and informational entropy for finding localized discriminative coordinates in the image space for face recognition. The identified coordinates are supplied to a Gabor filters based face recognition model for classification. The proposed system uses single image per subject for training database and is able to achieve a recognition rate of 92.5% with ORL face database.

Keywords: Discriminative coordinates · Face recognition · Gabor filters
Informational entropy

1 Introduction

Among the widely used biometric identity systems, physiological methods (i.e. fingerprint, face, DNA etc.) are usually more stable because of their non-mutable properties (except in the case of severe injuries or medical interference). Face recognition is one of the few biometric methods that possess the merits of both high accuracy and low intrusiveness. For this reason, since the early 70's [1], face recognition has drawn the attention of researchers in fields from security, psychology, image processing and computer vision [2, 3].

Face Recognition, generally, refers to the process of identification of individuals from a database of digital raster images. A face recognition system can be, generally, divided into three parts: (1) Face Detection, (2) Feature Extraction and (3) Classification [4]. The detection step is to determine - whether any human faces appear in a given image, and where these faces are located at. The output of face detection is supposed to be patches containing each face in the input image -effectively processed to justify the scales and orientations of respective faces. These face patches are then processed in feature extraction step to obtain a low-dimensional unique representation of each face. The output is usually a fixed dimension vector or a set of fiducial points (i.e. their respective locations in face image) corresponding to each face image. At last, the

P. Bhattacharyya et al. (Eds.): NGCT 2017, CCIS 828, pp. 640–650, 2018.
https://doi.org/10.1007/978-981-10-8660-1_48

classification step deals with the process of matching a test face in the database of previously processed input faces.

A recent survey of face recognition techniques can be found in [4, 5]. Generally, it has been observed that efficient feature extraction is crucial for satisfactory accuracy and recall of a face recognition system. Various techniques have been devised over time to find the most significant representation of face images that could be used for supervised or unsupervised classification. These techniques may be further categorized as statistical approaches, structural approaches, feature-based approaches, template based approaches etc. [6].

In this paper, author has proposed a feature extraction approach that utilizes localized entropy calculations to select most prominent features in the image space. In the feature extraction phase, entropy calculations are used to identify the coordinates that contribute maximally to the entropy of the smaller subsets of input image i.e. provide maximum discrimination locally. Wavelet analysis has been used as a pre-processing step to remove high frequency components from the face image that could affect the entropy contribution of individual subspaces because of illumination and pose variations. Subsequently, a Gabor filters based face recognition model has been used for experimental analysis of the proposed system.

Basic computational steps of the proposed system are depicted in the flowchart shown in Fig. 1. Each component is further discussed in detail in the following sections. Section 2 provides introduction to wavelet decomposition and its application as a pre-processing step for proposed system. In Sect. 3, the proposed feature extraction

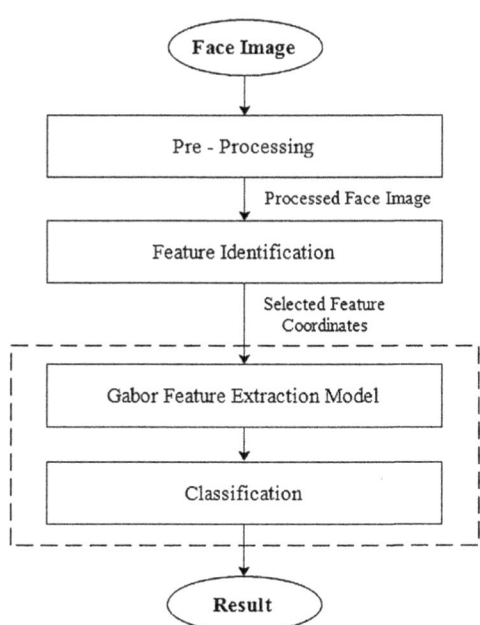

Fig. 1. Computational steps of the proposed face recognition system

algorithm is discussed which is further divided into two subsections. In Sect. 4, classification method used for experimental analysis is presented which is followed by experimental results and conclusion in Sects. 5 and 6 respectively.

2 Wavelet Decomposition and Dimension Reduction

Face images pose several challenges for identification of discriminative features [7]. Illumination changes and RST variations may cause sharp changes in intensity distribution of the face image. Generally, these sharp changes do not explicitly correspond to the facial structure of the subject and can be identified as high frequency components in the intensity spectrum of the input face image [8]. In the proposed approach, localized entropy calculations have been used for extracting eligible features for classification. The sharp intensity variations in the input image may alter entropy contribution of the affected region and, as a result, may cause false feature selection. It is therefore required to pre-process input images to discard such components.

Discarding the high frequency components from input image can be achieved using low pass filtering operation. It is to be noted that after applying a half-band low pass filter on the image spectrum, the maximum frequency in the image space is reduced to half. Therefore, following Nyquist's rate criterion, the image can now be subsampled as half of the data is now redundant. The subsampling process increases the scale and thereby, reduces the resolution of the image without affecting the low frequency spectrum of the image which is of most interest for our application.

Wavelet transform provides good frequency resolution of the input signal without losing significant time domain information. Discrete wavelet transform employs a technique known as sub-band coding to recursively apply low pass and high pass filtering operations on input signal to analyze frequency information of the signal at different resolutions [9, 10]. This allows us to identify high frequency components within the image spectrum and subsample the data post removal. But reconstruction of the input signal after removal of high frequency components using this phenomenon is theoretically possible using only ideal half band filters. Ingrid Daubechies developed certain filters that provide perfect reconstruction in certain conditions [11]. These filters are vastly known as Daubechies' wavelets.

The proposed system uses Fast Wavelet Transform (FWT) [12] for performing the desired operations on two-dimensional images. Output of 2-dimensional FWT is a set of four images (WD, WV, WH and W), of which, former three represent the high frequency components of the input image. The last one is a coarse approximation of the input image and is particularly desirable for our application. Moreover, this approximate image is relatively smaller (lesser number of pixels) than the input image due to subsampling. Using this image in later steps also reduces processing effort of the system significantly.

The intensity spectrum of a face image taken from ORL face database is shown in Fig. 2. Correspondingly, the intensity spectrum of the respective approximation image obtained after applying the wavelet transform is shown in Fig. 3. It can be observedfrom

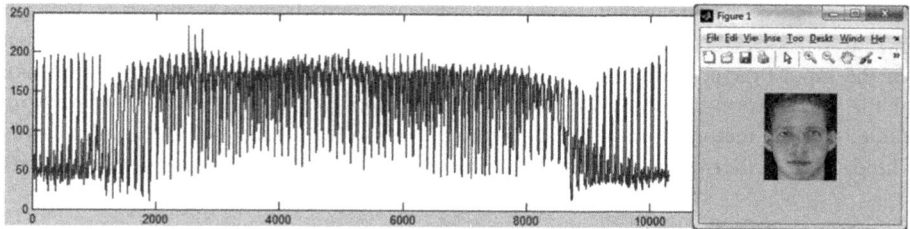

Fig. 2. Frequency representation of original ORL face image (shown on the right)

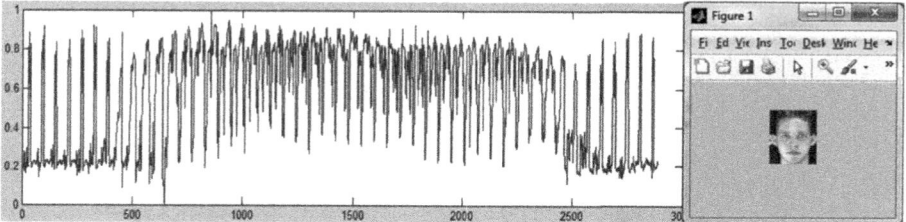

Fig. 3. Frequency representation of processed ORL face image (shown on the right)

these images that, after the removal of high frequency components, the approximation spectrum still resembles an identical distribution as the original spectrum.

3 Identification of Feature Coordinates

The process of feature extraction can be distributed into two parts – identification of feature coordinates in input face image and preparation of feature vector for classification. In the proposed method, author has used localized calculations to find those coordinates in the image space that maximize the respective entropy.

Entropy, in information theory, represents the amount of randomness available in any sample outcome of a finite stochastic process. If we consider intensity spectrum as stochastic representative of any image, then by assigning entropy value of corresponding neighborhood (for e.g. 9×9 window) of each pixel in the input image to intensity value of respective pixel in the output image, we get a new intensity mapped image that can be used to identify the most discriminative (or eventually most eligible) coordinates in the input image for feature extraction. The above phenomenon is illustrated in Fig. 4.

On the left in Fig. 4, low resolution image obtained by removing high frequency components in pre-processing phase is shown. Now, using a 5×5 window, localized entropy values are calculated by shifting the window at all possible locations in the face image. At each shift, entropy value of the area covered by the current window is assigned to intensity value of the output pixel respective to the center pixel of the current window. The resultant image after intensity normalization is shown on the right in Fig. 4. As can be seen from the figure, this new image depicts an information map for the input image. Intensity of the pixels in this image represent the localized notion of the information available in that region. By applying a threshold on the entropy value, eligible feature points (that contribute most to the entropy of the image) can be found. This further refines the feature selection and reduces the dimensionality of data.

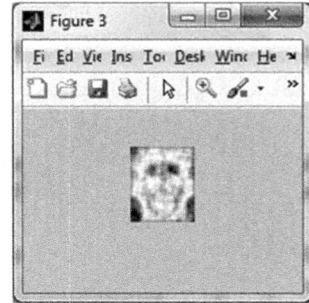

Fig. 4. (From left to right) (a) Pre-processed face image from ORL database (b) Respective localized entropy map obtained using a 5 × 5 window

By experimentation, it has been observed that most of the discriminative properties of the faces can be represented only by the pixel coordinates respective to more than 90% of the energy (or randomness). Therefore, only these pixel coordinates can be chosen as the features of interest.

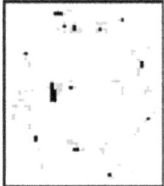

Fig. 5. (From left to right) (a) The face image (b) Entropy image at 96% threshold (c) Inverted entropy image

This threshold value can be termed as Entropy Threshold and denoted by E_t. We will designate a term "Entropy image" for the image obtained after applying the specified threshold. Figure 5 shows the corresponding entropy image for the face image used in pre-processing phase (see Fig. 4). Total number of features eligible for selection after discarding the feature coordinates below 96% Et comes out to be 595, which is a considerably low count than the original dimensions of the image (112 × 92) or features selected by many major feature based algorithms.

4 Preparation of Feature Vector

Gabor filters are extensively used in computer vision applications because of their close approximation to the simple cells in human visual cortex [13]. It has been shown that these filters provide some fairly reliable parameters for classification [14–16].

The responses obtained by applying Gabor filters of different scales and orientations at feature coordinates obtained in the selection step are used for preparation of feature vectors. For experimental analysis, a combination of 40 Gabor filters varied over 5 scales and 8 orientations have been used [17]. Magnitude and orientations of these filters are illustrated in Fig. 6(a) and (b) respectively.

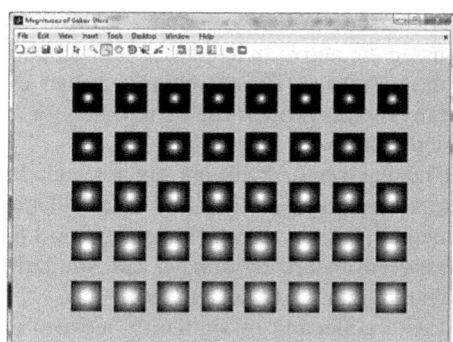 

Fig. 6. (From left to right) (a) Magnitude and (b) orientation of 40 Gabor filters used for proposed system

Feature vector of a face image is composed of Gabor responses and their respective location index (i.e. index of the selected coordinate in row-vectored representation of face image) at each of the selected feature coordinates. A feature vector corresponding to a selected feature coordinate can be defined as:

$$V_i = \{i, GR_{i,j} \ldots\}; \quad j \in \{1, 2, \ldots 40\} \tag{1}$$

where,

i = Index of feature coordinate in row-vectored image space
$GR_{i,j}$ = Gabor response for i^{th} index corresponding to j^{th} Gabor filter

Now, a face image I can be represented as –

$$F_I = \{V_i, \ldots V_k\} \tag{2}$$

Here, $i, \ldots k$ are feature locations selected in feature selection process and V_i is feature vector corresponding to location index i.

5 Classification

For classification task, a similarity measure based setup has been used as proposed in [18]. Similarity function used to derive a relationship between any two feature vectors *a* and *b* (possibly representing a test face and a database face respectively) is given below:

$$S_{a,b} = \frac{\sum |V_a||V_b|}{\sqrt{\sum |V_a|^2 |V_b|^2}} \tag{3}$$

where, $|V_i| = L^2$ Norm of the feature vector *i*.

To perform a similarity comparison on two faces (a test face and one from the database), we calculate the similarity values using the above function between all pairs of the feature vectors in the face matrix of the two faces. These similarity values are then used to construct a similarity matrix. Iteratively this process can be repeated for all pairs of test face and the face images in system database.

Now, it can easily be observed that all feature vector pairs are not relevant for similarity calculation. Irrelevant feature vectors need to be discarded from calculation of similarity between faces. In the proposed method, two parameters have been used for elimination of such pairs - spatial distance between feature coordinates and similarity threshold value i.e. similarity below which feature pairs may be ignored.

Now, a similarity matrix can be defined as a collection of similarity between all remaining relevant pairs of feature vectors. It can be denoted as,

$$Sim_{I,T} = \left[S_{i,j} \right]_{n,m} \tag{4}$$

where,

I = Input image,
T = Test image,
$S_{i,j}$ = Similarity of input feature vector i to test feature vector j,
n = Number of input feature vectors,
m = Number of test feature vectors.

It is to be noted here that $S_{i,j} = 0$, for all feature vector pairs that are eliminated.

Now, for obtaining a scalar value, say Similarity Quotient Q_s, the number of feature vectors having similarity greater than or equal to some statistical value is recorded for each pair. Note that, Q_s represent a metric for measurement of similarity between the test face image and database face image. The statistical value to be used can be chosen as a percentage of maximum similarity, mean of similarities above a certain threshold etc. In the proposed system, all the three mentioned statistical values were used for experimentation and the best results were obtained by using maximum similarity i.e.

$$Q_s = \arg max(Sim_{I,T}) \tag{5}$$

6   Experimental Analysis

The proposed system was implemented modularly using MATLAB and the test were performed on a 32-bit machine with Intel Pentium(R) Dual Core CPU clocked at 3.00 GHz and 2 GB DDR3 RAM. For experimental analysis, the ORL face database (now renamed as The Database of Faces) has been used. Currently hosted in joint collaboration by AT&T Laboratories, Cambridge and Computer Laboratory, Cambridge University as a public repository, it provides a small but fairly variant dataset for testing the performance of face recognition systems.

As per the description available on database homepage [19], it contains ten different images of each of 40 distinct subjects. For some subjects, the images were taken at different times, varying the lighting, facial expressions (open/closed eyes, smiling/not smiling), facial details (glasses/no glasses) and head pose (tilting and rotation up to 20 degrees). All the images were taken against a dark homogeneous background with the subject in an upright, frontal position (with tolerance for some side movement).

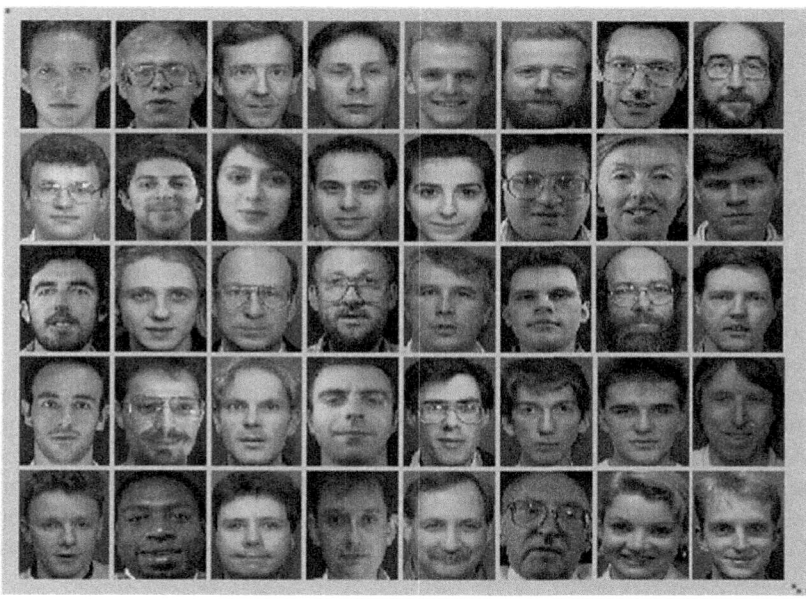

Fig. 7. Face images from ORL database used as training set for experimental analysis

For performing the tests, one frontal face image with neutral pose of each individual was used to build the system database and the others were used for testing. Figure 7 shows the set of face images used to build the system database. The system is tested against variations in entropy threshold and size of the window used for feature selection. Experimental results are formulated in Tables 1 and 2.

Table 1. Experimental results w.r.t. variations in entropy threshold

Entropy threshold (E_t)	Avg. number of features selected	Avg. number of comparisons	Average recall	Mean recognition accuracy
0.90	1519.40	84832.52	100%	**94%**
0.92	1246.60	52534.37	100%	**92.5%**
0.94	921.10	29651.96	100%	**90%**
0.96	539.10	11235.61	100%	**88%**

Table 2. Experimental results w.r.t. variations in entropy window

Entropy window	Avg. number of features selected	Avg. number of comparisons	Average recall	Mean recognition accuracy
All ones 5 × 5	1246.60	52534.37	100%	92.5%
All ones 7 × 7	599.40	11786.44	100%	91.5%
All ones 3 × 3	1087.30	40421.63	100%	92%
Sparse 3 × 3	1847.30	119288.40	100%	90%

7 Experimental Results

Through experimental analysis on the ORL face database, it is found that features corresponding to entropy values greater than 92% of the maximum value are suitable for recognition. Reducing the threshold further causes a significant increase in the selected number of features and degrades recognition speed to an unacceptable value. Whereas, increasing the threshold beyond 96% causes a significant decrease in recognition accuracy. On the other hand, deviation in entropy window does not have much impact on system accuracy but can be used to improve the performance of the system. It is also found that the classification method used is susceptible to the number of features selected for individual images and normalizing the feature extraction process to select a fixed number of features can improve system accuracy even further.

8 Conclusion

We have proposed a new hybrid approach using Gabor filters and localized entropy calculations to extract most significant features from a face image that can be used for face recognition. Proposed method achieves a maximum accuracy of 92.5% with ORL face database which is better than PCA (80%), Fisherfaces (76%), KPCA (88%), elastic graph matching (80%) and Gabor face recognition (90%) but lags behind neural network (96%), line (97%) and KECA (96%) based methods [18, 20, 21]. It is to be noted here that the proposed system uses only one image per subject for preparation of training database and when compared to the statistical and learning based methods, can provide a better accuracy if sufficient training data is not available.

A normalization method or a flexible classifier that can dynamically adjust the classification parameters with respect to number of features extracted will be developed consequently to further improve the system performance.

References

1. Kelly, M.D.: Visual identification of people by computer. Technical report, Stanford AI Project, Stanford, CA (1970)
2. Chellappa, R., Wilson, C.L., Sirohey, S.: Human and machine recognition of faces: A survey. Proc. IEEE **83**, 705–741 (1995)
3. Zhang, J., Yan, Y., Lades, M.: Face recognition: eigenfaces, elastic matching, and neural nets. Proc. IEEE **85**, 1423–1435 (1997)
4. Chao, W.L.: Face recognition. Technical report, National Taiwan University (2012)
5. Ding, C., Tao, D.: A comprehensive survey on pose-invariant face recognition. ACM Trans. Intell. Syst. Technol. (TIST) **7**(3), 37 (2016)
6. Khade, B.S., Gaikwad, H.M., Aher, A.S., Patil, K.K.: Face recognition techniques: a survey. Int. J. Comput. Sci. Mob. Comput. **5**(11), 65–72 (2016)
7. Jain, A.K., Klare B., Park U.: Face recognition: Some challenges in forensics. In: IEEE International Conference on Automatic Face and Gesture Recognition and Workshops (FG 2011), Proceedings, Santa Barbara, CA, USA (2011)
8. Ramesha, K., Raja, K.B.: Face Recognition System Using Discrete Wavelet Transform and Fast PCA. In: Das, V.V., Thomas, G., Lumban Gaol, F. (eds.) AIM 2011. CCIS, vol. 147, pp. 13–18. Springer, Heidelberg (2011). https://doi.org/10.1007/978-3-642-20573-6_3
9. Polikar, R.: The wavelet tutorial - the engineer's ultimate guide to wavelet analysis. Department of Electrical and Computer Engineering, Rowan University, Glassboro, NJ (2006)
10. Lin, P.Y.: An introduction to wavelet transform. Technical report, National Taiwan University, Taipei, Taiwan, ROC (2009)
11. Daubechies, I.: Ten lectures on wavelets. Society for industrial and applied mathematics SIAM, Philadelphia (1992)
12. MathWorks Fast Wavelet Transform (FWT) Algorithm Description Page. http://in.mathworks.com/help/wavelet/ug/fast-wavelet-transform-fwt-algorithm.html. Accessed 10 May 2017
13. Daugman, J.G.: Two dimensional spectral analysis of cortical receptive field profile. Vision. Res. **20**, 847–856 (1980)
14. Manjunath, B., Chellappa, R., Von der Malsburg, C.: A feature based approach to face recognition. In: IEEE Conference Proceedings on Computer Vision and Pattern Recognition, pp. 373–378. IEEE (1992)
15. Duc, B., Fisher, S., Bigün, J.: Face authentication with gabor information on deformable graphs. IEEE Trans. Image Process. **8**, 504–515 (1999)
16. Wiskott, L., Fellous, J.M., Krüger, N., Von der Malsburg, C.: Face recognition by elastic bunch graph matching. In: Intellignt Biometric Techniques in Fingerprint and Face Recognition, pp. 355–396 (1999)

17. Haghighat, M., Zonouz, S., Abdel-Mottaleb, M.: Identification Using Encrypted Biometrics. In: Wilson, R., Hancock, E., Bors, A., Smith, W. (eds.) CAIP 2013. LNCS, vol. 8048, pp. 440–448. Springer, Heidelberg (2013). https://doi.org/10.1007/978-3-642-40246-3_55
18. Kepenekci, B., Tek, F.B., Akar, G.B.: Occluded face recognition based on gabor wavelets. In: International Conference on Image Processing 2002 Proceedings, vol. 1, pp. I-I, IEEE (2002)
19. AT&T Laboratories Cambridge, The Database of Faces Homepage. http://www.cl.cam.ac.uk/research/dtg/attarchive/facedatabase.html. Accessed 25 June 2017
20. Bhati, D., Gupta, V.: A comparative analysis of face recognition technique. Intl J. Eng. Res. Gen. Sci. 3(2), 597–609 (2015)
21. Özdil A., Özbilen M.M.: A survey on comparison of face recognition algorithms. In: IEEE Conference Proceedings on Application of Information and Communication Technologies (AICT) 2014, Astana, Kazakhstan. IEEE (2014)

Vision-Based Gender Recognition Using Hybrid Background Subtraction Technique

Gourav Takhar[1], Chandra Prakash[1,2(✉)], Namita Mittal[1], and Rajesh Kumar[1]

[1] Malaviya National Institute of Technology, Jaipur 302017, Rajasthan, India
connectgourav@gmail.com, cse.cprakash@gmail.com,
mittalnamita@gmail.com, rkumar.ee@gmail.com
[2] University of Petroleum and Energy Studies,
Dehradun 248007, Uttarakhand, India

Abstract. Gait-Based Gender Classification (GBGC) is a relatively new field in gender classification based applications. Lots of work has been done on gender classification using voice and face. However, little, on the effect of background subtraction on gender classification. This paper focuses on analyzing the effects of background subtraction techniques used to obtained gait energy for GBGC and consider cases where the subject is injured or changes walking behavior intentionally. No prior research has been done on datasets containing walking behavior and effect of background subtraction on GBGC. ViMO and MOG2 are used as background subtraction techniques and applied on the dataset collected at MNIT- Jaipur containing 50 subjects (17 Female and 33 Male) with a total of 590 video sequences. The selected video sequences contained normal walk and unhealthy walk (both left and right) pattern. This paper shows ViMO technique performs better than state of the art MOG2 technique and effect of changing walking behavior is negligible.

Keywords: Gait based gender classification (GBGC) · Background subtraction
MOG2 · ViMO

1 Introduction

Gait-based gender classification is a relatively new field of gender classification based applications. GBGC is used to classify a person's gender based on walking behavior. It is different from fingerprint, face or iris based classification as It is not obtrusive, easy to obtain features, low image resolution requirement, etc. Long range security surveillance system makes it an attractive method for gender classification. Research work and study shows that GBGC is an efficient way for gender recognition with the far distance surveillance system. Li et al. [1] in 2008 studied the effect of seven parts (arm, trunk, head, thigh, back lower leg, front lower leg and feet) of the body on gender classification. Classification is based on Support Vector Machine (SVM) applied on 122 subjects from University of South Florida (USF) gait database. The study shows the effects of different parts of the body on gender recognition either positively or negatively.

© Springer Nature Singapore Pte Ltd. 2018
P. Bhattacharyya et al. (Eds.): NGCT 2017, CCIS 828, pp. 651–662, 2018.
https://doi.org/10.1007/978-981-10-8660-1_49

Lu et al. [2] in 2014 proposed a point to set metric learning approach on averaged gait images to GBGC in an unconstrained environment. It uses cluster-base averaged gait image as features and used a sparse reconstruction based metric learning technique. They constructed Advanced Digital Sciences Center- Arbitrary Walking Directions gait database and is now publically available online. This approach resulted in 98% correct classification rate on CASIA-B data set.

Yu et al. [3] in 2009 proposed GBGC using weighted GEI (5 regions with different weights). A classification rate of 95.97% was obtained using SVM classifier on features obtained after applying ANOVA for feature reduction. To find suitable features, the classification method is applied to features obtained after PCA and before PCA for comparison.

1.1 Dataset

For this study, the dataset is collected at MNIT-Jaipur containing 50 subjects (33 Males and 17 Females), containing normal and injured walk (both left and right side of frames) pattern. Each subject has multiple videos with a total of 590 videos (203 Females and 387 Males). Subjects walk at 90° from the camera. The videos work at 50 frames per second. The dataset is divided into three sub-datasets namely Normal, Injured and Combined. Injured contains datasets of subjects walking while injured, and combined is the collection of both. The CASIA-B dataset also has been used to analyze the effect of PCA on GBGC.

2 Feature Extraction

This paper uses Gait Energy Images (GEI) as features for the classification purpose. To obtain GEI from a video following steps are followed.

2.1 Silhouette Extraction

Various Background subtraction techniques are available to obtain silhouettes from a frame. For this paper, we have selected a state of the art MOG2 and ViMO.

The background subtraction techniques can be divided into four classes: Basic Techniques, Statistical Techniques, Machine Learning Techniques, and other techniques [4]. Any BS technique has three basic steps: (1) Initialization of background Model (2) Classification of each pixel as background or foreground and (3) updating of background model as shown in Fig. 1. State of art background subtraction techniques are discussed in this section for quantitative analysis with the proposed technique.

Basic Techniques. Most BS techniques assume a video sequence (I) with the static background (B), devoid of any moving object and foreground pixel value differentiated from B. Each pixel value is classified into foreground and background:

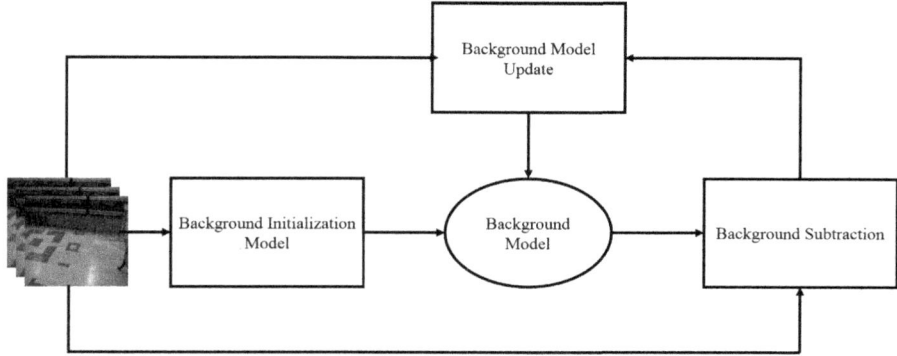

Fig. 1. Basic flow diagram of background subtraction technique

$$Foreground\ (I_{xi,yi}\ :\ d(I_{xi,\,yi},\ B_{x,y}) > T) \tag{1}$$

$$Background\ (I_{xi,yi}\ :\ d(I_{xi,\,yi},\ B_{x,y}) < T) \tag{2}$$

Where T is a threshold, $I_{xi,yi}$, $B_{x,y}$ is the pixel value at (x,y) in i^{th} frame and background respectively. d() is the distance between both pixel values. BST can be classified based on how background and foreground are classified.

The background is modeled using mean and median [5, 6] on last few temporal frames. Mean approach uses the average of last N frames and uses the result as background. It is also known as an average filter. Median chooses the middle value of the last N sorted pixel values and Histogram uses the mean of most occurring pixel value-bin as the background pixel. Using this background model a threshold can be applied over the distance between corresponding pixel values of I and B. Here Euclidean distance are used, but depending on the conditions Manhattan, Mahalanobis or any other distance method can be applied. This technique is faster than all other techniques and works better in constrained environments (static background, no shadow, No intermittent object motion and noiseless images) [4].

Visual Background Extractor (ViBe). It was proposed by Barnich and Van Droogenbroeck [7]. For every pixel, the background model is defined as a collection of pixel values chosen from past pixel values at the same position or its neighbors. To distinguish this pixel value as background or foreground it is compared with values from the collection corresponding with this pixel, and update the collection by selecting a random value from collection to replace with the background. The background model is initialized from a single frame assuming that pixels present in neighborhood share alike temporal distribution. Pixel model is initialized with values present in the neighborhood of each pixel. Each new pixel value is compared with closest pixel model values, within a Euclidean distance of R from new pixel value. The number of pixel values within the radius of R is stored as the cardinality of the pixel. The pixel is identified as background if cardinality is equal or greater than given threshold. Pixel model update uses random selection policy that assures an exponentially decaying lifespan for the values constituting the background models. ViBe gives good detection results in the dynamic background, Object introduction and removal from the background, camera jitter, and illumination changes but fails to detect shadow, unsatisfactory results in the dark background and bootstrap videos.

MOG2. It is a Gaussian-Mixture based BS technique. It is derived from papers by Zivkovic in 2004 [8] and 2006 [9]. K Number distributions for each pixel is selected dynamically. Hence providing better flexibility to changing images due to illumination changes. MOG2 gives a choice of deciding shadow be identified or not. If (detectShadows = True), it identifies and marks shadows, but increases the computing time. Shadows will be indicated in grayscale (127-pixel value). MOG2 gives good detection results in cases other than intermittent object motion or very slow moving object. OpenCV library provided this function which is compared with other techniques provided by OpenCV for background subtraction.

ViMO: Proposed Background Subtraction Technique to overcome the limitations of the above-mentioned state of art BSTs, a new hybrid technique has been proposed in this section. A hybrid background subtraction techniques ViMO, combining the properties from both MOG2 and ViBe has been proposed. ViBe performs poor in the presence of shadow and when the moving object is present in the first frame. While MOG2 performs better in both cases, but with very slow moving objects MOG2 diffuses the moving object in the background. Algorithm 1 illustrates the proposed algorithm for ViMO.

Algorithm 1 Proposed ViMo Algorithm

---
procedure ViMo
    Initialize F_i = first frame
    Model1 ← Initialize ViMO background model using F_i
    Model2 ← Create MOG2 background model
    for Each particle i **do**
        Output1 ← Apply ViBe classification with Model1.
        MOG_out ← Apply MOG2 classification with Model2.
        Output ← Remove shadow using MOG_out
        Update ← ViMO background model using MOG_out
    end for
    Exit
end procedure

Figure 2 presents the workflow of the proposed ViMO background subtraction technique. It can be divided into three phases: (1) Background Model Initialization From a Single Frame (2) Pixel Model and Classification Process (3) Updating the Background Model Over Time.

1. **Background Model Initialization From a Single Frame:** A single frame does not consist of temporal data, so we apply the hypothesis that adjacent pixels share similar temporal distribution. It explains the point that we fill the pixel model with pixel data obtained in the spatial adjacency of every pixel. We choose the pixel values for background model at random from their adjacent pixels of the initial frame. Neighborhood pixels are required to be selected such that it is sufficient to

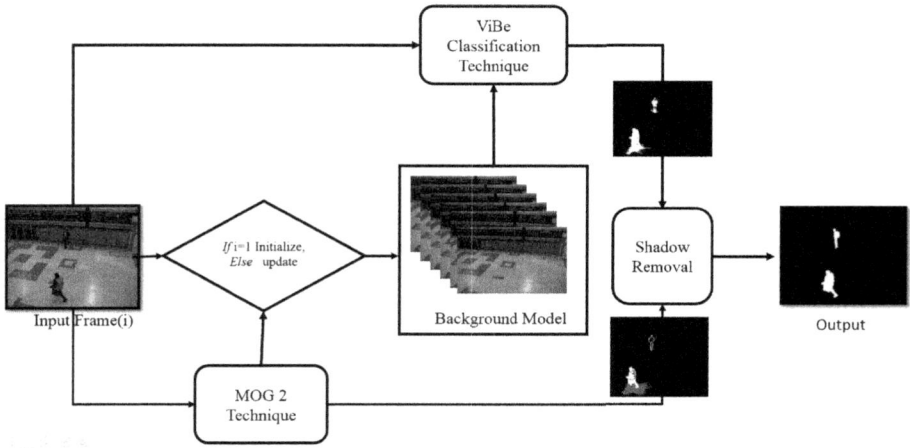

Fig. 2. Flow diagram of proposed ViMO: background subtraction technique

constitute a satisfactory number of diverse values while considering the analytic similarity among values at distinct locations lowers as the range of neighborhood rises. From [7], choosing values for background model at random from 8-adjacent neighborhood of every pixel has been confirmed to be adequate. Background model for each pixel is represented as a set of N values ($M_{(x,y)} = (V_1, V_2, ... V_N)$). V_1 to V_N are selected from $Ng_{(x,y)}$ which is a set of neighborhood pixel values for each $I_{(x,y)}$ pixel.

Where V_i are picked randomly from $Ng_{(x,y)}$ for each pixel. It is possible for a V_i to be picked numerous times or not to be picked at all, as it depends on N and number of values in $Ng_{(x,y)}$. Nonetheless, this is not a concern if one accepts that pixels in the neighborhood are wonderful background model value contenders.

This approach has determined to be fruitful. The only shortcoming is the attendance of foreground in the initial frame will inject a ghost. As per [24], a ghost is a set of connected points, detected as in motion but not corresponding to any real moving object. In this BST, the ghost is injected due to initialization of pixel models $M_{(x,y)}$ with pixel values chosen from the foreground. In following frames, the foreground leaves and reveals the actual background. This shortcoming is removed with the help of background model update, causing the ghost to dissolve after some frames. Luckily, as described in Sect. 2.1, ViMO update method assures a rapid model reconstruction in the existence of ghost as well as gradual fusion of moving objects (Part of the background) into the background model.

2. **Pixel Model and Classification Process:** For classification of a pixel $I_{(x,y)}$ as background or foreground, it is compared with each N values of V_i of background model $M_{(x,y)}$ ($M_{(x,y)} = V_1, V_2, ..., V_N$). For classification of $I_{(x,y)}$, Euclidean distance is calculated from V_i (i = 1-N). If the distance is less than a threshold of R (Taken 20) cardinality $C_{(x,y)}$ is increased by 1. $C_{(x,y)}$ is initialized as 0. $I_{(x,y)}$ is classified as background if $C_{(x,y)}$ is less than 18.

$$C_{x,y} = \sum_{i=1}^{n} \begin{cases} 0 & if \ Euc\big(I_{x,y}, V_i\big) \leq R \\ 1 & if \ Euc\big(I_{x,y}, V_i\big) > R \end{cases} \tag{3}$$

$$out_{x,y} = \begin{cases} background & if \ C_{x,y} \leq Th \\ foreground & if \ C_{x,y} > Th \end{cases} \tag{4}$$

Where $Euc(I_{(x,y)}, V_i)$ is Euclidean distance between two pixels, $out_{(x,y)}$ is classification output of $I_{(x,y)}$ and This the threshold value selected for background classification. Each pixel classification involves N Euclidean distance calculations The computation time depends on (N) and some pixels. The accuracy of the algorithm depends on Cardinality $C_{(x,y)}$ and (R). However, this approach is not able to distinguish shadow from BS. So we use output result obtained from MOG2 to identify shadow pixels and classify them as background.

3. **Updating the Background Model Over Time:** Classification step of our algorithm depends on background Model $M_{(x,y)}$. The concern for the update is which pixel values to memorize in $M_{(x,y)}$ and for how long. ViMO uses update method proposed in ViBe [7]. Which uses memory-less update policy ensuring smooth decaying lifespan for values stored in $M_{(x,y)}$, and random time sub-sampling to extend the time frame embraced by background pixel model. An approach that spreads background pixel values spatially to assure spatial consistency and to grant the adoption of the background pixel models that are hidden in the foreground. Update method provided in ViBe is not efficient in suppressing ghost, so we utilize Processed output provided by MOG2 technique to decide whether to update the background model or not.

Background model $M_{(x,y)}$ is updated randomly based on classification provided by MOG2 which suppresses ghost and shadow. For all pixels classified as background in MOG2, a random value is selected between 0 to 15. If the selected random value is 0 then a random Vi belonging to $M_{(x,y)}$ is replaced with $I_{(x,y)}$. This update method ensures memoryless property and time subsampling. To obtain GEI, these silhouette images are cropped and resized and normalized to fix the size of 240 × 240 images.

2.2   Normalized Cropped Silhouette (NCS)

The size of the silhouette obtained from methods mentioned under section: Silhouette Extraction, is not constant. To obtain GEI, these silhouettes need to be normalized because features used for classification needs to be of the same dimension.

Algorithm 2 Normalized cropped silhouette process

---
procedure NCS
    resized_sil ← resize the silhouette to 240-pixel height.
    t_image ← sub-image of resized_sil (top 1/6 portion of image)
    centroid ← Calculate centroid from t_image
    NCS ← pad resized_sil to make centroid (x coordinate) at pixel position 120 and make resized_sil of size 204X240
    Exit
end procedure

2.3   Gait Cycle

Gait cycle is the sequence of movement of a foot from the first touch on the floor to the next touch of the same foot on the floor, also known as stride. It is shown in Fig. 3. To obtain gait cycle, we collect a total number of foreground pixels in the lower half of cropped silhouette image. To obtain the gait cycle system selects two consecutive peaks as shown in the figure.

2.4   GEI

When obtaining GEI, it is necessary to use adjoining NCS over one gait cycle The normalized cropped silhouette frames over obtained gait cycle are averaged over to obtained GEI.

2.5   Features After PCA

PCA is a technique used to convert probably correlated features into linearly uncorrelated features. Called principle components. The dimension of components thus obtained are either equal to or less than the raw features. These components are arranged in descending order of variance. PCA is sensitive to the relative values of the variables hence the features have to be normalized. Therefore the GEI is obtained through the average of last n silhouettes (Fig. 4).

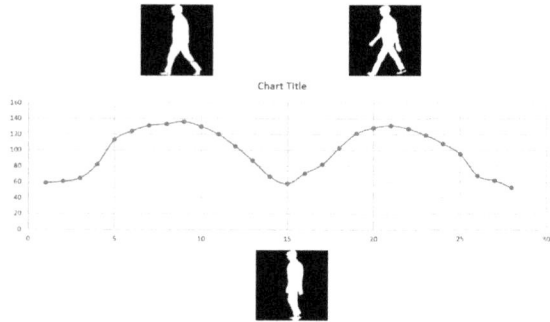

Fig. 3. Gait cycle based on NCS

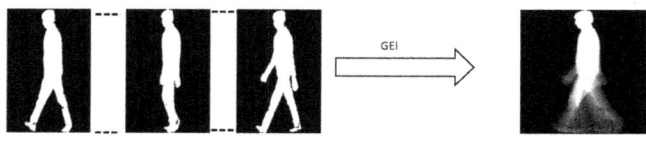

Fig. 4. GEI using NCS over a gait cycle

For each GEI mat (X1, X2,.., Xn)T First calculate mean matrix (m = m1, m2,.., mn) T, where mat is the GEI matrix, Xi is the ith row of mat containing K values and mi is the mean value of Xi vector.

$$m_i = \frac{1}{K} \sum_{k=1}^{K} X_k \tag{5}$$

Now we calculate new mat = mat m. After obtaining we calculate covariance (C) of the new mat as following

$$C = \sum_{i=1}^{n} (X_i - m_i)(X_i - m_i)^T \tag{6}$$

We calculate Eigenvalues and corresponding Eigenvectors. Eigenvalues are arranged in descending order, and Eigenvectors are arranged to correspond to the Eigenvalues and project them over the new mat and save it as F (feature after applying PCA).

Now we have two types of features, raw features (mat) and PCA processed features (F). To find appropriate reduced feature dimension, we ignore column features from right side one by one and find optimal no. of columns to select as features for classification techniques (Fig. 6a).

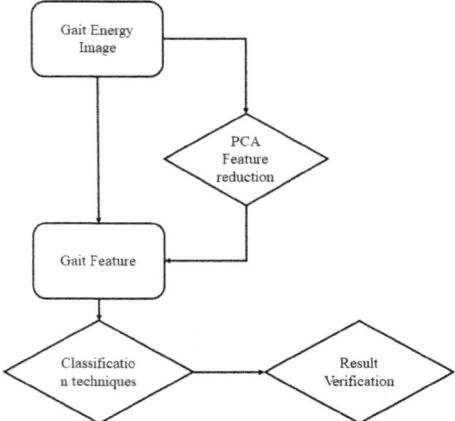

Fig. 5. Flow work of our study

3   Experimental Analysis

Standard CASIA-B dataset is used to analyze effects of PCA dimensional reduction using GEI provided by Zheng [10]. It contains a total of 124 subjects with 6 normal walks for each subject. A total of 196 Female and 558 male GEI are available.

Figure 6a shows that the performance of SVM decreases as we increase the dimension of the F. While Fig. 6b shows the relationship between training sample data and error rate. Figure 6c shows the effect of training sample size over SVM when GEI is used as features.

Maximum correct classification rate obtained using SVM after PCA is 96.7 corresponding to 142 training samples of each, male and female subjects. Maximum correct classification rate obtained using SVM on Gait Energy Images (GEI) is 98.3 corresponding to 158 training samples of each, male and female subjects.

3.1   GBGC on MNIT-Dataset with Different BST

State of the art BST MOG2 is compared with VIMO by GBGC results.

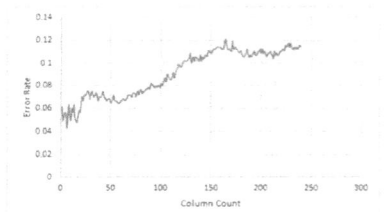

(a) Effect of PCA dimension reduction with 157 training sample

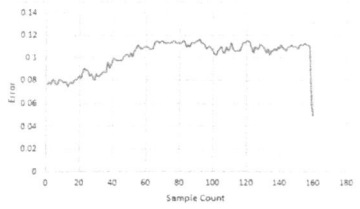

(b) Classification error rate with different size of training samples with column count of 3

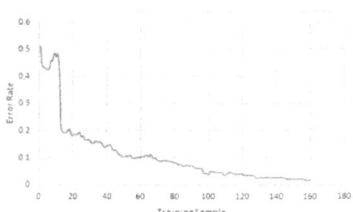

(c) SVM on Raw data (GEI)

Fig. 6. GBGC result with CASIA-B dataset

3.2   Silhouette Extraction

5 background subtraction techniques are applied on MNIT-Jaipur gait dataset to obtain silhouettes which are compared with each other. Figure 7 shows output obtained from Mean, Median, MOG2, ViMO and ViBe BST.

It shows that Mean, Median and ViBe cannot remove shadows which affect the gait cycle calculation, so MOG2 and ViMO are compared with each other.

3.3   GEI

The silhouettes obtained from MOG2 and ViMO are cropped and Normalized concerning its centroid which is used to calculate Gait Cycle and GEI. Figure 8 shows the effect of normalization on GEI.

From Fig. 8 it can be said that normalization plays a significant role in obtaining GEI and also removing the effect of distance of the subject from the camera.

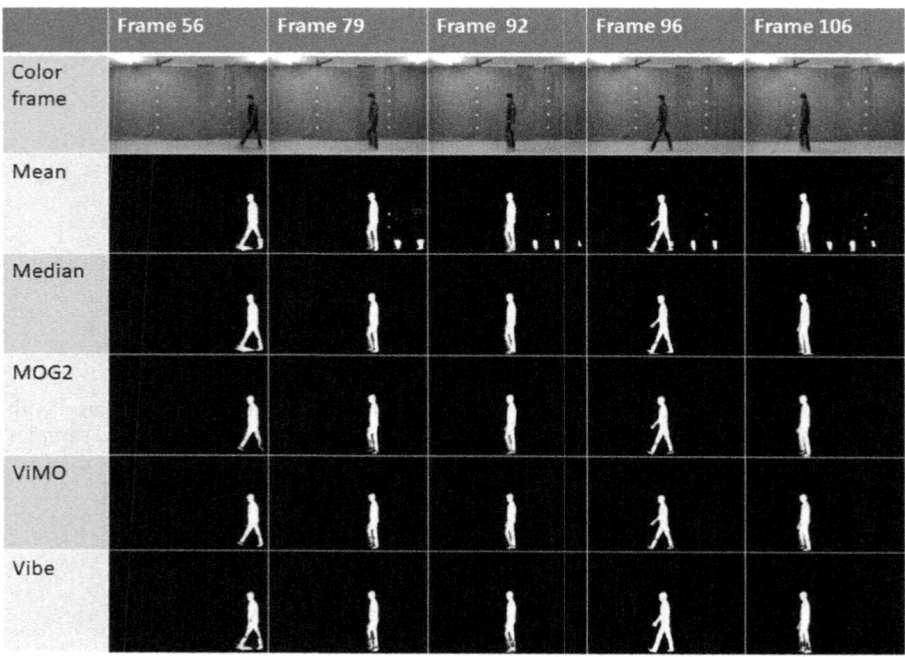

Fig. 7. Silhouette Extraction Based on Mean, Median, MOG2, ViMO, ViBe

3.4   Classification

The input features for training and testing are divided into multiple probes for each dataset. Each probe contains different training and testing data. Combined dataset contains largest GEI hence it is divided into 40 different probes. Experiment results are shown for all probes. Similarly normal and injured are also divided into 30 and 10 probes.

Figure 9c shows experiment result of 40 fold validation with different probes on combined dataset. ViMO BST gives an average of 90.1266025% classification rate. While MOG2 gives average classification rate of 87.8278925%. Normal and Injured dataset is also used for analysis. Figure 9 shows classification error rate using MOG2 and ViMO as BST, for injured and normal datasets. For Normal dataset, MOG2 gives 88.09% correct classification while ViMO gives 90.7% correct classification rate. For

Table 1. Average classification error rate with ViMO and MOG2 techniques

Method	Normal dataset	Injured dataset	Combined dataset
MOG2	0.1190636	0.213794	0.121721075
ViMO	0.092333033	0.1206894	0.098733975

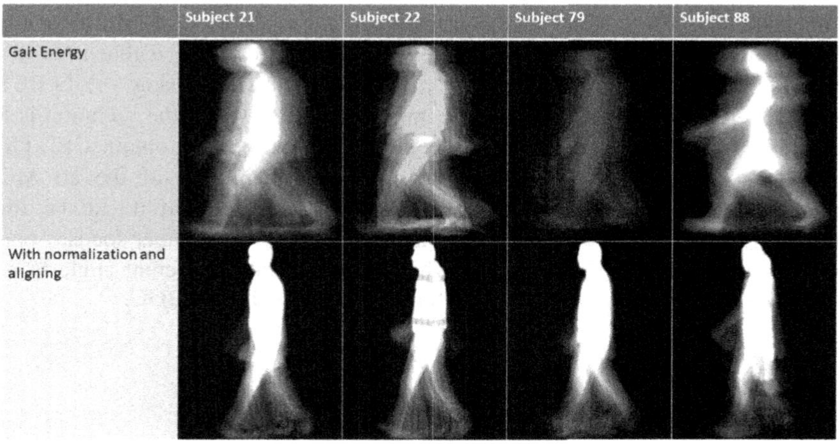

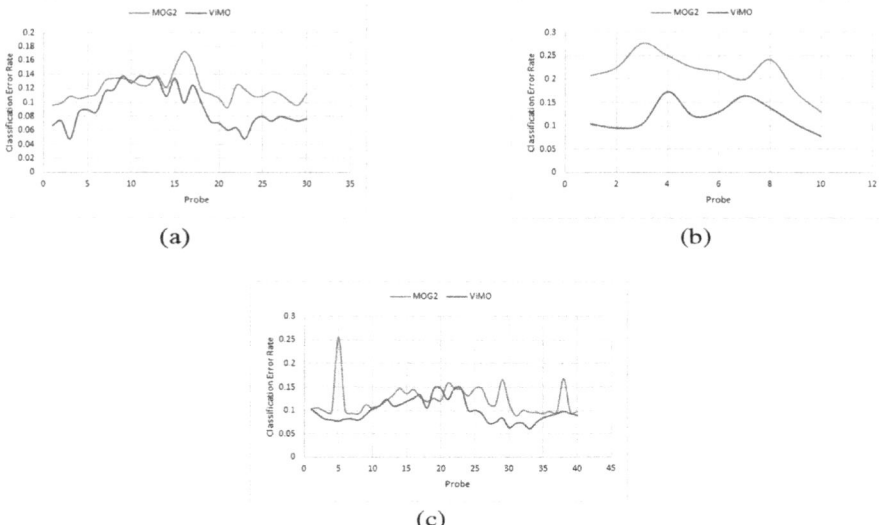

Fig. 8. Effect of Normalization on GEI

(a)

(b)

(c)

Fig. 9. GBGC result with MNIT-Jaipur dataset (a) Classification error rate for MOG2 and VIMO on normal dataset (b) Classification error rate for MOG2 and VIMO on injured dataset (c) Classification error rate for MOG2 and VIMO on the combined dataset

injured dataset, MOG2 gives 78.62% correct classification rate and ViMO gives 87.93% correct classification rate. Because the data is less for injured and normal datasets 10-fold and 30 fold validation are used respectively.

4 Conclusion and Future Work

Results show that when using ViMO correct gender classification rate does not change when the subject changes its walking style or changes its cadence. Table 1 shows that there is less difference between correct classification rate when using ViMO BST for GBGC, either using normal, injured or combined dataset. While the variation is large when using MOG2 for BST. ViMO is better suited for BST to obtain GEI. GBGC results obtained from the proposed BST are better than state of the art MOG2. Although the results obtained from VIMO are satisfactory, but it can be further improved by using better gait cycle calculation approach. This paper focuses on shadow challenges with all three datasets, while not including a different angle from the camera, distance from the camera or dynamic background for GBGC.

References

1. Li, X., Maybank, S.J., Yan, S., Tao, D., Xu, D.: Gait components and their application to gender recognition. IEEE Trans. Syst. Man. Cybern. Part C (Appl. Rev.) **38**(2), 145–155 (2008)
2. Lu, J., Wang, G., Moulin, P.: Human identity and gender recognition from gait sequences with arbitrary walking directions. IEEE Trans. Inf. Forensics Secur. **9**(1), 51–61 (2014)
3. Yu, S., Tan, T., Huang, K., Jia, K., Wu, X.: A study on gait-based gender classification. IEEE Trans. Image Process. **18**(8), 1905–1910 (2009)
4. Takhar, G., Prakash, C., Mittal, N., Kumar, R.: Comparative analysis of background subtraction techniques and applications. In: 2016 International Conference on Recent Advances and Innovations in Engineering (ICRAIE), pp. 1–8 (2016)
5. McFarlane, N.J., Schofield, C.P.: Segmentation and tracking of piglets in images. Mach. Vis. Appl. **8**(3), 187–193 (1995)
6. Elhabian, S.Y., El-Sayed, K.M., Ahmed, S.H.: Moving object detection in spatial domain using background removal techniques-state-of-art. Recent Pat. Comput. Sci. **1**(1), 32–54 (2008)
7. Barnich, O., Van Droogenbroeck, M.: Vibe: a universal background subtraction algorithm for video sequences. IEEE Trans. Image Process. **20**(6), 1709–1724 (2011)
8. Zivkovic, Z.: Improved adaptive Gaussian mixture model for background subtraction. In: Proceedings of the 17th International Conference on Pattern Recognition, ICPR 2004, vol. 2, pp. 28–31. IEEE (2004)
9. Zivkovic, Z., Van Der Heijden, F.: Efficient adaptive density estimation per image pixel for the task of background subtraction. Pattern Recogn. Lett. **27**(7), 773–780 (2006)
10. Zheng, S., Zhang, J., Huang, K., He, R., Tan, T.: Robust view transformation model for gait recognition. In: ICIP (2011)

Content Based Medical Image Retrieval System (CBMIRS) to Diagnose Hepatobiliary Images

Manoj Kumar[1($\boxtimes$)] and Kh. Manglem Singh[2]

[1] Department of ECE, NIT Manipur, Imphal, India
`manojara400@gmail.com`
[2] Department of CSE, NIT Manipur, Imphal, India

Abstract. This paper presents retrieval of hepatobiliary images based on content-based medical image retrieval techniques. Hepatobiliary images are related to hepatobiliary diseases. Hepatobiliary diseases include a group of diseases related to liver and biliary system. Different types of databases are constructed for storing hepatobiliary images. For feature extraction sift (scale invariant feature transform), Hu-moments and GLCM methods are used. Features extracted by these methods are combining to form a single feature vector. Feature extracted by query images and images which are stored in the database are compared using Euclidean distance method. Based on minimum distance images are retrieved. For performance measurement precision, recall and error rate are measured.

Keywords: Scale invariant feature transform (SIFT)
Content-based medical image retrieval (CBMIR) · GLCM · Hu-moment
Euclidean distance · Precision · Recall

1 Introduction

Today's medical imaging systems are widely used by physicians to get needed images to diagnose and treatment planning. We must organize these images for use. For efficient retrieval of images of particular interest, there must be a system which retrieves images from different modalities of medical images. Following are the examples of these modalities: Ultrasound (US), X-ray, Magnetic Resonance (MR), Positron Emission Tomography (PET), Computed Tomography (CT), Endoscopy (ENDO), Mammograms (MG), Digital Radiography (DR), Computed Radiography (CR), etc., Visual properties of the images are represented by these modalities [1]. These visual properties are used for image retrieval and to detect the anatomical and functional information about different body parts for the purpose of diagnosis, medical research, and education [2, 3]. Content-based medical image retrieval system (CBMIR) uses a visual feature of images such as texture, color, shape, and anything which can be derived from the image itself, for the image retrieval [4–6]. CBMIR is an automatic system designed to find images that are most similar to a given query. CBMIR is fast and more efficient compare to conventional text-based retrieval system by using visual

© Springer Nature Singapore Pte Ltd. 2018
P. Bhattacharyya et al. (Eds.): NGCT 2017, CCIS 828, pp. 663–676, 2018.
https://doi.org/10.1007/978-981-10-8660-1_50

features of the image. In text based approach, images are first annotated manually by keywords. Then these keywords are used for retrieval. For the larger database, text-based methods are extremely time- consume, laborious and insufficient. Figure 1 represents a general CBMIR system architecture. There are two major steps for CBIR system, 1. Feature extraction, and 2. Similarity comparison. The first one is the feature extraction, where a set of the feature is generated to represent the content of each image. Features which are extracted from the images are stored in the database. The second one is the similarity comparison where a distance between the query image and each image in the database is computed using their feature vectors. For similarity comparison, Euclidean distance is calculated between query and database images [7].

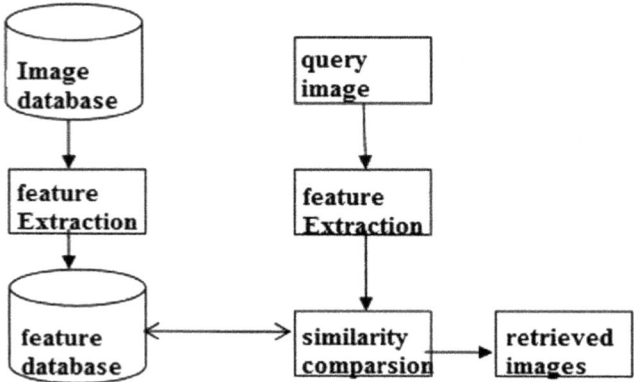

Fig. 1. General CBMIR system architecture

Relevance feedback In CBMIR explained in [8]. CBMIR based on multiple visual features is presented in [9]. Several CBMIR techniques are presented in [10–14]. CBMIR based on multidimensional feature Spaces is presented in [15]. Detection of lung cancer based on CBMIR is presented in [16, 17]. CBMIR for brain image retrieval are presented in [18–20]. SURF features are used image retrieval is presented in [21]. Images are invariant to scale, rotation, and translation by using SIFT. Nowadays sift are used to describe the content of images. Local features are presented by sift. Sift mainly detect keypoints and descriptors from the image. By using these keypoints feature vectors are constructed. By comparing with the query images, similar images are retrieved. In 2014, Bakar et al. had developed a CBIR system based on SIFT [22]. In this approach, authors show the excellent experimental result for the image retrieval. A CBIR system based on sift and PCA was presented by Reddy and Narayana [23]. In this paper author got better image retrieval performance compare to PCA approach. Alkhawlani et al. use SIFT approach for content-based image retrieval [24]. A survey research paper based on SIFT was presented in 2014 [25].

Meenu and Madaan proposed a CBIR system using the neural network and sift in 2015 [26]. In this paper, author has improved recall rate. Meshram and Bhombe proposed a CBIR system using sift and SVM in 2016 [27]. In this paper, the author has got higher precision and recall rate. Hu-moment is used for shape feature extraction. Using texture and shape feature for feature extraction was presented in 2015 [28]. In this paper, the author has used Hu-moment for shape feature extraction. Zhao et al. uses Hu-moment for shape feature extraction [29].

2 Methodology

The aim of this research is to retrieve hepatobiliary Images. Three types of database are created for storing hepatobiliary images.CBMIR approach is used to make the retrieval system. Different types of techniques are discussed to retrieve hepatobiliary images. Features are extracted based on texture, color, shape, and low-level features. These features are compared with query feature to retrieve similar images from the databases. For performance evaluation, common parameters are evaluated. Techniques for retrieving hepatobiliary images are given below.

SIFT and Hu-moment for Hepatobiliary Images
For feature extraction, SIFT and Hu-moment algorithm are used. Fig. 2 represents the proposed block diagram.

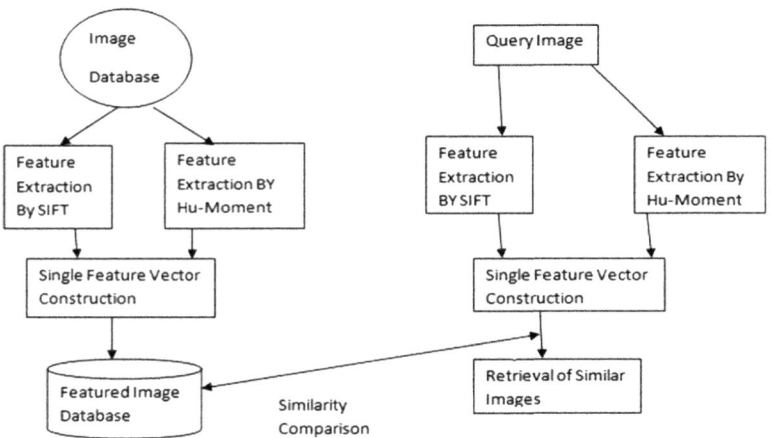

Fig. 2. System flow diagram

Algorithm

STEP1: Create a database containing various hepatobiliary images.
STEP2: Extract features using SIFT and Hu-moment.
STEP3: Single feature vector is constructed by using SIFT and Hu-moment feature vectors.
STEP4: Find the distance between feature vectors of query images and that of Featured database images.
STEP5: Based on minimum distance images are retrieved.

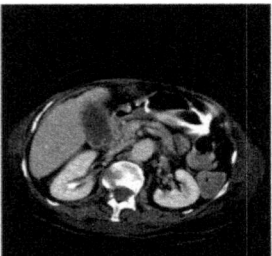

Fig. 3. Hepatobiliary diseases image

2.1   Feature Extraction by SIFT

Steps for SIFT algorithm are discussed below.

STEP1: Scale-space extrema detection Difference of Gaussian (DOG) function is used to detect extrema points. $L(x,y, \sigma) = G(x,y,\sigma) * I(x,y)$
Here $L(x, y, \sigma)$ represents the scale space of an input image $(I(x, y))$. $G(x, y, \sigma)$ is a variable scale Gaussian function. * Represents the convolution operator.

$$G(x,y, \sigma) = 1/2\pi\sigma2 \; e - (x^2 + y^2)/2\sigma^2$$

Stable keypoints are detected by using the formula given below [30].

$$D(x,y, \sigma) = L(x,y, k\sigma) - L(x,y, \sigma)$$

STEP2: Keypoint LocationTaylor expansion series are used to localize the stable keypoints.

$$D(x) = D + \frac{dD^t X}{dx} + \frac{1}{2} XTd \frac{DX}{dx^T}$$
Where D is the difference of Gaussian.
Then the extrema X is determined by
$$X = -\frac{d^2 D^{-1}}{dx2} \frac{dD}{dx}$$

Hession matrix is used to find local maxima.

$$H= \begin{matrix} Dxx & Dxy \\ Dxy & Dyy \end{matrix}$$
$$D_{xx} = D(x,y-1)-2D(x,y)+D(x,y+1)$$
$$D_{yy} = D(x-1,y)-2D(x,y)+D(x+1,y)$$
$$D_{xy} = D(x,y-1)-2D(x,y)+D(x-1,y)-D(x-1,y-1)$$

$Tr(H) = D_{xx} + D_{yy} = a + B;$
$Det(H) = D_{xx}D_{yy} - (D_{yy})^2 = a * B;$
$Ratio = (a + B)^2 / a * B;$
Hession matrix is calculated for each keypoint selected by second order derivative of D. Keypoints are removed which having a value less than ratio [31] (Fig. 4).

Fig. 4. keypoints for Fig. 3

STEP3: Orientation Assignment
Based on local image gradient directions one or more orientation is assigned to each keypoint.
STEP4: Keypoint Descriptor
At selected scale, local image gradients are measured for every keypoints.

2.2 Feature Extraction by Hu-Moment

Hu-moment gives seven- moments. These moments are invariant to rotation, scaling and translation.

Central moment is given by below formula

$$\mu_{p,q} = \sum (x - x_c)^p (y - y_c)^q f(x, y)$$

Here center of the object is given by (x_c, y_c). Normalized central moment is given by below formula

$$\eta_{pq} = \mu_{pq}/\mu_{00}^\gamma$$

$$\gamma = \left[\tfrac{p+q}{2}\right] + 1$$

Seven- moment formula is given below.

$$\emptyset 1 = \mu_{2,0} + \mu_{0,2}$$

$$\emptyset 2 = (\mu_{2,0} - \mu_{0,2})2 + 4\mu_{1,1}^1$$

$$\emptyset 3 = (\mu_{3,0} - 3\mu_{1,2})^2 + (\mu_{3,0} - 3\mu_{2,1})^2$$

$$\emptyset 4 = (\mu_{3,0} + \mu_{1,2})^2 + (\mu_{0,3} + \mu_{2,1})^2$$

$$\emptyset 5 = (\mu_{3,0} - \mu_{1,2})(\mu_{3,0} + \mu_{1,2})[(\mu_{3,0} + \mu_{1,2})^2 - 3(\mu_{2,1} + \mu_{0,3})^2]$$
$$+ (3\mu_{2,1} - \mu_{0,3})(\mu_{2,1} + \mu_{0,3}).[3(\mu_{3,0} + \mu_{1,2})^2 - (\mu_{2,1} + \mu_{0,3})^2$$

$$\emptyset 6 = (\mu_{2,0} - \mu_{0,2})[(\mu_{3,0} + \mu_{1,2})^2 - (\mu_{2,1} + \mu_{0,3})^2] + 4\mu_{1,1}(\mu)(\mu_{2,1} + \mu_{0,3})$$
$$\emptyset 7 = [(3\mu_{2,1} - \mu_{0,3})(\mu_{3,0} + \mu_{1,2})[(\mu_{3,0} + \mu_{1,2})^2 - 3(\mu_{2,1} + \mu_{0,3})^2]$$
$$- (\mu_{3,0} - \mu_{1,2})(\mu_{2,1} + \mu_{0,3})[3(\mu_{3,0} + \mu_{1,2})^2 - (\mu_{2,1} + \mu_{0,3})^2]$$

These seven moments are used to extract a feature from an image.

2.3   Feature Vector Construction

For combining one or more feature vector fusion methods are used. Sift features are fused to Hu-moment features to generate combined feature vector [32].

SIFT and GLCM for Hepatobiliary Images

For feature extraction, SIFT and GLCM algorithm are used. Fig. 5 represents the proposed block diagram.

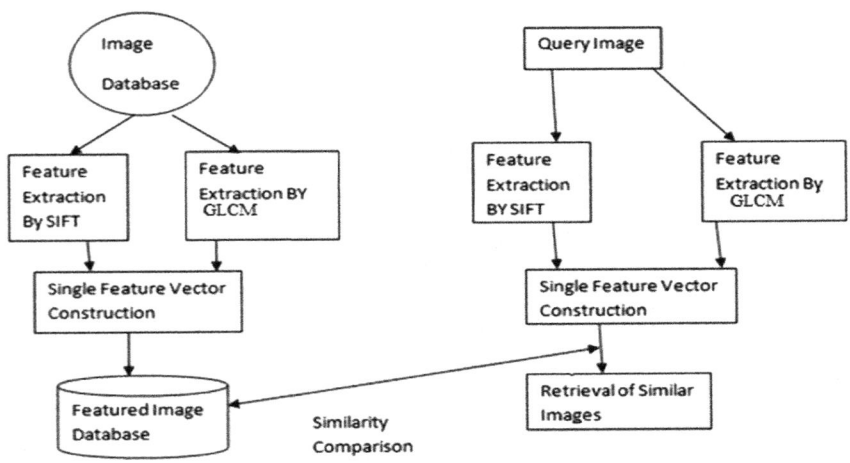

Fig. 5. System flow diagram

Algorithm

STEP1: Create a database containing various hepatobiliary images.
STEP2: Extract features using SIFT and GLCM.
STEP3: Single feature vector is constructed by using SIFT and GLCM feature vectors.
STEP4: Find the distance between feature vectors of query images and that of Featured database images.
STEP5: Based on minimum distance images are retrieved.

2.4 Feature Vector Extraction Using GLCM

A gray level co-occurrence matrix (GLCM) is used to extract texture feature from an image. It uses a statistical method to find texture feature. Contrast, Energy, Entropy, and Homogeneity etc. are an example of GLCM. Formulas are given in Table 1. Energy and homogeneity are used for extracting features from images.

Table 1. GLCM based feature formulas

Feature	Formula
Contrast	$\sum_i \sum_j ((i-j)*(i-j))p(i,j)$
Entropy	$\sum_i \sum_j p(i,j)log(p(i,j))$
Energy	$\sum_i \sum_j p(i,j)*p(i,j)$
Homogeneity	$\sum_i \sum_j \frac{p(i,j)}{1+|i-j|}$

2.5 Feature Vector Construction

For combining one or more feature vector fusion methods are used. Sift features are fused to GLCM features to generate combined feature vector.

- **Hu-Moment and GLCM for hepatobiliary images**

For feature extraction, GLCM and Hu-moment algorithm are used. Fig. 6 represents the proposed block diagram.

Algorithm

STEP1: Create a database containing various hepatobiliary images.
STEP2: Extract features using GLCM and Hu-moment.
STEP3: Single feature vector is constructed by using GLCM and Hu-moment feature vectors.
STEP4: Find the distance between feature vectors of query images and that of Featured database images.
STEP5: Based on minimum distance images are retrieved (Table 1).

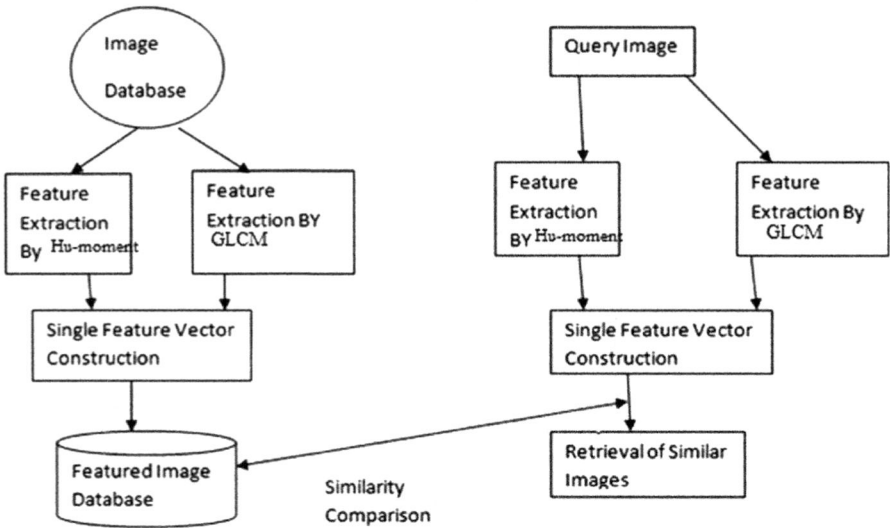

Fig. 6. System flow diagram

2.6   Feature Vector Construction

For combining one or more feature vector fusion methods are used. Hu-moment features are fused to GLCM features to generate combined feature vector.

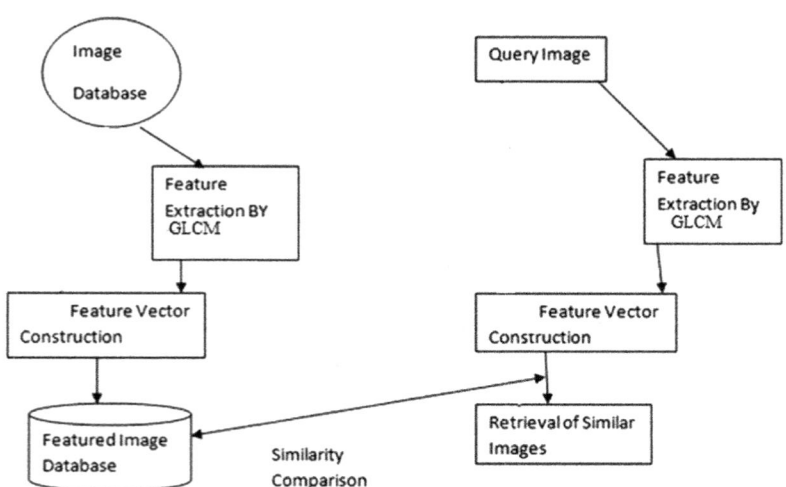

Fig. 7. System flow diagram

GLCM for Hepatobiliary Images

For feature extraction, GLCM algorithm is used. Fig. 7 represents the proposed block diagram.

Algorithm

STEP1: Create a database containing various hepatobiliary images.

STEP2: Extract features using GLCM.

STEP3: Feature vector is constructed.

STEP4: Find the distance between feature vectors of query images and that of featured database images.

STEP5: Based on minimum distance images are retrieved.

3 Results and Discussion

The image database is taken from PEIR digital library [33]. It is a multidisciplinary public access image database for use in medical education. The image database is of three types 1. Radiology 2. Pathology 3. Histlogy. Radiology database contains images related to hepatobiliary diseases which are taken by radiology imaging technique. Radiology database contains more than 200 images. Pathology database contains images related to hepatobiliary diseases which are taken by pathology imaging technique. Pathology database contains more around 300 images. Histology database contains hepatobiliary diseases which are taken by histology imaging technique. Histology database contains more than 200 images. The proposed methods have been implemented using Matlab (Figs. 8, 9, 10, 11, 12 and 13).

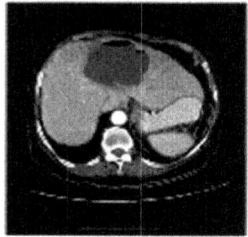

Fig. 8. Query image for the Radiology database

3.1 Image Retrieval Using Euclidean Method

By using Euclidean method distance between the query image and database image is calculated [34]. Euclidean distance method formula is given below.

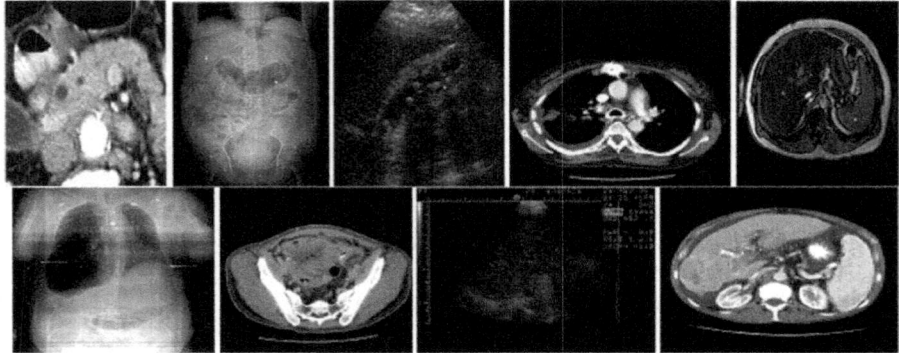

Fig. 9. Images in the Radiology database

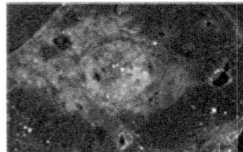

Fig. 10. Query image for the Pathology database

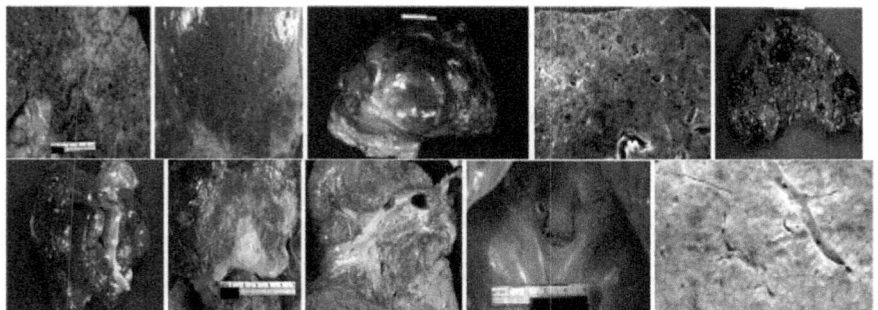

Fig. 11. Images in the Pathology database

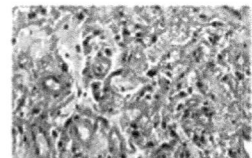

Fig. 12. Query image for the Histology database

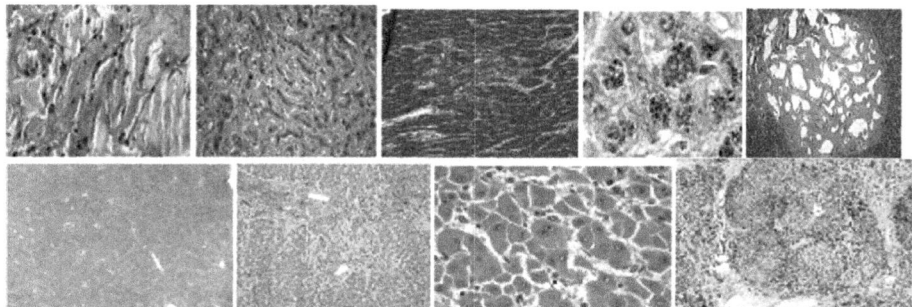

Fig. 13. Images in the Histology database

$$d(A^I, A^Q) = \sqrt{\sum_{i=1}^{n} (A_i^I - A_i^Q)^2}$$

Where,

AI-is the Image in the database
AQ-is the query image for retrieval.

3.2 Retrieval Efficiency

Precision, recall, and error-rate are measured for retrieval efficiency. Results are shown in below tables. For performance measurement retrieval time are measured for all databases.

Table 2. Experimental results for Radiology database

Methods	Precision (%)	Recall (%)	Error rate (%)	Time taken for retrieval in seconds
Sift + GLCM	98.20	60.96	1.79	1.3918
Hu-Moment + GLCM	97.43	56.50	2.56	441.208977
GLCM	98.03	18.58	1.96	5.2034
Sift + Hu-moment	94.71	100	5.28	3.6118

For radiology database, it is found that sift and GLCM approach gives better precision values compared with another approach. Also, error-rate and retrieval time values have been improved compared with another approach. For pathology database, it is found that sift and GLCM approach gives better result compared with another approach. For histology database, it is found that Hu-moment and GLCM approach gives better precision values compared with another approach. Error-rate has been improved for Hu-moment and GLCM approach. Image retrieval time for sift and GLCM approach is found to be less compared with another approach (Tables 2, 3 and 4).

Table 3. Experimental results for Pathology database

Methods	Precision (%)	Recall (%)	Error rate (%)	Time taken for retrieval in seconds
Sift + GLCM	96.77	20.83	3.22	1.579506
Hu-Moment + GLCM	95.16	20.48	4.83	1394.385511
GLCM	95.65	7.63	4.34	8.3483
Sift + Hu-moment	95.04	100	4.95	4.109085

Table 4. Experimental results for Histology database

Methods	Precision (%)	Recall (%)	Error rate (%)	Time taken for retrieval in seconds
Sift + GLCM	96.89	71.83	3.108	3.2108
Hu-Moment + GLCM	97.40	71.21	2.59	1260.923084
GLCM	95.31	23.10	4.68	8.7999
Sif + Hu-moment	94.58	100	5.41	3.6969

4 Conclusion

In this work, images are retrieved by using different CBMIR techniques. Features extracted by using SIFT, Hu moment and GLCM algorithm. Features vectors are combined to form a single feature vector. The experiment is conducted for three types of image database. For retrieval efficiency precision and recall, error-rate methods are used. By using combined features system performance has been improved.

Acknowledgment. I would like to thank Dr. Kh. Manglem Singh (Associate Professor), Computer Science and Engineering Department, National Institute of Technology Manipur for his support and valuable guidance.

References

1. Ranjidha, A., Kumar, A.R., Saranya, M.: Survey on medical image retrieval based on shape features and relevance vector machine classification. Int. J. Emerg. Trends Technol. Comput. Sci. (IJETTCS) **2**(3), 333–339 (2013)
2. Müller, H., Michoux, N., Bandon, D., Geissbuhler, A.: A review of content-based image retrieval systems in medical applications-clinical benefits and future directions. Med. Inform. **73**, 1 (2004)
3. Yao, J., Zhang, Z.F., Antani, S., Long, R., Thoma, G.: Automatic medical image annotation and retrieval. Neurocomputing **71**, 2012–2022 (2008)
4. Bhende, P., Cheeran, A.N.: Content based image retrieval in medical imaging. Int. J. Comput. Eng. Res. **03**(8), 10–15 (2013)

5. Parades, R., Keysers, D., Lehman, T.M., Wein, B., Ney, H., Vidal, E.: Classification of medical images using local representation. In: Workshop Bildverarbeitung fur die Medizin, pp. 171–174 (2002)
6. Zhang, W., Dickinson, S., Sclaroff, S., Feldman, J., Dunn, S.: Shape-based indexing in a medical image database. In: Biomedical Image Analysis, pp. 221– 230 (1998)
7. Ramamurthy, B., Chandran, K.R., Meenakshi, V.R., Shilpa, V.: CBMIR: content based medical image retrieval system using texture and intensity for dental images. In: Mathew, J., Patra, P., Pradhan, D.K., Kuttyamma, A.J. (eds.) ICECCS 2012. CCIS, vol. 305, pp. 125–134. Springer, Heidelberg (2012). https://doi.org/10.1007/978-3-642-32112-2_16
8. Rajalakshmi, T., Minu, R.I.: Improving relevance feedback for content based medical image retrieval. In: International Conference on Information Communication and Embedded Systems (ICICES 2014). IEEE (2014)
9. Jyothi, B., MadhaveeLatha, Y., Mohan, P.G.K.: An effective multiple visual features for content based medical image retrieval. In: 9th International Conference on Intelligent Systems and Control (ISCO). IEEE (2015)
10. Bharathi, P., Reddy, K.R., Srilakshmi, G.: Medical image retrieval based on LBP histogram fourier features and KNN classifier. In: International Conference on Advances in Engineering and Technology Research (ICAETR 2014). IEEE (2014)
11. Esther, J., Sathik, M.M.: Retrieval of brain image using soft computing technique. In: International Conference on Intelligent Computing Applications. IEEE (2014)
12. Rajkumar, S., Bardhan, P., Akkireddy, S.K., Munshi, C.: CT and MRI image fusion based on wavelet transform and neuro-fuzzy concepts with quantitative analysis. In: International Conference on Electronics and Communication Systems (ICECS). IEEE (2014)
13. Bhagat, A., Atique, M.: Web based medical image retrieval system using fuzzy connectedness image segmentation and geometric moments. In: International Conference on Computational Science and Computational Intelligence, vol. 1. IEEE (2014)
14. Ng, G., Song, Y., Cai, W., Zhou, Y., Liu, S., Feng, D.D.: Hierarchical and binary spatial descriptors for lung nodule image retrieval. In: 2014 36th Annual International Conference of the IEEE Engineering in Medicine and Biology Society. IEEE (2014)
15. Kumar, A., Nette, F., Klein, K., Fulham, M., Kim, J.: A visual analytics approach using the exploration of multidimensional feature spaces for content-based medical image retrieval. IEEE J. Biomed. Health Inform. **19**(5), 1734–1746 (2015)
16. Agarwal, R., Shankhadhar, A., Sagar, R.K.: detection of lung cancer using content based medical image retrieval. In: Fifth International Conference on Advanced Computing and Communication Technologies. IEEE (2015)
17. Tun, K.M.M., Soe, K.A.: Feature extraction and classification of lung cancer nodule using image processing techniques. Int. J. Eng. Res. Technol. (IJERT) **3**(3) (2014)
18. Esther, J., Sathik, M.M.: Fast and accurate brain image retrieval using gabor wavelet algorithm. Int. J. Eng. Technol. (IJET) **5**(6) (2014)
19. Faria, A.V., Oishi, K., Yoshida, S., Hillis, A., Miller, M.I., Mori, S.: Content based image retrieval for brain MRI. Science Direct, January 2015
20. Srilakshmi, G., Reddy, K.R.L.: Performance enhancement of content based medical image retrieval for MRI brain images based on hybrid approach. Int. Res. J. Eng. Technol. (IRJET) **02**(03) (2015)
21. Govindaraju, S., Kumar, G.P.R.: A novel content based medical image retrieval using SURF features. Indian J. Sci. Technol. **9**, 1–8 (2016)
22. Bakar, S.A., Hitam, M.S., Yussof, W.N.J.H.W.: Content-based image retrieval using SIFT for binary and greyscale images. In: IEEE International Conference Signal and Image Processing Applications (ICSIPA) (2013)

23. Reddy, K.R., Narayana, M.: A comparative study of sift and PCA for content based image retrieval. Inter. Refereed J. Eng. Sci. (IRJES) **5**(11), 12–19 (2016). ISSN (Online) 2319-183X, (Print) 2319-1821

24. Alkhawlani, M., Elmogy, M., Elbakry, H.: Content-based image retrieval using local features descriptors and bag-of-visual words. (IJACSA) Int. J. Adv. Comput. Sci. Appl. **6**(9), 212–219 (2015)

25. Velmurugan, K.: A survey of content-based image retrieval systems using scale-invariant feature transform (SIFT). Int. J. Adv. Res. Comput. Sci. Softw. Eng. 4(1) (2014)

26. Meenu, E., Madaan, S.: Content based image retrieval using neural network and SIFT. Int. J. Adv. Trends Comput. Appl. (IJATCA) **2**(3) (2015)

27. Meshram, K.S., Bhombe, D.L.: Implementation of content based image retrieval system using SIFT And SVM. IJMTER **03**(04), 666–672 (2016)

28. Bagri, N., Johari, P.K.: A comparative study on feature extraction using texture and shape for content based image retrieval. Int. J. Adv. Sci. Technol. **80**, 41–52 (2015)

29. Zhao, Z., Tian, Q., Sun, H., Jin, X., Guo, J.: Content based image retrieval scheme using color, texture and shape features. Int. J. Sig. Process. Image Process. Pattern Recognit. **9**(1), 203–212 (2016)

30. Lowe, D.G.: Distinctive image features from scale-invariant key points. Int. J. Comput. Vis. **60**(2), 91–110 (2004)

31. Implement of Scale-Invariant Feature Transform Algorithms Jing Li

32. Kavitha, C., Rao, B.P., Govardhan, A.: Image retrieval based on color and texture feature of the image sub block. Int. J. Comput. Appl. (0975– 8887) **15**(7) (2011)

33. PEIR digital library. http://peir.path.uab.edu/library/index.php?/category/117

34. Veni, S., Narayanankutty, K.A.: Image enhancement of medical images using gabor filter bank on hexagonal sampled grids. In: World Academy of Science, Engineering and Technology, vol. 65 (2010)

Robust Global Gradient Thresholds Estimation in Anisotropic Diffusion for Image Restoration Using DE

Nagaraj Bhat[1], U. Eranna[2], and Manoj Kumar Singh[3(✉)]

[1] Department of Electronics and Communication Engineering,
RVCE, Bangalore, India
nbhat437@gmail.com
[2] Department of Electronics and Communication, BITM Bellary, Bellary, India
jayaveer_88@yahoo.com
[3] Manuro Tech Research Pvt. Ltd., Bangalore, India
mksingh@manuroresearch.com

Abstract. The proposed method offers global parameterization of gradient threshold in anisotropic diffusion model to restore the different types of noises in the images. An optimization model has created to maximize the peak signal to noise ratio to restore the noisy reference image in terms of finding the optimal value of gradient threshold. Two different varieties of natural computing, evolution based differential evolution (DE) and swarm intelligence based particle swarm optimization (PSO), have applied to estimate the threshold values. Considering the diffusion process as a function of surrounding neighbors independently in each direction, two different possibilities have explored for threshold value. In the first case, all the neighbors share a same global threshold value and in second case each neighbor has their own global threshold value. The estimated threshold values have applied in two different types of diffusion function to restore the other noisy images. Proposed method saves lots of computational cost in comparison to approaches where estimation of the threshold value has done spatially in each iteration. Experimental results have shown that proposed restoring method is very effective and around 10 db improvement has observed in PSNR with different varieties of noise like Speckle noise, Gaussian noise and Poisson noise.

Keywords: Anisotropic diffusion · Gradient threshold · Conduction function
Particle swarm optimization · Differential evolution

1 Introduction

Captured real world images are usually corrupted by associate quantity of noise throughout the process of acquisition and transmission. The features like edges and corners are very important in the image analysis and machine vision based applications. But it is still very challenging task to reduce the noise deeply along with maintaining these feature available in the image. There are numbers of conventional image denoising techniques available, like averaging filter, median filter or Gaussian filter

© Springer Nature Singapore Pte Ltd. 2018
P. Bhattacharyya et al. (Eds.): NGCT 2017, CCIS 828, pp. 677–691, 2018.
https://doi.org/10.1007/978-981-10-8660-1_51

which can reduce the noise level in the image but a serious limitation in terms of blurring of the image edges also exist. This has motivated various researchers to find some alternative and in result, Partial Differential Equations (PDEs) based solution has been developed which support the quality of edge by controlling the diffusion process at the time of smoothing. In second section of this paper, mathematical models of diffusion-based image denoising algorithms and previous related works have presented. In third section, DE and PSO have discussed. Then, our planned PDE smoothing approach based on pre-estimated global diffusivity conductance is represented within the fourth section. A completely unique approach is presented to induce diffusivity conductance parameter automatically using differential evolution. Finally conclusion is presented.

2 Anisotropic Diffusion in Image Processing

PDE [12] based Images denoising process can represent by the diffusion equation as shown in Eq. 1.

$$\frac{\partial u}{\partial t} = div(C(x,y,t).\nabla u), (x,y) \in \Omega \subset R^2 \tag{1}$$

Where parameters u and C are the noised image and diffusion tensor correspondingly. Depending upon C characteristics either it is constant for entire image or having variability with space, diffusion process is considered as either homogeneous or inhomogeneous. It is also common in literature to consider, the homogeneous filtering as isotropic, while the inhomogeneous filtering as anisotropic process. From the homogeneous case,

$$div(C(x,y,t).\nabla u) = C(x,y,t).\Delta u + \nabla c.\nabla u \tag{2}$$

$$\text{We obtain } \frac{\partial u}{\partial t} = div(c.\nabla u) = c.\Delta u \tag{3}$$

The diffusion process is considered as linear if the process does not depend upon the image otherwise consider as nonlinear. Computationally $C(x,y,t) = g(u(t,x,y))$, hence, definition of g function is important for proper diffusitivity or edge stopping requirement. The linear diffusion models are the simplest PDE–based image denoising techniques. A 2D Gaussian smoothing process is equivalent to a linear diffusion filtering. Thus, if an degraded image is processed by convolving with a Gaussian kernel, the result

$$u(t,x,y) = G_t * u_0(x,y) \text{ where}$$
$$G_t(x,y) = \frac{1}{4\pi t} e^{\frac{-(x^2+y^2)}{4t}}, (x,y) \in R^2, t > 0 \tag{4}$$

represents also the solution of the heat equation given by the diffusivity coefficient $c = 1$. The linear PDE denoising process generate the blurr over the edges and lack of localization property in linear diffusion dislocate the edges when moving from finer to coarser scale. Such kind of difficulties can be removed from nonlinear diffusion. A nonlinear denoising solution is the directional diffusion, which is degenerate along the gradient direction, having the effect of smoothing the image along but not across the edges. Perona and Malik have proposed a well formulated nonlinear anisotropic diffusion process in [1]. Their approach reduces diffusivity at those locations having a larger likelihood to represent image edges. The Perona-Malik filter is characterized by the following nonlinear diffusion equation

$$u_t = \frac{\partial u}{\partial t} = div\big(g\big(\|\nabla u\|^2\big).\nabla u\big) \tag{5}$$

with the noisy image u_o as the initial condition. Obviously, the diffusivity coefficient that controls how much image smoothing is performed in (x, y) is

$$c(x, y, t) = g\big(\|\nabla u(t, x, y)\|^2\big) \tag{6}$$

The value of $C(x, y, t)$ should be lower when (x, y) is part of an edge, and higher when it is not. The function g that controls the blurring intensity should be monotonous decreasing for this reason. Perona and Malik considered two diffusivity function variants, $g : [0\,\infty] \rightarrow [0\,\infty]$, which are

$$g\big(s^2\big) = e^{\frac{-s^2}{k^2}}, g\big(s^2\big) = \frac{1}{1 + \big(\frac{s}{k}\big)^2} \tag{7}$$

where $k > 0$ represents the diffusivity conductance, being the parameter that controls the diffusion process (In this work the first function will consider as G1 while second function will consider as G2). They discretized the diffusion model provided by Eqs. 5 and 7, as following

$$u^{t+1} = u^t + \lambda\big[c_N^t.\nabla_N u^t + c_S^t.\nabla_S u^t + c_E^t.\nabla_E u^t + c_W^t.\nabla_W u^t\big] \tag{8}$$

$$\text{Where } \nabla_N u^t = u_{x-1,y}^t - u_{x,y}^t; \nabla_S u^t = u_{x+1,y}^t - u_{x,y}^t \tag{9}$$

$$\nabla_E u^t = u_{x-1,y+1}^t - u_{x,y}^t; \nabla_W u^t = u_{x-1,y}^t - u_{x,y}^t \tag{10}$$

$$c_N^t = g(|\nabla_N u^t|); c_S^t = g(|\nabla_S u^t|); c_E^t = g(|\nabla_E u^t|); c_W^t = g(|\nabla_W u^t|) \tag{11}$$

The Perona-Malik diffusion method produces smart smoothing results whereas preserving image edges.

2.1 Literature Review

The value of diffusitivity conductance 'k' plays very important role in denoising process. Various variation of anisotropic diffusion can be defined through the manner they opt for the diffusivity conductance. If gradient magnitude is more than "k" value, the available edge at that position enhanced. Perona-Malik [1] has suggested 'k' value can be determined through empirical observation. Another approach is to have 'k' value as function of time i.e. start with high value of 'k' and decrease this value with time as image smoothness get progress. In a different approach, depends upon the image smoothness status 'k' value has to estimated through various noise model. [2] has analyzed the behavior of the anisotropic diffusion model of Perona. [3] has planned a way for noise removal on color image sequences, supported coupled spacial and temporal anisotropic diffusions. [4] has proposed the method to restore the images and edge enhancement for cell phone device. [5] has discussed in detail of physical principle of transport coefficients within the PDE based image processing. Intensity, space position and gradient information have introduced into NLM model [6] to weakens the staircasing effect and preserves edge. In a medical image processing application, Spectral Domain Optical Coherence Tomography (SDOCT), [7] has applied anisotropic diffusion as pre-processing means for segmentation. Diffusion-shock filter coupling has applied in [8] for color image enhancement. [9] given scale-space interpretation of a category of diffusion filters that contains additionally many nonlinear anisotropic models. A system of nonlinear parabolic equation has applied to evolve the color image in [10]. Performance of anisotropic diffusion is heavily depending upon conduction function, gradient threshold and termination criteria of iterations. Different possibilities have been presented in [11]. For the image segmentation [13] has explored the Eigen value through anisotropic diffusion. In ultrasound image, to reduce the speckle noise cluster driven anisotropic diffusion (CDAD) has applied [14]. The problem of interpolation over sparse and discontinuous data have been handle in [15]. With help of diffusion tensor magnetic resonance electrical impedance tomography (DT-MREIT), anisotropic electrical conductivity tensor distributions inside canine brains has presented in [16].

3 Natural Computing: Swarm and Evolutionary Perspective

Among various method in SI, Particle swarm optimization (PSO) is one of the most successful and computational efficient method. In this approach, each member in population, get their new position value through adding the new velocity value with their existing position value as given in Eq. 12. The change is individual velocity value is the differential change with respect to the best member existing in the population at present and previously their own best achieved as given in Eq. 13.

$$S_i^{(k+1)} = S_i^k + V_i^{k+1} \tag{12}$$

$$V_i^{(k+1)} = \chi\left[wV_i^k + c_1 rand_1 \times \left(pbest_i - s_i^k\right) + c_2 rand_2 \times \left(gbest_i - s_i^k\right)\right] \tag{13}$$

where V_i^k : Velocity of 'ith' member at 'kth' iteration. W: Weight function. C_1 & C_2 are constants. S_i^k : Current position of 'ith' member at 'kth' iteration. pbest$_i$: previous their best has 'ith' member. gbest: best member present in the population at 'kth' iteration. χ is the constriction factor. In this dynamic weight value has been applied which is decrease with iteration progress as given by Eq. 14.

$$w = w_{max} \frac{(w_{max} - w_{min})}{iter_{max}} \times iter \tag{14}$$

where w_{max}: initial weight. w_{min}: final weight, $iter_{max}$: maximum iteration number, iter: current iteration number.

The differential evolution (DE) is one the most dominant method of natural computing which has background of evolutionary process. Functionally, each member of the population creates their own trial solution (offspring) and better one is survived for the next generation. The mutation process in the DE is a defined as the differential process. There are various strategies can be possible, in this research, strategies called DE/rand/1 as defined in Eq. 15 have taken. The crossover operator under probabilistic environment has applied to develop the trial vector as shown in Eq. 16. CR is a crossover control parameter and has value within the range of [0, 1] and presents the probability of creating parameters for a trial vector from the mutant vector. Index j_{rand} is a randomly chosen integer within size of population. Then a greedy selection operation selects between the parent and corresponding trial vectors to choose solution for the next generation as according to Eq. 17.

$$V_i^{(G)} = X_{r1}^{(G)} + F^*(X_{r2}^{(G)} - X_{r3}^{(G)}) \tag{15}$$

$$u_{ij}^{(G)} = \begin{cases} v_{ij}^{(G)} & \text{if } rand(0,\ 1) \leq CR \ or \ j = j_{rand} \\ x_{ij}^{(G)} & \text{otherwise} \end{cases} \tag{16}$$

$$x_{ij}^{(G)} = \begin{cases} u_i^{(G)} & \text{if } f(u_i^{(G)}) \leq f(x_i^{(G)}) \\ x_i^{(G)} & \text{otherwise} \end{cases} \tag{17}$$

4 Proposed Method and Experimental Results

Whole experimental model is shown in Fig. 1. There are two stages, in first stage it can be considered as training stage where DE/rand/1 and DWPSO has been applied to find the optimal value of 'K' so that PSNR of denoised image could be maximum. Fitness estimation of a particular 'K' value is established with PSNR value which is obtained after one scan of image through anisotropic diffusion. In second stage obtained optimal 'K' value is applied to conduction function in anisotropic function to denoise the image. We have considered the all possible direction neighbors for diffusion process i.e. 8 neighbors. In first experiment, all neighbors have same value of 'K', in result; we get one global value of 'K'. In the other experiment, each individual directional

Table 1. Mean & Std. Dev of estimated gradient threshold values and denoised image PSNR in learning phase with conduction function, G1 & G2 for 10 independent trials.

	G1				G2			
	PSO		DE		PSO		DE	
	DNI	K	DNI	K	DNI	K	DNI	K
Mean	31.65	103.48	31.65	103.90	31.62	96.46	31.58	94.33
SD	0.000	1.4934	0.000	0.0540	0.095	1.526	0.003	0.152

neighbor has their own value of 'K'. In result there are 8 different values of 'K' appears. In the phase of learning, for single global 'K' value, total 5 scanning iterations have given in denoising process while for the multiple values of 'K' total 15 scanning iterations have given. This is justified because there are more parameters needs to be explored. For both algorithms' population size is taken as 50. In DWPSO the parameters C1 and C2 are having value equal to 0.5, while constriction factor χ is equal to 0.72. The inertia weight is decrease linearly with iteration from 1.2 to 0.1. In DE/rand/1, the crossover factor is equal to 0.5 while mutation factor is 0.4. The whole experiment has developed under MATLAB environment.

In this work totally 12 images have been considered having different features in their contents. In the training phase the system is given with Lena image along with speckle noise having variance (V) equal to 0.01. For each conduction function as given in Eq. 7, 'K' value is estimated independently for 10 independent trials as shown in Table 1. The average value is considered as final 'K' value for denoising the other images and its results are shown in Table 2. For other noise variance, equal to 0.04 and 0.1, performances have shown in Tables 3 and 4 correspondingly.

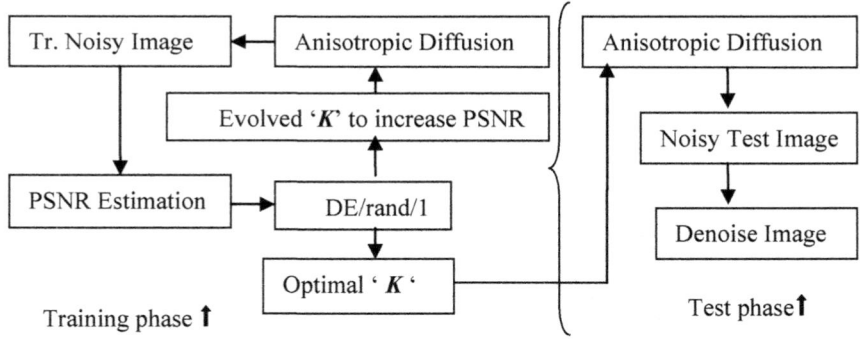

Fig. 1. Working flow for image denoising with global value of 'K'.

Table 2. Denoised test images performance with average gradient threshold obtained with speckle noise variance equal to 0.01.

Image name	PSNR(NI)	PSNR(DNI) (PSO-G1)	PSNR(DNI) (DE-G1)	PSNR(DNI) (PSO-G2)	PSNR(DNI (DE-G2)
Lena	25.2964	31.6575	31.6576	31.5802	31.5803
Alina	24.6266	30.6177	30.6148	30.4330	30.4513
Boat	25.3561	30.5103	30.5062	30.3750	30.3961
Vegetable	24.7619	30.8944	30.8873	30.7883	30.7905
Baboon	24.5850	25.6786	25.6656	25.4588	25.5196
Airplane	21.9622	29.4839	29.4771	29.2612	29.2969
Barbara	25.5833	28.0719	28.0601	27.8097	27.8651
Cameraman	25.5750	31.1809	31.1749	30.8423	30.8750
Earth	24.7069	30.6503	30.6507	30.6150	30.6135
House	22.9790	28.9631	28.9643	28.9109	28.9065
Tree	24.6210	29.4011	29.3999	29.3522	29.3593
Siyasha	28.1721	35.0662	35.0650	34.9271	34.9331

Table 3. Denoised test images performance with average gradient threshold obtained with speckle noise variance equal to 0.04.

Image name	PSNR(NI)	PSNR(DNI) (PSO-G1)	PSNR(DNI) (DE-G1)	PSNR(DNI) (PSO-G2)	PSNR(DNI) (DE-G2)
Lena	19.4191	28.5937	28.5900	28.3911	28.4128
Alina	18.8064	28.3243	28.3199	28.0031	28.0303
Boat	19.4081	27.2136	27.2135	27.0993	27.1073
Vegetable	18.8054	28.1827	28.1797	27.9923	28.0129
Baboon	18.5538	22.6630	22.6554	22.7663	22.7364
Airplane	16.4750	26.1679	26.1669	26.0176	26.0313
Barbara	19.7631	24.7199	24.7129	24.4858	24.5205
Cameraman	19.6204	27.6761	27.6648	27.3150	27.3328
Earth	18.7023	27.4870	27.4843	27.3683	27.3846
House	17.2301	25.7285	25.7263	25.5927	25.6101
Tree	18.9186	26.2204	26.2247	26.2487	26.2423
Siyasha	22.2052	31.2868	31.2807	31.0532	31.0806

In Table 5, average performance in denoising process with different noise variances has shown. It can observe from results that restored or reconstructed image is improved with increase in the noise density. As noise variance reach to 0.1, there is an improvement of nearly 10 db has obtained. It can also be seen that in comparison to conduction function G2, there is significant betterment being observed with conduction function G1 and also PSO has shown better results in compare to DE. Hence,

Table 4. Denoised test images performance with average gradient threshold obtained with speckle noise variance equal to 0.1.

Image name	PSNR(NI)	PSNR(DNI) (PSO-G1)	PSNR(DNI) (DE-G1)	PSNR(DNI) (PSO-G2)	PSNR(DNI) (DE-G2)
Lena	15.6501	26.3200	26.3172	26.1330	26.1462
Alina	15.0758	26.0324	26.0282	25.7403	25.7650
Boat	15.5477	25.1278	25.1263	24.9643	24.9809
Vegetable	15.0871	26.0065	26.0048	23.4445	25.8229
Baboon	14.7871	21.0823	21.0831	20.9818	21.0007
Airplane	13.2392	23.0971	23.0962	22.9356	22.9520
Barbara	16.0225	22.8903	22.8925	22.8191	22.8314
Cameraman	15.7773	25.4591	25.4550	25.0919	25.1210
Earth	14.9340	25.3996	25.4015	25.3603	22.6860
House	13.7818	23.4596	23.4585	23.3392	23.3429
Tree	15.4084	23.9928	23.9944	23.9681	23.9777
Siyasha	18.3398	28.8331	28.8279	26.1630	28.7222

Table 5. Mean performance of denoising with single global gradient threshold.

Noise variance	PSNR(NI)	PSNR(DNI) (PSO-G1)	PSNR(DNI) (PSO-G2)	PSNR(DNI) (DE-G1)	PSNR (DNI) (DE-G2)
0.01	24.8521	30.1813	30.0295	30.1770	30.0489
0.04	18.9923	27.0220	26.8611	27.0183	26.8752
0.1	15.3042	24.8084	24.5267	24.8071	24.4457

Table 6. Global gradient thresholds in all possible direction (8) with G1 conduction function.

Method	KN	KS	KW	KE	KNE	KSE	KSW	KNW
PSO	148.6169	126.4829	98.4710	88.0216	110.6983	82.6462	105.5434	91.5389
DE	153.9515	173.0398	94.8240	99.1471	82.6462	82.0430	91.3862	89.1219

estimation of multiple 'K' values is applied with only G1 conduction function. The results obtained with different approaches are shown in Table 6. Tables 7 and 8 have enclosed the performances of 12 denoised test images with noise variances equal to 0.04 and 0.1. In the tables below following nomenclature have applied, NI: Noisy Image, DNI: Denoised Image, PSNR: Peak Signal to Noise Ratio.

The average improved values in denoising process have shown in Table 9. It is observe that with 8 different value of 'K', there is high PSNR value in comparison with PNSR obtained with single value of 'K'. Performance of DE/rand/1 has shown some improvement over PSO. The required number of scanning iterations to denoise the

Table 7. Denoising the test images with obtained 8 global gradient thresholds in training using G1 conduction function and speckle noise with variance 0.01.

Image name	PSNR(NI)	PSNR(DNI) (PSO-G1)	PSNR(DNI) (DE-G1)
Lena	25.3149	31.6708	31.6698
Alina	24.6207	30.5884	30.5873
Boat	25.3483	30.6140	30.6411
Vegetable	24.7509	30.8637	30.8785
Baboon	24.5709	25.5385	25.5289
Airplane	21.9289	29.4697	29.5034
Barbara	25.6045	28.3009	28.3523
Cameraman	25.5848	31.1785	31.1977
Earth	24.7076	30.6614	30.6633
House	22.9518	28.9448	28.9599
Tree	24.6048	29.3679	29.3720
Siyasha	28.1424	34.9871	34.9699

Table 8. Denoising the test images with obtained 8 global gradient thresholds in training using G1 conduction function and speckle noise with variance 0.04 and 0.1.

Image name	PSNR (NI:0.04)	PSNR (PSO-DNI)	PSNR (DE-DNI)	PSNR (NI:0.1)	PSNR (PSO-DNI)	PSNR (DE-DNI)
Lena	19.4119	28.6035	28.5987	15.6516	26.3912	26.3901
Alina	18.8285	28.3415	28.3209	15.0730	26.0313	26.0045
Boat	19.4076	27.2615	27.2749	15.5435	25.1647	25.1845
Vegetable	18.8175	28.2484	28.2528	15.0921	26.0237	26.0381
Baboon	18.5928	22.6138	22.6409	14.8089	21.0261	21.0125
Airplane	16.4714	26.1427	26.1460	13.2485	23.1169	23.1207
Barbara	19.7384	24.8420	24.8609	16.0508	23.0184	23.0256
Cameraman	19.5975	27.7071	27.7138	15.7399	25.4459	25.4439
Earth	18.7109	27.4347	27.4610	14.9340	25.4096	25.4394
House	17.2295	25.7488	25.7617	13.7658	23.3999	23.3852
Tree	18.8988	26.1674	26.1701	15.3903	23.9995	24.0174
Siyasha	22.2071	31.3199	31.2819	18.3404	28.8433	28.7995

image has shown in Table 10. It is clear that within a few number of iterations only maximum PSNR is achieved and if applied over scanning PSNR has started to decrease as shown in Fig. 2. All the images which have applied in this paper are most commonly applied in image processing literatures and shown in Fig. 3. Images with speckle noise having variance equals to 0.1 have shown in Fig. 4, while, reconstructed images through DE/rand/1 and G1 conduction function have shown in Fig. 5. Estimated 'K'

Table 9. Denoising of speckle noise with various variances using 8 global gradient thresholds.

Noise variance	PSNR (NI)	PSNR (PSO-DNI)	PSNR Improv.	PSNR (DE-DNI)	PSNR Improv
0.01	24.8442	30.1821	5.3379	30.1937	5.3495
0.04	18.9927	27.0359	8.0432	27.0403	8.0476
0.1	15.3032	24.8225	9.5193	24.8218	9.5186

Table 10. Average no. of scan iterations required in denoising 12 test image case.

	V = 0.01	V = 0.04	V = 0.1
Avg. no. iteration	1.25	2.75	4.4167

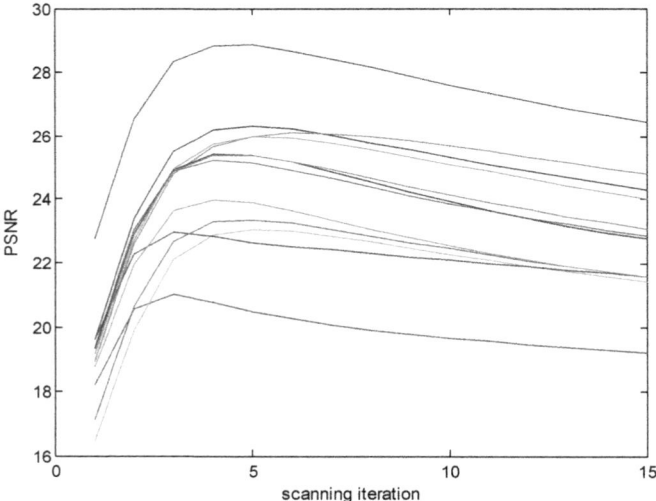

Fig. 2. Change in PSNR against the scanning iteration for different images with V = 0.1

values from speckle noise image, is applied with images suffering with different characteristics of noise like Gaussian and Poisson and obtained performance has shown in Table 11. Obtained denoised image for Alina has shown in Fig. 6. To understand the relative benefits of 'K' estimation with different type of noises, Gaussian and Poisson noise based corrupted images have applied for training and performances obtained with other test images have shown in Tables 12 and 13. The average benefit for all cases has shown in the Table 14. It is observed that speckle noise based estimation of 'K' has shown efficient denoising of the image corrupted with Gaussian and Poisson noise also. Not only that, this performance is nearly equal to the value of PSNR, when 'K' value has been estimated through Gaussian and Poisson noise respectively.

Fig. 3. Test image name: (1,1) Lena, (1,2) Alina, (1,3) Boat, (1,4) Vegetable, (2,1) Baboon, (2,2) Airplane, (2,3) Barbara, (2,4) Cameraman, (3,1) House, (3,2) Earth, (3,3) Tree, (3,4) Siyasha

Fig. 4. Test image with speckle nosie (variance = 0.1)

Fig. 5. Reconstructed images with DE/rand/1 and global 8 'K' values

Table 11. PSNR of reconstructed image through DE and Speckle noise based estimated 'k' over noisy image affected with Gaussian and Poisson noise along with mixture of both.

Image name	Gaussian		Poisson		Mix noise	
	NI	DNI	NI	DNI	NI	DNI
Lena	19.7052	28.8778	26.8369	32.6551	18.1211	27.9842
Alina	19.6821	28.8819	27.0095	31.3260	17.9499	28.0759
Boat	20.0975	27.7407	26.9972	31.3474	18.3995	26.7936
Vegetable	19.1588	28.2782	26.3608	31.7741	17.5475	27.4753
Baboon	19.1265	23.1562	26.1263	25.7396	17.4774	22.2739
Airplane	19.3368	27.9640	24.7748	31.2281	17.3005	26.6942
Barbara	19.8166	25.0025	27.1538	28.7758	18.3290	24.4164
Cameraman	20.3959	28.0867	27.3754	32.1981	18.6679	27.0923
Earth	18.3613	27.4127	25.3938	30.4142	16.9009	26.6746
House	19.4472	27.0985	25.3946	30.4374	17.4932	25.9369
Tree	19.6069	27.0016	26.6390	30.3174	18.0459	26.0154
Siyasha	20.7489	29.1042	29.1779	35.8259	19.5208	28.4770
Mean	19.6236	27.3837	26.6033	31.0033	17.9795	26.4925

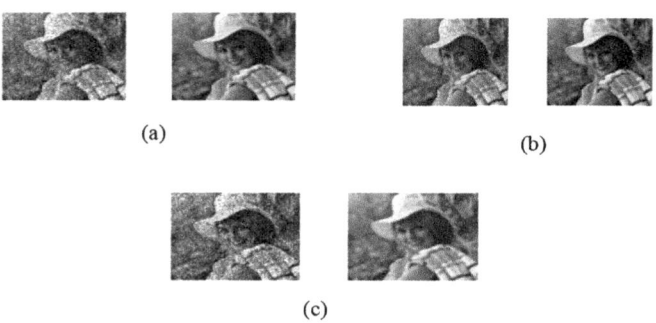

(a)

(b)

(c)

Fig. 6. Image denoising with (a) Gaussian (b) Poisson (c) Mixture of Gaussian, speckle and Poisson noise.

Table 12. All neighbors 'K' value from DE with image carry Gaussian and Poisson noise.

Noise model	KN	KS	KW	KE	KNE	KSE	KSW	KNW
Gaussian	71.8201	65.1750	16.3091	11.3330	94.1262	105.00	125.9563	82.3403
Poisson	69.1022	28.8566	23.4921	24.0623	45.3257	36.1232	19.3973	11.3989

Table 13. Performance of denoising

Image name	Gaussian		Poisson	
	NI	DNI	NI	DNI
Lena	19.7024	29.2164	26.8487	32.8787
Alina	19.6620	29.1584	26.4041	31.2345
Boat	20.0931	27.8174	27.0237	31.5671
Vegetable	19.1503	28.5031	26.3201	32.1514
Baboon	19.1407	22.7630	26.1223	27.6159
Airplane	19.3363	27.9376	24.7775	31.2592
Barbara	19.8075	25.4467	27.1174	30.2379
Cameraman	20.3804	28.2415	27.3715	33.1384
Earth	18.3576	27.3937	25.8551	30.6958
House	19.4636	26.9373	25.4122	30.2109
Tree	19.6101	26.8003	26.6486	30.2223
Siyasha	20.7508	29.2754	29.1832	36.1364
Mean	19.6212	27.4576	26.5904	31.4457

Table 14. Comparative improvement in PSNR performance under different learning reference condition of noise

Learning noise delmo	Gaussian		Poisson	
	NI	Improv.	NI	Improv.
Speckle	19.6236	7.7601	26.6033	4.4000
Gaussian	19.6212	7.8364		
poisson			26.5904	4.8553

5   Conclusion

In this paper auto estimation of global gradient threshold values have been done using differential evolution under influence of different types of conductance functions. Two different categories of global 'K' have been achieved in terms of having same or different values for all the surrounding neighbors. With the proposed method it is possible to decide the better conduction function among the others. With the experimental results it is shown that estimated 'K' value from speckle noisy environment works really well in restoration of images affected with different density of speckle noise as well other categories of noise environments like Gaussian noise or Poisson noise or a mixture of both. There is need of very few iterations to denoise the images hence proposed method is also computational efficient. From future work perspective, there are various challenges available, among them design of efficient conduction function is very important. It is possible to design the more efficient conduction function by exploring the solution space through evolutionary approach like genetic programming.

Acknowledgement. This research has done in Manuro Tech Research Pvt. Ltd., Bangalore, India, under Innovative solution for Future Technology program.

References

1. Perona, P., Malik, J.: Scale space and edge detection using anisotropic diffusion. In: Proceedings of IEEE Computer Society Workshop on Computer Vision, pp. 16–22. IEEE Computer Society Press, Washington, D.C. (1987)
2. You, Y.-L., Xu, W., Tannenbaum, A., Kaveh, M.: Behavioral analysis of anisotropic diffusion in image processing. IEEE Trans. Image Process. 5(11), 1539–1553 (1996)
3. Bourdon, P., Augereau, B., Olivier, C., Chatellier, C.: Noise removal on color image sequences using coupled anisotropic diffusions and noise-robust motion detection. In: 2004 12th European Signal Processing Conference, pp. 481–484 (2004)
4. Han, X., Lu, X., Wu, X., Liu, C.: An edge detection based anisotropic denoising method for mobile phone images. In: 2015 8th International Congress on Image and Signal Processing (CISP), pp. 876–881 (2015)
5. Kamgar-Parsi, B., Kamgar-Parsi, B., Kamgar-Parsi, K.: Notes on image processing with partial differential equations. In: 2015 IEEE International Conference on Image Processing (ICIP), pp. 1737–1741 (2015)

6. Yuan, J.: Improved anisotropic diffusion equation based on new non-local information scheme for image denoising. IET Comput. Vis. **9**(6), 864–870 (2015)
7. Padmasini, N., Abbirame, K.S., Yacin, S.M., Umamaheswari, R.: Speckle noise reduction in spectral domain optical coherence tomography retinal images using anisotropic diffusion filtering. In: 2014 International Conference on Science Engineering and Management Research (ICSEMR), pp. 1–5 (2014)
8. Bettahar, S., Lambert, P., Stambouli, A.B.: Anisotropic color image denoising and sharpening. In: 2014 IEEE International Conference on Image Processing (ICIP), pp. 2669–2673 (2014)
9. Weickert, J.: Theoretical foundations of anisotropic diffusion in image processing. In: Kropatsch, W., Klette, R., Solina, F. (eds.) Theoretical Foundations of Computer Vision. COMPUTING, vol. 11, pp. 221–236. Springer, Vienna (1996). https://doi.org/10.1007/978-3-7091-6586-7_13
10. Rossovskii, L.E.: Image filtering with the use of anisotropic diffusion. Comput. Math. Math. Phys. **57**(3), 401–408 (2017)
11. Tsiotsios, C., Petrou, M.: On the choice of the parameters for anisotropic diffusion in image processing. Pattern Recognit. **46**, 1369–1381 (2012). https://doi.org/10.1016/j.patcog.2012.11.012
12. Barbu, T.: Robust anisotropic diffusion scheme for image noise removal. Procedia Comput. Sci. **35**, 522–530 (2014)
13. Wang, J., Huang, W.: Image segmentation with eigenfunctions of an anisotropic diffusion operator. IEEE Trans. Image Process. **25**(5), 2155–2167 (2016)
14. Hu, Z., Tang, J.: Cluster driven anisotropic diffusion for speckle reduction in ultrasound images. In: 2016 IEEE International Conference on Image Processing (ICIP), pp. 2325–2329 (2016)
15. Abolhassani, A.A.H., Dimitrakopoulos, R., Ferrie, F.P.: Anisotropic interpolation of sparse images. In: 2016 13th Conference on Computer and Robot Vision (CRV), pp. 440–447 (2016)
16. Jeong, W.C., Sajib, S.Z.K., Katoch, N., Kim, H.J., Kwon, O.I., Woo, E.J.: Anisotropic conductivity tensor imaging of in vivo canine brain using DT-MREIT. IEEE Trans. Med. Imaging **36**(1), 124–131 (2017)

An AHP Based Automated Approach for Pole-like Objects Detection Using Three Dimensional Terrestrial Laser Scanner Data

Arshad Husain[✉] and R. C. Vaishya

Motilal Nehru National Institute of Technology, Allahabad, India
{rgi1501, rcvaishya}@mnnit.ac.in

Abstract. Pole-Like Objects (PLOs) situated along the corridor of street environment are critical roadway resources. They play major role in road safety inspection and road planning. Road side poles need to be relocated during rural and urban road widening. Road side objects including pole, street trees are among the most commonly struck road-side objects during road-side accidents. Use of Terrestrial Laser Scanning (TLS) technology for mapping of road side objects is a critical revolution in case of field surveying. Automatic detection of road side objects help in maintaining and managing of road surface. In present study a novel five-step method is proposed to detect PLOs along the roadway using TLS data. The first step, i.e. clustering of data, uses the K-means clustering method in order to divide the data into smaller chunks. Further, ground filtering is performed at each cluster of data in next step. Two dimensional projection and range search is used to extract the proximity points of selected seed point. In last step Analytical Hierarchy Process (AHP) is used to detect the PLOs. The proposed method is tested on a captured TLS point cloud data. Correctness and completeness, respectively of 98.18% and 96.42%, are achieved.

Keywords: Pole · PLOs · Terrestrial laser scanner · AHP · Lidar

1 Introduction

Terrestrial Laser Scanner (TLS) is turning into a prominent choice among the government and private agencies, working in the field of roadway planning, outlining and its administration. TLS is used to capture accurate, precise and dense geo-referenced three-dimensional (3D) point cloud data along the corridor in stationary mode. Extent of across the road coverage from the road boundary using TLS depends on the place at where the scanner is mounted and range of the device. A roadside is characterized as the zone beyond the edge line of the carriageway [1]. In the urban street condition, Pole-Like Objects (PLOs) mainly utility, street light poles and street side planted trees are found close-by street limit. In most of the roadside accidents, vehicle generally collapse with PLOs. In single vehicle crashes utility poles located along the corridor of street have consistently been a significant agent. Trees or other rigid vegetation seem to be most hazardous and utility poles are the second most hazardous roadside obstacles regarding fatal accidents [1] as compared to other roadside obstacles. Pole accidents in

© Springer Nature Singapore Pte Ltd. 2018
P. Bhattacharyya et al. (Eds.): NGCT 2017, CCIS 828, pp. 692–703, 2018.
https://doi.org/10.1007/978-981-10-8660-1_52

rural areas have higher impact severity than urban pole accidents as a result of higher impact speeds [2]. Therefore, identification of these PLOs plays significant role in road safety analysis. PLOs need to be removed and relocated during road widening from single-lane to multi-lane. So, their identification is useful to optimize the road planning having less destruction overhead. Captured data using TLS is generally bulky in nature, a couple of Giga Bytes (GB) per scans. In the last decade many researchers have been analyzing the importance of extracting PLOs from 3D lidar (light detection and ranging) point cloud data. It's become very tedious task to manually process and analyze tens or hundreds of kilometers of roads corridor data [3]. Therefore, several attempts have been performed in order to detect PLOs using terrestrial and mobile lidar point cloud.

Few researches have used the concept of voxelization to reduce the point cloud data size. Concept of voxelization has been used to reduce the data size for pole-like street furniture objects detection using mobile lidar point cloud data [4]. Voxel are created by generating a code for each laser scanner point, points having the same code are belongs to the same voxel. Further, two-dimensional analysis and tridimensional reconstruction are performed to detect pole like objects. The remedy of the proposed method is pole like objects located very close to other objects and partially occluded by other objects or are not detected. A voxel based method is also proposed for street tree detection [5]. The procedure of voxel creation and connectivity analysis of the voxels for tree detection is discussed.

Principle Component Analysis (PCA) for detection of PLOs is used by several researchers. PCA and k-nearest neighbor graph is used for the detection of pole-like objects from point cloud data [6]. The method is based on an assumption that input dataset do not have the ground points and method is not able to detect connected poles separately. El- Halawany and Lichti [7] have also proposed a PCA based pipeline for road pole detection. K-dimensional tree data structure for nearest neighbor search is used. Further, PCA has been used to detect the vertical linear objects. The accuracy of their algorithm is dependent on the point density of input point cloud data. Other extraneous information such as scanning pattern, type of point's distribution is also needed to detect the pole like objects. Therefore, poles having less point could not detected by their proposed pipeline.

A four phase algorithm namely scans line segmentation, clustering, merging of clusters and classification of clusters, have proposed in order to detect the PLOs [8]. The algorithm finds difficulty to identify tree trunks and utility poles surrounded by shrubs, bushes and wall structures. A percentile based method for the detection of poles is proposed by initially classifying the input data into on-ground and off-ground points [9]. Classification result is not accurate and many on-ground points are classified as off-ground points. It leads to some pole-like objects remains undetected, the method is also depends on additional information such as scanning pattern, point density and type of point's distribution. In year 2013 a method for road furniture (pole-like objects) detection is proposed by Li and Elberink [10]. To remove the points that do not belong to the area of interest, rough classification is performed. Tree detection is performed on the basis of defining rules based on different kind of attributes. To identify the pole-like objects percentile-based detection technique is used. Further, these detected PLOs are classified into traffic sign, traffic light or roadside furniture like lamp post. Along with the positional information, PCI (Pulse count Information) is also used in the case of tree detection. The limitation of the method includes, PLOs in the point cloud hanging in the air, partially occluded and having fewer points are not detected. Processing of huge size point cloud data processing is a major limitation in terms of time complexity. Therefore, methods for feature extraction should be fast and accurate. Some limitations of existing methods for PLOs detection are tried to remove by the proposed method including computational time efficiency, scanned poles in the TLS point cloud having very less number of non-uniformly distributed points and PLOs surrounded by shrubs and bushes. Automatic identification of PLOs is very beneficial and play critical role in the road safety analysis and road planning (lane wise widening of roads).

2 Proposed Method

Proposed method for detecting PLOs from TLS data is divided into five steps (see Fig. 1). The steps are namely clustering of input raw data, ground point filtering, two dimensional projection, range search and analytic hierarchy process. All these steps are discussed in detail in the following sections.

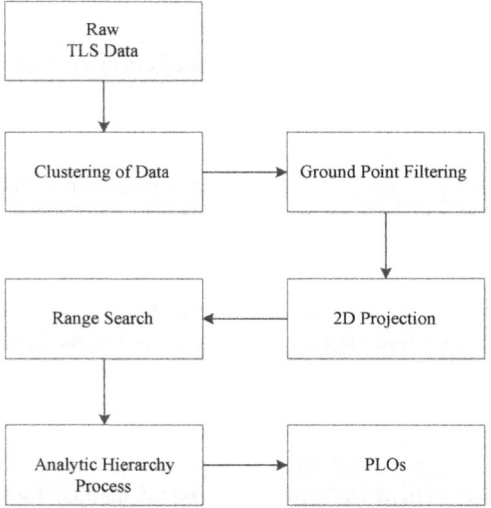

Fig. 1. Flowchart of proposed method

2.1 Clustering of Input Raw Data

X, Y and Z coordinate value of each TLS point is taken as input and K-means clustering is applied. The objective of clustering is to divide the input data into several smaller clusters. The input data is bulky in nature, it would be difficult to process the whole data at once therefore, K-means clustering is applied in order to cluster the input data into smaller pieces and process each cluster one by one. K-means clustering work on the basis of calculation of centroid, and is typically applied to object points scattered in a continuous n-dimensional space.

The K-means clustering uses conventional mathematical techniques, firstly K initial centroids are chosen by the user (user defined parameter), where K define the number of desired clusters. Each point is then assigned to the closest centroid among the K centroids. The centroid of each cluster is updated on the basis of Euclidian distance between the points and the centroids. Procedure of update is repeated until the centroids remain the same. The algorithm of K-means clustering is as follow.

1: Select K initial centroids.
2: repeat.
3: Form K clusters by assigning each point to its closest centroid (Euclidian distance).
4: Re compute the centroid of each cluster.
5: until Centroids do not change.

2.2 Ground Point Filtering

Each cluster is chosen one by one and ground point filtering is performed. In order to perform the ground filtering, vertical slicing at each cluster is performed. Two vertical slices are created for each cluster (see Fig. 2), first slice belongs to ground points and another slice belongs to the non-ground points. For performing vertical slicing, cluster data is organized on the basis of sorted Z coordinate values. Some (n) points having the lowest Z coordinate values are selected from the cluster points. Mean Z value of selected points is calculated. Similarly, mean of some (g) points having highest Z coordinate values is calculated. These two mean values are used as minimum Z and maximum Z values for further calculation at selected cluster. The reason of this calculation is to remove the effect of outliers. Points having the actual minimum Z and

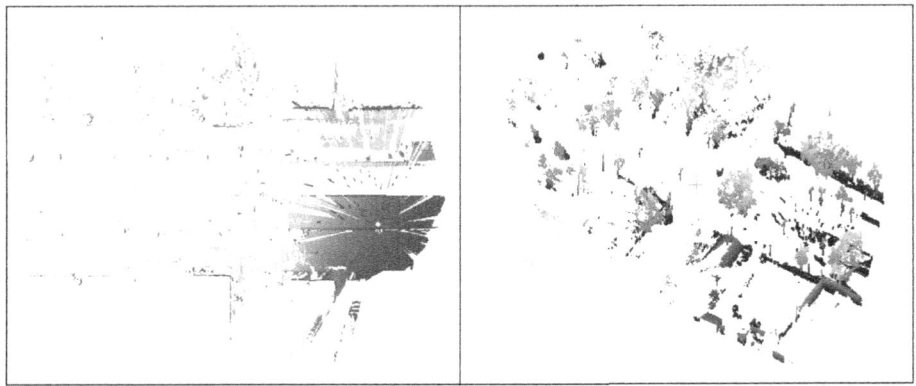

Fig. 2. Ground filtered points and non-ground points of a cluster

maximum Z value may belong from outlier. Two slices are created for each cluster. The Z value range of points belongs to first and second slice is given by (1) and (2).

$$(minimum\,Z)\,to\,(minimum\,Z + hl_1)\qquad(1)$$

$$(minimum\,Z + hl_1)\,to\,(maximum\,Z)\qquad(2)$$

Where, hl_1 represent the height of first layer.

2.3 Two Dimensional Projection

The ground filtered clusters are two dimensionally projected at XY plane. For projecting the ground filtered cluster, Z coordinate value of each point is ignored (set to zero). Now, each point has only X and Y coordinate values. The information of Z coordinate value of each point has been stored in such a way that it can be re-associated with the corresponding point. The reason for choosing the XY plane for projection is that, after projection, there is very less distortion in the area of the selected cluster.

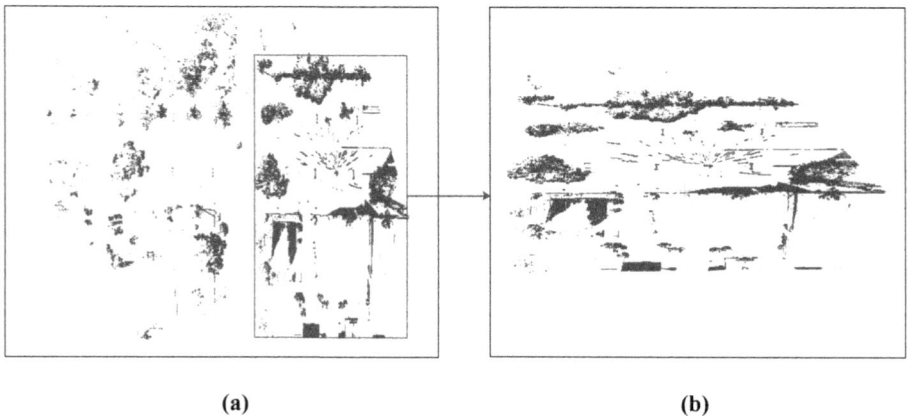

| (a) | (b) |

Fig. 3.   (a) 2D projected ground filtered cluster (b) closer view of 2D projected ground filtered cluster

Figure 3(a), shows a two-dimensional projected ground filtered cluster and Fig. 3(b), shows the closer view of projected cluster. The dark spots in Fig. 3(b), shows the two-dimensionally projected tree points, building facades, PLOs, etc.

2.4 Range Search

Each two dimensional projected cluster is chosen one by one and range search is performed. For performing the range search, first point of 2D projected cluster is selected as seed point. A circle with a user defined radius (r) is created and the points lying within the circle are extracted. K-d tree data structure is used in order to organize the points for range search. The objective of using k-d tree is to reduce the processing time associated with range search operation. The extracted points are analyzed with Analytic Hierarchy Process (AHP) in order to identify the pole like objects. If the extracted points are identified as pole like object, then these extracted points are removed from the cluster and placed in separate file otherwise, next point of the cluster is selected as seed point and similar procedure is applied. Likewise, the range search is performed for all the clusters (Fig. 4).

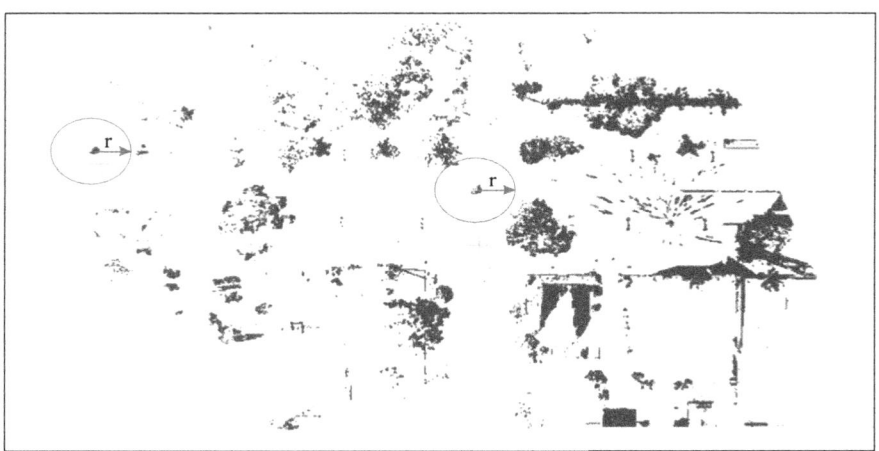

Fig. 4. Range search in ground filtered cluster

2.5 Analytic Hierarchy Process

Analytical Hierarchy Process (AHP) is one of the most widely used Multi-Criteria Decision Making (MCDM) approaches. In the context of the AHP, first hierarchical model was developed by Saaty in 1980 [11, 12]. AHP is a basic decision making approach that includes organizing various decision criteria into a progressive system, evaluating the relative significance of these criteria, contrasting options for every basis and deciding a general positioning of the choices [13]. AHP helps to capture both subjective and objective evaluation measures, providing a useful mechanism for checking the consistency of the evaluation measures and alternatives suggested by the team thus reducing bias in decision making [14]. Some of its applications are incorporate innovation decision [15], merchant choice of a broadcast communications framework [16], extend determination, spending portion etc.

In order to identify the PLOs, AHP is applied at the points extracted in range search operation. For identifying the PLOs, variance-covariance matrix of extracted points (points lying within the circle) is calculated. Further, the calculated variance-covariance matrix is taken as initial criteria matrix. The step of the AHP is as follow.

Step-1: Taking the pair wise comparison (variance-covariance (A1)) matrix for the criteria PLOs detection is as follow (Table 1).

Table 1. Pairwise comparison matrix for C1.

Criteria	X	Y	Z
X	0.0424	−0.0281	−0.2403
Y	−0.0281	0.0950	0.4129
Z	−0.2403	0.4129	3.6758

Step-2: Calculate the column sum $\sum_j C_{ij}$ for each column in the Table 2.

Table 2. Column sum for C1.

Criteria	X	Y	Z
X	0.0424	−0.0281	−0.2403
Y	−0.0281	0.0950	0.4129
Z	−0.2403	0.4129	3.6758
Sum	−0.2260	0.4798	3.8484

Step-3: Standardized each cell by $D_{ij} = \dfrac{C_{ij}}{\sum_j C_{ij}}$ (Table 3)

Table 3. Standardized matrix for C1.

Criteria	X	Y	Z
X	−0.1836	−0.0585	−0.0624
Y	0.1243	0.1979	0.1072
Z	1.0632	0.8605	0.9551

Step-4: Calculate row sum by $R_i = \sum_i D_{ij}$ and weight by $W_i = \frac{R_i}{n}$; n = 3(number of candidates) (Table 4).

Table 4. Calculate the row sum & weight.

Criteria	X	Y	Z	Sum	W
X	−0.1836	−0.0585	−0.0624	−0.3045	−0.1015
Y	0.1243	0.1979	0.1072	0.4294	0.1431
Z	1.0632	0.8605	0.9551	2.8788	0.9596

On the basis of weights of individual coordinates, a criterion (threshold) is established to detect the PLOs. For PLOs detection, a criterion is set on to the weight of Z coordinate value (Z_w).

3   Experimental Study

3.1   Test Data

The test data is captured from the Mahatma Gandhi Marg, Civil Lines, Allahabad city, Uttar Pradesh, India (25°27'03.8"N, 81°49'40.6"E) with the help of FARO Focus3D X 330 TLS. It offers a 360-degree field of view, a range from 0.6 m up to 330 m with distance accuracy up to ±2 mm, delivering high precision performance and coverage. It is easy to use as it has a dedicated touch screen Liquid Crystal Display (LCD) display that shows the status information and allows user to adjust the data capture parameters. The maximum elevation difference within the dataset is 24.59 m. There are very low slopes along the horizontal streets, and in some areas streets are heavily blocked by trees. Overall, the data set have an urban as well as nonurban behavior. The length of the street is 341.5 m. Some street floor points of captured dataset are missing due to the traffic at the time of data capturing. Figure 5, shows the Google Earth image of the corresponding location along with two different perspective view of captured dataset. Statistical specification of captured dataset is shown in Table 5.

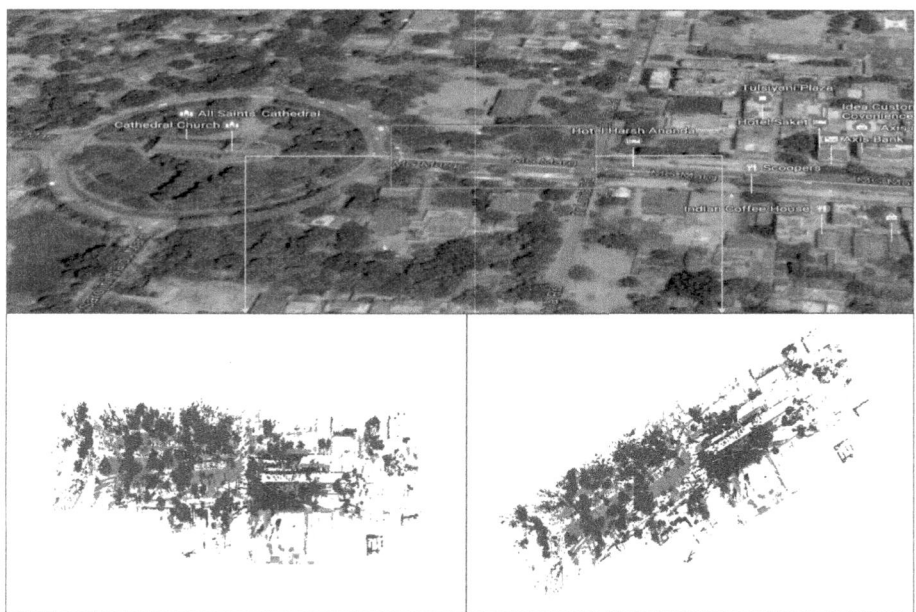

Fig. 5. Google Earth image along with captured dataset

Table 5. Statistical specification of captured dataset.

File size	No. of points	Street length (m)	Area (m^2)	Point density (per m^2)
2.1 GB	37490376	341.5	34029.690	1101.690

File size in Giga-Bytes (GB), point density is in per meter square (/m^2) and total covered area by the captured dataset is in meter square (m^2).

3.2 Results

Proposed method is tested on captured TLS point cloud dataset (see Fig. 5). Statistical specification of the same is shown in Table 5. The method uses the numerous parameters (K, hl$_1$, r, W$_z$) in different steps, the threshold (used) values of these parameters are shown in Table 6.

Table 6. Parameters and their used values in various steps of proposed method.

Step	Parameter(s)	Value(s)
Clustering of data	K	10
Ground point filtering	hl$_1$	0.1 m
Range search	R	0.5 m
Analytical Hierarchy Process	W$_z$	0.80

Reference Data
Visual inspection has been performed at captured dataset in order to collect the reference data. Quick Terrain Reader x32, v7.1.5 has been used to visualize the captured data. A video is also recorded of test site at the time of data collection; this video is also used to identify the particular PLOs.

Table 7. Completeness and Correctness of output dataset.

Name	Trees (detected/reference)	False positives	Completeness	Correctness
Captured dataset	56/54	1	96.42%	98.18%

Output Dataset
Total 56 numbers of PLOs are present in captured dataset. Out of 56, 54 trees are successfully detected by the proposed methodology (Table 7). Completeness and correctness of proposed methodology are 96.42% and 98.18% respectively. Figure 6, shows the output dataset.

$$Completeness = \frac{Number\ of\ PLOs\ detected}{Total\ number\ of\ PLOs\ in\ reference\ data} \times 100 \qquad (3)$$

$$Correcteness = \frac{Number\ of\ PLOs\ detected}{Number\ of\ PLOs\ detected + Number\ of\ False\ Postives} \times 100 \qquad (4)$$

Objects apart from the trees, detected by the method are called false positives.

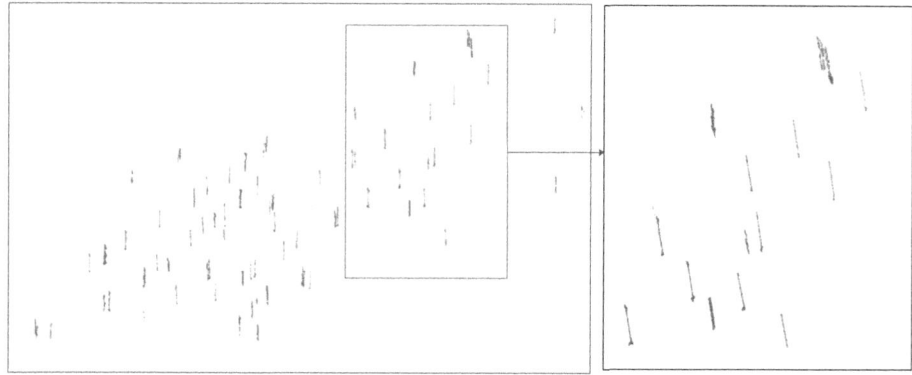

Fig. 6. Perspective view of detected PLOs

4 Discussion

Only X, Y, and Z coordinate of each TLS point are used by the proposed method. Therefore, the proposed method does not depend on additional information such as intensity, scan line, number of returns, return numbers, GPS time, etc. PLOs attached

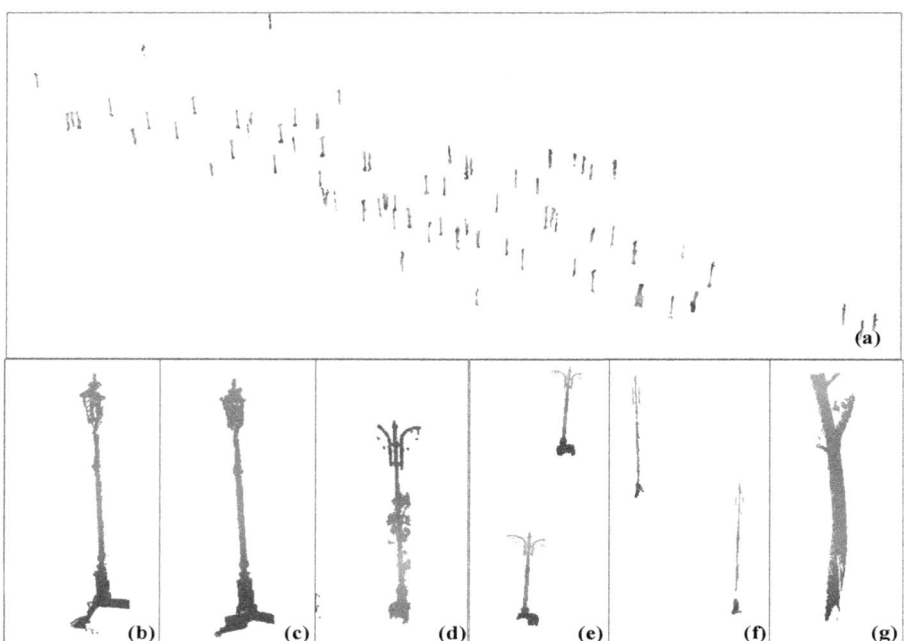

Fig. 7. (a) Detected PLOs (b, c, d, e) Street light and utility poles (f) detected poles having less point density (g) Tree trunks

with street bulbs are also detected by the proposed methodology (see Fig. 7(b, c, d)). Proposed method is also able to detect the utility poles and tree trunks (see Fig. 7(e, g)). Proposed method is independent of point density. Some PLOs with very few TLS points are present in captured dataset. These PLOs are also detected by the proposed method (see Fig. 7(f)). PLOs surrounded by shrubs and bushes are also detected (see Fig. 7(f)).

4.1 Execution Time

Proposed method has been coded at Matlab2013a installed on Sony Vaio E Series notebook (OS: Windows7 64bit, CPU: Intel Core i3@2.4 GHz, RAM: 3 GB). The execution time of the proposed method at standard parameters values (Table 6) is 186.14 s.

5 Conclusion and Future Recommendations

In the present study, a novel automated method for the detection of Pole-Like Objects (PLOs) using TLS data has been proposed. Proposed method incorporates five steps in order to detect the PLOs. Only the X, Y, and Z coordinate values each MLS point has been used by the method. Range search is implemented with the help of k-d tree data structure to determine the points which are lying within the circle. AHP has been used for identification of vertical linear objects. Proposed method does not use any training data. There is no initial assumption has been established in order to detect the PLOs. Proposed method has been implemented at Matlab2013a and run-time analysis is also performed. The method has been tested on a captured TLS dataset and corresponding PLOs are detected. Completeness and correctness of method are 96.42% and 98.18% respectively. Future work will be focused on developing such methodologies to automatically determine the optimized value of employed parameters.

References

1. Nitsche, P., Saleh, P., Helfert, M.: State of the art report on existing treatments for the design of forgiving roadsides. Project title: Improving Roadside Design to Forgive Human Errors, Project Nr. 823176, ERA-NET ROAD, Road research in Europe (2010)
2. Mak, K.K., Mason, R.L.: Accident Analysis-Breakaway and Non-Breakaway Poles Including Sign and Light Standards Along Highways, Volume 1: Executive Summary. U. S. Department of Transportation, National Highway Traffic Safety Administration, Federal highway Administration, Washington, D.C. (1980)
3. Kukko, A., Jaakkola, A., Lehtomki, M., Kaartinen, H., Chen, Y.: Mobile mapping system and computing methods for modeling of road environment. In: Proceeding of the Urban Remote Sensing Joint Event, pp. 331–338 (2009)
4. Cabo, C., Ordoñez, C., García-Cortés, S., Martínez, J.: An algorithm for automatic detection of pole-like street furniture objects from mobile laser scanner point clouds. ISPRS J. Photogramm. Remote Sens. **87**, 47–56 (2014)

5. Wu, B., Yu, B., Yue, W., Shu, S., Tan, W., Hu, C., Huang, Y., Wu, J., Liu, H.: A voxel-based method for automated identification and morphological parameters estimation of individual street trees from mobile laser scanning data. Remote Sens. **5**(2), 584–611 (2013)
6. Yokoyama, H., Date, H., Kanai, S., Takeda, H.: Detection and classification of pole-like objects from mobile laser scanning data of urban environments. Int. J. CAD/CAM **13**(2), 31–40 (2013)
7. El-Halawany, S.I., Lichti, D.D.: Detection of road poles from mobile terrestrial laser scanner point cloud. In: International Workshop on Multi-Platform/Multi-Sensor Remote Sensing and Mapping (M2RSM), Xiamen, China, Art. No. 5697364 0 (2011)
8. Lehtomäki, M., Jaakkola, A., Hyyppa, J., Kukko, A., Kaartinen, H.: Detection of vertical pole-like objects in a road environment using vehicle-based laser scanning data. Remote Sens. **2**(3), 641–664 (2010)
9. Pu, S., Rutzinger, M., Vosselman, G., Elberink, S.O.: Recognizing basic structures from mobile laser scanning data for road inventory studies. ISPRS J. Photogramm. Remote Sens. **66**(6), 28–39 (2011)
10. Li, D., Elberink, S.O.: Optimizing detection of road furniture (pole-like objects) in mobile laser scanner data. In: ISPRS Annals of the Photogrammetry, Remote Sensing and Spatial Information Sciences, vol. II-5/W2, pp. 163–168. ISPRS Workshop Laser Scanning, Antalya, Turkey (2013)
11. Saaty, T.L.: The Analytic Hierarchy Process. McGraw-Hill, New York (1980)
12. Saaty, T.L.: Priority setting in complex problems. IEEE Trans. Eng. Manag. **30**(3), 140–155 (1983)
13. Douligeris, C., Pereira, I.J.: A telecommunications quality study using the analytic hierarchy process. IEEE J. Sel. Areas Commun. **12**(2), 241–250 (1994)
14. Lai, V.S., Trueblood, R.P., Wong, B.K.: Software selection: a case study of the application of the analytical hierarchical process to the selection of a multimedia authoring system. Inf. Manag. **25**(2), 221–232 (1992)
15. Akkineni, V.S., Nanjundasastry, S.: The analytic hierarchy process for choice of technologies. Technol. Forecast. Soc. Change **38**, 151–158 (1990)
16. Tam, M.C.Y., Tummala, V.M.R.: An application of the AHP in vendor selection of a telecommunications system. Omega **29**, 171–182 (2001)

Human Identification by Gait Using Fourier Descriptor and Angle-Based Pseudo Anatomical Landmark Model

Mridul Ghosh[1(✉)] and Debotosh Bhattacharjee[2]

[1] Department of Computer Science, Shyampur Siddheswari Mahavidyalaya,
Howrah, India
mridulxyz@gmail.com
[2] Department of Computer Science and Engineering, Jadavpur University,
Kolkata, India
debotosh@ieee.org

Abstract. Feature extraction from Spatio-temporal movement characteristic for human gait recognition with respect to the surveillance camera has been a prime concern in this paper, and a very simple technique has been discussed to recognize the subject efficiently under surveillance. A new model has been proposed to extract features proficiently. For shape description, Fourier descriptor has been applied on the silhouettes. By the concept of anatomical landmarks on human figures, control point set has been created along with the Centre of Mass (C). Different angles, which play a very significant role in body movement, have been measured as features. Considering k features, thus found from each image in a sequence consisting of n images a total of k × n features are included in individual feature vectors. For recognition, Mahalanobis distance has been used on the feature vectors. It has been found that the recognition result of our approach is encouraging as compared to other recent methods. For CASIA-C, recognition rate obtained by our method is 93% and for OU-ISIR-D (DB$_{high}$), the rate is 93.6%.

Keywords: Gait recognition · Fourier descriptor · Centre of mass
Mahalanobis distance

1 Introduction

For reliable human identification Biometrics are a commanding mean. Commonly used biometric means used to identify human characteristics include fingerprint, face, iris, speech, etc., but there are some limitations to identify individuals using these biometrics. For example, face recognition techniques are able to recognize only a frontal face image or side face or with a different angle with respect to the surveillance camera, but it is impossible yet to recognize a person from the back. On the other hand, other biometrics like fingerprint, palmprint, iris is no longer pertinent when the person unexpectedly appears in the surveillance area. They perform badly at low image resolutions and need active user participation. Now-a-days, human identification using gait is very challenging which defines human characteristics of the systematic study of

© Springer Nature Singapore Pte Ltd. 2018
P. Bhattacharyya et al. (Eds.): NGCT 2017, CCIS 828, pp. 704–721, 2018.
https://doi.org/10.1007/978-981-10-8660-1_53

human walking styles and in due course of time it has drawn lots of attention to the people. Gait is a medical term to describe human locomotion i.e. the way people walk. Since gait can be measured at low resolution, it can be used in situations when a face or iris information does not have sufficient resolution for the recognition. The most advantageous part of this biometric recognition system is that it works without any intervention of any personnel or any intimation to the person under surveillance.

Another motivation is that as the surveillance cameras are reasonably low cost, video footage of suspects can be prepared, and can be installed in banks, railway stations, cinema hall, airport, most buildings, and shopping malls, different important areas of road, sacred places or different locations requiring a security presence. There are also some limitations in terms of level of uniqueness and covariate factors that change gait characteristics. These can be external like changes of view, direction, or speed of movement, illumination conditions, weather, clothing, footwear, terrain, etc. or internal like changes due to illness, injuries, ageing, pregnancy, etc.

2   Related Work

Gait features are very significant in improving the performance of gait recognition. In general, there are two different gait feature extraction methods: Model-based and model-free.

Model based approach is committed in recuperating the fundamental mathematical structure of gait with a construction model.

In model-free approaches, moments of shape or image template or the sequence of images are converted to a single image by averaging the silhouettes are used for feature extraction. Various research works have been conducted in the gait recognition system. This section reviews the related literature on gait feature extraction approaches.

Cunado [1] first proposed a model-based approach to gait biometric by a rotation pattern of hip, creating models of legs for gait motion, motion model of the thigh. By combining VHT (Velocity Hough transform) techniques with the FS (Fourier series) representation of the hip rotation, features have been extracted from the models. Cunado shows that the motion of the thigh is better represented as an FS rather than by polynomial fitting to the extracted data. This model-based approach uniquely gave a signature, which could be directly related to the original image sequence.

By linear regression analysis, hip and knee angles from the body contour are estimated by trigonometric-polynomial interpolation functions, which are fitted to the angle sequences [2] and the parameters, so obtained, are used for recognition.

Bhanu and Han [3] proposed a kinematic-based approach to recognize individuals by gait. The 3D human walking parameters are estimated by performing a least squares fit of the 3D kinematic model to the 2D silhouette extracted from a monocular image sequence. Human gait signatures are generated by selecting features from the estimated parameters.

Niyogi and Adelson [4] distinguished different subjects by extracting their gait signatures via curve-fitting of the walking patterns. These patterns were processed and recorded to identify the movements of the bounding contours and for a compact description a simplified stick model is fitted to the identified pattern.

In model free approach, Little and Boyd [5] used moments of a dense flow distribution as features from the shape of human motion. Collins et al. [6] selected key frames and applied template matching. Shutler et al. [7] used velocity into the traditional moments to obtain the so-called velocity moments (VMs). In another approach, the average of silhouettes are considered as GEI (gait Energy Image), Chrono gait energy image (CGI) by Chen et al. [8]

But the main problem lies in the feature extraction strategy depending on the movement of different body parts and these movements causes movements of different angles on different body parts with respect to each other. In this paper, the angle extraction technique has been proposed and a pseudo anatomical model is designed to fit various angles of human movement for proper representation of gait cycles of every individual uniquely.

3   Preprocessing Phase

The preprocessing phase of gait recognition involves capture of video sequences, frame generation, background subtraction and silhouette generation which is shown in Fig. 1. All the steps are discussed subsequently.

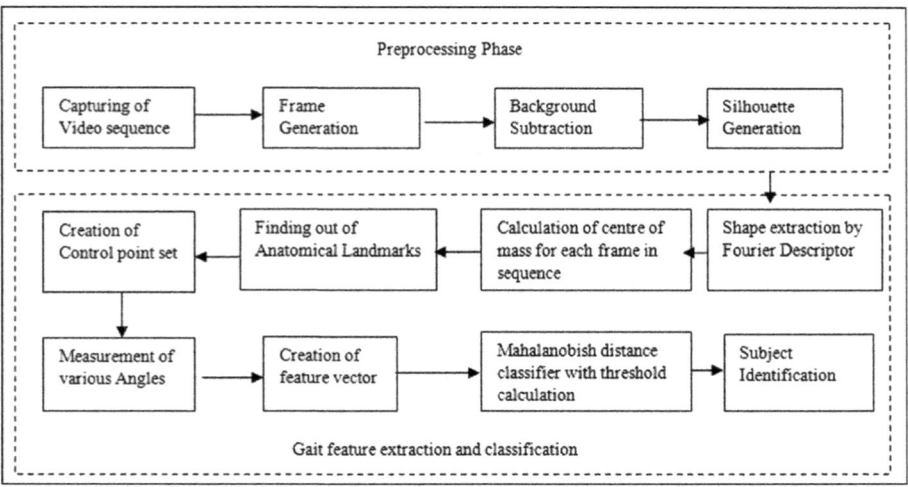

Fig. 1. Flowchart of the proposed method

3.1   Capturing of Video Sequences

From the raw video sequence, the movement of the moving subject has been captured considering the background as static. Although the main assumption made here is that the camera is static, and the only moving object in video sequences is the walker.

3.2 Frame Generation

Dividing the video sequences to a fixed time interval, still images are generated. After background modeling and moving object segmentation [9, 10], the segmented regions are smoothed using Gaussian filter and by morphological processing, namely erosion, the noisy pixels are removed and by dilation, the small holes are filled up to make the object as a single component. The segmented regions are tracked based on the overlapping of the centre of mass of the bounding rectangle [27] which encloses the region in consecutive frames.

3.3 Background Subtraction

To have the foreground object or the subject under consideration, the background is subtracted from the entire image. Background can be generated by LMedS (Least Median of Square) [11, 25, 26] method and differencing of background and foreground image can be obtained by the method described in [12, 25, 26] from the image sequence.

3.4 Silhouette Generation

Extracting the object and removing the background, all the constituent pixels of an object are replaced uniformly by intensity level, having 255 and background changes uniformly with intensity value 0 and thus the silhouette is generated. By applying morphological operations and binary connected component analysis single, highly compacted connected region with the largest size, silhouette of a person is obtained.

4 Gait Feature Extraction and Classification

In this section, the feature extraction technique has been discussed such as a Fourier Descriptor for shape extraction, Center of Mass Detection for the object under concern, anatomical landmarks, control points selection of pseudo anatomical landmarks, measurements of various angles of body part movement and in the classification part Mahalanobish distance has been exploited.

4.1 Fourier Descriptor for Shape Extraction

By Fourier descriptor [14] the boundary of any object can be described. The boundary points (say n) can be expressed as a complex function

$$T(n) = X(n) + jY(n) \tag{1}$$

The procedure of obtaining Fourier descriptor is as follows:
Apply the Fourier transforms to the K boundary points.

$$S(u) = \frac{1}{K}\sum_{n=0}^{K-1} T(n)e^{\frac{j2\Pi ux}{K}}, \text{ for } n = 0, 1, 2, \ldots K - 1 \tag{2}$$

The inverse transform can be applied to obtain the original points

$$T(n) = \frac{1}{K}\sum_{u=0}^{N-1} S(u)e^{\frac{j2\Pi ux}{K}}, \text{ for } u = 0, , 1, 2, \ldots K - 1 \tag{3}$$

The coefficients S(u) are called Fourier descriptors. Dividing all Fourier descriptors by the magnitude of the second Fourier descriptor (i.e. $|S(1)|$), scale invariance of Fourier descriptors can be achieved. Thus, the scale invariant vector (S(k)) may be written as

$$S(\text{k}) = \frac{S(k)}{|S(1)|} \tag{4}$$

The motive behind of using Fourier Descriptor [13, 14] for shape extraction is that the it can reduce the contour points by half keeping the shape of the original image intact, thus reducing the computational cost of feature extraction (Fig. 2) .

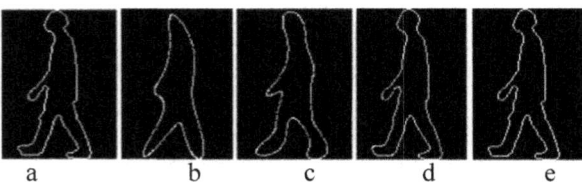

Fig. 2. (a) original contour points having 2^8 FDs (b) 2^4 FDs (c) 2^5 FDs (d) 2^6 FDs (e) 2^7 FDs

From the figure it has been seen 2^7 FDs gives same object shape as 2^8 FDs but with half contour points.

4.2   Detection and Normalization of the Bounding Rectangle and Center of Mass Detection

Making the aspect ratio fixed, images are cropped and resized to fit into a bounding rectangle to enclose the contours of the object.

2D Cartesian moment of a contour(r, s) can be defined as [15]

$$m_{r,s} = \sum_{i=1}^{n} I(x, y)x^r y^s \tag{5}$$

Here r is the x-order and s is the y-order. The 2D Cartesian coordinate of the center of mass C (x_c, y_c) is the ratio of the 1st order and 0th order of the contour moment

$$x_c = m_{10}/m_{00}, \quad y_c = m_{01}/m_{00} \tag{6}$$

Moment m_{00} is the length in pixels of the contours, when r = s = 0. m_{10} and m_{01} signify moments of x and y components correspondingly.

4.3   Anatomical Landmarks

From the theory of anatomical studies [13, 16, 17] the body segment lengths articulated as a percentage of body height was set by Drillis and Contini [16] to approximate the body segments proportions in the absence of enhanced data where the direct individual measurement is not viable. From this idea, the positions of ankle (an), knee (kn), hip (hip), wrist (r), chest (ch), shoulder (sh) and head (hd) are projected vertically as a division of the body height H (calculated as vertical height of the bounding rectangle) as 0.039H, 0.285H, 0.530H, 0.425, 0.720H, 0.818H and 0.870H calculated from the base of the subject i.e. highest y coordinate level. These points are called anatomical landmarks.

4.4   Control Point Selection

To generate the control points set from the boundary point set BP of the subject in the bounding rectangle, let the boundary point set BOUND = $\{b_k\}$, k is the number of boundary points. Each b_k has x and y coordinate named x_k, y_k. Perpendicular distances $\forall b_k(x_k, y_k)$ from the maximum y coordinate (say y_m) (bottom level) has been found out. Let it be D_k,

$$D_k = \{y_k - y_m \mid \forall k\} \tag{7}$$

The vertical distances of anatomical points an, kn, hip, ch, sh, hd from y_m as d_{Ak}, d_{Kn}, d_{Hp}, d_{Ch}, d_{Sl}, d_{Hd} have been calculated as the vertical height of the bounding rectangle. Comparing these distances (d_{Ak}, d_{Kn}, d_{Hp}, d_{Ch}, d_{Sl}, d_{Hd}) with D_k set, the index points have been found out. These index points are compared with $BOUND_{i-}$ (index of boundary point set) ($1 \leq i \leq k$). From the matched index value, x and y coordinates of corresponding anatomical points are extracted. From one anatomical landmark point, the opposite coordinate can be found out from the set BOUND. (E.g. the point on the hip marked as hip2 and the opposite is marked as hip1). From a landmark, comparing the y coordinate point with all corresponding x coordinate points from the set BOUND, the minimum x coordinate point will be taken from the set BOUND, this (x, y) point denotes the opposite point. Similar way points kn1-kn2, an1-an2, ch1-ch2, sh1-sh2 have been found out. The middle of y coordinate points between center of mass (C) and knee, shoulder and chest have been considered and corresponding x coordinate value has been extracted from the set BOUND and the opposite points are also obtained, say m1, m2, m3, m4 as shown in Fig. 3, which are basically pseudo anatomical landmarks and these points together with the anatomical landmarks are kept in the control point set named CONTROLP.

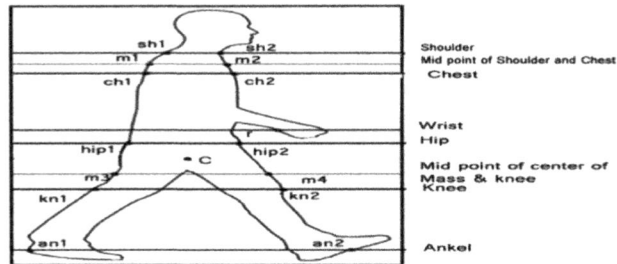

Fig. 3. Control points selection from Pseudo anatomical landmarks

Thus 16 control points have been obtained and out of 16, 6 points have been taken from the shoulder and the chest portion as it has been seen that shoulder and chest movement also help to distinguish individuals and 8 points have been considered from the lower portion of the body which covers all the body joints and play a very significant role in recognition. One point which has been taken from wrist to follow the wrist movement with respect to the body since it also varies from different individuals. Centre of mass point has been considered to find out the variations of some angle with respect to it (Figs. 5, 6, 7, 8, 9, 10, 11, 12, 13, 14, 15, 16, 17 and 18).

4.5   Measurement of Various Angles of Body Part Movement with Each Other

To find out the Ang1 (as shown in Fig. 4), two angles Th_1 and Th_2 need to be found out. From the chest point ch2, a horizontal line is drawn via ch1. A perpendicular line is

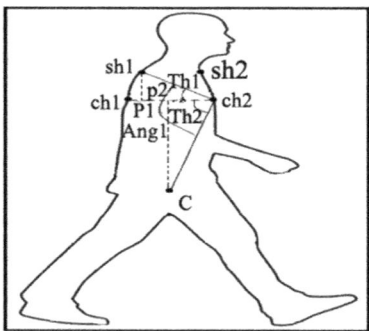

Fig. 4. Pictorial representation of finding out Angle-1

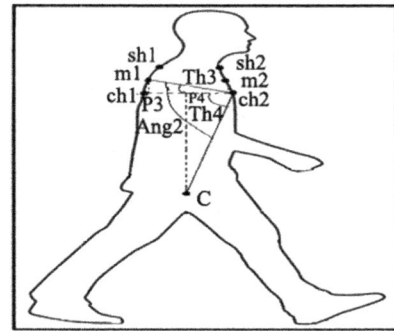

Fig. 5. Pictorial representation of finding out Angle-2

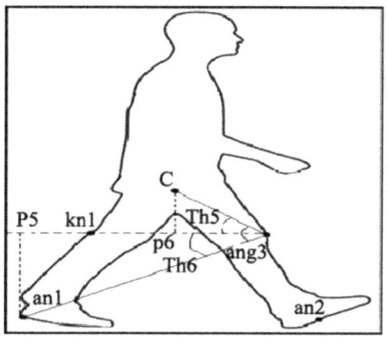

Fig. 6. Pictorial representation of finding out Angle-3

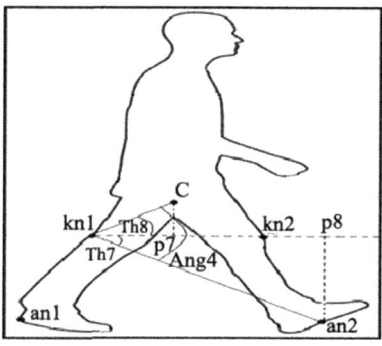

Fig. 7. Pictorial representation of finding out Angle-4

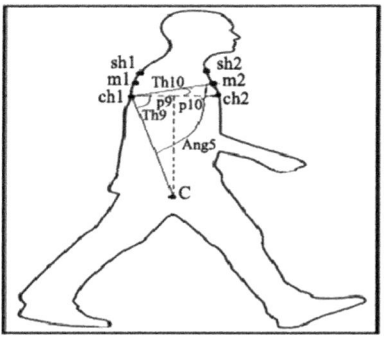

Fig. 8. Pictorial representation of finding out Angle-5

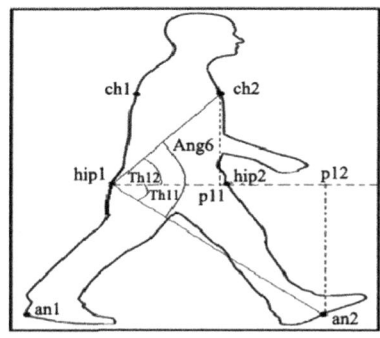

Fig. 9. Pictorial representation of finding out Angle-6

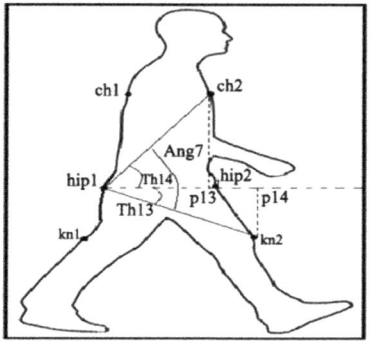

Fig. 10. Pictorial representation of finding out Angle-7

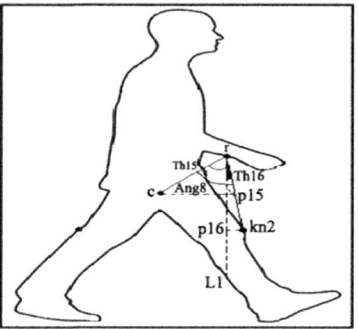

Fig. 11. Pictorial representation of finding out Angle-8

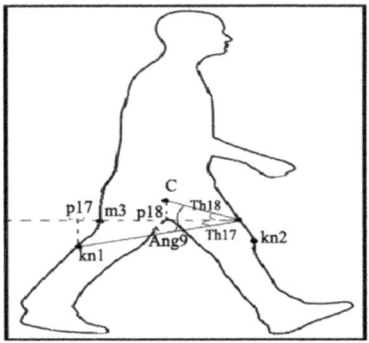

Fig. 12. Pictorial representation of finding out Angle-9

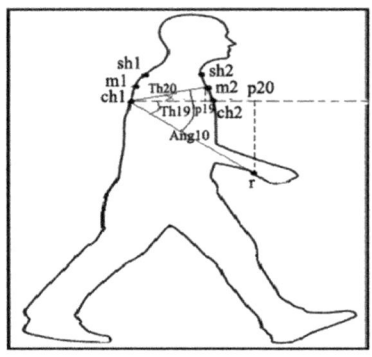

Fig. 13. Pictorial representation of finding out Angle-10

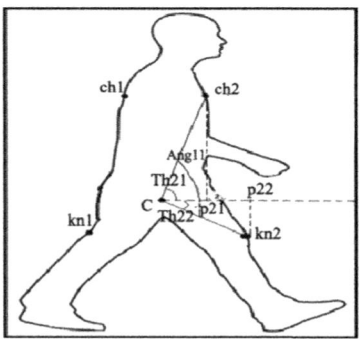

Fig. 14. Pictorial representation of finding out Angle-11

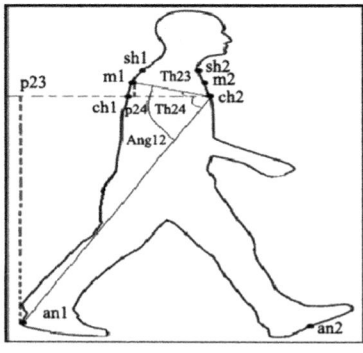

Fig. 15. Pictorial representation of finding out Angle-12

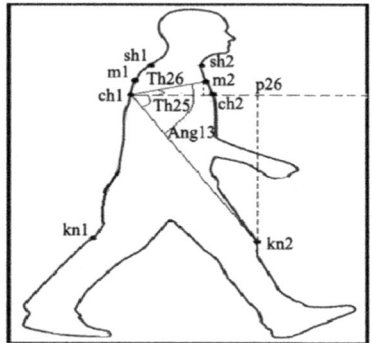

Fig. 16. Pictorial representation of finding out Angle-13

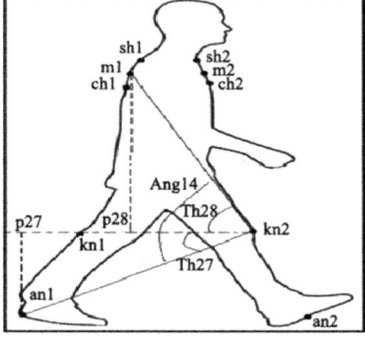

Fig. 17. Pictorial representation of finding out Angle-14

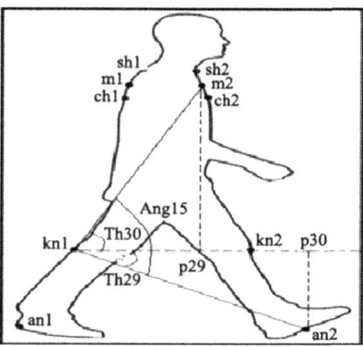

Fig. 18. Pictorial representation of finding out Angle-15

drawn from shoulder point sh1, which intersects the line ch1ch2 at p1. Another perpendicular line is drawn from the centre of mass(C) in such a way that it cuts ch1ch2 line at p2. Now, two angles $\angle$ sh1ch2ch1(i.e., Th1) and $\angle$ ch1ch2C(i.e., Th2) are formed. The coordinates of p1, p2 can be written as (xsh1, ych1) and (xc, ych1) respectively.

$$Th_1 = \tan^{-1}\left(\frac{ysh1 - ych1}{xch2 - xsh1}\right) \tag{8}$$

$$Th_2 = \tan^{-1}\left(\frac{yc - ych1}{xch2 - xc}\right) \tag{9}$$

$$\text{So, } Ang1 = Th_1 + Th_2 \tag{10}$$

In generic form the angles can be written as

$$Ang_i = Th_{i*2-1} + Th_{i*2} \tag{11}$$

$$\text{Where } Th_i = \tan^{-1}\left(\frac{(w_i - x_i)}{(y_i - z_i)}\right) \tag{12}$$

Where w_i, x_i, y_i, z_i denotes the coordinates of two end points of a line segment.
The following Table 1 shows the coordinate points to calculate Th_i.

In this proposed model (Fig. 19), to construct the feature vector by taking various angles during a walking sequence, 15 features (angles) were used to construct the features vector as shown:

F = {Ang1, Ang2, Ang3, Ang4, Ang5, Ang6, Ang7, Ang8, Ang9, Ang10, Ang11, Ang12, Ang13, Ang14, Ang15}

Here, only one pose has been shown in the figures to demonstrate different angles but these angles have been applied for all the 10 phases of walking i.e. initial contact, double support, mid-stance (3subphase(start of mid-stance, mid of mid-stance, end of mid stance)), propulsion, pre-swing, mid-swing (two sub phase (start of mid-swing,

Table 1. Parameter values to calculate Th_i

i	w_i	x_i	y_i	z_i	Ref fig
1	ysh1	ych1	xch2	xsh1	5
2	yc	ych1	xch2	xc	5
3	ym1	ych1	xch2	xm1	6
4	yc	ych2	xch2	xc	6
5	yc	ykn2	xc	xkn2	7
6	ykn1	yan1	xkn2	xan1	7
7	yan2	ykn1	xkn1	xan2	8
8	yc	ykn1	xkn1	xc	8
9	yc	ych1	xch1	xc	9
10	ym2	ych1	xch1	xm2	9
11	yan2	yhip1	xhip1	xan2	10
12	ych2	yhip1	xhip1	xch2	10
13	ykn2	yhip1	xhip1	xkn2	11
14	ych2	yhip1	xhip1	xch2	11
15	yc	yr	xr	xc	12
16	ykn2	yr	xr	xc	12
17	ykn1	ym4	xm4	xkn1	13
18	yc	ym4	xm4	xkn1	13
19	Yr	ych1	xch1	xr	14
20	ym1	ych1	xch1	xm2	14
21	ych2	yc	xc	xch2	15
22	ykn2	yc	xc	xkn2	15
23	ym1	ych2	xch2	xm1	16
24	yan1	ych2	xch2	xan1	16
25	ykn2	ych1	xch1	xkn2	17
26	ym2	ych1	xch1	xm2	17
27	yan1	ykn2	xkn2	xan1	18
28	ym1	ykn1	xkn1	xan2	18
29	yan2	ykn1	xkn1	xan2	19
30	ym2	ykn1	xkn1	xm2	19

mid of mid swing), ending swing and whenever any point will be obscured or the coordinate value cannot be obtained then the corresponding coordinate value will not be considered for angle calculation.

4.6   Classification Using Mahalanobish Distance

Mahalanobis distance [18] statistic has been exploited for classification purpose. For training and testing let, the mean vector μ_1 and μ_2 respectively and the sample variance-covariance matrices of the training and testing data V_1 and V_2 respectively.

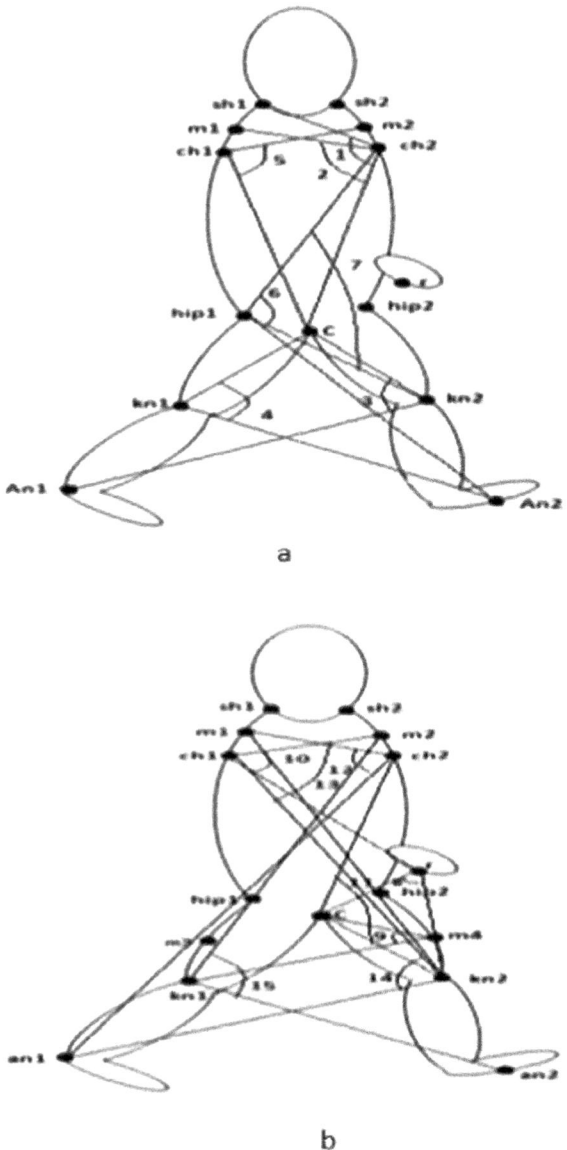

Fig. 19. Pseudo anatomical model of our proposed work considering fifteen angles. (a) Represents angles 1–7 and (b) represents angles 8–15

$$\text{Let, } U = (V_1 + V_2)/2 \tag{13}$$

Mahalanobis distance statistic says the statistical distance

$$D^2 = (\mu_1 - \mu_2)^T U^{-1} (\mu_1 - \mu_2) \tag{14}$$

For a person the of k sequences the distance metric become

$$D_{1k}^2 = \frac{1}{k}(D_1^2 + D_2^2 + \ldots \ldots + D_k^2) \tag{15}$$

The average distance for p persons

$$D_{avg}^2 = \frac{1}{p}(D_{1k}^2 + D_{2k}^2 + \ldots \ldots + D_{pk}^2) \tag{16}$$

Experimentally the precision value is chosen to have the threshold

$$\sigma = \frac{1}{p}((D_{avg}^2 - D_{1k}^2)^2 + \ldots \ldots + (D_{avg}^2 - D_{pk}^2)^2)^{1/2} \tag{17}$$

The threshold can be expressed as $D_{avg}^2 \pm \sigma$

5   Experiment and Results

The experiment has been conducted by using CASIA-C [19] and OU-ISIR Treadmill dataset D [20] (DB$_{high}$). Here, 15 different angles have been calculated. If in a sequence, there are n images, only 10 images have been considered according to 10 phases of walking to register in the database as the training and testing purpose and here 3 different sequences of walking has been taken and thus the size of the training feature set for each person becomes 15 × 10 × 3 (Fig. 21).

In this experiment, feature vectors have been generated for gait sequences of 100 persons from CASIA-C dataset and 50 persons from the OU-ISIR dataset. The gait sequences 1-2, 1-3 and 2-3 have been considered and corresponding D^2 values have been calculated and D_{avg}^2 and the precision value can be obtained by applying the Eqs. (16) and (17) have been calculated. For individual persons, the D^2 values, i.e. $D_1^2, D_2^2, \ldots \ldots, D_k^2$ (where k is the sequence number, in this case k = 3 have been considered) have been calculated. And for the 100 persons the D_{avg}^2 has been calculated, and it is 0.358 (Table 2).

The response of the false rejection rate (FRR), false acceptance rate (FAR) and the correct recognition rate (CRR) in accordance with the value of ± σ has been observed. It has been found out that this proposed method has shown better recognition rate than previous method [24–26].

The Fig. 20a and b show the recognition rates for both the +ve and –ve values of σ. It can be seen that in the –ve direction, the response of CRR and FRR, FAR is not

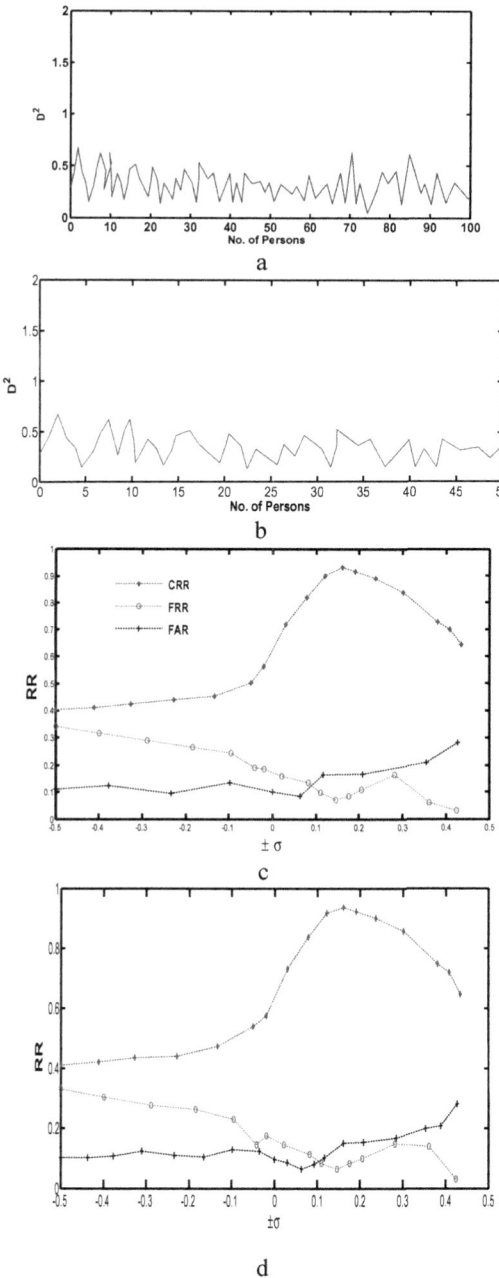

Fig. 20. (a)The D_{1k}^2, D_{2k}^2, ..., D_{pk}^2 values corresponding to 100 persons are mapped for CASIA-C dataset. (b) The D_{1k}^2, D_{2k}^2, ..., D_{pk}^2 values corresponding to 50 persons are mapped for OU-ISIR Treadmill dataset D (DB_{high}) (c) Plot with $\pm$ σ and the Recognition Rate (d) Plot with $\pm$ σ and the Recognition Rate

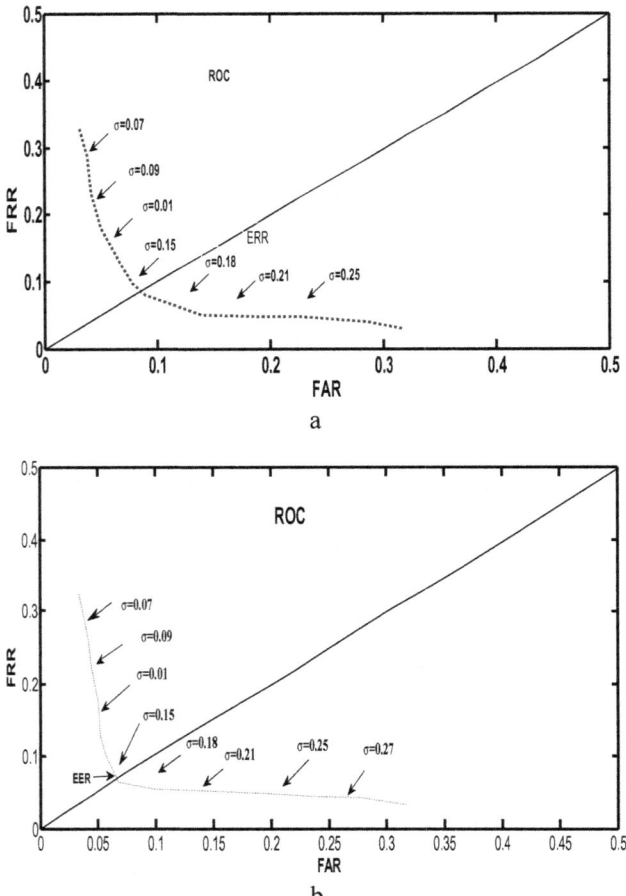

Fig. 21. (a) From the ROC curve, the ERR value is 0.07 for σ = 0.15 i.e. at this point FAR = FRR using CASIA-C dataset. (b) From the ROC curve, the ERR value is 0.06 for σ = 0.17 i.e. at this point FAR = FRR using OU-ISIR Treadmill dataset D(DB$_{high}$).

appreciable compared to the +ve direction and when = +0.15, CRR becomes maximum i.e. 93% and considering the trade of between FAR and FRR the value can be taken at 0.07 of RR i.e.7% and FAR value 0.69 i.e. 6.9% of RR using CASIA C database and CRR becomes 93.6% when FAR, FRR becomes 6% for σ = +0.17. So the threshold value becomes $D^2 avg + \sigma = 0.508 \approx 0.5$

To examine the performance of the proposed algorithm, comparative experiments have been conducted which is shown in Table 3. From Table 3, it is clear that the method, proposed here, has shown significant improvement in performance as compared to other recent methods for the same database.

Table 2. Different recognition parameters

Person	Correct recognition	Correct rejection rate	False acceptance rate	False rejection rate
100	93%	92%	6.9%	7%
50	93.6%	93.2%	6.8%	6.07%

Table 3. Comparison of different approaches with our methods

Method	Database	Recognition rate
$M_G^{ij}(x, y)$ + ACDA [21]	CASIA-C	34.7%
GEI [22]	CASIA-C	74%
2DLPP [23]	CASIA-C	88.9%
Method1 [24]	CASIA-C	84%
Method2 [25]		91%
Method3 [26]		92.3%
Proposed method	CASIA-C	93%
	OU-ISIR-D(DBhigh)	93.6%

6 Conclusion

Gait has a rich potential as a biometric for recognition, though it is sensitive to various covariate conditions, which are circumstantial and physical conditions that can affect either gait itself or the extracted gait features. The limitation of our technique is that only lateral view movement has been considered which may be applicable to many scenarios like banks, airports, shopping mall, sacred places, etc. So there is a scope to extend this technique on different view angles between camera and object.

Acknowledgement. The authors would like to thank Mr. Hongyu Liang for providing the database of the silhouettes named "CASIA Human Gait Database" collected by Institute of Automation, Chinese Academy Of sciences. Their thanks also go to those who have contributed to the establishment of the CASIA database [19]. Thanks to the Institute of Scientific and Industrial Research (ISIR) Osaka University for providing the OU-ISIR gait database [20].

References

1. Cunado, D., Nixon, M.S., Carter, J.N.: Automatic extraction and description of human gait models for recognition purposes. Comput. Vis. Image Underst. **90**(1), 1–41 (2003)
2. Yoo, J.H., Nixon, M., Harris, C.: Model-driven statistical analysis of human gait motion. In: Proceedings of the IEEE International Conference on Image Processing. vol 1, pp. 285–288 Sept. 2002
3. Bhanu, B., Han,. J.: Individual recognition by kinematic based gait analysis. In: Proceedings of the International Conference on Pattern Recognition. vol. 3, pp. 343–346 (2002)

4. Niyogi, S.A., Adelson, E.H.: Analysis and recognizing walking figures in XYT. In: Proceedings of the IEEE Conference on Computer Vision Pattern Recognition, Seattle, WA, pp. 469–474 June 1994
5. Little, J., Boyd, J.: Recognizing people by their gait: the shape of motion. Videre: J. Comput. Vis. Res. **1**(2), 1–32 (1998)
6. Collins, R.T., Gross, R., Shi. J.: Silhouette-based human identification from body shape and gait. In: International Conference on Automatic Face and Gesture Recognition (2002)
7. Kent, J.: New Directions in Shape Analysis, in the Art of Statistical Science: A Tribute to G. S. Watson, pp. 115–127. Wiley, New York (1992)
8. Chen, W., Junping, Z., Liang, W., Jian, P., Xiaoru, Y.: Human identification using temporal information preserving gait template. IEEE Trans. Pattern Anal. Mach. Intell. **34**(11), 2164–2176 (2012)
9. Horprasert, T., Harwood, D., Davis, L.S.: A statistical approach for real-time robust background subtraction and shadow detection. In: Proceedings of the International Conference on Computer Vision (1999)
10. Kim, K., Chalidabhongse, T.H., Harwood, D., Davis, L.: Real-time foreground- background segmentation using codebook model. Real-Time Imaging **11**, 172–185 (2005)
11. Rousseeuw, P.J.: Least median of squares regression. J. Am. Stat. Assoc. **79**(388), 871–880 (1984)
12. Kuno, Y., Watanabe, T., Shimosakoda, Y., Nakagawa, S.: Automated detection of human for visual surveillance system. In: Proceedings of the International Conference on Pattern Recognition, pp. 865–869 (1996)
13. Das Choudhury, S., Tjahjadi, T.: Silhouette-based gait recognition using Procrustes shape analysis and elliptic Fourier descriptors. Pattern Recogn. **45**(9), 3414–3426 (2012). ISSN: 0031-3203
14. Jain, A.K.: Fundamentals of Digital Image Processing: Information and Systems Science Series. Prentice Hall, Upper Saddle River (1989)
15. Nixon, M.S., Aguado, A.S.: Feature Extraction and image Processing, 2nd edn. Elsevier, London (2006)
16. Winter, D.A.: Biomechanics and Motor Control of Human Movement, 3rd edn. John Wiley & Sons, Hoboken (2004)
17. Drillis, R., Contini, R.: Body segment parameters. Rep. 1163-03, Office of Vocational Rehabilitation, Department of Health, Education and Welfare, New York (1966)
18. Mahalanobis, P.C.: On the generalised distance in statistics. In: Proceedings of the National Institute of Sciences of India, vol. 2, no. 1, pp. 49–55 (1936). Accessed 03 May 2012
19. CASIA gait database. http://www.sinobiometrics.com
20. Makihara, Y., Mannami, H., Tsuji, A., Hossain, M.A., Sugiura, K., Mori, A., Yagi, Y.: OU-ISIR gait database comprising the treadmill dataset. IPSJ Trans. Comput. Vis. Appl. **4**, 53–62 (2012)
21. Bashir, K., Xiang, T., Gong, S.: Gait recognition without subject cooperation. Pattern Recogn. Lett. **31**(13), 2052–2060 (2010)
22. Jungling, K., Arens, M.: A multi-staged system for efficient visual person reidentification. In: MVA2011 IAPR Conference on Machine Vision Applications, Nara, Japan, 13–15 June 2011
23. Zhang, E., Zhao, Y., Xiong, W.: Active energy image plus 2DLPP for gait recognition. Signal Process. **90**, 2295–2302 (2010)

24. Ghosh, M., Bhattacharjee, D.: Human identification by gait using corner points. I. J. Image Gr. Signal Process. **4**, 30–36 (2012)
25. Ghosh, M., Bhattacharjee, D.: An efficient characterization of gait for human identification. I. J. Image Gr. Signal Process. **7**, 19–27 (2014)
26. Ghosh, M., Bhattacharjee, D.: Gait recognition for human identification using fourier descriptor and anatomical landmarks. I. J. Image Gr. Signal Process. **7**(N2), 30–38 (2015)
27. Bradski, G., Kaehler, A.: Learning OpenCV Computer Vision with the OpenCV Library. O'Reilly Media, Sebastopol (2008)

Acute Myeloid Leukemia Detection in WBC Cell Based on ICA Feature Extraction

Jasvir Kaur[✉], Isha Vats, and Amit Verma

Department of Computer Science, Chandigarh Group of Colleges, Landran,
Mohali, Punjab, India
j.kaurjass92@gmail.com, cecm.cse.isha@gmail.com,
dramitverma.cu@gmail.com

Abstract. Leukemia Detection is planned in automatic advance. Such cancer is related to WBCs that affects the blood cells of body. Acute Myeloid leukemia is disease of the myeloid line of platelets described by the quick development of strange white platelets that development in the bone marrow. Generally acute leukemia influence adults and its affects maximizes with age. The symptoms of AML are occurred by replacement of genuine bone marrow by leukemia cells. A basic technique of LEUKAEMIA DETECTION, experts checks mini images. Leukemia identification delivers in the bone marrow. Leukemia is a kind of blood cancer. They develop quicker than ordinary cells, and they don't break expanding while they should. Above time, leukemia cells can mass out the typical platelets. Each bone contains a thin material inside is perceived bone marrow. The small scale scopic pictures of the platelets are testing to discover numerous ailments. Varieties in the blood circumstance demonstrate the development of maladies in a substance. Leukemia would central be able to end in the event that it is left indistinct. In view of an amount of information it is built up. The instruments of erythrocytes and leukocytes and platelets. Initiallly Leukemia is diagnosed only by investigating white blood cells. Active on WBC, Leukemia Detection framework examines the microscopic image and overcome such problems. Significant parts of pictures are removed and some strategies applied directly. K-mean collecting applies only to detect WBC. Its an active area of research and many strategies are proposed till date on automated differential blood count. Several experts are still researching in this area as mechanized difference blood counting framework contributions in identification of various diseases. From the writing on leukocyte picture division it's watched that the vast majority of plans push onto core extraction and not very many plans can extract the cytoplasm that too with lesser accuracy. In this research work, we implement the k-means clustering to identify the cell classification and ICA algorithm used for feature extraction algorithm and classifies the cancer detection and calculate the performance parameters like FAR, FRR and accuracy. Simulation tool used in this research work 2013a and compare the proposed performance parameters with existing parameters.

Keywords: Leukemia detection · Blood cell · Abnormal white blood cell
Leukocyte · Feature extraction (ICA)

© Springer Nature Singapore Pte Ltd. 2018
P. Bhattacharyya et al. (Eds.): NGCT 2017, CCIS 828, pp. 722–732, 2018.
https://doi.org/10.1007/978-981-10-8660-1_54

1 Introduction

Image Processing methods used for verification and the number of cells of interest opens a wide application for early detection of a huge number of ailments. The study of human blood samples gives data that could be used to perceive and expect various diseases [1], which could be treated positively if identified early. Acute Lympho-blastic leukemia is individual, such disorder, mostly affecting families of age minimum 5 years and younger age maximum 50 years. Acute Lympho-blastic leukemia is produced payable to the overproduction of im-mature WBCs [2]. The word "Acute" means Acute Lympho-blastic Leukemia could progress at a disturbing rate to another segments of human body like center nervous system. Liver, Spleen, lymph points and if left un-treated it could pose danger to-life in an insufficient months [3].

This creates early detection of the disease of the para-amount significantly to prevent further destroy to the whole body parts. Attendance of lympho-blasts in a blood sample is a complete path of knowing if the patient is tested positive for the disease. This paper defines that a method to automatically verify and count the lympho-blast cells in a defined blood sample so as to remove human exceptions and major significant facilitate earlier detect of ALL [4].

The major idea of the research work using the feature extraction approach is quite easy [6]. In applying independent Component Analysis to feature extraction, we add consequence class information in addition to input features. ICA method is classified as un-supervised learning since, it results a set of maximum independent component analysis. This approach by nature is regarded to the initial input distribution. But can't promise good performance in classification issues through the consequences independent variables might search some applications in such fields as visualization and source separation [5].

For example the benefit of this approach, consider the following issues :

Let, we have binary input features y1 and y2 uniformly divided in $[-1,1]$ for a twice classification and the result class z is calculated as follows:

$$Z = \ldots\ldots \tag{i}$$

Defining the issue in the 3D space (y1, y2, z) leads to Eq. (i) where the class data as well as the input features correspond to individual axis respectively. The point of data positions in the shaded fields in this issue. Issue is linear division and we could easily catch out y1 + y2 as a significant feature.

The clustering [7] issues comes in various applications i.e. data mining a knowledge discovery, medical processing and vector quantization. The idea establishes a better cluster depends on the applications and various approaches for searching clusters for different criteria and systematic.

The method consists of binary divisions steps:

Step 1: Choose k – centroid randomly,where the value k is fixed in new technology.

Step 2: Every object in the dataset is connected to the closest center.

ED is used to consider the distance between each data object and cluster-center.

Input:

KK = Number of anticipated clusters

DD = {e1,e2….. en} a data set containing m objects.

Output:

The set of kk cluster as quantified in input.

Method:

Arbitrarily select kk data stream from the DD dataset as start cluster centroid.

Repeat

Allocate each data item ddi to the cluster to which object is most same based on the object in the cluster,

Evaluate the novel mean-value of data items for each cluster and update the mean values.[8]

Then no change required

Stop

In k-means clustering method the inter cluster distance that is the least distance between the cluster centroid is considered as;….

Inter = …….. k-1 and kk = k+1…… k ……(i)

2 Related Work

Shankar et al. [9], Acute lympho-blastic leukemia is one of the most common cancer in the blood cells, which mostly occur with age below 5 years and more than 50. These are two categories where the chances of blood cancer are mostly found due to the abnormal increment of blood cell productions. The author proposed an automated system which working with digital image processing to find leukemia infected cells from the blood sample as input. The proposed method uses some distance and transformation techniques to count the abnormal increment of blood cells from a blood sample. The author did their work in Matlab platform and achieves more that 90%

accuracy for detection of infected blood samples from uploading dataset. Basima and Panicker [10], the accurate detection of blood samples is most important to find the stage of blood cancer. The perfect detection can also optimize the treatment process and increase the possibility to reduce the unwanted harmful effects. This process is measured with the better counting method and classification for blood cells to identify the infected samples. The existing methods are having some limitations which reduce the quality and features of classification as some of the tasks perform manually by the doctors. The proposed approach analysis the blood sample and classify the infected sample and the count of blood cells efficiently. The various parameters are used to verify the results of the proposed approach and perform a comparative study for result optimization. The performance of automated system achieve maximum accuracy rate for the used datasets. Rejintal and Aswini [11], author did their research on microscopic images to find infected samples from the upload dataset for the leukemia cancer detection system. Author proposed an automated system can help to find infected samples automatically and reduce the error probability as manual classification. The proposed approach used various steps to perform better classification for blood samples. Proposed approach used enhancement for uploaded image and apply clustering approach to achieve accurate results from uploading samples. The clustered data passed through the feature extraction process for calculating the unique values of cancer cells and compare the knowledge base to find the minimum distance of leukemia cells. Author test their system on various microscopic images to verify the stability of the system and calculate various parameters for comparative study. Saritha et al. [12], medical system needs an automated system which automatically finds the infected image from the uploaded samples for leukemia cancer detection. Acute Lymphoblastic Leukemia is mostly found in the age of 5 years. This type of cancer grows very fast due to the unwanted increment of blood cells. The most common cases are leading to death within a short time span. Here the automated system can help to find the minor chances of infected blood cells. The proposed approach used some classification techniques to find the infected sample and check the presence of leukemia blood cells. The comparison of various other approaches is also done with various calculations to ensure the working capability of the proposed approach. Singh et al. [13], the several diseases present in the world which affect the human life and also cause abnormal deaths. Leukemia is one of them, which occur due to abnormal growth of the infected cells in human blood in very small amount of time. When the bone-marrow produces the blood cells more than their limit, then the stage occurs as leukemia. The proposed method for leukemia detection is used with a classification technique which helps in efficient classification of infected blood samples. The process of detection and classification is depends upload the nearby distance and the count of blood cells. The proposed approach finds all this combined with the help of some feature extraction techniques to bind the feature values with the knowledge-base and achieve the maximum classification rate and accuracy for leukemia cancer detection.

3 Proposed Approach

Step 1: Search a microscopic blood smear image in the dataset from the UCI MACHINE REPOSITORY and ALL-DB site download it. Upload the Microscopic blood image from the database. To convert the original image to grayscale image cause of reduces the original image pixel size. Identify the noise level in the grayscale image and reduce the attack or noise in the image. Because of quality is maintained. Detect the RGB component (Red, Green and Blue) to grayscale conversion (Figs. 1, 2, 3, 4, 5, 6, 7, and 8).

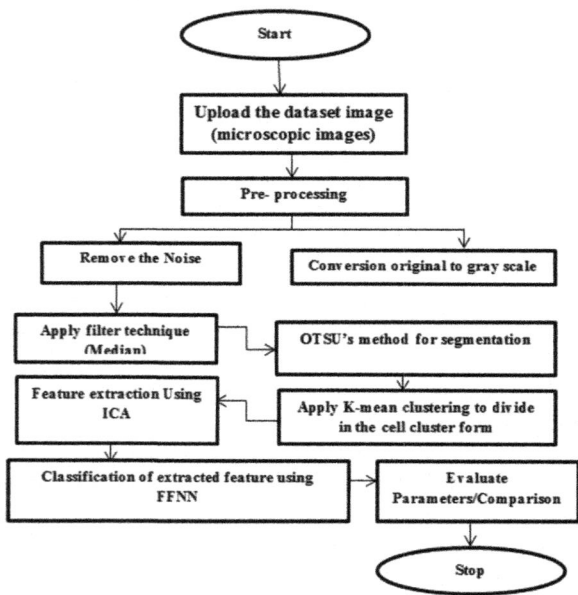

Fig. 1. Proposed flow chart

Step 2: After, to check the noise level in the microscopic images. Reduce the noise attacks in the image with the help of the median filter. Median filter removes the noise in the picture and convert images in 2D form background.

Step 3: Edge Detection: We implement the edge detection approach to calculate the edges in the particular microscopic model. An edge detector is also known as an optimal edge detector. In this edges describes boundaries and it is a problem of vital significance in image processing. Edges describe the area with robust intensity contrast that is a jump in intensity from one pixel to anotherpixel. Edges detect the image significantly. Filter out the useless information and reduces the amount of data.

Step 3: Feature extraction: we implement the Independent component analysis used to feature extraction algorithm used in microscopic images based on medical processing. In ICA algorithm used for extract the features in the form of Component.

Step 4: Classification: We implement the classification algorithm i.e. Feed Forward neural network. This algorithm used in two sections (Training and Testing Phases). These algorithms used to classify the microscopic images detect the cancer system and evaluate the performance parameters i.e. (FAR, FRR, MSE and Accuracy).

Step 5: Compare the performance parameters as existing performance parameters i.e. (FAR False Acceptance rate and Accuracy).

4   Result and Discussions

The implementation is complete in MATLAB 2016a by using the image processing toolbox. Furthermore, MATLAB is current programming language environment: comprised of complicated data structures, includes built-in debugs and editing tools, and aids object oriented programming. Due to such features MATLAB is an estimable tool for research and development and teaching. The input image database consists of 14 + 14 = 28 samples of images taken from healthy and infected patients considered with an optical lab microscope along with a G5 Digital Camera. The sample images are in.jpg format with a 24-bit colour depth and resolution of variables with more than 524288 elements or 512*512*3 pixels. The blood cell sample consists of three types of blood components: (i) Red Blood Cell (ii) White Blood Cells (iii) Platelets.

RBCs are also known as erythrocytes make-up around 40 Percentage of the blood's volume. WBCs are fewer in number associated with the red blood cells and are normally answerable in defending the body against external infections. The main purpose of this dissertation is to introduced a framework that helps to detect the leukemia cancer efficiently so that there will be no need of the manual recognition method that has an error rate between 30% and 40%.

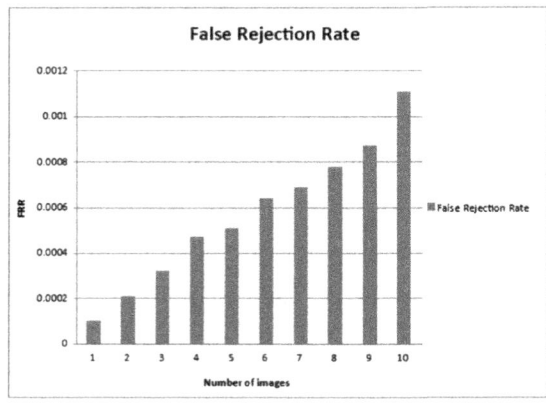

Fig. 2. False rejection rate test cases in proposed work

The above figure defines that the FRR means are the quantity of probability that biometric security framework will mistakenly dismiss an entrance endeavor by an approved client. A framework's FRR commonly is expressed as the proportion of the quantity of false dismissals partitioned by the quantity of recognizable proof endeavors.

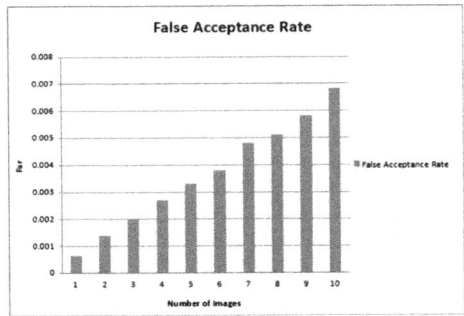

Fig. 3. False acceptance rate test cases in proposed work

The above figure defines that the FAR, is the consider of the likelihood that the growth identification framework will mistakenly acknowledge an entrance endeavor by an unapproved client. A framework's FAR commonly is expressed as the proportion of the quantity of false acknowledgments separated by the quantity of distinguishing proof endeavors.

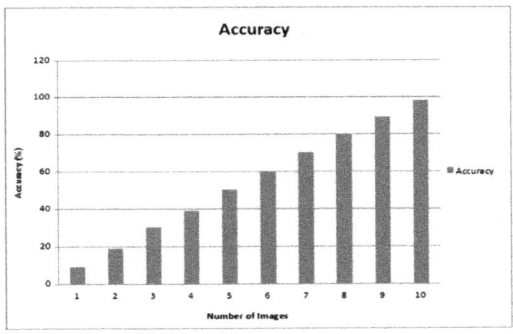

Fig. 4. Accuracy test cases in proposed work

The above figure represents the exactness of a test is its capacity to separate the patient and solid cases effectively. To appraise the precision of a test, we ought to figure the extent of genuine positive and genuine negative in all assessed cases.

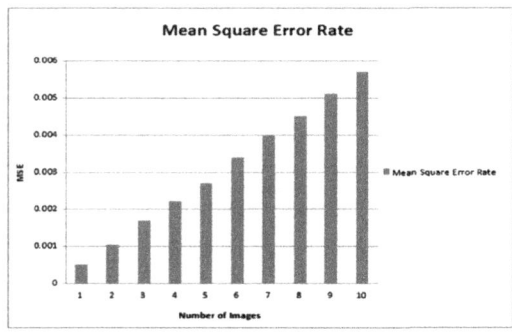

Fig. 5. Means square error rate

The above figure defined MSE is an every now and again utilized measure of the contrasts between values (test and populace esteems) anticipated by a model or an estimator and the qualities really watched (Tables 1 and 2).

Table 1. Accuracy, mean square error rate, FAR and FRR in introduced work

Images	False acceptance rate	False rejection rate	Mean square error rate	Accuracy
1	0.00062	0.0001007	0.0005	9
2	0.00138	0.00021	0.001044	19
3	0.0020	0.00032	0.00168	30
4	0.0027	0.00047	0.0022	39
5	0.0033	0.00051	0.0027	50
6	0.0038	0.00064	0.0034	60
7	0.0048	0.00069	0.004	70
8	0.0051	0.00078	0.0045	80
9	0.0058	0.00087	0.0051	89
10	0.0068	0.001108	0.0057	98

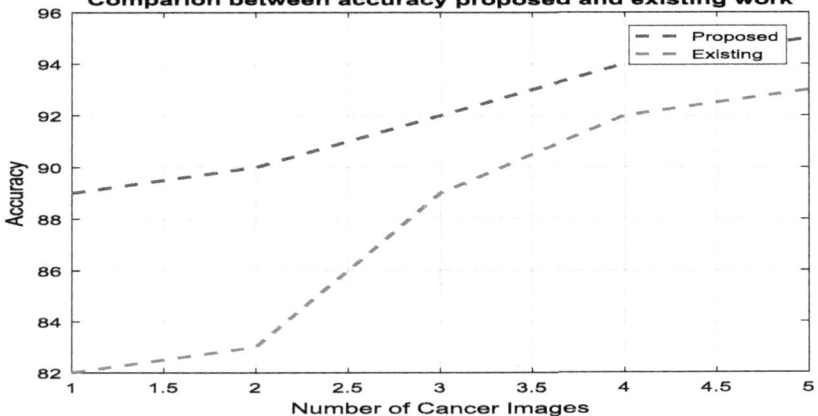

Fig. 6. Comparison between accuracy proposed and existing work

This is defined as a percentage of genuine users rejected by the Leukemia Detection. Accuracy is defined that test is its capacity to separate the patient and solid cases accurately. To gauge the precision of a test, we ought to ascertain the extent of genuine positive and genuine negative in all assessed cases.

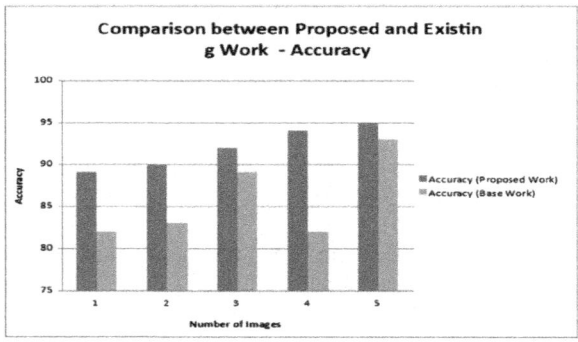

Fig. 7. Comparison between accuracy proposed and existing Work

The above figure represents that the comparison between the proposed and existing work in accuracy. We improve the performance parameters with the help of FFNN.

Table 2. comparison between comparison between accuracy (proposed and existing work)

Images	Accuracy (proposed work)	Accuracy (base work)
1	89	82
2	90	83
3	92	89
4	94	82
5	95	93

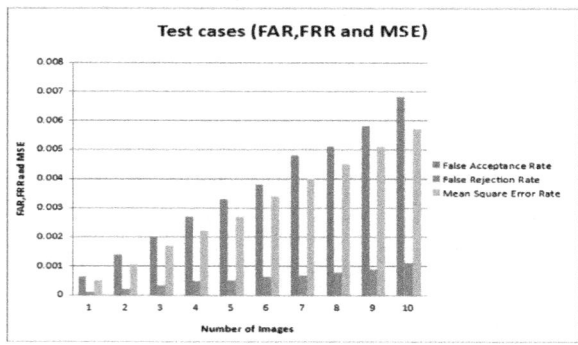

Fig. 8. Comparison between MSE, FAR and FRR error, test cases

The above figure shows that the mean square error rate is less as compared to FAR. The FRR is minimized similarly as false acceptance rate.

5 Conclusion and Future Scope

Lastly, we introduced a method to detect the nuclei and cytoplasm of AML cells. We use the change of gradient magnitude to filter the region of cytoplasm. It is applied to the threshold. We tested the proposed method with 301 images which total 643 AML cells. The suggested method was demonstrated to improve the detection performance when compared to another method. Experimental results confirmed that our method can efficiently segment the nuclei and cytoplasm of AML cells. We can also use this proposed method for another type of cell such as white blood cell, another type of leukemia cell. The proposed method is advantageous especially for the images which the difference between cytoplasm and background is low. However, in some case, we also segment some regions which are not the cytoplasm. In future work, we propose a method that eliminating the noiseless case. Another side, we will separate the group of AML cells to the single cell. Finally, we extract the features from the single AML cells and classify it into 4 subtypes.

The main part of this work is to segment the white blood cell for leukemia detect. The training module classifies the Feed Forward Neural Network's purpose. First, epochs mean, how many numbers of epochs to complete the training module, time considers and performance. The accuracy gets proposed system is 95.89%. We can also use the proposed system to find out the percentage of leukemia infection in microscope image. We hope this approach will be beneficial for today's fast life and early detection of leukemia without any need of costly tests and with a better accuracy.

In future, work can be additionally stretched out by precisely demonstrating highlight extraction procedures, wavelet change approach and dealing with the database all the more viably and assessing the coordinating philosophy and its execution of identifying the leukemia framework utilizing distinctive level of combination with the Fuzzy Interference framework.

References

1. Tran, V.N., Ismail, W., Hassan, R., Yoshitaka, A.: An automated method for the nuclei and cytoplasm of acute myeloid leukemia detection in blood smear images. In: 2016 World Automation Congress (WAC), pp. 1–6. IEEE (2016)
2. Tang, W., Cao, H., Wang, Y. P.: Subtyping of leukemia with gene expression analysis using compressive sensing method. In: 2011 First IEEE International Conference on Healthcare Informatics, Imaging and Systems Biology (HISB). IEEE (2011)
3. Jiang, Y., et al.: Extractives of rumex restrain the proliferation of leukemia cell THP-1. In: 2011 International Symposium on IT in Medicine and Education (ITME), vol. 2. IEEE (2011)
4. Madhloom, H.T., Kareem, S.A., Ariffin, H.: A robust feature extraction and selection method for the recognition of lymphocytes versus acute lymphoblastic leukemia. In: 2012

International Conference on Advanced Computer Science Applications and Technologies (ACSAT). IEEE (2012)

5. Supardi, N.Z., et al.: Classification of blasts in acute leukemia blood samples using k-nearest neighbour. In: 2012 IEEE 8th International Colloquium on Signal Processing and its Applications (CSPA). IEEE (2012)

6. Badea, L.: Unsupervised analysis of leukemia and normal hematopoiesis by joint clustering of gene expression data. In: 2012 IEEE 12th International Conference on Bioinformatics & Bioengineering (BIBE). IEEE (2012)

7. Tong, D.L., Ball, G.R.: Exploration of leukemia gene regulatory networks using a systems biology approach. In: 2014 IEEE International Conference on Bioinformatics and Biomedicine (BIBM). IEEE (2014)

8. Raje, C., Rangole, J.: Detection of leukemia in microscopic images using image processing. In: 2014 International Conference on Communications and Signal Processing (ICCSP). IEEE (2014)

9. Shankar, V., Deshpande, M.M., Chaitra, N., Aditi, S.: Automatic detection of acute lymphoblasitc leukemia using image processing. In: IEEE International Conference on Advances in Computer Applications (ICACA), pp. 186–189. IEEE (2016)

10. Basima, C.T., Panicker. J.R.: Enhanced leucocyte classification for leukemia detection. In: International Conference on Information Science (ICIS), pp. 65–71. IEEE (2016)

11. Rejintal, A., Aswini, N.: Image processing based leukemia cancer cell detection. In: IEEE International Conference on Recent Trends in Electronics, Information & Communication Technology (RTEICT), pp. 471–474. IEEE (2016)

12. Saritha, M., Prakash, B. B., Sukesh, K., Shrinivas, B.: Detection of blood cancer in microscopic images of human blood samples: a review. In: International Conference on Electrical, Electronics, and Optimization Techniques (ICEEOT), pp. 596–600. IEEE (2016)

13. Singh, G., Bathla, G., Kaur, S.P.: A review to detect leukemia cancer in medical images. In: 2016 International Conference on Computing, Communication and Automation (ICCCA), pp. 1043–1047. IEEE (2016)

Optimizing Rice Plant Diseases Recognition in Image Processing and Decision Tree Based Model

Toran Verma[(⊠)] and Sipi Dubey

RCET, Chhattisgarh Swami Vivekanand Technical University,
Bhilai, CG 490024, India
{toran.verma, dr.sipi.dubey}@rungta.ac.in

Abstract. The objective of this paper is to design rice plant diseases recognition system and optimize the recognition efficiency of the system for new test datasets. In this research, the images from rice plant field had been captured by Charged Couple Device digital camera in Joint Photographic Experts Group format in day lighting. The total 6 categories of images with 5 categories of disease infected and one category of non-infected images had been captured. These acquired images had been pre-processed and segmented using three-level of the threshold to extract hybrid features which are a combination of color, texture and discrete cosine coefficient. The hybrid features of each image represent unique feature pattern of individual categories. The inverse multi-quadrics radial basis function had been applied on extracted hybrid features to make features localized and non-singular to enhance the uniqueness of the feature patterns. These transformed features had been used to design rice plant diseases recognition system using a decision tree. The uses of radial function drastically optimize the average recognition efficiency of diseased and non-diseased rice plant from 16.67% to 83.34%. This method can be generalized to design a monitoring system for plant diseases to help farmers and government agencies for on-location inspection and assessment of severity of diseases and take precautionary measure to control the spread of diseases.

Keywords: Decision tree · Digital signal processing · Image processing
Radial basis function · Rice plant diseases · Pattern recognition

1 Introduction

1.1 Rice Diseases

Disease in the plant is a dynamic process induced by incitant factors which manifested at the micro and/or at the macro level (symptom). It impacts the survivability and production performance of the plants. The main causes of diseases in plants are microorganisms which differ widely in their size and shape [1]. The widely varying factors influencing the growth of rice in different parts of the world and during a different season of the year; causes extensive damage to straw yields and grain. Ashy center spots with Spindle-shape, and discolorations appear on leaf-sheaths and at the

© Springer Nature Singapore Pte Ltd. 2018
P. Bhattacharyya et al. (Eds.): NGCT 2017, CCIS 828, pp. 733–751, 2018.
https://doi.org/10.1007/978-981-10-8660-1_55

juncture. The cultivation practices, climatic conditions, soil properties, availability of water and crop varieties greatly influence the susceptibility of the variety to one or more diseases. Major diseases and symptoms of rice plants which had been considered in this research are given in Table 1. The main objective of this research is to create color image processing based rice crop diseases classification model.

Table 1. Rice crop diseases symptoms [2–4].

Rice diseases	Symptoms
Leaf blast	Whitish gray spot on the leaves with a brown margin
Panicle Blast	Whitish gray spot on the leaves with a brown margin
Brown Spot	Brown color oval shape spots appear on the leaves
Sheath Blight	Spots on the leaf sheath
Stem Borer	Brown and died centre leaves of tiller, panicle turns white

1.2   Color Image Processing

The digital image processing had been done in spatial domain and frequency domain to extract useful features. In the spatial domain, different methods are applied to manipulate pixels in an image directly on the image plane. An image is a two-dimensional function, $f(x, y)$ with spatial coordinates x, y and the intensity value of f are all finite with discrete quantities. The captured images by digital media support the compressed format of images such as TIFF, JPEG (JPG) etc. These formats use less byte to represent each pixel but many application developments require more dynamic range (byte) to represent the image pixels. The various system supports different types of images like the gray-scale image, binary image, indexed image, RGB color image and transformations of RGB color model to another color model like NTSC, YCbCr, HSV, CMY, CMYK, HSI and Lab etc. In this research, the joint photographic expert group (JPEG or JPG) images had been taken from the source. These JPEG (JPG) images are transformed in the form of binary images, gray images, RGB images and Lab images to extract spatial features of images after segmentation of a region of interest [5].

1.3   Discrete Cosine Transform (DCT)

Digital signal processing is done on images, to extract frequency domain features of the images. The images are a collection of discrete time, discrete amplitude signal. The vision of images plays very important role in human perception therefore image analysis at spatial domain and frequency domain applied in a varied field of application. Discrete Cosine Transform (DCT) of a digital image $f(x, y)$, is an image analysis technique to extract useful features of the images in the frequency domain. Discrete Cosine Transform (DCT) has the property to represent unique pattern by a few coefficient of the DCT of any image in the frequency domain. The DCT transform is a technique to represents an image as a sum of sinusoids of varying magnitudes and frequencies with invertible transform features. DCT is a Fourier-related transform and their coefficients are always real.

Let $f(x, y)$ for $x = 0, 1, 2, \ldots, M - 1$ and $y = 0, 1, 2, \ldots, N - 1$ denotes a digital image of size $M \times N$ Pixels. Frequency domain is the coordinate system spanned by $T(u, v)$ with u and v as (frequency) variables. DCT Transform $T(u, v)$ of image $f(x, y)$ is defined as (1),

$$T(u, v) = \sum_{x=0}^{M-1} \sum_{y=0}^{N-1} f(x, y)\alpha(u)\alpha(v)\cos\left[\frac{(2x+1)u\pi}{2M}\right]\cos\left[\frac{(2y+1)v\pi}{2N}\right] \tag{1}$$

where

$$\alpha(u) = \begin{cases} \sqrt{\frac{1}{M}} & u = 0 \\ \sqrt{\frac{2}{M}} & u = 1, 2, \ldots, M - 1 \end{cases}$$

and

$$\alpha(v) = \begin{cases} \sqrt{\frac{1}{N}} & v = 0 \\ \sqrt{\frac{2}{N}} & v = 1, 2, \ldots, N - 1 \end{cases}$$

The $M \times N$ often referred to as the frequency rectangle and it has the same size as the input image [5].

1.4 Decision Tree

The identification of the classes of data by various classification techniques is an important data analysis activity in decision making process. The classification methods are used to predict categorical (discrete, unordered) labels. It is a two-step process where a classifier is built by training with a predetermined set of a data classes and later; this trained model is used to predict the class of unknown dataset [6]. A decision tree is one of such model which performs classification and prediction. A Decision tree also looks like normal tree data structure which consists of a root, non-leaf or internal nodes and leaf or child nodes, but each node has a different purpose. Test condition of an attribute performed at the non-leaf node; outgoing branches from any node represent outcomes of the test on data sets and each leaf nodes hold predicted class labels. Topmost node defined as the root node in the decision tree. Attribute selection methods are evaluated to select the attribute to partition the input tuples into distinct classes during tree construction. To remove outliers, Tree pruning operation performed [7].

1.5 Radial Basis Function (RBF)

The radial-basis functions such as Multiquadrics, Inverse-Multiquadrics, and Gaussian etc. are used to approximate a smooth input-output mapping with optimum accuracy. The interpolation matrix Φ of radial basis function follows the property of non-singularity. The RBF may be localized or non-local in nature. The used

Inverse-Multiquadrics RBF is defined as (2), where c is some constant and R is set of hybrid extracted features of segmented images [8].

$$\Phi(r) = 1/(r^2 + c^2)^{1/2} \text{ for some } c > 0 \text{ and } r \in R \qquad (2)$$

1.6   Application of Image Processing in Plant Disease Recognition

High professional knowledge and rich experience are required for in-field visual identification of plant diseases. Disease diagnosis via pathogen detection requires satisfactory laboratory conditions and more professional knowledge due to the limitation of the human perception of visual symptoms interpretation of plant diseases. The pathogen detection methods based on the molecular biological techniques give more accurate results of disease recognition but it carries more time and high cost. Therefore, it is very necessary to find out a simple and fast plant disease identification method with high identification accuracy. Now image recognition of plant diseases is the widespread concern generated as a result of the development of visual technologies and the popularization of digital products [9]. The studies on the recognition and the automatic assessment of plant diseases based on image processing have been reported. The image processing is used to extract spatial and frequency of the infected images. The weeds had been recognized for precision farming soft computing after extracting features [10]. The plant diseases images had been recognized using principal component analysis and neural network [11]. The image features had been used to design model to recognize maize disease of corn leaf based on back propagation neural network [12]. Various classification and clustering techniques have been used to detect plant diseases using image processing [13, 14]. The image processing techniques had been also used to find the characteristics and varieties of the various plants [15, 16, 17]. Various image pre-processing techniques like cropping, morphing, segmentation etc. applied before extracting the plant features [18]. Computer automatic recognition and diagnosis based on symptom images of plant diseases could quickly and accurately provide disease information for agricultural technicians and farmers and thus reduce the dependence on agricultural technicians [19].The extracted features of the plant images mainly carry color, shape and texture features. These features represent unique feature patterns of plant/plant diseases. These features patterns are used to design recognizer by various method such as neural network [20, 21, 22], fuzzy logic [23, 24], neuro-fuzzy approach [25, 26], support vector machine [27].

The remaining paper divided into three sections. In Sect. 2, resources needed to perform the necessary experiments and applied methodologies have been discussed. The Sect. 3, enlightens about the experimental results and comprehensive discussion. These discussions lead to the Sect. 4, on which we will conclude the outcomes and future scope of work in detail.

2 Materials and Methods

In the first part, the decision tree based hybrid feature classification model had been designed, and in the second part, the performance of the model had been evaluated for unknown test feature pattern. The images in Joint Photographic Experts Group (JPEG or JPG) format had been captured by the Charged Couple Device (CCD) digital camera in an uncontrolled environment. These images were cropped and resized to avoid the limitations of space complexity. The pre-processed images were forwarded for the segmentation to extract a region of interest by using the algorithm 2.1. The spatial domain features; color and texture and frequency domain features: DCT had been extracted from the segmented images. Algorithm 2.2, 2.3 and 2.4 had been called for color, texture and DCT features extraction. Algorithm 2.5 used to divide hybrid features into training and testing data sets and further called algorithm 2.6, to convert this data sets in multidimension a space using the inverse multiquadrics radial basis function. The transformed data sets with the respective class label of diseases were passed in the algorithm 2.7, to create set of rules for disease classification (recognition) using a decision tree. Later, hybrid features of test images had been forwarded to pre-designed decision tree model in algorithm 2.8, which predicts class label of the test images. These results help to analyze about the disease type and accordingly help in decision making. Details of the each step are given below:

2.1 Image Segmentation

Images segmentation had been done to extract a region of interest of diseased image and non diseased images of the rice plant. The steps to perform segmentation are given in following Pseudo code:

Algorithm 2.1: *Color Image Segmentation of Cropped Images of 6 category*
Input: 30 cropped images of each category; Leaf Blast, Brown Spot, Panicle
        Blast, Sheath Blight, Stem Borer and Non-infected images
Output: 3 set of segmented images of each category for low, medium and
        high intensity level as $ISeg_1$, $ISeg_2$, and $ISeg_3$
Pseudo code
        for each image in each category *do*
i. Convert *RGB* images into *Lab* images.
ii. Extract component *a* of *Lab* images, apply 3-level threshold and quantize the same.
iii. Create 3 binary matrices according to 3-level of quantization as *B1*, *B2* and *B3*.
iv. Separate *R,G* and *B* components of each image and multiply each component with 3 binary matrix *R*B1*, *R*B2*, *R*B3*, *G*B1*, *G*B2*, *G*B3*, *B*B1*, *B*B2* and *B*B3*.
v. Concatenate *(R*B1, G*B1, B*B1)*, *(R*B2, G*B2, B*B3)* and *(R*B3, G*B3, B*B3)* to create 3 segments *$ISeg_1$, $ISeg_2$, and $ISeg_3$* of each images.
vi. Forward *$ISeg_3$* which contain infected parts of diseased images and important part of non infected images for Color, Texture and DCT feature extraction.
        end of for loop

2.2   Color, Texture and DCT Feature Extraction

In this research work, the segmented images stored in $ISeg_3$ are used for the feature extraction. The $ISeg_3$ collected images are the segmented parts of highest intensity level of all 6 categories of rice crop images. The color and texture features had been extracted in spatial domain and DCT features had been extracted in the frequency domain for each category of images individually. The pseudo code for feature extraction is given below:

Algorithm* 2. 2: *Extraction of color features in spatial domain
***Input*: $ISeg_3$;** 30 highest intensity level segmented images of each
    category: Leaf Blast, Brown Spot, Panicle Blast, Sheath Blight, Stem Borer and
    Non-infected images
***Output*:** Color features of size 30 × 4 for each categories of images as
LB_{col} for Leaf Blast, BS_{col} for Brown Spot, PB_{col} for Panicle Blast, SB_{col} for Sheath
Blight, STB_{col} for Stem Borer, NI_{col} for Non infected images
Pseudo Code
       for all segmented images of each category in $ISeg_3$ ***do***

i. Read RGB images as Img
ii. Seperate R, G and B components of RGB images
$$R = Img(:,:,1)$$
$$G = Img(:,:,2)$$
$$B = Img(:,:,3)$$

iii. Normalize the RGB components in range of $[0, 1]$ as
$$r = \frac{R}{255}, g = \frac{G}{255}, b = \frac{B}{255}$$

iv. Find $2 -$ dimensional standard deviation of r, g, b and correlation factor
between r and g components as
$R_{sd} = 2 -$ Dimensional Standard Deviation of (r)
$G_{sd} = 2 -$ Dimensional Standard Deviation of (g)
$B_{sd} = 2 -$ Dimensional Standard Deviation of (b)
$RG_{Corr} = 2 -$ Dimensional Correlation factor of r and g components
v. Merge the extracted features as
$$RGB_{ColFeat} = [R_{sd}\ G_{sd}\ B_{sd}\ RG_{Corr}]$$

end of for loop

Algorithm 2.3: *Extraction of Texture features in spatial domain*
Input: $ISeg_3$; 30 segmented images of each category: Leaf Blast, Brown Spot, Panicle Blast, Sheath Blight, Stem Borer and Non-infected images
Output: Texture features of size 30 × 4 for each categories of images as
$\quad$ LB_{Text} for Leaf Blast, BS_{Text} for Brown Spot, PB_{Text} for Panicle Blast, SB_{Text} for Sheath Blight, STB_{Text} for Stem Borer, NI_{Text} for Non infected images
Pseudo Code
$\quad\quad\quad\quad$ **for** all segmented images of each category in $ISeg_3$ **do**

i. Read RGB images as Img
ii. Convert Img to Gray image as
$$I_{Gray} = RGB - to - Gray\,of\,(Img)$$

iii. Create covariance matrix of I_{Gray}
$$I_{CoVar} = \text{Covariance}of(I_{Gray})$$

iv. Extract Contrast, Correlation, Energy and Homogeniety features by using I_{CoVar} as
$$I_{Contrast} = \text{Contrast}of\,(I_{CoVar})$$
$$I_{Correlation} = \text{Correlation}of\,(I_{CoVar})$$
$$I_{Energy} = \text{Energy}of\,(I_{CoVar})$$
$$I_{Homogeniety} = \text{Homogeniety}of(I_{CoVar})$$

v. Merge the extracted features as
$$RGB_{Texture} = [I_{Contrast}\ I_{Correlation}\ I_{Energy}\ I_{Homogeniety}]$$

$\quad\quad\quad\quad\quad$ **end of for loop**

Algorithm 2.4: *Extraction of DCT features in frequency domain*
Input: $ISeg_3$: 30 segmented images of each category: Leaf Blast, Brown Spot, Panicle Blast, Sheath Blight, Stem Borer and Non-infected images
Output: DCT features of size 30 × 3 for each categories of images as
$\quad$ LB_{dct} for Leaf Blast, BS_{dct} for Brown Spot, PB_{dct} for Panicle Blast, SB_{dct} for Sheath Blight, STB_{dct} for Stem Borer, NI_{dct} for Non infected images
Pseudo Code
$\quad\quad\quad\quad$ **for** all segmented images of each category in $ISeg_3$ **do**

i. Read RGB images as Img
ii. Seperate R, G and B components of RGB images
$$R = R(x,y) = Img(:,:,1)$$
$$G = G(x,y) = Img(:,:,2)$$
$$B = B(x,y) = Img(:,:,3)$$

iii. $[M, N] = \text{sizeof}(R(x,y)) = \text{sizeof}(G(x,y)) = \text{sizeof}(B(x,y))$
iv. Evaluate DCT features of $R(x,y), G(x,y),$ and $B(x,y)$ as
$$R_{dct} = \sum_{x=0}^{M-1}\sum_{y=0}^{N-1} R(x,y)\alpha(u)\ \alpha(v)\cos[\frac{(2x+1)u\pi}{2M}]\cos[\frac{(2y+1)v\pi}{2N}]$$

$$G_{dct} = \sum_{x=0}^{M-1}\sum_{y=0}^{N-1} G(x,y)\alpha(u)\,\alpha(v)\cos[\frac{(2x+1)u\pi}{2M}]\cos[\frac{(2y+1)v\pi}{2N}]$$

$$B_{dct} = \sum_{x=0}^{M-1}\sum_{y=0}^{N-1} B(x,y)\alpha(u)\,\alpha(v)\cos[\frac{(2x+1)u\pi}{2M}]\cos[\frac{(2y+1)v\pi}{2N}]$$

for

$$\alpha(u) = \begin{cases}\sqrt{\dfrac{1}{M}} & u=0 \\[2ex] \sqrt{\dfrac{2}{M}} & u=1,2,\dots,M-1\end{cases}, \alpha(v) = \begin{cases}\sqrt{\dfrac{1}{N}} & v=0 \\[2ex] \sqrt{\dfrac{2}{N}} & v=1,2,\dots,N-1\end{cases}$$

v. Extract average brightness (DC components) from R_{dct}, G_{dct} and B_{dct} as

$$RDC_{(0,0)} = R_{dct}(0,0)$$
$$GDC_{(0,0)} = G_{dct}(0,0)$$
$$BDC_{(0,0)} = B_{dct}(0,0)$$

vi. Merge the extracted fetures

$$RGB_{dct} = [RDC_{(0,0)}\ GDC_{(0,0)}\ BDC_{(0,0)}]$$

end of for loop

2.3   Training and Testing Data Sets Creation

Total 80% extracted features of each category had been used to create training datasets for the decision tree to form classification rules and remaining 20% datasets of each category had been used to test the performance of the decision tree.

Algorithm 2.5: *Training and Testing Datasets Creation*
Input: Color features of size 30 × 4 for each categories of images (LB_{col}, BS_{col}, PB_{col}, SB_{col}, STB_{col} and NI_{col}), Texture features of size 30 × 4 for each categories (LB_{Text}, BS_{Text}, PB_{Text}, SB_{Text}, STB_{Text} and NI_{Text}) and DCT features of size 30 × 3 for each categories of images (LB_{dct}, BS_{dct}, PB_{dct}, SB_{dct}, STB_{dct} and NI_{dct})
Output: Train datasets LB_{Train}, BS_{Train}, PB_{Train}, SB_{Train}, STB_{Train}, NI_{Train} of size 24 × 11 and testing datasets LB_{Test}, BS_{Test}, PB_{Test}, SB_{Test}, STB_{Test}, NI_{Test} of size 6 × 11, $DTree_{Train}$ of size 144 × 11 and $DTree_{Test}$ of size 36 × 11.
Pseudo Code
i. Merge color, texture and DCTfeatures of each category to create hybrid feature sets of size 30 × 11, seperately
   Leaf Blast merged hybrid features: $LB_{Hybrid} = [\ LB_{col}\ LB_{Text}\ LB_{dct}\ ]$
   Brown Spot merged hybrid features: $BS_{Hybrid} = [\ BS_{col}\ BS_{Text}\ BS_{dct}\ ]$
   Panicle Blast merged hybrid features: $PB_{Hybrid} = [\ PB_{col}\ PB_{Text}\ PB_{dct}\ ]$
   Sheath Blight merged hybrid features: $SB_{Hybrid} = [\ SB_{col}\ SB_{Text}\ SB_{dct}\ ]$

Stem Borer merged hybrid features: $STB_{Hybrid} = [\, STB_{col}\ STB_{Text}\ STB_{dct}\,]$
Leaf Blast merged hybrid features: $NI_{Hybrid} = [\, NI_{col}\ NI_{Text}\ NI_{dct}\,]$

ii. Seperate 80% datasets of each category for training and 20% datasets for testing purpose. The value 0.8 is just symbolic representation of 80% ration of hybrid features will be transferred into train datasets and reaming 20% will be transferred to test datasets

$LB_{Train} = LB_{Hybrid} \times 0.8$
$LB_{Test} = LB_{Hybrid} - LB_{Train}$
$BS_{Train} = BS_{Hybrid} \times 0.8$
$BS_{Test} = BS_{Hybrid} - BS_{Train}$
$PB_{Train} = PB_{Hybrid} \times 0.8$
$PB_{Test} = PB_{Hybrid} - PB_{Train}$
$SB_{Train} = SB_{Hybrid} \times 0.8$
$SB_{Test} = SB_{Hybrid} - SB_{Train}$
$STB_{Train} = STB_{Hybrid} \times 0.8$
$STB_{Test} = STB_{Hybrid} - STB_{Train}$
$NI_{Train} = NI_{Hybrid} \times 0.8$
$NI_{Test} = NI_{Hybrid} - NI_{Train}$

iii. Merge all train and datasets of each category to create final training and testing datastes of decision tree

$$DTree_{Train} = \begin{bmatrix} BS_{train} \\ LB_{train} \\ NI_{train} \\ PB_{train} \\ SB_{train} \\ STB_{train} \end{bmatrix}$$

$$DTree_{Test} = \begin{bmatrix} BS_{Test} \\ LB_{Test} \\ NI_{Test} \\ PB_{Test} \\ SB_{Test} \\ STB_{Test} \end{bmatrix}$$

2.4 Apply Inverse Multiquadrics Radial Basis Function on Training and Testing Datasets

The inverse multiquadric RBF had been applied on training and testing datasets to enhance the uniqueness of extracted features by transforming features in multi-dimensional space.

Algorithm 2.6: Training and Testing Datasets Creation
Input: Training datasets $DTree_{Train}$ **of size 144 × 11** and testing datasets $DTree_{Test}$ **of size 36 × 11**
Output: **High − dimensional space training datasets** $DTree_{TrainIM}$ **and testing** datasets $DTree_{TestIM}$
Pseudo Code
i. Read $DTree_{Train}$ and $DTree_{Test}$

ii. Apply inverse multiquadrics function on training and testing datasets

$$DTree_{TrainIM} = \frac{1}{(DTree_{Train}{}^2 + c^2)^{1/2}} \text{ for some } c > 0$$

$$DTree_{TestIM} = \frac{1}{(DTree_{Test}{}^2 + c^2)^{1/2}} \text{ for some } c > 0$$

2.5   Decision Tree Model Implementation

The high-dimensional datasets features of all images in each segment passed into a decision tree with corresponding category label. Decision tree model evaluates Gini index for all possible combination of attributes to break the forwarded set to the node for decision tree creation. An attribute with maximum Gini index considers as a splitting point to create a node. This process repeated till all class label defined into a decision tree. Pseudo code for decision tree formation is given below:

Algorithm 2.7: Decision Tree Classification Model Creation
Input: High $-$ dimensional space training datasets $DTree_{TrainIM}$
Output: Decision Tree model, $DTREE$, with decision rules for rice plant diseases classification
Pseudo code
i. Initialize $ClassLabel$ as
$ClassLabel_1 = BrownSpot$
$ClassLabel_2 = LeafBlast$
$ClassLabel_3 = Normal$
$ClassLabel_4 = PanicleBlast$
$ClassLabel_5 = SheathBlight$
$ClassLabel_6 = StemBorer$
ii. Initialize x_{ji} with high $-$ dimensional space training datasets $DTree_{TrainIM}$
  where
$$x_{ji} = DTree_{TrainIM}, j = 1,2,\dots,6 \text{ and } i = 1,2,\dots,m$$
iii. Combine extracted features $x_{ji}: j = 1,2,\dots,6$ and $i = 1,2,\dots,m$ for 6 groups
  of images with corresponding class label $ClassLabel_j | i = 1,2,\dots,6$ as
$$D = [x_{ji}: ClassLabel_j]$$
iv. Start root node (assume $t = 1$) with attribute D
  If the tuples in D are all of the same class, then node N becomes a leaf and
  is labeled with that class and exit.
v. Find $power\,set\,(D) = 2^{\{a_1, a_2, \dots, a_k\}}$ where $\{a_1, a_2, \dots, a_k\}$ are attributes of D and
  k is total number of attributes.
vi. Remove subset $\{a_1, a_2, \dots, a_k\}$ and empty set, $\{\ \}$ from $power\,set\,(D)$
$$D_{set} = powerset\,(D) - \{\{a_1, a_2, \dots, a_k\}, \{\ \}\}, \text{ where } |D_{set}| = 2^k - 2$$
vii. *for* each set of element, $D_j \in D_{set}, j = 1,2,\dots,2^k - 2 \ do$
  a.   Evaluate $p_i = \dfrac{|C_{i,D_j}|}{|D_j|}$
  b.   Compute impurity of D_i or Gini Index as

$$Gini(D_j) = 1 - \sum_{i=1}^{m} p_i^2$$

c. $$Gini_{split}(s, D_j) = Gini(D_j) - p_L Gini(D_L) - p_R Gini(D_R)$$

end of for loop

viii. Evaluate split attribute
$$s = maxof\left(Gini_{split}(s, D_1), Gini_{split}(s, D_j), \dots, Gini_{split}(s, D_{2^k-2})\right)$$
ix. Split node 1($t = 1$) into two nodes $t = 2$ and $t = 3$ using split attribute s
x. If there are no remaining attributes on which the tuples may be further partitioned or labeled then exit else goto step 4 to repeat perform split searching process in each of node $t = 2$ or/and $t = 3$ until at least one of the tree growing rules is met.

end of process

2.6   Decision Tree Model Testing

The testing datasets, $DTree_{TestIM}$ applied into decision rule which formed during decision tree creation, to identify the classes of test datasets.

Algorithm 2. 8: *Testing of Decision Tree*
Input: High − dimensional space Testing datasets $DTree_{TestIM}$ and decision tree $DTREE$ with decision rules
Output: Classification of testing datasets and classification accuracy
Pseudo Code
i. Read $DTree_{TestIM}$ and $DTREE$
ii. Evaluate test datasets classes by using $DTREE$ decision rules
$$TD_{Class} = DTREE\left(DTree_{TestIM}\right)$$

iii. Match TD_{Class} with desired class of each test dataset and calculate correctly classified sample $C_{Classified}$ and numble of total testing sample Tot_{sample}

iv. Evaluate classification accuracy of $DTREE$ as

$$\text{Classification Accuracy}(\%) = \frac{C_{Classified}}{Tot_{sample}} \times 100$$

3   Results and Discussion

The entire process is implemented in MATLAB version 8.4. Total 30 images were captured for each category by SONY/DSC-H300 digital camera, with size 5152 × 3864 in JPEG (JPG) format. The images were cropped in size of 205 × 410 to manually select a region of interest. The cropped images were further resized at 200 × 250 during segmentation process to overcome the limitation of space of the system. The image resizing in pre-processing steps are optional. The captured JPEG images were accessed in an RGB format for segmentation and feature extraction. The sample of each category of cropped resized image and the segmented image is shown in Figs. 1, 2, 3, 4, 5, and 6.

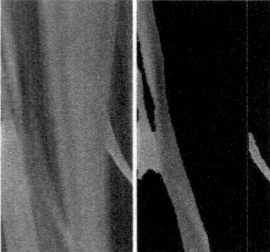

Fig. 1. Leaf Blast cropped image and segmented image

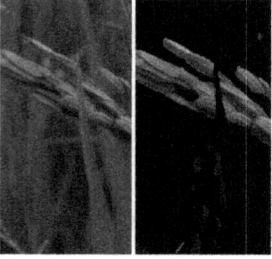

Fig. 2. Panicle Blast cropped image and segmented image

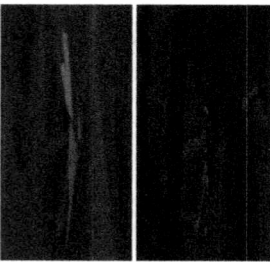

Fig. 3. Sheath Blight cropped image and segmented image

Fig. 4. Stem Borer cropped image and segmented image

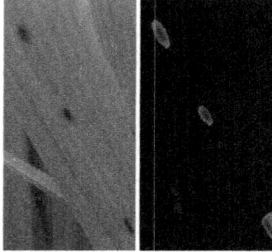

Fig. 5. Brown Spot cropped image and segmented image

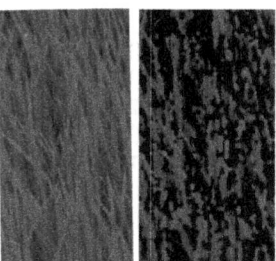

Fig. 6. Normal cropped image and segmented image

Total 4 color features, 4 textures features and 3 DCT features had been extracted from each segmented image of each category. The sample of the extracted features of 5 Brown Spot infected image is shown in Table 2. In the same way, features for Leaf Blast, Panicle Blast, Sheath Blight, Stem Borer, and Normal images had been extracted.

Table 2. Extracted features of Brown Spot infected rice crop images.

4 Color features	4 Shape features	3 Texture features
17.50,15.79,5.76,0.99	0.02,0.94,0.95,1.00	3.00,2.77,1.25
22.08,18.33,12.15,0.98	0.07,0.86,0.89,0.99	5.82,4.88,3.42
17.71,17.07,9.50,1.00	0.046,0.88,0.96,1.00	2.85,2.79,1.79
13.57,12.04,5.01,0.98	0.013,0.92,0.94,1.00	2.55,2.23,1.06
13.10,13.26,8.43,0.99	0.02,0.91,0.94,1.00	2.41,2.44,1.62

In the extracted features, 80% of features had been used to design decision tree and remaining 20% features had been used to evaluate the performance of decision tree based recognition model. To enhance the uniqueness of features, Inverse Multi Quadratic RBF function is used to transform training and testing datasets in multi-dimensional space. For different value of independent variable $r = 0.1, 0.2, 0.3,$ 0.4, 0.5, 0.6, 0.7, 0.8, 0.9, 1, 5, 10, 25, 50, 100, 200, 500, 700, 900, 1000, this transformation had been done. The sample of the first 10 transformed features of training datasets for $r = 1$ is given in Table 3.

Table 3. Inverse multi quadratic RBF conversion of training datasets

4 Color features	4 Shape features	3 Texture features
0.057,0.063,,0.171,0.709	1,0.728,0.726,0.708	0.316,0.34,0.624
0.045,0.055,0.082,0.714	0.998,0.759,0.748,0.711	0.17,0.201,0.281
0.056,0.059,0.105,0.709	0.999,0.75,0.723,0.709	0.331,0.338,0.488
0.074,0.083,0.196,0.713	1,0.735,0.73,0.708	0.366,0.409, 0.685
0.076,0.075,0.118,0.71	1,0.739,0.73,0.709	0.383,0.38,0.525
0.046,0.05,0.071,0.709	0.998,0.751,0.728,0.709	0.246,0.27,0.345
0.08,0.093,0.174,0.712	1,0.743,0.721,0.708	0.48,0.543,0.717
0.034,0.047,0.087,0.713	0.999,0.727,0.759,0.711	0.113,0.156,0.25
0.064,0.082,0.174,0.711	1,0.743,0.721,0.708	0.393,0.481,0.701
0.051,0.062,0.104,0.717	1,0.731,0.754,0.709	0.187,0.223,0.364

The result of designed decision tree after forwarding training datasets is given in Fig. 7. The set of if-then rules created by decision tree to classify test images into a particular category is given in Table 4. The symbol $\times 1$, $\times 2$, $\times 3$ and $\times 4$ represent 4 color features, $\times 5$, $\times 6$, $\times 7$ and $\times 8$ represents 4 texture features, $\times 9$, $\times 10$ and $\times 11$ represents 3 DWT features, forwarded during training of decision tree. When decision tree model designed with extracted feature directly; without converting the features into multi-dimensional space, during creation, decision tree gives 95.83% classification accuracy shown in Table 5. But the same result is not inferred for unknown test patterns and give 16.67% average recognition efficiency as in Table 6.

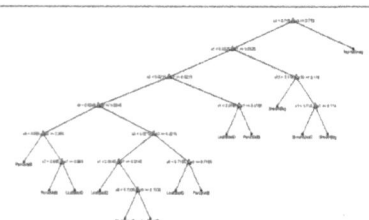

Fig. 7. A Decision tree for rice plant diseases classification

Table 4. Decision rules to classify rice plant diseases

Decision Rule
1 if x4<0.719 then node 2 elseif x4>=0.719 then node 3 else BrownSpotD
2 if x1<0.0325 then node 4 elseif x1>=0.0325 then node 5 else BrownSpotD
3 class = NormalImag
4 if x2<0.0215 then node 6 elseif x2>=0.0215 then node 7 else LeafBlastD
5 if x10<0.119 then node 8 elseif x10>=0.119 then node 9 else BrownSpotD
6 if x9<0.0245 then node 10 elseif x9>=0.0245 then node 11 else StemBorerD
7 if x1<0.0195 then node 12 elseif x1>=0.0195 then node 13 else PanickleBl
8 class = SheathBlig
9 if x1<0.114 then node 14 elseif x1>=0.114 then node 15 else BrownSpotD
10 if x5<0.955 then node 16 elseif x5>=0.955 then node 17 else LeafBlastD
11 if x3<0.0215 then node 18 elseif x3>=0.0215 then node 19 else StemBorerD
12 class = LeafBlastD
13 class = PanickleBl
14 class = BrownSpotD
15 class = SheathBlig
16 class = PanickleBl
17 if x7<0.865 then node 20 elseif x7>=0.865 then node 21 else LeafBlastD
18 if x1<0.0145 then node 22 elseif x1>=0.0145 then node 23 else StemBorerD
19 if x8<0.7155 then node 24 elseif x8>=0.7155 then node 25 else LeafBlastD
20 class = PanickleBl
21 class = LeafBlastD
22 class = LeafBlastD
23 if x6<0.7335 then node 26 elseif x6>=0.7335 then node 27 else StemBorerD
24 class = LeafBlastD
25 class = PanickleBl
26 class = StemBorerD
27 class = LeafBlastD

Table 5. Training performance of decision tree without Inverse Multi Quadratic RBF transformation

Brown Spot	Leaf Blast	Normal	Panicle Blast	Sheath Blight	Stem Borer	Average performance
100	95.83	100	79.17	100	100	95.83%

Table 6. Testing performance of decision tree without Inverse Multi Quadratic RBF transformation

Brown Spot	Leaf Blast	Normal	Panicle Blast	Sheath Blight	Stem Borer	Average performance
100	0	0	0	0	0	16.67%

The classification results after multidimensional space conversion using RBF of same training datasets used for designing of decision tree with different value of independent variable $r > 0$ is shown in Table 7.

Table 7. Training performance of decision tree with Inverse Multi Quadratic RBF transformation

r	Brown Spot	Leaf Blast	Normal	Panicle Blast	Sheath Blight	Stem Borer	Average performance
0.1	100	87.5	100	100	95.83	91.67	95.83
0.2	100	87.5	100	100	95.83	91.67	95.83
0.3	100	79.17	100	95.83	95.83	87.5	93.06
0.4	100	87.5	100	100	95.83	91.67	95.83
0.5	100	87.5	100	100	95.83	91.67	95.83
0.6	100	87.5	100	100	95.83	91.67	95.83
0.7	100	87.5	100	100	95.83	91.67	95.83
0.8	100	87.5	100	100	95.83	91.67	95.83
0.9	100	87.5	100	100	100	91.67	96.53
1	100	87.5	100	100	95.83	91.67	95.83
5	100	91.67	100	79.17	95.83	95.83	93.75
10	100	83.33	100	87.5	95.83	91.67	93.06
25	100	91.67	100	75	95.83	95.83	93.06
50	91.67	83.33	100	75	91.67	87.5	88.20
100	100	50	100	75	0	79.17	67.36
200	100	0	4.17	0	0	0	17.36
500	100	0	0	0	0	0	16.67
700	100	0	0	0	0	0	16.67
900	100	0	0	0	0	0	16.67
1000	100	0	0	0	0	0	16.67

Table 8 depicts testing results of a decision tree for unknown features which were not used during training of the decision tree. It has been observed that, for $r = 1$, average classification efficiency is 83.34% . This result reflect drastic enhancement in classification recognition efficiency with respect to decision tree model created by data features without multi-dimensional space conversion as shown in Table 11, where average classification efficiency is 16.67%.

Table 8. Testing performance of decision tree with Inverse Multi Quadratic RBF transformation

r	Brown Spot	Leaf Blast	Normal	Panicle Blast	Sheath Blight	Stem Borer	Average performance
0.1	100	66.67	83.33	66.67	100	66.67	80.56
0.2	100	66.67	83.33	50	100	66.67	77.78
0.3	100	16.67	83.33	50	100	66.67	69.45
0.4	100	66.67	83.33	66.67	100	66.67	80.56
0.5	100	66.67	83.33	50	100	66.67	77.78
0.6	100	66.67	83.33	50	100	66.67	77.78
0.7	100	66.67	83.33	50	100	66.67	77.78
0.8	100	66.67	83.33	50	100	66.67	77.78
0.9	100	50	83.33	50	100	66.67	75.00
1	**100**	**66.67**	**100**	**66.67**	**100**	**66.67**	**83.34**
5	100	50	66.67	66.67	100	66.67	75.00
10	100	33.33	66.67	66.67	100	66.67	72.22
25	100	16.67	66.67	33.33	16.67	50	47.22
50	0	66.67	100	0	100	0	44.45
100	100	0	0	0	0	0	16.67
200	100	0	16.67	0	0	0	19.45
500	100	0	0	0	0	0	16.67
700	100	0	0	0	0	0	16.67
900	100	0	0	0	0	0	16.67
1000	100	0	0	0	0	0	16.67

4 Conclusion

The decision tree based model had been successfully implemented to recognize rice plant diseases. Initially, the recognition efficiency of decision tree model was very meager but it had been optimized by using RBF. The classification accuracy for new test patterns depicts that; multi-dimensional space conversion based model enhances classification accuracy as a comparison to normal space based model. It has been observed that average recognition accuracy of a decision tree for the new test pattern, enhanced drastically from 16.67% in normal space to 83.34% in multi-dimensional space using inverse multi-quadric RBF. For independent variable r, the promising training and testing results achieved at $0 < r \leq 1$, but performance degrades at $r > 1$. The best recognition efficiency for new test pattern is achieved at $r = 1$.

In this research, some incidences of diseases are considered according to the availability of datasets. Total 30 images of each category had been considered in this research. The appearances of some plant diseases can be changed during the life cycle of plants. So, the training samples can be increased to enrich training datasets by considering other possible incidences of disease occurring. The entire approach for making decision tree based model to recognize diseases will be same but enhancing training feature patterns can help to optimize decision rules formed by a decision tree.

The decision tree based model can be also used to optimize fuzzy rules in the fuzzy based system. Most importantly, inverse multi-quadric RBF based multi-dimensional space conversion of feature pattern can be used to enhance pattern recognition efficiency for other models like a neural network, fuzzy inference system, and neuro-fuzzy system.

Acknowledgement. We are very thankful to Mr. Nalin Lunia (Secretary) and Dr. K.S.Pandya (Principal), Chhattisgarh Agriculture college, Durg, CG (India) for their kind support in this research to collect digital image data sets of rice plant under their esteemed guidance.

References

1. Chaube, H.S., Pundhir, V.S.: Crop Diseases and Their Management, 3rd edn. PHI Learning Private Limited, New Delhi (2012)
2. Rangaswami, G., Mahadevan, A.: Diseases of Crop Plants in India, 4th edn. PHI Learning Private Limited, New Delhi (2010)
3. USAID Technical Bulletin. http://pdf.usaid.gov/pdf_docs/PA00K8Z1.pdf Accessed 07 July 2017
4. Sarwar, M.: Management of rice stem borers (Lepidoptera : Pyralidae) through host plant resistance in early, medium and late plantings of rice (Oryza sativa L.). J Cereals Oil Seeds **3**(1), 10–14 (2012)
5. Gonzalez, R.C., Wood, R.E., Eddins, S.L.: Digital Image Processing Using MATLAB, 8th edn. McGraw-Hill Education (India) Private Limited, New Delhi (2013)
6. Duda, R.O., Hart, P.E., Stark, D.G.: Pattern Classifcation, 3rd edn. John Wiley and Sons Asia Private Limited, New Delhi (2007)
7. Han, J., Kamber, M.: Data Mining, 4th edn. Elsevier, Noida (2008)
8. Haykin, S.: Neural Networks A Comprehensive Foundation, 2nd edn. Pearson Education, New Delhi (2009)
9. Chahal, A.N.: A study on agricultural image processing along with classification model. In: 2015 IEEE International Advance Computing Conference (IACC), pp. 942–947 (2015)
10. Yang, C.C., Prasher, S.O., Landry, J.A., Perret, J., Ramaswamy, H.S., Yang, C.C.: Recognition of weeds with image processing and their use with fuzzy logic for precision farming. Can. Biosyst. Eng./Le Genie des biosyst. au Can. **42**(4), 195–200 (2000)
11. Li, G., Ma, Z., Li, X., Wang, H.: Image recognition of plant diseases based on principal component analysis and neural networks. In: International Conference on Natural Computation ICNC, pp. 246–251 (2012)
12. Kai, S., Zhikun L., Hang, S., Chunhong, G.: A research of maize disease image recognition of corn based on BP networks. In: 2011 3rd International Conference on Measuring Technology and Mechatronics Automation ICMTMA, vol. 1, no. 2009921090, pp. 246–249 (2011)

13. Khirade, S.D., Patil, A.B.: Plant disease detection using image processing techniques. Int. J. Innovative Res. Sci. Eng. Technol. **4**(6), 295–301 (2015)
14. Ying, G., Miao, L., Yuan, Y., Zelin, H.: A study on the method of image pre-processing for recognition of crop diseases. In: Proceedings of International Conference on Advanced Computer Control ICACC, pp. 202–206 (2009)
15. Güneş, E.O., Aygün, S., Kırcı, M., Kalateh, A., Çakır, Y.: Determination of the varieties and characteristics of wheat seeds grown in Turkey using image processing techniques. In: International Conference on Agro-Geoinformatics (2014)
16. Gastélum-Barrios, A., Bórquez-López, R.A., Rico-García, E., Toledano-Ayala, M., Soto-Zarazúa, G.M.: Tomato quality evaluation with image processing : a review. African J. Agric. Res. **6**(14), 3333–3339 (2011)
17. Kumar, R., Patil, J.K.: Advances in image processing for detection of plant diseases. J. Adv. Bioinf. Appl. Res. **2**(2), 135–141 (2011)
18. Huddar, S.R., Gowri, S., Keerthana, K., Vasanthi, S., Rupanagudi, S.R.: Novel algorithm for segmentation and automatic identification of pests on plants using image processing. In: ICCCNT 2012, Coimbatore, India, July 2012
19. El-Helly, M., Rafea, A.A., El-Gammal, S.: An integrated image processing system for leaf disease detection and diagnosis. In: Indian International Conference on Artificial Intelligence 2003, pp. 1182–1195 (2003)
20. Orillo, J.W., Cruz, J.D., Agapito, L., Satimbre, P.J., Valenzuela, I.: Identification of diseases in rice plant (oryza sativa) using back propagation Artificial Neural Network. In: 2014 International Conference on Humanoid, Nanotechnology, Information Technology, Communication and Control, Environment and Management, HNICEM (2014)
21. Biswas, S., Jagyasi, B., Singh, B.P., Lal, M.: Severity identification of Potato Late Blight disease from crop images captured under uncontrolled environment. In: 2014 IEEE Canada International Humanitarian Technology Conference - (IHTC), pp. 1–5 (2014)
22. Wang, H., Li, G., Ma, Z., Li, X.: Image recognition of plant diseases based on backpropagation networks. In: 2012 5th International Congress on Image and Signal Processing, CISP, pp. 894–900 (2012)
23. Rastogi, A., Arora, R., Sharma, S.: Leaf disease detection and grading using computer vision technology & fuzzy logic. In: 2015 2nd International Conference on Signal Processing and Integrated Networks SPIN, pp. 500–505 (2015)
24. Vinushree, N., Hemalatha, B., Kaliappan, V.K.: Classification, efficient kernel-based fuzzy c-means clustering for pest detection. In: World Congress on Computing and Communication Technologies, pp. 179–181 (2014)
25. Chaki, J., Parekh, R., Bhattacharya, S.: Recognition of whole and deformed plant leaves using statistical shape features and neuro-fuzzy classifier. In: 2015 IEEE 2nd International Conference on Recent Trends in Information Systems (ReTIS), pp. 189–194 (2015)
26. Rothe, P.R., Kshirsagar, R.V.: Adaptive neuro-fuzzy inference system for recognition of cotton leaf diseases. In: 2014 International Conference on Innovative Applications of Computational Intelligence on Power, Energy and Controls with their Impact on Humanity (CIPECH14), pp. 12–17 (2014)
27. Gavhale, K.R., Gawande, U., Hajari, K.O.: Unhealthy region of citrus leaf detection using image processing techniques. In: International Conference for Convergence of Technology (I2CT), pp. 2–7 (2014)

Real Time Hand Gesture Recognition Using Histogram of Oriented Gradient with Support Vector Machine

Saurav Dhakad[1]([⊠]) [iD], Jayesh Gangrade[1], Jyoti Bharti[2], and Antriksha Somani[1]

[1] IES IPS Academy, Indore 452001, India
{sourabhdhakad, jayeshgangrade,
antrikshasomani}@ipsacademy.org
[2] Maulana Azad National Institute of Technology, Bhopal 462003, India
jyotibharti@manit.ac.in

Abstract. Numerous applications use Hand gesture recognition (HGR) as an essential part of their system. One of the most important Human Computer Interaction (HCI) applications using HGR is to read and process sign language. There are various methods used for Hand Gesture Recognition. In this paper, we have used Kinect sensor to take real-time images of hand gestures. Then, we have applied Histogram of Oriented Gradients (HOG) on the images to extract hand features. A dataset of 3000 images from Kinect Sensor of 30 different people was created. Finally, we have applied Multi support vector machine to classify the hand gestures. This helped us to achieve an accuracy of 94.3% for real time hand gesture recognition in a cluttered environment.

Keywords: Hand gesture recognition (HGR)
HOG (Histogram of oriented Gradients) · Human Computer Interaction (HCI)
Kinect sensor · Support vector machine (SVM)

1 Introduction

Hand gesture recognition is vital for non-verbal human-machine interaction. Also, Gesture recognition is essential in replacing the need of devices such as mouse, joysticks, etc. that are used to interact with a machine.

Since human hand is very complex with varying shapes and sizes, therefore recognition of hand gestures has apparently become even more complex. Numerous researchers have proposed various methods for hand gesture recognition varying from data glove to vision based approach [1–7]. Albeit, it is reliable to use such sensors for hand gesture recognition, but it adds the burden of wearing the sensor which is not convenient to use in different scenarios. Also, adds extra cost to the user. Hand Gesture Recognition using conventional cameras such as web cameras, Tof Camera, 3D stereo camera, etc. have also been proposed by many researchers [13]. Conventional cameras reduce the system cost up to an appreciable level, but fails in cluttered environment. Conventional cameras are susceptible to light variations and the efficacy of such system drop drastically.

© Springer Nature Singapore Pte Ltd. 2018
P. Bhattacharyya et al. (Eds.): NGCT 2017, CCIS 828, pp. 752–760, 2018.
https://doi.org/10.1007/978-981-10-8660-1_56

With the advent of Depth Sensors such as Kinect Sensors, many researchers have used it for Hand Gesture Recognition [5–8]. It presented a much more feasible way to recognize hand gesture as sensors such as data glove were not further required. It works well in cluttered environment and is less susceptible to varying light conditions. Despite these advantages of Kinect Sensor for Hand Gesture Recognition, results are still not satisfactory. This is due to its resolution low resolution (640 × 480), which makes it hard to recognize small objects. Thus hand segmentation becomes very inaccurate making system less efficient.

In this work, we have presented an alternate technique to recognize hand gestures more efficiently using the depth image from Kinect sensor. Our method involves, background subtraction after acquisition of image by Kinect Sensor. By assuming that hand will be the closest object having the darkest shade. Therefore, clipping rest of the portion and binarizing image, hand segmentation is achieved. Later, features were extracted from our dataset using HOG (Histogram of Oriented Gradients) and classified hand gesture using Multi support vector machine. Experiment was performed in real time with cluttered environment to measure the efficiency of this method.

2 Related Work

Hand gesture can be recognized by various methods proposed by numerous scientists. But every methodology has some drawback that restricts it to be accepted widely.

Over years, researchers have divulged them into finding out new ways for hand gesture recognition. Hand gestures can be recognized using a sensor on the human body or by using the hand appearance to distinguish between gestures. Dipietro et al. [1] show how glove system technology can be used to recognize hand gestures more effectively. This method is effective, but it also adds the burden of wearing to user which makes the user uneasy. The calibration of data gloves and other sensor is also a complex process. Lamberti and Camastra [2] show how color segmentation can be used to detect gestures using a color glove. Still, user need to wear color glove and due to dynamic background efficiency of this system degrades. Yang et al. [3] proposed method to represent hand region by skin color model. This method does not work well in cluttered environment and hand segmentation is not achieved as required. Takimoto et al. [4] used arm movements features to define features for a gesture but this method results in contour distortions. Slight noise in the background results in serious inefficiencies for skeleton based methods.

RGB camera was prevalent in Hand Gesture Recognition methods until Depth Sensors were introduced. But, the main drawback of using the conventional webcam or RGB camera was that it is highly susceptible to light and varying background. RGB cameras alone cannot work well in the cluttered environment. But with the arrival of Kinect Sensor in 2010 it became a very dependable choice for hand gesture recognition. Marouf et al. [5] in their paper used the RGB and Depth Sensor of Kinect by doing a color depth calibration. But this is still not dependable since RGB camera cannot always be efficient. Ghotkar and Kharate [6] in their paper when worked without Kinect sensor in dynamic background the results were not satisfactory. But when Kinect sensor was used it worked well in dynamic background. Tara et al. [7]

proposed hand segmentation using Antropometric approach. This approach used depth image and by finding centroid of human body it divides the body into left and right. This approach suffers a drawback because hand cannot move freely which will affect the centroid of the body. Li [8] in his paper used Kinect Sensor for hand gesture recognition. But using an old version of Kinect Sensor reduces the efficiency of the system. Various algorithms can be used to extract features of an image such as Speed up robust features (SURF), Scale invariant feature transform (SIFT), Histogram of oriented gradients (HOG) and so on. Each method has its advantages and limitations. Sykora et al. [9] compared SIFT and SURF for use on Hand Gesture Recognition in which overall accuracy for SIFT and SURF was 81.2% and 82.2% respectively. Rublee et al. [10] in their paper provided ORB (Oriented FAST and Rotated BRIEF) as an efficient alternative to SIFT or SURF. Li et al. [11] in their paper used HOG with Kinect for hand gesture recognition. Even after achieving an accuracy of 93.5 for static images it has serious drawbacks because it only uses RGB image for gesture recognition which is susceptible to light and varying background.

3   Proposed Methodology

Overall process is represented above in the Fig. 1. The proposed methodology assumes that closest object to the Kinect sensor is the hand and nothing else is in between it. Hand is in front of the human body. Above given blocks represent individually occurring steps. First, the depth image is obtained by Kinect Sensor. Using depth image hand segmentation is done. There after features are extracted from segmented hand using HOG. These features now enable our classifier to detect the gesture correctly.

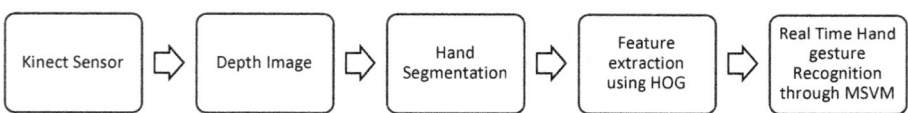

Fig. 1.   Overall process for hand gesture recognition

3.1   Hand Detection

As shown in Fig. 1, depth sensor (Microsoft Kinect) produces depth image of dimension 640 × 480. For hand detection hand must be clipped from other body parts as well as the background in the image. In order to do that we clipped the Depth image provided by the Kinect sensor as follows:

$$D_{max} < 2^{10} - 1$$

Where D_{max} is the maximum depth of an image. This restricts the depth image to have a maximum depth value of 1023. And then applying a right shift of 2 places making the leftmost 2 bits of the depth image zero. Finally, converting it into an 8-bit array which is a grayscale image. Gaussian blur is then applied to reduce the noise in the image. Gaussian blur uses Gaussian function which can be described as:

$$G(x, y) = \frac{1}{2\pi\sigma^2} e^{-\frac{x^2+y^2}{2\sigma^2}}$$

where x and y is distance from the origin in x-axis and y-axis respectively, and σ is the standard deviation of the Gaussian distribution. This gives the grayscale image which distinguish closer and farther object using shades, i.e. closest object with darker shade than the farther object with lighter shade as shown in the Fig. 2.

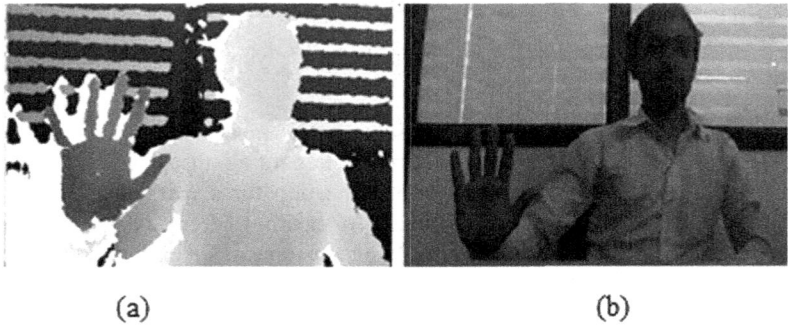

(a)   (b)

Fig. 2. (a) Grayscale image (b) RGB image

Now assuming that our hand is the closest object, we need to clip the rest of the portion since our objective is to recognize only hand gesture. Rest of the information is futile for us. To ensure the proper distance of the hand from the camera, we need to restrict darkest shade between black and mid grey. This is done as follows:

$$0 < S_D < 150$$

Where S_D represents darkest shade which is between 0(black) to 150(mid grey). After this, we binarize our image as follows:

$$\begin{cases} S_T > S_V : S_V = 255; \\ S_T < S_V : S_V = 0; \end{cases}$$

where S_T is the threshold value of the shade and S_V is the current shade value. S_V is changed to black (255) if it is less than our threshold value and white (0), if more. This will give us result as shown in the Fig. 3:

3.2 Feature Extraction

In this experiment image features were obtained using Histogram of Oriented Gradients. Histogram of Oriented Gradients is used to describe features of an image. Features

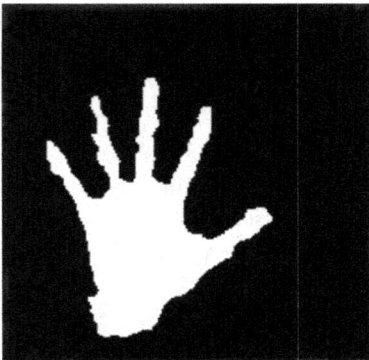

Fig. 3. Segmented Hand obtained after applying our algorithm

of an image can be considered as a representation of image or as a part of an image which only provide us the useful information regarding the image neglecting the superfluous information. This makes a generalization for a particular kind of image which in turn allow us to get same features (or nearby) of an image under different circumstances. Making classification of different gestures much easier and faster for our classifier algorithm to perform calculations.

HOG divides an image into different cells and then calculates gradient of each pixel in the cell. These cells combine to build a block. A HOG feature descriptor gives the information about the distribution of directions of gradients namely g_x and g_y gradients of an image. To find horizontal and vertical gradients we apply filtering on our image using Sobel operator. Where, the magnitude of gradient is defined by:

$$\sqrt{g_x^2 + g_y^2}$$

While, direction of gradients θ is calculated by the given formula:

$$\theta = arctan\frac{g_x}{g_y}$$

Image of hand gesture of size 64 × 128 after resizing was divided into 8 × 8 cells with a block size of 16 × 16, for which histogram was calculated for each cell. It gives 8 × 8 × 2 (gradient and direction value) numbers or values which can be represented on a 9-bin histogram as:

Histogram ranges from 0 to 180° as shown in Fig. 4. Each gradient can be calculated from histogram by its magnitude. To prevent our gradient from any light change that may result in serious inconsistencies, a 16 × 16 block was normalized using L2 norm. Given a n-dimensional vector x its normalization factor can be calculated as:

$$NormFac = \sqrt{x_1^2 + x_2^2 \dots \dots x_n^2}$$

Now we divide each element of the vector by *NormFac* to get the normalized vector which is less susceptible to light changes. Now finally concatenating all vectors into one big vector which gives the feature vector of the image (Fig. 4).

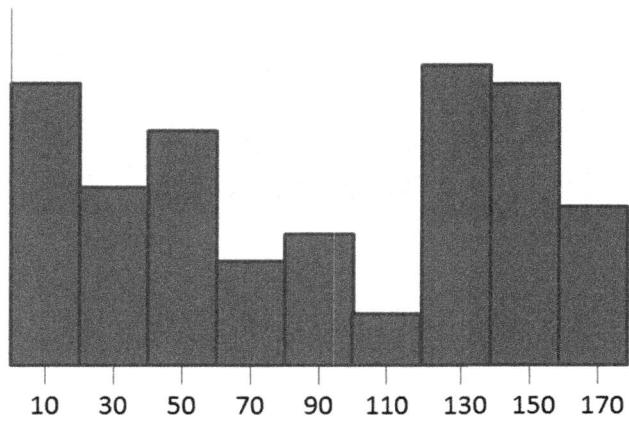

Fig. 4. Histogram representation for an image

3.3 Dataset

Dataset from 30 different people was created by taking 20 images that varies in angle, articulation etc. per person. Therefore, we were able to create 600 images per gesture. We have taken 6 gestures only of right hand that are as follows:

3.4 Classification

At last, descriptors extracted using histogram of oriented gradient must be fed into some acknowledgment framework in view of administered learning for hand gesture recognition. SVM is a binary classifier which means classifying given set into two classes. It finds an ideal hyperplane as a decision function. Once trained on images containing some particular object, the SVM classifier can settle on choices with respect to the nearness of an appropriate result by making decisions (Fig. 5).

SVM classifier can likewise be used for multi class classification. It builds a hyperplane in a high or unbounded dimensional space, which can be utilized for grouping. Clearly the grouping mistakes can be lessened if hyper-plane that has the biggest separation to the closest training data of any class otherwise called functional margin, as the margin and generalization error are indirectly proportional. In this paper we have used C-Support Vector Classification (SVC) for multiclass classification (Fig. 6).

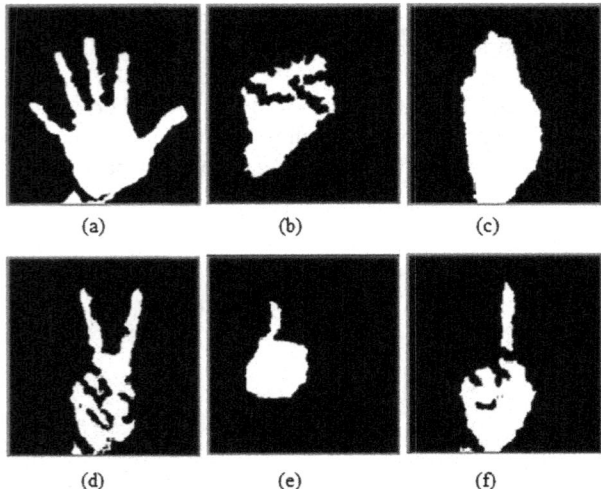

Fig. 5. All hand gestures. 5(a) Open hand 5(b) Closed hand 5(c) Flat hand 5(d) Victory sign 5(e) Thumbs up 5(f) Index finger

We trained our SVM using the Radial Basis Function kernel. Two parameters which decides the classification efficiency are C and gamma. C is common to all SVM kernels. A smaller value of C aims at making a smooth decision surface, on the other hand a high value of C classifies all training examples efficiently. Gamma describes influence of an individual training example. We have used the value of C as 2.67 and value of gamma as 5.383 for better efficiency (Fig. 7).

SVC with RBF kernel

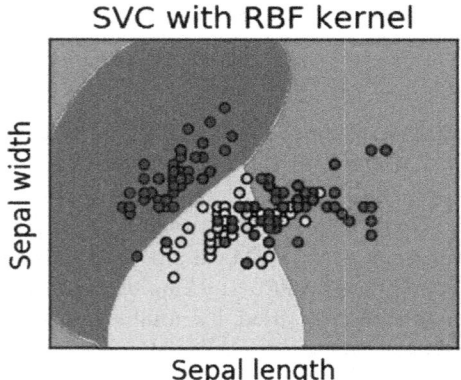

Fig. 6. Visualization of SVC with RBF kernel on IRIS dataset

4   Experiment Results

The experiment was performed on a PC with Linuxmint, 4 GB RAM and 2.1 GHz core i3 processor. The overall system achieves an accuracy of 94.3% (Table 1).

Table 1. Confusion matrix for hand gesture recognition using histogram of gradients

Gesture	Open hand	Closed hand	Flat hand	Victory sign	Thumbs up	Index finger
Open hand	98	1		1		
Closed hand		92	6		2	
Flat hand	2	1	97			
Victory sign				92	2	6
Thumbs up			1	4	94	1
Index finger			4		3	93

The accuracy of a particular gesture recognition was calculated as:

$$Accuracy(\%) = \frac{Correct\ Classification}{Total\ Test\ Data} \times 100$$

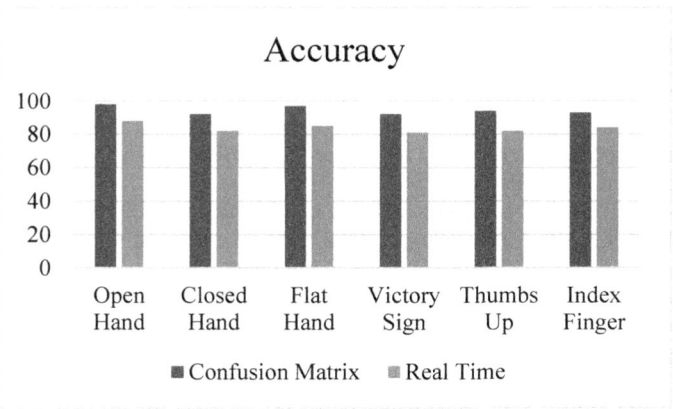

Fig. 7. Comparison chart for accuracy in confusion matrix and in real time

5   Conclusion

In this paper, we presented a method for hand gesture recognition using HOG and SVM. The method used depth image from the Kinect sensor. Segmented hand was obtained using our method from this depth image. Features of the segmented hand were extracted by Histogram of Oriented Gradients and these features were used to train our classifier. Multi Support Vector Machine was used as a classifier in this work. Using this method accuracy of 94.3% was achieved which is better than previously obtained accuracy in Hand Gesture Recognition systems.

Since hand gesture recognition includes gestures from both the hand as well as dynamic gestures. So the system presented in this paper could be used for developing various applications.

References

1. Dipieto, L., Sabatini, A.M., Dario, P.: Survey of glove-base systems and their applications. IEEE Trans. Syst. Man Cybern. **38**(4), 461–482 (2008)
2. Lamberti, L., Camastra, F.: Real-time hand gesture recognition using a color glove. In: Maino, G., Foresti, G.L. (eds.) ICIAP 2011. LNCS, vol. 6978, pp. 365–373. Springer, Heidelberg (2011). https://doi.org/10.1007/978-3-642-24085-0_38
3. Yang, M.H., Ahua, N., Tabb, M.: Extraction of 2D motion trajectories and its application on hand gesture recognition. IEE Tans. Pattern Anal. Mach. Intell. **29**, 1062–1074 (2002)
4. Takimoto, H., Yoshimori, S., Mitsukura, Y., Fukumi, M.: Hand posture recognition robust for posture changing in complex background. J. Signal Process. **14**(6), 483–490 (2010)
5. Marouf, A.A., Shondipon, S., Hasan, M.K., Mahmud, H.: 4Y model: a novel approach for finger identification using KINECT. In: IEEE 2nd International Conference on Recent Trends in Information System, pp. 183–188. IEEE, Kolkata (2015)
6. Ghotkar, A.S., Kharate, G.K.: Vision based real time hand gesture recognition techniques for human computer interaction. Int. J. Comput. Appl. **70**(16), 1–8 (2013)
7. Tara, R.Y., Santosa, P.I., Adji, T.B.: Hand segmentation from depth image using anthropometric approach in natural interface development. Int. J. Sci. Eng. Res. **3**(5), (2012)
8. Li, Y.: Hand gesture recognition using Kinect. (2012). Electronic Theses and Dissertations. Paper 823 (1989)
9. Sykora, P., Kamencay, P., Hudec, R.: Comparison of SIFT and SURF methods for use on hand gesture recognition based on depth map. In: AASRI Conference on Circuit and Signal Processing. vol. 9, pp. 19–24. ELSEVIER, UK (2014)
10. Rublee, E., Rabaud, V., Konolige, K., Bradski, G.: ORB: an efficient alternative to SIFT or SURF. In: ICCV 2011 Proceedings of the 2011 International Conference on Computer Vision, pp. 2564–2571. IEEE, Barcelona, Spain (2011)
11. Li, H., Yang, L., Wu, X., Xu, S., Wang, Y.: Static hand gesture recognition based on HOG with Kinect. In: 4th International Conference on Intelligent Human-Machine Systems and Cybernetics (IHMSC). Nanchang, China (2012)
12. Ren, Z., Yuan, J., Meng, J., Zhang, Z.: Robust part-based hand gesture recognition using Kinect sensor. IEEE Trans. Multimedia **15**(5), 1520–9210 (2013)
13. Shinde, V., Bacchav, T., Pawar, J., Sanap, M.: Hand gesture recognition system using camera. Int. J. Eng. Res. Technol. **3**(1) (2014). ISSN 2278-0181

A New Objective Function Based Multi-Level Image Segmentation Using Differential Evolution

Rupak Chakraborty[1(✉)], Rama Sushil[1], and M. L. Garg[2]

[1] Department of IT, DIT University, Dehradun 248001, Uttarakhand, India
rupak.jis@gmail.com, hod.it@dituniversity.edu.in
[2] Department of CSE, DIT University, Dehradun 248001, Uttarakhand, India
dr.ml.garg@dituniversity.edu.in

Abstract. This Paper represents a multi-level image thresholding approach based on the normalized index value of image and probability of pixel intensities. One new objective function proposed, which is the multiplication of normalized index value and probability, to obtain the scenario. This multiplication measure is then optimized to obtain the thresholds of the image. In order to solve an optimization problem, Differential Evolution (DE) as a meta-heuristic approach is used, which results a fast and accurate convergence towards the optimal solution. The performance of DE is compared to other well-known optimized algorithms like Particle swarm optimization (PSO), Genetic Algorithms (GA). The outcomes of images are compared with Kapur entropy, Tsalli entropy and Otsu method, both visually and statistically for establishing the perceptible difference in image.

Keywords: Multilevel image segmentation · Normalised index value
Probability · Differential Evolution · PSNR

1 Introduction

Image segmentation is the process of partitioning a digital image into multiple segments (sets of pixels), is an essential step for many advanced imaging applications. Image segmentation can be performed by recursively splitting the whole image until the total region is divided properly. The splitting technique generally considers intermediate level as its starting cutest, then recursive splitting approach is used to reach to the desired final cutest. Threshold selections of gray level images is the key for segmenting the images properly. Improper selection of threshold value can lead the segmentation to produce the wrong result. An unsupervised method of automatic threshold selection can be used [1]. Clustering is a technique to group up objects of similar properties. In bi-mean clustering two subsets of gray values can be formed which will ease segmentation further. Here mean value as a statistical parameter will be used with gray values of pixels to get the proper clusters [2]. Splitting and merging techniques on the basis of some

© Springer Nature Singapore Pte Ltd. 2018
P. Bhattacharyya et al. (Eds.): NGCT 2017, CCIS 828, pp. 761–770, 2018.
https://doi.org/10.1007/978-981-10-8660-1_57

parameters like density are also applied to get the proper clusters. Two phase splitting technique may be introduced, first one is on the basis of density parameter and next one is by using traditional K-means algorithm to form proper clusters [3]. Generally to find the population of pixels in a gray level image, a bi-modality technique is used to divide the regions into two subparts. Statistical parameters like mean, mode, median, entropy can be used. There are lots of techniques available, one of them is pyramid-based algorithm [4], other popular techniques of image segmentation are surface based segmentation, edge detection, fuzzy clustering etc. [5]. Proper segmentation of data intensive application depend on speed and economy of implementation. To achieve it properly iterative thresholding, histogram thresholding technique for converting gray value to binary value produce a good result [6,7]. Gray levels are determined at those points where the gradient is high, indicating probable object edges. Adaptive thresholding approach can be applied to get the segmented image [9]. Images can be considered as a two-dimensional function (x, y) in a gray-level space, like thresholding algorithms, more research conducted on split-merge techniques as well. One of the very popular approach was quad tree based approach. By using this technique determination of region uniformity in each iteration process calculated to identify the proper homogeneous regions [8]. As there was some deficiency of quad tree approach, a new improved quad tree method for splitting and merging developed to get the homogeneous regions identified properly. Top-down and bottom-up approach of region based segmentation helped to invent a technique named neighbor naming based image segmentation method to get the appropriate splitting results [12].

Researchers have attempted a lot of techniques to get the good segmentation results. When one particular approach can't produce the proper segmented value, then some hybrid techniques can also be applied where combination of region based technique, boundary based techniques, thresholding work altogether on the hierarchical watershed [10]. In medical image segmentation analysis, many researchers have produced different techniques to split the image and then form a cluster. But most of the techniques suffer from contour detection and as well as training samples should be adjusted manually for certain threshold parameters. Entropy based segmentation technique is more useful to get fast and efficient result of human X-ray images [14,15]. Some well-known entropy based techniques like Kapur et al. [21]; Tsalli [22]; Otsu [1]; available to find the gray level threshold value of gray-scale images which help to separate efficiently image objects from its background. Threshold values achieved by maximizing the total entropy by applying a global optimization technique, GA [20]. One important reason to use meta-heuristics is to minimize the computational time and complexity of algorithm as much as possible [23].

Different researchers have proposed different hard decision algorithms regarding traditional split-merge technique of image segmentation. In photogrammetry and computer vision automated reconstruction of images from different data source face a big challenge due to noise, low contrast, occlusion etc. to segment the images properly. A robust plane-fitting method has been applied to the splitting technique [11]. One of the successful and widely accepted split-merge technique for image segmentation is the bi-modality detection approach using frequency, standard deviation, threshold parameters. But after applying that approach it has been found that split regions are homogenous, so to overcome this problem merging has been done [13]. An automatic thresholding technique based on the normalized index value of image and probability of frequency of gray value with non-homogeneity criterion is applied in the splitting technique to get the image segmentation results. Since the proposed splitting technique depends upon homogeneity factor, so main focus in this algorithm is not to split the homogeneous regions.

To pursue with the current research interest a normalized index value (NIV) and probability (P) based multi-level image segmentation technique, encouraged by Differential Evolution (DE) is proposed in this paper. Now a days DE is the arguably best optimized and widely used technique. Several researchers showed that DE can outperform GA and PSO when it is used for multi-level image thresholding based segmentation technique [16–20,24]. Extensive surveys have been considered to demonstrate the efficiency and robustness of DE based approach in comparison with other popular optimization techniques like PSO and GA in terms of computational time, objective value and standard deviation. Results are tested against other available entropy techniques and final statistical comparison is done via peak signal to noise ratio (PSNR) maximization method.

This paper is represented in the following manner. In Sect. 2 we have described our mathematical foundation of our proposed objective function. In Sect. 3 we briefly described our meta-heuristic Differential Evolution (DE) approach. In Sect. 4 we have described our proposed segmentation algorithm. In Sect. 5 we have presented the comparative segmentation results of different images with other entropy based algorithms. In Sect. 5 we have concluded the future direction of our current work.

2   Mathematical Foundation of Proposed Objective Function Used in Segmentation Technique

The proposed segmentation technique based on objective function approach works in recursive way until a homogeneous region is found. Let R be the total population. It can be divided into two sub component populations, say $R_{m(i)}$, $R_{n(i)}$ such that:

(a) $R_{m(i)}$ contains all the pixels of gray value $\leq k$ and $R_{n(i)}$ contains all pixels of gray value $> k$.
(b) $R_{m(i)}$ and $R_{n(i)}$ are the smallest subset of R.

Now assume that NIV_i and p_i are the normalized index value and probability of i_{th} gray values of population R. We are now giving the mathematical definition of these two parameters in the following:

(i) $NIV_i = \frac{g_i}{g_{max}}$ where NIV_i denotes the normalised index value and g_i is the ith gray value and g_{max} is the maximum gray value of the population R respectively.

(ii) $p_i = \frac{h_i}{M \times N}$ where h_i is the total frequencies of g_i gray value and $M \times N$ is the total number of pixels in the population R and p_i is the probability measurement. The objective function can be defined in the following manner given in Eq. 1:

$$S(i) = \frac{\sum_{i=1}^{k} NIV_i \times p_i + \sum_{i=k+1}^{g_{max}} NIV_i \times p_i}{NIV \times P}, g_{min} \leq k \leq g_{max} \qquad (1)$$

Here g_{min} and g_{max} are the minimum and maximum gray values of populations R and finding out the splitting gray value for which $S(i)$ will be minimized. This objective function has been used to find out the optimal gray value of a region.

3   Differential Evolution (DE)

Differential search algorithm was proposed by Storn in 1997 and developed by Civicioglu [20] is one of the most popular population-based global optimization algorithm. In this algorithm, each point in the search space corresponds to an artificial- superorganism migration. With the help of the migration, an optimal solution can be found for a problem. A M-dimensional vector containing a set of D optimization parameters of the ith individual parameter of the population at generation time t can be described as:

$$\overrightarrow{W_i}(t) = [W_{i,1}, W_{i,2}, W_{i,3}........W_{i,M}] \qquad (2)$$

To change the population numbers $\overrightarrow{W_i}(t)$(say) of each generation, a donor vector $\overrightarrow{X_i}(t)$is created. In DE/rand/1 scheme (one of the DE version), for creating a donor vector $\overrightarrow{X_i}(t)$ for each ith member, three other parameter vectors (say p1, p2 and p3-th vectors such that p1, p2, p3 $\in$ [1,NP] and p1 $\neq$ p2 $\neq$ p3) are randomly chosen from the current population. Now to obtain donor vector $\overrightarrow{X_i}(t)$, a scalar number F is multiplied with the difference of any two of the three. So to get jth component of ith vector expression is:

$$\overrightarrow{X_{i,j}}(t) = W_{p1,j}(t) + F.(W_{p2,j}(t) - W_{p3,j}(t)) \qquad (3)$$

Next binomial crossover scheme is explained as it is used in the proposed method. The crossover is performed on each of the M variables by applying the control parameter Cr, also called crossover rate for DE. here the number of parameters inherited from a mutant has almost a binomial distribution. Now for each target vector $\overrightarrow{W_i}(t)$, a trial vector $\overrightarrow{S_i}(t)$ is created in the following manner:

$$R_{i,j}(t) = \begin{cases} X_{i,j}(t), & \text{if } rand_j(0,1) \leq Cr \| j = pn(i) \\ W_{i,j}(t), & \text{otherwise} \end{cases} \qquad (4)$$

where j=1,2....M and $rand_j(0,1) \in [0,1]$ is the jth evaluation of a random number generator and $pn(i) \in [1,2,...M]$ is a randomly chosen to ensure that $\overrightarrow{R_i}(t)$ gets at least one component from $\overrightarrow{W_i}(t)$. In order to select the resultant vector between target and trial vector which will survive in the next generation at time $t = t+1$, the selection is performed. If trial vector produces better value compare to target vector, it replaces its target vector in the next generation; otherwise, parent holds its position in the population:

$$\overrightarrow{W_I}(t+1) = \begin{cases} \overrightarrow{R_I}(t), & \text{if } f(\overrightarrow{R_I}(t)) > f(\overrightarrow{W_I}(t)) \\ \overrightarrow{W_I}(t), & \text{if } f(\overrightarrow{R_I}(t)) \leq f(\overrightarrow{W_I}(t)) \end{cases} \tag{5}$$

where f(.) is maximized function.

4   Proposed Segmentation Algorithm

Step 1: Initially the current region is the input image. N=0 (number of regions) and g_{min} and g_{max} are the minimum and maximum gray level values for the input image. Gray value frequencies are denoted as h_i

Step 2: Initially $g_{minimum} = g_{min}$ and $g_{maximum} = g_{max}$.

Step 3: Compute the thresholding value of homogeneity (T_{HOG}) using the following equation:

$$T_{HOG} = \sum_{i=g_{minimum}}^{g_{maximum}} (NIV_i \times p_i) \tag{6}$$

where NIV_i is normalized index value of image and p_i is the probability measurement are calculated in Sect. 2.

Step 4: If $T_{HOG} > T_H$ (where T_H is the predefined threshold) then go to Step 5. Otherwise, go to Step 7. T_{HOG} is called homogeneity factor.

Step 5: Apply Differential Evolution algorithm to detect the optimal splitting gray value g_{osgv} and split the current region by using g_{osgv}.

Step 6: $g_{maximum} = g_{osgv}$ and go to Step 3.

Step 7: Increment the number of region by 1 i.e. $N = N+1$

Step 8: If $g_{osgv} = g_{maximum}$ then go to Step 10. Otherwise, go to Step 9.

Step 9: $g_{minimum} = (g_{osgv} + 1)$ and $g_{maximum} = g_{max}$. Go to Step 3.

Step 10: STOP

Table 1. Comparison of computational time (t), objective value (f_t) and standard deviation (f_{std}) between DE, PSO and GA

Im		4 level			6 level			8 level		
		DE	PSO	GA	DE	PSO	GA	DE	PSO	GA
1	t	**3.838**	4.231	4.342	**7.617**	8.195	8.257	**12.851**	14.871	14.923
	f_t	**20.5879**	20.5674	20.5543	**26.5478**	26.3452	26.1256	**31.4434**	31.1209	30.9807
	f_{std}	**0**	0.0876	0.0865	**0**	0.0923	0.0927	**0**	0.1089	0.1076
2	t	**3.762**	3.957	4.012	**7.623**	8.217	8.436	**12.968**	14.012	14.332
	f_t	**19.8552**	19.8467	19.8356	**25.9784**	25.5678	25.4590	**31.4974**	30.0976	30.0470
	f_{std}	**0**	0.0723	0.0754	**0**	0.0844	0.0865	**0**	0.1108	0.1102
3	t	**3.787**	3.989	4.056	**7.679**	7.890	7.945	**12.891**	14.876	14.910
	f_t	**20.9759**	20.8590	20.8467	**26.9446**	26.2045	26.1089	**32.7039**	32.5545	32.4590
	f_{std}	**0**	0.0567	0.0578	**0**	0.0870	0.08745	**0**	0.1109	0.1130
4	t	**3.821**	4.083	4.120	**7.645**	8.650	8.784	**12.845**	14.609	14.981
	f_t	**20.741**	20.726	20.701	**26.795**	26.546	26.457	**31.964**	31.409	31.244
	f_{std}	**0**	0.0678	0.0673	**0**	0.0980	0.07884	**0**	0.1056	0.1046
5	t	**3.868**	4.230	4.497	**7.542**	7.667	7.809	**12.791**	14.560	14.789
	f_t	**20.385**	20.210	20.101	**26.844**	26.760	26.580	**32.721**	32.709	32.670
	f_{std}	**0**	0.0709	0.0809	**0**	0.0880	0.07874	**0**	0.1036	0.1016

5   Experimental Results

The operations are performed with MATLAB R2017a in a workstation with Intel Core i3 2.9 GHZ processor. We have got computation time after applying our objective function with DE/rand/1 optimization scheme to compute threshold values efficiently. The parameter set up of DE, PSO and GA have been taken using the guideline set up by different literatures. Optimization algorithm runs 50 independent times where each run continued till the exhaustion of D × 1000 numbers of fitness parameters, where D represents the search space dimensionality. In Table 1 we have shown the comparison of computational time (t), objective value (f_m), and standard deviation (f_{std}) between DE, PSO and GA and we can observe that DE optimization algorithm performs better in all aspects compare to other optimization techniques.

For testing and analysis, we have considered 5 gray scale images. Table 2 shows the result of $4th$ and $6th$ level threshold values and Table 3 displays corresponding level-wise computation times of Kapur, Otsu and Tsalli techniques along with proposed approach. The effectiveness of our proposed technique is clearly visualized in terms of threshold values as well as computation times over other entropy based techniques. Table 4 holds the original 5 gray scale images with $4th$ and $6th$ level results of our proposed algorithm including results of other renowned techniques. This qualitative comparison of segmented images further mapped by Figs. 1 and 2 graphs which clearly indicate the better computation time of our proposed algorithm.

Finally, we have calculated peak signal to noise ratio (PSNR) of all outcomes of segmented images to assure the better visual effectiveness of our proposed

Table 2. Threshold values obtained by DE for 4 and 6 level thresholding

Im	Lv	Threshold values			
		Our algo	Kapur	Otsu	Tsalli
1	4	$51, 94, 139, 220$	$55, 109, 178, 215$	$10, 36, 98, 183$	$40, 49, 119, 196$
	6	$34, 70, 100, 154, 192, 226$	$2, 53, 87, 148, 221, 249$	$100, 113, 144, 157, 194, 216$	$80, 112, 157, 180, 205, 230$
2	4	$34, 93, 132, 180$	$34, 136, 178, 202$	$47, 130, 184, 246$	$77, 140, 187, 249$
	6	$26, 59, 90, 128, 156, 192$	$15, 111, 146, 206, 219, 238$	$51, 71, 131, 218, 230, 241$	$77, 89, 149, 221, 239, 251$
3	4	$55, 111, 139, 211$	$28, 105, 184, 232$	$57, 135, 171, 205$	$56, 98, 178, 245$
	6	$47, 86, 109, 148, 174, 219$	$36, 77, 102, 163, 184, 219$	$13, 69, 104, 151, 208, 237$	$49, 87, 123, 190, 223, 249$
4	4	$38, 101, 138, 202$	$48, 99, 170, 198$	$59, 134, 166, 240$	$74, 140, 180, 240$
	6	$33, 66, 96, 127, 156, 217$	$20, 68, 104, 149, 188, 225$	$28, 51, 121, 178, 211, 235$	$45, 67, 130, 190, 224, 249$
5	4	$34, 93, 132, 180$	$34, 136, 178, 202$	$47, 130, 184, 246$	$77, 140, 187, 249$
	6	$26, 59, 90, 128, 156, 192$	$15, 111, 146, 206, 219, 238$	$51, 71, 131, 218, 230, 241$	$77, 89, 149, 221, 239, 251$

Table 3. Computational time obtained by DE for 4 and 6 level thresholding

Image	Lv	Computation time in seconds			
		Our algo	Kapur	Otsu	Tsalli
Cameraman	4	8.527	8.601	8.571	8.604
	6	13.791	13.909	13.879	13.981
House	4	8.881	8.951	8.929	8.955
	6	14.002	14.221	14.171	14.304
Mosque	4	8.545	8.665	8.61	8.672
	6	13.927	14.101	14.075	14.275
Peeper	4	8.53	8.581	8.565	8.585
	6	13.795	13.998	13.841	14.001
Ship	4	8.891	8.934	8.912	8.927
	6	14.009	14.316	14.22	14.375

algorithm with DE optimization technique compare to other meta-heuristic techniques like PSO, GA. PSNR is used to maintain the similarity of an original image against the segmented image based on the produced root mean square error (RMSE). RMSE and PSNR are defined as:

$$RMSE = \sqrt{\frac{\sum_{i=1}^{ro} * \sum_{j=1}^{co} (I_o(i,j) - I_{th}(i,j))}{r_o \times c_o}} \tag{7}$$

$$PSNR = 10 log_{10} \frac{(MAX_i^2)}{RMSE} dB \tag{8}$$

where I_o is the original image and I_{th} is the thresholded image, r_o and c_o are the total number of rows and columns. Table 5 concludes that as a meta-heuristic optimization technique DE performs better even it is applied to all other entropy based techniques as well.

Table 4. Qualitative comparison of proposed method with other existing method

Original					
Level − 4					
Level − 6					
Kapur					
Otsu					
Tsalli					

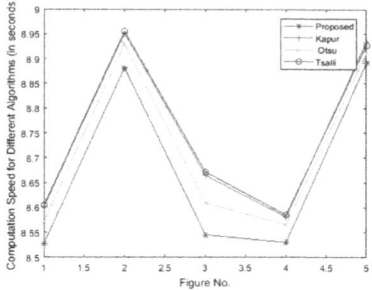

Fig. 1. 4th level graph

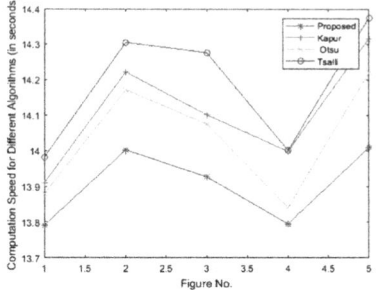

Fig. 2. 6th level graph

Table 5. PSNR values obtained from different optimization techniques (6 level)

Im	Proposed method			Kapur method			Otsu method			Tsalli method		
	DE	PSO	GA	DE	PSO	GA	DE	PSO	GA	DE	PSO	GA
1	18.372	18.351	18.218	15.564	15.439	15.390	16.219	16.198	16.065	15.890	15.798	15.587
2	17.746	17.509	17.465	15.102	15.045	15.010	15.908	15.809	15.470	15.798	15.609	15.540
3	21.409	21.201	21.102	18.309	18.278	18.109	19.391	19.210	19.102	18.781	18.671	18.560
4	20.980	20.763	20.451	16.095	16.050	16.031	17.870	17.698	17.450	16.908	16.709	16.563
5	19.769	19.654	19.230	17.690	17.552	17.321	18.321	18.209	18.126	17.670	17.560	17.431

6 Conclusion and Future Scope

We can conclude from the above discussion that our $NIV \times P$ technique can produce a better result with less computation time with the help of optimization technique DE. It can be considered as a useful method for computing multi-level threshold values for effective visualization and statistical analysis over entropy based techniques and other global thresholding techniques. According to the statistical analysis of DE over PSO and GA it takes less computation time as well as produces better objective value and effective visualization. Further, we have a scope to modify our techniques in future so that it produces more less time and better qualitative visualization compare to some fuzzy entropy based techniques. There is also some scope to modify DE parameters for choosing scaling factor as well as dimension parameters so that it produce the speedy and accurate result. Further modified DE based fuzzy technique will be proposed in order to get improved outcomes.

References

1. Otsu, N.: A threshold selection method from gray-level histograms. IEEE Trans. Syst. Man Cybern. **9**, 62–66 (1979)
2. Dunn, S., Janos, L., Rosenfeld, A.: Bimean clustering. Pattern Recogn. Lett. **1**, 169–173 (1983)
3. Chaudhuri, D., Chaudhari, B.B., Murthy, C.A.: A new split-and-merge clustering technique. Pattern Recogn. Lett. **13**, 399–409 (1992)
4. Bongiovanni, G., Cinque, L., Levialdi, S., Rosenfeld, A.: Image segmentation by a multiresolution approach. Pattern Recogn. **26**(12), 1845–1854 (1993)
5. Pal, N.R., Pal, S.K.: A review on image segmentation technique. Pattern Recogn. **26**(9), 1277–1294 (1993)
6. Perez, A., Gonzalez, R.C.: An iterative thresholding algorithm for image segmentation. IEEE Trans. Pattern Anal. Mach. Intell. **9**(6), 742–751 (1987)
7. Arifin, A.Z., Asano, A.: Image segmentation by histogram thresholding using hierarchical cluster analysis. Pattern Recogn. Lett. **27**(13), 1515–1521 (2006)
8. Lorenzo-Navarro, J., Hernandez-Tejera, M.: Image segmentation using a modified split and merge technique. Cybern. Syst. **25**, 137–162 (2006). https://doi.org/10.1080/0196972940890231
9. Yanowitz, S.D., Bruckstein, A.M.: A new method for image segmentation. Comput. Vis. Graph. Image Process. **46**, 82–95 (1988)

10. Jalba, A.C., Wilkinson, M.H.F., Roerdink, J.B.T.M.: Automatic segmentation of diatom images for classification. Microsc. Res. Tech. **65**, 72–85 (2004)
11. Khoshelham, K., Li, Z., King, B.: A split-and-merge technique for automated reconstruction of roof planes. Photogramm. Eng. Remote Sens. **71**(7), 855–862 (2005)
12. Kelkar, D., Gupta, S.: Improved quadtree method for split merge image segmentation. In: First International Conference on Emerging Trends in Engineering and Technology (2008)
13. Chaudhuri, D., Agarwal, A.: Split-and-merge procedure for image segmentation using bimodality detection approach. Def. Sci. J. **60**(3), 290–301 (2010)
14. Szenasi, S.: Medical image segmentation using split-and-merge method. In: 5th IEEE International Symposium on Logistics (2013)
15. Cao, F., Liang, J., Jiang, G.: Automatic segmentation of bones in x-ray images based on entropy measure. Int. J. Image Graph. **16**(1), 1650001–1650032 (2016)
16. Sarkar, S., Paul, S., Burman, R., Das, S., Chaudhuri, S.S.: A fuzzy entropy based multi-level image thresholding using differential evolution. In: Panigrahi, B.K., Suganthan, P.N., Das, S. (eds.) SEMCCO 2014. LNCS, vol. 8947, pp. 386–395. Springer, Cham (2015). https://doi.org/10.1007/978-3-319-20294-5_34
17. Sarkar, S., Das, S., Chaudhuri, S.S.: A multilevel color image thresholding scheme based on minimum cross entropy and differential evolution. Pattern Recogn. Lett. **54**, 27–35 (2014). https://doi.org/10.1016/j.patrec.2014.11.009
18. Ayala, H.V.H., dos Santos, F.M., Mariani, V.C., dos Santos Coelho, L.: Image thresholding segmentation based on a novel beta differential evolution approach. Expert Syst. Appl. **42**, 2136–2142 (2014). https://doi.org/10.1016/j.eswa.2014.09.043
19. Kotte, S., Kumar, P.R., Injeti, S.K.: An efficient approach for optimal multilevel thresholding selection for gray scale images based on improved differential search algorithm. Ain Shams Eng. J. (2016). https://doi.org/10.1016/j.asej.2016.06.007
20. Civicioglu, P.: Transforming geocentric Cartesian coordinates to geodetic coordinates by using differential search algorithm. Comput. Geosci. **46**, 229–247 (2012)
21. Kapur, J.N., Sahoo, P.K., Wong, A.K.C.: A new method for gray-level picture thresholding using the entropy of the histogram. Comput. Vis. Graph. Image Process. **29**, 273–285 (1985)
22. Jiulin, D.: Property of Tsallis entropy and principal of entropy increase. Bull. Astr. Soc. India **35**, 691–696 (2007)
23. Cao, L., Bao, P., Shi, Z.: The strongest schema learning GA and its application to multi-level thresholding. Image Vis. Comput. **26**, 716–724 (2008)
24. Zhao, M., Fu, A.M.N., Yan, H.: A technique of three level threshholding based on probability partition and fuzzy-3 partition. IEEE Trans. Fuzzy Syst. **9**(3), 469–479 (2001)

Target Tracking in WSN Using Dynamic Neural Network Techniques

Moxanki A. Bhavsar[1] ⓘ, Jayesh H. Munjani[2(✉)] ⓘ,
and Maulin Joshi[1] ⓘ

[1] Sarvajanik College of Engineering and Technology, Surat, Gujarat, India
moxmahi@ymail.com, maulin.joshi@scet.ac.in
[2] Chhotubhai Gopalbhai Patel Institute of Technology, Surat, Gujarat, India
jayeshecl2@gmail.com

Abstract. Wireless Sensor Networks (WSN) are increasingly being envisioned for the collection of data, such as physical or environmental properties. Unlike detection of an event, tracking requires ensuring continuous monitoring. Resource constrained nature of wireless sensor networks makes energy efficient tracking a challenging task. Prediction based approaches try to save energy by reducing an avoidable communication. A Kalman-based approach has been widely used for target tracking but is inaccurate in the case of maneuvering target due to its inability to incorporate nonlinearity. In this paper, dynamic neural network based approaches called Time Delay Neural Network (TDNN) and Nonlinear Autoregressive network with Exogenous inputs (NARX) are proposed for non-cooperative target tracking application. The performance of NARX is compared with Kalman based approach and TDNN in terms of tracking accuracy. Simulation results show that NARX outperforms both Kalman approach and TDNN for target tracking applications.

Keywords: Wireless Sensor Network · Target tracking · Neural networks
Nonlinear autoregressive network with exogenous inputs (NARX)
Time Delay neural network (TDNN) · Kalman filtering · Prediction mechanism

1 Introduction

The smart cities without sensors can't be predicted in near future. An auto configurable sensor network made up of small but powerful sensors, which can work without any human intervention, can be utilized effectively to save human efforts and time. Wireless Sensor Network has been widely utilized in civic and military industries, especially for tracking targets in critical areas of some fields such as intruder detection, vehicle location tracking, logistics management and anti-terrorism etc.

In literature, many static and dynamic duty cycle based methods are proposed that try to adjust sleep time of sensor motes when the target is not likely to be nearby [1]. To save power, sensor nodes can be put into sleep mode but it increases chances to miss the target. The sleep mode power consumption of sensor mote still increases as the product of time and per second sleep mode power consumption becomes larger. Deep

P. Bhattacharyya et al. (Eds.): NGCT 2017, CCIS 828, pp. 771–789, 2018.
https://doi.org/10.1007/978-981-10-8660-1_58

sleep mode can be effectively utilized in which process like an internal timer, etc. can be stopped to save power of sensor mote [2, 3].

Prediction algorithm can save the power by reducing avoidable communication. Prediction works as a sensor selection problem. Sensor selection problem is to choose a sub set of nodes nearer to predicted target location so that energy can be saved. The kalman-based approach [4] been widely used in target tracking, but fail when the target moves with acceleration. The kalman-based approach is appropriate to predict the next state of vehicles traveling at almost zero acceleration. The acceleration appears as an ample noise in target model and hence single kalman filter leads to divergence while tracking a maneuvering target. The performance of prediction algorithm depends on a selection of target state transition matrix. If state transition matrix is not able to characterize the behavior of target movement, it fails to give a correct prediction. Neural network being model free estimator, can be alternate to kalman-based approaches due to its generalization ability [4]. Target movement is considered as evolving time series due to changes in coordinates with respect to time. This necessity puts a requirement of memory while deciding the type of neural network i.e. Dynamic neural networks.

Dynamic modeling and Multi-step ahead prediction is assumed more complex to solve problem of one-step-ahead prediction, and in this kind of complex tasks, artificial neural networks based models like recurrent neural architectures, play an important role. Recurrent networks may have more than one feedback loop. There are many tasks that require learning a temporal sequence of data. In Sequence prediction by temporal association, it produces a particular output sequence in response to a specific input sequence.

To incorporate short term memory, many models consider memory in form of time delays. Time Delay Neural Network is one of the simplest ways of performing time series prediction [5, 6]. It allows conventional back propagation algorithms to be extended to use memory presented by a length of tapped delay line. Time Delay Neural Network performance can be optimized based on information available in training date.

In the real world, there are number of nonlinear systems whose behavior is dynamic and may depend on their past or current state. The dynamic neural networks like recurrent neural network (RNN), nonlinear autoregressive (NAR), and nonlinear autoregressive neural network with exogenous inputs (NARX) can be very useful in these cases [7, 8].

In TDNN, time aspect is only inserted through its inputs, unlike NARX that also needs past output value as an input. This feature makes TDNN less potent than NARX for predicting values, but takes less processing and is easier to train. However, the limitation of the TDNN is, it cannot learn or adapt time delay values. Time delays are decided initially and remain unaltered during training, but for tracking applications time delays must be variable to adapt acceleration characteristics. Any enemy object like vehicle, weapons, target maneuvers and human can be tracked using target tracking application for military surveillance. Target tracking application used for monitoring wild animals and also used in environmental applications.

This paper proposes an algorithm that is able to efficiently track a single moving object, which inherently is non-cooperative target. The paper compares kalman-based approach and soft computing techniques TDNN/NARX with the scope limited to tracking accuracy of a target and compare the intended results in terms of root mean square error. The proposed tracking algorithm overcomes drawbacks of kalman-based approaches as it does not rely on the selection of state transition matrix. The proposes algorithm is an extended work of our TDNN based tracking approach to track a target [21]. This algorithm also takes care of target acceleration. Obtained results are compared with kalman-based approach which shows that better tracking accuracy is achieved in terms of mean square error.

The rest of the paper proceed as follows: Sect. 2 presents brief survey about state of art pertaining to target related aspects. Section 3 discusses target motion model and linear prediction. Section 4 introduces kalman-based approach for one step ahead prediction. Section 5 highlights our earlier work based on Time Delay Neural Network [21] and introduces the proposed Nonlinear Autoregressive Network with Exogenous Inputs approach to predict future location of a target. Section 6 shows extensive simulation results and Sect. 7 contains conclusion and further scope in research work.

2   Literature Review

Prediction algorithm can significantly save the power of sensor mote by avoiding unnecessary communication. Figure 1 shows a prediction based tracking mechanism. In a sensor network, the majority of sensor motes are kept in deep sleep mode to save energy except for border area nodes.

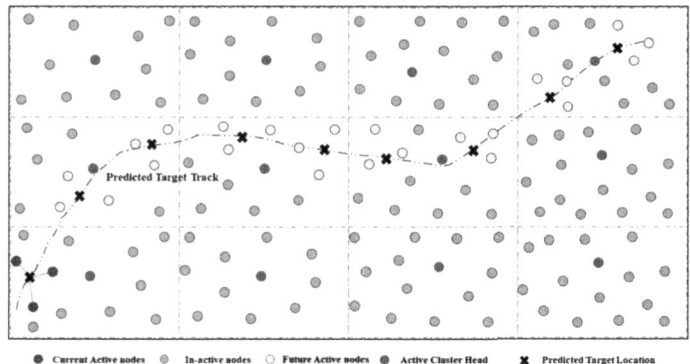

Fig. 1. Sample pattern of a prediction-based scheme

In deep sleep mode processor and sensing units are turned off to save energy. In the prediction based scheme, previously active nodes localize the target, communicate with neighbor nodes and predict the future location using prediction algorithm. The previously active nodes send awaken signal to the nodes which are nearer to predicted location.

To save processing power of sensor motes, prediction algorithm should be distributed and light weight and should consider following aspects [9]

1. The configuration space of a target as a state model (linear or nonlinear).
2. The noise model of sensor readings.
3. The target sensing modality (one or more than one modalities) and
4. The optimized resources of sensor nodes.

An appropriate state transition matrix only can increase the performance of prediction filter. The states to be estimated are typically the kinematic quantities like position, velocity, and acceleration. The state of a target space can be assumed in 1-dimensional or 2-dimensional. Based on target, space state transition matrix can be defined.

One dimensional model like constant velocity model, constant acceleration model and two-dimensional models like constant turn rate and velocity (CTV), constant turn rate and acceleration (CTA), constant steering rate and velocity (CSV), constant steering rate and acceleration (CSA) can be used for target tracking [10]. Traditional Kalman approach uses constant velocity model, hence inappropriate in the case of acceleration. Extended Kalman filter has been extensively used in a nonlinear system which incorporates Jacobian of a state tarnation matrix and observation matrices [11]. In addition, if the initial state estimation is wrong, or if the process is modeled incorrectly, the filter may quickly diverge, paying to its linearization. A nonlinear Kalman filter named Unscented Kalman filter shows great improvement over EKF [11]. To track a maneuvering target is a challenging task. A motion model must be able to accurately reassemble target trajectory and must contain term mechanism to detect acceleration. Kalman filter with input estimation in which maneuverer is taken as constant unknown input. It tries to correct state estimate based on estimated maneuverer magnitude and onset time [12]. Singer [13] proposed a target model in which a maneuvering motion is included as Markov first order process with zero mean and correlation time constant. This model shows great performance in case of low maneuverer but fails in case of high maneuvering target. Bogle [14] proposed modified input estimation method which takes long windows time to incorporate the effect of maneuverer, which is further modified by Wang [15] to reduce windows time.

The "current" statistical model for maneuvering target is proposed by Dr. Zhou Hongren which uses acceleration mean and modified Rayleigh Markov process to characterize maneuverer of a target. This model accurately models target maneuvering range and maneuvering intensity in real time. But it depends on the predetermined minimum and maximum range of acceleration. In practical, it is very difficult to know the range of acceleration.

Interacting Multiple Model (IMM) utilize the advantage of two Kalman filter working in parallel with different state transition matrix [16]. The output of both Kalman filter is combined together with prior to the state update using a set of conditional model probabilities. The conditional model probabilities are computed using the model probabilities from the previous update and a state switching matrix selected a priori. IMM filter gives accurate results as compared to KF, but at the cost of high processing power.

The neural network has been widely used in system identification problems. Stubberd proposed a Neural Extended Kalman Filter (NEKF) which uses an Extended Kalman filter to estimate the states by using dynamic system model and parallelly, the neural network is trained online to calculate nonlinearities, miss-modelled dynamics and other unknown parameters of the target motion [17]. NEKF learns the function that approximates the error between a priori motion model and the actual target dynamic, and apply a correction to the predicted state by extended Kalman filter.

The noisy observation may lead to the wrong prediction and can degrade tracking efficiency. Kalman-based approach and its variants consider process noise as well as observation noise variance to do efficient prediction, but it fails in case of non-Gaussian noise. The conventional EKF, as well as UKF algorithms, also incorporate observation noise that is additive, identically distributed normal variables with constant covariance. But if measurement noise become signal dependent, this assumption becomes false. The multiplicative measurement noise is roughly linearly increasing function of the sensor to target distance [18]. Noise may also affect localization of a target, which may lead to the wrong prediction of next target location, leads to full or partial death of sensor network.

Active nodes, who has detected a target, try to extract features of a target. Extraction of features is called sensing modality. A sensor can calculate the distance to vehicle or can find a reference or accurate position of the target. Many different measurement methods are proposed in the literature based on Time of arrival (TOA), Time Difference of Arrival (TDOA), Angle of arrival (AOA), Received Signal Strength (RSSI) etc. which are used to find the distance between target and sensor [19].

The Time of Arrival and Time Difference of Arrival methods uses time-based measurements to estimate distances between nodes. Based on the relationship between distance and propagation time distance between two nodes can be calculated.

The Angle of Arrival (AoA) methods calculate the relative angles between received radio signals. The method is highly accurate, but main requires additional hardware which consumes more sensor resource.

According to basic propagation models, the received signal strength is inversely proportional to the square of distance between the sender and receiver [20]. A known appropriate radio propagation model can be used to calculate distance based on received signal strength. This method is simple and cheap as it does not require dedicated hardware. However, in real time, signal strength may vary highly because of obstacles, noises, type of antenna, which makes it difficult to model mathematically.

As sensor nodes are having limited resource and hence prediction algorithm should be light enough so that it consumes less battery and less computational resources. In this paper, it is assumed that all processing like trilateration, prediction of target etc. are done at cluster head only.

3   Target Motion Model

The state of a target, moving in a X-Y plane field can be may contain its position and velocity [10].

$$x_n = [x(n)\ y(n)\ v_x(n)\ v_y(n)\,] \tag{1}$$

Where $(x(n), y(n))$ are the position coordinates of the target while $(v_x(n), v_y(n))$ are the velocities of the target in X and Y directions respectively. One can also consider acceleration and angle in target model.

The association between next target state and current target state is given by Eq. (2).

$$x_n = F * x_{n-1} + \Gamma * w_{n-1} \tag{2}$$

Where F define state transition matrix, Γ is process noise matrix and w_n state a process noise vector with distribution N (0, Q).

The observation vector y_n is the data observed as a function of state vector. The observation of sensor is given by Eq. (3).

$$y_n = H * x_n + n_n \tag{3}$$

Where H state observation matrix and n_n is an observation noise vector with probability distribution N (0, R).

The efficiency of prediction algorithm relies on state transition matrix. If target state transition matrix (F) is able to mimic target movement accurately, then the accuracy can be achieved. A prediction of next target state becomes difficult in the case of maneuvering target.

In linear prediction method uses current location (x_n, y_n) and previous location (x_{n-1}, y_{n-1}) of the target in order to predict next locations. One can estimate the target's speed as Eq. (4).

$$v = \frac{\sqrt{(x_n - x_{n-1})^2 + (y_n - y_{n-1})^2}}{t_n - t_{n-1}} \tag{4}$$

Based on this information and assuming that angle theta is with respect to positive x axis, the predicted location of target, after a given time t is given by

$$x_n = x_{n-1} + t * v * \cos\theta \tag{5}$$

$$y_n = y_{n-1} + t * v * \sin\theta \tag{6}$$

4   Kalman Based Approach

Kalman filter is generally applied in tracking applications that contain two steps (1) prediction in which prediction of the next state will be done and (a) Correction in which predicted value will be corrected based on a current observation [4].

4.1   Kalman as Predictor

The predicted position $\overline{x_{n+1}}$ and error covariance matrix $\overline{P_{n+1}}$ are given as follows.

$$\overline{x_{n+1}} = F * x_n \tag{7}$$

$$\overline{P_{n+1}} = F * P_n * F^T + \Gamma Q \Gamma^T \tag{8}$$

Where, P_n is the error covariance between actual and predicted state vector. The current observation y_{n+1} is used to correct the prediction.

4.2 Kalman Updating/Correction Equations

After receiving the correct observation of a target, the predicted value is corrected using Eq. (10) and Kalman gain as well as error portability matrix will be updated.

$$K_{n+1} = \overline{P_{n+1}} H^T \left(H \overline{P_{n+1}} H^T + \mathbf{R} \right)^{-1} \tag{9}$$

$$\widehat{x_{n+1}} = \overline{x_{n+1}} K_{n+1} \left(y_{n+1} - \mathbf{HH} \overline{x_{n+1}} \right) \tag{10}$$

$$P_{n+1} = \left(\mathbf{I} - K_{n+1} H \overline{P_{n+1}} \right) \tag{11}$$

Where K_n is the Kalman gain, $\widehat{x_n}$ is the state estimate, P_n is the error covariance. Further details on above and other kalman-based approaches can be found in [4].

5 Neural Based Approaches for Target Tracking

Neural Network being the model free estimator, can capture any nonlinearity between different states of a target and hence it has been a preferred choice than Kalman or other mathematical based approaches. During tracking, various wireless sensors are deployed to sense moving target in a 2D field. Selected cluster head node serves as the center of information processing. Selected sensors pass range information to the cluster head and cluster head uses NN based mechanism to perform prediction. The neural network approach for time series prediction is nonparametric, hence it is not required to know any source of information which generates it. An example of neural network based prediction approach is shown in Fig. 2.

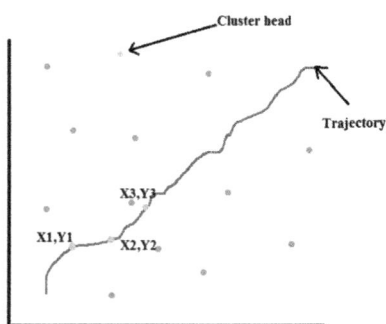

Fig. 2. Computation of distance using neural network based approach

A cluster head will awaken minimum set of nearest nodes to the target location. These active nodes compute distance to the target and send it to cluster head(CH). The CH will do time series prediction and initiate process to awaken minimum set of nodes nearer to predicted location.

Time series prediction is similar to system identification problem. Recurrent Neural Network (RNN) system can easily capture non-linearity available in target movement [8]. The RNN incorporate time significance by utilizing weighted feedback connection between intermediate layers of neurons. Therefore, RNN is the most suitable candidate for time series analysis.

The time series models are explored using Feed Forward Neural network (FFNN) approaches in both feedforward and recurrent model representation. The FFNN predictors have the following features [4]:

(1) Can model complex time series;
(2) Dynamic structure and parameter learning;
(3) Learning speed is fast;
(4) Generalization and computational efficiency is high.

Time Delay neural network and Nonlinear autoregressive with exogenous output are well-known RNN dynamic neural network used in time series prediction are explained in next subsections.

5.1 Time Delay Neural Network (TDNN)

A common approach for time series analysis is to use feed forward neural network (FFNN) trained with conventional back propagation. FFNNs responds a given input regardless of past values. Traditional back propagation algorithm needs error gradient, has slow convergence, can stick in local minima and hence fails to respond efficiently.

Back propagation is free from time series and for the dynamic network it should have memory. The memory can be included using dynamic models in terms of tap or time delays. A target movement can be considered as time varying random process. Figure 3 shows basic building block of Time delay neural network.

The previous p states are related and important for the next state of a target (x_n) as shown in Fig. 3. Neural network is provided with delayed inputs time series and each of them are connected with hidden layer neuron. Time delay neural networks (TDNN) are FFNNs with delayed input. TDNN tries to learn relationship between delayed input samples and current samples.

Algorithm: TDNN for Target Tracking

Assume $x_1(n)$ to $x_l(n)$ are inputs of network. $\mathbf{W}$ is representing weight matrix of delay time. P represent time delay. The output of neuron is $y_1(n)$ given as below.

$$
\begin{aligned}
y_1(n) = {} & w_{10}x_1(n) + w_{11}x_1(n-1) + w_{12}x_1(n-2) + \ldots + w_{1p}x_1(n-p) + w_{l0}x_l(n) \\
& + w_{l1}x_l(n-1) + w_{l2}x_l(n-2) + \ldots + w_{lp}x_l(n-p)
\end{aligned}
$$

$$(12)$$

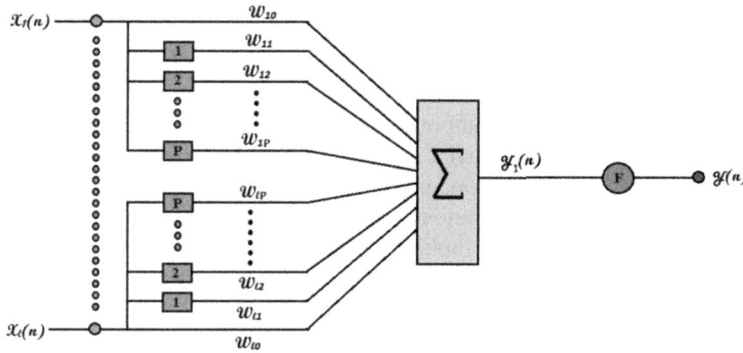

Fig. 3. Basic time delay neural network architecture

Equation (12) includes delay as P is connected to the hidden network. Here l indicates number of inputs and according to that inputs we get l *number* of weight delays denoted here as w_{10} to w_{l0}. Generalized equation can be written as Eq. (13).

$$y_1(n) = \sum_{i=1}^{l} \sum_{j=0}^{p} w_{ij} x_i(n - j) \tag{13}$$

The activation function used for neural network can be a Sigmoidal or Tansig function. The sigmoidal function is given by the following Eq. (14).

$$f = \frac{1}{1 + e^{-\lambda[y_1(n)]}} \tag{14}$$

With the help of activation function, output of neural network can be derived using Eq. (15).

$$y(n) = F(y_1(n)) \tag{15}$$

Implementation steps of TDNN can be summarized as follows:

Step 1: *Define target state dimensions and create a Time delay neural network.*
Step 2: *Initialize network with input delays and weights.*
Step 3: *Divide data for training, testing, and validation*
Step 4: *Train the network with training data.*
Step 5: *Test the network using testing data set.*
Step 6: *Compute the Mean Square Error.*
Step 7: *Perform till the goal is achieved (Go to Step 2).*

5.2   Non-linear Autoregressive Network with Exogenous Input (NARX)

Recurrent neural networks (RNN) are used in similar applications as TDNNs but have the advantage that the neurons send feedback signals to each other giving it a short-term memory. Nonlinear autoregressive with exogenous output (NARX) are examples of RNNs with time delayed input. NARX models are typically more robust and can be trained by Backpropagation Through Time (BPTT). The nonlinear autoregressive network with exogenous inputs (NARX) is an imitating network, with feedback connections connecting multiple layers of the network.

Algorithm: NARX for Target Tracking
NARX model and TDNN network differ in terms of network types. NARX has closed loop structure. As shown in Fig. 4, ℓ indicate a number of inputs to network, P is a number of delays which is fed into the hidden layer.

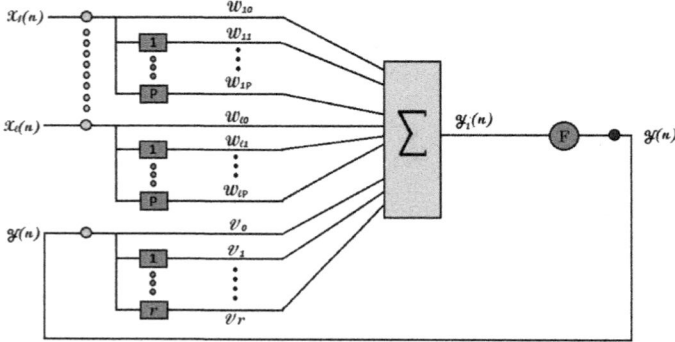

Fig. 4. Architecture of NARX neural network

As shown in NARX architecture, the next stage output also depends on the previous value of network's output. The output of hidden layer neuron is given by Eq. (16).

$$
\begin{aligned}
y_1(n) = {} & w_{10}x_1(n) + w_{11}x_1(n-1) + w_{12}x_1(n-2) + \ldots w_{1p}x_1(n-p) + w_{l0}x_l(n) \\
& + w_{l1}x_l(n-1) + w_{l2}x_l(n-2) + \cdots + w_{lp}x_l(n-p) + v_1 y(n-1) \\
& + v_2 y(n-2) + \cdots + v_r y(n-r)
\end{aligned}
$$

$$(16)$$

As in above Eq. (16), W_{ij} and V_r are the weights of input layer and feedback of output layer respectively. Output of output layer neuron is calculated with the help of present and past values of input and past values of output of network. Past values of input are carried out as $x(n)$ to $x(n-l)$ and the output value of network which is fed back as $y(n-1)$ to $y(n-r)$. where r denoted as number of delay at output side. Generalized equation can be written as Eq. (17).

$$y_1(n) = \sum_{i=1}^{l} \sum_{j=0}^{p} w_{ij} x_i(n-j) + \sum_{k=1}^{r} v_k y(n-k) \qquad (17)$$

From the activation function (F), final output of network $y(n)$ can be carried out using output of output neurons.

$$y(n) = F((y_1(n))) \qquad (18)$$

Implementation steps of NARX can be summarized as follows:

Step 1: Define target state dimensions and create an NARX neural network.
Step 2: Initialize network with input delays, output delays, and weights.
Step 3: Divide data for training, testing, and validation
Step 4: Train the network with training data.
Step 5: Test the network using testing data set.
Step 6: Compute the Mean Square Error.
Step 7: Perform till the goal is achieved (Go to Step 2).

6 Simulation Results

MATLAB 2014a is used to simulate and compare approaches Kalman filter, TDNN, and NARX. Different trajectories are used to find the accuracy algorithm i.e.: the ability to track an object by prediction.

6.1 Simulation Environment

In order to mimic actual environmental conditions, the creation of 2D environment plays an important role. In this simulation, the area of 100 m × 100 m is assumed in which sensor nodes are placed in particular positions and identified as fixed nodes in a 2D environment. A single moving target is assumed with a minimum velocity of 0.01 m/sec and maximum velocity of 0.3 m/sec. For target movement, different test paths including linearity, nonlinearity are generated in MATLAB to mimic real world examples like highway type, steep path, etc.

6.2 Implementation Using Kalman Approach

Kalman-based approach predicts next location using state variables position (x, y) and velocity (v_x, v_y) of a target. For simulation, Kalman approach with constant velocity model is taken. Process noise matrix is $10^{-5} * diag[0.5, 1, 0.5, 1]$. Measurement noise variance is 0.2. For target trajectory path-2, the output of Kalman filter is shown in Fig. 6.

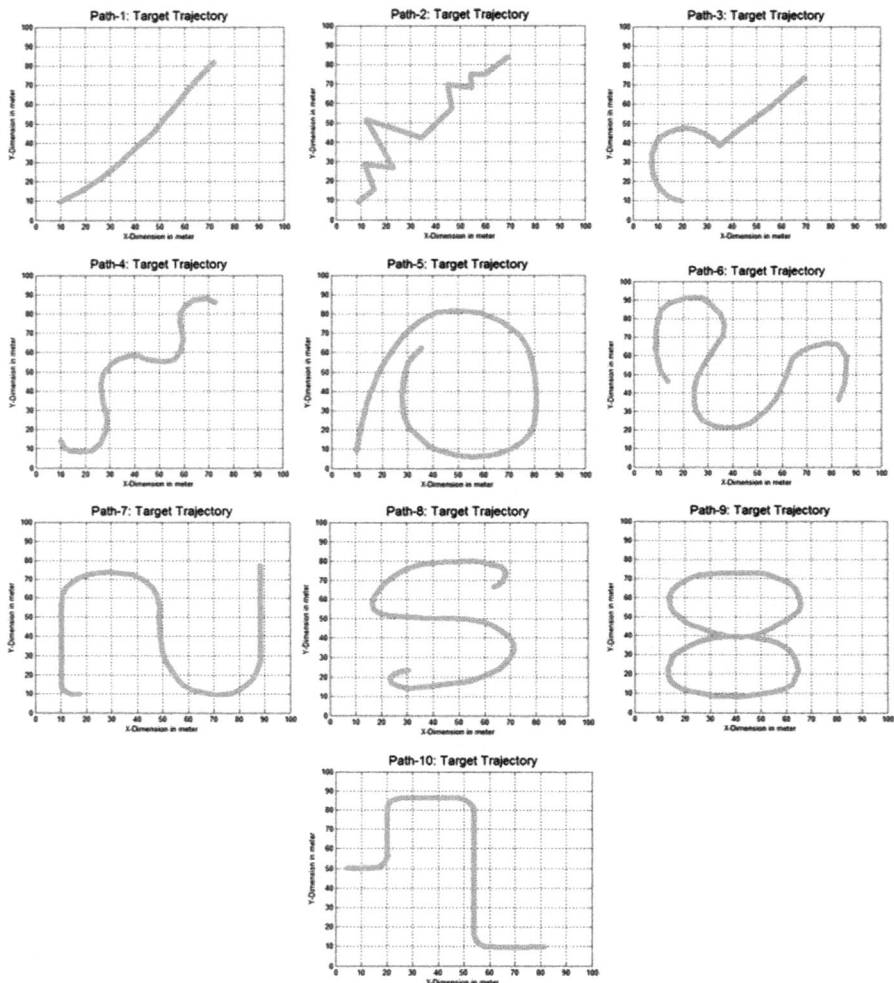

Fig. 5. Different target trajectories used in simulation

In Fig. 6(a) line (magenta) displays desired path and a blue dot shows the current position of a vehicle. While Fig. 6(b) shows, the path already traveled by an object on a specific trajectory with Kalman based predictor. It is worth to note that that path shows as a reference to track accuracy but it is not known to the vehicle in real scenarios. Figure 7 shows the path to be tracked and a journeyed path by an object with Kalman estimator under different tracks.

It can be observed from the Figs. 7, that Kalman filter is able to track an object efficiently in case of linear motion of a target, but fails when nonlinear motion is followed by a vehicle that is because of state transition matrix. The constant velocity state transition matrix fails in case of motion with acceleration, that is obvious.

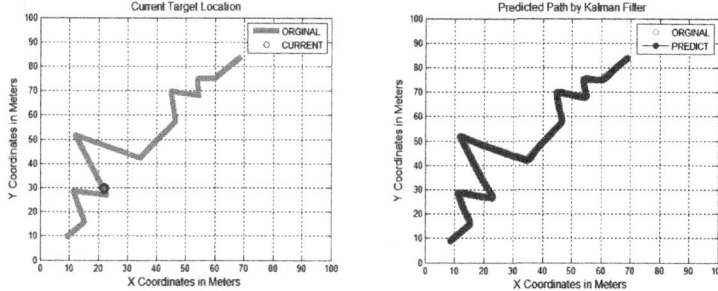

Fig. 6. (a) Current location of a target (b) Predicted track by Kalman filter in case of Path-2. (Color figure online)

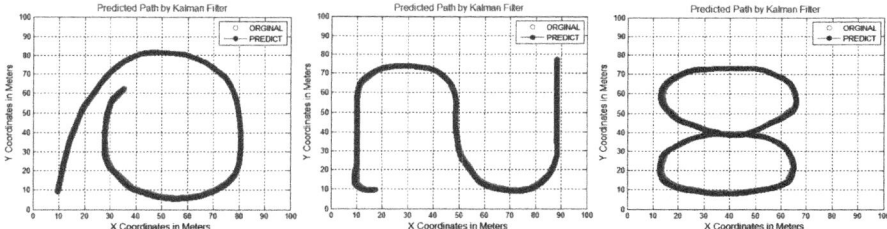

Fig. 7. Predicted track by Kalman filter in case of (a) Path-5 (b) Path-7 (c) Path-9.

6.3 Implementation of Time Delay Neural Network (TDNN)

TDNN is used to estimate next position of a moving vehicle. The prediction accuracy is tested for many different trajectories. Time delay neural network is trained for all values of velocity and acceleration with two hidden layer neurons. Figure 8 shows the TDNN architecture in which two tap/delays are available at input layer. Based on past two positions, TDNN will predict the next location of a vehicle. Because of simple architecture, it can save computational power of sensor mote.

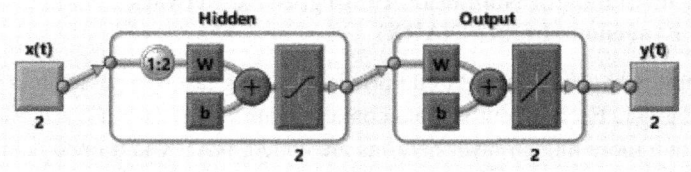

Fig. 8. TDNN neural network with two delays at input layer

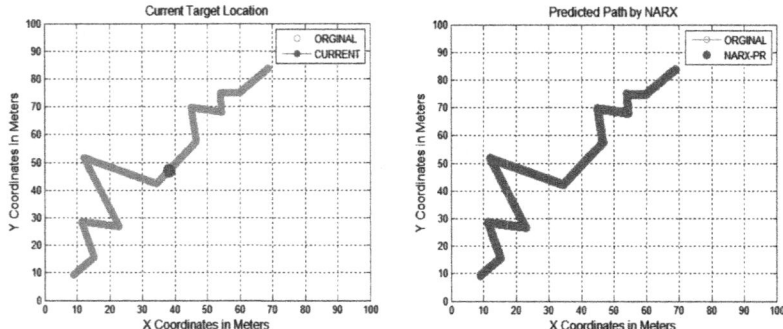

Fig. 9. (a) Current location of a target (b) Predicted track by TDNN in case of Path-2

Figure 9 shows the combined path including lines and triangles. Figure 9(a) shows the original targeted path for a mobile vehicle. The blue dot is representing the movement of the vehicle on the track.

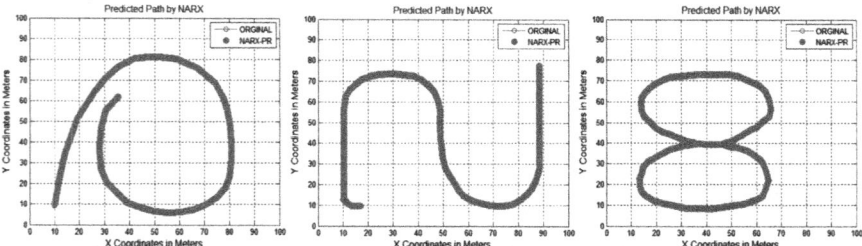

Fig. 10. Predicted track by TDNN approach in case of (a) Path-5 (b) Path-7 (c) Path-9

Similarly, one can see and analyze the performance of TDNN under a different environment in Figs. 10, that endorses ability of TDNN for target tracking. TDNN based approach is able to track moving target even in the case of maneuverer.

6.4   Implementation of Nonlinear Autoregressive Network with Exogenous Inputs (NARX)

NARX neural network is trained to do prediction using last two past output samples as shown in Fig. 11. Each output sample contains four values $[x, y, v_x, v_y]$. As compared to TDNN, two more hidden layer neurons are added. NARX is trained using the same training data set that was used in case of TDNN neural network.

In Fig. 12(a) line (magenta) is target path on which the object will be tracked and the red dot shows object movement. Figure 12(b) show the tracked path with NARX predictor. Other complex paths are created and have been examined by NARX model. Nearer to a circular path, numeric '8' typed path, alphabetic 'N' typed paths are tested.

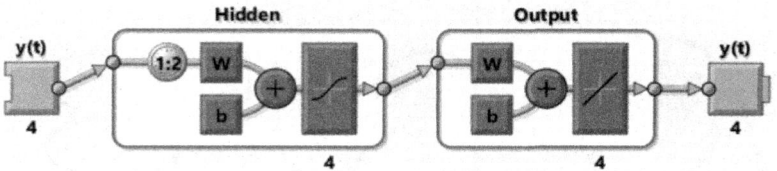

Fig. 11. The architecture of NARX neural network with a delay of 2 at the output layer.

The actual path to which target need to be traveled and this actual traced path are obtained here in Fig. 13(a), (b) and (c). As a result of NARX estimation technique, tracked paths look like an original path. It can be seen from traced path that NARX based approach follows the original path with almost zero error in case of maneuverer and non-maneuverer. It can be seen that NARX based approach is able to track an object very beautifully even in the case of turn and abrupt change in velocity at different locations as shown in Fig. 12. As compared to TDNN, NARX gives good results because of output feedback available in NARX which tries to reduces error in prediction.

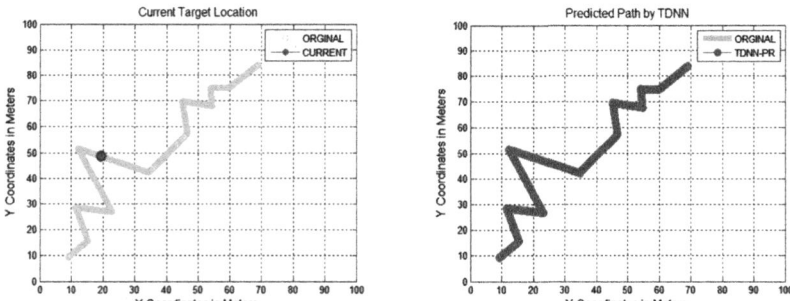

Fig. 12. (a) Current location of a target (b) Predicted track by NARX in case of Path-2 (Color figure online)

6.5   Comparison of Kalman, TDNN and NARX

To find accuracy, the average mean square error is used as a performance measure. The Prediction accuracy (average mean square error) of an algorithm can be calculated using Eq. (19).

$$MSE_{app} = \frac{1}{n} \sum_{i=0}^{n} \sqrt{\left(X_i - X_{app}\right)^2 + \left(Y_i - Y_{app}\right)^2} \tag{19}$$

Where, X_i and Y_i are actual data from trajectory. X_{app} and Y_{app} are predicted data by each approach. Approaches used are Kalman Filter, TDNN and NARX.

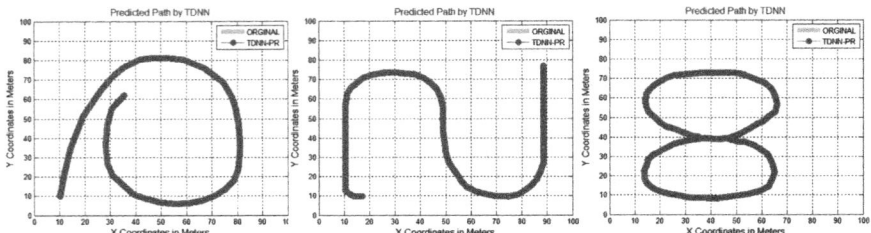

Fig. 13. Predicted track by NARX approach in case of (a) Path-5 (b) Path-7 (c) Path-9

Figures (14), (15) and (16) shows a comparison of Kalman, TDNN and NARX plots of error at each sample point for different paths. It is clear from the results that Kalman approach is not able to prediction accurately whenever nonlinearity is encountered. TDNN approach shows moderate accuracy. The accuracy of TDNN is very good as compared to Kalman approach. It shows that error value in the acceptable range and the average of these values is closer to zero but far from the value expressed in NARX model. NARX gives the best response with respect to Kalman and TDNN estimators. The average MSE value is nearly about to zero which means that final output is an almost replica of the input path.

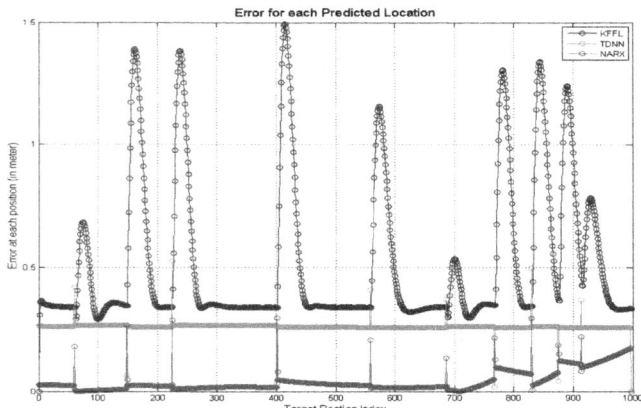

Fig. 14. Error plot of KF filter, TDNN and NARX neural network for Path-5

The Table 1 summarizes MSE values of approaches under different target trajectories. All these three different approaches, Kalman, TDNN, and NARX are examined for ten different tracks, which are linear, nonlinear or complex in nature. For all these paths, the average mean square value of Kalman filtering is comparatively high. TDNN outperforms Kalman filter and error overshoot is also less. The least value is expressed by NARX model at the cost of little bit more computation. TDNN uses two hidden layer neurons while NARX uses four hidden layer neurons. TDNN technique gives

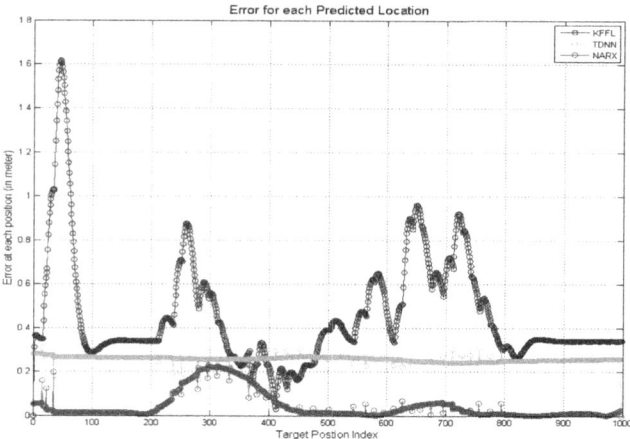

Fig. 15. Error plot of KF filter, TDNN and NARX neural network for Path-7

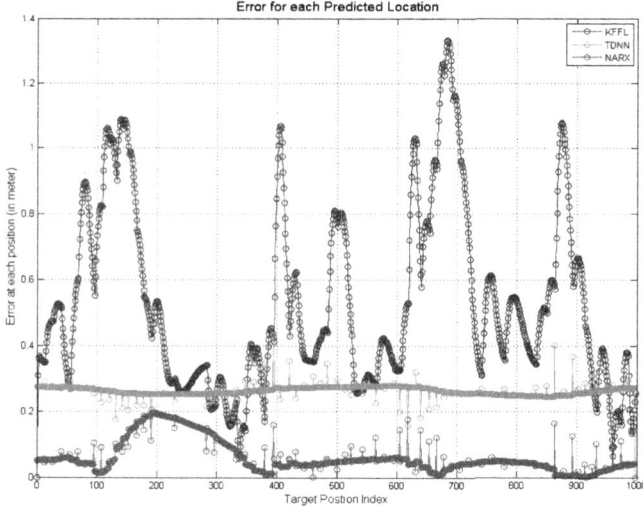

Fig. 16. Error plot of KF filter, TDNN and NARX neural network for Path-9

weakened values in accordance with NARX strategy. The performance of prediction algorithm totally depends on state transition matrix. Kalman filter is not able to resemble maneuvering target motion as it default uses constant velocity model. Selection of state transition matrix is also crucial as target motion is never known in advance. TDNN and NARX are state transition matrix free methods which give good results as compared to Kalman filter.

Table 1. Performance of KF, TDNN, and NARX under different Trajectories in terms of RMSE

Track	Average mean square error (in meter)		
	Kalman	TDNN	NARX
Path 1	0.34089	0.21014	0.0219
Path 2	0.52573	0.24224	0.0402
Path 3	0.37349	0.22851	0.0167
Path 4	0.39287	0.23021	0.0509
Path 5	0.41939	0.20998	0.0618
Path 6	0.48756	0.24881	0.0381
Path 7	0.45862	0.14202	0.0780
Path 8	0.46306	0.13883	0.0728
Path 9	0.53384	0.14290	0.0692
Path 10	0.40302	0.13968	0.0357

7 Conclusion

Computer vision applications like vehicle navigation, surveillance, etc. in which selection of tracking method plays a crucial role. This research was aimed to investigate target tracking for moving objects like non-cooperative - enemy vehicle. Current literature survey enabled us to implement target tracking using Kalman filter and dynamic neural network based methods. All methods are efficient enough to solve the issue of tracking a moving target. In Kalman Filter, tracking error increases with the increase of nonlinearly in the movement. TDNN outperforms Kalman filter. This is due to the ability of TDNN to incorporate nonlinearity which is not available in traditional Kalman filter. NARX model gives better results than both Kalman and TDNN approaches in terms of accuracy due to close loop structure that governs the smoothness in the controlled output. A reason for the significant improvement in accuracy for NARX model compared to TDNN is due to recursive nature of the architecture. That enables NARX model to remember not only past inputs but also past output as well. For real time operations, one may consider the trade-off between computation time vs. tracking accuracy. Adaptive time delay neural network and adaptive NARX model are still scopes of research in target tracking applications.

References

1. Wang, L., Xiao, Y.: A survey of energy-efficient scheduling mechanisms in sensor networks. Mob. Netw. Appl. **11**, 723–740 (2006)
2. Unterassinger, H., et al.: A power management unit for ultra-low power wireless sensor networks. In: IEEE Africon, pp. 1–6 (2011)
3. Sinha, A., Chandrakasan, A.: Dynamic power management in wireless sensor networks. IEEE Des. Test Comput. **18**, 62–74 (2011)

4. Haykin, S.: Neural Networks: A Comprehensive Foundation, 2nd edn. Pearson Education, Canada (2005)
5. Lang, K.J., Waibel, A.H.: A time-delay neural network architecture for isolated word recognition. Neural Netw. **3**(1), 23–43 (1990)
6. Lin, D.T., et al.: Trajectory production with the adaptive time-delay neural network. Neural Netw. **8**(3), 447–461 (1993)
7. Diaconescu, E.: The use of NARX neural networks to predict chaotic time series. WSEAS Trans. Comput. Res. **3**(3), 182–191 (2008)
8. Menezes Jr., J.M., Barreto, G.A.: Long-term time series prediction with the NARX network: an empirical evaluation. Neurocoumputing **71**(16), 3335–3343 (2008)
9. Demigha, O., et al.: On energy efficiency in collaborative target tracking in wireless sensor network: a review. IEEE Commun. Surv. Tutor. **15**(3), 1210–1222 (2013)
10. Li, X.R., Jilkov, V.P.: Survey of maneuvering target tracking: dynamic models. In: Proceedings of SPIE Conference on Signal and Data Processing of Small Targets, vol. 39, no. 4, pp. 212–235 (2000)
11. Wan, E.A., Van Der Merwe, R.: The unscented Kalman filter for nonlinear estimation. In: Proceedings of the IEEE Adaptive Systems for Signal Processing, Communications, and Control Symposium, pp. 153–158 (2000)
12. Chan, Y.T., Hu, A.G.C., Plant, J.B.: A Kalman filter based tracking scheme with input estimation. IEEE Trans. Aerosp. Electron. Syst. AES **15**(2), 237–244 (1979)
13. Singer, R.: Estimating optimal tracking filter performance for manned maneuvering targets. IEEE Trans. Aerosp. Electron. Syst. **6**(4), 473–483 (1970)
14. Bogler, P.L.: Tracking a maneuvering target using input estimation. IEEE Trans. Aerosp. Electron. Syst. **25**(2), 298–310 (1987)
15. Whang, I.H., et al.: A modified input estimation technique using pseudoresiduals. IEEE Trans. Aerosp. Electron. Syst. **30**(2), 591–598 (1994)
16. Bar-Shalom, Y., Chang, K.C., Blom, H.A.P.: Tracking a maneuvering target using input estimation versus the interacting multiple model algorithm. IEEE Trans. Aerosp. Electron. Syst. **25**(2), 196–300 (1989)
17. Owen, M.W., Stubberrud, A.R.: A neural extended Kalman filter multiple model tracker. In: Proceeding of OCEANS, pp. 2111–2119 (2003)
18. Hu, X., et al.: Generalised Kalman filter tracking with multiplicative measurement noise in a wireless sensor network. IET Sig. Process. **8**(5), 467–474 (2014)
19. Wang, L., Xiao, Y.: A survey of energy-efficient scheduling mechanisms in sensor networks. Mob. Netw. Appl. **11**, 723–740 (2006)
20. Oka, A., Lampe, L.: Distributed target tracking using signal strength measurements by a wireless sensor network. IEEE J. Sel. Areas Commun. **28**(7), 1006–1015 (2010)
21. Munjani, J.H., Joshi, M.: Target tracking in WSN using Time Delay neural network. In: IEEE Region 10 Conference TENCON, pp. 3839–3845 (2016)

Color Image Segmentation of Disease Infected Plant Images Captured in an Uncontrolled Environment

Toran Verma[1]([✉]) [iD], Sipi Dubey[1] [iD], and Hiteshwari Sabrol[2] [iD]

[1] Rungta College of Engineering and Technology, CSVTU,
Bhilai 490024, CG, India
vermatoran24@gmail.com, dr.sipi.dubey@rungta.ac.in
[2] DAV University, Jalandhar 144012, Punjab, India
hiteshwarisabrol@gmail.com

Abstract. In the field of an automated vision system for integrated disease control in plants, accurate identification of plant diseases is very important. The symptoms of the occurrences of diseases appear in different parts of the plant. The analysis of segmented images of infected parts in plant images helps to take curative and/or corrective measures for the diseases. In this paper, we present a threshold-based segmentation using RGB-L*a*b* hybrid color space features to segment the plant diseases from the digitally acquired images. In this proposed method, without interfering with spatial features of the color image, the quantization and binarization had been done in L*a*b* color space image and it applied to RGB color image for the segmentation of the image. Initially, the acquired RGB color images had been transformed into L*a*b* color images. Then multilevel threshold had been applied on the a* component of L*a*b* image. On the basis of threshold value a*, components of a* had been quantized, and equivalent binary matrices had been created. These binary matrices had been applied individually to the R, G, and B components of RGB images separately and concatenated to perform color image segmentation of infected part of the disease in the plant image. Our calculation gives the prominent result to segment diseased part of the plant images captured in an uncontrolled environment.

Keywords: Plant image · Color transformation · Multilevel threshold
Segmentation

1 Introduction

Integrated Plant Disease Management (IPDM) is a composite of Integrated Disease Management (IDM) and Integrated Crop Management (ICM). It is a hybrid structure of man, machine, and material. The advancement of technologies helps to automate many parts of the IPDM. It includes creating a database about diseases symptoms, automatic identification of the diseases by image processing and machine vision, giving options for protective and curative measures. The diseased plant's performance to produce or survive is compromised. The overall aim of IPDM is to improve quality and quantity of the yield. The image processing and computer vision play very important role to realize

© Springer Nature Singapore Pte Ltd. 2018
P. Bhattacharyya et al. (Eds.): NGCT 2017, CCIS 828, pp. 790–804, 2018.
https://doi.org/10.1007/978-981-10-8660-1_59

these goals by accurate quantification and identification of the diseases in plants. Plant disease is a dynamic process induced by an incitant that disturbs the energy utilizing the system in plants. According to the types of diseases, the symptoms (visual observation) of plant diseases appear in plant's Leaf, branch, twigs, trunk, root, and stump [1, 2].

It is estimated that the total intensity range over which the human visual system can sense colors is around 10^8:1. While the cones themselves respond only over 1000:1 intensity range [3]. The digital color input device captures the images in the controlled/ uncontrolled environment for further processing. Scanners and digital camera are two main type of image capturing device. Scanner capture reflected light through a medium and digital camera directly capture light from a scene by using a set of color filters, sensed by an array of charge-coupled devices (CCDs). Digital still cameras (DSCs) is a common source for digital imagery under an uncontrolled and varying condition which has in-built image processing algorithm to control and correct flare, exposure, color balance, etc. [4]. The color imaging systems use some form of color management which is a way to predict, control, and adjust color information from capturing to displaying of the image. The dedicated software handles this entire process. The digital color encoding has been done for a digital representation of colors in an image [5]. The color encoder is defined with the help of various device dependent or device independent color models. Some of the device-dependent color models are NTSC, YCbCr, HSV, CMY, CMYK, and HSI. The most widely used device-independent tristimulus color models are CIE XYZ, CIE xyY, L*u*v*, L*a*b* and sRGB [6].

After capturing the images by CCD camera, images are transformed according to chosen/supported a color model of the capturing device and stored in the compressed format to save bandwidth, memory, and disk space. The most common color image compression format is JPEG. During color image processing, the image of plants is captured by CCD camera in machine-dependent color model RGB and stored in JPEG compressed format. This image has been preprocessed to enhance the quality of image and segmented to find the region of interest. This segmented part is further analyzed by various machine learning process. Entire image processing has been done in decompressed JPEG images. Before processing of the image, it decompressed into the captured color model.

In image processing, both inputs and outputs are images or input is an image but outputs are extracted color, shape or texture features extracted from images. These extracted features are further used to analyze/design model based on specific application. The region of interest has been extracted from any input images in the segmentation process. It subdivides the image into its constituent regions. The computerized analysis mainly depends upon the successful segmentation of images.

The researchers are mainly focusing on two fields of image processing; first, improve the efficiency of various image processing algorithm [7, 8] and enhance the application area in a variety of discipline and fields. Image processing techniques are used to solve problems in a wide variety of disciplines and fields of science and technology, with applications such as 2D/3D image [9] and video processing, Photoshop [10], medical image processing for diagnosis [11, 12], character/pattern recognition [13], satellite image processing, robotics, integrated disease control management, quality control/inspection in industrial production, object detection [14] etc.

Today image processing and machine learning techniques are used in plant management and precision farming. Various digital devices are used to captures images of crop/plant from the field, analyze the pictures and make the appropriate decision. The image analysis is performed after preprocessing and segmentation of images. The Pre-processing step involves original captured image to select a region of interest, enhance contrast and/or noise filtering. The image segmentation in plants can be implemented for a different application. It can help to identify the plant as crop or weed, diseases on the crop, analysing disease affected area in the plant etc. Effective action based on plant management and/or precision farming is mainly based on segmented image features.

The segmentation stage involves the segmentation of plant against the background or fore-ground images according to various methods such as color indexed segmentation, threshold based segmentation and learning-based segmentation [15]. In color indexed segmentation, color is used to discriminate plants from background clutter in computer vision or foreground images are divided into multiple segments. Several researchers have used color to separate plant from soil to estimate leaf area [16, 17, 18]. In threshold technique, pixel intensity ranges are manually/automatically defined to categorize image pixels and accordingly segmentation is performed. Thus, numerous researchers have applied different threshold technique to address these problems. The threshold of histogram entropy used for segmentation [19]. Otsu's method is a threshold technique widely used in many applications of image processing based-segmentation. Otsu's method demonstrated the higher segmentation accuracy as a comparison to many other methods. Otsu's method was applied to separate the plant vegetation from the background [20]. The RGB images had been converted into a grayscale image which further processed to derive binary images according to homogeneity threshold [21]. The automatic threshold value is chosen by combined R and G pixel values, to differentiate soil and vegetation. Another threshold technique had been applied to automatically segment plant pixels from soil pixels based on the transformed RGB image (nearly grayscale image) [22]. Several machine learning techniques with color transformation had been used to improve the segmentation under varying illumination conditions. The fuzzy clustering approach [23], Environmentally Adaptive Segmentation Algorithm (EASA) with hue saturation [24] had been used to produce robust and fast plant image segmentation under complex field conditions. The Support Vector Machine [25], Back Propagation Neural Network [26] had been used for classification.

2 Materials and Methods

Many diseases infected color images of rice, tomato and brinjal plant in JPEG (JPG) format with a size of 5152 × 3864 had been captured from the field by digital camera SONY/DSC-H300 in an uncontrolled environment. In a pre-processing step, the image had been cropped and resized at 205 × 410 and manually selected images which carry disease infected region in each category. These collected images had been forwarded for segmentation. The captured JPEG images had been decompressed in RGB color model. RGB color transformed images had been transformed into L*a*b* color model. The global thresholding technique had been applied in a* components of L*a*b* color images. Accordingly, three binary matrices had been created. This binary matrix had been used to create color image segmentation to access the disease infected part of the image. Algorithm 2.1 presents the steps to required for color transformation from RGB to L*a*b*. Algorithm 2.2 give approaches used to find two optimized global thresholds using Otsu's method and Algorithm 2.3 explain the steps needed for binarization and segmentation of the images of the RGB images.

Algorithm 2.1: RGB to $L*a*b*$ color space conversion of image
Input: RGB linear matrix, Chromaticity coordinates of an RGB system (x_r, y_r), (x_g, y_g) and (x_b, y_b) and its reference white (X_W, Y_W, Z_W).
Output: $L*a*b*$ transformed matrix
Pseudo Code
  i. Evaluate following intermediate result
$X_r = x_r/y_r, X_g = x_g/y_g, X_b = x_b/y_b$
$Y_r = Y_g = Y_b = 1$
$Z_r = (1 - x_r - y_r)/y_r, Z_g = (1 - x_g - y_g)/y_g, Z_b = (1 - x_b - y_b)/y_b$

$$\begin{bmatrix} S_r \\ S_g \\ S_b \end{bmatrix} = \begin{bmatrix} X_r & X_g & X_b \\ 1 & 1 & 1 \\ Z_r & Z_g & Z_b \end{bmatrix}^{-1} \begin{bmatrix} X_W \\ Y_W \\ Z_W \end{bmatrix}$$

  ii. Find transformational matrix

$$M = \begin{bmatrix} S_r X_r & S_g X_g & S_b X_b \\ S_r & S_g & S_b \\ S_r Z_r & S_g Z_g & S_b Z_b \end{bmatrix}$$

  iii. If the RGB values are in the nominal range [0.0, 1.0] then go to (iv) else normalize RGB by dividing each component with 255, then go to (iv).
  iv. Evaluate XYZ color space transformation from RGB color space

$$\begin{bmatrix} X \\ Y \\ Z \end{bmatrix} = [M] \begin{bmatrix} R \\ G \\ B \end{bmatrix}$$

  v. Transform XYZ color space to $L*a*b*$ color space
$x_1 = \dfrac{Y}{Y_W}, x_2 = \dfrac{X}{X_W}, x_3 = \dfrac{Z}{Z_W}$

$if\ x_1 > 0.008856$
$f_1 = \sqrt[3]{x_1}$
$else\ \ f_1 = 7.787 x_1 + \dfrac{16}{116}$

$$if\ x_2 > 0.008856$$
$$f_2 = \sqrt[3]{x_2}$$

$$else\ f_2 = 7.787x_2 + \frac{16}{116}$$
$$if\ x_3 > 0.008856$$
$$f_3 = \sqrt[3]{x_3}$$

$$else\ f_3 = 7.787x_3 + \frac{16}{116}$$
$$L^* = 116f_1 - 16$$
$$a^* = 500(f_2 - f_1)$$
$$b^* = 200(f_1 - f_3)$$

Algorithm 2.2: Optimal threshold calculation k_1^* and k_2^*

Input: a^* component of $L^*a^*b^*$ color features with intensity level $I = [0, 1, ..., L - 1]$

Output: Optimal threshold value k_1^* and k_2^*

Pseudo Code

i. Calculate histogram of the each intensity values as

$$P_I = \frac{n_I}{n} \qquad I = [0,1,2,...,L-1]$$

Where n is the total number of pixels in the image, n_q is the number of pixels that has intensity level q and L is the total number of possible intensity levels in the image.

So

Intensity level: $I = [0, 1, ..., k_1, k_1 + 1, ..., k_2, k_2 + 1, ..., L - 1]$
Histogram: $P = P_I = [P_1, P_2, ..., P_{k_1}, P_{k_1+1}, ..., P_{k_2}, P_{k_2+1}, ..., P_{L-1}]$

ii. Repeat (iii) to (viii) for all combination n of threshold value $[k_1^i, k_2^i]$
where $k_1^i = \{0,1 ..., L - 1\}$, $k_2^i = \{0,1 ..., L - 1\}$,
$i = \{1 ..., n\}$ and $k_1^i < k_2^i$ to calculate between-class variance $\sigma_B^2(k)$
where $\sigma_B^2(k) = \{\sigma_1^2(k), \sigma_2^2(k), ..., \sigma_i^2(k), \sigma_{i+1}^2(k), ..., \sigma_n^2(k)\}$.

a. Find maximum of between-class variance σ_{Bmax}^2 where
$\sigma_{Bmax}^2(k) = maxof(\sigma_B^2(k)) =$
$maxof\{\sigma_1^2(k), \sigma_2^2(k), ..., \sigma_n^2(k)\} = \sigma_i^2(k)$ where $1 \le i \le n$.

b. Otsu's optimum threshold value will be ith combination of $[k_1^i, k_2^i]$.
Hence $[k_1^*, k_2^*] = [k_1^i, k_2^i]$

Exit

iii. Choose two threshold $[k_1^i, k_2^i]$ such that G_1 is the set of pixels with levels $[0,1,2, ..., k_1^i]$, G_2 is the set of pixels with levels $[k_1^i + 1, k_1^i +$

$2, ..., k_2^i]$ and G_3 is the set of pixels with levels $[k_2^i + 1, k_2^i + 2, ..., L - 1]$.

iv. Calculate $P_1(k)$ as the probability of occurring of G_1, $P_2(k)$ as the probability of occurring of G_2, and $P_3(k)$ as the probability of occurring of G_3 where

$$P_1(k) = \sum_{j=0}^{k_1^i} p_j$$

$$P_2(k) = \sum_{j=k_1^i+1}^{k_2^i} p_j$$

$$P_3(k) = \sum_{j=k_2^i+1}^{L-1} p_j$$

v. Calculate $m_1(k)$, $m_2(k)$, and $m_3(k)$ as the mean intensities of the pixels in sets G_1, G_2 and G_3 where

$$m_1(k) = \sum_{j=0}^{k_1^i} jp_j$$

$$m_2(k) = \sum_{j=k_1^i+1}^{k_2^i} jp_j$$

$$m_3(k) = \sum_{j=k_2^i+1}^{L-1} jp_i$$

vi. Calculate the global mean m_G (the mean intensity of the entire image) where

$$m_G = \sum_{j=0}^{L-1} jp_j$$

vii. Evaluate between-class variance $\sigma_{G_1 G_2}^2(k)$ between (G_1, G_2) and between-class variance $\sigma_{G_2 G_3}^2(k)$ between (G_2, G_3) where

$$\sigma_{G_1 G_2}^2(k) = P_1(k)[m_1(k) - m_G]^2 + P_2(k)[m_2(k) - m_G]^2$$
$$\sigma_{G_2 G_3}^2(k) = P_2(k)[m_2(k) - m_G]^2 + P_3(k)[m_3(k) - m_G]^2$$

viii. Evaluate total between-class variance $\sigma_i^2(k)$ where
$$\sigma_i^2(k) = \sigma_{G_1 G_2}^2(k) + \sigma_{G_2 G_3}^2(k)$$

Algorithm 2.3: Quantization, binarization and color image segmentation of RGB images

Input: RGB image, components of *Lab*(or L*a*b*) transformed image and multi-level threshold value $[T_1, T_2]$ where $T_1 < T_2$

Output: Three segmented images Seg_1, Seg_2 and Seg_3 for each RGB image

Pseudo Code

i.   Find size of *a*

$$[m_1, n_1] = sizeof(a)$$

ii. Create quantized matrix for *a* with three label values $\in \{l_1, l_2, l_3\}$

$$for\ i = 1\ to\ m_1\ do$$
$$for\ j = 1\ to\ n_1\ do$$
$$if\ a(i,j) \leq T_1$$
$$a_{Quantize}(i,j) = l_1$$
$$if\ a(i,j) > T_1\ and\ a(i,j) \leq T_2$$
$$a_{Quantize}(i,j) = l_2$$
$$if\ a(i,j) > T_2$$
$$a_{Quantize}(i,j) = l_3$$
$$end\ of\ n_1\ for\ loop$$
$$end\ of\ m_1\ for\ loop$$

iii. Create **3** binary matrices according to quantized matrix $a_{Quantize}$ with 3 label values $\in \{l_1, l_2, l_3\}$

a.   Find the size of $a_{Quantize}$ matrix

$$[m_1, n_1] = sizeof(a_{Quantize})$$

b.   Initialize three binary matrices $Bin_1, Bin_2,$ and Bin_3 with zeros of size $m_1 \times n_1$

$$Bin_1 = zeros(m_1, n_1)$$
$$Bin_2 = zeros(m_1, n_1)$$
$$Bin_3 = zeros(m_1, n_1)$$

c.   Creation of binary matrices

$$for\ i = 1\ to\ m_1\ do$$
$$for\ j = 1\ to\ n_1\ do$$
$$if(\ a_{Quantize}(i,j) == l_1)$$
$$Bin_1(i,j) = 1$$
$$elseif(\ a_{Quantize}(i,j) == l_2)$$
$$Bin_2(i,j) = 1$$
$$elseif(\ a_{Quantize}(i,j) == l_3)$$
$$Bin_3(i,j) = 1$$
$$end\ of\ n_1\ for\ loop$$
$$end\ of\ m_1\ for\ loop$$

iv. Color image segmentation of JPEG image in RGB format to create 3 segmented images for each RGB image

a. RGB= Read input JPEG image (imagename.jpeg)

b. Separate red component R, green component G, and blue component B from RGB

$$R = \text{RGB}(:,:,1)$$
$$G = \text{RGB}(:,:,2)$$
$$B = \text{RGB}(:,:,3)$$

c. Create 3 segments Seg_1, Seg_2 and Seg_3 of image

$$R_a = multiply(Bin_1, R)$$
$$R_b = multiply(Bin_2, R)$$
$$R_c = multiply(Bin_3, R)$$
$$G_a = multiply(Bin_1, G)$$
$$G_b = multiply(Bin_2, G)$$
$$G_c = multiply(Bin_3, G)$$
$$B_a = multiply(Bin_1, B)$$
$$B_b = multiply(Bin_2, B)$$
$$B_c = multiply(Bin_3, B)$$

$$Seg_1 = concatenate(R_a, G_a, B_a)$$
$$Seg_2 = concatenate(R_b, G_b, B_b)$$
$$Seg_3 = concatenate(R_c, G_c, B_c)$$

3 Results and Discussion

For this research work, total 5 categories of the rice disease infected plant, 4 categories of tomato and 4 categories of the brinjal disease infected plant had been captured by CCD camera in an uncontrolled environment in day lighting from the field. Each image had been converted from RGB color model to L*a*b* color model, correspondingly threshold had been evaluated according to a* component, and binary matrices had been created. The acquired binary matrix had been super imposed on RGB images, and different segments of images had been created including disease infected part and non-infected part of the plants. The entire process had been implemented in MATLAB 8.4. The RGB color space is platform dependent. The RGB color space to L*a*b* conversion is a three step process. First RGB image is transformed from platform dependent to platform independent color space conversion sRGB. Each sRGB image was converted into XYZ color space which in final step convert into L*a*b* color space. The chromaticity coordinates of an RGB system (x_r, y_r), (x_g, y_g) and (x_b, y_b) are auto generated by processing machine and its reference white $(X_W, Y_W, Z_W) =$

(0.9504, 1.0, 1.0889) had been taken according to CIE standard illuminant D65 for both RGB to XYZ conversion and finally XYZ to L*a*b*. The spatial features of RGB images and L*a*b* images had not been altered during quantization and binarization process. Only preprocessing steps which were applied on captured images were cropping and resizing of images to select region of interest and overcome the limitation of system related to space complexity.

The Figs. 1, 2, 3, 4, and 5 shows the sample of a pre-processed cropped image of original captured images and three segmented and equivalent binary matrices of 5 categories of rice plant diseases infected images.

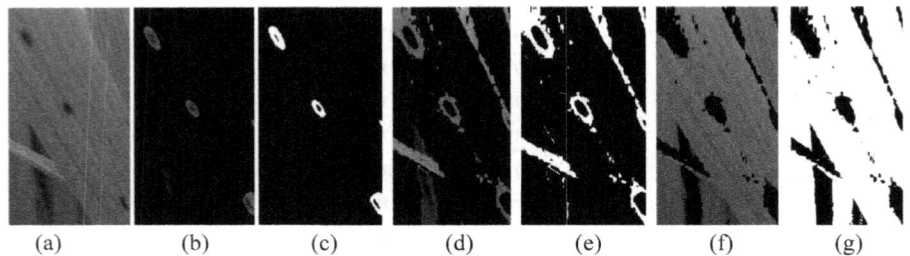

(a)   (b)   (c)   (d)   (e)   (f)   (g)

Fig. 1. Brown spot infected rice plant image (a) captured image (b & c) segmented images with high intensity threshold and equivalent binary image (d & e) segmented images with medium intensity threshold and equivalent binary image (f & g) segmented images with low intensity threshold and equivalent binary image (Color figure online)

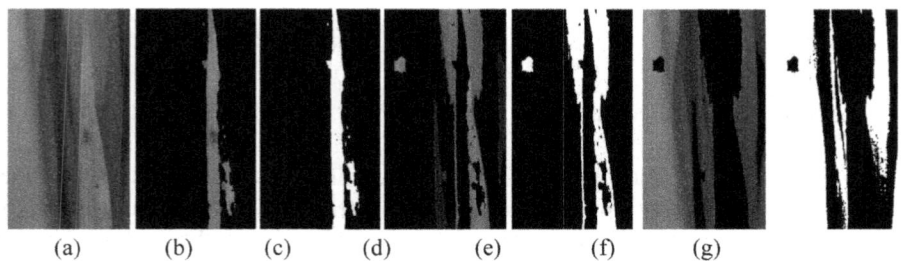

(a)   (b)   (c)   (d)   (e)   (f)   (g)

Fig. 2. Leaf Blast infected rice plant image (a) captured image (b & c) segmented images with high-intensity threshold and equivalent binary image (d & e) segmented images with medium intensity threshold and equivalent binary image (f & g) segmented images with low-intensity threshold and equivalent binary image (Color figure online)

The Figs. 6, 7, 8, and 9 shows the sample of a pre-processed cropped image of original captured images and three segmented and equivalent binary matrices of 4 categories of brinjal plant diseases infected images.

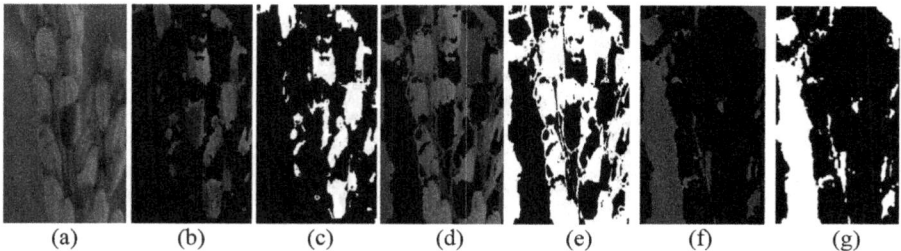

(a)   (b)   (c)   (d)   (e)   (f)   (g)

Fig. 3. Panicle Blast infected rice plant image (a) captured image (b & c) segmented images with high intensity threshold and equivalent binary image (d & e) segmented images with medium intensity threshold and equivalent binary image (f & g) segmented images with low intensity threshold and equivalent binary image (Color figure online)

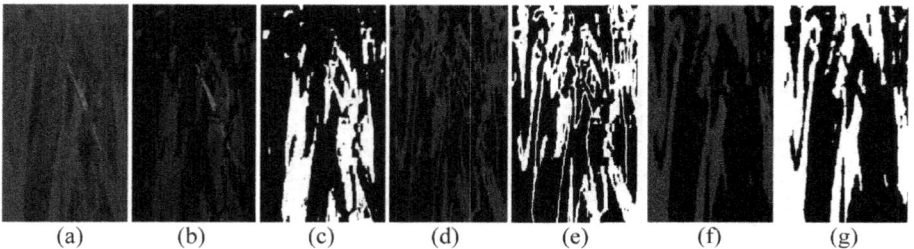

(a)   (b)   (c)   (d)   (e)   (f)   (g)

Fig. 4. Sheath Blight infected rice plant image (a) captured image (b & c) segmented images with high intensity threshold and equivalent binary image (d & e) segmented images with medium intensity threshold and equivalent binary image (f & g) segmented images with low intensity threshold and equivalent binary image (Color figure online)

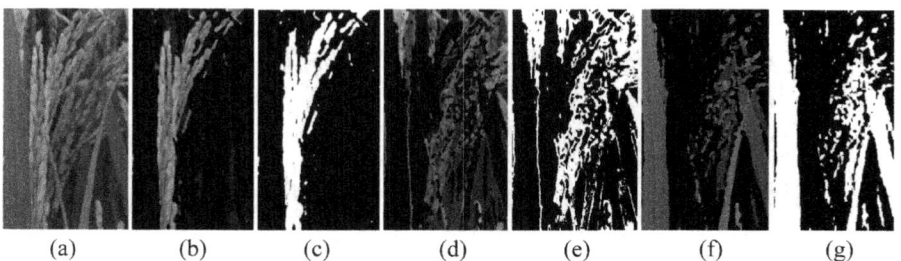

(a)   (b)   (c)   (d)   (e)   (f)   (g)

Fig. 5. Stem Borer infected rice plant image (a) captured image (b & c) segmented images with high-intensity threshold and equivalent binary image (d & e) segmented images with medium intensity threshold and equivalent binary image (f & g) segmented images with low-intensity threshold and equivalent binary image (Color figure online)

The Figs. 10, 11, 12, and 13 shows the sample of a pre-processed cropped image of original captured images and three segmented and equivalent binary matrices of 4 categories of tomato plant diseases infected images.

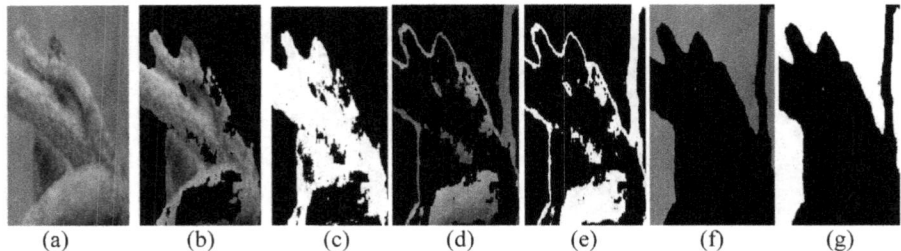

(a)   (b)   (c)   (d)   (e)   (f)   (g)

Fig. 6. Bacterial Wilt infected Brinjal plant image (a) captured image (b & c) segmented images with high intensity threshold and equivalent binary image (d & e) segmented images with medium intensity threshold and equivalent binary image (f & g) segmented images with low intensity threshold and equivalent binary image (Color figure online)

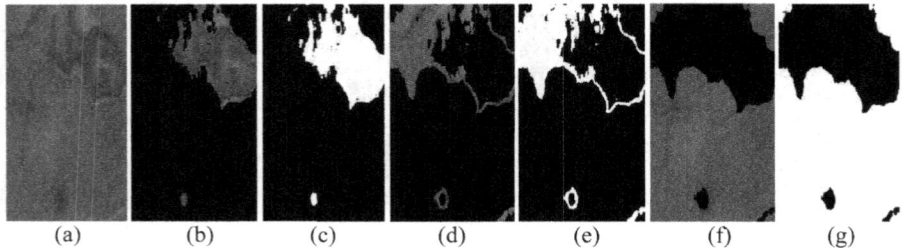

(a)   (b)   (c)   (d)   (e)   (f)   (g)

Fig. 7. Fungal Leaf Blight infected Brinjal plant image (a) captured image (b & c) segmented images with high intensity threshold and equivalent binary image (d & e) segmented images with medium intensity threshold and equivalent binary image (f & g) segmented images with low intensity threshold and equivalent binary image

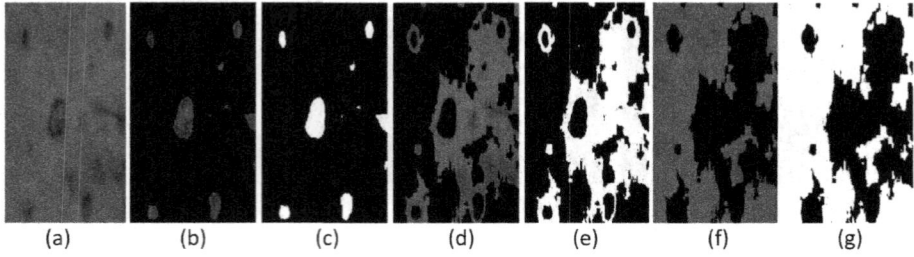

(a)   (b)   (c)   (d)   (e)   (f)   (g)

Fig. 8. Fungal Leaf Spot infected Brinjal plant image (a) captured image (b & c) segmented images with high intensity threshold and equivalent binary image (d & e) segmented images with medium intensity threshold and equivalent binary image (f & g) segmented images with low intensity threshold and equivalent binary image (Color figure online)

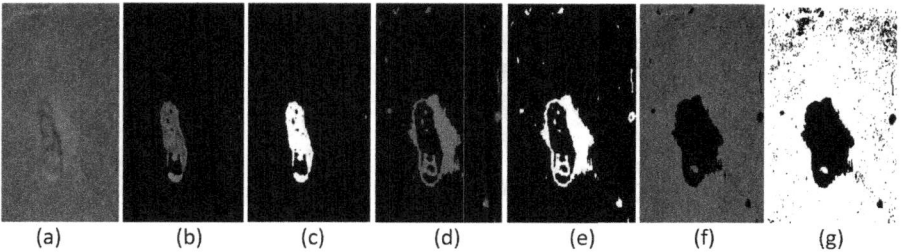

Fig. 9. Viral infected Brinjal plant image (a) captured image (b & c) segmented images with high intensity threshold and equivalent binary image (d & e) segmented images with medium intensity threshold and equivalent binary image (f & g) segmented images with low intensity threshold and equivalent binary image (Color figure online)

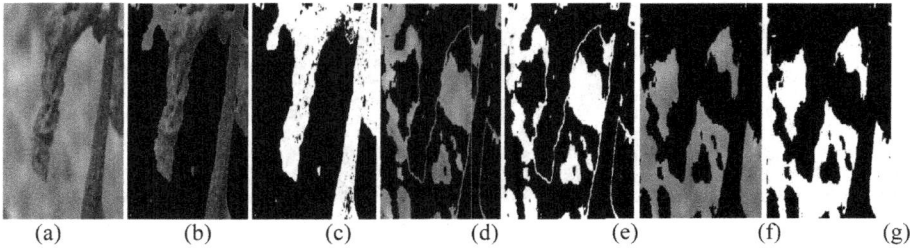

Fig. 10. Bacterial Canker infected Tomato plant image (a) captured image (b & c) segmented images with high intensity threshold and equivalent binary image (d & e) segmented images with medium intensity threshold and equivalent binary image (f & g) segmented images with low intensity threshold and equivalent binary image (Color figure online)

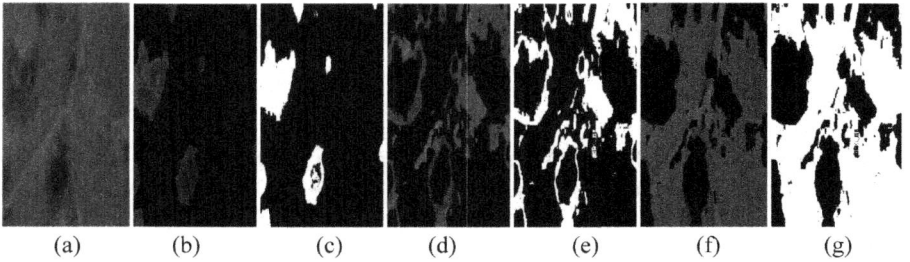

Fig. 11. Bacterial Leaf Spot infected Tomato plant image (a) captured image (b & c) segmented images with high intensity threshold and equivalent binary image (d & e) segmented images with medium intensity threshold and equivalent binary image (f & g) segmented images with low intensity threshold and equivalent binary image (Color figure online)

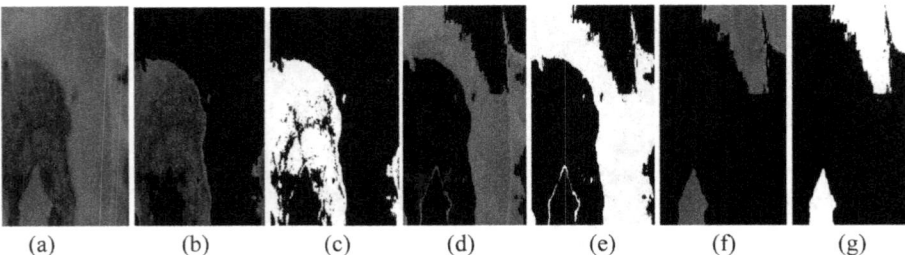

(a)   (b)   (c)   (d)   (e)   (f)   (g)

Fig. 12. Late Blight infected Tomato plant image (a) captured image (b & c) segmented images with high-intensity threshold and equivalent binary image (d & e) segmented images with medium intensity threshold and equivalent binary image (f & g) segmented images with low-intensity threshold and equivalent binary image (Color figure online)

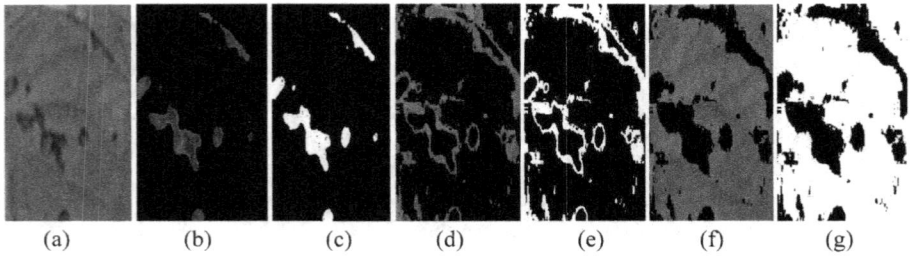

(a)   (b)   (c)   (d)   (e)   (f)   (g)

Fig. 13. Septorial Leaf Spot infected Tomato plant image (a) captured image (b & c) segmented images with high-intensity threshold and equivalent binary image (d & e) segmented images with medium intensity threshold and equivalent binary image (f & g) segmented images with low-intensity threshold and equivalent binary image (Color figure online)

These segmented parts are used for computerized analysis with specific features and algorithm.

4   Conclusion

In this paper, we had implemented a hybrid approach for segmentation of plant images. The color indexing technique had been used to reduce the variability of RGB color range by converting into perceptually uniform L*a*b* transform, without altering the spatial features of the RGB color space. The L*a*b* color space more clearly separate gray color information (L* values) from color information (a* and b* values). These features of L*a*b* color images help for better quantization and binarization after applying optimum thresholding. The spatial features of RGB color space and L*a*b*color space images were same, henceforth binary matrices were directly used with RGB images for segmentation. The displayed results are shown the prominence of the proposed method for the segmentation of plant images.

References

1. Chaube, H.S., Pundhir, V.S.: Crop Diseases and Their Management, 3rd edn. PHI Learning Private Limited, New Delhi (2005)
2. Rangaswami, G., Mahadevan, A.: Diseases of Crop Plants in India, 4th edn. PHI Learning Private Limited, New Delhi (2010)
3. Sharma, G.: Color fundamentals for digital imaging. In: Digital Color Imaging Handbook. CRC Press LLC (2003)
4. Balasubramanian, R.: Device characterization. In: Digital Color Imaging Handbook. CRC Press LLC (2003)
5. Giorgianni, E.J., Madden, T.E., Spaulding, K.E.: Color management for digital imaging systems. In: Digital Color Imaging Handbook. CRC Press LLC (2003)
6. Gonzalez, R.C., Woods, R.E., Eddins, S.L.: Digital Image Processing Using MATLAB, 2nd edn. McGraw Hill Education (India) Private Limited, New Delhi (2010)
7. Deokate, S., Uke, N.: Various traditional and nature inspired approaches used in image preprocessing. In: Pawar, P.M., Ronge, B.P., Balasubramaniam, R., Seshabhattar, S. (eds.) ICATSA 2016, pp. 345–352. Springer, Cham (2018). https://doi.org/10.1007/978-3-319-53556-2_34
8. Naidu, M.S.R., Kumar, P.R., Chiranjeevi, K.: Shannon and fuzzy entropy based evolutionary image thresholding for image segmentation. Alex. Eng. J. 1–13 (2017). https://doi.org/10.1016/j.aej.2017.05.024
9. Rakesh, Y., Sri Rama Krishna, K.: Wavelet based saliency detection for stereoscopic images aided by disparity information. In: Satapathy, S.C., Bhateja, V., Raju, K., Janakiramaiah, B. (eds.) Data Engineering and Intelligent Computing. AISC, vol. 542, pp. 473–482. Springer, Singapore (2018). https://doi.org/10.1007/978-981-10-3223-3_46
10. Wang, T., Lee, K., Wang, Y.F.: Partial image blur detection and segmentation from a single snapshot. In: ICASSP. IEEE, pp. 1907–1911 (2017)
11. Attia, M., Hossny, M., Nahavandi, S., Yazdabadi, A.: Skin melanoma segmentation using recurrent and convolutional neural networks. In: ISBI. IEEE, pp. 292–296 (2017)
12. Tareef, A., Song, Y., Feng, D., Chen, M., Cai, W.: Automated multi-stage segmentation of white blood cells via optimizing color processing. In: ISBI. IEEE, pp. 565–568 (2017)
13. Abbood, A.A., Sulong, G., Razzaq, A.A.A., Peters, S.U.: Segmentation and enhancement of fingerprint images based on automatic threshold calculations. In: Saeed, F., Gazem, N., Patnaik, S., Saed Balaid, A.S., Mohammed, F. (eds.) IRICT 2017. LNDECT, vol. 5, pp. 400–411. Springer, Cham (2018). https://doi.org/10.1007/978-3-319-59427-9_43
14. Acosta, B.M.T., Basset, A., Bouthemy, P., Kervrann, C.: Multi-scale spot segmentation with selection of image scales. In: ICASSP. IEEE, pp. 1912–1926 (2017)
15. Hamuda, E., Glavin, M., Jones, E.: A survey of image processing techniques for plant extraction and segmentation in the field. Comput. Electron. Agric. 125, 184–199 (2016)
16. Rasmussen, J., Norremark, M., Bibby, B.: Assessment of leaf cover and crop soil cover in weed harrowing research using digital images. Weed Res. 47, 299–310 (2007)
17. Meyer, G.E., Camargo-Neto, J.: Verification of color vegetation indices for automated crop imaging applications. Comput. Electron. Agric. 63, 282–293 (2008)
18. Kirk, K., Andersen, H.J., Thomsen, A.G., Jorgensen, J.R.: Estimation of leaf area index in cereal crops using red–green images. Biosyst. Eng. 104, 308–317 (2009)
19. Tellaeche, A., Burgos-Artizzu, X.P., Pajares, G., Ribeiro, A.: A vision-based method for weeds identification through the Bayesian decision theory. Pattern Recogn. 41(2), 521–530 (2008)

20. Shrestha, D.S., Steward, B.L., Birrell, S.J.: Video processing for early stage maize plant detection. Biosyst. Eng. **89**(2), 119–129 (2004)

21. Gebhardt, S., Schellberg, J., Lock, R., Kaühbauch, W.A.: Identification of broadleaved dock (Rumex obtusifolius L.) on grassland by means of digital image processing. Precis. Agric. **7** (3), 165–178 (2006)

22. Jeon, H.Y., Tian, L.F., Zhu, H.: Robust crop and weed segmentation under uncontrolled outdoor illumination. Sensors **11**(12), 6270–6283 (2011)

23. Meyer, G.E., Camargo-Neto, J., Jones, D.D., Hindman, T.W.: Intensified fuzzy clusters for classifying plant, soil, and residue regions of interest from color images. Comput. Electron. Agric. **42**, 161–180 (2004)

24. Ruiz-Ruiz, G., Gómez-Gil, J., Navas-Gracia, L.M.: Testing different color spaces based on hue for the environmentally adaptive segmentation algorithm (EASA). Comput. Electron. Agric. **68**, 88–96 (2009)

25. Guerrero, J.M., Pajares, G., Montalvo, M., Romeo, J., Guijarro, M.: Support vector machines for crop/weeds identification in maize fields. Exp. Syst. Appl. **39**, 11149–11155 (2012)

26. Zheng, L., Zhang, J., Wang, Q.Y.: Mean-shift-based color segmentation of images containing green vegetation. Comput. Electron. Agric. **65**, 93–98 (2009)

Intelligent Vulnerability Analyzer – A Novel Dynamic Vulnerability Analysis Framework for Mobile Based Online Applications

D. Jeya Mala[1(✉)], M. Eswaran[2], and N. Deepika Malar[3]

[1] Thiagarajar College of Engineering, Madurai, Tamil Nadu, India
djeyamala@gmail.com
[2] Zoho Corporation, Chennai, India
[3] Amazon, Chennai, India

Abstract. As per the survey taken by Computer Security Institute (2002), due to the evolution of internet technology and application popularization, security has become the key issue for implementing web based applications which have crucial online transactions. The surveys indicated that highly secured online applications accessed through the web are frequently experiencing several kinds of threats when compared to other conventional applications. If the vulnerable areas of such highly secured online applications are left undetected, inadvertent effects will happen ranging from erroneous operations, software failure and resource wastage to life threatening attacks such as leaking of sensitive information during crucial online transactions. In the proposed approach, the external attacks occurred due to dynamic user inputs are identified using heuristic guided intelligent graph searching performed by the Intelligent Vulnerability Analyzer Agent (IVA). To achieve this, each SQL query that accesses the SQLite data base information is converted into a graph and the agent compares each node in this graph against the SQL Master Graph (SQLMG) for potential threat areas. This is done by analyzing the pre and post conditions during the path exploration process from one node to another. For this, the agent performs both static source code as well as dynamic execution based analysis. Further, the queries are analyzed for percentage of false positives and false negatives based analysis.

Keywords: Software testing · Vulnerability analysis
Intelligent Vulnerability Analyzer Agent (IVA)
Structured query language injection attack (SQLIA)
SQL Master Graph (SQLMG)

1 Introduction

Most of the m-Commerce applications are real-time applications that include online sales, online auctions, online banking etc. These applications have to be deployed with higher degree of reliability, confidentiality and efficiency. As these applications are vulnerable to various kinds of attack, protecting such applications from them is essential. The vulnerabilities of m-Commerce applications are classified as Remote

© Springer Nature Singapore Pte Ltd. 2018
P. Bhattacharyya et al. (Eds.): NGCT 2017, CCIS 828, pp. 805–823, 2018.
https://doi.org/10.1007/978-981-10-8660-1_60

code executions, Cross Site Scripting (XSS), SQL injection attack, Format string vulnerabilities, Username enumeration.

SQL injection is an older approach but popular among attackers. This allows attackers to retrieve information from the SQLite database. Exploiting such vulnerabilities helps the attacker to use different usernames and identify the valid one with the help of error messages. Format string vulnerabilities result from the use of unfiltered input from the user as the format string parameter in certain functions that perform formatting (Siddarth and Doshi 2010).

Among these vulnerabilities, SQL Injection is more common and critical. Depending on the security measures of the application, the risk of this attack can vary from remote code execution and total system compromise to basic information disclosure. So we propose an approach to static analysis of SQL Injection vulnerabilities. The research problem here is to identify the potential SQL queries that are vulnerable to attack and provide alternate mechanism to rewrite them in order to prevent SQLIA type of attacks using an intelligent agent with heuristic guided graph searching technique.

2   Literature Survey

John et al. (2015), have surveyed various techniques applied to prevent SQL injections and also they have proposed an adaptive algorithm to prevent such attacks. Their approach applied parse tree evaluation and only static query analysis. But in dynamic queries case, the vulnerability of SQLIA will be high which is not considered in this approach.

Kar and Panigrahi (2013), they applied a hashing based technique to find out SQL injection attacks. For evaluation, they took only a single application as a prototype and evaluated their approach. Thus the results and efficiency of their approach cannot be generalized.

Inyong et al. (2012), have removed the SQL query attribute values of web pages when submitting the parameters and then it is compared with a predetermined one. This method focuses only on queries and not on stored procedures.

Tajpour et al. (2010) have evaluated the techniques proposed by various researchers to handle and prevent SQL injection types of attacks. Their conclusion states that there should be some improvement over current techniques to stop SQLIA attacks.

Petukhov and Kozlov (2008) applied dynamic analysis in penetration testing to detect security vulnerabilities in web applications.

Kemalis and Tzouramanis (2008) proposed an approach that uses the specifications to check the query's vulnerability. These are then used to evaluate the correctness of the web pages.

Bisht and Madhusudan (2007) proposed a mining based technique on programmer intended queries by dynamic evaluation of test runs using candidate inputs. Their approach targeted on protection of Java based web applications by modifying JVM without the need for retrofitting.

Wassermann and Su (2004) presented a static source code analysis to check whether the queries generated dynamically contain type errors or not. They described their technique and provided a static analysis algorithm to identify SQLIAs.

Muthuprasanna et al. (2006) proposed a defensive technique to protect web applications from SQLIAs that combines static code analysis with dynamic validation done at run time to detect the presence of the attacks.

Halfond et al. (2006) proposed a tool called AMNESIA which is able to detect and prevent SQLIA by means of both static source code based analysis along with monitoring being done at runtime.

Cook and Rai (2005), presented a technique in which the queries are represented as statically typed objects. These will be executed both at the time of current server side execution as well as in remote execution by means of a server.

McClure and Krüger (2005) have identified the drawbacks of using Call Level Interface(CLI) in terms of constructing SQL statements as they checked for correctness only not for their vulnerability/Hence, they applied SQL DOM based vulnerabilities detection to resolve the drawbacks.

Halfond et al. (2006) proposed an approach in which initially a set of correct input strings are provided to detect SQLIA. This execution identifies the un-trusted strings that are passed on to the next level and categorizes input strings based on the initialization only at runtime. After that, a 'syntax aware evaluation' is performed to evaluate the strings that are passed to the next level. Based on this the un-trusted strings are identified early and the queries that have these as part are restricted from entering into the database server for processing. The issue in this method is the trusted strings are initialized by the developers hence will have problems in trusted and un-trusted.

Pietraszek and Berghe (2006) proposed an idea to find out the basic reason for SQLIA. The basic reason will be identified by means of the metadata of the query. Here, the data is classified as trusted if it is provided by the application itself and is classified as un-trusted if it is provided by the user. The issue in this approach is elimination of unsafe characters restricts the functionality of the application.

Su and Wassermann (2006) proposed an approach to block the queries generated from the input given by the users that does not meet the syntax of the query. Also, the queries generated at runtime are tested based on the pre-defined grammar. The problem here is the queries are evaluated based on the pre-defined grammar only and so the dynamically formed queries correctness will become a stalk.

Jovanovic et al. (2006) proposed a Static Analysis approach for detecting vulnerabilities. It is based on the approach which uses data flow analysis. The data that causes the problems will be identified by checking the parameters and removing them from the queries will make the application free from SQLIA. A major issue is that Pixy is an open source tool; an attacker has a scope to bypass it by exploiting the features in it.

PQL is developed by Anekar (2012) for web application, which incorporates a static technique to find the solutions to vulnerable queries. Here, the static analysis part finds the vulnerable queries by means of a collective technique that has both context-sensitive as well as flow analysis. The major issues of this method are resolving the attack related queries, based on the output which is mostly developer dependent.

Shahriar and Zulkernine (2008) proposed a Mutation based SQL Injection Vulnerabilities Checking to analyze the vulnerabilities based on mutation of SQL statements. The major issues of this method are types of mutant generation are static and all types of mutated and injected query are generated for each SQL statements in the web applications.

3 Proposed Work - Intelligent Dynamic Vulnerability Analysis for SQLIA

A major issue in the existing system is the specification of un-safeness among the trusted string and characters are purely dependent on the m-Commerce developers. Due to the usage of temporary repository to store the vulnerable strings may cause second order attack. In mutation-based, approach number of mutation and injected query generation takes higher execution time. Mutation of all types of attack should be created to analyze the vulnerability and execution of each mutated query and malicious input injected query on SQLite database and comparison of both results will lead to high execution time.

The types of mutants generate method are static and are not able to identify the new types of attack. And, another major issue is, the mutation-based approach generates all type of mutants for each query, as it is unable to identify its type. The proposed strategy for SQLIA is a graph-based approach works along with the source code analysis for the post generated method.

In the proposed intelligent agent based approach, the SQL statements in functions and stored procedures are extracted which uses the user input dynamically to construct SQL statements. Then identify the relation between the input parameters and queries, query-to-query dependency. The relationship table and dependency table are constructed to identify the impact of user input on the query when it is attacked by malicious input. Prioritize the user input parameter by its impact on stored procedure control structure and construct the SQLGraph using relationship table and dependency table of SQL Mapper.

Next, SQL Parser evaluates the grammar of SQL statement and finds any mismatch in syntax of SQL statement. Then tokenize the SQL statement and identify the SQL keywords and user input parts. SQL Graph Generator generates a graph of SQL statement for both with and without malicious crafted input by using the SQL Master Graph (SQLMG), where in SQLMG all nodes are the generalized set of SQL keywords and operators which are connected according to the grammar of SQL statements.

Each node in SQLMG has specific attributes and its predefined values according to the grammar. SQLMG is used to identify the pre-conditions and post-conditions of SQL statement. Intelligent Vulnerability Analyzer Agent evaluates the pre-conditions and post-conditions of the graph of attacked type and analyzes the result generated from pre-condition and post-condition evaluation. The queries can be added either vulnerable or non-vulnerable list according to the result of Intelligent Vulnerability Analyzer Agent. Then test cases will be generated queries of both the list and execute on the SQLite database server and lists will be updated based on the execution result.

3.1 Proposed Framework for Intelligent Analysis for Vulnerability of SQLIA

The framework of the proposed intelligent agent based analysis for SQLIA vulnerability is shown in Fig. 1.

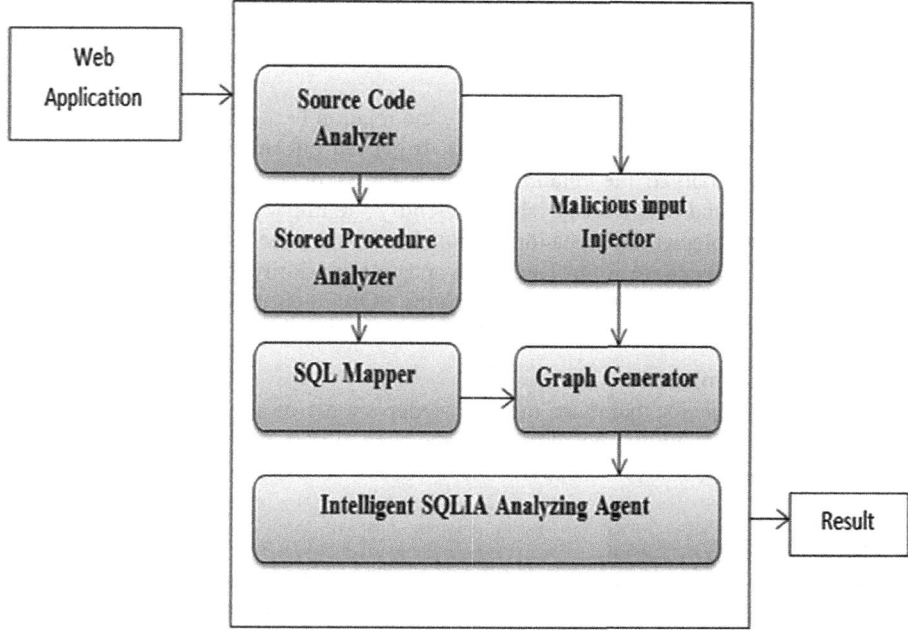

Fig. 1. Proposed dynamic vulnerability analysis framework for SQLIA

The internal components in the proposed framework are detailed below:

Source Code Analyzer
Source Code Analyzer receives the source code of m-Commerce application as input, so as to analyze the vulnerabilities of SQLIA in the source code. It identifies the functions that have SQL statements and passing parameters to SQL statements. It extracts the SQL statements which receive the user inputs dynamically to construct the SQL statement. And it eliminates the SQL statements which cannot be constructed dynamically. On another hand, it also extracts the stored procedures from the source code as they receive the user input dynamically. It passes the extracted selected SQL statements to SQL Parser and passes selected stored procedures to Stored Procedure Analyzer. It keep on monitoring the source code for changes in SQL statements. If any changes made then the SQL statements are extracted and passed to SQL parser.

Stored Procedure Analyzer
Stored Procedure Analyzer receives the stored procedure names from the source code and gets the SQLite database server connection parameters to obtain the details of the stored procedure. It reads the definition of stored procedure from the SQLite database server and identifies the input parameters and their types. Then it select the input parameters of string type and extracts the SQL statements which use those input parameters dynamically to construct SQL statements structure and pass those SQL statements to the SQL Parser. Stored procedure has n number of SQL statements and our analyzer identifies the SQL statements which consist of function EXEC or

EXECUTE. Our approach analyzes the control flow of SQL statements and inputs parameters in stored procedure and transfers the information to the SQL Mapper.

SQL Mapper

The major tack of SQL Mapper is to identify the relation between the input parameters and queries and query-to-query dependency. It get the information of input node and query node and analyze the relationship as well as dependency, it constructs the relationship table and dependency table to identify the impact of the user input on the query when it is injected by malicious input. It identifies the inputs which have high impact on stored procedure control structure and assign priority to each input parameter according to its impact. Finally, it constructs the SQLGraph, based on the relationship table and dependency table of the SQL Mapper.

Malicious Input Injector

Malicious input Injector maintains the knowledge source of all possible attack inputs. For each SQL statements extracted from source code, it injects all possible attack inputs from the knowledge source and passes all malicious crafted SQL statements to graph generator.

Graph Generator

Graph generator tokenizes the malicious crafted SQL statements and identifies the SQL keyword. It evaluates the grammar of the SQL statements and finds any mismatches in the syntax of SQL statements. It generates the graph for tokenized SQL keywords according to SQL master graph SQLMG which contains all SQL keywords as nodes and are connected according to the grammar corresponding to SQL statements.

As shown in Fig. 2, the nodes present in the master graph for the SQL statement contains the generalized set of keywords and operators of same behavior. The syntax of malicious input crafted graph is evaluated to identify whether the syntax matches with the default SQL syntax. If it mismatches, then SQL statements are blocked from further

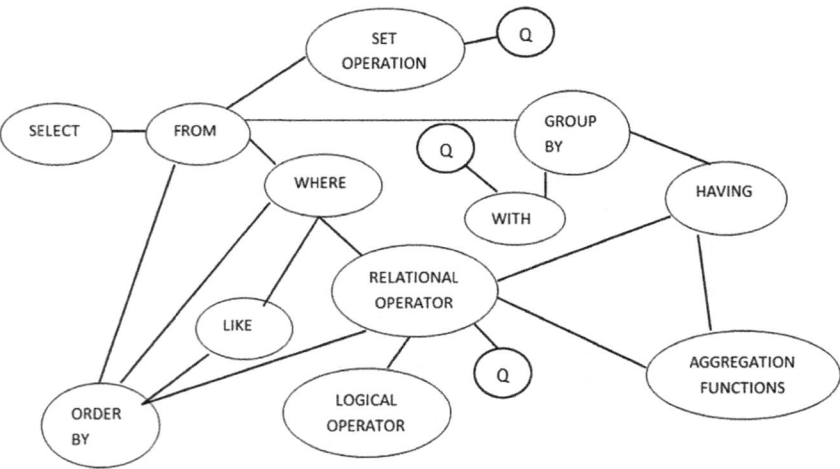

Fig. 2. SQL master graph for the select statement

testing. The syntax evaluation is performed by selecting each tokenized keyword to generate the source node and generate destination node by next tokenized keyword. Each source node has a set of possible destination nodes in SQLMG. If the generated destination node is not one of the possible destination nodes of the generated source node then the edge between the generated source and destination nodes cannot be created. Then selected malicious input crafted SQL statement is syntactically incorrect. If the graph generated successfully then it is passed to Intelligent SQLIA analyzing agent.

Example 1. "SELECT account FROM employee WHERE empId='" + employeeID +"'" this can be injected as "SELECT account FROM employee WHERE empId=''; SHUTDOWN;". Here SHUTDOWN is the SQL keyword but it is not the one of the possible destination nodes of the source node "=" so the Graph Generator cannot generate the graph for this injected query according to the SQLMG.

Example 2. "SELECT account FROM employee WHERE empId = (SELECT empId FROM login WHERE username=' +username+'" AND password='" + password+"')" this query can be changed as follow "SELECT account FROM employee WHERE empId = (SELECT empId FROM login WHERE username='' OR 'x='x' AND password='' OR 'x='x'")". In this case, the malicious input crafted SQL statement syntax matches the default SQL select statement syntax therefore the query can be tested further by IVA.

Intelligent Vulnerably Analyzer Agent (IVA)
The proposed IVA first identifies all condition and operator nodes in the syntactically correct malicious input crafted SQL statements. Here the agent use the pre-condition knowledge source and takes decisions based on the pre-condition of the given node. The pre-condition is the information required by the current condition node to get evaluated by agent. The knowledge source is updated through reasoning by means of forward chaining and verifying by means of backward chaining. In forward chaining all nodes needed for the condition and operator nodes to evaluate are obtained. In backward chaining the status of the condition and operator nodes are determined. Usually, knowledge source embody two elements:

- Preconditions
- Actions

   The pre-condition knowledge source has the following:
Logical operators

- Precondition – Both left and right hand relational operation should be safe.
- Action – The safeness value for the logical operator node is assigned.

Relational operators, HAVING, LIKE

- Precondition – Both left and right hand values should not be in the blocked list and should not be equal.
- Action – The safeness value for the relational operator node is assigned.

SET operators

- Precondition – Both left and right hand queries should be safe.
- Action – The safeness value for the SET operator node is assigned.

The abstract syntax tree is generated for all condition and operator nodes in the graph.

Example. SELECT account FROM employee WHERE empId = (SELECT empId FROM login WHERE username = 'aaa' OR 'x='x' AND password='' OR 'x='x''). The abstract syntax tree for the sub query is generated initially and is represented as Q1. In this query SELECT empId FROM login WHERE username = 'aaa' OR 'x='x' AND password='' OR 'x='x'' followings are the conditions (Tables 2 and 3).

Table 1. Conditions present in the query

Condition ID	Conditions
CO1	Username
CO2	aaa
CO3	X
CO4	X
CO5	Password
CO6	''
CO7	X
CO8	X

Table 2. Relational operators of the query

Relational operator ID	Relational operators
R1	=
R2	=
R3	=
R4	=

Table 3. Logical operators of the query

Logical operator ID	Logical operators
L1	OR
L2	AND
L3	OR

From Table 4, the pre-conditions for Relational operator R1 is CO1, CO2 and post-condition of R1 is L1. Similarly pre-conditions for L1 is R1, R2 and L3 is R3, R4 and post-condition of L1, L3 is L2. IVA evaluates each node in the condition Table 1. IVA maintains the blocked list knowledge source for the conditions, if the condition

Table 4. Logical operators of the query

ID	Pre-conditions
R1	CO1, CO2
R2	CO3, CO4
R3	CO5, CO6
R4	CO7, CO8
L1	R1, R2
L3	R3, R4
L2	L1, L3

Table 5. Safeness value of the conditions

Condition ID	Conditions	Status	Safeness value
CO1	username	Safe	1
CO2	aaa	Safe	1
CO3	X	Safe	1
CO4	X	Safe	1
CO5	Password	Safe	1
CO6	' '	Unsafe	0
CO7	X	Safe	1
CO8	X	Safe	1

Table 6. Safeness value of pre-conditions

ID	Pre-conditions	Status	Safeness value
R1	CO1, CO2	Safe	1
R2	CO3, CO4	Unsafe	0
R3	CO5, CO6	Unsafe	1
R4	CO7, CO8	Unsafe	0
L1	R1, R2	Unsafe	0
L3	R3, R4	Unsafe	0
L2	L1, L3	Unsafe	0

has a match in blocked list then the status of the node is updated as unsafe. The 'blocked list' knowledge source contains the conditions which satisfies dummy SQL query (Table 6).

The vulnerability of the query is based on the value of the probability of vulnerability (μ). The μ is calculated from the following

$$\mu = \text{Total number of safe nodes/Total number of nodes.} \tag{1}$$

In Eq. (1), if μ value is 1 the query in non-vulnerable, if 0.5 the query is minimum vulnerable, if 0 the query is maximum vulnerable. Here the value of μ for Q1is 0.1428. So the sub query is identified as maximum vulnerable. Now the agent evaluates the pre-condition of main query "SELECT account FROM employee WHERE empId = Q1". Here condition CO1 is empId, CO2 is Q1. And R1 is "=". Status of CO1 is Safe and status of CO2 is Unsafe therefore status of R1 is updated as Unsafe. The value of μ is 0, therefore the query is identified as maximum vulnerable. The agent updates the 'attack' knowledge source.

The agent evaluates the injected query by using the 'attack' knowledge source. The agent receives an injected query and searches the attack knowledge source for similar pattern by using pattern matching. If similar pattern exists then, the inputs used for testing the query in knowledge source is also applied to the received query to evaluate the vulnerability. The graph path of query evaluation is checked against the graph path of the query in knowledge source. If the paths are equal then the safeness values are checked. If the safeness value of the received query is less than the safeness value of query in knowledge source then the query is reported as vulnerable in log else update the attack knowledge source. If the paths are not equal then the graph paths of received query is updated in the knowledge source. If similar pattern does not exist in knowledge source then the received query is tested in possible ways by agent and updates the graph path, safeness value in knowledge source.

4 Algorithm for the Proposed Work

4.1 Algorithm for Intelligent Vulnerability Analyzer Agent (IVA)

(1) Read the source code and extract all SQL statements.
(2) Validate the extracted SQL statements.
   (a) If the query receives the user input dynamically then it will add to Selected Query List.
   (b) If not, reject the query.
(3) Generate the Graph for the each SQL Statements to evaluate the syntax of SQL statements
   (a) If it is syntactically correct go to step 4.
   (b) If not, block the SQL statement.
(4) Each SQL statement is pattern match with SQL statements present in Attack Knowledge Source.
   (a) If it already exists then the SQL statement is tested with existing attack input.
   (b) If it is not exists go to step 5.

(5) Generate the Abstract Syntax Tree for each graph to evaluate pre and post-conditions.
(6) Calculate the cumulative safeness value for each graph.
(7) Calculate the probability of vulnerability (μ) for each graph.
    (a) If $\mu = 1$ then the SQL statement is non-vulnerable.
    (b) If $\mu = 0.5$ then it is average vulnerable.
    (c) If $\mu = 0$ then it is maximum vulnerable.
(8) Update the Attack Knowledge Source
(9) Report the Vulnerable and Non-vulnerable SQL Statements.

4.2 Analysis of Stored Procedure

This model is a static analysis that works along with the graph based approach. The basis of this model is mapping the SQL commands and the user input parameters along with their relationship. Stored procedure analyzer identifies the SQL statements in stored procedure which uses the user input dynamically to construct the SQL statement. These SQL statements are known as Query Nodes. Identify all the user inputs used in the Query Nodes and the inputs are known as Input Nodes. Next the mapping function maps the Query Nodes and Input Nodes depending upon their relationship. Then the dependency graph is generated. Using this graph it is easy to identify the Input node which may attack many number of SQL statements. Using this SQL mapping technique, we can reduce the set of SQL queries to a smaller sub-set and generate test cases or Malicious crafted input for those sub-sets. This will reduce the execution time and identifies the set of queries which get affected by each user inputs dynamically. If more than one Input Nodes are mapped in single Query node then any one of those Input node can be crafted instead of all. The stored Procedure Parser will extract all queries which hold user inputs along with their control structure.

Algorithm for Analysis of Stored Procedure

Step 1: Read source code and extract the stored Procedure name
Step 2: Select the Stored Procedures name for analysis
Step 3: Get Stored Procedures details and their definitions from SQLite database
Step 4: Extract the SQL statements from the Stored Procedure definition
Step 5: Identify the Query Node, Input Node, and mapping their relations into SQLGraph
Step 6: Identify the inputs which affect queries which are the major sub set of SQLGraph
Step 7: Create the malicious crafted Queries from SQLGraph
Step 8: Analysis the Queries using Intelligent SQLIA Analysis Agent
Step 9: Display the result

4.3   Pseudo Code for Intelligent Vulnerability Analyzer Agent (IVA)

Input

      S: Source Code.

Output

      V: Vulnerable Query List.

      NV: Non-Vulnerable Query List.

Begin

```
[1]      SQL_List[] := extract_SQL_form_Source_code(S)
[2]      SQL_List[] := validate(SQL_List)
[3]      for each Query € SQL_List
[4]              exists := search_Attack_Knowledge_Source(Query)
[5]              if exists = flase then
[6]                      Injected_List.add(inject_Malicious_Input(Query))
[7]              else
[8]                      Injected_List.add(inject_Existing_input(Query))
[9]              end if
[10]     end for
[11]     for each Query € Injected_List
[12]             flag := create_Graph(Query)
[13]             if flag = flase then
[14]                     block_SQL(Query)
[15]                     continue()
[16]             else
[17]                     μ_value := evaluate_pre_post-condition(Query)
[18]                     if μ_value = 1 then
[19]                             V.add(Query)
[20]                     else
[21]                             NV.add(Query)
[22]                     end if
[23]             end if
[24]     end for
end
```

5   Performance Evaluation

Overall, it is observed that this novel approach is easier to implement moreover, it is every effective in identifying vulnerabilities and preventing from SQLIA. The evaluation of Intelligent Vulnerability Analyzer Agent and SQLIA Checker results in high detection rate and no false positive cases are found. The average run-time taken by our work is very low when compared to mutation-based approach (Shahriar and Zulkernine 2008) and XML-based approach (Das 2010).

In the proposed approach, Intelligent Vulnerability Analyzer Agent generates only the malicious crafted SQL Statements, not the mutations. Since while evaluating the graph, only the sub set of selected queries will be executed others are rejected from the graph itself. But in the case of mutation- based approach, both mutation and injected queries would be executed on the SQLite database server and analyze the result. This approach reduces the time and execution cost highly when compared to mutation-based approach (Table 7).

Table 7.   Result of intelligent vulnerability analyzer agent

Applications	No of stored procedures	No of SQL statements	Execution time in seconds		
			Mutation-based approach	XML SQL tree	Proposed approach
Bank automation for mobile	4	40	650	440	270
Bookstore website	3	17	335	187	114
Blood bank web portal	4	20	360	220	136
Virtual learning env.	5	35	480	365	236
Ecops website	2	35	516	385	244

Similarly in the case of stored procedures also selection of user input parameter and SQL statements are based on their SQLGraph generated by using mapping function. It selects the input parameters which are used by maximum number of SQL statements in the stored procedure. This reduces the test case generation of malicious input for stored procedures and reduces the execution time and cost. We have implemented both mutation and XML SQL- Tree based approaches and proposed approach as separate tools and analyzed the results. Table 5 shows the result of execution time of static analysis source code for sample case studies and is shown in Fig. 3.

The false positives and false negatives are analyzed and the result is given in Table 8.

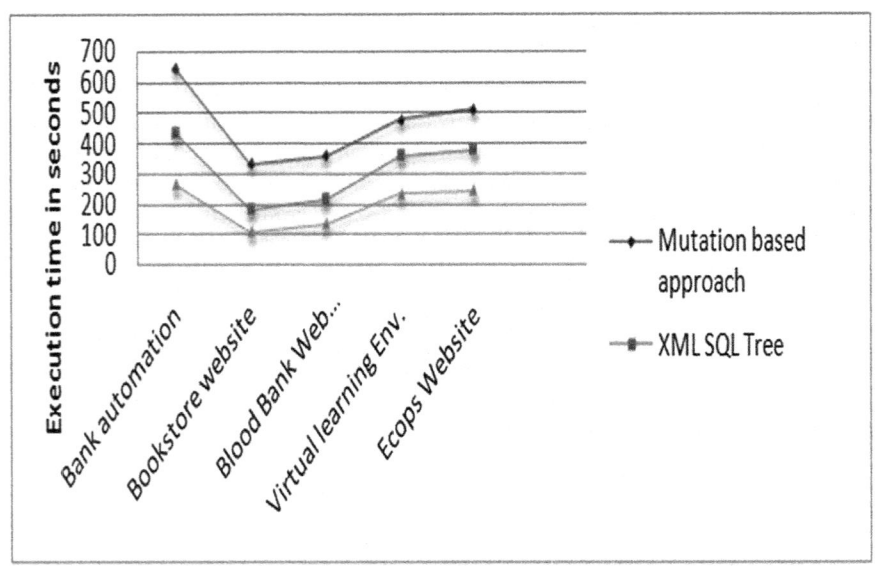

Fig. 3. Execution of intelligent vulnerability analyzer agent

Table 8. Result of false positive and false negative for virtual learning environment. (A mobile based online application)

SQLIAs	No of attacks made	Mutation-based approach		XML SQL tree based approach		Positive tainting		Proposed approach	
		No of false positives	No of false negatives	No of false positives	No of false negatives	No of false positives	No of False Negatives	No of false positives	No of false negatives
Use of tautology	20	0	0	0	0	0	0	0	0
Additional SQL statements (union)	10	0	8	0	0	3	10	0	0
Valid user input of (')	30	0	10	0	15	0	15	0	0
Piggy backed	20	0	2	0	8	0	10	0	0
Others SQLIAs	10	0	0	0	0	0	0	0	0

6   Conclusion

In this paper, we proposed a vulnerability analysis framework to detect the SQLIAs using intelligent graph searching based approach. By using this proposed approach, the developers and testers can easily find out the SQLIAs even when they appear in complex SQL queries. The proposed intelligent agent based vulnerability analysis of SQLIA proved to be an efficient technique as it applies intelligent approaches in learning and decision making processes. The proposed approach not only checked the queries in web pages but also the queries inside stored procedures. The technique has been compared with existing approaches and it proves to be an efficient technique in detection of SQLIA and analysis of vulnerability. Also, it is ease to implement as it accesses the SQLite database server at minimum cost and lower execution time. In future it is proposed to apply evolutionary algorithm for generating the test cases for the SQL queries to detect for vulnerabilities based on our approach.

Appendix

See Figs. 4, 5, 6, 7 and 8.

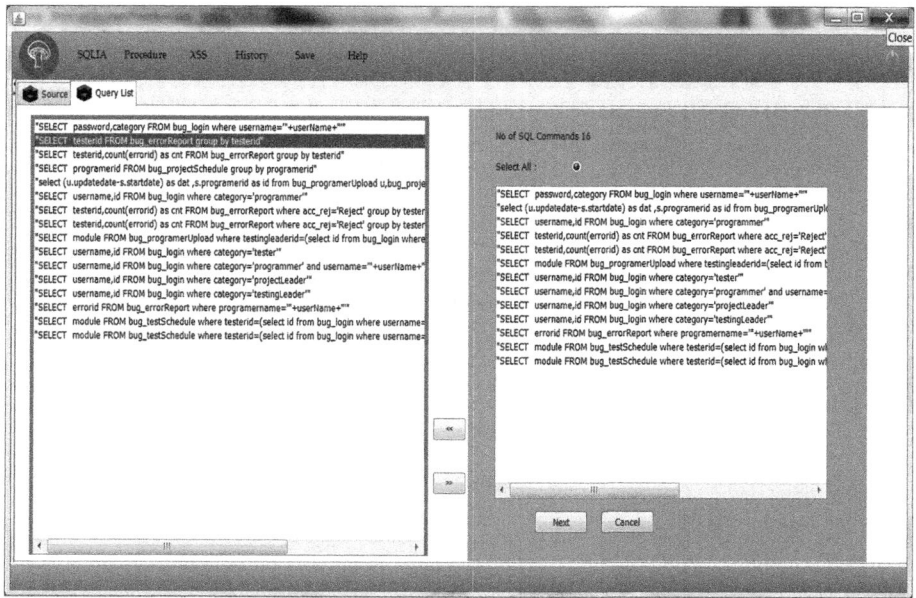

Fig. 4.   IVA – Extract the queries from source code and get query to check list.

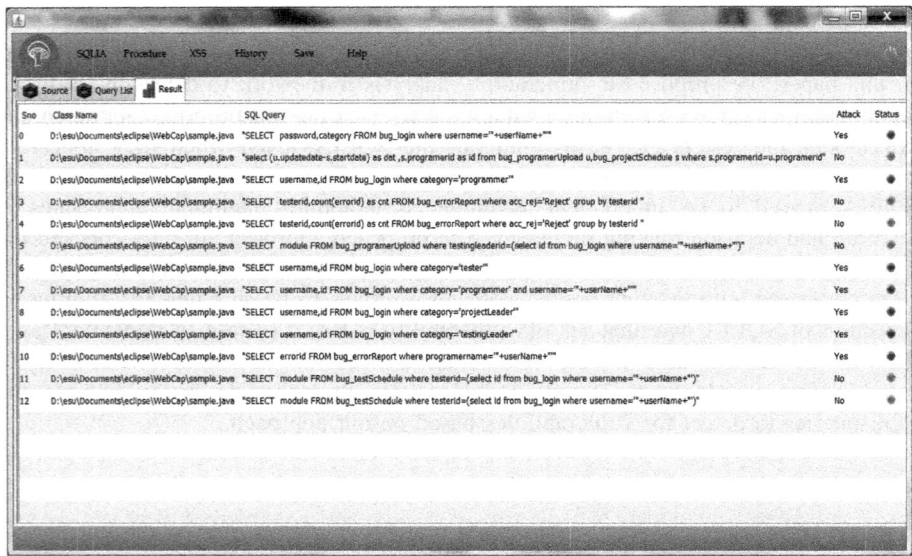

Fig. 5. IVA – Report the vulnerable status of the selected queries.

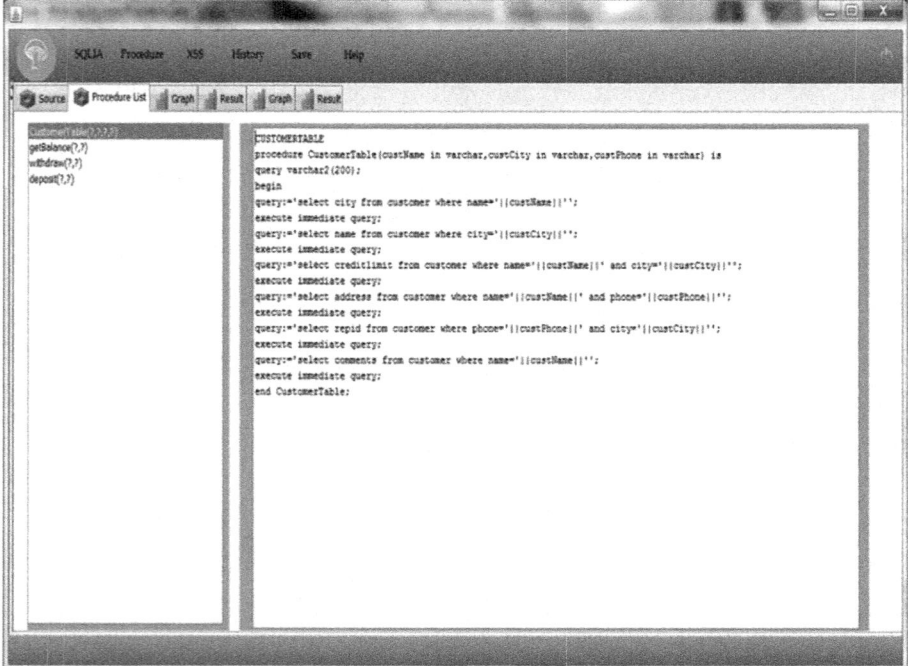

Fig. 6. IVA – Extract stored procedures from source code and get its details and definitions from SQLite database

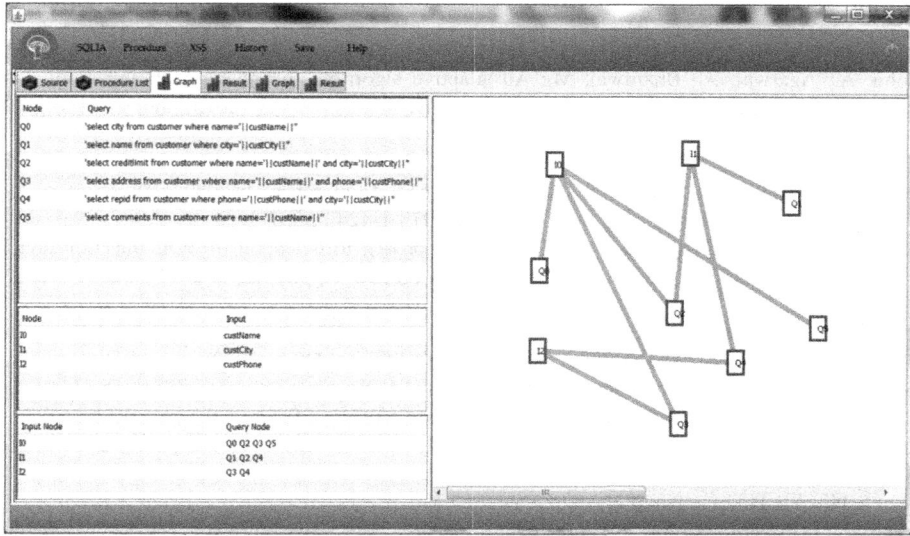

Fig. 7. IVA – Mapping the queries nodes and inputs nodes and display the SQLGraph

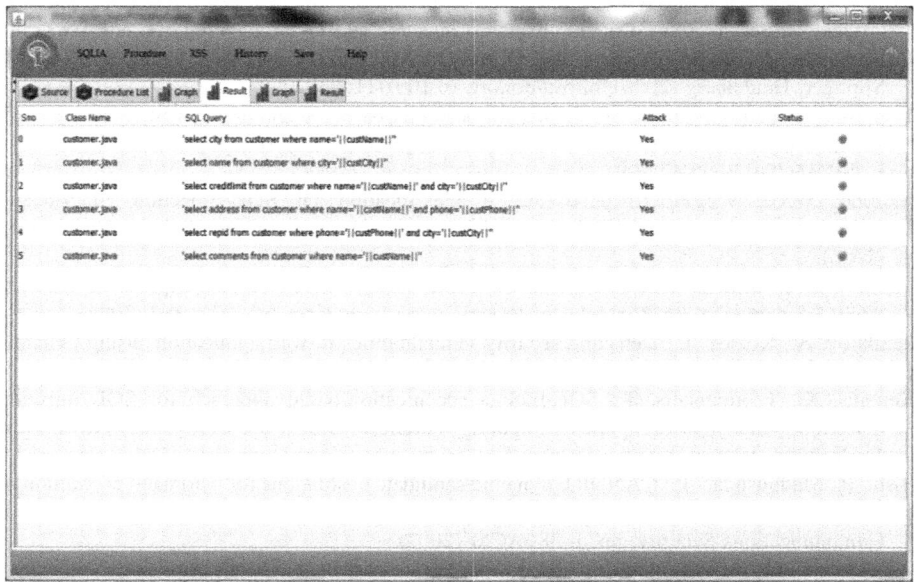

Fig. 8. IVA – Analyze the queries and display the result.

References

John, A., Agarwal, A., Bhardwaj, M.: An adaptive algorithm to prevent SQL injection. Am. J. Netw. Commun. Spec. Issue: Ad Hoc Netw. **4**(3–1), 12–15 (2015). https://doi.org/10. 11648/j.ajnc.s.2015040301.13

Tajpour, A., Heydari, M.Z., Masrom, M., Ibrahim, S.: SQL injection detection and prevention tool assessment. In: 2010 3rd IEEE International Conference on Computer Science and Information Technology, vol. 9 (2010). ISBN 978-1-4244-5537-9

Das, D., Sharma, U., Bhattacharyya, D.K.: An approach to detection of SQL injection attack based on dynamic query matching. Int. J. Comput. Appl. **1**(25), 28–34 (2010). ISSN 0975-8887

Anekar: Finding application errors and security flaws using PQL: a program query language. In: Opsla 2005, 16–20 October 2005, San Diego, California, USA (2012)

Shahriar, H., Zulkernine, M.: Music: mutation based SQL injection vulnerability checking. In: The Eighth International Conference on Quality Software (2008)

Inyong, L., Soonki, J., Sangsoo, Y., Jongsub, M.: A novel method for SQL injection attack detection based on removing SQL query attribute values. Math. Comput. Modell. **55**(1–2), 58–68 (2012)

Kar, D., Panigrahi, S.: Prevention of SQL injection attack using query transformation and hashing. In: 2013 IEEE 3rd International Advance Computing Conference (IACC) (2013)

Wei, K., Muthuprasanna, M., Kothari, S.: Preventing SQL injection attacks in stored procedures. In: Software Engineering Conference (2006)

Siddarth, S., Doshi, P.: Five Common Web Application Vulnerabilities (2010). www.Symantec. Com/Connect/Articles/Five-Common-Web-Applicaions-Vulnerabilities

Pietraszek, T., Berghe, C.V.: Defending against injection attacks through context-sensitive string evaluation. In: Valdes, A., Zamboni, D. (eds.) RAID 2005. LNCS, vol. 3858, pp. 124–145. Springer, Heidelberg (2006). https://doi.org/10.1007/11663812_7

Tian, W., Yang, J.-F., Xu, J., Si, G.-N.: Attack model based penetration test for SQL injection vulnerability. In: Computer Software and Applications Conference Workshop (2012). E-ISBN 978-0-7695-4758-9

Halfond, W.G., Viegas, J., Orso, A.: A classification Of SQL injection attacks and countermeasures. In: 2006 IEEE International Symposium on Secure Software Engineering (2006)

Su, Z., Wassermann, G.: The essence of command injection attacks in web application. In: 33rd Annual Symposium on Principles of Programming Languages, pp. 372–382 (2006)

Petukhov, A., Kozlov, P.: Detecting security vulnerabilities in web applications using dynamic analysis with penetration testing. In: OWASP Application Security Conference (2008)

Kemalis, K., Tzouramanis, T.: SQL-IDS: a specification-based approach for SQL injection detection symposium on applied computing, Fortaleza, Brazil, pp. 2153–2158. ACM, New York (2008)

Bisht, P., Madhusudan, P.: CANDID: dynamic candidate evaluations for automatic prevention of SQL injection attacks. In: Proceedings of the 14th ACM Conference on Computer and Communications Security, pp. 1–38. ACM (2007)

Wassermann, G., Su, Z.: An analysis framework for security in web applications. In: Proceedings of the FSE Workshop on Specification and Verification of Component-Based Systems (SAVCBS 2004), pp. 70–78 (2004)

Cook, W.R., Rai, S.: Safe query objects: statically typed objects as remotely executable queries. In: Proceedings of the 27th International Conference on Software Engineering (ICSE 2005) (2005)

McClure, R., Krüger, I.: SQL DOM: compile time checking of dynamic SQL statements. In: Proceedings of the 27th International Conference on Software Engineering (ICSE 2005), pp. 88–96 (2005)

Detection of Leukemia in Human Blood Samples Through Image Processing

Ravi Raj Choudhary, Savita Sharma, and Gaurav Meena[✉]

Central University of Rajasthan, Rajasthan 305817, India
{raviraj,2015mscs017,gaurav.meena}@curaj.ac.in

Abstract. This paper proposed a automated approach for leukemia detection in human blood samples. In this fast growing technology, the method of manual counting of WBCs under a microscope affords a time-consuming and its accuracy depends on the skill of the person. This paper proposed an image processing technique for the detection of leukemia in a human blood sample. Proposed work overcome the problem of k-means clustering and thresholding method by using the image enhancement techniques and some arithmetic operation for the segmentation of nucleus from the white blood cells. Segmentation based on LAB color space (luminosity, chromaticity layer a and chromaticity layer b) color space will be used in order to eliminate the white blood cells (WBC) from the background. The segmented image is used to calculate the shape based feature of the nucleus of the WBCs. K-NN classifier has been utilized to classify blast cells from normal lymphocyte cells. The system is applied to 108 images available in public image dataset for the study of leukemia.

Keywords: Leukemia · Chromaticity · Thresholding · Segmentation

1 Introduction

More than 1 Million North America are fighting against blood cancer and this is third leading cause of cancer death. Early detection is rare for blood cancer, there is no measure that can be taken to prevent the onset of these diseases. Leukemia is the most common cancer in children less than 20 years old and death rate for children 0–14 years old in united state has declined 76% over the last 30 years.

The body have different processes done by the different cells. Blood cells are one of the most important cells made in the bone marrow as shown in Fig. 1. Human body made billions of blood cells in which have WBCs fight against the infection, RBCs carry oxygen and platelets. The blood cells formed in the bone marrow and release into the blood stream to take part running in the body. Due to some causes, there is the rapid amplification of types of WBCs with the result the amount of number of WBCs in our body is start to rise and the result regulation is lost then the cell division is rapid. These are the cancerous cells.

© Springer Nature Singapore Pte Ltd. 2018
P. Bhattacharyya et al. (Eds.): NGCT 2017, CCIS 828, pp. 824–834, 2018.
https://doi.org/10.1007/978-981-10-8660-1_61

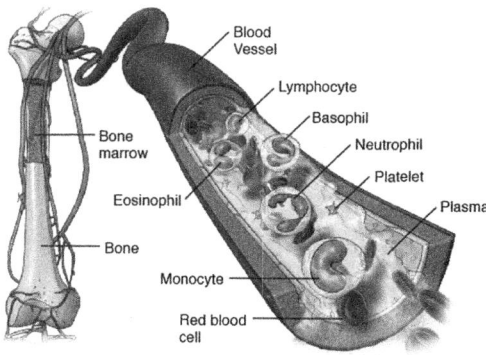

Fig. 1. Result of classification

Leukemia is a type of blood cancers, occur in all age groups.In the fast growing technology, the laboratory test takes a longer interval of time to detect the disease, which is time-consuming and the accuracy depends on the experience of the hematologist. The ratio of white blood cells is 1000:1 in our body. It means only 1 white cell between the 1000 red cells.

White blood cells rapidly grow in our body then it causes an effect on the other cells [1]. Leukemia plays a vital role to extract information associated with them which help us to detect many types of diseases. So we need a system which is helpful for the detection of leukemia in human blood samples images at an early stage so it can be diagnosed at right time and this is done by the image processing techniques. This paper proposed a CAD system for extracting information associated with WBCs. It consists of four modules: Image pre-processing, Image segmentation, Feature extraction, Classification.

Segmentation play the main role in these processes because the accuracy of the feature extraction and classification algorithms depend on correct segmentation of the nucleus and cytoplasm of WBCs. There are so many methods used in the literature of segmentation like k-means clustering algorithm, watershed transform, histogram equalization and contrast stretching and many other morphological operations based are used. All method are quite good but the problem occurs like in k-means clustering algorithm the chosen of initial centroid play a crucial role for the resultant cluster with the varying centroid the resultant clusters should different. To overcome this problem Patel and Mishra [2] introduce a subtractive cluster algorithm to choose the optimal data points for the centroid based on the density of surrounded data points. But it is very helpful if we have simple segmentation algorithm which gives us the segmented nucleus and cytoplasm of the WBCs which do not depend on the thresholding or some other. In this paper introduced a new segmentation technique based on the arithmetic and morphological operator. Types of Leukemia: Leukemia can be classified based on how fast it becomes severe. Leukemia is classified as chronic or acute. Acute Leukemia - cancerous cells do not perform like normal blood cells and growing very fast and shows its symptoms with in a week comes from immature cells. Chronic Leukemia - cancerous cells perform like normal cells and grow very slow and shows its symptoms in years comes from little bit mature cells. The whole process by which leukemia occurs still the same so we have mature cells loses its ability to mature and divide rapidly out of control that's still going on.

2   Literature Review

Dhanachndra et al. perform k-means clustering algorithm by using attractive clustering method where centroid is generated based on the potential value of data points to find out the white blood cells nuclei. Joshi et al. [3] proposed automatic otsu thresholding blood cell segmentation method along with image enhancement and arithmetic for WBCS segmentation.

Dipti et al. [4] proposed a lymphocyte segmentation method in two stages in which first identified the WBCs nucleus from the background by applied k-means clustering on the LAB color space and in the second stage perform Nearest Neighbor classification for undesirable overlapping of regions.

Savkare et al. [5] find that the k-means algorithm does not work efficiently in the case of low contrast images of cells. To overcome this problem in his proposed work used k-means clustering and global threshold in HSV color space and morphological operation to segment the cells.

Patel et al. [1] proposed a segmentation method based on HSV color space will be used in order to separate the white blood cells (WBC) from the background of the images.A morphological operator such as erosion plays importance role, especially for the overlapping cells. but the system is not so robust for the counting of WBCs.

Nimesh Patel et al. [2] applied k-means clustering algorithm for the detection of WBCs from the background of the image and then applied histogram equalization and Zack algorithm for the grouping of the lymphocytes and myelocytes and also use some techniques for the identification of the grouped lymphocytes and finally we get the segmented image in which the nucleus and cytoplasm are extracted.

Vaghela et al. [1] in this work eliminate the WBCs by using otsu thresholding and some morphological operator like area opening to remove connected component, dilation to remove pixel on object boundaries and then hole filling operator is performed and finally we get the segmented image and then find the shape based features is more accurate than other methods and the result is quite good.

2.1   Problem Statement

1. Proposed a image segmentation method to segment the nucleus of lymphocyte and lymphoblast cells by using arithmetic and morphological operations.
2. Also explore use of Lab color space other than RGB color space.
3. without using k-means clustering and thresholding method which improve the accuracy of the classification of lymphocyte and lymphoblast cells.

3   Proposed Work

This propoed work is based on four main processes Image pre-processing, Image segmentation, Feature Extraction, and Classification as shown in Fig. 2.

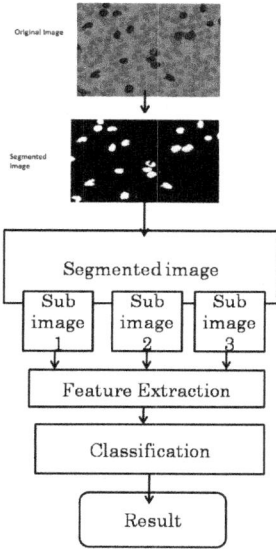

Fig. 2. Flow diagram of proposed system

3.1   Image Pre-processing

Some time input images may contain some noise. There may be blurriness in the image that's may causes some problems in accuracy of the system. The noise is removed from the image by applying some filters. For example Wiener filter is used to remove the blurriness in the image. Image cleaning also performed to clean the leukocytes which are present at the edges and other objects which are not useful for us. Solidity need to be measured for image cleaning. First, area and the convex area of each leukocyte need to be measured and then only we can find solidity for the image cleaning. The image we have got is in the RGB form which is needed to be converted into the grey scale image for further processing (Fig. 3).

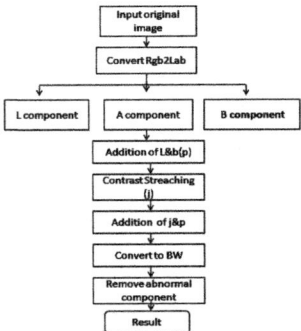

Fig. 3. Proposed Segmentation process

3.2   Image Segmentation

This algorithm procedure is applied to each and the resultant of segmentation is then achieved. As mentioned above through the study of the existing method we conclude that each and every method of segmentation either depend on the value of k or on the threshold value. There is no such a very simple and efficient which can easily segment the nucleus and cytoplasm of the lymphocyte and lymphoblast efficiently without the dependency of any other thing.

1. Step 1: Input the color blood slide image to the system.
2. Step 2: Convert the color image into CIE LAB image because it highlights the visual difference among colors, and it provides accuracy and a perceptual approach in the color difference calculation.
3. Step 3: Separate only L and B component because we need to segmentation of nucleus.
4. Step 4: Obtain the image $I_1 = L + B$ to brighten all other image components except cell nucleus.
5. Step 5: To adjust image intensity level apply linear contrast stretching to the image (I1) and we get the image I2.
6. Step 6: Obtain the image $I_3 = I1 + I2$ to remove all other components of blood with minimum effect of distortion Over nucleus.
7. Step 7: Find the gradient magnitude of I3 image.
8. Step 8: Convert I3 image to BW.
9. Step 9: To remove small pixel groups use morphological opening.

In this proposed segmentation algorithm we gives the input microscopic image as an input is shown in Fig. 6(a) then system convert the RGB to Lab color space because it has only two component is designed to approximate the human vision and then we take only two component L and b and add them which shown in Fig. 6(d) then applied the linear contrast stretching and perform some morphological function and we get the result as shown in Fig. 6(e) and the find the gradient magnitude of the resultant image and convert it into BW image as shown in Fig. 6(f) and finally we get the segmented images as shown in Fig. 6(h). Which represent the segmented human blood cells image. This is all done in segmentation phase. This proposed method is tested by the different microscopic human blood samples images. Applied this segmentation method on all these images and the result is quite good.

3.3   Identification of Grouped Leucocyte

One of the main problem in analyses the features of blood cells is the overlapping cells if the cells are overlapped or grouped together then we can not measure its features individually because the features of the cells grouped to each other. We can not find the find out the feature of the nucleus of the cells properly. So, in that case, our system considered that cells as a single cell and find the features and that will lead to the great impact on the accuracy of the classification of cells. We have to find the grouped lymphocyte and we can easily eliminate it or separate it for the further study. There are different kinds of methods available which are helpful to find out this grouped lymphocyte from the blood images. We can measure the roundness to separate the grouped lymphocyte by analyzing the shape of the lymphocyte. In mostly cases, the shape of the individual cell is rounded but that was not in a case of grouped cells. In rounded measure, we check the shape of the nucleus is circular or not. Roundness was checked by dividing the area of a circle to the area of an object by using the convex perimeter. If the object is circular then the value of roundness is 1 and if the object is not circular than the value of the roundness is less than 1. Roundness is not sensitive to the irregular boundaries because it disbars the local irregularities. After the observation, we find a threshold value i.e 0.80 which can be used properly to distinguish between the single lymphocyte and the grouped lymphocyte. The objects having the roundness value greater than the value of the threshold are considered as the individual lymphocyte and on the other hand, if the value of the roundness is less than the threshold value is considered as grouped lymphocyte. So we get the result the individual cells are sent for the further processing and the grouped cells are remove for the further study to separate the cells [2].

3.4   Image Cleaning

The main area of interest for the further study of the microscopic images of blood cells is the lymphocyte. So we have to focus on only the lymphocyte in the image we neglect the other than the lymphocyte from the images. The images which we take as the input images of the blood so there may occur that images contain some of the lymphocyte on the edges of the image. The presence of the partial lymphocyte image creates error in the study so we have eliminated those partial lymphocyte from the edges to get the better result. The operations we have to perform for image cleaning are to remove the abnormal objects and cleaning the edges of an image. The size of the area is an important to measure which we have to calculated. To discard the irregular component. We have to calculate the mean area from the size of the area. The objects which are on the edges having a very small area and the objects having the large area might be the grouped cells of lymphocyte. So we calculate the area and the convex area for the removal of the small and large area component, then we measure the solidity to find out the density of a component. We calculate the solidity by dividing the area to the convex hull of each component. The object is solid if the solidity value is 1 and component having irregular boundaries if the solidity is less than 1. After the observation, 0.90 value is use to find out abnormal component for the image. So 0.90 is considered as a threshold value for the solidity. The component whose value is less than the threshold value should be eliminated because these are the component that is on the edges of the image that should be discarded. Figure shows the cleaned image which can be obtained by eliminated the lymphocyte on the edges [2].

3.5   Feature Extraction

Feature extraction process find the feature of the nucleus of the lymphocytes. This process redefining a large set of redundant data into the set of features, the selection of features greatly influences the performance of the classifier, therefore the choice of a correct feature is very important and crucial step. In order to select the feature to construct an effective feature set, several published articles were studied and observed their methodology of the feature selection and then implemented their feature on the different images in our system and we get the effective features and this feature was widely used as they gave a good classification. The feature which is used in this proposed system that considered to boost the classifier performance and finally we can differentiate between the cancerous and non-cancerous data [2].

Proposed work find the geometric and textual features using statistical method of examining the texture of the segmented images that considered the spatial relationship of pixels is the gray-level co-occurrence matrices(GLCM). GLCM functions characterize the texture of the nucleus by calculating how often the pairs of pixel of the nucleus image with specific values and in a specified spatial relationship occurs in an image, creating a GLCM and then extracting statistical measure from this matrix. By using second-order statistics to described the Gray-level pixel distribution such as the probability of two pixels which have the particular gray levels at particular spatial relationships. This information can be given in 2-D gray-level co-occurrence matrices, various distances, and orientation can be computed for this matrices. So to use the information that is contained in the GLCM which is given by hard lick defined some statistical measure which is used for the extraction of the textual characteristics [6]. Some of the features are listed below:

Contrast: Measures the local variations in the gray level co-occurence matrix.

$$contrast = \sum_{n=0}^{N_g-1} n^2 \sum_{i=1}^{N_g} \sum_{j=1}^{Ng} p(i,j) \tag{1}$$

Correlation: Measures the joint probability occurence of the specified pixels pairs.

Energy: provide the sum of squarred elements in the GLCM. Also known as uniformity or the angular second moment.

$$Energy = \sum_{i,j=0}^{n-1} P_{i,j} \tag{2}$$

Homogeneity: Measures the closeness of the distribution of elements in the GLCM to the GLCM diagonal.

$$Homogeneity = \sum_i \sum_j (1/1 + (i,j)^2) p(i,j) \tag{3}$$

Area: Means the total number of pixels in the regions. IT means it measures the number of pixels in the nucleus of lymphocytes.

$$Area = \sum_{x=1}^{x} \sum_{y=1}^{y} f(x,y) \tag{4}$$

Perimeter: It measures the number of at the boundary of the regions.

$$perimeter = 2 * pi * Area \tag{5}$$

Centriod: Measure the co-ordinate with respect to the center of mass, in which the centroid1 is the horizontal co-ordinate of the center of mass and the centroid 2 is the vertical co-ordinate(y coordinate) of the center of mass.

Diameter: The diameter of the circle with the same area as the region of interest.

$$Diameter = sqrt(4 * Area/Pi) \tag{6}$$

MajorAxisLength: It is a scalar value,in which the pixels of the major axis of the sllipse that has the same second-moments as the region of interest.

$$MajorAxisLength = (\sum_{i=1}^{n} x_i/n, \sum_{i=1}^{n} y_i/n) \tag{7}$$

MinorAxisLength: It is a scalar value,in which the pixels of the minor axis of the sllipse that has the same second-moments as the region of interest.

Eccentricity: Eccentricity of the ellipse which has the same second-moments as the region and measured as the ratio of distance between the foci of the ellipse and its major axis length.

$$Eccentricity = \sqrt{(a^2 - b^2)}/a \tag{8}$$

Orientation: It is measured as the angle between the x-axis and the major axis of the ellipse that has the same second-moment as the region.

Solidity: is measured as the ratio of the area and convex Area.

$$solidity = area/convexarea \tag{9}$$

4   Dataset of Images

The ALL-IDB image dataset is used which is provided by Fabio Scotti to test and compare the algorithm for segmentation of the WBCs cells and classification of the ALL. These are two types of data sets are available the ALL-IDB1 used for testing and comparing the segmentation algorithm and also for the capability of algorithms and ALLIDB2 used to test the classification algorithm of the blast cells or to check the accuracy of different algorithm .The example of ALL-IDB1 and ALL-IDB2 images are shown in Figs. 4 and 5

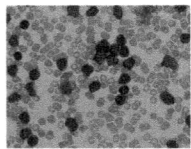

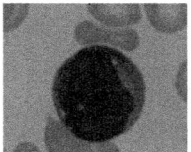

Fig. 4. ALLIDB1   **Fig. 5.** ALLIDB2

5   Experimental Result

The microscopic images have been given to proposed system as an input. The system convert RGB to Lab color space, it has only two component (Luminance and Chroma) approximate the human vision. L and b component and add them shown in Fig. 6(d). Result of linear contrast stretching and perform some morphological function are as shown in Fig. 6(e) and final segmented images as shown in Fig. 6(h). Figure 6(h) shows segmented human blood cells image. The proposed method is tested by the different microscopic human blood samples images and the data set which used here is ALL_IDB1 contains 108 images. Applied this segmentation method on all these images and the result is quite good. some of the segmented images from them is shown as: Shape and texture feature from segmented images are extracted for NN model. Initially extract the GLCM feature like correlation, energy, contrast and homogeneity are calculated from the nucleus region of the lymphocyte. The classification accuracy of lymphocyte and lymphoblast based on the texture and shape feature of the nucleus. Similarly, a shape based feature like area, perimeter, centroid, diameter, eccentricity, solidity, orientation, major axis length and minor axis length are calculated. We extract the shape-based feature of all the segmented images. Firstly we calculate the number of lymphoblast cells in an image and then extract the feature of the all these sub-images and finally we get the data set of these cells in the images which contain the features of 456 lymphocyte and lymphoblast cells. KNN classifier to classify these data set as a cancerous and non-cancerous cell, the achieved accuracy is 86.59% shown in Table 1.

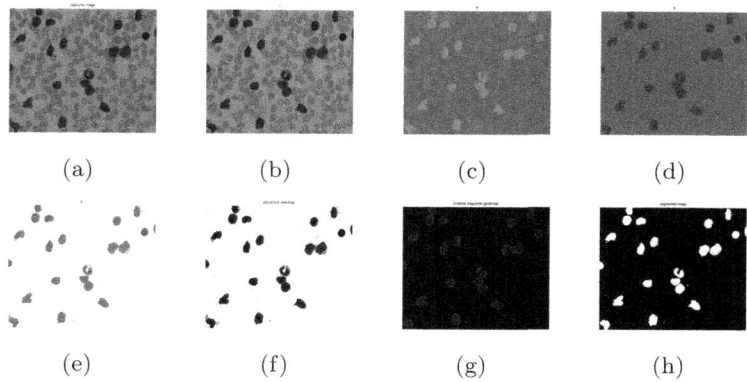

$$
\begin{array}{cccc}
\text{(a)} & \text{(b)} & \text{(c)} & \text{(d)}
\end{array}
$$

$$
\begin{array}{cccc}
\text{(e)} & \text{(f)} & \text{(g)} & \text{(h)}
\end{array}
$$

Fig. 6. (a) Original image (b) L component (c) B component (d) Addition of A and B(p) (e) Contrast stretching(j) (f) Additon of J and p (g) Gradient image (h) Segmented image

Table 1. Comparison of proposed results

Methods	Merits/demerits	Accuracy
Watershed transform	Merit: Easy method for detection of white cell. Demerits: It cannot give accurate result and cannot implement on each and every image	72.2%
K means clustering	Merits: It is used for clustering and separate the data based on value of K.	72%
	Demerits: It does not give classification with labeled data and also not applicable on incremental data	
Edge detection using histogram equalizing method and linear contrast stretching	Merit: This is very useful method to detect white cell and for contrast enhancement.	73.7%
	Demerit: It is hard to define boundary of overlapping cell	
Proposed work	Merit: A very easy and simple approach for the segmentation of cell.	86.59%
	Demerit: It cannot separate the overlapping cells	

6   Conclusion and Future Work

This proposed work presented a methodology to achieved a fully automated segmentation techniques. The methodology is based on the image enhancement and simple arithmetic operation method to extract the nucleus and cytoplasm of the lymphocyte. Then segmented images are used for the morphological study of the cells and finds the features of the normal lymphocyte and lymphoblast which help us to classify the normal cells and the cancerous cells. Results shows the presented methodology is achievable and it provide accuracy 86.59%. The research finding made out of this project work by open several fallback research direction which can be further explore. The segmentation scheme can be enhanced by some other techniques that can lead to the color based segmentation and can also lead to segmentation of overlapping cells as well. This proposed work, which deals with computer aided detection and classification of ALL can extended to the classification of all types of leukemia. Further we can also enhanced the efficiency of learning classifier system, which can executed in parallel for the better response time and for better accuracy.

References

1. Vaghela, H.P., Modi, H., Pandya, M., Potdar, M.B.: Leukemia detection using digital image processing techniques. Int. J. Appl. Inf. Syst. **10**(1), 43–51 (2015). Published by Foundation of Computer Science (FCS), NY, USA.
2. Patel, N., Mishra, A.: Automated leukaemia detection using microscopic images. Procedia Comput. Sci. **58**, 635–642 (2015)
3. Joshi, M., et al.: White blood cells segmentation and classification to detect acute leukemia. IJETTCS **2**(3), 147–151 (2013)
4. Mohapatra, S., Patra, D., Kumar, S., Satpathy, S.: Lymphocyte image segmentation using functional link neural architecture for acute leukemia detection. Biomed. Eng.Lett. **2**, 100–110 (2012)
5. Savkare, S.S., Narote, A.S., Narote, S.P.: Automatic blood cell segmentation using K-Mean clustering from microscopic thin blood images. In: Proceedings of the Third International Symposium on Computer Vision and the Internet, VisionNet'16, pp. 8–11, ACM. New York, NY, USA (2016)
6. Rawat, J., Singh, A., Bhadauria, H.S., Virmani, J.: Computer aided diagnostic system for detection of leukemia using microscopic images. Procedia Computer Science **70**, 748–756 (2015)

Automatic Screening Method for Bone Health Diagnosis

Punal M. Arabi[✉], Gayatri Joshi[✉], Tejaswi Bhat,
and Varini Chinnabhandar

ACS College of Engineering, Bangalore, India
arabi.punal@gmail.com, gayitrijoshi@gmail.com,
tbhat1995@gmail.com, vc_aus@yahoo.com

Abstract. Bone is a composite material consisting of both inorganic and organic components. The estimation of bone strength is an important risk factor in the clinical assessment of osteoporosis. There are several bone diseases that cause abnormalities of bone such as osteoporosis, rickets, osteomalacia, osteogenesis imperfecta, osteopenia, fibrous dysplasia etc. About 300 million people are affected annually by osteoporosis worldwide. Osteoporosis is a metabolic bone disorder that causes loss of bone mass and strength. Osteopenia refers to bone density that is lower than healthy bone density. Femur trabecular bone is a complex dynamic structure which represents porosity and stiffness. The evaluation of osteoporosis is developed by using the DXA (Dual-energy x-ray absorptiometry) imaging technique and computed tomography (CT). In this paper, a method is proposed to categorise healthy, osteopenia and osteoporosis bones based on 4-connectivity and the ratio of the number of 4 connected objects in every ROI to the reference value. The mean value of these ratio values of healthy, osteopenic and osteoporotic bone images are calculated and the decision rule is framed. This method experiments on a total of twenty bone images; ten healthy, five osteopenic and five osteoporotic categories. The result obtained shows that the proposed system gives 100% accuracy.

Keywords: Bone · CT · DXA · Femur · Osteoporosis · Osteopenia
4 connectivity · MATLAB 2013a

1 Introduction

Bone is a tough and rigid form of connective tissue. Various organs of the body are protected by bones. They produce red and white blood cells, store minerals and enable mobility as well as support for the body.

Bone density is the amount of bone mineral in bone tissue. Clinically, it is measured according to optical density per square centimeter of bone surface upon imaging. By a procedure known as densitometry, it is measured as an indicator of fractures and primarily osteoporosis. Usually the lumbar spine or the hip bone is considered but our study makes use of the femur trabecular bone. The hip bone can't be used to measure bone density for people weighing over 300 pounds. The disadvantage of bone density measurement along the lumbar spine is the overlapping effect caused by certain

© Springer Nature Singapore Pte Ltd. 2018
P. Bhattacharyya et al. (Eds.): NGCT 2017, CCIS 828, pp. 835–843, 2018.
https://doi.org/10.1007/978-981-10-8660-1_62

calcifications and aortic calcifications. Therefore, DEXA method used on the femur trabecular bone is more feasible apart from its reasons of accuracy. Trabecular bone has a complex dynamic structure and is porous.

Osteoporosis is a skeletal disorder characterized by decreased bone strength that may lead to the susceptibility of fracture. Osteoporosis can also be termed as a metabolic condition that causes loss of bone mass and strength. Osteopenia refers to a condition in which bone density is lower than healthy bone density but not low enough to classify as osteoporosis. It is difficult to diagnose osteoporosis at the early stages. Most often people suspect the symptoms of osteoporosis as a bone fracture.

Spine bone fracture is which called as compression fracture will cause severe pain over the entire spinal region; Osteoporosis also causes severe spine pain and this pain often mistaken as compression fracture pain.

1.1   Literature Survey

Lin et al. [1] presented two-Compartment model for calculating bone volume fractions and bone mineral densities of computed tomography images for diagnoses of osteoporosis disease. Wu et al. [2], reviewed meta-analysis of patients with osteoporosis-related fractures managed through a fracture liaison service (FLS) programmer. Danopia and Bhargava [3], prsented the geometry of femur bone with plate and screws to identify the location of maximum and minimum stresses of femur bone which is having no crack on the static condition. Analyzing the cracked femur bone and identification of fractured femur bone. Zeljkovic et al. [4], proposed visual and numerical functions. Visual function is detected and indicated the potential bone tissue by marking it in a different color and distinguishing it from the background. Numerical function enables the amount of detected skull bone by calculating its numerical content value.

Impulse response test was carried out by Tejaswini et al. [5] on a tibial bone for detection and prediction of osteoporosis using Labview. The vibrations generated by the tibial bone were analyzed and natural frequency of vibration was found to be much lesser in osteoporosis subjects due to the fact that the bone mineral density of osteoporosis bones is low. A decision making system is proposed in this work using ANN in MAT LAB to predict osteoporosis. Afsarimanesh et al. [6] presented non-invasive sensor system to detect CTX-I in order to detect bone loss at earlier stages by the technique of Electrochemical Impedance Spectroscopy (EIS). An equivalent circuit is tested using Complex Non-linear Least Square (CNLS).

Zheng and Makrogiannis [7] suggests the use of high-dimensional textural feature representations obtained from the study of radiographs. This was done to separate healthy subjects from osteoporotic subjects using the obtained data. Thus a texture classification technique was proposed for effective diagnosis of osteoporosis in bone radiography data. Ribagin et al. [8] presented an example of application of generalized nets in orthopedics and traumatology thus proposing a novel approach for the diagnosis of asymptomatic osteoporosis in elderly patients.

Reshmalakshmi and Sasikumar [9] proposed diagnosis of osteoporosis disease through medical imaging i.e. X-ray imaging density calculates bone intensity, Fuzzy edge directed image interpolation (FEDI) along with different membership functions for detecting osteoporosis. Arunkumar et al. [10] proposed osteoporosis can be detected by BMD (Bone mineral density). Trabecular region is studied by the use of Digital calcaneus radiographic images. Tafraouti et al. [11] suggested the use of fractal analysis of X-ray images for characterizing osteoporosis disease. This method involves steps based on the fractional Brownian motion (fBm) model. SVM classifier is used to distinguish two groups of patients, resulting in 95% accuracy classification between the two groups.

Lei [12] developed a method of pulse transmission system of quantitative ultrasound parameters. An ultrasound signal is transmitted in the bone. The message obtained by detection of the above signal can be used to diagnose and forecast the bone mass loss, thus giving a better picture of the effects of osteoporosis. Singh and Kim [13] proposed the use of biomarkers in clinical proteomics for early detection of osteoporosis. Various techniques such as BMD (Bone Mineral Density) testing, optical testing and electrochemical testing have been studied for comparison. The electrochemical technique was found to be the most suitable for the development of a Bio-MEMS chip due the achievement of high sensitivity in this method.

In this paper, a method is proposed to categorize healthy, osteopenia and osteoporosis bones based on 4-connectivity and the ratio of the number of 4-connected objects in every ROI to the reference value. The mean value of these ratio values of healthy, healthy, osteopenia and osteoporosis bone images are calculated and decision rule is framed. This method experiments on twenty bone images as ten images of healthy, five sets of osteopenia and osteoporosis category. The result obtained show that the proposed system is giving 100% accuracy.

1.2   Methodology

In the proposed method, ten images of healthy, three sets of osteopenic and osteoporotic CT femur bone images are taken for experimentation [14]. The acquired images are converted in to gray. The acquired RGB images are three-channel color images which takes three times as long as processing a grayscale image. Hence RGB to gray conversion is done to speed up the process. Preprocessing is applied for the converted gray images. The preprocessing is done by using the following steps.

1. Image filtering by high pass filter.
2. Image enhancement by Histogram Equalization.

The formula for Histogram Equalization is as follows:

$$\sum\nolimits_{i=1}^{k} = m_i \tag{1}$$

Where, Total number of observations is 'i' and k be the total number of bins, the histogram is m_i.

After Pre-processing, the ROI is selected and then it is converted to binary. For the obtained binary image 4-connectivity region property is applied and fixing threshold value for identifying healthy, osteopenic, osteoporotic bone structures (Fig. 1).

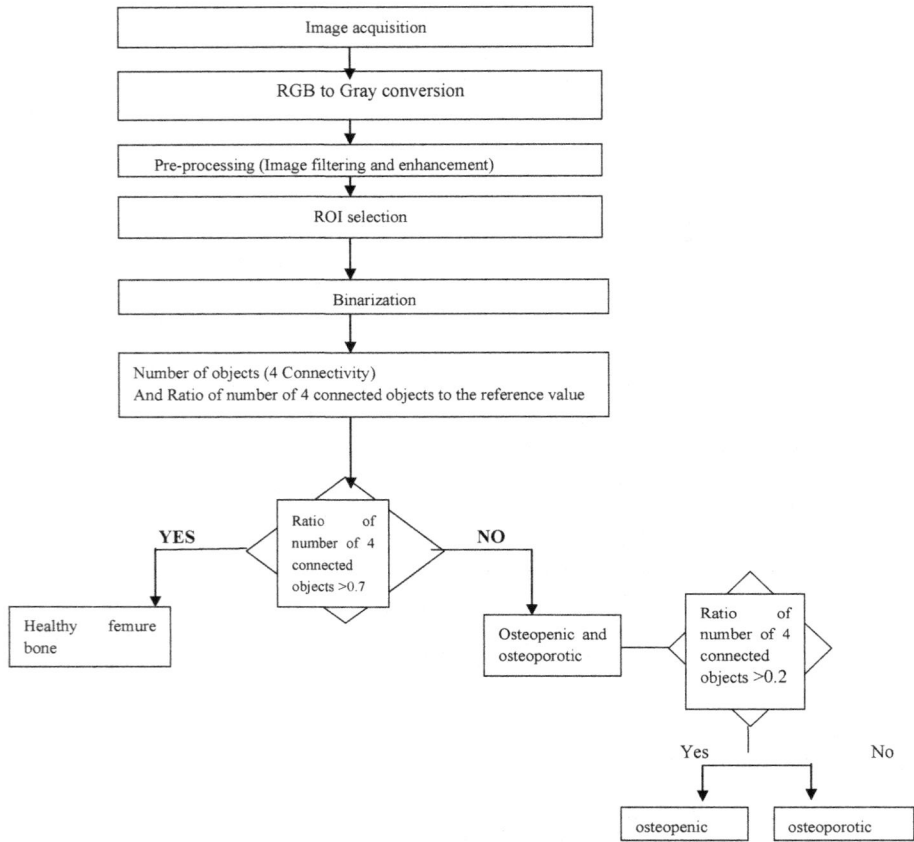

Fig. 1. Flow diagram

1.3   Results

Figure 2 shows the set of healthy femur CT bone images; Figs. 3 and 4 show the set of Osteopenic femur CT and the set of Osteoporotic femur CT bone images respectively. Table 1 shows the number of objects with 4-connectivity in the selected ROI regions of the images under analysis where as Table 2 shows the ratio of number of objects with four connectivity in the selected ROI regions of the images under analysis to the reference value 1294.1.

1.4   Discussion

A set of twenty bone images as ten in category of healthy, five sets of images in osteopenic and osteoporotic CT femur bone groups are taken for experimentation. A region of interest (ROI) is selected in each image. High pass filtering for noise removal and histogram equalization for Enhancement are done in the pre-processing

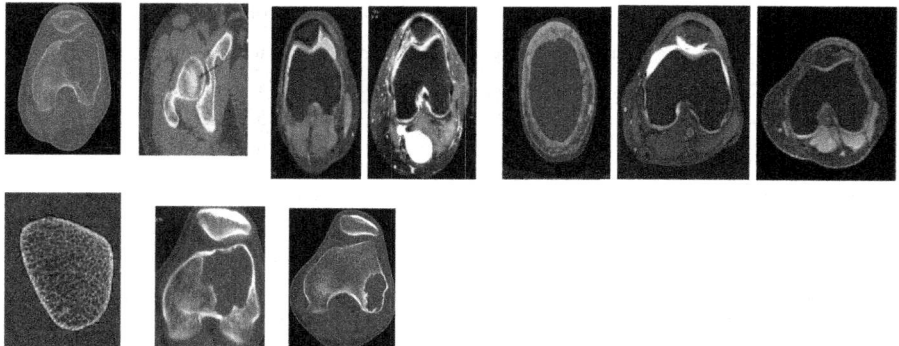

Fig. 2. Set of healthy femur images

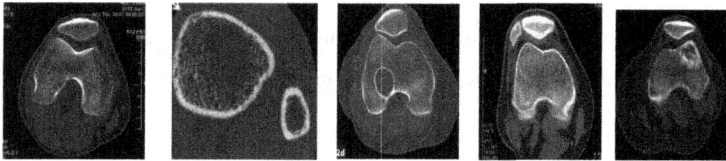

Fig. 3. Set of osteopenic femur bone images

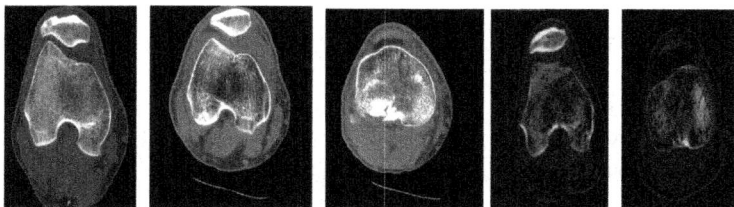

Fig. 4. Set of osteoporotic femur bone images

stage. The number of objects in the region of interest for 4-connectivity is calculated for all the healthy, osteopenic and osteoporotic CT femur bone images. The results obtained are tabulated. The reference value is arrived from a group of ten healthy bone images. For every healthy bone a ROI is identified and the number of 4-connected components in that region is calculated. The average of these 4-connected components (objects) in that region is then found and is taken as the reference value. The ratio of the number of objects in every ROI to the reference value is then calculate and tabulated. Table 2 shows these values. The mean values of these ratio values of healthy, osteo-penic and osteoporotic bone images are obtained and found to be equal to 0.99 for healthy, osteopenic it is equal to 0.3612 and osteoporotic it is equal to 0.051. Using these values a decision rule is framed as the average value for healthy bone is 0.7, threshold value for osteopenic and osteoporotic is 0.20.

Table 1. Number of connected components (4-connectivity)

Images	Healthy femur bone	Osteopenic femur bone	Osteoporotic femur bone
Image 1	1309	408	88
Image 2	1183	622	65
Image 3	1481	316	125
Image 4	1100	550	79
Image 5	1565	450	68
Image 6	1400		
Image 7	1676		
Image 8	1010		
Image 9	1001		
Image 10	1216		
AVG	1294.1		

Table 2. Ratio of number of 4 connected objects to the reference value

Images	Healthy femur bone	Osteopenic femur bone	Osteoporotic femur bone
Image 1	1.011	0.31	0.068
Image 2	0.9141	0.48	0.032
Image 3	1.144	0.244	0.044
Image 4	0.8500	0.425	0.061
Image 5	1.209	0.347	0.052
Image 6	1.081		
Image 7	1.2951		
Image 8	0.780		
Image 9	0.7735		
Image 10	0.9396		
AVG	0.999	0.3612	0.051

1.4.1 Calculation

Average value:

$$\frac{(1309 + 1183 + 1481 + 1100 + 1565 + 1400 + 1676 + 1010 + 1001 + 1216)}{10}$$
$$= 1294.1 \tag{2}$$

Ratio of number of 4 connected components

$$\frac{1309}{1294.1} = 1.011 \tag{3}$$

Average value of ratio of number of 4 connected components for healthy bone

$$\frac{1.011 + 0.9141 + 1.144 + 0.8500 + 1.209 + 1.081 + 1.2951 + 0.780 + 0.7735 + 0.9396}{10}$$
$$= 0.999$$

$$(4)$$

Average value of ratio of number of 4 connected components for osteopenic bone

$$\frac{0.31 + 0.48 + 0.244 + 0.425 + 0.347}{5} = 0.3612 \tag{5}$$

Average value of ratio of number of 4 connected components for osteoporotic bone

$$\frac{0.068 + 0.032 + 0.044 + 0.061 + 0.052}{5} = 0.051 \tag{6}$$

Average mean of ratio value for fixing threshold value (healthy and osteopenic)

$$\frac{0.999 + 0.3612}{2} = 0.7 \tag{7}$$

Average mean of ratio value for fixing threshold value (osteoporotic and osteopenic)

$$\frac{0.3612 + 0.051}{2} = 0.2 \tag{8}$$

Based upon above calculations the following decision rules have made.

(1) If the number of objects are greater than 0.7 then that bone is categorized as healthy bone, if it is lesser than 0.7 those bone structures are categorized as, osteopenic and osteoporotic bone structures from Tables 1 and 2.
(2) If the number of objects is greater than 0.20 then it is categorized as osteopenic, if it is lesser than 0.20 i.e. osteoporotic bone structures.

Based upon on the reference value an accuracy analysis is done and the proposed method is found to be g 100% accurate for the group of 20 images (10 healthy and five set of osteopenic, osteoporotic).

1.5 Conclusions

The proposed system is tested on a total of twenty images which include ten sets of healthy, five sets of osteopenic and osteoporotic CT femur bone images each. Based on the number of 4-connected components and ratio of 4-connected components to the average value of healthy bone, the decision rule is framed that the ratio value is greater than 0.7 then that bone is categorized as healthy bone, if it is lesser than 0.7 those bone structures are categorized either osteopenic or osteoporotic bone. For further classification of osteopenic and osteoporotic second decision rule applied. The second decision rule states that if the 4 connectivity ratio is greater than 0.2 the bone is categorized as osteopenic or if it is lesser than 0.2 the bone is osteoporotic one. The results obtained show that the proposed method of bone health monitoring and classification is 100% accurate. However the proposed method is tested only on twenty images hence the 100% accuracy cannot be confirmed, only after carrying out the test on several more images and also after the clinical studies the accuracy of the method can be confirmed.

Acknowledgment. The authors thank the Management and Principal of ACS College of Engineering, Mysore road, Bangalore for permitting and supporting to carry out the research work.

References

1. Lin, H.-H., et al.: A novel two-compartment model for calculating bone volume fractions and bone mineral densities from computed tomography images. IEEE Trans. Med. Imaging **36**(5), 1094–1105 (2017)
2. Wu, C.-H., Tu, S.-T., Chang, Y.-F., Chan, D.-C., Chien, J.-T., Lin, C.-H., Singh, S., Dasari, M., Chen, J.-F., Tsai, K.-S.: Fracture liaison services improve outcomes of patients with osteoporosis-related fractures: a systematic literature review and meta-analysis. Osteoporos. Sarcopenia 3(3 Suppl.), S51–S52 (2017)
3. Danopia, A., Bhargava, M.: Finite element analysis of human fractured femur bone implantation with PMMA thermoplastic prosthetic plate. In: 11th International Symposium on Plasticity and Impact Mechanics (2017). Procedia Eng. **173**, 1658–1665 (2017)
4. Zeljkovic, V., Tameze, C., Vucenik, I., Stains, J.P., Druzgalski, C., Mayorga, P.: Algorithmic quantification of skull bone density. In: International Conference on High Performance Computing and Simulation, pp. 791–795. IEEE (2017)
5. Tejaswini, E., Vaishnavi, P., Sunitha, R.: Detection and prediction of osteoporosis using impulse response technique and artificial neural network. In: International Conference on Advances in Computing, Communications and Informatics (ICACCI), pp. 1571–1575 (2016)
6. Afsarimanesh, N., Mukhopadhyay, S.C., Kruger, M., Yu, P.-L., Kosel, J.: Sensors and instrumentation towards early detection of osteoporosis. In: Instrumentation and Measurement Technology Conference Proceedings (I2MTC), pp. 1–6 (2016)
7. Zheng, K., Makrogiannis, S.: Bone texture characterization for osteoporosis diagnosis using digital radiography. In: IEEE Engineering in Medicine and Biology Society (EMBC), pp. 1034–1037 (2016)
8. Ribagin, S., Roeva, O., Pencheva, T.: Generalized net model of asymptomatic osteoporosis diagnosis. In: IEEE 8th International Conference on Intelligent Systems (IS), pp. 604–608 (2016)
9. Reshmalakshmi, C., Sasikumar, M.: Fuzzy inference system for osteoporosis detection. In: Global Humanitarian Technology Conference (GHTC), pp. 675–681 (2016)
10. Arunkumar, R., Vishnu, T., Saranya, K., Gayathri Devi, M.: Efficient and early detection of osteoporosis using trabecular region. In: Green Engineering and Technologies (IC-GET), pp. 1–5 (2015)

11. Tafraouti, A., El Hassouni, M., Toumi, H., Lespessailles, E., Jennane, R.: Osteoporosis diagnosis using fractal analysis and support vector machine. In: Signal-Image Technology and Internet-Based Systems (SITIS), pp. 73–77 (2014)
12. Lei, Z.: System development of quantitative ultrasonic detection for osteoporosis. In: Electrical and Control Engineering (ICECE), pp. 2221–2224 (2010)
13. Singh, K., Kim, K.C.: Investigating new BioMEMS techniques for early detection of osteoporosis. In: Engineering in Medicine and Biology Society, pp. 2265–2268 (2007)
14. https://radiopaedia.org/

Robust Face Recognition Using Sparse and Dense Hybrid Representation with Local Correlation

M. A. Sahla Habeeba[1] , Philomina Simon[2(✉)], and R. Prajith[3]

[1] NIT Calicut, Kozhikode, Kerala, India
sahla.m.a@gmail.com
[2] Department of Computer Science, University of Kerala, Kariavattom,
Thiruvananthapuram 695581, Kerala, India
philomina.simon@gmail.com
[3] Mobilexion Technologies Pvt. Ltd., Thiruvananthapuram, Kerala, India
prajithr85@gmail.com

Abstract. Face Recognition is one of the biometrics that can be used to uniquely identify an individual based on the matching performed against known faces. The real world face recognition is very challenging since the face images acquired may vary with illumination, expression and pose. No existing system can claim that they have handled all these issues well. This work particularly focus on addressing the problems of face images taken in challenging environments. A more efficient Face Recognition system based on a combination of Sparse and Dense representation (SDR) along with Local Correlation is proposed. While considering the efficient methods for classification, Sparse Representation (SR) is the best one. Here a Supervised Low Rank (SLR) decomposition of dictionary is used to implement the SDR framework in the initial step. Then we apply Local Correlation to the cases where SDR-SLR method fails to distinguish competing classes properly. Usually due to changes in illumination and pose, variations can be seen to occur in different face parts. Correlation is calculated between the query image and the images of top matches that are obtained from the SDR-SLR method. Since we compute local correlation of relevant points only within a small dictionary, computation time of the proposed method is very less. Challenging benchmark datasets such as AR, Extended Yale and ORL databases are used for testing the proposed method. Experimental analysis shows that performance of the proposed method is better than the state-of-art face recognition approaches and the performance gains are very high.

Keywords: Robust face recognition · Biometrics · Illumination
Occlusion · Sparse coding · Local correlation · Landmarks
Dictionary learning

© Springer Nature Singapore Pte Ltd. 2018
P. Bhattacharyya et al. (Eds.): NGCT 2017, CCIS 828, pp. 844–853, 2018.
https://doi.org/10.1007/978-981-10-8660-1_63

1   Introduction

In today's digital era security breaches and fraudulent transaction increases day by day. Thus a secure, reliable and simple system for personal verification is becoming a great concern. The use of face images provide a highly-secure identification and personal verification system. The main objective of face recognition is to detect and recognize face images in any challenging situations. The major challenges encountered in machine vision are the huge dimension data and lack of identifying efficient features for accurate data classification. Since lot of challenging test databases are available, Face Recognition (FR) can be used to solve several machine vision problems [6]. It addresses many challenging real world applications such as duplication of identity documents, access control, person tracking, surveillance and in online scenarios such as image tagging and image search. The images taken in unconstrained environment have very low quality. Images of a single face become very different due to variations in poses illuminations, Occlusion and different human facial expressions, hence the recognition problem becomes more complex.

There are different approaches for extracting the features or reducing the dimensions of the data which includes PCA, LDA, ICA [5–7,9,11] and probability based subspace learning [8]. Usually Nearest Neighbourhood (NN) Classifier is applied. But these classifiers cannot perform well and the images are corrupted by noise and occlusions.

To represent a query image Sparse representation based classifier (SRC) [10] use training samples of all classes collaboratively. The representation error is minimized through l_1-norm, hence SRC can recognize face images when heavily corrupted by noise and occlusions. These lead to very motivating face recognition results. But if the training images are not carefully controlled and sufficient samples of each class is not present, then the method may fail or performance may affected badly.

1.1   Sparse and Dense Hybrid Representation Using Dictionary Decomposition

A dictionary based method for face recognition based on Sparse and Dense hybrid representation and low rank dictionary decomposition based on supervised learning [3] is used as the initial step in this proposed work. The class specific dictionary is sparse based and intra class variation dictionary is dense based. This sparse and dense based combination is used to represent a face image. The class sparse representation works well with specified class membership, since a query face image is represented with different variations of face images from other classes [3].

In SLR dictionary decomposition, the raw training data is decomposed into class-specific dictionary (A), a common intraclass variation dictionary (B) and a sparse corruption matrix. SDR of the query image is

$$y = A\alpha + BX + e \tag{1}$$

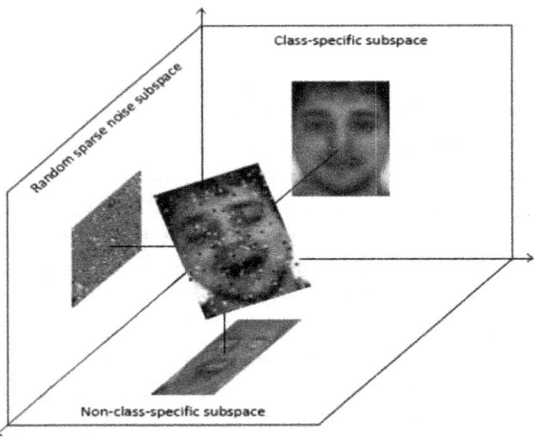

Fig. 1. Image decomposition [3]

Figure 1 denotes image of face projected to class specific dictionary (spanned by A), and intra class variation subspace (spanned by B) and the residual.

Inorder to make the method robust to corruptions by outliers and occlusions, l_1-norm minimization of the error e is applied. The equation can be applied to solve optimization problem to obtain the solution of SDR, α, X and e:

$$\min_{\alpha,X,e} \| \alpha \|_1 +\gamma \| X \|_2^2 +\beta \| e \|_1 \qquad s.t \quad y = A\alpha + +BX + e \qquad (2)$$

Although SDR-SLR gives a good result in face recognition problem the method obtains mis classification for many of the slightly varying images. For some test images, the difference between residual values produced by different classes is computed as very low and in such cases face images are wrongly classified.

2   Proposed Method - Sparse and Dense Hybrid Representation with Local Correlation (SDR-SLR-LC)

There are some cases of mis recognitions of the face images in SDR-SLR method due to the comparatively same residual values produced by different classes for a query image. These cases can be called as constituting weak classification. By analysing the mis recognitions over multiple datasets, we found out that these weakly classified images had significant local variations. This happens because SDR-SLR values are computed for full images. The result of SDR-SLR could be significantly improved if these weakly classified cases are verified through another method which addresses, the shortcomings of SDR-SLR (Fig. 2).

So a new method is proposed where the local correlation is applied as a refining step, after the SDR-SLR method, only in cases where SDR-SLR fails to

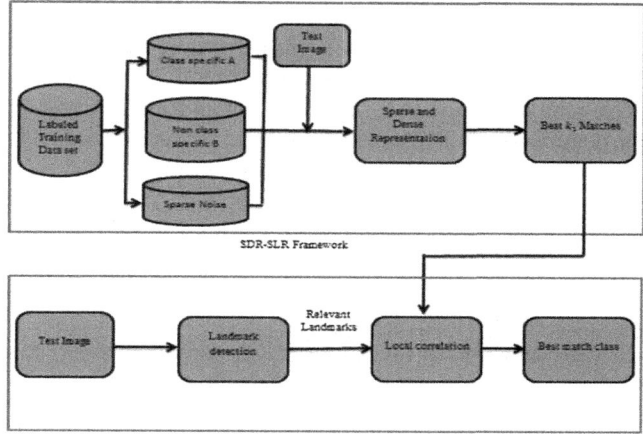

Fig. 2. Block diagram of SDR-SLR-LC

distinguish competing classes properly. Correlation based techniques are widely used for face detection, recognition and related tasks. [1, 2, 4] Their negative side being the time taken for computation if the dataset is large. But we can see that correlation is a viable method for refining SDR-SLR since by their very nature sparse coding is used with only a few samples for each person. So applying an additional step of correlation as a refining step only over weakly classified cases, will not consume any more significant time. Correlation of relevant landmarks of the query image and the training images of top matches, identified by SDR, is calculated. The person whose training image gives the highest correlation value is identified as the class to which the query image belongs to.

Now we consider the experimental analysis of SDR-SLR method conducted in AR database. From the 700 images tested in challenging situations such as variations in pose, illumination and occlusion in AR database, 28 face images got mis recognized. SDR-SLR classify the face image into the class which produce the least residual value. In this experiment, average difference between residuals produced by second match and best match is 0.11. It is a very low value compared with the average obtained from accurate matches. Because of this very small difference between the residual values produced by different classes, SDR-SLR fails to recognize the face images correctly. So we further validate the accept/reject result of SDR-SLR by using the reliability index [4]. Inspired from [12], we apply Local Correlation where the error difference between best match and second best match is less than a threshold. Using extensive empirical studies over different datasets it was found that most of the incorrect matches occur when *interclassvariation* < 2 * *avg.threshold*. The threshold is calculated based on residual difference, and it is fixed as twice the average Residual Difference [12] (between top 2 matches) for mismatches in dataset.

In order to compute the correlation, landmarks in the query face image are detected. Landmarks are the specific points in the face. For landmark point localization, we use Face Recognition based algorithm on Landmark Localization presented by Zhu and Ramanan [13]. Then the correlation of these landmarks and images of each person in the top k_1 matches and the sum of correlation indexes for all landmarks for each class is calculated. The query image is recognized as the class with highest correlation value.

The algorithm for the proposed method (SDR-SLR-LC) is outlined below.

Algorithm 1. SDR-SLR with Local Correlation for Face Recognition

Input: Training dataset, Probe image y
1. Apply SDR-SLR algorithm in the Training Data and find top k_1 matches.
   if the difference of residual values produced by top two matches is $< k_2$
   1. Identify the Landmarks in the face using Landmark Detection algorithm on probe image y and select 8 relevant landmarks
   2. Find Correlation of each landmark in Probe image y with different images of each person in top k_1 matches.
   3. Probe image y is recognized as the class which gives highest correlation value.
   else
   Probe image y is recognized as the class which gives the least residual value.
   end
Output: Recognized class

After performing empirical studies over different datasets, we have found that values of $< k_1 = 7, < k_2 = 0.22$ give good detection accuracy as the correct class of the query image is obtained either within the top 7 matches or within the top 1% of the number of training images available for all cases. The variable values are quite robust and small variation in its value do not affect the detection accuracy.

Extensive experiments on benchmark face databases demonstrate that the performance gains of the proposed method is far better than state-of-art SR based approaches.

Although SLR-SDR-LC method has given good results, there is still room for improvement. During empirical studies, it was found that extreme cases like faces with masks, sunglasses sometimes provide wrong results. This happens since local correlation of such images can give high correlation score even between different persons. This limitation can be solved by removing these odd cases from the refining step (Local Correlation step). If the correlation score is almost equal in all images for a particular landmark then remove that landmark and take the next relevant landmark point detected for the local correlation calculation. This will improve the accuracy for highly occluded images significantly.

3   Experimental Analysis

Both SDR-SLR and the proposed SDR-SLR-LC are evaluated on three face databases: Extended Yale B database [14], AR database [15] and ORL database

[16]. Comparitive analysis of the performance of the algorithm is done with SRC [10], ESRC [17] and LR and structural coherence based LR (LRS) [18] and using nearest neighbour classifiers and LRC [19]. Extended Yale B face database (cropped) contains 2414 images of 38 persons with 192×168, captured under different illumination conditions. In AR database, 2600 images of front-face of size 165×120 from 100 persons are present. Seven undisguised face image affected by different lighting conditions and expression, three face images wearing sunglasses and scarf each are taken from each subject. Face images of 40 distinct subjects captured in different time with variations in illumination, facial expression and glasses are in the **ORL database**. There are no restrictions imposed on the expression but the side movement or tilt is controlled within $20°$. Through extensive experimental analysis, the values of β and γ are set as 10 for all experiments.

3.1 Face Recognition on Mixed Variations

– Case 1 - undisguised images from AR database
  From AR database, all undisguised face images from session 1 are trained and those images from session 2 are tested. Undisguised images means that they do not contain any accessories that may change the person's identity. Images down-sampled to two different sizes are tested.
  700 images of 100 persons are taken for training and another 700 images of 100 persons are taken for testing (7 images per person). Images are down sampled to 27×20 (for dimension 540) and in another Images are down sampled to 55×40 (for dimension 2200). The face recognition algorithms LR, ESRC, SSRC didnot perform better than SRC even though the dataset images are containing lighting and expression variations. Nevertheless, SDR-SLR and proposed SDR-SLR-LC approach exhibits superior performance than other methods for all image sizes. As the image dimension increases, the recognition rate is also increased.
  The significant improvement in the recognition rate for the SDR-SLR method and the proposed SDR-SLR-LC can be understood clearly from the bar charts below (Fig. 3).

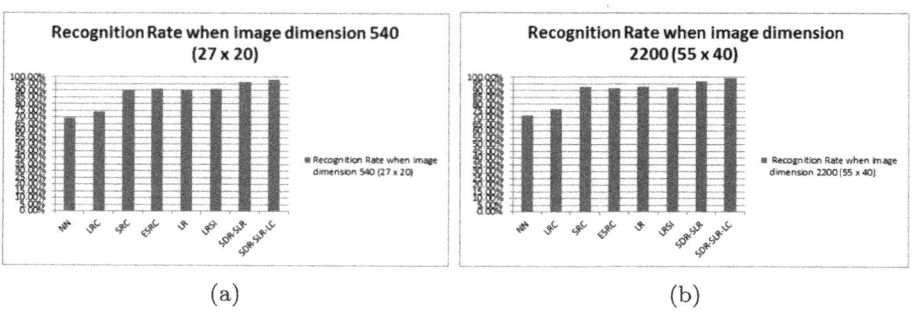

(a)   (b)

Fig. 3. Comparitive analysis of all undisguised images from AR dataset with dimension 27×20 and 55×40

– Case 2 - Fewer Training Samples from AR database
The above experiment is repeated for different 2200 dimensions of face images
with reduced training samples per person to 6, 5, 3. The final result is calculated by averaging the results of 10 runs. Table 1 illustrates that LR and LRS1
under perform SRC as the training data is not corrupted. For 3 training samples, the best accuracy of ESRC is 85% where as the proposed SDR-SLR-LC
gains 97%.

Table 1. Performance analysis of Fewer Training Samples from AR dataset

Method	Recognition rate	
	5 Training samples per person	3 Training samples per person
NN	60.4%	46.1%
LRC	67.4%	53.7%
SRC	88.7%	82.3%
ESRC	89.4%	85.1%
LR	87.8%	79.5%
LRSI	88.6%	79.7%
SDR-SLR	96.4%	95.2%
SDR-SLR-LC	97.2%	97.1%

Except SDR-SLR and the proposed method, for all other methods, recognition rate reduces badly as the number of training samples per person decreases
(Fig. 4).

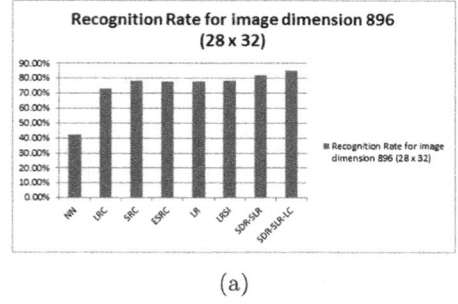

(a)

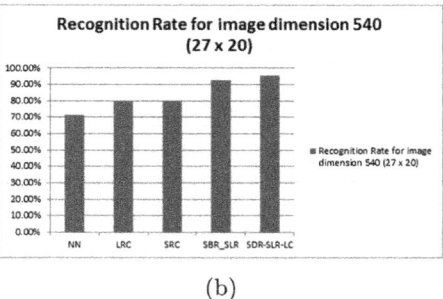

(b)

Fig. 4. Face recognition rate on Extended Yale and ORL database

3.2   Face Recognition on Corrupted Data

A random image is taken from six disguised images per person for training, all
remaining images are used for testing. Images may contain Sunglasses or Scarf.

There are 3 training and 18 testing images per person. Image Dimension 2200 ie, 55×40 Results are shown in Table 2.

Results demonstrates that the proposed SDR-SLR-LC significantly outperforms all other algorithms consistently for all levels of corruption.

Table 2. Face recognition rate on AR database with malicious occlusions

Method	Recognition rate
NN	35.8%
LRC	47.3%
SRC	79.9%
ESRC	84.5%
LR	79.9%
LRSI	80.2%
SDR-SLR	93.0%
SDR-SLR-LC	94.1%

In AR Database, 28 images out of 700 are misclassified using SDR-SLR method. But in the proposed method, SDR-SLR with Local Correlation, only 7 images out of 700 are misclassified. So the proposed method drastically reduces the misclassification and there by improving the recognition rate and accuracy.

In Extended Yale B database, eight images per sample selected randomly for training and testing. Images are down sampled to 28×32 (image dimension is 596). Total 228 (6 images per a person) images of 38 persons are tested. For SDR-SLR method, 186 images out of 228 are recognized correctly. In SDR-SLR-LC method, 193 images recognized correctly and 94.1% recognition rate is obtained.

For SDR-SLR algorithm, tested in ORL database, 10 images out of 120 are misrecognized. But for the proposed SDR-SLR-LC method, only 6 images out of 120 are misrecognized.

4   Conclusion

In this work a robust face recognition system based on Sparse and Dense hybrid Representation with Local Correlation is proposed. In SDR approach, the class specific component and non class specific component collaboratively competes against other samples. But there are some cases of misrecognitions of the face images in SDR-SLR method due to comparatively same residual values produced by different classes for a query image.

Here a method is proposed where the local correlation is applied to the SDR-SLR method, only in cases where SDR-SLR fails to distinguish competing classes clearly, so that the recognition rate is improved. Correlation of relevant landmarks of the query image and the training images of top matches, identified by SDR, is calculated. The person whose training image gives the highest correlation value is identified as the class to which the query image belongs to. Since we are computing local correlation of only relevant points within a small dictionary, the proposed method require very less computation time. SDR-SLR-LC method demonstrates superior performance compared to traditional face recognition algorithms, SRC and related extensions irrespective of whether the training data is corrupted or not and whether training samples for every class is sufficient or not. In the challenging datasets of AR database, the proposed method gives an accuracy of 98%.

References

1. Haghighat, M., Abdel-Mottaleb, M.: Lower resolution face recognition in surveillance systems using discriminant correlation analysis. In: 12th IEEE International Conference on Automatic Face and Gesture Recognition (FG 2017), pp. 912–917 (2017)
2. Wang, Q., Elbouz, M., Alfalou, A., Brosseau, C.: Designing a composite correlation filter based on iterative optimization of training images for distortion invariant face recognition. Opt. Lasers Eng. **93**, 100–108 (2017)
3. Jiang, X., Lai, J.: Sparse and dense hybrid representation via dictionary decomposition for face recognition. IEEE Trans. Pattern Anal. Mach. Intell. **37**(5), 1067–1079 (2015)
4. De Marsico, M., Nappi, M., Riccio, D., Wechsler, H.: Robust face recognition for uncontrolled pose and illumination changes. IEEE Trans. Syst. Man Cybern. Part A Syst. Hum. **43**(1), 149–163 (2013)
5. Turk, M.A., Pentland, A.P.: Face recognition using eigenfaces. In: Proceedings of the IEEE Computer Society Conference on Computer Vision and Pattern Recognition, pp. 586–591 (1991)
6. Jiang, X.D., Joshi, N., Kadir, T., Brady, M.: IEEE Trans. Pattern Anal. Mach. Intell. 31(5) (2009)
7. Belhumeur, P.N., Hespanha, J.P., Kriegman, D.J.: Eigenfaces vs. fisherfaces: recognition using class specific linear projection. IEEE Trans. Pattern Anal. Mach. Intell. **19**(7), 711–720 (1997)
8. Moghaddam, B.: Principal manifolds and probabilistic subspaces for visual recognition. IEEE Trans. Pattern Anal. Mach. Intell. **24**(6), 780–788 (2002)
9. Jiang, X.D., Mandal, B., Kot, A.: Enhanced maximum likelihood face recognition. Electron. Lett. **42**(19) (2006)
10. Wright, J., Yang, A.Y., Ganesh, A., Sastry, S.S., Ma, Y.: Robust face recognition via sparse representation. IEEE Trans. Pattern Anal. Mach. Intell. **31**(2), 210–227 (2009)
11. Cands, E.J., Li, X., Ma, Y., Wright, J., Candes, E.J.: Robust principal component analysis? J. ACM **58**(3), 137 (2009)
12. De Marsico, M., Nappi, M., Riccio, D., Tortora, G.: NABS: novel approaches for biometric systems. IEEE Trans. Syst. Man Cybern. Part C Appl. Rev. **41**(4), 481–493 (2011)
13. Zhu, X., Ramanan, D.: Face detection, pose estimation, and landmark estimation in the wild. In: CVPR, pp. 2879–2886 (2012)
14. Lee, K., Ho, J.: Acquiring linear subspaces for face recognition under variable lighting. IEEE Trans. Pattern Anal. Mach. Intell. **27**(5), 684–698 (2005)

15. Martinez, A.M.: The AR face database. CVC Technical report (1998)
16. Samaria, F.S., Harter, A.C.: Parameterisation of a stochastic model for human face identification. In: Proceedings of the 1994 IEEE Workshop on Applications of Computer Vision, pp. 138–142 (1994)
17. Deng, W., Hu, J., Guo, J.: Extended SRC: undersampled face recognition via intraclass variant dictionary. IEEE Trans. Pattern Anal. Mach. Intell. **34**(9), 1864–1870 (2012)
18. Chen, C.F., Wei, C.P., Wang, Y.C.F.: Low-rank matrix recovery with structural incoherence for robust face recognition. In: Proceedings of the IEEE Computer Society Conference on Computer Vision and Pattern Recognition, pp. 2618–2625 (2012)
19. Naseem, I., Togneri, R., Bennamoun, M.: Linear regression for face recognition. IEEE Trans. Pattern Anal. Mach. Intell. **32**(11), 2106–2112 (2010)

CIELch Color Space Based Satellite Image Segmentation Using Soft Computing Techniques

P. Ganesan[1(✉)], B. S. Sathish[2], L. M. I. Leo Joseph[3], and V. Kalist[4]

[1] Department of Electronics and Communication Engineering, Vidya Jyothi Institute of Technology, Aziz Nagar, C.B. Post, Hyderabad, India
gganeshnathan@gmail.com
[2] Sri Krishna Polytechnic College, Arakkonam, Tamilnadu, India
subramanyamsathish@yahoo.co.in
[3] Department of Electronics and Communication Engineering,
S.R. Engineering College, Warangal, India
leojoseph@srecwarangal.ac.in
[4] Faculty of Electrical and Electronics, Sathyabama University, Chennai, India
kalist.v@gmail.com

Abstract. Image segmentation is the process of partitioning or dividing an image into a number of sub images, segments, regions or clusters with similar attributes. This is the initial but most important step in the image analysis to gather necessary information. There are number of methods for the segmentation of satellite images such as region growing, threshold based methods, edge detection based methods, fuzzy based methods, neural based methods, genetic based methods etc. For the segmentation and extraction of information from satellite images, various approaches have been proposed. Both soft and non-soft computing methods have been applied on satellite images to obtain meaningful clusters. Even though, many literatures are available for non-soft computing methods, only a limited number of authors have proposed soft computing based segmentation of satellite images. In this work, soft computing based approaches have been discussed and applied on CIELch color space transformed satellite images.

Keywords: Color space · CIELch · Segmentation · Soft computing
FCM · PFCM · MFCM · SOM

1 Introduction

Image segmentation is a method in which the image pixels are grouping according to any one attributes of the input image [1, 8]. There are number of methods for the segmentation of satellite images such as region growing, threshold based methods, edge detection based methods, soft computing based neural, fuzzy and genetic algorithm based methods etc. The segmentation algorithm developed for one application is not well suited for other applications. For example, an algorithm developed for medical image segmentation is not well suited for satellite image segmentation.

© Springer Nature Singapore Pte Ltd. 2018
P. Bhattacharyya et al. (Eds.): NGCT 2017, CCIS 828, pp. 854–861, 2018.
https://doi.org/10.1007/978-981-10-8660-1_64

For the segmentation and extraction of information from satellite images, various approaches have been proposed. Both soft and non-soft computing methods have been applied on satellite images to obtain meaningful clusters. Even though, many literatures are available for non-soft computing methods, only a limited number of authors have proposed soft computing based segmentation of satellite images. In this work, soft computing based approaches have been discussed and applied on CIELch color space transformed satellite images. An overview of color space for image segmentation is given the Sect. 2. The CIELch color space for image segmentation is described in the Sect. 3. The Sect. 4 explains the experiments on satellite images using soft computing approaches and as a final point the Sect. 5 concludes the paper.

2 CIELch Color Space

Color space can be explained as a mathematical tool to characterize color details as three dissimilar color signals or components [12]. CIEXYZ color model proposed by Commission on Illumination (CIE) based on human eye sensitivity as a substitute to RGB color space [2, 11]. The renovation of image from RGB to CIEXYZ space is specified in (2) (3) and (4) respectively

$$X = 0.412453 * R' + 0.35758 * G' + 0.180423 * B' \tag{1}$$

$$Y = 0.212671 * R' + 0.71516 * G' + 0.072169 * B' \tag{2}$$

$$Z = 0.019334 * R' + 0.119193 * G' + 0.950227 * B' \tag{3}$$

The conversion from Lab to Lch space is as follows

$$L = L \tag{4}$$

$$C = \sqrt{a^2 + b^2} \tag{5}$$

$$H = 0 \ whether \ a = 0$$

$$H = \frac{180}{\pi} \left\{ \pi + arctan\left(\frac{b}{a}\right) \right\}. \tag{6}$$

3 Segmentation Based on Soft Computing Approach

Fuzzy C-Means (FCM) clustering algorithm divides a data set (collection of n data points) into c number of fuzzy clusters [9]. Euclidean distance is used to determine the distance between the cluster center and data points. The objective of this clustering algorithm is minimizing its objective function as given in (7).

$$J_m(U, V) = \sum_{i=1}^{c} \sum_{k=1}^{n} \mu_{ik}^m \|x_k - v_i\|^2 \tag{7}$$

where m is the weighting exponent parameter which determines the fuzziness of the resulting clusters. When m = 1, FCM algorithm tends to a hard c-means algorithm. In general, m = 2 is the preferable choice. The cluster centers and membership is computed as

$$V_i = \frac{\sum_{k=1}^{n} \mu_{ik}^m X_k}{\sum_{k=1}^{n} \mu_{ik}^m} \tag{8}$$

$$\mu_{ik} = \left\{ \sum_{j=1}^{c} \left\{ \frac{\|x_k - v_i\|}{\|x_k - v_j\|} \right\}^{2/(m-1)} \right\}^{-1} \tag{9}$$

Possibilistic C-Means (PCM) clustering algorithm is minimizing its objective function as given in (10)

$$P_m(T, V; X, \gamma) = \sum_{i=1}^{n} \sum_{k=1}^{c} t_{ik}^m d_{ki}^2 + \sum_{i=1}^{c} \gamma_i \sum_{k=1}^{n} (1 - t_{ki})^m \tag{10}$$

Where γ is the weighting exponent parameter and it controls the extend of membership sharing the clusters [5]. The following two conditions are necessary to for the objective function to reach the final optimum (minimum) value [4].

$$t_{ki} = 1 \left/ \left(1 + \frac{d_{ik}}{\gamma_i} \right)^{1/m-1} \right. , \qquad 1 \leq i \leq c; 1 \leq k \leq n \tag{11}$$

$$v_i = \frac{\sum_{k=1}^{n} x_k t_{ki}^m}{\sum_{k=1}^{n} t_{ki}^m} \tag{12}$$

Possibilistic–Fuzzy C-Means (PFCM) clustering is a mixture of fuzzy c-means (FCM) clustering and possiblistic c-means (PCM) clusteing [7, 10]. The objective of this clustering algorithm is minimizing its objective function as given in (13)

$$\begin{aligned} PF_m(T, V, U; X, \gamma) &= \sum_{i=1}^{n} \sum_{k=1}^{c} \left(a\mu_{ik}^m + bt_{ik}^\eta \right) d_{ki}^2 \\ &+ \sum_{i=1}^{c} \gamma_i \sum_{k=1}^{n} (1 - t_{ki})^\eta \end{aligned} \tag{13}$$

In Modified FCM (MFCM), the spatial information in the neighborhood of each pixel under consideration is incorporated [6].

$$S_{ij} = \sum_{k \in W(x_j)} U_{ik} \alpha_{k1} + \frac{\sum_{k \in (x_j)} U_{ik} \alpha_{k2}}{\sum_{t=1}^{c} \sum_{k \in W(x_j)} U_{tk}} \tag{14}$$

The new membership function after incorporating the spatial information is given by (15)

$$U_{ij(new)} = \frac{U_{ij}^p * S_{ij}^q}{\sum_{k=1}^{c} U_{kj}^p * S_{kj}^q} \tag{15}$$

In an image, every pixel has a weight (W_{ji}) in relation to every cluster.

$$W_{ji} = \frac{1}{1 + e^{-\left\{ \frac{\|x_j - v_i\|^2}{\sum_{j=1}^{n} \|x_j - v_i\|^2 \left(\frac{c}{n}\right)} \right\}}} \tag{16}$$

Now, the objective function of the new and modified FCM clustering algorithm can be formulated as given in (17)

$$J_{Mod} = \sum_{k=1}^{n} \sum_{i=1}^{c} \left(U_{ik}^m W_{ji}^m \right) \|X_k - V_i\|^2. \tag{17}$$

4 Experimental Result

The unsupervised clustering methods applied in this work are Fuzzy C-Means (FCM), Possiblistic C-Means (PCM), Possiblistic Fuzzy C-Means (PFCM), Self Organizing Map (SOM). Incorporating the spatial information, the conventional Fuzzy C-Means clustering is modified and is called modified Fuzzy C-Means Clustering (MFCM) in this work. The main function of the clustering algorithms is to determine the cluster centers and assign each pixel to its nearest neighboring cluster centers.

In image processing, the image quality parameters can be applied for the evaluation of the imaging system. In this work, the segmentation results have been evaluated using sixteen image quality measures. The quality measures used are Mean Square Error (MSE), Average Difference (AD), Maximum Difference (MD), Normalized Absolute Error (NAE), Root Mean Square Error (RMSE), Peak Mean Square Error (PSNR), Structural Content (SC), Normalized Cross Correlation (NCC), Laplacian Mean Square Error (LMSE), Mean Bias (Bias), ERGAS, Structural Similarity index Measures (SSIM), Normalized Mean Square Error (NMSE), Error Image, and Computation Cost (Execution Time). Image quality parameters measure the difference or similarity between the input image and its segmented version on the basis of comparing the corresponding pixels of the image [3].

Figure 1 shows Fuzzy and Neural Network based segmentation result for Ferrari World satellite image in CIELch color space. The evaluation of performance measures of Ferrari world satellite image segmentation in CIELch color space using fuzzy and neural network based technique is given in Table 1.

Fuzzy and Neural Network based segmentation result for Rim Fire satellite image in CIELch color space is illustrated in Fig. 2. The evaluation of performance measures

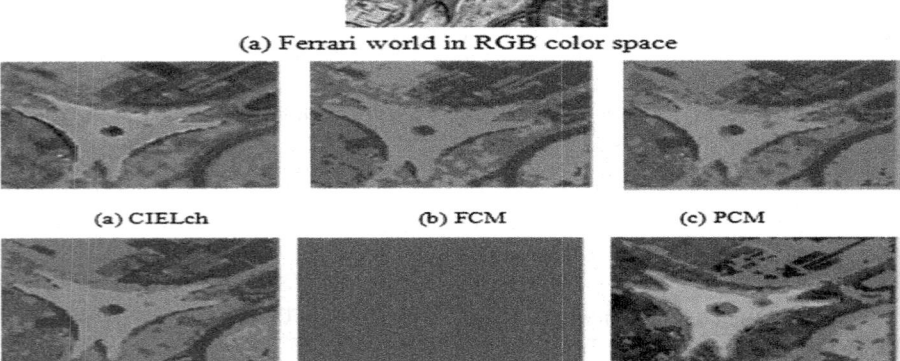

(a) Ferrari world in RGB color space

(a) CIELch   (b) FCM   (c) PCM

(d) PFCM   (e) SOM   (f) MFCM

Fig. 1. Fuzzy and Neural Network based segmentation result for Ferrari World satellite image in CIELch color space

Table 1. Evaluation of performance measures of Ferrari World satellite image segmentation in CIELch color space

Technique	No. of cluster	Cluster centers			No. of iteration	Execution time (Sec)
FCM	5	183.6837	176.2442	58.89234	15	26.6093
		223.8281	119.5783	10.14826		
		153.0359	65.64838	12.42357		
		207.0807	78.98678	8.396327		
		191.0154	137.4324	30.45501		
PCM	5	253.8525	250.8525	240.4	15	3.6668
		226.3081	140.9396	16.70872		
		212.4826	92.39205	7.355897		
		157.1263	63.88499	10.58947		
		179.9257	161.7528	41.69593		
MFCM	5	253.8367	250.7153	240.7399	15	16.6735
		216.1181	117.7553	9.56054		
		147.5216	64.33016	12.26202		
		208.0672	70.44659	6.681583		
		187.5396	170.6638	45.00041		
PFCM	5	177.9153	173.7887	52.09457	15	0.0934
		223.8127	117.5351	6.053463		
		157.2147	66.15626	9.968275		
		207.7885	83.82376	4.271965		
		188.7547	134.3795	22.45145		
SOM	2	253.6684	251.3128	241.5952	10	4.4493
		183.532	96.8106	17.12662		

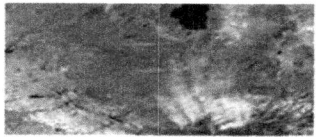

(a) RIM Fire Satellite image in RGB color space

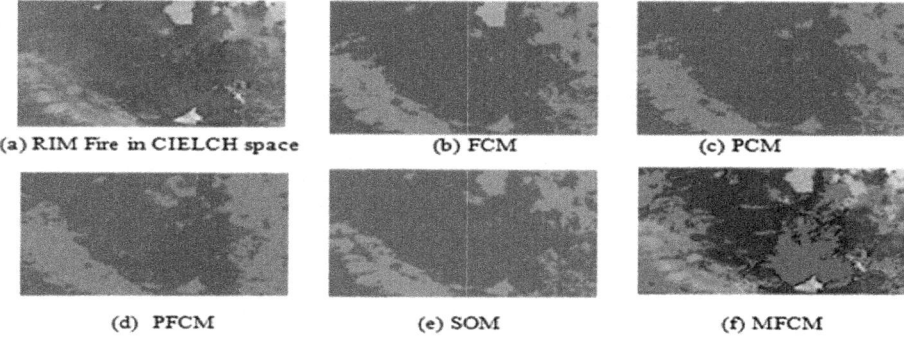

(a) RIM Fire in CIELCH space   (b) FCM   (c) PCM

(d) PFCM   (e) SOM   (f) MFCM

Fig. 2. Fuzzy and Neural Network based segmentation result for Rim Fire satellite image in CIELch color space

of Rim Fire satellite image segmentation in CIELch color space using fuzzy and neural network based technique is given in Table 2.

The performance analysis of soft computing based segmentation of Ferrari world e satellite CIELch color image using image quality measures is presented in Table 3.

Table 2. Evaluation of performance measures of Rim Fire satellite image segmentation in CIELch color space

Technique	No. of Cluster	Cluster centers			No. of iteration	Execution time
FCM	3	204.235	155.382	26.379	14	15.541
		184.368	101.167	68.139		
		198.710	76.811	26.406		
PCM	3	200.197	149.194	27.079	15	7.446
		183.938	101.362	70.022		
		204.561	60.952	22.565		
MFCM	3	43.437	216.708	121.039	15	30.139
		207.237	157.682	29.017		
		191.604	88.161	45.645		
PFCM	3	208.395	147.562	22.567	14	1.729
		184.669	97.067	68.194		
		192.763	84.320	29.330		
SOM	2	195.244	175.300	33.094	10	25.586
		187.422	111.093	22.309		

Table 3. Performance analysis for Ferrari World satellite image

Measures	FCM	PCM	PFCM	SOM	MFCM
MSE	125.81	431.69	332.89	774.15	**97.991**
RMSE	11.216	20.777	18.245	27.823	**9.8992**
PSNR	27.133	21.779	22.907	19.242	**28.218**
NCC	0.9992	0.9529	0.9651	0.9258	**0.8256**
AD	0.8789	3.2292	2.0702	6.8441	**0.0048**
SC	**0.9956**	1.0793	1.0568	1.1252	1.0041
MD	52	98	94	94	**51**
NAE	0.0634	0.0930	0.0754	0.1623	**0.0537**
LMSE	3.8679	7.9372	6.1604	14.454	**3.6470**
Bias	**0.0015**	0.0700	0.0443	0.0361	0.0073
NMSE	0.9537	0.8606	0.9019	0.7672	0.9511
ERGAS	1455.0	3465.8	3111.1	2793.9	**1306.3**
SSIM	0.8501	0.8334	0.8865	0.7471	**0.9478**
RASE	14.550	34.658	31.111	27.939	**13.063**

The performance analysis of soft computing based segmentation of Rim Fire satellite CIELch color image using image quality measures is illustrated in Table 4.

Table 4. Performance analysis for Rim Fire satellite image

Measure	FCM	PCM	PFCM	SOM	MFCM
MSE	358.72	464.83	290.70	752.40	**119.03**
RMSE	18.94	21.56	17.05	27.43	**10.91**
PSNR	23.81	22.19	24.26	17.71	**28.67**
NCC	0.9718	0.9945	0.9575	0.9318	**0.6823**
AD	1.561	3.817	0.9617	7.9141	**0.0812**
SC	**0.9402**	0.9941	10093	1.0007	0.9841
MD	62	58	52	101	**44**
NAE	0.0831	0.09531	0.08571	0.1529	**0.0674**
LMSE	6.2743	6.9051	5.0614	19.831	**4.4192**
Bias	**0.0027**	0.0823	0.0531	0.0674	0.0158
NMSE	0.7841	0.7123	0.75841	0.8101	0.3631
ERGAS	1679.3	1548.3	1878.3	3288.8	**426.91**
SSIM	0.8123	0.7641	0.8544	0.8341	**0.9324**
RASE	16.793	15.483	18.783	32.888	**4.2691**

5   Conclusion

This work analyzed the performance of satellite image segmentation in CIELch color space using fuzzy and neural network based soft computing techniques. The performance evaluation of segmentation methods is evaluated using 14 image quality measures (parameters). On the basis of this work, the following conclusions are drawn. MFCM method had produced the good cluster centers and excellent result. The execution time is very less for PFCM segmentation followed by PCM, SOM and MFCM segmentation. The execution time depends on the number of clusters, complexity of image and color space.

References

1. Thoonen, G., Mahmood, Z., Peeters, S., Scheunders, P.: Multisource classification of color and hyper spectral images using color attribute profiles and composite decision fusion. IEEE J. Sel. Top. Appl. Earth Obs. Remote Sens. **5**, 510–523 (2012)
2. Ganesan, P., Rajini, V.: Segmentation and edge detection of color images using CIELAB color space and edge detectors. In: 2010 IEEE International Conference on Emerging Trends in Robotics and Communication Technologies (INTERACT), pp. 393–397 (2010)
3. Sheikh, H.R., Sabir, M.F., Bovik, A.C.: A statistical evaluation of recent full reference image quality assessment algorithms. IEEE Trans. Image Process. **15**, 3440–3451 (2006)
4. Krishnapuram, R., Keller, J.: A possibilistic approach to clustering. IEEE Trans. Fuzzy Syst. **1**, 98–110 (1996)
5. Kurnaz, M., Dokur, Z., Olmez, T.: Segmentation of remote sensing images by incremental neural network. Comput. J. Pattern Recognit. Lett. **26**, 1096–1104 (2006)
6. Ganesan, P., Rajini, V.: A method to segment color images based on modified fuzzy possibilistic c-means clustering algorithm. In: RSTSCC 2010, pp. 157–163 (2010)
7. Kwok, N.M., Ha, Q.P., Fang, G.: Effect of color space on color image segmentation. In: 2nd IEEE International Congress on Image and Signal Processing, pp. 1–5 (2011)
8. Awad, M.: An unsupervised artificial neural network method for satellite image segmentation. Int. Arab J. Inf. Technol. **7**, 199–205 (2011)
9. Pal, N.R., Pal, K., Bezdek, J.C.: A possibilistic fuzzy C Means clustering algorithm. IEEE Trans. Fuzzy Syst. **13**, 517–530 (2005)
10. Ibraheem, N.A., Hasan, M.M., Khan, R.Z., Mishra, P.K.: Understanding color models: a review. ARPN J. Sci. Technol. **2**, 265–275 (2011)
11. Paschos, G.: Perceptually uniform color spaces for color texture analysis: an empirical evaluation. IEEE Trans. Image Process. **10**, 932–937 (2013)
12. Ganesan, P., Rajini, V.: HSV color space based segmentation of region of interest in satellite images. In: IEEE International Conference on Control, Instrumentation, Communication and Computational Technologies (ICCICCT), pp. 101–105 (2014)

Despeckling Filter Evaluation Using Image Quality Metrics and Coefficient of Variation

R. J. Hemalatha[1](✉) and V. Vijayabaskar[2]

[1] Department of Biomedical Engineering,
Sathyabama University, Chennai, India
rjhemalatha@gmail.com
[2] Department of Telecommunication and Engineering,
Sathyabama University, Chennai, India

Abstract. In the current trend of imaging ultrasound is one of the most preferred non-invasive tools for diagnosis. Generally medical images are corrupted by noise during acquisition. Speckle noise which is inherent in ultrasound images highly degrades the quality of the image there by decreases the diagnostic accuracy. Thus speckle reduction is significant and primary step in pre-processing of ultrasound images. The objective of this study is to evaluate the performance of ten different despeckle filters based on the image quality metrics and coefficient of variation, in ultrasound image of arthritis after filtering. The performance analysis of *DsFlsminsc, DsFlsmv, DsFsrad, DsFmedian, DsFwiener, DsFhomog, DsFlecasort, DsFgf, DsFad, DsFls* filters on ultrasound image was analysed by comparing the established seven image quality metrics like PSNR, SRMSE, SSI, LMSE, UQI and SNR for the filtered image. In addition the coefficient of variation (CV) was computed for the seven image quality metrics parameters and for the filtered images based on the statistical parameters like mean and standard deviation. Further the correlation coefficient value ρ was calculated for the CV value which is positively correlated, thus it provides a validation measure for the filter evaluation process using CV value. The result of the study shows that DsFlsmv and DsFmedian filters gave best results and can be used for despeckling the ultrasound arthritis image.

Keywords: Despeckling filter · Image quality
CV value and ultrasound imaging

1 Introduction

In the recent years advancement in the technology has led to many imaging modalities for the clinical diagnosis. The most common diagnostic imaging modalities used in the orthopaedics are X-ray, computed tomography (CT), magnetic resonance imaging (MRI). However these instruments use radiation as their source for imaging which raises several safety concerns for human beings [1]. To overcome this use of ultrasound in orthopaedics is preferred as it is cost effective, non-invasive, portable and safe. Due to wide availability the physicians readily integrate US in their clinical diagnosis [2]. The musculo skeletal ultrasound (MSUS) has been used for real time assessment of pathology related to musculo skeletal system.

© Springer Nature Singapore Pte Ltd. 2018
P. Bhattacharyya et al. (Eds.): NGCT 2017, CCIS 828, pp. 862–869, 2018.
https://doi.org/10.1007/978-981-10-8660-1_65

US with fast scan time make it a preferable imaging modality for musculo skeletal system. The first use of ultrasound in musculoskeletal system was reported in 1972. In 1978 Peterson and Cooperberg has reported the use of US to demonstrate synovitis [3]. The high resolution MSUS has become a major tool for arthritis diagnosis as it provides the visualization of abnormalities in the joints. DelCura has stated US which does not involve radiation makes it an ideal imaging modality for guidance procedures and injection in joints which increases local therapy accuracy and prevents patients from repeated needle pricks [4]. This makes it an ideal tool for therapy. The real time dynamic imaging helps in revealing the tendon pathologies. Mastos et al. showed that detection of synovitis in hand and feet has improved the diagnosis of seronegative arthritis [5]. In 2013 EULAR congress Kelly et al. presentation showed that early diagnosis and therapy of rheumatoid Arthritis (RA) can be made by the regular use of MSUS for patients with suspected inflammatory arthritis. It can detect even small erosions that are not revealed in X-rays.

However the qualities of ultrasound images are limited by speckle noise which is multiplicative in nature. Visual observation and interpretation of the ultrasound image is highly affected by the presence of speckle noise. The accuracy of the methods that involve computation is also affected by speckle noise [6]. In ultrasound the echogenic areas have granular appearance due to speckle which affects the image texture and the anatomical features of the organs. The texture and anatomical features gives quantitative details for better diagnosis [7]. The use of despeckling algorithms suppresses speckle noise and improves the visual perception. The despeckling algorithms should preserve the boundary information while suppressing the speckle noise. Despeckling filters are used as preprocessing step for segmentation. The structure of this paper is as follows: In Sect. 2. Materials and Methods used Sect. 3. Results of various methods followed by Sect. 4. Discussion and Sect. 5. Conclusion.

2   Materials and Methods

Speckle is a noise which creates black and white spots in the image. These spots are due to interference of the waves travelling from the point scatterers towards the probe. These point scatterers originates in a homogeneous tissue which cannot be resolved by the ultrasound machine [8]. The magnitude of the speckle noise is proportional to the strength of the signal. The speckle noise model is given as follows

$$F(x, y) = G(x, y) * n(x, y) \tag{1}$$

Where F(x, y) is the original image G(x, y) is the noise free image n(x, y) is the noise (x, y) is the pixel location.

The multiplicative speckle noise is transformed into additive noise by applying logarithmic transform.

$$\begin{aligned} \log[f(x, y)] &= \log[g(x, y)\, n(x, y)] \\ &= \log[g(x, y)] + \log[n(x, y)] \end{aligned} \tag{2}$$

2.1 Despeckling Filters

Since 1980 the speckle reduction filters which originated from SAR community was applied to ultrasound images [9]. Most of the despeckling filters described in the literature are summarized in the following Table 1.

Table 1. Different speckle reduction filters

S. No.	Filter name	Filtering technique
1	Median filter	*median*
2	Anisotropic diffusion filter	*AD, DPAD, SRAD, CED (ad, lsmedcd, lsmedc, adsr, nldif)*
3	Geometric filter	*gf4d, gfminmax*
4	Local statistics filter	*lsmv_leelsmv_frost, lsminsc, lsminv1d, wiener*
5	Linear filter	*ls, ca, lecasort*
6	Homogeneity	*homog*
7	Lograthmic	*lslog*
8	Homomorphic	*homo*
9	Wavelet	*waveltc*
10	Fourier	*FIF, FBF, HFIF, HFBF*
11	Multi-scale technique	*GLM,MBR,PSBE*

It is noted that removing speckle noise always is not desirable as it contains additional information about the region imaged. Loizou et al. has compared 10 different despeckling filters for ultrasound carotid artery images. In this paper we have applied despeckling filters like DsFlsminsc, DsFlsmv, DsFsrad, DsFmedian, DsFwiener, DsFhomog, DsFlecasort, *DsFgf,* DsFad, DsFls for ultrasound arthritis images. To make comparison of the filters a common image is used for all the filters.

Linear Despeckling Filter *(DsFlsmv, DsFlsminsc)*

DsFlsmv utilizes the mean and variance of neighbourhood pixel. This filter increase optical perception evaluation by preserving the mean and median value and decreases the variance of speckle noise in US images. *DsFlsminsc* is 2D filter which searches the homogeneous area in the neighbourhood around each pixel and substitutes the center pixel with the average value. It smoothens the image there by edge details are not preserved [10].

Geometric Despeckle Filter *(DsFgf,* DsFmedian)

DsFgf utilizes non linear noise reduction technique where the intensity of the centre pixel is compared with its neighbours and the intensity is increased or decreased. This filter reduces speckle index which provides better results. DsFmedian computes the median of the image with different window sizes. It enhances the edges and preserves it in the US images [11].

Anisotropic Diffusion Filtering (DsFad)

Perona and Malik introduced diffusion equation in 1990 for image smoothing. The filter function uses diffusion coefficient which controls intra region smoothing by applying diffusion at the edges thereby preserves the edge information [12].

Speckle Reducing Anisotropic Diffusion Filter (DsFrad)

The filter function uses diffusion coefficient by combining normalized gradient magnitude and normalized laplacian operator to act like an edge detector. The overall image quality is improved by this filter [13].

Wiener Despeckle Filter (DsFwiener)

It uses pixel by pixel adaptive wiener method. This filter improves image visualization but edges are not preserved when compared to linear despeckling filter [14].

Homogenity Filter (homog)

The most homogeneous neighborhood around each pixel is estimated by this filter. This filter doesn't involve any parameters to be set thus it makes an automatic interpretation. The filter deals with maximum homogeneity over a pixel neighborhood filtering concept [15].

Linear Scaling Filter (DsFlecasort, DsFls)

DsFlecasort is a linear scaling filter. The filter considers the gray level value of the neighboring pixel surrounding the center pixel whose pixel values are similar. It assigns mean value of this neighboring pixel to the center point. In DsFls the maximum and minimum value in a filter window is scaled. The filter replaces the center pixel value by maximum and minimum value [15].

2.2   Evaluation of Filter Performance

To quantitatively assess the performance of different despeckled filters, image quality metrics (IQM) and statistical parameters were applied to the original and despeckled images [16]. Different IQM parameters like signal to noise ratio (SNR), peak signal to noise ratio (PSNR), universal quality index (UQI), structural similarity index (SSI), structural content (SC), Laplacian mean square error (LMSE), square root of mean square error (SRMSE) were evaluated for the original and filtered images. The IQM mainly provides information about the filter quality, suppression of speckle noise and edge preservation [17].

Statistical parameters like mean, median, standard deviation (SD), variance, coefficient of variation (CV) were calculated for image quality metrics parameters and for the filtered images [18–20]. The main purpose of calculating the CV is to study the quality assurance by determining the content of the data. CV is considered as an important parameter as it provides the best suitable filter for despeckling. CV is calculated by measuring ratio of standard deviation to mean multiplied by hundred. The CV value with lowest value for IQM parameters and filtered images provides the stable and suitable filter type for despeckling [21].

3   Results and Discussions

3.1   Application of Different Despeckling Filters

In this paper we have considered a common B-mode gray scale ultrasound image of the thumb extensor affected by arthritis for filter application. The region of interest is selected and normalized using image normalization algorithm. The different despeckling filtered image is represented in Fig. 1.

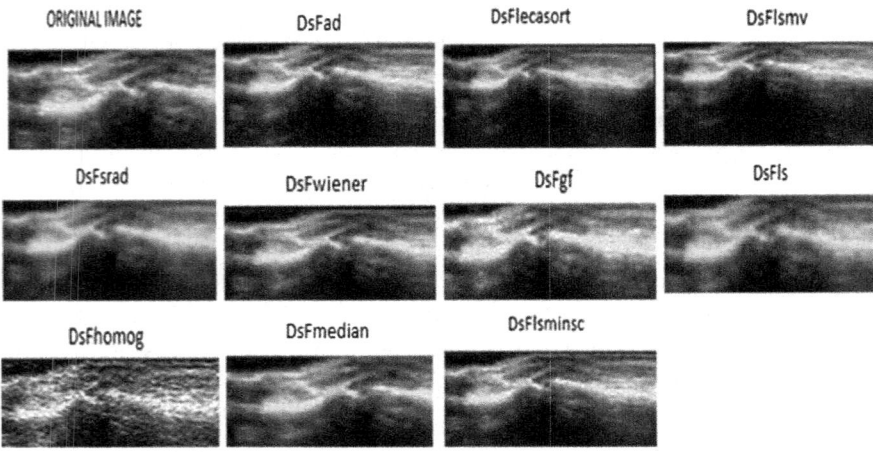

Fig. 1. Filtered ultrasound images

The filter performance was evaluated using different measures like statistical features and image quality metrics. Image quality metrics assess the difference in quality of original and despeckled image. The image quality metrics like PSNR, SRMSE, SSI, LMSE, UQI and SNR of all the despeckled filters are tabulated in Table 2.

Table 2. Image quality metrics of despeckled filters

Despeckling filters	Image quality metrics parameters						
	PSNR	SRMSE	SSI	LMSE	UQI	SNR	SC
DsFlsminsc	11.66	82.33	0.35	2.04	0.04	8.16	0.70
DsFlsmv	14.60	57.2	0.31	1.50	0.02	10.34	0.97
DsFsrad	14.2	61.13	0.39	1.62	0.14	13.53	0.93
DsFmedian	14.70	57.62	**0.309**	1.52	**0.01**	9.0	0.94
DsFwiener	14.3	60.72	0.38	1.15	0.06	10.24	1.10
DsFhomog	12.39	75.70	0.45	5.64	0.03	8.96	0.83
DsFlecasort	12.69	73.14	0.34	1.99	0.08	9.42	0.89
DsFgf	13.77	64.58	0.39	1.23	0.06	9.7	0.72
DsFad	14.4	59.9	0.38	1.74	0.05	9.42	0.82
DsFls	14.06	62.44	0.40	2.29	0.07	11.07	0.81

Statistical approach towards image quality metrics parameters was performed. Statistical parameters like Mean, Standard Deviation, Variance values for the image quality metrics parameters and for filtered images is calculated and tabulated in Table 3. Further coefficient of variation (CV) is calculated for the image quality metrics parameters and for the filtered images. The CV value provides the best suitable filter for despeckling the ultrasound images. The selection of CV value as a parameter to evaluate the filter performance is validated by finding the correlation of coefficient ρ value between the two CV values displayed in Table 3. The obtained ρ value is 0.365 which shows the two CV values are positively correlated.

Table 3. Statistical parameters

Despeckling filters	Statistical features for image quality metrics parameters				Statistical parameters for the despeckled images			
	Mean	SD	Variance	CV value	Mean	SD	Median	CV value
DsFlsminsc	15.03	30.0	900	200	86.7	64.5	68.7	74.3
DsFlsmv	12.3	21.1	**448**	**169**	87.4	61.3	65.5	**70.1**
DsFsrad	13.12	22.05	486	178	86.3	61.4	70.86	70.9
DsFmedian	12.1	20.01	402	**160**	89.4	62.8	78.0	**70.5**
DsFwiener	12.56	21.9	482	179	78.9	63.3	57.0	80.2
DsFhomog	14.8	27.2	743	180	80.16	65.7	60.5	81.9
DsFlecasort	14.07	26.5	702.7	190	80.66	62.4	60.5	77.4
DsFgf	12.9	23.4	547	180	98.5	70.1	86.9	71.4
DsFad	12.48	21.6	468	180	97	69	84.3	71.1
DsFls	13.2	22.5	506	180	92.4	66.1	85.05	71.7

4   Discussion

Different image quality metrics are tabulated in Table 2. From these values it is clear that filter DsFlsmv and DsFmedian filters have better noise suppression. The structural similarity index (SSI) value of the DsFlsmv is better than other filters. The universal quality index (UQI) is also well maintained by both the filters. All the metrics represents despeckling while preserving the overall image quality and structural similarity. These filters can be used as a pre-processing step for image segmentation.

For the quantitative analysis of filters coefficients of variation (CV) for all the filters were calculated. The CV value analyses whether the given filter is best suited for despeckling purpose. The minimum CV value represents the filter is more stable and suitable for filtering. From Table 3 its clear that DsFlsmv and DsFmedian have low CV values hence they are best suited for despeckling. The CV values for *DsFgf*, DsFad, DsFls are similar and has a difference of one when compared to DsFlsmv and DsF-median. The variance value is also maintained low for DsFlsmv filter. In addition to this correlation coefficient represented by r is calculated. The ρ value gives the measure of degree of dependence between two samples. The correlation coefficient has been used as a validation method for implementing the CV value as parameter of measure to evaluate the performance of despeckled filters.

5 Conclusion

In the enhancement of ultrasound images despeckling filters are considered as an important primary step. The despeckling filters for ultrasound arthritis image is analysed in this paper in terms of image quality metrics and statistical approach using CV value. Various filters are available but it is difficult to choose the suitable filter for clinical images. The major contribution of this paper is to select the best suitable filter for ultrasound image by evaluating the performance of the filters using image IMQ and CV value. The speckle suppression of each filter is studied by speckle suppression index value and the quality of the image with structural content are analysed by universal quality index and structural content parameter. The correlation coefficient ρ for the CV values is 0.365 which shows positively correlated between both the CV values. From the results it was shown that filters like DsFlsmv and DsFmedian can be used for despeckling and these filters can be used as preprocessing step in automatic image segmentation. The despeckling algorithm for ultrasound images is further investigated in the field of ultrasound video recordings and telemedicine. The future work focuses on application of different despeckling algorithms to ultrasound video recordings and incorporation of improved image quality assessment measures are to be investigated.

References

1. Loizou, C., Christodoulou, C., Pattichis, C.S., Istepanian, R., Pantziaris, M., Nicolaides, A.: Speckle reduction in ultrasound images of atherosclerotic carotid plaque. In: Proceedings of the IEEE 14th International Conference on Digital Signal Processing, vol. 2, pp. 525–528, July 2002
2. Hemalatha, R.J., Vijayabaskar, V.: Analysis of despeckling filter on rheumatoid arthritis affected ultrasound images. Biomedicine 37(1), 101–106 (2017)
3. Peterson, L.R., Cooperberg, P.L.: Ultrasound demonstration of lesions of the gastrointestinal tract. Gastrointest. Radiol. 3, 303–306 (1978)
4. DelCura, J.L.: Ultrasound-guided therapeutic procedures in the musculoskeletal system. Current Probl. Diagn. Radiol. 37(5), 203–218 (2008). https://doi.org/10.1067/j.cpradiol. 2007.08.001
5. Mastos, M., Miller, K., Eliasson, A.C., Imms, C.: Goal-directed training: linking theories of treatment to clinical practice for improved functional activities in daily life. Clin. Rehabil. 21 (1), 47–55 (2007)
6. Burckhardt, C.B.: Speckle in ultrasound B-mode scans. IEEE Trans. Sonics Ultrason. SU-25 (1), 1–6 (1978)
7. Wagner, R.F., Smith, S.W., Sandrik, J.M., Lopez, H.: Statistics of speckle in ultrasound B-scans. IEEE Trans. Sonics Ultrason. 30, 156–163 (1983)
8. Goodman, J.W.: Some fundamental properties of speckle. J. Opt. Soc. Am. 66(11), 1145–1149 (1976)

9. Christodoulou, C.I., Loizou, C., Pattichis, C.S., Pantziaris, M., Kyriakou, E., Pattichis, M.S., Schizas, C.N., Nicolaides, A.: Despeckle filtering in ultrasound imaging of the carotid artery. In: Proceedings of the Second Joint Engineering in Medicine and Biology/Biomedical Engineering Society (EMBS/BMES), pp. 1027–1028 (2002)

10. Loizou, C.P., Pattichis, C.S.: Despeckle Filtering Algorithms and Software for Ultrasound Imaging. Synthesis Lectures on Algorithms and Software for Engineering. Morgan & Claypool Publishers, San Rafael (2008)

11. Nieminen, A., Heinonen, P., Neuvo, Y.: A new class of detail-preserving filters for image processing. IEEE Trans. Pattern Anal. Mach. Intell. **9**, 74–90 (1987)

12. Perona, P., Malik, J.: Scale-space and edge detection using anisotropic diffusion. IEEE Trans. Pattern Anal. Mach. Intell. **12**(7), 629–639 (1990)

13. Yongjian, Y., Acton, S.T.: Speckle reducing anisotropic diffusion. IEEE Trans. Image Process. **11**(11), 1260–1270 (2002)

14. Devi, M.S., Radhika, V.: Comparative approach for speckle reduction in medical ultrasound images. IJART **1**, 7–11 (2011)

15. Loizou, C.P., Theofanous, C., Pantziaris, M., Kasparis, T.: Despeckle filtering software toolbox for ultrasound imaging of the common carotid artery. Comput. Methods Programs Biomed. **114**, 109–124 (2014)

16. Loizou, C.P., Pattichis, C.S., Christodoulou, C.I., Istepanian, R.S.H., Pantziaris, M., Nicoliades, A.N.: Comparative evaluation of despeckle filtering in ultrasound imaging of the carotid artery. IEEE Trans. Ultrason. Ferroelectr. Freq. Control **52**(2), 1653–1669 (2005)

17. Wang, Z., Bovik, A.C.: A universal image quality index. IEEE Sig. Process. Lett. **9**(3), 81–84 (2002)

18. Christodoulou, C., Pattichis, C., Pantziaris, M., Nicolaides, A.: Texture-based classification of atherosclerotic carotid plaques. IEEE Trans. Med. Imag. **22**(7), 902–912 (2003)

19. Altman, D.G. (ed.): Practical Statistics for Medical Research. Chapman & Hall, London (1991)

20. Haralick, R.M., Shanmuggam, K., Dinstein, I.: Texture features for image classification. IEEE Trans. Syst. Man. Cybern. **SMC-3**, 610–621 (1973)

21. Reed, G.F., Lynn, F., Meade, B.D.: Use of coefficient of variation in assessing variability of quantitative assays. Clin. Diagn. Lab. Immunol. **9**(6), 1235–1239 (2002). PMC.Web, 27 July 2017

Not Too Deep CNN for Face Detection in Real Life Scenario

Sanjoy Chowdhury[1], Parthasarathi Mukherjee[2], and Ujjwal Bhattacharya[2(✉)]

[1] Heritage Institute of Technology, Kolkata, India
schowdhury671@gmail.com
[2] CVPR Unit, Indian Statistical Institute, Kolkata, India
parthosarothimukherjee@gmail.com, ujjwal@isical.ac.in
http://www.isical.ac.in/~ujjwal

Abstract. This article presents our recent study of a moderately deep neural network architecture for detection of faces of widely variable sizes and orientations. One of the goals of this work is to achieve sufficiently low latency and acceptable true detection rates on low resolution video or still image data. Several attempts over the years have been made to design a robust and generic face detection system. But due to the inherent complexity of the problem, localization of face in complex and low quality images still remains an open problem. Moreover, the existing state-of-the-art systems usually involve very large network architectures requiring significantly high computational resources for their training. Typical challenges with this data include visual variations due to lighting condition, facial expression, occlusion etc. In the present work, we have designed a moderately deep architecture of Convolutional Neural Network (CNN) suitable for its use on commonly available computing devices. Also, we have proposed some simple strategies for calibration of bounding box that is trained to localize a face even in poor lighting condition and various typical occlusion scenarios. The CNN of the proposed framework receives an input image at three different resolutions to detect faces of various sizes. Simulation results of the proposed approach on publicly available "WIDER FACE" database and another database of 27,576 images/video frames collected by us establish its effectiveness in certain real life scenarios.

Keywords: Face detection · Deep neural network
Convolutional neural network · Deep learning

1 Introduction

Research on face detection has received a considerable amount of attention in the field of Computer Vision. Its goal is the localization of human faces in still images or video frames. A face detection algorithm reports the positions of faces in an input image. Automatic detection of face has a number of important applications

© Springer Nature Singapore Pte Ltd. 2018
P. Bhattacharyya et al. (Eds.): NGCT 2017, CCIS 828, pp. 870–886, 2018.
https://doi.org/10.1007/978-981-10-8660-1_66

such as video surveillance, human computer interface, face recognition, face verification, facial expression recognition, head pose tracking, landmark detection such as left eye, right eye, nose etc. Due to its enormous application potentials significant amount of research studies have been conducted on this face detection problem. Surveys of the existing face detection studies can be found in [1–3]. Although due to such extensive studies tremendous progress in this area of Computer Vision has been achieved, further studies are necessary because of the extremely challenging nature of the appearance of face in an image.

State-of-the-art face detectors can quite easily detect faces in relatively less difficult situations. Prime sources of difficulties of face localization are the large search space of positions of face in the entire image, widely variable size of faces, possible poor quality of input image, occlusion, complex background etc. Thus, the goal of current face detection research is to devise a system which can efficiently detect the exact location of the face in an image irrespective of image quality, size of face, its orientations, amount or fraction of its visible portion etc. Since the seminal work, popularly known as Viola-Jones face detector [4], was published, face detection research received significant thrust due to the effectiveness of the algorithm. Haar feature-based cascade classifiers of Viola-Jones face detector is extremely good at detecting faces as far as the input image has only limited or no complexity in terms of its lighting condition, pose, orientation of face, size of the face etc. However, as a matter of fact due to the simplistic nature of the Haar feature, it often fails on images captured in uncontrolled situations. Subsequently, many a study has been published [5,6] beyond the works of Viola-Jones to achieve a more robust face detection system resulting in very high computation cost.

There has been remarkable improvements in the domain of automatic face detection of late, thanks to the introduction of efficient deep learning models [7] supported by extremely powerful GPU based computing devices. In spite of the availability of such sophisticated learnable machines, one can't really claim even today that face detection is at least a nearly solved problem. However, till in recent past due to severe limitations of computational speed, various powerful deep learning tools like Recurrent Neural Network (RNN) [8], Convolutional Neural Network (CNN) [9] could not be experimented extensively whereas now a days the speed of data processing has gone a few notches higher making it conducive for the induction of such powerful learning models based on 'Deep Learning' strategy in various computation intensive tasks such as detection of face. In the present study, we have focussed mainly on a few challenging situations of face detection problem to improve the state-of-the-art in detecting faces in similar extremely difficult real-life scenarios involving issues like occlusion, poor lighting condition, multiple orientations, widely variable size of the face etc.

In the next section, we have discussed further details of the challenges of face detection in real-life scenarios. Recent advancements in the domain of automatic face detection have been described in Sect. 3. The proposed 'not too deep network' model and various strategies used to achieve acceptable performance in the above described difficult scenarios of face detection have been provided in Sect. 4. The strategy used for training of the proposed network has been described in Sect. 5. Simulation results have been provided in Sect. 6. Section 7 concludes the present article.

2   What Makes Face Detection in Real-Life Scenario a Challenging Task

It is true that face analysis technologies has improved a lot during the last decade. Still law enforcing officers cannot expect that existing technology could instantly match a suspect's face in a video from a gas station surveillance camera or a police CCTV camera on some lamppost against a drivers' license photo database. This is what happened exactly in case of Boston (USA) bombing manhunt of the year 2013. Photos of both the alleged perpetrators were present in a relevant image database available to the police but the automatic system failed to come up with a match and identifications were possible using other sources of information. Despite the significant advances in the technology, systems are efficient only on good quality high resolution image data whereas images from real life scenarios cannot be expected to comply with similar standards. So, although the face image analysis research has achieved significant success in recent times, it is still in nascent stage requiring further research in this area. So, several groups of researchers all over the world are working to contribute more and more in this domain for producing more robust technologies. Some typical challenging scenarios of face detection are discussed below.

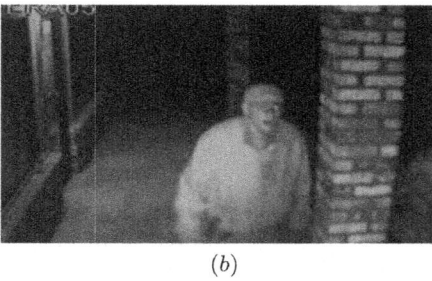

(a)   (b)

Fig. 1. Samples from our database with low contrast

- **Poor contrast image**
  Most of the prevailing face detection systems work satisfactorily when they are fed with good quality images. However, in real-life scenarios, there are situations where image quality is considerably poor posing serious challenge to an automatic face detection algorithm. Two such sample images are shown in Fig. 1.

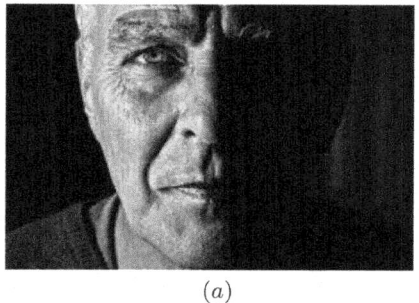
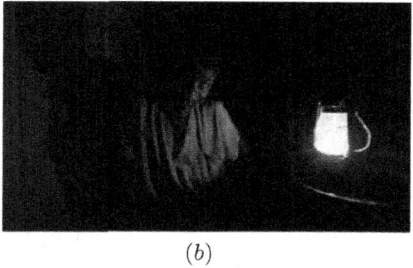

(a) (b)

Fig. 2. Samples from our database where only a part of the face is visible due to non-uniform lighting condition

- **Poor lighting condition**
  Another reason of difficulty of detection of faces in real life scenario is non-uniform lighting condition. Two such examples of faces captured under non-uniform/poor lighting sources are shown in Fig. 2.

(a) (b)

Fig. 3. Two samples from our database with faces in multiple orientations and scales

- **Variation in orientation and scale**
  Situations similar to the examples of Fig. 3 are not uncommon in real life where different faces are aligned in different orientations and/or have different resolutions. In a large majority of the available literature, face detection was studied for fronto-parallel or lateral view of face images without considering other possible variations in pose.

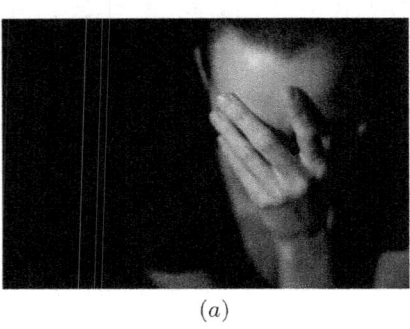

(a)   (b)

Fig. 4. Two examples from our face image collection where major parts of the faces are covered

- **Occlusions**
  Occlusion often poses a great challenge to any face detection algorithm because due to such incidents, vital information of the face remains hindered from the detection system and it needs to perform using only a small part of the usual information. Figure 4, shows two such examples. Although in Fig. 4(b), eyes are present but in Fig. 4(a), no such eye is available. In such cases, a face detection system is provided with only a small fraction of the constituents of the structure of a face.

(a)   (b)

Fig. 5. Camouflage reducing separability of face from background.

- **Poor separability from background**
  There are situations, particularly in the battle fields, people remain camouflaged to hide themselves in the background. Detection of faces in similar scenarios is a difficult task. Two such examples are shown in Fig. 5. Detection

of the human face in Fig. 5(b) is difficult even for human eyes while the same in Fig. 5(a) is comparatively less difficult.

In our work we have applied CNN [9] as the backbone of our model for the purpose of face localization. Given the fact that deep CNNs [10] are extremely computationally expensive it is difficult to scan the image in multiple resolutions and keep enjoying the benefit of low latency at the same time. So instead of scanning the image in multiple resolutions we have resized the image in 3 different scales maintaining its aspect ratio and used those images for our investigation. The idea behind using three separate resolutions for the same image is the potential variation in the size of the face in an individual image, *i.e.* an image can contain multiple faces each lying in different scales. After the initial training phase incremental learning is used in the form of hard negative mining. Where the term negative mining can be loosely described as the technique of re-training the wrongly detected facial regions as non face. We show that this extremely simple network is almost at par with the state-of-the-art methods of face detection. Main contributions of the present study can be summarized as follows.

1. Collection of a moderately large number of image/video frames containing faces of a wide variety of real life challenging situations.
2. Development of a moderately lightweight face detection system involving a not too deep CNN which is capable of performing in challenging scenarios.
3. Use of Non Maximal Suppression and/or Maximum Confidence score (for images containing a single face) to decide a single frame detecting a face among several such overlapping frames.
4. Use of a single CNN architecture instead of using 3 different CNN architectures to perform the detection task at 3 coarse to fine resolutions.
5. Use of hard negative mining to minimize false positive detection.

3   Related Works

Neural networks as a tool of face detection is being used from early 1990's. One of the most pioneering works in the domain of face detection dates back to 1994 by Vaillant *et al.* [11]. They proposed to train a CNN by scanning the entire image at all possible locations. A few other work too followed mainly aimed at detecting frontal faces in less fuzzy backgrounds. In 1998 Rowley *et al.* [12] described a face detection system again using neural nets. Garcia and Delakis [13] in 2002 proposed a system to detect semi lateral images. However, lately deep learning has taken the centre stage when it comes to Computer Vision related problems. Following are the successful methods used recently in face detection:

3.1   CNN Cascade Based Face Detection System

The works by Li *et al.* [14] has thrown light on a CNN cascade based system to detect faces. They have almost extensively worked on using different scales of

CNN cascade to scan the image. Initially the CNN layer scans the entire image densely across different scales to quickly reject a considerable amount of detection windows. To deal with the remaining detection windows there is a calibration network (alternatively after each convolution layer) which is used to adjust the location of the same. Finally after a set of three such convolution-calibration layers the output detection windows are generated. Thus their proposed CNN cascade operates in multiple resolutions to reject the background regions. To improve the detection quality the proposal of calibration setup has been made.

3.2   Region Based CNNs for Object Detection

One of the most recent breakthroughs in face detection is by Girshick *et al.* [15] using Region based CNN system where the authors have proposed a technique which includes pooling the region of interest and then mining only those regions to detect faces. Initially selective search in varied scales is performed to get the regions of interest in the image. Which is then propagated to the actual CNN layers to detect objects. Further developments on the same model has yielded two new variants of R-CNN namely, Fast R-CNN [16] and Faster R-CNN [17] all fairly successful in their own right. The original R-CNN method achieves excellent object detection accuracy albeit having notable drawbacks like multiple stages for training, slow detection rates, extensive requirement of space and time to train etc. Though the revamped model of Fast R-CNN by the same author has tried to address all the aforementioned issues and it was subsequently obliterated by Faster R-CNN.

3.3   Recurrent CNN for Object Detection

Another interesting work by Liang and Hu [18] in 2015 has proposed to use recurrent connection in each convolutional layer. Although the input is static, the fundamental activities of the recurrent units is dynamic in nature as opposed to being static and draws the attention of the subsequent layers. By doing so it is very naturally able to extract patterns and confine contextual information which is delicately used in the stages to come.

3.4   ResNet Based Model

Recently a work proposed by Hu and Ramanan [19] has used a pre-trained ResNet [20] based system to detect tiny faces. Though the network performs exceedingly well for images with (preferably) tiny faces, it fails to detect faces in some cases which has been discussed in the later section.

However, none of the prior works have emphasized on the issue of detecting faces in difficult backgrounds and especially poor lighting conditions. In the following section we have illustrated in detail the working principle of our proposed system.

4   Network Architecture

Here, we present the detailed architecture of our network starting with the stacked CNN setup used as a binary classifier followed by the decision layer which decides which one among multiple predicted windows to keep as the final predicted bounding box for the face. To train the CNN module we have used Keras [21] a high level python API with Tensorflow [22] at backend.

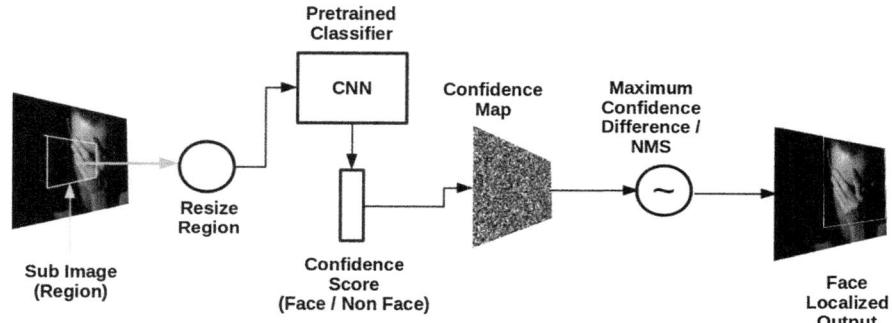

Fig. 6. Schematic diagram of the proposed face detector

4.1   CNN Structure

In the proposed scheme, we use a single CNN architecture. The idea is to use the same CNN module as the classifier in three different scales by adjusting the size of the input image. The sole requirement of iteratively using the stacked CNN is to detect faces of multiple resolutions. In these CNNs we have used our own customization to apply ReLU non linearity function. The proposed workflow and the structure of the CNN involved in this workflow are shown respectively in Figs. 6 and 7. In the training phase, dropout [23] has been used in order to avoid the common problem of overfitting.

It is a very shallow binary classification CNN which is used to scan the image rapidly. Every single image, in addition to being in it's original form, is resized to two other scales half and quarter to it's original dimension. A single CNN then scans the image densely with a sliding window. The scanning of an image of size $W \times H$ is done at a stride of 8 pixels along both the dimensions for 32×32 detection window. As a result from the fundamental working principle of a CNN we get $(\lfloor((W - 32)/8)\rfloor + 1) \times (\lfloor((H - 32)/8)\rfloor + 1)$ map of confidence scores. Where each and every point in this map is referring to a 32×32 detection window in the test image.

A major advantage of the proposed scheme is the use of only a single CNN classifier to achieve detection of face at three fine to coarse resolutions. When the image is being scanned in its original resolution, the detection window is able to detect small size faces as shown in Fig. 8 using blue colored rectangles; when

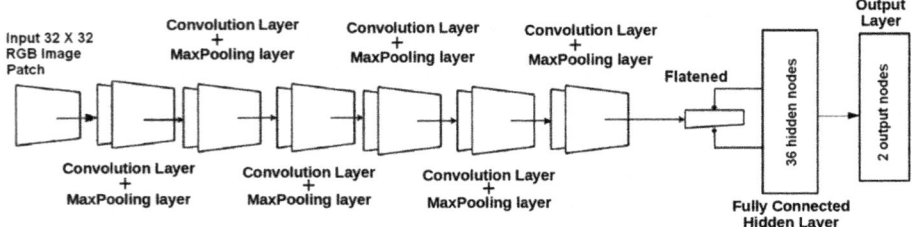

Fig. 7. Architecture of the CNN used in the present study. 32×32 3-channel image patches are input to this network. It consists of a stack of 6 sets of convolution and maxpooling layers. On the top of this stack, there is a fully connected layer with 36 hidden nodes and 2 output nodes. These two output nodes correspond to the two classes Face and Non-Face.

the image is resampled to half of its original size, the detection window is able to detect relatively larger faces as shown in the same Figure using green rectangles. Finally, when the image is resampled to one-fourth of its original size, the same 32×32 detection window efficiently detects further larger faces in the original image as shown in Fig. 8 using rectangles of red color. In the execution phase (test run), when presence of a face is detected by scanning a resampled image, simple computation is performed to locate the region of the face on the original image.

4.2 Decision Layer

4.2.1 Using Non-maximum Suppression (NMS) Strategy

Non-maximum suppression [24] is used as an intermediate step in many Computer Vision algorithms. The problem of using a detection window in face recognition problem is it will generate multiple bounding boxes surrounding the facial region in the image. The example in Fig. 9 illustrates the problem. It is quite evident that there exist a solitary face in the image but the system has drawn 3 windows in Fig. 9(a) surrounding the face. Considering the fact that there are parts of the face in each window still we don't want our system to predict multiple boxes for the same face. To alleviate this situation we use NMS. After applying NMS it produces only a single detection window as shown in Fig. 9(b).

4.2.2 Using Maximum Confidence Difference (MCD) Based Strategy

Here, a simple decision making technique has been applied. To single out one among many detection windows the detection with maximum difference in confidence score is taken *i.e.* the window having maximum score difference among the class probabilities is finally chosen as the bounding box. Figure 9 illustrates the decision making scheme. Figure 9(a) displays all detection windows. On the contrary in Fig. 9(b) only a single detection window has been chosen. The limitation of this process lies in the fact that it is useful only when we are dealing with

Fig. 8. Proposed system detects faces of widely varied resolutions. Blue, green and red rectangles show detected faces at the original, $\frac{1}{2}$ of the original and $\frac{1}{4}$ of the original resolutions respectively. The sample is taken from the 'Wider Face' database. Proposed algorithm detects larger face at a lower resolution.

images having solitary face. So the cases in which we have an a priori knowledge of the number of faces we can apply this simple yet efficient technique.

5   Training of the CNN

The CNN used in the present study has been trained using a sample database which is obtained by combining the training set of publicly available WIDER FACE dataset [25] and another crucial dataset of face images which particularly includes various difficult real life scenarios.

5.1   WIDER FACE Dataset

WIDER FACE dataset, a face detection benchmark dataset developed by Yang *et al.* [25], is a large image database containing faces of wide variations with respect to occlusion, pose, event category and size. It consists of 32,203 image samples and 393,703 labelled faces. This whole database is randomly divided into training, validation and test sets containing 40%, 10% and 50% of the samples respectively.

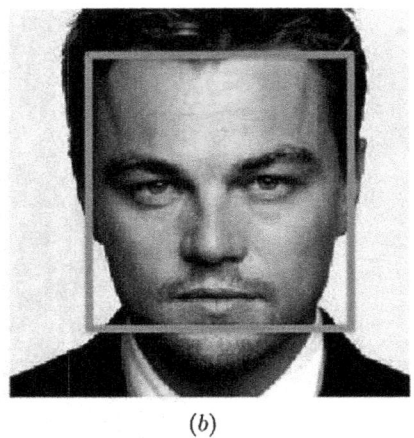

(a)   (b)

Fig. 9. Effect of non-maximal suppression: (a) before the application of decision layer, (b) after the application of decision layer

5.2   Face Dataset Developed by Us

For the purpose of the present study, we have created an annotated database of sample images/video frames consisting of instances of faces of various real life scenarios described in Sect. 2. We have randomly selected 8,000 images/video frames from the database of 27,576 samples collected by us for their use as test samples and the remaining 19,576 sample images/video frames have been used as training samples. We used a rudimentary classification system based on Haar-like features [5] for initial annotation of face regions in the sample images of our database and finally we have manually checked those detected face regions and incorporated necessary adjustments, additions and deletions into this initial set of annotated face regions. Remaining portions of these training image/video frame samples have been used to form the training set of non-face samples. Proper actions were taken so that the training set contains samples of three different resolutions as described in Sect. 4.1 and the sample windows of non-face regions should represent the wide variations in the non-face class. This is an important issue for the success of the proposed strategy and for the achievement of a good solution of the same, we opted for manual intervention.

Our database of image patches (windows) extracted from the above training samples consists of 90,050 patches from face regions and another set of patches of equal number from non-face regions. These two sets of training image patches consist of samples of three successive fine to coarse resolutions achieved through the process of sub-sampling the original images. Thus, here we have used a training set of 181,100 image patches. On the other hand, a distinct set of 8,000 samples of images/video frames have been used for the purpose of obtaining experimental results on the database developed by us.

 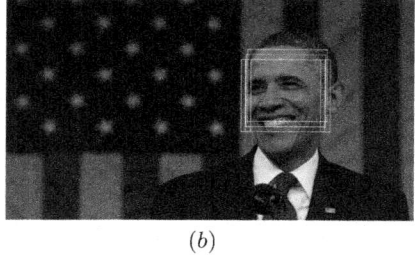

(a)   (b)

Fig. 10. Detection performance gets improved by negative mining: (a) without negative mining, (b) with negative mining.

Training of the present CNN was performed using a combined training set of the two databases described in the above. Training samples of the WIDER FACE database provide representations of realistic variations with respect to size, pose and occlusion while the training samples of our database mainly represent poor image quality of real life applications.

5.3   Effect of Hard Negative Mining

Hard negative mining is the process of identification of wrongly detected 'face' patches by the initial trained network and augmentation of the initial training set through inclusion of the windows corresponding to false positive responses of the network for next round of training. As a result, after the incremental learning phase of the classifier, it helps to outperform the initial learned network with the additional amount of information, and not come up with as many false positives. Figure 10(a) shows certain false positive regions but after execution of the negative mining based incremental learning, the system has improved by a significant margin which can be clearly understood from the Fig. 10(b).

The single 32×32 CNN setup is used to function as the face - non face binary classifier as described previously. The network being relatively simple in comparison to the state-of-the-art architectures takes negligible time to train however to reduce training latency batch normalization was done to speed up the training process.

6   Experimental Results

We have obtained experimental results of the proposed face detector on the test sets of benchmark WIDER FACE database and the database developed by us. The performance of the proposed system consisting of a CNN architecture of very modest size is comparable to the performance of the state-of-the-art methods. Moreover, the detection speed of the proposed system could be made significantly faster by increasing the stride from 8 pixels to 16 pixels at a cost

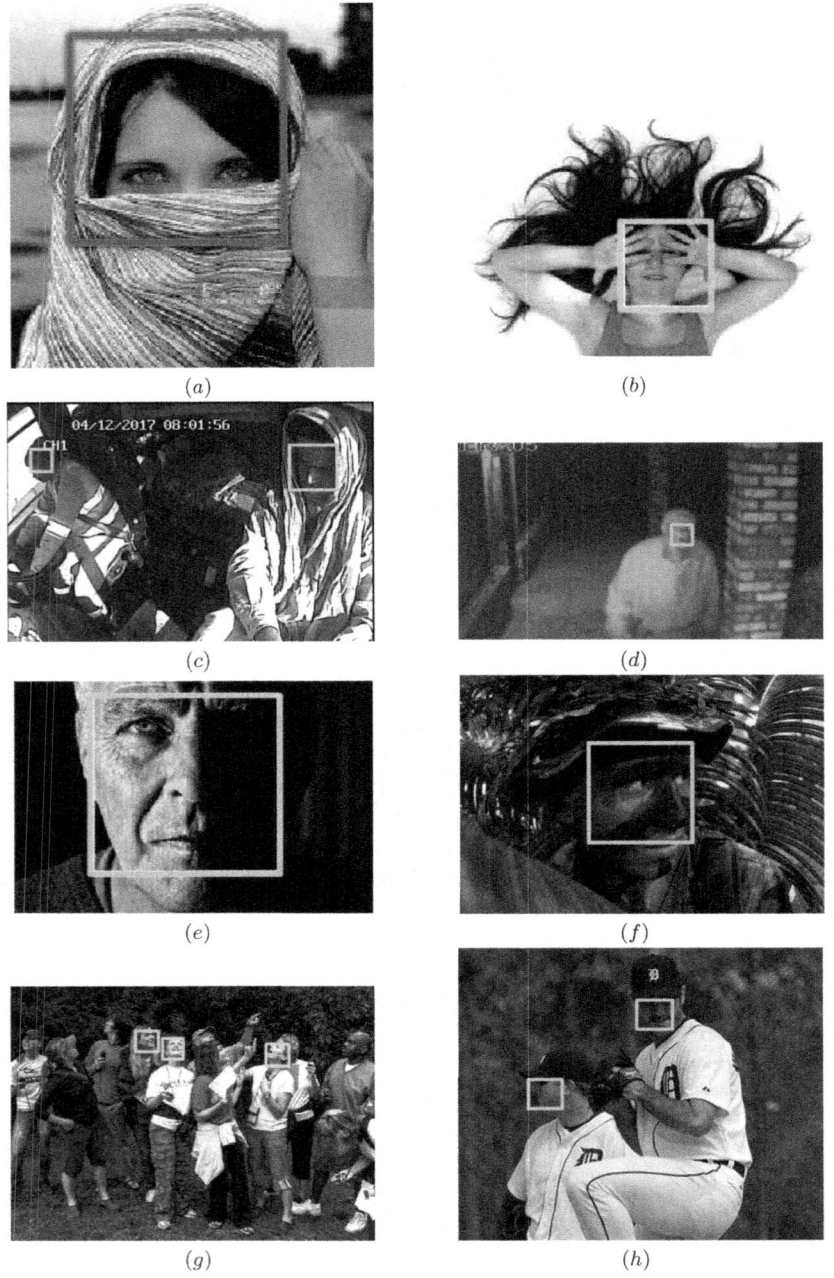

Fig. 11. Examples of successful performance of the proposed approach in various typical situations: (*a*) partially covered (both the eyes are uncovered) face, (*b*) eyes are partially covered, (*c*) face against complex background, (*d*) low contrast face image, (*e*) half of the face is under dark shadow, (*f*) camouflaged face, (*g*) faces are in different orientations (only few of them could be detected), (g) upper part of the face covered by caps.

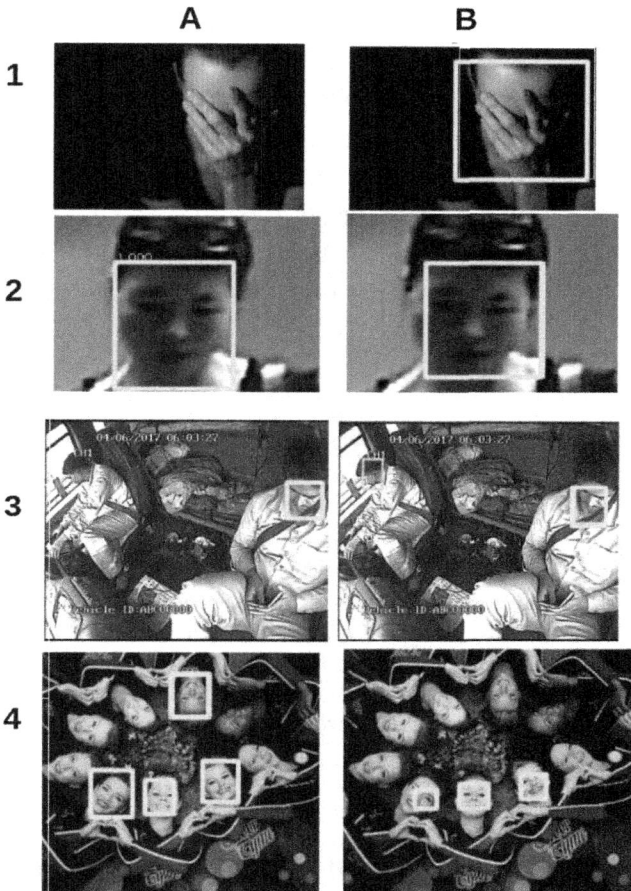

Fig. 12. A comparative study between the model proposed by Hu and Ramanan [19] and our proposed system. Images in column A show the results produced by the ResNet of Hu and Ramanan [19] and column B exhibits performance of the proposed system.

of 2.8% degradation in the performance of the network accuracy. Results of face detection of the proposed system on a few typical samples are provided in Fig. 11.

For the purpose of comparative study, we have shown results on a few typical images in Fig. 12. The results produced by the system proposed by Hu and Ramanan [19] in their system is in Fig. 12[A1, A3], whereas our system comes out with considerable amount of success Fig. 12[B1, B3]. Despite the fact that our system is not even half the size in terms of number of layers with respect to the referred system it performs modestly in the illustration shown below. In Fig. 12[A2] the performance of the ResNet based model is shown whereas Fig. 12[B2] shows face tracking by our detector. However, there are cases where our system fares comparatively poorly than the existing work [19]. As for

Table 1. Comparative performance of the proposed face detector.

System	Network type	No. of layers/classifiers	Test database	Accuracy (%)
Hu and Ramanan [19]	Resnet-50	50	Wider Face	82
Yang et al. [26]	Multi view detection	8192 weak classifiers	AFW	96.8
Proposed system	CNN	6 pairs of conv. & sub-sampling layers	Wider Face	79.8
Proposed system	CNN	6 pairs of conv. & sub-sampling layers	Our database	93

example, the illustration in A4 of Fig. 12 shows 4 faces have been detected by the system of Hu and Ramanan [19] while the corresponding output B4 of Fig. 12 shows that our system could detect only 3 of these faces. The possible reason for our system of not being able to localize the rotated face in Fig. 12[B4] is the lack of such training samples. Since we have hardly trained the system to detect faces in geometric transformation of rotation it is highly unnatural to expect the system to do so. Finally, the Table 1 provide some further comparative results.

7   Conclusions

Our aim, as we have duly emphasized in several contexts of the present article, was to explore a light weight yet robust system for automatic face detection in various possible difficult scenarios encountered in real life applications such as video surveillance. The proposed solution for the problem is significantly lightweight and it is capable of execution at a very low latency even on limited computational resources compared to the present day standard. On the other hand, the proposed face detection framework overcomes the limitations of the existing state-of-the-art in detecting faces under several challenging situations of uncontrolled imaging. Although the proposed face detection framework outperforms existing systems on various difficult image samples, its performance on existing standard benchmark datasets is comparable to the performance of the state-of-the-art algorithms.

The proposed strategy does not employ multiple networks to process the given image at multiple resolutions. Rather it employs only one network and the input image is fed to the network at three different resolutions consisting of original resolution and two low resolution images obtained through sub-sampling of the original image. Such a strategy helps us to detect faces of widely variable sizes using a single CNN architecture.

References

1. Yang, M.H., Kriegman, D.J., Ahuja, N.: Detecting faces in images: a survey. IEEE Trans. Pattern Anal. Mach. Intell. **24**(1), 34–58 (2002)
2. Lu, Y., Zhou, J., Yu, S.: A survey of face detection, extraction and recognition. Comput. Inform. **22**(2), 163–195 (2003)
3. Zafeiriou, S., Zhang, C., Zhang, Z.: A survey on face detection in the wild. Comput. Vis. Image Underst. **138**(C), 1–24 (2015)
4. Viola, P., Jones, M.J.: Robust real-time face detection. Int. J. Comput. Vision **57**(2), 137–154 (2004)
5. Pavani, S.K., Delgado, D., Frangi, A.F.: Haar-like features with optimally weighted rectangles for rapid object detection. Pattern Recogn. **43**(1), 160–172 (2010)
6. Ramanan, D.: Face detection, pose estimation, and landmark localization in the wild. In: Proceedings of the IEEE Conference on Computer Vision and Pattern Recognition (CVPR 2012), Washington, DC, USA, pp. 2879–2886 (2012)
7. LeCun, Y., Bengio, Y., Hinton, G.: Deep learning. Nature **521**(7553), 436–444 (2015)
8. Sutskever, I., Vinyals, O., Le, Q.V.: Sequence to sequence learning with neural networks. In: Ghahramani, Z., Welling, M., Cortes, C., Lawrence, N.D., Weinberger, K.Q. (eds.) Advances in Neural Information Processing Systems (NIPS 2014), vol. 27, pp. 3104–3112 (2014)
9. Lawrence, S., Giles, C.L., Tsoi, A.C., Back, A.D.: Face recognition: a convolutional neural-network approach. IEEE Trans. Neural Netw. **8**(1), 98–113 (1997)
10. Krizhevsky, A., Sutskever, I., Hinton, G.E.: Imagenet classification with deep convolutional neural networks. In: Advances in Neural Information Processing Systems, pp. 1097–1105 (2012)
11. Vaillant, R., Monrocq, C., Le Cun, Y.: Original approach for the localisation of objects in images. IEE Proc. Vis. Image Sig. Process. **141**(4), 245–250 (1994)
12. Rowley, H.A., Baluja, S., Kanade, T.: Rotation invariant neural network-based face detection. In: Proceedings of IEEE Computer Society Conference on Computer Vision and Pattern Recognition, pp. 38–44. IEEE (1998)
13. Garcia, C., Delakis, M.: Convolutional face finder: a neural architecture for fast and robust face detection. IEEE Trans. Pattern Anal. Mach. Intell. **26**(11), 1408–1423 (2004)
14. Li, H., Lin, Z., Shen, X., Brandt, J., Hua, G.: A convolutional neural network cascade for face detection. In: Proceedings of the IEEE Conference on Computer Vision and Pattern Recognition (CVPR 2015), pp. 5325–5334 (2015)
15. Girshick, R., Donahue, J., Darrell, T., Malik, J.: Region-based convolutional networks for accurate object detection and segmentation. IEEE Trans. Pattern Anal. Mach. Intell. **38**(1), 142–158 (2016)
16. Girshick, R.: Fast R-CNN. In: Proceedings of the IEEE International Conference on Computer Vision (CVPR 2015), pp. 1440–1448 (2015)
17. Ren, S., He, K., Girshick, R., Sun, J.: Faster R-CNN: towards real-time object detection with region proposal networks. In: Advances in Neural Information Processing Systems, pp. 91–99 (2015)
18. Liang, M., Hu, X.: Recurrent convolutional neural network for object recognition. In: Proceedings of the IEEE Conference on Computer Vision and Pattern Recognition (CVPR 2015), pp. 3367–3375 (2015)
19. Hu, P., Ramanan, D.: Finding tiny faces. arXiv preprint arXiv:1612.04402 (2016)

20. He, K., Zhang, X., Ren, S., Sun, J.: Deep residual learning for image recognition. In: Proceedings of the IEEE Conference on Computer Vision and Pattern Recognition (CVPR 2016), pp. 770–778 (2016)
21. Chollet, F., et al.: Keras (2015). https://github.com/fchollet/keras. Accessed 25 Sept 2017
22. Abadi, M., Agarwal, A., Barham, P., Brevdo, E., Chen, Z., Citro, C., Corrado, G.S., Davis, A., Dean, J., Devin, M., et al.: Tensorflow: large-scale machine learning on heterogeneous distributed systems. arXiv preprint arXiv:1603.04467 (2016)
23. Srivastava, N., Hinton, G.E., Krizhevsky, A., Sutskever, I., Salakhutdinov, R.: Dropout: a simple way to prevent neural networks from overfitting. J. Mach. Learn. Res. **15**(1), 1929–1958 (2014)
24. Neubeck, A., Van Gool, L.: Efficient non-maximum suppression. In: 18th International Conference on Pattern Recognition, vol. 3, pp. 850–855. IEEE (2006)
25. Yang, S., Luo, P., Loy, C.C., Tang, X.: Wider face: a face detection benchmark. In: Proceedings of the IEEE Conference on Computer Vision and Pattern Recognition, pp. 5525–5533 (2016)
26. Yang, B., Yan, J., Lei, Z., Li, S.Z.: Aggregate channel features for multi-view face detection. In: IEEE International Joint Conference on Biometrics (IJCB), pp. 1–8. IEEE (2014)

Feasibility Study of NIR, DSLR Imaging Techniques for Automatic Diabetic Foot Screening

Punal M. Arabi$^{(\boxtimes)}$, T. P. Prathibha, and Surekha Nigudgi

ACSCE, Bangalore, India
arabi.punal@gmail.com, Prathi.tp@gmail.com,
sursanju@gmail.com

Abstract. Diabetes is a group of metabolic diseases, characterized by high sugar levels in the blood and caused due to improper production of insulin in the pancreas or cells not responding coherently to insulin production. The earlier leads to Type 1 diabetes whereas the latter leads to Type 2 diabetes. It has become just as prevalent as an epidemic all around the globe although it is not infectious or pathogenic and statistics are estimated as 422 million people being affected globally and 69.2 million people in India, every year. Diabetes, if left untreated can cause serious health complications such as peripheral nerve dysfunction, diabetic retinopathy, diabetic foot and also doubles the risk of early death, thus making early diagnosis very essential for better disease management, thus improving the quality of life of the patient. If diabetic foot is not detected at an early stage, it may lead to gangrene and foot amputation of the patient. This paper presents comparison of NIR and DSLR images for diagnosis of diabetic foot images with the thermoregulatory behavior of a patient's feet. A total of 10 sets of images (120 images) of 10 subjects were obtained and analyzed statistically using pixel intensity matrix parameters and compared. The results obtained show that there is a distinct variation in the image parameters between the healthy and diabetic person's foot images and NIR Images are better suited for machine vision feasibility when compared to that of the DSLR images.

Keywords: Cold stress · Diabetic foot impairment · DSLR images
NIR images · Statistical image analysis

1 Introduction

Diabetes is fast gaining the status of a potential epidemic in India with 69.2 million people currently diagnosed with the disease [1]. An addition of 2.2 million deaths are caused by the risks of cardiovascular diseases resulting from high glucose levels resulting from high glucose increasing Higher blood glucose [2]. Diabetes, a metabolism disorder which causes high blood sugar level, due to inadequate insulin production as in the case of type-I diabetes or due to the body cells inability to properly respond to insulin as in the case of type2 diabetes; or it might due to both of these cases. The gestational diabetes is the metabolism disorder which is developed during pregnancy. Prediabetes is a stage at which the patients blood sugar level is higher than

P. Bhattacharyya et al. (Eds.): NGCT 2017, CCIS 828, pp. 887–898, 2018.
https://doi.org/10.1007/978-981-10-8660-1_67

normal but not high enough to be labeled as diabetes. Prediabetes are at the increase risk of getting type 2 diabetes. Diabetes is recognized as the world's fastest growing chronic condition. The number of type 2 diabetic people is increasing globally.

Statistics show that 8.8% of the global adult population has been diagnosed with diabetes as of 2015 and is expected to rise to up to 10.4% by 2040. It is predicted that count of 422 million people are affected by diabetes and the resulting annual fatality is 1.5 million people. The count in India is that 69.2 million are currently diagnosed with this disease.

2 Literature Survey

One of the only practical and feasible way of management of diabetes is by constant monitoring of the condition. Apart from the currently existing invasive glucose meter method, study on blood glucose monitoring in recent times has been improved by the proposal of non-invasive methods based on voltage intensity [2]. And Non-invasive blood glucose measurement [3].

Increased thirst, hunger, frequent urination, weight loss or gain that has no obvious cause, fatigue, blurred vision, wounds that heal slowly, nausea etc. are the common symptoms of diabetes. Chronic wounds are increasing problem as the world's population ages and the prevalence of diabetes increases. Diabetes needs to be managed or rather monitored on a routine basis, if left uncared for, it can cause serious problems, results of which may be life threatening. Temperature monitoring of diabetic foot [4]. Diabetes leads to peripheral nerve dysfunction which leads to the loss of sensitivity of nerves with respect to functions like clotting and healing. In such cases, on exposure of the wound to external conditions, for example in the foot region, healing will not take place and hence the affected region gets infected. This infection may cause the foot to rot which gradually progresses to gangrene. Alternately this may also cause diabetic ulcers. Increase ulcers that are associated with Hyperthermia, if the temperature higher than 2.2°C in a given region of one of the foot compared to the temperature of the same region of the contra lateral foot is diagnosed as hyperthermia present [5]. The probability of distribution of heat that could generate an ulcer in the foot can be determined using the finite element method [6]. Diabetic Foot Ulcers can be assessed with Diffuse near Infrared Methodology [7]. Diabetic person get affected twice than non diabetic person by which lower extremity amputation Ultimately is the results of gangrene. These situations are distressing and affect the patient psychologically. Also, these procedures are very expensive. Hence, diabetes also affects the quality of life physically, mentally and financially. The treatment of diabetes also affects the Indian economy at large.

Here, images of the foot are taken for the analysis. This method, in principle, is in accordance to the thermoregulation activity of the body upon cold provocation in comparison to normal body temperature, similar in procedure to temperature changes or diabetic foot hyperthermia [8]. This paper proposes a novel method for diagnosis of diabetic foot using NIR and DSLR images by the thermoregulatory behavior of patient's feet. The statistical analysis carried out on the pixel intensity matrix of these NIR and DSLR images show that there is a possibility of developing an automatic screening method for early diabetic foot diagnosis. Punal et al. proposed suitable enhancement techniques such as contrast stretching and histogram equalization for identification of thermal and non thermal diabetic foot images using signal to noise ratio [9]. Zaffar et al. proposed early diagnosis of diabetic peripheral neuropathy using low cost non-invasive patient centric device. By detecting hot, and cold vibration sensation of a diabetic patient and calibration it with respect to healthy person the device provides evaluation of level of neuropathy [10]. Vilcahuaman et al. proposed a method to detect a hyperthermia using an infrared camera, an image analysis method is composed of contour detection of the left and right foot using contour detection method [11].

3   Methodology

To acquire foot images of the subject, a corrugated box is fabricated with dimensions 1'9" × 1'5" × 1. The box is painted with dark black color to avoid external interferences for clarity of images taken. On 1 side of the box is a small door like opening that enables the insertion of the subject's feet at an elevated platform for taking images from a DSLR and an NIR camera. Inside the box, a platform was made to place the cameras at a distance of "xxx" in order to align and focus the cameras properly for images to be taken. The top of the box is covered with door like panels to enable opening and closing of the covers when images are taken in light and darkness.

The corrugated box is kept on the work table and a chair of the same height is placed as shown in the Fig. 1 The subject is made to sit on the chair with the legs stretched so as to insert the feet in the opening made in the box. The patient was advised to be relaxed and the feet to be placed in "V" shape, to acquire the images of the entire feet. A camera is kept on the opposite side of the feet aligned in such a way that focusing of the feet is accurate.

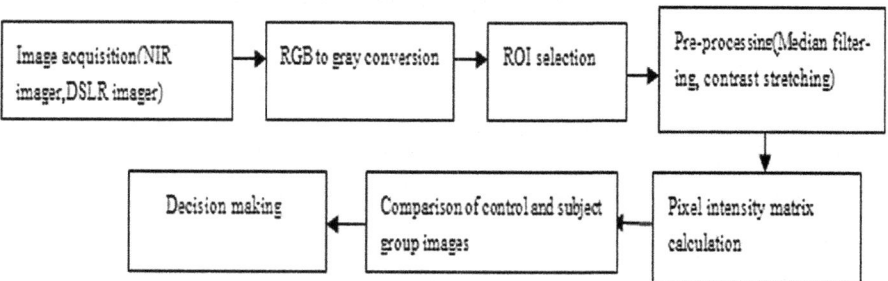

Fig. 1. Block diagram

Before the images were taken, the patient's feet were cleaned with soap and water and sanitized using a sanitizer. An image of the feet was taken in normal light at room temperature. The feet were subjected to cold stress using ice block for ten seconds. After ten seconds the subject's feet were wiped dry and 6 images were captured in series at an interval of 2 s using DSLR camera. The same is repeated with the NIR camera as well. The imaging was done in complete darkness by closing the lid. The same procedure was repeated for the other subject group (Figs. 2, 3, 4, 5, 6 and 7).

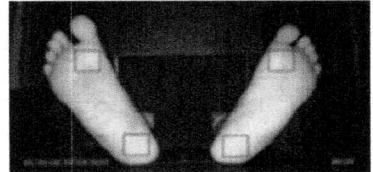

Fig. 2. Experimental setup   **Fig. 3.** ROI selection.

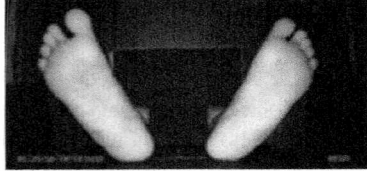
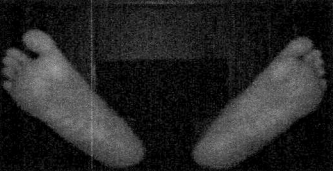

Fig. 4. (a) Feet of a control person using NIR. (b) Feet of a control person using DSLR.

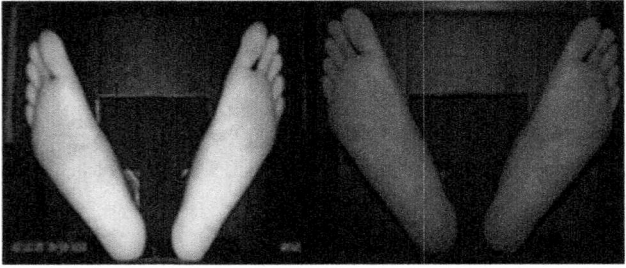

Fig. 5. (a) Feet of a control person using NIR. (b) Feet of a control person using DSLR.

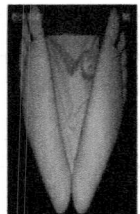
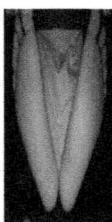
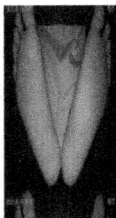
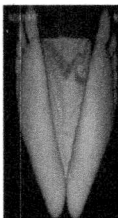
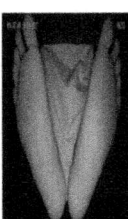

Fig. 6. The same process was repeated for obtaining the images of the remaining four diabetic patients and five healthy subjects using NIR imager.

A total of 120 images (6 * 10) NIR and (6 * 10) DSLR images of five diabetic patients and five healthy individuals were obtained and analysed. These images were then converted from RGB to grey and the regions of interest (ROI) was selected. The

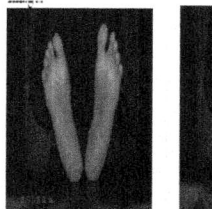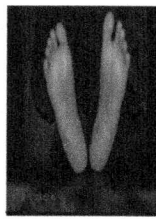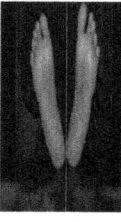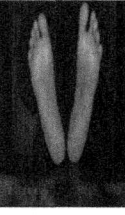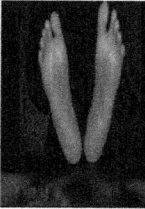

Fig. 7. The same process was repeated for obtaining the images of the remaining four diabetic patients and five healthy subjects.

region beneath the big toe and heel region of the feet were taken as the regions of interest as shown in figure. Median filtering and contrast stretching was accomplished towards pre-processing for noise removal and image enhancement. Pixel intensity matrix parameters namely covariance, standard deviation and mean of the ROI were calculated. The formulae for covariance, standard deviation and mean are given below:

$$\text{Covariance: } \text{cov}(A, B) = 1 N - 1 \sum (Ai - \mu A) * (Bi - \mu B) Ni = 1 \qquad (1)$$

where μA is the mean of A, μB is the mean of B, and * denotes the complex conjugate.

$$\text{Standard deviation: } S = \sqrt{1N - 1} \sum |Ai - \mu|2 \, Ni = 1 \qquad (2)$$

where μ is the mean of $A \, \mu = 1 \sum = 1$
  mean: $\mu = 1 \, N \sum AiNi = 1$

Using these parameter values obtained by DSLR and NIR imagers, thermoregulatory and the control groups is studied to evaluate the efficiency of the imagers is analyzed. The analysis is carried by comparing the impact of thermoregulatory over the pattern of changes in the GLCM values obtained by the above set of images.

4 Results and Discussion

Ten people, 5 healthy and 5 diabetics were taken for experimentation. The 5 healthy individuals were named as control group (C1-C5) and the 5 diabetic patients were named as subject group (S1-S5).

Table 1 shows the pixel intensity values namely covariance, standard deviation and mean of the left toe region of 6 NIR images. The values of covariance, standard deviation and mean of each image is averaged and represented by N C1(ALT1) and N S1(ALT1) for control and subject group respectively. N C1(ALT1) represents the average value pixel intensity parameters of left toe region of the control person using NIR. Similarly, N S1(ALT1) represents the average value of pixel intensity parameters of left toe region of the subject person. N C1(ALT1) has the average covariance = 0.0032, average standard deviation = 0.0562 and average mean = 0.9169. Similarly, for the subject group the average covariance = 0.0043, average standard deviation = 0.0651 and average mean = 0.9041. N C1(ALT1)...N C5(ALT1)

Table 1. Time vs pixel intensity matrix parameters of left toe region of control and subject using NIR imager.

TIME(S)	COV	STD_DEV	MEAN	TIME(S)	COV	STD_DEV	MEAN
0	0.0032	0.0568	0.9139	0	0.0031	0.0553	0.9209
2	0.0036	0.0597	0.9017	2	0.0031	0.0558	0.9154
4	0.0042	0.0646	0.9001	4	0.0031	0.0561	0.9173
6	0.0046	0.0676	0.904	6	0.0032	0.0563	0.9137
8	0.005	0.0709	0.8998	8	0.0032	0.0567	0.9186
10	0.0051	0.0711	0.9053	10	0.0032	0.0569	0.9157
N S1(LT1)	0.0043	0.0651	0.9041	N C1(ALT1)	0.0032	0.0562	0.9169

    DIABETIC   NORMAL

Note:N C1(ALT1)- average value of covariance, standard deviation and mean of left toe of control 1 using NIR.

Note: N S1(ALT1)- average value of covariance, standard deviation and mean of left toe of healthy subject 1 using NIR.

represents the average value of the pixel intensity matrix parameters covariance, standard deviation and mean of the left toe of each control group individual using NIR.

Similarly, N S1(ALT1)...N S5(ALT1) represents the average value of the pixel intensity matrix parameters covariance, standard deviation and mean of the left toe of each subject group individual using NIR.

$$NC1(ALT1) = \frac{C01 + C02 + C03 + C04 + C05 + C06}{6} \tag{3}$$

Where C01...C06 represent the covariance values of the images taken at 0th...10th second.

Similarly, the other values for standard deviation and mean are calculated for the control and subject group.

Table 2 shows the pixel intensity values namely covariance, standard deviation and mean of the left toe region of 6 DSLR images. The values of covariance, standard deviation and mean of each image is averaged and represented by D C1(ALT1) and D S1(ALT1) for control and subject group respectively.

D C1(ALT1) represents the average value pixel intensity parameters of left toe region of the control person using DSLR. Similarly, D S1(ALT1) represents the average value of pixel intensity parameters of left toe region of the subject person. D C1(ALT1) has the average covariance = 0.0014, average standard deviation = 0.0372 and average mean = 08695. Similarly, for the subject group the average

Table 2. Time vs pixel intensity matrix parameters of left toe region of control and subject using DSLR

TIME(S)	COV	STD_DEV	MEAN
0	0.0032	0.0568	0.9139
2	0.0036	0.0597	0.9017
4	0.0042	0.0646	0.9001
6	0.0046	0.0676	0.904
8	0.005	0.0709	0.8998
10	0.0051	0.0711	0.9053
N S1(LT1)	0.0043	0.0651	0.9041

DIABETIC

TIME(S)	COV	STD_DEV	MEAN
0	0.0013	0.0367	0.8705
2	0.0013	0.0367	0.8705
4	0.0013	0.0367	0.8705
6	0.0013	0.0367	0.8705
8	0.0014	0.0376	0.8674
10	0.0015	0.0391	0.8676
DC1(ALT1)	0.0014	0.0372	0.8695

NORMAL

Note:DC1(ALT1)- average value of covariance, standard deviation and mean of left toe of control 1 using DSLR.

Note: D S1(ALT1)- average value of covariance, standard deviation and mean of left toe of healthy subject 1 using DSLR

covariance = 0.0 D C1(ALT1)...D C5(ALT1) represents the average value of the pixel intensity matrix parameters covariance, standard deviation and mean of the left toe of each control group individual using DSLR.

Similarly, D S1(ALT1)...D S5(ALT1) represents the average value of the pixel intensity matrix parameters covariance, standard deviation and mean of the left toe of each subject group individual using DSLR.

$$DC1(ALT1) = \frac{C01 + C02 + C03 + C04 + C05 + C06}{6} \qquad (4)$$

Where C01...C06 represent the covariance values of the images taken at 0th...10th second.Similarly, the other values for standard deviation and mean are calculated for the control and subject group using DSLR.

Table 3 shows the average value of the pixel intensity matrix parameters of the left toe of each control group and subject group individual along with the average of these averaged values using NIR. N C(ALT) represents these average values of the pixel intensity matrix parameters of each individual of control group using NIR.

Similarly, N S(ALT) represents these average values of the pixel intensity matrix parameters of each individual of subject group.

N C(ALT) covariance = 0.00278, N C(ALT) standard deviation = 0.05212 and N C(ALT) mean = 0.93562 represent the average covariance, standard deviation and mean values of the left toe of each individual of the control group using NIR. Similarly, N S(ALT) covariance = 0.00374, N S(ALT) standard deviation = 0.06058 and N S

Table 3. Average value of pixel intensity parameters of control and subject group using NIR imager

SL NO.	COV	STD_DEV	MEAN
N S1(ALT1)	0.0043	0.0651	0.9041
N S2(ALT1)	0.0032	0.057	0.9179
N S3(ALT1)	0.004	0.0634	0.9173
N S4(ALT1)	0.0052	0.0723	0.8804
N S5(ALT1)	0.002	0.0451	0.8914
N S (ALT)	0.00374	0.06058	0.90222

DIABETIC

SL NO.	COV	STD_DEV	MEAN
N C1(ALT1)	0.0032	0.0562	0.9169
N C2(ALT1)	0.0019	0.0437	0.942
N C3(ALT1)	0.0031	0.0559	0.9268
N C4(ALT1)	0.0018	0.0427	0.9532
N C5(ALT1)	0.0039	0.0621	0.9392
N C (ALT)	0.00278	0.05212	0.93562

NORMAL

Note: N C1(ALT1)…N C5(ALT1) average pixel intensity parameter values of left toe region of control 1…control 5

Note: N C(ALT) average pixel intensity parameter value of the left toe region of control group i.e. group average.

Note:N S1(ALT1)…N S5(ALT1) average pixel intensity parameter values of left toe region of subject 1…subject 5

Note: N S(ALT) average pixel intensity parameter value of the left toe region of subject group i.e. group average.

(ALT) mean = 0.90222 represent the average covariance, standard deviation and mean values of the left toe of each individual of the subject group.

$$NC(ALT) = \frac{C1(ALT1) + C2(ALT1) + C3(ALT1) + C4(ALT1) + C5(ALT1)}{5} \quad (5)$$

Here each parameter namely covariance, standard deviation and mean are considered individually during

N C(ALT) calculations.

Table 4 shows the average value of the pixel intensity matrix parameters of the left toe of each control group and subject group individual along with the average of these averaged values using DSLR. D C(ALT) represents these average values of the pixel intensity matrix parameters of each individual of control group using DSLR. Similarly, D S(ALT) represents these average values of the pixel intensity matrix parameters of each individual of subject group using DSLR. D C(ALT) covariance = 0.00198, D C (ALT) standard deviation = 0.04407 and D C(ALT) mean = 0.85154 represent the average covariance, standard deviation and mean values of the left toe of each individual of the control group using DSLR. Similarly, D S(ALT) covariance = 0.00418, D S(ALT) standard deviation = 0.062156 and D S(ALT) mean = 0.72948 represent the

Table 4. Average value of pixel intensity parameters of control and subject group using DSLR

SL NO.	COV	STD_DEV	MEAN	SL NO.	COV	STD_DEV	MEAN
D S1(ALT1)	0.0038	0.0619	0.7893	D C1(ALT1)	0.0014	0.0372	0.8695
D S2(ALT1)	0.0018	0.0428	0.6076	D C2(ALT1)	0.0015	0.0385	0.785
D S3(ALT1)	0.0093	0.0963	0.7135	D C3(ALT1)	0.0023	0.0481	0.8751
D S4(ALT1)	0.003	0.055	0.7357	D C4(ALT1)	0.0022	0.0465	0.897
D S5(ALT1)	0.003	0.05478	0.8013	D C5(ALT1)	0.0025	0.05005	0.8311
D S(ALT)	0.00418	0.062156	0.72948	D C(ALT)	0.00198	0.04407	0.85154

DIABETIC   NORMAL

average covariance, standard deviation and mean values of the left toe of each individual of the subject group using DSLR.

$$D\ C(ALT) = C1(ALT1) + C2(ALT1) + C3(ALT1) + C4(AL回皖\ 1) + C5(ALT1)\ldots\ldots\ldots \quad (6)$$

Here each parameter namely covariance, standard deviation and mean are considered individually during

D C(ALT) calculations.

Table 5 shows the standard deviation and variance for the control and subject groups using NIR. N C(ALT), N C(ALH), N C(ART) and N C(ARH) represents the group average of pixel intensity parameters for the five members of the control group using NIR. Where N C(ALT), N C(ALH), N C(ART), N C(ARH) represents these average values of the pixel intensity matrix parameters of left toe, left heel, right toe, right heel region respectively. Similarly, N S(ALT), N S(ALH), N S(ART) and N S(ARH) represents the group average pixel intensity parameters for the five members of the subject group using NIR. Where N S(ALT), N S(ALH), N S(ART), N S(ARH) represents these average values of the pixel intensity matrix parameters of left toe, left heel, right toe, right heel region respectively. Standard deviation and variance for these four values is calculated using the formula given below

$$\text{Variance } \sigma 2 = 1N - 1 \sum (xi - \mu) 2 N i = 1 \quad (7)$$

where N is the population size and μ is the population mean.

Using NIR, the obtained values of variance of covariance is 2.17E-07 for healthy person and 1.30E-06 for the diabetic person. The values of variance of standard deviation is 2.38E-05 for healthy person and 1.17E-04 for the diabetic person. The values of variance of average mean pixel intensity is 3.07E-05 for healthy person and 5.84E-04 for the diabetic person.

Table 5. Standard deviation and variance of the group average parameters using NIR imager.

SL NO.	COV	STD_DEV	MEAN
NS(ALT)	0.00374	0.06058	0.90222
NS(ARH)	0.00212	0.04466	0.9456
NS(ART)	0.00378	0.05942	0.90364
NS(ARH)	0.00154	0.03886	0.9439
NS(STD_DEV)	0.00114	0.010804	0.02416172
NS(VAR)	1.30E-06	0.000153	0.00058379

DIABETIC

SL NO.	COV	STD_DEV	MEAN
NS(ALT)	0.00278	0.05212	0.93562
NS(ARH)	0.00196	0.04388	0.94482
NS(ART)	0.00266	0.05092	0.94038
NS(ARH)	0.00188	0.04246	0.94842
NS(STD_DEV)	0.00046562	0.00488	0.00554
NS(VAR)	2.17E-07	2.38E-05	3.07E-05

NORMAL

Table 6. Standard deviation and variance of the group average parameters using DSLR.

SL NO.	COV	STD_DEV	MEAN
DS(ALT)	0.00418	0.06216	0.72948
DS(ARH)	0.01046	0.09057	0.6626
DS(ART)	0.01193	0.09136	0.67615
DS(ARH)	0.00626	0.07774	0.71636
DS(STD_DEV)	0.0036	0.0137029	0.03186
DS(VAR)	1.30E-05	0.0001878	0.001015

DIABETIC

SL NO.	COV	STD_DEV	MEAN
DC(ALT)	0.00198	0.04407	0.85154
DC(ALH)	0.00375	0.06077	0.75814
DC(ART)	0.13934	0.04434	0.84471
DC(ARH)	0.004234	0.06432	0.76862
DC(STD_DEV)	0.06802	0.01069	0.04919334
DC(VAR)	0.00463	0.00011	0.00241998

NORMAL

Table 6 shows the standard deviation and variance for the control and subject groups using DSLR. D C(ALT), D C(ALH), D C(ART) and D C(ARH) represents the group average of pixel intensity parameters for the five members of the control group using DSLR. Where D C(ALT), D C(ALH), D C(ART), D C(ARH) represents these average values of the pixel intensity matrix parameters of left toe, left heel, right toe, right heel region respectively. Similarly, D S(ALT), D S(ALH), D S(ART) and D S (ARH) represents the group average pixel intensity parameters for the five members of the subject group using DSLR. Where D S(ALT), D S(ALH), D S(ART), D S(ARH) represents these average values of the pixel intensity matrix parameters of left toe, left heel, right toe, right heel region respectively.

Using DSLR, the obtained values of variance of covariance is 0.00463 for healthy person and 1.30E-05 for the diabetic person. The values of variance of standard deviation is 0.0001142 for healthy person and 0.00019 for the diabetic person. The values of variance of average mean pixel intensity is 0.002419 for healthy person and 0.001015 for the diabetic person.

From this we infer that the variance of covariance, standard deviation and the average mean pixel intensity of the pixel intensity parameters of the diabetic persons are more than that of healthy persons in NIR images, but for the DSLR images the variations in the parameter do not follow any pattern and this results in a difficult situation to frame the decision rule. Hence it is concluded that NIR imaging modality is better suited for developing an automated screening system for diabetic foot.

5   Conclusion

A set of 120 NIR and DSLR foot images of diabetic and non-diabetic people were analyzed. Pixel intensity matrix parameters are calculated for both NIR and DSLR images. The thermoregulatory response of the person's feet for cold stress was considered. The values of the pixel intensity parameters namely variance, Standard deviation, covariances and mean of the diabetic persons were found to be significantly greater than that of the NIR images of the healthy individuals, this is due to the blood vessls impairement caused by the diseases. There is a definite pattern of changes observed over the DSLR images obtained for the cold stress lead to the diabetic and non diabetic classification. This shows that the DSLR images are not reliable as it results in a difficult situation to frame the decision rule. By analyzing the NIR images after subjecting the feet to a cold stress, the diabetic feet impairment of the subject could be found. Hence, there is a possibility of developing an automatic screening system for early diabetic foot diagnosis using NIR images and thermoregulatory behavior of feet.

Acknowledgement. The authors thank the Management and Principal of ACS College of Engineering, Mysore road, Bangalore for permitting and supporting to carry out the research work.

References

1. Brodal, P.: The Central Nervous System: Structure and Function, 3rd edn. Oxford University Press, Oxford (2010)
2. Hodges, G.J., Traeger, J.A., Tang, T., Koshiba, W.A., Zhao, K., Johnson, J.M.: Role of sensory nerves in the cutaneous vasoconstrictor response to local cooling in humans. Am. J. Physiol. Heart Circ. Physiol. **293**, 784–789 (2007)
3. Gelao, G., Marani, R., Carriero, V., Perri, A.G.: Design of a dielectric spectroscopy sensor for continuous and non-invasive blood glucose monitoring. Int. J. Adv. Eng. Technol. **3**, 55 (2012)
4. Ashok, V., Nirmalkumar, A., Jeyashanthi, N.: A novel method for blood glucose mesurement by noninvasive technique using laser. World Acad. Sci. Eng. Technol. **51**, 672–682 (2011)
5. Abdallah, O., Bolz, A., Hansmann, J., Walles, H., Hirth, T.: Design of a compact multi-sensor system for non-invasive glucose monitoring using optical spectroscopy. In: International Conference on Electronics, Biomedical Engineering and its Applications (ICEBEA 2012), 7–8 January (2012)
6. Burmeister, J.J., Arnold, M.A., Small, G.W.: Noninvasive blood glucose measurements by near-infrared transmission spectroscopy across human tongues. Diab. Technol. Ther. **2**, 5–16 (2000)
7. Tang, F., Wang, X., Wang, D., Li, J.: Non-invasive glucose measurement by use of metabolic heat conformation method. Sensors **8**, 3335–3344 (2008)

8. Shinde, A.A., Prasad, R.K.: Non invasive blood glucose measurement using NIR technique based on occlusion spectroscopy. Int. J. Eng. Sci. Technol. (IJEST), **3**(12), 8325–8333 (2011). ISSN 0975-5462

9. Arabi, P.M., Joshi, G., Bhat, T., Singh, H.L.: Identifying suitable enhancement technique for thermal and non thermal diabetic foot Images. Int. J. Adv. Netw. Appl. (IJANA). ISSN: 0975-0282. 1st International Conference on Innovations in Computing & Networking (ICICN16). CSE, RRCE

10. Zaffar, M., Tariq, M.T., Arsalan, M.A., Qureshi, N.K., Cheema, H.M.: A low-cost, non-invasive sensory device for early diagnosis of diabetic peripheral neuropathy. IEEE (2016). ISBN 978-1-5090-2455-1/16/©2016

11. Vilcahuaman, L., Harba, R., Canals, R., Zequera, M., Wilches, C., Arista, M.T., Torres, L., Arbañil, H.: Detection of diabetic foot hyperthermia by infrared imaging. IEEE (2014). ISBN 978-1-4244-7929-0/14/2014

Feature Extraction and Classification of X-Ray Lung Images Using Haralick Texture Features

N. Vamsha Deepa, Nanditha Krishna, and G. Hemanth Kumar[(✉)]

Department of BME, ACSCE, Bangalore, India
vamshi.deepa@gmail.com, nanditha13@gmail.com,
hemumanju@gmail.com

Abstract. According to a survey given by world health organization pneumonia is the leading cause of death. Pneumonia is a disease caused due to bacteria, virus, or fungus infection in one or both the lungs [1]. Before the antibiotics were introduced, one third of all people who suffered from pneumonia died from the disease. Currently world wide about 3 million people develop pneumonia every year. Conventional chest radiograph is the widely used tool for the detection and diagnosis of lung disorders such as pneumonia, tuberculosis and lung tumors. Mortality rate due to late diagnosis of lung disorders is in millions, thus an early diagnosis of these diseases can reduce the death rate. This paper presents a novel system for the detection and classification of lung infected with pneumonia from the normal lung of the x-ray images by extracting various texture parameters like Haralick texture features. This method is tested on a set of 11 normal and pneumonic affected lung images. The results obtained show that the proposed method has an accuracy of 86%.

Keywords: Pnemonia · Chest radiograph · Diagnosis
Haralick texture features

1 Introduction

Pneumonia is the leading cause of death among children under the age of five, where at least 2,500 children die everyday [1]. According to a survey in 2015, pneumonia accounts for 15% of all deaths of children below five years and mostly were less than 2 years old. Pneumonia causes swelling in lung's alveoli or lung's air sacs. Pneumonia is the accumulation of fluids or pus in the alveoli causing respiratory problems. The severity of pneumonia generally depends on – the source of inflammation, the kind of organism causing the infection, age and general well being. Few specific types of pneumonia based on affected portions of lung are- bronchial pneumonia, lobar pneumonia, bilateral pneumonia, eosinophilic pneumonia, hypostatic pneumonia, lipoid pneumonia. The general symptoms of pneumonia include chest pain, fever, dry Cough, wheezing, rapid and difficulty in breathing. The different methods for diagnosing pneumonia are blood test, chest radiograph, lung ultrasound, CT scan, pulse oximetry and bronchoscopy.

© Springer Nature Singapore Pte Ltd. 2018
P. Bhattacharyya et al. (Eds.): NGCT 2017, CCIS 828, pp. 899–907, 2018.
https://doi.org/10.1007/978-981-10-8660-1_68

2   Literature Survey

Khobragade et al. proposed a method for the detection and classification of lung diseases such as tuberculosis, pneumonia and lung cancer in chest radiographs based on segmentation; feature extraction and artificial neural networks [2]. Ebrahimian et al. proposed a novel algorithm to solve the difficult problem of discriminating two similar diseases, pulmonary tuberculosis (PTB) and lobar pneumonia (PNEU) using phase congruency. The phase congruency parameter estimation was studied to obtain the best values that has the ability to differentiate between normal, PTB and PNEU. Eight texture measures of values were then investigated as global measures for differentiation of diseases [3]. Noor et al. attempted to discriminate three types of lung diseases pair-wise, namely lobar pneumonia (PNEU), pulmonary tuberculosis (PTB) and lung cancer (LC) using chest radiograph. A modified principal component method applied to wavelet texture measures yielded feature vectors for the pair-wise statistical discrimination procedure. The combination of mean of energy and maximum value texture measures gave good pair-wise discrimination rate and classification rate [4]. Karargyris et al. developed a approach for detecting ribs in chest radiographs. This approach computes wavelet features in terms of region-based features along with different orientation of anatomic structures for classification [5]. Khalid and Akbar focused on techniques of segmentation, feature extraction and classification of X-ray images as normal and diseased based on the classifier that is trained on number of features [6]. Barrientos presented a method for automatic diagnosis of pneumonia using ultrasound imaging of the pneumonic lungs based on the analysis of patterns present in rectangular segments from the ultrasound digital images, some specific features from the characteristic vectors were obtained and classified with standard neural networks [7]. Barrientos proposed a method to recognize and eliminate the portion of the skin in lung ultrasound images as the noise introduced by the image portion of the skin complicates the processing and interpretation of pneumonic lung ultrasound images [8]. Cisneros-Velarde proposed an application for the detection of pneumonia using ultrasound video analysis by processing and analyzing of small video fragments to achieve an overall video statistics for the findings of pneumonia in the video analyzed [9]. Zenteno developed an algorithm for the detection of pneumonia based on fundamental frequency downshift measurement over a depth of ultrasound RF signals obtained from samples of children aged between six months to five years [10]. Liu described a prevention method for pneumonia in the hospitals by automatically measuring how often and how much the subject is active out-of-bed using Microsoft Kinect V2. Hospital Acquired Pneumonia (HAP) deals with subject activities during their hospital stay. With regard to the healthcare staff, it is required to know the quantity of the subject's active time, mainly when the subject is alone. The described model recognized the out-of-bed activities using the features extracted from Kinect model. The observation on the detection results provide information to healthcare staff for better understanding the HAP formation and also to adjust the treatment process in time [11].

3 Methodology

The proposed method involves the texture based classification between normal lung X-ray images and pneumonia infected lung X-ray images. The steps involved in the identification of pneumonic infected lung is as shown in Fig. 1.

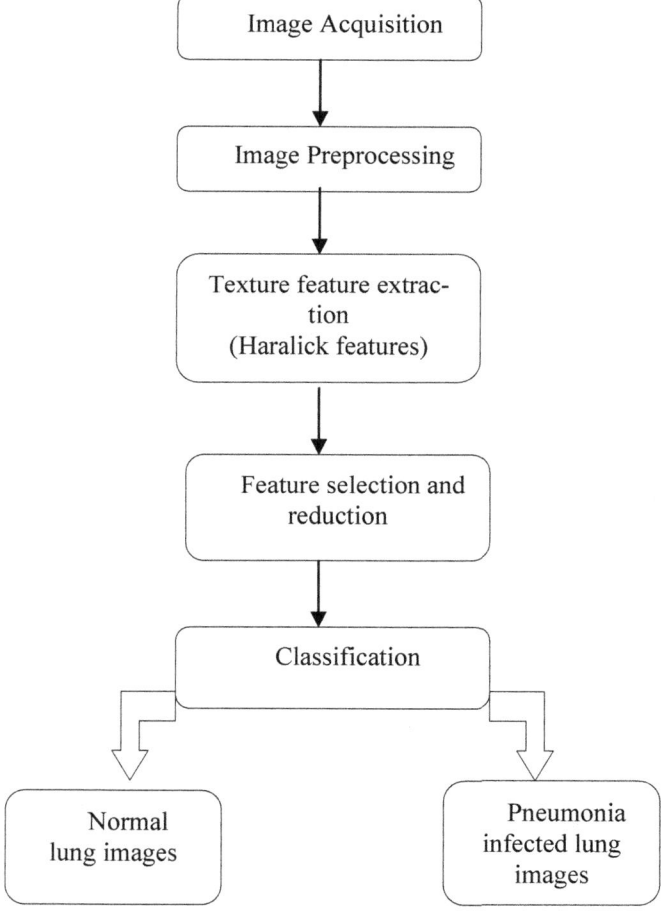

Fig. 1. Flow diagram

The images are collected from Rajarajeshwari medical college and hospital, Bangalore. The collected images undergoes preprocessing stage which includes selection of region of interest and resizing to a standard size of 512×512. The region of interest is the white mass of the pneumonic infected lung. Texture analysis is applied for detecting details of an image that are not rotationally variant. The co-occurrence matrix can measure the texture of the image depending on the grayscale values or intensity of the image and for different color dimensions. These co-occurrence matrices are huge and scattered, different measurements of the matrix are analyzed for certain set of features. The two similar co-occurrence matrices are rotated at various degrees (0, 45, 90 and 135°) and various features are evaluated; these features are referred to as Haralick features (14 features) and are extracted from the resized image. The gray-level co-occurrence (GLCM) matrix with dimension Ng is a square matrix, where Ng is the number of intensity levels in the image. Element (i, j) of the matrix is generated by counting the number of times a pixel with value I is adjacent to a pixel with value J and then dividing the entire matrix by the total number of comparisons made. Each entry is considered to be the probability that a pixel with value I to be adjacent to a pixel of value J. The 14 Haralick texture features are-

1. Angular second moment (ASM)- measures image homogeneity

$$f1 = \sum_{i=1}^{Ng} \sum_{j=1}^{Ng} p(i,j)^2 \tag{1}$$

2. Contrast- measures difference between maximum and minimum pixel values

$$f2 = \sum_{n=0}^{Ng-1} n^2 \{ \sum_{i=1}^{Ng} \sum_{j=1}^{Ng} p(i,j) \} \tag{2}$$

where $n = |i-j|$

3. Correlation-Linear dependency of gray levels of neighboring pixels of the image

$$f3 = \frac{\sum_i \sum_j (ij)p(i,j) - \mu_x \mu_y}{\sigma_x \sigma_y} \tag{3}$$

where μ_x, μ_y, σ_x, σ_y are the means and standard deviations of p_x and p_y, the partial probability density functions

4. Variance- average of squared differences from the mean of the image

$$f4 = \sum_{i=1}^{Ng} \sum_{j=1}^{Ng} (i-j)^2 p(i,j) \tag{4}$$

5. Inverse Difference Moment(IDM)- local homogeneity of the image

$$f5 = \sum_i \sum_j \frac{p(i,j)}{1 + (i-j)^2} \tag{5}$$

6. Sum average- sum of all the mean values in the given image

$$f6 = \sum_{i=2}^{2Ng} i p_{x+y}(i) \tag{6}$$

where x, y are the row and column coordinates of an entry in the co-occurrence matrix coordinates summing to x + y

7. Sum variance-sum of variance values of the image

$$f7 = \sum_{i=2}^{2Ng} (i - f8)^2 p_{x+y}(i) \tag{7}$$

8. Sum entropy- total amount of information which must be coded for an image

$$f8 = -\sum_{i=2}^{2Ng} p_{x+y}(i)\log\{p_{x+y}(i)\} \tag{8}$$

9. Entropy- amount of information which must be coded for an image

$$f9 = -\sum_{i=1}^{Ng} \sum_{j=1}^{Ng} p(i,j)\log(p(i,j)) \tag{9}$$

10. Difference variance- difference among the variance values of an image

$$f10 = \sum_{i=0}^{Ng-1} i^2 p_{x-y}(i) \tag{10}$$

11. Difference entropy- difference among the entropy values of an image

$$f11 = -\sum_{i=0}^{Ng-1} p_{x-y}(i)\log\{p_{x-y}(i)\} \tag{11}$$

12. Information measure of correlation 1&2- function of joint probability density distribution of variables which reduces the classical correlation coefficient

$$f12 = \frac{HXY - HXY1}{\max(HX, HY)} \tag{12}$$

   where HX, HY are the entropies of px and py
13. Maximal correlation coefficient- linear interdependence of pixels in the image

$$Q(i,j) = \sum_k \frac{p(i,k)p(j,k)}{Px(i)Py(k)} \tag{13}$$

After extracting the Haralick texture features the values obtained are compared between normal and pneumonic lung images; the difference among those values are verified. There was no considerable differences in the eleven features out of fourteen features extracted and the contribution of those features was less for classification and so were neglected. The remaining three features variance (f4), sum average (f6) and sum variance (f7) showed a significant difference in values between normal and pneumonic lung images. Thus these features were chosen for identification and classification of pneumonic lung images. From the selected features (f4, f6, and f7) a decision rule is made based on average, minimum and maximum values.

4   Results

Figures 2a and b shows a set of normal and pneumonic lung images.

(a)

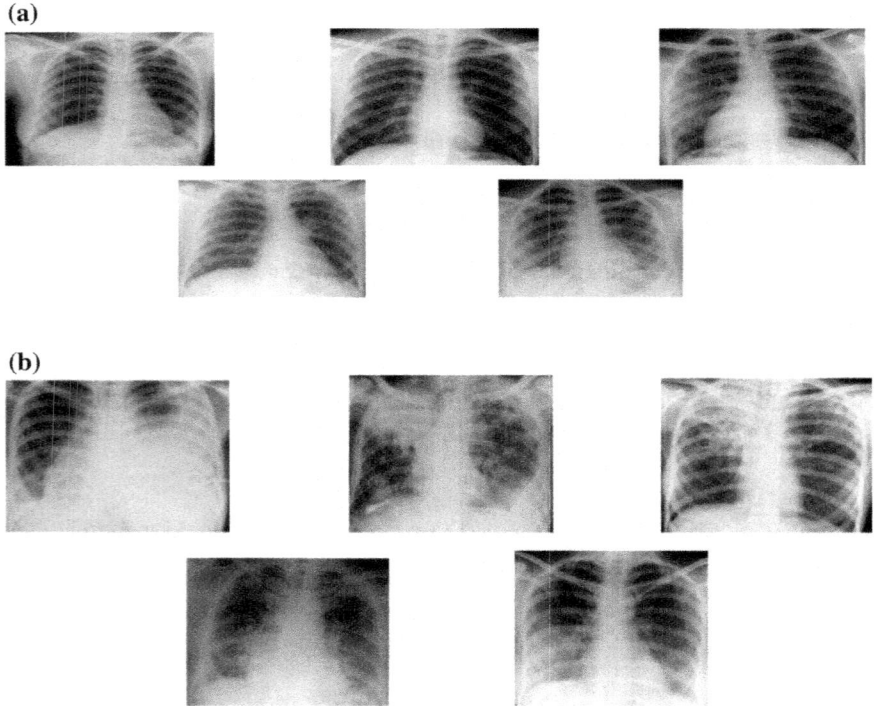

(b)

Fig. 2.   a. A set of normal lung images b. A set of pneumonia lung images

Tables 1 and 2 shows the 14 Haralick features for normal and pneumonic x-ray lung images

Table 1.   Haralick features for normal x-ray lung images

Images	f_1	f_2	f_3	f_4	f_5	f_6	f_7	f_8	f_9	f_{10}	f_{11}	f_{12}	f_{13}	f_{14}
1	.1658	.1031	.9896	32.81	.9504	10.58	131.8	2.1572	3.2242	.0938	.3294	.8038	.9934	.1471
2	.1781	.0786	.9809	29.62	.9607	10.53	119.19	1.8921	2.8082	.0746	.2755	.8135	.9892	.2141
3	.1304	.0798	.9937	30.46	.9603	9.86	122.50	2.2431	3.3159	.0756	.2782	.8485	.9962	.1781
4	.2287	.0639	.9913	35.00	.9682	11.23	140.80	1.9364	2.8550	.0636	.2374	.8534	.9929	.1236
5	.1628	.0642	.9920	26.53	.9682	9.53	106.75	2.0399	3.0056	.0639	.2380	.8583	.9946	.2295
6	.2158	.0508	.9893	32.13	.9746	10.94	129.23	1.7820	2.6215	.0537	.2009	.8637	.9907	.2360
7	.1354	.0787	.9880	33.06	.9607	10.95	133.00	2.1657	3.2005	.0747	.2756	.8350	.9950	.1659
8	.1718	.0485	.9924	28.26	.9757	10.04	113.53	1.9455	2.8543	.0520	.1942	.8777	.9942	.2330
9	.1979	.0490	.9877	30.58	.9755	10.74	123.10	1.8155	2.6648	.0523	.1954	.8694	.9918	.2487
10	.2452	.0463	.9927	22.85	.9769	8.915	92.03	1.7140	2.5151	.0504	.1875	.8768	.9901	.1972
11	.1729	.0671	.9861	28.40	.9666	10.33	114.18	1.9412	2.8681	.0660	.2459	.8406	.9926	.2262
Average	.1828	.0663	.9894	29.97	.9670	10.32	120.55	1.9666	2.9030	.0655	.2416	.8490	.9927	.1999

Here the mean values were calculated and are indicated at the bottom of each column of Tables 1 and 2 for each of the features extracted. The minimum and maximum values for the selected features variance (f4), sum average (f6) and sum variance (f7) are tabulated in Table 3.

Table 2. Haralick features for pneumonic x-ray lung images

Images	f_1	f_2	f_3	f_4	f_5	f_6	f_7	f_8	f_9	f_{10}	f_{11}	f_{12}	f_{13}	f_{14}
1	.1436	.0947	.9884	35.89	.9529	11.32	144.28	2.1531	3.2025	.0868	.3134	.8719	.9940	.2034
2	.1873	.0471	.9923	40.82	.9765	12.32	164.04	1.9219	2.8200	.0510	.1898	.8832	.9942	.1841
3	.2329	.0546	.9918	41.06	.9728	12.33	165.01	1.8547	2.7282	.0566	.2118	.8618	.9920	.1793
4	.1759	.0631	.9927	39.78	.9686	11.94	159.91	2.0437	3.0105	.0630	.2353	.8646	.9949	.2672
5	.1481	.0635	.9930	36.42	.9653	11.26	146.51	2.1686	3.1948	.0678	.2523	.8602	.9960	.2013
6	.1772	.0659	.9917	38.46	.9671	11.78	154.54	1.9869	2.9325	.0650	.2429	.8560	.9938	.2637
7	.2964	.0648	.9879	36.57	.9676	11.68	147.01	1.7224	2.5499	.0642	.2400	.8312	.9867	.1363
8	.3452	.0397	.9914	50.88	.9801	13.99	204.56	1.5084	2.2123	.0454	.1670	.8739	0.9840	.2174
9	.2900	.0477	.9890	46.64	.9761	13.37	187.21	1.5980	2.3512	.0514	.1918	.8565	.9852	.2899
10	.1778	.0926	.9892	37.08	.9545	11.46	148.97	2.0979	3.1234	.0854	.3079	.8188	.9934	.1765
11	.1886	.0625	.9880	42.18	.9689	12.62	169.51	1.9287	2.8450	.0625	.2336	.8515	.9927	.2138
Average	.2148	.0638	.9905	40.52	.9682	12.18	162.87	1.9076	2.8154	.0635	.2350	.8523	.9915	.2096

Decision Rule

From Table 3 a decision rule is framed to classify pneumonic infected lung and normal lung images. The decision rule for an image to be normal has to satisfy below three conditions -

1. $22.85 < f(4) < 35$
2. $8.9 < f(6) < 10.9$
3. $92 < f(7) < 140$

If f(4), f(6) and f(7) of any image does not lie in the above range then such a image is classified as pneumonic infected lung image.

Table 3. Features with significant difference in their values

Texture feature	Lung type	Mean value	Minimum value	Maximum value
f4	Pneumonic lung	40.5273	35.8974	50.8838
	Normal lung	29.9745	22.8507	35.0030
f6	Pneumonic lung	12.1853	11.2592	13.9814
	Normal lung	10.3236	8.9153	10.9535
f7	Pneumonic lung	162.8759	144.2782	204.5568
	Normal lung	120.5575	92.0365	140.8075

5   Discussion

A set of 22 images in total were taken for experimentation, out of which 11 images were of the normal lung images and 11 images were of pneumonic infected lung images. For all the 22 images, 14 Haralick texture features were calculated. From Tables 1 and 2 based on the differences of the obtained values between normal and pneumonic lung images eleven features were discarded as there was no significant differences between them. The remaining three features variance, sum average, and sum variance were selected for classification. The average, minimum and maximum values were identified for each of the selected three features and a decision was framed based on these values. From the tabulation it is observed that the feature variance (f4) had a minimum values of 22.85 and a maximum value of 35; feature sum average (f6) had a minimum values of 8.9 and a maximum value of 10.9; feature sum variance (f7) had a minimum values of 92 and a maximum value of 140 for normal lung images. If the input images satisfy the above range for all the three texture features then they were classified as normal lung images else were classified as pneumonic infected lung images. The proposed method is a quantitative analysis which may help in reducing the ambiguity between the radiologists as they classify based on visual perception such as contrast, size and echogenecity.

6   Conclusion

The proposed quantitative method classifies normal and pneumonic lung based on the Haralick texture features. Among the calculated 14 texture features only three features (variance, sum average and sum variance) showed a remarkable differences in values between normal and pneumonic lung. Thus the average, minimum and maximum value of these three features were considered for classification. The experimental results obtained show that the proposed method has an accuracy of 86%. However more number of images are to be tested to confirm the accuracy. The accuracy can be improved by extracting other texture parameters gray level co-occurrence matrix, statistical feature matrix and law's texture energy measures.

Acknowledgment. The authors thank the doctors and technical staff of radiology department, Rajarajeshwari medical college and hospital, Bangalore for providing images of their patients required to carry out this work

The authors also thank the Management and Principal of ACS College of engineering, Mysore road, Bangalore for permitting and supporting to carry out the research work.

References

1. Ghimire, M., Bhattacharya, S.K., Narain, J.P.: Pneumonia in South-East Asia region: public health perspective. Indian J. Med. Res. **135**, 459–468 (2012)
2. Khobragade, S., Tiwari, A., Patil, C.Y., Narke, V.: Automatic detection of major lung diseases using chest radiographs and classification by feed-forward artificial neural network

3. Ebrahimian, H., Rijal, O.M., Noor, N.M., Yunus, A., Mahyuddin, A.A.: Phase congruency parameter estimation and discrimination ability in detecting lung disease chest radiograph
4. Noor, N.M., Rijal, O.M., Yunus, A., Mahayiddin, A.A., Peng, G.C., Ling, O.E., Abu Bakar, S.A.R.: Pair-wise discrimination of some lung diseases using chest radiography
5. Karargyris, A., Antani, S.: George Thomas segmenting anatomy in chest x-rays for tuberculosis screening
6. Khalid, S., Akbar, M.U.: A review on automatic tuberculosis screening using chest radiograph
7. Barrientos, R.: Automatic detection of pneumonia analyzing ultrasound digital images. IEEE, 08 June 2017
8. Barrientos, F.: Filtering of the skin portion on lung ultrasound digital images to facilitate automatic diagnostics of pneumonia. IEEE, 08 June 2017
9. Cisneros-Velarde, P.: Automatic pneumonia detection based on ultrasound video analysis. IEEE (2016). ISBN 978-1-4577-0220-4/16
10. Zenteno, O.: Spectral-based pneumonia detection tool using ultrasound data from pediatric populations. IEEE (2016). ISBN 978-1-4577-0220-4/16
11. Liu, L.: Detecting out-of-bed activities to prevent pneumonia for hospitalized patient using Microsoft Kinect V2. IEEE (2016). ISBN 978-1-5090-0943-5/16

Human Activity Recognition Using Local Motion Histogram

Awadhesh Kumar Srivastava[1,2(✉)] and K. K. Biswas[3]

[1] UTU Dehradun, Dehradun, India
srivastava_awadhesh@yahoo.co.in
[2] KIET Group of Institutions, Ghaziabad, India
[3] Bennett University, Greater Noida, India
kanad.biswas@bennett.edu.in

Abstract. Human activity recognition is an important problem in computer vision with multiple challenges. In this paper we have proposed a method for human activity recognition based on local estimation of motion in RGB videos. Background subtraction method is used on pair of consecutive frames to determine local motion, and for a small bundle of frames, the maximum magnitude of motion at a pixel is utilized to create a Projected Motion Matrix. The matrix is segmented into horizontal and vertical strips and binned histograms of each strip serve as feature descriptors. We have used these descriptors in a random forest based classification scheme and evaluated the performance on JHMDB, a publicly available human action RGB dataset.

Keywords: Human activity · Histogram · Motion projection matrix
Random forest

1 Introduction

Human activity Recognition from video has been an active area of research for more than a decade. It is a challenging problem to detect humans in video streams due to variations in pose, appearance, clothing, background clutter and illumination. Camera movement or background clutter makes it even more difficult. Potential applications include surveillance, assisted care for the elderly, monitoring of children in daycare, crowd monitoring, sports training, detection of abnormal activities and content based video retrieval. Although image based features have made considerable advances in recent years [1–4], they are not yet mature enough for many practical applications. On the other hand, most movements are characteristics of human actions, so classification accuracy can potentially be improved by paying more attention to motion information. Many researchers in this area have assumed that the camera and the background scene are essentially static. This greatly simplifies the problem because the mere presence of motion information can help us identify the action class. Towards this end, Colque et al. [13] proposed a model for capturing anomalies in human activities using orientation, velocity, and entropy. Authors calculated histogram as a feature based on optical flow. Viola *et al.* [5] point out that including motion features markedly increases the overall performance of their system.

© Springer Nature Singapore Pte Ltd. 2018
P. Bhattacharyya et al. (Eds.): NGCT 2017, CCIS 828, pp. 908–917, 2018.
https://doi.org/10.1007/978-981-10-8660-1_69

Lot of work has been done for activity detection from RGB videos based on pose estimation and motion components. Ni et al. [6] analyzed human action through discovering the most discriminative dense trajectories group. Vrigkas et al. [7] clustered the motion trajectories and the clustered motion trajectories are used to represent human action.

Ma et al. [8] extracted video segments for partial or complete human motion. They constructed a tree based vocabulary of similar actions. Fernando et al. [9] exploited temporal ordering in videos to enumerate human actions in chronological order. They used ranking learning framework for summarization of relevant information. Zhang et al. [10] used Gaussian mixture model for modeling human action and a transfer ranking approach was used for recognizing unseen classes.

In this paper, we propose a set of features based on local estimation of *significant motion* in RGB videos. Many researchers use grid splitting of video frames for histogram calculation to generate feature descriptors [12, 14–16], To come up with features which are less sensitive to relative positioning of camera and the human in the scene, we propose to divide the motion matrix into independent horizontal and vertical strips and use the histograms of each strip as part of the feature descriptor. We show that this helps to better discern between various human actions. We use random forest classification technique as the machine learning tool, and present results on a publicly available dataset to illustrate the superiority of our method. The rest of the paper is organized as follows: Sect. 2 summarizes some related work in the area. In Sect. 3 we indicate the specific descriptors which we propose to extract from RGB video. Section 4 describes the experimental results and comparison with other state of art methods and finally Sect. 5 concludes the work.

2 Related Work

Chun and Lee [14] estimate motion flow using dense optical flow, then divide the estimations into grid cells and calculate histograms for each cell in the grid as feature descriptors. Zhang and Parker [15] proposed CoDe4D features using multi-channel orientation histogram for RGB-D data. Luo et al. [16] proposed to model the motion dynamics with robust linear dynamical systems and histograms of oriented gradients (HOG). Cheng et al. [17] proposed a framework for activity awareness using surface electromyography and accelerometer (ACC) signals. They used histogram of negative entropy to detect the starting and end point of the activity. Mukherjee et al. [18] proposed a graph theoretic technique for recognizing human actions. They used histogram of oriented optical flow and a bag-of-word approach to calculate the descriptor. Zhou and Zhang [19] proposed to encode the movements of local parts of human action. To discover elementary actions with stable states, the authors used multiple-instance formulation. Dogan et al. [20] proposed 3D volume motion templates (VMTs). To make the method view independent, the authors make a rotation with respect to a canonical orientation. Colque et al. [13] proposed Histograms of Optical Flow Orientation and Magnitude (HOFM) to detect anomalous events in videos. Tripathi et al. [12] used histogram of gradient (HOG) for detecting abnormal activity in ATM cabins.

In this paper we divide the video volume into row volumes and column volumes separately and calculate corresponding intensity histograms to reduce the sensitivity of feature vector toward the relative position of camera and object. This is described in the next section.

3 Proposed Method

RGB color frames are extracted from the action video clip, and converted to gray scale as depicted in Fig. 1a, b. The frames are bundled into small sized groups, such that each bundle contains B frames. In order to capture significant motion information, difference of consecutive frames is computed at each pixel. For each bundle, the magnitude of maximum difference at each pixel is stored in a matrix P, hereafter named as *Motion projection matrix*. Appropriate scaling of gray values at each pixel is carried out to depict the range of motion for the specific bundle. Regions having no motion will appear completely black, and areas with significant motion will appear bright gray. For a M × N frame, the difference matrix is computed using pair of consecutive frames as shown below:

$$d_i(m, n) = |f_{i+1}(m, n) - f_i(m, n)| \tag{1}$$

where m = 1, 2, ...; = 1, 2, ...
    and i takes on values 1, 2, ..., B − 1

Next, we consider the differences at each pixel across the bundle and select the maximum d_i to create the Motion projection matrix P:

$$P(m, n) = \max(d_1(m, n), d_2(m, n), \ldots\ldots, d_{B-1}(m, n)) \tag{2}$$

Figure 1c depicts a typical Motion Projection Matrix.

To capture region wise movements of the video bundle, the motion projection matrix P is independently examined along both horizontal and vertical directions. Firstly P is segmented into R rows $r_1, r_2, \ldots, r_R$ where the height of each row is chosen as 5 or 10 pixels. Histogram of each horizontal strip (row) is computed and stored into 15 bins. The histogram is divided into 15 bins. Histogram of ith horizontal strip is denoted by H_{r_i} which is a vector of size 15. For the R rows, we get 15 * R feature descriptors.

In a similar manner, the Motion Projection Matrix P is now segmented into C columns $c_1, c_2, \ldots, c_C$, each of width 5 or 10. Histogram of each vertical strip is computed and binned into 15 groups. H_{c_i} represents histogram of ith vertical strip as depicted in Fig. 3. Each histogram H_{r_i} or H_{c_i} is in form of a vector of size 15. Correspondingly, we obtain our next set of feature descriptor with 15 * C elements.

We could have divided P into R × C grid and computed histogram of each cell. However, it turns out that cell to cell feature matching in grid splitting is highly sensitive to relative position of camera and object (i.e. if an object is performing same activity 'near to' or 'away from' camera then grid based feature matching could not perform well because the movements reside in a particular set of grids for 'near to

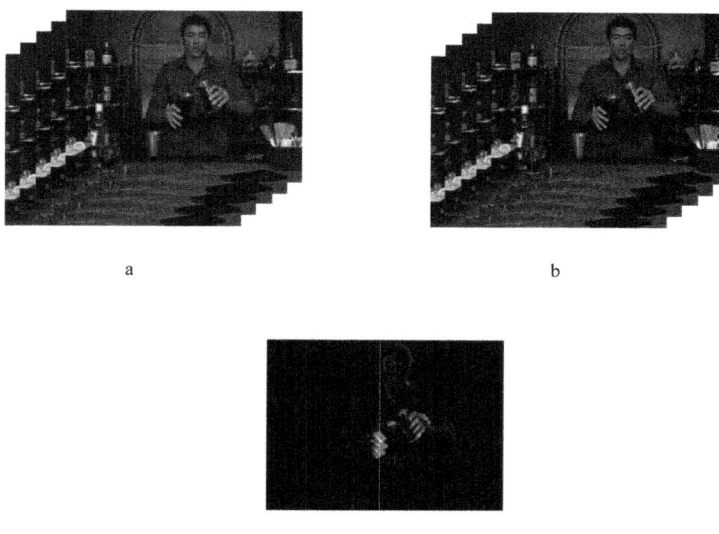

a   b

c

Fig. 1. (a) RGB video frames for *pour* activity, (b) gray scaled video frame with clubbing and(c) motion projection matrix for one club of frames

camera' case and other set of grids for 'away from camera' case. The same phenomenon will happen in case of left/right, up/down and various other compositions of relative positions.).

While row by row feature matching is less sensitive to the horizontal relative positions, while being more sensitive to vertical relative movements. Column by column feature matching is less sensitive to the vertical relative positions while more sensitive to horizontal relative movements of camera and object. The Proposed approach will also take care of 'near to' and 'away from' cases as shown in Fig. 2a and b.

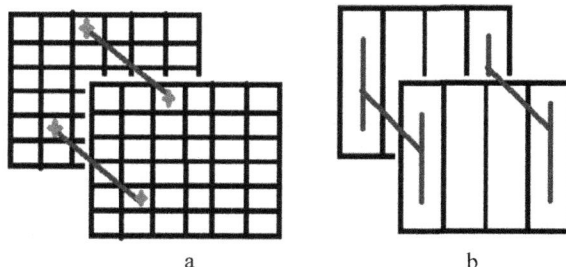

a   b

Fig. 2. Splitting of P for feature creation and matching (a) grid splitting and matching of features, (b) column splitting and matching of features

The proposed feature vector H is formed by concatenating horizontal and vertical histogram bins as shown below

$$H = [H_{r_1}, H_{r_2}, \ldots \ldots, H_{r_R}, H_{c_1}, H_{c_2}, \ldots \ldots, H_{c_C}] \tag{3}$$

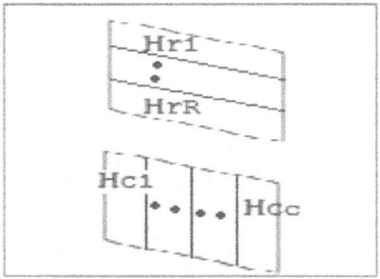

Fig. 3. Histogram calculation for horizontal and vertical regions in motion projection matrix

Algorithm 1: Feature-set Extraction
Input: video V with F frames of size NxM
1. Convert all f_i's of F from RGB color space to grayscale color space
2. Form Bundles $w_1, w_2, \ldots$ by clubbing B frames of F (in non overlapped fashion)
3. For every w_i
a. Calculate motion projection matrix P_{w_i} as per equations (1) and (2)
b. Divide P_{w_i} into R equal sized row segments
c. Calculate histogram H_{R_i}'s as $[H_{r_1}, H_{r_2}, \ldots \ldots, H_{r_R}]$
d. Divide P_{w_i} into C equal sized column segments
e. Calculate histogram H_{C_i}'s as $[H_{c_1}, H_{c_2}, \ldots ., H_{c_C}]$
f. Calculate feature vector H for w_i by concatenating all histograms as equation (3)
g. Associate activity label with H
h. Dataset=Dataset + H   :(column wise concatenation of H in to Dataset)
4. End For
Output: feature set

The size of proposed feature vector H is $15 * (C + R)$.

The output of Algorithm 1 is a set of feature vectors associated with corresponding activity labels. The outputs for various bundles are column wise concatenated to make a training dataset of features.

While the size of the various video clips in the dataset might differ for various activities, and the bundle size chosen arbitrarily, the proposed method ensures that number of feature descriptors remain fixed at $15 * (C + R)$ for each bundle, as it essentially extracts the histogram information.

4   Classification

Support Vector machine could be used for classification purposes. However, for large number of classes, the use of one-against-all technique creates an unbalanced dataset – usually the Positive class has very small share (5%–6%) while the negative class has the lion share (94%–95%). This may result in underperformance of the SVM algorithm because it would try to minimize the overall error. To circumvent this issue, we propose to use "random forest" for activity classification.

The method creates number of classification trees by selecting random feature vectors. The feature set is chosen randomly for training each tree in the Random Forest. Bagging is used to decrease correlation between randomly chosen trees. This makes it more immune to noise. For testing the query dataset, it is run on all the trees of the forest and the final classification is established through voting on the outcomes. We have chosen a publicly available dataset named JHMDB [11] for evaluating our proposed method.

This dataset is a joint-annotated human motion database consisting of 21 activities: (a) *brush hair,* (b) *catch,* (c) *clap,* (d) *climb stairs,* (e) *golf,* (f) *jump,* (g) *kick ball,* (h) *pick,* (i) *pour,* (j) *pull-up,* (k) *push,* (l) *run,* (m) *shoot ball,* (n) *shoot bow,* (o) *shoot gun,* (p) *sit,* (q) *stand,* (r) *swing baseball,* (s) *throw,* (t) *walk,* and (u) *wave.* The dataset consists of 36–55 clips per action class with each clip containing 15–40 frames. There are 31,838 annotated frames in total. Figure 4 illustrate some of the activities of JHMDB dataset, columns of the figure representing *catch, jump, wave* and *push* activity respectively. While first row of the figure shows the 10th frame, the second row shows the 20th frame of the corresponding activities.

| catch | jump | wave | Push |

Fig. 4. Frames of *catch, jump, wave* and *push* (column wise) activity of JHMDB dataset. First row is 10th frames and second row is 20th frames of the corresponding activities.

We have performed experiments on the JHMDB dataset for different values of B (number of frames in a bundle), R (number of horizontal strips in matrix P), C (number of vertical strips in matrix P) and number of trees in random forest. Typically R = C has been chosen in our experiments. Overall Classification accuracy of various experiments are shown in Table 1.

Table 1. Classification accuracy on various parameters of the experiments for JHMDB dataset

Experiment number	Number of frames in a bundle (B)	Number of trees in Random forest	Number of rows or column segment in a motion projection matrix (R or C)	Accuracy
1	5	100	10	51.75
2	7	100	10	51.43
3	5	50	10	51.1
4	3	50	10	50.16
5	3	100	5	49.52
6	3	50	5	49.52
7	7	100	5	48.89

In the rest of the paper our discussion is based on the values of the parameters chosen as in experiment 1 of Table 1.

JHMDB dataset is a challenging dataset, since scenes are taken from movies, youtube channel etc. without imposing any constrains on light illumination, camera movements, object orientation and relative position of object with camera.

The proposed method performed well for many activities while some activities are classified with low accuracies. *Pull-up* and *shoot bow* activities are classified with accuracy of 89% and 83%. There are four more activities which have been classified with accuracy more than 70%. Activities of *sit, run, walk* and *kick ball* are classified with lower accuracies. The reason for low accuracies can be attributed to high similarity amongst some of the activities resulting in greater number of misclassifications. The proposed method's overall classification accuracy comes out to 51.75%.

Activity wise classifier accuracy is shown in Fig. 5 and the confusion matrix for activity recognition on JHMDB dataset is shown in Fig. 6.

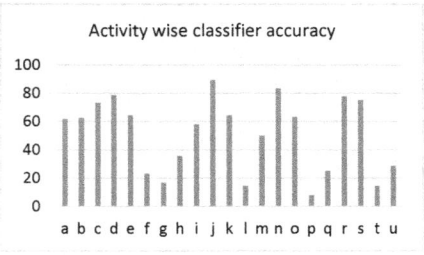

Fig. 5. Activity wise classifier accuracy for JHMBD dataset

	a	b	c	d	e	f	g	h	i	j	k	l	m	n	o	p	q	r	s	t	u
a	0.62			0.08					0.08	0.08					0.08				0.08			
b		0.63		0.06	0.13									0.06		0.06		0.06			
c		0.07	0.73	0.07				0.07						0.07							
d			0.07	0.79		0.07					0.07										
e				0.07	0.64						0.07			0.14				0.07			
f	0.15	0.15			0.08	0.23	0.08	0.08			0.08			0.08				0.08			
g	0.08	0.08			0.08	0.17	0.17		0.08	0.08				0.08				0.08	0.08		
h					0.07			0.36		0.07	0.14	0.07		0.14		0.07		0.07			
i		0.11		0.05					0.58				0.05	0.05	0.05			0.05			0.05
j									0.11	0.89											
k		0.07	0.07						0.07		0.64	0.07		0.07							
l			0.14		0.14		0.07				0.07	0.14		0.07	0.07		0.14	0.07		0.07	
m	0.14	0.14		0.07				0.07			0.07		0.50								
n	0.06												0.06	0.83	0.06						
o				0.05					0.05		0.16			0.11	0.63						
p		0.23									0.15				0.15	0.08	0.08	0.15		0.08	
q	0.08		0.08	0.08							0.00	0.08			0.08	0.17	0.25	0.08	0.08		
r		0.06							0.06	0.06	0.06							0.78			
s			0.06											0.06		0.06	0.06	0.06	0.75		
t			0.14	0.14							0.29			0.07	0.14			0.07		0.14	
u			0.07						0.07		0.21	0.07		0.07	0.07			0.07		0.07	0.29

Fig. 6. Confusion matrix for JHMDB dataset

Results of proposed method are compared with other state of art techniques in Table 2. It can be seen that our approach is performing better than all the histogram and trajectory based approaches of Jhuang et al. [11].

Table 2. Comparison with other methods.

Sr No	Author	Approach	Feature			
			Traj.	HOG	HOF	L. M. Histogram
1	Jhuang et al. [11]	(1) baseline	40.0	32.9	40.1	
		(2) of pmask	38.5	31.9	46.0	
		(3) pf pmask	36.4	32.8	48.0	
		(4) pf Dmask	38.0	32.2	46.4	
		(5) pf pmask of outside pmask	43.0	36.1	44.1	
		(6) (4) + (5)	46.2	35.2	51.7	
		(7) bbox F w. [21]	37.7	33.9	39.0	
		(8) bbox F	38.5	34.9	42.2	
		(9) bboxIm	42.7	46.9	44.5	
		(10) DmaskIm	41.4	47.0	45.6	
2	Proposed	Row and column wise splitting				**51.75**

5 Conclusion

In this paper we have proposed a method for human action recognition based on local estimation of motion in RGB videos. Background subtraction method is used on pair of consecutive frames to determine local motion, and for a small bundle of frames, the maximum magnitude of motion at a pixel is saved to create a Projected Motion Matrix. The matrix is segmented into horizontal and vertical strips and binned histograms of each strip serve as feature descriptors. We have used these descriptors in a random forest based classification scheme and evaluated the performance on a publicly available human action RGB dataset.

References

1. Aggarwal, J., Ryoo, M.: Human activity analysis: a review. ACM Comput. Surv. **43**, 16 (2011)
2. Dalal, N., Triggs, B.: Histograms of oriented gradients for human detection. In: Proceedings of the Conference on Computer Vision and Pattern Recognition, San Diego, California, USA, pp. 886–893 (2005)
3. Leibe, B., Seemann, E., Schiele, B.: Pedestrian detection in crowded scenes. In: Proceedings of the Conference on Computer Vision and Pattern Recognition, San Diego, California, USA, pp. 876–885, June 2005
4. Mikolajczyk, K., Schmid, C., Zisserman, A.: Human detection based on a probabilistic assembly of robust part detectors. In: Pajdla, T., Matas, J. (eds.) ECCV 2004. LNCS, vol. 3021, pp. 69–82. Springer, Heidelberg (2004). https://doi.org/10.1007/978-3-540-24670-1_6
5. Viola, P., Jones, M.J., Snow, D.: Detecting pedestrians using patterns of motion and appearance. In: Proceedings of the 9th International Conference on Computer Vision, Nice, France, vol. 1, pp. 734–741 (2003)
6. Ni, B., Moulin, P., Yang, X., Yan, S.: Motion part regularization: improving action recognition via trajectory group selection. In: Proceedings of IEEE Computer Society Conference on Computer Vision and Pattern Recognition (CVPR), pp. 3698–3706 (2015)
7. Vrigkas, M., Karavasilis, V., Nikou, C., Kakadiaris, I.A.: Matching mixtures of curves for human action recognition. Comput. Vis. Image Understand. **119**, 27–40 (2014). https://doi.org/10.1016/j.cviu.2013.11.007
8. Ma, S., Sigal, L., Sclaroff, S.: Space-time tree ensemble for action recognition. In: Proceedings of IEEE Computer Society Conference on Computer Vision and Pattern Recognition (CVPR), pp. 5024–5032 (2015)
9. Fernando, B., Gavves, E., Oramas, J.M., Ghodrati, A., Tuytelaars, T.: Modeling video evolution for action recognition. In: Proceedings of IEEE Computer Society Conference on Computer Vision and Pattern Recognition (CVPR), pp 5378–5387 (2015)
10. Zhang, Z., Wang, C., Xiao, B., Zhou, W., Liu, S.: Robust relative attributes for human action recognition. Pattern Anal. Appl. **18**, 157–171 (2015). https://doi.org/10.1007/s10044-013-0349-3
11. Jhuang, H., Gall, J., Zuffi, S., Schmid, C., Black, M.: Towards understanding action recognition. In: ICCV (2013)
12. Tripathi, V., Mittal, A., Gangodkar, D., Kanth, V.: Real time security framework for detecting abnormal events at ATM installations. J. Real Time Image Process. (JRTIP), 1–11 (2016). https://doi.org/10.1007/s11554-016-0573-3

13. Colque, R.V.H.M., Caetano, C., de Andrade, M.T.L., Schwartz, W.R.: Histograms of optical flow orientation and magnitude to detect anomalous events in videos. IEEE Trans. Circ. Syst. Video Technol. **27**(3), 673–682 (2017). https://doi.org/10.1109/TCSVT.2016.2637778

14. Chun, S., Lee, C.-S.: Human action recognition using histogram of motion intensity and direction from multiple views. IET Comput. Vis. **10**, 250–257 (2016)

15. Zhang, H., Parker, L.E.: CoDe4D: color-depth local spatio-temporal features for human activity recognition from RGB-D videos. IEEE Trans. Circ. Syst. Video Technol. **26**(3), 541–555 (2016)

16. Luo, G., Yang, S., Tian, G., Yuan, C., Hu, W., Maybank, S.J.: Learning human actions by combining global dynamics and local appearance. IEEE Trans. Pattern Anal. Mach. Intell. (PAMI) **36**(12), 2466–2482 (2014)

17. Cheng, J., Chen, X., Shen, M.: A framework for daily activity monitoring and fall detection based on surface electromyography and accelerometer signals. IEEE J. Biomed. Health Inf. **17**(1), 38–45 (2013)

18. Mukherjee, S., Biswas, S.K., Mukherjee, D.P.: Recognizing human action at a distance in video by key poses. IEEE Trans. Circ. Syst. Video Technol. **21**(9), 1228–1241 (2011)

19. Zhou, W., Zhang, Z.: Human action recognition with multiple-instance Markov model. IEEE Trans. Inf. Forensics and Secur. **9**(10), 1581–1591 (2014)

20. Dogan, E., Eren, G., Wolf, C., Baskurt, A.: Activity recognition with volume motion templates and histograms of 3d gradients. In: 2015 IEEE International Conference on Image Processing (ICIP), pp. 4421–4425 (2015)

21. Bourdev, L., Maji, S., Brox, T., Malik, J.: Detecting people using mutually consistent poselet activations. In: Daniilidis, K., Maragos, P., Paragios, N. (eds.) ECCV 2010. LNCS, vol. 6316, pp. 168–181. Springer, Heidelberg (2010). https://doi.org/10.1007/978-3-642-15567-3_13

Feature Based Multiple Vehicle License Plate Detection and Video Based Traffic Counting

P. L. Chithra[✉] and B. Prashanthi

University of Madras, Chennai 600005, Tamil Nadu, India
chithrasp20001@yahoo.com,
prashanthi.bhaskaran@gmail.com

Abstract. Traffic in the world is a vast problem which creates some inconveniences to the environment. Road traffic and traffic congestions have become a big mess in the society. So to monitor this issue video surveillance came into existence. With current technology, License Plate identification is in experimental from past few decades. Recognizing of license plate plays a noteworthy role in a few applications like Crime Investigation when the vehicles are stolen and when a vehicle met with some accident, for the Authorities to distinguish their own particular vehicle, for Security control, for Toll Enrolment, and identification of vehicle in parking slot. The proposed system accords with vehicle detection, traffic vehicle count and extracting of the license plate in an image which is obtained from a video sequence. The proposed method for license plate extraction copes with K-nearest neighbor classifier for training the input image and Contour Hierarchy technique is to identify and extract the license plate. This present strategy likewise it finds the closest match of the identified license plate number if the plate number already exists, then it produce the exact match of that license plate number. The Experimental outcomes license plate extraction creates exactness of the proposed work which can recognize around 99% times in case of 850 complex background images. The detection of vehicle is implemented using cascade classifier and background subtraction techniques and moment method is being used to count the vehicle in a motion video. In case of video detection and counting it produces 97.2% of accuracy.

Keywords: License Plated Number Extraction (LPNE) · Vehicle classification
Contour hierarchy · K - nearest neighbor classifier

1 Introduction

Intelligent Traffic System is one of the key parts. Traffic monitoring can pave a path to find solutions for people. A vision-based traffic analysis framework could comprise of numerous parts, for example, foreground segmentation, shadow removal, feature extraction, and tracking. For most traffic observation frameworks have fewer stages of traffic parameters, like vehicle location, counting, tracking, and classification. Every year, around million vehicle injuries happen on the road and more than a thousand is pushed to death. On monitoring traffic count and detecting vehicle and its license plate can reduce traffic congestion at peak hours and can avoid accidents. This monitoring

© Springer Nature Singapore Pte Ltd. 2018
P. Bhattacharyya et al. (Eds.): NGCT 2017, CCIS 828, pp. 918–931, 2018.
https://doi.org/10.1007/978-981-10-8660-1_70

helps in limiting the conceivable outcomes of folk activities in toll accumulation and rule violation. It is important to give better traffic surveillance to diminish the accidents. So the primary goal of this paper is to provide better traffic surveillance system.

The license plate extraction has four processes that include the following steps, image acquisition, locating license plate, fetching characters in the license plate and extracting the license plate. The main contribution of this research is to produce the clear view of the detected license plate number. In the case of crime the video extracted images plays and major role. The obtained images are blurred and not visible. In order to resolve this issue we have come out with this method to extract the license plate number and display them using an enhanced threshold technique. The rest of the paper is organized as follows. Section 1.1 describes related work. Section 2 elaborates proposed methods for real time vehicle detection, count and license plate extraction. Section 3 provides Experimental results and analysis. Section 4 gives the conclusion of the research work performed.

1.1 Related Work

In literature, there are lots of methods, which use specific features for detecting the license plate. In all countries there are standardized rules for the license plates, for their characters and colors. All the license plates are rectangular in shape and hence the aspect ratio is known, then it is possible to detect the plate using edge information. Multinational vehicle license plates have been detected based on rear-lights and Heuristic Energy Map of vertical edge information and using a unique histogram approach [1]. Using Sobel edge detector the license plates character and the border of the plate is detected [3]. Another method based on the Hough Transform which is only able to detect the straight plates [4]. Based on neural network a conversion of the image in the LAB color space to detect the license plate and it performs using level set methods to locate its contour. The license plate is detected in both day and night time using the line and clip functions in addition to Gaussian analysis [2]. A method for recognizing the vehicle number plate based on template matching using modified Otsu's method algorithm for threshold partitioning with normalized cross correlation [5].

Real-time traffic flow parameter estimation based on KLT tracker, intersection point analysis using k-means clustering, traffic flow theory and connected graphs able to achieve count, density and speed of moving vehicles [6]. Shorter processing time traffic congestion method performed on non-adaptive traffic light scheduling algorithm with minimum destination distance first algorithm [7]. Vehicle detection and tracking based on UAV-based transportation traffic estimation is achieved by KLT feature and a particle filter [8, 9].

2 Proposed Method

2.1 License Plate Number Extraction (LPNE)

The proposed LPNE approach for multi-national and various vehicles works in two stages: (i) Training images using KNN classifier and Pre-processing of input images and (ii) Plate Recognition and Extraction of License Plate. The dataset holds different vehicle images with different brightening condition both on Day and Night time, the few pictures are not precisely the full picture of the vehicle, pictures that are taken through some other vehicle mirror and pictures that are acquired from video casings and pictures with shadow, pictures that are dim and pictures with more content are additionally incorporated into the preparation and testing. The challenging images from dataset outperforms well with the proposed method. Algorithm for License Plate Detection is as follows,

> Step 1: **Image acquisition**: Images of different vehicles are obtained as saved as a dataset.
> Step 2: **Training** all the input images using KNN classifier.
> Step 3: Fix different **Aspect ratio** based on image samples.
> Step 4: **Pre-process** the input image.
> Step 5: **Apply Contour Hierarchy** method for the input image.
> Step 6: Finds the **Location of plate** and **possible characters** of the license plate.
> Step 7: Find the **extract** or **the nearest match** of the detected license plate.
> Step 8: Extract the Plate and displays the number using a threshold.

Training and Pre-processing: As first part detection of the license plate is to train images using K-nearest neighbor classifier and obtain the gray-level co-occurrence matrix (GLCM) features to classify the vehicles. After training with KNN based on the feature classification the values in the number plate find the exact match or the nearest match, this method is useful in some application of crime investigations of stolen vehicle or accidental vehicle when on a backend, some of the old list of vehicles in the database can be cross validated and produce the matches to find a solution for the case. After extracting the number of the license plates, the extracted number is passed as input to the KNN classifier to produce the best match relevant from the plate number given as input. In the proposed method the contour hierarchy function is used. The input passed to the contour hierarchy must be of black background and white text, to satisfy this condition the input image is pre-processed to a gray-scale and then adaptive threshold is applied.

Contour Hierarchy Method: The hierarchy of the contour is a parent-child relationship. When few shapes are in different shapes, they are called as nested figures. In this situation, external read line is called as a parent and an internal red line is called as a child. Contour in the picture has some relationship to each other. It is associated with each other, as offspring of some other shape, or is it a parent and so on. The portrayal of this relationship is known as the Hierarchy.

In Fig. 1 Contours 0, 1, 2 are the external or outermost layers. The contour 2a, it is considered as a child of contour 2. Similarly, contour 3 is the child of contour 2. Finally, Contours 4, 5 are the children of contour 3a. In Fig. 2 Contour Hierarchy algorithm is explained.

The Significance of Proposed Work: The proposed technique distinguishes and extracts license plate number of any vehicle in complex background. The license plate is recognizable in different images like front, back, side perspectives and furthermore

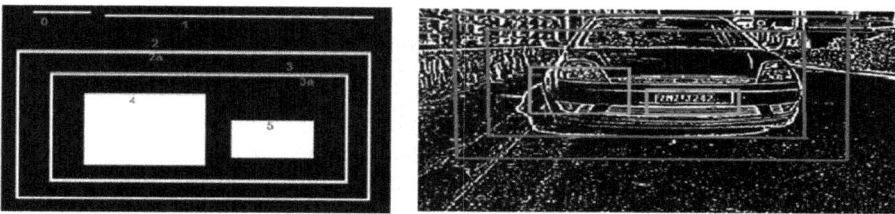

Fig. 1. (a) The contour hierarchy method, (b) the contour hierarchy method applied to the car. (Color figure online)

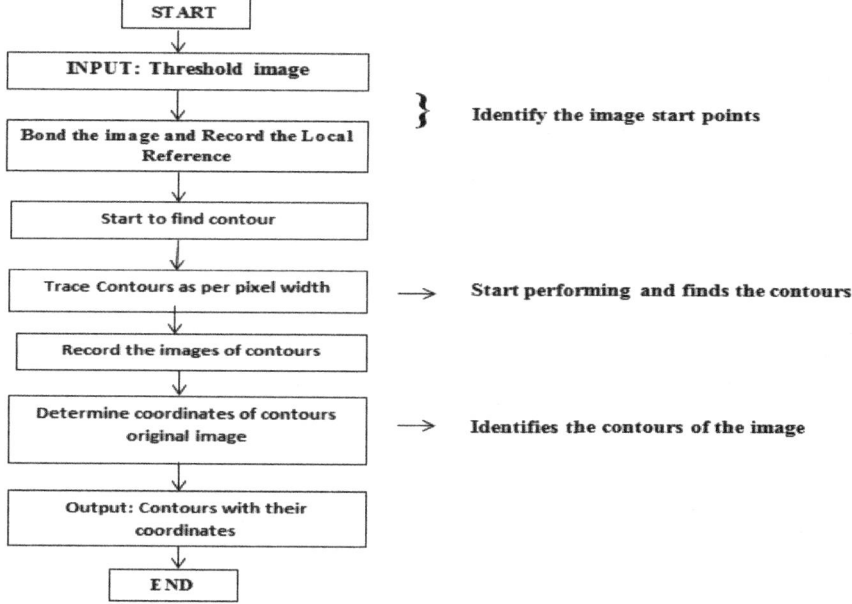

Fig. 2. Contour Hierarchy algorithm

for crop images also creates the best outcome. Nearly three cars in a path are also able to detect and extract license plate number. Accident car image has been tested in the proposed method, which also out performs best and extracts the license plate number.

2.2 Video Based Detection and Counting

In this paper other technique is designed to detect the vehicles and count the number of vehicles in the motion video. To detect vehicle the method used is based on feature extraction and training based on KNN classifier. In order to classify the vehicle and detect them, it is mandatory to train with test images of different type of vehicles to detect vehicle correctly. While the video classifier worked decently well at detecting all cars during both day and night other vehicles like bus and trucks were also detected successfully. The video is captured with a digital camera and tested on the current method which provides a better result of detecting vehicle and counting them.

Real Time Background Subtraction: In motion the pixels keep changing over time. In order to recognize the background and foreground, first identify the static object in the frame called as the background image and the foreground image is the one which keeps changing or in motion.

Step 1: Estimate the background time proposition t,
Step 2: Subtract the background image from each frame,
Step 3: Apply threshold and obtain the foreground mask.

The Gaussian Mixture Model: It is sufficient and flexible to deal with variation in multiple moving objects, lighting and other arbitrary objects. It utilizes a technique to display each background pixel by an optimized mixture of K Gaussian distribution in Eq. (1). The weights of the mixture speak to the time extents that every pixel is divided by its intensity in RGB color space. For every frame we must compute the probability, since it is multiple surface pixels is named as mixture model.

$$P\left(X_{t,}\right) = \sum_{i=1}^{k} \omega_{i,t}.\eta\left(X_t, \mu_{i,t}, \sum_{i,t}\right) \qquad (1)$$

X_t is the current pixel in frame t, K: the number of distributions in the Gaussian mixture, $\omega_{i,t}$: the weight of the kth distribution in frame t, $\mu_{i,t}$: the mean of the kth distribution in frame t, $\Sigma_{i,t}$: the standard deviation of the kth distribution in frame t, Where $\eta(X_t, \mu_{i,t}, \Sigma_{i,t})$ is probability density function.

Vehicle Detection Using KNN: The K Nearest Neighbor includes scanning for the nearest match of the test data in the component space of historical input data. Background mask using KNN when a larger region of pixel is detected, with and without motion the discern class produces the closest neighbor. The KNN mask works well on large area of motions like buses. The background mask using KNN gives the best balance between rapid response to changing of backgrounds, robustly recognizing vehicle motion, and not being triggered by external disturbance. The KNN classifier produces the best result of detecting vehicles.

Vehicle Counting: The Vehicle counting is performed on Contour Extraction. The area and the perimeter for each frame are founded and based on the moments the counting output is produced. The active contour model is the famous method in computer vision, and snakes are colossally used in applications like object tacking, segmentation, edge detection, shape recognition and stereo matching. The active contour method is also called as snake model. The energy function is used in current method in Eq. (2). s(t) = x(t), y(t) where t is the parameter of the curve.

$$E_{snake} = E_{snake} = \int\limits_{snake} E(s(t))dt = \int\limits_{snake} [E_{int}(s(t)) + E_{ext}(s(t))]dt \qquad (2)$$

After the subtraction of the updates background of the current frame the edge information is obtained to calculate the external force of the active contour model. Since different noise influence from external sources can lead to disintegration of edge appropriation, on calculating the moments of the input can improve robustness. The Moment method of a snake with M is defined as,

$$C = \sum_{i=1}^{M} \frac{Z_i}{M} \qquad (3)$$

Where $z_i = (x_i, y_i)$ is the 2D-coordinates of i contour. Figure 3 shows Vehicle detection and counting algorithm.

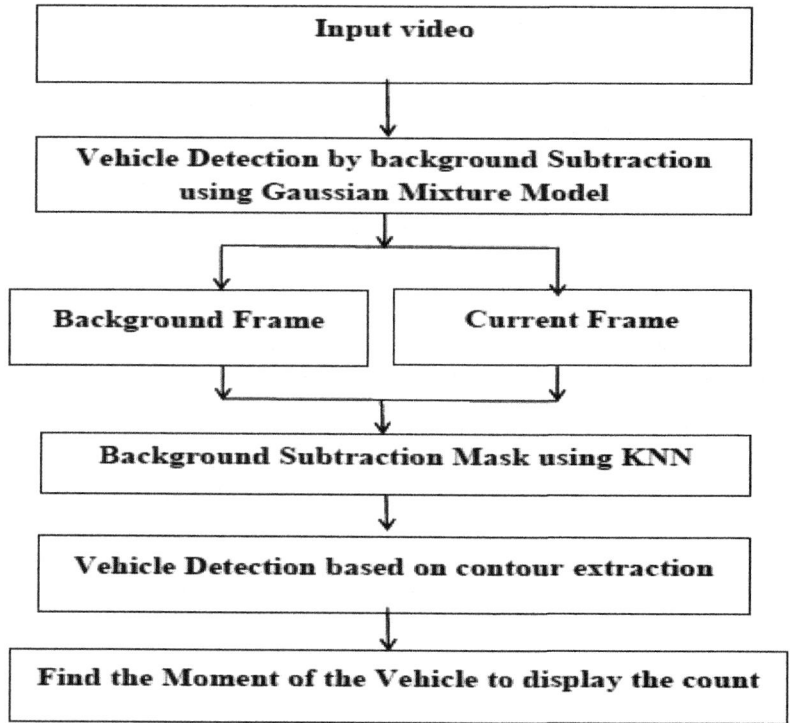

Fig. 3. Vehicle detection and counting algorithm

As a result the current method successfully detects and counts the vehicle in motion. The video data consist of various video and the current method is tested with four different video and one video is captured using a digital camera is and pre-processed then tested with current method. The video data are bidirectional traffic flow, single lane view, the motion of the video can be on either left or right. The vehicles like truck, bus, van and car are detected. The current method using KNN classifier and Contour extraction provides the most exact detection, nearest detection. The error rate associated with each video is about minimum average and the accuracy is better than the related method. The following section shows the experiment result for both license plate and video based detection and counting of vehicles.

3   Experiment Result and Analysis

3.1   License Plate Number Extraction

The experiment for License Plate Number Extraction has been tested standard 850 challenging images with low quality, high quality and blurry images. Most of the vehicles are from different part of the country. The proposed method is compared with other latest and the classical method. Images with various backgrounds and various color plates are included in the dataset. The images that are taken in shadowed and dark are included to verify the adaptability of the proposed method.

In order to find the vehicle license plate number the current method is discussed with its output of images. In Fig. 4 the image (a) is taken as the test image, the next step as per algorithm is Preprocessing of image (b) image is converted into the grayscale image (c) The output of adaptive threshold (d) Execution of Contour hierarchy. The Fig. 5 is the trace of contour method and Fig. 6 is an output of license plate. The extraction of number is shown in Fig. 7 The multinational vehicle output is displayed in the next sections.

The Fig. 8 shows, parking slot image where the extraction of a number plate is possible with the proposed method. Figure 9 shows the extraction of the number plate with very tilled license plate. Figure 10. Is the Image obtained through other vehicle's mirror, and the extracted license plate number shows the exact match of the detected number.

The Fig. 11 shows the image of tourist bus with an extracted license plate number are nearest match. Figure 12 holds the Tamil Nadu government bus with extract license plate. Figure 13 proves the best of the proposed method by exactly locating the license plate and extracting it because the car also holds the similar number like a license plate number on the left most but the license plate number is correctly located and extracted.

The Fig. 14 is most challenging images with headlight where the license plate is not much visible, But the novel algorithm produces the best output for this input image. The vehicle license plate is located accurately and the extracted plate is displayed (Fig. 15).

The accuracy rate is evaluated using statistical methods based on true and false rates. Each image is checked manually, if the detection and extraction of an LP of vehicle cover all areas, the output characters of plates are missing or partially detected, all the detection is effectively recognized. The images of video sequences are also tested, that can also able to extract license plate number.

(a) Test Image for LPNE

(b) Gray scale Image

(c) Output of adaptive Threshold

(d) Output of external Contour hierarchy

Fig. 4. Vehicle license plate detection

(a) Inner child output of contour hierarchy

(b) Trace the contour

Fig. 5. Trace of contour method

(a) Extracted License Plate Number

(b) Threshold output of plate number

Fig. 6. The output of contour hierarchy method extracted license plate

(a) the output KNN training of obtained plate (b) This is the final output with nearest match

Fig. 7. Identifying the region of interest

Fig. 8. (a) parking slot image. (b) Extracted license plate and threshold output.

Fig. 9. (a) Image of a military vehicle produces best result in spite of tilled characters (b) extracted license plate and threshold output.

3.2   Video Detection and Counting

To validate the accuracy video detection and counting of vehicles in a video of our proposed method is based on average speed per pixel by frames and vehicle count for each travel direction. The Figs. 16, 17 show the performance of current methods of video captured on a real time near University of Madras (Fig. 18).

Fig. 10. (a) Image obtained through other vehicles mirror, the input image finds exact match of the detected license plate (b) extracted license plate and threshold output.

Fig. 11. Image of a tourist bus with relevant output of license plate number

Fig. 12. Tamil Nadu Bus with its extracted license plate number

Proposed Method Output

The graph shows the number of vehicle's counting by number of frames in Fig. 19. It portrays that number of count keep increasing as the number of frames increases. The video based detection and works well when compared to other recent method. The output of this method gives better accuracy.

Fig. 13. Ancient car, produce best result in spite of some number displayed on left of car

Fig. 14. Poor lighting image with headlight

Fig. 15. The image with headlight dark image

Fig. 16. (a) Output of bidirectional road (b) detection of single direction road.

Fig. 17. Output of various vehicle detected in the video

Fig. 18. Output of various vehicle counting in video

Count of Vehicles

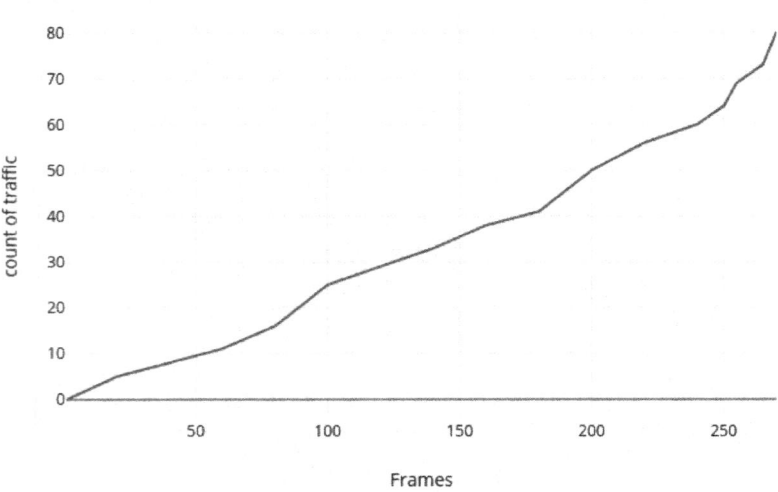

Fig. 19. The graph shows the count of the vehicle

4   Conclusion

The experimental results mainly focus on multinational license plate number extraction. In this paper, the attempt is made to detect and extract the number of the license plate of vehicle of various countries both on day and night. Thus, this paper use contour hierarchy method with KNN classifier tends to produce better output. The proposed method was tested on various vehicles like car, bus, van, bike, truck and auto. The proposed method is found to be robust and effective even under bad weather condition. The video based traffic count detection can detect and count various vehicles on bidirectional flow in the video. The current method works based on contour extraction and moment method. KNN is used to train the various images in order to detect multiple vehicles. The proposed method yields 98.4% for the vehicle license plate number extraction and 96.2% of accuracy for video based traffic vehicle count and detection.

References

1. Rizwan Asif, M., Chun, Q., Hussian, S., Fareed Sadiq, M., Khan, S.: Multinational vehicle license plate detection in complex backgrounds. Vis. Commun. Image Represent. **46**, 176–186 (2017)
2. Bhusan, N.: Automatic traffic surveillance using video tracking. In: 7th International Conference on Communication, Computing and Virtualization, vol. 79, pp. 402–409 (2015). Procedia Comput. Sci.

3. Tan, J.-L., Abu-Bakar, S.A., Mokji, M.M.: License plate localization based on edge geometrical features using the morphological approach. In: 20th IEEE International Conference on Image Processing (ICIP), pp. 4549–4553 (2013)
4. Prabhakar, P., Anuparma, P.: A novel design for vehicle license plate detection and recognition. In: 2nd IEEE International Conference on Current Trends in Engineering and Technology (ICCTET), pp. 7–12 (2014)
5. Ghazl, M., Hajjdiab, H.: License plate automatic detection and recognition using, level sets and neural networks. In: 1st IEEE International Conference on Communications, Signal Processing and their Applications (ICCSPA), pp. 1–5 (2013)
6. Ke, R., Li, Z., Ash, J., Cui, Z., Wang, Y.: Real time bidirectional traffic flow parameter estimation from aerial videos. IEEE Trans. Intell. Transp. Syst. 1524–9050 (2016)
7. Ahmed, F., Mahmud, S.A., Yousaf, F.Z.: Shortest processing time scheduling to reduce traffic congestion in dense urban areas. IEEE Trans. Syst. Man Cybern. Syst. **47**, 2168–2216 (2016)
8. Zhao, T., Nevatia, R.: Car detection in low resolution aerial images. Images vis. Comput. **21**(8), 693–703 (2003)
9. Gaszczak, A., Brackon, T.P., Han, J.: Real time, people and vehicle detection from UAV imagery In: Proceedings of SPIE International Society for Optics Photonics, Article No. 7878OB (2011)
10. Hycogsoon, I, Bonghee, H, Seungwoo, J, Jaegi, H.: Bigdata analytics on CCTV images for collecting traffic information. In: IEEE BigComp (2016). ISBN 978-1-4673-8796-5
11. Hong, G.S., Eom, T.J., lim, B.G.: Development of vision-based monitoring system technology for traffic analysis and surveillance. J. Inf. Secur. **11**(4), 59–66 (2011)

Automated Detection of Epileptic Seizure Using Histogram of Oriented Gradients for Analysing Time Frequency Images of EEG Signals

N. J. Sairamya, S. Thomas George[(⊠)],
D. Narain Ponraj, and M. S. P. Subathra

Karunya University, Coimbatore, India
thomasgeorge@karunya.edu

Abstract. This paper presents a computer aided methodology for automated detection of epileptic seizure activities using the histogram of oriented gradient (HOG) descriptor for analysing the time-frequency(t-f) representation (image) of EEG signals. The proposed approach for classifying epileptic signals is based on transforming the EEG signal into a t-f image and the features related to t-f structures and shapes are extracted using HOG descriptor. The obtained feature is fed into SVM classifier with Gaussian kernel function for classification process. Further, the computationally efficient techniques based on local binary patterns(LBP) namely center symmetric LBP(CS-LBP) and local binary count (LBC) are also proposed to analyse the t-f representation of EEG signals. The histogram features extracted from CS-LBP and LBC are fed into SVM classifier. The performances of the proposed techniques are compared in terms of computational performance and detection rate of the classifier. Experimental evaluation on publicly available EEG dataset suggests that features extracted using HOG technique are more powerful in classifying epileptic and non-epileptic signals with an accuracy rate of 100%. Further, the obtained result suggests that proposed HOG technique outperforms the existing technique in the literature and attains better classification accuracy with an improved computational performance.

Keywords: EEG signal · Time-frequency representation
Histogram of oriented gradients · Epileptic seizure detection
Support vector machine

1 Introduction

Epilepsy is a calamitous neurological disorder caused due to an abnormal hyperactivity of the neurons in the brain, affecting different parts of the central nervous system [7]. Electroencephalographic (EEG) is a most frequently used method to diagnose epileptic seizure disorder, which measures the electrical communication between the neurons in the brain and constructs a signal to represent the electrical activity of the brain [1]. Conventional diagnostic approach awaits on skilled neurophysiologist to visually

© Springer Nature Singapore Pte Ltd. 2018
P. Bhattacharyya et al. (Eds.): NGCT 2017, CCIS 828, pp. 932–943, 2018.
https://doi.org/10.1007/978-981-10-8660-1_71

examine the long(protracted) EEG signal, which is tedious, unreliable, time consuming and fatigue. Hence, an automated diagnostic tool to assist the neurophysiologist in diagnosing epileptic seizure disorder is at major demand.

Two main parts feature extraction and classification are associated with the automated diagnosis of epileptic seizure disorder. In feature extraction, the EEG signals are generally characterised in frequency [3], time [2] or t-f domain [4–6] and various features are extracted from it for detecting epileptic seizure activities. Recently image processing methods like local binary pattern (LBP) [7], local neighbour descriptive pattern (LNDP) and local gradient pattern technique (LGP) [8] are applied to one dimensional EEG signal for better classification of epileptic and non-epileptic signal. Various methods based on t-f representation of EEG signals are also proposed [9–14].

Haralick features were extracted from t-f image to classify seizure signals using support vector machine and obtained an accuracy rate of 99.125% [14]. In [9], the author combined the t-f image features with the features obtained from the t-f signal to enhance the performance of automatic epileptic detection. The texture pattern techniques like gray-level co-occurrence matrix(GLCM), LBP and texture feature coding method (TFCM) techniques were proposed to analyse the t-f image obtained using spectrogram of Short-Time Fourier Transform (STFT) [12]. Classification of epileptic signals were carried out by using SVM technique and obtained a classification accuracy of 100%. The t-f image obtained using quadratic time frequency distribution was analysed using LBP technique and obtained an accuracy of 99.3% in classifying epileptic and non-epileptic signals using SVM classifier [11].

The t-f image represents the energy distribution of non-stationary EEG signal in a two-dimensional space. The energy distribution of epileptic and non-epileptic EEG signals in different frequency bands consists of inequitable texture patterns. Hence, in [12], the author proposed LBP texture features with a higher dimension is suitable for characterizing the t-f image of epileptic and non-epileptic signals. This motivates the authors to use HOG descriptors to obtain features with high discriminative power and reduced feature vector dimensions to analyse the t-f image of the EEG signals. To the author's knowledge, this is the first work implementing HOG technique to analyse the t-f image of the EEG signals to detect epileptic seizure activities.

In this study, an effective HOG descriptor is used to analyse the t-f image of EEG signal to obtain features with high discriminative power to categorize epileptic and non-epileptic signals. HOG is insensitive to illumination and shadowing effect and its one of the widely used effective method in face recognition. Further, computational performance of the HOG technique is improved by reducing the feature vector dimensions. There are two stages in the HOG descriptor operation and in first stage, histogram based features are extracted from the image. The obtained histogram features are classified in the second stage. SVM classifier performance for classifying epileptic and non-epileptic EEG signals using HOG features were analysed based on 10-fold cross validation for 100 repetitions. The classification performance was evaluated based on accuracy, sensitivity and specificity. Similarly, computational performance is evaluated by measuring feature vector dimensions and the computational time. An extensive experimental study was conducted on the publicly available data and the proposed HOG method obtained a classification accuracy of 100% with improved computational efficiency. The proposed method was also compared with the existing methods, and the results show that proposed HOG technique outperforms the existing techniques.

Rest of the paper is organised as follows: Methodology and the related theories are explained in Sect. 2. Experimental results and discussions are provided in Sect. 3. In Sect. 4 the work is concluded.

2 Methodology

A brief discussion about the t-f representation of EEG signal, HOG feature extraction technique, Center symmetric LBP(CS-LBP), local binary count(LBC) and the SVM based classification technique has been done in this section. The performance of proposed technique is compared with the performance of LBP technique. Hence, LBP technique is also briefly discussed in this section.

2.1 Short Time Fourier Transform Spectrogram

A spectrogram of STFT represents the normalized, squared magnitude of STFT coefficients [12]. Hence, the energy in the t-f signal is equal to the energy in the spectrogram of STFT. In STFT, the time domain signals are divided into smaller parts (window) and Fourier transform is computed to each windowed section to obtain the frequencies. The window location is slided through entire data to obtain STFT coefficients. Based on [12] Mathematically STFT is given as,

$$X = (n, \omega) = \sum\nolimits_{m=-\infty}^{\infty} x(m)w(n - m)e^{-j\omega n} \tag{1}$$

where $x(n)w(n - m)$ is a short-time part of the input signal $x(n)$ at time n. In addition, a discrete STFT is defined as,

$$X = (n, k) = X(n, \omega)|_{\omega=(2\pi k/N)} \tag{2}$$

where, N shows the number of discrete frequencies. Thus the spectrogram in logarithmic scale is defined as

$$S(n, k) = \log|X(n, k)|^2 \tag{3}$$

2.2 Local Binary Pattern

LBP is an effective texture pattern descriptor introduced by Ojala et al. [17] to describe the local texture patterns of an image. It is widely used in the applications based on image processing. The LBP works in a block size of 3 * 3, in which the center pixel is used to threshold the neighbouring pixel and the LBP code of a center pixel is generated by encoding the computed threshold value into a decimal value. Mathematical expression of LBP is given as,

$$LBP = \sum_{i-0}^{p-1} s(n_i - c)2^i \tag{4}$$

$$S(x) = \begin{cases} 1 & \text{if } n_i \geq c \\ 0 & \text{otherwise} \end{cases}$$

where, P is the number of neighbourhood pixels, n_i represents the ith neighbouring pixel and c represents the center pixel. The histogram features of size 2^P is extracted from the obtained LBP code. Hence, for 8 neighbouring pixels obtained histogram feature vector length is 256.

2.3 Center Symmetric Local Binary Pattern

CS-LBP is a computationally efficient method of LBP, in which the size of the histogram features are reduced by comparing the center symmetric pairs of the pixels. In CS-LBP, due to the comparison of centre symmetric pairs of pixels, the better gradient information than LBP are obtained. The CS-LBP [16] is expressed as,

$$CS\text{-}LBP = \sum_{i=0}^{p/2-1} s(n_i - n_{i+(P/2)})2^i \tag{5}$$

$$S(x) = \begin{cases} 1 & \text{if } x \geq T \\ 0 & \text{otherwise} \end{cases}$$

where, P is the number of neighbourhood pixels, where n_i and $n_{i+(P/2)}$ correspond to the gray values of center-symmetric pairs of neighbouring pixels(P). The P pixels are equally spaced on a circle of radius R. The threshold value of T is taken as 0.01. In CS-LBP, for a radius of 2 with 8 neighbourhood pixels a feature vector length of 16 is obtained.

2.4 Local Binary Count

In LBC, the neighbouring pixels are thresolded based on the center pixel and the LBC code of a center pixel is obtained by counting the number of ones in the thresholded neighbouring pixel. Due to which the histogram feature vector length of LBC code is reduced to P + 1. The LBC code [15] is given as,

$$1D\text{-}LBC = \sum_{i=0}^{P-1} s(n_i - c) \tag{6}$$

$$S(x) = \begin{cases} 1 & \text{if } n_i \geq c \\ 0 & \text{otherwise} \end{cases}$$

where, P is the number of neighbourhood pixels, n_i represents the ith neighbouring pixel and c represents the center pixel. In LBC, for eight neighbourhood pixels a feature vector length of 9 is computed.

2.5   Histogram of Oriented Gradients

HOG is a powerful technique used for human detection in images. In HOG, the distribution of intensity gradients is used for the better characterization of local object appearance and shape in a given image [18]. To achieve this images are divided into smaller cells and the total number of edge orientations is calculated. The magnitude $|G(x, y)|$ and orientation $\theta(x, y)$ are computed as

$$|G(x, y)| = \sqrt{\left(G_x(x, y)^2 + G_y(x, y)^2\right)} \tag{7}$$

$$\theta(x, y) = \arctan\left(G_y(x, y)/G_x(x, y)\right) \tag{8}$$

where, $G_x(x, y)$ is the horizontal gradient and $G_y(x, y)$ is the vertical gradient computed by using the gradient filter $[-1, 0, 1]$ with no smoothing. To obtain better illumination invariance, histogram for larger spatial regions (block) is computed to normalize the cells in each block and histogram is computed for 9 orientation bins. HOG descriptor is obtained by combining all the histogram entries and it is used for classifying the epileptic signals.

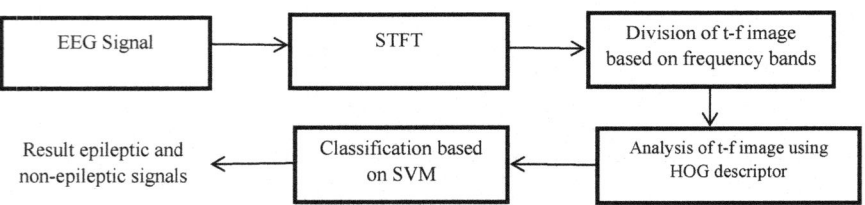

Fig. 1.   Frame work of the proposed method

2.6   Employed Methodology

The methodology is explained in the block diagram format in Fig. 1. All the five blocks are briefly explained as follows,

> **Block 1** A standard single channel epileptic and healthy EEG data obtained from Bonn University database is used for evaluating the proposed method.
> **Block 2** In this block, STFT is used to convert the EEG signal into a t-f image.
> **Block 3** The obtained t-f image is divided into sub-images based on frequency band of EEG signals (Delta, theta, alpha, beta and gamma).
> **Block 4** The HOG descriptor is applied to obtain features based on histogram to discriminate the epileptic and non-epileptic signals.
> **Block 5** The obtained features are fed into standard SVM classifier to classify the EEG signals. 10-fold cross validation with 100 repetitions was employed in this work. The parameters like accuracy, specificity and sensitivity were used to analyse the classifier performance. Apart from this, the feature vector dimensions and

computational time was computed to analyse the computational performance of the proposed technique.

2.7 Support Vector Machine

SVM is a powerful classifier used for both linear and non-linear classification by changing the kernel function utilized [20]. In SVM, by using the kernel functions the datas are mapped into a higher dimensional feature space, in which a hyperplane separating the classes are found. The general solution for finding the hyperplane with kernel functions are given as,

$$f(x) = \sum\nolimits_i a_i y_i K(x_i, x) \tag{9}$$

where, $\{x_i, y_i\}$ is the training data with classes y_i belonging to $\{-1, 1\}$, K is the kernel function.

The standard SVM classifier with Gaussian kernel function was first trained in this work and used for epileptic classification. The SVM model was built using the MATLAB functions.

3 Result and Discussion

The experiments were run on Intel core i3-7100U (2.40 GHz) processor with 4 GB RAM using MATLAB (Math Work R2016b) software. The widely accepted publicly available epileptic EEG dataset contributed by Bonn University, Germany is used for the evaluation of proposed techniques. The EEG dataset is divided into five groups namely A collected from five healthy volunteers with eyes open condition, B recorded from five healthy volunteers with eyes close condition, C and D collected from epileptic patients before the epileptic seizure occurrence and E represents the EEG data measured during the epileptic seizure occurrence. 100 single channel EEG signals are presented in each group which are measured with a sampling frequency of 173.6 Hz for 23.6 s and each signal consists of 4097 samples. Further details of the dataset are available at [19]. The EEG signals from group A (healthy) and group E (epileptic) are considered in this study and the illustration of both these groups of EEG signal is as shown in Fig. 2.

The STFT spectrogram of corresponding EEG signals are obtained and its shown in Fig. 3. Visually the qualitative difference between the epileptic and non-epileptic spectrograms can be noticed. Further the obtained t-f image is converted into a gray scale image and sub grouped into five images based on frequency band of EEG signals (Fig. 4) namely,

- Delta band with frequency 0–4 Hz
- Theta band with frequency 4–8 Hz
- Alpha band with frequency 8–12 Hz
- Beta band with frequency 12–30 Hz
- Gamma band with frequency 30 to 50 Hz.

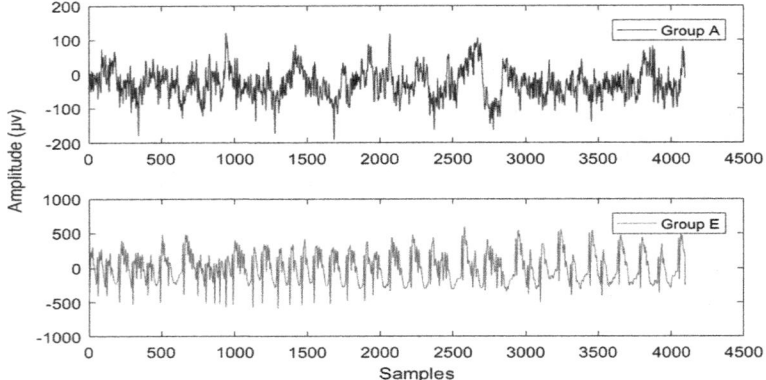

Fig. 2. Illustration of EEG dataset for group A and group E

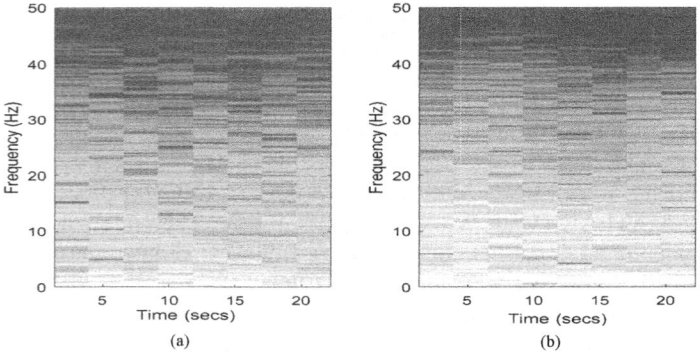

Fig. 3. STFT spectrogram of EEG signal (a) healthy and (b) epileptic

Feature extraction technique based on HOG descriptor is applied to each sub images for a block size of 3 * 3 and a histogram of 9-bit was used to analyse the t-f images. Hence, the dimension of HOG feature vector was 81.

The performance of other texture pattern techniques like CS-LBP [16], LBP [17] and LBC [15] were also analysed for the epileptic seizure detection using t-f image. In CS-LBP, the pixels which are symmetric to centre pixels are compared to obtain feature vector with dimensions 0–15. In LBC, the binary pattern obtained using LBP technique is encoded into a decimal value by counting the number of ones present in the pattern. Hence a feature vector dimension of 0–8 is obtained. Feature vector obtained from all the sub-images using various techniques are combined to form a single feature vector and their dimensions are as shown in Table 2. Further, the classifier performance time for LBP, CS-LBP, LBC and HOG are shown in Table 2. The extracted features are fed into SVM classifier with Gaussian kernel function and Table 1 shows the classifier performance using proposed and existing techniques.

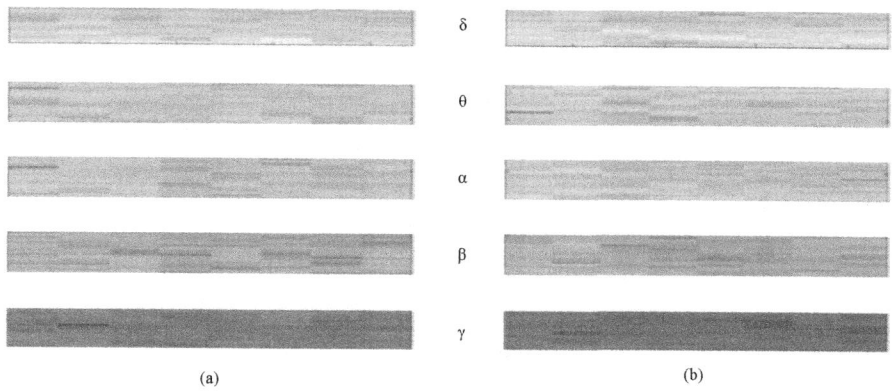

Fig. 4. Sub images of EEG signals (a) healthy (b) epileptic. δ-delta, θ-theta,α-alpha, β-beta, γ-gamma.

Table 1. Obtained classification result using SVM classifier

S. no	Techniques	Accuracy	Sensitivity	Specificity
1	LBP	100	100	100
2	CS-LBP	93.28	92.49	94.08
3	LBC	73.76	67.59	79.94
4	HOG	100	100	100

From Tables 1 and 2 it is evident that HOG descriptor attained a maximum classification accuracy of 100% with the highest computational efficiency than other techniques like CS-LBP, LBP and LBC. CS-LBP and LBC technique attained an accuracy of 93.28% and 73.76%, which is lesser than the accuracy of HOG descriptor. Şengür et al. reached an accuracy of 100% by using LBP descriptor in analysing a t-f representation of EEG signals. Comparison of SVM classification accuracy for different techniques are as shown in Fig. 5.

Table 2. Computational efficiency for all the techniques with SVM classifier

S. no	Techniques	Feature vector dimension for single sub-image	Feature vector dimension for 5 sub-images	Computational time for 5 images
1	LBP	256	1280	2.4417
2	CS-LBP	16	80	0.3415
3	LBC	9	45	0.3156
4	HOG	81	405	0.8375

From Table 2, it is noticeable that the concatenated feature vector dimensions of five sub images of LBC, CS-LBP, LBP and HOG are 45,80,1280 and 405. As, the

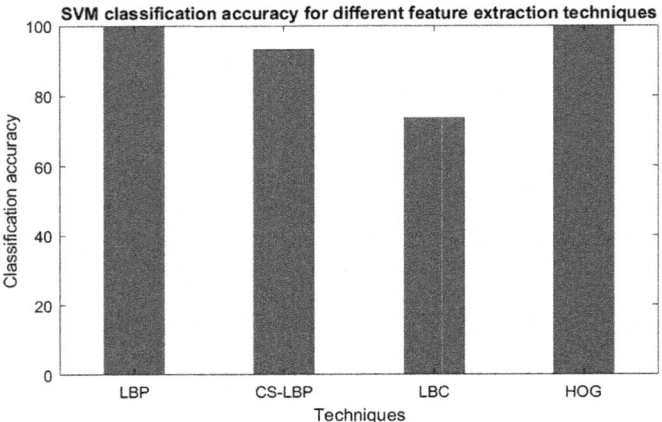

Fig. 5. Illustration of SVM classifier performance for LBP, CS-LBP, LBC and HOG

feature vector length of CS-LBP and LBC are lesser, the computational time of SVM classifier to execute the features of the same are 0.3415 s and 0.3156 s respectively. The time required to execute the SVM classifier using LBP and HOG are 2.4417 s and 0.8375 s. Although the execution time of SVM classifier using the histogram features based on LBC and CS-LBP are much faster than HOG based features, the accuracy achieved by them is lesser than the later. In contrary, the execution time of SVM classifier using HOG features is much lesser than LBP method. Thus highest classification accuracy with improved computational efficiency is achieved using HOG features.

The performances of the proposed technique with the existing technique for epileptic detection using t-f representation of EEG signals are compared in Table 3. The existing technique handling the classification problem with the same dataset A and E is considered. From Table 2 it is clear that the proposed technique outperforms the existing technique with highest classification accuracy of 100%. The histogram features obtained from grayscale image attained an accuracy of 99.125% and 95.33% [10, 13] which is comparatively lesser than proposed method. It is evident that the maximum accuracy of 100% for classifying epileptic and non-epileptic signals are achieved by using LBP and GLCM method [12]. But the proposed method outruns the existing method in terms of computational performance with high classification accuracy.

Over all, the experimental results indicate that the features based on proposed HOG descriptor is more informative and are suitable for detecting epileptic seizure activities. Hence, HOG method with highly improved computational performance can be employed for classifying epileptic and non-epileptic signals.

Table 3. Comparison with existing techniques for the dataset {A, E} using t-f image of EEG signal

Author	Method			Accuracy
	t-f image	Feature	Classification	(%)
Boashash (2012)	Quadratic time-frequency distributions	t-f signal features and t-f image features are combined	SVM classifier	95.33
Boubchir (2015)	Quadratic time-frequency distributions	t-f image features based on LBP technique	SVM classifier	99.33
Şengür (2016)	STFT	t-f image features based on LBP technique	SVM classifier	100
		t-f image features based on GLCM technique	SVM classifier	92.5–100
		t-f image features based on TFCM technique	SVM classifier	87
Fu (2014)	Hilbert–Huang transform	t-f image based on histogram features of grayscale image	SVM classifier	99.125
Boubchir (2014)	Quadratic time-frequency distributions	t-f image based on GLCM features	SVM classifier	99.09
Proposed method	STFT	t-f image based on HOG features	SVM classifier	100

4 Conclusions

In this study, a methodology for automatic detection of epileptic seizure activities using t-f representation (image) of EEG signals is proposed. The t-f image of EEG signal is obtained using STFT spectrogram and the attained t-f image is divided into five sub-images based on the EEG frequency bands. The features based on HOG, CS-LBP and LBC are computed from each sub-image. The obtained features of each sub image are concatenated into a single feature vector and the concatenated features were fed into SVM classifier with Gaussian kernel function for epileptic seizure detection.

Additionally, the performance of LBP technique in analysing the t-f image of EEG signal was studied along with the proposed techniques. Experimental result suggests that the proposed techniques are computationally efficient in detecting epileptic signals with a good accuracy rate. Compared with LBP technique, HOG descriptor obtained an accuracy rate of 100% with improved computational performance. Result also suggests that features based on HOG technique obtain better computational and classification performance than other techniques. In future, the proposed techniques will be validated for EEG signal for different cases with a better feature selection algorithm.

References

1. Noachtar, S., Rémi, J.: The role of EEG in epilepsy: a critical review. Epilepsy Behav. **15**(1), 22–33 (2009)
2. Joshi, V., Pachori, R.B., Vijesh, A.: Classification of ictal and seizure-free EEG signals using fractional linear prediction. Biomed. Sig. Process. Control **9**, 1–5 (2014)
3. Srinivasan, V., Eswaran, C., Sriraam, A.N.: Artificial neural network based epileptic detection using time-domain and frequency-domain features. J. Med. Syst. **29**(6), 647–660 (2005)
4. Upadhyay, R., Padhy, P., Kankar, P.: A comparative study of feature ranking techniques for epileptic seizure detection using wavelet transform. Comput. Electr. Eng. **53**, 163–176 (2016)
5. Riaz, F., Hassan, A., Rehman, S., Niazi, I.K., Dremstrup, K.: EMD-based temporal and spectral features for the classification of EEG signals using supervised learning. IEEE Trans. Neural Syst. Rehabil. Eng. **24**(1), 28–35 (2016)
6. Peker, M., Sen, B., Delen, D.: A novel method for automated diagnosis of epilepsy using complex-valued classifiers. IEEE J. Biomed. Health Inform. **20**(1), 108–118 (2016)
7. Kaya, Y., Uyar, M., Tekin, R., Yıldırım, S.: 1D-local binary pattern based feature extraction for classification of epileptic EEG signals. Appl. Math. Comput. **243**, 209–219 (2014)
8. Jaiswal, A.K., Banka, H.: Local pattern transformation based feature extraction techniques for classification of epileptic EEG signals. Biomed. Sig. Process. Control **34**, 81–92 (2017)
9. Bajaj, V., Pachori, R.B.: Automatic classification of sleep stages based on the time-frequency image of EEG signals. Comput. Methods Progr. Biomed. **112**(3), 320–328 (2013)
10. Boashash, B., Boubchir, L., Azemi, G.: A methodology for time-frequency image processing applied to the classification of non-stationary multichannel signals using instantaneous frequency descriptors with application to newborn EEG signals. EURASIP J. Adv. Sig. Process. **2012**(1), 117 (2012)
11. Boubchir, L., Al-Maadeed, S., Bouridane, A., Chérif, A. A.: Classification of EEG signals for detection of epileptic seizure activities based on LBP descriptor of time-frequency images. In: IEEE International Conference on Image Processing (ICIP), Quebec City, QC, pp. 3758–3762 (2015)
12. Şengür, A., Guo, Y., Akbulut, Y.: Time–frequency texture descriptors of EEG signals for efficient detection of epileptic seizure. Brain Inform. **3**(2), 101–108 (2016)
13. Fu, K., Qu, J., Chai, Y., Dong, Y.: Classification of seizure based on the time-frequency image of EEG signals using HHT and SVM. Biomed. Sig. Process. Control **13**, 15–22 (2014)
14. Boubchir, L., Al-Maadeed, S., Bouridane, A.: Haralick feature extraction from time-frequency images for epileptic seizure detection and classification of EEG data. In: ICM Conference, 14–17 December 2014, pp. 32–35 (2014)
15. Zhao, Y., Huang, D.S., Jia, W.: Completed local binary count for rotation invariant texture classification. IEEE Trans. Image Process. **21**(10), 4492–4497 (2012)
16. Heikkilä, M., Pietikäinen, M., Schmid, C.: Description of interest regions with center-symmetric local binary patterns. In: Kalra, P.K., Peleg, S. (eds.) ICVGIP 2006. LNCS, vol. 4338, pp. 58–69. Springer, Heidelberg (2006). https://doi.org/10.1007/11949619_6
17. Ojala, T., Pietikainen, M., Maenpaa, T.: Multiresolution gray-scale and rotation invariant texture classification with local binary patterns. IEEE Trans. Pattern Anal. Mach. Intell. **24**(7), 971–987 (2002)

18. Dalal, N., Triggs, B.: Histograms of oriented gradients for human detection. In: IEEE Conference on Computer Vision and Pattern Recognition (CVPR), San Diego, CA, vol. 1, pp. 886–893. IEEE (2005)
19. Andrzejak, R.G., Lehnertz, K., Rieke, C., Mormann, F., David, P., Elger, C.E.: Indications of nonlinear deterministic and finite dimensional structures in time series of brain electrical activity: dependence on recording region and brain state. Phys. Rev. E **64**, 061907 (2001)
20. Nicolaou, N., Georgiou, J.: Detection of epileptic electroencephalogram based on permutation entropy and support vector machines. Expert Syst. Appl. **39**(1), 202–209 (2012)

Detection of Lung Cancer with the Fusion of Computed Tomography and Positron Emission Tomography

Jaspreet Kaur[1(✉)], Sidharth Pancholi[2], and Amit M. Joshi[2]

[1] Thapar University, Patiala, Punjab, India
jass.jaspreet33@gmail.com
[2] Malaviya National Institute of Technology, Jaipur, Rajasthan, India

Abstract. In this paper, a wavelet fusion based cancer detection methodology has been presented. The database includes 200 samples of CT scan, and 200 PET scans out of which 50% samples of each were normal. Decomposition of CT scan and PET scan images have been performed by using wavelet transform (using haar as a mother wavelet) of depth 5 and combining the details of decomposed images by using averaging fusion rule and inverse wavelet transform. Further, 200 fused images have been segmented by manual cropping method to extract the useful information or region of interests (ROIs). 17 features of each of 200 ROIs have been extracted using GLCM and feature vectors are prepared. Subsequently, the features have been classified using two classifiers support vector machine (SVM) and k-nearest neighbors algorithm (k-NN) using their different kernels. The accuracy of SVM vary from 95.5%–98% and accuracy of k-NN vary from 69.5%–95.5%. This indicates that fused images can be a more powerful tool to diagnose the lung cancer.

Keywords: CT scan · PET scan · Image fusion · Feature extraction
SVM · K-NN

1 Introduction

Computed Tomography (CT) is an imaging technique which gives the structural information of the internal parts of the body. Positron Emission Tomography (PET) provides the functional information of internal parts of the body. Both PET and CT images individually contain an important information of human body. However, the combination of both images is a useful aspect for diagnosis purpose. Image fusion is a procedure which combines the information from different sources to make a single image to have more detail information. It sums up the information from different sensors (CT and PET) to a single image [1]. There are various techniques to fuse image such as principal component analysis (PCA), high pass filtering technique (HPF), Intensity Hue Saturation (IHS) sharpening technique and discrete wavelet transform technique. Out of these, first three techniques are based on spatial domain approach while the last one, discrete wavelet transform is frequency domain analysis which is based on multi-resolution [2]. DWT has been preferred choice at fusing technique because it accomplishes the target of the distortionless fused image [3, 4]. Because the

© Springer Nature Singapore Pte Ltd. 2018
P. Bhattacharyya et al. (Eds.): NGCT 2017, CCIS 828, pp. 944–955, 2018.
https://doi.org/10.1007/978-981-10-8660-1_72

fused images are intelligible and have concentrated information, the medical field is going to be benefited with such type of approaches [5, 6]. Image fusion using wavelet transform is attempted by many researchers, and various have been derived. The wavelet transforms based image fusion mainly used due to some distinct advantages over other techniques which include [7–9]:

- During decomposition of images, the redundancies don't exist in the reconstructed image.
- There is an isolation of frequencies in both space and time to extract detail information.
- It tends to produce better results over other techniques like PCA, IHS, etc.
- It is better to extract the sub frequency features.

It differs from the Fourier transform in the way that it represents features in both frequency and time domain [10]. The purpose of image fusion is to detect lung cancer with greater accuracy and precision. Also, fused images are helpful in locating any lesion or cancer easily while operating it. However, image fusion can be obtained with the help of different fusion in rules such as maximum fusion rule, minimum fusion rule, and average fusion rule. The maximum value out of two pixels is acquired in maximum fusion rule. In average fusion rule, the average of two pixels is obtained, and in minimum fusion rule, the minimum value pixel is retrieved. The average fusion rule is considered in the paper; it provides better quality as it reflects the weight of both pixels equally.

Various researches on fusion had been carried out in the past decades. The previous techniques were based on averaging or maximum/minimum fusion rule. Further, with the growth of the medical industry, techniques like IHS, PCA, DWT, had been proposed to fuse the medical images. Kuruvilla and Gunavathi [11] proposed a technique to detect cancer with the help of CT images. In this technique, classification has been performed by feed forward and feed backward neural network algorithms. The maximum classification accuracy has been achieved, is 91.1%. However, CT gives only structural details of the organ. Kumar et al. [12] suggested a new methodology for early cancer detection through CT images. They have developed a Computer-aided diagnosis (CAD) system for radiologists. In this work, they used deep feature extraction method for classification by decision tree algorithm. However, accuracy was achieved 75.01% for classification with the 83.35% sensitivity. Bi et al. [13] worked on PET-CT images and extracted class-driven feature extraction process for the classification of the PET-CT images. The classification accuracy was achieved, 91.73%. Shirke et al. [14] performed classification on MRI images. In this work, they have extracted features using GLCM method and after this reduction of feature vector has been performed by PCA method. For the classification, PNN-RBF classifier has been selected.

The organization of the paper is defined as follows: Sect. 2 covers the methodology section and some useful materials covered in the paper. Section 3 elaborates on the obtained results and conclusion is derived in Sect. 4.

2 Methodology and Materials

The database consists of 200 abnormal and 200 normal CT scan and PET scan. Database has been acquired from PET Center, Postgraduate Institute of Medical Education & Research (PGIMER), Chandigarh, India.

2.1 Discrete Wavelet Transform (DWT)

Discrete Wavelet Transform has been used for decomposition at level 5 using haar as a mother wavelet on CT scan and PET scan [15, 16]. It decomposes the images into four sub parts, approximation details, horizontal details, vertical details and diagonal details [17]. 2-D DWT has been used to 2-dimensional color images. In DWT, rows of images are passed through high pass filter and low pass filter, then down sampling is performed. After this, columns are also passed through high pass and low pass filter and further down sampling is done to achieve four sub parts of an image, i.e., approximation, horizontal, vertical and diagonal details [18]. It offers the image analysis with different resolutions. Figure 1 shows the detailed process of DWT decomposition into four sub frequencies.

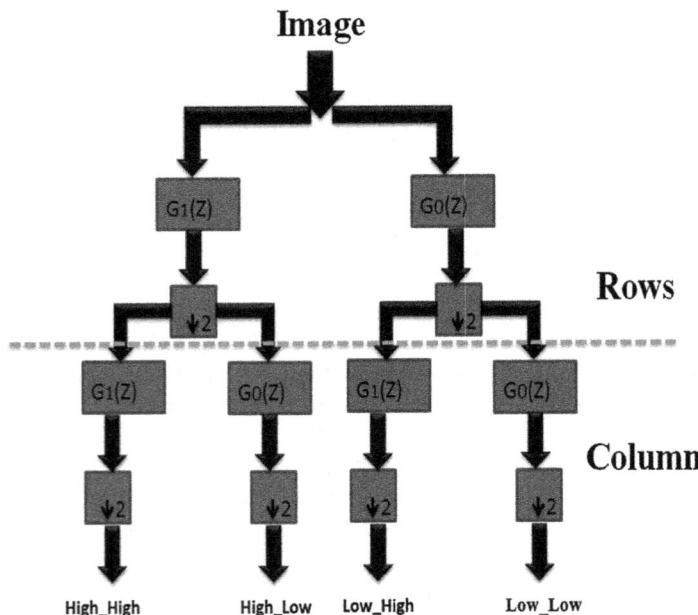

Fig. 1. Decomposition of a 2-D image into four details using high pass and low pass filters across rows and columns and down sampling.

Figure 1 shows the whole process of decomposition of PET and CT images. PET and CT images are obtained, and discrete wavelet transform (DWT) has been applied on both images. Both images have been broken into four main parts out of which contains the approximation details, horizontal details, vertical details and diagonal details [19]. It has been observed that, 5th level wavelet decomposition of image provides better separability for the features. So in this work 5th leavel wavelet decomposition has been selected.

2.2   Fusion Decision Map

To achieve the fused image, average fusion rule has been selected (out of maximum, average and minimum fusion rule). In maximum fusion rule, the pixel which has higher intensity value is retrieved and similar is the case with minimum fusion rule, minimum value out of two pixels is received [20–22]. In the proposed work, average fusion rule has been used in which simple average of two pixels is evaluated, and discrete wavelet coefficients have been attained.

2.3   Inverse Discrete Wavelet Transform (IDWT)

After fusion rule, the details of both images have been combined to form a single image. This is accomplished by using discrete inverse wavelet transform to reconstruct the fused image from discrete wavelet coefficients [8]. In IDWT, as the name suggests, it is exactly the reverse of discrete wavelet transform. Up sampling of pixels have been done by doubling the lengths of pixels, moreover, after filtering the pixels, reconstruction of pixels takes place by adding to get a single reconstructed image. The detailed block diagram of the whole process of fusion is depicted below in Fig. 2.

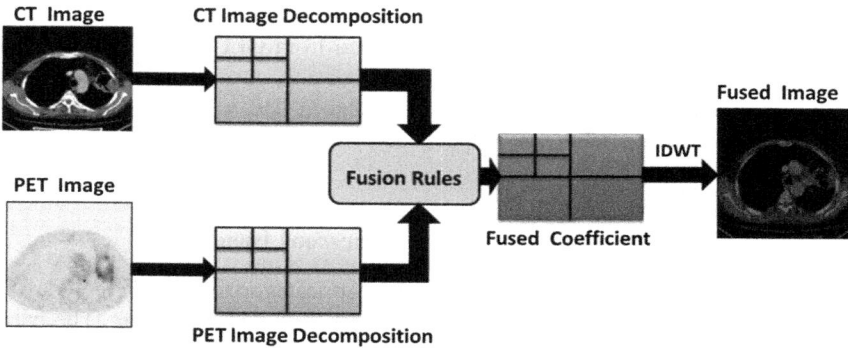

Fig. 2. Algorithm for fusion and decomposition of CT and PET scan and receiving fused PET/CT using inverse discrete wavelet transform.

2.4   Image Segmentation

It is a process of breaking a digital 2-D image into multiple segments [17, 23]. The aim of segmentation is to extract specific information from the image by segmenting Region of Interests (ROIs). It is a process in which labels are assigned to each element in a specified pixels with a similar label to share some characteristics. It is based on the fact that every pixel is similar to its nearby pixel to some extent in color, intensity, or texture (Fig. 3).

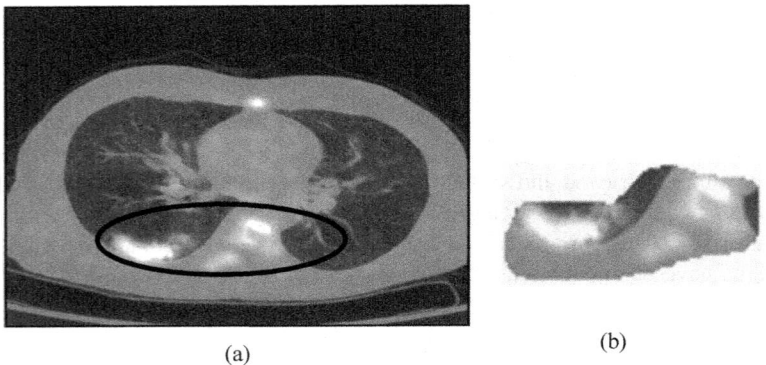

(a)   (b)

Fig. 3. (a) Shows the fused PET/CT colored image, (b) shows the segmentation of an image using manual cropping method in MATLAB.

2.5   Texture Features

Texture features are being extracted to obtain the meaningful information from PET/CT images [24]. These features are helpful in verifying the fusion methodology. These are further used to classify the normal and cancerous PET/CT image, and hence abnormality can be predicted. Gray Level Co-occurrence Matrix (GLCM) has been used to calculate the features of images. Features extracted from GLCM are explained below (Table 1):

Where: R = number of gray levels in an image μ_x, μ_y = Means of x and y. σ_x, σ_y = Standard deviation of P_x, P_y respectively, a = number of rows, b = number of column.

2.6   Classification of Non-cancerous and Cancerous Images

In the process of classification, objects and ideas are categorized in different classes. It is considered as an example of supervised learning, in machine learning. The basis of the classification is that the set of training data that contains the features, and its category is to be analyzed. With the help of training data, test data is classified. Classifier is the algorithm which classifies the data into different classes [25–28]. Support Vector Machine (SVM) and k-NN classifier have been used in this research. It is a type of learning model, which is based on supervised learning [28, 30]. It identifies the pattern and evaluates data which used for classification. Although SVM can classify nonlinear data, it is suitable for linear data set. Classification in SVM and k-NN has been done by taking the training data of known classes and by separating them into classes.

Table 1. Computed features for image classification

S.No.	Feature	S.No..	Features
1.	Mean	9.	Sum of squares
2.	Energy	10.	Inverse Difference movement
3.	Variance	11.	Sum Average
4.	Skewness	12.	Sum Variance
5.	Kurtosis	13.	Sum Entropy
6.	Angular Second Moment	14.	Entropy
7.	Contrast	15.	Difference Variance
8.	Correlation	16.	Difference Entropy

17.   17. Information measures of correlation

$$\frac{\left[-\sum_a \sum_b P(a,b) \, \log\left(P(a,b)\right)\right] - \left|-\sum_a \sum_b P(a,b) \, \log\left(P_x(a)P_y(b)\right)\right|}{max\left[\left[-\sum_a \sum_b P(a,b) \, \log\left(P(a,b)\right)\right],\left[-\sum_a \sum_b P(a,b) \, \log\left(P_x(a)P_y(b)\right)\right]\right]}$$

$$\left(1 - exp\left[-2.0\left(\left[-\sum_a \sum_b P_x(a)\,P_y(b)\log(P_x(a)\,P_y(b)\right] - \left[-\sum_a \sum_b P(a,b)\log(P_x(a)\,P_y(b)\right]\right)\right]\right)^{\frac{1}{2}}$$

3 Results

In this research, discrete wavelet transform has been used to fuse CT scan and PET scan. Classification of PET/CT is done after fusing the PET and CT images by wavelet transform, using haar as a mother wavelet. In fusion, first, both PET and CT images are decomposed into four parts as, approximation, horizontal, vertical and diagonal details. Further, decomposing, corresponding details are combined by using the averaging rule of fusion followed by inverse wavelet transform, which converts the details back to a single image. The detailed description of decomposition of PET lung and CT lung image is shown in Figs. 4(a), (b), 5(a), (b) and 6.

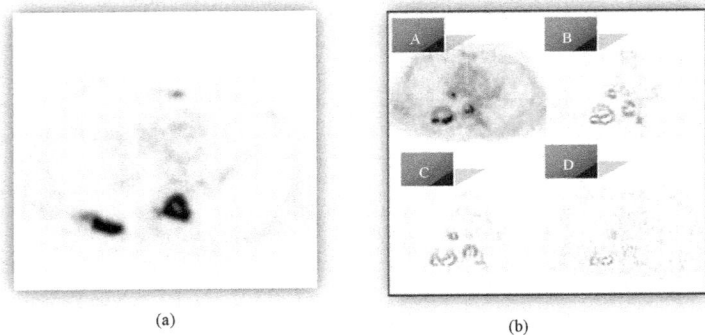

Fig. 4. (a) Depicts the original PET scan, (b) shows the four details after wavelet decomposition in which A shows the approximation details, B shows horizontal details, C shows Vertical details, D shows diagonal details.

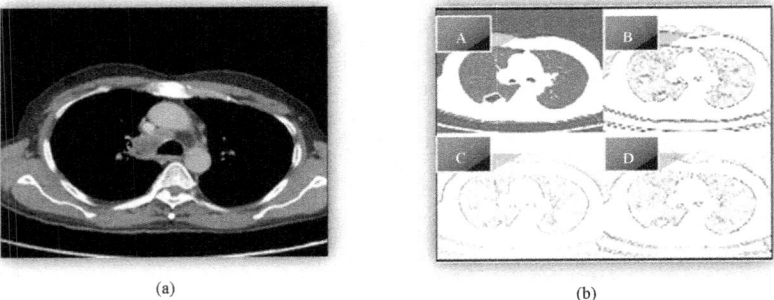

Fig. 5. (a) Depicts the original CT scan, (b) shows the four details after wavelet decomposition in which A shows the approximation details, B shows horizontal details, C shows vertical details, D shows diagonal details.

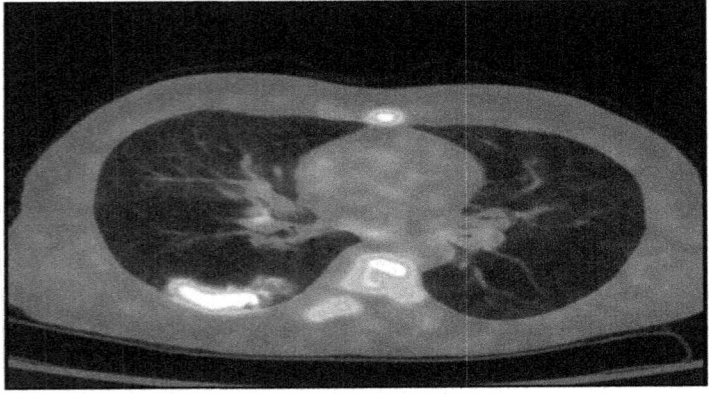

Fig. 6. Depicts the fused PET/CT image obtained by fusing the decomposed details using fusion rule and then taking inverse discrete wavelet transform.

Fusion of two images has been shown in Fig. 7(a), (b), (c), (d), (e) and (f). Abnormalities have been highlighted in Fig. 7(g) which helps to determine the location of cancer. It can be seen that PET/CT images are easy to analyze and it is comparatively easier to determine the location of any cancer or lesion. Moreover, fused PET/Ct images have been classified using different kernels of SVM and k-NN classifiers. Different kernels of k-NN and SVM classifiers are shown in Tables 2 and 3 with their specifications. The accuracy of fine k-NN classifier has been come out to be 95.5%, medium k-NN - 94.5%, coarse k-NN - 69.5%, cosine k-NN - 93.5%, cubic k-NN - 94.5% and weighted k-NN - 95.5%. Similarly, SVM classifier has been analysed with its different kernels like linear SVM - 96%, quadratic SVM - 96.5%, cubic SVM - 98%, fine Gaussian SVM - 94%, medium Gaussian SVM - 95%, coarse Gaussian - 95.5%.

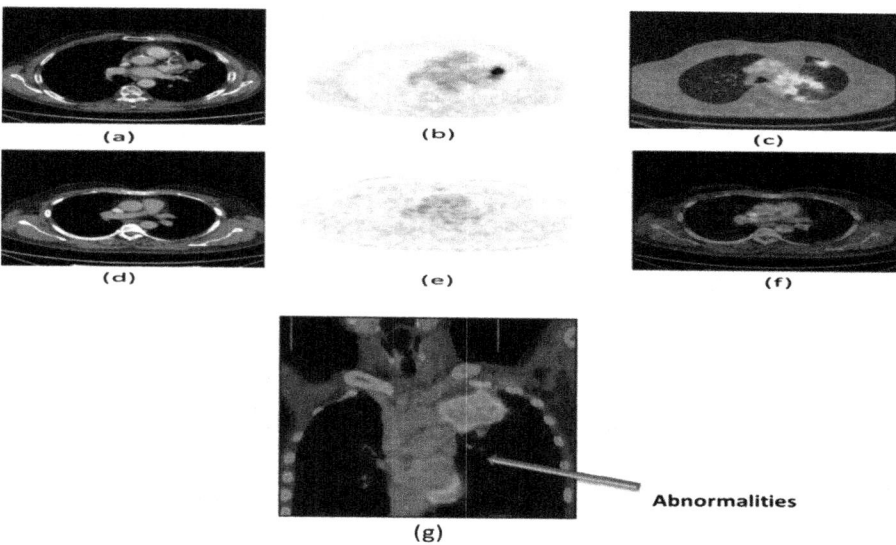

Fig. 7. (a) Shows the CT scan (b) shows the PET scan (c) depicts the fused PET/CT (d) CT scan (e) PET scan (f) Fused PET/CT (g) depicts the PET/CT scan in which abnormalities have been shown.

The accuracy of SVM varies from 95.5%–98% with fine Gaussian SVM having lowest accuracy and cubic SVM having highest accuracy. The accuracy of k-NN varies from 69.5%–95.5% with coarse k-NN having lowest and fine k-NN along with weighted k-NN having same highest accuracy. Comparison of accuracies of these classifiers has been displayed by plotting bar graphs shown below in Figs. 8 and 9.

Table 2. Different k-NN kernels and their specifications

S.no.	Classification kernel	Specification		
		No. of neighbours	Distance weight	Distance metric
1	Fine k-NN	1	Equal	Euclidean
2.	medium k-NN	10	Equal	Euclidean
3.	coarse k-NN	100	Equal	Euclidean
4.	cosine k-NN	10	Equal	Cosine
5.	cubic k-NN	10	Equal	Cubic
6.	weighted k-NN	10	Squared inverse	Euclidean

Table 3. Different SVM kernels and their specifications

S.no.	Classification kernel	Specification		
		Kernel Function	Box constraint level	Multiclass method
1	Liner SVM	Liner	1	One vs one
2.	Quadratic SVM	Gaussian	1	One vs. one
3.	Cubic SVM	Cubic	1	One vs. one
4.	Fine Gaussian SVM	Gaussian	1	One vs. one
5.	Medium Gaussian SVM	Gaussian	1	One vs one
6.	Coarse Gaussian SVM	Gaussian	1	One vs. one

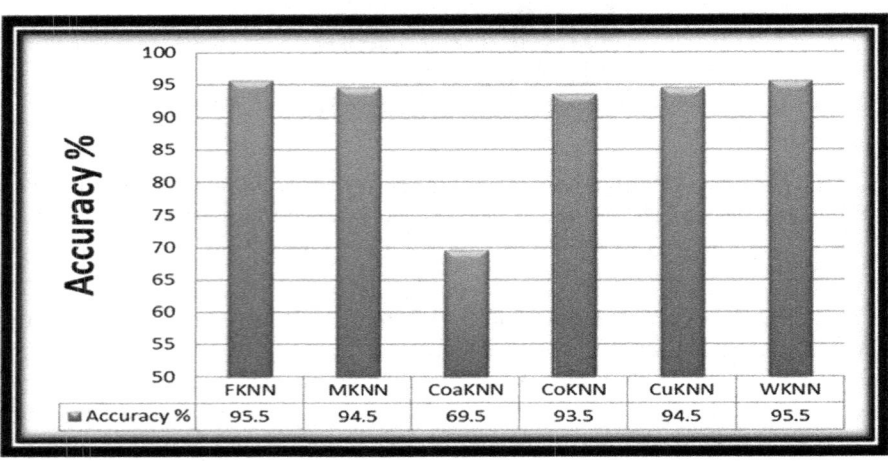

Fig. 8. Classification comparison of different kernels of K-in classification Fine KNN, Medium KNN, Coarse KNN, Cosine KNN, Cubic KNN, Weighted KNN

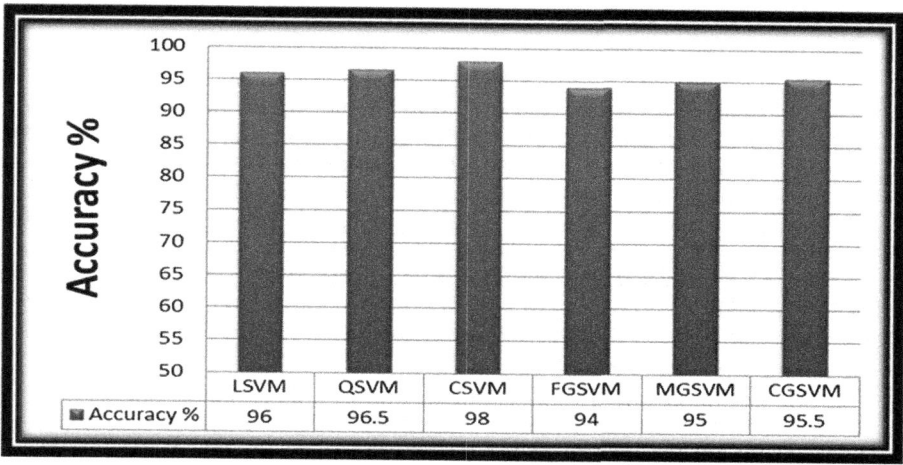

Fig. 9. Classification comparison of different kernels of SVM classification liner SVM, Quadratic SVM, Cubic SVM, Fine Gaussain SVM, Medium Gaussian SVM, Coarse Gaussian SVM.

4 Conclusion

The paper covers wavelet transform based fusion technique of PET/CT images. The fused image reveals more information as compared to an individual image. The proposed technique is an automatic cancer detection technique capable of acquiring fusion pictures with useful information. This sort of image is in a position to create a reliable foundation for the doctor's designation and treatment. Segmented images have been classified using two classifiers support vector machine (SVM) and k-nearest neighbors algorithm (k-NN) using their different kernels. From the observational solutions, SVM classifier with cubic kernel gives more reliable accuracy (98%) as compared to k-NN. This leads to the conclusion that the fused image has additional details and also the texture is additionally clear. Thus, the technique proposed in this paper is an effective technique for the combination of medical images.

5 Future Scope

The automated based fusion technique may be implemented through Field Programmable Gate Array (FPGA) to apply the real-time fusing of two captured images as PET and CT. The real-time fusion would help to speed the fusing which results in an early diagnosis of a patient. This can be useful for some critical condition of patients.

Acknowledgement. The authors are thankful to Postgraduate Institute of Medical Education and Research (PGI), Chandigarh, India to provide Dataset for this research.

References

1. Gonzalo, P., de la Cruz, J.M.: A wavelet based image fusion tutorial. Pattern Recogn. (2004)
2. Joshi, A., Bapna, M., Malpani, A., Goyal, A.K., Meena, M.: Hardware implementation of image and video watermarking for ownership verification. Sci. Gate Publ. **5**, 59–82 (2016)
3. Amolins, K., Zhang, Y., Dare, P.: Wavelet based image fusion techniques—an introduction, review, and comparison. ISPRS J. Photogramm. Remote Sens. **62**(4), 249–263 (2007)
4. Gangwar, J., Kumar, A., Jaiswal, A.K.: Image fusion of PET and CT images based on wavelet transform. Int. J. Comput. Appl. **121**(4) (2015)
5. Carriero, A., et al.: Image fusion: a new diagnostic and therapeutic tool. La Radiol. Med. **109** (4), 297 (2005)
6. Qu, G., Zhang, D., Yan, P.: Medical image fusion by wavelet transform modulus maxima. Opt. Express **9**(4), 184–190 (2001)
7. Joshi, A.M., Darji, A.: Efficient dual domain watermarking scheme for secure images. In: International Conference on Advances in Recent Technologies in Communication and Computing, ARTCom 2009, pp. 909–914. IEEE (2009)
8. Li, H., Manjunath, B.S., Mitra, S.K.: Multisensor image fusion using the wavelet transform. Graph. Models Image Process. **57**(3), 235–245 (1995)
9. Joshi, A.M., Darji, A., Mishra, V.: Design and implementation of real-time image watermarking. In: 2011 IEEE International Conference on Signal Processing, Communications and Computing (ICSPCC), pp. 1–5. IEEE (2011)
10. Bhatt, U., Singh, A., Bhadauria, H.S.: Performance analysis of wavelet filter bank for an image super-resolution algorithm. In: 2016 1st India International Conference on Information Processing (IICIP), pp. 1–4. IEEE (2016)
11. Kuruvilla, J., Gunavathi, K.: Lung cancer classification using neural networks for CT images. Comput. Methods Programs Biomed. **113**(1), 202–209 (2014)
12. Kumar, D., Wong, A., Clausi, D.A.: Lung nodule classification using deep features in CT images. In: 2015 12th Conference on Computer and Robot Vision (CRV). IEEE (2015)
13. Bi, L., Kim, J., Kumar, A., Wen, L., Feng, D., Fulham, M.: Automatic detection and classification of regions of FDG uptake in whole-body PET-CT lymphoma studies. Comput. Med. Imaging Graph. **60**, 3–10 (2016)
14. Shirke, S.S., Kendule, J.A., Vyaware, S.G.: An approach for PCA and GLCM based MRI image classification. In: Pawar, P.M., Ronge, B.P., Balasubramaniam, R., Seshabhattar, S. (eds.) ICATSA 2016, pp. 265–274. Springer, Cham (2018). https://doi.org/10.1007/978-3-319-53556-2_26
15. David, S., et al.: A multi-observation fusion approach for patient follow-up using PET/CT. In: 2010 IEEE IEEE Nuclear Science Symposium Conference Record (NSS/MIC) (2010)
16. Mane, S., Sawant, S.D.: Image fusion of CT/MRI using DWT, PCA methods and analog DSP processor. Int. J. Eng. Res. Appl. **4**(2(Version 1)), 557–563 (2014). ISSN 2248-9622
17. Pajares, G., Cruz, J.M.D.L.: A wavelet-based image fusion tutorial. Pattern Recogn. **37**(9), 1855–1872 (2004)
18. Indhumadhi, N., Padmavathi, G.: Enhanced image fusion algorithm using Laplacian pyramid and spatial frequency based wavelet algorithm. Int. J. Comput. Sci. Eng. **1**(5), 298–303 (2011)
19. Madanala, S., Rani, K.J.: PCA-DWT based medical image fusion using non sub-sampled contourlet transform. In: 2016 International Conference on Signal Processing, Communication, Power and Embedded System (SCOPES). IEEE (2016)
20. Boussion, N., et al.: Contrast enhancement in emission tomography by way of synergistic PET/CT image combination. Comput. Methods Programs Biomed. **90**(3), 191–201 (2008)

21. Jafarpour, S., Sedghi, Z., Amirani, M.C.: A robust brain MRI classification with GLCM features. Int. J. Comput. Appl. **37**(12), 1–5 (2012)
22. Rao, R.M., Bopardikar, A.: Wavelet Transform Introduction to Theory and Application
23. Haihui, W.: A new multiwavelet-based approach to image fusion. J. Math. Imaging Vis. **21**, 177–192 (2004)
24. Flusser, J., Sroubek, F., Zitova, B.: Image Fusion; Principles, Methods and Application (2007)
25. Gonzalo p and Jesus M. A wavelet based image fusion tutorial-Pattern recognition, 2007
26. Wong, K.P., Feng, D., Meikle, S.R., Fulham, M.J.: Segmentation of dynamic PET images using cluster analysis. IEEE Trans. Nucl. Sci. **49**(1), 200–207 (2002)
27. Udupa, J.K., Samarasekera, S.: Fuzzy connectedness and object definition: theory, algorithms, and applications in image segmentation. Graph. Models Image Process. **58**(3), 246–261 (1996)
28. Mohanaiah, P., Sathyanarayana, P., GuruKumar, L.: Image texture feature extraction using GLCM approach. Int. J. Sci. Res. Publ. **3**(5), 1 (2013)
29. Waske, B., Benediktsson, J.A.: Fusion of support vector machines for classification of multisensor data. IEEE Trans. Geosci. Remote Sens. **45**(12), 3858–3866 (2007)
30. Zhou, T.: Classification of hyperspectral data using support vector machine. In: Proceedings 2001 International Conference on Image Processing (Cat No 01CH37205) ICIP, January 2001

Multi Minimum Product Spanning Tree Based Indexing Approach for Content Based Retrieval of Bio Images

Meenakshi Srivastava[1]([⊠]), Sanjay Kumar Singh[1], and S. Q. Abbas[2]

[1] Amity Institute of Information Technology,
Amity University, Lucknow, Uttar Pradesh, India
msrivastava@lko.amity.edu, sksinghl@amity.edu
[2] Computer Science Department, Ambalika Institute of Information Technology,
Lucknow, Uttar Pradesh, India
sqabbas@yahoomail.com

Abstract. Similarity computation between bio images is very different from the similarity computation between routine images as the information about bio images are not completely in the form of textual nature. Like in case of bio-images (viz. protein structures) similarity can be computed on the basis of their sequence similarity and their structural similarity. In the previous work AMIPRO, has been proposed which takes both structural and sequential similarity into the consideration. Intelligent Vision Algorithm has been applied on the protein images and the sequence information present in the PDB file has been used to determine the sequential similarity. The proposed model minimizes the time taken in the online similarity determination by storing the pre calculated ranked results. In present manuscript a storage efficient index structure Multi Minimum Product Spanning Tree has been proposed and applied on AMIPRO. Our results shows that MMPST based implementation of index structure can easily map similar records on the basis of their level of similarity computed on multiple features.

Keywords: Content based retrieval · Minimum spanning tree
Multi Minimum Product Spanning Tree · Indexing · Graph based indexing

1 Introduction

Content based retrieval of information such as 3D images is the demand of today's scenario. With the growth of access to various Internet available data bases, it has become a foremost challenge for researchers of computer science to develop such algorithms which can retrieve the information from these databases in fast and efficient manner [1]. The application of 3D (Three-dimensional) images has emerged in various domains like bioinformatics, medicines and drug designing, archeology, cultural heritage, computer-assisted design (CAD), 3D face recognition etc. Various domains have developed individual 3D repositories for research purposes such as Protein Data Bank for biological macromolecules [2], AIM@SHAPE shape repository, INRIA-GAMMA 3D Database [3], and CAESAR for Anthropometry. The scientific community is

© Springer Nature Singapore Pte Ltd. 2018
P. Bhattacharyya et al. (Eds.): NGCT 2017, CCIS 828, pp. 956–963, 2018.
https://doi.org/10.1007/978-981-10-8660-1_73

devoted on development of algorithms that can be used in order to analyze the data and draw useful conclusions [4]. In case of biological databases, due to the huge amount of data many of the existing algorithms became inefficient due to their computational complexity. In case of bio-molecules, such as proteins similarity search are very important and are required for many purposes such as for designing new drugs, annotation of genome sequences, mutation of an organism etc. Similarity search is structural biology is basically done via two ways, one is sequential and other one is structural comparison [5]. Structural comparison is very vital because a clear relationship of functional similarity can be inferred between two structurally similar proteins [6]. Now while searching in a bio molecular database for similarity, instead of keyword based queries, dedicated sequences matching/alignment algorithms will be run on the sequence specified in the query [7]. These multiple sequence alignment algorithms use dynamic programming which is NP complete. One solution of this runtime complexity could be that, objects are stored in the database according their similarity of content (structural similarity as well as sequential similarity). Presently there exists humongous number of tools that can perform either structural or sequential alignment of the proteins but are not good at doing both simultaneously. This leads to a major problem for the bio-informaticians i.e. developing competent and precise algorithms to enable content based searching of proteins. In [8] authors have presented a content based search engine "AMIPRO" for similarity search in protein structures in time efficient manner. In the present manuscript a Multi Minimum Product Spanning Tree based index structure has been implemented on the visual and sequential features extracted in "AMIPRO" [8].

2   State of Art

Many researchers have discussed that in Structural Genomics it's very important to set a permanent relation between structures to structure. Most of the current web portals for structure correlation are either committed to a database scan or for match savvy structural arrangements [5]. DALI, the structural alignment server does the pairwise structure examination; it analyzes one query structure against those predefined by the user [9]. All against all structure correlation - restores an auxiliary closeness dendrogram for an arrangement of structures determined by the user. Combinatorial Extension (CE) and FATCAT are methods for calculating pairwise structure alignments [10]. Sequential Structure Alignment Program (SSAP) method uses double dynamic programming to produce a structural alignment based on atom-to-atom vectors in structure space [11]. MAMMOTH (Matching Molecular Models Obtained from Theory) is a sequence-independent protein structural alignment method [12]. One of the major goals of computational biology is to develop competent and accurate tools which can extract knowledge from these databases.

3   Overview of AMIPRO

Content based search engine AMIPRO consist of five main blocks. The first one is query block, the second one is feature extraction block, the third one is database block, and the fourth one is search engine block and finally the result block [8]. A block diagram representation of different components of AMIPRO is shown in the Fig. 1.

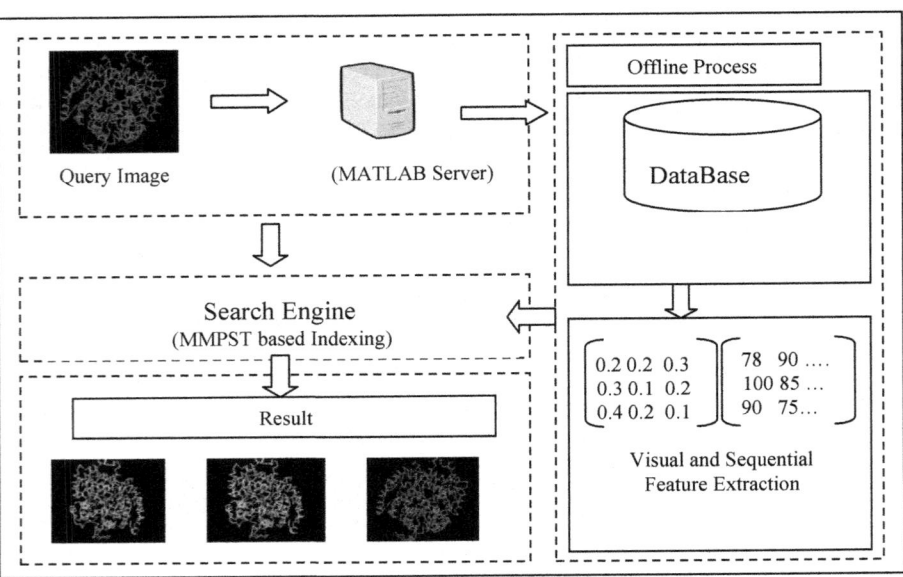

Fig. 1. The block diagram of AMIPRO [8]

3.1   Query Block

Query block is developed by using Query by example approach. Combination of three visualization method i.e. Backbone, ribbon and rocket have been used. Sample of various visualizations used in the experiments are shown in Fig. 2.

(a) Backbone   (b) Rocket   (c) Ribbon

Fig. 2. Various visualizations of protein structures

3.2 Visual Feature Extraction Block

Visual features from protein images have been selected by applying High Order Local Autocorrelation feature extraction [8, 13, 14]. The query image is rotated in its prime axis and HLAC features are extracted. HLAC features are Shift invariant, hence are used by many researchers for shape based feature representation [15].

3.3 Database Block

SQL server is used for storing 200 randomly collected proteins. RCSB PDB [16] was used for collection of proteins and the protein images were synthesized using JMOL [17] and Bioinformatics toolbox of Matlab [18].

3.4 Search Engine Block

Query Interface is implemented as Query by Example interface. Our proposed method involves a combination of semantic relation identification and graph indexing techniques to index image objects. The image database is indexed on visual similarity and content based similarity by combining both features. The image similarity has been represented in one matrix A and content based similarity is represented in matrix B with total weights n^2 each [19]. Expected Minimum Product Spanning Tree has been generated and afterward, using product operation Multi Minimum Product Spanning Tree based index structure has been created.

3.5 Image Retrieval and Visualization Block

Images on top node of MMPST are shown as result.

4 Minimum Product Spanning Tree Based Index Structure

A spanning tree of a graph G = (V, E) is a subset of edges from E that forms a tree connecting all vertices of V [20, 21]. The minimum product spanning tree of graph G is defined to be a spanning tree of G that minimizes the product of tree edge weights [22, 23]. In the minimum product spanning tree problem, the cost of a tree is the product of all the edge weights in the tree, instead of the sum of the weights [24, 25].

4.1 Building MMPST Based Index Structure

In minimum product spanning tree is basically a minimum spanning tree of a graph where the weights on the edges are the log-values of the initial weights [26, 27]. Here we will take the image similarity matrix A and content based similarity matrix B with total weights n^2 each for creating a graph structure and finally the minimal spanning tree and Minimum Product Spanning Tree will be created.

MMPST Steps involved in creation of MMPST index are:

STEP 1: Find the no. of vertices and key values and make the tree.
STEP 2: Generation of graph using adjacency matrix.
STEP 3: Construction of MST and evaluate minimum products.
STEP 4: Generation of MPST using Prim's algorithm.
STEP 5: Find the product matrix P of the two MPSTs.
STEP 6: Find the average of the product of the weights obtained and categorize on the basis of

    a. All product weights above average will come in group A (Homo)
    b. All product weights below average will come in group B (Hetero)

In Fig. 3. Structure of MMPST index is shown.

Fig. 3. Structure of MMPST index

5 Results and Discussions

Experiments have been conducted on SQL Server 2008 and MATLAB R2015a. For computing visual similarity 2DHLAC features protein images from four classes of SCOP database has been collected randomly. PDBID is used for calculating sequence based similarity in bioinformatics toolbox of MATLAB [17].

Performance of MPST is evaluated, on the savings of MST query processing time assuming the **MST nodes as most essential/cardinal nodes and the connections/ weights between these nodes as cardinal connection/weight** on new query processing on the number of isomorphism tests. However, its runtime becomes better with an increasing number of queries. The computational complexity of searching online similar protein has been reduced more than twice, by using MMPST based index structure as compared to performing online comparisons.

5.1 Query Evaluation on MMPST

In set of experiments, queries like "List protein entries which are 70% structurally similar and 90% sequentially similar" can be executed in time efficient manner. Performance of MMPST is compared with Inverted index algorithm. The most commonly used indexing algorithm by the search engines are the Inverted Index algorithm. The best case time complexity comparison for Prim's algorithm (MPST) and Inverted Index is given in Table 1. The comparison shows clearly that retrieval time taken by MMPST index is lesser that the time taken by Inverted Index.

Table 1. Best case time complexity comparison of MMPST and inverted index

	MMPST	Inverted index
Time Complexity	O(V2) and O(E + V log V)	O(I qI * D * IDI), q – length of query, IDI is the length of the document

A set of 200 protein images have been used for performance evaluation of MMPST. Total 80 queries have been executed using interface (Fig. 4) for finding structurally and sequentially similar proteins. Table 2 shows sample of queries executed on MMPST.

Table 2. Samples of Queries on MMPST

Query	Description	Answer	Time in msec.
Q2	Structural Similarity = 90% Sequential Similarity = 80%	8	54
Q10	Structural Similarity = 80% Sequential Similarity = 90%	5	48
Q15	Structural Similarity = 70% Sequential Similarity = 80%	6	34

The GUI based interface is designed in ASP using Java script Fig. 4. Best three results of each executed query is shown to user. In Figs. 5 and 6 result of Query no 2 and Query no 10 has been shown.

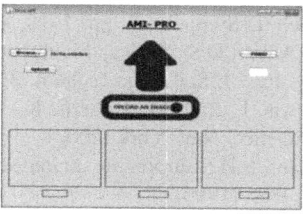

Fig. 4. Main page

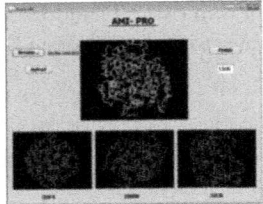

Fig. 5. Result of query no. 2

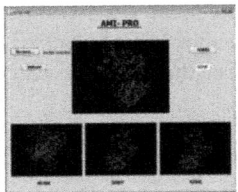

Fig. 6. Result of query no. 10

6 Conclusion and Future Work

To overcome the semantic gap in content based image retrieval it is very much required that similarity between two images is determined on the basis of multiple features instead of one. Now for retrieval based on multiple features a quick mapping/index structure is very much essential. In present manuscript a novel solution to the problem of similarity mapping on different features, has been proposed. The proposed algorithm can accelerate feature vector based query as well as composite feature vector based queries. The proposed algorithms composed of (i) a MST based index, (ii) a MPST based index and (iii) a method for efficiently maintaining the index. The MMPST based index structure has been implemented for bio-images and a significant performance gain and negligible space overhead has been experienced. In future the performance of MMPST index will be evaluated on different multimedia objects like videos and audios.

References

1. Yasmin, M., Mohsin, S., Sharif, M.: Intelligent image retrieval techniques: a survey. J. Appl. Res. Technol. **14**, 87–103 (2014)
2. Wiwie, C., Baumbach, J., Röttger, R.: Comparing the performance of biomedical clustering methods. NCBI, Nat. Methods **12**(11), 1033–1038 (2015). https://doi.org/10.1038/nmeth.3583
3. Min, V.P., Halderman, J.A., Kazhdan, M., Funkhouser, T.A.: Early experiences with a 3D model search engine. In: Web3D Symposium, pp. 7–18, March 2003
4. Srivastava, M., Singh, D.S., Abbas, D.S.: Web archiving: past present and future of evolving multimedia legacy. Int. Adv. Res. J. Sci. Eng. Technol. **3**(3), 44–46 (2015)
5. Alberts, B., Johnson, A., Lewis, J., Raff, M., Roberts, K., Walter, P.: Molecular Biology of the Cell, 4th edn. Garland Science, New York (2002)
6. Gibrat, J.F., Madej, T., Bryant, S.H.: Surprising similarities in structure comparison. Curr. Open Struct. Biol. **6**(3), 377–385 (1996)
7. Srivastava, M., Singh, S.K., Abbas, S.Q.: A novel model for fast and robust retrieval of 3D bio-images using intelligent vision algorithm. Int. J. Control Theory Appl. **9**, 617–627 (2016)

8. Srivastava, M., Singh, S.K., Abbas, S.Q., Neelabh: *AMIPRO*: a content-based search engine for fast and efficient retrieval of 3D protein structures. In: Somani, A., Srivastava, S., Mundra, A., Rawat, S. (eds.) Proceedings of First International Conference on Smart System, Innovations and Computing. SIST, vol 79, pp. 739–748. Springer, Singapore (2018). https://doi.org/10.1007/978-981-10-5828-8_70

9. http://ekhidna2.biocenter.helsinki.fi/dali/

10. http://source.rcsb.org/ceHome.jsp

11. Orengo, C.A., Taylor, W.R.: SSAP: sequential structure alignment program for protein structure comparison. Methods Enzymol. https://doi.org/10.1016/S0076-6879(96)66038-8

12. https://ub.cbm.uam.es/software/mammoth.php

13. Otsu, N., Kurita, T.: A new scheme for practical flexible and intelligent vision systems. In: IAPR Workshop on CV - Special Hardware and Industrial Applications, Tokyo, 12–14 October 1988

14. Shibuya, T., Kashima, H., Sese, J., Ahmed, S.: Pattern Recognition in Bioinformatics. Springer, Heidelberg (2012). https://doi.org/10.1007/978-3-642-34123-6

15. Suzuki, M.T.: Texture image classification using extended 2D HLAC features. In: International Conference On Kansai Engineering And Emotion Research Texture, KEER 2014 (2014)

16. Berman, H.M., Westbrook, J., Feng, Z., Gilliland, G., Bhat, T.N., Weissig, H., Shindyalov, I.N., Bourne, P.E.: The protein data bank. Nucleic Acids Res. **28**, 235–242 (2000)

17. Herráez, A.: Biomolecules in the computer: Jmol to the rescue. Biochem. Mol. Biol. Educ. **34**(4), 255–261 (2006)

18. MATLAB and Statistics Toolbox Release 2015a. The Math Works, Inc., Natick, Massachusetts, United States

19. Sorensen, K., Janssens, G.K.: An algorithm to generate all spanning trees of a graph in order of increasing cost. University of Antwerp; Hasselt University, Belgium (2005)

20. Sakr, S., Al-Naymat, G.: Graph indexing and querying: a review. Int. J. Web Inf. Syst. https://doi.org/10.1108/17440081011053104. Source: DBLP

21. Huan, J., Wang, W., Prins, J.: Comparing graph representations of protein structure for mining family-specific residue-based packing motifs. J. Comput. Biol. (JCB) **12**(6), 657–671 (2005)

22. Lončar, V., Škrbić, S., Balaž, A.: Parallelization of minimum spanning tree algorithms using distributed memory architectures. In: Yang, G.-C., Ao, S.-I., Gelman, L. (eds.) Transactions on Engineering Technologies, pp. 543–554. Springer, Dordrecht (2014). https://doi.org/10.1007/978-94-017-8832-8_39

23. Horowitz, E., Sahani, S., Rajasekaran, S.: Fundamentals of Computer Algorithms, 2nd edn. Universities Press (India) Pvt. Ltd., Hyderabad (2008)

24. Xu, Y., Olman, V., Xu, D.: Minimum spanning trees for gene expression data clustering. Genome Inf. **12**, 24–33 (2001)

25. Deo, N.: Graph Theory with Applications to Engineering and Computer Science. Prentice Hall of India Pvt. Ltd., New Delhi (2005)

26. Hasuikea, T., Katagirib, H.: Interactive decision making for uncertain minimum spanning tree problems with total importance based on a risk-management approach. Appl. Math. Model. **37**(6), 4548–4560 (2013)

27. Afrati, F.N., Fotakis, D., Ullman, J.D.: Enumerating subgraph instances using Map-Reduce. In: Proceedings of IEEE ICDE, pp. 62–73 (2013)

Author Index